BUD COLLINS'

Edited by **BUD COLLINS**

& ZANDER HOLLANDER

an Associated Features book

VISIBLE INK PRESS

DETROIT • WASHINGTON D.C. • LONDON

BUD COLLINS' MODERN ENCYCLOPEDIA OF TENNIS, 2ND EDITION

Published by **Visible Ink Press**™
a division of Gale Research Inc.
835 Penobscot Bldg.
Detroit MI 48226-4094

Visible Ink Press is a trademark of Gale Research Inc.

ISBN 0-8103-9443-X

FRONT COVER PHOTO OF JIM COURIER: Ron Angle, Photo Images
BACK COVER PHOTO OF BUD COLLINS: John Russell, Team Russell

ART DIRECTOR: Cynthia Baldwin
COVER DESIGN: Mark C. Howell
PAGE DESIGN: Kathleen A. Hourdakis

10 9 8 7 6 5 4 3 2 1
second edition

For the heroic Arthur Ashe, who showed us that sportsmanship even in a highly competitive game

goodness, initiated me:

Ed Costello, my first sports editor, at the long-departed *Boston Herald*; Greg Harney, my first TV producer, at WGBH, Boston; Mike ("Keep-it-short") Vickers, my first copy editor at the *Herald*; Harold "Big Z" Zimman, USTA publisher.

Because of them, I never had to go to work for a living.

ALSO FROM VISIBLE INK PRESS:

THE COMPLETE ENCYCLOPEDIA OF HOCKEY

"Crammed with interesting facts and figures." —*TORONTO STAR*

Completely revised fourth edition of this bestselling sports reference takes the hockey fan step-by-step from the beginning of the NHL to the events of the 91-92 season. Chock full of stats! 7 x 10. Paperback. 625 pp. $22.95

THE WORLD ENCYCLOPEDIA OF SOCCER

Comprehensive coverage of the World Cup, Olympic soccer and women's soccer. Look for histories, biographies, rules, rivalries and riots. 7 1/4 X 9 1/4. Paperback. 500 pp. $14.95

THE OLYMPICS FACTBOOK: A SPECTATOR'S GUIDE TO THE WINTER GAMES

Up-close and personal with hopefuls and heroes from previous games as well as an insider look at Lillehammer, Norway. Also provides facts and figures for each sport, schedules, medal history, rules and much more. 6 x 9. Paperback. 250 pp. $9.95

To order, call 1-800-776-6265.

CONTENTS

ix

PREFACE

If that is the confession of a junkie, a tennis degenerate—so be it.

Not that I drink lemonade whenever I watch tennis. A double fix? Hardly ever. But the two are inextricable in thought. A quenching of a thirst on a summer day. Especially since 1972, when the yellow ball was introduced to general play, and for me, life became: Follow the bouncing rubber lemon.

Tennis is no longer a game strictly for sunny, summery afternoons. But that original fresh-air form, hostage to the elements, remains the best. Even so, tennis has thrilled me beneath floodlights or, in the gloom of winter, bunkered in an arena such as Palais des Sports in Lyon the last weekend of November 1991. With 7,000 inmates jubilantly rocking and rattling their cage, the Palais became a cauldron of excitement and elation as France—in the left-handed persons of Guy Forget and Henri Leconte—made an unlikely grab of the Davis Cup from the U.S.

France hadn't won for 59 years and no one, whatever nationality, could begrudge the French a country-enveloping paroxysm of *joie*. One of the men—the Four Musketeers, they were called—who upheld France's Reign of Terror during the 1920s and '30s was happily present. Musketeer Jean Borotra (his comrades were René Lacoste, the late Jacques Brugnon and Henri Cochet) had anchored the Cup winners of 1927 through 1932.

"I couldn't wait much longer," said Borotra, understandably. However spry, Jean was 93. Yes, it was a long wait between his sips of champagne from the sterling crock (née 1900) nearly as old as he. I drank from the Davis Cup only vicariously that night, though the champagne tasted like *lemonade*.

Either the lemon flies over the net or it doesn't.

That's the essence of tennis, the simple and obvious requirement: Take a racket—an instrument that looks like an oversized magnifying glass, but with a network of strings in place of the lens—and hit a rubber ball over a rampart of netting three feet in height. Hit the ball over the net within a rectangular court one more time than your opponent, and you win a point. Win enough points and you defeat that opponent.

Should such a rudimentary exercise hold any fascination at all, or for very long? Spencer W. Gore remarked in 1880 that any gamesplayer worth his sweat wouldn't find tennis a satisfactory pastime for any length of time. No sour grapesman Gore, for he, an athletic Englishman, had in 1877 won the first recognized tennis tournament, one that continues highest in general esteem more than a century later: Wimbledon (properly titled, then and now, The Lawn Tennis Championships). If Gore were a Wimbledon champion at large today, his agent would censure him for deprecatory talk about their livelihood. "Don't knock the game that feeds us, Spencer," the agent would scold. "How do you expect me to get you any more endorsement contracts if you keep saying tennis is a bore?"

The first champion's doubting statements clearly had as much impact as the *Titanic* on its icy opponent. Gore sank from view quickly, but the game flourished in the cradle— Britain, and spread throughout the planet so that today it enthralls millions upon millions of hackers (recreational players) and a few thousand heroes/heroines (the professional elite) as well as millions more tennis addicts who attend tournaments and take the free fix from television.

The one and only James Scott Connors, the irrepressible American pro, who played his 22nd U.S. Open at age 40 in 1992 (he'd been an amazing semifinalist the year before) could look back on five U.S. titles and almost $9 million in career prize money. He wouldn't agree with Gore at all—if Jimmy could even identify the late, grumbling Gore.

"I think people play and watch tennis because it's exciting," Connors says. "I know that's how I feel."

Amen to that, James, even though the game's a living for us both.

It has been fascinating to watch the growth of tennis over the last four decades, to be part of the spectacular surge transforming it from a game of a relative few to a point where in 1992 a Gallup poll showed tennis as No. 4 in sports Americans prefer to watch, behind football, baseball and basketball.

My old sports editor would never have believed it. He was actually apologetic in sending me on my first tennis assignment for the Boston *Herald* in 1955, taking pains to let me know he wasn't being punitive. The boss assiduously devoted as little space as possible to "these clubby types running around in their underwear chasing a little white ball."

Certainly then the chances that I would rove the world writing and telecasting tennis— 22 Wimbledons for NBC, as I write—were as likely as the little white ball becoming the little yellow ball or players making 100 grand for a few hours of swatting those balls. The odds against were about as long as those facing the Newport Bolshevik, Jimmy Van Alen, who sought to chip the barnacles of ages off the game by introducing tie-breakers. Those overtimes eliminated endless deuce sets and made tennis more compatible with TV. Yet all these things happened.

The Boston *Globe*, where I moved in 1963, and editor Tom Winship encouraged me to take a worldwide view of the game for its readers. Station WGBH-TV in Boston, inspired by producer-director Greg Harney, launched the Public Broadcasting Service's thorough and thoughtful pioneering of tennis telecasting in the U.S., well ahead of the commercial networks. That was in 1963, when I soloed as commentator at the U.S. Doubles Championships at Longwood Cricket Club in Boston, and our "network" was three stations in New England. It was rewarding to do the first PBS national telecast in 1968, the U.S. Amateur Championships, also at Longwood, as a skinny young man named Arthur Ashe made a breakthrough—the first black male to win a significant championship.

Two Sundays later, Arthur was in the winner's circle again at Forest Hills, and Jack Kramer and I were describing his victory in the first U.S. Open for the CBS. Ashe was mak-

intriguing physical and mental battle between distinct personalities, the stress and exhilaration, the anxiety and sheer fun. There was no danger of Gore getting hooked, becoming a tennis degenerate.

For some of us degenerates, whether bearing witness or playing—or both—tennis can be a way of life, even a religion.

But let's never get solemn about something that is so much fun and can be stripped down to this: Either the rubber lemon goes over the net or it doesn't...

One man's lemonade may be another man's ulcer.

—*Bud Collins*

Acknowledgments

national Tennis Federation) have never quite gotten their acts together—even though all are involved in the same sport.

Nevertheless, we have tried to make sense of it all, and pack more than a century of organized tennis—as accurately as possible—into this volume.

Sometimes this has been frustrating. Unlike, say, baseball, where virtually everything is recorded (you can find out how many balls a St. Louis Browns infielder booted in the second game of a Fourth-of-July double-header in 1923), tennis history commands a woeful lack of authoritative data and records. No official record book. No complete record even of all the major championships. Conflicting reports and statistics abound.

Maybe that's part of the charm of this delightful, at times chaotic, sport, even in this, the so-called age of tennis professionalism. Take one example: The game is even played by different rules, depending on where you are. At the U.S. Open, ultimate sets (fifth for men, third for women) are settled by a tie-breaker at 6–6 in games. At the other three majors (Australian, French and Wimbledon), such sets are played out in the old fashion, which requires a two-game margin.

Take another. The ITF says Pete Sampras, David Wheaton and Michael Stich won the $2-million first prizes at its Grand Slam Cups of 1990–91–92. The ATP, preferring its own ATP World Championship as the season-concluding championship of champions, counters that the Grand Slam Cup doesn't exist. Thus on its prize-money lists the ATP doesn't credit Sampras, Wheaton and Stich with their GSC winnings (Pete, David and Michael's bankers know better). The ITF wonders, reasonably, why the ATP doesn't include the most difficult form of men's tennis—Davis Cup—in its computer rankings. So it merrily goes.

The computer, an invention of fairly long standing, and the relative youth of open tennis (born 1968), would lead you to think that at least the 1968–92 quarter-century of the game is thoroughly documented. But, think again.

Even though the ATP, WTA, USTA and ITF are trying to get up to date, they still can't provide the complete records of a couple of fairly consequential characters named John McEnroe and Chris Evert. Ah well, then imagine the pre-open era—"Back in the Stone Age"—as one of our aides, Suzanna Collins, characterizes much of tennis history. Has anybody ever compiled the career records of Don Budge or Alice Marble? Forget it. Another aide, Anita Ruthling Klaussen, with her usual organizational and inspirational verve, did piece together the fantastic records of pioneer pros Rosie Casals and Billie Jean King.

All this isn't meant to cop a plea or complain or point fingers. But just to say that we and our collaborators have tried to find our way through a thicket (and have had fun doing so). While prying, tracking, seeking, as, we believe, it's never been done before, we unearthed facts, records and performances previously unpublished. We fleshed out a considerable cast—the greats, the very goods, and even the ordinary—whose deeds are not to be overlooked. While granting that there is more digging to be done, we hope we have served the needs and curiosity of every player and fan.

A couple of discoveries especially tickled us. For example, it was believed that Maud Barger Wallach was the oldest U.S. female champ—38 years old in 1908. But, it seems that Molla Mallory (hardly alone in such matters) had been fibbing about her age. She was actually 42—not 34—when she won her record eighth title at Forest Hills in 1926. That finding came from invaluable researcher/historian Frank V. Phelps. Sorry, Molla.

"Help!" we cried. Often. And we got it from willing sources who deserve more but will have to settle for acknowledgments. We salute the memory of those good men, so devoted to the game, Allison Danzig of *The New York Times* and Lance Tingay of the *Daily Telegraph* of London, both Hall of Fame journalists, who have died since the first edition of the *Encyclopedia*, published in 1980.

We are also indebted to contributors Barry Lorge of *Tennis* magazine, Steve Flink of *Tennis Week* and CBS Radio, Marty Lader of UPI and Stan Isaacs, formerly of *Newsday*. And to Joe Gergen, sports columnist of *Newsday*; Ram Ramnath, distinguished academician at MIT; Phyllis Hollander of Associated Features, who helped get the manuscript through many a tie-breaker; historian George Alexander, who, in the first documented account, pinpointed the unlikely site—a remote U.S. Army post in Arizona—where the first games of tennis were played.

Honorable mention goes as well to super editor Becky Nelson and David Salamie of Gale Research Inc.; Eric Compton of *Newsday*; Jan Armstrong of the International Tennis Hall of Fame; Alan Little of the Wimbledon library; Ed Fabricius, Art Campbell, Lesley Poch, Paige Crosland of the USTA; Barbara Travers of the ITF; Ana Leaird, Jean Beckwith, Renee Block Shalouf, Robin Reynolds, Susan Vosburgh, Tracey Robinson, Toni Waters Woods, Doug Clery of the WTA; Greg Sharko, Giorgio Rubenstein, Billy Singh of the ATP; Jim Fuhse, Peter Land, Bettina Pettersen of Kraft; Harold and Helen Zimman and Adam Scharff of H.O. Zimman, Inc.; Bob Paul of the U.S. Olympic Committee; Kirko Klaussen, R.B.D.H. Wogan, Joe Johnson, Giovanni Clerici, Rino Tommasi, Pop Merrihew, Bill Talbert, C. Gene Mako, Giselle Marrou Asplundh, Gladys Heldman, Alan Trengove, Pat Henry Yoemans and indexer Terry Murray....

—*Bud Collins and Zander Hollander*

INTRODUCTION

25th anniversary of the advent of "open" tennis—the integration of amateurs and pros with cash payments offered on the basis of winning performance—more than $80 million was available throughout the world to male and female professionals. The total for the dawning season of opens, 1968, was about $400,000.

Grandest financially of the first open championships in that inaugural year was the U.S. Open at Forest Hills. A $100,000 pot held $14,000 and $6,000 as first prize for man and woman, respectively. By 1992 the pot had sweetened to $8,556,600 and the singles first prize (sexually equal since progressive 1973) amounted to $500,000.

Despite all the gold, this diversion is yet a game that is sometimes raised to an art form—a competitive ballet—by the splendor in movement of such acrobatic zephyrs as Maria Bueno and Ken Rosewall, Evonne Goolagong and Ilie Nastase, Martina Navratilova and John McEnroe, Steffi Graf and Pete Sampras.

Often it is sublime drama. Never more so than on a chilly, grim October afternoon in Bucharest in 1972 when nationalism and personal pride, strength of

ment. Slipping on the slow, salmon-hued European clay, he was assaulted by a canny, dark-maned lion while a feverish crowd and unfailingly patriotic officials gave him a thumbs-down treatment. Never mind the tennis match, Smith sometimes wondered whether he'd get out of town alive.

At stake was the Davis Cup, that huge silver basin from which world conquerors have swilled victorious champagne since 1900. It is the most difficult prize to win in tennis, a reward for the team title, pursued each year by more than 90 countries. In 1972 the United States and Romania were the finalists. The Cup would be decided by the Smith–Tiriac match, and this fact made a boiling tea kettle of an intimate 7,000-seat wooden stadium that was hastily hammered together for what amounted to a state occasion in Romania. Though Tiriac, a deceptively plodding and unstylish player, wasn't in Smith's league, he lifted himself as high as his native Carpathians with one thought: His tiny homeland, producer of few world-class players besides himself and teammate Ilie Nastase, could score a fantastic victory over the mighty U.S. if he beat Smith. "I know only one way to play—to win. If I lose," Tiriac said, "then it is nothing. We don't win the Cup."

Ion orchestrated the chanting crowd and deferential line judges into a united front for himself and against Smith. He stalled, he emoted—and he played like a madman, forcing the excruciating match all the way into a fifth set. It seemed a morality play in short pants, the exemplary sportsman Smith, tall and fair-haired, against the scheming Tiriac, hulking and glaring. Somehow Smith held together amid chaos to play to his utmost, too, and win the last set in a run of six games. Considering the adverse conditions and the magnitude of the prize, Smith's triumph was possibly the most extraordinary in the history of the game. "I concentrated so hard I got a headache," he said.

While Tiriac was chastised outside of Romania for a pragmatic approach to tennis, avoiding the accepted behavior, he was merely doing the best he could to seize a rare day for his homeland. It was only a game of tennis, but it had assumed a far greater significance for a few hours that afternoon.

The significance was global, and this internationality is a source of much of the appeal of tennis. By this, of course, I mean the established worldwide tournament game to which this encyclopedia is primarily devoted. The advance of the game since the tennis court was patented in London in 1874 by Major Walter C. Wingfield has been so complete that all continents are routinely represented in any tournament of consequence. Australians, Asians, Europeans, Africans, and North and South Americans populate a family of tournament players who work their way around the globe on an unending trek among the continents. They flit between Melbourne and Münich, Bombay and Buenos Aires, Johannesburg and Jacksonville as casually as commuters, aware that jets have made it possible to compete on one continent today and another tomorrow.

Tennis players have been ocean-hoppers almost since the beginning, but the year 1900 seems special: A British team showed up in Boston to launch the Davis Cup by challenging the U.S. Five years later a robust Californian, May Sutton, became the first foreigner to win Wimbledon. Two years after that Norman Brookes journeyed all the way from Melbourne to London to win the singles, showing the way to the Big W for Australians, who would one day be more awesome there than any other aliens. The next year, 1908, an American, Fred Alexander, was the first outsider to win the Australian title.

The game may have been restricted to a 78-by-27-foot plot, but the players were operating on a planetary playground. Don Budge presented striking evidence in 1938 when he circumnavigated the initial Grand Slam by winning the Australian, French, Wimbledon and U.S. titles all within that year. Budge traveled more leisurely, by ocean liner, but players would become winged rugbeaters in a few years, and no tournament was too far off the beaten path.

Major Wingfield's attempt to fire a tennis boom and cash in on it by patenting a set of equipment and instructions in 1874 is a convenient event in marking the start of the game we know as tennis—lawn tennis to sticklers (mostly Britons), who wish to distinguish this game from its parent, *real* (court or royal) tennis. Real tennis, a complex and beguiling game, is played with lopsided rackets in an erratically walled concrete court where the balls—hard as baseballs—rattle around on sloping roofs and disappear into arcane apertures. The game is still to be found in a few private clubs (seven in the U.S.) where members presumably have to pass a blood test: blue-positive required.

Real tennis dates back to the Middle Ages, called *jeu de paume* in France because the hand was used to smack the ball before the instrument called racket was conceived. Numerous kings, who had the court-building wherewithal and leisure time, were enthusiastic players, the first probably Louis X of France (1314–16). Poor Louis may have been a mite too enthusiastic. The story is that he became overheated at play, drank cold water immediately, developed a chill and died. Where was Gatorade when he needed it?

A more famous playboy monarch, old London Fats (aka King Henry VIII of Eng-

personal scorekeeper, one Anthony Angeley. What opponent would question a call by the royal umpire on the king's behalf?

If you think John McEnroe was the champ at unleashing passions on court, he was really a pussycat compared with another master stroker, the Italian painter Caravaggio. Enraged during a match in Rome in 1606, he killed his opponent, and had to leave town for a while.

According to Shakespeare, yet another English tennis-playing king, Henry V, also had a temper. He was not amused by a gift of tennis balls from the Dauphin of France.

Taking it as a "Balls to you, pal!" message, Henry declared: "When we have matched our rackets to these balls, we will, in France, by God's grace, play a set...." He proceeded to invade France to backhand the locals at the Battle of Agincourt in 1415.

Since kings and millionaires aren't numerous enough to carry a popular sport, real tennis never came very far out of its curiously constructed closet. Actually Major Wingfield wasn't the originator of an outdoor version. He was among several

who tried their hands at fresh-air tennis prior to 1874, but it was Wingfield who codified a game and envisioned commercial possibilities. When he set out to market equipment and rules for his game, Wingfield realized that a profitable volume of sales would rest on attracting a broader public than that involved in real tennis and very expensive indoor courts. Not the masses, certainly, but the affluent with

game was once and forever lawn tennis to the Brits, who would rather break their necks than tradition.

Although grass courts hold firm at Wimbledon as well as at a few other tournaments in Britain, they are scarce in number elsewhere. Steadfastly resisting the trend away from the sacred sod is Newport Casino at Newport, R.I., birthplace of the American tournament game. The world's oldest tennis patch, the Casino (1880), is a hardy survivor, a gingerbread architectural gem, scene of the first recognized U.S. tournament, on grass, the men's National Championships of 1881, and the last, an annual pro tour stopover called the Hall of Fame Classic. Like Wimbledon, Newport has no intention of forsaking God's own greenery.

Lawn tennis or just-plain-tennis—whatever it is called, however the ball bounces on whichever surface—has caught on in the U.S. more widely than anywhere else. Shortly after Wingfield started peddling tennis it reached the U.S. In 1876, Dr. James Dwight, a Bostonian, won a baptismal tourney of sorts, a sociable get-together he arranged in the yard of the Appleton estate at Nahant, Mass.

Dr. James Dwight: Father of U.S. tennis. • *USTA*

Americans were swinging rackets in numerous locales in 1874, and Dr. Richard Dwight of Boston, the son of "The Father," an active player himself in his 90s, had this to say:

"In 1874, just after Major Wingfield patented the game, and the first tennis sets were sold in London, a Sears relative named Beebe brought one to Nahant. There was a good lawn at the Appleton place and Father and his cousin, Fred Sears, set up a court. They didn't care much for the game the first time they played. But the second time—ah, they were caught."

However, nobody declared that tennis had landed in America. Or much noticed.

For many years afterwards, it was assumed, and written in numerous histories that one Mary Outerbridge, of a prominent Staten Island (N.Y.) family, in bringing a set of tennis equipment home from Bermuda in 1874, had planted the game in the United States on Staten Island. Thus feminists may have been dismayed in 1979 when an English historian, Tom Todd, asserted that it was Dwight—not Outerbridge—who introduced tennis to the States earlier that year. Founding mother or father? Both Outerbridge, long hailed, and Dwight have their backers.

A century later (1974), an American historian, George Alexander, uncovered evidence of the first recorded play in the U.S. Not in New York or Massachusetts, but—holy half-volleys! —in the wilds of Apache country in the Arizona Territory, also 1874. And a brand new name enters the game's literature: Ella Wilkins Bailey. Was Ella, wife of a U.S. Army officer, the champ of Camp Apache? Unknown. But it has been documented that she played on the court there that year, possibly with her sister, Caroline Wilkins.

Fair Ella may or may not have been the first American player—Doc Dwight and Sears, his cousin, get this guesser's nod— but according to the thorough Alexander, Ella Wilkins Bailey is the first for whom a reliable reference has been found.

While some may keen, "Say it ain't so, Doc!" and charge Alexander and Todd with revisionism, Dr. Dwight the younger is, as ever, gracious. "Even my father got mixed up as to the date when he later wrote about it," he says. "The main thing is that people did start to play and Mary Outerbridge was important in giving the push in New York. The fact seems to be that both my father and Outerbridge imported sets at about the same time, and nobody can be quite sure who was first."

Papa Dwight, however, has a much more solid position in tennis annals than

Early action at the Seabright (N.J.) Tennis Club. *•Fischer Collection/SPS*

Mama Outerbridge. A graduate of Harvard Medical School, he was not one to let his profession stand in the way of something as important as tennis. Dwight didn't work as a physician, excusing himself on the grounds of "poor health." Instead he devoted himself to tennis, teaching the game to the first U.S. singles champion, a fellow Bostonian, Dick Sears, and accompanying Sears to the national doubles championship five times between 1882 and 1887.

Although tennis drifted across the country from Staten Island and Nahant, the power remained in the Northeast. Three decades after Sears began his American championship dynasty in 1881, the American men's championship was still the property of an Ivy League crowd. Exceptions popped up among the women. Best known were Californians May Sutton, champ in 1904 (a year prior to butting into the homebodies' monopoly at Wimbledon), and Hazel Hotchkiss, 1909. But the Northeast's early stranglehold had actually been broken by Irishwoman Mabel Cahill (1891–92) and defied by Californian Marion Jones (1899 and 1902) and Myrtle McAteer from Pittsburgh in 1900.

At least, in 1912, the men's National Championships began to go truly national on the tail of the California Comet, hyperaggressive Maurice "Red" McLoughlin, and the general sporting public would soon become aware of tennis.

It was too good a game to be cloistered at Newport as an amusement of the swells, and in 1915 the National Championships for men moved to the metropolis, New York, and the West Side Tennis Club at Forest Hills. There would be a country-club tinge right up to the present day of heavy money and professionalization, but at Forest Hills tennis gained exposure to larger, more diverse crowds, and a national press.

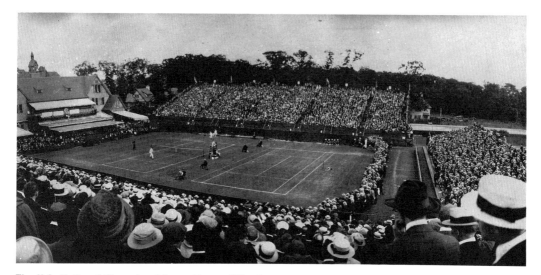

The U.S. National Championships at Forest Hills, N.Y. in 1920. • *Fischer Collection/SPS*

Once peacetime arrived, following World War I, the press had a tennis hero to hype—and a heroine. Big Bill Tilden, the gangling Philadelphian with a blowtorch serve, and Suzanne Lenglen, a flying Frenchwoman, worked their respective sides of the Atlantic with irresistible flair and shotmaking. Not only were Tilden and Lenglen virtually invincible champions, but also they were regal figures and somewhat mysterious. Theirs was a magnetism that pulled crowds and sold tickets, and tennis became a commercial venture. With Tilden as strong man, the U.S. went on a record rampage of seven straight Davis Cups, and it was necessary to construct a 13,000-seat stadium at Forest Hills to hold the throngs following Davis Cup matches and the National Championships.

Because of Lenglen, never beaten in singles at Wimbledon, the place seemed to shrink. It became too small for all the customers who wanted in. Thus the All England Lawn Tennis & Croquet Club, needing more space and seats, moved in 1922 to the present Wimbledon grounds with a Centre Court accommodating nearly 14,000.

Tennis joined other sports as a business game, but, unfortunately, not as a profession. By 1926 it was apparent that the athletes who sold the tickets deserved to be paid. It was not apparent, however, to those volunteer officials who controlled the game and, for generations past its time, they would keep alive the fiction of "amateurism" at the upper level of tennis. Instead of prize money, the subsidy for careerists was "expenses," paid beneath the table in proportion to a player's value as a gate attraction. During the 1920s Tilden made more out of tennis as an amateur than some of the better pros today. He earned it. But Tilden, a supreme individualist, showed neither gratitude nor obeisance to the amateur authorities and was eventually driven to the wilderness of outright professionalism in 1930, to take his place brilliantly on the treadmill of one-nighters.

Until 1926 the only professionals were instructors, ineligible for customary tournaments. Occasionally they played small tournaments among themselves for pin money. Even though open tennis was discussed wistfully by progressives among play-

The legendary Bill Tilden early in his career. • *Fischer Collection/SPS*

ers, officials and aficionados, such a sensible arrangement was well in the future—1968. From time to time a motion to approve open tennis was even introduced within the International Tennis Federation, but the governing body was much too narrow and steeped in the so-called gentlemanly tradition of "amateurism." The motion always failed, and "shamateurism" was maintained until 1968. Amateurs who traveled the world swinging at tennis balls, living and eating well, were nicknamed "tennis bums."

However, those who decided to accept their money above the table were considered outlaws traveling under that dirty label, "professionals." At least that was the view of amateur officials who barred pros from traditional championships. Forced to scrape for their living outside of the usual framework of private clubs, the pros appeared

Suzanne Lenglen was the wonder woman of the Golden Twenties. • *UPI*

mainly in public arenas, moving constantly as nomads, folding their canvas court and jaunting to the next night's location.

This way of life began in October 1926 when La Belle Suzanne Lenglen defected from amateurism to roam North America with a troupe that included her nightly foe, Mary K. Browne, the U.S. champion of 1912–14, and Vinnie Richards, the American second to Tilden. Their stopovers

were regarded as exhibitions, but the pay was all right. Lenglen reportedly collected at least $75,000—a fortune in 1927 dollars—for her four months on the road.

A few months after the debut of the original wandering pros, the first U.S. Pro Championships for men was thrown together at a small club in Manhattan in the summer of 1927 and won by Richards, whose reward was $1,000 from a purse of

Australia's Lew Hoad (right) has just slammed the ball en route to a clinching doubles victory (with Rex Hartwig) over Tony Trabert (left) and Vic Seixas in the 1955 Davis Cup challenge round at Forest Hills. • *UPI*

$2,000. His 1992 successor, at Boston's Longwood Cricket Club, Ivan Lendl, won $50,000, and the tournament was worth $400,000, another startling piece of inflationary evidence in men's pro tennis.

The U.S. Pro Championships went along year after year, precariously and unprosperously, the longest-lasting of a few tourneys, but life as a pro meant barnstorming, and there wasn't enough money to support more than a handful of outlaws. The tournaments that mattered were restricted to amateurs, whose game had structure, continuity, and the attention of the press and tennis public. Interest in amateur sport was high during the 1920s and 1930s, as a reader of newspapers [preserved] from that time quickly ascertains.

But after World War II that interest declined. The emphasis shifted to professional sport, particularly in the U.S., and tennis, stocked with phony amateurs, didn't keep pace. While other sports gleamed in television's red eye, tennis languished away from the cameras. Three events maintained an eminence: Wimbledon, Forest Hills, and the Davis Cup finale, which became the postwar preserve of the U.S. and Australia.

As the 1950s dawned, a tidal wave swept from the Antipodes at the bottom of the world: It was the Aussies, the most dynastic force ever in tennis. Their muscle lasted for more than two decades, between the Davis Cup seizure spearheaded by Frank Sedgman in 1950 and John Newcombe's U.S. Open triumph of 1973. In between were 16 Davis Cups and 14 Wimbledons for the men, two Grand Slams by Rod Laver, and a male record of 28 Big Four titles by Roy Emerson, as well as the rise and fall of Lew Hoad, and the rise and rise of ageless Kenny Rosewall.

Directed by a martinet named Harry Hopman, the Aussies were hungry and superbly conditioned, and gave the impression that the primary occupations at home were tennis and beer drinking. They were world champs at both. Their women were not as pervasive successes as American females, but one of them, Margaret Smith Court, outdid everyone else: Mighty Maggie rolled up 62 major titles in singles, doubles and mixed, bracketing the singles championships of Australia, France, Wimbledon and the U.S. in 1970 for her Grand Slam. Only Martina Navratilova with 54 majors has come close to Court's accomplishments.

Midway through the 1960s, a period of rising acclaim for sport in general, tennis was sagging at both the amateur and professional levels. The best players were pros, but the best tournaments were amateur. Agitation for open play increased, especially in England, where Wimbledon officials, tiring of exorbitant "expense" payments to amateurs, sought to present the finest possible tennis. This was impossible as long as the professional elite—Rod Laver, Ken Rosewall, Pancho Gonzalez, Lew Hoad, Butch Buchholz and Andres Gimeno—were off in limbo as outlaws.

An impetus for the decisive move toward opens was provided startlingly in 1967 by a man unknown within tennis—Dave Dixon of New Orleans. Buoyed by Texas money supplied by petrocrat Lamar Hunt, his partner in a wildcat tennis venture, Dixon signed up amateurs John Newcombe, Tony Roche, Roger Taylor, Cliff Drysdale and Nikola Pilic plus pros Butch Buchholz, Pierre Barthes and Dennis Ralston as his World Championship Tennis troupe. Since another promoter, George

Australia's Rod Laver serves against Arthur Ashe as rain falls in the semifinals of the U.S. Championships in 1969. Laver won the match and then beat Tony Roche for the title. • *UPI*

MacCall, had enlisted amateur Roy Emerson to blend with pros Laver, Gonzalez, Rosewall, Gimeno and Fred Stolle in his National Tennis League, the amateur game was abruptly depleted of its top resources, the six best players.

Even with those players entered, the 1967 Wimbledon had been dull. Now the outlook for the ultimate championship was

...tional Tennis Federation, led by the USTA and its enlightened president, Bob Kelleher—fell into line.

Bournemouth, England, was the scene of the first open, the British Hard Court Championships in April 1968. Kenny Rosewall won the men's title. Virginia Wade the women's. And curly-headed Englishman Mark Cox wrote his footnote in sporting history as the first amateur to beat a pro at tennis. Cox, a left-hander, knocked off Pancho Gonzalez and Roy Emerson on successive afternoons to upstage all else on Britain's front pages.

The Tennis Epidemic to come in the 1970s had been set in motion. In 1971 financial pioneer Rod Laver crossed the million-dollar mark in prize money after nine years as a pro. But by 1979, 15 other men and three women had followed, making their [million]s in shorter spans. And in 1977 Guillermo Vilas had a year that would seem a splendid career for most athletes: $800,642.

This was just walking-around money, as the upward-and-on-ward finances of the '80s and '90s would show. In 1990, 20-year-old Pete Sampras carted off a flabbergast-ing first prize of $2 million for winning the newly minted Grand Slam Cup tournament, and wound up the season with men's record winnings of $2,900,057. That mark wouldn't last long. Two years later, 18-year-old Monica Seles set the women's season record, $2,622,352. By 1993, Ivan Lendl had won more than $19 million for his career, and Martina Navratilova in excess of $18 million. While career millionaires

...mutual, warm handshake. The U.S. Pro was rescued by Longwood Cricket Club and a sponsoring Boston bank.

Laver, in his sophomore year as a pro, got $2,200 as first prize and would say only a few years afterwards, "It seemed like a million then."

At first the boom in prize money benefitted principally the men. As in so many areas of life, the women were left behind. However, the tennis-playing women refused to stand at the back of the game. Guided by brainy Gladys Heldman, publisher of *World Tennis* magazine, and inspired by the liberation-minded firebrand, Billie Jean King, the women divorced themselves from the conventional tournament arrangement, which had been shared unequally by the sexes. Top billing (and top dollars) had always gone to the men. Carrying the banner of Virginia Slims cigarettes, the women crusaded on a separate tour and made good artistically and economically. The Slims tour began haltingly in 1970 and picked up steam in 1971, when Billie Jean won $117,000, the first woman to earn more than 100 grand in prize money. The tour was solid by 1972, when ingenue Chrissie Evert won the first eight-woman playoff at the climax. In 1973 the women demanded and got equal prize money at Forest Hills, one of the few remaining tournaments staging both men's and women's events.

Television didn't rush to hug tennis when the open era began, although network interest picked up. Two telecasts in particular aided in lifting the game to wide public notice: Rosewall's sensational victory over Laver for the World Championship Tennis title of 1972 in Dallas, and Billie Jean King's put-down of 55-year-old Bobby Riggs in the bizarre "Battle of the Sexes" in 1973.

Creating one of the greatest matches, Laver and Rosewall flailed away at each other brilliantly for three-and-a-half hours. It came down to a fifth-set tie-breaker where the 37-year-old Rosewall, seemingly beaten as Laver served at 5 points to 4, took the last three points and the championship in the closest finish of a significant tourney until Boris Becker beat Ivan Lendl in a 7–5 fifth-set tie-breaker for the 1988 Masters title. Rosewall won $50,000, the richest prize in tennis at the time.

Bobby Riggs, well past his prime—"one foot in the grave" was one of the lines amid his con and corn—had challenged and beaten a nervous Margaret Court in what he termed the "Mother's Day Massacre" earlier in 1973. Glowing with hubris and newfound celebrity, Riggs then challenged 29-year-old Billie Jean King. "Nobody knew me when I was the best player in the world in 1939, when I won Wimbledon," he said. "Now I'm over the hill but I'm a star. Everybody recognizes me—the old guy who can beat the best women."

Publicity was tremendous. Super schlock blanketed the Astrodome in Houston, where a record tennis crowd, 30,472, assembled for the oddest couple's encounter. Though a meaningless match in one sense, it seemed to mean everything

Billie Jean King consoles Bobby Riggs after defeating him in straight sets in their $100,000 "Battle of the Sexes" at the Houston Astrodome in 1973. • *UPI*

to millions everywhere: mankind against womankind. Billie Jean was the defender of her sex against His Piggishness, Bobby. She won easily. Tennis was the beneficiary. Laver and Rosewall had showed a TV audience how majestically the game could be played. King and Riggs lured a much larger audience because their gimmick caught the fancy of many unaware of the existence of tennis.

Tennis began to appear regularly on TV, prize money accelerated for the stars, equipment sales and participation accelerated for the hackers. Construction of public courts as well as private clubs increased, particularly in the United States, where the proliferation of indoor courts was a sporting phenomenon.

Tennis was big business, and the professional performers involved, following the example of brethren in other sports, unionized to gain a stronger position in the management of their business. The male ATP (Association of Tennis Pros) and

theless, WCT continued its annual championship playoff in Dallas, the event that had electrified the game with the $50,000 payoffs to Rosewall for his 1971 and 1972 victories over Laver. But after John McEnroe beat Brad Gilbert in the last of those in 1989, WCT sadly expired.

As the brainchild of Hall of Famer Jack Kramer, the Grand Prix commenced in

Those who thought the war was over when the forces of open tennis triumphed over those upholding amateurism in 1968 soon realized that strife would become a way of life in this sport. Revolution and evolution continued to change the face of the professional game. Though for a long time the U.S. was the financial base, the stronghold for pro tennis, Europe has taken the lead, holding more events, offering greater incentives.

Interestingly it was another non-tennis figure, Hamilton Jordan, who launched a revolution on behalf of the ATP as Dave Dixon had done in founding WCT. Taking over as chief executive of the ATP in 1988, Jordan, former chief of staff for President Jimmy Carter, performed a political tour de force in bringing all the men's tourneys (except the four majors) under the umbrella of the ATP Tour in 1990.

This maneuver destroyed the MIPTC and the Grand Prix structure, which had embraced and administered the men's game for almost two decades, and WCT as well. WCT, which had led the way into professionalization, operated its own circuit until absorbed by the Grand Prix. Never-

Britain, the U.S., France and Australia, raised extraordinary prize money for their "Grand Slams"—the majors: Wimbledon and the U.S., French and Australian Opens. Furthermore, in 1991 the ITF added to the usual confusion and overcrowded calendar by instituting the $6-million Grand Slam Cup, admitting the top finishers in those four tourneys, as the season's closing event. The obvious attempt was to upstage the ATP/Masters Championship by amassing a substantially richer purse.

Considerably more orderly have been the women. Their tour, generally much easier to follow, has been underwritten by several sponsors over the years, but climaxes with the Virginia Slims Championships in New York's Madison Square Garden. Since 1990, in cooperation with the ITF, the Kraft Tour has connected all the top-line events en route to the Virginia Slims Championships.

In 1974 an ill-starred venture called World Team Tennis began in the U.S., a league of city franchises comprising teams of men and women. Most of the leading women took part, and once more the crusader, Billie Jean King, was a driving force.

She was the player-coach of Philadelphia in 1974, another first: a woman in charge of a team containing [of] male professionals. As a player she led New York to the 1976–77 titles. General lack of television and spectator interest, coupled with unrealistically high payrolls, caused the league to fold after the 1978 season.

Unwilling to accept that defeat, the resilient King revived the concept under the banner of Team Tennis in 1981 and it continues today with a shorter summer schedule and lesser known players, although Jimmy Connors and Martina Navratilova played in 1991 and 1992 for Los Angeles and Atlanta, respectively.

The U.S. has led in all facets of the game's development, but tennis is truly universal and well received in tournament locations in more than 30 countries. Growth continues, and Forest Hills was finally outgrown after 63 years. In 1978 the U.S. Open was relocated a few miles away, in Flushing Meadow, where the U.S. National Tennis Center is the largest of all tennis playgrounds. The main court, Louis Armstrong Stadium, surrounded by 20,000 seats, enabled the Open to set a tournament attendance record of 520,868 in 1992. Construction of the center, shepherded by the USTA's resourceful president, W.E. "Slew" Hester, produced a third style in the evolution of the game: hard courts of asphalt base.

The championships, begun in the grass period in 1881, switched to clay in 1975 as tennis lawns vanished as an American tournament surface. For a while, clay was predominant on the summer circuit. But the paving of Flushing Meadow led to regrettable conformity and a stony greentopping of America. By 1988, Australia had gone the way of the U.S., forsaking God's own greensward for hard courts at the splendid new center for its Open, Flinders Park, with a retractable-roof stadium in Melbourne. Of course then the Aussie circuit's grass also gave way to the bulldozers and pavement.

Martina Navratilova at Wimbledon in 1991, where she has won the singles crown nine times.
• *Russ Adams*

The Grand Slam route, once three-quarters turf and, at Paris, one-quarter clay, was now more diverse. But more than 50 percent of professional tournaments are currently contested indoors on thin green or blue toupees—artificial plastic rugs—covering bare floors.

Whatever the surface and wherever it is played, will the game ever be at peace? Probably not, particularly with player agents behind the scenes, guiding the greed and cluttering the calendar with exhibitions and pseudo tournaments called "special events."

Despite all the conflict and obfuscation, I believe the comment of Hall of Famer Bill Talbert, onetime director of the U.S. Open: "Tennis will survive in spite of itself. It's too good a game not to."

—*Bud Collins*

1: Roots: 1874–1918

are shrouded in mystery, as are the name—tennis—and the scoring terms, passed down from real tennis to our game which is properly named lawn tennis. This much is clear: it began on an English lawn—and remains there for its most exalted occasion, Wimbledon.

Love? How can you take seriously anything in which love means nothing? Probably it derives from the French, l'oeuf: the old goose egg. The quartered face of a clock seems the likely source of the game, and point scores—15, 30—but why 40 instead of the original 45? Was it a cuckoo clock? Probably modified over time. Nobody really knows. Deuce is the clearest, from the French a deux.

"Tennis" itself? There are many theories which historian George Alexander discusses, and have appeared elsewhere before, not conclusively. George has his own idea, on "tens" from the German, different from all the rest, as will be seen.

Lawn tennis reached an early high point of national prestige during the presidency of Theodore Roosevelt (1901–09), who formed a "tennis cabinet." The players, headed by the vigorous president, were

match of "Teddy, the hero of San Juan Hill."

The ambassador was a serious player of both court tennis and lawn tennis and a student of the history of those games. Among the studies he undertook was the derivation of the English word "tennis." His was not the first search for the origin of the word, nor was it the last. Then, as now, the usual explanation was that "tennis" was derived from the French tendere meaning "to hold." The etymologists rationalized that the server called out tendere as a warning to his opponent just prior to serving. At first glance this has an authentic ring, for it carries the approval of scholars of repute. The problem was that it did not make sense to Jusserand.

Jusserand made an extensive study of old French literature and he found much shouting by players, mostly profane, but no one ever seemed to have called out tendere or anything like it. The several studies on the subject made before and since the French ambassador have come to the same findings.

In 1878 Julian Marshall in his monumental Annals of Tennis addresses the matter and he lists 10 spellings of tennis through the years, but he leaves the decision as to the origin of the word "tennis" to others, finding no answer that satisfied him.

Tennis historians E. B. Noel and A. E. Crawley wrote on the subject but they offered no additional information. In *Bailey's* magazine of August 1918, C.E Thomas offered a slightly more logical explanation. According to him, the derivation is from the French *Tenez*, meaning "take it." Again a call of warning from the server. No one has come forth with evidence of such ever being done, let alone ever having been the custom.

Tennis Origins and Mysteries by Malcolm Whitman, U.S. champion (1898–1900), devotes a chapter to the subject and covers most of the theories that have been put forth through the years by tennis players with an interest in etymology. Most of these theories have a common root in French words that have "ten" as the start of words meaning variously "hold," "taut," "tense," "tendon," and several other similar words. Another idea was that tennis like the name Tennyson was derived from Saint Denis.

Two towns, widely separated, one on the Nile River in Egypt, the other in Northern France, having "Tennis" as their name, are thought to be possible origins of the name. Tennis in France was known for its lace, Tennis in Egypt for its fine long staple cotton. Since balls were often cloth bound, some have thought that was connection enough.

Alexander offers a more logical derivation. First, why was a new name for the game necessary when it came to England (some evidence indicates it came earlier to Scotland)? The French name then and now is *jeu de paume* (hand ball). By the time it reached the British Isles (the date not known with certainty), implements such as battledores and forerunners of

rackets were replacing the hand. Some of the French was retained such as "deuce" and "love," so no strong aversion to French words existed. The game needed a name to differentiate the game of playing across a net from those played against a wall.

The root stem of "tens" has given us many words including those such as *tendere*, which is the often listed parent of "tennis." One of the meanings of "tens" is the "weaver's shuttle" and other to-and-fro motions. Whitman had previously come across this, but he chose not to pursue it and he dropped it short of the shuttle meaning.

The naming of the game with a descriptive word is more logical than one requiring a tortured explanation. The logic of naming the game after some "shout" or ball material would have us call golf "fore" and the games of football "pigskin" and baseball "horsehide." The back-and-forth motion further lent its name to the missile that we know as the shuttlecock in badminton.

While the explanation may satisfy a few, more evidence is needed to support the theory, even though none has been offered to support the usually accepted *tendere*. It is like the unauthenticated story of Mary Outerbridge introducing the game to the U.S.: Once in place and repeated a few times, it takes on the position of presumed fact.

But this is part of the intrigue of tennis. We aren't quite sure of the origin and meanings of many aspects—even the name.

Even though the beginnings of tennis and many other sports and games are unknown and lost in the distant past, the history of modern (lawn) tennis is clearly documented. Its arrival was publicly announced on March 7, 1874, in two papers, the *Court Journal*, read by almost all of the British upper class as well as those

Major Walter Clopton Wingfield pioneered the game. • *Fischer Collection/SPS*

French and Co., 46, Churton Street, London, S.W. The price: five guineas.

Sales literature noted that "the game is in a painted box, 36 x 12 x 6 inches and contains poles, pegs, and netting for forming the court, 4 tennis bats, by Jeffries and Mallings, a bag of balls, mallet, and brush and *The Book of the Game.*"

The daily sales book for almost a year

agriculturist Ward Hunt, First Lord of the Admiralty, renowned for his girth which caused a semicircle to be cut from the Admiralty board table.

The records of French and Co. are not the complete list, for many sales went to unnamed parties and the company did much wholesale business with several London retailers and, as so often happens, competing sets were soon on the market despite patent protection.

There were several reasons for this great and widespread success. There was a need for a game which afforded vigorous exercise for both sexes and all ages. That was how Wingfield described his new game. Croquet had been the fad during the 1860s and it inspired the construction of many well-rolled, level courts with close-clipped grass. The least standard croquet court measured 30 yards by 20 yards. Such courts were ubiquitous and were ready-made for lawn tennis, and "The ground need not even be turf; the only condition is that it must be level."

This was not today's marvelous game, for it was quite simple. It used the scoring of 1,2,3 etc. of the game of rackets, but it

who aspired to join, and the *Army & Navy Gazette*, read by the military, which was stationed worldwide; for then the sun truly never set on the vast British Empire.

These notices followed the British patent office issuing Major Walter Wingfield provisional letters of patent (No. 685) for "A Portable Court of Playing Tennis" dated Feb. 23, 1874. English-speaking sportsmen around the world who read *The Field* of March 21, 1874 were informed in detail of the new game, for it reproduced much of *The Major's Game of Lawn Tennis*. It contained a short history of tennis, instruction and notes for the "erection of the court," and the six rules of the game.

The game was an immediate success and spread throughout Great Britain and Ireland in a matter of weeks and around the English-speaking world soon thereafter. The necessary equipment to play was sold by the inventor's agents, Messrs.

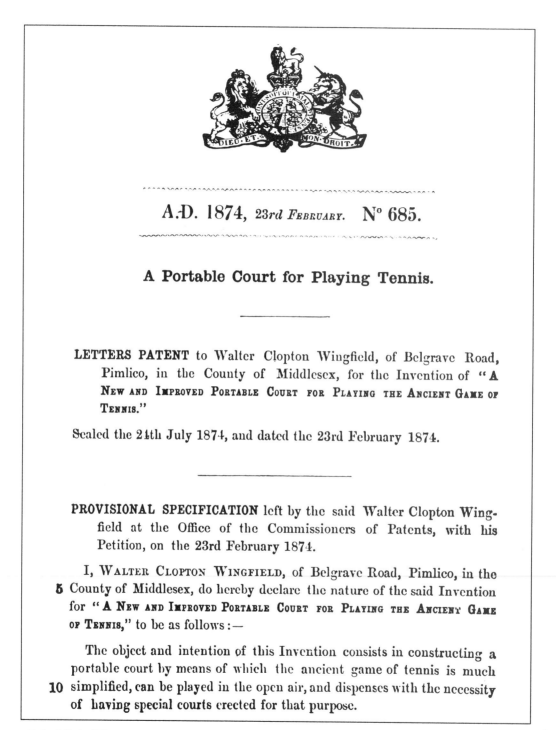

A·D. 1874, *23rd February.* N° 685.

A Portable Court for Playing Tennis.

LETTERS PATENT to Walter Clopton Wingfield, of Belgrave Road, Pimlico, in the County of Middlesex, for the Invention of "A NEW AND IMPROVED PORTABLE COURT FOR PLAYING THE ANCIENT GAME OF TENNIS."

Sealed the 24th July 1874, and dated the 23rd February 1874.

PROVISIONAL SPECIFICATION left by the said Walter Clopton Wingfield at the Office of the Commissioners of Patents, with his Petition, on the 23rd February 1874.

I, WALTER CLOPTON WINGFIELD, of Belgrave Road, Pimlico, in the
5 County of Middlesex, do hereby declare the nature of the said Invention for "A NEW AND IMPROVED PORTABLE COURT FOR PLAYING THE ANCIENT GAME OF TENNIS," to be as follows :—

The object and intention of this Invention consists in constructing a portable court by means of which the ancient game of tennis is much
10 simplified, can be played in the open air, and dispenses with the necessity of having special courts erected for that purpose.

bore the more refined name "tennis" rather than "rackets," which was associated with taverns and prisons. The game could also be played without buying the set, for items were sold separately. Rackets were 15 shillings, balls were 5 shillings a dozen, and *The Book of the Game* was 6 pence. People with rackets of other sports could easily try out the new game at little or no expense.

edged by Wingfield, as even the title of his patent and the game indicate.

Outdoor racket, ball and net play go back to the time of Queen Elizabeth I. Earlier in England and France, a game called long tennis (*longue paume*) was played, and it is still played in France. The other previous such games, at best neighborhood games, were without formal rules and they never traveled, soon dying out. The name Harry Gem is associated with just such a game. He wrote in *The Field* of Nov. 28, 1874: "He (J.B. Perera) first introduced the game fifteen years ago, and it recently has received the name of Pelota ..." After (lawn) tennis arrived, Gem wrote rules for "Pelota," which he sent to *The Field* and to his club, the Leamington Club, which added "Lawn Tennis" to it name.

Wingfield wrote to Gem in the fall of 1874 that he had worked on the game for a year and a half. After Wingfield's death an acquaintance wrote that Wingfield's thoughts of a game went back to his service in India. He wrote in *The Book of the Game* that the game was "tested practically at several country houses during the past few months."

Since all five editions of the book are "dedicated to the party assembled at Nantclwyd [in Wales] in December 1873," it has been assumed that was where it was introduced. There is no evidence that it was, for that party was a housewarming given by the new owner of the estate Nantclwyd, Major Naylor-Leyland, for his friends in the area. It featured the presentation of two plays and a grand ball. The

family, would be one of the test sites. It is more likely a test site than Wingfield's own Rhysnant Hall, which was at that time leased. The one country house which has a written record as a test site is Earnshill in Somerset. In May 1881, Wingfield's first cousin, R.T. Combe of Earnshill, wrote to the *Daily Telegraph,* "It is now some seven or eight years since Major Wingfield first put up a lawn tennis court here."

Several other places have been put forth as being sites of early play but confirming evidence is lacking. The first public exhibition occurred the Saturday following *The Field* announcement of May 4, 1874, which read in part, "It (lawn tennis) may be seen and played next week, on and after the opening of the Princes Cricket Ground, and also at the Polo Club, Lillie-bridge."

In the *Whitehall Review* (Nov. 14, 1896), Wingfield's good friend, Clement Scott, wrote in his column, "Wheel of Life," that the exhibition was in 1869. Such is an example how fallible the human memory is and how important "the palest ink" is to true history.

The closing of the Haymarket court tennis courts and the outdoor racket courts at taverns in several neighborhoods undoubtedly caused Wingfield to bring forth the new game. It was also helped by the development of the thin-wall rubber ball in Germany.

Besides private homes with croquet lawns becoming places to play tennis, it immediately became a game played at public parks and other common lawns and the great clubs. Among the London clubs to take up the sport quickly were M.C.C.— The Marylebone Cricket Club (Lords)— Hurlingham Club and Princes Club, as well as many others throughout the land. A club that waited until 1875 to accept a rival sport was the then five-year-old All England Croquet Club, which was located off Worple Road in the London suburb, Wimbledon.

Henry Jones, the editor of the Pastimes section of *The Field,* which covered card games, Jones' forte, as well as lawn tennis, was a founder, along with his publisher, John Walsh, of the All England Croquet Club. Jones introduced lawn tennis to the club. He wrote under the *nom de plume* of "Cavendish." Jones and Walsh were both doctors who had given up the practice of medicine to pursue their greater love, games and sports. Jones earned Wingfield's enmity by presuming to take over his game. It was Jones' nature to assume he had greater knowledge of all matters concerning games, and this included lawn tennis.

To Wingfield the remarkable success of the game was evidence of the rightness of it, and that you should not change a winning game. However, in the fall of 1874 he issued a second edition of *The Book of the Game.* There were now twelve rules and a larger court, and it also made more use of the alternate name of *Sphairistike,* Greek for ball games. These changes and complications could be added, for now the game had taken root. By that time some confusion existed, at least on the pages of *The Field* because Perera's game, pelota, and a

rival game, Germains Lawn Tennis, by J.H. Hale, with Jones' help, had been put forth. In reality nothing came of either; they were more complicated with no added redeeming features.

Through the winter, there was continued confusion. J.M. Heathcote, who with his wife had introduced the Melton cloth-covered ball, wrote to Fitzgerald, secretary of M.C.C., suggesting a meeting of the factions. With the cooperation of Wingfield, the other interested parties agreed to a general meeting with the M.C.C.'s rules committee to establish rules for lawn tennis as they recently had done for court tennis. This was done and the rules were announced in *The Field* of May 1875. There were now 25 rules and they appeared in subsequent editions of Wingfield's book.

Before the M.C.C. rules came out on May 2, 1875, Wingfield wrote Fitzgerald that he would execute any legal document "for the public good," canceling "en masse" his rules. A similar letter appeared in *The Field* a week after *The Field* published the M.C.C. rules. With the letter agreeing to the M.C.C. rules, Wingfield withdrew from the tennis scene.

In the spring of 1877 under the leadership of Henry Jones, the All England Club decided to hold a tennis tournament. *The Field* carried the announcement and a call for competitors and the promise "if entries are sufficiently numerous, prizes: Gold Champion Prize and the Silver Prize.... Also a Silver Challenge Cup, value 25 guineas ...."

The tournament committee worried about infringing on Wingfield's patent. This was unnecessary, for Wingfield had allowed his patent to expire on Feb. 23, 1877, the patent's third anniversary, by not paying the £50 fee to extend the patent seven years. It was public information, being published in the *Official Journal (Patents).* This was to the game's long-term benefit for it caused new rules to be drawn.

The hourglass court, as illustrated in Major Wingfield's book. • *Fischer Collection/SPS*

These were written by a committee of Jones, Julian Marshall and C.G. Heathcote. They established much of our present game. The tournament—the original Wimbledon—was a success. There were 22 entries. Spencer Gore, a rackets player, beat W.C. Marshall, a court tennis player, in the final, 6–1, 6–2, 6–4.

The new rules used tennis scoring and a rectangular court (78 x 27 feet), abandoning Wingfield's hourglass shape with baselines wider than the net and tapering to the net posts. The service lines were 26 feet from the net and the 33-foot wide net extended 3 feet on each side and was 5 feet on each side, 5 feet at the posts and 3½ feet at the center.

The championships became an annual fixture with Jones as referee. For several years he adjusted the net height and the service line according to the total of points won and lost on service until 1882, when the net heights arrived at today's 3½ feet at the posts and 3 feet at center with the service line at 21. The rules then became essentially today's rules except for two rules which were troublesome for several years. The changing-of-ends rule went through many alterations until the simple and fair changing sides after each odd game of each set was established in the rules of 1890. Foot-faulting has been more difficult to control and may still be further changed. Through the years the policy has been to make legal the past infringements, only to have the aggressive servers take that and a little more.

In the matter of tournament control two improvements were brought forth. R.B. Bagnal-Wild of Bath in 1883 proposed the present system of having byes in the first round so as to have the number of remaining players be of a power of two. This prevented three players arriving in the semifinals as happened in the first Wimbledon. This was accepted for the 1885 Championships. The other improvement took longer. In 1883 C.L. Dodgson, a mathematician who wrote under the name of Lewis Carroll (*Alice in Wonderland*), wrote a pamphlet, *Lawn Tennis Tournaments*—"The true method of assigning prizes, with proof of the fallacy of the present method." It was seeding that he envisioned, but he died before it was first permitted in the 1922 tournament.

In 1880 a Northern Lawn Tennis Association (of England) was founded and in 1883 the formation of a Lawn Tennis Association was attempted, but it failed for want of All England Club cooperation. The All England Club became the premier organization in tennis, supplanting the M.C.C. in those matters, and has remained a powerful tennis body, as witness its ability to lead the world to open tennis. The game owes much to the M.C.C. for its guidance and lending its name and prestige to the infant tennis during its early critical years.

On the courts, tennis made great strides in the 1880s. This progress in the level of play was led by the Renshaw twins. They had grown up with the game and were not handicapped with styles formed for rackets or court tennis. Willie Renshaw won the Wimbledon championships of 1881 through 1886 and 1889. Ernest won in 1888. Herbert Lawford won in 1887 when Willie did not defend his title. The Renshaws also dominated the doubles, winning in 1880–81–84–85–86–88–89.

Doubles was introduced in 1879 and ladies' singles made the scene in 1884. Ladies' doubles and mixed doubles began in 1913. The draws were small, only 16 players in 1887 for the men's tournament and six ladies in 1888. Attendance grew from 200 in 1877 to 3,500 in 1885. This growth of tennis ended in 1890 with interest switching to bicycle activities which were much enhanced by the invention of the modern bicycle. The 90s were also a time of recession in the business world.

With the cooperation of the A.E.C. (All England Club) the L.T.A. (Lawn Tennis Association) was formed in 1888. It was agreed the A.E.C. and the L.T.A. would share the funds raised by the Championships. However, the fall of popularity of tennis brought small draws and reduced attendance. The tournament of 1895 had a £35 loss. By the turn of the century tennis regained its popularity and went on to greater crowds and more players.

It was natural that tennis would come quickly to North America for there were close relationships, both social and commercial, with the motherland. British periodicals, including *The Field,* came to many in the United States and Canada. The date the first set arrived is not known but its arrival was inevitable. The earliest found recorded play is Oct. 8, 1874 in the then remote Camp Apache, Arizona Territory, north of Tucson.

In Martha Summerhayes' book, *Vanished Arizona,* she reports tennis being played by an Army officer's wife, Ella Wilkins Bailey. The date is confirmed by her husband's records. The trip to Apache

called "Nationals" at Staten Island Cricket and Baseball Club. Dwight's questioning of the balls used as not being proper was turned aside by the tournament officials by showing the "Regulation" marked on each ball.

That unsatisfactory tourney caused the formation of the U.S. National Lawn Tennis Association in 1881. It was the first

dently at several places: Boston, Newport, New York and Philadelphia as well as New Orleans and San Francisco. The game did not spread from only one center.

While both Miss Mary Outerbridge of Staten Island, N.Y., and Dr. James Dwight of Boston have their adherents as "the introducer" of the game to the United States, there is no clear-cut certainty for either. It is certain that neither was trying to be first, and made no claim to that effect. However, leadership of the game in the U.S. clearly fell to Dr. Dwight, who became known as "the father of American lawn tennis."

He may also have been a "first" player, but regardless he was associated with almost all important tennis events during the first quarter-century of tennis in the United States. Dr. Dwight, while summering at Nahant, Mass., outside of Boston, organized a tournament in 1876. With his cousin, Fred Sears, he held a formal and handicapped round-robin tournament for 15 entries, Dwight beating Sears in the final.

In 1878 the Nahant tournament used the A.E.C. rules. In 1880 Dr. Dwight and cousin Richard Sears played in the so-

tion, the first national tournament was held at Newport and a 19-year-old Harvard student, Dick Sears, another Dwight cousin, was the winner, retaining the title through 1887. The "other guy" in that original final was an Englishman, William E. Glyn, who was 20 or 21, summered at Newport, and has pretty much been lost in history, not even being accorded celebrity as the first flop. Did he choke?

In the 1881 doubles, Sears and Dwight were surprised losers in the third round to Philadelphia's team of Clarence Clark and Fred Taylor, who went on to win the championship. Sears and Dwight won the doubles five of the next six years. In 1883, following matches between Dwight and Sears versus the winning Clark brothers— Clarence and Joe—the Clarks went off to England. There in exhibition they lost to the Renshaws 6–4, 8–6, 3–6, 6–1, and a week later the Renshaws won in straight sets.

Later that year, following the U.S. Championships, Dr. Dwight went over and spent the fall, winter and spring competing against the best English players, including the Renshaws, playing indoors at Maida Vale and outdoors at Cannes. In 1885 he lost in the Wimbledon semifinals to Herbert Lawford in straight sets. As the most successful of the first Americans to play Wimbledon in 1884, Dwight was beaten in the second round of singles, 6–1, 2–6, 6–3, 3–6, 7–5, by Herbert Chipp. Dick Sears, kept out of the singles by injury, then joined him to reach the doubles semifinals where they lost to the champion Renshaws, 6–0, 6–1, 6–2.

Dwight won the Northern England Championship in 1884, and with Willie Renshaw the 1885 Buxton doubles Tournament. During these years he ranked just below the very best of England. He was much respected and through his instructional articles and two books, *Lawn Tennis* in 1886 and *Practical Lawn Tennis* in 1893, did much for the level of play in the U.S. His books were the standard instruction until 1920 when Bill Tilden's *The Art of Lawn Tennis* was published. The 1890s found tennis losing players to both the bicycle and to the newly arrived game of golf. Dwight saw the game and the USNLTA through those lean years. It was through his contacts with English players that the Davis Cup was launched in 1900, for which he drew up the rules. This helped restore the game to popularity.

As the 20th century came, tennis had weathered its first recession and had come back stronger than ever. It would not be the last time the sports taste of some would stray to the newest fad. But a faithful band of lovers of this exquisitely fair and always challenging game of a lifetime would remain true and preserve their love for those who once strayed later to return once again. The game was firmly attached to sportsmen and sportswomen in all the English-speaking countries and making inroads throughout the rest of the world.

By 1900 all the strokes, tactics and strategies had become part of the game. The Renshaws brought the net game, Lawford topspin, and Holcombe Ward and Dwight Davis the American twist serve

(kicker). All these have been improved, but a few, like the reverse twist serve are no longer used.

Then as now most of the play took place on the public courts. This is not to gainsay the importance of the great tennis clubs. In the mid-1880s Prospect Park in Brooklyn, N.Y., had over 100 clubs using its facilities. Sports clubs have often been targets as havens of snobs and bigots. Clubs, as other groups of people, have their share, but they have done much good for tennis and other sports. They established standards of play, deportment, and facilities which elevated the game everywhere. Almost all the greats of the game have started on the public courts, but they refined their games at clubs and colleges.

The year of that seminal tournament at Nahant, 1876, with Dr. Dwight free-forming the format and rules, was also that of the founding of the first tennis club in the U.S., the New Orleans Lawn Tennis Club.

Founded in 1877, Boston's Longwood Cricket Club, then situated near Fenway Park at the corner of Brookline and Longwood Avenues, adopted lawn tennis in 1878. An older institution, the Merion Cricket Club, in Philadelphia, which was founded in 1865, took up the new game in 1879. In that year a concrete court, making the name "lawn tennis" less than descriptive, was built in Santa Monica, Cal. The Orange Lawn Tennis Club in New Jersey had its beginnings in 1880.

The inaugural Wimbledon embraced only one event, the men's singles. An entry of 22 was received, and on Monday, July 9, 1877, a fine, sunny day, The Lawn Tennis Championships began. One entrant, C. F. Buller, was absent, so there were only 10 instead of the expected 11 matches.

The 11 survivors were reduced to six on Tuesday, then to three on Wednesday. The notion of restricting byes to the first round was still eight years off. On

The Longwood Cricket Club had lawn tennis as early as 1878 at its original site in Boston. • *Fischer Collection/SPS*

Thursday William Marshall had a free passage into the final while Spencer W. Gore beat C.G. Heathcote, 6–2, 6–5, 6–2. Advantage sets had been adopted but only for the final.

The title match was held over until the following Monday. Such delay had been indicated in the prospectus to allow for the Eton and Harrow cricket match at Lords. This was the ultimate sporting event so far as the fashionable London world was concerned, and lawn tennis, itself a fashionable sport, did not dream for many years of coming into conflict with that important fixture.

Monday turned out wet, and the final was postponed until Thursday, July 19. That day was also damp, but rather than disappoint 200 spectators, each of whom had paid one shilling (then about 25 cents) to see Wimbledon's baptismal final, Gore and Marshall sportingly agreed to play. Gore, came up to the net and volleyed. Whether this was entirely sporting was a matter of some debate, as was his striking the ball before it had crossed the net. He won, 6–1, 6–2, 6–4.

Gore, an old Harrovian of 27, had played rackets at school and was a keen cricketer. He did not think much of the new game. He defended his title the next year, losing in the challenge round to Frank Hadow, another old Harrovian on leave from coffee planting in Ceylon, who circumvented the volleyer by lobbing. Gore later wrote:

"That anyone who has really played well at cricket, tennis, or even rackets, will ever seriously give his attention to lawn tennis, beyond showing himself to be a promising player, is extremely doubtful; for in all probability the monotony of the game as compared with the others would choke him off before he had time to excel at it."

Those were the views of the world's first champion. Gore died in 1906, still a keen cricketer.

Competing in 1878 was a former Cambridge court tennis player, A. T. Myers. He was an innovator. He served overhead. Yet it is clear that at the time there was more of the vicarage lawn than athleticism about the infant game. In 1879 the Wimbledon champion was in fact a vicar. He was the Reverend John Hartley, yet another old Harrovian. He kept his title in 1880, and his ability to go on returning the ball was notorious.

In 1881 the game took on a new dimension. Two wealthy young twins from Cheltenham, in the west of England, initiated a dominance that endured for nearly a decade. They were Willie and Ernest Renshaw. In that year Willie won the first of his seven singles titles at Wimbledon. In the final he beat Hartley, 6–0, 6–1, 6–1, in an extraordinarily brief and devastating 37 minutes.

Its brevity is partly explained by the fact that at that time players changed ends only after each set. It is also explained by the difference in style. Hartley was a gentle retriever. Renshaw served hard, volleyed hard, smashed hard and went for fast winners all round. He and Ernest created modern lawn tennis. Crowds flocked to see them play.

The Scottish Championships in Edinburgh was inaugurated in 1878. The Irish Championships in Dublin began in 1879 and was notable for initiating a women's singles as well as a mixed-doubles event. The women's events, however, were restricted in some degree. While the main part of the tournament was played on courts prepared in Fitzwilliam Square and open to the public, the women were confined to the relative privacy of the Fitzwilliam Club itself. Only members and their guests were permitted the sight of

well-turned ankles on display. The first woman champion of the world was 14-year-old May Langrishe.

The men's singles champion in the first Irish Championships was V. St. Leger Goold. In the same year he became finalist in the all-comers' singles at Wimbledon, losing to the gentle Hartley. Many years later Goold wrote a unique chapter for himself in the history of the game by being convicted of murder by a French court and getting sent to Devil's Island, where he died.

A "Championship of America" was staged in 1880. It began on Sept. 1 on the courts at the Staten Island (N.Y.). Cricket and Baseball Club. The prize was a silver cup valued at $100. Rackets scoring was used, with the results turning on the aggregate number of aces.

An Englishman, O.E. Woodhouse, wrote from Chicago asking if he could enter. He was a member of the West Middlesex Club, Ealing, England. He had played that year in the Wimbledon Championships and reached the all-comers' final before losing to Herbert Lawford. Woodhouse's overhead service was a novelty to American players. With this advantage he reached the final, where he beat a Canadian, J. F. Helmuth, 15–11, 14–15, 15–9, 10–15, victory based on a score of 54 points to 50.

In October 1880 there was a tournament played in Beacon Park, Boston. The winner was Dick Sears. Tennis scoring was used. The nonstandardization of the game, both in its equipment and scoring, brought increasing difficulties as it grew. There was controversy about the correct way to play lawn tennis.

With the need for standardization in mind, a meeting was arranged at the Fifth Avenue Hotel in New York on May 21, 1881, in the name of three prominent clubs: the Beacon Park Athletic Association of Boston, the Staten Island Cricket and

Baseball Club of New York, and the All Philadelphia Lawn Tennis Committee.

There were 33 clubs represented, and the U.S. National Lawn Tennis Association, as it was then named, came into being. A constitution was drawn up. The rules of the All England Club and the M.C.C. were adopted. R. S. Oliver of the Albany Lawn Tennis Club was elected president, and

gurate the National Championships of the United States, men's singles and men's doubles. As a venue it settled on the Newport Casino, Newport, R.I., probably without equal at that time as the resort of wealth and fashion.

It began on August 31, 1881, with a singles entry of 26. Except for the final, the best of three sets, not of five, was played. Dick Sears won without losing a set. He was 19 years, 10 months, and the first U.S. champion would have a remarkable career. He won seven times in all, playing through in both 1882 and 1883 without losing a set. In 1884 the challenge round was instituted, and in the title match Sears yielded a set for the first time, to Howard Taylor. After three further victories he did not defend in 1888. Sears' singular singles record: matches played, 18; matches won, 18. From 1882 through 1887 he also won the doubles six times—five with James Dwight and once with Joseph Clark.

Sears learned to volley in 1881, the same time that the Renshaw twins were introducing their arts of aggression in England. They did so independently of each other.

In 1884 the Wimbledon meeting was enlarged to include a women's singles and a men's doubles. The doubles cups were passed on from the tournament, which had been staged, albeit with failing interest, at Oxford since 1879 and where originally the distance was over the best of seven sets.

The other new Wimbledon event, the women's singles, was staged at the same

The losing semifinalist to Watson, Blanche Bingley (later Mrs. George Hillyard), became one of the most indefatigable champions of all time. She won the singles six times between 1886 and 1900 and played for the last time in 1913 when she was 49 years old.

Before winning at Wimbledon in 1884, Watson beat the first woman champion in the world, May Langrishe, the Irish winner of 1879, in Dublin. There was coincidence in the deaths of the two women players, who have enduring fame as pioneer champions. Langrishe died at a house called "Hammersmead" in Charmouth, a small seaside resort in Devonshire, England, in 1939. Seven years later Watson died in the same house.

The women, recognized first by the Irish in 1879, made their early efforts in England and Ireland in concert with the men. In the U.S. the women came forward independently, at least in the beginning.

In 1887 the first U.S. women's championship, held at the Philadelphia Cricket Club, was an outgrowth of the first (1886) Chestnut Hill Tennis Club Ladies Open. The second "open" became the first U.S. Championship when the Wissahickon Inn offered the Wissahickon Cup as the singles prize. Arrangements for the 1886–87 tournaments were conducted by the Chestnut Hill T.C., and play was at the Philadelphia C.C., leased for the occasion. In 1888 the Cricket Club took over sponsorship of the national championship, and continued until the 1921 move to Forest Hills.

Seven women entered the singles in 1887, all from the greater Delaware Valley area, and the champ, Ellen Hansell, a 6–1, 6–0, victor over Laura Knight, represented Philadelphia's Belmont Cricket Club. The 1888 tourney included New Yorkers Adeline Robinson and the Roosevelt sisters, Ellen and Grace, but was won by another Philadelphian from the Belmont Club, Bertha Townsend, over Hansell, 6–3, 6–5, in the challenge round.

On February 9, 1889,, the USNLTA carried a motion that "its protection be extended to the Lady Lawn Tennis players of the country."

Ireland's Mabel Cahill won in 1892 and again one year later. She beat Elisabeth Moore in 1891, 5–7, 6–3, 6–4, 4–6, 6–2. For eight of the next nine years the women played the best of five sets, but only in the all-comers finals and challenge rounds. It was not unknown in Britain, though the women at Wimbledon at no time competed over such a distance.

The growth of lawn tennis round the world was fast. Clubs were founded in Scotland, Brazil and India in 1875. It was played in Germany in 1876. In 1877 the Fitzwilliam Club was started in Dublin, Ireland, and the Decimal Club was the first in France, in Paris. Australia, Sweden, Italy, Hungary and Peru had lawn tennis courts in 1878, and the first tournament in Australia was the Victorian Championship meeting in 1879. Denmark and Switzerland date their beginnings from 1880, Argentina from 1881. The first club in the Netherlands was in 1882; in Jamaica

in 1883; and in 1885 in both Greece and Turkey. Lawn tennis came to Lebanon in 1889, to Egypt in 1890 and to Finland in the same year. South Africa's first championship was staged in 1891.

After the successful intervention of Britain's O.E. Woodhouse, in the unofficial American championship of 1880, an Irishman, J.J. Cairnes, was refused entry to the 1881 Championships at Newport. But he was permitted to play in the Ladies Cup tourney there immediately afterwards, and Cairnes, a semifinalist in the initial Irish Championships of 1879, won the event easily, beating the newly crowned U.S. champ, Dick Sears, in the final.

In 1889 E. G. Meers, who was one of the top British players, was the first overseas challenger in the Nationals at Newport. He lost in five sets to Oliver Campbell, 18. The following year Campbell became champion for the first time and, at the age of 19½, was the youngest to do so until Pete Sampras, 19 years, 1 month, won in 1990.

It was evidently a time that favored youth. One year later, in 1891, Wilfred Baddeley won the men's singles championship at Wimbledon at 19 years, 6 months, a record lowered by 17-year-old Boris Becker in 1985.

A "pro tour" of sorts even took brief form in 1889. George Kerr, billed as the Irish professional champ, came to the U.S. to battle Tom Pettit of Boston, the teaching pro at Newport Casino and regarded as the New World's leading professional. They played at Springfield, Mass., Boston and Newport, and Kerr was the victor in three of four matches.

Manliffe Goodbody, one of the many Irishmen prominent in the game in the British Isles, gained notable success at Newport in 1893. He beat Clarence Hobart and Bill Larned, both players of championship ilk, and failed only in the challenge round, to Robert Wrenn.

In 1895 what almost amounted to a representative contest between the Americans and the British took the form of a round-robin tournament at the Neighborhood Club, West Newton, Mass. The British were from Ireland, Joshua Pim, the Wimbledon champion of 1893 and 1894,

The British challenge at Newport in 1897 was formidable, comprising Mahony, Harold Nisbet and Wilberforce Eaves, who was Australian-born but living in England. The British spectators, if there were any among the wealthy and fashionable who came to the Newport Casino, must have held their heads high. Eaves and Nisbet made an all-British final in the all-comers' singles. Eaves was the winner and challenged Wrenn. American pride was restored. Wrenn won in five sets as he took the title for the fourth time. It was the second occasion he had to thwart a cross-Atlantic challenge.

Anglo-American rivalry was channeled into a team instead of an individual exercise in 1900. Dwight Davis put up his famous Davis Cup for competition in that year. He had been inspired 12 months earlier by a tennis-playing tour he undertook with Holcombe Ward, Malcolm Whitman and Beals Wright, all keen players in their early 20s. Accompanied by George Wright, the father of Beals, they traveled some 8,000 miles, from the Atlantic Coast to the Pacific and up to British Columbia.

The USNLTA accepted Davis' offer and the International Lawn Tennis

Dwight Davis (right), donor of the Davis Cup in 1900, won the U.S. Doubles Championship with Holcombe Ward in 1899, 1900 and 1901.
• *Fischer Collection/SPS*

Challenge Trophy was offered to the world. They had the British primarily in mind and the British, despite the Boer War then taking place in South Africa, took up the challenge.

Davis was named as the U.S. captain for the inaugural. He was then 21 and had reached the all-comers' singles final at Newport in 1899. Whitman, 23, the champion of 1898, and Ward, 22, doubles partner of Davis, were the other members, Harvard men all. The venue chosen was the Longwood Cricket Club, still at its original Boston site, and the matches were arranged for early August, well before the Newport meeting at the end of the month.

The British team comprised Arthur Gore, Ernest Black and H. Roper Barrett. The 32-year-old Gore still had a lot of tennis life in him and had not yet won any of his three Wimbledon singles titles. The Scot,

Black, did not achieve the distinction of reaching the last eight at Wimbledon. Barrett was noted as a player of subtle abilities. It was not the best British team—the preeminent Doherty brothers were unavailable—since it was selected not only on playing ability but also on a capacity to spare both the time and the money for the trip.

After the British arrived in New York, they took the opportunity to pay a visit to Niagara Falls and eventually turned up at the Longwood Club in the best of spirits, though without having had much practice.

They found the courts too soft and the balls not hard enough either. They also found they had underestimated American playing skill. The American twist service, particularly that of Holcombe Ward, confounded them utterly.

The first two singles were played side by side on adjoining courts. Whitman beat Gore in three easy sets. Davis beat Black after losing the opening set. Black and Barrett could not take a set in the doubles against Ward and Davis the following day. On the last day Davis was one set up and 9–9 each in the second against Gore when it rained and further play was abandoned. The U.S. had won by a mile.

Later, by the sea at Newport, Gore and Black made an effort to retrieve British honor. They clashed in the quarterfinals and Gore survived, only to lose to George Wrenn in the next round. Whitman revealed the temper of his steel. He thrust back the challenge of Larned to keep his title.

Anglo-American rivalry continued to be the international aspect of tennis for some years. There was no challenge for the Davis Cup in 1901, but in 1902 the British renewed their effort, sending Reggie and Laurie Doherty, the finest British players of the time, with Joshua Pim. They played against Whitman, Davis and Larned at the Crescent Athletic Club in Brooklyn, N.Y. As in 1900 the two singles were played at the same time on adjacent courts. Fearful of Laurie's fitness, the British played Pim with Reggie Doherty in the singles. The doubles was scheduled to take place on the third day. By that time it was over, for Pim lost both his singles and Reggie was beaten by Whitman. The British plan to reserve Laurie's strength for the doubles had lost its point.

The classic powers of the Dohertys, which had captivated the crowds at Wimbledon and elsewhere in Britain, were again displayed to American audiences later in the month at Newport. The brothers reached the semifinals and should have played one another. Laurie gave a walkover to his elder brother and Reggie went on to beat Whitman in the final. Reggie, though he had beaten Larned in the singles in the Davis Cup, could not repeat his success when the U.S. title was at stake.

The year 1903 was a turning point and the British challenge in the United States was as effective as it was formidable. In the Davis Cup, where the British Isles were again the only challengers, the venue was again Longwood in Boston. Reggie and Laurie Doherty were put forward as a two-man side and made a gambling start, giving a match away. Because Reggie was the weaker physically and feeling unwell, the Brit defaulted his opening singles to Larned while Laurie beat Robert Wrenn. Then providence butted in—two days of rain. Reggie felt better, accompanying his brother to doubles victory over the brothers Wrenn, Robert and George, and finished up the next day by beating Robert Wrenn as Laurie stopped Larned to make it, 4–1, and the Cup left the U.S. for the first time.

The Doherty brothers achieved something more. In the Nationals at Newport they were again cast against one another in the quarterfinals. This time Laurie was given the walkover. He went on to reach the challenge round, where he dispossessed Larned of his title, 6–0, 6–3, 10–8, rather more easily achieved than his win in the Davis Cup, where his measure had been 7–5 in the fifth set.

Laurie Doherty, the first man to take the U.S. National Championship in singles overseas, was then 27 and perhaps at his peak. Reggie, three years older, won the Wimbledon singles.

equally so for Wimbledon. An American woman had entered for the first time in 1900. Marion Jones, then the U.S. champion, got as far as the quarterfinals. Five years later a chubby, robust 18-year-old from California with an intimidating forehand made a memorable appearance. She was May Sutton and she, too, was the American title-holder. She was, as it happened, English-born, having seen the light

If 1903 was a momentous year for the U.S. Championships, that of 1905 was

championships when only 15 years old, the youngest ever to win a major. There was

The British-born May Sutton, the first American to win at Wimbledon, in 1905 and again in 1907, won the U.S. Singles in 1904. • *Fischer Collection/SPS*

Blanche Hillyard, six times the champion. Dorothea Douglass (later Mrs. Lambert Chambers) had, when the uninhibited Sutton appeared, already won twice and was on the way to making herself a legend.

Sutton carved through all opposition and had the temerity to stop Douglass from winning for the third time. Sutton was the first overseas player to take a Wimbledon championship. This was in a year of the biggest invasion to date, for in 1905 there were among the men five Americans, two New Zealanders, three Australians, three Belgians, two Danes and a South African.

Tennis was in fact assuming an international role. The Davis Cup in 1905 enlarged to six nations. With the British Isles as holders, Belgium and France had challenged in 1904. So did Austria, only to withdraw before taking the court. The

United States, in the position of challenger for the first time, did not then do so, for the difficulties of finding a team to cross the Atlantic proved overwhelming.

But in 1905 teams from the U.S., France, Austria and Australasia converged on London. Belgium should have done so but in the event conceded a walkover to the U.S. At Queens Club in July, after the Wimbledon meeting was finished, the four nations played a knock-out competition to decide the best fitted to challenge the British Isles for the trophy. The U.S. beat France, 5–0. Australasia beat Austria, 5–0. The U.S. then beat Australasia, 5–0. In the challenge round the Doherty brothers and Sid Smith beat the U.S. —Larned, Ward, Beals Wright—5–0. It all took place in 12 days, July 13–24.

The Australasian side (until 1924 New Zealand and Australia functioned as a sin-

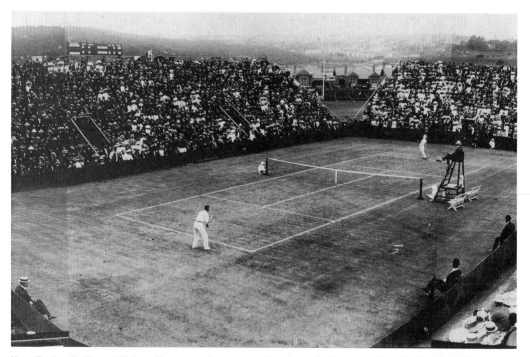

New Zealand's Tony Wilding (foreground), representing Australasia, vanquishes England's M.H. Long in 1909 Davis Cup play at Sydney, Australia. • *Fischer Collection/SPS*

gle entity for tennis) included Norman Brookes and Tony Wilding. Each was to impress himself deeply in the history of the game. New Zealand's Wilding combined athletic skill, good looks, and a personality that made him a teen-age idol.

In 1907 the men's singles at Wimbledon was won by Brookes. He was one of the world's all-time great volleyers, a

brought a new dimension to the game and so, perhaps, did his background. He was the first public parks player to take a title that had been dominated by club men from wealthy families. With McLoughlin's game, serve-and-volley came first. "The California Comet," as he was known, electrified tennis prior to the First World War.

He was a precociously skilled player.

in the history of lawn tennis.

In the U.S., the championship meeting at Newport settled back after the Doherty sortie of 1903 to control its own destinies. The outstanding player of the first decade of the century was Larned. In 1892 this Cornell man won the Intercollegiate Championship, a title established in 1883. A New York stockbroker, he won the U.S. singles for the first time in 1901 when he was 28. He equaled the record of Dick Sears taking it seven times, the last in 1911.

He played 74 singles in all and won 62. Tilden, the other seven-time winner along with Sears, did better (71–7), and Jimmy Connors (98–17), Ivan Lendl (72–11) out-did both while John McEnroe is up there (65–12). Larned had an unbroken sequence of 11 victories from 1907, when he played through and won, to his success in his last challenge round of 1911.

The popularity of the Newport singles reached unprecedented heights during his career. The entry passed 128 for the first time in 1908. It peaked at 202 in 1911, and this was the last year of the challenge round.

The winner in 1912 was a Californian, Maurice McLoughlin. His dynamic serving

Maurice McLoughlin (left) won his first U.S. Singles title against Bill Johnston in 1912.

• *Fischer Collection/SPS*

ing to Larned in the challenge round of 1911.

In 1913 McLoughlin made his only appearance in Europe. Wimbledon spectators were awestruck by his serving, and the word "cannonball" was used for the first time. His reputation preceded him and he did not disappoint. Before record crowds he came through the all-comers' singles and challenged Wilding, the title-holder since 1910, for the crown. "The history of the match," it was written at the time, "may be succinctly stated by saying that McLoughlin ought to have won the first set and was very near to winning the third. He lost both of them, and the second into the bargain, and so Wilding retained the honors." The score: 8–6, 6–3, 10–8.

Wilding's invincibility at Wimbledon was brought to an end in 1914 by his Davis Cup colleague, Norman Brookes. The great Australian was 36 years old when he won his second Wimbledon singles championship. Later that year he and Wilding were in America challenging the U.S. for the Davis Cup. They played at the West Side Tennis Club, Forest Hills, a few days after the start of World War I. (Wilding was killed, at 31, on May 9, 1915, at Neuve Chapelle on the Western Front.)

McLoughlin won both his singles against Australasia. In the first, he beat Brookes, 17–15, 6–3, 6–3, and the strength of his serve and volley had never been so devastatingly displayed. Nonetheless, Australasia won, 3–2. The International Team trophy had been in contention 13 times, with three successes for the U.S., five for the British and five for Australasia.

The West Side Tennis Club staged its first Davis Cup in 1911 when America beat the British Isles, 4–1. The famous club was founded in 1892, when 13 founder members rented three clay courts on Central Park West between 88th and 89th Streets, Manhattan. By the end of that season there were 43 members, five courts, and the initiation fee was $10, with a yearly subscription of the same amount.

A move was made to a site near Columbia University at 117th Street between Morningside Drive and Amsterdam Avenue in 1902. Six years later a further move took the club to 238th Street and Broadway, where there was room for 12 grass and 15 or more clay courts. The shift to Forest Hills in Queens was made in 1913. Until the building of the concrete stadium in 1923 the main courts were in front of the clubhouse, flanked by temporary stands.

The West Side Tennis Club became the host of the National Men's Singles Championship in 1915. In 1914, the last year at Newport, Dick Williams reversed the outcome of the final of the preceding year and beat McLoughlin to take the title. In the first meeting at Forest Hills, McLoughlin was again the losing finalist, this time to Bill Johnston.

The Newport Casino, after 34 years as the home of America's most prestigious event, had outlived that purpose, though it remains in the game as a tourney site and home of the Hall of Fame. The age it represented, of wealth and fashion and leisure, was passing. The victory by McLoughlin, the public parks player, had been significant.

In due course—1921—the West Side Tennis Club became the home of the U.S. Women's Championships as well. Until that time the Philadelphia Cricket Club was the site. The champion of 1908, Maud Barger Wallach, took a special place in the roll of winners. She was 38 when she won the title, having taken up the game as late as 30. When she was 45 she still ranked No. 5 in the U.S.

The successor to Mrs. Wallach was Hazel Hotchkiss, who became Mrs. George W. Wightman in 1912 and in the course of her career the winner of 45 national titles. Her name would have survived as a valiant and stalwart champion even without the Wightman Cup she later founded.

Hazel Wightman was succeeded as national singles champion in 1915 by the

Tennis was featured as part of the Olympic Games from the first in Athens in 1896 to the Paris event of 1924, then

restored in 1988. At the prewar Games, British players predominated except for those at St. Louis in 1904. Only men took part and the gold medalists were exclusively American, Beals Wright taking one for the singles and, with Edgar Leonard, the doubles.

In international administration 1913 was an important year. It marked the

the associations of Australasia, Belgium, Bohemia, Ceylon, Chile, Finland, Hungary, Ireland, Jamaica, Mauritius, Netherlands, Norway, the Riviera, Russia, South Africa,

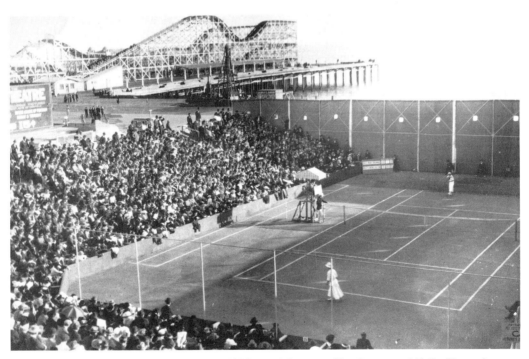

A roller coaster serves as a backdrop for a 1914 match between May Sutton and Molla Bjurstedt on the Hotel Virginia Courts at Long Beach, Cal. • *USTA*

Spain and Switzerland, as well as 26 individual clubs from 15 countries.

The ILTF had its inaugural meeting in Paris on March 1, 1913. Its founder members were Australasia, Austria, Belgium, the British Isles, Denmark, France, Germany, Netherlands, Russia, South Africa, Sweden and Switzerland. The U.S. was voteless and was only informally represented—by one of the British delegates, H. Anthony Sabelli, secretary of the BLTA.

The absence of the U.S. resulted in the Davis Cup organization developing along different lines from ILTF, parallel but separate. (The merger between the two international bodies did not take place until 1978, and even then the difference of voting procedure was left to mark the original reluctance of the U.S. to yield any of its independence to the world's governing body.)

This reluctance to join the ILTF was occasioned by the allocation of various "World Championship" titles. The Wimbledon meeting was granted ("in perpetuity") the description of "The World Championships on Grass." There was a "World Championships on Hard Court," which was staged mainly in Paris, and also a peripatetic "World Championships on Covered Courts." When these grandiose titles were abolished soon after World War I, the U.S. found its way clear to become a member of the ILTF.

An early winner of the women's singles in the World's Hard Court Championships in Paris was a promising French girl who was only 15 years old. She won the women's doubles with an American, Elizabeth Ryan. She was from Picardy and her name was Suzanne Lenglen, perhaps the greatest player in the history of the women's game.

Ryan's name was also to echo reverberatingly in the annals of tennis. Even before 1914 this Californian had laid the founda-

tion of her career as an assiduous, effective competitor.

The doubles events at Wimbledon, the women's and mixed, became full championship competitions in 1913 when officially the World title on grass belonged to it. In 1914, the indefatigable Ryan partnered Agatha Morton to win the women's doubles, the first of 19 titles she was to gain at Wimbledon, a record that stood until 1979 when Billie Jean King won her 20th, the doubles, with Martina Navratilova.

The Riviera season was by then a well-established feature of the game, reflecting the world of fashion, wealth, and leisure of which tennis had become as much a part in Europe as it had in the U.S., where Newport had been for so long a center.

Immediately prior to World War I, however, it was perhaps Imperial Russia that represented the high point of tennis in its smart social context. A party of British men who played in St. Petersburg in the Russian Championships of 1913 recorded that the ball boys were footmen in ornate uniforms who passed the balls on silver salvers. Ryan was the last women's champion of Imperial Russia, a title she was never able to defend.

Ryan was overshadowed at this time, like all other women, by Dorothea Lambert Chambers, as Dorothea Douglass had become. She made 13 attempts to win the Wimbledon singles between 1902 and 1920, and was beaten only six times. At the age of 24 she won for the first time, in 1903. Her seventh success was in 1914. She was the precursor of great, near-invincible players.

Yet at this period it was still possible to be near invincible and excel at other sports. Mrs. Lambert Chambers was one such, for she was a champion at badminton and a top-class field hockey player.

The Davis Cup strongly helped boost tennis as an international sport. Prior to

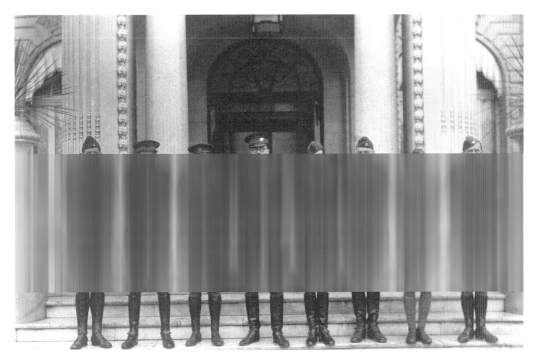

Tennis players all (left to right): Lt. Col. Dwight Davis, Maj. R.D. Wrenn, Maj. Bill Larned, Capt. Watson Washburn, Capt. Dick Williams, Capt. O.S. Walters, Lt. Dean Mathey, Col. Wallace Johnson. • *USTA*

1914, when the war brought the competition to a temporary halt, nine nations participated: the U.S., the British Isles, Belgium, France, Australasia, Austria, Germany, Canada and South Africa.

The Australian Championships was staged first in 1905. Four years earlier the former British colonies of Victoria, New South Wales and others united in a federal government.

A notable woman champion of New Zealand was K. M. Nunneley. She took the title first in 1895 and for the 13th successive year in 1907. Rodney Heath won the first Australian title in 1905; the women's event didn't begin until 1922, Mall Molesworth the victor.

The French, prior to the war, made an impact on the world with men of high cal-

iber, Andre Gobert and Max Decugis most notably. They won the men's doubles at Wimbledon in 1911, but it was not until 1925 that the French Championships was open to non-citizens. A German pair, Heinrich Kleinschroth and Friederich Rahe, were runners-up for the Wimbledon title in 1913. In 1912 Kleinschroth competed in the U.S. Nationals at Newport but did not survive the opening round.

The German Championships was an event favored by British players and among the fashionable happenings of season. They were staged in Hamburg from 1892.

Canada's first championships was held two years earlier, in 1890. The first tournament staged was on the turf of the Montreal Cricket Club in 1878. Like those in the U.S., the first official championships followed the founding of the Canadian Lawn Tennis Association in Toronto in

Mary K. Browne (left) was U.S. Singles champion in 1912, 1913 and 1914, and with Louise Williams (right) won the doubles in 1913, 1914 and 1921. • *Fischer Collection/SPS*

1890. The first women's championship was in Toronto in 1892.

In Europe the outbreak of the war in 1914 brought a halt to competitive tennis.

Australia, more remote, staged its championships for the 1914–15 season, and a Brit, Gordon Lowe, was the winner.

In the United States the game was affected to a lesser degree. Inevitably the international field dried up. In 1917, when America became directly involved in the war, there was a break. The National Championships was not staged as such that year, though the continuity of the events was not broken. The events were known as "Patriotic Tournaments," with the winners eventually taking full championship status.

In 1918 a tall, somewhat ungainly man from Philadelphia, William Tatem Tilden II, did well on his third attempt in the National singles at the West Side Tennis Club. He reached the final, where he was beaten by R. Lindley Murray, a left-hander with a big serve. Murray had revealed his aggressive qualities by taking the patriotic event the year before.

Tilden was not all that young to make his mark. He was, in fact, 25 years of old. He was a late developer. His record was to surpass, by far, that of Larned and Sears.

2: WAS IT REALLY GOLDEN? 1919-45

came on strong in the Roaring Twenties as never before, held high by such highly publicized stars as Babe Ruth in baseball, Jack Dempsey in boxing, Red Grange in football, Bobby Jones in golf, Man o' War in horse racing. Tennis was right up there, too, with players whose names had a broad public impact: Big Bill Tilden, Suzanne Lenglen, Helen Wills Moody. World War I was over, the trenches silent, and a prosperous period, with more leisure, seemed ripe for games-playing heroes and heroines who could be colored gold.

1919

This was the year of the arrival of Suzanne Lenglen on the world tennis stage she would dominate until she turned pro in 1926. A product of constant drilling by her father, Charles Lenglen, a well-to-do Frenchman, she had style as well as ability and would come to be ranked with Helen Wills Moody among the greatest women players of all time.

Lenglen appeared in her first tournament at 12 and won the singles and dou-

for the first time, Lenglen won the title in a match that is still regarded as one of the greatest Wimbledon women's finals.

Lenglen was no beauty. She had a long, Gallic nose, a large mouth and a prominent chin. She was stocky and swarthy, with thick shoulders. She also possessed a fiery disposition. She was 20 and advanced to the challenge round to play the seven-time champion, Britain's Mrs. Dorothea Lambert Chambers, who had won her first Wimbledon title in 1903, and was two months from her 41st birthday.

Lenglen's dress created a sensation. The British had been accustomed to seeing their women in tight-fitting corsets, blouses and layers of petticoats. When Suzanne stepped onto the center court in a revealing one-piece dress, with sleeves *daringly* just above the elbow, her hemline *only* just below the knee, reaction ranged from outrage on the part of many women spectators—some reportedly walked out during her matches, muttering "shocking"—to delight among most of the men.

Attending the matches were King George V and Queen Mary. Everybody was impressed by the young French women's grace and disciplined shotmaking. She won the match, 10–8, 4–6, 9–7; it wasn't until Margaret Court beat Billie Jean King, 14–12, 11–9, in 1970, that a Wimbledon women's final saw more games. After losing the second set, Lenglen sipped brandy during the interval. She took a 4–1 lead in the final set, then Lambert Chambers fought back to lead, 6–5, with two match points at 40–15. A lucky wood shot and slashing backhand winner pulled Lenglen back to deuce and she went on to win the set, the last game to love.

In the Wimbledon men's championship, Australian Gerald Patterson advanced to the challenge round by beating Britain's Algernon Kingscote and then met countryman Norman Brookes, who'd won the title in 1914, the last Wimbledon before the war. As champion, Brookes did not have to play until the challenge round. Patterson beat him, 6–3, 7–5, 6–2.

In the 1919 resumption of Davis Cup play after a four-year hiatus, Australasia, a combination of Australia and New Zealand, retained the Cup it had won in 1914, beating the British Isles, 4–1. The U.S. did not enter. Patterson was the dominant player, winning both singles and combining with Brookes to win the doubles. The Australian title went to Kingscote.

The U.S. Nationals final at Forest Hills between the 1915 champion, 5-foot-8, 120-pound William "Little Bill" Johnston, and 6-foot-2, William "Big Bill" Tilden, was billed in *The New York Time* as the battle for the title, "William the Conqueror." It was the first of six meetings between the two Bills in the Nationals final, the only one Johnston would win. Tilden had first played in the Nationals in 1916 and lost in straight sets in the first round to Harold Throckmorton. In 1918 he lost in the finals to R. Lindley Murray. By 1919 he was already being called the greatest player of all time. Johnston, however, spotted a weakness in

"Little Bill" Johnston was the first post-World War I U.S. champion. He defeated "Big Bill" Tilden in the 1919 final. • *UPI*

Tilden, a backhand that was totally defensive, hit invariably with underspin. Johnston pounded away at the weakness and won relatively easily, 6–4, 6–3, 6–3.

Tilden would go to the indoor court of a friend, Arnold Jones, in Providence, R.I., later in the year, work for months to correct the flaw, and come away with an improved backhand that would enable him to become the dominant tennis figure over the next decade.

For the women's championship the challenge round was abolished and Mrs. Hazel Hotchkiss Wightman won the title, interrupting a seven-year reign by Molla Bjurstedt of the United States, who had won in 1915, 1916, 1917 and 1918 and who would, as Mrs. Franklin Mallory, win in 1920, 1921, 1922 and then again in 1926. Marion Zinderstein eliminated the defending champion in the semifinals and was beaten in the final by Wightman, 6–1, 6–2.

1920

William Tatem Tilden II, born in 1893, the son of a Philadelphia wool merchant and prominent civic figure, came of age at 27 when he won at Wimbledon and Forest Hills and helped the United States win the Davis Cup for the first time since 1913.

In the all-comers final at Wimbledon against the Japanese Zenzo Shimizu,

for the Davis Cup in 1920. • *Fischer Collection/SPS*

to give lesser opponents a head start." Tilden had whipped Shimizu, 6–1, 6–1, in a tournament prior to Wimbledon. In the challenge round final, Tilden defeated the defending champion, Australian Gerald Patterson, 2–6, 6–3, 6–2, 6–4. The Associated Press reported that "Tilden in the first set opened with experiments all around the court and then settled down mercilessly to feeding his opponent's backhand, and, as the game progressed, Patterson got worse and worse....Tilden exploited his famous cut-stroke to his opponent's backhand again and again."

The British marveled at Tilden, acclaimed him the greatest of all time, and one observer rhapsodized, "His silhouette as he prepares to serve suggests an Egyptian pyramid king about to administer punishment."

In the U.S. championships, Tilden beat Bill Johnston in a dramatic five-set final, 6–1, 1–6, 7–5, 5–7, 6–3, that was regarded as the greatest championship final up to that time. During the match a Navy photographic plane crashed while making passes over Forest Hills and disrupted the match momentarily. Two aviators were killed.

It was the first of six straight national titles for Tilden, a flamboyant, controversial figure who dominated any match, win or lose.

Tilden, who would not lose an important match until 1926, teamed with Johnston in a 5–0 Davis Cup sweep of Australasia. He and Johnston each took a pair of singles matches and a doubles over Norman Brookes and Gerald Patterson.

In the women's championship at Wimbledon, Mrs. Dorothea Lambert Chambers defeated Elizabeth Ryan and Molla Mallory of the United States on the way to a return match with Suzanne Lenglen in the challenge round. Lenglen beat her, 6–4, 6–0. Mallory won the American title, defeating Marion Zinderstein, 6–3, 6–1.

1921

Suzanne Lenglen, who hadn't lost a match to anyone since the end of the war, came to the United States for the first time, and lost a match on a default. It was one of the most stunning results in tennis up to that time, and was long talked about and cited whenever Lenglen was discussed.

The position occupied by Lenglen at the time of the great default was described by Al Laney, the eminent tennis writer: "She probably did more for women's tennis than any girl who ever played it. She broke down barriers and created a vogue, reforming tennis dress, substituting acrobatics and something of the art of the ballet where decorum had been the rule. In England and on the Continent, this slim, not very pretty but fascinating French maiden was the most popular performer in sport or out of it on the postwar scene. She became the rage, almost a cult... Even royalty gave her its favor and she partnered King Gustav of Sweden in mixed doubles more than once."

Lenglen was beaten by the defending champion, Molla Mallory, in the second round of the first women's championships played at Forest Hills, six years prior to the advent of seeds. Lenglen lost the first set, 6–2, seeming weak and nervous, coughing from time to time, causing some concern to those who had seen her play before. Then, when she lost the first point of the second set and double-faulted to trail, 2–6, 0–30, she started weeping. She went to the umpire's chair and, speaking French, said she was too ill to go on. As she and the disappointed Mallory walked off the court, there was a faint hissing sound in the stands from the crowd of 8,000, the largest ever to witness a women's match in the United States.

The newspapers reported she told the umpire that she was unable to breathe and that she coughed the night before. Others

Molla Mallory (left) won her sixth U.S. Singles title in 1921. Along the way she ousted Marion Jessup (right). • *UPI*

recalled her saying she did not feel like playing and had been listless in a practice session. If she were suffering from menstrual cramps, that was not mentioned because it was a taboo subject in the public prints at the time. It was also pointed out that she had arrived in the United States only four days before her first scheduled match. Her opponent defaulted, so she did not have a warmup before her match with Mallory.

was current in New York; in France there were accusations of mistreatment by the Americans and the charge that her first-round opponent had purposely defaulted to help set up Lenglen for defeat.

Mallory went on to win the U.S. Championship, her sixth, with a 4–6, 6–4, 6–2 victory in the final over Mary K. Browne. Lenglen had breezed to her third Wimbledon title with a 6–2, 6–0 victory over Elizabeth Ryan of the United States.

Bill Tilden retained his Wimbledon Championship, coming out of a sickbed to defend against South African Babe Norton in the challenge round. Tilden won, 4–6, 2–6, 6–1, 6–0, 7–5. After losing the first two sets, Tilden gave up his normal hard-hitting game, took to chops and slices, and turned the match around. This displeased the crowd, which booed Tilden despite the remonstrations of the umpire that he was playing quite fairly and within the rules. Norton recovered in the last set, led 5–4 with two match points, but Tilden rallied and prevailed. F.P. Adams wrote: "He is an artist, more of an artist than nine-tenths of the artists I know. It is the beauty of the game that Tilden loves; it is the chase always, rather than the quarry."

In the Nationals, moved to Germantown Cricket Club in Philadelphia, Tilden won over Wallace Johnson in straight sets and teamed with Bill Johnston to dominate a 5–0 Davis Cup victory over Japan. Tilden lost the first two sets and was within two points of defeat before beating Japan's Zenzo Shimizu in five sets in the first singles match. Dick Williams and Watson Washburn took the doubles. Rhys

moved to its present site in a picturesque hollow at the foot of Church Road near Wimbledon Common. King George V and Queen Mary attended the opening on June 22 at the new Centre Court holding 14,750 seats (the previous arena had 8,500) and saw the first match, played by Leslie Godfree and Algernon Kingscote of Great Britain.

The challenge round was abolished. Bill Tilden did not choose to make the Atlantic crossing to defend his title, and it was won by Australian Gerald Patterson, whom Tilden had dethroned in 1920. Patterson defeated Great Britain's Randolph Lycett in the final, 6–3, 6–4, 6–2.

Suzanne Lenglen avenged her controversial default to Molla Mallory at Forest Hills the year before when she trounced Mallory in the Wimbledon final, 6–2, 6–0. Lenglen's appeal was such that before her first-round match with Kitty McKane, "a line stretched more than a mile and a half from the underground station to the entrance to the All England Club," Wimbledon official Duncan Macaulay wrote. "People used to call it the 'Leng-len trail a-winding' after the famous war song of those days ['a long, long trail'...]."

Australia's Gerald Patterson won Wimbledon for the second time in 1922. • *Fischer Collection/SPS*

Lenglen won three Wimbledon titles for the second time. She teamed with Pat O'Hara Wood to win the mixed doubles and with Elizabeth Ryan to take the doubles.

After her loss to Lenglen at Wimbledon, Mallory, 38, returned to Forest Hills to win her seventh U.S. Nationals, defeating 16-year-old Helen Wills in the final, 6–3, 6–1. It was the greatest disparity in ages for a final in the history of the Championships.

The meeting between perennial rivals Bill Tilden and Bill Johnston in the U.S. Nationals at the Germantown Cricket Club was called "a match for the Greek gods." They played for a coveted championship bowl, which each had won twice and which would be retired permanently by any three-time winner. Tilden advanced to the final, beating Wimbledon champion Gerald Patterson, while Johnston defeated a promising newcomer, Vincent Richards. Tilden lost the first two sets, then came back to win the match 4–6, 3–6, 6–2, 6–3,

6–4. The trophy gained by Tilden had on it the names of previous winners William Larned and R. Lindley Murray (once) and Maurice McLoughlin, R. Norris Williams and Johnston (twice each).

In the Davis Cup, Australasia advanced past Spain to the challenge round, where it was beaten by the United States, 4–1. In those days of unusual interest in Davis Cup, something of a stir was created by the loss of the doubles by the U.S. team of Tilden and Richards to Gerald Patterson and Pat O'Hara Wood. Tilden and Johnston swept Patterson and James Anderson in the singles.

1923

A new stadium was constructed at the West Side Tennis Club grounds in Forest Hills, but the men's Nationals wouldn't return from Philadelphia until 1924. Built at a cost of $250,000, the concrete bowl that would eventually seat 14,000 opened on August 10 with the inauguration of the Wightman Cup matches.

The competition was the brainchild of Hazel Hotchkiss Wightman, a champion in pre-World War I days who would compete until she was past 70, winning the last of her 45 national titles (senior doubles) at the age of 67. She had conceived the idea of a women's competition equivalent to the Davis Cup in 1920 and donated a silver vase. But the idea lay fallow until it was seized upon by Julian Myrick, a USTA official, as a way of launching the new Forest Hills stadium.

The competition between Great Britain and the United States consisted of five singles matches and two doubles, and though Wightman hoped to make it an international tournament by bringing in France, that never came to pass. With Wightman as a captain, the American team of Molla Mallory, Helen Wills and Eleanor

Helen Wills serves to Kitty McKane in the inaugural match at the new stadium in Forest Hills in 1923. • *UPI*

Goss scored a 7–0 sweep, starting with an inaugural match before 5,000 in which Wills beat Kitty McKane, 6–2, 7–5.

Wills won the first of her seven U.S. national titles, defeating Mallory, 6–2, 6–1. Suzanne Lenglen breezed through the Wimbledon field, losing only 11 games in the 12 sets she played defeating McKane in the final 6–2, 6–2.

With Bill Tilden, universally regarded as the kingpin of tennis, absent again from Wimbledon, Bill Johnston won for the only time . In straight sets he swept past countryman Vincent Richards, South Africa's Babe Norton and then Frank Hunter of the United States in a final that was completed in 45 minutes. Johnston's success at Wimbledon could not carry over to the U.S. Nationals where he was crushed by

Flanking the Wightman Cup won by the U.S. in 1923 are (left to right): Helen Wills, Molla Mallory, Hazel Hotchkiss Wightman (the donor), Geraldine Beamish and Mrs. R. Clayton. • *UPI*

Tilden in the final, 6–4, 6–1, 6–4. Pat O'Hara Wood won the Australian title.

In a Davis Cup field increased to 17 countries from 11, Australia beat France to challenge the U.S. The U.S. won, 4–1, with Tilden winning both singles and Johnston losing one of his singles to James Anderson. In the doubles, Tilden and Dick Williams won the first set, 17–15 (longest set for a Davis Cup finale), lost the second, 11–13, and the third, 2–6, before winning the final two sets from Anderson and John Hawkes, 6–3, 6–2.

It is hard today to realize how significant the Davis Cup used to be before open tennis, when there were not so many tournaments that players could choose to skip Cup play to chase big money. After World War I an atmosphere of international good fellowship took hold and the Davis Cup acquired tremendous significance, partly because of the U.S. dominance of the competition. It was front-page news then and controversies such as Tilden's threats to quit were looked upon as almost national calamities.

1924

In the latter part of the 1920s, when the French would dominate men's tennis, each of the three great Frenchmen would win two Wimbledon championships, and it started this year with the French final (French nationals only) in which 25-year-old Jean Borotra defeated 19-year-old René Lacoste, 6–1, 3–6, 6–1, 3–6, 6–4.

Borotra, the colorful "Bounding Basque" who wore a beret while playing, and Lacoste, the "Crocodile," were two of the Four Musketeers along with 22-year-old Henri Cochet and 29-year-old Jacques

Bill Tilden won the U.S. crown for the fourth year in a row and led the Americans' Davis Cup triumph in 1923. • *UPI*

The Crocodile, René Lacoste, one of the Four Musketeers, lost to fellow Frenchman Jean Borotra in an all-French Wimbledon final in 1924.
• *Fischer Collection/SPS*

"Toto" Brugnon, who was essentially a doubles specialist. Wimbledon Secretary Duncan Macaulay wrote in *Behind the Scenes at Wimbledon:* "They were all very different in style and temperament, and they sometimes clashed bitterly with one another on the courts. But whenever they felt they were playing for France...they always put France first. Thus it was the combined pressure of Lacoste and Cochet which began to rock the great Bill Tilden on his pedestal, and which finally toppled him off it."

Tilden, increasingly at odds with the tennis establishment, sent a letter of resignation to the USTA, bowing out of the Davis Cup because of a proposed ban on his writing for newspapers about tennis. That was a conflict with amateur rules. The threat of not having Tilden's gate appeal in the Davis Cup competition forced the tennis body to cave in. Tilden and Bill Johnston swept the Australian

team of Gerald Patterson and Pat O'Hara Wood, 5–0.

Underdog rooters hopeful that Little Bill Johnston would break the spell held over him by Tilden had reason to believe that Johnston would crash through in the U.S. Championships, the first played in the new West Side Tennis Club Stadium at Forest Hills. Tilden's feud with the USTA and the increased time he was devoting to a theatrical career led to charges that he was out of shape. He came to the final with a desultory five-set victory over Vincent Richards, while Johnston routed Australia's Gerald Patterson. In the final, however, Tilden crushed Johnston, 6–1, 9–7, 6–2, in a stunning display that tennis savant Al Laney later called "Tilden at his absolute peak, and I have not since seen the like of it." Patterson said, "Tilden is the only player in the world... the rest of us are second-graders."

President Calvin Coolidge makes the 1924 Davis Cup draw at the White House. • *Fischer Collection/SPS*

Suzanne Lenglen, a five-time winner at Wimbledon, weakened by an attack of jaundice earlier in the year, was forced to drop out after winning a quarterfinal match over Elizabeth Ryan of the United States in which Lenglen was extended, 6–2, 6–8, 6–4. That was the first singles set she lost—except the one to Molla Mallory in her great default at Forest Hills in 1921—since 1919. Britain's Kitty McKane got a walkover in the semifinals and then defeated Helen Wills in the final, 4–6, 6–4, 6–4, from 1–4 in the second, Helen's lone loss in 56 Wimbledon matches.

They had met only a few days earlier in Wightman Cup play at Wimbledon, McKane winning, 6–2, 6–2. The British evened the series at one-all, winning the competition, 6–1. The United States' only point came on a doubles triumph by Wills and Hazel Wightman over McKane and Evelyn Colyer. The 18-year-old Wills won her second successive U.S. title, defeating Molla Mallory, 6–1, 6–2.

In Australia, the men's championship was won by James Anderson, the women's by Sylvia Lance. Norman Brookes, the 47-year-old Australian immortal who had first played at Wimbledon 20 years before, highlighted early-round Wimbledon play with an upset victory over Frank Hunter, who had been a finalist in 1923.

1925

The French dominated Wimbledon as it never had been dominated before. They scored almost a clean sweep of the championships, winning the men's singles and doubles, the mixed doubles and women's singles—and half of the women's doubles.

Suzanne Lenglen, reaching the zenith of her career, lost only five games in sweeping through five opponents. She scored a 6–0, 6–0 triumph over Kitty McKane, who had won the title when Lenglen was incapacitated the previous year, and defeated

Joan Fry in the final, 6–2, 6–0. Lenglen combined with American Elizabeth Ryan to win the women's doubles for the sixth time, and Lenglen won the mixed doubles with Jean Borotra for Lenglen's third Wimbledon triple crown.

The men's final was a rematch of the previous year. This time, René Lacoste scored a 6–3, 6–3, 4–6, 8–6 victory over

Helen Wills made it three in a row in U.S. Singles in 1925. • *Fischer Collection/SPS*

Australian title and Daphne Akhurst the first of her five Australian championships.

Bill Tilden achieved the distinction of winning 57 straight games during the summer. The stage was set for another Big Bill-Little Bill confrontation in the U.S. Nationals at Forest Hills after semifinals in which Tilden beat Vincent Richards and Bill Johnston advanced past Dick Williams. Despite an injured shoulder, which prevented him from holding hardly more than half his service games in a long, five-set match. Tilden defeated Johnston, 4–6, 11–9, 6–3, 4–6, 6–3.

Johnston said immediately afterward, "I can't beat him; I can't beat the sonofabitch, I can't beat him." It was the last of Tilden's six straight U.S. titles and the last time he and Johnston would contest the title. Tilden, like most tennis people, admired Johnston greatly, and after Johnston's premature death from tuberculosis in 1946, dedicated his memoirs to him.

The French made their first breakthrough into the Davis Cup challenge round. Though the Four Musketeers—Lacoste and Borotra in singles, and Cochet and Jacques Brugnon in doubles—were swept by Tilden and Johnston in sin-

gles and Dick Williams and Vincent Richards in doubles, both Frenchmen extended Tilden to five sets. Tilden rallied for a 3–6, 10–12, 8–6, 7–5, 6–2 victory over Lacoste. Borotra extended him 4–6, 6–0, 2–6, 9–7, 6–4.

Helen Wills won her third straight U.S. Championship, defeating Kitty McKane of Great Britain, 3–6, 6–0, 6–2, in the final. Wills won both her matches in Wightman Cup play at Forest Hills, but Great Britain won the competition for the second straight year, 4–3. Dorothea Douglass Lambert Chambers, 46, who lost an epic singles confrontation with Suzanne Lenglen in the 1919 Wimbledon final, won a singles match over No. 5 American Eleanor Goss, 7–5, 3–6, 6–1, and participated in one of Britain's two doubles victories.

1926

Suzanne Lenglen and Helen Wills met in what would be the only confrontation between the two women generally recognized as two of the greatest players of all time. One writer called this match "the most important sporting event of modern times exclusively in the hands of the fair sex"—this five decades before two of the fair sex met Bobby Riggs.

Wills took off early in the year for a trip to southern France to participate in invitation tournaments on the Riviera and what some observers regarded as a chance for a showdown with Lenglen. "This gal must be mad," Lenglen told a close friend. "Does she think she can come and beat me on my home court?"

In a dramatic match played at the Carleton Club in Cannes, Lenglen, the favorite of the European crowd, won, 6–3, 8–6. Wills, who had appeared nervous in the first set, began moving her opponent around the court and was leading, 5–4, at

set point when she hit what appeared to be a winner. It wasn't called in her favor, however. Lenglen recovered, went on to win, and broke down in tears afterward. Wills said, "She is terrific, I think it was one of my greatest matches."

Lenglen's brilliant amateur career came to a sad end amid controversy and incriminations at Wimbledon when she failed to show up on time for a women's doubles match at which King George V and Queen Mary were present. Due to a mixup after a scheduling change, Lenglen arrived at Centre Court after the King and Queen had left. This drew a reprimand and she became hysterical. She never quite recovered, though the officials agreed to postpone her match. Meeting hostility from the crowds and in the press, Lenglen lost her doubles match. She won a first-round singles match and an opening mixed doubles, but then withdrew from

Spectators unable to purchase tickets for the Lenglen-Wills match in Cannes found a view from the ladder. • *UPI*

the tournament. She never played amateur tennis again, signing on as a pro with American promoter C.C. "Cash and Carry") Pyle. She went on a North American tour, winning nightly (38–0) over ex-U.S. champ Mary K. Browne, 35.

Unable to entice Bill Tilden to professionalism, Pyle settled for the next best American, Vinnie Richards, 23. He com-

about $80,000 while putting pro tennis into operation.

With Lenglen out of Wimbledon, the title was won by Kitty McKane Godfree of Great Britain over Lili de Alvarez of Spain, 6–2, 4–6, 6–3. The U.S. National title, which had been the property of Helen Wills, was opened to others when Wills was sidelined after an appendicitis operation.

the tour was a success. It was reported that Lenglen was paid a $25,000 bonus beyond her $50,000 guarantee, and that Pyle, who had no interest in tennis as such, made

The six-year reign of Bill Tilden came to an end in the U.S. Championships when he was eliminated in the quarterfinals by Henri Cochet, 6–8, 6–1, 6–3, 1–6, 8–6.

Football immortal Red Grange (left) and promoter C.C. "Cash and Carry" Pyle welcome Suzanne Lenglen as she turns pro in September 1926. • *UPI*

This broke Tilden's record U.S. run of 42 matches.

In many ways Tilden came to be more popular in defeat than he had been as the kingpin of the sport. Allison Danzig wrote of the Tilden-Cochet match: "The climax of the match, the point at which the gallery broke into the wildest demonstrations, was during the final set when Tilden, trailing at 1–4, rallied to volley Cochet dizzy with one of the most sensational exhibitions he ever gave at the net and pull up to 4–all. Every winning shot of the American was greeted with roars of applause. Tilden, 33, then led, 15–40, on Cochet's serve, but then fell back."

Bill Johnston also lost in the same round, to Jean Borotra in five sets. Borotra

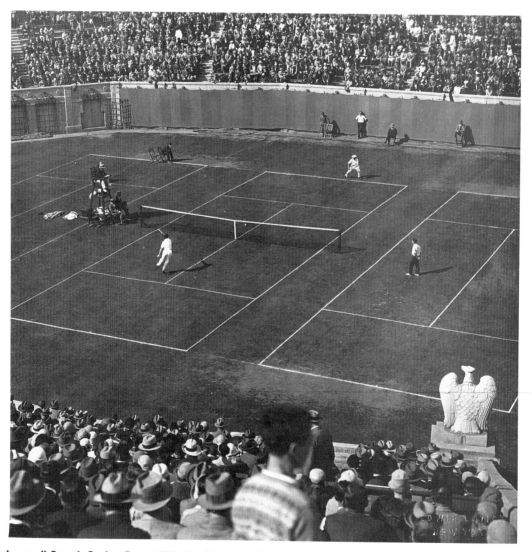

In an all-French final at Forest Hills, René Lacoste (far court) won the U.S. crown in 1926 in straight sets over Jean Borotra. • *Fischer Collection/SPS*

advanced to make it an all-French final by eliminating Vincent Richards. René Lacoste eliminated Henri Cochet in the semifinals and then beat Borotra for the title, 6–4, 6–0, 6–4.

It was the first time since 1917 that Tilden did not make the U.S. final, the first time since 1920 he didn't win; it was the first of three years in which Forest Hills

ranking, reached the finals of the singles, doubles and mixed doubles and lost in all. He would turn pro, joining the Lenglen tour. The men's doubles was notable for the entry of the Duke of York, later King George VI, teamed with Louis Grieg. They lost in the first round. Leslie and Kitty Godfree won the mixed doubles crown, the only time a married couple won that competition at Wimbledon.

In Davis Cup play at the Germantown Cricket Club, the U.S. extended its winning streak to seven, a record that still stands. The U.S. won, 4–1. Tilden suffered the only loss, to Lacoste, 4–6, 6–4, 8–6, 8–6, his first defeat in an important match since 1919. Johnston won both his singles, over Lacoste and Borotra, and Dick Williams and Vincent Richards beat Cochet and Jacques Brugnon in the doubles. The French championships went to Cochet. John Hawkes won the Australian title.

Though playing without Helen Wills, the U.S. tied the Wightman Cup competition at 2–all, defeating Great Britain at Wimbledon, 4–3, with a pair of doubles and singles triumphs. Elizabeth Ryan split in singles and won her doubles match teamed with Mary K. Browne. She and

Browne also won the Wimbledon women's doubles, and Ryan teamed with Eleanor Goss to win the U.S. crown.

1927

One of the most astounding turnarounds in the history of tennis occurred in the semifinals at Wimbledon. Bill Tilden at 34 was no longer the supreme

any outstanding tennis figure would ever experience. On Cochet's service Tilden hit out on three drives and lost the game. Cochet then won 17 consecutive points and went on to win, 2–6, 4–6, 7–5, 6–4, 6–3.

Tilden later wrote: "I have heard many interesting, curious, quite inaccurate accounts of what happened. One ingenious explanation was that King Alfonso of Spain arrived at 5–1 in the third set and I decided to let him see some of the match... Ridiculous! I didn't even know he was there. Another was that a group of Hindus hypnotized me. If they did, I didn't know it, but they certainly did a swell job. Personally, I have no satisfactory explanation. All I know is my coordination cracked wide open and I couldn't put a ball in court."

Before surprising Tilden, Cochet had come from behind a two-set deficit to beat Frank Hunter. Cochet added a third sensational comeback by losing the first two sets in the final to Jean Borotra and then rallying from 5–2 in the fifth set, surviving six match points, to win his first Wimbledon title. The score: 4–6, 4–6, 6–3, 6–4, 7–5.

Wimbledon Secretary Duncan Macaulay wrote, "Cochet was incredibly cool in a crisis—so much that I sometimes wondered

Henri Cochet overcame two-set deficits against Frank Hunter, Bill Tilden and Jean Borotra to capture Wimbledon in 1927. • *UPI*

whether he really knew what the score was." Footnote: In the doubles final, Cochet and Jacques Brugnon led Tilden and Frank Hunter, two sets to love, 5–3, 40–15, on Cochet's serve for the match, only to be up-ended, 1–6, 4–6, 8–6, 6–3, 6–4.

René Lacoste (the Crocodile) won three great matches over Tilden this year to establish his own supremacy in the sport. He won the French and U.S. Champion-ships in extraordinary finals and also beat Tilden in a crucial Davis Cup match. The French finale was a tourney-record 61-game, five-set duel with Lacoste winning the last set, 11–9. In the Forest Hills final, Lacoste may have played the best tennis of his life, defeating Tilden, 11–9, 6–3, 11–9.

"It was a match," Allison Danzig wrote, "the like of which will not be seen again soon. On one side of the net stood [Tilden], the perfect tactician and most ruthless stroker the game probably has ever seen, master of every shot and skilled in the necromancy of spin. On the other side was the player who has reduced defense to a mathematical science; who has done more than that, who has developed his defense to the state where it becomes an offense, subconscious in its workings but nonetheless effective in the pressure it brings to bear as the ball is sent back deeper and deeper and into more and more remote territory."

Lacoste, whose career was cut short by ill-ness and who became famous for his sports-shirt line with the crocodile emblem on the chest, never played at Forest Hills again.

America's record seven-year reign came to an end in the Davis Cup. France broke through in its third challenge with a 3–2 vic-tory over the U.S. team that included the two men who had brought America the Cup in 1920, Tilden and Johnston. Lacoste beat Johnston, then Tilden beat Cochet, then the Americans took a 2–1 lead on a doubles victory by Tilden and Frank Hunter over Jean Borotra and Jacques Brugnon. Tilden could not come through with another victory, however. He fell to Lacoste, 6–3, 4–6, 6–3, 6–2, and the Cup moved to France when Johnston was beaten by Cochet, 6–4, 4–6. 6–2. 6–4 in a dramatic match. The

Tilden's writing newspaper articles about tennis, a violation of amateur rules. Tilden was suspended, missing the interzone Davis Cup matches against Italy. As the finale with France approached, other members of the American team threatened to strike. René Lacoste announced he would not defend his title at Forest Hills. He said, "We would rather lose the Davis Cup than retain it where there may be

Miss Poker Face because of her lack of expression on the court) assumed complete dominance of the women's ranks at 22. She began a string of four Wimbledon titles with a 6–2, 6–3 victory over Lili de Alvarez. Wills won her fourth straight U.S. Championship, defeating 19-year-old Helen Jacobs in the semifinal and 16-year-old Betty Nuthall of England in the final, 6–1, 6–4.

The United States went ahead in Wightman Cup play, 3–2, beating the British, 5–2, at Forest Hills. Wills and Molla Mallory both won a pair of singles matches, and Wills teamed with Hazel Wightman for a doubles triumph. Gerald Patterson won an 18–16 fourth set in a five-set victory over defender John Hawkes for the Australian title. The women's Championship went to Esna Boyd.

The first U.S. Pro Championships was played in New York, Vinnie Richards winning over Howard Kinsey.

1928

Controversy raged much of the year between Bill Tilden and the USTA over

Helen Wills (left), with Lili de Alvarez, her victim in the Wimbledon final, also won the U.S. and French titles in 1928. • *UPI*

permit Tilden to play, though it would later keep him out of the U.S. Championships.

Tilden then went out and played what teammate George Lott called his greatest match of all time. He defeated Lacoste on clay—the first time grass hadn't been the surface for the Cup deciding round—1–6, 6–4, 6–4, 2–6, 6–3. Afterward, Lacoste said, "Two years ago I knew at last how to beat him. Now, he beats me. I never knew how the ball would come off the court, he concealed it so well. I had to wait to see how much it was spinning—and sometimes it didn't spin at all. Is he not the greatest player of all time?"

That victory was not enough. Tilden lost to Henri Cochet. Both Lacoste and Cochet beat John Hennessey, and the Cochet-Jean Borotra team beat Tilden and Frank Hunter for a 4–1 French triumph. The ranks of the Davis Cup, which was contested for by six countries in 1920, had now swelled to 33 participants.

French supremacy carried to the major championships where, for the first time, one country's representative swept all four major championships. Cochet won the U.S. and French crowns, Lacoste won his second Wimbledon title and Borotra won the Australian Championship.

With Tilden and Lacoste missing from Forest Hills, Cochet won by beating Frank Shields in the semifinal and Frank Hunter in the final, 4–6, 6–4, 3–6, 7–5, 6–3. It was the third straight victory by a Frenchman at Forest Hills, and it would turn out to be the last. Except for Cochet, who would be runner-up in the 1932 U.S. final, there would be no outstanding Frenchman to play in the United States, let alone win, after the retirements of Lacoste and Borotra. At Wimbledon, a Lacoste-Cochet final was set up when Lacoste scored a five-set victory over Tilden, and Cochet beat countryman Christian Boussus. Lacoste won, 6–1, 4–6, 6–4, 6–2.

In the Wightman Cup matches Great Britain evened the series again, 3–all, with

Time marches on: An electronic scoreboard was installed at Wimbledon in 1929. • *UPI*

a 4–3 victory gained on two doubles triumphs. The Americans' victories came as Helen Wills won both her singles and Helen Jacobs won in Wightman Cup play for the first time. Both lost in separate doubles matches, and 44-year-old Molla Mallory lost twice in the singles.

Wills won both at Wimbledon and Forest Hills for the second straight year and also won the French title. She beat Lili de Alvarez in the Wimbledon final and, in the first final of their classic rivalry, trounced Jacobs at Forest Hills, 6–2, 6–1. Wills so dominated the sport that as much attention was given to her reserved manner as her skills. W. O. McGeehan wrote in the New York *Herald Tribune*, "She is powerful, repressed and imperturbable. She plays her game with a silent, deadly earnestness, concentrated on her work. That, of course, is the way to win games, but it does not please galleries. Of course, there is no reason why an amateur athlete should try to please galleries." Wills did not play in the Australian Championships won by Daphne Akhurst.

Vinnie Richards succeeded C.C. Pyle as a promoter of professional matches and imported Karel Kozeluh, a Czech who was being acclaimed as a great player even though he had not played long on the amateur circuit. In a head-to-head duel with Richards, Kozeluh proved superior on clay

opponents as well as his spectators. Tilden, even when beaten, always leaves the impression on the public mind that he was superior to the victor."

The French had broken Tilden's six-year dominance at Forest Hills, and now Tilden ended the three-year French reign. He won the U.S. title for the seventh time, coming back from 2–1 deficits against John

was still the most dynamic figure in the sport. René Lacoste wrote, "He seems to exercise a strange fascination over his

beating Jean Borotra, 6–4, 6–3, 6–4, after defeating Tilden in the semifinals. Great Britain's future great, Fred Perry, made his

Czechoslovakia's Karel Kozeluh (left) is congratulated by Vinnie Richards after Kozeluh won the pro championship at Forest Hills in 1929. • *UPI*

Wimbledon debut, losing in the third round to John Olliff.

France was extended in winning a third successive Davis Cup competition over the United States. Cochet beat Tilden, 6–3, 6–1, 6–2, then Borotra beat American newcomer George Lott, 6–1, 3–6, 6–4, 7–5. The U.S. doubles team of John Van Ryn and Wilmer Allison beat Cochet and Borotra, 6–1, 8–6, 6–4, and then Tilden beat Borotra, 4–6, 6–1, 6–4, 7–5, tying the competition at 2–all. In the deciding match, Cochet defeated the 22-year-old Lott, 6–1, 3–6, 6–0, 6–3.

Helen Wills was never more supreme. She swept Wimbledon and Forest Hills for the third straight year and the French Championships for the second. In the first of four Wimbledon finals she would win over Helen Jacobs, she romped, 6–1, 6–2. At the U.S. Championships, Jacobs was eliminated in the semifinals by Britain's Phoebe Watson, and Wills shut out 45-year-old Molla Mallory, 6–0, 6–0. Wills then beat Watson, 6–4, 6–2. South African Billie Tapscott caused an echoing wave of criticism by being the first player to be seen at Wimbledon without stockings.

Wills led the American team to a 4–3 Wightman Cup victory on the strength of singles superiority. Wills beat Watson and Betty Nuthall, Jacobs beat Nuthall, and Edith Cross beat Mrs. Peggy Michell. The English won two doubles matches, and Watson beat Jacobs in the other singles. The U.S. led in the series, 4–3, no team having taken a more than one-match lead since the Wightman Cup inaugural in 1923.

Colin Gregory of Britain and Australian Daphne Akhurst won the Australian singles titles.

In what still was a minor aspect of the sport, the U.S. Pro Championship was contested for again by Vinnie Richards and the Czech Karel Kozeluh. This time Kozeluh won.

1930

Bill Tilden's magnificent career as an amateur came to an end on the last day of the year when he officially announced he was turning professional. He bowed out after one of the most glorious victories of his career. He won his third Wimbledon, becoming at 37 years, five months, the second oldest man to win the Wimbledon singles title. Arthur Gore won at 41 in 1909.

Tilden beat Texan Wilmer Allison 10 years and six days after he had defeated Gerald Patterson to win his first Wimbledon. Before defeating Allison, 6–3, 9–7, 6–4, Tilden had to survive a tough five-set match with Jean Borotra in which Tilden trailed, 3–1, in the final set. The London *Daily Mail* reporter called this the greatest match he had seen at Wimbledon, one of many matches in Tilden's career that struck some observers as the "greatest."

Tilden had his most successful European tour, winning the Austrian, Italian and Dutch Championships, losing to Henri Cochet in the French final. Ranked first in the United States for the 10th time, Tilden wanted badly to break a tie with Bill Larned and Richard Sears by winning the U.S. title for an eighth time. He came a cropper against 21-year-old California John Doeg, a big left-hander with a powerful serve, a formidable opponent when he had control of his ground game. Doeg made 20 aces, 12 in the final set, losing his serve only once in 29 games, and beat Tilden, 10–8, 6–3, 3–6, 12–10. Doeg hit his serve so hard, it was reported that he turned the ball into an ellipse; it was called his "egg ball." The loss marked the first time Tilden had been beaten by a countryman in a U.S. Championship since Bill Johnston 11 years earlier. Doeg then beat Frank Shields in the final, 10–8, 1–6, 6–4, 16–14.

Tilden's record in U.S. Championships showed 78 matches, at least one every year

Bill Tilden's valedictory as an amateur in 1930 included his third Wimbledon title in singles, over Wilmer Allison (right). • *UPI*

sequence, the umpire, an Englishman, finally just got up and departed when Tilden kept fussing. Once, at Orange, New Jersey, he rudely informed the tournament chairman that Big Bill Tilden was not accustomed to competing on grass that had the texture of cow pasture, and had to be coaxed back onto the court."

Earlier in the year, Tilden played in his

Jacques Brugnon beat Wilmer Allison and John Van Ryn for a 4–1 victory, France's fourth in a row.

The year marked the first appearances in the U.S. Top Ten rankings of Sidney Wood, fourth; Ellsworth Vines, eighth; and Bitsy Grant, 10th.

Queen Helen, now Mrs. Helen Wills Moody, won Wimbledon for the fourth straight year without working up too much of a sweat in a 6–2, 6–2 final triumph over Elizabeth Ryan. She and Ryan teamed to win the doubles over Edith Cross and Sarah Palfrey, making her Wimbledon debut at 17. Wills did not play at Forest Hills, and Britain's 19-year-old Betty Nuthall won. Daphne Akhurst won the Australian women's title for the third straight year and Gar Moon defeated Harry Hopman for the men's crown.

For the fifth time in the eight-year rivalry, Wightman Cup competition ended in a 4–3 score, Great Britain evening the series at 4–all. Moody won her two singles matches, Helen Jacobs split her two matches, and the pair suffered one of the two doubles defeats when they played together in a loss to Phoebe Watson and

since 1916, except for 1928, when he was suspended. He won 71, lost seven. He won 203 sets and lost 59.

Tilden, who had a long love-hate relationship with crowds that admired his gallant efforts in the face of defeat and his sportsmanship, but didn't like some of his showboating, now had no great goals to achieve as an amateur. Frank Deford wrote in his biography of Tilden:

"Frustrated by the reductions of age, appearing more effeminate in his gestures (Tilden would die a lonely, broken figure at 60 after two convictions on morals charges), he became testier, even petty, on the court. Once, on the Riviera, in a match of no con-

Kitty Godfree. Watson and Phyllis Mudford won singles matches over Jacobs and Palfrey, respectively.

Women's dress continued to be less cumbersome. Lili de Alvarez was wearing a pagodalike trouser dress. Eileen Bennett and Betty Nuthall showed up at Wimbledon with open-backed tennis dresses, and necklines continued to drop.

1931

Sidney Wood first appeared at Wimbledon as a 15-year-old wearing white knickers on the Centre Court and losing to René Lacoste. Wood returned at 19, became the youngest player in this century (until 17-year-old Boris Becker in 1985) to win and the only one ever to win a Wimbledon final in a walkover.

Wood, who was seeded seventh, advanced to the final with a four-set victory over 22-year-old Fred Perry, a winner in an early round over a promising young German, Gottfried von Cramm. The other semifinal went to American Frank Shields over Jean Borotra, who had won the French Championship for the first time. Shields strained a leg muscle against Borotra, however, and had to scratch out of his final with Wood.

Ellsworth Vines, who had been ranked eighth in 1930 and hadn't been picked for the Davis Cup team early in the year, came into his own at 19 when he won the United States Championship in September. Vines, from Pasadena, Cal., was a lanky 6-foot-1, weighing only 145 pounds, who had a great cannonball serve. Analyst Julius Heldman wrote, "He had the flattest set of ground strokes ever seen and they were hit so hard, particularly on the forehand, that they could not clear the net by more than a few inches without going out."

He had a scare in the semifinal, losing the first two sets to Fred Perry before rally-

Nineteen-year-old Sidney Wood made history when he won Wimbledon in 1931. • *UPI*

ing. In the final Vines met George Lott, who advanced by eliminating defending champion John Doeg. Vines won, 7–9, 6–3, 9–7, 7–5. Jack Crawford took the Australian title.

Playing without Bill Tilden, the U.S. failed to appear in the challenge round of the Davis Cup for the first time since 1914. It appeared the U.S. would have a crack at the French in the challenge round when, in the inter-zone final, after a loss by Sidney Wood to Great Britain's Bunny Austin, the U.S. took a 2–1 lead as Shields beat Perry, and the American doubles team of Lott and John Van Ryn beat George Hughes and Perry. Britain prevailed, however, as Perry beat Wood, and Austin defeated Shields. In the challenge round,

France won, 3–2, for the fifth straight time, on a doubles victory and two singles triumphs by Henri Cochet, the second over Perry in the climactic match.

With Helen Wills Moody choosing not to play at Wimbledon, it appeared that Helen Jacobs would have an excellent opportunity to win, particularly after she beat Betty Nuthall, the 1931 Forest Hills

Hills Nationals without a major title because she had not played there in 1930 and had skipped Wimbledon and the French championships earlier in 1931, rectified that by winning the U.S. crown, 6–4, 6–1, over Britain's Eileen Bennett Whittingstall. By the end of the year Moody had gone four years without losing a set of singles.

As the U.S. and Great Britain prepared for the Wightman Cup matches, they were tied at 4–all. The U.S. won 5–2, with both Moody and Jacobs winning a pair of singles. This was the start of a 21-year string of U.S. Wightman Cup victories that would not be broken until 1958.

Bill Tilden made his long-awaited debut as a professional in the midst of the Depression. Co-promoter of his tour with entrepreneur William O'Brien, Tilden opened against Czech Karel Kozeluh at Madison Square Garden on Feb. 18 before a crowd of 13,000 paying $36,000. Tilden won his debut, 6–4, 6–2, 6–4, then ran off 16 straight victories and went on to beat Kozeluh before big galleries at almost every stop of a cross-country tour that grossed $238,000.

Frank Hunter, Robert Seller and Emmett Pare played subordinate roles on the tour. Other professionals at the time were Roman Najuch of Germany, the three Burke brothers—Albert, Thomas, Edward—of France; and Major Rendell of England. At Forest Hills during the summer, the U.S. Pro Championships drew a field of 44, Tilden trouncing Richards, 7–5, 6–2, 6–1 in the final.

him the greatest player of all time.

He defeated Australia's Harry Hopman in an early round and sailed through Australia's Jack Crawford and Britain's Bunny Austin in the last two rounds in straight sets. Vines scored 30 service aces against Austin, who broke his serve only once. Vines' match point was a service ace and Austin said, "I saw him swing his racket and I heard the ball hit the back canvas. The umpire called game, set and match, so I knew it was all over, but I never saw the ball." Vines' serve was timed at 121 miles per hour (Pancho Gonzalez' serve was later measured at 118 miles per hour).

Crawford, the winner of the Australian Championship, had beaten Fred Perry in the quarterfinals. An oddity of the tournament was Henri Cochet losing in the second round, then entering the All England Plate competition for also-rans eliminated in the first two rounds, and winning. He became the first ex-champion to win the Plate.

Americans were so impressed with Vines at Wimbledon that hopes were high the U.S. would win back the Davis Cup

The U.S. Championship and Wimbledon were 21-year-old Ellsworth Vines' conquest in 1932. • *UPI*

the third singles against Allison. Borotra lost the first two sets, then rallied to take the next two. Allison went on to hold a commanding 5–3 lead in the final set, but blew three match points, once when a Borotra shot hit the tape and fell over safely. The final blow came on a match point against Borotra's serve. Borotra hit his first ball into the net and his second seemed long, so long that Allison didn't hit it, and most observers thought the ball was out and the match completed. But the linesman said it was good, Borotra was saved again, and he came on to give France her third victory of the competition. Fans were left to debate whether Cochet, who won the first two sets and then lost the final match to Vines, would have been able to pull through if France needed that point. This was the sixth straight Davis Cup triumph for France, and her last.

Vines, who often wore a white cap, had a curious windmill stroke in which the racket made an almost 360-degree sweep. Starting on high as though he were going to serve, he brought the racket head back almost to the ground and swept up to the ball. He put no spin on it, however, thereby hitting a flat shot with tremendous force that made him unbeatable when he was on.

Opponents came to realize that the way to beat Vines was to keep the ball in play, hitting him soft stuff until he started making errors. A harbinger of all that came in one of the memorable semifinals at Forest Hills, when Cliff Sutter of New Orleans won the first two sets before losing in an exhausting two-and-a-half-hour match that had a packed stadium roaring. As Vines made error after error, Sutter kept the ball in play, avoiding deep shots as much as possible because he knew Vines was unbeatable at the base line. Because of the length of that match, the other semifinal, in which Cochet beat Allison, was postponed because of darkness.

When they resumed the next day, Cochet completed a five-set victory, then

after the U.S. had advanced past Great Britain in the inter-zone final. Vines showed himself to be less than invincible, however, losing to Jean Borotra in the first singles, 6–4, 6–2, 3–6, 6–4. When Cochet beat Wilmer Allison in the second singles, it looked as if France would win easily. A doubles triumph by Allison and John Van Ryn over Cochet and Jacques Brugnon, however, tightened things and set up one of the most controversial episodes in Davis Cup history.

First, the groundskeepers heavily watered the clay at Stade Roland Garros in the hope of slowing the court down to hamper Vines in his final match. The slow court served instead to bother Borotra in

complained bitterly that he had to compete on the same day in the final against Vines, who disposed of him in straight sets, 6–4, 6–4, 6–4. Cochet was tired. Twice he was unable to move out of the way in time to avoid being hit by Vines' blinding serve. The last two aces of the match by Vines were so hard that they bounced into the stands. Cochet never returned to Forest Hills.

With Wills Moody absent from Forest Hills, Jacobs won the U.S. Championship for the first time, defeating third-seeded Carolin Babcock in the final, 6–2, 6–2. Alice Marble made her first appearance in the U.S. rankings at No. 7 and was a finalist in the women's doubles at Forest Hills. Mrs. Coral Buttsworth won her second successive Australian title.

The U.S. took a 6–4 lead in Wightman Cup play on a 4–3 victory. Wills Moody won two singles matches, Jacobs and Mrs. Anna Harper one each. Bill Tilden continued to dominate the thin professional ranks with a mixture of tennis skill and theatrical showmanship. He and Vinnie Richards grossed $86,000 on their tour.

1933

Helen Wills Moody and Suzanne Lenglen are regarded by many long-time observers as two of the greatest women players of all time. It is an irony that both are best remembered for matches they lost—in which they defaulted and walked off the court. Lenglen defaulted to Molla Mallory at Forest Hills in 1921, and Moody

quit in the middle of her final with Helen Jacobs in 1933.

The two Helens—Moody, almost 28, tall, dark-haired, and coldly methodical, and Jacobs, 25, stocky and outgoing—were natural rivals. They both came from the San Francisco Bay area. Both had the same coach, Pop Fuller. When they met for the second time in this U.S. final, Moody had

Though Jacobs insisted there was no feud, she wanted badly to beat Moody. She went to none other than Lenglen, who drilled her in hitting crosscourt so that she would avoid giving Moody the backcourt dominance she liked best. Jacobs, being faster, was determined to play the net as often as possible.

In the semifinal Moody had lost her first set in seven years at Forest Hills to Betty Nuthall. Jacobs proceeded to take her first set ever from Moody, 8–6. Moody won the second, 6–3, using drop shots to tire her opponent. Given a respite in the intermission, Jacobs broke Moody's service in the opening game and then again for a 3–0 advantage. In his history of tennis, Will Grimsley wrote: "At this point Moody strode to the umpire's chair and put on her sweater. 'I am sorry, my back pains me. I cannot go on,' she said tersely. That was all she said. Wearing a long coat, her familiar eyeshade pulled low, she strode to the dressing room. She declined an interview."

It was reported that Jacobs pleaded with her to continue. Jacobs denied this, saying she merely inquired if she would

Helen Wills Moody's default to Helen Jacobs (left) in 1933 marked Moody's last appearance in a Forest Hills final. • *New York Herald Tribune*

like to rest. Moody said no and walked away without shaking hands. The fans were stunned. The press lambasted her for not trying to finish the match. She was accused of being a poor sport, a quitter, ungracious. Later she said, "I feel that I have spoiled the finish of the National Championships and wish that I had followed the advice of my doctor and returned to California. I still feel I did right in withdrawing because I was on the verge of collapse on the court."

The loss was her first since she had been beaten by Lenglen in 1926. Earlier, Moody had won the Wimbledon final over Dorothy Round, 6–4, 6–8, 6–3, for her sixth title. Joan Hartigan won the Australian championship, Britain's Margaret Scriven the French crown.

Playing without Moody, who injured her back, and Alice Marble, the U.S. defeated Great Britain in Wightman Cup play, 4–3, as Jacobs won singles matches over Round and Scriven, Sarah Palfrey scored a key victory over Scriven, and the doubles team of Jacobs and Palfrey beat Round and Mary Heeley.

Before Don Budge was to come along

Vines' serve. The score: 4–6, 11–9, 6–2, 2–6, 6–4.

The crowd exulted over the first victory by a player from the British Empire since another Australian, Gerald Patterson, won 10 years earlier. Macaulay wrote, "The cheering of the spectators went on and on, and their enthusiasm was so great there appeared to be a distinct danger that the

Wimbledon: Jack Crawford was one of the most popular champions who ever appeared at Wimbledon. Although he was only 25 when he won the title, he always seemed much older. Perhaps it was the effect of his hair, parted in the middle, the sleeves of his cricket shirt buttoned at the wrist (though he was known to roll them up in moments of crisis) and, most of all, the old-fashioned square-headed racquet with which he always played. In a long match he liked to have a pot of tea, complete with milk and sugar, and reserves of hot water, by the umpire's chair, instead of the iced beverages and other revivers favored by the moderns."

English authority Max Robertson wrote in 1974 that if a poll were taken about the best men's singles final at Wimbledon, "the Crawford-Ellsworth Vines match in 1933 would probably head it; certainly it would have to be included in the top six." Vines' service earned him 13 aces and he ran out 11 service games at love. Crawford played a defensive game against Vines' power, concentrating on Vines' relatively weak backhand. They split the first two sets, then the next two. Then Crawford changed tactics, rushing the net. He broke Vines at the end, winning the last game at love on

mixed doubles, and his opponent, Norman Farquharson, rolled up his trousers.

A big disappointment at Wimbledon was fourth-seeded Fred Perry, who lost in the second round to Farquharson, a South African. Perry finally achieved his first major title, at Forest Hills, when he outlasted Crawford in a grueling match, 6–3, 11–13, 4–6, 6–0, 6–1. Defending champion Vines lost in the fourth round in straight sets to Bitsy Grant in what was called a Mutt & Jeff match.

Perry spearheaded Britain's first Davis Cup triumph since 1912. The British ended France's six-year reign by a 3–2 margin. Perry won in five sets over Henri Cochet and then defeated 19-year-old André Merlin in the climactic singles. Austin beat Merlin and lost to Cochet; Jean Borotra and Jacques Brugnon won the doubles over Harry Lee and Pat Hughes.

Bill Tilden's opponent on the professional tour was Hans Nusslein of Germany. Tilden dominated, though gross receipts dropped from $86,000 the year before to $62,000. Henri Cochet also turned pro and was beaten by Tilden in his debut in Paris.

His leap says it all for Fred Perry, winner over Jack Crawford in the 1933 U.S. final. • *New York Herald Tribune*

1934

Fred Perry brought England its first Wimbledon Championship since 1909, the year he was born. He won the Australian and U.S. Championships and teamed with Bunny Austin to spearhead a successful defense of the Davis Cup.

In his history of Forest Hills, Robert Minton wrote, "Perry combined speed with a wristy forehand developed from first play-ing table tennis, of which he became the world champion. He was an enormous crowd pleaser; handsome enough to be a movie star, and a cocky showman in a white blazer and an unlit pipe, as though he were a Lord, and not the son of a Labor Party member of Parliament. He never ruffled anyone with a display of temper, for he was phlegmatic and won his matches by outlast-ing his opponents. His physical condition was second to none."

Perry's opponent in the Wimbledon final was Jack Crawford, who had lost to Perry in the final of the Australian Championships and to Gottfried von Cramm in the French final. Reporter Ferdinand Kuhn said of Perry's 6–3, 6–0, 7–5 triumph: "Perry was always the complete master. He didn't make a half-dozen bad shots in the whole match. He was lithe as a panther, always holding the opponent in check and beating

Australia's Jack Crawford, No. 1 in the world rankings in 1933 after missing a Grand Slam, lost to Fred Perry in the 1934 Wimbledon final. • *UPI*

into the net, the first time anybody could remember a Wimbledon final ending on a double fault.

Britain's joy was complete when Dorothy Round won the women's title, and afterward, to a tumultuous ovation, she and Perry were summoned to the Royal Box to be presented to King George and Queen Mary.

The women's final had come to down to a meeting between Round, who had been beaten in the 1933 final by Helen Wills Moody, and Helen Jacobs, who had lost to Moody in the 1929 and 1932 finals. Playing before the King and Queen in a scene much like Virginia Wade's Wimbledon Centenary victory in 1977, Round won the first set, 6–2, lost, 7–5; then triumphed in the finale, 6–3.

By now shorts and bare legs were much in evidence at Wimbledon. The Prince of Wales said, "I see no reason on earth why any woman should not wear shorts for lawn tennis. They are very comfortable and quite the most practical costume for the game; and I don't think the wearers lose anything in looks."

Elizabeth Ryan teamed with France's Simone Mathieu to win the women's doubles crown, her 19th at Wimbledon, a record that Billie Jean King later would tie and surpass. Ryan won 12 doubles and 7 mixed-doubles titles. Wimbledon official Duncan Macaulay discussed why Ryan, so strong in doubles, never won a major singles championship: "Firstly, her era coincided with that of two superlative singles champions, Suzanne Lenglen and Mrs. Moody; and secondly, Miss Ryan's only stroke on the forehead was a sizzling chop, very effective in doubles—particularly against women—but not so effective in singles as a good flat or topspin drive such as Lenglen or Moody played to perfection."

At Forest Hills, Perry won in the semifinals over Vernon Kirby, who earlier had eliminated 19-year-old Don Budge, making his first appearance in the Nationals. Wilmer Allison beat Sidney Wood in the other semi, then put Perry to the test before losing, 6–4, 6–3, 3–6, 1–6, 8–6.

George Lott won his fifth U.S. doubles title, teaming with Lester Stoefen. That pair gave the U.S. its only point in a 4–1 Davis Cup loss to the British. In singles Perry and Austin swept Wood and Frank Shields.

The United States increased its Wightman Cup lead to 8–4 with a 5–2 triumph powered by Helen Jacobs and Sarah Palfrey. Each won singles over Dorothy Round and Peggy Scriven, and they combined to win a doubles match.

The pro tour needed some new blood and got it with the arrival of Ellsworth Vines. With much fanfare before a Madison Square Garden crowd of 14,637, the largest ever to see a tennis match in the United States, Vines, 23, made his debut against Bill Tilden, 41. The match grossed $30,125 and Tilden won, 8–6, 6–3, 6–2. They went on a tour of 72 cities, grossing $243,000, the most ever for the pros, and Vines beat Tilden, 47 matches to 26. Vines won a match in Los Angeles, 6–0, 21–23, 7–5, 3–6, 6–2. Another memorable match between old adversaries Tilden and Henri Cochet took place at the Garden before a crowd of 12,663 paying $20,000, and Tilden outlasted the 32-year-old Cochet, 7–9, 6–1, 4–6, 6–3, 6–3.

1935

Probably no player ever suffered as much frustration against an arch-rival as Helen Jacobs did against Helen Wills Moody. The only time Jacobs beat Moody, the victory was less than fully satisfying because it came as a result of a default when back trouble forced Moody to quit the 1933 final at Forest Hills while losing. All other times Jacobs lost to her, and among the toughest setbacks was the 1935 Wimbledon final.

Moody had played little the year before and was seeded only fourth in pursuit of

her seventh Wimbledon title. Early in the season she had lost a set to Mary Hardwick, had lost a match to Kay Stammers, and in an early Wimbledon round against unknown Czech Slenca Cepkova she lost the first set and was within a point of trailing 4–1 in the second set before rallying.

In the final Jacobs, seeded third, fell behind, 4–0, almost tied at 4–4, then faltered and lost the first set 6–3. Of the second set British authority Max Robertson wrote, "Jacobs' length improved; her favorite forehand chop became as dangerous as a scimitar. Mrs. Moody tried to come to the net but she was never able to run up and down the court as well as she could cover it from side to side." Jacobs won the second set.

Jacobs took a 4–2 lead, knocking the racket from Moody's hand on one powerful serve. She then broke Moody to lead, 5–2, but Moody broke to 3–5, where she faced a match point at 30–40, and flicked a desperation lob with Jacobs at the net. It looked like a simple smash, but a gusty wind caused the ball to sink swiftly, so that Jacobs had to drop to her knees to hit it— into the net. That turned the match around. Jacobs went down fighting, serving two aces when trailing, 5–6, but lost the set and match, 6–3, 3–6, 7–5. It was her fourth loss to Moody at Wimbledon, the third time in a final. She also lost to her in the 1928 Forest Hills final.

With Moody again absent from Forest Hills, Jacobs went on to win the title for the fourth successive year, beating Sarah Palfrey, 6–1, 6–4. Jacobs had a hand in a 4–3 Wightman Cup victory by the United States over Great Britain, winning in singles over Dorothy Round and teaming in the doubles with Sarah Palfrey. Palfrey and Ethel Burkhardt Arnold also won in singles, as did Stammers (over Jacobs) and Round (over Arnold) for the British.

In the second year of Fred Perry's three-year reign over the men he won the

French and Wimbledon Championships, lost the Australian final to Jack Crawford and to Wilmer Allison at Forest Hills in the semifinals when hampered by a kidney injury. He led Britain to a 5–0 sweep over the U.S. in the Davis Cup.

At Wimbledon, Perry beat Crawford in four sets, then trounced Gottfried von Cramm. the first German male to make the

Wilmer Allison won his only U.S. Singles title in 1935. • *UPI*

grew that Budge even said, "Hi, Queenie," and Budge took pains in his autobiography to point out that he did not wave, that he did wipe his brow, a reflex gesture with him. Two years later, though, when Budge was again at Wimbledon and met the Queen, she told him, he said, "You know, Mr. Budge, I did not see you a few years ago when you waved to me, but had I, I want you to know that I would have waved back."

The Wimbledon mixed finals was marked by the appearance of Mr. and Mrs. Harry Hopman—she the former Nell Hall—of Australia. They were beaten by Perry and Dorothy Round.

At Forest Hills, Perry fell heavily on his side at 3–3 against Allison in the semifinals. A doctor was brought to the sidelines to keep an eye on Perry, who kept putting his hand to his back (it turned out to be a displaced kidney). He lost to Allison, whom he had beaten the previous year, and in the Davis Cup, in straight sets. Allison then beat Sidney Wood, 6–2, 6–2, 6–3 for the title, and thereafter confined himself to doubles.

The United States was shut out for the first time in the Davis Cup since 1911, losing to Great Britain as Perry and Austin

swept Allison and Budge in singles, and Pat Hughes and Raymond Tuckey defeated Allison and John Van Ryn.

George Lott and Lester Stoefen joined the professional ranks. Tilden beat Lott 6–4, 7–5, before a crowd of 16,000 in Madison Square Garden, and Tilden and Ellsworth Vines defeated the newcomers in their specialty, doubles. The pros' cross-country tour grossed $188,000.

1936

Fred Perry turned pro late in the year after dominating tennis in the four previous years as few men have over such a span. He won three successive Wimbledon titles, three U.S. titles, a French and an Australian title, and nine out of 10 Davis Cup challenge round victories.

Perry had laid off for seven months after his injury at Forest Hills in 1935, and when he was beaten in the French final by Gottfried von Cramm, there was some question that he could retain his old form. At Wimbledon, however, he quickly established that he would be formidable by sailing through early-round opponents. He beat Bitsy Grant in straight sets, then had what would turn out to be his only difficult moments of the tournament, losing the first set to fifth-seeded Don Budge in the semifinals. Perry rallied to win in four sets, 5–7, 6–4, 6–3, 6–4. He then had an easy time in the final when von Cramm hurt his leg in the second game of the first set. Von Cramm continued on a bad leg and Perry won, 6–1, 6–1, 6–0, the widest margin of victory in a Wimbledon final.

It was the first time since the pre-World War I days that somebody had won three

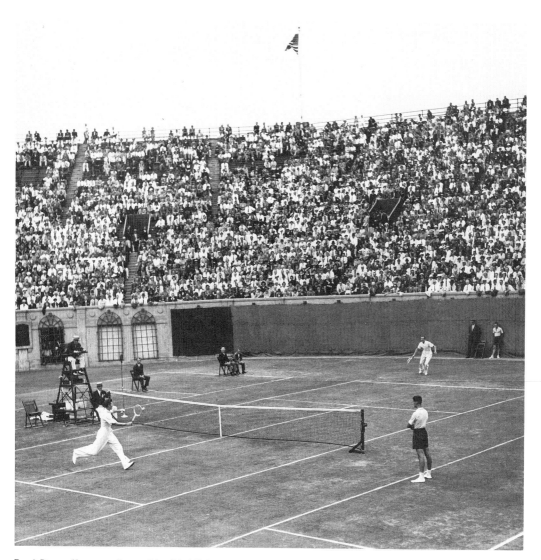

Fred Perry (far court) won his third U.S. Singles championship in 1936, defeating Don Budge. • *UPI*

straight Wimbledons, and Perry was on hand in 1978 as a radio commentator when Bjorn Borg did the same.

Perry and Budge met again in a Forest Hills final that represented Budge's last chance to beat Perry in a major international tournament before Perry turned pro. They played a classic five-set match twice interrupted by rain. Budge won the first set, 6–2. Perry the second by the same

my country against the No. 1 player in the world. All I had to do was hold my serve one more time. I could not. I was so exhausted in reaching up to hit my serve that I felt as if I were leaning on the ball. There was no life in my shots. The stretching and reaching for the serve particularly wore on me. He broke me again—our fourth loss of service in a row—held his own serve at last, and tied the set at 5–all."

Budge came to within two points of victory at 8–7, but couldn't break through, and Perry finally won, 10–8, for his third Forest Hills title. Nobody won the U.S. at Forest Hills three times since. Budge later beat Perry on concrete in Los Angeles. Only Perry beat him on grass.

A loss to Australia in the inter-zone final knocked the United States out of the Davis Cup final for the first time since 1933. Great Britain defended successfully, though pressed. After Bunny Austin beat Jack Crawford and Perry beat Adrian Quist, the Aussies rallied to take the doubles, Crawford and Quist over Pat Hughes and Raymond Tuckey, and Quist beat Austin. Perry prevailed, however, whipping Crawford in straight sets.

Helen Jacobs' quest for a Wimbledon Championship finally was successful after

10 years. She and Hilde Krahwinkel Sperling split the first two sets and were tied at 5–all in the third before Jacobs broke through for a 6–2, 4–6, 7–5 triumph that brought an ovation from an approving Wimbledon crowd. Sperling had won the French title.

Jacobs did not win a fifth straight U.S. Championship because she ran into 22-

woman player. Joan Hartigan won the Australian crown.

The Wightman Cup competition came down to its closest finish ever. The U.S. was hard-pressed because Jacobs was beaten by both Kay Stammers and Dorothy Round. Victories by Sarah Palfrey Fabyan and Carolin Babcock in singles, and a doubles win by Babcock and Marjorie Gladman Van Ryan evened the match at 3–all. Jacobs and Fabyan then teamed to beat Stammers and Freda James in a match that went to 5–all in the final set before the Americans won, 7–5.

The pros continued to struggle in their quest for gate attractions. Promoter Bill O'Brien brought women back for the first time since 1926, and Ethel Burkhardt Arnold defeated Jane Sharp at Madison Square Garden. Bruce Barnes was added to the troupe led by Tilden, but the tour lost $22,000.

1937

The line of dominant players, which started with Bill Tilden in the 1920s and continued through the French trio of René

Lacoste, Henri Cochet and Jean Borotra, then Ellsworth Vines and Fred Perry, added the imposing red-headed figure of Don Budge. Budge, 22, swept Wimbledon and Forest Hills and sailed through all Davis Cup competition, winning what many rate as the greatest Davis Cup match ever played.

With Perry moving to the professional ranks, it was obvious that Great Britain would yield the Davis Cup to the strong challenger that emerged from the inter-zone final. Budge spearheaded United States victories over Japan and Australia, beating Aussies Jack Crawford and John Bromwich, to set up a showdown against Germany.

Before Davis Cup play came the Wimbledon in which Budge was seeded first and Gottfried von Cramm second. On his way to the final Budge lost only one set,

to Frank Parker in the semifinals, while von Cramm was extended to five sets by Crawford. Budge then defeated von Cramm, 6–3, 6–4, 6–2. Budge also became the first man ever to score a Wimbledon triple, adding the men's doubles title with Gene Mako and the mixed doubles with Alice Marble.

On to the Davis Cup and a match that had implications beyond the tennis court. "War talk was everywhere." Budge recalled. "Hitler was doing everything he could to stir up Germany. The atmosphere was filled with tension although von Cramm was a known anti-Nazi and remained one of the finest gentlemen and most popular players on the circuit."

On the first day von Cramm beat Bitsy Grant, and Budge beat Henner Henkel, the Australian champion, in straight sets. Budge and Mako then defeated von

Princess Helena Victoria presents the Davis Cup to non-playing captain Walter Pate in 1937 as (left to right) Don Budge, Gene Mako, Frank Parker and Bitsy Grant look on. • *Fischer Collection/SPS*

Cramm and Henkel in four sets. Henkel, however, defeated Grant easily, setting up the concluding match on the Wimbledon Centre Court, July 30, with Queen Mary in attendance. Just before Budge and von Cramm went out to the court, von Cramm was called to the telephone. It was a long-distance call from Adolf Hitler exhorting von Cramm to win for the Fatherland. Budge recalls that "Gottfried came out pale

the Germans, the crowd slightly favored von Cramm. An oddity of the competition was that the Germans were coached by Bill Tilden. It was not unusual for a pro in one country to coach another country's Davis Cup team, but it was uncommon for a coach to hold the post when it meant working against his own nation. At one point Tilden was so animated in his rooting he infuriated American show-business celebri-

Attacking von Cramm's service and going to the net behind it, he got the matching break in the seventh game, making the score, 3–4, and held service to tie, 4–all. The score went to 5–5, then 6–6. In the 13th game Budge achieved another break. He then reached match point five times on his own service only to see von Cramm fight back to attain the sanctuary of deuce. "The crowd was so quiet I am sure they could hear us breathing," Budge recalled.

"On the sixth point, there was a prolonged rally," Will Grimsley wrote. "Von Cramm sent up a lob. Budge raced back and returned it. Von Cramm then hit a forehand crosscourt. Budge tore after the ball, got his racket on it and took a desperate swing, sprawling to the court. It was a placement—game, set, match and the Davis Cup series. The final score was 6–8, 5–7, 6–4, 6–2, 8–6. The match ended at 8:45 P.M. in semi-darkness. The two players went to their dressing rooms, relaxed, dressed and returned more than an hour later to find most of the crowd still on hand, buzzing over the spectacular final."

Because von Cramm was the underdog and the British thought they might have a better chance in a Davis Cup final against

and Bunny Austin, Budge teamed with Mako in the doubles for another point, with Frank Parker splitting his singles assignments.

The Americans returned with the trophy to a ticker-tape parade in New York, and Budge later was greeted with a parade in his hometown of Oakland, receiving a signet ring that featured the city seal flanked by diamonds. At Forest Hills Von Cramm had a third crack at Budge, but only after he survived an 0–6, 8–6, 6–8, 6–3, 6–2 semifinal over Bobby Riggs, who had gained a place in the Top Ten rankings at No. 6 the previous year. Von Cramm extended Budge to five sets, yet Budge said he felt none of the trauma he found at Wimbledon, which he had won in straight sets. The score this time: 6–1, 7–9, 6–1, 3–6, 6–1. The packed crowd of 14,000 (5,000 were turned away) roared all the way for Budge. He was voted athlete of the year and became the first tennis player to win the Sullivan Award, annually presented to the outstanding amateur athlete in the U.S. Viv McGrath won the Australian, Henkel the French.

Despite the victory by Alice Marble over Helen Jacobs at Forest Hills the year before,

Jacobs was seeded first at Wimbledon and Marble fifth. Neither player reached the final. Marble lost in the semifinals to Jadwiga Jedrzejowska of Poland; Jacobs went out in the quarterfinals against Britain's Dorothy Round, who went on to beat Jedrzejowska in the final, 6–2, 2–6, 7–5.

At Forest Hills, Jedrzejowska beat Jacobs in the semifinal, then lost, 6–4, 6–2, to startling No. 2 foreign seed Anita Lizana of Chile, making her only appearance in the championships. The French title having been won by Hilde Sperling of Denmark and the Australian title by Nancye Wynne of Australia, this marked the first time since the end of World War I that no American woman had won any of the four major championships.

International success came in Wightman Cup play with a 6–1 victory over Great Britain, the United States' seventh straight for an 11–4 edge in the series. Marble and Jacobs won twice in singles from Kay Stammers and Mary Hardwick; Sarah Palfrey Fabyan defeated Margot Lumb; and Marble and Fabyan won a doubles point. Interest in professional tennis revived with the debut of Fred Perry playing a cross-country tour against Ellsworth Vines, promoted by Frank Hunter, Bill Tilden's old doubles partner, and S. Howard Voshell. Perry opened at Madison Square Garden in fine fashion, defeating Vines, 7–5, 3–6, 6–3, 6–4, before a crowd of 17,630 paying $58,120, a record for the tour. Perry won the first six matches, but Vines finished strong, winning the series, 32–29. The tour grossed $412,181. Perry, under his guarantee, receiving the bigger slice, $91,335, while Vines got $34,195.

Though Vines was regarded as the "official" pro champion at this time, Tilden scheduled himself against Perry in the Garden later in the year. Tilden was 44, Perry 28, and though the crowd of 15,132 cheered mightily for the old guy, he was outclassed. He lost in the Garden for the first time, 6–1, 6–3, 4–6, 6–0. Al Laney wrote in that period, "All they can do is beat him, they cannot ever be his equal." It was estimated that Tilden had netted $500,000 (in Depression dollars) since turning pro six years before.

In October, a premature—31 years before its time—and rather plaintive event advertised as the "first open championship" was held in the West Virginia Hills at the posh Greenbrier resort. Prize money was offered, but no amateurs of note rushed in to test the waters, and the few unknowns who did were suspended by the USTA. Vines, Tilden and Perry stayed away, too. The event was dominated by the second-line pros, Karel Kozeluh beating Bruce Barnes, 6–2, 6–3, 4–6, 4–6, 6–1, for America's allegedly first open title.

1938

Don Budge at 23 had the single most successful year of any player in tennis history to that time. He won the four major championships—Australia, France, Wimbledon and the U.S.—a feat that came to be known as the Grand Slam after Budge accomplished it. He also won the triple crown at Wimbledon for the second straight year and he helped the U.S. retain the Davis Cup.

Budge had received his first substantial offer to go professional in 1937. He turned it down because he felt he owed a debt to amateur tennis to the extent of helping defend the Davis Cup the U.S. had won in 1937 for the first time since 1926. "The Grand Slam then occurred to me as something of an afterthought," Budge said. He laid his plans carefully, telling only his friend Gene Mako, resolving not to extend himself at any time, so that he shouldn't tire along the way, as Jack Crawford had in 1933 when he won the first three titles, but lost in the final at Forest Hills.

Budge won the four majors in 1938. • *UPI*

Budge started in Australia, after losing frequently in leisurely tune-ups, and he swept through the championships, beating John Bromwich, 6–4, 6–1, 6–1. Shortly after the players' return to their home countries, Gottfried von Cramm of Germany, Budge's friend, was arrested and thrown into jail, charged with homosexuality, but probably imprisoned because of his opposition to Nazi rule. Budge led a committee of athletes appealing without success for von Cramm's release.

In the French Championships, though Budge suffered from diarrhea, he had a fairly easy time. Extended to five sets by a Yugoslavian lefty, Franjo Kukuljevic, Budge was never behind and said later he never felt threatened. Where von Cramm might have been his opponent in the final, he faced 6-foot-4 Czech Roderich Menzel, an outstanding clay-court player. Budge romped, 6–3, 6–2, 6–4, in less than an hour. He recalled best about that feat the party afterward at which cellist Pablo Casals gave a concert in Budge's honor in Casals' apartment within view of the Eiffel Tower.

At Wimbledon, Budge won without losing a set, yet there was a time in the tourna-ment when he said he was near panic because he had been having trouble with his backhand, his most celebrated weapon, considered by many to have been the great-est backhand of them all. He had been undercutting the stroke, and only while watching an older woman member of the All England Club on a side court, hitting with topspin on her backhand, did he real-ize his error. He won his second successive

The U.S. won, 3–2, as Bobby Riggs beat Adrian Quist in a key four-set opening vic-tory, and Budge beat Bromwich in four sets and Quist in straight sets. The Budge-Mako team lost to Bromwich-Quist, and Bromwich beat Riggs.

Budge had been suffering from the flu and a loss of voice off and on during the year. But he proceeded to romp through the U.S. championships, defeating Welby Van Horn, Bob Kamrath, Charlie Hare, Harry Hopman and Sidney Wood to reach the final against his pal Mako, who had become the first unseeded player ever to reach the finals at Forest Hills.

To some it looked like a setup for Budge, but he responded, "Gene was as likely to roll over and play dead for me as peace was to come in our time." Mako actually won the second set, only the sec-ond one Budge lost in the four tourna-ments. Budge then had to explain that he did not intentionally throw a set to his friend, certainly not at Forest Hills with so much at stake. "And I had too much respect and affection for Gene to treat him as if he were an inferior player who could be given a set for his troubles, rather like a condescending pat on the head."

They had to wait a week to play the final, sitting out a hurricane that struck the northeast. Then Budge won, 6–3, 6–8, 6–2, 6–1. Budge's season record: won seven of nine tournaments on a 44–2 match record.

Aside from Budge's heroics, Wimbledon was marked by one of the strongest women's fields of all time, featuring the return after a two-year absence of 32-year-old Helen Wills Moody, seeking a record eighth title. Though she had been extended by Kay Stammers in Wightman Cup play and had lost in a minor tournament to Hilde Sperling, she was seeded No. 1. Behind her came Alice Marble, Jadwiga Jedrzejowska of Poland and Sperling. Sarah Palfrey Fabyan was seeded seventh; not seeded at all was Helen Jacobs.

The semifinals came down to these match-ups: Moody vs. Sperling, and Marble vs. Jacobs. Had Moody and Marble won, it would have brought a meeting of the long-time queen of tennis, Moody, and the bright new face who had succeeded her and Jacobs. Despite a struggle, Moody prevailed, 12–10, 6–4, but Marble lost to Jacobs, 6–4, 6–4, giving Jacobs what would be her fourth and last chance in a Wimbledon final against her lifelong nemesis.

The day before the final Jacobs worked out with Bill Tilden, who had been cultivating a flat forehand drive in her game, and she came up with a slight strain of her Achilles tendon. She came on the court with her ankle bandaged, had trouble with it during the match, stopping to change the bandage at one point, and after holding even at 4–4 in the first set, she eventually deteriorated and lost, 6–4, 6–0. It was Moody's 50th successive match win, a record, and 55th in 56 matches at Wimbledon, concluding her career in major events. During the tournament, word came that Suzanne Lenglen had died from pernicious anemia. She was 38.

The Australian Championship went to Dorothy Bundy of the United States, the French title to Simone Mathieu of France. With Moody absent from the U.S. Championships, Marble won for the second time. She beat Sarah Palfrey Fabyan in the semifinals after losing the first set, then won the final over Australian Nancye Wynne.

An eighth straight Wightman Cup success for the United States over Britain, this time 5–2, consisted of two singles triumphs by Moody in her first appearance since 1932, a split in singles by Marble, a singles triumph by Fabyan and a doubles victory by Marble and Fabyan. Moody lost with Bundy in doubles, Moody's seventh defeat in 10 Wightman Cup doubles matches. Moody's overall singles record: 18–2.

A pro tennis pattern had been set. The tour would flourish with the arrival of a new amateur champion, then taper off until a new face appeared. Fred Perry, in his second year, became co-promoter with Ellsworth Vines, the champion. Vines won 48 matches, Perry 35 on a tour that brought in $175,000, considerably less than the previous year, and the pair split $34,000.

1939

With the departure of Don Budge to the professional ranks, amateur tennis turned up another great player in Bobby Riggs, though his cocky attitude served to overshadow for a long time the fact that he was a quality player.

Riggs was a key figure in the Davis Cup challenge by Australia, and at Wimbledon and Forest Hills. In the Davis Cup competition at the Merion Cricket Club in Philadelphia, the United States won the first two singles, then lost the doubles and the final two singles, enabling Australia, captained by Harry Hopman, to reclaim the Davis Cup for the first time since 1919.

Riggs, instrumental in winning the Cup for the U.S. the previous year by beating Adrian Quist, failed this time by losing to Quist, a heavy underdog. Riggs beat Australian champion John Bromwich in straight sets and then Frank Parker came through with a big victory with a five-set success over Quist to open a 2–0 lead. Two kids, Joe Hunt, 20, and Jack Kramer, 18, who had yet to gain a Top Ten ranking, lost the doubles to Quist-Bromwich, so a Riggs victory over Quist was needed

ninth game. Quist wouldn't break, however, and he then held serve to win the match. Bromwich defeated Parker, 6–0, 6–3, 6–1, and for the only time in Cup history a team had come back from 0–2 to win the finale.

Riggs was a wily player, compact, versatile, a great all-court retriever and completely self-confident. He preferred to play from the baseline, but he had a better serve than many people thought, and it kept getting better. He also could play the net, particularly when his opponent least expected it. He was a compulsive gambler. At Wimbledon, he reportedly won more than $100,000 from English bookies in 1939 when he bet on himself to win the singles, doubles and mixed doubles. In the singles, he trailed two sets to one before rallying to beat his doubles partner, Elwood Cooke. After he and Cooke won the men's doubles, Riggs paired with Alice Marble to win the mixed doubles, becoming the only man other than Budge and Frank Sedgman in 1952 to win a Wimbledon triple. Marble became the only woman to win a triple other than Suzanne Lenglen before World War II. Louise Brough (1948 and 1950), Doris Hart (1951) and Billie Jean King (1967 and 1973) followed.

Marble won Wimbledon for the first time, and in such convincing fashion that the British experts were ready to accord her a place with the all-time greats. She beat Hilde Krahwinkel Sperling, 6–0, 6–0, then romped in the final, 6–2, 6–0, over Kay Stammers, who had eliminated Helen Jacobs and Sarah Palfrey Fabyan. Marble and Fabyan won their second Wimbledon doubles crown.

Horn, an unseeded player who beat Bromwich, Wayne Sabin and Cooke on his way into the final. Riggs eliminated Joe Hunt in the semis. Van Horn opened with two aces, and the supportive crowd roared with approval. Riggs then took charge. As Robert Minton wrote in *A History of Forest Hills,* "Serving a high twist ball to Van Horn's backhand, keeping the ball down the middle of his forehand, to increase the youngster's tendency to crowd his powerful drive, interspersing drop shots, throwing up lobs and constantly mixing his speed and length, Riggs won the match not so much on his ability to finish off the rallies as on his success in prodding Van Horn into mistakes." The score: 6–4, 6–2, 6–4.

In the women's championship, Marble, completing one of the most powerful seasons ever enjoyed by a woman, was threatened by Helen Jacobs, the 32-year-old four-time champion who reached the final by overcoming Stammers, her conqueror at Wimbledon. After losing the first set, 6–0, Jacobs won the second , 10–8, and took a 3–1 lead in the third set before Marble recovered to win.

Allison Danzig wrote in *The New York Times:* "Here was one of the most dramatic battles that women's tennis had produced in years, fought out for an hour-and-a-half in gusty cross-currents of wind that raised havoc with the strokes, while the gallery roared and screamed its encouragement at Miss Jacobs. The crescendo of the enthusiasm was reached in the final game, a furiously disputed 20-point session in which Miss Jacobs five times came within a stroke of 5–all and twice stood off match point, only to yield finally to Miss Marble's more powerful attacking weapons."

Thus, Marble completed her second straight U.S. triple, having won in Boston the women's doubles with Sarah Palfrey Fabyan for the third straight year and then the mixed doubles, not with Riggs, but with the 33-year-old Australian, Harry Hopman.

When Don Budge made his pro debut in Madison Square Garden in January, he was a slight underdog to Ellsworth Vines, the champion. A crowd of 16,725, paid $47,120, and many of them were USTA officials who showed their devotion to Budge for his loyalty in putting off his departure from the amateur ranks a year in order to defend the Davis Cup. Budge trounced Vines, 6–3, 6–4, 6–2, and it may have been because Vines had played only eight matches with Fred Perry in South America that summer.

Later, Budge made a second Garden appearance against Perry, who had been his master as an amateur. Budge won easily, 6–1, 6–3, 6–0. On the tour played mostly in big cities, Budge asserted his superiority, beating Vines, 21–18, and Perry, 18–11. Budge collected more than $100,000, including a $75,000 guarantee from the $204,503 gross. Vines got $23,000, then deserted tennis for a successful pro golf career.

Holcombe Ward, president of the USTA, presents the U.S. Singles trophy to Bobby Riggs, victor over Welby Van Horn in 1939. • *UPI*

1940

Bombs fell on Wimbledon. The start of World War II a year earlier forced the cancellation of Wimbledon and the French Championships between 1940 and 1945, though the French held a tournament that was closed to non-nationals. The Australian Championships was halted in 1941. Bombs first hit Wimbledon on October 11, causing

the postwar years.

Defending champion Bobby Riggs suffered a costly loss in the U.S. Championships because his defeat by Don McNeill in the final took some of the luster off his record and he had to wait a year before turning pro. McNeill, a 22-year-old Oklahoman, fought one of the great come-from-behind battles against Riggs in a match marked by some outstanding sportsmanship. McNeill won, 4–6, 6–8, 6–3, 6–3, 7–5.

With the score tied at 4–all and deuce in the final set, McNeill hit a shot to Riggs' sideline that the linesman first called out. As Riggs turned his back and prepared to serve, the official reversed his call, declaring it good. Riggs did not know of the change until he heard the call, "Advantage McNeill." Allison Danzig wrote, "The defending champion, who rarely questions a decision, turned at the call and then walked back toward the linesman, asking him why he had changed his ruling. The official maintained that the ball was good and Riggs, without further quibbling, accepted the costly decision and lost the next point and the game."

Then, in the opening rally of the final game, Riggs had to hit a ball that was falling just over the net and he gingerly endeavored to keep from touching the tape as he made his volley. The umpire instantly announced his foot had touched the net and he lost the point. "At that critical state," Danzig wrote, "it was a bitter pill to swallow, but Riggs took it without arguing. McNeill, however, apparently did not like to win the point that way, even though the ruling was correct, and when he knocked Riggs' next service far out of court, the stadium rang with applause."

After losing the first set, McNeill rallied from 1–5 and 15–40 in the second set to tie, saved four set points, went on to take a 6–5 lead, but then dropped the set anyway. Down by two sets, he still came back, and with the crowd almost completely behind the valiant underdog, he pulled out the final set and the match.

Alice Marble won the singles, doubles and mixed doubles for the third straight year, equalling the feat of Hazel Hotchkiss in 1909–11 and Mary K. Browne in 1912–14. In the singles final she won a return match with Helen Jacobs, 6–2, 6–3; she and Sarah Palfrey Fabyan won a third straight doubles, and she and Riggs won the mixed. She turned pro at the end of the year. In Australia, Adrian Quist won the men's title, Nancye Wynne Bolton the women's.

There was little pro tennis action of any note in 1940, although Don Budge won his first U.S. Pro title, over Fred Perry in Chicago.

1941–45

The United States Championships at Forest Hills was the only major tournament outpost during the World War II years. Old champions went off to war, new ones emerged and though there were no sellout crowds, there were outstanding matches among fine players.

The Top Ten rankings for 1941 give some indication of the names that would dominate the sport during the war years: The men: 1. Bobby Riggs, 2. Frank Kovacs, 3. Frank Parker, 4. Don McNeill, 5. Ted Schroeder, 6. Wayne Sabin, 7. Gardnar Mulloy, 8. Bitsy Grant, 9. Jack Kramer, 10. Bill Talbert. The women: 1. Sarah Palfrey Cooke, 2. Pauline Betz, 3. Dorothy Bundy, 4. Margaret Osborne, 5. Helen Jacobs, 6. Helen Bernhard, 7. Hope Knowles, 8. Mary Arnold, 9. Virginia Kovacs, 10. Louise Brough.

1941— Riggs regained the title he had won in 1939 and then relinquished in 1940 to Don McNeill. In the semifinals Riggs beat Ted Schroeder in five sets, while McNeill was eliminated by the colorful Kovacs. Riggs then took apart Kovacs' game after the first set, winning 5–7, 6–1, 6–3, 6–3.

Sarah Palfrey Fabyan, divorced and newly remarried as Sarah Palfrey Cooke, won the women's title, the first Easterner

Sarah Palfrey Cooke displays the form that won her the U.S. crown over Pauline Betz in 1941. • *UPI*

to achieve that distinction since Maud Barger Wallach in 1908. Cooke was 28, a year older than Bill Tilden when he won his first U.S. crown. She had been a contender for the championship since she was 14; she had been a runner-up to Helen Jacobs in 1934 and 1935. Victory came by a 7–5, 6–2 score over Pauline Betz. She also won the women's doubles with Margaret Osborne, her ninth title with her fourth partner in this competition. She won with Betty Nuthall in 1930 and 1933, Jacobs in 1934 and 1935, and with Alice Marble from 1937 through 1940.

Jack Kramer and Ted Schroeder won their second straight doubles championship.

Marble joined the pros and beat Britain's Mary Hardwick, 8–6, 8–6, in their debut at Madison Square Garden. Bill Tilden, 48, came out of semi-retirement to face Don Budge and lost, 6–3, 6–4. The tour was a relative bust, Budge winning 51 of 56 matches. Budge wrote: "Tilden was still capable of some sustained great play that could occasionally even carry him all the way through a match. Most of the time he could, at his best, hang on for at least a set or two. Despite his age, he was no pushover. The people came out primarily for the show—to see me at my peak, and to see Tilden because they might never have the chance again. Bill could invariably

out of bed for the final, in which Navy Lieutenant Joe Hunt beat him, 6–3, 6–8, 10–8, 6–0. It was Hunt's last major tournament. He was killed in an aircrash in pilot training in February 1944.

Pauline Betz won her second straight women's title, again downing Brough in the final, 6–3, 5–7, 6–3. Kramer and Frank Parker won the doubles, Bill Talbert and

7–5, 3–6, 4–6, 6–2. Early favorite Jack Kramer, who had not lost a match all year, missed the tournament with appendicitis. A few weeks later, Kramer was inducted into the U.S. Coast Guard.

Betz defeated 19-year-old Louise Brough, 4–6, 6–1, 6–4; Brough and Margaret Osborne won the doubles for the first time. Gardnar Mulloy and Bill Talbert won the men's doubles (shifted from Longwood to Forest Hills), Schroeder and Brough the mixed.

Bobby Riggs and Frank Kovacs turned pro in late 1941, but the entrance of the U.S. into the war cut down the scope of the tour. Budge won, finishing ahead of Riggs, Perry and Kovacs in that order. They played 71 cities, drew only 101,915 customers, and that was the end of the pro tour for the remainder of the war, although Budge won his second U.S. Pro title over Riggs at Forest Hills.

1943— Kramer, on leave, was topseeded at Forest Hills, but he ate a plateful of bad clams the night before the semifinals and came down with food poisoning. He managed to beat Pancho Segura in the semis but was so sick he could hardly get

6–4, 3–6, 6–3, 6–3. It was the only tournament in which he competed. Betz won her final over Margaret Osborne, 6–3, 8–6. Osborne and Brough won the women's doubles, McNeill and Bob Falkenburg the

Sgt. Frank Parker was the U.S. champ in 1944 and 1945. •*New York Herald Tribune*

Lt. (J.G.) Don McNeill (left) and Pvt. Frank Kovacs appeared at Forest Hills in a tennis benefit for the Red Cross Victory Fund in 1944.

• *New York Herald Tribune*

men's doubles, and Talbert and Osborne their second mixed doubles.

Though there was no pro activity, pro champion Don Budge and cadet Jack Kramer played a war charity exhibition at Madison Square Garden. Kramer won, 6–3, 6–2.

1945— In a repeat of the previous men's final, Sergeant Frank Parker defeated Bill Talbert, and Sarah Palfrey Cooke ended Pauline Betz' three-year reign. Parker beat Mrs. Cooke's husband, Elwood, in the semifinals and then defeated Talbert, 14–12, 6–1, 6–2. Talbert had eliminated Pancho Segura. Talbert and Gardnar Mulloy won the men's doubles, Brough and Osborne the women's doubles, and Talbert and Osborne the mixed.

3: The 25 Greatest Players: 1914–45

wearing a white cap, still another wore a white eyeshade. They had nicknames such as the Wizard, Big Bill, Little Miss Poker Face, the Baron. They all had one thing in common: They were champions, the best tennis players in the years 1914 to 1945.

To select the 25 top players from this period is a challenging task, for there was an unusually large number of performers of first class in the world. Tennis had its full share of all-time greats during the Golden Twenties and in the '30s, too.

There are no such things as computer points and professional earnings by which to rank these players. The professional game carried small weight and small money except for the top two or three touring pros. More important to prestige was amateur competition in the major national tournaments and in Davis and Wightman Cup play. When a woman wins Wimbledon eight times, when a man becomes the first to complete the Grand Slam, there can be little doubt of his or her

It is much harder for me to draw the line and leave out so many of the following who deserve mention but who did not make the top 25, players like Mary K. Browne and Hazel Hotchkiss Wightman, both trailblazers in women's tennis, both national champions before World War I, and both prominent afterward ... Elizabeth Ryan, one of the best volleyers in the 1920s ... Lili de Alvarez of Spain, whose carefree style of playing in the late 1920s was so captivating ... Cilly Aussem, the only German to capture the Wimbledon crown (prior to Steffi Graf), winning in 1931 ... Simone Passemard Mathieu of France, six times a Wimbledon semifinalist ... Anita Lizana of Chile, who won the 1937 U.S. title ... Jadwiga Jerdrzejowska, the hard-hitting Pole of the '30s and '40s.

Among the men left out were Wilmer Allison, the 1935 U.S. champion and a formidable doubles player with John Van Ryn ... John Bromwich and Adrian Quist, the tough Australian duo of the late '30s and

'40s ... Vivian McGrath, the 1937 Australian champion and the first of the two-handed hitters to win renown ... Bunny Austin, a Davis Cup mainstay for Great Britain in the 1930s ... Frank Parker, a U.S. Davis Cupper in the late 1930s who blossomed into the U.S. singles champion in 1944 and 1945 ... Sidney Wood and Frank Shields, native New Yorkers who both advanced to the 1931 Wimbledon final round...Vincent Richards, a great volleyer of the 1920s and one of the first pros... George Lott, a dynamic doubles player in the 1930s... Frank Hunter, a late bloomer born in 1894 who didn't make his big tennis moves until the late 1920s and the 1930s... and John Doeg, the smooth lefty who was 1930 U.S. champion.

—Allison Danzig

Jean Borotra
France (1898–)

In many ways, Jean Borotra fit the image of the cosmopolitan Frenchman: a spectacular, debonair personality, a gallant kissing ladies' fingertips, a host of elegant parties aboard the *Ile de France* or at his fashionable residence in Paris.

Borotra, a right-hander, was spectacular, too, on the tennis court in the 1920s and early '30s. He won Wimbledon in 1924 and 1926 and was runner-up in 1925 and 1927. He won the championship of France in 1924 and 1931 and the Australian title in 1928. And he was a demon in international play, a member of the Four Musketeers who in 1927 broke the U.S. grip on the Davis Cup and brought it to France for the first time.

Born on Aug. 13, 1898, at Arbonne, Basque Pyrenees country near Biarritz, France, he first attracted wide attention when he played in the 1921 covered-court championship in Paris. Standing out with a dramatic, aggressive style of play—and with the blue beret he always wore—Borotra became known as the "Bounding Basque from Biarritz."

His energy on the court was limitless, marked by headlong assaults and dashes for the net, both on his service and return of ser-

Jean Borotra: Bounding Basque in blue beret. • *Fischer Collection/SPS*

vice, then a stampede back to retrieve lobs. No player could start faster or dash so madly. His service was not a rifled cannonball, but it was not to be trifled with. His backhand return of service and backhand volley were vividly individual, thrusts for the kill.

Borotra was named to France's Davis Cup team in 1922, and in 1923 he assem-

U.S. He defeated Ellsworth Vines, the winner of Wimbledon and the U.S. Championship that year. On the final day, Borotra lost the first two sets to Wilmer Allison, and with the Texan holding a sixth match point in the fifth set, Borotra's second serve appeared to be out. Allison ran forward for the handshake, thinking he had won, but the linesman insisted the serve was good and play resumed. Borotra pulled out the victory and France retained the Cup.

With his dazzling performances, Borotra was popular everywhere. This included the Seventh Regiment Armory in New York, where he was in his element on the fast board courts and four times won the National Indoor Championships. He was not rated quite the player that Cochet and Lacoste were, but Borotra's celebrity endured and the legs that ran like fury kept him active in tennis into his 70s as a competitor in the veterans' division at Wimbledon. He was among the champions honored at the 1977 Wimbledon Centenary a year after he was enshrined with the three other Musketeers in the Hall of Fame.

He was ranked in the World Top Ten nine straight years from 1924, No. 2 in 1926.

character to command respect and win honors.

And win honors he did. Born on Nov. 14, 1877, in Melbourne, Australia, he became in 1907 the first male from overseas to win the championship at Wimbledon. He won Wimbledon again in 1914 and was runner-up in 1919 after returning from World War I. Long ranked as the best of left-handed players, he was a member of the Australasian and Australian Davis Cup teams between 1905 and 1920 and played in eight challenge rounds.

World rankings were instituted after his best days, but he was in the Top Ten 1914–19–20, the last at 43.

He was an exponent of the serve and volley game, the "big game" that was supposed to have originated after World War II. Brookes played that type of game in 1914, but he had more than a serve and volley. He had ground strokes adequate to hold his own from the back of the court. Because his serve was so big an asset and he volleyed so much, his methods were characterized as unorthodox when he was in his prime.

MAJOR TITLES (7)—*Australian singles, 1911; Wimbledon singles, 1907–14; Australian doubles, 1924; Wimbledon doubles, 1907–14; U.S. doubles, 1919.* DAVIS CUP—*1905–07–08–09–11–12–14–19–20; record: 18–7 in singles, 10–4 in doubles.*

Don Budge
United States (1916–)

In sheer achievement, John Donald Budge accomplished what nobody before 1938 had been able to do—he won the Grand Slam of tennis, capturing the championships of Australia, France, Wimbledon and the United States in the same year. People were suddenly speaking of Budge in the same breath with the already immortal Bill Tilden.

Born on June 13, 1915, in Oakland, Cal., Budge had been less interested in tennis than in baseball, basketball and football while growing up in the California city, where his Scottish-born father, a former soccer player, had settled.

When the 6-foot-2 right-hander turned to tennis, his strapping size enabled him to play a game of maximum power. His service was battering, his backhand considered perhaps the finest the game has known, his net play emphatic, his overhead drastic. Quick and rhythmic for his size, he was truly the all-around player and, what is more, was temperamentally suited for the game. Affable and easygoing, his concentration could not be shaken from the objective of winning without any fuss or waste of time, with the utmost application of hitting power.

The red-haired young giant was a favorite wherever he played, and he moved quickly up the tennis ladder. At the age of 19, he was far enough advanced to be named to the Davis Cup team. The next year, 1936, he lost at Wimbledon and Forest Hills to Fred Perry, the world's No.1-ranked amateur, but beat Perry in the Pacific Southwest tournament.

Norman Brookes: An unorthodox southpaw. • *UPI*

Germany's Otto Froitzheim, a player of skill and quickness, put Brookes to a severe test in an 8–6 fifth set in the 1914 Wimbledon championships, the Australian's first appearance there since his 1907 victory. Brookes demonstrated the all-around strength of his game preparatory to wresting the championship from Tony Wilding of New Zealand in straight sets with a display of faultless ground strokes. Brookes' durability was demonstrated again in 1924 at Wimbledon when, at 46, he ousted Frank Hunter, finalist in 1923 and 17 years his junior.

The honors didn't stop for the man who seemed to command them. In 1926, he was named president of the Lawn Tennis Association of Australia, a post he held until 1955. He was decorated with the French Legion of Honor for his services in World War I as a captain in the British Army and, in 1939, he was knighted.

He died Sept. 28, 1968, in Melbourne and entered the Hall of Fame in 1977.

the French championship he beat Roderich Menzel of Czechoslovakia in the final and yielded three sets in the tournament. At Wimbledon he did not lose a single set, beating Bunny Austin of Britain for the title, and at Forest Hills he gave up but one set—to Gene Mako in the final—in winning the U.S. crown.

Budge had won the Grand Slam and

In 1937 Perry turned pro and Budge earned the world's No. 1 ranking. He won at Wimbledon and Forest Hills and led the U.S. to the Davis Cup challenge round with a comeback victory over Gottfried von Cramm in one of Budge's many classic matches with the German ace. In a culmination to a fantastic year, Budge received the Sullivan Award as America's top amateur athlete, the first tennis player to be so honored.

The high regard in which Budge was held by fellow players, spectators and officials was reflected by the loyalty he demonstrated in 1937. He was a big attraction for pro tennis but decided against leaving the amateur ranks for another year. The United States had the Davis Cup and he decided that, in return for all tennis had done for him, he must help in the defense of the Cup for at least another year.

So he turned down the professional offers, aware that poor fortunes in 1938 could hurt, if not end, his earning power as a pro. As it turned out, 1938 would be his most glorious year. He defeated John Bromwich in the Australian final, losing only one set in the entire tournament. In

He made his professional debut at Madison Square Garden in New York early in 1939 and, before a crowd of 16,725, defeated Ellsworth Vines, 6–3, 6–4, 6–2. On tour, Budge defeated Vines, 21 matches to 18, and also defeated Perry, 18–11. On tour with the 47-year-old Tilden, Budge beat him, 51-7.

Budge conquered Bobby Riggs, 6–2, 6–2, 6–2, for the U.S. Pro title at Forest Hills in 1942, the same year Budge enlisted in the Air Force. After the war, his playing career slumped due to a shoulder injury suffered in military training, but he reached the U.S. Pro final again in 1946, 1947, 1949 and 1953, and left little doubt as to his greatness. "I consider him," said Bill Tilden, "the finest player 365 days a year who ever lived."

He was elected to the Hall of Fame in 1964.

MAJOR TITLES (14)—*Australian singles, 1938; French singles, 1938; Wimbledon singles, 1937–38; U.S. singles, 1937–38; Wimbledon doubles, 1937–38; U.S. doubles, 1936–38; Wimbledon mixed, 1937–38; U.S. mixed, 1937–38.* OTHER

U.S. TITLES—*Clay Court doubles, 1934, with Gene Mako; Pro singles, 1940–42; Pro doubles, 1940–41, with Fred Perry; 1942–47, with Bobby Riggs; 1949, with Frank Kovacs; 1953, with Richard (Pancho) Gonzalez.* DAVIS CUP—*1935–36–37–38; record: 19–2 in singles, 6–2 in doubles.*

Dorothea Chambers
Great Britain (1878–1960)

What a clash of eras and customs it was in the Wimbledon final of 1919 when the sturdily conformed, long-skirted 40-year-old matron, Dorothea Douglass Lambert Chambers, seven times champion between 1903 and 1914, faced the slim new kid half her age, audacious, skimpily dressed (for the time) Suzanne Lenglen. They battled through the longest final up to that time, 44 games, Mrs. Robert Lambert Chambers narrowly missing two match points in the third set of the 10–8, 4–6, 9–7 decision, the first of six titles for Lenglen, never beaten at Wimbledon.

With King George, Queen Mary, and the Princess Royal in the committee box, one of the finest matches to be played at Wimbledon, by men or women, was enacted.

Against the all-court game of Lenglen, the right-handed Lambert Chambers delighted the gallery with superb resistance. She drove with such power and length from both forehand and backhand, passed so accurately, put up lobs so irretrievable, and had so much touch on her drop shot that her youthful opponent was showing signs of physical distress and found herself in danger of losing.

After two sets, the match was even and Lenglen was sipping brandy to ease her peril. In the third set, trailing, 4–1, Lambert Chambers put on a remarkable comeback and seemed to have the victory in hand at 6–5, 40–15, on her service at double match point. But, just as remarkably, Lenglen rallied and pulled out the match, 10–8, 4–6,

Dorothea Lambert Chambers: Ageless champion.
• *UPI*

9–7. Both players were so exhausted that when asked to come to the Royal Box, they said they were physically unable to do so. It had been an epic struggle between the past and the future in tennis.

Despite the interruption of World War I, she was in 11 Wimbledon singles finals, the last in 1920 when she lost again to Lenglen, and, at 41, was the oldest female finalist. Continuing to play the Big W through 1927, she played 115 matches in all there: 32–8 in singles, 29–11 in doubles, 24–11 in mixed. Dolly as some called her, won two of her Wimbledons after the birth of her first child, two more after the birth of her second.

As Britain's Wightman Cup captain in 1926, at 47, she helped her side win, 4–3, at Forest Hills by beating 30-year-old Eleanor Goss, 7–5, 3–6, 6–1. She also captained the team in 1927. She was born Sept. 3, 1878, in Ealing, England and died in 1960. She entered the Hall of Fame in 1981.

MAJOR TITLES (7)—*Wimbledon singles, 1903–04–06–10–11–13–14.* WIGHTMAN CUP—*1926; record: 0–1 in doubles.*

Henri Cochet
France (1901–87)

It could be said that Henri Jean Cochet had as pronounced a gift for playing tennis as anyone who attained world supremacy. A racket in his hand became a wand of magic, doing the impossible, most often in a position on the court considered untenable, and doing it with nonchalant ease and fluency. He took the ball early, volleys

Henri Cochet: The Little Musketeer.

• *Fischer Collection/SPS*

sister when nobody was using the courts. In 1921 he went to Paris where he and Jean Borotra, both unknowns, reached the final of the covered-court championship. Cochet was the winner.

The next year, he and Borotra played on the Davis Cup team, and in 1923 they joined with René Lacoste and Jacques Brugnon in the origin of the Four Musketeers. Cochet won 10 successive Davis Cup challenge round matches from the time the Musketeers wrested the Cup from the U.S. in 1927.

A sensitivity of touch and timing, resulting in moderately hit strokes of genius, accounted for the success the little Frenchman had in turning back the forceful hitters of the 1920s and early '30s. Following a stunning victory over Bill Tilden in the quarterfinals of the 1926 U.S. Championships, ending Tilden's six-year sway, and a triumph over William Johnston in the 1927 challenge round, the right-handed Cochet established himself in 1928 as the world's foremost player. Winner of the U.S. and French Championships that year, and runner-up at Wimbledon, he became more of a national hero than ever

as he scored three victories in the Cup challenge round.

With Lacoste's retirement from international play in 1929, Cochet was France's indispensable man. He led his country to victory over the United States in the challenge round in 1929 and 1932, and over the British in 1931.

He was champion of France five times (four times after it was opened to non-French citizens in 1925) and won the Wimbledon and U.S. titles once. His triumph over Bill Tilden in the 1927 Wimbledon semifinals, after losing the first two sets and trailing by 1–5 in the third, was one of the most remarkable comebacks in tennis. "In these inspired moments of his," said Tilden, "Cochet is the greatest of all the Frenchmen and in my opinion is possibly the greatest player who has ever lived."

He ranked No. 1 from 1928 through 1931 and was in the World Top Ten 10 times between 1922 and 1933. After France lost the Davis Cup to Great Britain in 1933, Cochet turned professional. He did not have much of a career as a pro, however, and after the war, in 1945, one of the most naturally gifted tennis players in history received reinstatement as an amateur, a role in which he had once ruled the tennis world, and continued playing well. Elected to the Hall of Fame in 1976, he died April 1, 1987, in St. Germain-en-Laye, France.

MAJOR TITLES (15)—*French singles, 1926–28–30–32; Wimbledon singles, 1927–29; U.S. singles, 1928; French doubles, 1927–30–32; Wimbledon doubles, 1926–28; French mixed, 1928–29; U.S. mixed, 1927.* DAVIS CUP—*1922– 23–24–26– 27–28–29–30–31–32–33; record: 34–8 in singles, 10–6 in doubles.*

Sarah Palfrey Cooke
United States (1912–)

If any player may be said to have been the sweetheart of tennis, as Mary Pickford was of the movies, her name was Sarah Palfrey.

Twice U.S. champion, Sarah Hammond Palfrey Fabyan Cooke Danzig was twice a runner-up for the title to Helen Jacobs, nine times U.S. doubles champion, and twice doubles champion at Wimbledon, and she was an international attraction on both sides of the Atlantic and west to the Pacific.

Born Sept. 18, 1912, in Sharon, Mass., she was a carefully reared girl of upper-register Boston and a protege of Hazel Hotchkiss Wightman. The galleries loved her radiant smile and her unfailing graciousness in triumph and defeat alike, and they marveled at the cleverness and dispatch she used in the volleying position and at the execution of her sweeping backhand. She was one of the most accomplished performers around the net, thanks in part to the instruction of Wightman, a pioneer in

Sarah Palfrey Cooke: The sweetheart of tennis.
• *USTA*

introducing the volley as a major component of the women's game. A slip of a girl, Sarah was remarkable in the way she stood up to the more powerful hitters.

Sarah was so prized as a doubles partner in the 1930s and 1940s that she had the pick of the best. Seven times in Wightman Cup play she teamed with Jacobs, three times with Alice Marble, and once with Helen Wills Moody. But prestige comes from superiority in singles play, and in this the artful right-hander ranked no fewer than 13 times in the U.S. Top Ten. She was No. 1, No. 2 or No. 3 seven times. She was in the World Top Ten six times between 1933 and 1939.

After her playing career she was a successful business executive and (as Mrs. Jerry Danzig) was available for committee work in the tennis associations, the International Tennis Hall of Fame and for organizations devoted to public service and charity. Her writings appear in books and magazines. In 1963 she was voted into the Hall of Fame. Although the women's pro tour was 21 years down the road, she and Pauline Betz turned pro to barnstorm against each other in 1947, making about $10,000 apiece, a nice sum in that day.

MAJOR TITLES (18)—*U.S. singles, 1941–45; Wimbledon doubles, 1938–39; U.S. doubles, 1930–32–34–35–37–38–39– 40–41: French mixed.*

Jack Crawford
Australia (1908–91)

Few players so completely won the gallery as did John Herbert Crawford, called by one commentator the "most popular Wimbledon winner in history."

Indeed, Crawford, a right-hander, was an exemplary sportsman, as well as a handsome figure on the court in his long, white flannels and long-sleeved shirt. And he moved easily, gracefully, over the turf with his flat-topped racket, a model of early vintage. He was in the World Top Ten six times, 1932–37, No. 1 in 1933.

Crawford, born March 22, 1908, in Albury, Australia, was a masterful player from the back of the court, driving the ball with length and pinpoint control with seemingly little strain. He played the classical game of solid, fluent strokes, and he played it so well that he came within one set of completing a Grand Slam five years before Don Budge accomplished the feat of winning the four major championships in one year.

Crawford's bid came in 1933, a year after he won 16 tournaments, starting with a victory over Keith Gledhill in the Australian final. Next Crawford won the French Championship, beating Henri Cochet for the title. At Wimbledon came a legendary final against Ellsworth Vines that Crawford won, 4–6, 11–9, 6–2. 2–6. 6–4.

So Crawford moved on to Forest Hills and the United States Championship with an opportunity to complete the ultimate sweep. After defeating Frank Shields in the semifinals, Crawford faced Fred Perry as the last obstacle in his path. Crawford lost the first set, but then won the next two, 11–9, 6–4, and was one set away from a Slam. But his strength faded, owing in part to the asthma and insomnia he had at the time. Perry went on to victory in the next two sets, dashing Crawford's hopes.

Still, the gallery loved this man— "Gentleman Jack," they called him—from Down Under. He won the championship of his country four times, and he did it all his way, seemingly never hurried, his every move appearing effortless, his serve belonging in a picture book. Jack Crawford was one of the greats of his time while playing tennis in the style of a gentleman of the old school.

He died Sept. 10, 1991, in Sydney.

MAJOR TITLES (17)—*Australian singles, 1931–32–33–35; French singles, 1933; Wimbledon singles, 1933; Wimbledon doubles, 1935; Australian doubles, 1929–30– 32–35; French doubles, 1935; Australian mixed, 1931–32–33; French mixed, 1933; Wimbledon mixed, 1930.* DAVIS CUP— *1928–30–32–33–34–35–36–37; record: 23–16 in singles, 13–5 in doubles.*

Kitty Godfree
Great Britain (1896–1992)

Kathleen McKane Godfree, a sturdy, good-natured competitor, may have been the best female player Britain has produced. In winning Wimbledon for the first time in 1924, she charged back from 1–4 in the second set to hand Helen Wills her lone defeat in nine visits to the Big W, 4–6, 6–4, 6–4. She also beat Wills in the British Wightman Cup victory that year at Wimbledon. Who else could boast of royal-flushing "Little Miss Poker Face" twice in a season?

Kitty won Wimbledon again two years later over Lili de Alvarez, who was within a stroke of a 4–1 lead in the decisive third, 6–2, 4–6, 6–3. Thus Kitty and Dorothy Round (1934–37) were the only Brits to win twice since World War I. She was one of a select group to play more than 100 matches (147) at Wimbledon, 19th on the list: 38–11 in singles, 34–12 in doubles, 40–12 in mixed between 1919 and 1934.

In 1923 Kitty had reached her third Wimbledon final by beating Elizabeth Ryan, 1–6, 6–2, 6–4, but lost to Lenglen, 6–2, 6–2. In the U.S. Championships that year, Kitty offered a dangerous challenge to Wills, coming from 2–5 to 5-all in the third set before losing. In 1925 she pushed Wills in the final of the U.S. Championships, losing 3–6, 6–0, 6–2, after eliminating Molla Mallory and Ryan. Two years before, 1923, she fell to Wills in the quar-

Kitty McKane Godfree: Dynamic Britisher. • *UPI*

terfinals, coming from 2–5 to 5–5 in the third, only to lose, 2–6, 6–2, 7–5.

She was a member of the British team that played the United States for the Wightman Cup in the inaugural matches in 1923 in the Forest Hills stadium. She lost to Wills and Mallory, both members of the host team. But the following year, in the first of these international team competitions held in Britain, Kitty beat Mallory as well as Wills, and the home team won by a surprising margin of 6–1. Then in 1925 the British won again in a close series, with Kitty defeating Mallory and losing to Wills. In 1926 she beat both Mary K. Browne and Ryan, but the British lost the series at Wimbledon despite Kitty's heroics.

In 1925 she arrived in the French final but was beaten by Lenglen.

Speedy, smart and a fighter with an all-around game, she was her country's most successful Olympian, gathering five medals in the 1920 and 1924 Games. In 1920 she won a gold in the doubles with Winifred McNair, a silver in mixed doubles with Max Woosnam and a bronze in singles. Four years later, a silver in doubles with Phyllis Covell and a bronze in singles. Active throughout her long life, she was a 92-year-old spectator at the 1988 Games in Seoul, and approved the entry of professionals, saying, "It's a sign of the times if you want the best in the Olympics."

She was among the champions of the past who received Centenary medallions on Wimbledon's Centre Court in 1977 and was inducted into the Hall of Fame in 1978. Born May 7, 1896, in London, she died there at the age of 96, June 19, 1992.

MAJOR TITLES (7)—*Wimbledon singles, 1924–26; U.S. doubles, 1923–27; U.S. mixed, 1925; Wimbledon mixed, 1924–26.* WIGHTMAN CUP—*1923–24–25–26–27–3034; record: 5–5 in singles, 2–5 in doubles.*

Helen Jacobs
United States (1908–)

Helen Hull Jacobs had the misfortune to be a contemporary of Helen Wills Moody. Four times in the battle of Helens in the final round at Wimbledon, Jacobs lost. She also lost to her arch-rival at Forest Hills in the 1928 U.S. Championships.

On top of all those defeats to Helen the First, Jacobs was beaten in a Wimbledon final by Dorothy Round of Britain, and three times she was turned back in a U.S. final by Alice Marble.

Particularly bitter for her to take was a defeat in the 1935 Wimbledon final.

Helen Jacobs: Artist at the net. • *New York Herald Tribune*

Moody that season was struggling, and in the final round Jacobs led at match point, 5–3. Victory seemed at hand when Wills threw up a lob that barely got to the net, and Jacobs waited to smash it for the final point. But a wind current caught the ball and Jacobs, off balance, hit it into the net. Moody rallied and went on to her seventh Wimbledon title. At the time, Jacobs had none.

In spite of so much adversity, Jacobs, a right-hander, born Aug. 6, 1908, Globe, Ariz., was as stout of heart as any champion. She won at Forest Hills four years in a row, 1932–35, a rare achievement, and she was finally crowned at Wimbledon in 1936, beating Hilde Sperling.

Jacobs' unflagging courage, her iron will to win, was her biggest asset. She had little of the power that Moody applied, and Jacobs' forehand stroke was so unsatisfactory that she forsook it for a sliced cut at the ball, not too effective either to stand off a full-blooded drive or to repel a volleyer. Her backhand, while not severe, was steadfast, reliable against any amount of pressure, and she won heavily with it.

It was at the net where she was most effective. She was not as conclusive with her volley or her smash as Marble, but she was a determined, skilled foe at close quarters, and her fighting traits counted most, whatever her position on the court. Even when afflicted with injuries, she refused to be discouraged. Her admirable qualities, including sportsmanship and great self-reliance, had a strong appeal for tennis galleries.

A feud was built up in publications between the two Helens that Jacobs said never existed. Moody was pictured as resenting Jacobs following in her footsteps. Both played at the Berkeley (Cal.) Tennis Club, had the same coach, won national junior championships two years in a row and attended the University of California. The Jacobs' family lived in the Wills' former home. The two Helens did not see each other except in connection with tennis.

Jacobs, after eight losses to Moody, finally got the victory she was after in the 1933 U.S. Championships, although even then it was not a complete one. She won the first set against Moody, 8–6, and lost the second, 6–3. When the score went to 3–0 in Jacobs' favor in the third set, Moody walked to the umpire's stand, informed the official that because of pain in her back she was unable to continue, and conceded the match. Jacobs had dealt Moody her first big defeat since 1926. It would be Jacobs' lone win in an 11-match rivalry.

She was ranked in the World Top Ten 12 straight times from 1928, No. 1 in 1936, and in the U.S. Top Ten 13 times between 1927 and 1941, No. 1 in 1932–33–34–35.

She was elected to the Hall of Fame in 1962.

MAJOR TITLES (9)—*Wimbledon singles, 1936; U.S. singles, 1932–33–34–35; U.S. doubles,* *1932–33–34–35; U.S. mixed, 1934.* WIGHTMAN CUP—*1927–28–29–30–31–32– 33–34–35–36– 37–39; record: 14-7 in singles, 5-4 in doubles.*

Bill Johnston
United States (1894–1946)

William M. Johnston's name is inevitably associated with Bill Tilden's. Tilden was "Big Bill" (6-2) and Johnston "Little Bill" (5-8½) and they were the twin terrors who turned back the Australasians, French and Japanese in the Davis Cup challenge round from 1920 through 1926, a seven-year span of invincibility unequaled in those international team matches.

Big Bill and Little Bill were teammates and they were also rivals. It was Johnston's bad luck that his career was contemporaneous with the player commonly regarded as the greatest ever. Otherwise Johnston might have won the U.S. Championships most of the years it fell to Tilden, from 1920 to 1925. As it was, Little Bill won it twice, in 1915 and in 1919, defeating Maurice McLoughlin the first time and Tilden in the 1919 final. Johnston was runner-up six times, and in five of those years it was Tilden who beat him in the final.

Until the French began to catch up to Big Bill and Little Bill in 1926, Johnston had been winning his Davis Cup matches with the loss of few sets. In seven challenge rounds, he won 11 of 14 matches in singles. He lost only once until 1927, when his age and his health began to tell. He ranked in the World Top Ten eight straight years from 1919 and in the U.S. Top Ten 12 times between 1913 and 1926, No. 1 in 1915 and in 1919.

The topspin forehand drive he hammered with the western grip was one of the most famous and effective shots in tennis history. No other player executed it as well as he did, taking the ball shoulder high and leaping off the ground on his fol-

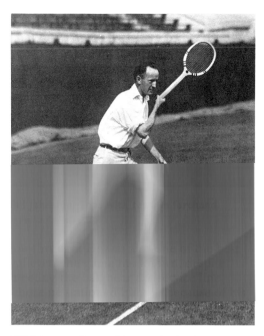

Bill Johnston: Tops with topspin forehand.
• *Fischer Collection/SPS*

3–0 in the fourth. It seemed that every spectator in the stands was cheering for Johnston, the favorite of galleries virtually every time he went on the court. Both he and Tilden had two legs on the challenge trophy, and Little Bill had his heart set on retiring it for his permanent keeping in this match. It was a crushing disappointment when he lost in five sets.

1923; U.S. singles, 1915–19; U.S. doubles, 1915–16–20; U.S. mixed, 1921. OTHER U.S. TITLES—*Clay Court singles, 1919–20; Clay Court doubles, 1919, with Sam Hardy.* DAVIS CUP— *1920–21–22–23–24–25–26–27; record: 14–3 in singles, 4–0 in doubles.*

low-through. He was also one of the best volleyers the game has known, despite meeting the ball near the service line, where he stationed himself because of his short height.

Johnston a right-hander, was born Nov. 2, 1894, in San Francisco and developed many of his skills on public parks courts. His whole game was aggressive and he played to win on the merit of his strokes rather than on the opponent's errors. Though he did not have a big serve, overhead he was secure and angled his smash effectively. He had as much fight as anyone who was ever champion, and many times when he came off the court, dripping with perspiration after a prolonged struggle, he was five to eight pounds below his usual weight of 125.

Such was the case in his U.S. National final with Tilden in 1922 at the Germantown Cricket Club in Philadelphia in which Johnston won the first two sets and led by

René Lacoste
France (1905–)

He was not particularly athletic in build or in his movements, and as a reserved and rather shy youth he seemed to be more fitted for the world of education, law or medicine than for athletic achievement. But Jean René Lacoste, known as the Crocodile, would win Wimbledon twice and the French and U.S. titles twice and would become a member of the Four Musketeers, the scourges of the tennis world in the 1920s. He was in the World Top Ten six straight years from 1924, No. 1 in 1926–27.

Lacoste would be a self-made champion, a player who won world renown through sheer hard work and devoted application rather than through the benefit of natural talent. Born in Paris, July 2, 1904, he did not go onto a court until he was 15 years old, while on a trip with his

René Lacoste: Relentless as a crocodile. • *Fischer Collection/SPS*

father to England. His development after that was slow.

His father, a wealthy manufacturer of motor cars, agreed to his son's devoting himself to tennis, but with the understanding that he must set himself the task of becoming a world champion and must achieve his goal within five years or drop it.

In his determination to excel, Lacoste trained faithfully and read and observed everything, even keeping a notebook on the strengths and weaknesses of his contemporaries. He became a master of the backcourt game, choosing to maintain a length of inexorable pressure to exact the error or the opening for the finishing shot, and repelling the volleyer with passing shots and lobs.

His successes began to build. He joined the French Davis Cup team, forming the Four Musketeers with Jean Borotra,

Henri Cochet and Jacques Brugnon. He lost to Borotra in the 1924 Wimbledon final, then avenged the defeat the next year to win Wimbledon. The French title fell to Lacoste in 1925 and also in 1927 and 1929. He won Wimbledon for the second time in 1928.

But perhaps his most stirring victory came in the 1927 U.S. championships, where the efficiency of his backcourt game thwarted the great Bill Tilden in the final. The 34-year-old Tilden attacked for close to two hours and volleyed far more than was his custom, but despite efforts that brought him to the point of exhaustion, he could not win a set. The sphinx-like Lacoste, 22 years old, kept the ball going back the full length of the court with the inevitability of fate and hardly an inexcusable error. The scores of the fabulous match were 11–9, 6–3, 11–9, enabling Lacoste to retain the U.S. title he had won the previous year against Borotra.

Lacoste also defeated Tilden two other times in 1927—in the French Championships and in Davis Cup play in which French beat the U.S. In 1928 Lacoste lost the opener in Davis Cup play to Tilden and it marked the Frenchman's last appearance in international team matches, owing to his health. After winning the French title in 1929, he withdrew from competition, having more than fulfilled the goal he once never seemed suited for—that of a tennis champion.

MAJOR TITLES (10)—*French singles, 1925–27–29; U.S. singles, 1926–27; Wimbledon singles, 1925–28; French doubles, 1925–29; Wimbledon doubles, 1925.* DAVIS CUP—*1923–24–25–26–27–28; record: 32–8 in singles, 8–3 in doubles.*

Suzanne Lenglen
France (1899–1938)

In the days of ground-length tennis dresses, Suzanne Rachel Flore Lenglen played at Wimbledon with her dress cut just above the calf. She wept openly during matches, pouted, sipped brandy between sets. Some called her shocking and indecent, but she was merely ahead of her time, and she brought France the greatest global sports renown it had ever known.

Right-hander Lenglen was No. 1 in 1925–26, the first years of world rankings.

Suzanne Lenglen: The magnificent swinger. •
Fischer Collection/SPS

high-necked shirtwaist, and a long skirt that swept the court. The young Lenglen was in her revealing dress that shocked the British at the sight of ankles and forearms. After the second set, Lenglen took some comfort from her brandy and won, 10–8, 4–6, 9–7, in a dramatic confrontation.

After her victory, Lenglen became easily the greatest drawing card tennis had known, and she was one of those who made it a major box-office attraction. Along with a magnetic personality, grace and style, she was the best woman player the world had seen.

Lenglen, born May 24, 1899, in Paris, played an all-court game such as few had excellence at. She moved with rare grace, unencumbered by the tight layers of garments others wore. She had extraordinary accuracy with her classical, rhythmic ground strokes. For hours daily her father had her direct the ball at a handkerchief he moved from spot to spot. Her control was so unfailing that she thought it shameful to hit the ball into the net or beyond the line. In addition, she had so keen a sense of anticipation that she invariably was in the right position to meet her opponent's shot.

Her 1926 match against Helen Wills in a tournament at Cannes, France, caused a sensation. Tickets brought unheard-of wealth to scalpers, and the roofs and windows of apartments and hotels overlooking the court were crowded with fans. Lenglen, on the verge of collapse during the tense match, but saved by smelling salts and brandy, defeated the 20-year-old Wills, 6–3, 8–6.

Lenglen's career was not free of setbacks, however. In the 1921 U.S. Championships, having lost the first set badly to Molla Mallory, Lenglen walked weeping and coughing to the umpire and said she could not continue, defaulting the match. She made up for it the next year at Wimbledon by defeating Mallory in the final and did not lose another match for the remainder of her amateur career.

In the 1926 Wimbledon, Lenglen had a terrifying ordeal. She kept Queen Mary waiting in the Royal Box for her appearance when, owing to a misunderstanding or a failure of communications, Lenglen did not have the correct information about the time she was to be on court. The ghastly error was too much. She fainted and Wimbledon saw her no more as a competitor. She withdrew from the tournament, and that year went on a tour for money in the United States under the management of C.C. Pyle. It marked the start of professional tennis as a playing career.

At the age of 39, Lenglen died of pernicious anemia July 4, 1938 in Paris. She was elected to the Hall of Fame in 1978. There was speculation that her health had been undermined by her long hours of practice as a young girl. But she had brought the glamour of the stage and the ballet to the court, and queues formed at tennis clubs where before there had been indifference. She had emancipated the female player from layers of starched clothing and set the short-hair style as well. She had brought the game of tennis into a new era.

MAJOR TITLES (21)—*French singles, 1925–26; Wimbledon singles, 1919–20–21–22–23–25; French doubles, 1925–26; Wimbledon doubles, 1919–20–21–22–23– 25; French mixed, 1925–26; Wimbledon mixed, 1920–22–25.*

Molla Mallory
Norway/United States (1884–1959)

Anna Margarethe"Molla" Bjurstedt Mallory had less in the way of stroke equipment than most players who have become tennis champions. But the sturdy, Norwegian-born woman, the daughter of an army officer, had the heart and pride of a gladiator, could run with limitless endurance, and was a fierce competitor. She won the U.S. Championship a record eight times and she administered the only post-World War I defeat that Suzanne Lenglen suffered as an amateur.

It was her match with Lenglen in the second round of the U.S. Championship at

Molla Mallory: A striking force out of Norway.
• *UPI*

Forest Hills in 1921 that won Mallory her greatest celebrity. She won the first set, 6–2, playing with a fury that took her opponent by surprise, running down the ball interminably to wear out the French girl in long rallies, and hitting her mighty topspin forehand down the line for blazing winners. Lenglen, the Wimbledon queen, out of breath from running, coughing and weeping, walked to the umpire's stand after two points of the second set and informed the official that she was ill and could not continue. This was as sensational a reversal as ever recorded on the courts.

Mallory, a right-hander, whose game was developed in Norway, where she was born March 6, 1884, came to the United States as Molla Bjurstedt in 1914 and won the U.S. tournament, 1915–16–17–18–20–21–22 and in 1926 at 42, as the elder among all major champions.

She was a player of the old school. She held that a woman could not sustain a volleying attack in a long match and she put her reliance on her baseline game. That game amounted to a forehand attack and an omnivorous defense that wore down her opponents. She took the ball on the rise and drove it from corner to corner to keep her rival on the constant run and destroy her control. The quick return made her passing shots all the more effective.

MAJOR TITLES (13)—*U.S. singles, 1915–16–17–18–20–21–22–26; U.S. doubles, 1916–17; U.S. mixed, 1917–22–23.* OTHER U.S. TITLES—*Indoor singles; 1915–16–18–21–22; Indoor doubles, 1916, with Marie Wagner; Indoor mixed, 1921–22, with Bill Tilden; Clay Court singles, 1915–16; Clay Court mixed, 1916, with George Church.* WIGHTMAN CUP—*1923–25–27–28; record: 5–5 in singles, 1–1 in doubles.*

strong volleyers, like Mrs. Wightman, but neither could win a set against the Norwegian native.

Mallory yielded her title to Helen Wills in 1923, after defeating her in the 1922 final, and lost to her again in 1924. In 1926 Mallory hit one of the heights of her career when she came back from 0–4 in the third set of the final against Elizabeth Ryan and won her eighth championship. Never had a gallery at Forest Hills in the years of her triumphs cheered her on as it did in this remarkable rally.

Mallory reached the final at Wimbledon in 1922 and lost to Lenglen, 6–2, 6–0. Mallory was twice a semifinalist at Wimbledon, and she played on the Wightman Cup team in 1923, 1924, 1925, 1927, and 1928.

She was in the World Top Ten in 1925–26–27, its first three years, and the U.S. Top Ten 13 times between 1915 and 1928, No. 1 in 1915–16–18–20–21–22–26. She bade farewell to the U.S. Championships as a 45-year-old semifinalist in 1929. She entered the Hall of Fame in 1958 and died Nov. 22, 1959.

approximated the game of Don Budge or Ellsworth Vines than it did the game of any woman.

There had been women before her who could volley and hit overheads— Suzanne Lenglen and Helen Wills Moody among them—but none played the "big game," the game of the big serve and volley, as it was to be called years later, as their standard method of attack the way Marble did regularly. No woman had a stronger service. Her first serve was as severe as any, and she delivered the taxing American twist serve as few women have been able to do. She followed it to the net for emphatic volleys or the strongest kind of overhead smash.

A right-hander pressing the attack without a letup, she could win from the back of the court as well as at the net. Her ground strokes, made with a short backswing and taking the ball on the rise, were not overpowering, and her forehand was not always steadfast against the many fine backcourt players of her day, in part because of her daring in playing for winners. But in the aggressive all-court game she played, with her speed and agility and

Alice Marble: The lady was a tiger. • *UPI*

tournament at East Hampton, N.Y., she had to play the semifinals and finals of singles and doubles in one day with the temperature on the court more than 100 degrees. She played an almost unbelievable 108 games, and then collapsed. She was so weakened that she had to withdraw from the Wightman Cup team.

In the spring of 1934, playing in a Franco-American series near Paris, she was taken ill and removed to a hospital, where her illness was diagnosed as pleurisy. She was cautioned not to play more tennis that year when she left. It was feared her career might be at an end. But in 1935 she began to play again in California and changed to the eastern grip. In 1936 she returned to the East. Officials of the USTA were fearful that she might jeopardize her health permanently if she returned to serious competition. But she was determined, and with the assistance of her coach, Eleanor Tennant, she undertook to re-establish herself and get back to the top.

At Forest Hills in 1936 she came up against Helen Jacobs in the U.S. final. Jacobs had held the title four years in a row, raising serious doubts about Marble's chances. But Marble won the match, 4–6, 6–3, 6–2, to attain the No. 1 ranking. In 1937 she lost in the quarterfinals but again was ranked No. 1, and she held the top spot in 1938, 1939 and 1940, winning the U.S. crown all three years and winning all three titles at Wimbledon in 1939. In four years of Wightman Cup play she lost but one match in singles and one in doubles.

She made her bow as a professional late in 1940, touring with Mary Hardwick, Don Budge and Bill Tilden. When the United States entered the war, she enlisted in the Hail American movement and played exhibitions in training stations and camps. She was elected to the Hall of Fame in 1964 and was among the past champions present at Wimbledon in 1977 to receive Centenary medallions on the Centre

with her skill in the use of the drop shot, they served to carry her to four U.S. titles and to the Wimbledon Championship. World War II brought about French, Wimbledon and Australian tournament suspension or she might have added appreciably to her major conquests.

Her dominance is evidenced by her record of invincibility in 1939 and 1940. She did not lose a match of consequence either year. In winning her fourth U.S. title in 1940, she did not yield a set. She was voted by sportswriters the Woman Athlete of the Year in 1939 and 1940.

She was in the World Top Ten 1933–36–37–38–39, No. 1 the last year, and in the U.S. Top Ten those years, plus 1932 and 1940, No. 1 from 1936 through 1940.

Born Sept 28, 1913, in Plumas County, Cal., she achieved a place high among the world's best after she had been stricken with an illness that threatened to end her career before the age of 21. In 1933 at a

Court, where she had defeated Kay Stammers in the 1939 final. No one there seemed happier or was more joyously greeted by the other champions than was the attractive woman who had once played tennis like a man.

She died Dec. 13, 1990, in Palm Springs, Cal.

Maurice McLoughlin
United States (1890–1957)

He came out of out the West with a cannonball service, spectacular volleys and overhead smashes. He created great excitement in the East and abroad at Wimbledon with the violence of his attack. And more than anything else, Maurice Evans "Red" McLoughlin, known as the California Comet, opened the eyes of the public to tennis as a demanding game of speed, endurance and skill.

Tennis at the turn of the century was a moderately paced game contested from the back of the court. But McLoughlin, a right-hander, carried this attack forward, projecting the cannonball serve and rushing in behind it to meet the return near the net with a cataclysmic overhead or a masterful volley. The volley was not new to the game (it had been used in the first championship in 1881), but it had not nearly been the finishing stroke that Red Mac made it.

Born Jan. 7, 1890, in Carson City, Nev., McLoughlin polished his game on the public parks courts of northern California, and this in itself was a departure in the direc-

Maurice McLoughlin: California Comet. • *USTA*

tion of democratizing the game. Most of the top-ranking players had developed their games on the turf of exclusive clubs in the East or their own private family courts.

At 19 he had developed sufficiently to be named to the Davis Cup team to play against Australasia in the 1909 finale.

He won the U.S. championship in 1912 and 1913 at Newport, but the Comet lost in a hard fight at Wimbledon against the champion, Tony Wilding. McLoughlin's style of play created a big stir at Wimbledon, however, and brought out large crowds. An attendance record was set at his match with Wilding, and McLoughlin's sunny disposition made him something of a favorite with the British gallery.

McLoughlin reached his peak the next year in 1914 Davis Cup play at Forest Hills. The matching of McLoughlin and Norman Brookes of Australasia brought forth tennis that was a revelation to the thousands who attended. The match was characterized as "never been equaled." McLoughlin won, including a first-set victory of 17–15. The matches attracted 14,000 people daily, and McLoughlin was given much of the credit for the large crowds.

After the Davis Cup success, the 1915 *Tennis Guide* said, "In McLoughlin America undoubtedly has the greatest tennis player of all time." Yet he never again attained that form. Absent from the East for several years, he returned after Army duty in World War I and was hardly recognizable. He had lost his cannonball and his punch. Gone was his whirlwind speed. After he was defeated by Dick Williams decisively in a tournament, he left the tennis scene for golf, where he soon was shooting in the low 70s. His tennis career had come to a premature end. Some said he was burned out from his violent exertions on the court.

On Dec. 10, 1957—the year of his entry into the Hall of Fame—the Comet died. But in the short time that he had lighted the tennis firmament, as no one before him, he had started the sport on its way to becoming a popular game for Americans. He ranked No. 1 in 1915, the first year of world rankings, and was in the U.S. Top Ten seven straight years from 1909, No. 1 in 1912–13–14.

MAJOR TITLES (5)—*U.S. singles, 1912–13; U.S. doubles, 1912–13–14.* DAVIS CUP—*1909–11–13–14; record: 9–4 in singles, 3–4 in doubles.*

Helen Wills Moody
United States (1905–)

It scarcely seems possible that two players of the transcendent ability of Helen Newington Wills Moody and Suzanne Lenglen could have been contemporaries. They were ranked for close to half a century as the two best female tennis players of all time. Their records are unmatched and hardly have been approached.

While indeed contemporaries, they were rivals in only one match, played in 1926 and won by Lenglen, 6–3, 8–6, at Cannes, France. Lenglen, not yet 27, was at the crest of her game, with six Wimbledon championships in her possession. Wills' game at 20 had not quite attained full maturity, though she had won Wimbledon one of the record eight times she was to triumph there. Their rivalry was limited to the single meeting, for later that same year Wills was stricken with appendicitis and Lenglen turned pro.

It would be difficult to imagine two players of more different personalities and types of game. Between 1919 and 1938 Wills won 52 of 92 tournaments on a 398–35-match record, a .919 average, and had a 158-match winning streak (27 tournaments to the 1933 U.S. final, the only time she lost to Helen Jacobs in 11 meetings).

Quiet, reserved, and never changing expression, Wills, known as Little Miss Poker Face, played with unruffled poise and never exhibited the style, the flair or the emotional outbursts that Lenglen did. From her first appearance in the East in 1921, when she was national junior champion, Wills' typical garb on the court was a white sailor suit, white eyeshade and white shoes and stockings.

The game she played right-handed was one of sheer power, which she had developed in practice against men on the West Coast. From both forehand and backhand she hammered the ball almost the full length of the court regularly, and the speed, pace and depth of her drives, in conjunction with her tactical moves, sufficed to subdue her opponents. She could hit winners as spectacularly from the baseline on the backhand as on the forehand.

She went to the net occasionally, not nearly as often as Lenglen, and Wills was sound in her volleying and decisive overhead with her smash. Her slice service,

Helen Wills Moody: Little Miss Poker Face. • *USTA*

Wimbledon and four French championships without loss of a set until Dorothy Round of Britain extended her to 6–4, 6–8, 6–3 in the 1933 Wimbledon final.

In Wightman Cup play from 1923 to 1938, she won 18 singles matches and lost two, both in 1924. She won the Olympic singles and doubles in Paris in 1924. When she scored her first Wimbledon victory, in

snips. The third remarkable match was in the 1935 Wimbledon final in which Jacobs led, 5–2, in the third set and stood at match point, only to see the then Mrs. Moody rally and add one more victory to her astounding record. She later become Mrs. Roark and was inducted into the Hall of Fame in 1969.

MAJOR TITLES (31)—*French singles, 1928–29–30–32; Wimbledon singles, 1927–28–29–30–32–33–35–38; U.S. singles, 1923–24–25–27–28–29–31; French doubles, 1930–32; Wimbledon doubles, 1924–27–30; U.S. doubles, 1922–24–25–28; Wimbledon mixed, 1929; U.S. mixed, 1924–28* WIGHTMAN CUP—*1923–24–25–27–28–29– 30–31–32–38; record: 18–2 in singles, 3–7 in doubles.*

breaking wide and pulling the receiver beyond the alley, was as good as any female player has commanded.

Her footwork was not so good. She did not move with the grace and quickness of Lenglen, and opponents fared best against her who could use the drop shot or changes of length to draw her forward and send her running back. Anchored to the baseline, she could run any opponent into the ground. Because of her exceptional sense of anticipation, she seemed to be in the right spot, and it was not often that she appeared to be hurried in her stroking.

She was born Oct. 6, 1905, in Centreville, Cal., and the facts of her invincibility are stark. She won the Wimbledon title a record eight times (surpassed by Martina Navratilova's nine in 1990) in nine tries, her only loss coming in her first appearance, in 1924. She won the U.S. championship seven times. From 1927 to 1932 she did not lose a set in singles anywhere. She won seven U.S., five

Betty Nuthall
Great Britain (1911–)

Until Betty Kay Nuthall came along from England, no one in the 20th century had taken the women's national championship out of the U.S. It was a far less widespread and organized game when Irishwoman Mabel Cahill won at Philadelphia in 1891–92. In 1927, the 16-year-old Nuthall, a prodigy who had won the British Hard Court title in the spring (a quarterfi-

Betty Nuthall: Serving with distinction. • *USTA*

and Mrs. Anna McCune Harper, 6–1, 6–4. Defending the title, she reached the 1931 semis, losing, 6–4 in the third, to Wightman Cup teammate Eileen Bennett Whitingstall. Nuthall again was a semifinalist in 1933, startling onlookers by taking the first set from the champ, Helen Wills Moody. As the youngest to play for Britain when she joined the team in 1927, she was a Wightman Cupper eight years, beating the redoubtable Helen Jacobs in her debut.

She had a fine French in 1931, beating Jacobs before having to contend with the Germans who would clash for the Wimbledon title weeks later. Betty beat Hilde Krahwinkel in the semis to prevent a preview of Wimbledon's all-German final, but lost the title match to the tiny woman who ruled Paris and London, 5-footer Cilly Aussem, 8–6, 6–1. But she took the doubles with Whitingstall.

The main strength of Betty's game was her forehand. Holding the racket out with extended right arm, she used it as a flail, and hit with great power. Speed was the essence of her game; there was no temporizing. She hit with length and discernment, and was resourceful and wise in tactics.

Born May 23, 1911, in Surbiton, Surrey, she took up the game at seven with her father's guidance. She accomplished little in 1928 after her success the previous year, which included a beating of reigning U.S. champion Molla Mallory at Wimbledon to gain the quarters. It was not until she was bypassed for the Wightman Cup team in 1930 that she decided to take matters into her own hands and campaign alone. Packing her trunk, and accompanied by her brother, Jimmy (the English junior champ), she sailed for the U.S., and her perseverance, initiative and faith in herself were rewarded. This time, serving overhanded, she came through, the only Brit to rule Forest Hills until Virginia Wade in 1968, thus establishing herself as one of the

nalist there at 14), was not only threatening a long-lived American monopoly at Forest Hills but a record of Bessie Moore, the 16-year-old finalist to Cahill in 1892.

Still serving underhanded, as she had all her life—a habit she would soon change—Betty might have been the youngest of all U.S. champs. But Helen Wills took care of that in the U.S. final, 6–1, 6–4. Nevertheless, Nuthall, exactly the same age, to the day, as Moore had been, shared the "youngest finalist" record with her until Pam Shriver, a younger 16, displaced both of them in 1978.

Three years later, 1930, and still a teenager, Nuthall did get the U.S. title, beating in succession the 2–1 seeds, Midge Morrill

most distinguished performers, ranking in the World Top Ten, 1927–29–30–31–33.

Selected for the Hall of Fame in 1977, she died Nov. 8, 1983, in New York, where she had been a resident, as Mrs. Franklin Shoemaker.

MAJOR TITLES (9)—*U.S. singles, 1930;*

Fred Perry: Britain's finest. • *UPI*

stroke that was the making of Fred Perry as a world champion—and as a tennis player considered the best Great Britain has produced.

The knack of making the stroke baffled the promising Briton for so long that he was on the verge of giving up in despair. He had been advised that to get very far he would have to learn to take the ball early on his continental forehand, the racket making impact instantly as the ball rose from the court.

For months he could not master the timing. Then suddenly, like riding a bicycle, it came to him and he was on his way— on his way to the net on a running forehand, going forward with the swing of the racket to gain good volleying position if the drive did not win outright. And on his way to three Wimbledon Championships, three U.S. Championships, an Australian, a French and a lucrative pro career.

Born May 18, 1909, in Stockport, England, the right-handed Frederick John Perry did not take up tennis until he was 18 years old. But he had good coaching and

took to the game quickly, for he had been playing table tennis for years and winning tournaments and recognition.

Perry developed an undercut backhand that came off with surprising pace. He hit the ball smartly with good length and regularity on the service, was sharp and sound with his smash, perfect in his footwork and timing, and volleyed with dispatch. None of his strokes was overpowering, but his attack was impetuous and relentless, ever challenging, and he ran like a deer in retrieving.

He was the completely equipped and efficient adversary, jaunty, a bit cocky in his breezy self-assurance, with gallery appeal. He could be sarcastic and some thought him egotistical, but it was a pose and he had an ever-ready grin. He cut a handsome figure with his regular features, raven black hair, and physique that was perfection for the game. Once he developed the stroke that had eluded him, he was virtually unstoppable.

In 1933 Perry led the British Isles to a 4–1 victory over the United States in the inter-zone final and to the glorious victory over France that brought the Davis Cup back to Britain after a wait of 21 years. Britain retained the Cup through 1936 as Perry won every singles match he played in the four challenge rounds. England had not produced a Wimbledon singles champion for a quarter-century, but Perry took care of that, too. He won three straight Wimbledon finals without loss of a set, defeating John Crawford in 1934 and Gottfried von Cramm in 1935 and 1936.

Perry was also impressive elsewhere, winning the U.S. Championship in 1933, 1934 and 1936, an assault interrupted only in 1935, when he suffered a painful kidney injury and lost in the semifinals. In 1934 he won the Australian Championship and in 1935 the French Championship, one of only four men to take all four majors.

When Perry joined the professional tour, he drew huge crowds to see him play Ellsworth Vines and Bill Tilden. Perry won the U.S. Pro Championship in both 1938 and 1941.

After his playing career, he became associated with the manufacture of tennis clothes, was a tennis correspondent for a London newspaper and took part in radio and television coverage of tennis. He was elected to the Hall of Fame in 1975. He ranked in the World Top Ten from 1931 through 1936, No. 1 the last three years.

MAJOR TITLES (14)—*Australian singles, 1934; French singles, 1935; Wimbledon singles, 1934–35–36; U.S. singles, 1933–34–36; Australian doubles, 1934; French doubles, 1933; French mixed, 1932; Wimbledon mixed, 1935–36; U.S. mixed, 1932.* DAVIS CUP—*1931–32–33–34–35–36; record: 34–4 in singles, 11–3 in doubles.*

Bobby Riggs
United States (1918–)

Though he had little of the power of Don Budge and Jack Kramer, and though his physique was hardly comparable to that of these six-footers, right-hander Bobby Riggs was one of the smartest, most calculating and resourceful court strategists tennis has seen, particularly in his defensive circumventions. He had a temperament that was unruffled in all circumstances and he hung in the fight without showing a trace of discouragement other than a slight shake of the head. He won the championship at Wimbledon and twice at Forest Hills.

Budge, with his vast power, usually had to work his hardest to turn back the little Californian, whose forte was to subdue the fury of the big hitters. Riggs had both the brains and the shots to quell the cannonaders, particularly the drop shot from both forehand and backhand, and a lob matched by few in the way he masked it and his control of its length. Most often Budge required four sets, if not five, to win when they were amateurs. When they met as pros, Riggs won his full share.

Born Feb. 25, 1918, in Los Angeles, Robert Larimore Riggs first began to make tennis progress at the age of 12, when Dr. Esther Bartosh saw him hitting balls and took over his instruction. In 1934, at 16, he beat Frank Shields, a finalist at Wimbledon and Forest Hills. Two years later Riggs was ranked fourth in the country, and he was second to Budge in 1937 and 1938.

Riggs had the best record of any amateur in the world in 1939 in winning a rare bag of three titles at Wimbledon and the U.S. Championships. After yielding his U.S. title to Don McNeill in the 1940 final, he regained it in 1941, beating Frank Kovacs, a spectacular shotmaker. His career as an amateur soon ended. Riggs was in demand on the pro circuit.

In 1942 he competed in the U.S. Pro Championships and lost in the final to Budge. But the next time they met was

manners and sportsmanship in the years when he was playing serious tennis.

He made the World Top Ten, 1937–38–39, No. 1 the last year, and the U.S. Top Ten, 1936 through 1941, and was named to the Hall of Fame in 1967.

MAJOR TITLES (6)—*Wimbledon singles, 1939;*

after World War II, in 1946, and this time Riggs beat Budge in the U.S. Pro final at Forest Hills. They went on tour and Riggs won 23 matches to 21 for Budge. Again in 1947 they met in the final of the Pro Championships and Riggs won in five long sets. Late in the year Jack Kramer made his pro debut at Madison Square Garden in New York and Riggs beat him before a crowd of 15,114 who had plowed through 25 inches of snow in a blizzard. However, Kramer won the tour.

After losing to Kramer in the final of the U.S. Pro at Forest Hills and regaining the title in 1949 against Budge, Riggs began to taper off as a player and tried his hand as a promoter when Gussy Moran and Pauline Betz made their debuts as pros in 1950. Years later, 1973, after fading into virtual obscurity as a senior player who would make a bet on the drop of a hat, Riggs was back, taking on first Margaret Court and then Billie Jean King in mixed singles matches that gave tennis much publicity. He defeated Court, but King made him look like Humpty Dumpty. Few things ever fazed Riggs, though, or made him unhappy. And nothing ever made him forget his good

Dorothy Round
Great Britain (1909–82)

Dorothy Edith Round Little was the leading British female player at the time Helen Wills Moody ruled the courts in the 1930s. Round distinguished herself on several counts, among them that she was the only British player besides Kitty McKane Godfree to win Wimbledon twice since World War I, and she was in 1935 the only player from overseas to win the Australian Championship.

Born July 13, 1908, in Dudley, Worcestershire, England, she developed a right-handed groundstroke game of power and precision and volleying ability equaled by few. She won the Wimbledon crown in 1934 and repeated in 1937. Her play at the net was a factor in her victory over Helen Jacobs in the 1934 final, 6–2, 5–7, 6–3. In the 1937 final, she defeated the strong Polish player, Jadwiga Jedrzejowska, 6–2, 2–6, 7–5, overcoming a 1–4 deficit in the final set.

To get to the Wimbledon final of 1937, Round defeated Jacobs and Simone Mathieu, France's leading player. Round

Dorothy Round: All-round game. • *UPI*

appeared to rise to her best form when confronted by Jacobs or Moody. In 1933 Round got to the final at Wimbledon and gave Moody one of the most challenging fights of her career, yielding at 6–4, 6–8, 6–3. That same year in the U.S. Championships, she lost to Jacobs, 6–4, 5–7, 6–2, in the semifinals.

Round was not as successful, however, in Wightman Cup matches as in tournaments for the championship of England, U.S. and Australia.

She was a member of the British team from 1931 to 1936. She lost to Jacobs four times before defeating the American in 1936, in her final appearance in the international team matches, 6–3, 6–3. Round (later Mrs. Little) probably relished that victory particularly, for it was the year Jacobs finally achieved her ambition of winning Wimbledon.

She was in the World Top Ten from 1933 through 1937, No. 1 in 1934, and was named to the Hall of Fame in 1986. She died Nov. 12, 1982, in Kidderminster, England.

MAJOR TITLES (6)—*Australian singles, 1935; Wimbledon singles, 1934–37. Wimbledon mixed, 1934–35–36.* WIGHTMAN CUP—*1931–32–33–34–35–36; record: 4–7 in singles, 0–2 in doubles.*

Bill Tilden
United States (1893–1953)

If a player's value is measured by the dominance and influence he exercises over a sport, then William Tatem "Big Bill" Tilden II could be considered the greatest player in the history of tennis.

From 1920 through 1926, he dominated the game as has no player before or since. During those years he was invincible in the United States, won Wimbledon both times he competed there, and captured 13 successive singles matches in the Davis Cup challenge round against the best players from Australia, France and Japan.

As an amateur (1912–30) he won 138 of 192 tournaments, lost 28 finals and had a 907–62 match record—a phenomenal .936 average.

When he first won Wimbledon, in 1920, he was 27 years old, an advanced age for a champion. But he had a long and influential career, and at the age of 52, in 1945, he was still able to push the 27-year-old Bobby Riggs to the limit in a professional match.

Tilden, a right-hander, born Feb. 10, 1893, in Philadelphia, had the ideal tennis build, standing over six feet tall, with thin shanks and big shoulders. He had speed and nimbleness, coordination and perfect balance. He also had marked endurance, despite smoking cigarettes incessantly when not playing. In stroke equipment, he had the weapons to launch an overpowering assault and the resources to defend and confound through a variety of spins and pace when the opponent was impervious to sheer power.

Bill Tilden: Greatest of all? • *UPI*

ished playing tennis as a game of chess, matching wits as well as physical powers. The drop shot, at which he was particularly adroit, and the lob were among his disconcerting weapons.

His knowledge and mastery of spin has hardly ever been exceeded, as evidenced not only on the court but also in his *Match Play and the Spin of the Ball*, a classic written

intelligent and opinionated, he was a man of strong likes and dislikes. He had highly successful friends, both men and women, who were devoted to him, and there were others who disliked him and considered him arrogant and inconsiderate of officials and ball boys who served at his matches. He was constantly wrangling with officers and committeemen of the USTA on Davis Cup policy and enforcement of the amateur rule, and in 1928 he was on the front pages of the American press when he was removed as captain and star player of the Davis Cup team, charged with violating the amateur rule with his press accounts of the Wimbledon Championships, in which he was competing. So angry were the French over the loss of the star member of the cast for the Davis Cup challenge round—the first ever held on French soil— that the American ambassador, Myron T. Herrick, interceded for the sake of good relations between the countries, and Tilden was restored to the team.

Nobody had a more devastating service than Tilden's cannonball, or a more challenging second serve than his kicking American twist. No player had a stronger combination of forehand and backhand drives, supplemented by a forehand chop and backhand slice. Tilden's mixture of shots was a revelation in his first appearance at Wimbledon. Gerald Patterson of Australia, the defending champion, found his backcourt untenable and was passed over and over when he went to the net behind his powerful service. Tilden won, 2–6, 6–3, 6–2, 6–4.

The backcourt was where Tilden played tennis. He was no advocate of the "big game," the big serve and rush for the net for the instant volley coup. He rel-

When Tilden, in the opening match, beat René Lacoste, the French gallery suffered agony and cursed themselves for insisting that "Teel-den" be restored to the team. It all ended happily for them, however, as the French won the other four matches and kept the Davis Cup. On Tilden's return home, he was brought up on the charges of violating the rule at Wimbledon. He was found guilty and was suspended from playing in the U.S. Championships that year.

Eligible for the U.S. title again in 1929, after the lifting of his suspension, he won the crown for the seventh time, defeating his doubles partner, Frank Hunter. In 1930 he won Wimbledon for the third time, at the age of 37. After the U.S. Championships, in which he was beaten in the semifinals by John Doeg, he notified the tennis association of his intention to make a series of motion pictures for profit, thus disqualifying him for further play as an amateur. He was in the World Top Ten from 1919 through 1930, No. 1 a record six times (1920–25), and in the U.S. Top Ten 12 straight years from 1918, No. 1 a record 10 times (1920–29). He was named to the Hall of Fame in 1959.

In 1931 he entered upon a professional playing career, joining Vincent Richards, Hans Nusslein and Roman Najuch of Germany and Karel Kozeluh of Czechoslovakia. Tilden's name revived pro tennis, which had languished since its inception in 1926 when Suzanne Lenglen went on tour. His joining the pros paved the way for Ellsworth Vines, Fred Perry and Don Budge to leave the amateur ranks and play for big prize money. Tilden won his pro debut against Kozeluh, 6–4, 6–2, 6–4, before 13,000 fans in Madison Square Garden.

Joining promoter Bill O'Brien, Tilden toured the country in 1932 and 1933, but the Depression was on and new blood was needed. Vines furnished it. Tilden and O'Brien signed him on, and in 1934 Tilden defeated Vines in the younger man's pro debut, 7–9, 6–1, 4–6, 6–3, 6–3. That year Tilden and Vines went on the first of the great tennis tours, won by Vines, 47–26.

The tours grew in the 1930s and '40s, and Tilden remained an attraction even though he was approaching the age of 50. For years he traveled across the country, driving by day and sometimes all night and then going on a court a few hours after arriving. At times, when he was managing his tour, he had to help set the stage for the matches.

Tragically, his activity and fortunes dwindled after his conviction on a morals charge in 1951. He died of a heart attack under pitiful circumstances, alone and with few resources, on June 5, 1953, in Los Angeles. His bag was packed for a trip to Cleveland to play in the U.S. Pro Championships when perhaps the greatest tennis player of them all was found dead in his room.

MAJOR TITLES (21)—*Wimbledon singles, 1920–21–30; singles, 1920–21–22–23–24– 25–29; Wimbledon doubles, 1927; U.S. doubles, 1918–21–22–23–27; French mixed, 1930; U.S. mixed, 1913–14–22–23.* OTHER U.S. TITLES— *Indoor singles, 1920; Indoor doubles, 1919–20 with Vincent Richards; 1926, with Frank Anderson; 1929, with Frank Hunter; Indoor mixed, 1921–22, with Molla Mallory; 1924, with Hazel Hotchkiss Wightman; Clay Court singles, 1918–22–23– 24–25–26–27; Pro singles, 1931–35; Pro doubles, 1932, with Bruce Barnes; 1945, with Vincent Richards.* DAVIS CUP—*1920–21–22–23–24–25– 26–27– 28–29–30; record: 25–5 singles, 9–2 in doubles.*

Ellsworth Vines
United States (1911–)

One night in 1930, an 18-year-old lad sat in a rocking chair on the porch of the Peninsula Inn in Seabright, N.J., looking out to sea and thinking that his tennis dreams were shattered. "I guess I'm just a flash in the pan like they say," said Henry Ellsworth Vines, Jr.

Weeks earlier they had been calling him another California Comet. He had come out of the West, a lanky youth who had the kick of a mule in his cannonball service and who terrorized the Eastern grass-court circuit.

Vines, a right–hander, born Sept. 29, 1911, in Los Angeles, ambled along mournfully like slow molasses when not in hot pursuit of a tennis ball. But on the court he was devastating, wherefore came

Ellsworth Vines: Master gambler. • *UPI*

moderate strokes. Vines could never get his confidence or control against Wood's tactics, and some were saying the new Comet had burned out already.

Vines didn't settle for being a flash in the pan, however. A year later, after practicing all winter and spring back in California against slow-ball strategy, Vines came East again. In 1931 he was the U.S. champion and No. 1 in America, and Wood was Wimbledon champion. In 1932, Vines won at Wimbledon and Forest Hills. He had become No. 1 in the world.

Vines played amateur tennis on the grass circuit only five years, 1929–33, making the World Top Ten the last three years, and the U.S. Top Ten in 1930–31–32, No. 1 the last two years. But in those five years he established at Forest Hills and Wimbledon that he had one of the best serves, if not the very fastest serve ever turned loose, with almost no spin. He also had as fast and as risky a forehand as ever seen, a murderous overhead, and a skill in the volleying position to compare with the best.

Moreover, his disposition and temperament were foolproof. Where others might explode in protest against a line call, Vines

would slowly turn his head and grin under his white cap at the linesman.

He was a gambler on the court. He hit his forehand flat, with all his whizzing might, and closer to the net and the lines than anyone dared. At his best he was equal to beating any player, but his margin of safety was so thin that on days when he did not have the feel and touch, his errors could be ruinous.

Wimbledon crowds marveled at the devastating fury of his attack in beating Bunny Austin in the 1932 Wimbledon final, which ended with a service ace. The ball catapulted by Austin so fast that the Briton said afterward he did not know whether it went by him to the left or to the right. Yet, the very next year, Vines lost to both Fred Perry and to Austin in Davis Cup play and to Bitsy Grant in the fourth round at Forest Hills. Disgusted, Vines could not wait to cut the gut out of his rackets and leave for home, his tennis career as an amateur soon at an end.

He signed a professional contract to go on tour with Bill Tilden and won their opening match, 8–6, 6–3, 6–2, before 14,637 fans at Madison Square Garden. Vines beat the aging Tilden, 47 matches to 26. A match in the Garden between Vines and Perry drew 17,630.

Near the end of the decade, Vines' interest in tennis waned. He turned to golf and became the best golfer who was ever a top tennis player. For years he prospered as a teaching pro, and he was good enough to reach the semifinals of the 1951 Professional Golf Association Championship.

He was enshrined in the Hall of Fame in 1962. In 1977 he attended the Wimbledon Centenary as one of the former champions receiving commemorative medals. He had turned out to be much, much more than a flash in the pan.

MAJOR TITLES (6)—*Wimbledon singles, 1932; U.S. singles, 1931–32; Australian doubles, 1933; U.S. doubles, 1932; U.S. mixed, 1933.* OTHER U.S. TITLES—*Clay Court singles, 1931; Clay Court doubles, 1931, with Keith Gledhill; Pro singles, 1939.* DAVIS CUP—*1932–33; record: 13–3 in singles.*

Baron Gottfried von Cramm
Germany (1909–76)

If any player was the prince charming of tennis, he was Gottfried von Cramm, a baron of the German nobility, six feet tall, with blond hair, green eyes, and a magnetism that, in the words of Don Budge, "made him dominate any scene he was part of."

The most accomplished tennis player Germany had known, von Cramm must be one of the finest players never to have won the Wimbledon Championship, for which he was runner-up three years in a row—to Fred Perry in 1935 and 1936, and to Budge in 1937.

Von Cramm, who was known as The Baron, was also runner-up to Budge for the

Gottfried von Cramm: The Baron. • *Fischer Collection/SPS*

U.S. Championship in 1937 and runner-up yet again to Budge in what has been termed the greatest Davis Cup match ever played, the fifth and deciding match in the 1937 inter-zone final between the United States and Germany. Budge came from 1–4 and had match point five times before he hit the final shot, racing across the court beyond the alley, and he lay sprawled on the ground as the umpire declared the United States to be winner. The score of the match: 6–8, 5–7, 6–4, 6–2, 8–6.

Said The Baron at the end, when he stood at the net waiting for Budge to pick himself up from the ground: "Don, this was absolutely the finest match I have ever played in my life. I'm very happy I could have played it against you, whom I like so much. Congratulations." The next moment, their arms were around each other.

Von Cramm, a right-hander, born July 7, 1909, at Nettlingen, Hanover, Germany, was noted on the court for his endurance and tenacity. In recalling their thrilling Cup match, Budge related how he put four successive first serves in play, his very best, and all four came back as winners for von Cramm.

When von Cramm won the French Championship in 1936, he was carried to five sets in round after round, and in the

of his outstanding seasons was in 1935 when was 11–1 in singles, 4–1 doubles. He was in the World Top Ten from 1932 through 1937.

Von Cramm, at the height of his career when Hitler was preparing for Germany to launch World War II, declined to speak for Nazism in his tennis travels and was imprisoned by the Gestapo in 1938. After the war, during which he was a hero on the Russian front, he had a successful business career and was an administrator in tennis, serving as president of Lawn Tennis Club Rot-Weiss in Berlin. The Baron died in an automobile crash near Cairo, Egypt, Nov. 8, 1976, and a year later was enshrined in the Hall of Fame.

MAJOR TITLES (5)—*French singles, 1934–36; French doubles, 1937; U.S. doubles, 1937; Wimbledon mixed, 1933.* DAVIS CUP—*1932–33–34–35–36–37–51–52–53; record: 58–10 in singles, 24–11 in doubles.*

Tony Wilding
New Zealand (1883–1915)

The British idolized Tony Wilding. He was a superb figure of a man, his sports-

Tony Wilding: Wimbledon hero. • *UPI*

manship was exemplary, and, besides, he learned his tennis at Cambridge University.

Anthony Frederick Wilding, born Oct. 31, 1883, in Christchurch, New Zealand, stood with Norman Brookes as two of the foremost players in tennis for nearly a decade. Four straight times, 1910–13, he won the Wimbledon Championship. In the 1913 Wimbledon final, beating Maurice McLoughlin, the formidable California Comet, Wilding was particularly impressive. "He was in prime physical condition," wrote distinguished British tennis authority A. Wallis Myers. "All his best fighting instincts were aroused, his tactics were as sound as his strokes and he won a great victory, the greatest of his career, in three sets."

Wilding a right-hander, lost his title to Brookes in 1914 and joined with the Australian "Wizard" to win the Davis Cup back from the United States that very year. Wilding's triumph over Dick Williams of the U.S. on the first day of the Cup was a shock. Williams was one of the most daring and brilliant shotmakers in history, but Wilding, playing almost unerringly, won quickly.

Wilding played the classic game in vogue at the time. His drives were the strength of his attack and his defense was outstanding. He could hit with immense pace and overspin, but when prudence and judgment dictated security of stroke rather than speed, as against a player of Williams' daring, Wilding could temper his drives and play faultlessly from the baseline.

Wilding made his debut on the Australasian Davis Cup team at the age of 21 in 1905. In 1906 he won the Australian Championship and a year later he and Brookes won the Davis Cup for Australasia for the first time, defeating the British Isles. Wilding-Brookes retained the Cup in 1908 against the United States, and repeated in 1909, a year in which Wilding won the Australian Championship a second time.

Wilding's 1914 appearance in the Davis Cup was his last. Following their victory at Forest Hills, he and Brookes went to war. Wilding never came back. At the age of 31, on May 9, 1915, he was killed in action at Neuve Chapelle, France. He had been No. 3 in the world ranking in 1914, and was named to the Hall of Fame in 1978.

MAJOR TITLES (11)—*Australian singles, 1906–09; Wimbledon singles, 1910–11– 12–13; Australian doubles, 1906; Wimbledon doubles, 1907–08–10–14.* DAVIS CUP—*1905–06–07–08–09–14; record: 15–6 in singles, 6–3 in doubles.*

Dick Williams
United States (1891–1968)

Richard Norris Williams II survived the sinking of the Titanic, and after that harrowing experience, tennis must have seemed easy, for he became one of the outstanding players of his time. Born of American parents in Geneva, Switzerland, Jan. 29, 1891, he left for the United States in 1912 aboard the *S.S. Titanic,* which struck an iceberg and sank. His father went down with the ship, but young Williams was rescued from the icy North Atlantic.

He lived a long life, until 77, and for that the tennis world was always grateful.

Williams, a right-hander, had learned to play in Switzerland, using the continental grip and hitting his ground strokes with underspin. He developed his game further as a Harvard University undergraduate, winning the Intercollegiate championship in 1913 and 1915, and he was accepted for the U.S. Championships at Newport in 1912, getting to the quarterfinals.

The next year, he was runner-up at Newport, but in 1914 he won, defeating Maurice McLoughlin, 6–3, 8–6, 10–8, in a stirring final before a large crowd on the new championship court at the Casino. Throughout the three sets Williams maintained a terrific pace and marvelous control, averting the loss of the final set several times with bursts of speed and master strokes that thwarted even so aggressive and courageous a foe as the Comet.

In 1916 he won the U.S. title again, this time over Little Bill Johnston, and attained the No. 1 ranking. Williams was in the U.S. Top Ten 10 times between 1912 and 1925. He played on Davis Cup teams from 1913 to 1926 and was captain of six victorious teams, 1921 through 1926, as well as the team of 1934. He played doubles on four of the winning sides he captained, partnering Bill Tilden, Watson Washburn and Vinnie Richards.

In 1924 he won an Olympic gold in mixed with Hazel Wightman. Williams had a daring style of play taking every possible ball (when not in volleying position) on

Dick Williams: Unsinkable. • *UPI*

the first and second ball. He did not know what it was to temporize.

On occasion, his errors caused by his gutsy tactics might bring defeat by opponents of inferior ability. But it was the commonly held opinion that Williams, on his best days, when he had the feel and touch and his breathtaking strokes were flashing on the lines, was unbeatable

the rise with hair-trigger timing. Always he hit boldly, sharply for the winner, and that included serving for the winner on both

MAJOR TITLES (6)—*U.S. singles, 1914–16; Wimbledon doubles, 1920; U.S. doubles, 1925–26; U.S. mixed, 1912.* OTHER U.S. TITLES—*Clay Court singles, 1912–15; Intercollegiate singles, 1913–15; Intercollegiate doubles, 1914–15 with Dick Harte.* DAVIS CUP—*1913–14–21–23–25–26; record: 6–3 in singles, 4–0 in doubles.*

4: UNDER THE TABLE: 1946–67

two parts: the amateur fixtures, and a struggling band of gypsy professionals who wandered rather anonymously from city to city and continent to continent, playing one-night stands. They may have been the best

Ashore at last, Jack Kramer won the U.S. Singles, defeating Tom Brown in 1946. • *UPI*

"Big Four" tournaments (Australian, French, Wimbledon, U.S.) and the Davis Cup and Wightman Cup competitions— were ostensibly amateur. Only a handful of top stars made a living playing tennis; the rest were "tennis bums" on a lark for several years before settling down and getting jobs. All were paid, according to previously established reputation, "under the table" by an Establishment of amateur officials. Major-league tennis was not big-time at all; it was very much a game of country club and old school tie.

1946

The year 1946 was one of reconstruction for international tennis. The French and Wimbledon championships and the Davis Cup had last been played in 1939, the Australian Championships in 1940. The U.S. Championships had continued uninterrupted.

Jack Kramer, who had entered the Coast Guard as a seaman and was discharged as a lieutenant after seeing action in the Pacific, returned at the age of 24 to claim the No. 1 U.S. ranking that had been predicted for him since 1942. Ted Schroeder was No. 1 in 1942, Joe Hunt in 1943 and Frank Parker in 1944–45.

It was comparatively easy restarting championships in countries that had not been ravaged by the war. In Australia, John Bromwich—a highly unorthodox player who hit a two-fisted forehand—re-established a thread with the prewar era. He had been the 1939 singles champion and regained the Australian title with a five-set victory over countryman Dinny Pails, 5–7, 6–3, 7–5, 3–6, 6–2. In doubles, it was as if the war had never occurred: Adrian Quist, the last prewar singles champion, who had won his national doubles title with Don Turnbull in 1936–37 and with Bromwich in 1938–39–40, successfully teamed with Bromwich once again, re-establishing a monopoly that lasted through 1950.

In Paris, French tennis fans crowned the first native champion since Henri Cochet in 1932: left-hander Marcel Bernard. He upset Czech Jaroslav Drobny, 3–6, 2–6, 6–1, 6–4, 6–3, and teamed with countryman Yvon Petra to win the doubles.

More startling was Petra's triumph in the singles at Wimbledon, the first Frenchman to win there since Cochet beat Jean Borotra in the all-French final of 1929. (Borotra was refused entry to Wimbledon in 1946 because he had been Minister of Sport in the Vichy government of France, though he was later a Nazi prisoner.)

Kramer, though seeded second, was the favorite, but he was done in by a nasty blister on his right hand that had caused him to default at the Queen's Club tune-up tournament the week before. Drobny beat him in the round of 16, 2–6, 17–15, 6–3, 3–6, 6–3, after Kramer had lost only five games in the three previous rounds despite his handicap.

Pails, 25, was the top seed, but he got lost on the London Underground on his way to Wimbledon for his quarterfinal match and arrived late. Unsettled, he lost to Petra in four sets. Petra—a tall, lanky player with less than polished strokes—then reached the final by beating San Franciscan Tom Brown after losing the first two sets. Petra did not figure to have a chance in the final against Australian Geoff Brown, a player of medium build with a devastating serve and great pace on the rest of his shots, but Brown made the curious tactical miscalculation of trying to slow-ball during the first two sets. He did win the third and fourth, but by that time was psychologically exhausted, and when he dropped his serve in the opening game of the fifth set, Petra ran out the match, 6–2, 6–4, 7–9, 5–7, 6–4.

Kramer, playing with his damaged racket hand encased in bandages and a glove, dominated the doubles final, teaming with Tom Brown for a straight-set victory over Geoff Brown and Pails.

There had been some reluctance on the part of the All England Lawn Tennis & Croquet Club to stage the Championships at all in 1946. The club had been heavily damaged by German bombs, and a gaping hole in the Centre Court competitors' stand and adjacent seats had to be cordoned off. The organizing committee did not want to have a tournament if Wimbledon's prewar standards of preeminence could not be maintained. Colonel Duncan Macaulay, who returned as the club's full-time secretary after the war, summarized the obstacles in his book *Behind the Scenes at Wimbledon:*

"The groundsmen were not back from the war, the mowers wouldn't work, the rollers wouldn't roll, nothing would function. We were surrounded by bomb-shelters, improvised buildings and huts of every sort. The back part of the club was covered with broken glass as a result of flying bombs. Britain was under a tight wartime economy and nothing could be obtained without a license or a coupon. There was the difficulty of supplies of balls and rackets and the printing of tickets. Paper was very short . . . Soap, too, was strictly rationed—and we needed a lot of it. Clothes were rationed and tennis flannels and costumes were almost non-existent. And of course, food was rationed, too—

that resulted from the wartime hiatus.

One fact that was amply demonstrated was the superiority of American women players, who put a stranglehold on the distaff game in the immediate postwar years and maintained it through the 1950s, until Australia, Latin America, and Europe again began producing champions in the early 1960s.

Macaulay explained the phenomenon quite logically. "Least upset by the war of all the lawn tennis-playing nations was the United States. America's young tennis-playing men were, of course, called up for service in the armed forces. But whereas lawn tennis in Britain and on the Continent closed down completely during the war and only started up again with many creaks and groans, with ruined courts and grave shortages of equipment, the American lawn tennis courts and clubs remained in being and the American Championships continued all through the war. It was in the sphere of women's tennis that the United States gained such a tremendous advantage during these years."

Few non-Australian women ventured Down Under in those days, so the Australian

Championships remained a native affair, but American women won just about every title of consequence, setting the pattern for ensuing years.

Margaret Osborne defeated Pauline Betz, 1–6, 8–6, 7–5, in the French final, and the two of them teamed with Louise Brough and Doris Hart to rout Great Britain in the resumption of the Wightman

ning her first Wimbledon title, and overcame net-rusher Brough in the final, 6–2, 6–4. Betz had won the U.S. Championship in 1942–44, beating Brough the first two years and Osborne the third, but had been runner-up to Sarah Palfrey Cooke in 1945. In 1946, Betz won Forest Hills again, for the fourth and last time, beating Patricia Canning, 11–9, 6–3.

Brough and Osborne teamed to win the first of their three French and five Wimbledon doubles titles. They also maintained an incredible streak in the U.S. Doubles they had started in 1942; they won the title nine straight years, until Shirley Fry and Doris Hart took over in 1951–54, and then won three more in a row for a total of a dozen titles together.

Osborne and Billy Talbert won their fourth consecutive U.S. Mixed Doubles title (Osborne had teamed successfully with Tom Brown at Wimbledon), and the tactically astute Talbert and Gardnar Mulloy defended the U.S. Men's Doubles crown they had won in 1942 and 1945, and would again in 1948.

Don Budge and Bobby Riggs, the best players in the world immediately before

Gardnar Mulloy (left) and Billy Talbert took their third U.S. Doubles at Longwood in 1946. • *UPI*

the war, were now teamed up again on the pro circuit. Riggs, who had succeeded Budge as Wimbledon and Forest Hills champ in 1939 and won the U.S. crown again in 1941, was signed by promoter Jack Harris when he got out of the service. In an abbreviated tour against Budge, Bobby won, 18 matches to 16, lobbing incessantly to take full advantage of Budge's ailing shoulder. He trounced Budge, 6–3, 6–1, 6–1, in the final of the U.S. Professional Championship, which went virtually unnoticed at the West Side Tennis Club.

The tournament that did draw attention at Forest Hills, naturally, was the "amateur" Nationals—as America's premier tennis event was called before it became the U.S. Open in 1968. It was here that Jack Kramer finally assumed the crown and top ranking that had been more or less reserved for him, as Hannibal Coons intimated in an article in Collier's in August 1946:

"Six-feet-one, powerfully built and a natural athlete, Jack Kramer has been the logical heir to the American tennis throne since he was fourteen. Successively

National Boys' champion, National Interscholastic champion, a Davis Cup veteran at 18, and three times National Doubles champion, twice with Schroeder and once with Parker, Kramer has for four years been shoved away from the singles title only by the whim of circumstance."

Kramer had re-established himself as a force in the game after his three-year military service by winning the singles, doubles (with Schroeder), and mixed doubles (with Helen Wills Moody Roark) without losing a set at the Southern California Championships at Los Angeles in May. His Wimbledon blisters had extended his reputation as "the hard-luck kid," but at Forest Hills there was no stopping him. Kramer had developed his aggressive, hard-hitting game on the concrete courts of the Los Angeles Tennis Club under the watchful eye of the longtime iron-handed developer of Southern California junior talent, Perry T. Jones, and his coach and onetime idol, Ellsworth Vines. Kramer always had a thunderous serve and forehand, and with the formidable backhand he developed on a South American exhibition tour in 1941 also in harness, he ravaged Tom Brown—who had beaten defending champ Frankie Parker and Gar Mulloy—in the Forest Hills final, 9–7, 6–3, 6–0.

There was one task left for Kramer in 1946: recovery of the Davis Cup. He had been an 18-year-old rookie for the U.S. in 1939, playing only doubles, teaming with Joe Hunt in a four-set loss to Adrian Quist and John Bromwich as Australia won, 3–2. Now Kramer and his friend Schroeder, 12 days his senior, went to Kooyong Stadium (the name, in the aboriginal tongue, means "haunt of the wild water-fowl") in December and socked it to the Aussies, 5–0, inaugurating a four-year U.S. reign. Kramer beat Dinny Pails and Bromwich, and teamed with Schroeder for revenge against Bromwich and Quist in the deciding match, all in straight sets.

Kramer and Schroeder were the first Davis Cuppers to fly to Australia—then a four-day trip in a propeller-driven aircraft, complete with sleeping berths. Prior to 1946, tennis players had gone to Australia by boat, making the journey in a leisurely month, stopping off and playing exhibitions at ports en route to stay sharp. Kramer and Schroeder were the first airborne tennis stars, but they could hardly

to him by King George VI and Queen Elizabeth after he won Wimbledon in 1947. • *UPI*

in 1947. Of the nine countries (Germany, Italy, Japan, Bulgaria, Finland, Hungary, Romania, Thailand and Libya) that had been expelled from the ITF at its first postwar meeting in 1946, four (Italy, Hungary, Finland, and Romania) were readmitted, reflecting a cooling of hatreds that had been kindled by the war. This trend would continue.

If 1946 had marked Jack Kramer's emergence, 1947 verified his greatness. He dominated the amateur game, paving the way for the most significant pro-contract signing of the era. Kramer did not play the Australian or French Championships, but he won the singles and doubles titles of Wimbledon and the United States, and won both his singles (over Dinny Pails and John Bromwich) in straight sets as the U.S. defended the Davis Cup with a 4–1 victory over Australia at the West Side Tennis Club.

Pails and Bromwich were again the finalists in the Australian Championships, but this time Pails reversed the decision of the previous year in another five-setter, 4–6, 6–4, 3–6, 7–5, 8–6, for his only Grand Slam singles title. Nancye Bolton beat Nell

Hopman, wife of the Australian Davis Cup captain, 6–3, 6–2, for the fourth of her six Australian singles titles (1937–40–46–47–48–51). She also teamed with Thelma Long for the sixth of their 11 doubles titles together, re-grasping the championships they had captured from 1936 through 1940 under their maiden names of Nancye Wynne and Thelma Coyne.

Readmission of Hungary to the ITF permitted Josef Asboth, an artistic clay court specialist, back into the international fixtures, and he won the French Championship over South African Eric Sturgess, a slim but accomplished player with superbly accurate ground strokes. Pat Canning Todd, a statuesque and graceful Californian who was largely overshadowed by her American contemporaries, beat Doris Hart for the French women's title, 6–3, 3–6, 6–4.

Hart, a remarkable player who had been stricken with a serious knee infection at age 11 and took up tennis to strengthen her right leg, beat Louise Brough, 2–6, 8–6, 6–4, in the semifinals at Wimbledon, but had little left for Margaret Osborne in the final and was relegated to being runner-up, 6–2, 6–4. Brough and Osborne had successfully defended their French doubles title, but were dethroned in the Wimbledon final by Hart and Todd.

The U.S. Wightman Cup team—again a powerhouse with Brough, Osborne, Hart and Todd replacing Betz (who had been suspended by the USTA merely for *talking* about turning pro)—overwhelmed Great Britain, 7–0, at Forest Hills, but this time conceded a couple of sets in the process.

Kramer's domination of Wimbledon was so great that John Olliff, longtime tennis correspondent of London's *Daily Telegraph,* referred to him as "a presence of unutterable awe." In his book *The Romance of Wimbledon,* Olliff recalls: "It became almost boring to watch him mowing down his victims when it was so obvious that nothing short of a physical injury could possibly prevent him from winning.... He was an automaton of crushing consistency."

Kramer lost only 37 games in seven matches. In the quarterfinals he beat Geoff Brown, the 1946 runner-up, 6–0, 6–1, 6–3; in the semis, Dinny Pails, 6–1, 3–6, 6–1, 6–0, and in the final, Tom Brown, 6–1, 6–3, 6–2, in just 48 minutes. King George VI and Queen Elizabeth were in the Royal Box, and His Majesty presented the champion's trophy to Kramer, the first titlist to have worn shorts instead of long white flannels. It was the King's first visit to Wimbledon since, as the Duke of York, he had played in the men's doubles in 1926.

Ted Schroeder did not play Wimbledon, but Kramer teamed with Bob Falkenburg—another tall American with a big serve—to win the doubles without losing a set. In the Davis Cup challenge round, Kramer and Schroeder won all four singles but lost the doubles to Bromwich and Colin Long. Jack and Ted then teamed to win the National Doubles for the third time at Longwood.

And so on to Forest Hills, Kramer was again top-seeded and considered a cinch winner; in fact, he had already signed on Sept. 3, 1947, with promoter Jack Harris to play a tour against Bobby Riggs in 1948. Riggs had beaten Don Budge on a short tour for the second consecutive year, 23 matches to 21 this time, and had edged Budge for the U.S. Pro title, 3–6, 6–3, 10–8, 4–6, 6–3. Kramer was to be the new challenger for pro king Riggs, but the deal had to be hushed up until after the U.S. Nationals, which ended Sept. 14.

Everything went according to plan until, as Kramer recalled in a *Sports Illustrated* article, "I almost blew the whole thing sky high. Here I was, signed and sealed for delivery to Riggs, and I lost the first two sets in the final to Frankie Parker. He was playing his best, but I did my best to help him. I can still remember looking up into the first row of the stadium seats and seeing the top of Jack Harris' bald head. The reason I could look up and see the top of his bald head was because he had it bowed forward in despair." But Kramer pulled himself together, starting the third set with two aces and the first of many winning drop shots. He purged the errors from his game and brought Harris back to life by winning the last three sets easily.

Allison Danzig, the venerable tennis writer of *The New York Times,* reported on the final: "Not since Sidney Wood tamed the lethal strokes of Ellsworth Vines at Seabright in 1930 with his soft-ball strategy and reduced the Californian to a state of helplessness, has so cleverly designed and executed a plan of battle been in evidence on American turf as Parker employed in this match.

"In the end, the plan failed, as the challenger's strength ebbed and the champion, extricating himself from a morass of errors, loosed the full fury of his attack to win at 4–6, 2–6, 6–1, 6–0, 6–3. But the gallery will long remember the thrill and the chill of those first two sets and also the tense final chapter as the 31-year-old Parker gave his heavily favored and younger opponent the scare of his life."

1948

Perhaps the most unforgettable event

Kramer, the top amateur of 1947, had been signed to face 1946–47 pro champ Riggs on a long tour. Francisco "Pancho" Segura of Ecuador and Australian Dinny Pails came along as the preliminary attraction—"the donkey act," in the vernacular of the tour. As was customary, the long and winding road of one-night stands began in the Garden, then the American Mecca of pro tennis.

New York Times 50 years later. "Yet with taxis, buses, commuter trains and private cars stalled and the subways limping, 15,114 customers found their way into the big barn at Eighth Avenue and 50th Street."

rushing the net on virtually every point and hammering away at Riggs' backhand.

"I began to really get comfortable with this new style around the time our tour

Jack Kramer (far right) joins Pancho Segura, Bobby Riggs and Dinny Pails on the pro circuit. • *UPI*

Twenty-year-old Pancho Gonzalez (right) was the victor, Eric Sturgess the vanquished, in the 1948 U.S. Singles. • *UPI*

Club. He had a tough match against Welby Van Horn in the quarterfinals, then beat aging but still formidable Don Budge in the semifinals, 6–4, 8–10, 3–6, 6–4, 6–0. Al Laney, who covered tennis for 50 years, many of them for the New York *Herald Tribune,* made no secret of his low regard for the pros "because for so many years they have preferred exhibitions to real tournaments," but he begrudgingly put this one on his list of all time memorable matches. The next day Kramer put away Riggs, 14–12, 6–2, 3–6, 6–3, becoming the undisputed ruler of the pros as he had been of the amateurs.

With Kramer out of the amateur ranks, three other Americans took major titles. Frankie Parker won the French over Jaroslav Drobny in four sets; Bob Falkenburg startled Wimbledon by taking the men's singles over John Bromwich, 7–5, 0–6, 6–2, 3–6, 7–5, saving three match points; and Richard "Pancho" Gonzalez stormed to the first of his back-to-back U.S. titles, over Eric Sturgess, 6–2, 6–3, 14–12.

Adrian Quist, the last prewar champ, had regained the Australian singles title over doubles partner Bromwich, but was able to win only one set in the Davis Cup challenge round as Australia fell to the United States 5–0, at Forest Hills. Parker— who had been denied a singles berth in 1946–47—and Ted Schroeder beat Quist and Bill Sidwell to sweep the four singles matches. Bill Talbert-Gardnar Mulloy won the clinching doubles point over Sidwell and Colin Long.

Falkenburg, 23, was a tall and skinny Californian who dawdled between points sometimes apparently stalling to upset opponents; and threw games or whole sets to grab a breather and pace himself. He later moved to Rio de Janeiro and played in the Davis Cup for Brazil. Seeded seventh, he beat Frank Sedgman in the fourth round, Lennart Bergelin (conqueror of Parker in five sets) in the quarters, and Mulloy in an acrimonious semifinal. Then

reached San Francisco, when we were tied at 13 matches apiece," Kramer reminisced in *Sports Illustrated.* "I won there, and then we flew to Denver, and Bobby got something started with the stewardess, and that gave me Denver, and then we went into Salt Lake City, where we played on a tremendously slick wood surface. Bobby couldn't handle my serve there, and all of a sudden it was 16–13. And that was it. Now he had to gamble on my serve. He had to take chances or I could get to the net, and he was dead. He was thoroughly demoralized."

By the time the tour worked its way through the hinterlands, Riggs was "tanking" matches. Kramer won 56 of the last 63, finishing with a 69–20 record, the last amateur to overthrow the pro king. Kramer, whose cut of the opening-night receipts at the Garden had been $8,800, earned $89,000. Riggs made $50,000.

Kramer also won the U.S. Pro Championships at the West Side Tennis

he met Bromwich, 29, in the final. Lance Tingay, in his book *100 Years of Wimbledon,* described the match-up:

"Bromwich was a much-loved player. Not only did he have a gentle personality but a persuasively gentle game. Craft and skill and guile were his all, never muscle and pace. His racket was lightweight, the grip small and could have been a girl's. He

New York Herald Tribune

6–3. By then the effectiveness of Falkenburg's big serve had declined. And he was missing much with his forehand volley.... Bromwich controlled the fifth set decisively, so much so that he led 5–2, 40–15, on his own service. On the two match points Falkenburg played shots that were pure gambles, screaming backhand returns of service. Bromwich had his third match point at advantage and Falkenburg repeated his performance. The Australian 'died' as an effective player from that stage. Falkenburg devoured the remaining games. If Bromwich was heart-broken he shared the sentiment with nearly every spectator round the court."

Bromwich never did win the Wimbledon singles, but he salvaged some consolation by taking the doubles title with the 20-year-old Sedgman, and successfully defended the mixed doubles title with Louise Brough.

After all the Wimbledon surprises, Forest Hills in 1948 was considered a wide-open affair. Ted Schroeder, generally regarded as Kramer's heir apparent, did not play. Frank Parker was the top-seeded American, ahead of Falkenburg. Virtually

ignored was Gonzalez, 20, one of seven children of a poor Mexican-American family from Los Angeles. His father wished he would give up tennis and get an education, but Pancho preferred to be a truant, going to movies or developing the blazing serve that was his hallmark.

Gonzalez—a lean 6-foot-3, 185-pounder whose theatricality, smoldering Latin temper, sex appeal, and combination of power and touch gave him a kind of animalistic magnetism—upset Parker in the quarterfinals, Drobny in the semis, 8–10, 11–9, 6–0, 6–3, and the South African Sturgess in the final. A friend had once described Gonzalez as "even-tempered—he's *always* mad." The fact that his worthiness as champion was questioned because Schroeder had not played made him an even angrier young man.

American women continued to rule international tennis, although Nancye Bolton recovered the Australian title and Frenchwoman Nelly Adamson Landry won in Paris, beating Shirley Fry by the bizarre score of 6–2, 0–6, 6–0, the only non-American to win between 1946 and 1958.

The U.S. clobbered Great Britain again in the Wightman Cup, 6–1, at Wimbledon. Louise Brough won her first major singles title overseas, starting a three-year Wimbledon reign by beating Doris Hart, 6–3, 8–6. Margaret Osborne, who had become Mrs. William duPont, beat Brough in a scintillating Forest Hills final, 4–6, 6–4, 15–13, the first of her three consecutive triumphs there.

Hart and Pat Todd dethroned Brough-duPont at the French Championships, as they had at Wimbledon the year before, but Brough-duPont turned the tables at Wimbledon. When Brough left the Centre Court at 8:15 P.M. on the final Saturday of Wimbledon, after defending her title with Bromwich over Sedgman and Hart, she was the reigning singles, doubles, and mixed champion of both the United States and Great Britain, a feat previously achieved only by Alice Marble in 1939.

1949

Ted Schroeder won the Wimbledon singles on his first and only attempt, and Pancho Gonzalez proved that he was not the "cheese champion" some had called him. But 1949 will always be remembered as the year of "Gorgeous Gussy" Moran and the lace-trimmed panties that shocked Wimbledon.

Couturier Teddy Tinling, a tennis insider since he umpired matches for Suzanne Lenglen on the Riviera decades earlier, had waged a one-man battle against the unflattering white jersey and skirt that pretty much constituted women's tennis attire. He had experimented with touches of color on the dresses he made for Englishwoman Joy Gannon in 1947, without objection, but ran into problems in 1948 when Mrs. Hazel Wightman, captain of the U.S. team playing for the cup she had donated, objected to bits of color on the Tinling frock of British No. 1 Betty

Gussy Moran's lace-trimmed panties stirred staid Wimbledon in 1949. • *UPI*

Hilton. This resulted in Wimbledon officials issuing an "all-white" rule.

In 1949, unable to use color as requested by the attractive and sexy Gertrude Moran of Santa Monica, Cal., Tinling put a half inch of lace trim around her panties, trying to satisfy Gussy's wish for some distinctive adornment. This was done innocently, but when the flamboyant Gussy posed for photographers at the pre-Wimbledon garden party at the Hurlingham Club, she caused a sensation. The first time she twirled on Centre Court a tremor went through the staid old arena. "Tennis was then suddenly treated to the spectacle of photographers lying flat on the ground trying to shoot Gussy's panties," Tinling remembered in a 1953 interview. The "coquettish" undergarment became the subject of Parliamentary debate and photo-stories on front pages around the world.

"No one in their wildest dreams could have foreseen the furor, the outcry, the sensation..." Tinling wrote in the 25th anniversary issue of *World Tennis*. "Wimbledon interpreted the lace as an intentional device, a sinister plot by Gussy and myself for the sole purpose of guiding men's eyes to her bottom. At Wimbledon I was told that I had put 'vulgarity and sin' into tennis, and I resigned the Master of Ceremonies job I had held there for 23 years." Fortunately, he continued designing for and dressing most postwar women champions.

The year had begun with Frank

women's doubles, but Doris Hart ended Bolton's quest for a fifth consecutive singles title. Her 6–3, 6–4 triumph in the final made Hart the first overseas champion since Californian Dodo Bundy in 1938.

Frank Parker defended his French singles title over the elegant Budge Patty, 6–3, 1–6, 6–1, 6–4, and teamed with Gonzalez to win the doubles. Margaret duPont recovered the singles title she had won in Paris in 1946, dethroning Nelly Landry, 7–5, 6–2, and teamed with Louise Brough to regain the doubles title they had won in 1946–47.

At Wimbledon, spectators were anxious to see the man Americans called "Lucky" Schroeder. Though almost 28, he had never played the world's premier championship, but was well-known worldwide for his Davis Cup exploits. "Rather stocky, he had a rolling gait which made him look as though he had just got off a horse," remembered Lance Tingay. "Except when he was actually playing he always seemed to have a pipe in his mouth, a corn cob as often as not." Britons found him an intriguing character.

Seeded No. 1, Schroeder lost the first two sets of his first-round match to the dan-

gerous Gardnar Mulloy, whom he had beaten in the final at Queen's Club just two days earlier. In the quarters, he was again down two sets to Frank Sedgman, trailed 0–3 in the fifth, and had a match point against him at 4–5. He was called for a foot fault, but coolly followed his second serve to the net and hit a winning volley off the wood. He saved another match point at 5–6, this time with a bold backhand passing shot, and

after being within a point of a 0–2 deficit in the final set. "Lucky" Schroeder, indeed; he was always living on the edge of the ledge.

The women's final came down to a memorable duel between the No. 1 seed, Louise Brough, and the No. 2, Margaret duPont. Brough won the first set, 10–8, duPont the second, 6–1, and at 8–all in the third the difference between them was no more than the breadth of a blade of Wimbledon's celebrated grass. Brough served out of a 0–40 predicament like a champion, and then broke for the match and successful defense of her title.

Parker and Gonzalez added the Wimbledon doubles title to the French they had won earlier, while Brough and duPont joined forces to defend their title over Pat Todd and Gussy Moran. The scores were 8–6, 7–5—close enough to prevent anyone from quipping that the champs had beaten the lace panties off Gorgeous Gussy.

The American women continued their relentless domination of the Wightman Cup, drubbing Great Britain, 7–0, at Philadelphia. Schroeder and Gonzalez

Ted Schroeder had his day at Wimbledon in 1949, but Forest Hills was spoiled for him by Pancho Gonzalez. • *UPI*

gave the U.S. all four singles points as the U.S. men made it four straight victories over Australia in the Davis Cup challenge round at Forest Hills. Schroeder was up to his usual five-set high-jinks in the opening match, beating Bill Sidwell, 6–1, 5–7, 4–6, 6–2, 6–3, but he put away Sedgman in straight sets to clinch. The Americans lost only the doubles. Sidwell and Bromwich, who also won the 1949 U.S. National Doubles at Longwood, beat Bill Talbert and Gar Mulloy in a long five-setter.

There was keen interest in a Schroeder-Gonzalez showdown at Forest Hills. Because Gonzalez, seeded second at Wimbledon, had gone out to Geoff Brown in the round of 16, there was speculation that his 1948 U.S. victory had been a fluke. One writer flatly called him a "cheese champ"—which is how Gonzalez got his nickname of "Gorgo." It was short for "Gorgonzola."

Gonzalez was taken to five sets by Art Larsen and by Parker, who let him off the hook in the semis. Schroeder was pushed to the limit by Sedgman in the quarters and Billy Talbert in the semis. But finally

the men people wanted to see arrived safely in the final.

The old 15,000-seat horseshoe stadium at the West Side Tennis Club was packed and tense as Schroeder and Gonzalez fought to 16–all in the first set. Gonzalez fell behind 0–40, but three big serves got him back to deuce. A net-cord winner gave Schroeder another break point, and Gonzalez lost his serve on a volley that he thought was good. A linesman called it wide. Schroeder served out the set, then donned spikes on the slippery turf and quickly ran out the second set, 6–2. Gonzalez seethed.

But "Gorgo" always had a knack of channeling his temper, and he turned the rage surging within him to his advantage. Serving and attacking furiously, he achieved one of the great Forest Hills comebacks, 16–18, 2–6, 6–1, 6–2, 6–4.

Margaret duPont, meanwhile, won her second "Big Four" title of the year with an easy 6–4, 6–1 victory over Doris Hart in the women's final.

Jack Harris had quit the promotional game after the successful Kramer-Riggs tour. The new promoter was Riggs, who had won the U.S. Pro title at Forest Hills over Don Budge, 9–7, 3–6, 6–3, 7–5, while Kramer sat out, awaiting a new amateur king.

That was supposed to be Schroeder, who actually had signed after winning Wimbledon but then changed his mind, deciding that his intense constitution was not suited for the nightly grind of the tour. If he had won Forest Hills, Schroeder undoubtedly would have signed so as not to leave his old friend Kramer in the lurch; Kramer thought that in the back of his mind, Schroeder wanted to lose to Gonzalez for that reason.

But in any event, Gonzalez—as two-time Forest Hills champ—became the only viable alternative, and Riggs signed him for the longest head-to-head tour yet. Frank Parker came along to play Segura in the prelims. The tour stretched from October 1949 to May 1950, and Kramer clobbered the talented but surly and immature Gonzalez, 96 matches to 27. Both players made $72,000, but the future seemed a dead end for Gonzalez, who was only 21 years old.

new crop of Yanks was coming along—led by touch artists Art Larsen and Herbie Flam, the expatriate Californian Budge Patty and the forthright Tony Trabert and Vic Seixas. But Frank Sedgman, Ken McGregor and Mervyn Rose signaled a powerful new line of Australian resistance.

Germany and Japan were readmitted to the ITF, indicating that wartime wounds had healed. The Italian Championships was played for the first time since 1935, revived by the energetic promotion of Carlo della Vida, who was intent on building it into one of the international showcases. Despite rains that threatened to flood the sunken *Campo Centrale* (center court) at Rome's Il Foro Italico, the tournament was a success, won by the clay court artist, Jaroslav Drobny.

The self-exiled Czech, who traveled on an Egyptian passport until becoming a British citizen in 1959, also won the German championship, which had started to rebuild slowly as a Germans-only affair in 1948–49. The elegant and sporting prewar star, Baron Gottfried von Cramm, had won both years. The Hamburg and Rome tournaments were destined to rise simultaneously to a stature just below the French

Championships as the most important clay court events of Europe.

Sedgman, an athletic serve-and-volleyer with a crunching forehand, defeated McGregor for his second straight Australian singles title, while Adrian Quist and John Bromwich won their record eighth doubles title.

clay.

Patty was a great stylist, fluent on all his strokes and mesmerizing with the effortlessness of his forehand volley. He was also a painter and patron of the arts—"I have a way to go to catch Rembrandt, but Renoir doesn't stand a chance," he commented once, upon the opening of an exhibition of his canvases in Paris. "He gave the impression," noted Tingay, "of being the most sophisticated champion of all time."

Unsophisticated, flaky, eccentric, and totally original was Art "Tappy" Larsen, so nicknamed because of his habit, one of many superstitions, of tapping objects from net posts to opponents in ritualistic "good luck" sequences. Patty was known as a suave playboy who only occasionally trained; Larsen was an eager if unpolished ladies' man who never trained. But he had a great gift for the game, and magnificent touch, as he amply demonstrated in winning the Forest Hills title over his pal Flam in a lovely match of wits and angles, 6–3, 4–6, 5–7, 6–4, 6–3.

In doubles, Bill Talbert partnered his athletic Cincinnati protégé, Tony Trabert, also a star basketball guard, to the French

Southpaw Art "Tappy" Larsen outplayed fellow Californian Herbie Flam for the U.S. Singles title in 1950. • *UPI*

Hart as champion with a 6–4, 3–6, 6–4 victory over the defender. They then teamed to win the doubles, interrupting the long reign of eight-time champions Nancye Bolton and Thelma Long.

Hart won her first French singles, over Pat Todd, 6–4, 4–6, 6–2. Brough won her third straight Wimbledon title, beating Margaret duPont, 6–1, 3–6, 6–1, while duPont took her third straight Forest Hills crown, dispatching Hart in the final, 6–3, 6–3.

An historic footnote at Forest Hills was the appearance of a future champion and Hall of Famer, 23-year-old Althea Gibson, the first black American to play in the U.S. Championships. It was a leap of the color bar in tennis as Jackie Robinson's debut with the Brooklyn Dodgers had been three years before, a breakthrough that was almost sensational since Gibson nearly toppled the Wimbledon champ, fourth-seeded Louise Brough, in the second round.

Starting off with a prophetic victory over Barbara Knapp, 6–2, 6–2, Gibson overcame nerves and a 1–6 opening set against Brough to seize the second, 6–3. As the sky darkened, Gibson battled to a 7–6 lead in the decisive set. At that moment Brough may have been reprieved: Forest Hills was struck by a thunderstorm so fierce that lightning knocked one of the brooding concrete eagles from the upper rim of the stadium. Resuming the following afternoon, Gibson may have had too much time to think about victory lying within her long reach—four points away. Brough held serve, and won the next two games to escape.

"When lightning put down that eagle," Gibson laughed, "maybe it was an omen times was changing. Brough was a little too experienced for me in that situation — but my day would come." So it did with titles in 1957 and 1958.

Brough had also teamed with Eric Sturgess for her fourth Wimbledon mixed

title. Quist and Bromwich won their only Wimbledon title together, outlasting Geoff Brown and Bill Sidwell, 7–5, 3–6, 6–3, 3–6, 6–2. Bromwich and Sedgman won the U.S. Doubles over four-time champs Bill Talbert and Gardnar Mulloy.

Australia ended the four-year American grip on the Davis Cup with a 4–1 victory in the challenge round at Forest Hills. Sedgman walloped Tom Brown, 6–0, 8–6, 9–7, and McGregor ambushed Ted Schroeder, 13–11, 6–3, 6–4, in the opening singles, and then Sedgman and Bromwich sealed the Aussie triumph by beating Schroeder and Mulloy in the doubles, 4–6, 6–4, 6–2, 4–6, 6–4.

America's women extended their monotonous superiority over Great Britain with another 7–0 Wightman Cup Wimbledon, and hoarded all the "Big Four" titles in singles and doubles. The Australian final was an unusual all-American affair, Brough succeeded Doris

doubles title in five years, with three different partners. Hart and Shirley Fry began a four-year rule in the French doubles, while duPont and Brough won their third consecutive Wimbledon and ninth consecutive U.S. doubles crowns.

Jack Kramer again passed up the U.S. Pro Championships, and Pancho Segura won the title over Frank Kovacs, who

percent of the gate. Kramer got 25 percent. Unfortunately, the cunning "Segoo" simply could not handle Kramer's big serve on fast indoor courts, and the tour was not

competitive. Riggs tried to spice it up by signing Gussy Moran to a lucrative contract—$35,000 guaranteed, against 25 percent of profits—to play Pauline Betz. Gussy got tremendous publicity as the glamour girl of the lace pants, but she was not in the same class with Betz, who was overwhelming even after Riggs suggested she try to "carry" her fashionable but outclassed opponent.

1951

The new era continued to take shape on the world's tennis courts in 1951.

In 1950 Althea Gibson became the first black to play in the U.S. Championships and came within one game of defeating Louise Brough in the second round. • *UPI*

American Dick Savitt surprisingly won the Australian and Wimbledon singles titles, but Frank Sedgman and Ken McGregor helped forge the foundation of a new Australian dynasty, holding onto the Davis Cup and fashioning the first Grand Slam of doubles. Meanwhile, American women continued their postwar supremacy, but the dominance of Louise Brough, Margaret Osborne duPont, Doris Hart and Shirley Fry was challenged by a stirring new teen-age talent: Maureen Connolly.

Savitt, 24, a rawboned and hulking competitor from Orange, N.J., and Cornell University, sported a big serve, a solid ground game, and an impressive, hard-hit backhand. He was the first American to win the Australian singles—in fact, the first non-Australian finalist—since Don Budge in 1938.

Like Ted Schroeder two years earlier, Savitt won Wimbledon on his first attempt. He was aided by Herb Flam's defeat of Sedgman from two sets down in the quarters, Englishman Tony Mottram's third-round upset of Jaroslav Drobny, and defending champion Budge Patty's demise in the second round, at the hands of former Tulane star, Rhodes scholar Ham Richardson.

Savitt also had a narrow escape from Flam, whom the BBC's extraordinary radio commentator Max Robertson called "the Paul Newman of tennis players, with hunched and self-deprecating look." Savitt trailed 1–6, 1–5 in the semifinals before salvaging the second set, 15–13, to turn the match a round. "A couple of points the other way and my whole life might have been different," Savitt mused on the occasion of Wimbledon's Centenary "parade of champions" in 1977. As it happened, he lost only five games in the third and fourth sets against Flam and then chastened McGregor in the final, 6–4, 6–4, 6–4.

Drobny—the crafty left-hander with the sad countenance, spectacles, and wonderful repertoire of touch and spin to go with his tricky serve—defeated Eric Sturgess, 6–3, 6–3, 6–3, to win the French singles for the first time after being runner-up in 1946, 1948 and 1950.

Sedgman, the personification of robust Australian fitness with an unerring fore-hand volley, atoned for his Wimbledon failure by winning the first of back-to-back Forest Hills titles.

He was the first Australian player to win the U.S. Nationals, the first in the final since Jack Crawford in 1933. Sedgman got there in devastating form, ravaging defending champion Art Larsen in the semifinals, 6–1, 6–2, 6–0, in just 49 minutes, the worst beating ever inflicted on a titleholder. Wrote Allison Danzig in *The New York Times,* "The radiance of the performance turned in by the 23-year-old Sedgman has not often been equaled. With his easy, almost effortless production of stabbing strokes, he pierced the dazed champion's defenses to score at will with a regularity and dispatch that made Larsen's plight almost pitiable."

In the final against Philadelphian Vic Seixas, Sedgman was nearly as awesome, winning 6–4, 6–1, 6–1. Seixas had played superbly until then, beating McGregor, Flam, and then Savitt in the semifinals, 6–0, 3–6, 6–3, 6–2. Savitt was the No. 1 seed, but severely hobbled by an infected left leg, which had to be lanced the day before he faced Seixas.

Savitt had played zone matches against Japan (readmitted to the Davis Cup, along with Germany, for the first time since the war) and Canada. But captain Frank Shields passed him over—angering him and many supporters—for the challenge round in Sydney. Seixas handled Mervyn Rose, and Sedgman beat Ted Schroeder to

Dick Savitt, Australian and Wimbledon champion in 1951, wore a bonnet to withstand the heat in a Davis Cup match against Japan's Jiro Kumamaru in Louisville. • *UPI*

make it 1–1 after the opening singles, but the match hinged on the doubles. Schroeder had one of his worst days—"I wanted to cry for him, he was so bad," recalls old friend Jack Kramer—and he and Trabert were beaten by Sedgman and McGregor, 6–2, 9–7, 6–3. Schroeder did pull himself together after a nervous, sleepless night and beat Rose with a courageous performance, but Sedgman rolled over Seixas in the fifth match, 6–4, 6–2, 6–2, for a 3–2 Australian victory.

It was appropriate that Sedgman-McGregor won the pivotal doubles, for this was their year as a tandem. They swept the Australian, French, Wimbledon and U.S. doubles titles, the only male pair ever to do so. They ended the eight-year monopoly of Adrian Quist-John Bromwich in the Australian final, beating the champions, 11–9, 2–6, 6–3, 4–6, 6–3, then went on to

capture the French over Savitt and Gardnar Mulloy, and Wimbledon over Drobny and Sturgess, 3–6, 6–2, 6–3, 3–6, 6–3. They completed the Slam by taking the U.S. title over countryman Don Candy and Merv Rose, 10–8, 4–6, 6–4, 7–5, the final having been moved to Forest Hills after heavy rains at Longwood.

U.S. women—Doris Hart. Shirley Fry.

from the backcourt, beat Hart in the French final, 6–3, 3–6, 6–3, but got her comeuppance at Wimbledon, where Hart thrashed her, 6–1, 6–0. This was Hart's only singles title—she had been runner-up in 1947–48—and she parlayed it into a triple, taking the women's doubles with Fry (starting a three-year rule) and the mixed doubles with Sedgman (first of her five successive triumphs, two with Sedgman and three with Vic Seixas).

In fact, Hart-Fry and Hart-Sedgman swept the women's and mixed doubles titles of France, Wimbledon, and the U.S. in 1951. Hart was the No. 1 seed at Forest Hills and thought she was the best woman player in the world, but she was given a rude jolt in the semifinals by 16-year-old Maureen Connolly of San Diego. Blasting her flawless ground strokes from both wings, Connolly overcame a 0–4 deficit to win the first set on a drizzly, miserable day, 6–4. Hart asked several times that the match be halted. It was, but Connolly won the second set the following afternoon. In the final, the tenacious and mentally uncompromising Connolly beat Fry, 6–3, 1–6, 6–4, for the first of three straight championships. "I later kidded Maureen that she was lucky to beat me in '51," Hart has said. "But after that she became, unquestionably, the greatest woman player who ever lived."

A distasteful Forest Hills outburst by seventh-ranked American Earl Cochell brought swift retribution from the USTA, a demonstration of the arbitrary power national associations held over players prior to the open era and the forming of player unions. Clearly Cochell was out of line in the fourth-rounder, a four-set loss to Gar Mulloy. He argued many line calls, erupted in bursts of temper, argued with the umpire and spectators, tried to climb the umpire's chair and grab his microphone to lecture the crowd, and blatantly threw a number of games, batting balls into the stands or playing left-handed (he was right-handed). What really did him in was his abusive verbal attack on the referee, Dr. Ellsworth Davenport, who reprimanded him.

The upshot was that the USTA suspended Cochell for life. No agent, lawyer or union to protect him then. Some years later the sentence was lifted, but Cochell, unfairly unranked for 1951 (he was 29) lost perhaps his best years.

1952

Another patch in the nearly complete postwar reconstruction of tennis was put in place in 1952 when the King's Cup, a European team competition for a trophy donated by Swedish monarch and tennis patron Gustav V in 1936, was resumed. But other than Jaroslav Drobny's second straight French title, Europe had little impact on the world tennis stage. Australian men and American women dominated the major championships.

Maureen Connolly, at 16 the youngest until 1979 to win the U.S. title, is shown in 1951 in Los Angeles (after capturing the Pacific Southwest crown) with former U.S. champions May Sutton, Helen Wills Moody and Marian Jones. • *UPI*

Frank Sedgman prevailed at Wimbledon and here against Gardnar Mulloy (far court) in the final at Forest Hills in 1952. •*UPI*

Among the men, it was Frank Sedgman's year. The aggressive, diligent Aussie was in all of the "Big Four" finals, singles and doubles, and led Australia's successful Davis Cup defense.

He was on the losing end of the first two singles finals, however, beaten by his partner McGregor in the Australian, 7–5, 12–10, 2–6, 6–2, and by the ever-dangerous Drobny on the salmon-colored clay of Paris, 6–2, 6–0, 3–6, 6–3.

Sedgman got his revenge on "Old Drob" in the final at Wimbledon, 4–6, 6–2, 6–3, 6–2, becoming the first Aussie champ there since Jack Crawford in 1933. Two other Aussies—Lew Hoad (who, with Ken Rosewall, was making his first overseas tour, the 17-year-olds reaching the semifinals in doubles) and McGregor—gave Drobny trouble en route. Hoad took him to four tough sets in the fourth round, and

McGregor came within two points of beating him in the quarters. American Herbie Flam also pushed him to the five-set limit in the semis.

Drobny took the first set of the final, but Sedgman seized control of the match in a swirling wind on Centre Court when he tuned in his crushing overhead smash. Sedgman, in fact, lost only two sets at Wimbledon, underscoring his superiority, and rolled impressively to his second straight Forest Hills title. He crunched countryman Merv Rose in the semis and made the final against surprising 37-year-old Gardnar Mulloy look as easy as one, two, three—6–1, 6–2, 6–3.

Sedgman, who also won the Italian Championship in his last year as an amateur, defended his Wimbledon doubles title with McGregor and the mixed with Doris Hart, becoming one of only three

Lew Hoad and Maureen Connolly reach for the ball in mixed doubles against Rex Hartwig and Julie Sampson at Forest Hills. The championship went to Frank Sedgman and Doris Hart in 1951 and 1952.
• *New York Herald Tribune*

men to achieve such a triple. (The others were Don Budge in 1937–38 and Bobby Riggs in 1939.) Sedgman-McGregor again won the Australian and French doubles but were denied a second consecutive doubles Grand Slam when the unusual Australian-American alliance of Merv Rose and Vic Seixas beat them in the final of the U.S. National Doubles at Longwood. Since Sedgman had won the 1950 U.S. title with John Bromwich, his record run of eight straight doubles majors was ended.

Sedgman-Hart did defend their U.S. mixed title, however, as they had the French and Wimbledon.

Sedgman beat both Seixas and Tony Trabert in straight sets, and partnered McGregor to a four-set triumph in doubles, as Australia won the Davis Cup challenge round for the third year in a row, 4–1. Seixas salvaged the only point for the

United States, beating McGregor in the meaningless fifth match.

American women again avoided the long journey to Australia, allowing Thelma Long to win her first singles title and team with Nancye Bolton for their 10th doubles title together. (Long later won two more.)

But U.S. women were oppressive in the other major championships, as had become their custom. Doris Hart won her second French singles title, reversing the final-round result of a year earlier to beat Shirley Fry, 6–4, 6–4. Maureen Connolly ascended to the world No.1 ranking at age 17 by beating three-time champ Louise Brough, 7–5, 6–3, in the Wimbledon final, and Hart 6–3, 7–5, to defend her Forest Hills crown.

Connolly's first appearance at Wimbledon, seeded No. 2 behind Hart, was a celebrated event. "The pressures under which she played were enormous," noted Lance Tingay. "There was the basic pressure of being expected to win. There was a blaze of publicity because Miss Connolly, for reasons of her skill, her charm and achievement, was 'news' in everything she did. And her guidance went sour at this her first Wimbledon challenge. Her coach—the strong-willed,

Connolly lost sets to Englishwomen Susan Partridge, who slow-balled her, giving neither the pace nor angle on which Maureen thrived, and to Thelma Long in the quarterfinals. Partridge, the Italian champion, proved her toughest foe, taking her to 6–3, 5–7, 7–5. Hart was beaten in a long quarterfinal by Pat Todd, leaving Connolly to mow down Fry and Brough in straight sets in the final two rounds. Connolly's scythelike strokes were as deadly as the British had heard; in fact, in three years she never lost a single match in Great Britain.

Hart and Fry extended their streaks in the French, Wimbledon and U.S. doubles, and the U.S. again rolled over Great Britain in the Wightman Cup, losing only one set in a 7–0 triumph at Wimbledon.

Bobby Riggs had tried to sign Sedgman and McGregor to tour as pros with himself, Pancho Gonzalez and Pancho Segura in 1952, dismissing Jack Kramer by saying he had retired. Riggs struck a deal, but later Gonzalez wanted to change the agreed-upon terms, and Riggs—who was about to re-marry—got disgusted and left the promoting business.

There was no pro tour in 1952, but Segura startled Gonzalez in the final of the

U.S. Pro Championships, 3–6, 6–4, 3–6, 6–4, 6–0, at Lakewood Park in Cleveland. Kramer, who had no intention of retiring, took over as player-promoter, signing Sedgman to a contract ($75,000 guarantee) that was announced right after the Davis Cup challenge round. McGregor also turned pro to face Segura in the prelims on the 1953 tour.

Missouri ("Big Mo"), swept the Australian, French, Wimbledon and U.S. singles, and won 10 of 12 tournaments, compiling a 61–2 record. This was the crowning year of an abbreviated career that was to end through injury, after three-and-a-half awesome seasons, in 1954.

Meanwhile, Kenneth Robert Rosewall, 21 days older than his fellow Australian "Whiz Kid" Lew Hoad, took the Australian and French singles titles, the first major accomplishments of a career matchless in its longevity. Rosewall would still be going strong a quarter of a century later, nine years after Connolly's death from cancer at age 34.

Connolly, at 18, was the first woman to emulate Don Budge, who took the "Big Four" singles titles in 1938 and popularized the feat by calling it the Grand Slam. In doing it, she trampled 22 opponents, losing just one set and 82 games.

"Little Mo" started in Australia, demolishing her partner Julie Sampson, 6–3, 6–2, before they teamed up to win the doubles. In the quarterfinals at Paris, Connolly lost that lone set—to Susan Partridge, her toughest rival at Wimbledon the year before, who by this time had married France's Philippe Chatrier. She slow-balled again, but Connolly hit her way out of trouble, blasting her ground strokes even harder, deeper, and closer to the lines than usual, prevailing by 3–6, 6–2, 6–2. Then she drubbed Doris Hart in the final, 6–2, 6–4.

Hart was also her final-round opponent at Wimbledon and Forest Hills. "The Wimbledon final was the finest match of the Slam: 8–6, 7–5. The two great players called it the best of their life," noted a silver anniversary tribute to Little Mo's wondrous 1953 record. "In the homestretch at Forest Hills, Connolly won driving, as they say at the racetrack, 6–2, 6–3 over Althea Gibson in the quarters; 6–1, 6–1 over Shirley Fry; and 6–2, 6–4 over Hart."

In fact, Connolly lost only two matches during the year: to Hart in the final of the Italian Championships, and to Fry in the Pacific Southwest at Los Angeles.

Connolly and Hart teamed for the French doubles title, but Little Mo—never a great doubles player because of her distaste for net play—was not destined for a doubles Slam. Hart and Fry won their fourth consecutive Wimbledon doubles, whitewashing Connolly and Sampson, 6–0, 6–0, minutes after Maureen had gotten a telephone call from her fiancé, Olympic equestrian Norman Brinker, telling her he was being sent to Korea by the U.S. Navy. Hart and Fry also won the third of their four successive U.S. National doubles titles.

Rosewall, 18, a 5-foot-7, 145-pounder with an angel face and neither a hair nor a footstep out of place, took the first of his four Australian singles titles, spanning 19 years, by beating left-hander Mervyn Rose, 6–0, 6–3, 6–4. Rosewall beat Vic Seixas, 6–3, 6–4, 1–6, 6–2, in the French final, the first tournament covered by a new magazine, *World Tennis*, which debuted in June 1953 and would become an influential force in the game. It was edited and pub-

lished by New Yorker Gladys Heldman. The story under Gardnar Mulloy's by-line described Rosewall as "a young kid with stamina, hard-hitting groundstrokes and plenty of confidence."

The Wimbledon and U.S. titles came back into American possession, property of Vic Seixas and Tony Trabert.

Seixas, according to Lance Tingay's official history of Wimbledon, was "hardly the prettiest player in the world, for his strokes smacked more of expediency than fluency and polish, but he gave the impression of being prepared to go on attacking forever." He edged Hoad in the quarters and Rose in the semis, both in five long sets. In the final, he beat Dane Kurt Nielsen—whose chopped forehand down the middle of the court had upset top seed Rosewall in the quarters—9–7, 6–3, 6–4.

The match of the tournament was the third-round classic in which Jaroslav Drobny defeated his good friend and constant touring companion, Budge Patty, 8–6, 16–18, 3–6, 8–6, 12–10. The herculean epic began at 5:00 P.M. and ended in dusk some 4½ hours later. Its 93 games, played at a consistently high standard, were the most in any Wimbledon singles to that time. But Drobny had ruptured a blood vessel, and after limping through victories over Australian Rex Hartwig and Swede Sven Davidson, lost to the surprising Nielsen in the semis.

Trabert did in Rosewall, and Seixas beat Hoad in the semifinals at Forest Hills, and then Trabert—serving and volleying consistently and returning superbly whether Seixas charged the net or stayed back—beat the Wimbledon champ in the final, 6–3, 6–2, 6–3, in just one hour. Trabert was less than three months out of the U. S. Navy, but he had trained hard to regain his speed and match fitness, and he leveled Seixas with a vicious onslaught from backcourt and net, off both wings— especially his topspin backhand.

themselves from rain, Trabert lost his serve at love at 5–6 in the desperate final set, double-faulting to 0–40 and then netting a half volley off a return to his shoetops.

Meanwhile Frank Sedgman, the Davis Cup hero of a year earlier, lost a pro tour to Jack Kramer, 54 matches to 41, but earned $102,000, the highest total to date. The tally was closer than it might have

Jaroslav Drobny (left) and Budge Patty wearily leave the court at Wimbledon after their 93-game marathon match in 1953. • *UPI*

Hoad and Rosewall captured the Australian, French, and Wimbledon doubles titles, but their countrymen Hartwig and Rose took the U.S. title over popular oldies Bill Talbert, 35, and Gar Mulloy, 38.

Australia was favored in the Davis Cup challenge round at Melbourne but nearly threw it away when the team selectors ordered captain Harry Hopman to nominate Hartwig and Hoad, both right-court players, as his doubles team instead of either of the experienced pairs available: Rosewall-Hoad or Hartwig-Rose. The confused Aussie duo lost to Trabert-Seixas, 6–2, 6–4, 6–4.

Hoad had beaten Seixas, and Trabert had stomped Rosewall the first day. But Australia won from 1–2 down, Hoad beating Trabert, 13–11, 6–3, 2–6, 3–6, 7–5 in the pivotal fourth match—one of the greatest in Davis Cup history. As a huge crowd huddled under newspapers to protect

1954

The quotation that hangs above the competitors' entrance to the Centre Court at Wimbledon, and was also adopted for a similar exalted position in the marquee at the Forest Hills stadium, is from a poem by Rudyard Kipling. It says, "If you can meet triumph and disaster, and treat those two impostors just the same..." The words seldom seemed more appropriate than in 1954, for it was a year of continued triumph and then sudden disaster for Maureen Connolly.

"Little Mo" did not go to Australia to try for another Grand Slam—in her absence, the experienced 35-year-old Thelma Long won her second Aussie singles title—but Maureen successfully defended her French and Wimbledon titles, and also took the Italian crown that had eluded her in 1953. At Wimbledon she defeated Louise Brough in the final, 6–2, 7–5. Historian Lance Tingay wrote, "The whole event was accounted a trifle dull because of the inevitability of the eventual winner. Miss Connolly, without losing a set, won 73 games and lost but 19."

Little did anyone know that this would be Little Mo's last major title. Between Wimbledon and Forest Hills, she was riding her horse, Colonel Merryboy—a gift from a group of San Diegans after her 1952 Wimbledon triumph—and was struck by a truck. Most people thought she would return in 1955, but in her autobiography Maureen wrote that she knew she was finished: "My right leg was slashed to the bone. All the calf muscles were severed and the fibula broken. Eventually, I got on-court again, but I was aware that I could never play tournament tennis."

It was the shortest of great careers, but few got more done in many more years. During those three-and-a-half years when she was undisputed No. 1, Maureen won Wimbledon in 1952–54, Forest Hills in 1951–53, all seven of her Wightman Cup singles in 1951–54, the Irish singles of 1952 and 1953, and the U.S. Clay Courts in 1953–54.

Mervyn Rose won his only Australian singles title in 1954, over countryman Rex Hartwig, 6–2, 0–6, 6–4, 6–2. Rugged Tony Trabert—firing like the big guns that adorned the aircraft carrier on which he had served the year before—blasted fellow American Art Larsen in the French final, 6–4, 7–5, 6–1. But the year ultimately belonged to three players who savored sentimental triumphs that came when they were seemingly a shade past their prime: Jaroslav Drobny, Vic Seixas, and Doris Hart.

Drobny, age 34, still had a punishing serve, though not as oppressive as it had been before a shoulder injury. He was seeded only No. 11 in his 11th appearance at Wimbledon, but upset Lew Hoad in the quarterfinals and beat old rival Budge Patty in the semifinals. In the final Drobny defeated Ken Rosewall, 13–11, 4–6, 6–2, 9–7, in two hours, 35 minutes, becoming only the second left-handed champion. No one could have imagined that Rosewall, in

the final for the first of four times at age 19, would never win the singles title he coveted most. The galleries loved Drobny, the expansive Czech refugee in dark glasses. "No better final had been seen since Crawford and Vines 21 years before," judged Lance Tingay. "The warmth of Drobny's reception as champion could not have been greater had he been a genial Englishman. In a sense he was, for he had married an Englishwoman and lived in Sussex."

The triumphs of Vic Seixas and Doris Hart at Forest Hills were just as popular with the American audience. Seixas, age 31 and competing in his Nationals for the 13th time, finally won in his third appearance in the final. He stopped Rex Hartwig, who had upset defending champion Tony Trabert and Rosewall, 3–6, 6–2, 6–4, 6–4. Hart, runner-up five times in 13 appearances but never champion, survived three match points and outlasted Louise Brough, 6–8, 6–1, 8–6.

Vic Seixas, 31, in his 14th try, won his first U.S. Singles in 1954. • *UPI*

Seixas, according to Allison Danzig's report in *The New York Times,* "made the most of his equipment and he never lagged in carrying the attack to his opponent. His speed and quickness, the effectiveness of his service, his strong return of service and his staunch volleying all contributed to the victory. Too, he found a vulnerable point in his opponent's game and exploited it by directing his twist service to Hartwig's back-

Jack Kramer retired as undefeated pro champion and promoted a round-robin tour involving Pancho Gonzalez, Frank Sedgman, Pancho Segura and Don Budge. Gonzalez won it, narrowly defeating Sedgman, and thus gained a previously unheard-of second life in the head-to-head pro tour. He also won the U.S. Pro title over Sedgman, 6–3, 9–7, 3–6, 6–2, at the Cleveland Arena.

Hart and Seixas teamed for the mixed doubles title of the U.S. as they had at Wimbledon. Both also won the doubles, Hart with Shirley Fry for the fourth consecutive year and Seixas with Trabert, whom he had also partnered to the French title. Elsewhere, Hartwig and Rose won the Australian and Wimbledon men's doubles; Connolly and Nell Hopman took the women's doubles at the French, while at Wimbledon, Brough and Margaret duPont recaptured the title they had won in 1948–49–50.

Connolly, in her last Wightman Cup appearance, led the United States to a 6–0 frolic over Great Britain at Wimbledon. The U.S. also recovered the Davis Cup after four straight losses, captain Bill Talbert's duo upsetting Australia, 3–2, in the challenge round at Sydney. Trabert and Seixas, who earned his spot because of his Forest Hills form, were the conquering heroes. Trabert beat Hoad, and Seixas upset Rosewall, both in four tough sets, and they combined to beat Hoad-Rosewall, 6–2, 4–6, 6–2, 10–8, in the decisive doubles. The largest crowds ever to watch men play tennis at the time, 25,578, jammed White City Stadium each day.

siderable legacy—Louise Brough and Doris Hart—took their final bows as soloists in the world tennis arena.

Ken Rosewall beat Lew Hoad, 9–7, 6–4, 6–4, for his second Australian singles title, but Trabert—the All-American boy from Cincinnati with his ginger crewcut, freckles, and uncompromisingly aggressive

Tony Trabert soared in 1955, winning the French, Wimbledon and U.S. • *UPI*

game—won the French, Wimbledon and U.S. singles.

In the Italian Championships, two of the most unorthodox but combative clay-court specialists of Europe—tall and gangly Fausto Gardini ("The Spider") and tiny, gentle Beppe Merlo ("The Little Bird")—met in an all-native final before a raucous Roman crowd. They had their customary epic battle—"We were always like a dog and a cat," Merlo recalls—with Gardini claiming victory as Merlo collapsed with cramps. To make sure his opponent could not recover and win, Gardini counted off one minute while Merlo writhed in pain, then rolled down the net and raised his arms triumphantly.

There were no such histrionics in Paris, where Trabert bulled his way to the French title over Swede Sven Davidson, 2–6, 6–1, 6–4, 6–2. At Wimbledon, Trabert eliminated defending champion Jaroslav Drobny in the quarters and Budge Patty (conqueror of Hoad) in the semis.

In the final Trabert expected to meet Rosewall, but instead came up against 1953 runner-up Kurt Nielsen, who beat the Australian champ in the semis. "Nielsen clearly remembered his success against the Little Master in 1953, when he hit his approach shots down the middle and came to the net, making it difficult for Rosewall to play his favorite passing shots decisively," wrote Max Robertson in *Wimbledon, 1878—1977*. "He pursued the same tactics and with the same result; for the second time he had reached the final unseeded—a record which could stand forever." Trabert denied him a more satisfying immortality, however, 6–3, 7–5, 6–1.

The only real stain on Trabert's record for the year in which he won 18 tournaments came in late August, in the Davis Cup challenge round at Forest Hills. After Rosewall had beaten Vic Seixas, 6–3, 10–8, 4–6, 6–2, Trabert went down in straight sets to Hoad in the critical second match;

Hoad, it must be said, played with immense power and brilliance.

The next afternoon, Hoad and Rex Hartwig—who two years earlier had been thrown together as first-time doubles partners, with disastrous results—blended beautifully to clinch the Cup with a 12–14, 6–4, 6–3, 3–6, 7–5 victory over Seixas and Trabert that had 12,000 spectators howling with delight through five scintillating sets. The Aussies had their cake and put frosting on it too, running up a 5–0 final margin the next day.

Trabert had the last laugh, though, banishing Rosewall in the final of Forest Hills, 9–7, 6–3, 6–3. That set him up as the new amateur champ. Actually, promoter Jack Kramer had signed Hoad and Rosewall as well, to tour with him and Trabert playing a Davis Cup-style format, but the deal fell through. Slazenger, the racket company that Rosewall represented, gave him a bonus, and Jenny Hoad persuaded her husband to make one more grand tour as an amateur. So Trabert's indoctrination into the pros in 1956 wound up taking the more conventional form of a head-to-head tour against the champ, Pancho Gonzalez.

On the women's side, new singles champions were crowned in Australia, where Beryl Penrose defeated Thelma Long, 6–4, 6–3, and in France, where England's Angela Mortimer topped Dorothy Head Knode, 2–6, 7–5, 10–8.

At Wimbledon, 1948–49–50 champion Louise Brough, seeded second, defeated demonstrative newcomer Darlene Hard in the semis, reaching the final for the seventh time. Her opponent was ambidextrous, a non-backhanded racket-switcher, Beverly Baker Fleitz, who upset top seed Doris Hart in the semis.

"Louise was always prone to tighten up at important points but had a greater breadth of stroke and experience at her command, which just saw her through a keenly fought struggle," reported Max Robertson. "In the sixth game of the second set, for example, it was only after nine deuces and five advantages to Fleitz that Louise wrong-footed her near exhausted opponent with a backhand slice down the line to lead 4–2. This was the turning point and Louise went on to win her fourth singles, 7–5, 8–6."

best amateur tennis players in the world. They smothered the United States in the Davis Cup challenge round, 5–0, for the second straight year, and played each other in three of the "Big Four" singles finals. Ultimately, on the last day of Forest Hills, it was Rosewall who prevented his three-weeks-younger countryman from pulling off the Grand Slam.

1955 as the U.S. defeated Great Britain, 6–1, at Westchester Country Club in Rye, N.Y. She had been on the U.S. team since 1946, compiling a record of 14–0 in singles and 8–1 in doubles. She became a teaching pro at the end of the year.

As for doubles titles in 1955, Brough and Margaret duPont, who had reigned nine successive years between 1942 and 1950, regained the U.S. title, starting a new three-year run. Seixas and Trabert won the Australian and French titles, but Hoad and Hartwig, presaging their Davis Cup heroics, won Wimbledon. The little-known team of Kosei Kamo and Atsushi Miyagi won the U.S. National Doubles, primarily because they were willing to hang around Longwood Cricket Club through Hurricane Diane as most of the favored teams fled Boston. When the waters that turned the grass courts into ponds finally receded, the Japanese pair triumphed. World War II truly was a long time past.

the Australian measuring up to the caliber of a truly great player they were dispelled by his play in the championship," wrote Allison Danzig in his vivid and authorita-

Ken Rosewall lost to Lew Hoad in the Wimbledon and Australian finals, but Rosewall repulsed his countryman in 1956 at Forest Hills. • *UPI*

1956

In 1956, the 21-year-old former "Whiz Kids" of Australia, Lew Hoad and Ken Rosewall, had clearly grown up into the

tive story, "A Grand Slam Trumped," in *The New York Times*. "His performance in breaking down the powerful attack and then the will to win of the favored Hoad was even more convincing, considering the breezy conditions, than his wizardry in his unforgettable quarterfinal round match against Richard Savitt.

"Against the powerful, rangy Savitt, Rosewall's ground strokes were the chief instruments of victory in a crescendo of lethal driving exchanges seldom equaled on the Forest Hills turf. Yesterday's match between possibly the two most accomplished 21-year-old finalists in the tournament's history was a madcap, lightning-fast duel. The shots were taken out of the air with rapidity and radiance despite a strong wind that played tricks with the ball.

"The breakneck pace of the rallies, the exploits of both men in scrambling over the turf to bring off electrifying winners, their almost unbelievable control when off balance and the repetition with which they made the chalk fly on the lines with their lobs, made for the most entertaining kind of tennis. In time the gallery was so surfeited with brilliance that the extraordinary shot became commonplace, particularly by Rosewall."

So it had been much of the year, the blond-haired, blue-eyed, muscular, and positively engaging Hoad rousing galleries around the world with his remarkable weight of shot and free-wheeling attack; the immaculate, compact, and quicksilver Rosewall challenging him but constantly being rebuffed, until now.

Hoad had beaten Rosewall in the finals of the Australian, 6–4, 3–6, 6–4, 7–5, and Wimbledon, 6–2, 4–6, 7–5, 6–4. He had beaten Sven Davidson in the French final, 6–4, 8–6, 6–3. He had won the Italian and German titles on clay as well. But finally Rosewall got him, and with Hoad changing his mind again about signing a pro con-

tract with Kramer, it was Rosewall who signed on to face Pancho Gonzalez the following year.

Doris Hart, who had climaxed 15 appearances with back-to-back Forest Hills titles in 1954–55, had, like Trabert, turned pro to give lessons at the end of the year. In her absence, her old doubles partner, Shirley Fry, took the Wimbledon and Forest Hills singles titles for the first and only time. At Wimbledon, Shirley beat Englishwoman Angela Buxton, 6–3, 6–1, and at Forest Hills, her final victim was Italian and French champion Althea Gibson of New York's Harlem. Gibson's 6–0, 12–10 victory in Paris over Angela Mortimer was the first major title for a black.

Fry, who attained her first singles title, on her 16th attempt, had beaten Gibson at Wimbledon and the U.S. Clay Court. This time Fry maintained her mastery by attacking the net constantly in the first set, then staying back and thwarting Gibson's attack with deep, accurate ground strokes in the second.

The addition of Buxton, Shirley Bloomer and Mortimer (runner-up to Gibson in the French) made the British Wightman Cup team more competitive than it had been at any time since the war, but the U.S. still prevailed, 5–2, at Wimbledon.

Gibson teamed with Buxton to win the French and Wimbledon doubles titles, but Louise Brough and Margaret duPont continued their unmatched supremacy in the U.S. National Doubles.

Hoad and Rosewall won the Wimbledon and U.S. doubles titles, and single-handedly achieved the Davis Cup shutout of the United States in the challenge round at Adelaide. Hoad beat Herbie Flam easily, Rosewall kayoed Vic Seixas in four sets, and Hoad and Rosewall thumped Seixas and Texan Sammy

Giammalva in a four-set doubles to make sure that the contest was decided before the third day.

Pro promoter Jack Kramer would have liked to sign Hoad, who had won 15 tournaments, but Rosewall was a fine attraction to oppose Pancho Gonzalez in 1957. Kramer had started training to play 1955 amateur king Tony Trabert in 1956, but was persuaded by Gonzalez' wife to let Pancho face Trabert on the head-to-head tour. Kramer, now badly afflicted with arthritis, was just as happy to do the promotion and let the strong and hungry Gonzalez play.

Gonzalez, very likely the best player in the world even though few realized it, crushed Trabert, 74 matches to 24. Gonzalez also won the U.S. Pro Championships over Pancho Segura at Cleveland, and beat Frank Sedgman, 4–6, 11–9, 11–9, 9–7, in a match remarkably of high quality at Wembley.

"Wembley, a London suburb of fast-fading respectability, is a shrine of English soccer. In those days its indoor arena was also

a shrine of pro tennis," wrote Rex Bellamy in *World Tennis* more than two decades later. "That night, public transport ceased long before the match did. Stranded spectators did not much mind. They were unlikely to see such a match again."

1957

~~The~~ ...

... ~~designs Hoad may have on the~~ Grand Slam he had come within one match of achieving in 1956 were shattered quickly. The "baby bull" was upset in the semifinals of the Australian singles by a promising young left-hander, Neale Fraser, son of a prominent Labor politician. Cooper—a rather mechanical but solid and determined player who, with Fraser and Anderson, represented the new products off Harry Hopman's Australian Davis Cup assembly line—then won his first major title by beating Fraser in the final, 6–3, 9–11, 6–4, 6–2. Hoad and Fraser took the doubles.

Shortly after the pro tour between Pancho Gonzalez and Ken Rosewall—which Gonzalez would win, 50–26—had begun in Australia at the New Year, Hoad had a friend contact promoter Jack Kramer and tell him that he was again interested in turning pro. Kramer was baffled, since Hoad had recently refused his entreaties. Later Kramer figured that Hoad was starting to encounter the back problems that eventually cut short his career, and decided he'd better get his payday while he still could.

Kramer signed Hoad—sending Ted Schroeder to the bank with him to make sure he cashed a $5,000 advance, which would provide proof of a contract if Hoad changed his mind again—but agreed to keep the pact secret until after Wimbledon.

Sven Davidson, the Swedish Davis Cup stalwart who was runner-up the previous two years, won the French singles over Herbie Flam, the last American man in the Paris final for 19 years, 6–3, 6–4, 6–4. Anderson and Cooper were the doubles titlists.

Hoad, whose season had been erratic, made his last amateur tournament a memorable one. At Wimbledon he lost only one set, to fellow Aussie Merv Rose in the quarters. Then he routed Davidson, the only non-Australian semifinalist, while Cooper won a tougher semifinal in the other half over Fraser. In the final, Hoad was brilliant, humbling Cooper, 6–2, 6–1, 6–2, in a mere 57 minutes. "It was a display of genius and it is to be doubted if such dynamic shotmaking was sustained with such accuracy before. If Cooper felt he had played badly, he had no chance to do anything else," wrote Lance Tingay in *100 Years of Wimbledon*. "Hoad was superhuman. It never began to be a contested match."

Gardnar Mulloy, age 43, and Budge Patty, 10 years younger, won their only Wimbledon doubles title—an exciting and sentimental occasion—over Fraser and Hoad, 8–10, 6–4, 6–4, 6–4.

Hoad joined the pros, Kramer carefully trying to get him ready for a serious run at Gonzalez the following year. "I used him in a couple of round-robins in the States, and then I made myself into a sparring partner and, with Rosewall and [Pancho] Segura, we took off on an around-the-world tour to get Hoad in shape for Gonzalez," Kramer recalled in *Sports Illustrated*. "If Hoad could beat Gonzalez, that was my chance to get rid of that tiger. Gonzalez knew what I was doing, too, and he was furious. We played a bru-

tal death march, going to Europe, then across Africa, through India and Southeast Asia, all the way to Manila. I was impressed by how strong Hoad was. He was personally as gentle as a lamb, but on the trip his body could tolerate almost anything."

With Hoad gone, the 20-year-old Cooper was the top seed and heavy favorite to win Forest Hills. But he was upset by Anderson, the first unseeded champion of the U.S. Nationals.

Anderson, a country boy from a remote Queensland cattle station, had lost to Cooper in five of six previous meetings. But in the month before Forest Hills, the thin, quick, dark-haired lad of 22 had become an entirely different player. Early in the year he had suffered from nervous exhaustion and heat prostration. At Wimbledon he broke a toe. But at Newport, R.I., on the U.S. Grass Court circuit, he beat U.S. No. 1 Ham Richardson and got a confidence-boosting title under his belt.

At Forest Hills, he clobbered Dick Savitt, who had a cold, 6–4, 6–3, 6–1, then put on a dazzling display of piercing service returns and passing shots to crush Chilean Luis Ayala, 6–1, 6–3, 6–1. In the semifinals, he overcame Sven Davidson—conqueror of Vic Seixas at Wimbledon—from a 1–2 deficit in sets, 5–7, 6–2, 4–6, 6–3, 6–4.

In his 10–8, 7–5, 6–4 triumph over Cooper, Anderson was so good that he inspired rhapsodic prose and superlatives from Allison Danzig in the next day's *New York Times*: "Anderson's performance ranks with the finest displays of offensive tennis of recent years. His speed of stroke and foot, the inevitability of his volley, his hair-trigger reaction and facileness on the half-volley, the rapidity of his service and passing shots and the adroitness of his return of service, compelling Cooper to volley up, all bore the stamp of a master of the racket. It was offensive tennis all the way, sustained without a letup. The margin of safety on most shots was almost nil. The most difficult shots were taken in stride with the acme of timing, going in or swiftly moving to the side."

Less artistically satisfying, but just as dramatic, was Althea Gibson's 6–3, 6–2 victory

Althea Gibson made it to the top in 1957. • *UPI*

only one of the Grand Slam singles titles she had not previously won, over Gibson, 6–3, 6–4. They teamed to win the doubles; these were Fry's last big titles before retiring to become a housewife and teaching pro in Connecticut.

Englishwoman Shirley Bloomer, whose victory in the Italian Championships had been overshadowed by the first men's title of the stylish Nicki Pietrangeli, took the French over Dorothy Knode, 6–1, 6–3, and teamed with Darlene Hard for the doubles crown. But thereafter Gibson reigned supreme, clobbering Californian Hard, 6–3, 6–2, in the Wimbledon final, winning two singles and a doubles as the U.S. defeated Great Britain, 6–1, in the Wightman Cup, and then winning Forest Hills. Althea also won the Wimbledon doubles with Hard, but they lost in the U.S. Doubles final to Louise Brough and Margaret duPont, who took their last title—the third straight and 12th in all.

Fifteen years earlier, Gibson had been playing paddle tennis on the streets of Harlem. She had as difficult a path to the pinnacle of tennis as anyone ever did. She had to stare down bigotry as well as formidable opponents. Some tournaments had

gone out of existence rather than admit her. But finally, at age 30, she was standing on the stadium court at Forest Hills, already the Wimbledon champion, accepting the trophy that symbolized supremacy in American women's tennis from Vice President Richard Nixon. The cup had white gladiolus and red roses in it, and "Big Al" had tears in her eyes.

There was one other important piece of silverware at stake in 1957. With Hoad and Rosewall gone, Australia was vulnerable to a U.S. raiding party invading Melbourne for the Davis Cup challenge round. But Anderson edged big-serving Barry MacKay, 6–3, 7–5, 3–6, 7–9, 6–3; Cooper bumped 34-year-old Vic Seixas in a similarly tortuous match, 3–6, 7–5, 6–1, 1–6, 6–3; and Anderson and Merv Rose—chosen even though Cooper and Fraser had won the U.S. Doubles—combined to demoralize MacKay and Seixas, 6–4, 6–4, 8–6.

Seixas beat Anderson and MacKay edged Cooper, both in five sets, to make the final score respectable, 3–2 for

Australia, but it all had been decided on the second day. The second-largest Davis Cup crowds—22,000 a day at Kooyong—witnessed the four singles marathons and the decisive, straight-sets doubles. There were no flowers in the cup, but for the third straight year Aussies drank libations of victory beer from it.

1958

In 1958, Australians Ashley Cooper, Mal Anderson and Mervyn Rose were the top men in amateur tennis, and American Althea Gibson the outstanding woman. By the end of the year, they had all turned professional, underscoring the rapidly growing distance in quality between the small band of pros who wandered around the world playing one- and two-night stands as unsanctioned outcasts and the amateurs who basked in the limelight of the traditional "fixtures."

The previous year the issue of "open competition" between amateurs and pros was raised formally within the councils of the USTA for the first time since the 1930s. A special committee report favored open tournaments. This document was promptly tabled since the leadership of the USTA was not nearly as progressive as the committee, but the ferment that ultimately led to the open game a decade later had started, and not only in America.

With Hoad and Rosewall touring professionally with Jack Kramer's World Tennis, Inc., Cooper took over the top amateur ranking by winning the three legs of the Grand Slam played on grass courts: the Australian, Wimbledon and Forest Hills.

He reversed the result of the 1957 Forest Hills final and took the Australian singles by beating Mal Anderson, 7–5, 6–3,

Ashley Cooper, netting the ball against Neale Fraser in the 1958 semifinals at Forest Hills, proceeded to win the championship in his finest year. • *New York Herald Tribune*

6–4, and then teamed with Neale Fraser for his only U.S. doubles title.

At Wimbledon, Anderson injured himself in the quarterfinals, and Cooper very nearly stumbled in the same round, probably coming within one point of defeat against Bobby Wilson, the pudgy but talented Englishman who delighted British galleries with his deft touch. Wilson had a

Cooper and Fraser were beaten in the doubles final, however, as the title went to an unseeded pair for the second straight year, the strapping Sven Davidson and Ulf Schmidt becoming the first Swedes to have their names inscribed on a Wimbledon championship trophy.

At Forest Hills, Cooper and Anderson advanced to the final for the second consecutive year, but this time Cooper prevailed in the longest final since Gonzales-Schroeder in 1949, 6–2, 3–6, 4–6, 10–8, 8–6. Gardnar Mulloy, reporting the match for *World Tennis,* wrote that the final set had "all the drama of a First Night," and suggested that Cooper merited an Oscar for his theatrics. The even-tempered Anderson served for the match at 5–4, but lost his serve at love. At 6–6, 30–15, Cooper apparently twisted an ankle, writhed in pain, hobbled to the sideline, and finally went back out to play after several minutes, to tumultuous applause. He "ran like a deer and served as well or better than he had all afternoon," opined Mulloy, a bit skeptical about the "injury." Cooper promptly held serve and then broke Anderson for the match. "Cooper is strong, tenacious, smart, and merciless," wrote Mulloy. "And don't forget his famous one-

act play, 'The Dying Swan,' a real tear-jerker which clinched the championship for him."

Ham Richardson and Alex Olmedo foreshadowed a U.S. revival in the Davis Cup by winning the National Doubles at Longwood in their first tournament together, beating Sammy Giammalva and Barry MacKay in the final after bumping

urrection from 0–5, 0–40 down in the fifth set to beat Budge Patty. Cooper and Fraser won the doubles, as they had in Australia, but were to advance no farther toward a Grand Slam.

Australia was heavily favored to defend the Davis Cup at the end of the year, but the United States had a potent and somewhat controversial weapon—the sleek, bronze-skinned, outgoing Alejandro "Alex" Olmedo, 22, from Arequipa in the snow-capped Peruvian Andes. The nimble 6-foot, 160-pounder was a student at the University of Southern California, and a protégé of Perry Jones, czar of tennis in the Southern Cal section. Jones was also U.S. Davis Cup captain and he lobbied successfully for Olmedo's inclusion, permissible since Peru did not have a Davis Cup team. "The Chief," as he was called because of his regal Inca appearance, had lost a tough five-setter to Fraser at Forest Hills, but in the Davis Cup Olmedo was magnificent.

In the opening singles, before a capacity crowd of 18,000 at the Milton Courts in Brisbane, Australia, Olmedo stunned Anderson, 8–6, 2–6, 9–7, 8–6. Cooper beat MacKay in four sets to make it 1–1, but on the second day Olmedo teamed with

Richardson to outlast Fraser and Anderson, 10–12, 3–6, 16–14, 6–3, 7–5—82 games, a record for final-round doubles.

Olmedo, the U.S. Intercollegiate champion, then capped his heroic performance by clinching the Cup with a 6–3, 4–6, 6–4, 8–6 victory over Cooper. Anderson beat MacKay to make the final margin for the U.S. 3–2, Olmedo was rewarded with the No. 1 ranking.

No. 1 among the women, in the U.S. and the world, was clearly the 5-10½, 145-pound Gibson, who used her thunderous serve and overhead, long reach and touch on the volley, and hard, flat, deep ground strokes to defend the Wimbledon and U.S singles titles. At Wimbledon she beat Angela Mortimer—who had won the Australian title over Lorraine Coghlan—in the final, 8–6, 6–2. At Forest Hills, Gibson's final victim was Darlene Hard, 3–6, 6–1, 6–2. Gibson teamed with Maria Bueno—an enchanting Brazilian who, making her first overseas tour at age 18, had won the Italian title—for the Wimbledon doubles title. But they were beaten in the final of the U.S. Doubles by Jeanne Arth and Hard. This was the first of Hard's five successive National women's titles; she won six in all, with four partners.

Gibson lost only four matches during the year, three in the early season (to Beverly Baker Fleitz and Janet Hopps twice), but the one that hurt was to tall Englishwoman Christine Truman in the pivotal match of the Wightman Cup. The British had a fine young team with Truman, Shirley Bloomer (runner-up to Hungarian Suzi Kormoczi in the French Championships), and left-hander Ann Haydon, even though Angela Mortimer didn't play. To the glee of the crowd at Wimbledon's Court 1, the British won the Cup for the first time since 1930, 4–3. Truman's 2–6, 6–3, 6–4 upset of Gibson paved the way, and the left-handed

Haydon's scrambling 6–3, 5–7, 6–3 triumph over Mimi Arnold was the clincher.

After Forest Hills, Gibson announced her retirement "to pursue a musical career." She needed a source of income. The next year she accepted an offer to turn pro and play pregame exhibitions at Harlem Globetrotters' basketball games against Karol Fageros, a popular glamour girl noted for her gold lamé panties, but not a player of Gibson's standard. Gibson won the tour with an 114–4 record.

Lew Hoad found pro tennis much more lucrative. Even though he lost his 1958 tour against Gonzalez, 51–36, Hoad made $148,000. Gonzalez, who rallied from a 9–18 deficit after Hoad developed a stiff back in Palm Springs, Cal., made over $100,000.

"That was the last tour to make any real money, though," promoter Kramer later said. It had been a doozy. In Australia at the start of the year, Hoad was awesome, winning eight of 13 matches against a stale and overweight Gonzalez. In San Francisco, on a canvas court indoors, Hoad won, 6–4, 20–18, to inaugurate the U.S. segment of the tour. The next night Gonzalez won in his hometown of Los Angeles, 3–6, 24–22, 6–1. Before a crowd of 15,237 at Madison Square Garden, Gonzalez won the only best-of-five-setter, 7–9, 6–0, 6–4, 6–4.

Then Hoad, strong as an ox and beating Gonzalez in every department—serve, overhead, volley, ground strokes—surged to an 18–9 lead. But the bad back got him, and he was never again the factor he had been. Gonzalez won the tour and beat Hoad in the U.S. Pro Championships at the Arena in Cleveland, 3–6, 4–6, 14–12, 6–1, 6–4. Gonzalez was the best in the world, and the next year—when Cooper, Anderson, and Rose came aboard for a round-robin—he proved it decisively.

1959

The folly of the uneasy arrangement between amateur officials and pro promoter Jack Kramer during the "shamateur" days of the late 1950s and early 1960s was apparent in this passage from a 1958 *Sports Illustrated* story on Kramer by Dick Phelan:

" 'I look on the amateurs as my farm

the amateur tennis officials, whose own tournaments sometimes follow Kramer's and don't draw nearly so well, to lambaste him afresh. But they let him come back. Their share of his gate receipts helps support the Australian amateurs."

After the heady peak of the Pancho Gonzalez-Lew Hoad tour in 1958, the profits of Kramer's World Tennis, Inc., started to dwindle, despite his personal flair for promotion. Anderson and Cooper joined the vanquished Hoad and the victorious Gonzalez in a round-robin tour, but the thrill was gone. They did not draw well, nor did similar tours with other personnel. If they had, it might have hastened the willingness of the amateur officials to consider open tennis. With Cooper, Anderson, and Mervyn Rose gone, Alex Olmedo and Neale Fraser ruled the amateur roost, sharing the world stage with the fiery Latin grace of Maria Bueno.

Olmedo, still buoyed by his herculean accomplishment in the Davis Cup challenge round at the end of 1958, stayed and took the 1959 Australian singles title over southpaw Fraser, 6–1, 6–2, 3–6, 6–3. Rod Laver and Bob Mark took the first of their three straight Aussie doubles titles.

Olmedo then returned to the United States and won the U.S. Indoor at New York, 12–10 in the fifth set over Dick Savitt. Olmedo did not play the Italian Championship, where Luis Ayala prevailed over Fraser, or the French, where the great Italian artist Nicola Pietrangeli beat Fraser in the semis and then South African Ian Vermaak in the final, 3–6, 6–3, 6–4, 6–1. Pietrangeli and Italian Davis Cup teammate

Jones—and the Cup itself. Olmedo added to his skyrocketing reputation by winning Wimbledon, beating Emerson in the semifinal, and Laver, a left-hander of enormous but as yet unconsolidated talent, in the

Dick Savitt (left) congratulates Alex Olmedo after the transplanted Peruvian won the U.S. Indoor in 1959. • *New York Herald Tribune*

Barry MacKay makes the return to Rod Laver in the course of winning their Davis Cup match in 1959, but Australia regained the Cup when Neale Fraser vanquished MacKay in the deciding duel. • *UPI*

final, 6–4, 6–3, 6–4. Emerson took the first of his eventual record 16 Grand Slam men's doubles titles, alongside Fraser.

Wimbledon was the peak of Olmedo's year, however. Fraser beat him in the final of Forest Hills, 6–3, 5–7, 6–2, 6–4, the Chief's serve lacking its customary zip because of a shoulder strain he had suffered in a mixed doubles match the night before.

Australia regained the Davis Cup at Forest Hills, 3–2, Olmedo never finding the form to which he had risen in the previous December. Fraser beat him again in the opening match, 8–6, 6–8, 6–4, 8–6. Barry MacKay, the hulking "Bear" of Dayton, Ohio, served mightily in beating Laver, 7–5, 6–4, 6–1, but in the doubles Emerson and Fraser outclassed Olmedo and Buchholz, 7–5, 7–5, 6–4. The Aussies had prevailed in the U.S. National Doubles

by the breadth of their fingernails, 3–6, 6–3, 5–7, 6–4, 7–5, but this time the nails became claws.

Olmedo raised his game to beat Laver, 9–7, 4–6, 10–8, 12–10, to tie the series at 2–all, but Fraser clinched by beating MacKay in a match that was played over two days. They split sets before darkness forced a postponement, but after a long rain delay, Fraser won the last two sets easily for a soggy 8–6, 3–6, 6–2, 6–4 victory.

On the women's side, Mary Carter Reitano won the Australian singles over South African Renée Schuurman, who teamed with her countrywoman Sandra Reynolds for the doubles crown. Englishwoman Christine Truman won both the Italian and French titles, dethroning clay-court specialist Suzi Kormoczi in the Paris final, 6–4, 7–5. Reynolds and Schuurman won the doubles.

Thereafter the season belonged to the incomparably balletic and flamboyant Bueno. Volleying beautifully, playing with breathtaking boldness and panache, the lithe Brazilian became the first South American woman to win the Wimbledon singles, beating Darlene Hard in the final, 6–4, 6–3. Hard did team with Jeanne Arth to add the Wimbledon doubles to the U.S. crown they captured the previous year, and

her countrywoman Jan Lehane, 7–5, 6–2, for the first of seven consecutive Australian titles and 24 Big Four singles titles in all—both records.

It would have been much more of a landmark year but for five votes at the annual general meeting of the ITF. By that slim margin, a proposal calling for sanction of between eight and 13 "open" tourna-

Wightman Cup from Great Britain with a 4–3 victory at the Edgeworth Club in Sewickley, Pa. The British won the final two matches, but only after Hard's 6–3, 6–8, 6–4 victory over Angela Mortimer and Beverly Baker Fleitz's 6–4, 6–4 conquest of Truman had given the Americans an unbeatable 4–1 lead.

Gonzalez remained the pro champion. He beat Hoad for the second straight year in the final of U.S. Pro Championships at Cleveland, 6–4, 6–2, 6–4, after romping in the round-robin tour against Hoad, Cooper, and Anderson.

1960

Once again, the start of a new decade was the dawn of a new era in tennis. As 1950 had been, so 1960 was an eventful year.

It began with an Australian Championships that heralded a man and woman who would be king and queen of tennis. Rod Laver beat fellow Aussie left-hander Neale Fraser in an epic final, 5–7, 3–6, 6–3, 8–6, 8–6, to take the first of his eventual 11 Big Four singles titles. Margaret Smith, who would later become Mrs. Barry Court, beat

Another proposal put forth by the French Federation calling for creation of a category of "registered" players who could capitalize on their skill by bargaining with tournaments for appearance fees higher than the expenses allowed amateurs, was tabled. The USTA had voted to oppose this resolution on the basis that "registered player" was just another name for a pro.

Maria Bueno did not reach the semifinals of the Australian singles, but she teamed with Christine Truman to win the doubles over Margaret Smith and Lorraine Coghlan Robinson, 6–2, 5–7, 6–2. That was the first leg of a doubles Grand Slam by Bueno. She went on to win the French, Wimbledon and U.S. titles with American Darlene Hard, losing only one more set along the way—to Karen Hantze and Janet Hopps in the semifinals at Wimbledon.

Hard won her first Big Four singles title at Paris, struggling through three three-set matches in the early rounds and then whipping Bueno in the semis and the quick little Mexican Yola Ramirez in the final, 6–3, 6–4. Hard also won her first U.S. National singles at Forest Hills, beating Bueno, 6–4, 10–12, 6–4, after the final was postponed nearly a week by Hurricane Donna.

Darlene Hard and Neale Fraser made off with the silverware at the 1960 U.S. Championships. • *USTA*

At Wimbledon, where American women had been so dominant for more than a decade after the war, not one of the 10 Americans who entered reached the semifinals. This had not happened since 1925. Hard, the best U.S. hope, lost in the quarterfinals to South African Sandra Reynolds, who reached the final but lost to Bueno, 8–6, 6–0. A year earlier, journalist Lance Tingay had pointed out that the difference between being very good or very bad was, for Bueno, a thin line based on her timing. "Mundane shots did not exist for her." he observed. "It was either caviar or starvation." For the second year in a row it was mostly caviar, and a feast for the spectators. Her Wimbledon performance was good enough to earn Bueno the No.1 world ranking by a shade over Hard.

Britain won the Wightman Cup for the second time in three years, snatching a 4–3 victory at Wimbledon by winning the final two matches. Hard had given the U.S. a 3–2 lead with a 5–7, 6–2, 6–1 triumph over

Ann Haydon, but Angela Mortimer beat Janet Hopps, 6–8, 6–4, 6–1, and Christine Truman paired with Shirley Bloomer Brasher to beat Hopps and Dorothy Head Knode, 6–4, 9–7.

Nicki Pietrangeli defended his French singles title over Luis Ayala, runner-up for the second time in three years, 3–6, 6–3, 6–4, 4–6, 6–3. Ayala was also second best in Rome, where Barry MacKay served and volleyed on the slow clay, winning the final by a most peculiar score: 7–5, 7–5, 0–6, 0–6, 6–1. MacKay had won the U.S. Indoor in February in a splendid five-set final over Dick Savitt, so within four months he took titles on just about the fastest and slowest court surfaces in the world. Roy Emerson and Neale Fraser combined for the French doubles title, the first of six straight for Emerson, with five partners.

Fraser took over as the No.1 man in the amateur ranks by winning Wimbledon and the U.S. Championship.

As with the women, no American man got to the semis at Wimbledon. MacKay was beaten in the quarterfinals by Pietrangeli, and Butch Buchholz, 19, led Fraser by 6–4, 3–6, 6–4 in the same round and had six match points in the fourth set before being seized with cramps that left him unable to continue. Fraser, 26 and playing for the seventh time, was a sporting and popular champion. His left-handed serve had a wicked kick, and he was a daring and resourceful volleyer. He beat Laver, five years his junior, in the final, 6–4, 3–6, 9–7, 7–5.

A small measure of U.S. pride was saved when Dennis Ralston, 17, teamed with agile 21-year-old Mexican Rafael Osuna to win the men's doubles, the second-youngest team to win Wimbledon. They beat Britons Humphrey Truman and Gerald Oakley in the first round, 6–3, 6–4, 9–11, 5–7, 16–14, and second-seeded Laver and Bob Mark, the Australian champions, 4–6, 10–8, 15–13, 4–6, 11–9, in the semifinal. After that pulsating contest, the final was comparatively easy: 7–5, 6–3, 10–8 over Welshman Mike Davies and Englishman Bobby Wilson.

Laver foreshadowed greatness to come by ripping up the U.S. Eastern grass court circuit, winning consecutive titles at

attack of cramps and losing 7–5 in the fifth. Fraser beat the precocious Ralston and then, after sitting around through a week of hurricane rain and wind, slogged to the title over Laver, 6–4, 6–4, 10–8.

For the first time since 1936, the United States failed to reach the challenge round of the Davis Cup, falling to Italy, 3–2 in the inter-zone semifinals at Perth, Australia, in December.

Buchholz beat the lanky Orlando Sirola in the opening match, and MacKay gave the U.S. a 2–0 lead in an all-time classic, saving eight match points in beating Pietrangeli, 8–6, 3–6, 8–10, 8–6, 13–11. But Sirola and Pietrangeli beat Buchholz and Chuck McKinley in a long four-set doubles, Pietrangeli beat Buchholz in five sets to even the series, and then Sirola— definite underdog on grass instead of his preferred clay—served and played like a dream to upset MacKay, 9–7, 6–3, 8–6.

Italy's first appearance in the challenge round a couple of weeks later was less auspicious. Australia won, 4–1, Fraser and Emerson clinching the doubles point over Pietrangeli-Sirola for an unbeatable 3–0 lead. Pietrangeli beat Fraser in four sets in

the final match, but the Australian No.1 had started things off with a decisive four-set win over Sirola.

This time the Aussies suffered no defections to the pro tour immediately after the Davis Cup, but the Americans did. MacKay and Buchholz, undoubtedly thinking that open tennis was near and wanting a piece of Jack Kramer's checkbook before

champ a year before, beat Trabert in the U.S. Pro final, 7–5, 6–4, at Cleveland.

1961

In 1961, the amateur tennis Establishment was stunned and smarting from a wholesale raid on its ranks by pro promoter Jack Kramer, who in 1960 signed to contracts several middling players: Spaniard Andres Gimeno, Welshman Mike Davies, Frenchman Robert Haillet and Dane Kurt Nielsen, as well as young Americans Butch Buchholz and Barry MacKay. Kramer tried without success to lure into his fold Australian Neale Fraser, the Wimbledon and Forest Hills champion; Italian Nicki Pietrangeli, champion of France; and Chilean Luis Ayala, runner-up in the 1960 Italian and French Championships.

When a proposal for introducing "open tournaments" was unexpectedly stymied by just five votes at the 1960 ITF annual meeting, there was relatively little official grieving among the member national associations and their officials. However Kramer's response of taking out his wallet and waving it in front of practically every player of moderate reputation—which the amateur pow-ers-that-be thought both irresponsible and reprehensible—started alarm bells sound-ing. Suddenly the national associations saw their tournaments, and hence their rev-enues, in grave danger. Kramer became Public Enemy No. 1.

But if his motive was to force the ITF into open competition by his mass signings, as most suspected, he failed. Amateur offi-cials did not like being bullied. A new "open tournament" proposal was rejected at the 1961 ITF annual meeting at Stockholm. Delegates approved a resolution agreeing "to the principle of an experiment of a lim-ited number of open tournaments," but referred the matter to a committee for another year of study to see how the experi-ment might be conducted. A U.S.-spon-sored "home rule" resolution, which would have permitted national associations to stage open tournaments at their own discre-tion, was defeated. The ITF was able to stand up to Kramer because he had been able to sign only two of the previous year's top handful of players: No. 3, MacKay, and No. 5, Buchholz. The amateurs still had Fraser, Rod Laver, Pietrangeli, Roy Emerson and Ayala. But the battle lines had been drawn. Instead of the uneasy coexistence of the past, the amateur associations and Kramer were now at war.

Emerson—a magnificently fit and affa-ble fellow with slick black hair that shone like patent leather and a smile that sparkled with gold fillings—served and volleyed relentlessly to defeat his fellow Queenslander Laver in the Australian final, 1–6, 6–3, 7–5, 6–4. This was the first of six Australian titles in seven years for "Emmo," the first of 12 major singles titles in all. Laver and Bob Mark annexed the doubles crown for the third straight year. On the women's side, "Mighty Margaret" Smith beat Jan Lehane again in the singles final, 6–1, 6–4, and teamed with Mary Carter Reitano for the first of Smith's eight Australian doubles titles.

In Paris, the two greatest European vir-tuosi of the '60s met in the final. English writer Rex Bellamy was there and remem-bered it some years later:

"Nicola Pietrangeli, the favorite to win for the third consecutive year, was beaten by the young Manuel "Manolo" Santana, the first Spaniard to win a major title. The match lasted five sets. Santana and Pietrangeli were like artists at work in a stu-dio exposed to a vast public in the heat of the afternoon. Each in turn played his finest tennis. The flame of Pietrangeli's inspiration eventually died, his brushstrokes overlaid by Santana's flickering finesse. But long before that, these two Latins had established a close rapport with a Latin crowd enjoying a rare blend of sport and aesthetics. At the end there was a tumult of noise. Santana, his nerves strung up to the breaking point, dropped his racket and cried. And Pietrangeli, disappointed yet instantly responsive to the Spaniard's feel-ings, went around the net, took Santana in his arms, and patted him on the back like a father comforting a child."

The scores were 4–6, 6–1, 3–6, 6–0, 6–2, but bald numbers could hardly convey the emotion of this long afternoon, espe-cially for the toothy Santana, who got to the final by upsetting cannonball-serving Englishman Mike Sangster, Emerson and Laver (runner-up to Pietrangeli in Rome).

A vivid contrast in style to the gliding and caressing strokes of the singles finalists was provided by Laver and Emerson, who bore in on the net for murderous volleys in winning the doubles. Ann Haydon showed the legs, heart, and brain of a clay-court stalwart in beating agile volleyer Yola Ramirez, 6–2, 6–1, for the women's title. South Africans Renée Schuurman and Sandra Reynolds won the doubles.

Maria Bueno, who had beaten Austra-lian Lesley Turner in the Italian final, lost to Suzi Kormoczi in the quarterfinals at Paris and then was bedridden with hepatitis. Lacking funds to pay for hospital care, she was confined to a tiny hotel chamber for a month, with the rest of the floor quarantined, until she was able to go home to Brazil.

Bueno was thus unable to defend her Wimbledon title. Darlene Hard, her doubles partner and the Forest Hills champ, also withdrew and stayed in Paris to care

Billie Jean Moffitt won the women's doubles at Wimbledon. • *UPI*

The crowd adored Truman, a tall and smiling lass with a big forehand and attacking game who epitomized all the best British sporting traits, and they moaned when she fell awkwardly on a rain-slicked court in the third set of the final. That tumble cost her the momentum she had built up against the more defensive Mortimer, who didn't hesitate to lob and drop-shot in a 4–6, 6–4, 7–5 victory.

Hantze, age 18, and bouncing, bubbly Billie Jean Moffitt, 17, won the doubles unseeded, the youngest pair ever to seize a Wimbledon crown. Eighteen years later, Billie Jean Moffitt King's 10th doubles title would give her the all-time record for career Wimbledon titles in all events: 20.

Laver, the red-haired Queenslander called "Rocket," won the men's title for the first time, over American Chuck McKinley, 6–3, 6–1, 6–4. This was the start of an unprecedented reign: Laver would win 31 singles matches without a defeat at Wimbledon in five appearances to the fourth round in 1970, winning four singles titles plus a BBC-sponsored pro tournament in 1967. Fraser, who had lost his title in the round of 16 to Englishman Bobby Wilson, captured the doubles with

Emerson, but then returned home to Australia to tend an ailing knee.

Great Britain had both Wimbledon singles finalists and the French champion on its team, but was startlingly ambushed in the Wightman Cup by a "mod squad" of eager American juniors. Hantze beat Haydon and Truman, Moffitt beat Haydon, and 18-year-old St. Louis lefty Justina Bricka shocked Mortimer, the first British Wimbledon champ since 1937. Hantze-Moffitt clobbered Truman-Deidre Catt, and the U.S. won the final doubles when Mortimer defaulted with foot cramps. Truman's singles win over Moffitt was the only one the shell-shocked English could salvage in the 6–1 massacre at Chicago's Saddle and Cycle Club.

Texan Bernard "Tut" Bartzen won his fourth U.S. Clay Court singles since 1954, beating Donald Dell, who earlier in the year had gone with doubles partner Mike Franks on a State Department tour of South Africa, the Middle East and the Soviet Union, the first Americans to play in Russia since the 1917 Revolution.

McKinley and Dennis Ralston won the rain-delayed U.S. Doubles over Mexicans Rafe Osuna and Antonio Palafox. Hard teamed with Turner for her fourth successive women's doubles title, and was supposed to play with Ralston against Margaret Smith and Bob Mark in the mixed final, at Longwood instead of Forest Hills. But rain postponed it until after Forest Hills, and Ralston, unfairly treated by the USTA, was unable to play because he was suspended for his behavior earlier, in a Davis Cup match against Mexico.

At Forest Hills, Whitney Reed—a spacy, unorthodox player who never trained, partied all night, but had such a wonderful touch that he earned the No. 1 U.S. ranking—upset McKinley in the third round. He fell to Osuna, and Dell to Laver, leaving no Americans in the men's semis. Emerson just got by the catlike and clever Osuna, 6–3, 6–2, 3–6, 5–7, 9–7, in a rousing semifinal. Emerson grabbed the first two sets in just 35 minutes, but Osuna kept scrambling for every ball, even making shots from flat on his back. He saved two match points in the fourth set and leveled after trailing 0–3 in the fifth. Finally three fine passing shots brought Emerson to match point again at 8–7, and this time he wouldn't let it get away. Then the speedy and powerful Emerson overwhelmed Laver in the final, 7–5, 6–3, 6–2, to lay claim to the No. 1 ranking among the amateurs.

Darlene Hard, the only American in the women's quarterfinals, battled past Ramirez, 6–3, 6–1; Smith, 6–4, 3–6, 6–3; and Haydon in the final, 6–3, 6–4, for her second straight title.

With MacKay and Buchholz professionals, U.S. Davis Cup captain David Freed named a 14-man squad that accented youth. The U.S. beat British West Indies, Ecuador, Mexico (losing Ralston via suspension) and India, but again lost to Italy in the inter-zone semifinals, 4–1. Jon

Douglas astonishingly upset Fausto Gardini on the clay at Rome's Il Foro Italico, 4–6, 3–6, 7–5, 10–8, 6–0, but Pietrangeli beat Whitney Reed—who trained for the occasion, and later said that spoiled his game—2–6, 6–8, 6–4, 6–4, 6–4. Orlando Sirola and Pietrangeli beat Reed and Dell in the doubles, and Pietrangeli spanked Douglas in straight sets to clinch. Gardini came from behind to beat Reed, 3–6, 7–5, 3–6, 8–6, 6–4, as a raucous Italian crowd exulted in his adding to the margin of victory.

Gardini refused to go to Australia for the challenge round unless he was assured of a singles berth. However, he wasn't, and Pietrangeli and Sirola never got a set on the grass at Melbourne until Emerson and Laver in singles and Emerson and Fraser in doubles had closed out the Aussie defense of the Cup. The final score was 5–0.

Kramer's expanded traveling circus—Pancho Gonzalez, Lew Hoad, Frank Sedgman, Tony Trabert, Ashley Cooper, Alex Olmedo, Gimeno, MacKay and Buchholz as principals, plus the others—did not make enough to cover his vastly increased overhead. Gonzalez beat Sedgman, 6–3, 7–5, in Cleveland for his eighth and last U.S. Pro title, but the pros were in trouble, and Kramer's grandstanding of the previous autumn had not helped the cause of open competition.

1962

The Australian grip—both hands firmly around the throat of players of any other nationality—was in vogue in 1962, the season of Rod Laver's first Grand Slam and Margaret Smith's first near-Slam.

Laver duplicated Don Budge's supreme feat of 1938, sweeping the singles titles of Australia, France, Great Britain (Wimbledon) and U.S. He also won the Italian and German titles, not to mention the less prestigious Norwegian, Irish and

Rod Laver: Grand Slam in 1962. • *UPI*

Swiss, and led Australia to a 5–0 blitz of upstart Mexico in the Davis Cup challenge round. In all, Laver won 19 of 34 tournaments and 134 of 149 matches during his long and incomparably successful year.

Smith was staggered in the first round of Wimbledon by the pudgy chatterbox who would grow up to be her arch-rival—Billie Jean Moffitt—but otherwise won just about everything in sight. Smith's only other loss was to another young American, Carole Caldwell, but "Mighty Maggie" won 13 of 15 tournaments, including the Australian, French and U.S., and 67 of 69 matches.

Laver, the "Rockhampton Rocket" from that Queensland town, started his Slam at White City Stadium in Sydney, beating Roy Emerson, 8–6, 0–6, 6–4, 6–4. Emerson and Neale Fraser took the doubles.

Laver lived precariously in Paris, the only leg of the Slam on slow clay. He saved a match point in beating countryman Marty Mulligan in the quarterfinals, 6–4,

3–6, 2–6, 10–8, 6–2. He also went five sets with Fraser in the semis, 3–6, 6–3, 6–2, 3–6, 7–5, and with Emerson again in the final, 3–6, 2–6, 6–3, 9–7, 6–2. Emerson and Fraser racked up another doubles title.

At Wimbledon, Laver lost only one set to Manolo Santana in a 14–16, 9–7, 6–2, 6–2 victory. There were no Americans in the quarterfinals for the first time since 0–1. With Emerson sidelined, Aussies Bob Hewitt and Fred Stolle won the doubles.

At Forest Hills, Laver lost only one set again en route to the final—to gangly American Frank Froehling in a 6–3, 13–11, 4–6, 6–3 quarterfinal victory. The athletic Emerson was back, but Laver repelled him as he had in Sydney, Rome and Paris. Laver hit four fearsome backhand returns to break serve in the first game and dominated the first two sets with his varied backhand, either bashed or chipped, a topspin forehand, and ruthless serving and net play. Emerson, always barreling forward and battling, aroused a crowd of 9,000 by winning the third set, but Laver closed out the match and the Slam, 6–2, 6–4, 5–7, 6–4, and was greeted by Budge in the marquee.

Astonishingly, there were again no Aussies in the U.S. Doubles final at Longwood, where the "Mexican Thumping Beans," collegians Rafe Osuna and Tony Palafox, out-hustled temperamental Americans Chuck McKinley and Dennis Ralston, reversing the previous year's final result, 6–4, 10–12, 1–6, 9–7, 6–3.

Osuna and Palafox had scored a victory of much greater import over Ralston-

McKinley earlier in the year, in the pivotal match of Mexico's 3–2 upset of the U.S. in the Davis Cup. Palafox beat Jon Douglas in the rarefied atmosphere of Mexico City after McKinley had disposed of Osuna in three straight sets in the opener. The doubles point provided the impetus, and then Osuna was carried off on the shoulders of his jubilant countrymen when he out-nerved Douglas, 9–7, 6–3, 6–8, 3–6, 6–1, for the clinching 3–1 point. This was the first time Mexico had won the American Zone, and Osuna and Palafox lugged their adoring nation past Yugoslavia, Sweden and India to the challenge round. But Laver and Neale Fraser in singles and Laver-Emerson in doubles had too much serve-and-volley power on the slick grass at Brisbane, winning 5–0.

Margaret Smith drubbed Jan Lehane, 6–0, 6–2, in the final of the Australian, but had a much closer final in Paris against another countrywoman, Lesley Turner. Smith had shown she could play on clay too, however—she had won the Italian title as a tune-up—and she prevailed, 6–3, 3–6, 7–5, rescuing a match point at 3–5 in the third. By that time Smith, just shy of 20, must have been entertaining thoughts of duplicating the Grand Slam accomplished by only one woman previously, Maureen Connolly in 1953. But 18-year-old Billie Jean Moffitt, who had a premonition weeks earlier that she would draw Smith in her opening match at Wimbledon, rudely wrecked the dream. It was the only time that the No. 1 female seed had failed to survive one round, and established "Little Miss Moffitt" as a force to be reckoned with on the Centre Court that already was her favorite stage.

It was Karen Hantze Susman, with whom Moffitt repeated as doubles champion, who took the singles at age 19. An outstanding volleyer, Susman captured the title with a 6–4, 6–4 victory over unseeded Vera Sukova of Czechoslovakia, who had scored successive upsets over the defend-ing champ sixth-seeded Angela Mortimer, second-seeded Darlene Hard and third-seeded Maria Bueno.

Smith was back in form at Forest Hills. With her enormous reach, athleticism, weight of shot and solid arsenal from the backcourt and net alike, she beat Hard in a nerve-wracking match, 9–7, 6–4 to become the first Australian woman to win the U.S. singles. She saved a set point in the 10th game of the first, and benefitted from 16 double faults by Hard, who was perplexed by numerous close line calls and burst into prolonged tears in the sixth game of the second set.

Hard beat Christine Truman, 6–2, 6–2, and Ann Haydon, 6–3, 6–8, 6–4, as the United States edged Britain, 4–3 in the Wightman Cup at Wimbledon. Captain Margaret Osborne duPont, age 44, teamed up with Margaret Varner to show that she could still win at doubles.

While the interest generated by Laver and Smith signaled a banner year for amateur tennis, the pros were struggling. Pancho Gonzalez had retired for the time being, leaving Butch Buchholz to win the U.S. Pro title over Pancho Segura, 6–4, 6–3, 6–4, in Cleveland.

Jack Kramer had also given up the ghost as promoter. "We had all the best players, but the public didn't want to see them," he recalled in *Sports Illustrated.* "...there was no acceptance for our players. The conservative and powerful amateur officials were secure. Among other things, they had succeeded in making me the issue. If you were for pro tennis, you were in favor of handing over all of tennis to Jack Kramer. That was the argument."

That is vastly oversimplified, of course. Kramer in many ways had only himself to blame for antagonism. But name-calling aside, the pro game was in sorry shape.

Ken Rosewall was the top dog, but he had little flair for promotion, and the top amateurs no longer were tempted to turn pro and face an uncertain, anonymous future. Under-the-table payments afforded a comfortable if not lavish lifestyle for the top "amateurs." For the second time in the postwar era, there was no pro tour in the United States. Rosewall and Lew Hoad were contemplating retirement. Their only chance at reviving interest, they thought, was to induce Laver to join them.

and universally popular Roy Emerson of rural Blackbutt, Queensland—set his sights on the Grand Slam that Laver had achieved in 1962. Emerson won the first two legs, but was thwarted at Wimbledon as Australian supremacy waned. By the end of the year Latin America had scored a unique "double" at Forest Hills, and the United States had both recovered the Davis Cup and captured the inaugural Federation Cup, the women's equivalent.

Politically, it was not a progressive year. With Jack Kramer retired from promoting, amateur officials worldwide felt they had won a battle against some dark specter, and the movement for open competition lagged. In the United States, which had supported the principles of "self-determination" and experimentation with open tournaments, the Old Guard reasserted itself, repudiating USTA president Ed Turville, a supporter of open tennis. The USTA instructed its delegates to the ITF to oppose "opens" and "home rule."

Emerson, 26, romped to the Australian title over countryman Ken Fletcher, 6–3, 6–3, 6–1, while Bob Hewitt and Fred Stolle took the doubles. Margaret Smith ritually slaughtered two-fisted Jan Lehane, 6–2,

6–2, for the fourth straight year in the women's final and teamed with Fletcher to beat Lesley Turner and Stolle in the first leg of a mixed doubles Grand Slam. They took the French, Wimbledon and U.S. titles as well.

Emerson won the French over the first native to reach the men's final since 1964: the suave and sporting Pierre Darmon,

upset by the steadiness of Vera Sukova, the unseeded Wimbledon finalist of 1962, who was more at home on Parisian clay. The title did remain in Australian hands, however, Lesley Turner beating Ann Haydon

Chuck McKinley returned the U.S. to Wimbledon supremacy in 1963 after a long drought. • *UPI*

Jones, 2–6, 6–3, 7–5. Jones teamed with Renée Schuurman for the doubles trophy.

Wimbledon, which had seen five all-Australian men's singles finals in seven years, got its first American male champion (discounting the Peruvian Alex Olmedo in 1959) since Tony Trabert in 1955: 22-year-old Chuck McKinley, a Missourian attending Trinity University in San Antonio, Tex. He was the first since Trabert to win the title without losing a set, but it was a peculiar year. No seeded players wound up playing each other in the men's singles.

Emerson, the favorite, ran into Germany's Wilhelm Bungert on a hot day and was beaten in the quarters, 8–6, 3–6, 6–3, 4–6, 6–3. McKinley, a little but athletic man who charged the net like a toy top gone wild, was too sure in his volleying for Bungert in the semis and Fred Stolle in the final, 9–7, 6–1, 6–4. This was the first of three straight years as runner-up for the tall, angular Stolle, who never did win the singles. Mexican Davis Cuppers Rafe Osuna and Antonio Palafox won the doubles.

Margaret Smith, who had already won four Australian, two Italian, one French and one U.S. title, became the first Australian woman to win the Wimbledon singles. In the final, she avenged her early defeat by Billie Jean Moffitt the year before, 6–3, 6–4. The title was not decided until the start of the third week because of rain, and thus Miss Smith did not get to dance the traditional champions' first foxtrot with McKinley at the Wimbledon Ball. He was perhaps relieved, since he was four inches shorter than Smith; instead, he guided his wife around the hardwood floor.

The Federation Cup was inaugurated to celebrate the 50th anniversary of the ITF. The U.S. blanked the Netherlands, Italy, and Great Britain, then upset Australia, 2–1, in the women's interna-

tional team competition, which drew 16 nations. It was set up to be more compact than the Davis Cup—played in best-of-three (two singles, one doubles) series instead of best-of-five, with all participating countries together at one site for one week. Smith blitzed U.S. No. 1 Darlene Hard, 6–3, 6–0, in the opening match, but then Moffitt upended Turner, 5–7, 6–0, 6–3, and teamed with Hard to take the excruciating doubles from Smith and Turner, 3–6, 13–11, 6–3, indoors because of inclement weather at London's Queen's Club.

The U.S. also beat Britain, 6–1, in the Wightman Cup at the Cleveland Skating Club. Ann Jones beat Hard in the opening match, 6–1, 0–6, 8–6, but Moffitt beat Christine Truman, 6–4, 19–17 (the second set a female record) to turn things around for teammates Hard, Nancy Richey and Donna Floyd Fales. Richey won the first of her six consecutive U.S. Clay Court titles.

For the first time, the U.S. did not have a woman in the semifinals at Forest Hills. Hard, a finalist the last three years and champion twice, was beaten by Jones in the quarters. Even more curious, Australia was shut out of the men's quarterfinals after having had both finalists in six of the previous seven years.

This was a south-of-the-border year, Rafe Osuna becoming the first Mexican to take the men's singles, and Brazilian Maria Bueno recapturing the women's title she had won in 1959 with a breathtaking display of shotmaking.

Osuna, a gallery favorite because of his quickness of hand, foot, and smile, ousted Wimbledon champ McKinley in the semis and unseeded Floridian Frank Froehling III in the final, 7–5, 6–4, 6–2. Froehling had served devastatingly to upset top seed Emerson, but Osuna cleverly neutralized his power with wonderfully conceived and executed tactics, especially lobbed service returns from 10 to 12 feet behind the baseline. Occasionally Osuna would stand in and take Froehling's serve on the rise, chipping the backhand, but more often he lobbed returns to disrupt Froehling's serve-volley rhythm and break down his suspect overhead. In fact, Osuna climbed the wall of the stadium to retrieve smashes and float back perfect lobs, frustrating Froehling with his nimble speed around the court, touch and tactical variations.

she hit blazing winners from the backhand and threw up lobs in an overwhelming assault."

At Longwood, Hard was not able to snag a sixth straight women's doubles title; she and Bueno fell in the final to Smith and Robyn Ebbern. McKinley and Dennis Ralston met Osuna and Palafox for the third straight year in the men's final, saving two match points in recapturing the title, 9–7, 4–6, 5–7, 6–3, 11–9, before a record crowd of 7,000.

That was immediately after they combined to beat Osuna and Palafox, 4–1, in a Davis Cup match at Los Angeles. Captained by Bob Kelleher and coached by Pancho Gonzalez, the Americans also conquered Iran, Venezuela, Britain and India to return to the challenge round for the first time in three years.

It had been a long campaign, taxing competitively and medically. Ralston nearly lost an eye in England, McKinley had dysentery in India, Froehling needed his abscessed backside lanced, and McKinley had back spasms. But the squad persevered and took the Cup back from

Australia, which had held it in a Melbourne bank vault 11 of the last 13 years.

Ralston beat 19-year-old Cup rookie John Newcombe in five sets in the opening match, and McKinley and Ralston took the key doubles over Emerson and Neale Fraser, 6–3, 3–6, 11–9, 11–9. Emerson kept the Aussies alive to the final match with his

was supreme, beating Laver in the final of the U.S. Pro Championships at Forest Hills, 6–4, 6–2, 6–2, but the tournament went bust, and at presentation time Rosewall got only a handshake from Laver.

1964

As if any additional evidence were necessary to prove the depth of tennis talent in Australia, the Davis Cup went back Down Under for the 11th time in 14 years even though three members of the Aussies squad fled to other countries because of an altercation with the autocratic Lawn Tennis Association of Australia.

Roy Emerson, Fred Stolle, Marty Mulligan, Bob Hewitt and Ken Fletcher were all suspended by the LTAA for the grievous offense of leaving for the overseas tournament circuit earlier than permitted. Emerson and Stolle were reinstated after reaching the Wimbledon final—Emerson beat Stolle in the singles finals of the Australian, Wimbledon and U.S. Championships in 1964 but had his notions of a Slam punctured by Nicki Pietrangeli at the French semis. 'Emmo' and Fred were the core of the raiding party that took the Cup back from the U.S. in Cleveland, the first time a challenge round in the U.S. was played out of the East and off grass. The battleground was clay.

The other three continued to have problems. Mulligan moved to Italy, where he married, became a successful businessman, and played in Davis Cup competition in 1968, nicknamed "Martino Mulligano." (He had been on the Australian squad but had never played, so he was eligible to play for Italy when he became a citizen.) Hewitt married a Johannesburg model and became a mainstay of the South African Davis Cup team, continuing to develop into one of the world's best doubles players. Fletcher took up residence in Hong Kong. It is a measure of the strength of Aussie captain Harry Hopman's production line that Australia won the Cup four years in a row, never missing this trio of talented players.

The affable Emerson—strong enough to quaff beer and sing choruses of "Waltzing Matilda" into the wee hours of the morning, then get up early to train and

Roy Emerson led the Aussie raiding party in 1964. • *UPI*

play magnificently athletic tennis—ruled the amateur world in 1964. He won 55 straight singles matches in one stretch, finishing the year with 17 tournament championships and a 109–6 record, including two singles victories in the Davis Cup challenge round.

Emmo thumped Stolle in the Australian final, 6–3, 6–4, 6–2; at Wimbledon, 6–4, 12–10, 4–6, 6–3; and at Forest Hills, 6–4, 6–1, 6–4. He also took the French doubles, practically an annual acquisition, with Fletcher. Hewitt and Stolle took the Australian and Wimbledon doubles, while Chuck McKinley and Dennis Ralston captured the U.S. title at Longwood for the third time in four years, the first three-timers since Bill Talbert and Gardnar Mulloy (1942, 1945–46, 1948).

A preview of America's Davis Cup fate was offered in the most dramatic match of the U.S. Nationals, a quarterfinal in which Ralston fought back from two sets down against Stolle, saved a match point at 3–5 in the fifth, and hauled himself back to 7–7 before the gripping encounter was halted by darkness. Ralston had two break points at 15–40 as Stolle served the first game of the resumption the next morning, but the lean Aussie with the pained gait and delightful wit held and broke Ralston in the next game for the match.

It was the 25-year-old Stolle's 7–5, 6–3, 3–6, 9–11, 6–4, triumph over Ralston on a clay court at newly built and jam-packed (7,000 a day, at top dollar) Harold T. Clark Stadium in Cleveland that broke America's back in the challenge round. On a gray day, after a long rain delay, they played a majestic match for a national television audience. Ralston saved one match point, serving at 4–5 in the fifth, but Stolle blasted a forehand crosscourt passing shot by him on the next. Emerson wrapped up a 3–2 Australian victory the next afternoon, running like a greyhound and whacking piercing ground strokes and volleys to sear

McKinley, 3–6, 6–2, 6–4, 6–4, sending the Davis Cup back to Melbourne.

The French, Italian and German titles, the three biggest on continental clay, all went to Europeans. Manolo Santana beat Pietrangeli, 6–3, 6–1, 4–6, 7–5, in a rematch of their more memorable meeting in the Parisian final three years earlier; Jan Erik Lundquist of Sweden won in Rome,

of the arms, face and hands, In the final, it was not the sun's rays but Bueno who blistered her, 6–1, 6–0, in just 25 minutes.

Bueno thus usurped Smith's throne as the No.1 player, even though her record of 82–10 and seven titles was not quite as formidable as Smith's 67–2 and 13 championships. Smith had a 39-match winning streak at one point in the season.

illness and Smith had slipped from her.

Smith beat her countrywoman Lesley Turner 6–3, 6–2, in the Australian singles, and Bueno, 5–7, 6–1, 6–2, at Paris. Bueno beat Smith only once in three meetings, but it was the most important: the final at Wimbledon, 6–4, 7–9, 6–3. This was a match of almost unbearable tension, a patchwork of glorious shots and awful ones, and Bueno ultimately controlled her nerves better. Smith seemed more serene beforehand, but her anxiety showed in her usually oppressive serve. She was a little tentative, and double-faulted badly on several key points. "I guess I beat myself. I felt pressure all the way," she said afterward. "It was like beating my head against a wall."

Karen Hantze Susman, the 1962 Wimbledon champion who was back for a fling after temporary retirement for childbirth, troubled Smith in the first round at Wimbledon and beat her in the fourth round at Forest Hills. That paved the way for Bueno, who raced through the championship without losing a set. In the final she met surprising Carole Caldwell Graebner, who had resolutely upset Susman and Nancy Richey despite suffering from painful second-degree sunburns

with Darlene Hard, the U.S. No.1 of the past four years, retired to a teaching pro career, the U.S. relinquished the Federation Cup to Australia, 2–1, in the final of a 24-nation assemblage in Philadelphia. Smith beat Moffitt, 6–2, 6–3, and Turner did in top-ranked American Nancy Richey, 7–5, 6–1, rendering Moffitt-Susman's three-set victory over Smith-Turner meaningless.

Richey and Moffitt won both their singles, over Deidre Catt and Ann Haydon Jones, and Carole Graebner added a victory over Elizabeth Starkie as the U.S. swept the singles and the Wightman Cup at Wimbledon, 5–2.

Most of the men pros were scattered around the globe, playing the odd exhibition here and there, badly disorganized. Ken Rosewall, the pro king, was observed playing Pancho Segura in a shopping-center parking lot in Los Angeles.

One who thought this was wrong was Ed Hickey of the New England Merchants National Bank in Boston, who convinced his boss to put up $10,000 in sponsorship money to revive the U.S. Pro Championships. John Bottomley, president of

Longwood Cricket Club, threw his support to the project. Jack Kramer was enlisted to contact the far-flung gypsies and put together a short summer tournament circuit with $80,000 in prize money. A dozen pros were assembled and Rod Laver won the climactic event at Longwood over Pancho Gonzalez, 4–6, 6–3, 7–5, 6–4, in a rainstorm that turned the grass into a quagmire.

It was a humble renaissance with a $2,200 first prize, but the U.S. Pro, the longest-running pro tourney, somehow stayed in business and was to become a fixture at Longwood, as was Laver. He won there four more times. It wasn't strawberries-and-cream. *à la* Wimbledon, but the pros were on the rocky road to a comeback.

1965

The gloom of a drizzly, gray September afternoon in Forest Hills was pierced by Spanish singing and dancing, and the unmistakable click of castanets filled the old concrete stadium of the West Side Tennis Club. There were loud choruses of *"Olé!"* and *"Bravo, Manolo!"* The discreet charm of the bourgeoisie that so long characterized tennis audiences gave way to unabashed Latin celebration as Manolo Santana beat South African Cliff Drysdale in four absorbing sets, 6–2, 7–9, 7–5, 6–1, to become the first Spaniard to win the U.S. singles title.

The balletic and crowd-pleasing Santana, age 28, provided other occasions for rejoicing in 1965, but few places came alive as Forest Hills did when a troupe of entertainers from the Spanish Pavilion at the nearby World's Fair arrived to urge him on with an up-tempo Latin beat. Santana was arguably the No. 1 amateur in the world, winning 10 of 16 tournaments, compiling a 71–7 record, and a 25-match winning streak, longest of the season. He did not enter Wimbledon, devoting his

The Spanish reign: Manolo Santana defeats South Africa's Cliff Drysdale for the 1965 U.S. Singles crown. • *UPI*

summer instead to Davis Cup preparation and duty on clay. Such diligence paid off. Santana and teammates Juan Gisbert and José Luis Arilla bumped off the United States in the inter-zone semifinals in Barcelona and carried Spain to the challenge round for the first time.

Not that Spanish music replaced "Waltzing Matilda" as the anthem of the world tennis empire. Australia won the Cup again, for the 14th time since 1950, as Roy Emerson and Fred Stolle gunned down Santana & Company, 4–1, at Sydney. Australians also captured the Federation Cup and all the other Grand Slam singles titles, men's and women's. Most of the finals were all-Aussie affairs.

Emerson outslugged Stolle, who seemed capable of beating anybody else, from two sets down in the Australian final, 7–9, 2–6, 6–4, 7–5, 6–1. John Newcombe and Tony Roche, the latest in a long line of great Aussie pairs, took their first major doubles title.

Roche, a ruggedly muscular left-hander with an unerring backhand volley, spoiled Emerson's latest vision of a Grand Slam in the French semifinals. With his chief nemesis out of the way, Stolle prevailed in Paris over Roche, 3–6, 6–0, 6–2, 6–3—winning his first major title after being runner-up in

This time it was easier than in 1964, 6–2, 6–4, 6–4. Newcombe and Roche won the first of their five Wimbledon doubles titles together.

At Forest Hills, where there had been all Aussie finals seven of the last nine years, none of the men from Down Under made the semis, however. Charlie Pasarell ambushed Stolle in the second round, and Arthur Ashe, who was to gain the No. 2 U.S. ranking behind Dennis Ralston, delivered big serves and fatal backhands in enough glorious clusters to topple Emerson.

Santana, shrewdly changing speeds and spins as he danced around the turf, erased Ashe in a four-set semifinal. Drysdale, who had beaten Ralston in a five-set quarterfinal, got by Mexican Rafe Osuna in the other half. Santana vs. Drysdale was thoughtful tennis, much of it from the backcourt, between two intelligent and stylish men. Two-fisted backhands would become common after Chris Evert arrived six years later, but Drysdale's was the first to be seen in a U.S. final. Rain interrupted the match and made the footing slick, but it couldn't dampen Santana's flashy shotmaking or the castanets.

Emerson and Stolle were unbeaten in doubles on the U.S. circuit, winning six tournaments and 31 matches, a run climaxed by a 6–4, 10–12, 7–5, 6–4 triumph over Pasarell and Frank Froehling in the National Doubles final at Longwood .

Emerson won seven of 22 tournaments in singles for an 85–16 record. He was 0–2 against Santana, demolished on clay in the

Spain had similarly won the first three matches against the U.S., heralding three years of nightmares for the *Americanos* on red clay in Latin countries. Chuck McKinley had retired to stockbrokering, leaving Ralston to head the U.S. contingent, and it was his demise to the inspired play of Gisbert after leading 6–3, 4–1 that paved the way for a 4–1 U.S. defeat. Santana jolted Froehling in three straight sets and joined with Arilla to break the hearts of Ralston and Clark Graebner, 4–6, 3–6, 6–3, 6–4, 11–9.

Australia beat the United States, 2–1, in the final of the Federation Cup at Kooyong in Melbourne. Lesley Turner beat Carole Graebner, 6–3, 2–6, 6–3, and Margaret Smith stopped Billie Jean Moffitt, 6–4, 8–6, in the singles.

Smith, 23, won three of the major singles titles in one season for the second time in her still ascending career. She beat Maria Bueno, who retired with an injury while trailing 2–5 in the final set in the Australian final; Bueno again at Wimbledon, 6–4, 7–5; and Moffitt at Forest Hills, 8–6, 7–5. The only match that prevented a Grand Slam was the final of the French, which she lost to Turner, 6–3, 6–4.

After that, Smith didn't lose another all year, piling up 58 consecutive victories for a season record of 103–7, including 18 titles in 25 tournaments.

Bueno, 25, won the Italian Championship and two other of the 11 tournaments she entered, finishing 40–8 in a year in which she was hampered by a knee injury that required surgery. She played Forest Hills against the advice of her doctor, losing to Moffitt in the semis.

Moffitt led Smith by 5–3 in both sets of the Forest Hills final, and had two set points in the second. Even though she lost, Moffitt later said this was a turning-point match in her career, adding a great deal to her self-awareness. She knew that the forehand she had gone to Australia to rebuild from scratch the previous year was coming around, complementing her exquisite backhand and volleying, and that she had the ability to rival Smith for No. 1. Billie Jean married Larry King shortly after Forest Hills, and she knew she was coming of age as a player.

She was co-ranked No. 1 in the U.S. with Nancy Richey, an unprecedented decision by the USTA ranking committee. Moffitt had shone on the grass court circuit, which Richey avoided after winning the U.S. Indoor and Clay Court. Both were 1–1 in singles in the 5–2 U.S. victory over Britain in the Wightman Cup.

Richey and Carole Graebner (whose husband, Clark, ranked No. 13 among the U.S. men and would return to the Top Ten the next year) earned the top U.S. ranking in doubles after winning the Nationals at Longwood. They beat defending champs Moffitt and Karen Susman in the final, 6–4, 6–4.

Turner teamed with Judy Tegart to win the Australian doubles and with Smith to take the French. Moffitt captured her third title at Wimbledon with her second

Maria Bueno (left) and Billie Jean Moffitt won the Wimbledon doubles in 1965, marking the fourth time that the Brazilian beauty had been a winner in this event. • *UPI*

partner, Maria Bueno. Smith and Ken Fletcher won the French, Wimbledon and U.S. mixed doubles. They might well have repeated their 1963 Grand Slam, but the mixed final of the Australian was abandoned because of bad weather.

The itinerant pros of tennis were still trying to organize. Mike Davies, Butch Buchholz and Barry MacKay were among the driving forces behind the International Professional Tennis Players' Association (IPTPA) formed in 1965 to try to give some structure to the amorphous, struggling pro game. The U.S. Pro Championships returned to Longwood, Ken Rosewall regaining the title he had won in 1963—and getting paid, albeit modestly, this time—by beating Rod Laver, 6–4, 6–3, 6–3.

Patrician scoring reformer Jimmy Van Alen of Newport, R.I., whose "Van Alen Streamlined Scoring System" (VASSS) became the basis for "sudden death" tie-breakers in 1970, hosted a pro tournament at famed Newport Casino, where the U.S. Championships had been played from their inauguration in 1881 until 1914. Van Alen put up $10,000 in prize money, on the condition that the pros use his radical VASSS round-robin, medal-play format, in which every point counted and each was worth $5. The players were happy to play

There were no one-man or one-woman gangs, as the game's major titles got spread around. For the first time since 1948, no

Australia's Fred Stolle, unseeded, defeated countryman Roy Emerson in the semis and John Newcombe in the final to win at Forest Hills in 1966. • *UPI*

player, man or woman, captured more than one of the four major singles crowns.

Fred Stolle, thought to be past his prime at age 27, didn't win a single tournament until August, then came on like the old Australian Mafia. He won the German Championship on clay and took the U.S. title at Forest Hills unseeded. There he routed nemesis Roy Emerson in the semifi-

Davis Cup challenge round. That was the climax of his amateur career as he turned pro at the end of the year.

Stolle's Davis Cup accomplice, Emerson, started the year by grabbing his national championship for the fourth consecutive time. In the final he extinguished Arthur Ashe—who had burned up the Australian circuit, winning four of seven tournaments—6–4, 6–8, 6–2, 6–3. Emmo teamed with Stolle to win the doubles, and they went on to post the year's best doubles record, adding the Italian, South African and U.S. Championships.

Emerson was perhaps never in better condition or form than at the start of Wimbledon, where he was keen to become the first man to win three successive singles titles since Fred Perry in 1934–35–36. He looked as if he would until fate and his own eagerness intervened during his quarterfinal against fellow Aussie Owen Davidson. Richard Evans described what happened in *World Tennis*:

"The first set took Emerson precisely 14 minutes to win 6–1. His first service was going in, his volleys were crisp and accurate, his ground-strokes laden with power and spin. There was no danger in sight unless it lay in the greasy, rain-slicked turf and of this, surely, Emerson was aware. So it surprised many people when he raced for a Davidson drop-volley in the third game of the second set. And it horrified us all when he skidded headlong into the umpire's chair and brought the BBC microphone crashing down on top of him. He was up in a moment, flexing his left shoulder and telling Davidson that he thought he had heard something snap. In fact he had torn the shoulder ligaments—an injury that, in a fatal second, had shattered a dream, ruined weeks of arduous preparation and deprived Wimbledon of its champion."

Manolo Santana, the clay-court artist who had proved himself a man for all surfaces by winning Forest Hills on grass the previous year, inherited the throne that Emerson abdicated, and he was a popular champion. Grinning and playing extraordinary shots when behind, he beat Ken Fletcher and then Davidson, both in deuced fifth sets, to get to the final. There he eliminated Dennis Ralston, who had more firepower but less control, 6–4, 11–9, 6–4.

But Santana had his own problems with injuries during the season—a bad shoulder that plagued him as Spain, the 1965 runner-up, went out to Brazil in the Davis Cup elimination rounds, and a bad ankle that reduced his Forest Hills' defense to a limp.

It was not Santana but Australian lefty Tony Roche who was the 1966 man of the year on clay. He won the Italian and French singles, beating Hungarian road-runner Istvan Gulyas in the Paris final, 6–1, 6–4, 7–5. Thereafter ankle problems sapped his effectiveness as well.

So who was the world's No. 1 amateur? Take your pick. Stolle won four of 19 tournaments, 70 of 85 matches; Emerson won eight of 16 tournaments, including the rising South African Championships, and 67

of 78 singles; Santana was 52–16, winning only two of 17 tournaments, but one of those was the biggest: Wimbledon; Roche played the most ambitious schedule, winning 10 of 29 tournaments and 106 of 125 matches.

Ralston, generally considered No. 5 in the world, was top-ranked in the U.S. for the third year in a row, the first man so honored since Don Budge in 1936–37–38, but frustrated by his failure to win a Grand Slam singles title. He turned pro with Stolle at the end of the year, leaving Ashe—a lieutenant in the U.S. Army—as heir apparent.

Ralston did have one particularly satisfying doubles triumph, teaming with Clark Graebner to become the first American champions of France since 1955. Their final-round victims, little known until later, were the hulking Romanian Ion Tiriac and his wet-behind-the-ears but gifted protégé, Ilie Nastase. Ralston and Graebner were runners-up for the U.S. title at Longwood to Emerson-Stolle, 6–4, 6–4, 6–4. Newcombe, separated from regular partner Roche, won the Wimbledon doubles anyway, with Ken Fletcher.

It was a dark year for the U.S. in the Davis Cup as captain George MacCall's team was bushwhacked, 3–2, by unheralded Brazil at Porto Alegre. Cliff Richey was upset in singles by both Edison Mandarino and Tom Koch, and Mandarino took Ralston in the fifth match, 4–6, 6–4, 4–6, 6–4, 6–1.

The most successful American player was the No. 1 woman, Billie Jean King, who won her first Wimbledon singles title at age 23 and spearheaded successful team efforts in the Federation and Wightman Cups. A virus infection diminished her effectiveness later, but Billie Jean won 10 of 16 tournaments and compiled a 57–8 record, best in the world.

Nancy Richey, co-ranked No. 1 with Billie Jean in 1965, slipped to No. 2 despite reaching the finals of the Australian, French and U.S. singles, and winning six of 14 tournaments, with a 55–9 record. She also won her fourth straight U.S. Clay Court title (her younger brother Cliff won the men's title for an unprecedented family "double"), and won three of the major doubles titles: the Australian with Carole Graebner, and Wimbledon and the U.S. with Maria Bueno.

semimals of Wimbledon, she announced her retirement at age 24 to open a clothing boutique in Perth—the first of several short-lived retirements, as it turned out.

Ann Haydon Jones won her second French singles over Richey, 6–3, 6–1, the American having been spent in a semifinal victory over Smith.

King was magnificently aggressive at Wimbledon. With grass staining her knees on the low volleys, she played better than anyone else, as her husband of less than a year sat nervously in the competitors' guest stand. Having dispatched one old rival, Smith, in the semis, she did in another, Bueno, in the final, 6–3, 3–6, 6–1, then tossed her racket high in the air and squealed with glee.

King, Julie Heldman and Carole Graebner carried the U.S. to a 3–0 victory over surprise finalist West Germany in the Federation Cup on clay at Turin, Italy. King, Richey, Mary Ann Eisel and Jane Albert were the Americans who played in a 4–3 Wightman Cup victory over Great Britain at Wimbledon. Richey and Eisel contributed the decisive point in doubles, over Elizabeth Starkie and Rita Bentley.

Maria Bueno captured her fourth Forest Hills title—the last of her seven major singles crowns—by beating Richey, 6–3, 6–1, with an all-court display of grace and shotmaking magic that completely thwarted Richey's backcourt game. They had teamed for the doubles title at Longwood, 6–3, 6–4, over the new but potent partnership of King and Rosemary Casals, but in the singles final Bueno treated

competition: Roger Taylor of Britain defeated Wieslaw Gasiorek of Poland, 27–29, 31–29, 6–4, on a slick wood surface in a King's Cup match that stretched until the early hours of a bitterly cold Warsaw morning; and American Kathy Blake outlasted Elena Subirats of Mexico, 12–10, 6–8, 14–12 on grass at the Piping Rock Country Club.

The pros had decided to cast their fate to small tournament-format events rather than head-to-head tours, as in the past, but the going was still rough. The U.S. Pro at Longwood remained an encouraging beacon, lighting the future, and Rod Laver signaled his takeover from Ken Rosewall as the pro king, beating "Muscles," 6–4, 4–6, 6–2, 8–10, 6–3.

1967

By sweeping the singles titles at Wimbledon and Forest Hills, Australian John Newcombe and Californian Billie Jean King reigned as the king and queen of amateur tennis in 1967, the last year of the amateur era. By the end of the year two professional troupes—World Championship Tennis (WCT) and the National

Tennis League (NTL)—had been formed, Newcombe and a half dozen other leading amateur men had turned pro, and a successful eight-man pro tournament had been played on the Centre Court at Wimbledon. These were all factors in a rebellion destined to change forever the old order in tennis.

The call to revolution was sounded in December 1967. Despite a threat of expulsion from the ITF which had again voted against Open Tennis at its midyear annual meeting, the British Lawn Tennis Association voted at year's end to remove the distinction between amateur and professional players in their country. It declared that tournaments in Britain in 1968, including Wimbledon, would be open to pros and amateurs alike. This hard-line stand by one of its oldest and most influential member nations ultimately forced the ILTF's hand on the "open" question that had been festering for four decades. Progressives, when they got the enormous prestige of Wimbledon behind them, finally carried the day.

Early in the year, such upheaval did not seem to be in prospect. The USTA hired Robert Malaga, a successful promoter of Wightman Cup and Davis Cup matches in his hometown of Cleveland, as its first full-time executive secretary and signed a product-endorsement agreement with Licensing Corporation of America.

The competitive year began the same way the previous four had, with Roy Emerson winning his native Australian singles title. Arthur Ashe was his victim in the final for the second straight year, this time in straight sets: 6–4, 6–1, 6–4. The triumph was Emerson's sixth in seven years, but he was unable to defend his doubles crown. Newcombe and Tony Roche, who would go on to win the French and U.S. doubles as well, beat Owen Davidson and Bill Bowrey in a rousing final, 3–6, 6–3, 7–5, 6–8, 8–6.

Billie Jean King and John Newcombe display their trophies in 1967 after winning the U.S. Singles. • *UPI*

Nancy Richey, runner-up as Margaret Smith won her seventh consecutive singles title the year before, took advantage of Margaret's temporary retirement to capture the women's title with a 6–1, 6–4 triumph over Lesley Turner. Turner and Judy Tegart captured the doubles.

Turner upended Maria Bueno, 6–3, 6–3, in the Italian final and won the first set of the French final before losing it to Francoise Durr, whose 4–6, 6–3, 6–4 victory was the first by a native woman at Paris since Simone Mathieu in 1939. Durr teamed with Australian Gail Sherriff, who was later to marry Frenchman Jean Baptiste Chanfreau and move to France, for the first of five consecutive doubles titles—two with Ann Jones and then two more with Mme. Chanfreau.

Emerson, fit as ever, powered his way to the French men's singles title, dethroning fellow Aussie Roche in the final, 6–1, 6–4, 2–6, 6–2. Roche had earlier lost his Italian title to Marty "Martino Mulligano" Mulligan.

Having cleared the troublesome hurdle of Parisian clay, Emerson set his sights again on the elusive Grand Slam, but his vision was shattered in the fourth round at Wimbledon by tall Yugoslav Nikki Pilic. Emerson was the favorite after the startling first-round ambush of Manolo Santana by American Charlie Pasarell in the curtain-raiser on Centre Court, the only time a defending champion and No. 1 seed was

nerve condition nearly cost him the U.S. Doubles championship, which was decided for the 46th and last time at Longwood Cricket Club, but he and Roche pulled through over Bowrey and Davidson. His lower back was still worrying "Newc" going into the U.S. singles, but he experienced no ill effects in plowing to victory at Forest Hills with the loss of but four sets.

rugged Yorkshireman Roger Taylor, both left-handers, were unseeded semifinalists, as was Germany's Wilhelm Bungert.

Bungert erased Taylor, but was spent by the final and offered only token, half-hearted resistance as Newcombe claimed the title, 6–3, 6–1, 6–1, equaling the most lopsided postwar men's finals (Lew Hoad over Ashley Cooper in 1957 and Rod Laver over Mulligan in 1962).

In doubles, Newcombe and Roche—reunited and favored to regain the title—fell in the quarters to Englishmen Graham Stilwell and Peter Curtis. The title went to the newly minted South African Davis Cup team of Bob Hewitt (who, as an Australian, had won twice with Fred Stolle) and Frew McMillan. They drubbed Emerson and Fletcher, winner the previous year with Newcombe, 6–2, 6–3, 6–4.

Cumulative attendance for the last amateur Wimbledon exceeded 300,000 for the first time, as 301,896 spectators went through the turnstiles.

Newcombe took the No. 1 world ranking at age 23 by winning eight of 24 tournaments and 83 of 99 matches. A sciatic

6–4, 7–5 semifinal victory over Jan Leschly, the clever and sporting left-handed Dane. Newcombe outslugged Graebner, seeking to become the first native champ since 1955, in a serve-and-volley final, 6–4, 6–4, 8–6.

Sharing attention with the winners at Forest Hills were the much-publicized steel rackets used by women's champ Billie Jean King, Rosemary Casals, Graebner and Gene Scott, among others. Wilson's equipment innovation, adapted from a French design pioneered by clothier and ex-champion René Lacoste, was the harbinger of a wave of new racket designs and materials that flooded the market in the next decade. Scott, then a 29-year-old Wall Street lawyer and part-time player who would later become the self-styled Renaissance Man of tennis in the '70s, fulfilled many a Walter Mitty fantasy by working mornings in his office and taking the train to Forest Hills, where he reached the semis before Newcombe jolted him back to reality. Scott predicted that wood rackets would soon be obsolete, but his accurate prophecy did not come to pass immediately.

Woman of the Year in tennis in 1967 was Billie Jean Moffitt King, 24, who scored triples—victories in singles, doubles and mixed doubles—at both Wimbledon and Forest Hills. Only Don Budge in 1938 and Alice Marble in 1939 had achieved this feat previously.

Billie Jean also won all her singles in leading the United States to victories in the Federation and Wightman Cups. She teamed with Rosie Casals to sweep past Rhodesia, South Africa, Germany and Great Britain without losing a match in the Federation Cup on clay at Berlin, and with Nancy Richey, Carole Graebner and Mary Ann Eisel for 6–1 triumph over Great Britain at Cleveland. Richey won the decisive fourth point with a gritty 3–6, 8–6, 6–2 victory over Virginia Wade despite a pulled muscle in her back that pained her through the last six games.

King compiled a 68–5 record during the ranking season and won 10 tournaments. In addition to seizing the Wimbledon and Forest Hills titles without losing a set, she won the U.S. Indoor and the South African Championship, and had the season's two longest winning streaks: 23 and 25 matches. In Johannesburg she scored another triple, teaming triumphantly with Casals (her partner in U.S. and Wimbledon doubles victories) and Aussie Owen Davidson (her partner in French, Wimbledon, and U.S. Mixed Doubles Championships). Davidson scored a Mixed Grand Slam, having first teamed with Lesley Turner to win the Australian title.

King beat Ann Jones, the tenacious British left-hander, in the Wimbledon final, 6–3, 6–4, and again in the Forest Hills title match, 11–9, 6–4. In the latter, Jones ignored a pulled hamstring and gallantly fought off nine match points before succumbing. Injuries had influenced the women's singles from the outset, four-time champion Maria Bueno pulling out with tendinitis in the right arm and Nancy Richey with the back ailment sustained in the Wightman Cup.

Richey had earlier won her fifth consecutive U.S. Clay Court title, gunning down Casals after little Rosie conquered King in the semis. Arthur Ashe, whose duties as a lieutenant in the U.S. Army kept him out of Wimbledon and Forest Hills, won the men's title for the only time, beating Marty Riessen. Ashe was ranked second in the U.S. behind Pasarell, who beat him twice in three meetings: in the finals of the U.S. Indoor and in the Richmond Indoor, in Ashe's hometown.

The U.S. outdoor season survived what is believed to be the longest (147 games) tournament match of all time, in the doubles of the Newport (R.I.) Casino Invitational. Dick Leach and Dick Dell defeated Len Schloss and Tom Mozur, 3–6, 49–47, 22–20. The marathon consumed six hours and 10 minutes over two days, and undoubtedly provided impetus for the scoring reform championed by Newport's Jimmy Van Alen—whose "sudden death" tie-breaker, designed to terminate such monster matches, was finally adopted in 1970.

For the third consecutive year under hapless captain George MacCall, the U.S. Davis Cup team was upset on foreign soil—slow, red clay. The 1967 loss to Ecuador at Guayaquil was the most ignominious of all, undoubtedly the most startling upset in the long history of Davis Cup competition. Ecuador's two players, Pancho Guzman and Miguel Olvera, were barely known internationally.

Cliff Richey, the most comfortable of the Americans on clay, won the first and inconsequential fifth matches, but the middle three spelled disaster for the United States. Olvera, a 26-year-old who had been sidelined by tuberculosis, beat Ashe—who had not lost a set in his 10 previous Cup matches—4–6, 6–4, 6–4, 6–2. Ecuadorian captain Danny Carrera was so thrilled he attempted to leap the net to embrace Olvera, tripped and broke his leg. Still, the

1–1 score did not seem too worrisome for the U.S. until the scrambling Olvera and his 21-year-old sidekick Guzman overcame a 0–6, 2–5, deficit and stunned Americans Riessen and Graebner, 0–6, 9–7, 6–4, 4–6, 8–6, setting the stage for a raucous third day. The giddy crowd of 2,200 at the Guayaquil Tennis Club cheered wildly for their sudden heroes and unsettled the Americans with a shower of abuse. Panic

and young Ray Moore gave the South Africans three formidable singles players, and Hewitt-McMillan was the doubles team of the year. (Their 53–1 record included victories in the Italian, Wimbledon and South African Championships, plus seven other tournaments. Newcombe-Roche won 12 of 19 tournaments, including the Australian, French and U.S.)

But Hewitt broke his ankle in the quarterfinal series against India and was unavailable for the semis, in which Spain eliminated South Africa, 3–2. In Australia for the challenge round for the second time in three years, Spain was outclassed again. Emerson took advantage of one of Santana's rare poor matches and won the opener in a rout, 6–4, 6–1, 6–1. Newcombe swamped 18-year-old Cup rookie lefty Manuel Orantes, 6–3, 6–3, 6–2, then teamed with Roche to scald Santana Orantes, 6–4, 6–4, 6–4, losing only 16 points in 15 service games. The 3–0 lead assured Australia's 15th Cup victory in 18 years.

Emerson blasted Orantes, ending a peerless Davis Cup career in which he won 11 of 12 singles matches plus six doubles matches in nine challenge rounds, eight of

them won by Australia. Newcombe's last match as an amateur was not as successful. He lost to Santana, making the final score 4–1.

Immediately after the challenge round, Newcombe, Roche, Emerson and Davidson turned pro. Newcombe and Roche signed with New Orleans promoter Dave Dixon, who—bankrolled by Texas oil-

England Club and Britain's national coach.

The formation of WCT's "Handsome Eight" barnstorming troupe had an enormous impact on the amateur tennis establishment. In one day, Dixon and his partner Bob Briner, a tennis neophyte who would later become executive director of the Association of Tennis Professionals, signed Newcombe, Roche, Nikki Pilic and Roger Taylor, accounting for three of the 1967 Wimbledon semifinalists. Dennis Ralston had been their first signee, and they soon added Cliff Drysdale, Butch Buchholz and Pierre Barthes.

"We had in one fell swoop taken all the stars out of the game. If anyone was ever going to see them again at Wimbledon and Forest Hills, the ITF had to make an accommodation," Briner remembers. "Open tennis came about so fast after that, it was pitiful."

The stage for the "British Revolution" that ultimately pierced the reactionary armor of the ILTF had been set for some time. The press was agitating against the hypocrisy of the "shamateur" system. For years Herman David, chairman of the All England Club, had denounced shamateurism as "a living lie" and urged open competition. He allowed Wimbledon's Centre Court to be used for an eight-man pro tournament sponsored and televised by the British Broadcasting Corporation in August 1967. Laver, who had won 14 straight singles matches at Wimbledon in his last amateur appearances (1961–62), beat Rosewall in a final of much higher standard than Newcombe's romp over Bungert a month earlier. This whetted the public's appetite for open tennis.

When the ITF, at its 1967 annual meeting in Luxembourg, turned down by a 139–83 vote a British proposal for a limited number of open tournaments in 1968, the British refused to accept the verdict.

"It seems that we have come to the end of the road constitutionally," said David, who vowed that Wimbledon would continue to be the world's premier tournament, with a field commensurate with that reputation, even if it had to "go it alone" as a pioneer of open competition. Britain's LTA took an unconstitutional, revolutionary step by voting overwhelmingly at its December meeting to make British tournaments open in 1968.

The ITF threatened to expel the British from the international organization, but its hand had been forced. A number of compromises later, open tennis became a reality in 1968, through in a much more limited and qualified way than the British had envisioned.

5: THE OPEN ERA: 1968–92

starched white flannel past and became a favored diversion of the modern leisure class—attired in pastels and playing tie-breaker sets in public parks and clubs. They were equipped with a bewildering variety of gear, from optic yellow, heavy-duty balls to double-strung graphite rackets.

All this was inspired by the advent of Open Tennis in 1968. If competition between amateur and professionals did not trigger the tennis boom single-handedly, it unquestionably fueled it. By making tennis at the top level professional, honest, and unabashedly commercial, open competition ushered in an era of dramatic growth and development.

For an expanding group of pros, this was boomtime, a veritable bonanza of opportunities. They enjoyed and reaped the benefits of a Brave New World of televised matches and two-fisted backhands, evolution of technique and technology, full-blown tours for women and over-45s, exposure and prize money undreamed of even by Wimbledon champions in the pre-open era.

1968 truly a watershed year for tennis.

The British "revolt" of December 1967, reinforced by the USTA's vote in favor of Open Tennis at its annual meeting in February 1968, led to the emergency meeting of the ITF at Paris and approval of 12 open tournaments for 1968.

Unfortunately, the hypocrisy and confusion of the "shamateur" period was not done away with quickly and cleanly. Rather than accept the British proposal that all competitors would be referred to simply as "players," abolishing the distinction between amateur and professional, the ITF bowed to heavy pressure from Eastern European countries and their voting allies and effected a compromise that called for four classifications:

1. Amateurs, who would not accept prize money.

2. Teaching professionals, who could compete with amateurs only in open events.

3. "Contract professionals," who made their living playing tennis but did not

accept the authority of their national associations affiliated to the ITF, signing guaranteed contracts instead with independent promoters.

4. "Registered players," who could accept prize money in open tournaments but still accepted the authority of their national associations and retained eligibility for amateur events including the Davis, Federation, and Wightman Cups.

The prime example of this strange and short-lived new breed was Dutchman Tom Okker, who won the Italian and South African Championships (not yet prize-money events) and was runner-up to Arthur Ashe in the first U.S. Open at Forest Hills. Okker pocketed $14,000 in prize money while Ashe, then a lieutenant in the U.S. Army and a member of the Davis Cup team, had to remain an amateur (the USTA had not yet adopted the "registered player" concept) and received only $28 per day expenses.

Other ludicrous examples abounded. Margaret Court, for instance, won and

It was a landmark year for tennis, and Army Lt. Arthur Ashe, winning the first U.S. Open in 1968, helped make it memorable. • *UPI*

accepted nearly $10,000 in open tournaments in Britain, then came to America and played in the U.S. Amateur in Boston for expenses only, beating old rival Maria Bueno in the final.

But despite such anomalies of the transition period, great progress had undeniably been made toward a more honest and prosperous international game.

The first open tournament, a month after the concept was approved at the conference table, was the British Hard Court Championships (in Europe, "hard court" refers to a clay surface, not concrete or similar hard surface as the term is used in the U.S.) at the coastal resort of Bournemouth. History was made on a drizzly, raw Monday, April 22. The "open era" began with an undistinguished young Briton, John Clifton, winning the first point but losing his match against Australian pro Owen Davidson—then the British national coach—on the red shale courts of the West Hants Lawn Tennis Club.

The field at Bournemouth was not as distinguished as the historic nature of the occasion warranted. The "Handsome Eight" of World Championship Tennis were off playing their own tour, leaving the professional portion of the field to come from George MacCall's National Tennis League, plus Davidson and former Chilean Davis Cupper Luis Ayala, then a coach in Puerto Rico, who paid his own way to take part. The top-line amateurs, wary of immediate confrontation with the pros, stayed away. None of the World Top Ten amateurs entered, and Englishman Bobby Wilson was the only amateur seeded. On the women's side, the only four pros at the time—Billie Jean King, Rosemary Casals, Francoise Durr and Ann Haydon Jones, who had just signed contracts with MacCall—were otherwise engaged.

The male pros were expected to dominate the amateur field of Englishmen and a few second-line Australians. But many of the pros were nervous; they knew their reputations were on the line, and the most discerning realized they were ill prepared, given long absence from best-of-five-set matches and exposure to new faces and playing styles.

Pancho Gonzalez particularly recognized the hazards posed by sudden emer-

Gonzalez, only a month from his 40th birthday, hadn't played a five-set match in five years, but his defeat sent shock waves through the tennis world. Buoyed by his instant celebrity, Cox ousted first-year pro Roy Emerson the next day to reach the semifinals.

Obviously the pros were not invincible—a notion that would be reinforced convincingly throughout the year. But the best of their number, Rod Laver and Ken Rosewall, proved they still inhabited the top echelon. Laver canceled Cox's heroic run in the semis, 6–4, 6–1, 6–0, and Rosewall—a man for all seasons whose longevity at the top level of international competition is unsurpassed—beat Laver in the title match, 3–6, 6–2, 6–0, 6–3.

Rosewall beat Laver again in the final of the second open, the French Championships, also on clay. The first of the traditional "Big Four" tournaments to be open, its field still lacked most of the top American men and Okker, but was stronger than Bournemouth had been.

The French was also memorable because it was played during the general

strike and student riots of 1968. Paris was a troubled, crippled city, without public transportation or essential services, but record crowds flocked to Stade Roland Garros on the western outskirts of the city—many by bicycle or on foot—because literally nothing else of a sporting nature was happening. Players, many of whom had harrowing true-life adventures getting to Paris, found accommodations within

a ladder.

"So the fortnight's excitement was two-edged: a revolution on the courts, and a whiff of revolution in the streets.... The first major open was played in the sort of environment that nightmares are made of. But the tennis was often like a dream."

In the quarterfinals, Laver was taken to five sets by the lumbering Romanian Ion Tiriac, one of numerous protracted struggles that kept the packed galleries gasping appreciatively. Laver then easily handled Gonzalez, who had enchanted spectators earlier, but in the final Rosewall again asserted his clay-court mastery, 6–3, 6–1, 2–6, 6–2.

The women's singles was also full of surprises. Amateurs Gail Sherriff (later Gail Chanfreau Lovera) and Elena Subirats eliminated pros Francoise Durr and Rosie Casals in straight sets. Nancy Richey, a clay-court specialist, beat Billie Jean King, who always preferred faster and more sure-footed surfaces, in the semifinals and won the title over the last of the four women pros, Ann Jones, who had been considered the world's leading lady on clay, 5–7, 6–4, 6–1. In the first set, Jones led, 5–1, but lost 11 of the next 13 points. In the second she led, 4–2, then lost 15 of the ensuing 16 points. "A fortnight earlier," Bellamy recalled of Richey, "she had asked anxiously: 'How do we get out of here?' Like the rest of us, she was glad she stayed."

There was more upheaval on the courts, amid the giddy jubilation of a once-in-a-lifetime occasion, at the first open Wimbledon. This was a richly sentimental fortnight, as legendary champions who had been stripped of their All England Club membership upon turning pro were welcomed back to the shrine of the game and again permitted to wear its mauve-and-green colors. Even old-time champions no longer able to compete came back for the festivities surrounding the enactment of a long-held dream. The tournament began with five days of intermittent rain, which held down crowds, but even this couldn't dampen soaring spirits.

Wimbledon was also the first of the open tournaments that every player of consequence entered. The seeding list for the men's singles read like a Who's Who of the present and immediate past: Laver, Rosewall, Andres Gimeno, defending champion John Newcombe, Emerson, Manolo Santana, Lew Hoad, Gonzales, Dennis Ralston, Butch Buchholz, Fred Stolle, Okker, Ashe, Cliff Drysdale, Tony Roche and Nikki Pilic.

There were numerous surprises, none more unsettling to the pros than the third-round defeat of Gimeno, the elegant Spaniard who was regarded as just a shade below Laver and Rosewall, by long-haired, unheralded, 21-year-old South African Ray Moore. Hoad was beaten by Bob Hewitt, and Gonzalez by Soviet Alex Metreveli in the same round, demonstrating again that the pros were unaccustomed to this Brave New World. Indeed, in the quarterfinals only two old pros—Laver and Buchholz—shared the stage with two recent pros (Ralston and Roche), three amateurs

(Clark Graebner, Ashe and Moore) and the lone "registered player," Okker.

Rosewall, who had won everything but Wimbledon as an amateur in the, '50s, was upset in the fourth round by the tricky left-handed spins of Roche, who went on to beat Buchholz and unseeded Graebner (conqueror of Santana, Stolle, and Moore) to reach the final. Laver got there by beating Gene Scott, Stan Smith, Marty Riessen, Cox, Ralston, and Ashe, then clobbered Roche, 6–3, 6–4, 6–2, in 59 minutes to again command the stage he had made his in 1961–62, and in the eight-man BBC pro event the summer before.

Having artfully made the pros' return to the premier championship of the game triumphant, Laver received $4,800, but said decisively that money had never entered his thoughts. "Wimbledon's first open tournament enabled this fine left-hander to prove his magnificent worth. Wimbledon endorsed his quality," wrote Lance Tingay of London's *Daily Telegraph*. "Equally, Laver endorsed Wimbledon's renewed status as the *de facto* world championship."

The cream also rose in the women's singles. Billie Jean King won her third consecutive singles title, equaling a feat last achieved by Maureen Connolly in 1952–54, over a surprise finalist: seventh-seeded Judy Tegart. An accomplished doubles player, this affable Australian earned her day in the sun by beating second-seeded Margaret Court in the quarters and third-seeded Nancy Richey in the semis, but King was not to be denied her throne. The scores of the final were 9–7, 7–5.

Billie Jean, weary and ill three weeks before the tournament, was pressed to three sets only in the semifinals. Ann Jones led her, 6–4, 5–4, 15–15, three points away from the match on her own serve. But BJK saved the next point with a lob and was off on a 13-point binge that carried her to 1–0 in the final set and out of trouble, 4–6, 7–5, 6–2, on a July 4 she could truly celebrate.

King also repeated her doubles triumph of 1967 with Casals, but was unable to defend the mixed doubles title with Owen Davidson for a second consecutive "triple." Australians Ken Fletcher (then playing out of Hong Kong) and Court ended their reign in the semis and went on

Graebner in four-set semis. Ashe simply had too much flashing firepower—26 aces, a lightning backhand, and superior volleying—for Okker in a superb final, 14–12, 5–7, 6–3, 3–6, 6–3. That was the first five-set final since Ashley Cooper over Mal Anderson a decade earlier, and produced the first native champion since Tony Trabert in 1955.

Hills, richest of the year's events, which was lavishly promoted by Madison Square Garden in the first year of an ultimately uneasy five-year contract with the USTA.

By the end of the summer, observers were no longer startled when amateurs knocked off pros, as Ray Moore did in repeating his Wimbledon victory over Andres Gimeno, this time in the first round. The biggest upsets were the fourth-round knockouts of the Wimbledon men's singles finalists: a badly off-form Laver by Cliff Drysdale, 4–6, 6–4, 3–6, 6–1, 6–1, and Roche by the clever and rejuvenated Gonzalez, 8–6, 6–4, 6–2.

Gonzalez, 40, the graying but still glorious "Old Wolf," was the darling of the crowds in the stadium where he had prevailed as a hungry young rebel with a cause in 1948–49, but the speedy "Flying Dutchman," Okker, was too fresh for him in the quarters. Gonzalez melted in a broiling sun, 14–16, 6–3, 10–8, 6–3.

Joining Okker in the semis were Rosewall (over Ralston), Ashe (over Drysdale), and Graebner (over defender John Newcombe). Okker was too quick for Rosewall, and Ashe was too powerful for

weeks earlier without losing a set, took the title, 11–9, 6–1, 7–5. They won 11 of 19 tournaments, 57 of 66 matches on the season, to claim the No. 1 U.S. doubles ranking for the first time.

Billie Jean King was unable to defend her title as she had done at Wimbledon. Like Laver, she was far from peak form and struggled three sets with Maryna Godwin in the quarters and Maria Bueno in the semis. Virginia Wade, a 23-year-old Englishwoman of regal bearing recently graduated from Sussex University with a degree in math and physics, beat BJK in the final, 6–4, 6–2. Wade had won at Bournemouth, but this was infinitely more impressive, as she beat Casals, Tegart, Jones and King in succession. Court and Bueno dislodged the defending champs, King and Casals, in the women's doubles finals.

There was only one other open tournament in the U.S., the Pacific Southwest at Los Angeles, and form held truer on concrete, Laver beating Rosewall in the final, 4–6, 6–0, 6–0. Casals beat Bueno for the women's title, 6–4, 6–1.

Despite Laver's Wimbledon triumph and No. 1 world ranking, Ashe was the

Man of the Year in tennis, winner of 10 tournaments to earn the No. 1 U.S. ranking for the first time after three straight years at No. 2. The first black male to win one of the Grand Slam titles, he triumphed at Forest Hills while commuting to his Army duties as a data processing instructor at West Point, N.Y. Ashe won 30 straight matches from the start of the Pennsylvania Grass Courts through the Inter-Service Championships (he beat Air Force Pfc. Pasarell, who plunged from No. 1 to No. 7 in the U.S. rankings, in the final), the U.S. Amateur, U.S. Open and the Las Vegas Invitational, to the semis of the Pacific Southwest. Also included were singles victories over Juan Gisbert and Manolo Santana in the 4–1 U.S. victory over Spain in the Davis Cup.

Ashe and Graebner were the singles players for the U.S. as it recaptured the Davis Cup for the first time since 1963 at Adelaide in December, recording a 4–1 victory over an Australian team depleted by the defection of Newcombe, Roche, Emerson and Davidson to the pro ranks. Imbued with great *esprit de corps* and dedication by 29-year-old captain Donald Dell, a former player, the Americans, (Ashe, Graebner, Smith, Lutz and Pasarell) trained hard and made winning back the Cup into, as Ashe called it, "a quest." They lost only three matches plowing through the West Indies, Mexico, Ecuador, Spain, India and Australia to end the three years of U.S. Davis Cup disaster.

Graebner beat Bill Bowrey (who had won the Australian Championships in January, before open competition was approved), and Ashe topped lefty Ray Ruffels, both after losing the first set, to give the U.S. a 2–0 lead. Smith and Lutz clinched the Cup by gunning down the makeshift pair of Ruffels and 17–year-old John Alexander, 6–4, 6–4, 6–2, in just 66 minutes.

There were a couple of other notable achievements during this landmark season.

Nancy Richey made one of the fantastic comebacks in tennis history to beat Billie Jean King, 4–6, 7–5, 6–0, in the semifinals of the Madison Square Garden International. BJK had a match point at 5–1 in the second set, and apparently had the match won with an angled overhead. Richey retrieved it and lobbed again, however, and this time King bungled the smash, then inexplicably collapsed. Richey ran 12 straight games thereafter, 39 of the last 51 points.

That was King's last match as an amateur. Within days she signed with George MacCall. Richey, who beat Tegart in the Garden final, took over the No. 1 ranking and finished 2–0 for the year over King by thwarting BJK's hoped-for revenge in the French. Richey also won her sixth straight U.S. Clay Court title, something only one player had previously achieved, Bill Tilden in 1922–27.

With King and Casals unavailable for duty in the still amateur women's team competitions, the U.S. relinquished both the Federation Cup (Netherlands beat the U.S. in the semis at Paris, then lost the final to Australia, 3–0) and the Wightman Cup (Wade and Christine Truman Janes led the British to a 4–3 victory at Wimbledon, their first since 1960).

The longest match on national championship record, in terms of elapsed playing time, took place at Salisbury, Md., when Englishmen Bobby Wilson and Mark Cox defeated Pasarell and Graebner, 26–24, 17–19, 30–28, in the U.S. Indoor doubles. The match consumed six hours, 20 minutes, and is the longest in terms of games, 144, in a U.S. Championship event.

1969

The second year of Open Tennis was one of continued progress but lingering confusion on the political front, and indis-

Australian Tony Roche in the 1969 Open final, took home the most money. • *UPI*

putably towering oncourt performances by Rod Laver and Margaret Court.

There were 30 open tournaments around the world and prize money escalated to about $1.3 million. Laver was the leading money-winner with $124,000, followed by Tony Roche ($75,045), Tom Okker ($65,451), Roy Emerson ($62,629) and John Newcombe ($52,610).

The Davis Cup and other international team competitions continued to be governed by reactionaries, however, and admitted only players under the jurisdiction of their national associations. This left "contract pros"—who were paid guarantees and committed by contract to play where scheduled by independent promoters—on the outs, while players who accepted prize money but remained under the aegis of their national associations were allowed to play. At the end of the year a proposal to end this silly double standard and allow "contract pros" back in was defeated by the Davis Cup nations on a 21–19 vote.

The "registered player" concept, borne of compromise a year earlier, persisted

until finally being abolished by a newly elected and more forward-looking ITF Committee of Management in July. Still, the public found it difficult to understand who was and who was not a pro. In the United States, those who took prize money but remained under the authority of the USTA were officially called "players." Under the leadership of captain Donald Dell, the members of the U.S. Davis Cup

Garden, U.S. Open, Pacific Southwest, Howard Hughes Invitational). This would have kept down spiraling overhead costs, a threat to the exclusive clubs, which resisted sponsorship but did not want to lose their traditional events. Dell and the Davis Cup team refused to play in tournaments that offered expenses and guarantees instead of prize money, however, and thus effectively forced a full prize-money circuit into being in the U.S.

Dell led the way by organizing the $25,000 Washington *Star* International in his hometown. It was a prototype tournament in many ways: commercially sponsored and played in a public facility for over-the-table prize money rather than under-the-table appearance fees. Other tournaments followed suit, and a new and successful U.S. Summer Circuit began to emerge. In all, 15 U.S. tournaments offered $440,000 in prize money, with the $137,000 U.S. Open again the world's richest event. In 1968, there had been only two prize-money open tournaments in the U.S., with combined purses of $130,000.

A few peculiar hybrid events—half amateur and half pro—remained. The most obviously unnecessary was the

$25,000 National Singles and Doubles at Longwood Cricket Club, which welcomed amateurs and independent pros but excluded the "contract pros." Stan Smith beat Bob Lutz, and Margaret Court prevailed over Virginia Wade for the singles titles, but the grandly named tournament was essentially meaningless and vanished from the scene the next year in a natural sorting-out process.

If the labels put on tournaments and players boggled the public mind, there was no doubt as to who the world's No. 1 players were: Australians Laver and Court were truly dominant.

Laver repeated his 1962 Grand Slam—something only he, Don Budge (1938) and Maureen Connolly (1953) had achieved—by sweeping the Australian, French, Wimbledon and U.S. titles the first year all four were open.

Laver also won the South African Open and finished the season with a 106–16 record for 32 tournaments, 17 of which he won. He didn't lose a match from the start of Wimbledon in June until the second round of the Pacific Southwest Open in late September, when Ray Moore ended the winning streak at 31 matches. During that stretch, Laver won seven tournaments, including his fourth Wimbledon (where he had not lost since the 1960 final), his second Forest Hills and his fifth U.S. Pro Championship. By the time he got to Los Angeles, Rod just wanted to get 45 minutes farther south to his adopted home of Corona Del Mar, Cal., where his wife, Mary, had just presented him with his first child, Rick Rodney.

The most difficult match for Laver of the 26 that comprised the Slam came early, in the semifinals of the Australian. He beat Tony Roche, 7–5, 22–20, 9–11, 1–6, 6–3, in a match that lasted more than four hours in the sweltering, 105-degree heat of a Brisbane afternoon. Both players got groggy in the brutal sun, even though they employed an old Aussie trick of putting wet cabbage leaves in their hats to help stay cool. It was so close that it could easily have gone either way, and a controversial line call helped Laver grasp the final set. Having survived, Laver beat Andres Gimeno in the final, 6–3, 6–4, 7–5.

His tall countryman, Dick Crealy, took the first two sets from Laver in a second-rounder at the French Championships, but the red-haired "Rocket" accelerated and ultimately played one of his best clay-court matches to beat Ken Rosewall in the final, 6–4, 6–3, 6–4.

An unheralded Indian named Premjit Lall similarly captured the first two sets in the second round at Wimbledon, but Laver awoke to dispose of him, 3–6, 4–6, 6–3, 6–0, 6–0. Stan Smith took Laver to five sets in the quarterfinals, and Arthur Ashe and John Newcombe to four in the semis and final, respectively. But despite Newcombe's thoughtful game plan of using lobs and changes of pace instead of the straightforward power for which he was known, Laver prevailed, 6–4, 5–7, 6–4, 6–4.

Then it was on to Forest Hills, where Philip Morris and its tennis-minded chairman of the board, Joe Cullman, had infused heavy promotional dollars into the U.S. Open and brought flamboyant South African promoter Owen Williams in from Johannesburg to run a jazzed-up show and foster corporate patronage. They drew record crowds until the weather turned surly. Rain inundated the already soft and uneven courts, played havoc with the schedule and pushed the tournament three days past its scheduled conclusion.

Despite the trying conditions and the imminent birth of his son on the West Coast, Laver remained intent on the task at hand. He was taken to five sets only by Dennis Ralston in the fourth round. After that Laver disposed of Roy Emerson in four sets, Arthur Ashe in three straight, and—after two days of rain—donned spikes in the second set to climb over Roche, 7–9, 6–1, 6–3, 6–2, on a gloomy Tuesday before a crowd of only 3,708 fans who sat through rain delays of 90 and 30 minutes.

The weather certainly dampened the occasion, but it was appropriate that Roche—clearly No. 2 in the world, and

The aging Pancho Gonzalez, still a crowd favorite, provided excitement in a new era. • *UPI*

Laver shed a few tears as USTA President Alastair Martin presented him the champion's trophy and check for $16,000, saying, "You're the greatest in the world… perhaps the greatest we've ever seen."

"I never really think of myself in those terms, but I feel honored that people see fit to say such things about me," said Laver shyly. "Tennis-wise, this year was much tougher than '62. At the time the best players—Ken Rosewall, Lew Hoad, Pancho Gonzalez—were not in the amateur ranks. I didn't find out who were the best until I turned pro and had my brains beaten out for six months at the start of 1963."

Now, in the open era, there was no question who was best.

Margaret Court, who had returned to action following a brief retirement (the first of several in her long career), was almost as monopolistic as Laver. She lost only five matches the entire season, winning 14 of 17 tournaments and 79 of 82 matches.

She won the Australian over Billie Jean King, 6–4, 6–1, after trailing Kerry Melville,

3–5, in the final set in the semis. In the French, Court beat Pat Pretorius Walkden, Melville, defending champ Nancy Richey and Ann Jones—all splendid clay-court players—in the last four rounds.

Court's dream of a Grand Slam ended at Wimbledon, however, where Ann Jones beat her in the semifinals, 10–12, 6–3, 6–2. To the unbridled joy of her British countrymen, the left-handed, 30-year-old Mrs. Pip Jones then won her first Wimbledon title after 14 years of trying, squashing Billie Jean King's bid for a fourth consecutive crown, 3–6, 6–3, 6–2. Billie Jean was shaken by the noisy partisanship of the customarily proper British gallery and what she thought were some dubious line calls, but the British extolled the popular Jones as a conquering heroine.

Court won the U.S. Open without losing a set. In fact, she lost more than two games in a set only twice in six matches, in beating fellow Aussie Karen Krantzcke in the quarters, 6–0, 9–7, and Virginia Wade in the semis, 7–5, 6–0. Nancy Richey—eschewing her usual baseline game for net-rushing tactics quite foreign to her—helped out by eliminating King in the quarters, 6–4, 8–6, but found herself passed repeatedly in the final by some of Court's finest groundstroking. The score was 6–2, 6–2.

But if Laver and Court clearly reigned supreme, there were other notable heroes and achievements in 1969.

Pancho Gonzalez, at 41, buried Peter Curtis, John Newcombe, Ken Rosewall, Stan Smith and Arthur Ashe in succession to win the $50,000 Howard Hughes Open at Las Vegas. Gonzalez also won the Pacific Southwest Open and had a 2–0 record over Smith, who was ranked No. 1 in the U.S. for the first time. Gonzalez was the top U.S. money-winner with $46,288, and might have returned to the No. 1 spot he occupied in 1948–49 if the USTA had included "contract pros" in its rankings.

Gonzalez' most dramatic performance, however, came at Wimbledon, where he beat Charlie Pasarell in the first round in the longest match in the history of the oldest and most prestigious of championships. It consumed 5 hours and 12 minutes over two days. Gonzalez lost a marathon first set and virtually threw the second, complaining bitterly that it was too dark to continue play. He was whistled and hooted by the normally genteel Centre Court crowd, but won back all his detractors the next day with a heroic display. Pasarell played well, but Gonzalez was magnificent. In the fifth set he staved off seven match points, twice serving out of 0–40 holes, and won, 22–24, 1–6, 16–14, 6–3, 11–9—112 games. Gonzalez lasted until the fourth round, when his protégé, Ashe, beat him in four sets.

Stan Smith won eight tournaments, including the U.S. Indoor, to replace Ashe atop the U.S. rankings. Ashe, bothered by

a nagging elbow injury and numerous non-tennis distractions following his big year in 1968, won only two tournaments but had an 83–24 match record and more wins than any other American. He was a semifinalist at Wimbledon and Forest Hills, losing to longtime nemesis Laver at both, and was ranked No. 2, ahead of Cliff Richey and Clark Graebner, even though they had more tournament victories—eight and seven, respectively.

The United States defeated long-shot Romania, 5–0, in the Davis Cup challenge round on a fast asphalt court at Cleveland, painted and polished to make it even slicker, to the home team's benefit. Ashe defeated Ilie Nastase in the opening singles, 6–2, 15–13, 7–5, and Smith escaped the hulking and wily Ion Tiriac, 6–8, 6–3, 5–7, 6–4, 6–4, in the pivotal second match. Smith and Lutz closed out the Romanians, 8–6, 6–1, 11–9.

President Richard M. Nixon, a bowler and golfer who secretly despised tennis, had both teams to a reception at the White House. This was a nice gesture, but the Chief Executive caused a few awkward stares when, as a memento of the occasion, he presented each player with a golf ball. Perhaps these were left over, some speculated, from the golf-happy Eisenhower administration.

Tiny Romania, with the lion-hearted Tiriac and the immensely talented Nastase its only players of international standard, was proud to have gotten past Egypt, Spain, the Soviet Union, India and Great Britain (which, with a heroic 10–2 singles run from unranked Graham Stilwell, reached the semifinals for the first time since relinquishing the Cup in 1937) to the final. Never before had Romania won more than two rounds.

Australia failed to reach the final for the first time since 1937—beaten in its first match by Mexico, 3–2, the first opening-round loss for the Aussies since falling to Italy in 1928. Rafael Osuna, Mexico's popular tennis hero, defeated Bill Bowrey in the fifth match, 6–2, 3–6, 8–6, 6–3, and was hailed triumphantly by his countrymen. This was the engaging Osuna's last hurrah, however; he died tragically shortly thereafter, at age 30, when a private plane carrying him on a business trip crashed into the mountains outside Monterrey.

female winning streak in a U.S. Championship event at 33 straight matches over seven years. She was trying to become only the second player to win seven consecutive titles, matching the feat of Richard Sears in the first seven U.S. Men's Championships (1881–87). Clark Graebner, winner of the Clay Court doubles three times with Marty Riessen and once with Dennis Ralston, teamed with Bowrey for Graebner's fifth

nals of the National Clay Courts by Gail Sherriff Chanfreau, ending her record

Jane "Peaches" Bartkowicz to regain the Federation Cup at Athens and the Wightman Cup at Cleveland.

The U.S. Wightman Cup winners: (Standing, from left)—Doris Hart, coach; Mary Ann Curtis, Hazel Wightman, captain Betty Pratt, Nancy Richey and Julie Heldman. (Kneeling)—Valerie Ziegenfuss and Peaches Bartkowicz. • *UPI*

Richey was undefeated in singles and Heldman lost only to Margaret Court as the U.S. defeated Bulgaria, Italy, Netherlands and Australia, 2–1, for the Federation Cup. Richey and Bartkowicz, an unlikely doubles team made up of two confirmed baseliners, upset the world's No. 1 team—Court and Judy Tegart—in the final match, 6–4, 6–4, Bartkowicz stayed in the backcourt throughout, even when Richey served, but the Americans astonishingly won the curious match with energetic retrieving and deft lobbing.

Heldman, a clever player who nicknamed herself "Junkball Julie," set the tone of the 5–2 Wightman Cup victory by upsetting Wade in the opening match. Ranked No. 2 nationally with eight victories in 20 tournaments and a 67–13 match record, Heldman also became the first American woman to win the Italian Championship since Althea Gibson in 1956, beating three outstanding clay-courters—Lesley Turner Bowrey (wife of Bill), Ann Jones and Kerry Melville.

One of the most remarkable and crowd-pleasing victories of the year was that of Darlene Hard and Francoise Durr in the U.S. Open women's doubles. They were a "pickup" team; Hard, by then a 33-year-old teaching pro, had entered as a lark. Out of tournament condition, she was an embarrassment in losing the first eight games of the final, but seemed suddenly to remember the skills and instincts that had made her the world's premier doubles player in her time, winner of five previous U.S. women's titles. As the crowd loudly cheered their revival, Hard and Durr stunned heavily favored Court and Wade, 0–6, 6–3, 6–4.

Forest Hills had begun with a match of record duration—F. D. Robbins defeated Dick Dell, younger brother of Donald, 22–20, 9–7, 6–8, 8–10, 6–4, the longest in number of games—100—in the history of the U.S. Championships. When the tournament ran three days over, the men's doubles finished in a disgraceful shambles, Ken Rosewall and Fred Stolle beating Denny Ralston and Charlie Pasarell, 2–6, 7–5, 13–11, 6–3, before a few hundred spectators on a soggy Wednesday. Pasarell-Ralston got defaults from Wimbledon champs Newcombe and Roche in the quarters and Australian Open winners Laver and Emerson in the semis.

Newcombe-Roche were urged to leave waterlogged New York by their employers, WCT, in order to meet other commitments, a decision that rankled the ITF in its increasingly uneasy dealings with the new pro promoters. After all, it was unseemly for the No. 1 team—they had repeated at Wimbledon, over Tom Okker-Marty Riessen, and won four other tournaments, including the Italian and French—to walk out on one of the "Big Four" showcase championships.

1970

As in 1950 and 1960, the beginning of a new decade also was, in many ways, the start of a new era for tennis. In 1970, the professional game for both men and women fitfully began to assume the structure that would characterize the decade of its most rapid growth.

This was the first year of the men's Grand Prix—a point system, under the aegis of the ITF, that linked together tournaments, leading to year-end bonus awards for the top finishers in the standings and berths in a new tournament at the end of the year: the Grand Prix Masters.

The brainchild of Jack Kramer, the Grand Prix was announced late in 1969 and sponsored by Pepsico. Players earned points, round by round, in the Grand Prix tournaments they entered, and at season's end the top men received cash awards scaled according to their order of finish.

Cliff Richey, for example, collected $25,000 for topping the standings; Arthur Ashe earned $17,000 for placing second; Ken Rosewall $15,000 for coming in third, etc. There were 19 tournaments in the Grand Prix in 1970. The "bonus pool" totaled $150,000 and another $50,000 was at stake in the six-man Masters.

The underlying intent of the Grand

players to contracts, then increasing its "stable" to 30 players by swallowing the NTL in May.

Mike Davies, executive director of WCT, became a member of the ITF scheduling committee, but wariness and distrust between the maneuvering giants continued. It became increasingly difficult for traditional tournaments to count on the participation of the WCT players because of the "management fees" demanded by WCT in order to cover their guarantees to the players.

In September, at the U.S. Open, WCT took the wraps off a Grand Prix-style competition of its own, announcing a "million-dollar circuit" for 1971. The first World Championship of Tennis, for 32 players to be selected by an international press panel, would consist of 20 tournaments with uniform prize money and point standings, leading to a rich, nationally televised play-off with a $50,000 first prize.

This was considered a declaration of war by WCT against the ITF, especially since Davies had never mentioned it to the ITF calendar committee. The battle intensified when, shortly thereafter, WCT

announced that it had signed Arthur Ashe, Charlie Pasarell and Bob Lutz to five-year contracts in a package deal.

The ITF went ahead and announced an expanded Grand Prix, worth $1.5 million, in 1971, but the battle lines had already been drawn.

The beneficiaries of the infighting, of

but still became the first tennis player to crack the $200,000 barrier in winnings. He collected $201,453, compared to the $157,037 won by Lee Trevino, top earner on the professional golf circuit. This had heretofore been considered unimaginable. But prize money was escalating at a rate no one had foreseen—nearly $1 million was up for grabs in U.S. tournaments alone—and three players (Laver, U.S. Open champ Ken Rosewall and Arthur Ashe) won more than $100,000.

Growing along with the total purses, however, was the disparity in prize money for men and women. Despite Margaret Court's fulfillment of a long-held ambition—a singles Grand Slam of the Australian, French, Wimbledon and U.S. titles—1970 was for the majority of women players the autumn of their discontent. A group of pioneers, led by the strong-willed Gladys Heldman—a tough, shrewd businesswoman who had founded *World Tennis* magazine in 1953—decided that the women would have to split away from mixed tournaments and found their own tour if they were ever to corner a significant share of the sport's mushrooming riches and publicity. This was a bold step, but the women decided to take it in September,

Margaret Smith Court, with her U.S. Open trophy, was the leading lady in 1970. • *UPI*

and from a little acorn—a $7,500 renegade tournament for eight women in Houston—there eventually grew a mighty oak: the women's pro tour in the U.S.

The political kettle was boiling, but 1970 was also a spectacularly eventful year on the court. It was made singularly exciting by the advent of the game's first major scoring innovation—tie-breakers—and towering performances by several players, notably Rosewall and Court.

"Mighty Margaret" had twice before won three of the "Big Four" singles titles in a season. In 1970, at age 28, she finally corralled the Grand Slam previously achieved by only one woman—Maureen Connolly in 1953. Court compiled a 104–6 record, winning 21 of 27 tournaments, and had the season's longest winning streak: 39 matches.

Court lost only three sets during the Slam, none in winning her ninth

Australian singles title. She defeated Kerry Melville—one of only four women to beat her during the season—in the final, 6–3, 6–1, and teamed with Judy Dalton to win the doubles by the same score over Melville and Karen Krantzcke.

In the French, only Russian Olga Morozova pushed Court to three sets, in the second round. Court's next four victories were all in straight sets, German Helga Niessen falling in the final, 6–2, 6–4. Francoise Durr won her fourth consecutive doubles title, alongside Gail Sherriff Chanfreau.

At Wimbledon, the tall, languid Niessen—not considered a threat on grass courts—took the first set from Court in the quarterfinals, but did not get another game. The final between Court and Billie Jean King was a masterpiece of drama and shotmaking under duress. Both players were hurt. Court had a painfully strained and swollen ankle tightly strapped as she went on court; she had taken a pain-killing injection beforehand. King was hobbling on a deteriorated kneecap, which required surgery immediately after Wimbledon.

Nevertheless, BJK broke service in the first set three times. Each time Court broke back. Their injuries partially dictated the pattern of play, but both players produced magnificent shots under pressure. It was the longest women's final ever at Wimbledon—46 games—Court finally winning by 14–12, 11–9, in 2½ hours, after the anesthetic effects of her injection had worn off. King saved three match points with gutsy shots worthy of the contest. "It was a bit like one of those 990-page novels that Trollope and Arnold Bennett used to write," suggested British journalist David Gray, who in 1977 would become general secretary of the ITF. "It started a little slowly, but had so many fascinating twists of character and plot that in the end it became a matter of utter compulsion to see how it all ended."

King took her sixth doubles title, her third with Rosemary Casals (who teamed with Ilie Nastase to win the mixed). Billie Jean was the only player who truly challenged Court, splitting their four matches during the year, but King was still recuperating from her post-Wimbledon surgery. In her absence, Court completed the Slam, losing only 13 games in mowing down Pam Austin, Patti Hogan, Pat Faulkner, Helen

Court won approximately $50,000 in prize money on the year, about one quarter of what Laver earned for a far less productive season. In most tournaments, the women's share of the prize money was one quarter or less that of the men's. In the Italian Open, for example, Billie Jean King received a mere $600 for beating Julie Heldman in the final, while Ilie Nastase earned $3,500 for whipping Jan Kodes in the men's final.

Court, never a crusader or champion of causes, wanted no part of a "women's lib" movement in tennis, but King and several others resented the growing inequity in prize-money ratio between men and women. They enlisted fiery activist Gladys Heldman as their negotiator and spokeswoman, and focused on the Pacific Southwest Open at Los Angeles—which favored men by an 8–to–1 ratio—as an example of their plight.

Heldman tried to get tournament chairman Jack Kramer to raise the women's purse. He would not. At a highly publicized Forest Hills press conference, a group of eight women declared they would boycott the Los Angeles tournament and

play in a $7,500 event in Houston, sponsored by Virginia Slims cigarettes. The USTA said it would not sanction this rebel event. The women said they would play anyway—and did. After signing token one-dollar contracts with Heldman, the Houston Eight (King, Casals, Kristy Pigeon, Peaches Bartkowicz, Judy Dalton, Valerie Ziegenfuss, Kerry Melville and Nancy Richey) competed in an event that was

win the Australian singles, the first since Dick Savitt 19 years earlier. Laver did not defend, and Dennis Ralston eliminated Newcombe in a marathon quarterfinal, 19–17, 20–18, 4–6, 6–4—94 games, the sixth-longest in history. Ashe took out Dick Crealy in the final, 6–4, 9–7, 6–2, while Stan Smith and Bob Lutz captured the doubles, the first American men to do so since Vic Seixas and Tony Trabert 17 years earlier.

• With Laver, Rosewall, and their fellow "contract pros" out of the French Championships because their bosses could not come to a financial accommodation with the French Tennis Federation for their appearance, Czech Jan Kodes, Yugoslav Zeljko Franulovic, American Cliff Richey, and Frenchman Georges Goven reached the semifinals of the richest ($100,000) tournament outside America. Kodes beat Franulovic, 6–2, 6–4, 6–0, for the $10,000 top prize. Romanians Ilie Nastase and Ion Tiriac took the doubles.

• At Wimbledon, Laver's 31–match winning streak (dating back to 1961) in the world's most important tournament was snapped when he came up badly off-form against Englishman Roger Taylor in the fourth round and tumbled, 4–6, 6–4, 6–2, 6–1. John Newcombe withstood five break points in the fifth set of an excruciating three-hour quarterfinal against fellow Aussie Roy Emerson, won it by 6–1, 5–7, 3–6, 6–2, 11–9, then crushed Spaniard Andres Gimeno (conqueror of Ashe) and beat Rosewall, 5–7, 6–3, 6–2, 3–6, 6–1. This was the first five-set final in 21 years, and the 10th all-Aussie men's final in 15 years.

Rosewall had beaten left-handers Tony Roche and Taylor to reach the final for the third time, 14 years after losing to fellow Aussie "Whiz Kid" Lew Hoad, but again failed at the final hurdle. Newcombe and Roche teamed for their third consecutive doubles triumph, the first to achieve this since Reg and Laurie Doherty, the English brothers in 1903–5.

• Rosewall, two months shy of his 36th birthday, reigned at Forest Hills, where 14 years earlier he had halted Hoad's Grand Slam bid, It was a wild tournament, the richest in the world with a $176,000 pot. Pastel clothing was permitted in lieu of the traditional "all white," and red flags flew every time a set reached 6–6 and went into the "sudden death" best-of-nine-points tie-breaker.

Record crowds totaling 122,996 came out to see all the revolutionary happenings, but Rosewall interjected a reactionary note. After Dennis Ralston had achieved one of his career high points, knocking off defending champ Laver in a five-set quarterfinal to lead a charge of four Americans into the last eight, Rosewall took over. He blasted Stan Smith and Newcombe in straight sets, then relegated Roche to the runner-up spot for the second consecutive year, 2–6, 6–4, 7–6, 6–3. Rosewall was the oldest champ at Forest Hills since Bill Tilden, who was 36 when he won for the seventh and last time in 1929.

The men's doubles event was notable for several reasons. Pancho Gonzalez, the oldest man in the tournament at 42, entered with a then unknown protégé, Jimmy Connors, who at 18 was the youngest man in the tournament. They reached the quarters. Nikki Pilic of Yugoslavia and Pierre Barthes of France slew Emerson and Laver in the final, 6–3, 7–6, 4–6, 7–6, to become the first European team ever to win the U.S. Doubles. The victors won eight of their 15 sets in tie-breakers, the scoring innovation by Jimmy Van Alen that was given its first widespread exposure in the U.S. Pro Championships and U.S. Open.

Players were skeptical—"It's like rolling dice," said Newcombe—but spectators, schedule-makers and television producers loved them, so tie-breakers were here to stay—although the more conservative 12–point, win-by-two method gradually won favor over nine-point sudden death in professional tournaments.

• Laver, at 32, did win five significant tournaments on four continents, but in addition to losing his Grand Slam titles, he gave up his four-year stranglehold on the U.S. Pro title. Roche beat him in the final at Longwood, 3–6, 6–4, 1–6, 6–2, 6–2. Laver also won the "Tennis Champions Classic," a series of head-to-head, winner-take-all challenge matches played in seven cities. He beat Rosewall for the $35,000 top prize at Madison Square Garden.

• Nastase underscored his emerging brilliance by winning titles on one of the world's fastest courts—the canvas of the U.S. Indoor at Salisbury, Md., where he escaped a two-set deficit and two match points in the fourth set to beat Cliff Richey, 6–8, 3–6, 6–4, 9–7, 6–0—as well as on one of the slowest, the red clay of Foro Italico in Rome.

Richey, a scrappy Texan with more tenacity than natural talent, earned the No. 1 U.S. ranking, thereby establishing a unique family achievement. His sister,

Nancy, had been the top-ranked U.S woman in 1964–65 and 1968–69.

Richey won eight of 27 tournaments he played during the season, was runner-up in five more and went farther than any other American man at Forest Hills—to the semi-finals. His match record for the year was 92–10.

Even so, he did not clinch the top

down to 4-points-all in the sudden-death tie-breaker: simultaneous match point for both players. Richey served to Smith's backhand and charged the net. Smith cracked a backhand return crosscourt that Richey could barely get his racket on. He nudged the ball crosscourt, and Smith lashed what appeared to be a winning passing shot down the line. Richey dived for the ball, throwing everything into a desperate last lunge and astonishingly volleyed a winner to seize the breaker, 5–4, and the match, 7–6, 6–7, 6–4, 4–6, 7–6.

Richey also was the unlikely hero of the lackluster 1970 Davis Cup challenge round. U.S. captain Ed Turville agonized over the selection, but finally chose Richey over Smith to face upstart Germany on a fast asphalt court at Cleveland. Richey, who felt he had been slighted by not being chosen in 1969, responded by clobbering Christian Kuhnke, 6–3, 6–4, 6–2, and Wilhelm Bungert, 6–4, 6–4, 7–5, to spearhead a 5–0 U.S. victory. Arthur Ashe beat Bungert, 6–2, 10–8, 6–2, in the opener and erased Kuhnke, 6–8, 10–12, 9–7, 13–11, 6–4, in the meaningless fifth match, the longest singles—86 games—ever in a Davis Cup final. Smith and Bob Lutz beat Bungert and Kuhnke, 6–3, 7–5, 6–5,

becoming the only doubles team to clinch the Cup three straight years.

It was a disappointing final, concluding a tarnished Davis Cup campaign. The exclusion of contract pros, even though all major tournaments were now "open," left the Davis Cup a second-rate event. Australia, denied the services of perhaps its 10 best players, fell pathetically to India.

apartheid racial policy of its government was considered disruptive to the competition, and Rhodesia withdrew to avoid political problems.

Largely because contract pros were excluded from the Davis Cup, a new competition—grandly misnamed the World Cup—was organized as a charity event in Boston. It put a two-man team of Australian pros—Newcombe and Fred Stolle—against U.S. Davis Cuppers Richey, Smith, Ashe and Clark Graebner for $20,000 in prize money. The Aussies won, 5–2, at Harvard University's indoor clay courts and, even though the ITF opposed the event, a new Australian-U.S. pro team rivalry had begun.

Australia won the Federation Cup at Freiburg, West Germany, even though Margaret Court opted not to play. Judy Dalton and Karen Krantzcke swept through the competition without losing a match, whitewashing West Germany—2–1, victors over Americans Peaches Bartkowicz, Julie Heldman and Mary Ann Eisel Curtis—in the final.

With Billie Jean King winning two singles and collaborating with Bartkowicz for the first time to win the decisive doubles, the U.S. scored a 4–3 Wightman Cup victory over Great Britain at Wimbledon. King beat Virginia Wade in the opening singles, but had to stop Ann Jones and then team with Bartkowicz for a 7–5, 3–6, 6–2 triumph over Wade and Winnie Shaw to salvage victory after Wade's singles win over Nancy Richey gave the British a 3–2 lead.

The season ended with the first Grand Prix Masters tournament, a six-man round-robin in Tokyo. Cliff Richey, who topped the Grand Prix point standings, was ill and could not participate. Stan Smith and Rod Laver both had 4–1 records in the round-robin, but Smith took the $15,000 first prize because of his head-to-head win over Laver.

The next year, because of the growing strain of the tug-of-war between WCT and the ITF, Smith and Laver would not be playing in the same season-ending playoff tournament. There were negotiations throughout the fall of 1970, trying to develop an accord, and in December WCT and the ITF issued a joint communique pledging that they would "work together toward the development and spectator appeal of the game throughout the world." An agreement in principle for the appearance of WCT contract pros in the 1971 French, Wimbledon, and U.S. Open Championships also was announced, but the cautious harmony turned out to be short-lived.

1971

In 1971, both men's and women's professional tennis were split into rival camps. It was an uneasy, acrimonious year politically, but the game prospered.

On court, there were many highlights: John Newcombe's second consecutive Wimbledon triumph, after he trailed Stan Smith by two sets to one in the final;

Evonne Goolagong, French and Wimbledon victor, ranked No. 2 in the World Top Ten in 1971. • *UPI*

Smith's impressive triumph at Forest Hills; the first "World Championship of Tennis," in which Ken Rosewall upset Rod Laver in the final; a new women's pro tour, dominated by the indefatigable Billie Jean King; and the emergence of Evonne Goolagong, who won the French Open and Wimbledon at age 19, and Chris Evert, who reached the semifinals of the U.S. Open at 16.

Rosewall, who in 1970 had captured his second U.S. Championship 14 years after the first, continued to perform geriatric marvels. He dethroned Arthur Ashe in the Australian Open final, 6–1, 7–5, 6–3, regaining a title he first held in 1953. Newcombe and Tony Roche won the third of their four Australian doubles titles.

Unfortunately, for much of the season the 34 men under contract to World Championship Tennis and the "independent pros" who remained under the authority of their national associations played separate tournaments.

WCT's new "World Championship of Tennis"—a million-dollar series of 20 tournaments in nine countries on four continents—got off to a promising start with the Philadelphia Indoor, where Newcombe beat Laver for only the second time in a dozen career meetings.

Meanwhile, the independent pros were playing on an expanding indoor circuit promoted by Bill Riordan under the aegis of the USTA. The highlight was the U.S. Indoor at Riordan's hometown of

ment series, but also open to noncontract pros. This made for a week of exceptional matches and excitement on the red clay of Il Foro Italico. Record crowds and profits were recorded before Laver defeated Czech Jan Kodes in the final, 7–5, 6–3, 6–3.

Only a few of the WCT players entered the French Open. After five months of a grueling travel and playing schedule, Ashe—never a factor on European clay—was the only one of WCT's top "names" who opted to go to Paris for two weeks of physically demanding best-of-five-set matches. The mass nonappearance of the "contract pros" infuriated the ITF and was a major factor in polarizing opposition to WCT. Meanwhile, the dour but energetically industrious Kodes won his second straight French title, beating the more gifted but less persistent Nastase, 8–6, 6–2, 2–6, 7–5, in an absorbing final. Ashe and Marty Riessen, the top two WCT players entered, won the doubles. (Both had been beaten in singles by surprising Frank Froehling, who survived a match point against Ashe in the quarterfinals.)

At Wimbledon, No. 1 seed Laver was ambushed by the inspired serving and volleying of American Tom Gorman in the

quarterfinals. The best match was an enchanting four-hour quarterfinal in which Rosewall finally outstroked Richey, 6–8, 5–7, 6–4, 9–7, 7–5. The final between Newcombe and Smith had fewer breathtaking rallies and was dominated by slam-bang points accentuating each's serve-volley power, but it also became gripping in the end. Smith seemed in control after a seven-game run that took him to 1–0 in the

The U.S. Open—minus Laver, defending champ Rosewall, and Emerson, who opted to rest—was less than three hours old when Wimbledon champ Newcombe was rudely dismissed by Kodes—who was unhappy about being unseeded, even though he said tennis on grass courts was "a joke" that he found totally unfunny. This was the first time in 41 years that a top seed failed to survive his opening match— No. 1 foreign seed Jean Borotra lost in the 1930 opening round to Berkeley Bell. In 1928 George King beat No. 1 American seed John Hennessey in the first round, but Borotra hadn't come in as Wimbledon champ, and Hennessey was no Newcombe.

But Kodes proved it was no fluke. He came back from two sets down against Pierre Barthes, and from two sets to one and a service break down in the fourth to beat Arthur Ashe in the semifinals. Kodes also won the first set of the final against U.S. Cpl. Smith, but the 6-foot-4 Californian had learned from his near miss at Wimbledon. Unflinching on the crucial points, he erased the "bouncing Czech," 3–6, 6–3, 6–2, 7–6.

Smith and Erik van Dillen were even at two sets apiece against Newcombe and

Englishman Roger Taylor in the doubles final when darkness forced a halt. Rather than resume the next day, it was agreed unorthodoxly that a nine-point sudden-death tie-breaker would decide the championship. Newcombe-Taylor won it, 5–3.

It was indeed a curious year for men's tennis, climaxed by separate playoffs for the leading "contract" and independent pros.

Laver, Tom Okker, Rosewall, Cliff Drysdale, Ashe, Newcombe, Riessen and Bob Lutz were the top eight men in the WCT standings. They had their playoffs in Houston and Dallas, Rosewall won two magnificent tie-breakers to seize the $50,000 top prize at Dallas Memorial Auditorium over Laver, 6–4, 1–6, 7–6, 7–6.

Smith, Nastase, Zeljko Franulovic, Kodes, Richey, Barthes and Gorman were the seven men who made the round-robin Grand Prix Masters at Paris. Smith collected the $25,000 top bonus prize from the season-long point standings, but Nastase went 6–0 in the Masters, whipping Smith, 5–7, 7–6, 6–3, and collected the tournament's $15,000 top prize. It was the first of Nastase's four victories in the Masters.

At year's end Newcombe and Smith shared Player of the Year honors, but there was no clear-cut No. 1.

The Italian was Laver's biggest title, but he won six of 25 tournaments, 78 of 86 matches, and was far and away the leading money winner with $292,717, which made him tennis's first career millionaire. His nine-year pro winnings: $1,006,974. His most astounding string came in the second and last Tennis Champions Classic, a series of head-to-head, winner-take-all matches in various cities, leading to a four-man playoff in Madison Square Garden. Laver incredibly swept all 13 of his matches, against top opponents, to win $160,000 in this one event.

Rosewall won six of 25 tournaments, including the Australian and South African Opens and his third U.S. Pro Championship, and 70 of 86 matches. He earned $138,371 and would have been unchallenged as "Old Man of the Year" had not Pancho Gonzalez—43, and already a grandfather—beaten Roscoe Tanner, Richey and Jimmy Connors (conqueror of Smith in the semis) in succession to win the $10,000 top prize in the Pacific Southwest Open at Los Angeles.

Newcombe captured five of 19 tournaments, 53 of 67 matches, and amassed $101,514. Smith, who missed the early season because he was in basic training with the U.S. Army, won six tournaments and compiled a 79–15 record that included beating Nastase in the opening match and Ion Tiriac in the decisive singles of the 3–2 U.S. Davis Cup challenge round victory over Romania. Smith earned $100,086. Nastase, who finished the season spectacu-

Despite Army duty, Stan Smith managed to cop the U.S. Open and winnings of more than $100,000 in 1971. • *UPI*

larly, was the top "independent" earner with $114,000 in winnings.

Relations between the ITF and WCT, strained at the start of the year and aggravated by the French Open, broke down completely at Wimbledon. In a bitter, turbulent press conference, fueled by misunderstanding over several WCT "points of negotiation" that were falsely interpreted

money. Billie Jean King, who energetically promoted the Virginia Slims Circuit—one observer suggested that she "single-handedly talked it into prominence"—won the lioness' share of the rewards: $117,000. She became the first woman athlete to break the $100,000-in-a-year milestone.

Publisher Gladys Heldman was the behind-the-scenes driving force, arranging

member national associations, effective at the start of 1972. After 3½ years of "open" tournaments, the contract pros were to be made outcasts again.

In November, new ITF president Allan Heyman announced that Commercial Union Assurance, a London-based worldwide insurance group, was taking over sponsorship of the Grand Prix from Pepsico, and expanding the financial commitment to more than $250,000. WCT, meanwhile, said that it would focus its attention on strengthening its own tournament series, which it shifted to a May windup in 1972 for maximum TV exposure in the U.S. In the first week of 1972, Ken Rosewall won his second consecutive Australian Open; ironically, the man who had won the first Open tournament in 1968 also won the last of the now interrupted Open era.

Meanwhile, women's tennis—which a year earlier seemed to be overshadowed by the men's game and suffering from a dearth of refreshing young talent—took a dramatically vibrant upturn. From the renegade Virginia Slims of Houston tournament the previous September sprang a new women's tour with $309,000 in prize

Chattanooga. She beat Rosemary Casals in the first four finals, then Ann Jones and teamed with Casals to win the doubles at the first seven Slims tournaments.

At Philadelphia—where word came that the USTA had lifted its suspension of the "rebel" women—Francoise Durr snapped King's singles streak in the semifinals, and Casals won the tournament. King, who had been ineligible as a "contract pro" for two years, then recovered the U.S. Indoor title she had held in 1966–68, beating Casals again in the final. Rosie, so long the whipping girl, got revenge in the tour's disappointing New York stop at the dingy old 34th Street Armory. In all, King won eight of the inaugural 14 tournaments. Ann Jones won the biggest prize ($9,000) at Las Vegas, and amateur Chris Evert was the most surprising winner, striking down Durr, Judy Alvarez, an ailing King, and Julie Heldman to capture her first of 157 pro tourney titles, at St. Petersburg, Fla.

The winter/spring tour—which captured a great deal of media attention, thanks to the clever and energetic promotion of Heldman and King and the emerging fascination with "women's liberation"—was so successful that the women's tour added five summer tournaments, starting with a $40,000 Virginia Slims International at Houston. King captured the $10,000 first prize there, beating Australian Kerry Melville in the final, and went on to take the $10,000 top bonus in the first women's Grand Prix. King's total of $117,000 in prize money was the highest sum for any American, male or female.

While King and Company were pioneering under the banner of "Women's Lob," Margaret Court and Evonne Goolagong dominated the traditional early season. Court beat Ann Jones in three tough sets, Goolagong walloped Virginia Wade, and Court teamed with hometown girl Lesley Hunt to beat Wade and Winnie Shaw as Australia won the 1971 Federation Cup at Perth (actually played the last week in 1970) with a 3–0 victory over Great Britain in the final. With most of the top U.S. players suspended as part of the new women's pro group, the USTA sent a young team of Patti Hogan and Sharon Walsh, who lost to Britain in the semis.

The Australian Open was played in March, three months later than usual, and Court beat Goolagong, 2–6, 7–6, 7–5, to take her sixth consecutive Grand Slam singles title (1969 Forest Hills, 1970 Australian, French, Wimbledon, and U.S., 1971 Australian). Margaret beat Evonne again in the final of the South African Open (Goolagong, of one-eighth aboriginal descent, was the first "nonwhite" woman to compete in Johannesburg). They teamed to win the doubles.

Virginia Wade won the Italian Open and Billie Jean King the German, both over Helga Niessen Masthoff in the finals, and then Court's Grand Slam winning streak was surprisingly terminated in the third round of the French by Gail Sherriff Chanfreau, who played the match of her life to win, 6–3, 6–4. She lost in the next round to Helen Gourlay, who went on to

beat 1968 titlist Nancy Richey in the semis. Goolagong came through the other half easily and beat Gourlay in the final, 6–3, 7–5, the first player since Althea Gibson in 1956 to win the tournament the first time she played. Durr, alongside Chanfreau, won her fifth consecutive doubles title.

Having won the most prestigious clay-court title, Goolagong cemented the No. 1 women's ranking for the year by winning Wimbledon in her second appearance on the grass of the All England Club. The most ethereal of tennis players, graceful, smiling, and free-spirited, she captivated the galleries in dismissing Nancy Richey Gunter in the quarters, 6–3, 6–2; Billie Jean King in the semis, 6–4, 6–4; and Court in the final, 6–4, 6–1. Couturier Teddy Tinling made Goolagong a special dress for the final, white with a scalloped hem and lilac lining and adornments; his staff worked through the night to get it ready, and sent it to Wimbledon with a "good luck" message sewn in, and a silver horseshoe. Such was the spirit of the occasion as Evonne became the youngest champion since Karen Susman in 1962. King and Casals collaborated on their fourth Wimbledon doubles title, and King-Owen Davidson took the mixed over Court-Marty Riessen, 3–6, 6–2, 15–13, the final set being the longest in any Wimbledon final to date.

Despite her triumphs in Paris and London, Goolagong's coach, Vic Edwards, adhered to his long-range plan of not having Evonne play the U.S. circuit until 1972. Therefore, she did not enter the U.S. Open. Neither did Margaret Court nor Ann Jones, both of whom were pregnant. But just when it appeared that Billie Jean King would have the stage to herself, another appealing young rival emerged: Chris Evert.

A 16-year-old high-school student from Fort Lauderdale, Fla., she had beaten Court on clay in Charlotte, N.C., the previous fall and won the Virginia Slims tournament at St. Petersberg on the same surface. But she gained national attention for the first time as the heroine of the 4–3 U.S. Wightman Cup victory over Great Britain on an ultra-slow rubberized court in Cleveland in August. Three months younger than Maureen Connolly had been in her debut 20 years earlier, Chris crunched Winnie Shaw, 6–0, 6–4, in the opener and a nervous and off-form

the Pacific Southwest Open, which they had boycotted the year before. It was one of the strangest episodes in U.S. tournament history and both players were later fined for their "double default." BJK finally went over the 100-grand mark at Phoenix, where she again beat Casals in the final. King celebrated with champagne in the dressing room, and at a news conference in New York the following week

Forest Hills, she immediately became the darling of the crowds, the star of the show since three prominent men were missing. Playing every match in the old concrete stadium, she beat Edda Buding, 6–1, 6–0; Mary Ann Eisel, 4–6, 7–6, 6–1, after Eisel had six match points; Francoise Durr, 2–6, 6–2, 6–3; and Lesley Hunt, 4–6, 6–2, 6–3, to supplant Little Mo Connolly as the youngest American semifinalist since 1951—16 years, 9 months, to 16, 11. Betty Nuthall of England had been 16, 3½ in 1927. Eisel, Durr and Hunt all departed in tears, intimidated by Chrissie's nerveless backcourt stroking and the wildly partisan crowds cheering for "Cinderella in Sneakers."

King had too much of a fast-court arsenal for Evert and ended her fairy tale in the semis, 6–3, 6–2. BJK wrapped up her second Forest Hills title by beating Casals, 6–4, 7–6, sealing the No. 1 U.S. ranking for the fifth time. Her record for the season was 112–13, including victories in 17 out of 31 tournaments.

King's persistent drive to the $100,000 landmark was slowed when she and Casals walked off the court because of a line call dispute at 6–6 in the first set of the final of

that the 1971 windup would be contested on clay, at Charlotte, N.C. Romania, on the backs of Ilie Nastase and Ion Tiriac, had come through six matches to reach the ultimate round for a second time. Two years earlier in Cleveland they had been blasted off a lickety-split asphalt court, and Turville felt it would be more entertaining and fairer to stage this one on clay. Richey felt it was treason, giving it away to the dirt-bred Romanians—and quit the team.

Turville contended it would be more exciting, and it certainly was, 3–2. Searching for a singles replacement for Richey, to accompany Smith, he came up with a surprise, 28-year-old Frank Froehling, III, who hadn't been on the team for six years. After Smith beat Nastase to give the U.S. 1–0 lead, long-legged Froehling called "Spider Man," had his own surprise for Tiriac: the greatest Cup-round comeback for an American in more than a half-century, 3–6, 1–6, 6–1, 6–3, 8–6. That was the critical point for the U.S. since Nastase and Tiriac snuffed Smith and Erik van Dillen in doubles, and Nastase beat Froehling. With little more than a forehand, and heart, Froehling survived seven break points, three in the opening game, to take the third set and begin turning it his way. Tiriac fought back from a break down, saved a match point in the fifth to 5–5; and darkness, at 6–6, pushed them to the next day, which was all the American's. He broke Tiriac on a second match point with a buzzing forehand, and the U.S. was on its way to a fourth straight Cup.

Tiriac's straight-set win over Edison Mandarino in the decisive fifth match at Sao Paulo had clinched a 3–2 victory over Brazil and landed the Romanians in Charlotte.

1972

In 1972, a peace agreement was reached between the International Tennis Federation and World Championship Tennis, reintegrating a men's game that had briefly and regrettably regressed into segregated "contract pro" and "independent pro" circuits, but not in time for the 32 WCT contractees to participate in the French Open or Wimbledon. Stan Smith's triumphs over Ilie Nastase in the Wimbledon final and the Davis Cup gave him the edge over the mercurial Romanian, who won the U.S. Open, for the No. 1 men's ranking. Meanwhile, Billie Jean King swept the French, Wimbledon and U.S. Open titles—she didn't enter the Australian—and again dominated the ascending Virginia Slims circuit, emphatically ruling women's tennis and giving the U.S. dual supremacy in men's and women's tennis for the first time since 1955.

Despite the unsatisfactory separate circuits for men most of the year, prize money kept spiraling, to more than $5 million worldwide. Nastase was the top earner at $176,000, with Smith second at $142,300, even though he was in the U. S. Army. Four other men (WCT employees Ken Rosewall, Arthur Ashe, John Newcombe and Rod Laver) and one woman, King, collected more than $100,000.

It also was a year of outstanding matches, none finer than the three-hour, 34-minute classic between Rosewall and Laver in the final of the WCT Championships at Dallas in May. Laver was favored to grab the $50,000 plum that had eluded him the previous November, but Rosewall—an enduring marvel at age 38—again stole it. Laver revived himself from 1–4 in the final set, saved a match point with an ace, and had the match on his racket at 5–4 in the "lingering death" tie-breaker, with two serves to come. He pounded both deep to Rosewall's backhand corner, but tennis' most splendid antique reached for vintage return winners. Laver failed to return the exhausted Rosewall's last serve and it was over, 4–6, 6–0, 6–3, 6–7, 7–6 (7-points-to-5 in the breaker). This had been a duel of torrid, exquisite shotmaking on a 90-degree Mother's Day afternoon, and the sell-out crowd at Moody Coliseum and a national television audience of 21 million were enthralled. Many old hands said it might have been the greatest match of all time, and it was certainly the one that put tennis over as a TV sport in America. It was the closest finish of an important tourney until 1988, when Boris Becker won the Masters final over Ivan Lendl, also a 7–5 fifth-set tie-breaker.

In order to restructure its season for a spring windup, the most advantageous time for U.S. television, WCT counted the last 10 tournaments of 1971 and 10 between January and April 1972 in its point standings. Laver won the Philadelphia opener, rechristened the U.S. Pro Indoor, and four more tournaments to top the point standings heading into the Dallas playoffs. Behind him were Rosewall, Tom Okker, Cliff Drysdale, Marty Riessen, Arthur Ashe, Bob Lutz and John Newcombe.

Meanwhile, the "independent pros" were playing the USLTA Indoor Circuit organized by Bill Riordan. Smith played only five of 13 events, but won four in a row, starting with the U.S. Indoor over Nastase, 5–7, 6–2, 6–3, 6–4. Also prominent were rookie pro Jimmy Connors—he dropped out of UCLA after becoming the first freshman to win the National Intercollegiate singles in 1971—and "Old Wolf" Pancho Gonzalez, who, at 43, beat Frenchman Georges Goven from two sets down to win the Des Moines Indoor. He was the oldest title winner of the open era.

The men's singles was dull until the final— the first ever played on Sunday, after a rain delay—when Smith and Nastase went after each other for five absorbing sets. It was Smith's serve-volley power and forthright resolve against Nastase's incomparable speed, agility and eccentric artistry. The fifth set was electrifying. Smith escaped two break points in the fifth game, which went to seven agonizing deuces, the first

between major championships.

Another veteran Aussie, 35-year-old Roy Emerson, saved a match point and beat Lutz, 4–6, 7–6, 6–3, to give Australia the pivotal point in a 6–1 victory over the U.S. in a World Cup marked by Laver's first appearance.

A contemporary of Laver and Emerson, the elegant Spaniard Andres Gimeno, nearly 35, who had left WCT to return to "independent pro" status, won his only Grand Slam singles title, taking the French Open, over surprising Frenchman Patrick Proisy, 4–6, 6–3, 6–1, 6–1. Gimeno became the event's oldest champ. Proisy had ended Jan Kodes' 17-match French winning streak and bid for a third successive title in the quarters, and had eliminated Italian and German champ Manuel Orantes in the semis. Bob Hewitt and Frew McMillan captured their first French doubles title, and within a month would add the Wimbledon crown.

Smith, runner-up to the now disenfranchised Newcombe (who went to court to try to break the ITF ban and get a crack at a third straight title) the previous July, was an overwhelming favorite at Wimbledon.

Pro Championship at Longwood, over Tom Okker, 6–4, 2–6, 6–1, 6–4, ending a nine-year Australian rule to become the first American champ since Butch Buchholz in 1962. But it was the U.S. Open that commanded the most attention.

Lamar Hunt, the Texas millionaire who bankrolled WCT, and Allan Heyman, the Danish-born English lawyer who was president of the ITF, had been meeting secretly throughout the winter and spring, prompted by Americans Donald Dell and Jack Kramer to find a solution to reunify the men's game. In April, they reached an accord to divide the season into two segments, starting in 1973. WCT would have free reign the first four months of the year, expanding to two groups of 32 players each that would play an 11–tournament series to qualify four men from each group for the May WCT finals in Dallas. During that period, no other tournaments with more than $20,000 would be sanctioned. The last eight months of the year would belong to the ITF for its Grand Prix and Masters.

With this agreement—later modified considerably, under pressure of an antitrust suit by Bill Riordan, who felt he had been sold down the river—the ban of

WCT players from the traditional circuit was removed in July, making Forest Hills the year's only big event open to everybody.

In turned out to be a wild tournament. No. 2 seed Rosewall was beaten by Mark Cox in the second round; No. 3 Laver by Cliff Richey in the fourth; No. 1 Smith by Ashe in the quarters; No. 5 Newcombe by Fred Stolle; No. 7 Tom Okker by Roscoe Tanner; and No. 8 Kodes by Alex "Sandy" Mayer, all in the third round. Three Americans (Ashe, Richey and Tom Gorman) made the semis for the first time in 21 years, but the lone foreigner, Nastase, won the tournament.

"Nasty" incurred the enmity of 14,690 spectators with temper tantrums early in the final but gradually won them over with his shot-making genius. He trailed by two sets to one, 1–3 and 2–4 in the fourth set, and had a break point against him for 1–4. Ashe failed to get a backhand return in play, and faded thereafter, Nastase running five straight games for the set and recovering quickly after losing his serve in the first game of the fifth. Nasty became the first European since Manolo Santana in 1965, and the first ever from Eastern Europe to triumph on the soft grass at Forest Hills, 3–6, 6–3, 6–7 (1–5), 6–4, 6–3. Roger Taylor, champ with Newcombe the year before, teamed up with Cliff Drysdale to whip Newcombe and Owen Davidson in the doubles final.

Smith sealed his No. 1 ranking in the fall, winning the Pacific Southwest Open, Stockholm and Paris Indoor and giving a towering performance in the Davis Cup final at Bucharest.

The Davis Cup nations had voted in 1971 to do away with the challenge round in which the defending nation sat out and waited for a challenger to plow through the Zone competitions. Thus the U.S. had to follow an unprecedented road for a

Romania's Ilie Nastase led the run to the bank in 1972, winning at Forest Hills, the first European to do so since Spain's Manolo Santana in 1965. • *UPI*

defending champion: five matches, all in the opponents' backyards. The U.S. didn't lose a match in sprinting past Commonwealth Caribbean, Mexico and Chile to the semifinals against Spain, but only a gritty five-set victory by Cup rookie Harold Solomon over Juan Gisbert in Barcelona salvaged a 3–2 U.S. victory and a trip to Bucharest for the final.

Romania, with the brilliant Nastase and the menacing Ion Tiriac at home on the red clay of the Progresul Sports Club, was a heavy favorite. Nastase boasted, "We cannot lose at home"—and his record of 19 straight Cup singles victories and 13 consecutive Romanian triumphs in Bucharest seemed to support his braggadocio. Slow clay, an adoring and vocal home crowd and notoriously patriotic linesmen all favored Nastase and Tiriac.

This was the first Davis Cup final in Europe in 39 years, and perhaps the greatest international sporting occasion ever in Bucharest, where likenesses of Nastase and Tiriac were everywhere. But the pressure of great expectations worked in reverse. Smith played undoubtedly his finest match on clay, while Nastase was high-strung and erratic as the American took the critical opener, 11–9, 6–2, 6–3, though Nastase served for the first set at 9–8. Tiriac, the brooding former ice hockey international who claims kinship with Dracula, used every ploy of gamesmanship, orchestrating the crowd and the linesmen, to come from

wiles and battled heroically in the fourth match, but Smith was too good for him and clinched the Cup, 4–6, 6–2, 6–4, 2–6, 6–0. Nastase beat Gorman in the meaningless fifth match.

It had been a wild weekend in Bucharest, made unforgettable by the fervor of the fans, the thievery of the linesmen, the machinations of Tiriac, and extraordinarily heavy security in the aftermath of the Olympic massacre at Munich. (There had been rumors of threats against two Jewish members of the U.S. team, Solomon and Brian Gottfried.) But in the end, captain Dennis Ralston's brigade could savor the finest victory ever by a U.S. team away from home.

Once again there were separate playoffs for "contract pros" and "independents" at the end of the year. WCT scheduled a makeshift "winter championship" in Rome for the top eight men in a summer-fall circuit that filled the gap before a new two-group format started in 1973. Ashe won the $25,000 first prize, beating Nikki Pilic, Okker and Lutz.

The Commercial Union Masters was played in Barcelona with the new format—

two four-man round-robin groups, with the two players with the best records in each advancing to "knockout" semis and final. Gorman had Smith beaten in one semi, but hurt his back and defaulted so as not to wreck the final. Nastase repeated as champion, beating Smith in a rousing final, 6–3, 6–2, 3–6, 2–6, 6–3, but it was his only victory in five meetings on the year with the tall Californian.

enlisted Jack Kramer as executive director. The urbane Cliff Drysdale was elected president and Dell became the Association's legal counsel. Other players' associations had come and gone in the past, but the ATP was carefully constituted and loomed as a major new force in the pro game's politics and administration.

The politics of women's tennis in 1972 began with conciliation and ended with a major new rift.

Early in the year Gladys Heldman, organizer of the rebel women's pro tour the year before, was appointed by the USTA as coordinator of women's tennis and director of the women's tour in a peace effort. Thus empowered, she expanded the winter tour to $302,000 in prize money. But by September the honeymoon was over. Heldman resigned her USTA post amid mutual mistrust and formed the Women's International Tennis Federation. She took the USTA to court for alleged antitrust violations. Meanwhile, the USTA appointed U.S. Wightman Cup captain Edy McGoldrick to form a women's tour in opposition to Heldman's in the winter-spring of 1973.

On the tennis court, there was no question who was boss in 1972. King did not play the Australian Open, but swept the rest of the Grand Slam singles titles with the loss of only one set, to Virginia Wade in the quarterfinals at Wimbledon. Billie Jean won 10 of 24 tournaments, compiled an 87–13 record, ran away with the women's Grand Prix top prize, and exceeded her prize money landmark of 1971, earning $119,000. Against her greatest career rivals, she was 3–2 over Margaret Court (back on the circuit after the birth of her first child, Daniel) and 4–3 over Nancy Richey Gunter for the year.

Wade won her first Australian Open title, over Goolagong, 6–4, 6–4. King won her first French Open title—joining Doris Hart, Maureen Connolly, Shirley Fry and Court as the only women to have won all four Grand Slam singles titles—with a 6–3, 6–3 triumph over Goolagong. (They would be joined by Chris Evert in 1982, Martina Navratilova in 1983 and Steffi Graf in 1988.) BJK also dethroned Goolagong at Wimbledon by the same scores, after Evonne had thrillingly won her first meeting with Chris Evert in the semis.

At the U.S. Open, King beat Wade in the quarters, 6–2, 7–5; Court in the semis, 6–4, 6–4; and Kerry Melville—who ripped Evert in the semis by skidding clever slices short, low and wide to Chrissie's two-fisted backhand—for the $10,000 first prize, 6–3, 7–5.

Dutchwoman Betty Stove was the Woman of the Year in doubles, teaming with King to win the French and Wimbledon and with Françoise Durr to take the U.S. Open. She was the first woman to win all three in a season since Darlene Hard and Maria Bueno did so in 1960.

Evert, still an amateur at age 17, was the only player with a winning record over King for the year: 3–1, including a 6–1, 6–0 victory in the final of the Virginia Slims tournament in her hometown of Fort Lauderdale. She also won the richest women's tournament, the inaugural season-climaxing $100,000 Virginia Slims Championship at Boca Raton, Fla.—beating King and Melville in the final two rounds after her 15-year-old sister, Jeanne, erased Court in the third round—but could not accept the $25,000 first prize.

Evert ranked third in the U.S. behind King and Gunter (who beat her all three times they played), compiling a 47–7 record, winning four tournaments. She spearheaded the 5–2 U.S. Wightman Cup victory over Great Britain at Wimbledon, beating Wade and Joyce Williams in singles; then beat Court and Goolagong for the only two U.S. victories in a 5–2 loss to Australia in the inaugural Bonne Bell Cup at Cleveland. Evert also won her first adult national title—the first of four consecutive U.S. Clay Court singles at Indianapolis—by beating Court in the semis and Goolagong in the final.

The Maureen Connolly Brinker Indoor at Dallas was the first tournament in which both Goolagong and Evert competed, but King delayed their first meeting. She fought off a 1–3, 15–40 deficit and later cramps in the final set to beat Evert in the quarters, and came from behind again to beat Goolagong in the semis. Exhausted, she fell easily to Gunter in the final.

The magical first encounter between the two radiant new princesses of women's tennis came, appropriately, in the semis at Wimbledon. It was a majestic match worthy of the occasion, Goolagong, winning, 4–6, 6–3, 6–4, after trailing 0–3 in the second and 2–3 (down a break) in the third. Evert promptly won the next two meetings, however, setting the tone for their career rivalry.

The Virginia Slims circuit continued to grow, offering $525,775 in prize purses for 21 tournaments, but the appeal of Evert and Goolagong—who could not be enticed by Heldman to side with her in a war against the ITF establishment—made them the cornerstones of the rival USTA circuit in 1973.

1973

A questionable Centennial was celebrated throughout tennis in 1973. It com-

In the "Battle of the Sexes" in 1973, Bobby Riggs cleared the net, and Billie Jean King cleared $100,000. • *UPI*

The landmark match of the year did not come in any of the traditional major tournaments. There was nothing traditional at all about the celebrated "Battle of the Sexes" between 29-year-old Billie Jean King and 55-year-old Bobby Riggs, the self-proclaimed "king of male chauvinist pigs," at Houston's Astrodome the night of September 20. But this spectacle—roughly equal parts tennis, carnival, and sociological phenomenon—captured the fancy of America as no pure tennis match ever had. The crowd of 30,472, paying as much as $100 a seat, was the largest ever to witness a tennis match. Some 50 million more watched on prime-time television. The whole gaudy promotion was worth perhaps $3 million, and King collected a $100,000 winner-take-all purse, plus ancillary revenues, for squashing Riggs, 6–4, 6–3, 6–3.

Riggs, the outspoken hustler who had won Wimbledon and the U.S. Championship in 1939, created the bonanza by a challenge proclaiming that women's lib was a farce and that the best of the female tennis pros couldn't even beat him, "an old man with one foot in the grave." He challenged Margaret Court to a winner-take-all challenge match on Mother's Day at a California resort he was plugging in Ramona. She was the ideal victim for his well-perfected "psych job" and assortment of junk shots. Margaret choked and Riggs won, 6–2, 6–1. That set the stage for the challenge against Billie Jean, the leading voice of women's lib in sports.

The whole ballyhooed extravaganza was just right for the times, and it became a national media event, front-page news in papers and magazines across the country. King exulted in her victory, not as a great competitive triumph but as "a culmination" of her years of striving to demonstrate that tennis could be big-league entertainment for the masses, and that women could play.

Tennis was clearly the "in" sport of the mid-'70s. Sales of tennis equipment, clothing and vacations were burgeoning, and though the pro game remained plagued with disputes—notably an antitrust suit in women's tennis and a boycott of Wimbledon by the men's Association of Tennis Professionals—it continued to grow quickly. Prize money in 1973 rose to nearly $6 million.

World Championship Tennis introduced the new format agreed to in its 1972 accord with the International Lawn Tennis Federation: a January-through-May series with a field of 64 players split into two groups of 32, playing parallel tours of 11 $50,000 tournaments. The top four men of each group (Stan Smith, Rod Laver, Roy Emerson and John Alexander of "A"; Ken Rosewall, Arthur Ashe, Marty Riessen and Roger Taylor of "B") went to Dallas for the $100,000 finals.

Smith, who had won a record four consecutive tournaments and six of 11 to top Laver (three victories) in his group, took the $50,000 top prize by beating Ashe, 6–3, 6–3, 4–6, 6–4. Ashe had ended Rosewall's bid for a third straight Dallas title in a five-set semi, and Smith waylaid Laver.

For the first time, WCT also conducted a doubles competition, using the same format as singles. Smith and Lutz won the $40,000 first prize in the playoffs at Montreal, beating Riessen and Tom Okker, 6–2, 7–6, 6–0.

Running concurrently with the WCT tour for three months was the USTA Indoor Circuit of Bill Riordan, who refused to be dealt out by the WCT-ITF deal dividing the season, and threatened restraint-of-trade proceedings if forced to limit the prize money in his tournaments. His headliners were Jimmy Connors and Ilie Nastase, both of whom he managed at the time. Connors won six of the eight events he played, including the U.S. Indoor over Germany's Karl Meiler.

John Newcombe made the winner's circle at the 1973 Open and helped bring the Davis Cup back to Australia. • *UPI*

John Newcombe started the year by winning his first Australian Open title over New Zealander Onny Parun, 6–3, 6–7, 7–5, 6–1, and sharing the doubles with countryman Mal Anderson. Newcombe also won the French doubles with Okker, but slumped badly until rededicating himself late in the year, winning the U.S. Open and teaming with Laver to return the Davis Cup to Australia in the first year it was open to "contract pros."

On balance, the No. 1 ranking had to go to Nastase, the volatile Romanian (he accumulated fines totaling $11,000) who won 15 of 31 tournaments, 118 of 135 matches, and led the money earning list with $228,750, including a $55,000 bonus for topping the Grand Prix standings. He clobbered Manuel Orantes in the Italian Open final, 6–1, 6–1, 6–1; swept through the French Open without losing a set (Nikki Pilic was his final victim, 6–3, 6–3, 6–0), topped the Grand Prix standings and won the Masters for the third straight year, beating Newcombe in the round-robin and personal nemesis Okker in the final, 6–3, 7–5, 4–6, 6–3, at Boston.

Nastase played indifferently at Wimbledon, where he was considered a shoo-in because of the boycott, but was beaten in the fourth round by Sandy Mayer, and at Forest Hills, where Andrew Pattison ambushed him in the second round. But his overall record was the best.

The No. 1 U.S. men's ranking was shared for the first time in history. The ranking committee could not choose

Bjorn Borg and Brian Gottfried (winner of the $30,000 first prize at the ATP's Alan King Classic in Las Vegas, over Ashe). Connors was the youngest man atop the American rankings since one of his mentors, Pancho Gonzalez, ruled at 20 in 1948, and Smith was the first to be No. 1 four times since Bill Tilden gained the top spot for the 10th time in 1929.

Connors, brimming with confidence after his fine showing on the less-strenuous-than-WCT U.S. Indoor circuit, knocked off top-seeded Smith in the first round of the U.S. Pro Championships and went on to whip Ray Moore, Dick Stockton, Cliff Richey and Arthur Ashe for the title. He saved a match point in beating Smith again at the Pacific Southwest and escaped another match point in beating out Smith for a semifinal berth in the Grand Prix Masters, giving him a 3–0 record against Stan for the calendar year. (Smith was the only player to reach both the WCT and Masters playoffs.)

The already turbulent political waters in tennis were muddied further by formation of a league called World Team Tennis, which planned to start intercity team competition using a unique, Americanized for-

mat in 1974. Dennis Murphy, who had helped found the American Basketball Association and the World Hockey Association, envisioned 16 teams with six players apiece under contract competing in a May-through-August season.

Jack Kramer and the ATP board came out staunchly opposed to WTT, saying it would harm the long-range players' inter-

series to which he had allegedly committed himself, ATP members objected, claiming that this was precisely the sort of arbitrary disciplinary power by a national association that the players' association had been formed to counteract. An ATP threat to withdraw all its 70 members from the French Open if Pilic was barred from the tournament was averted by a delaying tactic: an appeal hearing before the ITF Emergency Committee, which reduced Pilic's suspension from three months to one month.

This did not satisfy the ATP board, which contended that only their own association should have disciplinary authority over players. Many also felt that the one-month suspension, which included Wimbledon, was devised by the ITF to demonstrate its muscle because it believed the players would never support a boycott of the world's premier tournament. Thus "the Pilic Affair" became a test of the will and organization of the new association. Many ATP leaders felt that if they gave in on this first showdown, they would never be strong, whereas if they held firm and proved to the ILTF that even Wimbledon was not sacred, the ATP's unity and power would never be doubted in the future.

After days of tortuous meetings and attempts to find compromises, including the ATP's seeking an injunction in Britain's High Court forcing Wimbledon to accept Pilic's entry, ATP members voted to withdraw en masse if Pilic were barred from Wimbledon. Seventy-nine men did withdraw their entries, including 13 of the original 16 seeds; Ilie Nastase, Englishman Roger Taylor and Australian Ray Keldie were the only members who did not withdraw. (They were later fined by the ATP.)

Amid ferocious press criticism and bitterness, the tournament was played with a second-rate men's field. The British public, taking up the press crusade that "Wimbledon is bigger than a few spoiled players," turned out in near-record numbers. They made heroes of Nastase, Taylor and such bright newcomers as Connors and Swedish teen-ager Borg, who became the immediate heartthrob of squealing British schoolgirls.

Nastase, an overwhelming favorite, was beaten at the end of the first week by collegian amateur Mayer, who went on to reach the semifinals. Jan Kodes won the championship, the first Czech to do so since expatriate Jaroslav Drobny in 1954, beating Soviet No. 1 Alex Metreveli, 6–1, 9–8, 6–3, in a predicatably uninspiring final. Nastase and Connors clowned their way to a five-set victory over Australians John Cooper and Neale Fraser in the doubles final.

In one sense, the success of the boycotted Wimbledon was a triumph for the tournament, proving again what an unshakable institution it is, an important part of British summer life. But in the long run, the boycott made the ATP. The players' message to the ITF was clear. They were finally united in an organization to influence their own destiny. If they could stand up to Wimbledon, they could stand up to any authority. The ATP was established as a political force to be reckoned with in the future.

Meanwhile, with Wimbledon sacrificed for one year, the U.S. Open became the men's most important competitive test of 1973. Nastase, co-seeded No.1 with Smith, squandered a two-set lead and lost to journeyman Pattison. Kodes, who resented being downgraded as a "cheese champion" at Wimbledon, returned serve spectacularly in going all the way to the final, saving a match point at nightfall to outstroke Smith, 7–5, 6–7, 1–6, 6–1, 7–5, in the semifinals. Kodes almost repeated his 1971 upset over Newcombe, this time in the final instead of the first round, but the rugged Australian ultimately had too much firepower and won a spectacular finale, 6–4, 1–6, 4–6, 6–2, 6–3. Newcombe and Davidson beat countrymen Laver and Rosewall in the doubles final.

Newcombe and Laver also performed heroically in the Davis Cup. Laver, representing his country for the first time since 1962, won all his singles in a 4–1 semifinal victory over Czechoslovakia in Melbourne and a 5–0 whitewash of the United States in the final, ending the Americans' five-year reign. In the Cup's first indoor final, before disappointing crowds totaling about 10,000 for three days at Cleveland's Public Auditorium, Newcombe set the tone by beating Smith in the opener, 6–1, 3–6, 6–3, 3–6, 6–4. Artistically, this might well have been the match of the year, Newcombe—an enforced absentee from Davis Cup compensation since 1967—coming back from 1–3 and a break point in the fifth set with some sublime play. Laver beat Tom Gorman, 8–10, 8–6, 6–8, 6–3, 6–1, in the second match, then surprisingly teamed with Newcombe to pummel Smith and Erik van Dillen in the decisive doubles, 6–1, 6–2, 6–4. (Earlier in the year, in the American Zone final, Smith and van Dillen had beaten Chileans Jaime Fillol and Patricio Cornejo, 7–9, 37–39, 8–6, 6–1, 6–3—122 games, the longest Davis Cup match on record.)

Captain Neale Fraser's "Australian Antique Show" was so strong that evergreen

Ken Rosewall—whose brilliant singles victories over Marty Riessen and Smith and inspired doubles alongside John Alexander had spurred Australia to a 5–2 World Cup triumph over the U.S. at Hartford in March—couldn't crack the final-round lineup. Newcombe and Laver handled the stunned Gorman and Smith in the final singles for the 5–0 sweep, concluding the record U.S. streak of 17 match wins.

September 1973. Part of the compromise was that Heldman would not be involved.

Out of the wreckage of the WITF, a new women players' guild—the Women' Tennis Association—was formed at Wimbledon. With Billie Jean King as its first president, the WTA worked closely with the USTA's Edy McGoldrick in organizing a strong women's circuit for 1974

announced that it would begin operations in May 1974, and signed such prominent players as Newcombe, Rosewall, Billie Jean King and Evonne Goolagong to lucrative contracts.

In women's pro tennis, two separate tours were played in the winter and spring of 1973. The Virginia Slims Circuit consisted of 14 events, starring Billie Jean King and Margaret Court, conducted under the auspices of the Women's International Tennis Federation (WITF), incorporated as an autonomous body by Gladys Heldman. The USLTA—claiming that it had been hoodwinked and double-crossed by Heldman—hastily arranged a circuit of eight tournaments featuring Chris Evert, Evonne Goolagong and Virginia Wade.

In Heldman's suit against the USTA in Federal District Court in New York, Judge Milton Pollack ruled against her, rendering the WITF short-lived. The players who signed with WITF were declared ineligible for the 1973 Commercial Union Grand Prix (won by Chris Evert), but by June an agreement was reached between the USTA and Philip Morris, Inc., parent company of Virginia Slims, for a single women's tour under USTA/ITF auspices starting in

Circuit, and $204,000 in prize money, the female high. Dating from her loss to Jeanne Evert in Boca Raton the previous fall, Court won 59 consecutive matches. For the calendar year her record was 102–6, and she beat King in three of four meetings.

Court started the year by beating Evonne Goolagong in the final of the Australian Open for the third consecutive year, 6–4, 7–5. She then teamed with Virginia Wade to win the doubles for the eighth time in 13 years, with her sixth different partner.

Court was down 3–5, second set, in the final of the French, but recovered to beat Evert, 6–7 (5–7), 7–6 (8–6), 6–4, and became the only woman other than Suzanne Lenglen to win five singles titles in Paris. (Only two of Lenglen's six, 1925–26, count in the standings of all-time champs since non-French citizens couldn't enter their championships prior to 1925.) This was a battle of torrid ground-stroking, the most memorable women's match of the year. Court also won her fourth French doubles title, with Wade.

Only Wimbledon prevented Court from recording a second Grand Slam. All eight seeds advanced to the quarterfinals, and the only reversal of form was Evert's 6–1, 1–6, 6–1 defeat of top-seeded Court in the semis—as unexpected a result on the grass that Margaret liked so much as was her comeback in the French final on Chrissie's beloved clay. King, superbly conditioned physically and mentally and operating at a high emotional pitch, beat Goolagong in the semifinals, 6–3, 5–7, 6–3, and blasted Evert in the final, 6–0, 7–5. BJK became the first five-time singles winner since Helen Wills Moody four decades earlier and also teamed with Rosemary Casals to win the doubles and with Owen Davidson to capture the mixed, her second Wimbledon "triple." The women's doubles triumph was King's ninth, with four partners, and fifth with Casals.

At the U.S. Open, 1971–72 champion King walked off court while trailing Julie Heldman, 1–4, in the final set of a fourth-round match played in exhausting heat and humidity. Heldman complained, as was her right under the rules, that King was taking far more than the one minute allowed at changeovers. "If you want the match that badly, you can have it," seethed King, who later said she was suffering from a virus that had sapped her strength. King's defeat—3–6, 6–4, 4–1, ret.—recalled two other celebrated surrenders by champions: Suzanne Lenglen to Molla Bjurstedt Mallory in 1921, and Helen Wills Moody to Helen Jacobs in 1933.

Court beat Wade in two tie-breakers in the quarterfinals, avenged her Wimbledon defeat by Evert, 7–5, 2–6, 6–2, in the semis, and made Goolagong a bridesmaid again in the final, 7–6, 5–7, 6–2. For her victory Margaret received $25,000, the same as Newcombe, as the women achieved prize money parity with men in a major championship for the first time. The singles triumph was her 24th major and last in a Big Four event. Court teamed with Wade for Court's 18th and last Big Four doubles title.

King, despite being hampered by injuries in the early season, won eight of 19 tournaments and 58 of 68 matches. Including her $100,000 triumph over Riggs, she earned $197,000 for the year. In earning the No. 1 U.S. ranking for the seventh time, she equaled a feat previously achieved only by Mallory (between 1915 and 1926) and Moody (between 1923 and 1931).

Evert—who turned pro on her 18th birthday, December 21, 1972—earned $151,352 in her rookie season. She virtually monopolized the USTA winter tour, winning six of seven tournaments, beating Goolagong in the final of the last three. Evert went on to win 12 of 21 tournaments, 88 of 98 matches, including the Virginia Slims Championship at Boca Raton over her personal nemesis, Nancy Richey Gunter. Evert was disappointed to lose three big finals in a row at midseason—the Italian Open to Goolagong, the French to Court, and Wimbledon to King—but she took her first significant international title in the autumn, the South African Open over Goolagong. During this tournament she also announced her engagement to Jimmy Connors, later called off.

Evert also led the U.S. to a 5–2 victory over a young and, except for Virginia Wade, inexperienced British team in the Wightman Cup. This was the 50th anniversary of the competition, and was therefore played at Longwood Cricket Club, only yards from the home of Cup donor Hazel Hotchkiss Wightman, who was present and active in the celebrations at age 86.

Australia, led by Evonne Goolagong, defeated South Africa, 3–0, in the final of the Federation Cup at Bad Homburg, Germany, and Goolagong's 6–2, 6–3 victory over Evert and Kerry Melville's triumph over Julie Heldman spearheaded an Australian comeback and 6–3 victory over the U.S. in the second Bonne Bell Cup, at Sydney.

Other notable happenings during the year: Rosie Casals took the biggest check, $30,000, for beating King in the semis and Gunter in the final of the family Circle Cup at Hilton Head, S.C. Goolagong beat Evert in the final of the Western Championships at Cincinnati, Chris's last defeat on clay for nearly six years. Evert won her second U.S. Clay Court title the next week, beginning an astounding streak on her favorite sur-

The king and queen of Wimbledon: Jimmy Connors and Chris Evert in 1974. • *UPI*

having been unsuccessful on the tour, she applied for and was granted a return to amateur status in order to play college tennis.

Although Arthur Ashe was beaten by Connors in the South African Open final, he was the first nonwhite to reach the men's final there, and the first to win a men's title, the doubles with Tom Okker. Ashe's first appearance in South Africa was an emotional pilgrimage for him to a country he had long studied, but had heretofore been denied a visa to visit.

1974

Two young Americans—21-year-old Jimmy Connors and 19-year-old Chris Evert, who had announced their engagement late in 1973 but called it off before getting to the altar the next fall—reigned as the king and queen of tennis in 1974. And as the American game celebrated its Centennial, two startling surveys revealed just how popular the game had become in the United States.

The respected A. C. Nielsen Company made its first survey of tennis in 1970, esti-

mating that 10.3 million Americans played occasionally and projecting that the number would increase to 15 million by 1980. A second survey in 1973 indicated that the growth rate was much faster, and fixed the number of players at 20.2 million. A third study, released in September 1974, indicated a staggering 68 percent increase to 33.9 million Americans who said they played tennis "from time to time," and a more significant estimate that 23.4 million played at least three times a month.

Almost as surprising as the rate of the participation boom was a Louis Harris survey that indicated a substantial rise in tennis' popularity as a spectator sport. "The number [of sports fans] who say they 'follow' tennis has risen from 17 to 26 percent just in the last year, by far the most dramatic change in American sports preferences," the Harris organization said. This growth was reflected in the tennis industry, as new companies rushed in to offer a dizzying variety of equipment to the burgeoning market, and in the professional game, where prize money continued to sky-rocket. Four men and one woman exceeded the $200,000 prize money barrier, which had seemed unattainable just a few years earlier. Connors ($281,309) and Evert ($261,460) led the parade of six-figure earners.

Connors rampaged to the most successful season of any American man since Tony Trabert in 1955, and also became the center of a new political storm in men's tennis.

Connors won 99 out of 103 matches during the year, 14 of 20 tournaments, including the Australian Open, Wimbledon, U.S. Open, U.S. Indoor, U.S. Clay Court and South African Open. He was denied a chance at the Grand Slam when the French Tennis Federation, then led by the strong-willed Phillippe Chatrier, barred any player who had signed a contract to compete in the new World Team Tennis league in the U.S., which Europeans viewed as a threat to their summer tournaments.

Thus Connors, who had signed to play some matches with the WTT Baltimore Banners, and Evonne Goolagong, contracted to the Pittsburgh Triangles, were kept out of the world's premier clay-court championship after having won the Australian at the start of the year. Bill Riordan, the maverick Connors' maverick manager, knew there was no way he could sue the French Federation directly, but filed a $40 million antitrust suit against Association of Tennis Professionals officers Jack Kramer and Donald Dell (who had been anti-WTT activists) and Commercial Union Assurance, sponsor of the ITF Grand Prix, alleging a conspiracy to monopolize professional tennis and keep Connors (and other WTT players) out of the French.

Few envisioned what a world-beating year it would be for the brash left-hander Connors when he beat Australian Phil Dent, 7–6, 6–4, 4–6, 6–3, for the Australian title. Aussies Geoff Masters and Ross Case took the doubles at Kooyong in Melbourne, their first Grand Slam title.

Connors dominated Riodan's USTA Indoor Circuit—which was played at the same time as an expanded, three-group World Championship Tennis circuit—winning seven of the nine tournaments he played, including the U.S. Indoor, his second of a record seven such titles, over Frew McMillan.

At Wimbledon, Connors came within two points of defeat at the hands of Dent in the second round, but pulled away to win from 5–6, 0–30 in the fifth set. He beat Jan Kodes in five rugged sets in the quarterfinals, Dick Stockton (conqueror of Ilie Nastase) in a four-set semi, and then ravaged 39-year-old Ken Rosewall, 6–1, 6–1, 6–4, in the final.

Rosewall had masterfully beaten 1970–71 champ and top seed John Newcombe in the quarters and come from two sets and a match point in the third-set tie-breaker to beat 1972 champ Stan Smith, 6–8, 4–6, 9–8, 6–1, 6–3, in one of Wimbledon's most memorable comebacks.

But Connors' ferocious returns of Rosewall's unintimidating serves kept the old man constantly on the defensive, the young lion always on the attack. Consequently, Connors became the youngest champion since Lew Hoad beat Rosewall at age 22 in the 1956 final, and Rosewall—the sentimental choice who had been runner-up in 1954, '56 and '70—remained, along with Pancho Gonzalez, Gottfried von Cramm and Fred Stolle, "the greatest players who never won Wimbledon."

Meanwhile, Newcombe captured his sixth doubles title, the fifth with fellow Aussie Tony Roche.

Connors had a virus infection that left him doubtful for the last U.S. Open played on grass courts. He lost a great deal of weight, but turned out to be lean and mean as he barreled through the tournament without serious danger, beating Alex Metreveli in the quarters, Roscoe Tanner (who had stopped Nastase and Smith) in the semis and Rosewall again in the final.

also stayed in America, Smith and Bob Lutz regaining the prize they first won in 1968.

Connors was the main man, but there were other outstanding performers during the year. Bjorn Borg, the ascending "Teen Angel" from Sweden, became the youngest player to win the Italian and French Opens and the U.S. Pro Championship. He celebrated his 18th birthday during the French, where he lost the first two sets of the final and then stomped Manuel Orantes, 2–6, 6–7, 6–0, 6–1, 6–1. He had been 17 when he won the Italian, dethroning Nastase in the final, 6–3, 6–4, 6–2. At the U.S. Pro, Borg beat Tom Okker, 7–6, 6–1, 6–1, after resurrecting himself from 1–5 in the fifth set to beat Jan Kodes in an astonishing semifinal, 7–6, 6–0, 1–6, 2–6, 7–6.

Borg won nine tournaments and was runner-up in five more, including the WCT finals at Dallas. There he coolly beat Ashe and Kodes before running up against Newcombe, 30, who won this one for the older generation, 4–6, 6–3, 6–3, 6–2.

Borg was also runner-up to Connors in the U.S. Clay Court, their only meeting of the year. Borg had won their first meeting

Roscoe Tanner ousted Ilie Nastase and Stan Smith before losing to Jimmy Connors in the 1974 U.S. Open semifinals. • *Jack Mecca*

in the quarterfinals of the 1973 Stockholm Open, but now Connors was off on a seven-match run in what would develop into the rivalry of the '70s in men's tennis.

Newcombe was the dominant player of the WCT season, winning five of the 11 tournaments in his group (Nastase and Laver won four each in theirs). But the new format of tricolor groups (Red, Blue, Green), each playing 11 tournaments to qualify their two point leaders plus two "wild cards" for the eight-man Dallas finals, was not very successful. The product was too diluted, difficult to follow, and the zigzagging global travel schedule taxed the players. WCT, which two years before had the inside track in the men's pro game, had overexpanded and suffered in prestige in the process.

Bob Hewitt and Frew McMillan won the WCT doubles final at Montreal, sharing $40,000 for beating Newcombe and Owen Davidson in the final, 6–2, 6–7, 6–1, 6–2. A makeshift young doubles team of Brian Gottfried and Mexican Raul Ramirez was formed in the spring and immediately proved to be a successful partnership, winning the first of four consecutive Italian doubles titles and several other tournaments.

After Wimbledon, another 22-year-old left-hander arose and edged out Connors for the $100,000 top prize in the Commercial Union Grand Prix. Guillermo Vilas of Argentina, who had shown promise of things to come by knocking out defending champ Andres Gimeno at the French Open in 1973, ruled the U.S. Summer Circuit and won six of his last 15 tournaments.

The attractive and sensitive young South American, a former law student and part-time poet, also won the Grand Prix Masters at Melbourne, which Connors boycotted. (He claimed a dental problem, but most blamed his suit against sponsor Commercial Union for his absence.) Even though Vilas did not like grass courts, which were not well suited to his heavy topspin game, he beat Newcombe, Borg and Onny Parun to win his round-robin group, then Ramirez in the semis and Nastase in a brilliant final, 7–6, 6–2, 3–6, 3–6, 6–4, to claim his biggest title to date.

At season's end, Vilas was not far behind Connors on the money list, having earned $271,327. Newcombe was third with the $273,299, Borg fourth with $215,229. Laver won six tournaments, including the U.S. Pro Indoor over Ashe (his 15th consecutive victory over Arthur in 15 years) and the rich Alan King Classic, and temporarily remained the all-time

money winner with a career total of $1,379,454. Connors would catch him soon enough.

Meanwhile, World Team Tennis made its raucous debut in May, offering players a lucrative alternative to tournaments during the summer. Sixteen teams embarked on a schedule of 44 contests each, the format being five one-set matches (men's and women's singles and doubles, plus mixed doubles), with the cumulative games won in all five deciding the outcome.

The Philadelphia Freedoms, with Billie Jean King as player-coach, defeated Ken Rosewall's Pittsburgh Triangles in the ballyhooed opener at Philadelphia's Spectrum, 31–25. Philadelphia had the best season record, 39–5, but lost the playoffs in two straight to the Denver Racquets, who promptly moved to Phoenix. No team made money, and the average loss per franchise was estimated to be $300,000. The league was cut down to 12 teams in 1975, and only one came back for the second season with the original owners.

A more traditional team competition, the Davis Cup, continued to be tarnished by political problems and cumbersome scheduling that often left countries playing matches without their best players, who had conflicting commitments elsewhere. Such was the case with both the United States, which was ambushed by Colombia, 4–1, at Bogota in January, and Australia, which traveled to India undermanned and was beaten by the same score.

For the first time in the 74-year history of the competition, the Cup was decided by default. South Africa became the fifth nation to hold the sterling silver punchbowl when the Indian Government refused to let its team play the final, in protest of South Africa's apartheid racial policies.

Connors declined to play for the U.S. in either the Davis Cup or the World

Cup—won by Australia at Hartford, 5–2, with Newcombe spearheading the attack, beating both Ashe and Smith in singles and teaming with Roche to beat them in doubles.

Evert became the youngest woman to gain the No. 1 U.S. ranking since Maureen Connolly reigned supreme in 1951–52. Chrissie won 16 tournaments—including 55-match winning streak in midseason. Evonne Goolagong beat her in four of six meetings, including the finals of the Australian Open and the Virginia Slims Championship at Los Angeles, and the semifinals of the U.S. Open. Billie Jean King won the Open and took two of three from Evert, including the final of the U.S. Indoor, which BJK captured for the fifth time.

Goolagong played inspired tennis in celebrating the New Year with a 7–6, 4–6, 6–0 triumph over Evert at Melbourne, winning her native title for the first time after being runner-up the previous three years. Evonne also paired with American Peggy Michel, her Pittsburgh Triangles teammate and partner in WTT, to win the Australian and Wimbledon doubles.

With Goolagong, King, Kerry Melville (who would marry her Boston Lobsters teammate Raz Reid), and most of the other leading women playing WTT during the summer, Evert had the European clay-court season pretty much to herself. She beat Martina Navratilova, the promising young Czech left-hander who had played the USTA women's circuit at age 16 in 1973, in the Italian Open final, 6–3, 6–3, and Soviet No. 1 Olga Morozova in the French Open final, 6–1, 6–2. Evert and Morozova won both doubles titles.

Evert barely survived her opening match at Wimbledon—she squeezed by Lesley Hunt, 8–6, 5–7, 11–9, in a thrilling match that was delayed for several hours by rain, breathtakingly played despite a slippery court, and suspended overnight by Melville, 9–7, 1–6, 6–2. Evert beat Melville, and Morozova erased Virginia Wade in the semis, and Evert got to dance the champions' traditional first foxtrot at the Wimbledon Ball with her fiancè, Connors. The "lovebird double," a Connors-Evert parlay, paid bettors 33–1 in England's legalized gambling shops.

Evert won 10 consecutive tournaments after losing the U.S. Indoor to King, but her streak ended at 55 matches in the semifinals at Forest Hills. Goolagong raced to a 6–0, 4–3 lead before rain suspended their match. The next day, Evert pulled level after Goolagong served for the match at 5–4 in the second set, four times reaching deuce, and came within two points of victory twice more when she served at 6–5. Evert broke again, won the tie-breaker by 5 points to 3, but could not contend with Goolagong's outstanding volleying in relinquishing the excruciating final set, 6–3.

King avenged her bitter loss of the year before by beating Julie Heldman, 2–6, 6–3, 6–1, in the other semifinal, and toppled Goolagong, 3–6, 6–3, 7–5, in a final of thrilling shotmaking that delighted a Monday sellout crowd of 15,303. Vastly more entertaining than the massacre of a men's final, this one was alive until the very end; Goolagong broke at love when King served for the match at 5–4, but BJK won eight of the last nine points to seal her fourth singles title. She also collaborated with Rosemary Casals for their second U.S. doubles crown. Bulldozers moved into the stadium at the West Side Tennis Club the next day to dig up the grass courts, which were to be replaced with synthetic clay.

Goolagong beat Evert in the final of the Virginia Slims tournament at Denver and again in the Slims playoff, where she took the richest women's prize to date— $32,000—with a 6–3, 6–4 victory over the 1972–73 champ. That evened their career rivalry at 8–8 over three years.

Melville, who had been runner-up to Evert for the $30,000 top prize in the Family Circle Cup in the spring, won the South African Open, her biggest international title, over Australian 17-year-old Dianne Fromholtz, 6–3, 7–5. Fromholtz had eliminated Margaret Court, making a comeback after the birth of her second child.

America's top two players, Evert and King, sat out the Federation, Wightman and Bonne Bell Cups. Player-captain Heldman beat both Goolagong and Hunt in leading the U.S. to a shocking 5–4 victory over Australia in the third Bell Cup, at Cleveland, after which the competition was unfortunately abandoned.

Great Britain, psyched by player-captain Virginia Wade's 5–7, 9–7, 6–4 victory over Heldman, sprinted to a 6–1 victory in the Wightman Cup, only their eighth in 46 meetings with the U.S., at Deeside, Wales. Cup donor Hazel Wightman died at age 87 in December, shortly after the series.

Heldman and Jeanne Evert—Chrissie's younger sister, who ranked No. 9, making the first time since Ethel and Florence Sutton in 1913 that sisters were among the U.S. Top Ten simultaneously—got to the final of the Federation Cup at Naples, Italy, before falling to Australia, 2–1. Goolagong beat Heldman for her 13th straight Fed Cup singles without a loss and teamed with Janet Young for the clincher after Evert guttily beat Fromholtz, 2–6, 7–5, 6–4.

Chris Evert was elected to succeed the more activist King as president of the Women's Tennis Association at Wimbledon, where the women threatened to boycott in 1975 unless they received "equal parity" with the men in prize money, as Evert put it. That was about the only political story in the women's game, however, and it turned out to be no more than a mild tempest in a teapot, solved by teatime.

1975

Jimmy Connors joined world leaders as a cover subject for *Time* magazine in 1975, as he beat first Rod Laver and then John Newcombe (avenging a loss in the Australian Open final) in ballyhooed "Heavyweight Championship of Tennis" challenge matches in Las Vegas.

These extravaganzas—the focal point of a TV sports scandal two years later because of the CBS network's misleading "winner-take-all" hype—gained high ratings and massive exposure. Connors and his clever, prizefight-style manager Bill Riordan—who were to split bitterly before the end of the year as Connors dropped the controversial antitrust suit he filed in 1974—were the kings of hype. But the ruler of men's tennis was King Arthur Ashe.

At age 32, after nearly 15 years in the big time, Ashe finally fulfilled the promise that had been acclaimed for him in 1968 and gradually abandoned. Seemingly a perennial bridesmaid, loser of 14 of his last 19 final-round matches coming into the year, Ashe became the best by dedicating himself to training and positive thinking as never before.

In 29 tournaments he got to 14 finals, winning nine of them, including the two he really set out to win: the WCT finals at Dallas (over Bjorn Borg, 3–6, 6–4, 6–4, 6–0) and Wimbledon (over Connors in a stunner, 6–1, 6–1, 5–7, 6–4). Ashe's $338,337 earnings for the year boosted his

lenge matches at Caesar's Palace, the Las Vegas hotel-casino. The opponent was Laver, the Grand Slammer of 1962 and 1969—a "natural" pairing since they had never played each other. Connors won, 6–4, 6–2, 3–6, 7–5, seizing what was said to be a $100,000 "winner-take-all" purse, but it was widely reported that both players took home big checks from "ancillary" revenues.

on December 20, Chrissie defended her Italian and French Open titles, won the first U.S. Open, on clay, by outgritting archrival Evonne Goolagong, dethroned Goolagong to recapture the Virginia Slims throne, won 16 of 22 tournaments for the year and set an all-time single-season winnings record of $350,977. She didn't lose a match the last six months of the season after succumbing to King in the Wimbledon semis, and was never beaten before the quarterfinals of a tournament.

Ashe was the Man of the Year, but the season began with another self-reclamation project. John Newcombe, who was slowed by injuries after winning the WCT title in May 1974, and who was to miss Wimbledon and the U.S. Open with new ailments, flogged himself into shape for the Australian Open by doing miles of roadwork and charging countless times up the hill behind his attractive split-level home in the Sydney suburb of Pymble. He struggled to the final, but was ready for Connors, serving ferociously to win, 7–5, 3–6, 6–4, 7–5.

Already set before the loss to Newcombe was the first of Connors' chal-

onship prize fight, each player receiving a pre-agreed percentage, win or lose. Connors made $480,000; Newcombe, $280,000.

Although he won these indoor bouts amid the heavyweight hoopla on which he thrives, Connors lost in the finals of the three major championships he had swept the previous year. Newcombe set the tone in Australia. Ashe, considered a prohibitive underdog, came up with a tactical masterpiece at Wimbledon. He changed speed and spin smartly, fed junk to Connors' forehand, exposing the vulnerability of that wing to paceless shots, and sliced his serves wide to Connors' backhand, exploiting the slightly limited reach of his two-handed shot.

This was an extraordinary final, the first ever between litigants in a lawsuit since President Ashe, along with other officers of the Association of Tennis Professionals, were named in the $40-million antitrust suit Connors and Riordan had filed against attorney Donald Dell, Jack Kramer and Grand Prix sponsor Commercial Union. There were several other suits and counterclaims associated with this one, but all were quietly settled, out of court and without payment of damages, not long after Ashe's emotion-charged and enormously popular victory.

Ashe was not considered a serious threat at the U.S. Open after the grass courts at the West Side Tennis Club in Forest Hills were dug up immediately after the 1974 tournament, replaced with a synthetic clay called Har-Tru, which became the predominent surface of the U.S. Summer Circuit. Sure enough, clay specialist Eddie Dibbs—one of a group of scrappy young Americans coming up to succeed Ashe's generation—beat Arthur in the fourth round.

Forest Hills, previously dominated by grass-loving Americans and Australians, suddenly became a happy hunting ground for clay-reared Europeans and South Americans. The most successful was Manuel Orantes, the elegant left-hander from Barcelona. In the semifinals, he revived himself from two sets and 0–2 down, and from 0–5 in the fourth set, saving five match points to beat Argentinian left-hander Guillermo Vilas, 4–6, 1–6, 6–2, 7–5, 6–4. That three-hour, 44-minute marathon did not end until 10:40 P.M. on Saturday—the installation of all-weather courts permitted floodlighting and night play for the first time—and Orantes did not get to bed until 3:00 A.M. because of a plumbing failure in his hotel room. He was assumed to be a lamb going to slaughter in the final against Connors, who had hammered Borg in the other semifinal, 7–5, 7–5, 7–5, early the previous afternoon.

But taking his cue from Ashe's strategy at Wimbledon, Orantes slow-balled Connors and cleverly mixed up his game. He drop-shotted and lobbed, chipped and passed, traded ground strokes and sometimes dashed in to take away the forecourt, snaring Connors in his butterfly net.

It was 10 years to the day since Manuel Santana had become the first Spaniard to

Spain's Manuel Orantes overcame every obstacle in 1975, including Jimmy Connors at Forest Hills.
• *Peter Mecca*

win at Forest Hills, and again the old concrete stadium was filled with Latin chants and shouts of "*Bravo!*" as 15,669 spectators roared Orantes to an astonishing 6–4, 6–3, 6–3 victory. At the end, he fell to his knees, jubilantly, his toothy Latin face the definitive portrait of ecstacy. Why not? His last 24 hours had constituted the most remarkable feat of any player in a major championship since Wimbledon in 1927, when Frenchman Henri Cochet elevated himself from two sets and 1–5 down to beat Bill Tilden in the semifinals, then from two sets down to overhaul Jean Borotra in the final.

Connors lost his stranglehold on men's tennis, but did not have a bad year by anyone's standards except his own. He entered 19 tournaments and won nine—five of them on Riordan's USLTA Indoor circuit, including the U.S. Indoor over Vitas Gerulaitis, 5–7, 7–5, 6–1, 3–6, 6–0. Connors was runner-up in six others, including the Australian, Wimbledon and

U.S. Open. Connors compiled an 83–10 record and, made well over a half-million dollars with all his "special" matches, but Ashe was the prize-money leader with $306,712.

Connors also split with Riordan in the fall. He had prospered, financially and competitively, under Riordan's tutelage, but also had become the isolated man of

Ashe, who had been one of the first to recognize that a deep freeze by his peers would be the most effective way of ending the divisive lawsuits Connors fronted for Riordan, won four of eight tournaments in his group during the WCT season, while Connors was playing the smaller Riordan-organized tour. Laver set a WCT record by winning four consecutive tournaments and 23 straight matches, but Ashe earned a solid gold tennis ball, valued at $33,333, as the top point-winner on the tour, which was divided into three groups (Red, Blue and Green) playing a total of 25 tournaments. He won the $50,000 top prize in the WCT finals at Dallas by beating Mark Cox, John Alexander and Bjorn Borg.

Ashe also played a substantial number of events in the $4-million dollar Commercial Union Grand Prix, which embraced 42 tournaments in 19 countries during its May-through-December calendar, boosting the total prize money available in men's tennis to more than $8 million dollars. Ashe compiled a 16-match winning streak in the fall, winning tournaments at Los Angeles and San Francisco, and qualified for the eight-man Grand Prix Masters playoff at Stockholm. He had

visions of a unique WCT-Masters "double," but was upended in the semis of the Masters by Borg and concluded, "I don't think anybody is strong enough, mentally and physically, to win WCT and the Masters in the same year."

Borg was runner-up in both—to Ashe in Dallas and to Ilie Nastase (who came back from a disqualification against Ashe

he steamrolled Vilas again, 6–3, 6–4, 6–2, to defend his U.S. Pro crown. Borg won five of 23 tournaments on the year, amassed a 78–19 record, and carried Sweden to its first possession of the Davis Cup, winning all 12 of his singles matches against Poland, West Germany, the Soviet Union, Spain, Chile and Czechoslovakia. His record of 16 consecutive Davis Cup singles victories over three years eclipsed the all-time Cup record of 12 set by Bill Tilden between 1920 and 1926, and would stretch to 33 by his retirement.

Vilas didn't win any of the big international titles, but won six of 23 tournaments—including Washington and Louisville during a 16-match winning streak early in the U.S. summer circuit—and reached at least the quarterfinals of 21 to seize the $100,000 top prize in the Commercial Union Grand Prix for the second straight year. Orantes, who counted the German, Swedish, Canadian, British, U.S. Clay Court and U.S. Open titles among the seven tournaments he won, finished second in the Grand Prix standings.

Nastase won the Masters for the fourth time in five years, coming back from his opening disqualification. (Ashe, disgruntled by Nastase's behavior and stalling, uncharacteristically stormed off the court, but was declared the winner the following day.) "Nasty" beat Orantes and Adriano Panatta in his remaining round-robin matches, Vilas in the semifinals, and a badly off-form Borg in the final, 6–2, 6–2, 6–1. This was by far the biggest of Nastase's seven tournament victories for the year, but he set a dubious achievement record by being defaulted three times, quitting his semifinal match in the Italian Open to ultimate champion Raul Ramirez, and "tanking" the Canadian Open final to Orantes after getting upset by a line call in the first-set tie-breaker.

For this unprofessional conduct, Nastase was fined $8,000 by the newly formed Men's International Professional Tennis Council, a tripartite body made up of three representatives each of the male players, the ITF, and worldwide tournament directors. Nastase's lawyers appealed, and the fine was reduced, but the "Pro Council" had established itself as an important new administrative and judicial force in the men's game. It was designed to be legislative as well, and became the autonomous governing body of the Grand Prix circuit.

It was a peculiar year in men's doubles. Australians John Alexander and Phil Dent won their national title for the first time, but Brian Gottfried and Raul Ramirez were the Team of the Year. They began their reign in the U.S. Pro Indoor at Philadelphia, and won the WCT doubles title at Mexico City over Mark Cox and Cliff Drysdale. Gottfried-Ramirez also won a special "Challenge Match" during the WCT singles finals at Dallas, necessitated because South African Davis Cuppers Bob Hewitt and Frew McMillan had been rudely kicked out of Mexico shortly after their arrival for the doubles playoff—a clumsy power play by the Mexican Government to protest the apartheid racial policies of South Africa.

Gottfried-Ramirez also won the French title, over Alexander-Dent, and the U.S. Pro, but they came up flat at the end of the year, failing to win a match in the Masters as a four-man doubles playoff was inaugurated alongside the singles. The doubles was a round-robin affair, which proved to be an unsatisfactory format when three teams tied with identical 2–1 records. Spanish Davis Cuppers Orantes and Juan Gisbert were declared champions on the basis of having the best percentage of games won for their three matches, even though they were beaten head-to-head by the spirited new American tandem of Sherwood Stewart and Freddie McNair. (The Masters doubles was changed to a knock-out format in succeeding years.)

The Wimbledon doubles turned into a wildly unpredictable scramble as only one seeded team reached the quarterfinals. Sandy Mayer and Vitas Gerulaitis, who had not blended well earlier in the year, became the first American champions in 18 years with a 7–5, 8–6, 6–4 victory in the final over similarly unseeded Allan Stone of Australia and Colin Dowdeswell of Rhodesia, who had never even met each other until introduced in the tea room the first day of the tournament. Their regular partners were injured, so they formed a makeshift alliance and filled a late vacancy in the draw.

Connors got his only major title of the year by teaming with Nastase to win the U.S. Open doubles over Marty Riessen and Tom Okker. Connors seldom played doubles thereafter, a trend soon followed by Borg and Vilas as top players began to concentrate singularly on singles.

Connors also ended—only temporarily, as it turned out—his one-man boycott of the U.S. Davis Cup team. Former French, Wimbledon and U.S. champion Tony Trabert replaced Dennis Ralston as the American captain after Raul Ramirez led a 3–2 Mexican ambush of the U.S. at

Palm Springs in February 1975, ironically the same weekend that Connors was beating Laver in the first Las Vegas Challenge Match.

Trabert coaxed Connors, who had long feuded with Ralston (this was really a proxy fight between Riordan and Ralston's agent, former Cup captain Donald Dell), onto the American squad for a first-round conquest

at Baastad was kept almost empty except for thousands of police and troops; boats patrolled the harbor, aircraft hovered overhead, and huge nets around the stadium protected the players from projectiles hurled by anti-Chile demonstrators, who chanted and set off firecrackers a block away. In this unnerving atmosphere, Borg and Birger Andersson—who helped win four of Sweden's matches along the way,

two countries in the decisive fifth match, and Ramirez was as high as the 6,000-foot altitude of Mexico City as he beat Connors, 2–6, 6–3, 6–3, 6–4, in a match suspended overnight by darkness.

The 1975 final was played the same weekend at Stockholm's Kungliga Tennishallen. Borg whipped both Jiri Hrebec and Jan Kodes in singles and teamed with towering Ove Bengtson to dispatch Kodes and shaky Vladimir Zednik in doubles as Sweden defeated Czechoslovakia, 3–2, to become the sixth nation to hold the Davis Cup. Both teams were first-time finalists.

The Davis Cup continued to be plagued by political turmoil. Mexico, after eliminating the U.S., refused to play South Africa. Colombia similarly defaulted, putting South Africa—winner of the Cup by default the previous year—into the American Zone final without playing a match. But the South Africans were eliminated by Chile at Santiago. Chilean No. 1 Jaime Fillol received a death threat from opponents of the military junta in his homeland, and it was only with massive security precautions that Chile was able to play the semifinal In Sweden. The stadium

Nations Cup. The American team of Ashe and Tanner defeated Great Britain's Roger Taylor and Buster Mottram, 2–1, in Jamaica, but the competition was not a success. Meanwhile, Laver and 40-year-old Ken Rosewall helped Australia to a 4–3 victory over the U.S. in the World Cup at Hartford, showing that the Aussie dynasty was not entirely dead—though a group of younger Aussies was beaten by Czechoslovakia in the semifinals of the Davis Cup at Prague.

World Team Tennis, despite the huge financial losses of its inaugural season and a ludicrous player draft (numerous showbiz personalities were named by teams in a publicity stunt that made a mockery of the league), surprised many by coming out for a second season. There were 12 teams, four fewer than in 1974, and only one returned with the original ownership, but the league staggered along. Pittsburgh, led by Vitas Gerulaitis and Evonne Goolagong, beat the San Francisco Bay Area's Golden Gaters in the championship series.

Goolagong started the season by repeating as Australian Open champion, beating Martina Navratilova, 6–3, 6–2, in an emotional final. (Evonne's father had been killed in an auto accident, and Evonne cried on the shoulder of her coach and guardian, Vic Edwards, at the presentation ceremonies.) Goolagong also successfully defended her doubles title with WTT teammate Peggy Michel.

Evert won the biggest check for women in "special events"—$50,000 for winning the four-woman L'Eggs World Series over King at Lakeway, Tex., 4–6, 6–3, 7–6. She also won $40,000 for adding her third triumph in the Virginia Slims Championship at Los Angeles, over Navratilova, 6–4, 6–2. Navratilova won the U.S. Indoor at Boston, beating Virginia Wade, Margaret Court and Goolagong, but she lost again to Evert in the final of the rich Family Circle Cup at Amelia Island, Fla.

With most of the top women committed to World Team Tennis, Evert and Navratilova were the class of the women's field in the Italian and French Opens. They reached the singles finals of both, Evert winning in Rome by 6–1, 6–0 and in Paris by 2–6, 6–2, 6–1. Chris and Martina then teamed up to win both the doubles titles.

King always considered the Centre Court at Wimbledon her favorite stage, and she never performed more majestically there than she did in coming from 0–3 down in the third set to beat Evert in the semifinals, and burying Goolagong, 6–0, 6–1, in the most lopsided women's final since 1911. BJK's sixth singles title was her 19th in all at Wimbledon, tying the career record of Elizabeth Ryan, who never won the singles but captured 12 doubles and seven mixed crowns between 1914 and 1934. King said this was her last appearance in singles because of a deteriorating knee—"I want to quit on top," she said, "and I can't get much higher than this"— but she eventually returned, in 1977.

The women's doubles champions turned out to be as unlikely as the men's,

Kazuko Sawamatsu of Japan and Ann Kiyomura, an American of Japanese ancestry, teaming to upset Francoise Durr and Betty Stove in the final. Margaret Court teamed with Marty Riessen for the mixed doubles title over Stove and Allan Stone.

Evert won the U.S. Open, dropping only one set. That was in the final, where her 5–7, 6–4, 6–2 victory over Goolagong relegated Evonne to the record books as the first woman to lose three consecutive U.S. singles finals. Chris was just too formidable on the clay she loved so well, as she demonstrated by grinding out the last four games of the match in a baseline duel. Court and Wade took the doubles title over King and Casals; this was the last of Court's record 62 Big Four titles in singles and doubles.

More important than tennis was Navratilova's decision, announced at Forest Hills, to defect from her native Czechoslovakia and seek U.S. citizenship. She made the decision after the Czech tennis federation, chiding her for becoming "too Americanized," initially refused her a visa to compete in the U.S. Open. Navratilova felt she had to follow the lead of the great Czech player Jaroslav Drobny, who defected in 1949, if she were to develop as a tennis player and as a person, but the decision was painful. She knew that her action meant that it would be years before she would see her parents and younger sister Jana again.

Navratilova and Renata Tomanova had led Czechoslovakia past Ireland, Netherlands, West Germany, France and Australia to win the 30-nation Federation Cup at Aix-en-Provence in southern France. Australia beat the United States in the semifinals, Goolagong and Helen Gourlay stopping U.S. captain Julie Heldman and Janet Newberry, 11–9, 6–1, in the doubles that swung a 2–1 decision. That put the Aussies in the final for the 10th time, but Navratilova ended

Martina Navratilova made a big decision in 1975—she defected from Czechoslovakia. • *UPI*

Goolagong's 16-match unbeaten streak in Fed Cup singles, 6–3, 6–4, and Tomanova ambushed Gourlay, 6–4, 6–2. The Czechs then teamed to beat Gourlay and Dianne Fromholtz for a 3–0 verdict, clinching the Cup for the first time.

Great Britain also humbled the U.S. in the Wightman Cup for the second straight year, its first back-to-back wins since 1924–25. Evert won both her singles, over Wade and Glynis Coles, in straight sets, but with Heldman sidelined with a sore shoulder, the U.S. did not have the depth it needed to contend with Wade, Coles and Ann Jones, who returned to the battle at age 37. Coles' 6–3, 7–6 victory over Mona Schallau was the clincher in a 5–2 British victory at Cleveland's Public Auditorium.

The most spectacular comeback of the year belonged to Evert, who trailed Nancy Richey Gunter, 6–7, 0–5, 15–40—double match point—in the semifinals of the U.S.

Clay Court at Indianapolis. After that, Chrissie didn't make a mistake in roaring back to win, 6–7, 7–5, 4–2 ret. Gunter finally had to quit with cramps. Evert went on to thrash Fromholtz in the final for her fourth consecutive U.S. Clay Court crown.

A couple of administrative happenings during 1975 are worthy of note. Over the protests of tournament chairman and direc-

dance, to 210,083. This was also the year the U.S. Lawn Tennis Association voted to drop the "Lawn" from its name, becoming simply the USTA. It was the beginning of a fashion that would, in 1977, see the International Lawn Tennis Federation become the ITF.

1976

Jimmy Connors returned to the pinnacle of men's tennis in 1976 and Chris Evert consolidated her stranglehold on the women's game. But the most bizarre and compelling story of the year was the emergence of professional sport's first transsexual.

Richard Raskind, a 41-year-old ophthalmologist, enough player to captain the Yale University varsity in 1954, play at Wimbledon and Forest Hills, and reach the semifinals of the National 35-and-over championships in 1972. In August 1975, he had sex reassignment surgery and moved west to Newport Beach, Cal., to start a new life and practice as Dr. Renée Richards.

In July 1976, Dr. Richards—a 6-foot-2 left-hander—entered and won a local

Dr. Richard Raskind, an ophthalmologist, switched to a career in tennis as Renée Richards. • *Peter Mecca*

women's tournament in La Jolla, Cal. A former acquaintance noticed her resemblance in playing style to Richard Raskind, verified her identity and tipped off a San Diego television sportscaster, who broke the story.

Dr. Richards, who had sought a clean start in California, far from her former wife and four-year-old son in New York, decided to "go public" and put aside her brilliant career as an eye surgeon in order to play professional tennis.

"I started getting letters, poignant letters from other transsexuals who were considering suicide, whose friends and families won't see them," she explained to *Newsday* reporter Jane Gross. "I realized that this was more than just a tennis thing, my hobby; I could easily give that up. But, if I can do anything for those people, I will. I am in a position to try and make people

see that such individuals should be allowed to hold up their heads. I realize this is important from a social standpoint."

The Richards case caused an extraordinary, highly publicized stir in women's tennis. The Women's Tennis Association opposed her eligibility for tournaments, and sided with the USTA in its hasty ruling that women would have to pass an Olympic-style chromosome test before being accepted for women's national championships, including the U.S. Open. Dr. Richards refused to take the test, claiming that it was an unsatisfactory means of determining gender, given the advances of modern medicine.

Many women felt that Dr. Richards would have an unfair competitive advantage because of her size, strength and past experience in competition against men. Others feared that her acceptance would set a bad precedent, paving the way for a younger, stronger transsexual to dominate women's tennis in the future. Many WTA members liked Richards personally, admired her courage, but still opposed her acceptance in tournaments.

Dr. Richards was denied admission to the U.S. Open—she took her case to court, and was admitted in 1977 by court order—but did play in a pre-Forest Hills tournament at South Orange, N.J. Most WTA members withdrew in protest, but the tournament attracted national television coverage and massive publicity. Richards was beaten in the semifinals by 17-year-old Lea Antonoplis, early evidence that fears Dr. Richards would upset the competitive balance of the women's game were unfounded. Richards played several other tournaments, winning one at Kauai, Hawaii, at the end of the year over Kathy Kuykendall, ranked No. 10 in the U.S.

Along more conventional lines, Jimmy Connors recaptured the No. 1 world ranking even though he won only one major championship, the U.S. Open, in which he edged his major rival, Bjorn Borg, in a superlative final, 6–4, 3–6, 7–6, (11–9), 6–4.

Connors compiled a 100–12 record, winning 13 of 23 tournaments he played. He won the only two WCT events he entered, the two big prize-money events put on by the Association of Tennis

Championship of Tennis" Challenge Match at Las Vegas. (Orantes, guaranteed more than $250,000 just for showing up, did little more than that, winning three games in three pathetic sets.)

More important in deciding the global game of king-of-the-hill, Connors was 3–0 in head-to-head clashes with Borg. Connors vanquished the young Swede in the U.S. Pro Indoor final at Philadelphia, the American Airlines Games and the Forest Hills final.

Otherwise, Borg had an outstanding season, winning seven of 19 tournaments and 63 of 77 matches. He continued his domination of his good friend and some-times doubles partner, Guillermo Vilas, to win the WCT Finals at Dallas in May, 27 days before his 20th birthday. He failed in his bid for a third consecutive French Open title, but prepared diligently on grass courts and became the third youngest champion in the history of Wimbledon, the first man to sweep through the most presti-gious of championships without losing a set since Chuck McKinley in 1963. Borg pulled a muscle in his abdomen in a doubles

match the first week, but deadened the pain in his last four singles matches by tak-ing pre-match cortisone injections and spraying his abdomen at changeovers with an aerosol freeze spray. Despite the injury, he never served or smashed more authori-tatively than in routing Brian Gottfried, Vilas, Roscoe Tanner (quarterfinal con-queror of Connors) and Ilie Nastase in the final, 6–4, 6–2, 9–7.

which Connors escaped four set points and finally prevailed, 11–9, tilting an epic his way.

The year began with perhaps the most startling result ever in one of the Grand Slam championships, 21-year-old Australian Mark Edmondson—an anonymous serve-and-volleyer recently removed from employment as a janitor and odd-jobs man—winning the Australian Open. Lowest ranked to win a major, No. 212, he beat two former champions, 42-year-old Ken Rosewall in the semifinals and defender John Newcombe, 6–7, 6–3, 7–6, 6–1, in a final played in fierce winds and the eerie weather of a gathering storm.

Edmondson was hardly a Grand Slam threat. He quickly found his level again, losing in the first round of the French Open to Paraguayan Victor Pecci. Adriano Panatta, the handsome and dashing Italian No. 1, won the French during a dazzling 16-match winning streak that established him as the king of European clay for the year.

Panatta withstood 11 match points against Aussie Kim Warwick in the first

Harold Solomon ousted Arthur Ashe in the 1976 WCT playoffs and reached the French final against Adriano Panatta. • *Wide World*

round of the Italian Open, then went on to win the title before his adoring hometown fans in Rome, beating Vilas in the final, 2–6, 7–6, 6–2, 7–6. Panatta was nearly a goner in the first round in Paris, too, saving a match point against an unorthodox and virtually unknown Czech, Pavel Hutka, with a desperate, lunging volley winner. After that narrow escape, however, Panatta was superb, dispatching Borg in the quarterfinals, Eddie Dibbs in the semis, and gritty Harold Solomon, 6–1, 6–4, 4–6, 7–6, in the final. (Solomon, who roared from behind in five of his seven matches, was the first American finalist at Paris since Herbie Flam in 1957.)

Arthur Ashe, No. 1 in the world in 1975, got off to the best start of his career, winning five of his first six tournaments and 29 of 30 matches. He again topped the WCT point standings, earning a $50,000 bonus, but lost his crown in the first round of the WCT playoffs at Dallas,

beaten by Solomon, and did little thereafter. His fade was in part attributed to inflammation of a chronic heel injury that required surgery in February 1977.

A pinched nerve in his elbow slowed another of the 1975 heroes, Orantes, much of the season, but therapy and a switch to a lighter aluminum racket revived him in the autumn. The elegant left-hander won five of his last eight tournaments (including the year's longest winning streak: 23 matches), reached two other finals and resurrected himself from 1–4 down to win a stirring Grand Prix Masters final at Houston over Poland's Wojtek Fibak, the most improved pro of the year, 5–7, 6–2, 0–6, 7–6, 6–1.

The Houston Masters culminated five years of Grand Prix sponsorship by the Commercial Union Assurance group, which withdrew because of flagging profits in the insurance business and was replaced by Colgate-Palmolive, which already had undertaken sponsorship of the women's Grand Prix, known as the Colgate International Series. Commercial Union's swan song was soured when Connors decided to pass up the Masters for a third consecutive year (thereby forfeiting the $60,000 he already had earned from the Grand Prix bonus pool for finishing third in the season-long standings), and Borg and Nastase chose to play exhibitions in the fall instead of Grand Prix tournaments that could have qualified them for the eight-man Masters.

Mexican Raul Ramirez won only four of 32 tournaments, but he was a tireless and consistent campaigner. His diligence paid off as he earned both the $150,000 prize for topping the Grand Prix singles standings and the $40,000 award for heading the doubles standings, a unique accomplishment. In all, the Grand Prix encompassed 48 tournaments (and produced 23 different winners) in 22 countries, with more than $5 million in prize purses. With the WCT (24 16-man tournaments) and U.S. Indoor circuits added in, more than $9 million was available in men's tournaments worldwide.

The riches available were demonstrated graphically when Ilie Nastase collected $180,000 in a single tournament: the WCT-run Avis Challenge Cup, a series

In doubles, John Newcombe and Tony Roche won their fourth Australian championship, but team-of-the-year honors were shared by Ramirez-Brian Gottfried and Sherwood Stewart-Freddie McNair, who underscored the old axiom that the ordinary singles players can blend extraordinarily in doubles.

Stewart-McNair won the French Open, dethroning Gottfried-Ramirez, 7–6, 6–3, 6–1, and came back from 1–4 in the fourth set to stun the same team in the Masters doubles final, 6–3, 5–7, 5–7, 6–4, 6–4. Those triumphs earned Stewart-McNair the No. 1 U.S. ranking in doubles. (Connors was No. 1 in singles, regaining the spot he occupied in 1973–74.)

Fibak and Karl Meiler won the WCT doubles at Kansas City, after beating Gotffried-Ramirez in a five-set semifinal. Gottfried-Ramirez won their third straight Italian title, over Newcombe-Geoff Masters, even though completion of the final was delayed by darkness and continued four months later at The Woodlands, outside Houston. They also won Wimbledon, knocking off curiously unseeded

Newcombe-Roche (five-time champions) in the first round and Masters-Ross Case in a rousing final, 3–6, 6–3, 8–6, 2–6, 7–5, and the $100,000 ATP Doubles at The Woodlands. Tom Okker and Marty Riessen took the U.S. Open over surprising Aussies Paul Kronk and Cliff Letcher, 6–4, 6–4.

It was a quiet year politically, in men's

have disqualified him, caused this match to get out of control. Nastase was eventually fined $1,000, which increased his aggregate disciplinary fines for a 12-month period to more than $3,000 and triggered an automatic 21-day suspension, under provisions of a new Code of Conduct enacted by the Men's International Professional Tennis Council. The suspension was a joke, however, since it applied only to Grand Prix tournaments; Nastase played exhibition tournaments and earned more than $50,000 during the time he was supposed to be disciplined.

In the Davis Cup, Mexico—after upsetting the United States in the American Zone—refused to play South Africa for the second consecutive year, and defaulted. When the Davis Cup nations refused to take action against Mexico at its annual meeting, the United States led a walkout of the major Cup nations, including France and Great Britain, for 1977. A compromise was worked out within two weeks, however, and these nations returned. The Soviet Union defaulted its semifinal series to Chile in protest of the military junta that had overthrown the Marxist regime of Salvador Allende in Santiago in 1973. This was precisely the sort of political disruption

Captain Tony Trabert talks strategy with doubles players Bob Lutz (center) and Stan Smith, winners over Mexico in 1976 Davis Cup competition. Italy won the Cup for the first time. •*UPI*

that the U.S. was opposing, and a reconstituted Davis Cup Committee of Management threw the USSR out of the 1977 competition.

Italy, runner-up in 1960–61, won the Davis Cup for the first time, beating Chile, 4–1, in a final distinguished more by the enthusiasm and sportsmanship of the sellout crowds at Santiago than by the quality of play. Corrado Barazzutti upset Chilean No. 1 Jaime Fillol, and Panatta beat game but overmatched Patricio Cornejo, then teamed with Paolo Bertolucci to down Cornejo-Fillol for an unbeatable 3–0 lead as captain Nicola Pietrangeli, the star of the 1960–61 Italian teams, exulted at courtside. The political situation had been tense, Italian leftists opposing the matches, but the Italians' joy at winning was unrestrained.

Earlier in the year Connors had made his first appearance for the U.S. in the World Cup. Both he and Ashe thrashed Newcombe and Roche in singles, leading captain Dennis Ralston's American squad to a 6–1 victory over declining Australia before sellout crowds in Hartford.

World Team Tennis was more stable in its third season, but even with Chris Evert as a shining new attraction and the respected Butch Buchholz aboard as commissioner, all of the 10 franchises continued to operate in the red. The New York Sets—led by league most valuable player Sandy Mayer, Billie Jean King, Virginia Wade and Phil Dent—captured the league title with a 3–0 sweep of the Golden Gaters (San Francisco Bay Area) in the playoff final series. Evert, of the Phoenix Racquets, was the female MVP, her singles winning percentage (.700) the best of any player in WTT.

Evert was unquestionably the queen of tournament tennis as well. She won 75 of 80 matches, 12 of 17 tournaments, including Wimbledon, the U.S. Open and the rich Colgate Inaugural at Palm Springs in October, which launched the new Colgate International Series, and was to serve thereafter as its climactic playoff. Its $45,000 top prize was the biggest of the year in women's tennis. It boosted Evert's season winnings to $289,165 and her career winnings to $1,026,604, making her the first woman to earn more than $1 million in prize money.

Only four players—Evonne Goolagong Cawley (twice), Wade, Martina Navratilova and Dianne Fromholtz—were able to beat Evert during the year.

Goolagong started the year by winning her third straight Australian Open title, a 6–2, 6–2 rout of Czechoslovakia's Renata Tomanova, and teaming with Helen Gourlay to defend the doubles title she had won the previous two years with Californian Peggy Michel.

The lithe Australian was at her best during the January through April Virginia Slims circuit, winning 38 of 40 matches, dropping only 10 sets, and at one point running off 16 consecutive victories without loss of a set. She climaxed her record

$133,675 Slims season (en route to a $195,452 year) by beating Evert, 6–3, 5–7, 6–3, in a magnificent match at the Los Angeles Sports Arena, the final of the Virginia Slims championship. That was the high point of Goolagong's year.

On the season, Evonne won eight of 14 tournaments, 58 of 64 matches. She reached the final of every tournament she

as she announced at season's end that she was taking maternity leave, she was overshadowed by Evert.

After losing the Virginia Slims final, Chrissie won her next six tournaments in a dazzling 36-match winning streak, and lost only one more match the rest of the year.

Her streak began with her third consecutive triumph in the Family Circle Cup, over Australian Kerry Melville Reid, 6–2, 6–2, at Amelia Island, Fla.

At Wimbledon, where all eight seeds reached the quarterfinals, Evert beat Olga Morozova in the quarterfinals, Martina Navratilova in the semis, and Goolagong, 6–3, 4–6, 8–6, in a thrilling final that ended Evonne's 25-match streak. This was Evert's first triumph ever over Goolagong on grass. Then Evert and Navratilova took the doubles title over Betty Stove and Billie Jean King—who did not play singles, and was thwarted in her attempt to seize a record 20th career Wimbledon title—6–1, 3–6, 7–5. (King and her New York Sets teammate Sandy Mayer were upset in the second round of the mixed doubles by South Africans Bob Hewitt and Greer Stevens, leaving BJK tied with Elizabeth

Ryan, who never won the singles but captured 19 Wimbledon doubles and mixed titles between 1914 and 1934.)

Evert was at her dominating best on the clay at Forest Hills, winning her second consecutive U.S. Open title with the loss of only 12 games in six matches. (The only more devastating run through the field was accomplished by Helen Wills, who gave up

startlingly won the doubles title over Wade and Morozova, 6–1, 6–4, becoming the first South African women to win a U.S. title. King and another WTT teammate, Phil Dent, won the mixed doubles over Stove and Frew McMillan.

King came out of her self-imposed singles retirement in the Federation Cup at Philadelphia in August. Colgate assumed sponsorship of this women's team competition, and infused it with prize money for the first time: $130,000 for teams representing 32 nations, $40,000 to the winners. Unfortunately, a political hassle developed when the Soviet Union reneged on a previous promise and led a four-nation walkout (1975 champion Czechoslovakia, Hungary and the Philippines joined the USSR in refusing to play) to protest the inclusion of South African and Rhodesia in the draw. The defaulting nations were subsequently fined by the ITF, but they had succeeded in making the draw a shambles.

King filled in unexpectedly in singles for Evert, who withdrew with a sore wrist. King, playing for the U.S. for the first time since 1967, teamed with old doubles partner Rosie Casals in a two-woman *tour de force*. They sprinted through four 3–0 victories to a meeting with favored Australia in the final. Kerry Reid beat Casals, but King found a wellspring of her old inspiration to beat Goolagong, 7–6, 6–4, in a match of exceptionally high standard. King-Casals then toppled Reid-Gollagong, 7–5, 6–3, for the championship.

After rare back-to-back losses in 1974–75, the U.S. regained the Wightman Cup with a 5–2 victory over Great Britain, indoors at London's Crystal Palace. Evert led the way, beating Wade and then Sue Barker in the decisive match, 2–6, 6–2, 6–2. (In the absence of the leading women, who were contracted to WTT, Barker had won the German and French Opens, sharing with Italian Open champ Mima Jausovec preeminence on European clay for the year.)

Evert was ranked No. 1 in the U.S., of course, but Nancy Richey achieved a milestone in earning the No. 3 ranking. It was the 16th time she figured in the U.S. Top Ten, a record for consistency at the top previously held only by Louise Brough.

A major innovation in equipment was introduced in 1976. New rackets in a dizzying variety of designs and materials—wood, metal, fiberglass, alloys, composites—had been marketed over the previous decade, but the biggest stir since the introduction of Wilson's steel T-2000 in 1967 was created by the Prince racket, with its oversized head. Howard Head, founder of Head Ski and architect of that company's headlong plunge into tennis equipment, joined forces with the manufacturer of Prince ball machines to produce the revolutionary and subsequently imitated new racket, which had much the same balance as conventional rackets but twice the hitting area.

1977

By any standard, 1977 was a landmark year for tennis. Wimbledon, the oldest of

One hundred years after it began, Bjorn Borg won Wimbledon in 1977. • *Jack Mecca*

tournaments, celebrated its Centenary. The U.S. Open was played at Forest Hills for the last time. And a technological innovation, the "double strung" or "spaghetti" racket, caused such a stir that it was banned from tournament play several months after gaining notoriety, and led to the definition of a racket for the first time in the official rules of the game.

Three men—Bjorn Borg, Guillermo Vilas and Jimmy Connors—waged their own version of the year's hit movie, the science-fiction classic *Star Wars*. They were in a stratospheric super class, a galaxy above anyone else in tennis.

Borg won Wimbledon and had the most solid record, including winning margins against both his rivals. Vilas won the French and U.S. Opens and fashioned the longest winning streak of the 10-year-old Open era. Connors won the World Championship of Tennis in Dallas and the Grand Prix Masters, and was runner-up at

Wimbledon and Forest Hills. The debate as to who was No. 1 continued right through the Masters which, because of U.S. television considerations, was moved back by new Grand Prix sponsor Colgate-Palmolive to the first week of January 1978.

There was no similar disagreement as to who was the ruler of women's tennis. Chris Evert remained the indisputable

and their applause swelled. As the Band of the Welsh Guards, resplendent in scarlet uniforms and polished brass, played "The March of the Kings" from the opera *Aida*, a wonderfully nostalgic "Parade of Champions" began, the former winners striding out onto the most famous lawn in the tennis world to receive commemorative medals from the Duke of Kent in a brief, dignified ceremony.

In a touching final gesture, medals were presented to Elizabeth "Bunny" Ryan, 85, and Jacques "Toto" Brugnon, 82, "representing all the doubles champions." Ryan—winner of 12 women's doubles and seven mixed titles between 1914 and 1938—moved slowly, on walking sticks, but cast them aside to wave to the crowd. Brugnon—who won Wimbledon doubles titles twice each with fellow French "Musketeers" Henri Cochet and Jean Borotra—used a cane and later held the arm of the fourth "Musketeer," René Lacoste. Toto died the next winter, but for this moment he was ebullient. When the presentations were over, the band started to play again, softly. The champions posed for photos then joined arms and sang "Auld Lang Syne."

The tournament was also richly memorable. Left-hander John McEnroe, 18, of Douglaston, N.Y., became the youngest semifinalist in Wimbledon's 100 years, the first player ever to come through the qualifying rounds and get that far. He won eight matches in all before Connors brought him back to reality, 6–3, 6–3, 4–6, 6–4. In the other semifinal, Borg defeated the swift and flashy Vitas Gerulaitis, 6–4,

70s in tennis—batting each other from the baseline in torrid rallies seldom seen on grass courts. Connors seemed out of it at 0–4 in the fifth set, but roused himself for one last challenge and came back to 4–4 before a crucial double fault in the ninth game cost him his momentum, his serve and the match, 3–6, 6–2, 6–1, 5–7, 6–4.

In the women's singles, 14-year-old Californian Tracy Austin became one of the youngest players to compete at Wimbledon. She defeated Ellie Vessies Appel, then showed tremendous poise and groundstrokes in losing a Centre Court match to defending champion Evert, 6–1, 6–1. That match, and her first victory ever over Billie Jean King on grass—6–1, 6–2 in the quarterfinals—took an enormous emotional toll on Evert, and left her curiously flat for her semifinal against Wade.

"Our Ginny," as the British affectionately called Wade, had never prepared better for a tournament, nor felt more self-confident. She had never gone beyond the semifinals in 15 previous Wimbledons, but she kept the pressure on with bold approach shots and magnificent net play to beat Evert, 6–2, 4–6, 6–1. Wade was much more passive in the final against 6–foot, 160-pound Betty Stove—the first Dutch finalist at Wimbledon—but settled down and let her erratic opponent make the mistakes. Wade won nine of the last 10 games and the match, 4–6, 6–3, 6–1.

The tennis was commonplace, but the occasion unforgettable. Wade, the first Englishwoman to win her national title since Ann Jones in 1969, accepted the gold championship plate from Queen Elizabeth II, who was making her first appearance at Wimbledon since 1962 in honor of the Centenary and her own Silver Jubilee celebration. British reserve gave way to an unbridled outpouring of patriotic sentiment. The Duchess of Kent waved excitedly to Wade from the Royal Box, and thousands of delighted Britons broke into a spontaneous, moving chorus of "For She's a Jolly Good Fellow."

Stove wound up a triple loser, runner-up with Martina Navratilova in the women's doubles to unseeded JoAnne Russell and Helen Gourlay Cawley, 6–3, 6–3, and with Frew McMillan in the mixed doubles to Bob Hewit and Greer Stevens, 3–6, 7–5, 6–4. In the men's doubles, defending champions Brian Gottfried and Raul Ramirez fell to Jim Delaney and Sashi Menon in the first round, paving the way for an all-Australian final. Ross Case and Geoff Masters, runners-up in five sets the previous year, beat John Alexander and Phil Dent in another thriller, 6–3, 6–4, 3–6, 8–9, 6–4.

Wimbledon was the highlight of the year, but the most impressive achievement was the winning streak Vilas compiled the last six months of the year, after losing listlessly to Billy Martin in the third round at Wimbledon.

Vilas started the year as runner-up to Roscoe Tanner, the hard-serving left-han-

Only 14, Tracy Austin became a crowd favorite from Wimbledon to Forest Hills. • *Peter Mecca*

der, in the Australian Open, 6–3, 6–3, 6–3. By winning the French Open in the absence of Borg and Connors—Vilas lost only one set in seven matches and his 6–0, 6–3, 6–0 victory over Brian Gottfried in the final was the most decisive since the tournament went international in 1925—Vilas shed his image as "The Eternal Second" and removed an enormous psychological burden.

five-year, $10-million rights contract. Hester set in motion ambitious plans for building a new USTA National Tennis Center in nearby Flushing Meadow Park, site of the 1939–40 and 1964–65 New York World's Fairs.

Vilas helped make "the last Forest Hills" memorable. He lost only 16 games in five matches up to the semifinals, in which

streak was by far the longest since the advent of Open tennis, eclipsing Rod Laver's 31 straight matches of 1969, previously the male record. And he immediately launched another streak of 30.

The record streak ended controversially the first week in October in the final of a tournament at Aix-en-Provence, France, Vilas defaulting angrily after losing the first two sets to Ilie Nastase, who was using the "spaghetti" racket that had just been barred, effective the following week.

The crowning glory of Vilas' streak was winning the U.S. Open, which was played at the West Side Tennis Club in the Forest Hills section of New York's borough of Queens for the last time, after 73 consecutive years there as the Championships site. Clumsy last-ditch efforts by the club's officials to retain the Open could not compensate for their years of foot-dragging on making physical improvements. W. E. "Slew" Hester of Jackson, Miss., president of the USTA, decided that the West Side Tennis Club was too congested, its management too stubbornly old-fashioned, to accommodate America's premier tournament, which was given 28 hours of television coverage by CBS-TV under a new

many Latins in the crowd hoisted Vilas to their shoulders and carried him around the old horseshoe stadium like a conquering hero. Connors, furious at both the outcome and the reception given the victor,

Argentina's Guillermo Vilas made money, and Jimmy Connors furious, in 1977. • *Peter Mecca*

left in a huff, not bothering to wait for the trophy presentation ceremonies.

Vilas dominated the Grand Prix point standings, winning the $300,000 prize earmarked as the top share of the $1.5-million bonus pool put up by Colgate, which took over from Commercial Union Assurance as the Grand Prix sponsor. On the year, Vilas won a record 17 tournaments and $800,642 in prize money—more than he had earned in five previous pro seasons. He played the most ambitious tournament schedule of any of the top men and finished with a 145–14 record, including Davis Cup matches. (With Vilas and Ricardo Cano playing singles, Argentina upset the United States in the American Zone final to reach the Cup semifinals for the first time.) During his 50-match streak, Vilas won an astonishing 109 of 125 sets. Starting with the French Open, he won 57 consecutive matches on clay.

But even though *World Tennis* magazine declared him No. 1 for the year, most other authorities disagreed and bestowed that mythical honor on Borg, who defaulted in the fourth round of the U.S. Open with a shoulder injury. The 21-year-old Swede had the best winning percentage for the season—.920, on a record of 81–7. He won 13 of the 20 tournaments he played. Including the Masters—played in 1978, but considered the climax of the 1977 season—Borg was 3–0 over Vilas (two victories in the spring, the third in the semis of the Masters) and 2–1 over Connors, who beat him in the Masters final, 6–4, 1–6, 6–4, before a crowd of 17,150 at Madison Square Garden.

Connors may have had the season-ending last laugh, but he finished No. 3 after having been the best player in the world in 1974 and 1976 and No. 2 to Arthur Ashe in 1975. Connors won seven of 21 tournaments, 70 of 81 matches, and was in four big finals (winning the WCT playoffs over Dick Stockton, 6–7, 6–1, 6–3, 6–3, and the

Masters, losing to Borg at Wimbledon and to Vilas at Forest Hills). But Connors was 1–2 head-to-head against Borg and 0–2 against Vilas, including a gripping match in the round-robin portion of the Masters, won by Vilas, 6–4, 3–6, 7–5. This spellbinder kept a record tournament crowd of 18,590 riveted to their seats in the Garden until 12:42 A.M. on a Friday morning.

While Borg, Vilas, and Connors constituted the ruling triumvirate of men's tennis, there were other noteworthy performers. Spaniard Manuel Orantes underwent surgery to repair a pinched nerve in his left elbow in the spring, but came back splendidly to bedazzle Connors, 6–1, 6–3, in the U.S. Clay Court final at Indianapolis and to topple Eddie Dibbs in the 50th U.S. Pro Championships. Vitas Gerulaitis became the first American since 1960 to win the Italian Open, on slow clay, beating Tonino Zugarelli, and later demonstrated his versatility by winning the second Australian Open of the calendar year—the tournament was moved up to mid-December so that it could be included in the Grand Prix—on grass at Melbourne. Floridian Brian Gottfried won four tournaments in a six-week span early in the year and reached 15 finals during the season, winning five of them and compiling a 108–23 record.

In doubles, South Africans Bob Hewitt, 37, and Frew McMillan, 35, won 13 tournaments, even though separated for four months during the summer because McMillan played World Team Tennis. Their biggest victory came at Forest Hills, where they captured their first U.S. Open doubles title over Gottfried and Raul Ramirez, 6–4, 6–0. Hewitt and McMillan also won the Masters over Stan Smith and Bob Lutz, 7–5, 7–6, 6–3.

Gottfried and Ramirez won the Italian Open doubles for a record fourth consecutive year and recaptured the French Open title. Arthur Ashe and Tony Roche won the Australian Open title in January, and Aussies Allan Stone and Ray Ruffels took it in December. Vijay Amritraj and Dick Stockton made their only doubles victory together count, collecting $40,000 apiece for beating the makeshift pair of Adriano Panatta and Gerulaitis in the WCT doubles finals at Kansas City, 7–6, 7–6, 4–6, 6–3.

The Colgate Grand Prix embraced 76

career earnings mark, increasing the number of tennis millionaires to 13 since Laver first broke the milestone in 1971.

In team competitions, Australia recovered the Davis Cup for the first time since 1973 and tied the U.S. for the most possessions (24). John Alexander and Phil Dent spurred the Aussies past Argentina, 3–2, in the semifinals at Buenos Aires. For the finale at Sydney, captain Neale Fraser surprisingly called on veteran left-hander Tony Roche, who responded by toppling Adriano Panatta in the opening match, 6–3, 6–4, 6–4. Alexander beat Corrado Barazzutti in the second match and clinched a 3–1 triumph with an epic 6–4, 4–6, 2–6, 8–6, 11–9 triumph over Panatta.

The U.S., undermanned, was ambushed on the road again—this time by Argentina, 3–2, at Buenos Aires. Ricardo Cano beat Dick Stockton in the prophetic first match. This was the third consecutive year that the U.S. failed to survive the American Zone, eclipsing 1965–67 as the dimmest period in U.S. Davis Cup history.

World Team Tennis completed its fourth season, with the Boston Lobsters topping the East Division, and the Phoenix

Racquets the West Division. Ten teams played 44 matches each, and again all operated in the red. The New York Apples, led by Billie Jean King and Sandy Mayer, won the league championship, defeating Phoenix in the final round of the playoffs.

Chris Evert won three of the four biggest tournaments in women's tennis: her fourth Virginia Slims Championship,

Prix over Billie Jean King, 6–2, 6–2, at Rancho Mirage, Cal.

Evert represented the United States for the first time in the Federation Cup, which attracted 42 nations to the grass courts of Devonshire Park in Eastbourne, England, the week before Wimbledon. Chrissie did not lose a set in singles as the United States romped past Austria, Switzerland, France, South Africa and Australia. Evert defeated Kerry Reid, 7–5, 6–3, and King disposed of Dianne Fromholtz, 6–1, 2–6, 6–2, to clinch the championship before the Americans lost the meaningless final doubles.

Evert also led America's 39th victory in the 54-year-old Wightman Cup rivalry against Great Britain, played on the West Coast for the first time, at Oakland Coliseum. Chrissie opened with a 7–5, 7–6 victory over Wade, King blistered Barker, 6–1, 6–4, and a 7–0 rout was on. Even though the outcome was already decided, a record Wightman Cup crowd of 11,317 turned up on the final evening of the three-day event to see King beat Wade in a glorious match, 6–4, 3–6, 8–6.

In all, Evert at age 22 won 11 tournaments, 70 of 74 matches, and $453,134 in prize money. She was ranked No. 1 in the

U.S. for the fourth consecutive year and No. 1 in doubles for the first time, with Rosemary Casals. Evert won the U.S. Open without losing a set for the second straight year and stretched her remarkable clay-court winning streak to 23 tournaments and 113 matches, dating back to August 1973. Even though Fromholtz surprised her in the round-robin portion of the Colgate Series Championships, Evert reached the final with a bitterly fought 1–6, 6–4, 6–4 victory over Wade, and went on to claim the richest prize in women's tennis: $75,000.

Although Evert was the dominant force, and Wade the sentimental success story, there were other notable achievements in women's tennis in 1977:

• Tracy Austin, 5 feet tall and weighing 90 pounds, reached the quarterfinals of the U.S. Open, beating No. 4 seed Barker en route. The 14-year-old took enough time off from her eighth- and ninth-grade classes in Rolling Hills, Cal., to play 10 professional tournaments and wound up ranked 12th in the world on the computer of the Women's Tennis Association and No. 4 in the United States—the youngest ever to crack the Top Ten until Jennifer Capriati, a younger 14 in 1990.

• Martina Navratilova, starting the season slimmed down and determined to make up for a disappointing 1976, won four of 11 tournaments on the Virginia Slims circuit, beating Evert in the final of the season opener at Washington, D.C.

• Sue Barker, with an improved backhand to go with her already devastating forehand, won two Slims tournaments and lost three finals to Navratilova. Barker finished third on the circuit, but beat Navratilova to get to the final of the Slims Championships.

• Wendy Turnbull, so swift afoot she was nicknamed "Rabbit," emerged as a player to be reckoned with by upsetting

Casals, Wade and Navratilova to reach the U.S. Open final.

• Transsexual Renée Richards won her year-long legal struggle for acceptance in women's tournaments when a New York judge ruled that she could not be barred from the U.S. Open because she could not pass the Olympic chromosome test. The court ruled that medical evidence proved that Richards was "female," and the USTA and WTA dropped efforts to bar her. She lost in the first round of the Open singles to Wade, but reached the doubles final with Californian Bettyann Grubb Stuart before losing to Navratilova and Stove, 6–1, 7–6. (Stove also won the mixed doubles, with Few McMillan, over King and Gerulaitis, 6–2, 3–6, 6–3.) Thereafter, Richards became a regular competitor on the women's circuit, though several players defaulted against her to protest her inclusion in their tournaments.

• King, recovered from knee surgery the previous November, worked her way back into shape and won three consecutive tournaments and 18 straight matches in the autumn to reach the playoff finale of the $2-million Colgate Series, which carried a $600,000 bonus pool. She was 0–4 on the year against Evert, but 2–0 against WTT teammate Wade, 3–0 against Navratilova, 1–0 against Barker and 4–0 against Stove. King, winning six titles, finished the year with a 53–6 record, ranked No. 2 in the U.S. and again a major factor in the women's game. While the topcats were away, employed in WTT, lesser ladies were at play in Europe: Janet Newberry won the Italian, Mima Jausovec the first Yugoslav to win the French.

• Kerry Reid, at 29, won the Australian Open for the first time, over fellow Aussie Dianne Fromholtz, 7–5, 6–2. Fromholtz and Helen Gourlay Cawley captured the doubles.

• Evonne Goolagong Cawley, kept out of the January version of the Australian

Open because she was pregnant, gave birth to her first child—daughter Kelly—in May, and launched a comeback in the fall. She won the December version of the Australian Open over Gourlay (formally, it was Mrs. Cawley vs. Mrs. Cawley), 6–3, 6–0. This was Evonne's fourth Australian title and she extended her unbeaten streak in the tournament to 20 matches.

The controversial spaghetti racket, subsequently banned, was used by France's Christophe Roger-Vasselin in the 1977 Poree Cup finals in which he lost to Guillermo Vilas. • *UPI*

with fish line, adhesive tape, rope or other protuberances, including a plastic tubing called "spaghetti." While rackets thus strung generally had a very low tension— between 35 and 55 pounds—they were able to generate tremendous power because of a "trampoline effect," the ball sinking deep in the double layer of strings and being propelled out. Because the dual layer of strings also moved, they were able to "brush" the ball, artificially imitating a heavy topspin stroke. Thus, some players were able to hit the ball extremely hard from the backcourt and still keep it in play. The "spaghetti" racket was all the more maddening to play against because the ball came off it with a dull thud that made it difficult to judge.

The "double strung" racket was invented in West Germany by a former horticulturist named Werner Fisher, and it created a major scandal in club and national tournaments there as second- and third-line players became champions with it. An adaptation of the racket was first used in a major tournament by Australian lefty Barry Phillips-Moore in the French Open. A number of professional players used it in Europe during the summer and it gained further notoriety at the U.S. Open when an

obscure American player named Mike Fishbach used his homemade version to trounce Billy Martin and 16th-seeded Stan Smith in the first two rounds.

A couple of weeks later, Ilie Nastase was beaten by a player using a "spaghetti" racket in Paris and swore he would never play against it again. The following week he turned up with one and used it to win a tournament at Aix-en-Provence, ending Guillermo Vilas' long winning streak in the final. Vilas quit after two sets, claiming that playing against the exaggerated spin injured his elbow.

The ITF had already acted by that time, however, putting a "temporary freeze" on use of the double-strung rackets in tournaments, effective Oct. 2. The ITF based its decision on a report by the University of Brunswick in West Germany, which indicated that every hit with the racket was in fact a "double hit," in violation of the rules.

The ITF made its "ban" permanent the following June by adopting a definition of a racket for the first time: "A racket shall consist of a frame, which may be of any material, weight, size of shape and stringing. The stringing must be uniform and smooth and may be of any material. The strings must be alternately interlaced or bonded where they cross. The distance between the main and/or cross strings shall not be less than one quarter of an inch nor more than one-half inch. If there are attachments they must be used only to prevent wear and tear and must not alter the flight of the ball. They must be uniform with a maximum protrusion of .04 of an inch."

1978

In 1978, as Wimbledon began its second century, Stade Roland Garros in Paris—home of the French Championships—celebrated its 50th anniversary, and the U.S. Open moved to the new USTA National Tennis Center in Flushing Meadow, Queens, N.Y., the most important new arena for international tennis in half a century.

Bjorn Borg and Jimmy Connors continued their spirited battle of king-of-the-hill in men's tennis, Martina Navratilova and Chris Evert waged a similarly lovely little war for the No. 1 ranking among the women, and several precocious young talents blossomed—19-year-old John McEnroe starting to challenge the top men, and high-school girls Tracy Austin and Pam Shriver asserting themselves in women's tournaments.

Perhaps nothing better symbolized what happened to the once-elitist, white-flanneled sport of tennis in the 1970s than the fact that the U.S. Open, America's premier tournament, moved to a public park. The National Tennis Center was built, remarkably, in one year on 16 acres of city-owned land in Flushing Meadow Park, site of the 1939–40 and 1964–65 New York World's Fairs, and adjacent to Shea Stadium.

Conducted to Flushing by drawling, cigar-chomping W.E. "Slew" Hester, a 66-year-old wildcat oilman from Jackson, Miss., the U.S. Championships was retreating from 97 years in patrician clubs—first for the men at high society bastion Newport (R.I.) Casino, then (for the women) the Philadelphia Cricket Club and subsequently for both the West Side Tennis Club at Forest Hills, not to mention a three-year visit to Philadelphia's Germantown Cricket Club by the men.

Hester sounded like a Southern conservative, but proved in a memorable two-year term to be perhaps the most progressive president in the history of the USTA.

Many people second-guessed Hester in September 1977 when, fed up with the reactionary board of governors of the West Side Tennis Club, he announced that the Open would not be played again at Forest Hills. Few thought the new complex Hester envisioned a couple of miles away could be completed in 12 months, and many considered the project "Hester's Folly." But Hester's perseverance and leadership, despite arthritis so severe it was difficult for him to walk, enabled the USTA to cut through bureaucratic red tape, union disputes and cost overruns and get the splendid complex built in time for the 1978 Open.

The National Tennis Center was dedicated on Aug. 30, 1978. Its main arena—Louis Armstrong Stadium, site of the Singer Bowl for the 1964–65 World's Fair and named for the late jazz great who lived nearby—accommodated nearly 20,000 spectators, with barely a bad seat in the

The new home of the U.S. Open—The National Tennis Center in Flushing, N.Y. • *Jack Mecca*

house. In addition to the steeply banked, red, white and blue stadium, the complex included a 6,000-seat grandstand, 25 additional lighted outdoor courts, and nine indoor courts, all with the same acrylic asphalt surface that approximates the hard courts most Americans play on. Under a 15-year lease agreement between the USTA and the city of New York, the facility is open to the public year-round and is available to the USTA for tournaments and special events 60 days a year, at a modest fee. The USTA, in turn, spent $10 million to renovate and enlarge a stadium that was intended for concerts but that had fallen into terrible disrepair.

The result was the most significant new venue for world tennis since the modern All England Club was opened in the London suburb of Wimbledon in 1922 and Stade Roland Garros was dedicated as a

Bjorn Borg wins in 1978 for the third straight year at Wimbledon as Jimmy Connors, his victim, stonily departs the scene. • *UPI*

civic monument in Paris for the 1928 Davis Cup challenge round.

Roland Garros celebrated its golden anniversary during the 1978 French Open Championships. On balance, this was a dull tournament, but on a day when 32 past champions were honored in gala center court ceremonies, Bjorn Borg asserted himself as one of the greatest by winning the most important clay-court test of Europe for the third time, five days past his 20th birthday.

Two weeks after winning the Italian Open in five sets over Roman matinee idol Adriano Panatta, Borg repeated the arduous clay-court "double" he had first achieved in 1974. He swept through seven matches in Paris in 21 straight sets, dropping only 32 games. In the final, he trounced defending champion Guillermo Vilas, 6–1, 6–1, 6–3.

Borg went on to become the first man since Rod Laver in 1962 to sweep the Italian, French and Wimbledon singles titles in one season. In dominating the grass of Wimbledon as he had the clay in Rome and Paris, Borg also equaled a more important milestone. He became the first man since Englishman Fred Perry in 1934–36 to win the Wimbledon singles three successive years.

Borg's dream of duplicating Perry's feat nearly ended in the first round. Victor Amaya, a 6-foot-7, 220-pound left-hander with a thunderous serve, led him by two sets to one, 3–1, in the fourth, 30–40 on Borg's serve. Borg escaped a second service break only by the margin of a bold second serve, then broke Amaya and came back to win.

Thereafter, Borg grew increasingly sharper and stronger. He routed a rejuvenated Tom Okker in the semifinals and thrashed archrival Connors, 6–2, 6–2, 6–3, in the final. Never before had Borg served, volleyed and smashed with such authority, and he also displayed a new weapon—a sliced backhand approach shot to Connors' vulnerable forehand, which stayed low on the fast grass. "The way Borg played today," marveled Perry, who hustled down from behind his microphone in the BBC radio commentary booth to congratulate the young Swede on Centre Court, "if he had fallen out of a 45th-story window of a skyscraper, he would have gone straight up."

At the midpoint of the season, it seemed that Borg, with his beefed-up serve, had begun to dominate his grand rivalry with Connors. Despite a loss in the 1977 Grand Prix Masters the first week of the new year, Borg had won five of their last six meetings, giving up only 11 games in the last six sets, through Wimbledon.

But Connors immediately began to train for another showdown, vowing to "follow that sonofabitch to the ends of the

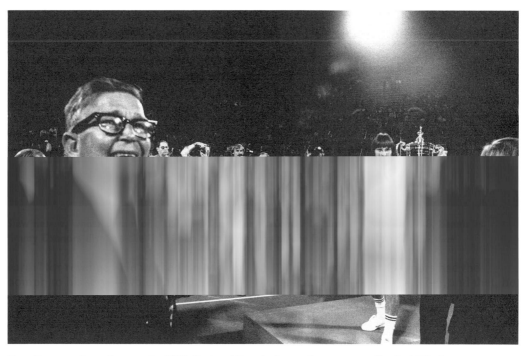

Slew Hester, whose dream of a USTA National Tennis Center became a reality in 1978, beams as Jimmy Connors displays the U.S. Open trophy he won at the facility's inaugural. • *Jack Mecca*

earth" for revenge. He worked on adding oomph to his serve—which had deserted him in the Wimbledon final—and shoring up his forehand. Having won 18 straight matches going into the Wimbledon final, he didn't lose another the rest of the summer, winning Grand Prix tournaments at Washington, Indianapolis (the U.S. Clay Court) and Stowe, Vt., as he groomed his game to peak at the U.S. Open.

Connors' moment of truth at the Open came in a fourth-round victory over Panatta, the dashing and talented Italian. Panatta served for the match at 5–4 in the fifth set of this 3-hour, 36-minute epic, came within two points of victory at 30–30, and later fended off four match points. Connors got to the fifth with an astounding shot: a backhand down the line on the dead run from 10 feet out of court, which he somehow reached and drilled one-handed around the net post for a winner.

Moments later, Connors had the match, 4–6, 6–4, 6–1, 1–6, 7–5, and that, he said later, gave him the impetus to steam-roll through the final three rounds without losing a set to Brian Gottfried, John McEnroe and Borg. Never before were Connors' skill, will and churning internal aggression better shown than in the final. He annihilated Borg, who had a blister on the thumb of his racket hand, almost as badly as he had been ravaged at Wimbledon, 6–4, 6–2, 6–2, ending the Swede's 39-match streak.

Connors, the first man since Bill Tilden in the 1920s to reach the singles final five consecutive years, thus became the first man since Perry in 1933–34 and 1936 to win three U.S. singles titles, and the first American to do so since Tilden. By quirk of history, Connors also gained the singular distinction of having won on grass (1974), clay (1976), and hard court (1978).

"The best player in the world the last four months of 1978," Arthur Ashe said of young John McEnroe. • *Peter Mecca*

The U.S. Open final was the last meeting of the year between Borg and Connors. The last four months of the season belonged to McEnroe, the brash left-hander from Douglaston, N.Y., who was the first man since Ken Rosewall, 19 in 1954, to have reached the semifinals at both Wimbledon and the U.S. Championships while still a teenager.

After losing to Connors in the Open, McEnroe won four Grand Prix tournaments (Hartford, San Francisco, Stockholm, London) in singles, seven in doubles, led the U.S. to its first possession of the Davis Cup since 1972 with a spectacular singles debut, and won both the singles and doubles titles at the Colgate Grand Prix Masters at Madison Square Garden the second week in January 1979. His singles record over that stretch was 49–7. In the six months since turning pro in June after winning the National Intercollegiate singles title as a Stanford

University freshman, McEnroe collected $463,866.

At Stockholm, on a fast tile court, he won his first meeting with Borg, 6–3, 6–4. His left-handed serve, sliced low and wide so that it skidded away from Borg's two-fisted backhand, was so effective that McEnroe lost only seven points in 10 service games. It was the first time that Borg, 22, had lost to a player younger than he.

McEnroe made his Davis Cup debut in doubles in September, partnering Brian Gottfried to the decisive point in America's 3–2 victory over Chile in the American Zone Final at Santiago. McEnroe made his singles debut in the Final at Rancho Mirage, Cal., and lost his serve only once in demoralizing John Lloyd, 6–1, 6–2, 6–2, in the opening match and Buster Mottram, 6–2, 6–2, 6–1, in the clincher of the 4–1 U.S. victory over Great Britain. This ended a five-year drought for the U.S. and gave it possession of the trophy symbolizing international team supremacy in tennis for a record 25th time. As for McEnroe's dominance, it should be noted that never before in 67 Davis Cup finals had a player lost as few as 10 games in two singles matches.

McEnroe went into the season-ending Masters playoff eager for a showdown with Connors, who had beaten him in all four of their career meetings. The Masters, designed to bring together the top eight finishers in the previous year's Grand Prix standings for a $400,000 shootout, had lost much of its luster because Borg and Guillermo Vilas declined invitations. They had not played the minimum 20 Grand Prix tournaments required to qualify for shares of the $2-million Grand Prix bonus pool, and so turned their backs on the showcase finale. Connors did not qualify for his bonus either, but was coaxed at the 11th hour into defending his title.

The Connors-McEnroe duel was seen as the savior of a disappointing tournament, but it also fizzled because Connors aggravated a blood blister on his foot in the first set of their meeting in the round-robin portion of the tournament, and defaulted while trailing, 5–7, 0–3. McEnroe went on to beat Eddie Dibbs in the semifinals and comebacking Arthur Ashe, 6–7, 6–3, 7–5, in a scintillating final, McEnroe reviving himself from 1–4 down and two match points in the final set.

Tennis magazine's ranking panel voted for Connors, but *World Tennis* and the International Federation—which instituted a "world champion" award—went for Borg.

The "World Champion" title was a new honor to be awarded annually by the ITF for men and women, intended to establish an official No. 1 player for each calendar year, eliminating the confusion caused by diverse and often contradictory sets of unofficial rankings.

Borg was the unanimous choice of the selection committee of three former champions: Fred Perry, Australian Lew Hoad and Californian Don Budge. Their decision was based primarily on his superior record in traditional major events, although Borg also held a 3–2 edge over Connors in head-to-head meetings, including three four-man "special events."

Borg's record for the entire season was 88–8, including a 10–0 singles record in spurring Sweden to the semifinals of the Davis Cup.

Connors was 84–7 overall. He monopolized the U.S. Indoors, Clay Court and

Open titles. Following the Wimbledon final, he compiled a 30-match winning streak.

Other notable achievements in men's tennis in 1978:

• "Broadway" Vitas Gerulaitis, the flamboyant 23-year-old New Yorker, got a

• Dibbs won four Grand Prix tournaments (Tulsa, Cincinnati, North Conway, Toronto), 84 of 111 matches in 30 tournaments, and finished third in the Grand Prix standings. Because Connors and Borg did not qualify, Dibbs received the top prize of $300,000 from the bonus pool and headed the Association of Tennis Professionals' "official money" list (tournament winnings and bonuses only) with $575,273. Borg ($469,441), Raul Ramirez ($463,866) and McEnroe were also over the $400,000 mark. Connors ($392,153) led a parade of six more players who won in excess of $300,000. Fourteen players were over $200,000 and a total of 34 collected over $100,000. In all, more than $12 million was at stake in 93 Grand Prix tournaments around the world.

• Guillermo Vilas won eight tournaments, including the German Open and the Australian Open, which ended Jan. 3, 1979. His 6–4, 6–4, 3–6, 6–3 triumph over unseeded John Marks, and a semifinal victory over Arthur Ashe in five sets gave him his third Big Four singles title, to go along with his French and U.S. Open crowns of 1977.

• Ashe, the Wimbledon champion and World No. 1 of 1975, started the year ranked only No. 257 on the computer printout of the Association of Tennis Professionals because he had missed almost the entire 1977 season after surgery on a chronic heel ailment. He won three Grand Prix tournaments (San Jose, Columbus, Los Angeles), reached the Masters final and finished the season ranked No. 11.

• Bob Hewitt and Frew McMillan won seven doubles titles, including their third at Wimbledon. Tom Okker and Wojtek Fibak also won seven tournaments, including the WCT finals at Kansas City, for which they split an $80,000 prize. Stan Smith and Bob Lutz captured their third U.S. Open doubles and won crucial Davis Cup matches in America's 3–2 victory over Sweden in the semifinals at Goteborg and the 4–1 victory over Great Britain. John McEnroe and Peter Fleming were the hottest team the second half of the season, winning six tournaments together between August and December, plus the 1978 Masters early in January. Brian Gottfried and Raul Ramirez, a standout team the previous four years, won only the U.S. Indoor at Memphis together in 1978 and split up their partnership after the French Open.

In women's tennis, the first half of the year belonged to Martina Navratilova, the second half to Chris Evert.

With Evert taking the first three months of the year as a vacation, Navratilova, at age 21, began to fulfill her rich promise. She dominated the Virginia Slims winter circuit—the last under the cigarette company's sponsorship—winning the first seven tournaments and the $150,000 final playoff at Oakland, Cal., over Evonne Goolagong, 7–6, 6–4. That was Navratilova's most important victory to date, an important psychological break-through for the expatriate Czech left-hander.

Evert returned to competition in the spring, but Navratilova, supremely fit and confident, beat her in the final of a pre-Wimbledon grass court tournament at Eastbourne, England, coming back from 1–4 in the final set and saving a match point.

They met again in the Wimbledon final, and this time Navratilova came back from 2–4 in the final set, serving magnificently and outsteadying as well as overpowering Evert to win, 2–6, 6–4, 7–5. Navratilova, whose emotions had regularly overwhelmed her abundant talent, won 12 of the last 13 points. She held at love the last two times she served, missing only one first serve, while Evert made three uncharacteristic unforced errors to lose her serve to 5–6 in the most crucial game of an absorbing match.

When it was over, Navratilova looked ecstatically toward her friend and manager, Hall of Fame golfer Sandra Haynie, an important stabilizing influence in her life who sat beaming in the competitors' guest box. Then Martina shed a flood of tears into a towel and was puffy-eyed when she received the championship trophy from the Duchess of Kent.

"I don't know if I should cry or scream or laugh. I feel very happy that I won, but at the same time I'm very sad that I can't share this with my family," said Navratilova, who had not seen her parents or her 15-year-old sister since defecting to the United States during the 1975 U.S. Open Championships. Her victory, predictably, was all but neglected in the government-controlled media of Czechoslovakia, but her parents watched it on German television by driving to a town near the German border.

Navratilova and Billie Jean King—again foiled in her attempt to win a record-setting 20th career Wimbledon title—were upset in the quarterfinals of the Wimbledon women's doubles by Mona Schallau Guerrant and Sue Barker, but they did win the U.S. Open title, over Wimbledon champs Kerry Reid and Wendy Turnbull, 7–6, 6–4. Australians Reid and Turnbull took the Wimbledon crown with a 4–6, 9–8, 6–3 thriller over French Open champs Mima Jausovec and Virginia Ruzici. Betty Stove and Frew McMillan won the mixed doubles at both Wimbledon and Flushing Meadow.

semifinalists—Austin, 15-year-old Pam Shriver of Lutherville, Md., and 18-year-old Anne Smith of Dallas. Goolagong, 26, eventually beat Austin in the final, 4–6, 6–0, 6–2. "Someday, that tournament may be looked upon as a landmark, the beginning of a new order," predicted women's tennis pioneer Billie Jean King.

Those words appeared prophetic as

both players.

The Dallas tournament produced several startling upsets and three teen-aged

Austin rose to No. 6 in the world before turning 16 on Dec. 12, 1978. She beat Shriver in the finals of the U.S. Girls'

Sixteen-year-old Pam Shriver had to settle for roses after a noble try against Chris Evert in the 1978 U.S. Open final. • *UPI*

16 and 18 Championships, increasing her record total of U.S. junior titles to 27. She turned pro in October, won her first tournament as a professional at Stuttgart, Germany, and collected $70,000 in prize money within three months.

Shriver, while 0–9 against Austin in their junior careers, one-upped her at the U.S. Open, becoming the youngest finalist in the tournament's history. Shriver upset Kerry Reid, an injured Lesley Hunt, and Navratilova, 7–6, 7–6, in a rain-interrupted semifinal. That was arguably the greatest upset in women's major tournament history. Playing nervelessly and aggressively with her Prince (oversized head) racket, Shriver used her serve-and-volley game to extend Evert to 7–5, 6–4 before losing an exciting final.

Both Austin and Shriver, who remained an amateur, were named to the U.S. Wightman Cup team, which was upset by Great Britain, 4–3, at London's Royal Albert Hall. Evert routed Sue Barker, 6–2, 6–1, and Virginia Wade, 6–0, 6–1, but the British preyed on the inexperience of the American teen-agers. Michele Tyler upset Shriver, Wade and Barker each beat Austin, and Wade and Barker teamed up to beat Shriver and Evert, 6–0, 5–7, 6–4, in the decisive doubles match.

Austin also joined Evert and captain Billie Jean King as the U.S. won the Federation Cup for the third straight year, at Melbourne, Australia. The U.S. nipped Australia, 2–1, in the final, Evert and King teaming for the decisive point over Reid and Turnbull, 4–6, 6–1, 6–4.

Evert did not lose a tournament match after the Wimbledon final, winning her last 34 of the year, including three over Navratilova. Evert finished with a 56–3 record, six victories in 10 tournaments, and $443,540 in prize money. She became only the third woman to win the U.S. singles four consecutive years, the first since Helen Jacobs in 1932–35. Evert won the U.S. Open without losing a set for the third consecutive year, an astonishing feat, especially since the surface was changed from clay (on which she had not lost since August 1973) to the medium-fast hard courts that were not ideally suited to her backcourt game.

Evert finished the year with a 3–2 record against Navratilova and was voted the ITF "World Champion" by unanimous vote of a panel of three former women champions: Ann Jones, Margaret Court and Margaret Osborne duPont.

Again devalued in the female precinct by the absence of the strength working in WTT, the Italian went to Czechoslovak Regina Marsikova, the French to Romanian Virginia Ruzici, the first women of their countries to win those titles.

Evert also was voted the Most Valuable Player in World Team Tennis, leading her Los Angeles Strings to their first championship of the intercity league. The Strings beat the Boston Lobsters in the playoff finale.

But after five years of financial losses, WTT was on shaky ground as the year ended. Half of the league's 10 teams announced that they were ceasing operations in the fall, and despite some optimistic noises from the commissioner's office in St. Louis, the chances of finding replacements appeared slim. Plans for a seven-week, $1-million women's tournament circuit in Europe in the spring gave Evert, Navratilova and the other women stars of WTT a lucrative alternative. The failure of the league to sign top players for 1979 caused several influential owners to give up the ghost, and the league seemed to unravel quickly after the Boston Lobsters and the New York Apples folded.

Virginia Slims, which had pioneered the promotion of women's tennis since 1971, startlingly departed from the sponsorship scene in April when the WTA board of directors voted not to renew its contract for the winter circuit. The WTA cited "differences in philosophy on the structure of the circuit" for the divorce from the company, which had poured more than $8 million into women's pro tennis over eight years.

Some women players thought the termi-

the Futures. Avon's $2.2-million annual commitment was to fund 11 "Championship" tournaments with purses between $125,000 and $200,000, leading to a $325,000 singles and doubles championship playoff, and an expanded circuit of $25,000 "Futures" tournaments.

Despite growing pains, sometimes acute, it was obvious that professional ten-

Martina Navratilova won Wimbledon in 1979 for the second year in a row. • *UPI*

nis was still on the rise as the 1980s approached.

1979

The United Nations designated 1979 as the "International Year of the Child," and in tennis, youth was well served. This was most evident at the U.S. Open, where

rankings, the "kids" were not ready to ascend the throne quite yet. The positions of honor in the last year of tennis' remarkable "growth decade" belonged to "old-timers" Martina Navratilova, 22, who won the Avon Championships climaxing the women's indoor circuit and her second consecutive Wimbledon title, and the irrepressible Bjorn Borg, 23, who captured his fourth French Open title and his fourth in a row at Wimbledon, a feat no man had accomplished since before World War I.

Still, it was an exceptional season for those young overachievers, Austin and McEnroe. In addition to her triumph in the Open, Tracy was runner-up to Navratilova in the Avon Championships and snapped Chris Evert Lloyd's six-year, 125-match clay-court winning streak en route to victory in the Italian Open, her first big international title. McEnroe, who had started the year by winning the 1978 Grand Prix Masters, added the World Championship of Tennis title, beating Jimmy Connors and Borg back-to-back, and teamed with Peter Fleming to win the Wimbledon and U.S. Open doubles. Prodigious in their successes, they were clearly the best doubles pair in the world.

The rapid ascendance of Austin and McEnroe did symbolize a significant change in the old order that had ruled much of the latter part of the decade.

Chris Evert and Jimmy Connors—who had reached the pinnacle of the game in 1974 as "the lovebird double," young champions engaged to wed—finally did get married. But not to each other. Evert became the bride of British Davis Cup player John Lloyd. A few weeks earlier, Connors revealed that he had secretly married former *Playboy* magazine Playmate-of-the-Year Patti McGuire in Japan the previous autumn. The couple's first child, Brett David, was born in August.

Meanwhile, though still formidable players, neither Evert Lloyd nor Connors was quite the force of before. Their marriages and apparent off-court happiness seemed to coincide with a slight but noticeable decline in their competitive fires.

Tracy Austin is a study in concentration during her straight-set victory over Chris Evert Lloyd in the U.S. Open final in 1979. • *UPI*

Evert Lloyd said she was no longer obsessed with the ambition to be the No. 1 player in the world. She did recapture the French Open title in the absence of Navratilova and Austin, but never really resembled her dominant and awesomely consistent form of the prior five years. She failed to reach the semifinals of the Avon Championships, was runner-up to Navratilova at Wimbledon for the second straight year and succumbed to Austin one hurdle short of an unprecedented fifth consecutive U.S. Open title.

Connors, after being in the finals at Wimbledon four of the five previous years and at the U.S. Open five straight times, fell in the semis of each and at the same stage in the WCT playoffs and French Open as well. Moreover, Borg established indisputable superiority in their long-running and splendid rivalry—crushing Connors in straight sets in four meetings on four different surfaces (clay at Boca Raton, Fla., concrete at Las Vegas, grass at Wimbledon, indoors in Tokyo), never losing more than three games in a set.

Connors did defend his titles in both the U.S. Pro Indoor at Philadelphia and the U.S. Indoor at Memphis, beating Arthur Ashe—who had made an impressive comeback from heel surgery, but shockingly suffered a mild heart attack at age 36 in August—in both finals. Connors romped in Philly, 6–3, 6–4, 6–1. Memphis was closer, Ashe fighting valiantly for the only U.S. National singles title he had never won, before losing, 2–6, 6–4, 6–4.

It was at Moody Coliseum in Dallas, at the end of the winter-spring men's indoor season, that McEnroe gave a convincing glimpse of great things ahead. Playing in the WCT final for the first time, he beat Australian John Alexander, 6–4, 6–0, 6–2; Connors, 6–1, 6–4, 6–4; and Borg, 7–5, 4–6, 6–2, 7–6, to win the $100,000 first prize with the kind of left-handed serve-and-volley attack—rich in variations of speed and spin, touch and improvisation—not seen since the salad days of Rod Laver.

Navratilova was the prevailing figure on the 12-week, $2.2-million Avon Championship Series, winning four of seven tournaments she played plus the showcase $275,000 finale at Madison Square Garden. In the climactic match,

successful first year for the cosmetics firm as heir to Virginia Slims in sponsoring the women's indoor circuit, was the failure of Evert to get through the round-robin portion of the playoffs to the semifinals. Until 1979, Chrissie had never lost two matches in a row in her professional career. That astounding landmark of consistency was broken when she was beaten by Navratilova in the final of an Avon tournament at Oakland and then by Greer Stevens in the first round at Hollywood, Fla. In the play-offs at New York, Evert—whose mind was obviously more on her upcoming wedding than on her tennis—lost listlessly on successive nights to Austin and Australian Dianne Fromholtz.

Evert did regroup to win her last tournament before her April 17 nuptials, coming from behind to beat Fromholtz (conqueror of Navratilova), 3–6, 6–3, 6–1, for the $100,000 first prize in the four-woman Clairol Crown special event at Carlsbad, Cal.

After a two-week honeymoon, Evert Lloyd teamed with Austin, Billie Jean King, and Rosemary Casals to give the U.S. its fourth consecutive triumph in the

Federation Cup, on clay at Madrid. In the final, the American juggernaut over-whelmed Australia (Fromholtz, Wendy Turnbull, Kerry Reid), 3–0. Later in the year, an expanded U.S. squad also white-washed Great Britain, 7–0, in the Wightman Cup at Palm Beach, Fla.

This was the year the Women's Tennis Association embarked on a bold experi-

tennis was traditionally lacking.

Attendance at the new women's-only events was generally disappointing. This was especially true in Rome, where the paid attendance was only about 5,000 for the week, despite the glorious semifinal in which Austin defeated Evert Lloyd, 6–4, 2–6, 7–6, 7 points to 4 in the final-set tie-breaker. This was on May 12 and it marked the first time Evert Lloyd had lost a match on a clay court since Aug. 12, 1973, when Evonne Goolagong beat her in the final of the Western Championships at Cincinnati. Evert Lloyd's incredible streak had covered 25 tournaments and 125 matches over nearly six years, only eight of which went to three sets. Evert Lloyd said she was more relieved than stunned when the streak finally ended. Austin was thrilled, and celebrated the next day by beating West German left-hander Sylvia Hanika—voted the most improved player of the year by the WTA—in the final.

It was a shame that the streak ended before such a sparse and seemingly disinter-ested audience, however. There were only about 1,500 spectators at Il Foro Italico, compared with a howling sell-out throng of more than 9,000 for the final of the men's Italian Open two weeks later. That was a glorious match, too. Vitas Gerulaitis, the flamboyant New Yorker, defeated Guillermo Vilas, 6–7, 7–6, 6–7, 6–4, 6–2, in an enthralling battle of wit and grit begun in the mid-afternoon sunshine and ended in the cool of the evening. At the time this was thought to be the longest final ever in big tournament history, in terms of playing time: 4 hours and 53 minutes.

Interest in the women's matches was also clearly secondary in the French Open at Stade Roland Garros, where the center court was enlarged to 17,000 seats as part of a major renovation targeted at producing a second "show" arena in 1980. Twelve of the tournament's 14 days were sold out, the French Open having become almost as much of an "in thing" in Paris as Wimbledon is in London, but only 10,000 spectators turned out on the final Saturday to view the women's singles final. This was a terribly tedious match in which Evert Lloyd monotonously ground down erring Wendy Turnbull, 6–2, 6–0. Evert Lloyd, the champion of 1974–75, lost only one set in regaining the title she had abdicated in order to play in World Team Tennis, the American intercity league which was gasping for breath at the end of 1978 and was pronounced officially dead early in 1979.

The men's singles in Paris was expected to produce another duel between Borg and Connors. Jimmy entered the premier clay-court championship of the world for the first time since 1973, ending his personal boycott, a reaction to the tourney barring him in 1977 for his WTT affiliation. Instead, it was exciting primarily because of Victor Pecci, a 6-foot-3 Paraguayan with a diamond in his right ear who entered the tournament ranked No. 30 in the world and unseeded. He knocked off four seeds in succession—15, 6, 3, 2: 1978 semifinalist Corrado Barazzutti, 1976 runner-up Harold Solomon and 1977 champion Guillermo Vilas in straight sets, and Connors in four.

Vital Gerulaitis won his second Italian Open in 1979. • *Jack Mecca*

In the final, Pecci stirred a capacity crowd on a drizzly day by coming back from two sets and 2–5 down to push Borg before bowing, 6–3, 6–1, 6–7, 6–4. Gene and Sandy Mayer won the men's doubles over Australians Ross Case and Phil Dent. The Americans were the first brothers to win a major since U.S. champs Bob and Howard Kinsey in 1924. Betty Stove and Wendy Turnbull won the women's doubles over Virginia Wade and Francoise Durr, 2–6, 7–5, 6–4.

McEnroe, who had missed Rome and Paris because of a pulled groin muscle, returned to action and won a Wimbledon tune-up tournament on grass at London's Queen's Club over Pecci—and was simultaneously grilled in the British press for his surly deportment. Dubbed "Superbrat," he dominated pre-Wimbledon publicity and was seeded No. 2 to Borg, largely because Connors did not reveal until after the draw was made whether he would play or remain at home with his expectant wife.

McEnroe, still bothered by the groin pull, was upset in the fourth round by Tim Gullikson, culminating a first week that was tumultuous for the men (10 of the 16 seeds were beaten in the first five days) and form-ful for the women. Most observers thought the semifinal between Borg and Connors, who had met in the previous two finals, would be the *de facto* title match, but Borg was in his most devastating form and anni-

order to enjoy the champion's traditional honor of playing the opening contest on Centre Court. She had good reason for making this decision: watching her from the competitors' guest box was her mother, whom she had not seen in nearly four years, since defecting from Czechoslovakia during the 1975 U.S. Open. Mrs. Jana Navratilova was granted a two-week tourist visa to visit her daughter in London with

absorbing final that kept 15,000 spectators and a live television audience in 28 countries spellbound for 2 hours, 49 minutes. Half an hour after his 6–7 (7–4), 6–1, 3–6, 6–3, 6–4 triumph, which made him the first man since New Zealander Tony Wilding in 1910–13 to win the Wimbledon singles four years running, Borg said: "I feel much, much older than when I went on the court. Especially at the end of the match, I have never been so nervous in my whole life... I almost couldn't hold my racket."

That was a revealing admission from the astonishing Swede who, after a narrow second-round escape against Vijay Amritraj, the only man in four years to have a match game against Borg at Wimbledon, had said he gets more relaxed when matches are at their tightest.

Coupled with Navratilova's 6–4, 6–4 victory over Evert Lloyd in the women's final the previous day, Borg's victory marked the first time that both the men's and women's singles champions had successfully defended their titles since Bill Tilden and Suzanne Lenglen won in 1920–21.

Navratilova was entitled to a first-round bye, but chose instead to play a match in

Fighting a cold, Navratilova struggled into the semifinals, losing sets to Greer Stevens and Dianne Fromholtz. But she did not lose a set in the last two rounds, beating Austin and Evert Lloyd. Her stepfather and 16-year-old sister, who were not granted visas, watched the match, live on West German television in the border town of Pilsen, as they had the year before. But this time, instead of ignoring the expatriate's victory, the government-controlled Czech media gave it prominent attention in newspapers and on television.

Navratilova had another thrill in partnering Billie Jean King to the women's doubles title, 5–7, 6–3, 6–2, over Turnbull and Stove. This was King's record 20th Wimbledon title, a 10th doubles to go with six singles and four mixed in the world's most prestigious tournament.

But the occasion was saddened by the death the previous day of 87-year-old Elizabeth Ryan, with whom King had shared the record since 1975.

Miss Ryan, a native Californian who lived in London, was stricken with a heart attack while watching the women's singles final, collapsed in a ladies room at the All England Club and died on the way to a hospital. Winner of 12 doubles and seven mixed doubles titles between 1914 and 1934, but never the singles, Ryan had told friends of a premonition that this would be the year King broke her cherished record. She dreaded the moment, but never saw it. She died less than 24 hours before being erased from the record book.

Back in the United States, Connors won the U.S. Clay Court singles for the fourth time, beating Vilas in the final, 6–1, 2–6, 6–4. Evert Lloyd—returning after a three-year absence—won her fifth title, extending her personal winning streak in the tournament to 26 straight matches. Both joined 16 other former champs in ceremonies dedicating a superb new 10,000-seat stadium at the Indianapolis Sports Center.

The U.S. Open was played for the second time at the National Tennis Center in Flushing Meadow, N.Y., and amid the cacophony of planes roaring overhead and spectators moving about during play, the youngsters came to the fore.

McEnroe's toughest battle came in the second round against Ilie Nastase, no longer the exquisite shotmaker he once was, but still a tempestuous personality. McEnroe won, 6–4, 4–6, 6–3, 6–2, in a stormy match that could be completed only after the crowd of 10,000 spectators at a night session—many of them heavily into their cups—had booed veteran umpire Frank Hammond from the chair amid a shower of beer cans, paper cups and other unidentified flying objects. After more than 2½ hours of tennis charged with a constant undercurrent of psychological warfare. Hammond lost his temper and control of the match in docking Nastase a "penalty game" for alleged stalling. The predominantly pro-Nastase crowd rebelled, objected vociferously when Hammond tried to default Nastase, and did not calm

down until the tournament director had overruled the default and replaced Hammond as the umpire. McEnroe—at home on the asphalt-based courts less than 15 minutes from his front door in Douglastown, N.Y., but never a favorite with the home crowds because of his incessant pouting and grousing—won two matches by default, including his quarterfinal over Eddie Dibbs. But he stayed sharp playing doubles, and in the semifinals routed Connors, who was inhibited by back spasms, 6–3, 6–3, 7–5. He won the final with similar ease over Long Island neighbor Gerulaitis, 7–5, 6–3, 6–3.

Gerulaitis had made a magnificent comeback from two sets and a service break down in the semifinals to beat Tanner, who had served magnificently in upsetting No. 1 seed Borg in the quarterfinals, 6–2, 4–6, 6–2, 7–6. Borg—who hated playing at night, especially against a big

The U.S. Open trophy was John McEnroe's after his straight-set conquest of Vitas Gerulaitis in 1979. • *UPI*

server like Tanner—was thus foiled for the second straight year in his attempt to nail down the third leg of a possible French-Wimbledon-U.S.-Australian Grand Slam, and failed to win his first U.S. Open.

In the women's singles, Pam Shriver—who a year earlier had become the youngest finalist in the tournament's history at 16 years, 2 months—lost in the first

became the youngest U.S. champion ever, three days younger than May Sutton in 1904 and several months younger than Maureen Connolly in 1951.

"I thought the title might intimidate her," said Evert Lloyd, who until a three-set victory over Sherry Acker in the fourth round had not lost a set in the U.S. Open since the 1975 final. "But she was out there like it was just another tennis match."

McEnroe and Fleming won the men's doubles over fellow Americans Stan Smith and Bob Lutz, 6–2, 6–4. The sentimental story of the doubles, however, was the reunion of Australians Roy Emerson, 42, and Fred Stolle, 40, who had last played together in the U.S. Doubles when it was played in Boston. They were the champions of 1965–66, and added four more victories to reach 15 in a row before Smith and Lutz toppled them in the semifinals, 7–5, 3–6, 7–5. Stove-Turnbull reversed the result of the Wimbledon final, beating King-Navratilova for the women's doubles title, while Greer Stevens and Bob Hewitt repeated their Wimbledon victory over Stove and Frew McMillan in the mixed doubles final.

In the Davis Cup final, McEnroe and Gerulaitis in singles and Smith-Lutz in doubles cinched the Cup with a 5–0 shutout of Italy. The U.S. team did not allow Italy a single set in 15 sets.

Not long after the U.S. Open, Volvo, the Swedish auto manufacturer, announced that it would assume and expand sponsorship of the men's Grand Prix of tennis, fol-

and battles for control of the men's game.

1980

For such a moment is the grass maintained with tender loving care. For such a moment are the vines trimmed and the roses tended. For such a moment are the stands of the All England Lawn Tennis & Croquet Club retouched every year in a somber shade of green.

The moment is everything. It is at the root of all this, beneath the ivy and the proper manners and even the hallowed lawns. Scratch deep enough at Wimbledon and a hundred matches of high drama rise from the earth. They are the foundation of the most significant tennis tournament in the world, the source of the tradition which sets the event apart from all others.

Wimbledon exists for Borg vs. McEnroe, Centre Court, July 5, 1980. The defending champion reeling. His opponent seeking to score the most memorable of upsets. And a huge crowd engrossed in great theatre.

That's Wimbledon at its best, the most marvelous of backdrops for a haunting match, perhaps the most gripping in the history of what club officials call simply The Championships. Bjorn Borg survived the loss of seven match points in the fourth set of the men's final and, finally, the set itself. Then he survived the loss of seven break points in the deciding set before defeating the American upstart, 1–6, 7–5, 6–3, 6–7 (16–18), 8–6, in a three-hour, 53-minute epic.

At the instant he fell to his knees in that signature ritual of triumph, the man was at the top of his game and at the peak of a career that challenged history for an equal. It marked his fifth consecutive Wimbledon title, following on the heels of a fifth French Open championship, all achieved at the tender age of 24. He would close out the year by winning the Volvo Masters for a second successive year and stand unchallenged as the leading figure in the sport.

But even in his most satisfying season, there were intimations that Borg's grip on tennis was loosening. He had won his last 13 five-set matches when he looked across the net at McEnroe at the start of yet another sudden-death encounter in the final of the U.S. Open. This time he couldn't summon the will to outlast the upstart American on his home turf.

McEnroe's 7–6 (7–4), 6–1, 6–7 (5–7), 5–7, 6–4 victory, which enabled him to claim a second consecutive U.S. title, canceled plans for a tennis migration to Australia for what would have been the concluding act of a quest for a men's Grand Slam, last achieved by Rod Laver in 1969. Without that added incentive, Borg and most of his major adversaries bypassed the Christmas season in Melbourne, leaving the Australian Open to lesser mortals. American Brian Teacher won the men's title by defeating Aussie Kim Warwick, 7–5, 7–6, 6–3.

Although overshadowed by the duel of titans on the male side, Chris Evert Lloyd starred in a drama of her own making by

On the ropes, Bjorn Borg came back to win Wimbledon for the fifth time in a row in 1980. • *Russ Adams*

dominating the spotlight on the women's tour. Suffering from fatigue, burnout or mid-life crisis—take your pick—she emerged from a three-month sabbatical to capture clay titles at Rome and Paris, reach the final of a Wimbledon which belonged, unexpectedly, to a blithe spirit from the past, Evonne Goolagong Cawley, and reclaim her U.S. Open birthright by overcoming, among others, Tracy Austin, her most recent nemesis.

Austin failed to add a Grand Slam title to her collection, yet she won a dozen others—including the Avon championship and the Colgate Series championship—and banked more than $600,000 in prize money, not bad for a high-school student. She also teamed with an older sibling, John, to become the first sister-brother team to capture the mixed doubles title at Wimbledon.

Another fast-rising teenager, the graceful Hana Mandlikova of Czechoslovakia,

Nine years after she'd earned the crown at Wimbledon, Evonne Goolagong Cawley won a second time in 1980. • *Russ Adams*

advanced to the final of the U.S. Open and climaxed an outstanding season by defeating Wendy Turnbull for the Australian title at 18. Precocious Andrea Jaeger, 15, was a quarterfinalist at Wimbledon and a semifinalist at Flushing Meadow. Martina Navratilova, suddenly caught in a time warp, had no majors to call her own. She compensated by leading all women in prize money with earnings of $749,250.

Still, it was the men who held the attention of the world, particularly in those instances when Borg and McEnroe shared a major stage. If the Swede added to his legend on the English grass, then the Yank confirmed his mettle by holding his

ground on American asphalt. Their two matches formed an exquisite set of mantelpieces that bracketed the summer of 1980.

As the Wimbledon Championships got underway, Borg was in a class of his own. In the French Open, he had ripped through a field that featured 17 of the top 20 players in the world, with consummate ease. The man dropped no sets and never more than

Amaya, who won the doubles in the company of Hank Pfister. "But some people don't realize this is the Borg Invitational. They think they can actually win the thing. What a joke!"

At Wimbledon, the Swede was busy establishing the Borg Invitational II. Unlike his experience in previous years, he needed no escape hatches in advancing to the men's final, losing only two sets along the way. Centre Court belonged to him as it did to no other.

Only McEnroe, jeered at the start of the tournament for intemperate outbursts, stood between Borg and a measure of immortality. Earlier in the week, when he was questioned about his motivation after having won so easily, the Swede said he would like the final "to be 12–10 in the fifth, but only if I know I win." McEnroe came perilously close to meeting that challenge, so much so that Borg actually doubted he would win.

It was in the 34-point fourth set tie-breaker that a battle for the ages was joined. At 5–4, Borg had only to serve it out for his 35th consecutive triumph on Wimbledon grass. He promptly rolled to a 40–15 advantage, double match point. But McEnroe saved both points and then broke service.

At 6–6, the combatants began a tie-breaker that lasted 22 minutes. It featured five championship points for Borg, seven set points for his opponent. Finally, on the 34th point, with the crowd exhausted from the emotion of the moment, the champion failed to execute a difficult drop volley and the match was tied at two sets apiece.

"I thought mentally he'd get down after that," McEnroe said. "It would've gotten me a little down, but it didn't seem to get to him. He's won it four times. You'd think he might let down and say forget it."

Indeed, Borg did admit to being discouraged at the start of the fifth set. "When I lost those match points, I couldn't believe it," the man conceded. "I was thinking then maybe I will end up losing the match. It is a terrible feeling."

The disappointment lasted two points into the fifth set. Borg fell behind 0–30 on his serve, then dipped deeply into his vast reserve of spirit. He won the next four points to take a 1–0 advantage. From that instant, McEnroe was waging an uphill fight.

Borg would serve 25 more times in the match and win 24 points, losing at 40–0 in the ninth game. He gained his break in the 14th game when, at 15–15, the Swede won the last three points with a return down the line, a volley McEnroe couldn't retrieve and a backhand passing shot. Then he fell to his knees in supplication, as ever, and added an impromptu collapse on the well-worn grass.

"At this rate," McEnroe said, "I don't know when he's ever going to lose here. He hits harder than when I first saw him. He volleys better."

And it was not out of the question then to consider him in the context of Tilden,

Budge, Laver. Not with 10 Grand Slam championships, not with the U.S. Open and a Grand Slam within his sights. "I want to be remembered as the greatest ever," Borg said.

In the afterglow of that triumph, Borg took a bride, the fair Mariana Simionescu, a Romanian player of modest accomplishment. His warmup for the U.S. Open was jeopardized by a knee injury which caused him to retire in the midst of the Canadian Open final against an ascending star, 20-year-old Ivan Lendl of Czechoslovakia. Earlier in the same tournament, McEnroe twisted an ankle and defaulted in the second round, then was beaten in the first round at Atlanta the following week.

Despite hysterical headlines suggesting that neither man might be able to walk—let alone run—on the court at Louis Armstrong Stadium, there was no stopping the two from an appointment in the Open finale. Their journeys, however, were not without obstacles. Borg's were psychological as well as physical.

Only the previous year, serving so hard that one of his missiles collapsed the net, Roscoe Tanner had ousted Borg from the Open in a quarterfinal match staged at night. When they met again, in the same round, it appeared that the only difference was the presence of daylight. Tanner continued to blast away—he was credited with 19 aces and 26 service winners—in building a lead of 2–1 in sets, 4–2 in games.

But Borg, displaying the same resilience that had been the hallmark of his Wimbledon success, rallied to salvage the fourth set, 7–5, and closed out the match, 6–3. Nor was that his last scare. He yielded the first two sets to Johan Kriek in the semifinals before overwhelming the expatriate South African, 4–6, 4–6, 6–1, 6–1, 6–1.

Kriek became the fifth player to take the first two sets of a best-of-five match against Borg. Not one of them—not Guillermo Vilas at the Italian in '74, not Manuel Orantes at the French in the same year, not Brian Gottfried at the Open in '76, not Mark Edmondson at Wimbledon in '77, not Kriek at the Open in '80—had been able to put away the Swede. The challenge of facing Borg was enough to make a man believe his heart rather than the scoreboard. And, in his heart, Borg

American said, "I thought my body was going to fall off."

Neither man played with the artistry that marked the historic match at Wimbledon two months earlier. The record Open crowd of 21,072 appeared not to notice. If it wasn't a classic, it still left people breathless with excitement.

They produced an amazing match that stretched more than four hours. Connors appeared to be in control when he took a 2–1 lead in sets, 2–0 in games. Instead, McEnroe rallied to win the fourth set and served for the match at 5–4 in the fifth, only to be broken. Mac finally prevailed in a tie-breaker, 6–4, 5–7, 0–6, 6–3, 7–6 (7–3), not the ideal preparation for a final against Borg scheduled to start less than 24 hours later.

This was the pairing everyone hoped to see, even McEnroe. "I just want to win the tournament," the defender said on the first day of the two-week event, "but if I knew beforehand that I'd win, I'd rather play Borg in the final. Say 22–20 in the fifth set." When a man noted they play fifth-set tie-breakers at the Open, Mac altered the score. "Okay," he said, "make it 7–0 in the tie-breaker."

As it developed, a decisive tie-breaker wasn't necessary. But that was about all the match lacked. Such was the pressure in what became a battle of survival that McEnroe felt like wilting after Borg squared the score at two sets apiece. "When I lost the fourth set," the 21-year-old

after breaking his racket on a serve and it was his best-looking shot in several games.

"I was trying my best," he said, "but I was not playing well. I had no feel for the ball."

And yet somehow the two staggered into an excruciatingly dramatic final scene, stumbling into a cliffhanger finish. Call it destiny. The tension was suffocating.

The fatal break occurred in the seventh game of the fifth set after Borg had committed two of his uncharacteristic nine double faults. McEnroe laid claim to the title with a sharp volley at 4–15 of the 10th game, four hours and 13 minutes after the initial serve. He became the first repeat champion since Australian Neale Fraser in 1959–60 and the first Yank to win national honors in consecutive years since Pancho Gonzalez in 1948–49.

"I think our Wimbledon match was much better," Borg said. "I think I can play much better and John can play much better. The two tie-breakers, that's why it was so exciting. In the future, I think John and I have some great matches. For as long as we play."

It wouldn't be as long as the public surmised. They met only twice more during the 1980 season, Borg triumphing in straight sets at the Stockholm Open in November and in three tight sets (two decided by tie-breaker) in the preliminary round of the Masters.

McEnroe enjoyed a superb year, leading the men in earnings ($972,369) and tournament victories (10). Despite his losses to Borg at Wimbledon and to Connors (2–6, 7–6, 6–1, 6–2) in the WCT Finals played at the brand new Reunion Arena in Dallas, he was a legitimate candidate for the top spot in the world when the leading players converged on Madison Square Garden for the Masters. There, he inexplicably lost all three preliminary round-robin matches, to Gene Mayer and Jose-Luis Clerc as well as Borg.

The latter overcame Connors in the semifinal and then whipped Lendl, 6–4, 6–2, 6–2, for the $100,000 top prize and the clear designation as No. 1. Lendl, who scored a season-high 113 victories in a gruelling 142 tournament matches, had his greatest satisfaction in team competition, leading Czechoslovakia to a 4–1 victory over Italy in Prague for its first Davis Cup title. In their previous match, the Czechs had upset Argentina in Buenos Aires, site of the U.S. demise in the American Zone final.

Comebacks marked women's play, the most remarkable being Goolagong's at Wimbledon. Her previous victory on the lawns had occurred nine years earlier as an ethereal teenager. "I just happened to win," she recalled. "I didn't think much of it at the time."

And the thought remained buried as she went on to lose her next seven appearances in a Wimbledon or U.S. final. But neither age, nor her marriage to Roger Cawley nor motherhood had dimmed the lustre of her strokes nor the effortless grace of her movement. She rose to the occasion one last time at 28.

Her career had been interrupted several times by injuries and illness but 1980 had been particularly trying. Before she returned to action in June, she had not hit a ball for seven weeks. Goolagong considered that a positive. "I get stale if I play too much," she said.

Goolagong played herself into shape at Wimbledon. She was down a set (Betty Stove) in her third-round match and trailed by a set and a break (Hana Mandlikova) in the fourth. That experience served her well in the semifinals when she faced Austin, who had won 35 of her previous 36 matches.

Despite the loss of seven consecutive games, Goolagong eliminated the young American, 6–3, 0–6, 6–4. Then she upset Evert Lloyd, 6–1, 7–6 (7–1), marking the only time in the tournament's history that a singles championship had been decided by a tie-breaker. She was the first mother to claim a Wimbledon singles title since Dorothea Lambert Chambers in 1914.

That represented one of the few setbacks suffered by Evert Lloyd after her return to competitive tennis in time for the European clay circuit. After being beaten by Austin in the opener of the Avon series at Cincinnati and losing to Navratilova at Chicago, Evert Lloyd had departed the tour in Seattle for what she later called a "leave of absence."

Apparently refreshed, she seized her third Italian title in Rome and then, in the absence of Austin, Navratilova and Goolagong, won her fourth French championship, thrashing 1978 champ Virginia Ruzici, 6–0, 6–3, in the final. Evert Lloyd increased her winning streak to 25 matches by dispatching Navratilova, 4–6, 6–4, 6–2, in a Wimbledon semifinal before falling to Goolagong.

She stepped up the pace back in the States, winning a U.S. Clay Court title for the sixth time and taking a second Canadian title. Evert Lloyd was primed to regain her Open crown and to defeat Austin, the clone who had whipped her five consecutive times. She got her opportunity in the semifinal round at Flushing Meadow.

A revived Chris Evert Lloyd captured all the majors except Wimbledon in 1980. • *Russ Adams*

she swept into the final by winning the last two sets convincingly, 6–1, 6–1.

What she called her "most emotional victory" preceded her most satisfying moment of the year. Evert Lloyd had invited her father and first teacher from Florida to witness the final. Jim Evert, preferring to stay far in the background and not engage his nervous system, had never seen his daughter win a major championship in person.

So Evert Lloyd's 5–7, 6–1, 6–1 conquest of Mandlikova represented a first of sorts even as it reestablished an old pattern. The Czech, who had upset her idol, Navratilova, and overcome Jaeger in a 6–1, 3–6, 7–6 (7–4) battle of prodigies, began strongly against Evert Lloyd but didn't have the concentration or will to withstand the relentless American. After claiming her fifth Open championship, Evert Lloyd had a 53–5 match record in the tournament.

Nor did she stop there. A month later, she annexed her 100th professional tournament title at Deerfield Beach, Fla.

Evert Lloyd also enjoyed remarkable success in team play. She captained the U.S.

team in the Wightman Cup. In the Federation Cup, she (5–0) and teammates won all 15 of their matches, including a 3–0 sweep of Australia in the championship round at West Berlin. Chris concluded a remarkable campaign by leading the U.S. over Britain in the Wightman Cup, 5–2.

The captain won both singles and teamed with Rosie Casals to win her doubles match in the event staged at Albert Hall in London. Furthermore, she recovered from double match point (at 15–40, 1–5 in the third) to defeat Virginia Wade, 7–5, 3–6, 7–5, in the deciding match. It was her 23rd overall victory in Wightman play, surpassing Louise Brough's record.

Another Brough standard, one she shared with Nancy Richey for most years ranked among the Top Ten in the U.S. (16), was eclipsed by Billie Jean King. The latter celebrated her 17th year among the elite with a fifth-place finish. King, who turned 37 in November, won three singles titles and 11 doubles titles, including the U.S. championship in partnership with Navratilova. It was her 39th—and last—Big Four title, second then only to Margaret Smith Court's 62. But it was Navratilova's ninth, and she was on her way to eclipsing King with 54 in 1990.

1981

In a land rich in ceremony, men's tennis staged a changing of the guard. Not only did John McEnroe topple Bjorn Borg from his Wimbledon throne in 1981 but he usurped the man's place as the ruler of his sport. By year's end, the former monarch relinquished all claims to the territories he once commanded.

Borg's decision to reduce his schedule so drastically that it resulted in virtual retirement from competitive tennis followed humbling four-set losses to McEnroe in the finals of both the Wimbledon and U.S. Open championships. It represented a stunning development in the wake of the Swede's victory at Paris, his sixth French Open title and his 11th in a Big Four event. There would be no others. At 25, the man decided to remove his headband and let down his hair after a decade of single-minded devotion.

He may have been suffering from burnout or come to the realization that he was never going to achieve a U.S. title, let alone the Grand Slam that seemed so close and yet so far. Clearly, the brash McEnroe, three years his junior, had gained sufficient composure and mental toughness to suggest he wasn't going to be easily dislodged.

At Wimbledon, the American had battled with linesmen, umpires, tournament officials and the tabloid press and still exhibited the poise to deprive Borg of a sixth successive title on his own personal lawn. Two months later, McEnroe completed his coup on the hard courts at Flushing Meadow. The defeat was the Swede's fourth in a U.S. Open final and marked him as the most accomplished player never to claim the U.S. championship.

There was no such seismographic activity in the women's ranks. Each of the four Grand Slam titles was claimed by a different player. Hana Mandlikova won her first French Open, Chris Evert Lloyd excelled at Wimbledon for the third time, Tracy Austin added a second U.S. Open championship and Martina Navratilova triumphed over a complete women's field in Australia.

Yet, there wasn't much doubt that Navratilova enjoyed the finest year of the four, and not only for the quality of her tennis. She won 10 tournaments playing singles, a circuit best, and she also combined with Pam Shriver to claim 11 doubles titles, including Wimbledon. Additionally, she was granted U.S. citizenship in midsummer and then bathed in the sustained applause of the crowd at the National Tennis Center, her National Tennis Center, following a loss to Austin in a brilliant Open final. She received the affection she craved with tears in her eyes.

If Borg cried following his loss to McEnroe the following day, it was on the inside. For the first time in memory, the well-mannered Swede ignored the protocol of the trophy presentation, spoke not a word to the fans or the media assembled at Flushing Meadow and left the grounds in a huff or, as one timekeeper noted, a minute and a huff. Only the previous day, while blasting Jimmy Connors in a men's semifinal, he had been the subject of a telephoned death threat. But for the man who had purchased a luxurious house on Long Island for the express purpose of establishing a home-court advantage at the previously inhospitable playground, it seemed the disappointment of the moment simply overwhelmed him.

Martina Navratilova became a U.S. citizen in 1981 and had an outstanding campaign that soared even in her U.S. Open defeat at the hands of Tracy Austin. • *Russ Adams*

Still, two weeks of serious practice had left him fit. "I feel strong," he said. "I can be out on the court for a long time if I have to."

It wasn't necessary, at least not until the final. The man mowed down his half of the draw until he came to Lendl, who had overcome Italian Open champ Jose-Luis Clerc in a five-set semifinal. The

That it would be the final picture of Borg at a championship event was perhaps the cruelest twist of fate. His season had started with such promise at Paris where his 6–1, 4–6, 6–2, 3–6, 6–1 triumph over Ivan Lendl left him tied with the great Rod Laver at 11 Grand Slam singles titles, one behind all-time male leader Roy Emerson. At the time, it appeared inevitable that the Swede would establish a standard of his own for men's tennis, perhaps before the year was out.

His performance in the French Open temporarily silenced questions about the man's future. Borg had reported to Paris following an absence from competition that extended nearly two months, the result of a tender right shoulder. Since he had played in only three tournaments since January and failed to advance past the second round in two of them, even he was uncertain of his form.

added to his résumé, he turned his attention to Wimbledon. A sixth consecutive championship in the London suburb would tie him with Willie Renshaw, who competed before the turn of the century (1881–86) when defenders were treated to a bye into the final, the challenge round. Borg prepared in his usual fashion, shunning warmup tournaments in favor of long practice hours on the grass with coach-adviser Lennart Bergelin and sparring partner Vitas Gerulaitis. There was no reason to believe the outcome would be any different this time.

While McEnroe did receive a greater share of attention at Wimbledon from the outset, it was for all the wrong reasons. On the occasion of his first match, versus Tom Gullikson, the man launched a verbal assault on umpire Ted James and tournament referee Fred Hoyles, whose presence at courtside he demanded. The tournament committee actually considered showing him the gate before settling on $1,500 in fines.

The hornet's nest he stirred quickly spread to the demon barbers of Fleet Street, ever alert to scandal. They reached for their sharpest blades and headlines of a size normally reserved for world wars and the royal

It was goodbye Bjorn Borg as John McEnroe (forecourt) hastened the Swedish master's abrupt exit following Wimbledon and U.S. Open setbacks in 1981. • *Russ Adams*

family. "Superbrat" was among the fondest of compliments they could muster.

McEnroe grumbled his way into the semifinals where he again dressed down Hoyles during an interminable victory over unseeded Australian Rod Frawley that was fraught with objections and unprintables. But the real brouhaha began in the interview room after the Yank had vented his spleen on the British tabloid press in the wake of some baiting by a gossip columnist. There followed a dialogue on the nature of journalism among emissaries from various countries and soon an Englishman and an American were rolling on the floor.

Through all the tumult, Borg kept rolling toward his appointment with destiny. He overcame a major challenge from Connors in the semifinals, rallying from yet another two-set deficit to oust his old adversary, 0–6, 4–6, 6–3, 6–0, 6–4, in a match that rivaled any the two had produced for quality and tension. "He had to play his best stuff to beat me," Connors said. And it was true.

But even a sharp and determined Borg wasn't enough to hold off a McEnroe who had learned to orchestrate his talents, if not his temper. Uncharacteristically, the defender started fast. Shockingly, he finished second. The American triumphed, 4–6, 7–6 (7–1), 7–6 (7–4), 6–4. The king was dead.

For all practical purposes, Borg lost his title in game 10 of the third set, where he enjoyed four set points for a 2–1 lead. First, McEnroe served out of a 15–40 hole, then overcame two Borg ads in the six-deuce game. He took control of the tie-breaker with two sensational passing shots after Borg served at 3–4.

In the fourth set, the one that terminated Borg's Wimbledon winning streak at 41, McEnroe attacked at every opportunity. He also continued to dominate with his big first serve, winning 79 percent of the points when he was on target. In the critical tiebreakers, he missed only one of 10 first serves.

"I was surprised that I served so well."

and call him McEnroney," telecaster Bud Collins observed—Superbrat closed out an era with a forehand volley winner on his second championship point.

Horrified officials of the All England Club had their revenge. They declined to tender McEnroe an honorary membership, a traditional spoil of victory. Not that the man had any desire to join an institution he labelled "the pits of the world."

If anything, the loss seemed to spur Borg to new heights of resolve. He settled into his mansion fronting Long Island Sound during the summer and stepped up his practice routine for the Flushing hothouse. "We don't have a tennis court," Bergelin noted, "but the house is on the water. Very nice. Very nice." And it wasn't far from the home of Gerulaitis, who did have a hard court in his backyard.

As usual, McEnroe practiced while playing, whipping Chris Lewis in the final of the ATP championship in Cincinnati in advance of the Open. The American circuit had been otherwise dominated by Clerc, who walked off with four clay-court

titles, including the U.S. Clay Court championship in Indianapolis, where he defeated Lendl, 4–6, 6–4, 6–2. But the lean Argentine would be no factor on the Open surface.

The field was reduced to the usual suspects in time for the semifinals. McEnroe, who had lost an opening set to the likes of

was matched against Roscoe Tanner in the quarterfinals. For the second straight Open, he survived, winning two of three tiebreakers required in the four-set match. "Could you have him win the tournament this year?" Tanner said to Bergelin afterward. "Then they'll stop writing that he's won everything but this and maybe I won't have to play him in the quarterfinals again."

It seemed a genuine possibility after Borg, serving as well as he ever had, demolished Connors in their semifinal meeting, 6–2, 7–5, 6–4,. He had 14 aces plus many unreturnable serves and all of them appeared to occur on the big points. "It seemed like every first serve was going in," he said. "I was a little surprised."

The victory extended Borg's streak over Connors to 10 matches. Shortly before the match, which began at dinnertime, the switchboard operator at the National Tennis Center received a call from a man threatening Borg's life. Additional security guards ringed the stadium court as a precaution but Borg was not informed until after he had vanquished Connors.

As he had at Wimbledon, Borg jumped out in front of McEnroe in the final. But the Yank swept the last three sets to post a 4–6, 6–2, 6–4, 6–3 victory, stamping him as the first man to capture a third successive U.S. singles title since the legendary Bill Tilden strung together six during the Roaring '20s.

Borg's best chance evaporated in the third set when, leading 4–3, he was broken in stunning fashion as McEnroe unleashed four winners, including a pair of spectacular running topspin lobs, to draw even. "I felt I could do anything," the American said. He won eight of the last 11 games as Borg's future flashed before his eyes. It did not include competitive tennis.

One month later, the former No. 1 player in the world said he was taking his first extended vacation from tennis until the following April. He also said he would participate in only seven tournaments, a number insufficient for placement in the main draw under the rules of the Men's International Professional Tennis Council. He would have to quality for every Grand Prix tournament he entered, a course he would pursue with apparent disinterest.

Suddenly, the stage was all McEnroe's. Although Johan Kriek—whom Mac had defeated in the WCT final at Dallas, 6–1, 6–2, 6–4—would emerge from a depleted field to take the Australian title by virtue of a 6–2, 7–6, 6–7, 6–4 victory over Steve Denton and despite Lendl's first-place finish in the Grand Prix standings and his subsequent 6–7 (5–7), 7–6 (8–6), 6–2, 6–4 triumph over Gerulaitis in the Masters final, McEnroe was the unchallenged leader of the pack.

Not only did the left-hander from the New York borough of Queens win nine of 17 singles tournaments but he teamed with Peter Fleming to win an equal number of

doubles titles, including both the Wimbledon and U.S. championships. Additionally, he won both his singles matches and, alongside Fleming, the doubles match in a 3–1 victory over Argentina that returned the Davis Cup to the States. No man had swept the singles at Wimbledon, the U.S. and in the Cup final since Don Budge in 1938, the year of his Grand Slam.

Furthermore, his facility in doubles marked him as the most complete champion since John Newcombe was lending his mustache to a line of tennis gear. Fittingly, the representatives of two generations held an improbable meeting on the stadium court at Flushing Meadow in the doubles semifinals. Newk, 37, and partner Fred Stolle, 42, both singles titlists at the Open in their salad days, had a merry romp through the first four rounds of the draw, in contrast to the grim attitude of Mac and Fleming.

Remarkably, it took a fifth-set tie-breaker for the youngsters to overcome the veterans. They won the match but not the crowd, which cheered and laughed as the old Aussies reprised a few vaudeville routines, sometimes sending one man to the other side of the net to help the grim Americans. "We always had a fair bit of fun playing doubles in my day," Stolle said.

To Newcombe, who chose not to live his life between the white lines, the current attitude was unfortunate. "I feel sorry for them," he said. "It's a sport. It's a living, too, yes, but they take it over the fringe."

The fine schedule for the year indicated just how much court conduct had deteriorated. McEnroe, Gerulaitis and Ilie Nastase all drew 21-day suspensions for exceeding $5,000 in fines. Of the three, Gerulaitis created the biggest stir, walking out of the Melbourne indoor final in a protest against officiating, an offense which earned him a record $10,000 penalty.

Tim Mayotte, the 21-year-old Intercollegiate champion from Stanford, made an auspicious professional debut and was honored as Rookie of the Year. He reached the quarterfinal round at Wimbledon in only his second pro tournament, won 28 of 43 matches in 15 events and finished the year at No. 31 on the computer.

The march of children into the

6–1, 6–3, in the quarters.

Having disposed of the latest princess, Mandlikova went after the queen. Now 19, she sent Evert Lloyd to her second defeat on clay in the last 191 matches, 7–5, 6–4, in the semifinals. Mandlikova closed out her first Grand Slam title by stopping Sylvia Hanika, a semifinal winner over Andrea Jaeger, 6–2, 6–4.

She carried her form onto the grass at Wimbledon, a tournament which lost its defending champion when Evonne Goolagong Cawley interrupted her career to give birth to a second child. That absence was offset by the return of Austin, who missed the first five months of the season with a sciatic nerve condition. In the presence of Rinaldi and Jaeger, Austin, 18, was perceived as a veteran. "I can't believe this is my fifth Wimbledon," she said.

Rinaldi became the youngest player to win a match at Wimbledon but advanced no farther. Jaeger, 16, was upset by Mima Jausovec and an unsteady Austin was stunned in the quarters by Pam Shriver,

whom she had dispatched in all 11 previous encounters.

The semifinals matched Mandlikova against Navratilova, and the younger woman—seeded second despite her ranking of No. 5 on the computer—justified her placement by tournament officials with a 7–5, 4–6, 6–1 victory, winning 11 of the last 13 points in the process. Now all she

Two in a row for Tracy Austin in the U.S. Open in 1981. •*Wide World*

6–3, 6–1 rout of Shriver in the semifinal was typical of her fortnight. So was the final.

After three consecutive defeats in the championship round, she took apart a nervous Mandlikova, 6–2, 6–2. "I told myself that if I played Hana at Wimbledon," she said, "I would beat her." And so she did, with relative ease.

Youth was served on the summer circuit. Most notably at Indianapolis, where Jaeger became the youngest winner of the U.S. Clay Court championship, thrashing the seasoned Romanian, Virginia Ruzici, in the final, 6–1, 6–0. Austin demonstrated she had regained her fitness by outlasting Shriver at San Diego, 6–2, 5–7, 6–2, and then dethroning Evert Lloyd at the Canadian Open, 6–1, 6–4.

It was ideal preparation for the U.S. Open, where she breezed through 12 effortless sets to reach the final. The path for the third-seeded Austin was smoothed by Jaeger's second-round collapse against Andrea Leand, an amateur who had never before qualified for a pro tournament. Leand, a 17-year-old headed for Princeton, rallied from far behind to leave the second-seeded Jaeger in tears following a 1–6, 7–5, 6–3 verdict.

Form prevailed in the other half of the draw where Evert Lloyd advanced to her 11th consecutive Open semifinal. Her opponent was Navratilova, who had been frustrated in the tournament since that September day in 1975 when she announced her defection to the U.S. at Forest Hills. After years of complaining about the noise, the constant movement of the crowds and all the other distractions that threw her off her game, she triumphed over all and dispatched Evert Lloyd, 7–5, 4–6, 6–4, in a marvelous and emotional match.

That qualified Navratilova for her first U.S final, where she seized the initiative in the first set, 6–1. But the gritty Austin fought back to win the last two sets in tie-breakers, 7–6 (7–4) and 7–6 (7–1), and claim the first major championship decided by an ultimate set artificial ending. The fans' reaction to the loser's efforts thrilled Navratilova as much as anything in her career.

Their warm applause interrupted her concession speech on several occasions. She cried from happiness as she turned to all four sides of the court and made a little bow, the kind expected at Wimbledon but seen so rarely in the New World. "I want to thank each and every one of you who was pulling for me today," she said. "I really didn't think that would happen." At long last love.

One month later, Navratilova snapped Austin's 28-match winning streak with a 6–0, 6–2 victory in the U.S. Indoor final at Minneapolis. She also annexed the Avon championship and won the final Grand Slam event of the year, overcoming Evert Lloyd, 6–7 (4–7), 6–4, 7–5, in the Australian final. That boosted her singles titles in 1981 to 10 which, combined with the 11 doubles titles she shared with Shriver, enabled her to set a one-season earnings record of $865,437.

Austin rebounded to win the Toyota Series championship that closed out the year. Evert Lloyd, who ran her singles records in the Wightman Cup and Federation Cup to 20–0 and 23–0, respectively, as the U.S. won all its matches in both competitions, raised her total of tournament singles titles to 110 with nine more and regained the top spot in the USTA rankings.

1982

It would have been out of place in such a proletarian celebration as the U.S. Open,

For Chris Evert Lloyd and Jimmy Connors, 1982 would mark the last time they would share the winner's circle at a major tournament. • *Russ Adams, Mitchell Reibel*

staged in a municipally-owned complex in a public park. After all, people at the National Tennis Center consider a sweater looped over the shoulders as evening wear. But just this once the tournament of the people, by the people and for the people deserved a formal conclusion.

Something on the order of the Wimbledon Ball would have been appropriate. And for one reason. So Jimmy Connors, men's champion, could get to dance the first dance with Chris Evert Lloyd, the women's champion.

What a picture that would have made. And what a fitting commentary on the state of the sport eight years after they reigned as the sweethearts of center court. They had taken divergent paths since 1974 and yet, before the eyes of enthralled spectators and in front of a worldwide television audience, they wound up in the same spot.

Champions of the New World, Connors at 30 and Evert Lloyd at 27.

They grew up before our eyes. The girl who was Chrissie, a beribboned semifinalist at the event at sweet 16, did so with considerably more grace but Connors got there nonetheless, maturing after his marriage to Patti McGuire and the birth of a son. They had first appeared in the tournament when it was staged at Forest Hills, when the surface was grass, when tennis players dressed only in white.

So Connors' 6–3, 6–2, 4–6, 6–4 victory over Ivan Lendl, which followed by a day Evert Lloyd's 6–3, 6–1 conquest of Hana Mandlikova, was—as much as anything—a triumph of the familiar. And it continued an all-American winning tradition in the singles since the tournament was shifted to the former World's Fair ground five years earlier. Czech-mate. Czech-mate.

Johan Kriek made headlines in 1982, winning the Australian championship and topping John McEnroe in the U.S. Indoor and in fines.

• *Wide World*

It was at the U.S. where Martina Navratilova's quest for a Grand Slam ended prematurely in a quarterfinal loss to her doubles partner, Pam Shriver. Evert Lloyd made the most of that opportunity, then defeated Navratilova in the Australian final, 6–3, 2–6, 6–3, to even the score in Big Four tournaments at two apiece. But the naturalized American still reigned as the foremost figure in women's tennis, winning 29 tournaments (15 in singles), earning a record of $1,475,055 and securing the season-closing Toyota Series playoffs, climaxed by a 4–6, 6–1, 6–1 triumph over Evert.

Among the men, Connors stood alone after completing a double that appeared beyond his reach at the age of 30. The irrepressible left-hander prevailed over John McEnroe in the first Wimbledon final of the post-Borg era, then turned back Lendl at Flushing Meadow, while climbing

back to the pinnacle from which he had been ousted by Borg and McEnroe.

Mats Wilander, from the first class of Swedish youngsters inspired by Borg, ascended to the French Open title at the tender age of 17 years, 10 months. In becoming the youngest man to annex a Grand Slam title—Borg was two months older when he won at Paris for the first time in 1974—Wilander outlasted 1977 champion Guillermo Vilas, 1–6, 7–6 (8–6), 6–0, 6–4, in his very first tournament on the Roland Garros clay. Before the year was over, he would finish first in four of 20 tournaments, compile a match record of 60–18 and walk off with rookie honors.

In what was a replay of the 1981 Australian Open final, Johan Kriek, a native South African resettled in Florida, routed hard-serving Texan Steve Denton, 6–3, 6–3, 6–2, at Melbourne. Earlier in the year, the man had stripped McEnroe of yet another prize, the U.S. Indoor championship, 6–3, 3–6, 6–4. Mac wasn't nearly as upset by Kriek's other coup, replacing the feisty left-hander atop the punitive standings: $11,500 to $2,060 in fines.

Lendl continued to outwork—and outearn—everyone else on the men's tour. Balancing his schedule between the Grand Prix and the more lucrative rival circuit, World Championship Tennis, the lean Czech captured 15 of the 23 tournaments he entered, won 107 of 116 matches and overpowered Yannick Noah, Connors and McEnroe to claim a second consecutive Masters title. He also threatened Vilas' Open-era record of 50 before Noah terminated his match-winning streak at 44 in February at LaQuinta, Cal.

For all of that, and despite a record one-season haul of $2,028,850 that almost doubled Connors' payoff of $1,173,850, Lendl was denied the No. 1 position by his failure to win a Grand Slam event. He didn't even bother to enter Wimbledon, claiming an allergy to grass while he worked on his golf game back in the States. Nor was he the only defector from the world's most prestigious tournament. No fewer than five of the top 10 males on the ATP computer skipped the event, including the mysterious Borg, and Vilas, whose country was at war with Great Britain over

in Monaco in conjunction with the Monte Carlo Open, which happened to mark the Swede's debut as a qualifier.

Sir Brian Burnett, chairman of the Wimbledon Championships, joined the discussions. He was eager for a compromise that would make it unnecessary for Borg to quality at Wimbledon. The council was willing. "But," said Arthur Ashe, a council member, "Borg wasn't. For him, it was a matter of principle."

Standing on principle, Borg won his three qualifying matches in Monte Carlo, where he made his home. But he performed strangely in the main draw. He prepared to serve from the wrong side of the court in one match. In another, he served underhanded after two double faults. And he whistled during a loss to Noah in the quarterfinals. This certainly was not the man of steely concentration who had exhausted the will of so many opponents.

Burnett announced the compromise proposal the following week in London. Borg would be accepted for the main draw

at Wimbledon if he agreed to play in 10 Grand Prix tournaments before March 31, 1983. Borg, who had taken his principle to Tokyo for a couple of lucrative exhibition matches, declined. He would play according to the dictates of his own schedule, and he would not play qualifying matches at Wimbledon. So much for tradition.

hand. Borg, observers recalled clearly, hits his backhand with two hands on the racket. "I don't think he had his heart in the qualifying," Stockton reported.

Following that experience, Borg stated he would play only exhibitions for the remainder of the year but return to the circuit in 1983. Months later, during the Masters, he amended that decision with the announcement he was retiring from competitive tennis.

No wonder it was so much easier to follow the fortunes of the women, especially given the dominant manner in which Navratilova started the season. She was unbeaten in five tournaments on the Avon circuit before the cosmetics company withdrew as winter sponsor, to be replaced by year-round angel Virginia Slims. No sooner had her 27-match winning streak been interrupted by Sylvia Hanika in the Avon finale at Madison Square Garden then she began a 41-match run that wouldn't be stopped until the U.S. Open in September. Her loss at Flushing Meadow marked the first time all year she had failed to reach a tournament final.

To her immense satisfaction, Navratilova proved as formidable on the clay as she had been on the grass by sweeping both the Family Circle Cup at Hilton Head, S.C., and the French Open. On both occasions, Andrea Jaeger had done the dirty work, eliminating perennial champion Chris Evert Lloyd in the semifinals.

Prior to her meeting with the Illinois high-school student, Evert Lloyd not only had won all six previous Family Circle Cups but all 64 sets in which she had participated. Jaeger showed her disrespect with a 6–1, 1–6, 6–2 triumph. A few weeks later, she gave herself a 17th-birthday present by stunning Evert Lloyd, favored to win a fifth French title, 6–3, 6–1.

In both cases, however, Jaeger received her comeuppance from Navratilova. She followed a 6–4, 6–2 victory at Hilton Head with a 7–6 (8–6), 6–1 decision at Paris, saving a set point in the tie-breaker. Thus ended the run of the youngest French finalist.

Although Navratilova carried her form onto grass, winning at Eastbourne, the major news of the pre-Wimbledon circuit was provided by Billie Jean King. After playing only a few matches in 1981, when she was buffeted by the agonizing, highly publicized law suit filed by ex-lover Marilyn Barnett, the 38-year-old Founding Mother of the women's tour returned with a vengeance. In the Edgbaston Cup at Birmingham, she defeated Rosalyn Fairbank, 6–2, 6–1, for her first tournament singles title in two years and her 66th as a pro. It was a most favorable omen for a Wimbledon desperately in need of an electric charge.

Wimbledon was inundated by so much rain during the first week that the vice chairman of the tournament was summoned to the interview room to discuss the weather. "Somebody once asked us," said Richard Holt, "why we didn't play the tournament in summer, and I thought that was pretty accurate." Of course, Wimbledon '82 had begun on the first day of the summer solstice. The only dry thing about the British on this occasion was their humor.

An underground strike only added to the gloom, flooding streets around the club with traffic. Into this dreary setting stepped a revitalized B.J. King and the old tennis shrine fairly glowed with her reflection. On the occasion of her first match, her 100th singles battle at Wimbledon, the club planned to present her with a centennial plate.

Officials didn't announce the ceremony in advance because they feared she would lose to 19-year-old Claudia Pasquale of Switzerland. They also sent her to Court 14, "out in the boondocks" according to King, because her seeding of 12th was based as much on sentiment as recent results. The gift appeared to be the British equivalent of a gold watch: Thanks for your contributions to the game and enjoy your retirement.

But the self-styled Old Lady had other plans. She hammered Pasquale, 6–3, 6–2, saved triple match point against South African Tanya Harford in a remarkable 5–7, 7–6 (7–2), 6–2 third-round triumph and then announced she was a genuine title contender by overcoming third-seeded Tracy Austin, 3–6, 6–4, 6–2 in the quarterfinals. She hadn't come back to Wimbledon, her favorite tennis haunt, just for a testimonial.

King knew what she wanted when she took a look in the mirror the previous fall. She lifted weights and she ran and she took the first steps back up the ladder, occasionally falling but getting back on her feet and climbing higher. Wimbledon was her goal and she had more than a trinket in mind when she walked onto the grounds.

She wanted the Duke and Duchess of Kent and everyone else who occupied the Royal Box to empty their pockets on the table. This was a holdup. "Unless you win the whole *woiks* " she said, flavoring the All England Club with a dollop of

But, in 1982, she was in superior physical condition. Despite five operations on her knees and one on her foot, King was the stronger of the two. Troubled by sciatica, Austin would win only one of the 11 tournaments she entered.

Still, the reigning U.S. Open champ had no excuses for her Wimbledon exit, only praise for her conqueror. She recalled a fifth-grade assignment that required a composition about a famous person. Austin chose King. "I was mad because I only got an A-minus," she said, "and I had pictures and everything."

King's victory catapulted her into a semifinal match against Evert Lloyd, one that was all anyone could have anticipated and more. They presented the tournament with a blast from the past. The younger woman prevailed, but not before King fought off four match points and performed a medley of her greatest shots, perfected over two decades. So small was the edge in Evert Lloyd's 7–6 (7–4), 2–6, 6–3 triumph that the two women split the 30 games and King achieved one more service break.

Meanwhile, Navratilova was cruising through an upset-strewn half of the draw, without the loss of a set. "I really can't believe I've won as easily as I have," she said. "I haven't been tested."

Her test came in the final when she found herself down a break in the third set. A finalist for the sixth consecutive year, Evert Lloyd won the last four games

come out better. But she won this match. She played well under pressure."

Indeed, Navratilova needed mental strength commensurate with her physical talents to beat Evert Lloyd, 6–2, 3–6, 6–2, for her third successive Big Four title, including the Australian Open championship she had claimed in December.

All went well until the second week of the U.S. Open where, Navratilova claimed, her condition was weakened by a case of toxoplasmosis, a viral condition transmitted by her cat. Ironically, she was victimized by Shriver who, at 16, had upset Navratilova to reach her only Open final in 1978. In this instance, Shriver rallied from a 1–6, 4–5, 15–30 predicament to oust her doubles partner, 7–6 (7–5) and 6–2 in the third. The two women then hugged at the net and both left the court in tears.

Shriver failed to survive the semifinals, beaten by Hana Mandlikova, who earlier had eliminated defending champ Austin competing in only her second tournament since Wimbledon. Evert Lloyd received her only real challenge in the quarters from an unlikely source, a 19-year-old former gymnast from Florida who had reached the finals at Monte Carlo against Virginia Ruzici. On her way to women's rookie honors, Bonnie Gadusek not only took the first set from Evert Lloyd but broke serve to begin the second.

Thereafter, it was no contest, Evert Lloyd sweeping the last 12 games for a 4–6, 6–1, 6–0 triumph. It was a harbinger of what was to come. The queen of Flushing overwhelmed Jaeger, 6–1, 6–2, in the semis and then dispatched Mandlikova, 6–3, 6–1, to clinch her sixth Open singles title.

She continued winning until Navratilova stopped her streak at 31 matches in the final at Brighton, England, in late October, 6–1, 6–4. Five weeks later, Evert Lloyd reversed the outcome, defeating Navratilova, 6–3, 2–6, 6–3, for her first Australian title. In that instant she became the 10th player of either sex to win all four Big Four singles championships.

The two rivals also teamed for the first time in Federation Cup play as the U.S. stretched its unbeaten streak to 34 rounds en route to its seventh consecutive team championship. Evert Lloyd also captained the American squad to its fourth consecutive Wightman Cup victory over Great Britain, winning both her singles and surpassing Helen Wills Moody's U.S. record for most matches entered with 32.

Connors' resurrection salvaged what had been a lacklustre Wimbledon among the men. With so many top players absent and with the rain pelting down, the primary topic of conversation was McEnroe's relationship with the All England Club. He complimented officials for their attitude following his opening match but he was not entirely pleased, noting that he had not yet received his trophies from the previous year.

Ted Tinling, the liaison between players and the club, explained that McEnroe had not picked up the silver replicas of the President's Cup, the Challenge Cup and the Renshaw Cup on his way out the door in 1981. Nor had he attended the champion's dinner that night. Tinling said the club considered shipping the silverware to New York but found the insurance prohibitive.

So there they sat until the player's father claimed the prizes later that day. As for membership in the club, which Mac also sought, Tinling said that was another matter entirely. "I explained to Mr. McEnroe," he said, "that it's not an automatic to become a member if you win. It's an elected privilege."

Unlike the previous year, his advance to the final was virtually free of controversy. He was warned once, for ball abuse, in a second-round victory over Eddie Edwards and drew a $500 fine for verbal abuse in his 6–3, 6–1, 6–2 semifinal thrashing of Tim Mayotte, the unseeded second-year pro who improved one round on his Wimbledon debut in 1981. McEnroe's first All-England title defense would be against Connors, who easily turned aside another surprise semifinalist, 12th-seeded Mark Edmondson, 6–4, 6–3, 6–1.

It had been eight years since Connors reigned as men's singles champion. He was a whiz kid of 21 when he demolished Ken Rosewall in the '74 final. Only Big Bill Tilden had gone a longer time between Wimbledon titles.

Brandishing a redesigned serve and hungry for another major championship, Connors outlasted McEnroe, 3–6, 6–3, 6–7 (2–7), 7–6 (7–5), 6–4, in a match that was distinguished more by its length (four hours, 15 minutes) than its brilliance. Despite 13 double faults, Connors grabbed hold of his seventh Grand Slam tournament victory. "I'm not a one-timer," he announced, "someone to be forgotten. I've had chances [in finals] three times since then. And I was going to do anything not to let the chance slip by today."

As a special consolation prize, McEnroe was granted the honorary membership denied the previous year. He was so advised between the singles final and doubles final, which he and Peter Fleming lost to Peter McNamara and Paul McNamee of Australia, relinquishing the title they won in 1981. "I guess I'm happy," Mac said after being welcomed to the club.

1983

Considering their backgrounds, their forehands and their achievements, one would not expect to mention them in the same sentence. But on May 28, Martina Navratilova and Kathy Horvath shared a court in Paris. In retrospect, it may have been the most significant match of the year.

baseline, he startled and demoralized the Czech with his returns in a 6–3, 6–2, 4–6, 6–4 triumph that returned the man to the top of the tennis world just when his career appeared to be in eclipse.

"When I won before," Connors said, "everybody thought I would. When I won now, everybody thought I wouldn't. And that's very satisfying." So was joining the likes of Tilden, Fred Perry, Don Budge and Rod Laver as the only men twice to win Wimbledon and the U.S. championship in the same year.

Although winning no major individual titles for the first time in four years, McEnroe did lead the U.S. to a second consecutive Davis Cup. The 4–1 final over France in Grenoble was notable mainly for the man's 12–10, 1–6, 3–6, 6–2, 6–3 victory over Yannick Noah on a clay court built inside the former Olympic ice rink. But even that superb 4-hour, 21-minute battle paled in comparison to Mac's extraordinary 9–7, 6–2, 15–17, 3–6, 8–6 triumph over Mats Wilander in a decisive fifth match of the U.S.-Sweden quarterfinal at St. Louis. Time of play: a Cup singles record of 6 hours, 32 minutes.

the tennis world for what happened at Stade Roland Garros.

The unseeded American, a pupil of Harry Hopman, posted a stunning 6–4, 0–6, 6–3 victory. The ramifications of that upset wouldn't be felt for months. Following the defeat, Navratilova won her next 50 matches and swept the field of Wimbledon, the U.S. Open and Australian Open championships. Not only had Horvath denied her the opportunity of achieving a Grand Slam but spoiled what might have been the first perfect campaign in the modern history of the sport.

Navratilova's domination among the women, marred only by that single loss, and Chris Evert Lloyd's subsequent march to a record-tying fifth French title, was the story of the year in tennis. It overshadowed a mad scramble on the men's circuit as the major championships were divided four ways for the first time in seven years and the race for No. 1 wasn't decided until the Masters in the 13th month of an exhausting season. At the end, the distinction belonged once again to John McEnroe, who boasted a second Wimbledon crown among his seven singles titles.

For breadth of accomplishment, however, Mats Wilander emerged as male Player of the Year. Not only did he win the most matches (82) and singles tournaments (9) but he went 8–0 in Davis Cup play while leading Sweden to second place behind Australia and he compiled the best record in the Grand Slam tournaments. He captured the Australian title, was runner-up at the French, reached the quarterfinals at the U.S. and the third round at Wimbledon. He also finished atop the Volvo Grand Prix standings, pocketing a $600,000 bonus which enabled him to finish third in prize money behind Ivan Lendl and McEnroe.

In terms of shock value and fan satisfaction, however, perhaps nothing compared to Yannick Noah's victory in Paris. By turning back defending champ Wilander in the final, the acrobatic athlete from Cameroon became the first French citizen in 37 years to hold the French title. He also became such a celebrity that he found it necessary to flee to Little Old New York for privacy.

On another national front, Jimmy Connors continued his mastery of the Flushing Meadow hard courts, claiming his fifth U.S. crown while denying Lendl a first Big Four title. The angular Czech also stumbled in the Masters final. He was consoled by checks totaling $1,747,128.

Lendl's earnings exceeded even those of Navratilova but the $1,456,030 she collected, more than triple the take of Evert Lloyd, was only one indicator of the success she enjoyed. At the very least, it was the most stellar female performance since Margaret Smith Court completed her Grand Slam in 1970. Suzanne Lenglen of France and Helen Wills Moody had posted unbeaten seasons earlier in the century but they didn't play in all Big Four championships or endure the same demanding schedule.

Viva le Frenchman Yannick Noah, winner of the French championship in 1983. • *Russ Adams*

Consider that Navratilova won 16 of the 17 singles events she entered and added 13 doubles championships, including 11 in the company of Pam Shriver. Her greatest satisfaction occurred in New York, where she annexed her first U.S. Open title. That brought to 11 the number of players, male and female, to have won all four of the Grand Slam championships.

But for the intervention of Horvath, it might have been a season unlike any other. Horvath at 17 was almost four years removed from her greatest moment of fame. She had advanced through the qualifying rounds to reach the main draw of the 1979 U.S. Open less than a week after her 14th birthday, the youngest ever entered, and received a first-round bye before being ousted, not without a struggle, by sixth-seeded Dianne Fromholtz, 7–6, 6–2.

After two years of consistent progress, Horvath received a setback in 1982 when she was sidelined for four months by a back injury. But she worked her way up to 33rd on the computer by the spring of 1983, winning an event on the satellite circuit, reaching the semifinals of the Italian Open and then defeating Bonnie Gadusek, Andrea Leand, Bettina Bunge and Andrea Jaeger en route to the final of the German Open, where she succumbed in straight sets to Evert Lloyd, 6–4, 7–6 (7–1).

Tracy Austin, 5–7, 6–1, 6–0. Limited by injuries to eight tournaments, the luckless Austin appeared in only the one final.

Entering the French, Navratilova appeared unbeatable. She was backstopped by a trainer and motivator (Nancy Lieberman), a strategist (Renée Richards) and even a nutritionist. "Team Navratilova" the entourage was called, and it made her appear even more formidable than she already was.

Against the biggest arsenal in the game, Horvath marshalled her resolve and an attack strategy that contrasted with her earlier years as a baseline mechanic. "To be in the rankings these days," she said, "you have to be really steady from the baseline but you also have to be able to finish up the point. Against a serve-and-volleyer, when it's close, it's important to get to the net first. They're used to being there, and if you take that away from them, they get shaky."

She did exactly as planned against Navratilova, and the defending champion was as bothered as Horvath had hoped. The youngster kept hitting to Navratilova's backhand and volleying her increasingly

Only one loss—to Kathy Horvath in the French—kept Martina Navratilova from a perfect 1983. • *Russ Adams*

weak returns. In the final game of the match, the favorite saved one match point only to net a forehand volley. Then she was wide on a backhand down the line to snap the winning streak.

"I was trying to outsteady her at the beginning instead of going for shots," Navratilova said . "Tactically, if I had to play the match over, I'd start off by going for broke. I think I played it too conservative at the start, and that's not my game. Once it gets close, it's hard to go for it."

The surprised loser attempted to be philosophical about the defeat. "Obviously, I'm not happy about it," Navratilova said, "but I knew I had to lose sooner or later. It's not a disaster."

Evert Lloyd didn't appear any more pleased than her rival when she heard the score. "All I thought was, 'Damn, I wish I'd been the one to beat her,'" she said.

In six meetings that year, Evert Lloyd failed to do just that but she never got the chance on her best surface. She had to be satisfied with beating Hana Mandlikova, Jaeger and Mima Jausovec in the last three rounds to clinch her fifth French title, tying Court's record. Jausovec, the 1977 champion who ended Horvath's dream in the quarterfinals with the loss of two games, succumbed in the final, 6–1, 6–2. It didn't take Navratilova long to start on a new streak. She prepared for Wimbledon by routing Wendy Turnbull in the final at Eastbourne and was at her devastating best at Wimbledon, where her average match lasted 47 minutes. Only Sherry Acker, in the second round, provided a semblance of a struggle, 7–6, 6–3.

The field was weakened notably by Evert Lloyd's dismissal in the third round. Suffering from the after-effects of flu, the three-time champion was eliminated by Kathy Jordan, 6–1, 7–6 (7–2). It marked the first time in 35 Grand Slam tournaments, dating back to 1971, that she had failed to reach the semifinals.

In her absence, Billie Jean King made another run at the championship at the age of 39. For the second consecutive year, she won the warmup at Birmingham and then advanced to the round of four with a 7–5, 6–4 triumph over Jordan in the quarterfinals.

The Old Lady, however, was no match for Jaeger in the semis. The 18-year-old, less than half King's age, passed and lobbed her opponent into submission, 6–1, 6–1, to become the youngest women's finalist at Wimbledon since Mo Connolly in 1952. She had little time or reason to savor the honor.

Navratilova, who had crushed unseeded Yvonne Vermaak, 6–1, 6–1, in the semifinals, overwhelmed Jaeger, 6–0, 6–3, and proudly accepted the mantle of No. 1 player in the world. "Is there any doubt in anybody's mind?" she said. Anything else would have been false modesty.

Not that she thought she had played to her full potential. "Today I didn't serve really well," she said. "I can still adjust better during the matches. I can improve my concentration. My thinking could be better. My backhand can be stronger."

Although no other female player on earth possessed her combination of strength and agility, there remained the faintest of doubts about her composure as she prepared for her final frontier, the U.S. Open. It was the mental edge to which Evert Lloyd clung, even after she fell to Navratilova at the Virginia Slims of Los Angeles and the Canadian Open in consecutive weeks. The defending champ seemed to be counting upon her rival to fall apart at Flushing Meadow once again. "Nerves might enter in," she decided.

Certainly, no other threat materialized in the course of the tournament. Navratilova waded through the field with almost as much dispatch as she displayed at Wimbledon. She failed to drop more than four games in any of her first five matches and she continued to limit her court time to under one hour through the semis, where she avenged her 1982 loss to Shriver in businesslike fashion, 6–2, 6–1.

Nor did Evert Lloyd struggle unduly. Her run of straight-set victories included a 6–3, 7–6 triumph over Jordan in the fourth round. In turning back Jo Durie of Great Britain, 6–4, 6–4, in the semifinals, she qualified to defend the title she had regained the previous year. If there was any stopping Navratilova, this was the time and, particularly, the place.

But Navratilova had come too far, had worked too hard to trip over her own anxieties. She took charge of the match at the outset, en route to a decisive 6–1, 6–3 victory, the most satisfying of her career. "If I don't win another tournament in my life," she said, "I can still say I've done it all."

With the last jewel in her crown, she silenced criticism of her emotional fortitude. In the second set, Evert Lloyd had rallied briefly for her lone break and then held serve at love for a 3–2 lead. It was as if she had read the writing in the sky—Good Luck Chrissie—fashioned by a squadron of

tough. But I've proved myself in three-set matches, too. Maybe I don't have that many close matches that I have to prove myself. If there's doubt in anybody's mind that there's a weakness in my mental outlook, this should tell them otherwise."

Evert Lloyd's only consolation, and it was minimal, was pushing Navratilova three minutes beyond an hour. Still, the first-time U.S. champion set a record for fewest games lost in a seven-match tournament (19 of 103). It was the decisive triumph she had longed for in the national championship of her adopted country and it pleased her so much she said the first prize money of $120,000 (and a $500,000 bonus from Playtex for winning at Hilton Head, Wimbledon and Flushing Meadow) was incidental.

"If I had been guaranteed a title," Navratilova said, "I would have been happy not to win a dime. You can't buy a U.S. Open championship."

Not that she was content to rest on it. Navratilova continued to cut a swath through the women's tour all the way to Melbourne. There, in the absence of Evert Lloyd, she was almost undone by a soggy

lawn and the eighth seed, Durie. The Englishwoman captured the first set before rain postponed the match but Navratilova rallied the following day to win, 4–6, 6–3, 6–4, taking five of the last six games.

She then turned back Shriver, 6–4, 6–3, and Jordan, 6–2, 7–6, completing the campaign with her 50th consecutive victory in her ninth successive tournament final,

three majors in a season since Court and Virginia Wade 10 years earlier. Their lone defeat, to King and Anne Smith at the Tournament of Champions final in April, ended a 40-match streak, so they started another that reached 31 by season's end.

Navratilova also assumed Evert Lloyd's former role as captain and chief assassin of the Wightman Cup team, leading the U.S. to a 6–1 victory over Great Britain. But neither was available for the Federation Cup in Zurich. Czechoslovakia, behind Hana Mandlikova and Helena Sukova, triumphed for the first time since 1975 when Navratilova was rising to prominence in her native country.

Only two women other than Navratilova won more than two tournaments all year. Evert Lloyd captured six titles and, aside from her six losses to Navratilova, slipped only twice—to Jordan at Wimbledon and to Lisa Bonder in the first round at Tokyo. Andrea Temesvari, a 17-year-old Hungarian lass, won three events, including the Italian Open and the U.S. Clay Court. And Kathy Horvath, the obstacle to perfection at Paris, won the Ginny championships at Honolulu in November and finished the year No. 9 in the U.S., the only time she would ever be ranked among the Top Ten by the USTA.

Although the men offered no transcendent figure, they were a lot more competitive from the start of the European season to the finish of a dandy Masters in January, 1984. In a year of new faces, the youngest and freshest belonged to Jimmy Arias, who cleaned up Italian clay both in Florence and Rome at the age of 18. A three-year pro who was in the first wave of coach Nick Bollettieri's baseline prodigies, Arias would go on to capture the U.S. Clay Court and Palermo, skyrocket to sixth place on the ATP computer and, besieged by injuries, fail to win another tournament in the decade.

Emotionally, no one made a more spectacular jump than Noah even though he was 23 and had been a steady winner on the tour for five seasons. Until this year, however, he hadn't advanced beyond the quarterfinal of a Grand Slam event. But on the occasion of the 1983 French Open, he was more than a gifted entertainer. He was a champion.

With a running start provided by his victory at the German Open, where he deposed Jose Higueras, Noah tore through Paris, dropping only one set, that to Lendl in the quarterfinals. The fans at Roland Garros were treated to the stunning sight of two Frenchmen in the semifinals after Christophe Roger-Vasselin, No. 230 on the computer, shocked the top-seeded Connors in straight sets. Noah easily disposed of his countryman, 6–3, 6–0, 6–0, and then ground down the defending champ, resourceful Mats Wilander, 6–2, 7–5, 7–6 (7–3).

It marked the culmination of a long journey by Noah, who left behind his family in the modest capital of Yaounde, Cameroon, at the age of 11 to study tennis in Paris. Afterward, he cried with joy, as did his father. The trophy was presented by Marcel Bernard, the last native to hold the title in 1946.

The aftermath wasn't nearly so inspirational. Noah was idled by a 42-day suspension for failing to represent France at the World Team Cup in Dusseldorf and by a knee injury. He played in only four more tournaments, including the U.S. Open where he lost to Arias in a splendid quarterfinal match.

But before Flushing Meadow, there was Wimbledon and a new cast of up-and-comers. These included Nduka "Duke" Odizor of Nigeria and the University of Houston, who bounced fourth seed Guillermo Vilas in the first round and reached the round of 16; hard-serving Kevin Curren of South Africa and the University of Texas, who dismantled Connors in the fourth round with the help of 33 aces and smashed his way to the semifinals; and, finally, Chris Lewis, a dashing Kiwi who didn't seem to know his place on the lawns of the All England Club.

Lewis was ranked No. 91 in the world at the start of the event. Although he had won the Wimbledon junior title in 1975, he had advanced beyond the semifinals of only three pro tournaments. But, once inside the gates on Church Road, he wouldn't leave. He scooted through the top half of the draw with amazing grace and grit, outlasting Curren in a brilliant five-set semifinal that left the participants applauding each other.

As a result, he became the first unseeded player to reach a Wimbledon final since Willy Bungert in 1967 and the first New Zealander in the championship match since matinee idol, Tony Wilding, won four consecutive titles from 1910–1913. There, however, reality struck in the form of McEnroe's impenetrable service and superb court sense. In three immaculate sets of serve-and-volley tennis, the American won easily, 6–2, 6–2, 6–2, to regain the honor he last held in 1981.

The surprise package at the U.S. Open was a skinny 16-year-old from Grosse Pointe, Mich., Aaron Krickstein, his country's youngest U.S. junior champion. Like Arias, he was a product of Bollettieri's school of double-fisted backhands in Florida. At Flushing Meadow, in his first Grand Slam event, Aaron won three matches, including a marvelous five-set triumph over Vitas Gerulaitis.

ber. • *Russ Adams*

...... The perennial contender defeated the teen-ager in straight sets.

Awaiting him in the final was the defending champion. Connors had repulsed 16th-seeded Bill Scanlan, who upset McEnroe in the fourth round, to reach the championship match. Since Connors had just turned 31, was playing with a bone spur on his right little toe, was suffering from diarrhea (he rushed to the men's room late in the second set) and was combating court temperatures in excess of 100 degrees, the time appeared ripe for Lendl.

After splitting the first two sets, the Czech expatriate served for the third set at 5–4. The title appeared within his reach. Then, inexplicably, he double-faulted at set point. After that, he said, "I could never recover." In a mysterious meltdown, the man who hadn't lost a set until the final never won another game. Connors whipped through the last nine games to win his fifth U.S. title, 6–3, 6–7 (2–7), 7–5, 6–0. Since an international statistical panel recently had ruled that some of his early achievements were of an exhibition nature and revised his total of career tournament victories to 99, Connors recelebrated his centennial in his favorite setting.

At the Australian Open, which Connors bypassed but which attracted the rest of the elite, the 19-year-old Wilander knocked off defending champion Johan Kriek, McEnroe and, finally, Lendl, 6–1, 6–4, 6–4, to become the youngest champion Down Under since Ken Rosewall won at 18 in 1953. It was his ninth victory of a season in which 10 players won three or more tour events and 46 men earned at least $100,000 in prize money.

Parity was in the air, and a handful of players had a chance to claim the No. 1 ranking when the Masters got underway at Madison Square Garden. There was only one notable absentee, 1974 champion Vilas, who had been hit with a one-year suspension by the MIPTC for allegedly accepting $60,000 illicit appearance money at Rotterdam. He subsequently lost an appeal and was fined $20,000. Although the suspension was waived in January 1984, he already had been sidelined for six months.

After reversing his fortune against Wilander, 6–2, 6–4, in the semifinal, McEnroe decisively whipped Lendl, 6–3,

6–4, 6–4, for the title and the top ranking. "John deserves to be No. 1," Lendl said. "He had the most consistent year."

For good measure, McEnroe and Peter Fleming, the best doubles team in the world, reprised their Wimbledon and U.S. championship performances by beating the second-best team of Pavel Slozil and Tom Smid, 6–2, 6–2. It was their sixth Masters doubles crown in as many years.

1984

Rare as it may be for any athlete to be identified as a genius, it's more unlikely still to be branded a tormented genius. But John McEnroe fit the billing, never more than in 1984. En route to the greatest season of his career, he jousted with the furies and toyed with his peers.

But for an occasional slip, it might have been said that the only man capable of beating McEnroe this year was McEnroe himself. Certainly, he had to be credited at least with an assist when he allowed himself to be distracted while holding a two-set lead over Ivan Lendl in the final of the French Open. Lendl went on to win the match for his first Grand Slam triumph.

Thereafter, McEnroe was magnificent in duplicating his 1981 feat of sweeping Wimbledon and the U.S. Open. He also counted the U.S. Pro Indoor, the WCT championship, the Canadian Open and the season-ending Masters among his 13 tournament victories. In addition to the loss in Paris, he suffered only two more singles defeats, to Vijay Amritraj in the first round at Cincinnati and to Henrik Sundstrom in the Davis Cup final at Goteborg.

McEnroe's 82–3 record produced a .965 winning percentage, highest of the Open era among men. In finishing at the top of the computer rankings for the

Until the French in 1984, Ivan Lendl had never won a Grand Slam crown. • *Russ Adams*

fourth consecutive year, he enjoyed the most dominant season since Jimmy Connors won the only three Grand Slam events he entered and compiled a 99–4 mark in 1974. The latter still was going strong 10 years after his big year, claiming five titles, reaching the final at Wimbledon and pushing McEnroe to five sets in a brilliant semifinal showdown at Flushing Meadow.

Andres Gomez, the finest player from Ecuador since Pancho Segura, ascended to the Top Ten by winning five tournaments, including the Italian Open and the U.S. Clay Court. But the biggest breakthrough occurred among the Swedes. Bjorn Borg's legacy was a nation of nine million swarming with tennis talent. Mats Wilander and four compatriots—Sundstrom, Anders Jarryd, Joakim Nystrom and Stefan Edberg—not only seized the Davis Cup for the first time in nine years but they accounted for 14 tournament victories.

Yet, the only individual to challenge McEnroe for supremacy and attention was Martina Navratilova, who continued her

only other loss of the year to Hana Mandlikova 11 months earlier in Oakland. Ironically, both women once had served as ballgirls at Navratilova's matches in Czechoslovakia.

Beyond her 13 tournament victories, the world's top female player posted the longest (74 matches) and third-longest (54) winning streaks of the Open era. And she also surpassed her great rival, Chris Evert Lloyd, in head-to-head competition by winning all six meetings, with the loss of only one set.

Evert Lloyd did claim the Australian Open title by beating Sukova, thereby extending to 11 years her streak of having won at least one major championship. She also amassed her 132nd professional tournament victory, a record for either sex, and increased her total of matches won to 1,003.

Manuela Maleeva, a 17-year-old Bulgarian, made the biggest jump among the women. She vaulted from No. 31 to No. 6 in the world rankings by winning four tournaments, among them the rain-plagued Italian Open, where she stunned five-time champion Evert Lloyd, 6–3, 6–3,

Helena Sukova upset Martina Navratilova and went on to take the Australian title in 1984.
• *Russ Adams*

Manuela's third victory of a strenuous last day. Headed in the opposite direction were Tracy Austin, who played in only one tournament before being sidelined again with a chronic back ailment, and Andrea Jaeger, who withdraw from the tour to enter college after lackluster efforts in six events.

But the year will belong forever to McEnroe and Navratilova, who never again would stand unchallenged. (Although only 25, McEnroe would not win another Grand Slam event.) The two shared a physical characteristic, left-handedness, and a love for doubles.

McEnroe won seven doubles titles. In six of those tournaments, including Wimbledon and the Masters, he was joined by his steady partner, Peter Fleming. Together, they raised their victory total to 52.

According to Fleming, "The best doubles team in the world is John McEnroe and whoever he plays with." As if to prove it, Mac took his 17-year-old brother Patrick, a top junior, to a WCT tournament in Richmond and they routed Kevin Curren and Steve Denton, the 1982 U.S. Open champions, in the final.

Navratilova enjoyed even greater success in doubles, losing one of 61 matches. But with Pam Shriver she was perfection. She and Pam completed the open era's first undefeated season by a team: 11 titles, 53 matches. Pam's personal doubles match record was 59–2. The pair also registered a Grand Slam. By beating Sukova and Claudia Kohde-Kilsch, 6–3, 6–4, they added the Australian title to the French, Wimbledon and U.S. championships. It was their 52nd career triumph.

Despite the parallel success of the two champions, however, there was a significant distinction in their approach to the sport. Having reshuffled her entourage midway through the 1983 season, Navratilova continued to improve her conditioning under coach Mike Estep and to digest only the proper foods. She was a disciple of Robert Haas, the nutritionist whose "Eat to Win" diet found favor among a number of tennis players, including Ivan Lendl.

That led a reporter to inquire of McEnroe, who played doubles in order to avoid tedious practice sessions and whose appetite was ruled by his taste buds, whether he had tried the Haas diet. "No," he smirked, "I prefer the Haagen-Daz diet."

Yet, when the man was in tune with himself, his dedication and his fitness seemed not to matter. McEnroe had such astonishing touch and such finely honed instincts for the game that the points just flowed off his racket. To Robert Green, a bright candidate for a masters degree in Soviet studies and a first-time opponent at the U.S. Open, "He almost anticipates the shot before you think of it. He gets to places you don't think he should be."

Wimbledon and the U.S. Open were among John McEnroe's many titles in 1984. • *Mitchell Reibel*

And McEnroe was never better than in 1984, which he began in spectacular fashion. Following his Masters victory, he thrashed Lendl at the U.S. Pro Indoor in Philadelphia, the Belgian Indoor in Brussels, the WCT Tournament of Champions at Forest Hills and the World Team Cup at Dusseldorf. He also dismissed Tomas Smid at the Grand Prix de Madrid and overwhelmed Connors at the WCT finals in Dallas. In reaching the championship round of the French Open for the first time, he extended his winning streak to 42 matches, an open-era high for an American man.

Not that his form left him serene. Paris was a struggle from the outset. There, in addition to opponents, Mac battled the usual suspects—courtside photographers, groundskeepers, linespersons—as well as the ambience of the tournament and city itself, of which he had once declared in full voice, "I hate this place."

McEnroe demanded court repairs during a third-round victory over Mel Purcell, drilled two balls into the photographers' pit while beating Jose Higueras in the next match and complained so much about calls in a semifinal rout of Connors that the latter offered some free advice while approaching the net. "Shut up," the onetime bad boy yelled. "Grow up. You're a baby."

only one set in reaching the final and blasted the steady Wilander, who had eliminated defending champion Yannick Noah, in the semifinals.

For the first two sets of their showdown on clay, McEnroe was completely in charge, granting only 10 points on his serve. He appeared certain to become the first American male since Tony Trabert (1954–55) to win at Roland Garros and given his form and past performances at Wimbledon and the U.S. Open, a Grand Slam was not out of the question. At that critical juncture of history, however, McEnroe snapped.

With Lendl preparing to serve at 1–1 in the third set, the American objected to a television cameraman's headset that was emitting a director's instructions and cast it aside. Once Lendl fell behind, 0–30, Mac began grousing at photographers, allowing his opponent to collect himself. Lendl held serve there but fell behind, 0–40, two games later.

By then, the crowd was hooting and whistling at the leader. McEnroe blew the triple-break point as well as another ad point and Lendl recovered, broke serve in the following game and ran out the set.

The result was what McEnroe later called "a snowball effect. I had gotten to such a high level early, when I went down I couldn't come back. Then the crowd got into it. It's frustrating."

Although the man held two service breaks in the fourth set, McEnroe could convert neither. And, as his first serve continued to wane, he became more and more

one match point at 15–40 in the 12th game but then mis-hit a shoulder-high forehand volley. "It feels great to finally answer some different questions," the new champion said after becoming only the 14th man in 107 years to overcome a two-set deficit in the final of a Big Four event.

McEnroe appeared to have learned his lessons from Paris and a subsequent squall at the Queen's Club in time for Wimbledon. Either that or the uncharacteristically benign weather left him mellow. The defending champ behaved impeccably at the All England Club and he performed brilliantly. Whether the one had anything to do with the other was pure conjecture.

He ceded only one set in the tournament—to Paul McNamee in the first round—and was mesmerizing in dismissing Connors, 6–1, 6–1, 6–2, in the final. Even McEnroe, the perfectionist, allowed that it was "maybe the best match of my life."

It had been 46 years since a Wimbledon championship was concluded in such decisive fashion (Don Budge over Bunny Austin, 6–1, 6–0, 6–3). Incredibly, McEnroe didn't commit the first of his two unforced errors until the 62-minute mark of Connors' hour-and-a-half ordeal. The champion served 75 percent, with 11 aces, and never permitted Connors a break point in becoming the second American male to win Wimbledon for a third time, following the lead of Bill Tilden, and the first to hold consecutive titles since Budge in 1937–38.

Although that would be the last Grand Slam final for Connors, the man had one more bullet in his gun. He saved it for the U.S. Open, where he seemed to feed on the energy of the crowds.

En route to the next duel of American titans, McEnroe suffered his second loss of the year. He was defeated by Vijay Amritraj, a budding film star, at Cincinnati on the day after he wrapped up his first Canadian Open championship with a straight-set conquest of Vitas Gerulaitis. Amritraj, who had slipped to 104th in the rankings, had won his first Grand Prix tournament in four years only a month earlier, overcoming Tim Mayotte on the grass at Newport.

Still, there wasn't any question but that McEnroe was poised to dethrone Connors at the U.S. Open. Not only was his form comparable to the level he displayed at Wimbledon but so was his approach.

"I understand how people get turned off by seeing a guy jumping around and screaming at the chair," he explained. "Of course, they don't understand that's a result of pressure. But I'm finding out life isn't fun when you're banging your head against a wall."

On the Flushing hard courts, McEnroe raced through his first five opponents, including the young Swede who had won an unofficial gold medal (demonstration class) at the Los Angeles Olympics. The 6–1, 6–0, 6–2 rout of Stefan Edberg was a barometer of how well he was playing. Meanwhile, Connors, back home on his favorite surface, also won all 15 sets in

advancing to the semifinal, including a victory over surprising quarterfinalist, John (Mr. Chris Evert) Lloyd.

Those who couldn't wait for the showdown of the perennial bad boys had a very long afternoon on Super Saturday at the National Tennis Center. They went on last following a men's 35 match between legends John Newcombe and Stan Smith, the first men's semifinal between Lendl and brash Pat Cash and the women's final between those rivals for the ages, Navratilova and Lloyd. All four matches were carried to the ultimate set and the tennis, which began at 11: A.M. didn't conclude until 11:14 P.M.

Even McEnroe, annoyed that he didn't strike his first ball until 7:28, allowed that "It had to be the best day (for fans) at the Open...ever." Certainly, the day's finale qualified as the match of the tournament, if not the year.

After 37 minutes, Connors had equalled the four games he won in the Wimbledon final. Within 90 minutes, he had won a set and broken McEnroe's serve for the fourth time for a 3–1 lead in the third set. In the end only a scant few shots separated the pair, perhaps none more important than a missed forehand by Connors on break point in the seventh game of the final set.

Connors finished with 45 winners, to 20 for the winner. But McEnroe's 19 aces pushed him over the top in a magnificent 6–4, 4–6, 7–5, 4–6, 6–3 victory. Both agreed the match was superior to their epic 1980 semifinal.

"We're both better players now," Connors said. "Four years ago, the match had great emotion. This had all that and better tennis."

Remarkably, the best server in the game had been broken seven times by the best service returner. Yet, McEnroe had produced the final break to emerge in a match devoid of animosity or histrionics. "I just don't see how either of us could play much better," he said.

Fortunately for him, he didn't have to the following afternoon. Lendl, who barely survived his semifinal with the help—at match point—of a running topspin lob course of a semifinal victory over Jarryd, he was fined for ball abuse, abuse of an official and unsportsmanlike behavior. The total pushed him over the $7,500 limit, triggering a 21-day suspension.

During his stay on the sidelines, he injured his left wrist in practice. That caused him to withdraw from the Australian Open, where Wilander had a clear path to his second consecutive title, bashing two-time champ Johan Kriek in the semifinals with the loss of three games and overcoming Curren in the final, 6–7 (5–7), 6–4, 7–6 (7–3), 6–2.

McEnroe was healed in time for the Davis Cup final in Goteborg, where he was joined by Connors. The latter had committed himself to the full year of Cup play for the first time but was distracted by the impending birth of his second child and as unprepared as McEnroe for the tough Swedes on a clay court inside the Scandinavium. He hadn't competed in six weeks.

In what was a dark day for American tennis, both Connors and McEnroe were drubbed on the first day and Connors embarrassed himself and his team by incur-ring a game penalty and adding a $2,000 fine for profane language. Wilander handled Connors easily, 6–1, 6–3, 6–3, but the real surprise occurred in the next match when McEnroe was upset by lanky 20-year-old Henrik Sundstrom, 13–11, 6–4, 6–3. The first set, in which McEnroe held four set points, consumed two hours.

One day later, Jarryd and Edberg

Although McEnroe's 6–3, 5–7, 6–3 third-day victory over Wilander was mostly cosmetic, it did spare the U.S. the ignominy of a 5–0 shutout and helped to prepare him for the season-ending Masters. Back in New York, McEnroe defeated both Jarryd and Wilander en route to the final, where he crushed Lendl, 7–5, 6–0, 6–4, raising his earnings to $2,026,109. For good measure, he then combined with Fleming to turn back Mark Edmondson and Sherwood Stewart, 6–3, 6–1, for their seventh consecutive Masters doubles title.

In the opinion of the International Tennis Federation, which ruled in 1982 that a player need only win four consecutive majors to claim a Grand Slam, Navratilova completed the quartet in early June at the French Open. In recognition, it awarded a $1-million bonus. Still, few were prepared to grant her admission to the select group of those who had won the Big Four in the course of a calendar year— Don Budge, Maureen Connolly, Rod Laver (twice) and Margaret Court.

After Navratilova routed Evert Lloyd, 6–3, 6–1, in Paris, however, few doubted that this would be the year for such a feat. She hadn't lost a match since her first tournament in January, the Virginia Slims of California, where Mandlikova prevailed, 7–6, 3–6, 6–4. And only Mandlikova, in the semifinals, took a set off her at Stade Roland Garros.

At Wimbledon, she was even more formidable. Her only persistent opposition in England came from the tabloid press, which outdid itself in pursuing Navratilova's relationship with her newest traveling companion, former Texas beauty queen Judy Nelson. On the court, she was tested only in the championship match when Evert Lloyd began with two service breaks for a 3–0 lead.

Not to worry. Navratilova stormed back for a 7–6 (7–5), 6–2 victory, handing Evert Lloyd her sixth final-round defeat. It marked the second consecutive Wimbledon in which she had failed to drop a set and her third successive title was the first for a female since Billie Jean King's 1966–68 run.

The pattern continued at Flushing Meadow, which produced one notable sidelight. Gabriela Sabatini, a 14-year, 4-month-old Argentine, introduced herself to the world. She became the youngest player ever to win a U.S. Open match. Dissatisfied with one, she actually won two matches before losing in straight sets to Sukova.

The latter reached the quarterfinals, where she was beaten by Navratilova, whom her mother once had coached back in Czechoslovakia. The top-ranked player in the world marched into the final without the loss of a set. Ditto her great rival, Evert Lloyd.

When they collided in Louis Armstrong Stadium on Sept. 8, their series stood at 30 victories apiece. Additionally, Navratilova had won 54 consecutive matches, one shy

of her opponent's record. With all that and an Open title at stake, Evert Lloyd played superb tennis, perhaps the best of any of her nine U.S. finals.

Still, it was insufficient. Navratilova rallied for a 4–6, 6–4, 6–4 victory. "It's just not enough to play a good match against her anymore," Evert Lloyd lamented.

The pair added to their friendship by sharing bagels while awaiting the outcome of the first men's semifinal and the delayed start of their match. Afterward, Navratilova gave a gracious acceptance speech in which she said, of their rivalry, "I wish we could have stopped at 30 [wins] all. She's a great champion and I'm sorry one of us had to lose."

With six majors in a row to her credit, the Australian Open appeared a formality. Navratilova had prepared herself for the grass at Kooyong Stadium by winning a doubles tournament at Brisbane and the singles at Sydney the following week. She dropped only one set (to Kathy Rinaldi) in advancing to the semifinals at Brisbane and raced through a 6–1 first set against Sukova.

But the 6-foot-2 19-year-old who had just notched her first important singles title at Brisbane, was not discouraged. She broke for 4–2 in the second set and, at 5–5 in the third set, achieved the deciding break. Navratilova did not go down without a fight, saving five match points with a series of admirable forehands before her backhand return sailed over the baseline.

"It hurts but I'm sure I'll get over it," she said after the 1–6, 6–3, 7–5 defeat that terminated her streak at 74 matches and ended the dream of a genuine Grand Slam. Sukova, the ninth seed, carried the momentum into the final but couldn't sustain it as the steady Evert Lloyd rallied for a 6–7 (4–7), 6–1, 6–3 triumph, her 16th Big Four singles championship.

Earlier, Evert Lloyd had led the U.S. to its sixth successive Wightman Cup triumph over Britain. In the absence of both Evert Lloyd and Navratilova, the American team was upended by Australia in a Federation Cup semifinal. The latter was beaten in the final by the Czech team of Mandlikova and Sukova, 2–1, marking that country's second consecutive championship.

Starting with Boris Becker at Wimbledon, youth took over in 1985. • *Russ Adams*

the brightest and most engaging belonged to a 17-year-old son of a West German architect, a teen-ager either too cool or too naive to know he had no business playing with grown men. At Wimbledon, a tournament that prizes tradition above all else, Becker challenged the past and won.

Never had anyone so young claimed a men's title at The Lawn Tennis Championships. Never had an unseeded player been fitted for a singles crown. Never had a German male ascended to the throne of tennis. Becker changed all of the above in the span of three hours, 18 minutes on one sunlit, summer afternoon. Game, set and match.

The youngster, who had won only one previous event on the men's tour (three weeks earlier at Queen's Club in London), climaxed a breathtaking rise to prominence by wearing down eighth-seeded Kevin Curren, 6–3, 6–7 (4–7), 7–6 (7–3), 6–4, in the Wimbledon final. By the end of the season, he had made a spectacular jump in the rankings from No. 65 to No. 6 and become the symbol of change sweeping over the sport.

When Stefan Edberg of Sweden, 22 months older than Becker, dethroned

countryman Mats Wilander at the Australian Open, this represented the first time two teen-aged males reigned as champions of Big Four tournaments in the same year. Following Wilander's victory in the French Open and Ivan Lendl's breakthrough in the U.S. Open, this also completed a Continental sweep of the Grand Slam events. Never before had European males held all major championships.

Although Lendl's presence was a familiar one and although he was a relatively old 25, he made a significant contribution to the new order by completing his long and arduous climb to the top of the ATP computer rankings. He posted the biggest triumph of his career by overwhelming John McEnroe, who hadn't lost in four previous U.S. finals, at Flushing Meadow, 7–6 (7–1), 6–3, 6–4. And he solidified his position at the season-ending Masters in January, 1986, where he didn't lose a set en route to his third title in five years.

Ivan Lendl broke John McEnroe's finals streak at the U.S. Open in 1985. • *Wide World*

Newcomers also made an impact on the women's circuits although none came away with major prizes. In what were portents of the future, 15-year-old Gabriela Sabatini reached the semifinals of her first French Open and 16-year-old Steffi Graf of West Germany advanced to the final four of the U.S. Open. Additionally, Katerina Maleeva, at 16 two years younger than older sister Manuela, won two tournaments and Floridian Mary Joe Fernandez became the most callow winner of a U.S. Open match (14 years, eight days).

While Martina Navratilova remained queen of the sport, she yielded two of her dominions. Chris Evert Lloyd unseated her at the French Open and Hana

Mandlikova did the honors at the U.S. Open. Navratilova even was separated from her No. 1 ranking by Evert Lloyd after 156 consecutive weeks at the top but she regained her place by the end of the season in which she added the Australian championship to her sixth Wimbledon singles title.

The stranglehold Navratilova and Pam Shriver had on women's doubles competition also was loosened. Their monumental 26-month winning streak, comprising 109 matches and 23 tournaments, ended on Centre Court in the Wimbledon final where they were beaten by the Aussie-American alliance of Liz Sayers Smylie and Kathy Jordan, 5–7, 6–3, 6–4. They later surrendered their U.S. title to the twin towers, 6–1 Claudia Kohde-Kilsch of West Germany and 6–2 Helena Sukova of Czechoslovakia.

Coincidentally, McEnroe and Peter Fleming abdicated after the better part of a decade atop men's doubles. Mac decided to put doubles aside after three tournaments, among them Wimbledon, where they faltered before Aussies Pat Cash and John Fitzgerald two rounds short of defending their title. Their lone victory, at Houston, raised their career total to 53.

The vacuum quickly was filled by a pair of young Americans. Ken Flach and Robert Seguso, both 22, inherited the U.S. Davis Cup role from the perennial team, compiled a match record of 62–22 and won eight tournaments, including the U.S. Open and U.S. Clay Court.

However, nowhere were the changing times better illustrated than at Wimbledon. None of the usual suspects even made it to the last day. Lendl, whose bid for a second successive French title was ended in the final by Wilander, 3–6, 6–4, 6–2, 6–2, was wiped out in the round of 16 by young Frenchman Henri Leconte. Curren, who became a U.S. citizen in March, demolished McEnroe, 6–2, 6–2, 6–4, in the quarterfinals and Jimmy Connors, 6–2, 6–2, 6–1, in the semifinals with an arsenal of powerful serves.

He was joined in the final by Becker, who added to his reputation as a wunderkind by outlasting Leconte and then Anders Jarryd of Sweden in four-set matches. In reaching the championship

"I should have had the advantage," Curren said. "Being older, being to the semifinals [in 1983], being on Centre Court. Maybe he was too young to know about all that stuff."

Or at least too young to rattle. He became such a sensation in the early stages of the tournament with his reckless dives— "Usually, he comes off the court with blood

Not Becker. He responded to every challenge like a man, yet still reacted with the infectious enthusiasm of a boy. After completing his semifinal victory over Jarryd on Saturday morning, he hung around to watch the Duke and Duchess of Kent present Navratilova with the women's singles plate after beating Evert Lloyd.

If his play belied his years, Becker acted his age as he peered around the backdrop separating Centre Court from the players' entrance after the women's match. He hurriedly removed a set of headphones from his ears and practically snapped to attention as the royal couple walked by, oblivious to his presence. Then he returned to his vantage point, looking for all the world like the tallest member of the knothole gang.

A day later, he appeared on the other side of the screen and walked off with the men's trophy. Before a capacity crowd that included a few assorted princes and princesses, the 6-foot-2 manchild answered Curren's serve with a bludgeon of his own and outsteadied his 27-year-old opponent from the baseline.

let anyone forget he was a German. Even the respectable broadsheets relentlessly used war analogies in describing the player. In *The Times*, the respected Rex Bellamy duly noted that scheduled television programming in Becker's homeland was interrupted to carry his quarterfinal victory over Leconte and added, "How odd it was that Germany should have such a personal interest in a court on which, in 1940, they dropped a bomb."

It's true a bomb did land on the roof of Centre Court in October 1940, destroying 1,200 seats. And no German was permitted to enter the tournament for four years after it was resumed in 1946. That represented a concession on the part of officials who had banned Germans for nine years after World War I.

Ironically, Becker's shining moment occurred on July 7, the birthdate of Baron Gottfried von Cramm. The latter, long acknowledged as Germany's greatest player, would have been 76 had he lived. For more than half of the century, he was regarded as one of the finest tennis players never to have won Wimbledon. It had been 50 years since he reached the final for the first of three consecutive years, 50 years since he was victimized by Fred Perry.

"He was a very good player," recalled Perry, the three-time champion who was an analyst for the BBC radio network. "He walked like an aristocrat. And he had a long, elegant swing. When he played Bunny Austin in the semifinals, it was like a picture book. You could turn the page and see one classical shot after another."

Perry, the finest British player of the modern era, was taken with Becker. "What impresses me," he said, "is that he's got no fear. I saw him in the juniors at Paris a few years ago and he'd hit four in and nine out. But he'll consolidate."

Already, he had combined with other teen-agers to energize the oldest of the Grand Slam events. "As far as the game itself is concerned," tournament chairman Buzzer Hadingham said, "it is most exciting to see the emergence of a new generation of talented, young players."

The new generation of males wasn't as successful in the cauldron that was Flushing Meadow. Becker made 64 unforced errors in bowing to Nystrom in four sets in the round of 16, which was where Edberg came to grief against Connors. Wilander, an old man of 21, did push McEnroe to five sets in the semifinals but couldn't put the 26-year-old codger away. The American survived, 3–6, 6–4, 4–6, 6–3, 6–3.

"That was a legitimate five-setter," McEnroe observed. "I was scrounging. And it was just so hot [115 degrees at courtside] that you couldn't keep your concentration all the time. In that kind of heat, you've got to go through cycles."

Two other familiar faces turned up in the other semifinal, where Lendl romped over Connors, 6–2, 6–3, 7–5. It had been a frustrating season for the 33-year-old campaigner. For the first time in his professional career, Connors failed to win a tournament all year. Yet, he reached the semis of the French, Wimbledon and the U.S., the latter for the 12th successive year.

For Lendl, the victory also was the continuation of a streak. This was his fourth consecutive final at Flushing Meadow. Alas, he had lost in all three previous trips. After their Saturday night match, Connors said he didn't expect the man to play well on Sunday. "Because he never has," the gracious loser said.

Certainly, there was little in the early going to indicate otherwise. Lendl was broken in his first service game and failed to get a single point off McEnroe's serve through seven games, creating a 2–5 deficit. But, at set point, the Czech who had moved into a comfortable estate in nearby Greenwich, Conn., hit a crosscourt backhand winner for deuce, held service and then broke McEnroe for the first time. He eventually won a 7–6 tie-breaker by a stunning 7–1 margin and raced through the next two sets, 6–3, 6–4, for the most satisfying triumph of his career.

"It's the biggest tournament in the world," the first-time titleholder said dryly. "And it is the championship of the country where I enjoy living so much. I have won the Czechoslovakian Open three times, in my native country, but I don't think that is the same."

McEnroe said that his energy was sapped from the five-setter in the previous day's heat and complained about the schedule of matches on consecutive days for the benefit of network television. But he also gave credit to Lendl. "He put a lot of pressure on me," the former No. 1 said. "It was one of the best matches he's ever played against me."

It was the climax of a superb year for the winner. He annexed the first of 11 titles by beating Tim Mayotte at the WCT finals in Dallas after McEnroe, the defender and four-time champ, had been bounced by Nystrom. In the Tournament of Champions, Lendl prevailed over Mac and he also stopped the lefty at Dusseldorf although a singles victory by Connors and a doubles triumph by Flach and Seguso over Lendl and Tom Smid lifted the U.S. to a 2–1 victory over Czechoslovakia and the World Team Cup.

After routing Schapers in the quarters, the teenager from Vastervik snapped Lendl's 31-match winning streak, 6–7 (3–7), 7–5, 6–1, 4–6, 9–7 and then overpowered defending champ Wilander, 6–4, 6–3, 6–3, in a rain-delayed final. It marked the first time two Swedes met for a Big Four championship.

Both McEnroe and Lendl argued so incessantly about the slippery condition of the courts and other distractions that they surpassed the fine limit, earning 21-day suspensions. Not that either was inclined to play any more in December. For the first time in a while, McEnroe didn't even have Davis Cup commitments.

He had declined to sign a so-called "behavior guideline" instigated by the U.S. team's sponsor, Louisiana Pacific, to guarantee there would be no repetition of the ruckus at Goteborg the previous year. Since Connors—the prime instigator—had no intention of returning, the U.S. squad was led by Eliot Teltscher and Aaron Krickstein, who turned 18 just in time for a second-round encounter against West Germany.

That was as far as the Americans went, Germany winning, 3–2, as Becker bashed Krickstein in the decisive fifth match, 6–2, 6–2, 6–1.

Becker carried the fatherland all the way to the final and nearly upset the Swedes as he defeated both Edberg and Wilander in singles. The fate of the Cup rested on the fifth and final match at

Masters, whose field was raised to 16 under the first-time sponsorship of Nabisco. But none of the Swedes was a major factor. Edberg lost in the first round to Johan Kriek, Wilander was beaten by Becker in the quarters and Jarryd, who had defeated Nystrom in a first-round match and later would team with Edberg to win the doubles, was stopped by Becker in the semifinals. The most resounding loss of all, however, involved McEnroe who, tired and out of sorts, went down in the first round to Brad Gilbert.

In the end, Lendl reverting to the form he had displayed in the U.S. Open, turned back Becker in commanding fashion, 6–2, 7–6, 6–3, and raised his earnings to $1,971,074. At last, he was clearly the top male player in the world.

For the first time in what seemed like ages, there actually was some doubt about the identity of the leading woman. The competition wasn't settled until Navratilova beat Mandlikova, her U.S. Open conqueror, in the semifinals of the Australian Open and then wore down French Open queen Evert Lloyd, 6–2, 4–6, 6–2 in the final at Melbourne. She concluded her season with 12 tournament victories and an

80–5 match record, slightly ahead of Evert Lloyd's 10 titles and an 81–8 mark. The latter also led the U.S. to its seventh consecutive victory over Great Britain in Wightman Cup play.

By defeating Navratilova in their thrilling French final, 6–3, 6–7 (4–7), 7–5, Evert Lloyd won the tournament for an unprecedented sixth time and extended to a dozen years her standard for winning at least one of the Big Four titles. It also marked the second time in five months she had overcome her nemesis, the first being at Key Biscayne in late January.

Following that loss and one to Mandlikova in the U.S. Indoor semis, Navratilova went to an eye doctor. She emerged with spectacles and promptly won 23 consecutive matches (and 46 sets), including the Virginia Slims Championship over Mandlikova and Sukova after Evert Lloyd was ambushed by Kathy Jordan. That string was interrupted at Paris, where her old rival held serve after falling behind 0–40 at 5–5 in the third set and then closed out the match in extraordinary fashion.

"I just hope she stays around a little bit longer," Navratilova said, "because, quite honestly, she's playing better tennis now than she ever did. It must be nice to know that you can still improve at 30."

Defeat cost Navratilova the honor of being the first player since Margaret Court in 1964 to hold three French titles simultaneously. She combined with Shriver to win the women's doubles, their eighth consecutive Grand Slam championship, and with Heinz Gunthardt to win the mixed.

Sabatini, who had created a sensation in April by beating three Top 10 players to reach the final at Hilton Head, where she lost to Evert Lloyd, advanced to the semifinals at Paris. Her victims included Ros Fairbank, Anne White and fourth-seeded Manuela Maleeva. Once again, it took a

woman twice her age to stop her. Evert Lloyd prevailed, 6–4, 6–1.

Sabatini's showing convinced her coach, Pato Apey, with whom she resided in Florida, that she should enter Wimbledon, where she became the youngest player ever to be seeded (15th at 15 in a masterstroke of British symmetry). Her presence caused an immediate stir. The tabloids dubbed her "Gorgeous Gaby" and the special eligibility Commission of the International Tennis Federation called for a "gradual, carefully monitored entry" into pro tennis, restricting the number of events in which a player can enter before reaching 16.

She won two matches on the grass, one fewer than the 11th-seeded Graf, who was denied a berth in the quarterfinals by Shriver. The most surprising of the final eight was No. 154 Molly Van Nostrand, a 20-year-old qualifier from New York who defeated fourth-seeded Manuela Maleeva and was only three games from a semifinal meeting with Navratilova before faltering against Zina Garrison. And Kathy Rinaldi, still only 18, made her deepest penetration in a Grand Slam event when she advanced to the semifinals.

Not that there was ever any doubt but that the women's competition was a two-horse race. In a most unusual move, the tournament committee jointly seeded Evert Lloyd and Navratilova No. 1. And their final was almost as close, with Navratilova rallying for a 4–6, 6–3, 6–2 victory.

She became only the third woman in history to win four singles titles in a row and the first since Helen Wills Moody in 1930. "This court," Evert decided, "is her court." It also marked Navratilova's sixth triumph in as many Wimbledon finals, equalling the feat of Suzanne Lenglen, the legendary French star of the Roaring '20s.

One of the most affecting moments of the tournament was Virginia Wade's 205th

Wimbledon match, her last in the singles draw. "Our Ginny," England's last great champion, was beaten by the fifth-seeded Shriver, 6–2, 5–7, 6–2, in an enthralling third-round match one week shy of her 40th birthday. She left to a standing ovation. "How can I feel sad?" Wade said. "I've had more out of tennis, more fun out of playing Wimbledon, than anybody..."

Hana Mandlikova made history as a European in winning the 1985 U.S. Open. • *Russ Adams*

the match of the tournament. It marked the only U.S. Open three-setter comprised entirely of tie-breakers and the longest women's struggle since the advent of such overtimes in 1970.

Still, it was Mandlikova who took home the prize. And she did it in remarkable fashion, beating two ex-champs—Evert Lloyd, 4–6, 6–2, 6–3, and Navratilova, 7–6 (7–3), 1–6, 7–6 (7–2)—the first time that had happened since 1962 when Margaret Smith (Court) won over 1959 champ Maria Bueno and defender Darlene Hard. Her victory was the first by a European citizen in the U.S. championship.

"I've been working on myself, my game, my head, everything," said Mandlikova, finally harnessing her immense talent. "I'm 23 now and I'm maturing slowly. I've been working very hard."

The Open title was one of two great rewards in 1985. The second occurred a month later in Nagoya, Japan, where she won all five of her singles and two deciding doubles in Czechoslovakia's third successive victory in Federation Cup play. She beat Kathy Jordan, 7–5, 6–1, in the 2–1 Cup-round defeat of the U.S.

It was at the Australian Open that order was restored. Navratilova dispensed with Mandlikova en route to another final showdown with Evert Lloyd. It was their 67th meeting and Navratilova's all-out attack won the day, 6–2, 4–6, 6–2, increasing her margin in the rivalry of the age to 35–32.

"Martina and I have pushed each other to get better and better," Evert Lloyd said. And they weren't planning to stop anytime soon.

1986

They got together on a Sunday in September at a public park. Two men and two women raised in Czechoslovakia met for an afternoon of tennis. Twenty years earlier, when the iron curtain and the sport both were closed, they might have been limited to a game of mixed doubles in Prague but now they gathered as professionals in New York to contest the most important singles championships in the New World.

What an extraordinary development not only for the U.S. Open but for the sport. When Ivan Lendl and Miloslav Mecir followed Martina Navratilova and Helena Sukova onto the stadium court of the National Tennis Center, they raised the profile of a nation whose government was young but whose culture was old. Theirs was an unprecedented achievement.

The presence of four finalists born in the same distant land had occurred only four times previously in the history of the Grand Slam tournaments, twice at Wimbledon and twice at the French Open. Never before had it happened at the U.S. Open and never before had the delegation hailed from Czechoslovakia. Suddenly, the country of 15-million inhabitants ranked as the first nation of tennis.

That Navratilova had received her citizenship papers in the U.S. and that Lendl was an aspiring Connecticut Yankee didn't diminish the impact. All had learned the game, had taken their first steps to prosperity on Czech clay. And, by virtue of their victories in the final major tournament of the year, the expatriates solidified their places at the top of the women's and men's rankings.

Better yet for the land of their youth, Prague welcomed the first significant international tennis event in Eastern Europe. The Federation Cup attracted teams from 40 nations to brand new Stvanice Stadium where the Czech defenders were denied a fourth successive triumph by the U.S. It so happened that Navratilova won her singles match and paired with Pam Shriver to win the doubles in a 3–0 victory that completed an emotional homecoming for the woman who had defected 11 years earlier.

"The whole experience," she said through tears after a heartwarming reception, "was beyond my wildest dreams."

Aside from the success of its foreign imports, the U.S. endured a desultory year. Chris Evert Lloyd, who won yet another French Open, was the only American-born player to reach the final of a Grand Slam event, whose number temporarily was reduced to three when the Australian Open was pushed to the front end of the calendar in time for the 1987 season. She also was the only native of either gender to be ranked among the top five players in the game.

Of course, as Navratilova pointed out at Flushing Meadow, if you stress only the country of origin, "... then John McEnroe was born in Germany but he's as red-blooded American as you can get." It's true that McEnroe was born in Wiesbaden, where his father was serving as an officer of the U.S. Air Force. But then McEnroe was not relevant to the discussion, having decided to take a sabbatical for the first six months of the year and having been bounced out of the Open in the very first round by Paul Annacone.

In his absence, Jimmy Connors was the highest-ranked American male, No. 8 on the computer at year's end. But, for a second consecutive season, he failed to win a tournament. Connors didn't even survive the first round at Wimbledon and was a third-round victim at Flushing Meadow.

Once again, the men's tour was dominated by Europeans. Lendl won both the French Open, defeating Mikael Pernfors of Sweden in the final, and the U.S., as well as capturing the Masters. He also reached the final at Wimbledon, only to be stopped one step short of his goal by defending champion Boris Becker. The latter also pressed Lendl at the Masters and rose to No. 2 in the world at the age of 18.

On the women's side, Navratilova continued her reign over Wimbledon by defeating another Czech, Hana Mandlikova. Her only major defeat of the year occurred in Paris, where Evert Lloyd prevailed in a bid for a record seventh singles championship. By the end of 1986, however, it was clear that Steffi Graf was prepared to challenge both women.

Fraulein Forehand, as the teen-aged German was known, won eight tournaments, two more than Evert, and almost denied Navratilova the U.S. Open title.

ment...I shouldn't be playing tennis now...I'm letting things affect me and I'm embarrassed. As a person I'll learn and grow from what is happening. I hope others do, too. They didn't seem to learn from Borg. Now they see it happening to me."

McEnroe was 26, one year older than Bjorn Borg when the latter walked away

This represented one of several schedule adjustments that finally brought tennis into line with the calendar. Back in March, Martina had won the first Virginia Slims, the one that purported to be the season-ending event of the 1985 circuit, with a 6–2, 6–0, 3–6, 6–1 triumph over Mandlikova. With a 7–6, 6–3, 6–2 victory over Graf, she clinched the designation of No. 1 for 1986.

The men also managed to cram their play into a 12-month season. For the first time since 1976, the Masters was given December dates. Lendl certainly didn't appear rushed. After reaching the final for the seventh consecutive year, he blasted an eager Becker, 6–4, 6–4, 6–4, forestalling the future a while longer.

Perhaps the most far-reaching development of the year occurred at the start. In the wake of a disappointing loss in the first round of the (1985) Masters in January, McEnroe decided to drop off the tour for at least 60 days. His long-standing relationship with actress Tatum O'Neal and impending fatherhood had become more important than his career.

"My attitude is very bad, very negative," he said. "I'm not happy with my move-

Boca Raton, Fla. Lendl was leading, 5–2, in the fifth set when Connors began arguing a linesman's call. He insisted that umpire Jeremy Shales overrule the call and, when that failed, demanded that Shales be removed from the chair.

Eventually, Connors was defaulted. Not only did he lose the match but he was suspended for 70 days, a period that carried through the French Open, where he had been a semifinalist in each of the two previous years. He was also fined a record $20,000.

With the field at Paris thinned by the abstention of the two top Yanks, Sweden was in position to take over the men's competition. Not only had a Swede won the 1985 edition and six of the previous eight but representatives of that nation were granted four of the top eight seeds. Ironically, the only Swede to make it to the quarterfinals and beyond was a total outsider.

Pernfors, a 22-year-old who had gone the American collegiate route, made his French Open debut a memorable one. The two-time Intercollegiate champion from the University of Georgia upset

Stefan Edberg, Becker and local favorite Henri Leconte en route to the final. Wilander, the defending champ. was stunned in the second round by Andrei Chesnokov of the Soviet Union, ranked No. 81 in the world.

Meanwhile, Lendl thundered through the top half of the draw with the loss of only one set, a tie-breaker against Andres Gomez of Ecuador which he repaid by winning the next two sets of their quarterfinal at love. With the same championship form he had displayed in winning his first Italian Open three weeks earlier, Lendl dispatched the scrappy Pernfors, 6–3, 6–2, 6–4.

Some uncertainty was injected into the women's competition by Mary Joe Fernandez. The Florida teen-ager, who had become the youngest player ever to win a match at the U.S. Open eight months earlier, overcame two seeds, No. 14 Andrea Temesvari and No. 4 Claudia Kohde-Kilsch, in advancing to the quarterfinals. There the 14-year-old was stopped by Sukova, 6–2, 6–4.

It was also in the quarters that Graf's 23-match winning streak—which included tournament victories at the WTA championships, the U.S. Clay Court and the German Open—came to an abrupt end. After holding a match point on Mandlikova, the German lass succumbed 2–6, 7–6 (7–3), 6–1. The final was one more reprise of the familiar, Navratilova vs. Evert Lloyd.

The world would never see its like again. Although no one realized it at the moment, it was the last time the two would meet in the championship round of a Grand Slam event. Evert Lloyd, in her last Big Four final, made the most of it with a commanding 2–6, 6–3, 6–3 victory. That raised her total of major singles titles to 18 and extended to 13 years her record of at least one major conquest.

The cosmetic changes at the 100th edition of Wimbledon included the introduction of yellow tennis balls, the unavailability of McEnroe, who was back in the States changing diapers, and the earliest departure on Connors' record. The two-time champion and five-time finalist was shown the gate by young Robert Seguso, known as a doubles specialist, in the first round.

"You don't know what you have until you lose it," said Connors, indicating Wimbledon would miss him more than he would Wimbledon, "and that's what you're feeling toward McEnroe right now." Other first-round losers included Kevin Curren, runner-up the previous year, and John Lloyd, who promptly announced his retirement.

Meanwhile, Lloyd's wife experienced unaccustomed difficulty of her own. A finalist in seven of the previous eight years, Evert Lloyd struggled through a difficult draw, dropping sets to Pam Casale and Sukova. She got no farther than the semifinals, where she was eliminated by Mandlikova, 7–6, 7–5.

The latter said she was much better prepared for her second Wimbledon final than her first, five years earlier against Evert Lloyd. On the night before the showdown against Navratilova, she said, "I slept very well. Maybe, as it turned out, too well," she decided afterward.

By contrast, Navratilova was particularly eager for the meeting after rolling unopposed through her first six matches. "I've never, ever been so excited about being in a final," she said. "I couldn't wait to go to sleep so I could get up and play."

Not since the reign of Suzanne Lenglen six decades earlier had a woman won five consecutive singles championships at Wimbledon. And history was no more prepared to stop her than was Mandlikova,

Fourteen-year-old Mary Joe Fernandez returns a shot from Chris Evert Lloyd in the first round at Wimbledon in 1986. • *Wide World*

Lendl, the top-seeded male, worked harder than any player in the tournament in his effort to secure a Wimbledon title. He struggled past Matt Anger in a 12–10 fourth-set tie-breaker, then overcame Tim Mayotte, 9–7, in the fifth set of their quarterfinal. He was pushed to the limit again by 6-foot-6 Slobodan Zivojinovic, 6–2, 6–7 (5–7), 6–3, 6–7 (1–7), 6–4 in the semifinal.

uccionly and would almost singlehandedly drive Australia to victory in Davis Cup competition later in the year. Becker's semifinal victim was Leconte.

One point illustrated the distinction in the opponents' approach to the grass. In the final game of the third set, with Becker serving for the match, Lendl hit what appeared to be a forehand winner down the line. The German knifed through the air to intercept with a backhand stop volley but the ball caught the net cord and crawled over after Becker had landed on his stomach. Without a moment's hesitation, he sprang to his feet and spontaneously shipped a backhand winner crosscourt.

He then pounded two more service winners at Lendl to formalize the 6–4, 6–3, 7–5 victory. No wonder Becker said Wimbledon "feels like my tournament." Lendl, fighting the grass and his allergies and the fans who rallied behind more graceful and flamboyant players, had never felt that.

although the latter served for the first set at 5–3. She got no closer to a title.

Beginning in the eighth game of that set, through the tie-breaker and into the third game of the second set, Navratilova put 22 consecutive first serves in play and won 14 points on those serves, including three aces. She finished off the challenger, 7–6 (7–1), 6–3, in 72 minutes. In five years of supremacy, she had dropped only two sets.

"Unbelievable," Mandlikova said. "It's like Bjorn Borg." But he, like Lenglen, no longer was around. Navratilova stood alone.

Two weeks after completion of Wimbledon, the top female players in the world assembled in Czechoslovakia for the most eagerly anticipated Federation Cup in the 24-year history of the event. From start to finish, it was Navratilova's show. Certainly, there was supreme irony in the idea of her leading an American team into Prague. It was shortly after she had contributed to Czechoslovakia's first Cup victory, in 1975, that she made the decision to seek political asylum in the U.S.

For the longest time, her success was not publicized in her native land. Her name did not appear in the Czech press, her matches were not seen on television. Yet, she was welcomed home as a returning heroine. She set out to demonstrate to her long-lost fans what they had missed.

"They may know about me," she said, "but they haven't actually seen me—not for a very long time, anyway. I want to show them what I can do."

Nor did she disappoint. Navratilova played brilliantly, winning every set in the course of carrying an unblemished record into her anxiously awaited final-round confrontation with Mandlikova, who made news of her own by marrying a Sydney restaurant owner in Prague's town hall.

The tournament produced one freak accident when an umbrella stand fell on Graf's foot, breaking her big toe, and one monumental upset, Evert Lloyd's loss to Anna Maria Cecchini of Italy in the quarterfinal round after 30 consecutive singles victories in Cup competition. Evert Lloyd was wearing a brace on a balky knee at the start of the event but, following the loss, she removed the brace and won her last two matches, against Bettina Bunge of Germany and Sukova, in straight sets.

Evert Lloyd scored the first point in the final round, leaving Navratilova in position to regain the Cup for the U.S., which she did by beating Mandlikova, 7–5, 6–1. Then she combined with Shriver, a pairing that won all three Grand Slam events con-

tested in 1986, to defeat Mandlikova and Sukova in doubles, 6–4, 6–2. Afterward, she cried tears of happiness.

The journey to her old neighborhood only intensified Navratilova's desire to win another U.S. Open which she now considered *her* national tournament. "I'll always be a Czech," she said at Flushing Meadow. "I'm not trying to deny it. I think I appreciate living here a lot more than people who have been born here and sort of take it for granted. I had to earn it. I had to learn and take a test."

The biggest test she would face in New York was administered by Graf after she breezed through the first five rounds. It happened in an epic semifinal match that required two hours and 16 minutes stretched over two days. Navratilova held a 4–1 lead in the first set when rain interrupted play on Friday night and she quickly closed out the set upon its resumption on Saturday.

Thereafter, however, it was a struggle, with both the second and third sets decided by tie-breakers. Graf had two match points in the 10th game of the third set and then a third at 8–7 in the tie-breaker. The champion weathered them all, with the help of the tape that barely denied Graf's attempted backhand pass for the upset.

"The last time I saved three match points [and won]," Navratilova said after the 6–1, 6–7 (3–7), 7–6 (10–8) victory, "I think I was 10 years old. I know I faced 15 match points once and I lost. Whenever it happened last, I know I was little."

Her great rival, Evert Lloyd, wasn't able to dig so deep against Sukova in their semifinal. The tall Czech hadn't beaten the American in 14 previous meetings but it took her only 70 minutes to dispose of the six-time Open champion, 6–2, 6–4. "Helena, Hana, Steffi, they're not intimidated by Martina or me anymore," said

Evert Lloyd, who rested her ailing knee for the remainder of the season, passing up another 7–0 Wightman Cup romp by the U.S.

Still, Navratilova held the hammer over Sukova, whose mother had once coached Martina back in Prague. In the final that was pushed back until Sunday and staged just before the men's championship, the

responsible for seven of the eight previous singles titles, failed to last the first week. McEnroe, in fact, didn't make it past sundown on the first day, drilled by Annacone's 25 aces in four sets.

To make matters worse, the former king of Queens and partner Peter Fleming arrived six minutes late for their first doubles start and were defaulted. McEnroe's subsequent profane tirade resulted in a $1,000 fine. Weeks later, after winning three fall tournaments, the man's intemperate outburst at the Paris Indoor Championships led to a $3,000 fine, pushing him beyond the $7,500 limit and triggering a 42-day suspension that removed whatever slim possibility existed of his qualifying for the Masters.

Those expecting Connors to ride to the rescue at Flushing Meadow were sadly disappointed. The five-time champion saved six match points but finally bowed to third-year pro Todd Witsken in straight sets in the third round. It was his earliest exit from his national since 1972.

Remarkably, no native reached the semifinals for the first time in two decades. The last of the Mohicans was the unlikely

One of the four Czechs in the U.S. Open finals in 1986, Helena Sukova fell before the onslaught of Martina Navratilova. • *Wide World*

Tim Wilkison, ranked No. 32 in the world, who was dusted by Edberg in the quarterfinals.

Fittingly, the mystery man of the Open was a Slovak. The 6–foot-3 Mecir, forever disinterested in appearance but astonishingly quick to the ball, knocked off the second-seeded Wilander, the seventh-seeded Joakim Nystrom and the third-seeded Becker in succession to arrive at the final. He had presented his credentials at Wimbledon, where he reached the quarterfinals, but at Flushing Meadow his performance stunned observers, especially considering how much he professed to dislike New York ("too big") and how much he missed his favorite form of entertainment ("fishing").

"He is maybe the fastest player I've ever played against," Becker said. Indeed, the 22-year-old was called "Gattone" (Big Cat) by Italians. And his assortment of junkballs and deceptive strokes befuddled some of the best players in the world.

But in Lendl he met his match. Lendl, who had dropped only one set, was not mesmerized by the sight of his former countryman. And Mecir, so fluid earlier in the tournament, seemed rooted to the ground, content merely to trade groundies with the steady Lendl. The match produced a lot of yawns in the crowd, which shrank steadily in size over the course of the 6–4, 6–2, 6–0 rout by the two-time champion.

Lendl finished the year with a match record of 74–6 and nine titles, second in the world only to Navratilova's 90–3 mark and 14 championships. In the race to the bank between the two practicing capitalists from Czechoslovakia, Lendl won by a nose—$1,987,537 to $1,905,841.

1987

In a year of mixed blessings for the most relentless campaigners on the world stage, Martina Navratilova and Ivan Lendl added to their collections of major tournament titles by two apiece. But there was a down side for both in 1987. She lost one of her most treasured possessions and he failed once again to win the prize that mattered most.

Navratilova's reign as the No. 1 female practitioner of tennis ended despite victories at Wimbledon and the U.S. Open. The queen was far from dead but, nonetheless, someone else was seated on her throne at the conclusion of the season. Her successor was Steffi Graf, who not only won her

first Grand Slam title at Paris but 75 of the 77 matches in which she participated.

Fortified by triumphs at the French Open and at Flushing Meadow, Lendl continued to hold the top spot in the men's rankings. But he would have traded all his trophies and perhaps thrown in a generous share of his $2,003,656 earnings for the great honor that eluded him for a second successive year. Once more, he lost in the final at Wimbledon. His nemesis was Pat Cash, who had beaten Lendl six months earlier in the last Australian Open played on grass.

But for those two flaws, the Czech native might have joined the list of Grand Slam immortals. As it was, Lendl forged the most victories (25) in Big Four tournaments by a male since Rod Laver went 26–0 in his 1969 sweep. Yet he had to stand by and watch forlornly as Cash joyously celebrated the first Wimbledon championship by an Aussie mate in 16 years with an unprecedented climb through the stands at Centre Court. "It's a miserable feeling," the losing finalist decided.

Before the year was out, Lendl would win eight tournaments, including a third consecutive Masters, for a total of 70. He surpassed John McEnroe for second place behind Jimmy Connors (105) in the all-time standings. Remarkably, neither American won an event in 1987 although the 35-year-old Connors did reach the semifinal round at both Wimbledon and the U.S. Open and rose to No. 4 on the ATP computer.

The shutout was the first in McEnroe's professional career. Not only was he afflicted by lapses in concentration and an aching back but he contributed to his demise with temper tantrums at the World Team Cup in May and at Flushing Meadow. For walking off the court in Dusseldorf, he defaulted the match to Miloslav Mecir and was fined $10,000. For

Wimbledon in 1987 belonged to the colorful Aussie, Pat Cash. • *Russ Adams*

old right-hander lost the opening match in five sets to No. 68 Eric Jelen and the deciding contest, also in five sets, to Becker. As a result of the 3–2 defeat by Paraguay in the relegation round, the U.S. dropped from the 16-entry World Group while Germany, a first-round loser to Mexico, stayed in. The trouble began for the U.S. in Asuncion, where an intimidating crowd and a revved-up Victor Pecci took a 3–2

ranked No. 265 and heard of neither before nor after, was out of it after a good start. He trailed Arias, 1–5, in the final set, but dodging three match points, somehow pulled out perhaps the most astounding victory ever against the U.S., 6–4, 6–1, 5–7, 3–6, 9–7. Pecci wrapped it up for Paraguay, and though there was a chance to avoid demotion against Germany, the U.S. plunged to the American Zone for 1988, ineligible to compete for the Cup for the first time.

Mats Wilander was the strength as the Swedes won a third Davis Cup in four years. He and Anders Jarryd handled the singles in the 5–0 final-round bogging down of upstart India on indoor clay in Goteborg. But the Indians made a nice story, the peerless sportsmen from the subcontinent seeming to be players from another, earlier era. It was a splendid career closer for the Flying Amritraj Brothers—Vijay and Anand—to play a final.

Thirteen years before, they'd lifted India to the same position where they were forced to default to South America, their government's anti-apartheid gesture. But in their 16th year of Davis Cup they'd made it again, along with another name in

a profane tirade during a third-round victory over Slobodan Zivojinovic at the U.S. Open he received point and game penalties, fines totaling $17,500 and a two-month suspension.

It was a measure of McEnroe's season that his most courageous and impressive performance came in defeat. In a Davis Cup relegation playoff to determine which nation would be banished to the boondocks (zonal competition) the following year, he played an historic five-set match on behalf of the U.S. against Boris Becker, representing West Germany, in late July. Becker's 4–6, 15–13, 8–10, 6–2, 6–2 victory consumed six hours and 20 minutes, 12 minutes shy of the Cup singles record set by McEnroe and Mats Wilander in a 1982 quarterfinal round match at St. Louis.

Tim Mayotte, whose five tournament victories topped U.S. players, teamed with McEnroe for America's last stand at the Hartford Civic Center. Alas, the 26-year-

their country's sporting history: Krishnan. This was Ramesh, son of the man—Ramanathan Krishnan—who had carried India to the Cup round in 1966, a gallant loss to Australia.

Never before had a father and son played in Cup finals. Incredibly they beat Australia in the semis, 3–2, on Sydney greensward. Vijay, nearly 34, stopped Wally Masur and Krishnan beat John Fitzgerald on the first day, and Ramesh enmeshed Masur in the deciding fifth match with delicate touch, 8–6, 6–4, 6–4. The Brothers Amritraj were the third such pair to grace a final, following the British Reg and Laurie Doherty of 1902–06 and Robert and George Wrenn of the U.S. in 1903.

American females weren't treated so badly, not with Navratilova still near the top of her form, but there was one jarring note. Chris Evert not only jettisoned her married name following a divorce from John Lloyd but she also relinquished her hold on the majors. For the first time since 1974, she failed to win any of the Big Four tournaments. In fact, she wasn't even a finalist.

Furthermore, her performance at Flushing Meadow signalled the beginning of the end of a remarkable career. For the first time since her debut at Forest Hills in the era of grass, she failed to reach the semifinals of the U.S. Open. At least, her conqueror was an American, 23-year-old Lori McNeil, up from the public parks of Houston.

By taking Evert's accustomed spot in the final four, McNeil provided "a shot in the arm" for minorities. Not since Arthur Ashe, in 1972, had a black advanced to a singles semifinal at the Open. Not since Althea Gibson won the tournament in 1958 had a black woman had such an impact. And McNeil did herself proud by pushing Graf to a third set before succumbing, 4–6, 6–2, 6–4.

In the end, of course, it was Navratilova's tournament. Not only did she defeat Graf for the singles title but she also won the women's doubles with Pam Shriver and the mixed doubles with Emilio Sanchez of Spain. Billie Jean King had scored the last triple, at Wimbledon, in 1973. No one had tripled at the U.S. Championships since Margaret Court in 1970.

Still, despite her brilliant Open, the fact she was a finalist in all four majors and the 36–1 record she and Shriver compiled in doubles (losing only in the fourth round at Wimbledon to Russians Larisa Savchenko and Svetlana Parkhomenko), it was a disappointing season for Navratilova. She won only four of the 12 tournaments she entered, fell short of the $1-million mark ($932,102) for the first time since 1981 and faltered in the season-ending Virginia Slims Championships. She never got to contest Graf's claim to No. 1, her 21-match winning streak in the event terminated in straight sets by Gabriela Sabatini.

Graf, whose only two defeats were inflicted by Navratilova in Grand Slam finals, overcame Sabatini, 4–6, 6–4, 6–0, 6–4, to win her first Slims title and confirm her place at the top of women's tennis. She also raised her earnings for the year to $1,063,785. "Steffi's No. 1, no doubt about that," Navratilova said.

The woman's slip began showing early. While Evert and Graf bypassed the resurrected Australian Open, staged for the last time on the grass at Kooyong Stadium, Navratilova journeyed Down Under and came away empty, beaten in the final by Hana Mandlikova, 7–5, 7–6. That curtailed a 58-match winning streak dating back to the 1986 French Open and sent her into a downward spiral.

Forced to contend with a persistent foot injury and a breakup with coach Mike Estep, she was beaten in straight sets by Graf at the International Players

Championship. "Today," Navratilova said, "she was the best player in the world and she will be until I play her again."

While she waited for the next meeting, Navratilova was overcome by Evert at the Virginia Slims of Houston and routed by Sabatini, 7–6 (7–2), 6–1, in the semifinals of the Italian Open in Rome, where the ladies at long last returned after being rele-

Steffi Graf won Paris and lost only two matches in 1987. • *Russ Adams*

7–5. Again, in a magnificent final, the German lass trailed 3–5 in the third. Again, Graf escaped with a 6–4, 4–6, 8–6 triumph for her second French crown. It ran her string of victories to seven tournaments comprising 39 matches.

Navratilova had to take solace in extending her record for most consecutive final appearances in Grand Slam tournaments (9). "Don't try to dethrone me," she instructed the press. Nonetheless, it was Graf she had to worry about.

Even the return to blessed English grass didn't reverse her fortunes, at least not instantly. At Eastbourne, where she had tuned her game for Wimbledon by winning in each of the five preceding years, she was denied by Helena Sukova, 7–6 (7–5), 6–3. Only the previous day, Sukova had outlasted Evert, 4–6, 6–4, 8–6, and she fell behind Navratilova 0–5 in the first set of their final before rallying.

Just when it seemed that her fall was complete, Navratilova dug in her heels at the All England Club. She defeated Evert, 6–2, 5–7, 6–4, in a match worthy of the great rivalry. Yet, it was a sign of the times that the 73rd meeting of the pair occurred

in the semifinal. Theirs had become a warmup act.

In the other half of the draw, Graf bludgeoned Shriver, 6–0, 6–2, in 51 minutes. "I can't believe Steffi is only 18 and is so strong," the loser said. "There is something there that is special. The ball comes off her racket with unbelievable force."

That force finally was blunted, at least temporarily, in the final when Navratilova needed all her athleticism and her experience to emerge with a 7–5, 6–3 victory. Not only did it stop Graf's 45-match streak but it elevated the winner to another plateau in the history of the sport. It was an unprecedented sixth consecutive Wimbledon singles championship and her eighth overall, tying the record established by Helen Wills Moody 49 years earlier.

"How many more Wimbledons do you want?" Graf asked as the players waited for the Duchess of Kent to present the trophies.

Replied Navratilova, "Nine is my lucky number."

She was invigorated by the outcome after 229 days without a tournament triumph and began mapping plans for another successful defense at Flushing Meadow. Meanwhile, Graf plunged on. She led West Germany into the final of the Federation Cup at Vancouver, where the U.S. was poised to defend.

Her 6–2, 6–1 rout of Evert offset Shriver's 6–0, 7–6 victory over Claudia Kohde-Kilsch and the two German ladies then rallied from a 1–6, 0–4 deficit to defeat Evert and Shriver, 1–6, 7–5, 6–4, in the decisive doubles. Thus did the Fatherland become the fifth nation to own a piece of the Cup. Two weeks later, after Evert posted a semifinal victory over Navratilova in Los Angeles, Graf dismissed her elder, 6–3, 6–4, in the final and ascended to No. 1.

So shaky was the game of the former Ice Maiden that she even lost to Shriver, in the semifinal round of the Canadian Open. After nine years and 18 unsuccessful attempts, Shriver defeated Evert, 6–4, 6–1, then followed with a 6–4, 6–1 triumph over Zina Garrison for her most significant singles title. She would finish a splendid season with four tournament victories, a match record of 67–13 and the honor of captaining the U.S. Wightman Cup team, which beat a British squad for the ninth straight year, by the score of 5–2.

The most touching moment of the U.S. Open didn't occur in the final or even during Evert's quarterfinal loss to McNeil. It took place in the round of 16, where McNeil was matched against Garrison, her friend since childhood. The two were protégés of John Wilkerson, a public parks coach in Houston who was teaching McNeil's mother, Dorothy, when the woman decided to entrust her 10-year-old to his care.

Garrison and McNeil, whose father once played defensive back for the San Diego Chargers, were doubles partners and virtually inseparable on the tour. One month older, Garrison had enjoyed the more successful career and had won two of her first three tournaments in 1987, at Sydney and Oakland. But this was McNeil's moment, her tournament, and she survived two match points and defeated Garrison in a third-set tie-breaker, 7–6 (7–0), 3–6, 7–6(8–6).

That boosted her into the quarterfinals, where her attacking game wore down Evert, 3–6, 6–2, 6–4, before an agonizing crowd. Needing only to hold serve to force a third-set tie-breaker, the former champion lost the last four points from 15–0. She called it a bad day. "And that happens," she said, "when you get older."

Evert started, stopped and interrupted herself as she tried to place the premature exit in perspective. "I think that anybody who plays...I don't want to say over 30...but when you get to a point at the end of your career...I've had some terrible days this year," she said. "I'm just not as consistent as I was when I was 17, 18 years old."

Without a clothing company to dress her or endorsements decorating her outfit, McNeil proved she belonged in such surroundings when she jumped on Graf to take the first set of their semifinal. She charged the net at every opportunity and defied the top seed, who was suffering from a cold and fever, to pass her. The definitive moment came in the seventh game of the third set, when McNeil held a break point for a 4–3 lead.

However, she netted a relatively easy volley and a relieved Graf took control. Navratilova, who won all 12 sets, awaited the German in the final. The defending champ was prepared to use the same tactics, but with the benefit of experience and a fierce determination to retain what she had.

Lori McNeil ousted Chris Evert and reached the U.S. Open semis in 1987. • *Russ Adams*

The match turned in the tie-breaker when, at 3–3, Graf missed two backhands. Navratilova assumed command and closed out the challenger, 7–6 (7–4), 6–1, in one hour, 17 minutes. "She was the champion," Graf said. "I knew it was going to be difficult to beat her."

As Navratilova held up the trophy, her fourth U.S. singles prize, both she and Graf were aware that the result wouldn't alter the computer ratings. "I'm not going to say anything against that," Graf said.

After convincing victories in the world's two biggest tournaments, Navratilova said, "I'd have to think I have the edge right now." She paused. "Nothing is worse than when people say you're washed up."

She was a long way from that but still she needed to outlast Graf at the Slims Championships if she hoped to reclaim her eminence for the year. Instead, she fal-

tered in the quarterfinal, bowing, to Sabatini, 6–4, 7–5. Her old rival had an even worse experience as Sylvia Hanika spanked Evert, 6–4, 6–4, in the opening round. A new generation made its mark as Graf closed out the season with her 11th title and the designation as best in the game.

There would be no change at the top

in his hometown of Melbourne, he became one of the finalists. Starting as the 11th seed, Cash advanced to the title match of the Australian Open by beating third-seeded Yannick Noah and then Lendl, 7–6, 5–7, 7–6, 6–4, in the semifinal round. In the championship match, Edberg prevailed, 6–3, 6–4, 5–7, 6–3, the first of six tournament victories that would boost him into second place in the rankings.

He followed with a victory at the U.S. Indoor in Philadelphia where Connors, a seven-time champion, suffered a knee injury and had to retire at 3–6, 1–2. Edberg's countryman, Mats Wilander, warmed up for Paris by beating McEnroe and Martin Jaite in the last two rounds of the Italian Open.

For McEnroe, his form on the clay was encouraging after a frustrating early season where he reached the finals of the U.S. Pro Indoor and the WCT finals, only to lose to Mayotte and Mecir, respectively. But it proved to be an illusion as he staggered in the very first round of the French Open, falling in four sets to 49th-ranked Horacio de la Pena. He flew home with a sore back, not to be seen again until the Davis Cup match, with West Germany.

So depressed was the state of American men's tennis that Connors, 34, was the only Yank to reach the quarters, where he was blown away by Becker. The final, between Lendl and Wilander, was an excruciatingly tedious exchange of groundstrokes that consumed four hours, 30 minutes. The first set alone took 100 minutes. Lendl emerged with a 7–5, 6–2, 3–6, 7–6 (7–3) victory.

But it was Wimbledon for which Lendl hungered. This looked like it might be the year after Peter Doohan, an Aussie ranked 70th in the world, stunned Becker, the two-time defending champ, in the second round. Lendl almost stubbed his toe in the same round, surviving a stiff challenge from Paolo Cane of Italy, but had smooth sailing thereafter. His four-set victory over Edberg in the semifinals was most impressive.

If his passage was relatively quiet, that was the result of some pyrotechnics in the other half of the draw, most of it caused by that old rabble-rouser, Connors. In the round of 16, the man staged one of the great rallies in the history of Grand Slam tennis by rising from a 1–6, 1–6, 1–4 deficit against Mikeal Pernfors to win the last three sets 7–5, 6–4, 6–2. "Phenomenal," Connors decided, "right?" Right.

Then the codger dodged the thunderbolt serves of Zivojinovic in a three-set quarterfinal triumph. It appeared he might really have a chance to win a third title but he was no match for Cash in the semifinal, losing in straight sets.

That wasn't the only indication the Aussie was ready to take the biggest step of his career. But grass was his best surface and he was fit after an injury-plagued season and he was a battler. Cash didn't grow up worshipping Laver, Lew Hoad, Ken Rosewall or John Newcombe, the last Digger to win Wimbledon in 1971. He favored the rough-and-tumble proponents of Australian rules football.

"We have footballers who'll go in all the time," said his coach, Ian Barclay. "We have players who hang back on the fringes. When we're cruel, we call them gutless. Patrick doesn't know how to hang back."

What he did know was how to play on grass. It was instinctive, the way he covered the net, the way he volleyed. For all his countless hours of practice, Lendl wasn't a natural. He was mechanical. And it showed as the 22-year-old Cash crushed his opponent's spirit, 7–6 (7–5), 6–2, 7–5.

There followed perhaps the most amazing victory celebration in the annals of the proper All England Club. Cash didn't wait to accept the congratulations of the Duke and Duchess of Kent. Instead, he clambered through the crowd massed at one corner of Centre Court and over the ledge to the second level of stands where were gathered his coach, psychologist, sister, father and girlfriend as well as the couple's 14-month-old son, not to mention his London pubmate. And Lendl, so formal, had to watch this riotous scene and force a smile. "I believe the second player shouldn't be there," said the man, who wanted to be anywhere else. "He should be allowed to leave."

Lendl tuned up for the green slabs of Flushing Meadow by winning at Washington, reaching the rained-out final at Stratton Mountain against McEnroe and beating Edberg in the Canadian Open. Cash continued to celebrate, which helped to explain his first-round loss to 47th-ranked Peter Lundgren at the U.S. Open. (Later, a knee injury limited him to doubles duty as Australia was upended in Davis Cup competition by India, which then lost 5–0 to Sweden in the final.)

The home team received a nice surprise when Michael Chang, the new junior champion at 15½, and the youngest male to compete in the U.S. Championships since Vinnie Richards in 1918, defeated

Paul McNamee in his first match. Duke Odizor sent him packing in the second round and it wasn't long before the American presence was reduced, once again, to McEnroe and Connors.

Alas, Mac caused a commotion not with his play but his behavior. He went ballistic, spewing curses at chair umpire Richard Ings and a courtside cameraman during the

French. Although the quality of tennis was higher, so was the quantity. Lendl's 6–7 (7–9), 6–0, 7–6 (7–4), 6–4 victory lasted a U.S. record four hours and 47 minutes.

Neither Lendl nor his new Connecticut neighbor was prepared to attack, resulting in a war of attrition. That was fine with the champ. "Probably because of not having as much talent as other players and working harder because of that," Lendl said, " I am steadier than others. But I'm not as flashy. It's tougher to be flashy all the time."

Three weeks after the Open, he was shocked by Lundgren at San Francisco, ending a 25-match winning streak. But he steadied himself for the Masters, where he dropped only a set in the round-robin and pounded Wilander, 6–2, 6–3, in the final for a record fifth title, topping Ilie Nastase (1971–72–73–75). Once again, Ivan was No. 1, with an asterisk that noted "except for Wimbledon."

1988

The trophy was not his to give but at least Don Budge had a hand in the presen-

tation. That made the man who first realized the achievement more than a bystander to history. Standing under the flags of four nations, he reached across a gulf of 50 years and offered his congratulations.

Steffi Graf made the Grand Slam a permanent part of her résumé in 1988, adding the U.S. Open title to the championships of Australia, France and Wimbledon. And

sive club in tennis, Budge whispered into her ear during the award ceremonies at Flushing Meadow. "He said he knew it all the way," she recalled later. "He said he thinks I'm going to do it a couple more times."

That would make Graf unique. Of the five persons who have claimed the four major titles in the same year, only Rod Laver did so twice. "She doesn't look behind," said Papa Peter Graf, her coach throughout her formative years. "She always looks forward. She wants to play in two-three years her best tennis."

But people would look back at 1988 from the perspective of the future and recognize the accomplishment. If Graf herself failed to comprehend the enormousness of what she had done, perhaps it was because, as her father said, "She doesn't know so many things from the history of tennis." What she knew about the Grand Slam was what other people had told her.

Graf lost but two sets in her triumphant march, the first to Martina Navratilova in the Wimbledon final and the second to Sabatini. Budge said he expected Graf to capture the Slam after watching her in

Australia. At the Wimbledon Ball, he told her, "Steffi, when you win the Grand Slam, I hope they let me present the trophy."

The USTA was too conscious of tradition to allow such a radical departure. But Budge was included in the ceremony on the golden anniversary of his achievement. He held one handle of the silver jug while Gordon Jorgensen, the USTA president, held the other. They were surrounded by the Stars and Stripes, the Union Jack, the Tricolor and the Southern Cross.

"I'm glad she did it," Budge said. "It's going to give the game a shot in the arm. There aren't any men now who I think are Grand Slam material. Sooner or later, a man will come along."

A man like Budge or Laver, who completed a Slam as an amateur in 1962 and repeated as a professional in 1969. Clearly, however, the sport's dominant player in 1988 was a teen-aged female who followed in the steps of Maureen Connolly and Margaret Smith Court. In fact, she took a few steps beyond when she added the Olympic title to her collection.

This marked the first time since 1924 that tennis had been included as a medal sport in the Olympic Games and Graf took full advantage of the opportunity to establish a new standard of excellence. Not only was she queen of the Big Four but, by Zeus, an Olympic champion in the same year. "There's nothing quite as special as winning a gold medal for your country," she exulted after earning the last of her Fab Five titles in Seoul, South Korea.

A slam of sorts was registered in men's competition as well. But this was national and not individual. As the result of Mats Wilander's victories at the Australian, French and U.S. championships and Stefan Edberg's ascendancy at Wimbledon, each of the major events was captured by a Swede. There hadn't been a male sweep

Mats Wilander racked up all the majors except for Wimbledon in 1988. • *Russ Adams*

by citizens of one country since Laver ran the table in 1969.

In the course of a season that would have been lionized if not for Graf's transcendent performance, Wilander also bumped Ivan Lendl from the top spot on the computer. In slipping from the No. 1 position for the first time in 156 weeks, Lendl reached only one Big Four final, at Flushing Meadow. He also surrendered his Masters title, which he had held for three years, to Boris Becker.

The latter, who was beaten by Edberg in the Wimbledon final, won seven tournaments and also led West Germany to its first Davis Cup title, dethroning Sweden, 4–1, at Goteborg. Miloslav Mecir, the enigmatic Czech, took home the Olympic gold medal. He also denied Wilander any chance of a Grand Slam by defeating the Swede in straight sets in the Wimbledon quarterfinals.

Neither foot-faults nor rain could keep Stefan Edberg from his destiny at Wimbledon in 1988.
• *Russ Adams*

It was another empty year for America's two controversial stars. Neither John McEnroe nor Jimmy Connors advanced beyond the quarters of a Grand Slam event and both sagged in the rankings, Mac to No. 11 and Connors to No. 7. Each won two tournaments, the first for Connors in four years.

Suddenly, however, the future appeared bright for men's tennis in the U.S. Andre Agassi, an 18-year-old graduate of Nick Bollettieri's groundstroke academy who had won his first Grand Prix tournament only the previous November at Itaparica, captured six titles, reached the semifinals at the French and U.S. Opens and shot from No. 25 to No. 3 in the world standings. He also won all three singles matches as the U.S. defeated Peru and Argentina in Davis Cup American Zone play, qualifying for a return to the World Group in 1989.

Two years younger than Agassi, Michael Chang also made great strides. By

defeating Johan Kriek at San Francisco in early October, he became the second-youngest winner of a men's professional tournament at 16 years, 7 months (Aaron Krickstein had been 16 years, 2 months when he triumphed at Israel five years earlier). Chang rose 133 places in the rankings, from No. 163 to No. 30, in his first full season on the circuit.

But Navratilova reached the final of only one Grand Slam tournament, Wimbledon. In the first Australian Open

Eighteen-year-old Andre Agassi burst on the scene in 1988, soaring to No. 3 in the World Top Ten. • *Russ Adams*

It was a Grand Slam for Steffi Graf in 1988.

• *Russ Adams*

played on hard courts in the sparkling new complex at Flinders Park, she was a straight-set, semifinal loser to Chris Evert. At the French, she was stunned by 17-year-old Russian Natalia Zvereva in the fourth round. Zina Garrison did the honors in a quarterfinal match at Flushing Meadow.

In doubles, Navratilova and Pam Shriver continued their successful pairing, winning 28 of 30 matches and five championships, including a sixth Australian and record-tying fourth French. Shriver later teamed with Garrison to win an Olympic gold medal for doubles, equalling the feat of the more experienced Ken Flach and Robert Seguso. Garrison had defeated Shriver in the quarterfinal round of the singles tournament and earned a bronze medal.

The first Olympic women's singles champion since Helen Wills in 1924, Graf lost but three matches all year. Sabatini triumphed twice, beating her for the first

time after 11 consecutive losses at Boca Raton in March and again at Amelia Island one month later. Shriver applied the final blemish to Graf's record in the semifinals of the Virginia Slims Championship, which the 18-year-old Sabatini won for her fourth title of the season.

Graf zipped through the Australian without the loss of a set but she was pressed in the final by Evert, who had been sharp in a 6–2, 7–5 semifinal victory over Navratilova. For Evert, it was the 34th Big Four final of her career but for tennis the match was unprecedented, a schizophrenic outdoor-indoor title bout made possible by the new stadium's sliding roof. It was, according to Evert, "the weirdest [final] I ever played."

Rain suspended the match with Graf ahead, 2–1 in the first. Officials decided to close the roof and, after a 91-minute delay, the outdoor tournament resumed indoors. Graf adapted better to the change, racing to a 6–1, 5–1 lead before Evert steadied herself. She won four of the next five games and came within two points of squaring the match before the German prevailed, 6–1, 7–6 (7–1).

Navratilova won five consecutive tournaments and 29 matches in the U.S. before she was again stopped by Evert at Houston in their 77th meeting. But Navratilova would win their final three matches, raising her record in the enduring rivalry to a concluded 43–37.

Any semblance of competition at the French vanished when Evert was dismissed in the third round by 16-year-old Arantxa Sanchez of Spain and Navratilova was surprised by 13th-seeded Zvereva in the round of 16. Zvereva then upset Helena Sukova and outlasted unseeded Nicole Provis of Australia, landing in her first Grand Slam final.

Graf, who had straight-setted Sabatini in the semifinals, was brutally efficient against her powerless opponent. Her 6–0, 6–0 rout lasted only 32 minutes, the most exciting feature of which was an hour rain delay. There hadn't been such a one-sided major tournament championship match since 1911 when Dorothea Lambert Chambers rang up two goose eggs over Dora Boothby in an all-English Wimbledon final.

championships at the All England Club and she prepared in her usual fashion, by winning at Eastbourne where she had the satisfaction of victimizing Zvereva, 6–2, 6–2. But Navratilova was less than commanding once the tournament got underway on Church Road. She struggled both in the quarterfinals and semifinals, edging both Ros Fairbank and Evert 7–5 in their third sets.

Indeed, after holding out through three match points in their 78th meeting, (6–1, 4–6, 7–5), Evert suggested Navratilova was "beatable" and picked Graf to win. The German, despite a 6–1, 6–2 rout of Shriver in the other semifinal, was more respectful. "This is her surface," Graf said of her opponent. "She can play so much better, so you've got to watch out."

Graf did more watching than playing in first set of the final. She appeared jumpy, served below her standard and committed a bundle of unforced errors. Before long, Navratilova had raced to a 7–5, 2–0 lead and appeared well on her way to another glorious moment. That's when Graf drew the line.

She broke Navratilova's second service of the second set. Remarkably, the defend-

ing champion would not hold service again in the match. Graf allowed Navratilova only one more game and the only delay in a 5–7, 6–2, 6–1 triumph was caused by rain after four games of the third set.

"I hit good volleys," Navratilova reasoned. "I hit good balls that other people wouldn't get to, and then she hits winners. I didn't succumb to pressure today. I suc

with Sabatini to win the Wimbledon doubles championship, defeating the Soviet pairing of Zvereva and Larissa Savchenko, who had stopped Navratilova and Shriver in the third round.

Fittingly, the only genuine competition Graf faced at the U.S. Open was contemporary in nature. Having failed to derail her at Wimbledon, Navratilova lost any opportunity at Flushing Meadow when she was ousted in an exciting three-set quarterfinal by Garrison, who had lost their previous 21 matches. Evert, recently married to former Olympic skier Andy Mill, earned a chance to thwart the Grand Slam in the semifinal round but had to withdraw on the day of the match with a stomach virus that left her so weak she could barely get out of bed.

That left Sabatini, Graf's doubles partner and the person responsible for the "2" in Graf's 61–2 record at that point. Sabatini became the first Argentine to qualify for a Big Four women's final with a straight-set victory over Garrison but she wasn't prepared to go further. In the end, although Sabatini did extend the fräulein to a third set, Graf's principal opponent may have been her nerves.

Playing conservatively, even tentatively, Graf nonetheless added the U.S. title to her necklace of jewels with a 6–3, 3–6, 6–1 victory. "Steffi wasn't herself," her father insisted. "Normally, she's not nervous. She has the best nerves of the whole tennis scene."

His daughter seemed more relieved than thrilled. She didn't jump for joy or kneel in supplication. Graf merely jogged to the stands to embrace her family and she barely smiled during the award ceremony. "Now I've done it," she said. "There's no more pressure. There's nothing else you can tell me I have to do."

She didn't have much time to savor the moment. By that evening, she was on a flight to her home in Bruhl. The Olympic tournament was scheduled to begin in a week.

Naturally, Graf was seeded first. Naturally, she won. In the final, she again bested Sabatini, this time by the definitive score of 6–3, 6–3. A sign of the times: Of the seven Americans representing the U.S. in tennis at Seoul, the only player not to medal was Evert, a third-round victim of Italy's Raffaella Reggi.

Neither Evert nor Navratilova survived the quarters at the season-ending Slims Championships in New York. Shriver, who had knocked off Evert, terminated Graf's 46-match winning streak with a 6–3, 7–6 decision in the semifinals. But Sabatini upheld the new order with a 7–5, 6–2, 6–2 victory.

Garrison, the captain, and her pal, Lori McNeil, starred in a 7–0 Wightman Cup victory over a woefully weak British squad that won only one set. But McNeil and Patty Fendick each dropped a singles match in a second-round loss to Sweden as the date and place of the Federation Cup—December in Melbourne—weakened the level of competition.

Czechoslovakia, whose Helena Sukova was one of the few elite players to make the trip, defeated the Soviet Union for the title at Flinders Park.

Eleven months earlier, at the ground's baptism, the three top male players in the world advanced to the Australian Open semifinals. Ironically, the only outsider was the native, Pat Cash. For the second consecutive year, he qualified for the final by beating Ivan Lendl and for the second consecutive year he lost his national championship in five sets to a Swede.

In 1987, Cash slipped on the grass against Edberg. This time, on hard courts, he was beaten by Wilander, 6–3, 6–7 (3–7), 3–6, 6–1, 8–6. By defeating Edberg and Cash back-to-back, Wilander not only eliminated the two previous champions but became only the second man to win major titles on three different surfaces–grass, clay, now hard—matching the achievement of Connors.

Memphis was the launch pad for Agassi, ranked No. 18 after winning his second career tournament, the U.S. Indoor Championships, over Mikael Pernfors. At 17 years, 10 months, he was the youngest player to win the second oldest of U.S. titles. He followed with victories over Jimmy Arias in the U.S. Clay Court and Slobodan Zivojinovic in the Tournament of Champions at Forest Hills. As a result, he was seeded ninth in the French Open.

Agassi reached the semifinals, the best American finish in three years, before he was worn down by Wilander in five sets. But the Yank who received the best reception was, of all people, McEnroe. The man, who returned from a seven-month hiatus (and a plunge to No. 25 in world rankings) to defeat Edberg in the final of the Japan Open, wowed the crowd in Paris with a reasonable facsimile of his championship form and three straight-set victories, the last over Chang.

He even won a first-set tie-breaker over Lendl before falling in four. Lendl, the defending champ, then was eliminated in straight sets by unseeded Swede Jonas Svensson, who in turn was beaten by Frenchman Henri Leconte. Wilander breezed in the final, missing only two of 74 first serves and committing only nine unforced errors in a 7–5, 6–2, 6–1 rout of the local hero, who had served for the first

But this time, Edberg was mentally prepared for the challenge, even after London's dismal weather interrupted play in the first set and delayed completion of the match until Monday. He served well and volleyed impeccably in scoring a 4–6, 7–6 (7–2), 6–4, 6–2 victory that fulfilled the Swede's immense promise. Edberg fell to his knees and then onto his back on match point. "I couldn't think of anything else to

match at the All England Club before being flattened by Aussie Wally Masur. Connors, the fifth seed, lasted until the fourth round where he was victimized by Patrick Kuhnen of West Germany. Tim Mayotte was the lone U.S. player to make the quarterfinals.

Any dreams Wilander had of a Grand Slam ended in the quarters, where he was tormented by Mecir, 6–3, 6–1, 6–3. "My style is not suited to this surface," Wilander said. "If we played three of the four majors on clay, maybe I'd have a chance for the Slam."

One Swede whose style was suited to grass was Edberg. He was down two sets to love and 3–3, 0–40 in the third against the crafty Mecir before staging the comeback of his young career. "It makes you feel really strong," he said, "that you should never give up."

That boosted him into the championship match against Becker. The two-time champion had slugged the incumbent, Cash, and Lendl en route to another final and decided that, in his mind, he already had won a third title. Two weeks earlier, Edberg had double-faulted away the final of the Queen's Club tournament to Becker.

blasted him in straight sets, securing the No. 1 U.S. ranking for the year, before bowing to Lendl, the hardy perennial.

McEnroe, seeded a lowly 16th, stumbled in the other half of the draw, falling to Mark Woodforde in the second round. The Aussie reached the quarterfinals where he was dispatched by Wilander. The second seed defeated two more unseeded players, Emilio Sanchez and Darren Cahill of Australia, who had knocked off Becker in the second round, to earn the other berth in the final.

Seeking to become the first man to win four consecutive U.S. championships since the era of Bill Tilden and closing in on Connors' record of 159 weeks at the top of the rankings, Lendl fell one set and three weeks short against his Connecticut neighbor. In the longest Open final on record (four hours, 54 minutes), Wilander soared to his third Grand Slam title of the year and to the top of the ATP ladder, 6–4, 4–6, 6–3, 5–7, 6–4. "I don't think I've ever felt better," he said.

Earlier in the tournament, he had served as a spokesman for the players' association which announced it was assuming control of the men's tour starting in the

1990 season. Nothing that happened in the final three months of 1988—not Mecir's 3–6, 6–2, 6–4, 6–2 victory over Mayotte in the Olympic gold-medal match, nor Becker's heroic 5–7, 7–6 (7–5), 3–6, 6–2, 7–6 (7–5) conquest of Lendl in the Masters final—altered the final standings. It equaled the finish of an important tournament: Ken Rosewall's 7–5 fifth set tie-breaker win over Rod Laver in the 1972 WCT final.

Ironically, neither Wilander nor Edberg, the major champions of the season, could stop Becker and West Germany from wresting the Davis Cup at Goteborg in the waning days of the old year. No fan of clay, Becker nevertheless beat Edberg in straight sets opening day on the formerly good earth within the Scandinavium, where Sweden had mired the U.S. in 1984 and India 12 months before. But it was No. 79-ranked Charlie Steeb who truly stunned the home folks by ducking a match point while leading off with a resurgent 8–10, 1–6, 6–2, 6–4, 8–6, triumph over Wilander. That was no left-handed compliment Steeb paid Wilander, whose No. 1 ranking (made with three majors and three other titles on a 53–11 mark in 15 tourneys) quickly vanished, like the Cup.

1989

At the end of a memorable decade, the world said hello to Michael Chang and goodbye to Chris Evert. If further proof were needed that a new era was at hand, it was to be found in the disposition of the Grand Slam events. Only one of the eight singles championships was awarded to a player older than 21.

That individual was Ivan Lendl, the fit Czech expatriate who captured his first Australian Open title at the outset of the season, regained his No. 1 ranking and, at the advanced age of 29, held off a late charge by Boris Becker. The latter added a first U.S. Open crown to his third

Wimbledon title and capped an outstanding year by leading West Germany to its second consecutive Davis Cup. However, it was Chang, the 17-year-old American, who provided the most distinctive victory on the men's tour with an improbable triumph at the French Open.

The California teenager was born in 1972, one year after Evert, then 16, made her sensational debut in the U.S. Open. At 34, Evert decided to make her final tournament appearance in the same event where she first rose to prominence. The last of her Grand Slam matches was a quarterfinal loss to Zina Garrison, 7–6 (7–2), 6–1, at Flushing Meadow. She concluded her

Seventeen-year-old Michael Chang was the toast of Paris—and his American followers—when he won the French Open in 1989. • *Russ Adams*

career one month later by teaming with Martina Navratilova in the U.S. drive to a Federation Cup title in Tokyo.

As she had the previous year, Steffi Graf dominated the women's tour. At 20, the German lass even surpassed her 1988 record by winning 86 of 88 matches and 14 of 16 tournaments. But she was denied an unprecedented second successive Grand

the youngest of any nationality, at 17 years, 6 months. At least, she had a reputation as a dogged competitor on clay, had risen to No. 10 on the computer before the start of the tournament and was seeded seventh in the event. By comparison, Chang was a nobody.

Well, that's not completely true. He also demonstrated the patience to play for-

Arantxa Sanchez Vicario took the French from Steffi Graf in 1989, spoiling the German wunderkind's quest for consecutive Grand Slams.

• *Russ Adams*

Not since Tony Trabert defeated Sven Davidson for his second consecutive title in 1955 had an American reigned in Paris. It was a drought that defied such U.S. champions as Arthur Ashe, Jimmy Connors and John McEnroe, as well as a legion of lesser players better suited to clay, among them Harold Solomon and Vitas Gerulaitis. And Chang's breakthrough heralded a reversal in the direction of U.S. tennis fortunes.

By the end of the season, no fewer than six Americans held places in the Top Ten, topped by McEnroe's climb to No. 4. For the first time since the advent of the computer in 1973, however, the elite group did not include Connors. The 37-year-old campaigner slipped to No. 11 despite increasing to 109 his record for tournament victories with triumphs at Toulouse (over McEnroe) and Tel Aviv.

Connors won his first major tournament in 1974, the same year Evert made her breakthrough. They were more than contemporaries. Once upon a time, they were engaged to be married. But whereas Evert formally bade farewell to the crowd at Flushing Meadow, Connors vowed to press on even after being eliminated in the same round.

Of course, there was a major difference in the amount of fight left in the player. The 37-year-old Connors forced 19-year-old Andre Agassi, the top-ranked American, to a fifth set before yielding in a men's quarterfinal. He never surrendered. "The people were excited," Connors decided. "You know what? I was excited, too."

Damn right, he was planning to continue. But Evert knew she had had enough after her first season without a single tournament victory, let alone a major championship. She lost three consecutive finals in the spring, to Graf at Boca Raton, to Gabriela Sabatini at Key Biscayne and, finally—did this convince her?—to 15-year-old Monica Seles of Yugoslavia (the female tour's newest sensation) at Houston, 3–6, 6–1, 6–4. Evert did manage to reach the semifinals at Wimbledon for the 17th time in 18 appearances and she bashed Seles, 6–0, 6–2, in her penultimate match at Flushing Meadow.

The symbol of athletic consistency finished on a high note, winning all five of her matches in Federation Cup play. Navratilova also was 5–0 as the U.S. won the team championship for the first time since the great rivals last pooled their talents in 1986 at Prague. They beat Spain, 3–0, Chris' valedictory: 6–3, 6–2, over Conchita Martinez. Sadly, Evert and Navratilova did not oppose each other at all in 1989 and the record of their meetings remained fixed in history at 43–37 in favor of Navratilova.

Although the latter retained her No. 2 ranking and won eight of 15 tournaments, Navratilova was frustrated by Graf in the two most significant tournaments she entered. The fraulein needed three sets on both occasions but nonetheless defeated Navratilova in the final at Wimbledon, 6–2, 6–7 (1–7), 6–1, and Flushing Meadow, 3–6, 7–5, 6–1. Graf also turned back the naturalized American in

the final of the Virginia Slims Championships, 6–4, 7–5, 2–6, 6–2.

Sanchez Vicario's victory at Paris upset the rankings as well as Graf. By the end of the year, she had scrambled from No. 18 to No. 5, one place ahead of Seles. The 15-year-old Yugoslav, operating out of her new home base in Florida, made a stunning professional debut at Washington. She beat Larisa Savchenko, Robin White and Manuela Maleeva to reach the semifinals where an ankle injury forced her to default to Zina Garrsion. Then she defeated Evert in the Houston final before taking a set from Graf in the French Open semifinals.

Another teen-ager, Spain's Conchita Martinez, also made inroads, zooming to No. 7 on the WTA computer as a result of three tour victories. And, in a brief promo of coming attractions, 13-year-old Floridian Jennifer Capriati blitzed Clare Wood, 6–0, 6–0, in the course of another 7–0 Wightman Cup wipeout of the Brits by the U.S. Still an amateur, Capriati was the youngest participant in the event by a full two years.

While Graf remained atop the women's rankings, Mats Wilander began a precipitous drop from first to No.13 at the Australian Open, one of three Grand Slam titles he had claimed the previous year. The Swede, a three-time champion in the event, stumbled in the second round against No. 51-ranked Ramesh Krishnan of India and never regained his equilibrium. Complaining of shin splints and a loss of motivation, Wilander failed to win a single tournament. He lost his only final, at the U.S. Pro in Boston, to Andres Gomez.

The other Swede with a Grand Slam title to his credit in 1988 also was shut out in the majors. But Edberg was a finalist both at Paris and Wimbledon and he actually climbed the ladder to No. 3 with a strong finish, culminating in a 4–6, 7–6, 6–3 (8–6), 6–1 victory over Becker in the

20th and final edition of the season-ending Grand Prix Masters. He, too, had his problems in Melbourne when he suffered a back injury in the course of a fourth-round victory over Pat Cash and had to withdraw.

With the field thinned, Lendl had a clear shot to one of the two Big Four titles that had eluded him and he made the most of the opportunity. He blasted 7th-

Navratilova a 6–2, 3–6, 9–7 quarterfinal defeat, recalling the 1984 semifinal upset that cost Martina a Grand Slam. Sukova outlasted unseeded Belinda Cordwell of New Zealand in the semis but received a 6–4, 6–4 spanking in the final from Graf, who had crushed Sabatini in the semis with the loss of three games.

It was at Paris that the season took an abrupt turn. After both Evert and Navratilova declined to enter—preferring to devote extra time on preparations for Wimbledon—and Sabatini was upset in the fourth round by Mary Joe Fernandez, a third French title for Graf appeared a mere formality. She ceded a set to Seles in the semifinal but it seemed unthinkable Steffi would lose to a 17-year-old appearing in her first Grand Slam final.

Not since the 1962 Wimbledon final (Karen Hantze Susman over Vera Sukova) had a woman seeded as low as seventh won a major against a world-class field. But Sanchez Vicario had the spunk, the shots and the determination to stay in a gruelling match against a woman primed for her sixth consecutive Big Four title. Their match consumed two hours, 58 minutes

and it was a riveting demonstration of championship tennis.

Sanchez Vicario achieved her upset with an extraordinary comeback from 3–5 in the third set, winning the last four games and 16 of the last 19 points. "This is a great day for me," she said. "This is the tournament I wanted to win all my life. This is the one I've been dreaming about."

ing," said her coach, Juan Nunez. "But when she gets on the court, she turns into a lion. What you saw out there was the lion."

Graf appeared pale and sad-eyed after failing to equal Navratilova's streak of six consecutive Grand Slam titles. "Arantxa is a wonderful girl and she played unbelievable to win," said the German, who suffered cramps in the third set. "But I did nothing at all. It wasn't me out there. It was another person hitting those balls."

It was the second and final loss of the year for Graf (following a three-set defeat by Sabatini at Amelia Island) but, for Sanchez Vicario, it was a peerless achievement. At the end of the match, she tossed her racket into the air and collapsed on the red clay. "It is the most joyous moment of my life," she said. "I cannot believe this. I have never been so happy."

No less remarkable was Chang's feat. If anything, it may have been more improbable. The 5-8, 135-pounder would have been unseeded if not for the absence of McEnroe and Muster, who suffered a serious knee injury when hit by a drunken driver on the eve of the Lipton final. The son of research chemists who had emigrated from Taiwan, the 17-year-old youngster seemed too small and too inexperienced for such a herculean task.

But he proved his stamina and his mettle in a fourth-round battle against the top-ranked Lendl, whom he trailed two sets to love. Instead of capitulating, he fought through debilitating cramps to oust the No. 1 player, 4–6, 4–6, 6–3, 6–3, 6–3. He was in such distress late in the fourth set and early in the fifth that he stood at changeovers, munched on bananas, staggered about the court between points and even served underhanded on one occasion.

"I've never seen a player show such courage on a tennis court," said Trabert. Chang's coach, Jose Higueras, called it "the most incredible match I've ever seen."

But that only earned him a berth in the quarterfinals, where he beat Ronald Agenor in four sets. Chang required another four sets to eliminate Andre Chesnokov of the Soviet Union for the right to meet Edberg, who had beaten Italian champ Albert Mancini and Becker in his previous two matches.

Realistically, that should have been the end of the road for Chang. But the youngster stretched the imagination once more, rallying from one set down and saving 13 straight break points over one stretch. He emerged with a shocking 6–2, 3–6, 4–6, 6–4, 6–2 victory. "Whatever happens from now on, good or bad," he said, "this will stay with me for the rest of my life."

Edberg, with three Big Four titles to his credit as well as a superior serve and volley, appeared rattled by his opponent's bottomless reserve. He had 26 break points in the match and converted only six.

"He just keeps coming back," the Swede said. "I have to admire him for it.

But you know these young guys. They just hit. They don't have to think."

With his victory, Chang surpassed Wilander (17 years, 9 months) as the youngest male winner in Paris and supplanted Becker (17 years, 7 months) as the youngest male winner of a Grand Slam event. One of the people who was happiest for him was Trabert, the last previous American to win the French title.

"Chang is a little bit different from other young players," said Trabert, now a television analyst. "Too many of them aren't patient and willing to play long points. I think it should be a personal point of pride to be a well-rounded player."

If that event offered an unlikely duo of titlists, the next major produced a seemingly inevitable pairing. Becker and Graf had been raised in nearby towns in the southeastern corner of West Germany and had known each other since they were children. "I used to be the worst in the boys and she was the best in the girls," Becker recalled with good humor. "So, when I was maybe nine and she was eight, I would have to hit with her."

Each had grown up to be a Wimbledon champion but not in the same year. In 1989, on the grass of the All England Club, they became the Teutonic Twosome. Even the weather cooperated, in a fashion. Rain pushed back the women's final one day so that Graf and Becker might receive their awards at Centre Court on the same afternoon.

Graf, the defender, had the tougher final. She dropped the first set of the tournament before subduing Navratilova, 6–2, 6–7 (1–7), 6–1. But she finished in championship form, firing an ace past the eight-time titleholder. Graf won 17 of 22 points on her serve in the final set and said she was playing so well. "... I was starting to laugh ... I was so loose out there and it showed in my tennis."

Earlier in the tournament, she had toyed with the opposition, including Evert. The latter struggled from 2–5 in the third set to defeat Laura Golarsa of Italy, 6–3, 2–6, 7–5, and earn the satisfaction of one last trip to the Wimbledon semifinals. At least, that gave her an opportunity to wave

Graf was severely tested twice, by Sabatini in the semifinals and, once again, by Navratilova in the ultimate match. Against the Argentine, she lost the first set and overcame leg cramps in the stifling heat to triumph, 3–6, 6–4, 6–2. Afterward, she had to be treated with liquids and an ice massage.

Navratilova appeared to have the final

cult semifinal and smooth sailing in the final. He was thankful for the 76-minute rain delay in the midst of the third set against Lendl, wherein he regained his composure and posted a 7–5, 6–7 (2–7), 2–6, 6–4, 6–3 victory. Taking the first set in 22 minutes, he then overpowered Edberg, 6–0, 7–6 (7–1), 6–4, to reverse the result of the previous year's final.

It was Becker's third Wimbledon title but, after two years of disappointment, he seemed to appreciate this one more than the others. "Then it was like a fairy tale," he said of the consecutive championships he won as a teen-ager. "It wasn't true. I didn't know what I was doing."

This was real. And the two champions from a country with no previous championship there shared the first dance at the Wimbledon Ball.

The U.S. Open lacks such a formal conclusion. Otherwise, the pair could have continued their dance in New York. Graf and Becker each left Flushing Meadow with another major title. They had to work harder than they had at Wimbledon and they had to share the spotlight with a departing champion.

"I was close," said Navratilova, her face streaked with tears. "I was as close as you get." Close but no trophy. Graf got that, for the seventh time in her last eight Grand Slam finals.

Becker almost didn't make it out of the second round, where he faced two match points against vagabond Derrick Rostagno in a fourth-set tie-breaker. On the second, his running forehand ticked the net and hopped over the Californian's waiting racket. Becker took that set and the fifth as well. "I've thought about that shot every day for 10 days," he said on the day he won his first U.S. Open Championship.

The man needed three hours and 21 minutes to defeat Lendl, 7–6 (7–2), 1–6, 6–3, 7–6 (7–4). The latter was appearing in his eighth consecutive final, a Tildenesque achievement. But once Becker got a full head of steam, neither Ivan nor the ghost of Big Bill could stop him. "He just has more power in his game than I do." Lendl said.

For Becker, the victory proved that the man was more than splendor in the grass, that he was able to beat a world-class field

The Davis Cup, Wimbledon and the U.S. Open made Boris Becker's hit list in 1989. • *Mitchell Reibel*

somewhere other than Wimbledon. He had filled in the gaps in his game since the summer of '85, had firmed his ground-strokes along with his tenacity. Now he was a worthy challenger for the honor of top-ranked men's player on the planet. "If I'm not No. 1," he said, "then I'm quite close to it."

But he couldn't close the narrow gap before year's end, despite his two majors and a 64–8 match record on winning six of 13 tournaments. Boris's magnificent year had included possibly the most remarkable win—6–7 (4–7), 6–7 (5–7), 7–6 (7–3), 6–3, 6–4, over Agassi in the Cup semis—and another Davis Cup, 3–2 over Sweden as he blasted Edberg and Wilander in singles

and held on with Eric Jelen for a 6–4 fifth-set decision over Anders Jarryd and Jan Gunnarson. Agassi had served for victory at 6–5, got as close as 30–15, and led by a break, 4–3 in the fifth.

With all his heroics, Becker was still second to Lendl, who won 10 of 17 starts on a 79–7 record and won record earnings of $2,334,367. Ivan lost the Masters semifinal to Edberg, who then cut down Becker the following day, 4–6, 7–6 (8–6), 6–3, 6–1.

Still, the Open was as notable for a dignified exit as for Becker's grand entrance into the circle of champions. Evert made her last stand on the stadium court in the quarterfinals against Garrison, an opponent who had lined up for her autograph 10 years earlier in Houston. In the end, her nerves betrayed her. Twice she served for the first set and was broken both times.

Afterward, Garrison was as spent as Evert. "It was the hardest match I've ever played," the winner said, "because it was so emotional." At the end, Evert's eyes were red but her voice was unshaken.

"This place is special to me," she said. "I knew my last match here would be sad, win or lose."

Evert departed with the records for most Open victories (101) and most career singles titles (157). Her 5–0 record in subsequent Federation Cup brought her lifetime record to 1,309–146, an astonishing percentage of .900.

"I really can't fathom it [her retirement] because we have been at it since 1973," Navratilova had said at Wimbledon. "So a piece of me will be gone with her." And a piece of tennis as well.

Also fading away was the men's Grand Prix format, a victim of the ATP revolt. For the record, the last GP event in history was the Masters Doubles at the Royal Albert Hall in London on Dec. 10. McEnroe's younger brother, Patrick, teamed with Jim Grabb to beat Wimbledon champions Anders Jarryd and John Fitzgerald in the match that brought down the curtain on two decades of play, 7–5, 7–6 (7–4), 5–7, 6–3.

1990

Fourteen-year-old Jennifer Capriati wasted no time in fulfilling her $5-million endorsement contracts. • *Mitchell Reibel*

another for the underaged. Although the gap wasn't quite so large among their male counterparts, Andres Gomez scored a stunning triumph for the 30-and-over crowd in Paris and Pete Sampras became a U.S. Open champion within a month of celebrating his 19th birthday. Ironically, each defeated Andre Agassi for his first major title.

This also was the year in which Stefan Edberg, the Wimbledon champion for a second time, dislodged from No. 1 Ivan Lendl, who successfully defended his Australian title. Graf continued at the top of the women's charts but, after losing the French and U.S. finals to Seles and Gabriela Sabatini, respectively, her reign was seriously threatened. And John McEnroe paid for his years of sins against the tennis establishment when he was defaulted in the midst of a Grand Slam tournament.

Perhaps the most encouraging development at the start of a new decade was the emergence of Jennifer Capriati, the 14-year-old American who received $5 million in endorsement contracts before playing her first professional match just days before her 14th birthday, and promptly demonstrated what all the fuss was about. She mowed

down five opponents in her first tournament before losing to Sabatini in the final at Boca Raton. Then she became the youngest semifinalist in any Grand Slam event when she reached the final four at the French Open, advanced to the fourth round both at Wimbledon and Flushing Meadow and finished the season as the No. 8-ranked player on the WTA computer.

Another prosperous rookie was the men's tour, managed for the first time by the players themselves. The ATP conducted 75 tournaments on six continents, culminating in season-ending singles and doubles championships. Agassi won the former, defeating Edberg in the final at Frankfurt, and the team of Guy Forget and Jakob Hlasek triumphed over Sergio Casal and Emilio Sanchez in the latter, staged at Sanctuary Cove, Australia.

Less successful was the Grand Slam Cup, inaugurated by the International

Tennis Federation in conjunction with officials of the four Grand Slam tournaments. Although the December event carried a staggering purse of $6 million, many elite pros—including German star Boris Becker—boycotted the competition in Munich because it detracted from the ATP Tour finals. Sampras defeated fellow American Brad Gilbert in straight sets for the $2-million first prize.

There were no melancholy retirement scenes such as that provided the previous year by Chris Evert but an historic event passed from the tennis calendar with the suspension of the Wightman Cup between U.S. and British women. The competition, first staged in 1923, had grown too one-sided to attract attention on either side of the Atlantic. The U.S. had won the last 11 contests.

America claimed each of the other major team championships. Capriati won the clinching match as the U.S. women retained the Federation Cup by defeating the Soviet Union, 2–1, in Atlanta. Agassi and Michael Chang were the stalwarts as the host country took possession of the Davis Cup for the first time in eight years by beating Australia, 3–2.

Agassi led off, struggling to beat young unknown giant, 6-foot-4 Richard Fromberg, 6–4 in the fifth, and Chang crushed Darren Cahill for a 2–0 lead, setting up Jim Pugh and Rick Leach for the clincher, 6–4, 6–2, 3–6, 7–6 (7–2) over Pat Cash and John Fitzgerald. It was a bizarre windup to the 29th Cup for the U.S., played indoors in Florida while sun baked the roof of St. Petersburg's Suncoast Dome. And on clay, so often the burial ground for U.S. teams. But the dirt, specially trucked in, was what the doctor—captain Tom Gorman—ordered to bog down the best Aussie, Cash, who thus wasn't even selected to oppose the American baseliners.

Aaron Krickstein, a last-minute stand-in for pouting Agassi, was the quarterfinal hero of Prague, beating Petr Korda and Milan Srejber to get his side past Czechoslovakia. But it was 18-year-old Chang, youngest American to play for a Cup winner, who gave the key push to the final in a screamer at Vienna. In the decisive fifth match, he lost the first two sets to Horst Skoff, then won the third before they were halted by darkness. On the following gloomy, soggy afternoon, gritty Michael wrapped up the semifinal, 3–6, 6–7 (4–7), 6–4, 6–4, 6–3.

For a topsy-turvy year, 1990 began in conventional fashion. Graf won an eighth major championship in her last nine attempts by bashing Mary Joe Fernandez, 6–3, 6–4, at the Australian Open. The latter had upset third-seeded Zina Garrison en route to her first Grand Slam final in a field that did not include Navratilova and Seles.

The top men turned out in greater numbers at Finders Park but the final ended in disappointment. Edberg, who played brilliantly in routing Mats Wilander in the semifinals, suffered a torn abdominal muscle in the midst of the third set of his showdown with Lendl and could not continue. Lendl was awarded a 4–6, 7–6 (7–3), 5–2 (ret.) victory and his second consecutive Australian title.

At Melbourne, the first of the Big Four tournaments was spiced by the spectacle of McEnroe's banishment. After the testy perfectionist received two code violations for racket abuse and intimidation of a linesman during his fourth-round match against Mikael Pernfors, he cursed umpire Gerry Armstrong and referee Ken Farrar. Under the new three-step code of conduct introduced at the start of the season, Mac was automatically disqualified.

Despite his history of misbehavior, it marked the man's first default. He was fined $6,500 and the setback was the first of many in an erratic year that saw him bounced in the first round at Wimbledon by Derrick Rostagno, reach the semifinals of the U.S. Open, post a lone tournament victory and drop from No. 4 to No. 13 in the ATP rankings.

As it had been the previous year, Paris was the site of two startling results.

ᴏꜰ Gᴀꜰ suggested a new order in women's tennis.

Before taking on the top-ranked German, Seles eliminated Capriati, 6–2, 6–2, in a match that was a preview of the future. For Capriati, who had dropped only 20 games in her five previous matches, the 62-minute rout was an educational experience, not unlike her first visit to Notre Dame. And her opponent was sure she would be back. "I have the feeling we're going to be playing many, many more times," Seles said.

Her current rivalry, however, was with Graf and, suddenly, they appeared to be equals. Although the German still had that booming forehand, her slice backhand left her vulnerable to Seles, who powers the ball from both sides. "She hits like she means it," Graf said.

Additionally, the favorite was bothered by allergies that plague her every spring in Paris and press reports from back home that charged her father with impregnating a German model only slightly older than Steffi. There was a vulnerability about her that no one had sensed since she ascended to the top.

Graf rallied from a 1–4 deficit to force a tie-breaker, where she won the first five points and led, 6–2. One point from the set, however, she dropped the next six, double-faulting on her fourth and final set point. "That's when I knew I had her," Seles said.

In her first major final, the latter saved two break points in the ninth game of the

them.

At the very least, the victory at Roland Garros made her famous for something other than her grunting on court, her cackle during press interviews and her unruly mane. "I didn't want to go into the history books 20 years from now," she said, and have people read, 'She was a great grunter, a great giggler and had a lot of hair.'"

Now she had one for the books, a major championship. Graf appeared wasted after the defeat, only the second in her last 74 matches. "I'm lacking a little bit right now," she said. "I'm not hitting the ball like I used to. There's something missing."

Among the missing in Paris were Navratilova and Lendl. Both were consumed with preparations for Wimbledon, a tournament where the woman would be seeking a record ninth title and the man a fulfilling first. Inadvertently, Lendl's decision not to enter the French had a major impact on the results.

Gomez, the man who would become king on the clay, was weighing an offer to serve as a commentator on Ecuadorian television at Paris until he learned that Lendl was bypassing the tournament to practice on grass. The Czech star had eliminated him in four previous French Opens. Gomez had taken a vacation from the tour in 1988 after the birth of his first son and even considered a permanent leave after his ranking plunged to No. 43.

At 30, he seemed an unlikely semifinalist, let alone champion. But, given his first chance at a final four in a Grand Slam event, he bulldozed Thomas Muster of Austria, 7–5, 6–1, 7–5. That earned him a berth opposite the outrageous Agassi, who appeared finally to be living up to his advertising image as the hottest thing on tour.

The youngster from Las Vegas, seeded third, emerged as the favorite in the draw after the top two seeds, Edberg and Becker, suffered unprecedented indignities for such elite: first-round losses to Sergi Bruguera of Spain and Goran Ivanisevic of Yugoslavia, respectively. Agassi also gained attention by engaging in a verbal battle with Philippe Chatrier, president of the ITF and the reigning potentate of the tournament, after the official took one look at Agassi's hot lava (pink) and black tennis ensemble and issued a statement that the French Open would consider requiring predominantly white clothing the following year. Agassi responded by calling the man a "bozo," an insult even in a country that reveres Jerry Lewis.

But the man brought more than bicycle shorts and a matching bandana to the event. He had the talent to whip his 1989 Paris conqueror, Jim Courier, defending champion Michael Chang and Jonas Svensson en route to what appeared to be a coronation. Gomez was one of the most popular players in the world among his peers but, Agassi pledged, "He's going to be in for a long afternoon because I want it bad."

Surprise. Gomez made relatively short work of the American, 10 years his junior.

In the match of his career, he dismissed Agassi, 6–3, 2–6, 6–4, 6–4, claiming the first Big Four title for Ecuador. "I've been coming here for many years," he said, "and I've been dreaming about this day."

The South American served 10 aces to his opponent's one and he demonstrated more bounce despite the age differential. Although Gomez had 72 unforced errors, he also hit 58 winners in becoming the oldest French singles champ in 18 years. "I don't think of this as a sunset," he said. "I think of it as a sunrise."

At 33, Navratilova was seeking a final sunrise of her own at Wimbledon. Three years without a Grand Slam victory, she trained diligently under her latest coach/motivator, Billie Jean King, for the triumph that would distance her from Helen Wills Moody, the eight-time champion from an earlier era. As it developed, she was virtually unchallenged.

Despite her problems in Paris, Graf still was favored. But from the moment she set foot in London, the German was under siege. If it wasn't the sinus problem that caused her to fly home for treatment during a weekend break, then it was the tabloid press which had a field day with the story of her father and the suddenly nefarious Nicole Meissner, whose provocative photos appeared almost daily in the sensational journals. Tournament officials limited questions to tennis at interview sessions although that failed to stop the gossip.

When they weren't harassing Graf, the arbiters of England's morals were going after the new generation of grunters, Seles in particular. *The Sun* unveiled a Grunt-o-meter, with which it allegedly measured the chief offender at 82 decibels—"between a pneumatic drill and a diesel train." As silly as this appeared, the new chairman of the tournament, John Curry, said he would "readily relax the all-white clothes rule if I could just get rid of the grunts."

"Gaby [Sabatini], [Anke] Huber and Jennifer grunt," Seles said. "But probably I'm the loudest. I don't know. I don't even realize I do it until I watch tape of myself on television. I think it's better than it was last year or in the French Open but I can't get rid of it."

Zina Garrison saved officials the trouble of silencing the teen-ager. Overcoming

called her more relaxed approach. And she laughed. "I'm 26," she explained. "Old person on the tour now."

From one standpoint, at least, she had been bypassed. Garrison spent years trying unsuccessfully to crack the ranks of the elite when Chris Evert and Navratilova ruled the sport. Then Graf had zoomed past, followed by Seles. Only last fall, after her loss to Navratilova at Flushing Meadow and her marriage to Willard Jackson, she said, "Since I was 16, I felt I would win Wimbledon and the U.S. Open. I still do."

It didn't seem to faze her that her next opponent would be Graf, who had ended Capriati's summer vacation with a 6–2, 6–4 decision in the fourth round. Although Garrison had beaten Graf only once in six matches—in their first meeting when the German was 16—the American was confident. "I've always wanted to play her on the grass," she said.

She made the most of the opportunity in what the normally understated Dan Maskell, who had been telecasting the championships for the BBC since the dawn of time, called an "epic match."

In denying Graf entry to a Grand Slam final after a record 13 consecutive appearances, Garrison overcame not only the German but her own nerves in a 6–3, 3–6, 6–4 triumph. She served out the match by winning the last four points in succession, capped by a glorious ace.

"My first thought was to hit it to the forehand," she said, "and right at the last

said. "It was not my day. She didn't make mistakes. She used to make much more errors, unforced errors especially, but she didn't do that today at all." Nevertheless, Graf decided, her conqueror had no chance in the final. "Zina doesn't have the game to beat Martina," she said.

Certainly, there was little in the head-to-head record that suggested a titanic struggle. Of the 28 matches between the two friends, Navratilova had won 27. Moreover, in her 6–3, 6–4 semifinal victory over Sabatini, she had demonstrated she was still near the top of her form.

Garrison, who didn't have a clothing deal and was wearing Navratilova's signature line, was compensated on the eve of the championship by a six-figure contract with Reebok, one of several the player landed for her attention-getting run. Additionally, her presence in the title match stirred Althea Gibson, the last black woman to win a Grand Slam event in 1958, to fly in from New York. "She came out and watched me practice," Garrison said. "She's a very nice lady."

But no amount of personal or financial support for her opponent was going to stop

Navratilova when she was this close to an historic accomplishment. In the match and the tournament that defined her career, Navratilova was more than triumphant. She was regal in a 6–4, 6–1 victory.

Her virtually flawless performance at Centre Court, where nerves can be stretched as taut as racket strings, was one to be preserved in a time capsule. "It was my match to win," Navratilova decided, "and I wasn't afraid of it."

Thus did she surpass Wills, who lost only one of 56 singles matches at Wimbledon in nine tournaments from 1924 through 1933.

"Little Miss Poker Face," as she was known, won her last Wimbledon final at the age of 32 years, 270 days, making her the oldest female champion since 1914. The 33-year-old Navratilova, 99–9 on the most famous lawns in the world, also took that distinction from Wills. Charlotte Cooper Sterry was 37 as the 1908 champ.

Navratilova was rewarded for her decision to train harder, to bypass Paris for additional practice on the grass. Lendl, who made a greater commitment, who journeyed to Australia during the winter for seven weeks of training under coach Tony Roche and who (after attending the birth of his first child, Marika) spent six weeks on the grass in England, did not. After playing brilliantly in the traditional warmup tournament at Queen's Club, blasting McEnroe and Becker among others, he wilted at Wimbledon.

Lendl used a Czech term to describe his obsession for the only major title he lacked. "Zazrany," he called it. "It means very much into it, almost stubborn." Alas, after weaving fitfully into the semifinals, he staggered out of the tournament following a crushing 6–1, 7–6 (7–2), 6–3 loss to Edberg. He promised to return.

Edberg earned his third trip to the final, all against Becker, who received a scare from 18-year-old hotshot Goran Ivanisevic—his conqueror at the French Open—before advancing, 4–6, 7–6 (7–4), 6–0, 7–6 (7–5). Not since 1894, when Wilfred Baddeley challenged Joshua Pim in their fourth consecutive championship match, had the title contest been an object of such familiarity.

This time they produced the longest men's final since Jimmy Connors—sidelined almost the entire 1990 season by a wrist injury that would require surgery—defeated McEnroe in 1982. However, the five-setter wasn't nearly as strained, partly because their similar serve-and-volley styles allowed for no rallies, partly because they were unable to play their best tennis at the same time. Edberg won, 6–2, 6–2, 3–6, 3–6, 6–4.

Pete Sampras aced Andre Agassi to death in the U.S. Open final in 1990 and capped the year by banking $2 million in Munich from the Grand Slam Cup. • *Russ Adams*

It was a match full of British civility, one in which each player attempted to hand the championship to the other. Becker made the final gesture when he lost his serve at 3–2 in the fifth set. The two hugged at the conclusion.

Inspired by the victory, Edberg won his next three tournaments, at Los Angeles, Cincinnati and Long Island, displacing

Gabriela Sabatini dethroned Steffi Graf in the U.S. Open in 1990. • *Russ Adams*

reach the final at Flushing Meadow for the first time since 1981. In fact, he didn't survive the quarterfinals, beaten in five sets by the eager Sampras, who was credited with 24 aces and 27 service winners.

Much of the crowd's attention at the Open was diverted by the restoration of the McEnroe legend. Unseeded for the first time since his Open debut 13 years earlier, the former champion went back to his old coach, Tony Palafox, prepared diligently and then won over the fans by beating seeded Andrei Chesnokov (10) and Emilio Sanchez (7) and David Wheaton to gain the semifinals for the first time in five years. But he couldn't cope with Sampras' power, the youngster finishing him off in four sets with his 17th ace. "It's been a great run," McEnroe decided.

It was an even more remarkable tournament for Sampras, the lanky and laid-back California who was ranked No. 81 as recently as January, who hadn't won his first pro tournament until February in Philadelphia. But the best was yet to come—against Agassi, who had overcome Becker in four sets, setting the stage for the first all-American men's final since 1979.

Agassi, who had changed to "electric lime" for this tournament, was nearly undressed in the championship match. Sampras fired 13 more aces, raising his tournament total to 100, added 12 service winners and never was broken in demolishing his opponent, 6–4, 6–3, 6–2 in one hour, 42 minutes. "It was a good old-fashioned street mugging," Agassi said.

Sampras, 28 days past his 19th birthday, was the youngest male player to win America's national championship, supplanting Oliver Campbell, an older 19 one century earlier. Sampras shrugged. "I'm just a normal 19-year-old with an unusual job, doing unusual things," he said.

At 20, Sabatini had been doing unusual things for five years, since her breakthrough season of 1985. But she had reached only one major final (U.S., 1988) until 1990 when, attacking boldly, she applied the finishing touch to Graf's unhappy Grand Slam year with a bold game plan and 6–2, 7–6 (7–4) victory. Nevertheless, the German retained her No. 1 position as a result of Linda Ferrando's victory over Seles in a third-round match, one of two huge upsets in the first week of the tournament (Navratilova was burned by Manuela Maleeva Fragnier in the fourth round).

Graf recovered to win four tournaments in the fall, including two at Sabatini's expense, but Seles served notice of future intentions when she became the youngest to win a Virginia Slims championship in November at Madison Square Garden. In the final, she defeated Sabatini, 6–4, 5–7, 3–6, 6–4, 6–2, in the first five-set women's match since the 1901 U.S. Nationals. A new day was at hand.

1991

Her talent was undeniable. After she won the three Grand Slam events she chose to enter, her credentials were impeccable. By the end of the year, only Monica Seles' judgment was considered suspect.

In her third season as a professional, Seles dislodged Steffi Graf as the No. 1 woman in the world and won more money ($2,457,758) than any previous practitioner of tennis, male or female. Not until she had wrapped a ribbon around 1991 by earning a second consecutive Virginia Slims Championship did she turn 18. The teen-ager pursued and embraced both fame and fortune.

It was the source of the former that the tennis establishment found distasteful, if not embarrassing. A professed admirer of pop singer Madonna and the glamour associated with movie stars, Seles gained a greater share of attention not for her victories at the Australian, French and U.S. Opens but for her mysterious withdrawal from Wimbledon without a suitable explanation. Her subsequent self-imposed exile

Her opponents grumbled while Monica Seles grunted her way to women's supremacy in 1991. • *Russ Adams*

created a rash of rumors popular in supermarket tabloids.

If her disappearance from public view revealed a fascination for Garbo, her return to tennis at an exhibition event for which she reportedly received a $300,000 appearance fee indicated she also had studied Gabor. On the day of her arrival at the Pathmark Tennis Classic in New Jersey, she posed for photographers with her dog tucked under her arm. Zsa Zsa would have been proud, darling.

In Seles' absence, Graf did manage to regain self-respect by claiming a third Wimbledon title. But the top ranking she had held for an unprecedented 186 weeks slipped away on March 10. The German did regain the No. 1 position for two brief periods during the summer but Seles zoomed back in front after her victory over Martina Navratilova at Flushing Meadow and opened a comfortable margin by winning three late-season tournaments and the Slims Championship, where Graf was upset by Jana Novotna in the quarterfinals.

Graf, in fact, failed to reach a final in any major outside of Wimbledon. She barely held off Gabriela Sabatini for second place. Although Navratilova fell to fourth and endured a drawn-out palimony suit brought by former companion Judy

man won more than one major. Boris Becker won the Australian Open for the first time but was a losing finalist at Wimbledon for the second consecutive year, bowing to countryman Michael Stitch in the first all-German title match at the world's most prestigious tournament. Jim Courier became the third young American in three years to win a Grand Slam event when he defeated Andre Agassi at the French but he was overwhelmed by Stefan Edberg in the final of the U.S. Open.

The last of the Big Four tournaments was energized by the spectacular comeback of Jimmy Connors. After losing all three of his matches the previous year before undergoing surgery on his left wrist, the man was reborn in 1991 when he celebrated his 39th birthday at Flushing Meadow with a sentimental journey to the semifinals. Over the course of a season in which he also earned standing ovations in Paris and London, Connors rose from No. 936 on the ATP computer to No. 48, a gain of 888 positions.

Courier, a Floridian who turned 21 in mid-August, had the most significant jump of all. With his first major title, the baseline basher with the baseball cap vaulted from No. 25 to No. 3 in the men's rank-

Jim Courier catapulted to No. 3 in the world in 1991 as he won the French and reached the finals of the U.S. and ATP championships. • *Russ Adams*

ings, the highest achievement by an American since John McEnroe in 1985. The latter fell from No. 13 to 28, his lowest finish as a pro, despite gaining his 77th career title. It occurred in Chicago at the expense of his younger brother, Patrick, who rose to No. 36 after he reached the Australian Open semifinals and achieved his first singles tournament final.

Edberg, who spent much of the year dueling Becker for the top spot, took command at the U.S. Open and became only the fourth player in the era to finish No. 1 for consecutive seasons, joining Connors, McEnroe and Ivan Lendl. He won six of eight finals, compiled a tour-best 76–17 match record and earned a men's record $2,363,575.

Tendinitis in the knee, however, caused the Swede to withdraw from the ATP championships at Frankfurt. Pete Sampras, whose hangover from his remarkable 1990 success lasted until August, added the season-ending title to three other tour victories in the second half of the season. But the Californian finished the year on a down note when he lost both his singles matches in an emotional Davis Cup final won by France at Lyon.

In a bizarre sideshow, Bjorn Borg attempted a comeback at Monte Carlo 10 years after his last Grand Slam event. He played with a wooden racket, and lost in the opening round to Jordi Arrese. After saying he would make an appearance at the French Open, he decided not to ask for a wild card into the main draw, and appeared not again.

Seles, born six months before Borg won his first major tournament, emerged as the youngest world champion in history. She began her climb to the top at the Australian Open, where she dropped only 12 games in the first five rounds. She qualified for the final by struggling past Mary Joe Fernandez, escaping a match point, 6–3, 0–6, 9–7, and then overcame the loss of the first set to beat Novotna, 5–7, 6–3, 6–1.

The Czech had upset Zina Garrison, Graf and Arantxa Sanchez Vicario to reach her first Grand Slam final. Her 5–7, 6–4, 8–6 victory over Graf marked the first time in the last 17 Big Four appearances that the German had failed to advance as far as the semifinals.

Graf's 1,310-day reign as No. 1 ended with her loss to Sabatini in the final at Boca Raton. She did have the satisfaction of defeating Seles at the U.S. Hard Court Championships in San Antonio three weeks later and at Hamburg five weeks after that. But Seles entered the French Open as the top-ranked player and emerged as the clearcut leader.

Both Graf and Sabatini had the opportunity to move to the top of the ladder with a victory in Paris. But Seles defeated Sabatini, 6–4, 6–1, in the semifinals shortly after Graf was humbled by Sanchez Vicario, 6–0, 6–2. The two games were the fewest won by Graf in a complete match since turning pro in October 1982, at the age of 13.

"That hasn't happened in a long, long time," Graf said. "And I hope it's going to be a long, long time until it happens again. I can't remember the last time I played that bad," she said.

Seles, who had dropped only one set in the tournament, defeated Sanchez Vicario in routine fashion, 6–3, 6–4, for her second consecutive French title. It was somewhere between Paris and London, at least in terms of the WTA schedule, that the season took a strange twist.

With the public considering the possibility of a second female Grand Slam in three years, Wimbledon officials were startled to receive a message that Seles had withdrawn from the event "due to an injury caused by a minor accident." There was no additional explanation, no contact with the player herself and the tournament was due to start in three days. Her whereabouts became the hottest topic in tennis.

She was undergoing treatment for a knee injury in Vail, Colo. Or she was having her legs checked in New York. Or she was in hiding at entrepreneur Donald Trump's vast estate in Florida.

Maybe it wasn't an injury at all, some tabloids speculated, coming to the conclusion that she was pregnant. Another report had her skipping the grass-court event to preserve her ranking and a $1-million bonus from the company that manufactures her racket. About the only possibility overlooked was that she had been spirited away by a UFO. Meanwhile, she could not be reached by reporters, her agents nor the WTA, which levied a $6,000 fine for a late withdrawal.

While she was away, Jennifer Capriati had the time of her life at Wimbledon. The

15-year-old not only became the youngest semifinalist in tournament history but she did so at the expense of Navratilova. Capriati stunned the most honored singles champion in the annals of the All England Club in the quarterfinals, 6–4, 7–5.

Against the person she called in her schoolgirl shorthand "the lege," as in legend, the youngster won the first set but was

from Wimbledon in 14 years and ended a record streak of nine consecutive finals. Capriati scored her first triumph over a player ranked in the top four and qualified for the semifinals against Sabatini. She got no further, losing to the Argentine, 6–4, 6–4.

Meanwhile, Graf took the opportunity to emerge from her personal cloud cover, whipping Zina Garrison and Mary Joe Fernandez en route to the final. The championship match was anything but stellar and the German was sufficiently shaky to double-fault away the ninth game of the third set, presenting Sabatini the chance to serve for the trophy at 5–4, again at 6–5, 30–15. Gaby failed to get the last two points and Graf went on to a 6–4, 3–6, 8–6 victory, the first extended women's final at Wimbledon since 1976.

"In many ways, it means a lot to me," Graf said. "It gave me so much pleasure to see myself getting through, winning a tough match, a close match, not letting up. I needed to win again. I needed it for myself."

Following that exercise in tennis, the Seles media circus was called to order one

week later in New Jersey. Underneath a hot tent on the campus of Ramapo College, the player made her first public appearance since her withdrawal from Wimbledon. Sixteen microphones and 13 television cameras were in place as she met the press.

The truth, she said, was that she had skipped the most prestigious tournament in the world because of "shin splints and

Her representative explained that she had hit herself in the leg with the racket during the French Open, aggravating her shin splints. She agreed that "maybe the wording [of her withdrawal] could have been better," but chose not to make any public statements. "I wasn't ready to talk to anyone," she said.

The site of her return certainly didn't mollify WTA officials. She chose an exhibition tournament, offering a huge guarantee, over an official tour event the following week in nearby Westchester County, N.Y. For that offense, she was fined $20,000, a penalty assumed by the local promoter, John Korff. He also paid the $2,500 fine assessed to Capriati, who defeated Seles in the final of the 16-woman event.

From there, Capriati flew to Nottingham, England, where the U.S. team qualified for the final of the Federation Cup. Despite her singles victory over Conchita Martinez, however, the Americans lost, 2–1, to Spain as Sanchez Vicario defeated Mary Joe Fernandez and the team of Garrison and Gigi Fernandez was thwarted in the doubles, 3–6, 6–1, 6–1.

Seles offered three reasons why she was not representing Yugoslavia in the international team competition. She said she didn't think it was good for her leg. She didn't think she was ready to play at that level of competition. And, she said, "Nobody asked me." She also suggested it would be a nice gesture if Yugoslav authorities apologized for not contacting her.

Returning to the tour at the end of July, Seles was upset by Capriati at San Diego in a match that boasted a pairing of the two youngest finalists in the open era. Two weeks later, Seles won in Los Angeles. Twice in August, however, Graf supplanted Seles at the top of the rankings and the German entered the U.S. Open in the familiar role of No. 1.

It was not to last. Graf was upset in the semifinals by the oldest woman in the draw. The 34-year-old Navratilova, playing a classic serve-and-volley game, ousted Graf, 7–6 (7–2), 6–7 (6–8), 6–4, advancing to her eighth U.S. final. Her opponent was Seles.

The mysterious one had overcome Capriati, 6–3, 3–6, 7–6 (7–3), in a memorable semifinal. Capriati twice had served for the match in the third set, twice had failed. Remarkably, neither player held serve in the tie-breaker until the eighth point. Tears flooded the loser's eyes.

On the following afternoon, Seles demolished Navratilova, 7–6 (7–1), 6–1, passing her elder at will from either end of the baseline. Navratilova won only 34 points on 76 approaches to the net and committed 26 unforced errors to the champion's five. Seles thus won her third Grand Slam title of the season in as many attempts. She did not win many new fans, especially after publicly thanking the controversial Trump in post-match ceremonies.

The victory restored her to the top spot on the computer, which she held for the remainder of the year. Seles said she didn't regret the decision to withdraw from Wimbledon. "I can't erase it," she said.

"But if I were to play Wimbledon, I don't think I could have played the Open (because of the time for recuperation)... There will always be that little emptiness."

Seles finished the season in style, defeating Navratilova, 6–4, 3–6, 7–5, 6–0, at Madison Square Garden in the final of the Slims Championships. Navratilova teamed with her old partner, Pam Shriver, to win the doubles title for the first time in three years, their 10th in this event.

The men's tour offered surprises as early as the first major tournament, where one of the semifinalists advised the press, "It's just like you all expected—Edberg, Lendl, Becker and McEnroe." Except that the speaker was Patrick McEnroe and it was the doubles specialist who had advanced to the final four, rather than older brother John. The latter hadn't even made the trip following his disqualification the previous year.

McEnroe, who had defeated Jay Berger, Mark Woodforde and Cristiano Caratti in his best Grand Slam showing, battled Becker for four sets before the German prevailed, 6–7 (2–7), 6–4, 6–1, 6–4. Becker went on to a 1–6, 6–4, 6–4, 6–4 victory over Lendl, who had survived a five-set marathon over Edberg.

Paris belonged to the Americans. For the first time since 1954, a pair of Yanks qualified for the final. But long before Courier and Agassi walked into Roland Garros to contest the championship, Connors stole the show. A wild-card entry in the only Big Four championship he hasn't won, the 38-year-old Connors eliminated Todd Witsken, outlasted No. 28 Ronald Algenor of France in five sets and forced 1989 champion Michael Chang to a fifth set before he had to retire with a stiff back and other ailments.

"I'm sorry," he said to umpire Bruno Rebeuh after more than three-and-one-half hours of play against a man half his age. "I did all I could. I just can't play anymore. Believe me, if I could stay out here and play, I would."

Certainly, that's what the public believed. The fans accorded him several standing ovations. "To be honest, I felt awful," Connors said after getting an ice massage and an intravenous solution. "I've

adventurous trip to his first Grand Slam title match, ousting top-seeded Edberg in the quarterfinals before beating Stich. It marked only the fourth all-American men's final in Paris and the first since Tony Trabert defeated Art Larsen 37 years earlier.

"I'd like to slap around the people who asked where American tennis was about five years ago," said Courier, a frustrated baseball player whose style was to swing for the fences. "This says, 'Here we are.'"

Both players had trained at the Nick Bollettieri Tennis Academy but Courier left when he decided Agassi was receiving most of the coach's attention. And Agassi had taken a faster track to the spotlight. But it was Courier who was the more poised in the end, ignoring a couple of rain delays and strong winds in a 3–6, 6–4, 2–6, 6–1, 6–4 victory.

It was Courier's fourth career triumph in as many finals and the $451,660 he pocketed exceeded his total prize money from 1990. He closed with an ace, then flopped backward onto the clay. "There have been lots of happy moments in my life and there will be lots more," the champion said, "but at the moment this is the happiest."

Agassi received greater attention just for showing up at Wimbledon than he did for any of his 1991 results. He hadn't made an appearance at the All England Club since a first-round loss to Henri Leconte in 1987. He said he wasn't ready for the grass and it wasn't clear if officials were ready for a peacock.

And then Agassi removed the white

Wheaton, a 22-year-old American with a big serve.

The unseeded Wheaton, who would cap his season with the $2-million first-place check at the Grand Slam Cup in December, was the only outsider in the semifinals of a tournament that, in an unprecedented move, opened the gates on the middle Sunday in order to clear a backlog of matches postponed by rain. Tickets were hastily printed after the announcement on Friday and all seats were unreserved, causing a mad dash from the turnstiles. So enthusiastic and unfamiliar with tradition were the fans at Centre Court that they even performed a wave.

Order was restored in time for the final between Becker, who had turned back Wheaton, and his countryman, who had upset Edberg without once breaking the defending champ's service. Stich—"I can say it but you can't spell it," he warned—won three successive tie-breakers after dropping the first set and prevented a fourth consecutive Edberg-Becker battle for the championship.

By winning his match after Edberg lost, Becker climbed to No. 1 in the rankings for the second time in the season. But the added stature did not intimidate Stich. Eleven months younger than Becker, the relatively anonymous German had only one tournament title (Memphis in 1990) to his name when he broke his more celebrated compatriot in the first game, slugged 16 aces (for a tournament total of 97) and overwhelmed the three-time champion, 6–4, 7–6 (7–4), 6–4.

"It's an incredible feeling," Stich said. To which Becker nodded in agreement. "I know the feeling," the loser said. "He was a nobody, but today he is a star."

Becker held onto the top spot in the rankings until the U.S. Open, where he was upset in the third round by Paul Haarhuis. Edberg, who had never reached the final at Flushing Meadow in the major tournament he liked least, made the most of the opportunity. He beat Chang, Lendl and, finally, Courier, 6–2, 6–4, 6–0, for his first U.S. title and the designation as the best player in the world.

Still, the star of the tournament was none of the above. It was Connors, the wild card with a No. 174 ranking, who owned the crowds in winning five matches against Patrick McEnroe, Michiel Schapers, 10th-seeded Karel Novacek, Aaron Krickstein and Haarhuis. He came from two sets down to eliminate McEnroe in the first round and rallied from a 1–2 set deficit and 2–5 in the fifth to beat Krickstein, who had stunned Agassi on the very first day of the event. Connors was a marvel and the fans couldn't contain themselves. "It was 20,000 people making the sound of 60,000," he said proudly.

Connors, who turned 39 the day he beat Krickstein, became the second-oldest semifinalist in history, behind Ken Rosewall, whom he drubbed in the 1974 final on grass at Forest Hills. He was also the first wild card to advance that far. Even competitors were caught up in the excitement he generated.

Michael Stich prevailed over Boris Becker in Wimbledon's all-German final in 1991. • *Russ Adams*

But he ran out of miracles against Courier. The latter scored a 6–3, 6–3, 6–2 victory that was coldly efficient and brutally quick. To that point, Courier hadn't dropped a set in the tournament, yet he proved unable to handle Edberg.

The new champion devoted part of his post-match interview to honoring Connors. "I think what happened here is great for tennis," Edberg said. "Jimmy Connors' performance here has created a lot of publicity. It has given the U.S. Open a boost. I thank him."

Courier also reached the final of the ATP World Championship, which Sampras won 3–6, 7–6 (7–5), 6–3, 6–4. In the doubles event, which reopened South Africa to the men's tour, John Fitzgerald and Anders Jarryd culminated an outstanding year in which they claimed the French, Wimbledon and U.S. Open titles by beating Ken Flach and Robert Seguso, 6–4, 6–4, 2–6, 6–4, at Johannesburg.

Still, the historic highlight of the season occurred at Lyon when a French team, fortified by Guy Forget and Leconte—the first pair of lefties to win the Cup—and motivated by captain Yannick Noah, posted an inspirational victory over the U.S., returning the Davis Cup to France for the first time since 1932. Forget, who enjoyed his finest year as a pro with six singles titles and his first Top Ten ranking, defeated

Stefan Edberg made it back-to-back titles at the U.S. Open in 1992. • *Russ Adams*

When the 3–1 victory was complete, the ecstatic players lifted Noah to their shoulders and, with Gallic pride, paraded him in front of the fans like a loving cup.

1992

In a year in which the U.S. regained the summit of men's tennis, Americans accounted for all but one of the Grand Slam singles titles. Ironically, the championship that eluded them was the one they prized most, the U.S. Open. Stefan Edberg, the Swede who discovered New York can be a nice place to visit, triumphed at Flushing Meadow for the second consecutive year.

Elsewhere, however, the U.S. reigned supreme. Jim Courier added a second French title to the Australian crown he won five months earlier and finished the season as the No. 1 player in the world, the first Yank to claim that honor since John McEnroe in 1984. Andre Agassi finally annexed his first major at Wimbledon, of all places. And Pete Sampras, a beaten finalist at the U.S. Open, compiled the best match record, 70–18, while gaining No. 3 in the final ATP rankings.

Then, in a classic melding of generations, Courier, Agassi and Sampras combined with McEnroe to reclaim the Davis Cup for the U.S. Courier, a loser on opening day to Olympic champ Marc Rosset, won the clinching singles match in a 3–1 decision over astonishing first-time finalist Switzerland at Fort Worth, Tex. Agassi had led off by beating Jakob Hlasek, and Courier finished it over Hlasek, 6–3, 3–6, 6–3, 6–4. Sampras, devastated by his two singles losses to France a year earlier, teamed with the 33-year-old McEnroe to defeat Rosset and Hlasek in a gripping five-set doubles match, 6–7 (5–7), 6–7 (7–9), 7–5, 6–1, 6–2. The victory was especially sweet for McEnroe, who had indicated it was his last season of full-time competition, and was the first such comeback since Alex Olmedo and Ham Richardson beat Aussies Mal Anderson and Neale Fraser from 0–2 in 1958 Cup play.

The American influence was apparent throughout the entire tour as players from

For Andre Agassi, it was sweet strawberries at Wimbledon in 1992. • *Russ Adams*

the States accounted for 24 of the 82 singles titles, triple the total of runners-up Spain and Germany. Five U.S. citizens ranked among the Top Ten men, including No. 8 Ivan Lendl, who ended a 14-month drought by winning the Seiko championships in Tokyo three months after receiving his naturalization papers. In all, 43 individuals from 18 countries captured at least one tournament and no player won more than five.

Of the three who shared that distinction—Courier and Sampras were the other two—Boris Becker finished the year on the highest note. The German, shut out of a Grand Slam final for only the second time in eight years, won the ATP World Championship by defeating Courier, 6–4, 6–3, 7–5, in Frankfurt on his 25th birthday. It marked his third victory in the final eight weeks of the season and raised his ranking to No. 5.

A somber note was Arthur Ashe's revelation in April that he had contracted AIDS

through a blood transfusion while undergoing surgery in 1988. Characteristically, he asked not for sympathy, but continued a heavy schedule of obligations in charitable work and TV commentary. He also became active in the fight against AIDS, raising funds for education, research and treatment.

Competition among the women was more one-sided. For the second successive year, Monica Seles captured the Australian French and U.S. Open titles, won the Virginia Slims Championship, finished atop the WTA rankings and established a record for tennis earnings ($2,622,352). But, in 1992, she was not denied a Grand Slam by an error of omission.

This time she entered Wimbledon and took her case to the final, where she was overwhelmed by Steffi Graf. The German woman, whose eight victories included a four-tournament winning streak in the fall, demolished Seles, 6–2, 6–1, equalling Martina Navratilova's 6–0, 6–3 conquest of Andrea Jaeger in 1983 as the second most lopsided Wimbledon of the Open era. Graf's singles title was her fourth in five years at Wimbledon and her 11th in a Grand Slam event.

Although Navratilova slipped to No. 5 on the computer and failed to reach a Big Four final, she won Chicago over Jana Hovotna to break the record for most tournament victories she had shared with Chris Evert at 157. After saving two match points in beating Novotna, 7–6 (7–4), 4–6, 7–5, Martina concluded the season with three more titles for a total of 161, the last achieved in the Porsche Grand Prix at Filderstadt, Germany, on the occasion of her 36th birthday. And the grande dame did reach the last round of the Virginia Slims Championship in New York, where she was drubbed by Seles, 7–5, 6–3, 6–1.

Two months earlier, in a gimmick-ridden sendup of the Battle of the Sexes waged by Billie Jean King and Bobby Riggs 19 years earlier, Navratilova had unraveled in a match against Jimmy Connors at Caesars Palace. She double-faulted on set point in the first set and lost, 7–5, 6–2, despite getting two serves to her opponent's one and hitting into a court four feet wider. Each player received $500,000 in appearance money and Connors, who had won his first-round match over Jaime Oncins in the U.S. Open on his 40th birthday, earned an extra

Three months later, when they next met in the semifinals at Philadelphia, Graf drubbed the American teen-ager, 6–0, 6–1, en route to her fourth consecutive tournament victory. The German, upset by Lori McNeil in the first round of the Slims showdown the following week, finished the season ranked No. 2 behind Seles.

Graf was not on hand when Seles took

season in which she reportedly balked at the heavy schedule arranged by her father and appeared to lose her zest for tennis.

In contrast, the French Open provided some of the finest moments and tightest matches of the year. Merely to qualify for

It didn't have the hoopla of Bobby Riggs vs. Billy Jean King and it wasn't ladies' day for Martina Navratilova, humbled by Jimmy Connors in their made-for-Caesars-Palace exhibition at Las Vegas in 1992. • *Wide World*

Olympic gold was Jennifer Capriati's harvest in the 1992 Olympics at Barcelona. • *Russ Adams*

who committed 29 unforced errors in the last two sets. The result was a final for which the Paris fans were clamoring.

Their match, the first between the two in more than a year, disappointed no one save the loser and her family. And even Graf conceded it was a remarkable experience after saving five championship points in Seles' 6–2, 3–6, 10–8 victory that consumed two hours and 43 minutes. "It definitely was a special match, no doubt about it," Graf said.

For Seles, who became the first woman to win three consecutive French singles titles since Hilde Sperling in 1935–37, the match culminated an exhausting tournament that merely confirmed what the world already suspected. Namely, that she was the most tenacious as well as most successful tennis player on the planet. "That's the hardest I've ever had to work for a Grand Slam title," she decided after amassing her sixth major (and fifth in the last five she had entered.)

Four times Graf was confronted with a match point on her own serve at 3–5 in the third set. Four times she withstood the pressure. Fraulein Forehand then broke Seles in the 10th game when her opponent, suddenly impatient, committed four unforced errors. They exchanged service breaks in the 15th and 16th games before Graf, after saving a fifth match point in the 18th game, netted a forehand. The two-hour, 43-minute ordeal was over.

"In a match like this when you are out there for so long and the last set is so close, in my opinion, both players deserve to win," the champion said.

On the following day, Courier joined Seles, a fellow Florida resident, halfway to a Grand Slam. In the Australian Open final, he avenged the blowout by Edberg in the 1991 U.S. Open four months earlier by beating the Swede, 6–3, 3–6, 6–4, 6–2. He

an epic final against Graf, Seles twice had to rally from third-set deficits. The first of her comebacks occurred in the fourth round when she trailed No. 150-ranked Akiko Kijimuta of Japan, 1–4, before running off five consecutive games for a 6–1, 3–6, 6–4 victory. Then, in the semifinals, she was down 2–4 against the eminently more formidable Sabatini before putting her away, 6–3, 4–6, 6–4.

When it was over, the loser was dumbfounded. "She seemed tired and then suddenly she started hitting the ball very hard," Sabatini said. "I don't know where she got the power."

Graf also passed a critical test in the semifinals by overcoming Arantxa Sanchez Vicario, who had demolished the German, 6–0, 6–2, in similar circumstances a year earlier. When Graf lost the first set at love, she couldn't help but recall the scenario of 1991. Yet, she rallied for a 0–6, 6–2, 6–2 triumph with the help of her opponent,

celebrated the victory, which enabled him to leapfrog Edberg in the rankings, by jumping into the Yarra River.

His ascent to the top, the first of five changes at the top in 1992, ended nearly a seven-year drought for Americans since McEnroe was toppled from No. 1 in mid-1985 by Lendl. At 21 years, five months, Courier was the third-youngest male to hold ~~the No. 1 spot, after McEnroe (21 and 15~~

on hard work and mental strength because "I don't think he has a lot of natural ability to fall back on." Courier saved his talk for after the match, which he won most convincingly, 6–3, 6–2, 6–2.

"I've been reading about how I don't have much talent," Courier said. "There are many different talents besides hitting a tennis ball. Having guts on the court is a talent; having desire is a talent; having courage to go for a shot when you are love-40 down is a talent. I may not hit the ball as cleanly as anybody out there, but I have got a few talents that are just as good as anybody else's."

That triumph pushed his winning streak to 22 matches, which he extended in the final by blasting seventh-seeded Petr Korda of Czechoslovakia, 7–5, 6–2, 6–1. Unlike the women's final, the men's match offered little drama. Courier finished off his nervous opponent in one hour, 59 minutes. The normally free-swinging Korda, who had never previously advanced beyond the third round of a Big Four event, had 49 unforced errors and nine double faults.

"I think I played big feet today," he said. "I tell you I was very nervous. My

hand is still tight. I couldn't play my game. My body didn't work too much today."

So routine was the decision that the two-time champion received greater attention for his post-match behavior. He paid an imaginary golf-swing tribute to Johnny Carson, the retired talk-show host who occupied a courtside box, and he flavored his acceptance speech with French, charm~~ing the crowd at Roland Garros.~~

~~...upset in the third round~~ when he stumbled against an obscure Russian, the No. 193-ranked Andrei Olhovskiy, a qualifier, 6–4, 4–6, 6–4, 6–4. That defeat opened the door for McEnroe, a first-round washout at the French who had gained impetus in what he said would be his last Wimbledon Championship by beating Pat Cash and David Wheaton. The unseeded Mac dismissed Olhovskiy in the fourth round and then whipped Guy Forget of France to reach the semifinals, becoming the talk of tennis and a crowd favorite at the tournament where so often he had played the boor.

Awaiting him was another surprise. In the midst of a sour season, Agassi had managed to overcome his fear of grass to win five matches, most notably over three-time Wimbledon champ Becker in the quarters, 4–6, 6–2, 6–2, 4–6, 6–3. The meeting of the old rebel and the young anarchist was a stunning development, enriched by their growing friendship. After being thrust together on the Davis Cup team, they played doubles in the French Open, became occasional dinner companions and frequently practiced against each other.

Indeed, Agassi asked McEnroe for his advice on coping with the Wimbledon grass and the flattered former champion readily agreed. "We hit it off well," McEnroe said. "He's young, he's really inquisitive and he's very, very smart. He asks good questions."

Agassi learned his lessons well. The only help he needed from McEnroe on, fittingly, the Fourth of July was a reminder to bow to the Duke and Duchess of Kent as he was departing the court. Then again, he had played with such command he didn't want to leave.

The shaggy-haired American required only one hour, 51 minutes to cut down McEnroe, 6–4, 6–2, 6–3. Agassi, returning brilliantly, converted all seven break points he held, lost his serve only twice and was in control from the very first game, which McEnroe double-faulted away. At No. 12, Andre was not only the lowest seed to advance to the Wimbledon final since the unseeded Becker in 1985 but he found himself as the senior member of the pairing.

In the other half of the draw, Goran Ivanesevic of Croatia had defeated Pete Sampras, 6–7 (4–7), 7–6 (7–5), 6–4, 6–2, in a battle of 20-year-old prodigies with fearsome serves. The winner's deliveries were the more lethal, accounting for 36 aces. The slender left-hander from a war-torn region of what used to be Yugoslavia won a remarkable 91 percent of the points on his first serves and captured eight of the last 10 games.

Ironically, maturity may have been Agassi's greatest advantage in the final. He failed to wither when confronted by Ivanisevic's serve, which produced 37 more aces for a stunning tournament total of 206, failed to lose serve until the second game of the fourth set and appeared much more calm than the easily-distracted eighth seed. The 22-year-old Yank persevered 6–7 (8–10), 6–4, 6–4, 1–6, 6–4 for his first Grand Slam title.

At the moment of triumph, Andre whose past displays had seemed as calculated as his television commercials ("Image is everything"), fell to his knees, sprawled face-first on the turf and appeared genuinely moved. "I've realized my dream of winning a Grand Slam tournament," he said. "To do it here is more than I could ever ask for. If my career was over tomorrow, I got a lot more than I deserved, than I could ever ask for."

Nor did McEnroe leave the All England Club empty-handed. Fitter and sharper than he had been in years working with new coach Larry Stefanki, he teamed with Michael Stich, the grass-court whiz of 1991, to claim the men's doubles prize. The unseeded pair defeated fourth-seeded Americans Jim Grabb and Richie Reneberg in a match that consumed five hours and one minute, was decided by a 19–17 fifth set—Wimbledon's longest ultimate set— and had to be completed on the day following the singles championship because of rain delays.

Seles was a lot more successful than Courier in her assault on the grass but she also endured greater frustration. The complaints about her grunting actually grew in volume and opponents joined in the controversy fueled by the tabloid press. Nathalie Tauziat of France raised the issue before her straight-set dismissal in the quarterfinals and Navratilova did her one better, reporting Seles to umpire Fran McDowell, who called her to the chair for an admonition in the midst of the ladies' semifinal. Seles still prevailed, 6–2, 6–7 (3–7), 6–4.

"It just gets loud and louder," Navratilova said. "You cannot hear the ball being hit...I am not saying I lost because of her grunting. I would have said this if I won...I know she is not doing it on purpose, but she can stop it on purpose."

That's exactly what Seles did in the final. She barely uttered a peep against

Graf. Whether that was a cause or an effect of her listless performance was a matter for conjecture. The German woman was crisp and dominating from the outset and Seles appeared as limp as the weather, which forced three delays. Although the match lasted 5½ hours, only 58 minutes were devoted to tennis.

"I didn't want to think about it," the

1991 Federation Cup, Seles was not eligible for the Olympic tournament. Neither was Navratilova nor Sabatini. But Graf, who had helped Germany to the 1992 Federation Cup title over Spain the previous month, arrived for Barcelona clay in pursuit of a second consecutive gold medal.

She was one match away from a repeat of Seoul when Capriati, who had terminated Seles' streak of 21 consecutive final appearances at the Lipton in March but who hadn't won a tournament herself, emerged from her growing pains to stun Fraulein Forehand, 6–3, 3–6, 6–4. She bubbled with delight on the medal stand. "I had chills the whole time," the youngster said. "Right now this means more to me than any of the Grand Slams."

The men's competition on the slow courts produced a bigger surprise. Edberg lost in the first round to Andrei Chesnokov while Becker and Courier both were defeated by outsiders Fabrice Santoro and Marc Rosset in the third round. Courier's conqueror, the No. 43-ranked Rosset, went on to win the gold, beating Jordi Arrese of the host nation, 7–6 (7–2), 6–3, 3–6, 4–6, 8–6, while pounding 38 aces in the deciding match.

Becker and Stich combined to win the men's doubles for a unified German team over South Africa's Wayne Ferreira and Piet Norval, 7–6 (7–5), 4–6, 7–6 (7–5), 6–3. Ferreira-Norval were their nation's first medalists since 1960 in Rome, when South Africa took a silver in track and field, and two bronze in boxing. The unrelated Fernandez women, Gigi and Mary Joe, captured the gold medal in doubles for the

and the U.S. Open.

At Flushing Meadow, Navratilova suffered a shocking second-round defeat administered by Magdalena, the third of the three Maleeva sisters on the circuit. One year after she became the oldest woman's finalist in open tournament history, she was ousted by a 17-year-old precisely half her age, 6–4, 0–6, 6–3. It marked her earliest exit from the Open since 1976 when she departed in tears following a first-round knockout by Janet Newberry at Forest Hills.

Maggie advanced to the quarterfinals, where she fell to the oldest of her sisters, Manuela Maleeva Fragniere. In the same round Sanchez Vicario eliminated Graf in straight sets and Mary Joe Fernandez toppled Sabatini. The wave of upsets cleared any major obstacles from Seles' path and she cakewalked to the title without the loss of a set, turning back Fernandez in a semifinal, 6–3, 6–2, and Sanchez Vicario in the final, 6–3, 6–3. Seles was slowed only by a nasty cold and a sore throat.

The men had much greater difficulty settling their differences. The played from here to "Infiniti," which happened to be the corporate sponsor of the men's singles. Although all four top seeds reached the semis, it was not without a struggle.

Twenty-one matches lasted five sets and six consumed more than four hours. Edberg, the eventual champion, participated in three consecutive five-setters—against Richard Krajicek, Lendl and Michael Chang—all of which surpassed the four-hour mark. His 6–7 (3–7), 7–5, 7–6 (7–3), 5–7, 6–4 semifinal duel with the indefatigable Chang endured for five hours, 26 minutes, a record for major events no one will be in a hurry to break. It surpassed the 5:12 monster won by Pancho Gonzalez over Charlie Pasarell at Wimbledon in 1969.

By comparison, the final was swift and decisive. Edberg overcame Sampras, 3–6, 6–4, 7–6 (7–5), 6–2 in a tidy 2:52, winning his second consecutive Open title and regaining the No. 1 ranking. Sampras had defeated Courier in a four-set semifinal just before racing to the bathroom with stomach problems. Had he beaten Edberg, U.S. men would have swept all four Grand Slam championships for the first time since Don Budge did it singlehandedly in 1938. Their last triple was accomplished by Connors (Australian, Wimbledon, U.S.) in 1974.

Edberg got his comeuppance two weeks later when he suffered two losses in a 4–1 victory by the U.S. over Sweden at the Davis Cup semifinals in Minneapolis. Stefan was defeated in singles by Agassi, 5–7, 6–3, 7–6 (7–4), 6–3, after Courier rallied to beat Nicklas Kulti, 4–6, 7–6 (7–1), 6–3, 7–5. Then he and Anders Jarryd were overtaken in a five-set doubles match by McEnroe and Sampras, 6–1, 6–7 (2–7), 4–6, 6–3, 6–3. The Swede also lost his place at the top of the computer in the fall and failed a final opportunity at the ATP

World Championship when he was eliminated in preliminary round-robin play. Nevertheless, Edberg finished the season as the leader in official earnings, with $2,341,804.

Of course, Stich almost equalled that total in one December weekend. Although he plummeted from the Top 10, the German managed to regain his singles form in time for the Grand Slam Cup in Munich, where he won the first-place prize of $2 million by defeating Chang in the final. Semifinalist Ivanesevic belted 25 aces while losing to Chang, ending the year with a record 1,017.

The men's season was notable for two other developments. Lendl posted his 1,000th tour victory, second only to Connors, by beating Brett Steven of New Zealand at the Sydney indoor championships in October, and Borg, 36, failed to capture a set in eight matches of a murky comeback attempt. The former legend did, however, win his first tournament of any kind since 1981 when he handled Roscoe Tanner, 6–4, 6–1, at the Advanta Tour of Chicago for players 35 and older. The Australian duo of Todd Woodbridge and Mark Woodforde won eight doubles titles, including the ATP World Championship in Johannesburg.

Among the women, Navratilova pledged to continue playing a full schedule through 1993 but she ended the 12-year doubles partnership with Pam Shriver in order to concentrate on singles. After 79 titles, 20 Grand Slam championships and 10 trips to the winner's circle at the Virginia Slims Championship, they went their separate ways following the season-ending event at Madison Square Garden. The defending champions lost in the Slims semifinals, 6–4, 7–5, to the champs, Sanchez Vicario and Helena Sukova.

6: THE 35 GREATEST PLAYERS: 1946-92

a few exceptions, I believe the best tennis players have appeared since World War II, and probably even better ones are coming. Thus a selection of the foremost 35 (21 men, 14 women) inevitably neglects some standouts.

I also feel that greats in one era would be greats if transposed to another. Big Bill Tilden and Helen Wills, benefiting from startling improvements in equipment, coaching and training methods, immersed in a highly professionalized environment, would be champions today. So would Jack Kramer and Maureen Connolly, Rod Laver and Billie Jean King. Nobody has played the game any better.

But they would find themselves surrounded by a deeper, more imposing cast, hitting the ball harder, battling for fantastic financial awards, ever monitored by the cold-hearted computer ratings.

My faith in the current crop—hundreds of very good pros—is high, and I have cho-

While narrowing the field, with difficulty, to 35, I recognized that numerous others made records that deserve accolades, possibly inclusion, and were so highly regarded that they landed in the International Tennis Hall of Fame at Newport, R.I. In singling out the outstanding, I must also salute:

Bill Talbert, who ranked in the U.S. Top Ten 13 times between 1941 and 1954, who won 21 American titles (including the U.S. doubles four times with Gardnar Mulloy), and who played on two winning Davis Cup teams... Nicola Pietrangeli of Italy, who won the French (1959–60) and Italian (1957 and 1961) singles twice each and played and won more Davis Cup singles (78–32) and doubles (42–12) than anyone else... Tony Roche, who won the Italian and French singles in 1966, the U.S. Pro singles in 1970 as well as five Wimbledon doubles with John Newcombe, and who helped Australia win five Davis Cups... Darlene Hard, who won Forest Hills twice

(1960–61), the U.S. doubles five straight years with three different partners, and who helped the U.S. win four Wightman Cups and one Federation Cup... Virginia Wade, who won the Wimbledon (1977), Australian (1972), U.S. (1968), and Italian (1971) singles and helped Britain seize four Wightman Cups... Nancy Richey, who ranked in the U.S. Top Ten 16 times between 1960 and 1976, won the U.S. Clay Court title a record six straight times as well as the Australian (1967) and French (1968) singles and played on eight winning Wightman Cup teams... Frank Parker, who added two French titles and U.S. finals to a glittering pre-war career... Ashley Cooper, another of the Aussie Mob, who notched Australian, Wimbledon and U.S. titles... The Rosebud—Rosie Casals—a 5-footer whose doubles record made her seem a one-woman team: 11 majors, and a helping hand in four each of Wightman and Federation Cups for the U.S.... Vic Seixas, victor at Wimbledon in 1953, and at Forest Hills in 1954 where he played a record 28 times between 1939 and 1969... Argentine strongman Guillermo Vilas, winner of the Australian in 1978–79 and the U.S. and French in 1977 when he strung together a record open-era streak of 50 matches... Spunky little Missourian Chuck McKinley, winner of Wimbledon in 1963, three U.S. doubles titles (as well as the '63 Davis Cup) with Dennis Ralston... Aussie lefty Neale Fraser, important element in four Davis Cup winners, and conqueror of Forest Hills in 1959–60, Wimbledon in 1960... Another Aussie Cup hero of three triumphs, Fred Stolle, winner at Forest Hills in 1966 and the French in 1965 as well as 16 majors in doubles... Jaroslav Drobny, the wily Czechoslovak-born lefty who, when almost 33, added Wimbledon '54

to three Italian and two French titles... Tracy Austin, who accounted for two U.S. titles, 1979 and 1981, during a brief, injury-concluded career... Czechoslovak Davis Cup pillar Jan Kodes, winner of Wimbledon in 1973, the French in 1970–71... Psychedelic strokeswoman Francoise Durr, winner of her native French in 1967 plus 11 major doubles... Aussie Lesley Turner with two French singles plus 10 major doubles...

—Bud Collins

Arthur Ashe
United States (1943–93)

A singular figure in the game's history as the only black male to win a major singles titles—three of them in fact—Arthur Robert Ashe, Jr., also in 1968 set a record most unlikely to be equaled as winner of both the U.S. Amateur and Open championships, the first time such a double was possible. No one has come remotely close since.

That first season of the open era was a whirlwind year for him, then 1st Lt. Ashe of the U.S. Army. In order to maintain Davis Cup eligibility and gain time away from duty for important tournaments, Ashe was required to maintain his amateur status. Determining that the traditional (and previously amateur) National Singles Championships at Forest Hills would become the inaugural U.S. Open in 1968, the USTA designated Longwood Cricket Club in Boston as the site for a U.S. amateur tournament. Seeded first in Boston, Ashe came through to the title by surging past teammate Bob Lutz in the exciting final, 4–6, 6–3, 8–10, 6–0, 6–4.

However, with pros introduced to Forest Hills, Ashe was a lightly regarded fifth seed. Nevertheless, at 25, he came of age as an internationalist. Unflappable

Arthur Ashe: More than tennis. • *UPI*

over the New York fortnight, he served-and-volleyed splendidly. In the final he clocked 26 aces, returned with precision, and held his cool in a five-set final-round victory over pro Tom Okker, 14–12, 5–7, 6–3, 3–6, 6–3.

An amateur would never do so well again. As the last remaining pro, Okker got the $14,000 first prize while Ashe was happy to settle for $28 daily expenses for his historic triumph, the first major for a black since Althea Gibson's Forest Hills triumph a decade before. Not only that but Ashe boosted American morale by ending the U.S. male championship drought that dated back 13 years to Tony Trabert's 1955 win.

That year Ashe was also a Davis Cup drought-buster, spearheading the U.S. drive to the sterling tub last won five years before. He won 11 straight singles (the most in one campaign for an American) in the drive to retrieve the Cup from Australia

in Adelaide. In the finale he beat Ray Ruffels easily on opening day, and, after the Cup was clinched by Bob Lutz and Stan Smith in doubles, finally gave way, losing to Bill Bowrey in a meaningless third-day match. The season closed with Ashe winner of 10 of 22 tournaments on a 72–10 match record.

He would win both his singles in 1969 and 1970 as the U.S. successfully defended the Cup against Romania, then West Germany, at Cleveland. In the latter his third-day defeat of Christian Kuhnke, 6–8, 10–12, 9–7, 13–11, 6–4, was the longest match (86 games) in a Cup-deciding round. Eight years later he reappeared for a vital cameo that led to another Cup for the U.S.; his singles victory over Kjell Johansson helped edge Sweden, 3–2, in the semifinal at Goteborg.

Ashe put in 10 years of Davis Cup, topped for the U.S. only by John McEnroe's

12 and Bill Tilden and Stan Smith's 11 each, and won 27 singles, second only to McEnroe's 41.

He returned in 1981 as captain for five years, piloting the victors of 1981 and 1982.

Ashe was born July 10, 1943, in Richmond, Va., where he grew up. Since racial segregation was the law there during his childhood and early youth, Ashe could not play in the usual junior tournaments. With the aid of the concerned Lynchburg, Va., physician, Dr. Walter Johnson (who had also befriended and helped Althea Gibson), Ashe finished high school in St. Louis, where he could get the necessary tennis competition.

In 1961, after Dr. Johnson's lobbying got him into the previously segregated U.S. Interscholastic tourney, Ashe won it for Sumner High. Four years later, leading man of his alma mater's (University of California at Los Angeles) varsity, he won the U.S. Intercollegiate singles.

Although Ashe was ever a winner, a man of strong character, poised and able to overcome racial blocks, it took him a while to harness his power, groove his groundstrokes and become a thoughtful player, comfortable on all surfaces. As one whose career overflowed the amateur and open eras, he followed the 1968 breakthrough with 11 sterling years as a professional that netted 33 singles titles including the 1970 Australian and the gloriously unexpected: Wimbledon '75. He won 35 amateur singles tournaments.

In 1975, days before his 32nd birthday, seeded sixth, he was a longer shot than he had been seven years earlier at Forest Hills. Defending champ Jimmy Connors, seemingly inviolable, was a 10-to-1 favorite in the final, but Ashe was too slick and cerebral in one of the momentous upsets, 6–1, 6–1, 5–7, 6–4. Changing pace and spin cleverly, startling Connors with a sliced serve wide

to the two-fisted backhand, Ashe foxed the man a decade his junior.

This was the centerpiece of Ashe's pre-eminent year, a heavy-duty season when he won nine of 29 tourneys on a 108–23 match record and wound up No. 1 in the U.S., No. 4 in the world. He reached No. 2 in 1976. Improving with age, he unfortunately was grounded prematurely, and permanently, by a heart attack in July 1979. In 1992 he revealed that he'd contracted AIDS through a 1988 blood transfusion.

For 12 years he was in the World Top Ten, and for 14 years, through 1979, in the U.S. Top Ten, No. 1 in 1968 and 1975. He was one of the founders of the ATP in 1972, served as president and had been a reasoned, intelligent spokesman for the game, served on numerous corporate boards and received several honorary degrees. He entered the Hall of Fame in 1985. He died Feb. 6, 1993, leaving his wife, Jeanne, and six-year-old daughter, Camera.

MAJOR TITLES (5)—*Australian singles, 1970; Wimbledon singles, 1975; U.S. singles, 1968; Australian doubles, 1977; French doubles, 1971.* OTHER U.S. TITLES—*Amateur singles, 1968; Clay Court singles, 1967; Hard Court singles, 1963; Intercollegiate singles, 1965; Indoor doubles, 1967, with Charles Pasarell; 1970, with Stan Smith; Clay Court doubles, 1970, with Clark Graebner; Intercollegiate doubles, 1965, with Ian Crookenden.* DAVIS CUP (As player)—*1963–65–66–67–68–69–70–75–77–78; record: 27–5 in singles, – in doubles; (As captain)—1981–82–83–84–85; record: 13-3, 2 Cups.*

Boris Becker
Germany (1968–   )

A redheaded phenomenon, Boris Becker illuminated 1985 and 1986 with his Wimbledon triumphs at the improbable ages of 17 and 18.

The records came tumbling down in 1985 when the unseeded German teenager beat eighth-seeded Kevin Curren, 6–3, 6–7

(4–7), 7–6 (7–3), 6–4, in the final. He was the first German champ, first non-seed to win—Boris was ranked No. 20—and the youngest male ever to win a major at 17 years, 7 months. (Michael Chang, at 17–3, lowered that four years later in winning the French).

A big man (6-foot-4, 180) playing a big, carefree game of booming serves, heavy

Boris Becker: A boomer. • *Mitchell Reibel*

ne carried his country to the 1985 final in Munich and beat both Stefan Edberg and Mats Wilander in the 3–2 loss to Sweden.

Three years after that he lifted the Fatherland to the Cup in a 4–1 victory over the Swedes in Goteborg. Boris beat Edberg, then paired with Eric Jelen for the clinching doubles win over Edberg and Anders Jarryd. In 1989 he won both his singles, the doubles again with Jelen at Stuttgart as Germany kept the Cup, 3–2, over Sweden. His third-day beating of Wilander, 6–2, 6–0, 6–2, was the clincher.

By the close of the 1992 season he had won 21 straight Cup singles, and had lost only two of 34 starts, both to Sergio Casal of Spain.

Becker beat Ivan Lendl in straight sets for his second Wimbledon title, and Edberg just as swiftly in 1989 for a third, developing the feeling that Centre Court was his special haunt. He and Edberg also contested the 1988 and 1990 finals, Edberg winning. They were the first men in almost a century, since Wilfred Baddeley and Joshua Pim split the finals in 1891–92–93–94, to monopolize the final for at least three successive years. In the only all-German final on Centre

Court, Michael Stich upset him in 1991. After the 1992 tourney, when Becker lost to champion Andre Agassi in the quarters, his Wimbledon match record was 46–6.

Boris Franz Becker, a right-hander, was born Nov. 22, 1967, in the small town of Leiman, Germany, and grew up there, not far from Bruhl, where the other German wunderkind, Steffi Graf, was raised. A promising junior, he dropped from high school to become a pro. An atypical European, he prefers faster surfaces to his native clay. His best finishes at the French have been semifinals in 1989 and 1991.

At the conclusion of 1988 he squashed Ivan Lendl's bid for a sixth Masters title by the narrowest possible of final-round margins—two points—on a net-cord dribbler that won the fifth-set tie-breaker, 7–5. It stands as one of the two closest significant tournament finishes, along with Ken Rosewall's 1972 WCT (World Championship Tennis) victory over Rod Laver, also a fifth-set tie-breaker, 7–5.

His marvelous 1989 season, during which he won six of 13 tournaments on a 64–8 match record, included his fourth major, the U.S. Open in a 7–6 (7–2), 1–6, 6–3, 7–6 (7–4) victory over No. 1-ranked Ivan Lendl. It was the lone major male final to conclude in a tie-breaker.

His fifth major (the third he won over Lendl) was the Australian at the outset of 1991, giving him the No. 1 ranking momentarily. During his nine years as a pro he has been in the World Top Ten eight times and won 36 singles titles, standing ninth on the all-time roll.

In 1992 he won an Olympic gold in doubles, alongside Stich, in a 7–6 (7–5), 4–6, 7–6 (7–5), 6–3 triumph over South Africa's Wayne Ferreira and Piet Norval. By the close of 1992 his prize money amounted to $11,670,442.

MAJOR TITLES (5)—*Australian singles, 1991; Wimbledon singles, 1985–86–89; U.S. singles, 1989.* DAVIS CUP—*1985–86–87–88–89–91–92; record: 32–2 in singles, 12–6 in doubles.*

Pauline Betz
United States (1919–   )

Many believe Pauline May Betz Addie was the finest of the post-World War II players of the U.S., even though her career was cut short in her prime by a controversial ruling by the USTA. In 1947 she was declared a professional for merely exploring the possibilities of making a pro tour.

There was no pro tennis as such for women at the time, but she did make two tours of one-night stands against Sarah Palfrey Cooke in 1947, and Gussy Moran in 1951, dominating both opponents. Then she became a teaching professional and married sportswriter Bob Addie.

Born Aug. 6, 1919, in Dayton, Ohio, she grew up in Los Angeles, and became noted for her extreme speed and mobility. She was quick to the net, a pleasure to

Pauline Betz: Speediest afoot. • *New York Herald Tribune*

watch as she attacked with sureness and a firm finishing touch.

World War II deprived her of the chance for much international play, but she won Wimbledon the only time she entered, in 1946, without losing a set. Her closest match was the 6–2, 6–4 final with Louise Brough. In Betz's only Wightman Cup match against Britain, in 1946, she helped the U.S. win by taking both her singles matches and her doubles.

Betz was first ranked in the U.S. Top Ten, at No. 8 in 1939, and stayed in that select group for seven more years, standing at No. 1 in 1942–43–44 and 1946, the years she won the U.S. Championship in singles at Forest Hills. She held the No. 1 world ranking in 1946.

Two other years, 1941 and 1945, she was runner-up, thus setting a Forest Hills record of six straight years in the final. In playing Forest Hills eight times, she won 33 of 37 matches.

She captured 19 U.S. titles on various surfaces, including the Clay Court singles in 1941 and 1943 and the Indoor singles in 1939–41–43–47. Twice she scored triples at the Indoor Championships, winning the singles, doubles and mixed doubles in 1941 and 1943, a feat equaled only by Billie Jean King in 1966 and 1968.

Tennis historian Jerome Scheuer

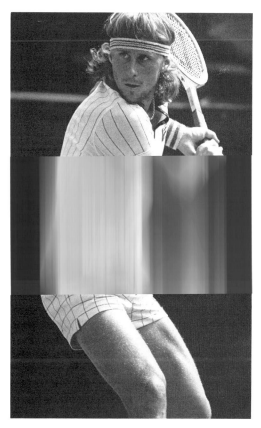

Bjorn Borg: Power without passion. • *Mitchell Reibel*

Dorothy Bundy; 1943, with Hazel Hotchkiss Wightman; Indoor mixed, 1939, with Wayne Sabin; 1940, with Bobby Riggs; 1941–43, with Al Stitt; Clay Court singles, 1941–43; Clay Court doubles, 1943, with Nancy Corbett; 1944–45, with Doris Hart. WIGHTMAN CUP—*1946; record: 2–0 in singles, 1–0 in doubles.*

Bjorn Borg
Sweden (1956–)

Before he was 21, Bjorn Rune Borg had registered feats that would set him apart as one of the game's greats—and before he was 26, the headbanded, golden-locked Swede was through. No male career of the modern era has been so brief and bright.

Tennis is filled with instances of precocious achievements and championships, but none is quite as impressive as those of the seemingly emotionless Borg. Just before his 18th birthday he was the youngest winner of the Italian Championship, and two weeks later he was the youngest winner of the French Championship (a record lowered by Mats Wilander, 17, in 1982, and subsequently by Michael Chang, a younger 17 in 1989). Eighteen months later, at 19, he climaxed a Davis Cup record winning streak of

19 singles by lifting Sweden to the 1975 Cup for the first time in a 3–2 final-round victory over Czechoslovakia. His Cup singles streak of 33 was intact at his retirement, still a record.

Although Lew Hoad and Ken Rosewall were a few months younger in 1953 when they won the Davis Cup for Australia, both were beaten during the final round. But Borg won both his singles and teamed with Ove Bengtson for the doubles win. Borg's Davis Cup debut at 16 in 1972 as one of the youngest ever in that competition was phenomenal: a five-set win over seasoned pro Onny Parun of New Zealand. Borg was also the youngest winner of the oldest professional championship, the U.S. Pro, whose singles he took in 1974 at 18 (and, subsequently, 1975 and 1976). Aaron Krickstein, 16, lowered that record in 1984.

A player of great strength and endurance he has a distinctive and unorthodox style and appearance. He is bowlegged, yet very fast. His muscular shoulders and well-developed torso give him the strength to lash at the ball with heavy topspin on both forehand and backhand. He uses a two-handed backhand, adapted from the slap shot in hockey, a game he favored as a child. By the time he was 13 he was beating the best of Sweden's under-18 players and Davis Cup captain Lennart Bergelin cautioned against anyone trying to change Borg's rough-looking, jerky strokes. They were effective. Through 1977 he had never lost to a player younger than himself.

Born June 6, 1956, in Sodertalje, Sweden, where he grew up, Bjorn was fascinated by a tennis racket his father had won as a prize in a ping-pong tournament. His father gave him the racket and that was the start.

Borg prefers to battle from the baseline, trading groundstrokes tirelessly in long rallies, retrieving and waiting patiently to outlast his opponent. Volleying, with his Western grip forehand and two-fisted backhand, was troublesome, and his serve was not impressive at first. He didn't do much on grass until 1976, when he was determined to win Wimbledon, and did so after devoting himself to two weeks of solid practice on serve-and-volley tactics. He won the most important tournament without loss of a set, beating favored Ilie Nastase in the final, 6–4, 6–2, 9–7. Borg was the youngest champion of the modern era at 20 years, one month, until Boris Becker, 17, won in 1985.

Borg repeated in 1977, although the tournament was more demanding. His thrilling five-set victories over Americans Vitas Gerulaitis in the semifinals and Jimmy Connors in the final were considered two of the best ever played at Wimbledon. By that time Borg had more confidence and proficiency in his volleying . Borg repeated over Connors in 1978, becoming the first to win three successive years since Fred Perry (1934–36). He made it four in a row with a five-set triumph over American Roscoe Tanner in the 1979 final, thus becoming the first player since Tony Wilding (1910–13) to win four straight years.

His fifth straight Wimbledon championship, in 1980, climaxed with an all-time great final, a 1–6 , 7–5, 6–3, 6–7 (16–18), 8–6 triumph over John McEnroe. During one of the most electrifying passages in tennis history, the 34-point tie-breaker, Borg was stymied on five match points and saved six set points before giving way. But his famous resolve brought him through in the brilliantly battled fifth.

Borg, a right-hander, was now flirting with the ancient Wimbledon record of six straight titles. That was the much less demanding feat of Willie Renshaw (1881—86) since in that day of the challenge round format, Renshaw needed to play only one match to win the last five titles. Thus his match winning streak was only 13, up to an 1888 defeat by Willoughby Hamilton.

While winning 1980, Borg also surpassed Laver's Wimbledon male match winning-streak record of 31. Bjorn built that to his own record 41 (Helen Wills Moody won 50 straight between 1927 and 1938) by reaching the 1981 final. There he was finally dethroned by McEnroe, 4–6, 7–6 (7–4), 7–6 (5–7), 6–4.

When he won his male record sixth French title in 1981, with another record, his 28th straight match win, it seemed that Borg, then 25, would surely surpass Roy Emerson's male record of 12 major singles titles. Borg had 11. But he would not win another, remaining tied with Laver.

His left-handed nemesis, McEnroe, followed up on Wimbledon by beating Borg in a second successive U.S. Open final to take over the No. 1 ranking that the Swede had held in 1979–80. That defeat, 4–6, 6–2, 6–4, 6–3, effectively ended Borg's career. He retired not long after with 62 tournament titles, including the Masters of 1978 and 1979, and was inducted into the Hall of Fame in 1987. Nevertheless, he did

Tribune

Tanner his conqueror in 1979.

Borg's career prize money was $3,609,896.

MAJOR TITLES (11)—*French singles, 1974–75–78–79–80–81; Wimbledon singles, 1976–77–78–79–80. DAVIS CUP—1972–73–74–75–78–79–80; record: 37–3 in singles, 8–8 in doubles.*

Louise Brough
United States (1923–   )

One of the great volleyers in history was Althea Louise Brough, whose handiwork at the net earned her 13 titles at Wimbledon alone, in singles, doubles and mixed, including a rare triple—championships in each—in 1950. Of the foremost U.S. females only Chris Evert (19 times) and Billie Jean King (18) lasted longer in the Top Ten. Brough was there 16 times between 1941 and 1957, No. 1 in 1947. She was in the World Top Ten 12 times, 1946 through 1957, No. 1 in 1955.

Louise Brough was born March 11, 1923, in Oklahoma City, Okla., but grew up in Southern California, where she came to prominence as a junior, winning the national 18-and-under title in 1940 and 1941.

Wimbledon was not held during World War II, but when the tournament reopened in 1946 Brough was ready to play a dominant role for a decade in the leading tournament, and is recalled by the British as one of the most overwhelming players to compete there. In the first postwar visit she appeared in every final and just missed out on a triple, losing the singles final to Pauline Betz. But the right-handed Brough won the doubles with Margaret duPont and the mixed doubles with Tom Brown. During the Brough decade a Wimbledon final without her was unusual. Between 1946 and 1955, she won her way into 21 of the 30 finals, taking the singles in 1948–49–50–55, the doubles also in 1948–49–50–54 with duPont, and the mixed doubles also in 1947–48 with John Bromwich and in 1950 with Eric Sturgess.

Although she won the U.S. Singles Championship at Forest Hills only in 1947, she was a finalist on five other occasions. Doubles was the stage for her utmost success in the U.S., allied with duPont in possibly the finest female team ever, certainly the most victorious in major events. They won 20 Big Four titles together (12 U.S., five Wimbledon, three French), a mark equaled by Martina Navratilova and Pam Shriver in 1989.

Included in their record dozen U.S. titles was the longest championship run in any of the Big Four Events: nine straight doubles between 1942 and 1950. (Max Decugis and Maurice Germot won the French doubles 10 straight times between 1906 and 1920, but competition then was restricted to French citizens.) Brough and duPont did not enter the U.S. doubles in 1951 and 1952, but they returned to increase their record match winning streak to 41 before narrowly losing the 1953 final to Doris Hart and Shirley Fry, 6–2, 7–9, 9–7, despite holding two match points. As a team in the U.S. doubles they won 12 of 14 times entered and 58 of 60 matches, losing but five sets.

Altogether, Brough won 35 of the major titles in singles, doubles and mixed doubles to rank fifth on the all-time list behind Margaret Court (62), Martina Navratilova (54), Billy Jean King (39) and Margaret duPont (37). Brough won the Australian singles in 1950. Her various U.S. titles amounted to 18, and she was inducted into the Hall of Fame in 1967.

A willowy blonde, she was quiet and diffident, but the killer in the left court when at play alongside duPont. Despite their close friendship and partnership, they were keen rivals in singles, and Brough's most difficult Wimbledon triumphs were the three-set wins over duPont in 1949–50, the most stirring the 10–8, 1–6, 10–8 decision in 1949.

After retiring from the amateur circuit she married Dr. A. T. Clapp, and later occasionally played in senior (over-40) tournaments, winning the U.S. Hard Court Doubles in that category in 1971 and 1975 with Barbara Green Weigandt.

MAJOR TITLES (35)—*Australian singles; 1950; Wimbledon singles, 1948–49–50–55; U.S. sin-* *gles, 1947; Australian doubles, 1950; French doubles, 1946–47–49; Wimbledon doubles, 1946–48–49–50–55; U.S. doubles, 1942–43–44–45–46–47–48–49–50–55–56–57; Wimbledon mixed, 1946–47–48–50; U.S. mixed, 1942–47–48–49.* OTHER U.S. TITLE—*Hard Court doubles; 1948, with duPont.* WIGHTMAN CUP—*1946–47–48–49–50–52–53–54–55–56–57; record: 12–0 in singles, 10–0 in doubles.*

Maria Bueno
Brazil (1939–)

Maria Esther Andion Bueno came swirling out of Brazil as a teenager to quickly establish herself as one of the world's most graceful and proficient athletes, a delight to watch and dangerous to deal with since she had a wide repertoire of shots and the skill and grace to deliver them constantly.

As the São Paulo Swallow, she was slim and quick, swooping to the net to conquer with piercing volleys. She was a blend of power and touch, a woman of superb movement and rhythms. Stylishly gowned by the tennis couturier, Ted Tinling, she was the frilly treasure of Wimbledon's Centre Court, where she was at her best and won eight titles: three in singles (1959, 1960, 1964), and five in doubles.

Grass was her favorite surface, suiting her attacking nature. Born Oct. 11, 1939, in São Paulo, she was clearly the best female player to come from Latin America, and was rated No. 1 in the world in 1959, 1960, 1964 and 1966, a member of the Top Ten 10 times between 1958 and 1968.

In her regal choreography, the versatile right-hander was one of a triumvirate of women—including Frenchwoman Suzanne Lenglen and Australian Evonne Goolagong—whose fluidity and artistry set them apart.

She was agreeable, but reserved, a private person who underwent a number of physical agonies, harming her career, with-

Maria Bueno: Fluidity and artistry. • *Peter Mecca*

out complaint. Her best days were as an amateur. By the time open tennis and prize money dawned in 1968 she was hobbled by a variety of arm and leg injuries. After a long retirement, she felt sufficiently well to try the pro tour in 1975, and returned to Wimbledon for a spiritual triumph in 1976 after a hiatus of seven years. There were glimpses of the wondrous Maria as she won three rounds, and most spectators were gratified to see her again. "In her day she was so marvelous to watch," said Billie Jean King, an old rival and doubles accomplice, after defeating Maria at Wimbledon in 1977. "But it was painful to play her today. I wanted to remember her as she was."

Bueno seemed undismayed to be a loser. "I have always loved tennis, and still enjoy playing. I've had my glory," she said.

At 18, in the company of Althea Gibson, Maria won her first Wimbledon prize, the doubles of 1958. In all she won 19 Big Four titles in singles, doubles and mixed, includ-

ing the U.S. Singles at Forest Hills in 1959–1963–64–66. She and American Darlene Hard were one of the best teams, taking the Wimbledon title twice and the U.S. twice. Maria's skill at doubles was such that she won her 12 majors with six partners and in 1960 scored one of three doubles Grand Slams, with two partners: Christine Truman in the Australian, Hard in the French, Wimbledon and U.S.

bles, 1960–62–66–68; French mixed, 1960.
FEDERATION CUP—*1965; record: 1–0 in singles, 0–1 in doubles.*

Maureen Connolly
United States (1934–1969)

A too brief flash on the tennis scene was that of Maureen Catherine Connolly, but it was of such incandescence that she may have been the finest of all female players.

Nicknamed "Little Mo" for her big-gunning, unerring ground strokes (it was an allusion to "Big Mo," the U.S. battleship *Missouri*), she was devastating from the baseline, and seldom needed to go to the net. A small and compact, right-hander (5-foot-5, 127 pounds), she won her major singles championships as a teenager: three successive Wimbledons, 1952–53–54, and U.S. Championships at Forest Hills, 1951–52–53. At 16 years, 11 months, she was the youngest U.S. champ ever until Tracy Austin won in 1979 at 16 years, 9 months. In addition, Connolly won three other American titles and held the No. 1 U.S. rankings of 1951–53. She was undisputed world leader in 1951–54.

Connolly was born Sept. 17, 1934, in San Diego, Cal., and grew up there. She

Maureen Connolly: The force of a battleship. • *UPI*

was a pupil of Eleanor "Teach" Tennant, an instructor who had guided a previous world champ, Alice Marble. Connolly first came East in 1949 to win the U.S. junior title and would soon dominate the world while still technically a junior, not yet 19.

A cheerful and sporting competitor, she crushed the opposition, never losing an important match, only occasionally losing a set. She helped the U.S. beat Britain in the Wightman Cup matches of 1951–54, winning all seven of her singles.

Fifteen years after Don Budge scored the first Grand Slam, Connolly traveled the same route in 1953, winning all the major singles championships (Australian, French, Wimbledon, U.S.) within a calendar year to achieve the first female Slam. She lost only one set in doing so. That season she won 10 of 12 tournaments on a 61–2 match record. By winning the three French titles in 1954 she became the fourth of five players to score a triple in Paris.

By 1954 her playing career was over, aborted by an unusual traffic accident: the horse she was riding was struck by a truck and she received a severe leg injury. By then she was Mrs. Norman Brinker. She recovered sufficiently to give tennis instruction, and helped a number of players with their games, but she died at 34 in 1969 of cancer.

She was inducted into the Hall of Fame in 1968 and is memorialized by the Maureen Connolly Brinker Cup, an international team competition between the U.S. and Britain for girls under 21.

"Whenever a great player comes along you have to ask, "could she have beaten Maureen?" That was the standard of Lance Tingay, the Hall of Fame tennis correspondent of the *Daily Telegraph* of London. "In every case the answer is, I think not."

MAJOR TITLES (12)—*Australian singles, 1953; French singles, 1953–54; Wimbledon singles, 1952–53–54; U.S. singles, 1951–52–53; Australian doubles, 1953; French doubles, 1954; French mixed, 1954.* OTHER U.S. TITLES—*Clay Court singles, 1953–54; Clay Court doubles, 1954, with Doris Hart.* WIGHTMAN CUP—*1951–52–53–54; record: 7–0 in singles, 2–0 in doubles.*

Jimmy Connors
United States (1952–   )

A marvel of longevity and self-motivation, he has been (as one-time agent Bill Riordan boasted) "the one and only James Scott Connors."

Fiery of temperament and shotmaking, this lefty with a two-fisted backhand has pounded foes for more than two professional decades in rip-roaring baseline style, a ragdoll throwing himself into his groundies with utter gusto. Often controversial, he fought verbally with opponents, officials and the crowd.

Considered a feisty wiseguy in his earlier days, he eventually became a respected elder. The championships, honors and prize money piled up, but not as high as his zeal as he continued to compete forcefully against much younger men into his 41st year and through the 1992 season when he roused galleries in Paris, London and New York and compiled a 17–15 match record, ending the season with a remarkable No. 83 ranking.

Jimmy Connors: Ageless, two-fisted backhander.
• *Wide World*

His particular feat has been the U.S. Open (five championships), where he was singular in winning on all three surfaces: grass (1974) and clay (1976) at Forest Hills, and hard (1978–82–83) at Flushing Meadow.

But he also won Wimbledon twice (1974 and 1982) and the Australian (1974) for a total of eight singles majors, second only to Bill Tilden's 10 among American men, and tied with Fred Perry and Ken Rosewall for fourth on the all-time roll.

Perhaps the most extraordinary year of his certain progression toward the Hall of Fame was 1991. His career had seemed ended. Troubled by a deteriorated left elbow he had played (and lost) only three matches in 1990, dropping to No. 936 in the rankings. However, surgery restored him, and he came back smoking, playing 14 tournaments and climaxing with a phenomenal semifinal finish (his 14th) at the U.S. Open.

His first- and second-round victories as a Wimbledon wild card raised his tournament male record to 84 match wins. Wild-carded again at Flushing, because of a No. 174 ranking, Jimmy exploded by beating

Patrick McEnroe from two sets down and 10th-seeded Karel Novacek, and celebrated his 39th birthday in a tumultuous victory over Aaron Krickstein, soaring from 2–5 in the fifth set to win in a stirring tie-breaker. Then he beat Paul Haarhuis from a set and a break down, stalling at last against Jim Courier. He was the oldest semifinalist since 39-year-old Rosewall lost the title match to none other than James himself 17 years before. Although Stefan Edberg won the title, it was Connors' Open in the public eye.

Ever a sensational celebrator of his own birthday (he has won 10 of 11 matches on that day at the U.S. Open), Jimmy took the cake on his 40th by beating Jaime Oncins, notching a tournament-record 98th match win.

He was raised to be a tennis player by his mother, a teaching pro named Gloria Thompson Connors. Connors grew up in Belleville, Ill., across the Mississippi from

St. Louis. Although he was always smaller than his contemporaries on his way up the ladder, he made up for that through determination and grit. He played in his first National Championship, the U.S. boys' 11-and-under of 1961, when he was only eight. He was born Sept. 2, 1952, in East St. Louis, Ill., and claimed to have begun playing when he was two. "My mother rolled balls to me, and I swung at them. I held the racket with both hands because that was the only way I could lift it."

Connors became known as a maverick when he refused to join the ATP (Association of Tennis Pros) in 1972, the then new union embracing most male professionals, and avoided the mainstream of pro tennis to play in and dominate a series of smaller tournaments organized by Bill Riordan, his manager, a clever promoter.

In 1974 he and Riordan began bringing lawsuits, eventually amounting to $10 million, against the ATP and its president, Arthur Ashe, for allegedly restricting his freedom in the game. It stemmed from Connors' banning by the French Open in 1974 after he had signed a contract to play WTT (World Team Tennis) for Baltimore. Connors had sought to enter the French, the only major championship he did not win that year, but because the ATP, and French administration, opposed WTT—conflicting with their tournament—the entries of WTT players were refused. The 1975 Wimbledon final, then, was unique, a duel between opponents in a lawsuit. Ashe won, and shortly thereafter Connors dropped the suits, and parted with Riordan.

Deprived unfairly by the French of a second leg on what might have been a Grand Slam, Connors nevertheless enjoyed in 1974 one of the finest seasons ever, the best by an American since Tony Trabert's 1955. Connors lost only four matches in 20 tournaments, while winning 99.

Among the 14 tournaments he won—a record for American male pros—were the

Australian, Wimbledon, South African, U.S. at Forest Hills, U.S. Clay Court and U.S. Indoor. He was clearly the No. 1 player in the world, a status he also held in 1975–76–77–78, an open-era record for continuous hegemony. He took over No. 1 in July 1974, held it 159 straight weeks and was there a total of 263 weeks, second only to Ivan Lendl's 269.

Although he trailed his foremost rivals head-to-head—Bjorn Borg, 7–10; John McEnroe, 13–20; Lendl, 13–22—he had great moments at their expense. He saved four set points to win a thrilling and vital 11–9 third-set tie-breaker while beating Borg in the 1976 Forest Hills final, and stunned the Swede (his conqueror at Wimbledon) to take the inaugural Flushing Meadow final in 1978. Three points from defeat in the fourth-set tie-breaker, he startled McEnroe to win Wimbledon in five sets in 1982, bridging a gap of eight years between titles there. Jimmy's incredible service returning jolted Lendl in the 1982–83 U.S. Open finals.

By winning the U.S. Indoor singles three straight (1973—75) he tied a record set by Gus Touchard (1913—15) He made this his most successful tourney, adding wins in 1978–79 and 1983–84 for a record total of seven. At the U.S. Clay Court in 1974–76–78–79, his four titles were the most since Frank Parker's five between 1933 and 1947.

Connors seemed to delight in keeping the public off-balance. He annoyed numerous tennis fans in the U.S. with his sometimes vulgar on-court behavior, and his refusal to play Davis Cup (except briefly in the 1976–81–84 seasons). He was booed at Wimbledon—a rare show of disapproval there—for snubbing the Parade of Champions on the first day of the Centenary in 1977.

After irritating sponsors and tennis officials by shunning the climactic Masters for three years, Connors entered and won the 1977 event over Bjorn Borg, having qualified by finishing among the top eight in the worldwide Grand Prix series.

His two crushing final-round victories over Ken Rosewall in 1974 (6–1, 6–1, 6–4 at Wimbledon, and 6–1, 6–0, 6–1, at Forest Hills) made Connors seem invincible. His manager, Riordan, proclaimed Jimmy

five successive U.S. finals, the first man to do so since Bill Tilden (1918–25). He was the first since Fred Perry (1933–34 and 1936) to win the U.S. title three years. Connors was beaten in the finals by Manolo Orantes in 1975 and by Guillermo Vilas in 1977, striking the last ball, an error, in championship play in Forest Hills Stadium.

Jimmy went to college one year at the University of California at Los Angeles, where he won the U.S. Intercollegiate Singles in 1971 and attained All-American status.

It was in 1973 that he made his first big splash by winning the U.S. Pro Singles, his first significant title, at 20, toppling Ashe, the favorite, in a five-set final. Ashe said, "I've played them all, and I never saw anybody hit the ball so hard for so long as Jimmy did." That year Connors was ranked co-No. 1 in the U.S. with Stan Smith, but was No. 1 alone seven other years, and in the U.S. Top Ten a record 20 times. During his 21 year-pro career he was in the World Top Ten 16 times. His prize money amounted to $8,471,435.

MAJOR TITLES (10)—*Australian singles, 1974; Wimbledon singles, 1974–82; U.S. singles,*

1974–76–78–82–83; French doubles, 1973; U.S. doubles, 1975. OTHER U.S. TITLES—*Indoor singles, 1973–74–75–78–79–83–84; Clay Court singles, 1974–76–78–82–83; Indoor doubles, 1974, with Frew McMillan; 1975, with Ilie Nastase; Clay Court doubles, 1974, with Nastase; Pro singles, 1973.* DAVIS CUP—*1976–81–84; record: 10–3 in singles.*

Margaret Smith Court
Australia (1942–   )

female Grand Slam. She is the only player to achieve a Slam in doubles as well as in singles; Margaret and Ken Fletcher won the four titles in mixed in 1963.

Her closest rivals statistically are not close: Martina Navratilova with 54 majors, and Roy Emerson heading the men with 28. Court has 24 alone in singles.

From the country town of Albury in New South Wales, where she was born July 16, 1942, Margaret was one of the first Australian notables to be developed outside of the principal cities. Tall and gangling, nearly six feet, she worked hard in the gym and on the road, as well as oncourt, to attain coordination and to marshal her prodigious strength. She was self-made through determination and training. Her power and incredible reach ("I call her the Arm," said rival Billie Jean King) first paid off and called international attention to her when she won the Australian singles at 18 in 1960. It was the first of her record 11 conquests of her homeland, the first seven in a row.

In 1961 she traveled abroad for the first time and played, in her first Wimbledon final, the doubles that she and

Margaret Smith Court: "The Arm" and the attack. • *UPI*

Court was primarily an attacker, basing her game on a heavy serve and volley, and relying on athleticism and endurance. She could conquer with ground strokes, though, as she demonstrated in stopping clay-court terror Chris Evert in the splendid French final of 1973. Sometimes Court fell prey to nerves, as in her 1971 Wimbledon final defeat by the crowd's favorite, Evonne Goolagong; or the bizarre televised challenge by 55-year-old Bobby Riggs in 1973, which she lost implausibly and badly. She couldn't reach the inspirational heights of her chief foe, King, but held a lifetime edge over Billie Jean, 22–10.

Her Grand Slam year, 1970, make those of Maureen Connolly, 1953 (12 tournaments) and Steffi Graf, 1988 (14 tournaments) seem almost leisurely. Court won 21 of 27 tournaments on a 104–6 match record, earning $14,800 for the four titles while Graf's prize money take for the four was $877,724. Connolly was an amateur, and certainly several of Court's best years were as such during an 18-year career. As an amateur she had such years as 1962 (winning 13 of 15 tournaments on a 67–2 match record) and 1964 (13 of 16 on 67–2, including a 39-match winning streak).

She won 79 pro singles titles, had her last sensational season in 1973, winning 18 of 25 tourneys on 102–6, among them the Australian, French, and U.S.

Representing Australia six times in the worldwide Federation Cup team competition, she played in the first in 1963 (a final-round defeat by the U.S.) and spearheaded Cup victories in 1964–65–68 and 1971.

Tapped for the Hall of Fame in 1979, Court was born a left-hander. She was transformed to a right-handed player (like two other Famers, Maureen Connolly and Ken Rosewall), as frequently happened in that era. She had the best two-season run in history, 1969–70, with seven majors, missing out only at Wimbledon, 1969,

countrywoman Jan Lehane lost to Karen Hantze and a budding star, Billie Jean Moffitt.

Margaret was to win three Wimbledon, five French, and seven U.S. singles championships, and the greatest of those victories was probably the 1970 Wimbledon final. In considerable pain with a sprained ankle, she held off Billie Jean, 14–12, 11–9, in possibly the finest of female finals there, and certainly the longest in point of games, 46 (two more than the Suzanne Lenglen-Dorothea Lambert Chambers record in 1919).

She retired briefly upon marrying Barry Court in 1967, but was soon back on the trail of championships. Margaret was remarkable in that she continued to win major titles, such as the U.S. of 1973, after the birth of her first of three children, and was still competing at 34 in 1977. She was shy, soft-spoken, and late in her career, extremely religious.

where she lost in the semis to champion Ann Jones. That defeat, as well as a first-round loss at Wimbledon to King in 1962, a final-round loss to Lesley Turner at the French in 1965, and a semifinal loss at Wimbledon to Evert in 1973, were her only major defeats and those years may have cost her four additional Grand Slams.

She scored triples (singles, doubles,

eras, yielded $550,000 in prize money.

MAJOR TITLES (62)—*Australian singles, 1960–61–62–63–64–65–66–69–70–71–73; French singles, 1962–64–69–70–73; Wimbledon singles, 1963–65–70; U.S. singles, 1962–65–69–70–73; Australian doubles, 1961–62–63–65–69–70–71–73; French doubles, 1964–65–66–73; Wimbledon doubles, 1964–69; U.S. doubles, 1963–68–70–73–75; Australian mixed, 1963–64; French mixed, 1963–64–65–69; Wimbledon mixed, 1963–65–66–68–75; U.S. mixed, 1961–62–63–64–65–69–70–72.* FEDERATION CUP—*1963–64–65–68–69–71; record: 22–0 in singles, 15–5 in doubles.*

Margaret Osborne duPont
United States (1918–   )

One of the most cerebral players, Margaret Evelyn Osborne duPont was a collector of major championships topped only by Margaret Court (62), Martina Navratilova (54) and Billie Jean King (39). In two decades duPont accumulated 37 in singles, doubles and mixed, although never entering the Australian.

Peerless at doubles, she was the canny right-court player, superbly complementing Louise Brough in the most successful team prior to Navratilova and Pam Shriver. Together they won a record 20 major titles:

Margaret Osborne duPont: Wise playmaker. • *UPI*

12 U.S., five Wimbledon, three French, a mark tied by Navratilova and Shriver in 1989. She won the U.S. doubles first with Sarah Palfrey Fabyan (later Mrs. Cooke) in 1941, and the next time with Brough in a record streak that ran from 1942 through 1950. Their record match-win streak of 41 ended in the 1951 final, a 6–2, 7–9, 9–7 defeat by Shirley Fry and Doris Hart. As a team in the U.S. Championships, Brough and duPont won 12 of the 14 times they entered and 58 of 60 matches. DuPont, a right-hander, was the playmaker, utilizing a devilish forehand chop and a variety of other spins that kept the ball low. She lobbed and volleyed excellently, and set up her volley with an effective serve.

Although 31 of her major titles were doubles and mixed doubles, she was just as tough in singles, reaching the U.S. final at Forest Hills five times and Wimbledon three times, the French twice. Her rivalry with Brough was as close as their friendship and partnership. They split two of the more spectacular finals at the two top championships. Brough won the 1949 Wimbledon final, 10–8, 1–6, 10–8, and duPont the 1948 Forest Hills, 4–6, 6–4, 15–13—48 games, the longest female final played there.

She won Forest Hills in 1948–49–50, Wimbledon in 1947 and the French singles in 1946 and 1949. In the U.S. Mixed Doubles Championship she set a record by winning nine times; 1943 through 1946 with Bill Talbert; 1950 with Ken McGregor; 1956 with Ken Rosewall, and 1958 through 1960 with Neale Fraser. In the 1948 semifinal she and Talbert won the longest mixed doubles played until 1991, 71 games, over Gussy Moran and Bob Falkenburg, 27–25, 5–7, 6–1. Forty-three years later, Brenda Schultz and Michiel Schapers exceeded that in a 77-game Wimbledon win over Andrea Temesvari and Tom Nijssen.

Born March 4, 1918, in Joseph, Ore., Margaret grew up in San Francisco. She made her initial appearance in the U.S. Top Ten in 1938 at No. 7 and set a longevity record for U.S. females, ranking No. 5 two decades later at the age of 40 in 1958. Over the 20 years she was ranked in the Top Ten 14 times, No. 1 in 1948—50. Between 1946 and 1957 she was in the World Top Ten nine times, No. 1: 1947–48–49–50.

She married William duPont in 1947 and later interrupted her career to give birth to a son. She was one of the few women to win a major title after childbirth.

Hers was one of the finest Wightman Cup records. In nine years of the British-U.S. series, she was unbeaten in 10 singles and nine doubles, and did not play on a losing side between 1946 and 1962. She also captained the U.S. team nine times, presiding over eight victories.

In 1967 she was inducted into the Hall of Fame.

MAJOR TITLES (37)—*French singles, 1946–49; Wimbledon singles, 1947; U.S. singles, 1948–49–50; French doubles, 1946–47–49; Wimbledon doubles, 1946–48–49–50–54; U.S. doubles, 1941–42–43–44–45–46–47–48–49–50–55–56–57; Wimbledon mixed, 1962; U.S. mixed, 1943–44–45–46–50–56–58–59–60.* OTHER U.S. TITLE—*Hard Court doubles, 1948, with Louise Brough.* WIGHTMAN CUP—*1946–47–48–49–50–54–55–57–61–62; record: 10–0 in singles, 9–0 in doubles.*

Stefan Edberg
Sweden (1966–   )

A stylistic misfit among the Swedish legion that rose in Bjorn Borg's sneaker-steps and image, Stefan Edberg has ever been an extraordinarily graceful attacker. A serve-and-volleyer, he has done superbly with only one hand propelling his backhand.

Clay, on which he was reared, hasn't been his favorite surface although he nearly beat Michael Chang in a five-set French final in 1989.

A splendid junior career led to great expectations which he has fulfilled with six major singles—two each, Australian (1985–87), Wimbledon (1989–90), U.S. (1991–92). In 1983 he became the lone achiever of a junior Grand Slam, winning the Australian, French, Wimbledon and U.S. 18-and-under singles.

Making his Davis Cup bow in 1984, at 18, he was the youngest to play for a Cup winner (until Chang, a slightly younger 18 in 1990). Edberg performed a consequential one-day role in Sweden's startling upending of the U.S. in the final at Goteborg. He and Anders Jarryd clinched the 4–1 victory by stunning Peter Fleming and John McEnroe, unbeaten in 14 previous Cup starts, 7–5, 5–7, 6–2, 7–5.

In successfully defending the Cup the following year in Munich, a 3–2 victory over Germany, Edberg won it at the wire, a

Stefan Edberg: Super server-and-volleyer.

• *Russ Adams*

thrilling, rebounding fifth-match decision over Michael Westphal, 3–6, 7–5, 6–4, 6–3. Though he didn't play in the final, he had an earlier hand in winning the 1987 Cup.

Stefan Edberg, a right-hander, was born in Vastervik, Sweden, Jan. 19, 1966, and was reared there. He lives in London with his Swedish wife, Annette. He has a hammering serve, as well as a difficult kicker, a raking backhand and is one of the finest of all volleyers. His groundstrokes continue to improve. Outwardly unemotional, he dispelled doubts about his competitiveness by winning Wimbledon in 1988. He charged from two sets down to beat Miloslav Mecir in the semis, and a set down to overcome favored Boris Becker, 4–6, 7–6 (7–2), 6–4, 6–2, for the title.

His rivalry with Becker has been a highlight of the '80s and '90s. Becker leads, 20–10.

Beating the 1983–84 champ, countryman Mats Wilander, in the final, 6–4, 6–4,

6–3, Stefan took the Australian in 1985, his first major. He repeated two years later, the last man to win it on grass, 6–3 in the fifth set over Patrick Cash.

Flushing Meadow was almost the mystery to him that it had been for Borg (no titles in 10 tries). But on his ninth, Edberg came through for the U.S. title in one of the most devastating final-round perfor-

he overcame Chang, 6–7 (3–7), 7–5, 7–6 (7–3), 5–7, 6–4, the longest-lasting major match—five hours, 26 minutes.

During 10 professional seasons he was in the World Top Ten eight times, No. 1 1990–91–92. He has won 36 pro singles and $13,339,075 in prize money.

Edberg represented Sweden in the 1988 and 1992 Olympics, winning a bronze in singles in the former.

MAJOR TITLES (8)—*Australian singles, 1985–87; Wimbledon singles, 1988–90; U.S. singles, 1991–1992, Australian doubles, 1987; U.S. doubles, 1987.* DAVIS CUP—*1984–85–86–87–88–89– 90–91–92; record: 22–9 in singles, 11–8 in doubles.*

Roy Emerson
Australia (1936–   )

In the grand days for Australia of domination of the tennis world, nobody played as large a role as the country boy out of Black Butt in Queensland, Roy Stanley Emerson.

Emerson, a slim, quick, athletic farm kid who strengthened his wrists for tennis by milking innumerable cows on his father's property, played on eight winning

Davis Cup teams between 1959 and 1967, a record. He won 28 of the major singles and doubles championships—a record for men—including two Wimbledon singles in 1964–65 and two U.S. singles at Forest Hills in 1961 and 1964. His accomplishments as a right-court doubles player who could make anybody look good amounted to 16 Big Four titles with five different partners, the last in 1971 at Wimbledon with his old Queensland pal, Rod Laver. His best-known alliance was with Aussie left-hander Neale Fraser, with whom he won Wimbledon in 1959 and 1961, the U.S. title in 1959–60 and the doubles of the Davis Cup triumphs of 1959–60–61.

Known as "Emmo" to his wide circle of friends on the circuit, he was a rollicking, gregarious six-foot right-hander who could lead the partying and singing without jeopardizing his high standards of play. Fitness was his hallmark. He trained hard and was always ready for strenuous matches and tournaments. Although primarily a serve-and-volleyer, he could adapt to the rigors of slow courts, winning the French singles in 1963 and 1967, and leading the Davis Cup victory over the U.S. on clay in Cleveland in 1964. That year he was unbeaten in eight Davis Cup singles as the Aussies regained the Cup. Emmo had a singles winning streak of 55 matches during the summer and autumn while establishing himself as No. 1 in the amateur game by winning 17 tournaments and 109 of 115 matches. The only prize to elude him in that majestic 1964 was the French on a quarters loss to Nicola Pietrangeli. Between 1961 and 1967, he won a male record six Australian singles titles, the last five in a row.

An outstanding team player who could fire up his teammates, Emerson also took part in two Australian victories in the World Cup, a since disbanded annual competition against the U.S.

He exemplified the Aussie code of sportsmanship and competitiveness, stating

Roy Emerson: Fittest of the fit. • *UPI*

it as, "You should never complain about an injury. We believe that if you play, then you aren't injured, and that's that."

Emerson was born Nov. 3, 1936, in Black Butt, a crossroads, and his family moved to Brisbane, where he could get better competition and coaching when his tennis talent became evident.

After resisting several professional offers, he turned pro in 1968 just before open tennis began, and was still competing in 1978 as player-coach of the Boston Lobsters in World Team Tennis, directing them to the semifinals of the league playoffs. Of all Australia's Davis Cup luminaries under captain Harry Hopman, Emerson made the best record. While helping win the eight Cups, he won 22 of 24 singles and 13 of 15 doubles. When the Cup was on the line, the score tied 2–2 with one match to be played in 1964, he beat American Chuck McKinley, 3–6, 6–2, 6–4, 6–4, to ice the 3–2 decision.

Beginning in 1959, he was ranked in the World Top Ten nine straight times, No. 1 in 1964–65.

Emerson was elevated to the Hall of Fame in 1982 after a career that bridged the amateur and open eras and was credited with three pro titles in singles and 30 in doubles, and $400,000 in prize money. His son, Antony, was All-American in ten-

1900–61–62–63–64–65, Wimbledon doubles, 1959–61–71; U.S. doubles, 1659–60–65–66. Davis Cup—1959–60–61–62–63–64–65–66–67; record: 21–2 in singles, 13–2 in doubles.

Chris Evert
United States (1954–   )

In 1970, at a small, insignificant tournament in North Carolina, 15-year-old Christine Marie Evert gave notice to the world that a dynamo was on the way up. Chrissie defeated Margaret Court, who had recently completed her singles Grand Slam and was the No. 1 player of the world.

A year later in the U.S. Open at Forest Hills, Evert reconfirmed by marching resolutely to the semifinals—at 16 years, 8 months, 20 days, the youngest at that time to reach that stage. Before losing to Billie Jean King, the eventual champion, schoolgirl Evert bowled over a succession of seasoned pros—Edda Buding, Mary Ann Eisel, Francoise Durr, Lesley Hunt—captivating the American sporting public and filling the Forest Hills stadium day after day. Against Eisel, the No. 4 American, Evert thrilled a national television audience by rescuing six match points with bold shot-making while converting what seemed a certain defeat.

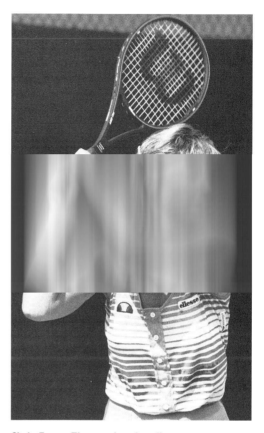

Chris Evert: The peerless baseliner. • *Mitchell Reibel*

Although essentially a slow-court baseline specialist, raised on clay in Fort Lauderdale, Fla., where she was born Dec. 20, 1954, the right-handed Evert showed that booming groundstrokes could succeed on the fast Forest Hills, Wimbledon and Australian grass. She was the Little Ice Maiden, a pony-tailed kid, deadpan, with metronomic strokes that seldom missed. Her two-handed backhand, a powerful drive, stimulated a generation of newcomers to copy her, even though her father, teaching pro Jimmy Evert, advised against it. "I didn't teach the two-hander to her," said her father, who had won the Canadian singles in 1947. "She started that way because she was too small and weak to swing the backhand with one hand. I hoped she'd change—but how can I argue with this success?"

It was such a success that by the time she completed a 20-year career in 1989 she had won $8,896,195 in prize money and a record 157 pro singles titles on a 1,309–146 won-lost record. That's an .8996 winning average, highest in pro history.

Martina Navratilova would overtake her in singles titles in 1992. Evert also was runner-up for 72 singles titles, which meant she made it to 76 percent of the finals of 303 tournaments entered.

An amateur until 1973, she was the first to reach $1 million in career prize money, in 1976.

Her major titles numbered 21–18 of them in singles, six behind Margaret Court, one behind Helen Wills Moody, tied with Navratilova. Phenomenally, Chris won at least one major singles for 13 consecutive years, a record. She started in 1974 and ended in 1986 at the French where she was the all-time champ with seven championships on a 72–6 match record, a tourney high.

By winning the U.S. title a fourth consecutive time in 1978 she was the first to do so since Helen Jacobs' run of 1932—35. Between 1973 and 1979 she won 125 consecutive matches on clay, including 24 tournaments. The streak came to an end in the semifinals of the Italian Open in Rome when she lost, 6–4, 2–6, 7–6, to Tracy Austin.

Her introduction to Goolagong was the 1972 Wimbledon semifinal, an exciting three-set struggle won by Goolagong, the defending champion. That was the start of one of the two most compelling female rivalries of the open era, one in which Evert held a 21–12 edge. The other, perhaps the most renowned in the game's history, was Chris' friendly feud with Martina Navratilova. From 1973 through 1988 it stretched, 80 matches. Evert won the first meeting in Akron, Ohio, and took a big

early lead, but Navratilova overtook her, and came out ahead, 43–37, winning nine of 13 of their major final engagements.

During the open era the Virginia Slims circuit and its championship became prominent in women's tennis. Evert won the first of her four Slims championships in 1972 at 17. In choosing to preserve her amateur status until her 18th birthday that year, she disdained more than $50,000 in prize money, including the $25,000 Slims award.

Once she entered tennis for a living, she was a thorough exemplary professional in her relations with colleagues, press and public, and perennially a hard but sporting competitor. Fairly soon she lost her status as the darling little girl. Her style was based on flawless barrages from the backcourt, and her constant winning seemed monotonous to many. Nevertheless she was a smart player, able to maneuver a foe cleverly, scoring decisively with a well-disguised drop shot. She was also a better volleyer than given credit for, after overcoming an early distaste for the net. "I realize that a lot of fans think my game is boring, and they want to see me lose, or at least for somebody to give me a good fight all the time. But this is the game I played to win," she said. "Losing hurts me. I was always determined to be the best."

She was No. 1 in the world 1975–76–77–80–81 and in the World Top Ten 17 years, a paragon of consistency in that she entered 57 of the Grand Slam tourneys, winning 18, and was at least a semifinalist 53 times. Her worst efforts were two quarterfinal (U.S.) and two third-round losses (French and Wimbledon).

Ranking No. 1 in the U.S. 1974–75–76–77–78 and 1981, she was the first since Alice Marble (1936–40) to be on top five straight years. Her 19 years in the U.S. Top Ten were one better than Billie Jean King, although Navratilova subsequently held onto No. 1 11 straight years through 1992.

As one of five tennis-playing Evert children, she was clearly the star, but her sister, Jeanne, three years younger, was also a pro.

In 1974 Jeanne ranked No. 9 in the U.S. and they were the first sisters to be ranked in the Top Ten since Florence (No. 3) and Ethel Sutton (No. 2) in 1913. Chris and Jeanne were teammates on the victorious U.S. Wightman Cup team of 1973, the

riage to English player John Lloyd ended in divorce. She then married ex-Olympic skier Andy Mill, by whom she has a son, Alexander Mill.

MAJOR TITLES (21)—*Australian singles, 1982–84; French singles, 1974–75–79–80–83– 85–86; Wimbledon singles, 1974–76–81; U.S. singles, 1975–76–77–78–80–82; French doubles, 1974–75; Wimbledon doubles, 1976.* OTHER U.S.

of Navratilova in 1985, 6–3, 6–7 (4–7), 7–5, and—at age 33—1986, 2–6, 6–3, 6–3.

Her farewell to Flushing Meadow was a quarterfinal defeat by Zina Garrison, leaving her with a record 101 match wins in that event. She closed her career by winning all five singles matches as the U.S. won the Federation Cup in 1989. It was her ninth year and eighth Cup-winning team. She was undefeated in Wightman Cup singles (26–0), helping the U.S. win 11 Cups in the 13 years she played.

Evert was the first player to win more than 1,000 singles matches as well as 150 tournaments, the only one other than Court and King to win more than 100 matches in a season, that during a mammoth 1974 when she won 16 of 24 tournaments on a 103–7 record. Her 55-match winning streak in 1974 (ended at the U.S. Open by Goolagong) was an open-era record until eclipsed by Navratilova's 74 in 1984.

Three seasons of World Team Tennis included 1976–77 with Phoenix and 1978 with champion Los Angeles.

She played in the 1988 Olympics, but did not win a medal. Her eight-year mar-

One of the elite dozen men and women to win each of the major championships in singles, Shirley June Fry Irvin is also one of only five to win them all in doubles as well. The French was the first to fall to her, in 1951, the Australian the last, in 1957, after which she retired to become Mrs. Karl Irvin and live in Hartford, Conn.

She won Wimbledon and—on the 16th and last try—the U.S. in 1956, beating, respectively, Angela Buxton and Althea Gibson. A right-hander, born on June 30, 1927, and raised in Akron, Ohio, she was in 1941 the youngest ever to play in the U.S. Championships until slightly younger fourteens, Kathy Horvath (1979) and Mary Joe Fernandez (1985).

As a 15-year-old, she became, unseeded, the Championships' youngest quarterfinalist. She lost the 1951 final to Maureen Connelly, 6–3, 1–6, 6–4, but came through five years later, outsteadying Gibson, 6–3, 6–4. She had a solid groundstroking game, but showed her volleying skills in doubles alongside Doris Hart. They were the only team to win four straight French (1950–53). They won three straight Wimbledons (1951–53) and four straight U.S. (1951–54).

Shirley Fry: Ultimate in doubles. • UPI

In their hard-fought 1953 final-round victory, 6–2, 7–9, 9–7, despite two match points, over Louise Brough and Margaret Osborne duPont, they ended the Brough–duPont record streaks of nine straight titles (1942–50) and 41 matches. Their own streak, until losing the 1955 final to Brough–duPont, was 20 matches.

Shirley ranked in the U.S. Top Ten 13 straight years (1944–56), No. 1 in 1956, and in the World Top Ten nine times between 1946 and 1956, No. 1 the last year. She played Wightman Cup for the U.S. six times, never on a loser, winning 10 of her 12 matches. She entered the Hall of Fame in 1970.

MAJOR TITLES (17)—*Australian singles, 1957; French singles, 1951; Wimbledon singles, 1956; U.S. singles, 1956; Australian doubles, 1957; French doubles, 1950–51–52–53; U.S. doubles, 1951–52–53–54; Wimbledon doubles, 1951–52–53; Wimbledon mixed, 1957.* OTHER U.S. TITLES— *Clay Court singles, 1956; Clay Court doubles, 1946, with Mary Arnold Prentiss; 1950, with Doris Hart;*

1956, with Dorothy Head Knode. WIGHTMAN CUP—*1949–51–52–53–55–56; record: 4–2 in singles, 6–0 in doubles.*

Althea Gibson
United States (1927–   )

No player overcame more obstacles to become a champion than Althea Gibson, the first black to win at Wimbledon and Forest Hills.

Her entry in the U.S. Championships of 1950 at Forest Hills was historic: the first appearance of an American black in that event. It took seven more years for Gibson to work her way to the championship there, in 1957.

Tennis was pretty much a segregated sport in the U.S. until the American Tennis Association, the governing body for black tournaments, prevailed on the U.S. Tennis Association to permit the ATA female champion, Gibson, to enter Forest Hills. Two years earlier, in 1948, Dr. Reginald Weir, a New York physician, was the first black permitted in a USTA championship, playing in the U.S. Indoor event.

Althea's first appearance at Forest Hills was not only a notable occasion, it was nearly a moment of staggering triumph. In the second round she encountered third-seeded Louise Brough, the reigning Wimbledon champion, and came within one game of winning. Recovering from nerves, Althea led, 1–6, 6–3, 7–6, when providence intervened: a rainstorm struck Forest Hills, curtailing the match until the following day, when Brough reaffirmed her eminence by winning three straight games.

Born Aug. 25, 1927, in Spring, S.C., Gibson a right-hander, grew up in a New York City ghetto in Harlem. Her family was poor, but she was fortunate in coming to the attention of Dr. Walter Johnson, a Lynchburg, Va., physician who was active in the black tennis community. He became her patron, as he would later be for Arthur

Althea Gibson: Breakthrough for a big hitter. • *UPI*

Ashe, the black champion at Forest Hills (1968) and Wimbledon (1975). Through Dr. Johnson, Gibson received better instruction and competition, and contacts were set up with the USTA to inject her into the recognized tennis scene.

Tall (5-foot-11), strong, and extremely athletic, she would have come to prominence earlier but for segregation. She was 23 when she first played at Forest Hills, 30 when she won her first of two successive U.S. Championships, in 1957. During the two years she won Wimbledon, 1957 and 1958, she was ranked No. 1 in the U.S. and the world, but she was never completely at ease in amateur tennis for she realized that, despite her success, she was still unwelcome at some clubs where important tournaments were played. She was ranked No. 9 in 1952, her first of six inclusions in the U.S. Top Ten.

A mark of general acceptance, however, was her 1957 selection to represent the U.S. on the Wightman Cup team against Britain. She played two years, winning three of four singles, and two of two doubles.

Gibson was a big hitter with an awesome serve. She liked to attack, but developed consistency at the baseline eventually, and won the French—the first major for a black—and Italian Singles Championships on slow clay in 1956.

Louise Brough in the Forest Hills final to at last rule her own country.

It was in doubles that Gibson accomplished the first Wimbledon championship by a black, in 1956 alongside Englishwoman Angela Buxton.

After winning Forest Hills for a second time in 1958, Althea turned pro. She played a series of head-to-head matches in 1960 against Karol Fageros, who had been ranked No. 8 in the U.S. Their tour was played in conjunction with the Harlem Globetrotters, the matches staged on basketball courts prior to Trotter games. Gibson won 114 of 118 matches. She said she earned over $100,000 in one year as her share of the gate, but there was no professional game in tennis for women then, and she turned to the pro golf tour for a few years. She showed an aptitude for that game, but was too late in starting.

Althea tried to play a few pro tennis events after open tennis began in 1968, but by then she was too old. She was married briefly to W. A. Darben, and worked as a tennis teaching pro after ceasing competition. She was inducted into the Hall of Fame in 1971.

MAJOR TITLES (11)—*French singles, 1956; Wimbledon singles, 1957–58; U.S. singles, 1957–58; Australian doubles, 1957; French doubles, 1956; Wimbledon doubles, 1956–57–58; U.S. mixed, 1957.* OTHER U.S. TITLES—*Clay court singles, 1957; Clay Court doubles, 1957, with Hard.* WIGHTMAN CUP—*1957–58; record: 3–1 in singles, 2–0 in doubles.*

Pancho Gonzalez
United States (1928–)

Very much his own man, a loner, and an acerbic competitor, Ricardo Alonso Gonzalez was probably as good as anyone who ever played the game, if not better. Most of his great tennis was played beyond wide public attention, on the nearly secret pro tour amid a small band of gypsies of whom he was the ticket-selling mainstay.

His rages against opponents, officials, photographers, newsmen and even spectators were frequently spectacular—but they only served to intensify his own play, and didn't disturb his concentration, as fits of temper do to most others. Pancho got mad and played better. "We hoped he wouldn't get upset; it just made him tougher," said Rod Laver. "Later when he got older, he would get into arguments to stall for time and rest, and we had to be careful that it didn't put us off our games."

Gonzalez, a right-hander, born May 9, 1928, in Los Angeles, was always out of the tennis mainstream, a fact that seemed to goad him to play harder. Because he came from a Chicano family, he was never acceptable in the supposedly proper upper circles of his city's tennis establishment. And because he was a truant he wasn't permitted to play in Southern California junior tournaments. Once he got out of the Navy in 1946 there was no preventing him from mixing in the game, and beating everyone. He had a marvelously pure and effortless service action that delivered thunderbolts, and he grew up as an attacker on fast West Coast concrete.

Pancho Gonzalez: Thunderbolt server. • *UPI*

Although not regarded as anything more than promising on his second trip East in 1948, he was at age 20 ready to win the big one, the U.S. Championship at Forest Hills. Ranked 17th nationally at the time, and seeded eighth, he served and volleyed his way to the final, where he beat South African Eric Sturgess with ease, 6–2, 6–3, 14–12. The following year Gonzalez met the favorite, a Southern California antagonist, top-seeded Ted Schroeder. It was one of the gripping finals. Schroeder won the first two sets as expected, but they were demanding and exhausting, 18–16, 6–2, and after that Gonzalez rolled up the next three, 6–1, 6–2, 6–4, for the title. In 1949 Pancho also helped the U.S. hold the Davis Cup against Australia, then went for the money, turning pro to tour against the monarch, Jack Kramer. Gonzalez was too green for Kramer, losing, 96–27, and he faded from view for several agonizing years.

When Kramer retired, Gonzalez won a tour over Don Budge, Pancho Segura and Frank Sedgman in 1954 to determine Jack's successor, and stood himself as Emperor Pancho, proud and imperious, for a long while, through the challenges of Tony ~~Trabert, Ken Rosewall, Lew Hoad, Ashley~~

~~reaching their zeniths during the mid- and~~ late-1960s the aging Gonzalez hung on as a dangerous foe, still capable of defeating all. In 1964, his last serious bid for his ninth U.S. Pro title, he lost the final to Laver in four hard sets. Yet there was still much more glory ahead. In 1968, at 40, he beat second-seeded Tony Roche (Wimbledon finalist) to reach the quarters of the initial U.S. Open. A year later, this grandfather literally electrified Wimbledon by overcoming Charlie Pasarell in the tournament's longest match, 112 games, a first-rounder that consumed 5 hours, 12 minutes, a major tourney record that stood until 1992, eclipsed by 14 minutes by Michael Chang and Stefan Edberg at the U.S. Open.

The marathon with Pasarell began one afternoon and concluded on the next after darkness intervened. In winning, 22–24, 1–6, 16–14, 6–3, 11–9, Gonzalez saved seven match points.

Later that year, he beat John Newcombe, Rosewall, Stan Smith and Arthur Ashe in succession to win a rich tournament at Las Vegas. Early in 1970, in the opener of a series of $10,000 winner-take-all challenge matches leading to a grand final, he toppled Laver. The Aussie, just off his second Grand Slam year (and

the eventual winner of this tournament), was clearly No. 1 in the world, but Pancho warmed a crowd of 14,761 at New York's Madison Square Garden with a 7–5, 3–6, 2–6, 6–3, 6–2 victory.

Three months before his 44th birthday, in 1972, he was the oldest to record a tournament title in the open era, winning Des Moines (Iowa) over Georges Goven. ~~That was also a No. 2 in the U.S. Open.~~

In 1968, though still active, he was named to the Hall of Fame and he was a consistent winner on the Grand Masters tour for the over-45 champs beginning in 1973. Although his high-speed serve, so effortlessly delivered, was a trademark, Gonzalez, a 6-foot-2, 180-pounder, was a splendid athlete and tactician , who excelled at defense, too. "My legs, retrieving, lobs and change-of-pace service returns meant as much or more to me than my power," he once said, "but people overlooked that because of the reputation of my serve." He won $911,078 between 1950 and 1972, and crossed the million mark as a Grand Master. He has been married six times.

MAJOR TITLES (4)—*U.S. singles, 1948–49; French doubles, 1949; Wimbledon doubles, 1949.* OTHER U.S. TITLES—*Indoor singles, 1949; Clay Court singles, 1948–49; Indoor mixed, 1949, with Gertrude Moran; Pro singles, 1953–54–55–56–57–58–59–61; Pro doubles, 1953, with Don Budge; 1954–58, with Pancho Segura; 1957, with Ken Rosewall; 1969, with Rod Laver.* DAVIS CUP— *1949; record: 2–0 in singles.*

Evonne Goolagong
Australia (1951–   )

The most improbable of a long line of champions from Down Under, Evonne Fay

Goolagong Cawley is the only native Australian, an Aborigine, to become a tennis internationalist.

Born July 31, 1951, in Griffith, New South Wales, she grew up in near poverty. As one of eight children of an itinerant sheep-shearer, Ken Goolagong, and his wife, Melinda. She spent her formative years in the small country town of Barellan in wheat and sheep territory west of Sydney. Her father, long-armed and limber, knew nothing of tennis. It's unlikely that she would have left Barellan if a kindly resident, Bill Kurtzman, hadn't seen her peering through the fence at the local courts and encouraged her to play.

She was a natural, a free-flowing right-hander blessed with speed, lightning reflexes and a carefree temperament. Tipped off to this by two of his assistants, Vic Edwards, proprietor of a tennis school in Sydney, journeyed upcountry to take a look. He immediately spotted the talent that would eventually result in two Wimbledon, one French and four Australian championships and a 1988 posting to the Hall of Fame.

Edwards, knowing that she couldn't develop in the bush, convinced her parents to allow Evonne to move to Sydney and live in his household, where he could coach her. This she did in 1967 at age 13, becoming one of the family and an early doubles partner of Edwards' daughter, Patricia.

Her rise was swift. On her second world tour, 1971, Goolagong, just before turning 20, beat countrywoman Helen Gourlay to win the French. A month later, in her last act as a teenager, seeded third, she stunned defending champion, and her girlhood idol, Margaret Court, in the Wimbledon final, 6–4, 6–1.

Called Sunshine Supergirl in London, she captivated crowds wherever she played with her graceful movement and gracious manner. Three more times she got to the final, losing to Billie Jean King in 1972 and 1975 and Chris Evert in 1976, and it appeared that her Wimbledon title days were over. However, a unique success was to be hers: victory again at the end of a nine-year gap, in 1980—her last tournament triumph. Seeded fourth, Evonne made a spirited run through 1977 runner-

Evonne Goolagong: Lightning on the loose. • *UPI*

up Betty Stove, Hana Mandlikova (No. 9 seed), Wendy Turnbull (No. 6), Tracy Austin (No. 2), 6–3, 0–6, 6–4, and Evert (No. 3), 6–1, 7–6 (7–1), the only Wimbledon singles championship to end in a tie-breaker.

By then she had married Englishman Roger Cawley and had the first of their two children. Thus she was the first mother to

Overall Evert led 21–12, but in the majors her edge was only 5–4, Chris winning three of their five finals. Goolagong took their initial championship encounter, the 1974 Australian, 7–6, 4–6, 6–0. She beat Martina Navratilova to repeat in the Australian in 1975.

For a decade Evonne, refreshing as a zephyr, illuminated the World Top Ten, retiring after the 1983 season. She won the season-climaxing Virginia Slims championship in 1974 and 1976, both over Evert, and had career totals of 43 singles and nine doubles titles, and $1,399,431 in prize money.

Although she won the U.S. Indoor in 1973, she couldn't quite make it at the Open, the only woman to lose the final four successive years, 1973 through 1976, at Forest Hills, falling to Court, King then twice to Evert. Her most winning seasons: 1973 with nine titles, including wins over Evert in the Italian and Cincinnati finals; 1976, eight titles.

A seven-year mainstay of Australia's Federation Cup team, she led the way to Cups in 1971–73–74 and finals in 1975–76.

MAJOR TITLES (13)—*Australian singles, 1974–75–76–77; French singles, 1971; Wimbledon singles, 1971–80; Australian doubles, 1971–74–75–76; Wimbledon doubles, 1974; French mixed, 1972.* FEDERATION CUP—*1971–72–73–74–75–76–82; record: 21–3 in singles, 11–2 in doubles.*

Steffi Graf
Germany (1969–   )

attain heights unimaginable before 1988. That year she registered the sixth Grand Slam (third female) and topped it off with a gold medal at Seoul as tennis returned to the Olympics after a 64-year absence. It was a quintessential quintuple for "Fräulein Forehand," a right-handed proprietor of that feared weapon.

Born June 14, 1969, in Bruhl, she became one of the fastest of all female players, a nimble retriever who prefers the baseline but volleys ably. She runs and plays speedily, hardly pausing, impatient to win the next point. She and Martina Navratilova are the greatest players produced in Europe since the 1920s heyday of Suzanne Lenglen.

Once she'd stunned Evert (the eight-time champ) at Hilton Head, 6–4, 7–5, Steffi began to roll up titles at an incredible pace: 11, 11, 14, 10, 1987 through 1990. In seven years, at the close of 1992, she had 68 singles titles—11 majors, numbering four Wimbledon, three Australian, two French and two U.S.

Days before her 18th birthday she grabbed her first major, the 1987 French, over Navratilova, 6–4, 4–6, 8–6. But it was in Paris three years later that she stumbled while strongly bidding for Navratilova's open-era record (74) for consecutive match victories. Steffi was stopped at 66 in the final by Monica Seles.

As a pro she has won matches at a .884 clip. Evert was .899, Navratilova .878. By mid-1987 she deposed Navratilova at No. 1, and hung on to the top spot for four years (a record 186 weeks) until displaced in 1991 by Seles.

Her Grand Slam year amounted to 11 singles titles in 14 tournaments on a 73–3 match record. In navigating the Australian, French, Wimbledon and U.S. finals, she beat Evert, 6–1, 7–6 (7–3); Natalia Zvereva, 6–0, 6–0; Navratilova, 5–7, 6–2, 6–1, and Gabriela Sabatini, 6–3, 3–6, 6–1, to close it out at Flushing Meadow. Then she beat Sabatini, 6–3, 6–3, for the 1988 Olympic crown, but relinquished it to Jennifer Capriati, 3–6, 6–3, 6–4, in 1992 at Barcelona.

Steffi Graf: "Fraulein Forehand." • *Mitchell Reibel*

Almost as impressive was 1989 with 14 wins in 16 tournaments on a 86–2 match record. Twice she won the season-climaxing Virginia Slims Championship (1987–89).

She led Germany to two victories in the Federation Cup (1987 and 1992), an event in which she hasn't been beaten in singles (17–0). After 10 years as a pro and $10,332,673 in prize money, she has not reached her peak.

MAJOR TITLES (12)—*Australian singles, 1988–89–90; French singles, 1987–88; Wimbledon singles, 1988–89–91–92; U.S. singles, 1988–89; Wimbledon doubles, 1988.* FEDERATION CUP— *1986–87–89–91–92; record: 17–0 in singles, 8–1 in doubles.*

Doris Hart
United States (1925–   )

As a child Doris Jane Hart was certainly not a candidate for sports immortality. She was stricken by a serious knee infection later erroneously publicized as "polio," and faced the prospect of being crippled for life. She began to play tennis at six as therapy, and recovered so successfully that, despite bowed and uncertain-appearing legs, she became one of the all-time champions.

"One of the first newspaper stories on me described me as having recovered from polio," she once said. "It was a good story that just caught on. But it wasn't so."

Her total of 35 major (Australian, French, Wimbledon and U.S.) championships in singles, doubles and mixed ties her with Louise Brough, behind only Margaret Court (62), Martina Navratilova (54), Billie Jean King (39) and Margaret duPont (37). Hart and Court are the only players in history, male or female, to win all 12 of the Grand Slam titles at least once, and she is one of 12 to win all four singles within her career.

For 15 successive years between 1942 and 1955 she was ranked in the U.S. Top Ten, standing at No. 1 in 1954–55.

Doris Hart: The complete performer. • *UPI*

Fla. She was an intelligent and solid all-around player whose strokes were crisp and stylish. She moved very well, despite the early handicap of her legs, and had an excellent disposition. She was effective at the net, or in the backcourt, as attested by her championships in the French singles of 1950 and 1952, and the U.S. Clay Court singles in 1950.

Possibly her finest tournament was Wimbledon of 1951, when she scored a triple—championships in singles, doubles, and mixed—and lost only one set, that in the mixed. After handing her good friend and partner, Shirley Fry, one of the worst beatings in the tournament's history (6–1, 6–0), Doris united with Shirley for the doubles title, then annexed the mixed with Frank Sedgman. Doris won the mixed the following year with Sedgman, and the next three years with Vic Seixas, a Wimbledon record of five straight years.

After being a runner-up at Forest Hills for the U.S. Singles Championship four times, including 1952–53 to Maureen Connolly, Hart finally was rewarded on her 15th try at the title, beating Brough in a thriller, 6–8, 6–1, 8–6, in the 1954 title match. She retained that title, 6–4, 6–2, over Pat Ward, then retired to become a teaching pro.

Born June 20, 1925, in St. Louis, Hart, a right-hander, grew up in Coral Gables,

avoided two match points at 2–5 in the third. In turn their own streak of four championships and 20 matches was stopped in the 1955 final by Brough and duPont.

During a decade of U.S. supremacy over Britain (1946—55) in the Wightman Cup, Hart won all 14 of her singles and eight of nine doubles. She captained the winning U.S. team in 1970.

Her U.S. championships on various surfaces amounted to 21 singles and doubles. In 1969 she was enshrined in the Hall of Fame.

Beginning in 1946 she was in the World Top Ten 10 successive years, No. 1 in 1951.

MAJOR TITLES (35)—*Australian singles, 1949; French singles, 1950–52; Wimbledon singles, 1951; U.S. singles, 1954–55; Australian doubles, 1950; French doubles, 1948–50–51–52–53; Wimbledon doubles, 1947–51–52–53; U.S. doubles, 1951–52–53–54; Australian mixed, 1949–50; French mixed, 1951–52–53; Wimbledon mixed, 1951–52–53–54–55; U.S. mixed, 1951–52–53–54–55.* OTHER U.S. TITLES—*Clay Court singles, 1950; Hard Court singles, 1949; Indoor doubles,*

1947–48, with Barbara Schofield; Clay Court doubles, 1944–45, with Pauline Betz; 1950, with Shirley Fry; 1954, with Maureen Connolly; Indoor mixed, 1947–48, with Bill Talbert WIGHTMAN CUP—*1946–47–48–49–50–51–52–53–54–55; record: 14–0 in singles, 8–1 in doubles.*

Lew Hoad
Australia (1934–   )

During his quarter-century career as a professional, Pancho Gonzalez faced a vast array of first-rate players, and the one he considered the most devastating was Lewis Alan Hoad.

"When Lew's game was at its peak nobody could touch him," said Gonzalez, who cited Hoad as his toughest foe during his years of head-to-head one-night-stand pro tours. Hoad, who turned pro in 1957, after winning his second successive Wimbledon singles, was one rookie who seemed able to dethrone Gonzalez as the pro king. They were just about even when Hoad's troublesome back gave way during the winter of 1958. Gonzalez won the tour, 51–36 but felt threatened all the way. It was Pancho's closest brush with defeat after taking over leadership in 1954.

Hoad, a strapping 175-pounder with a gorilla chest and iron wrists, may have been the strongest man to play tennis in the world class. He blistered the ball and became impatient with rallying, preferring to hit for winners. It was a flamboyant style, and made for some bad errors when he wasn't in tune. But when his power was focused along with his concentration, Hoad came on like a tidal wave. He was strong enough to use topspin as an offensive drive. He was assault-minded, but had enough control to win the French title on slow clay in 1956.

Born Nov. 23, 1934, 21 days after Ken Rosewall, in the same city, Sydney, the right-handed Hoad was bracketed with Rosewall throughout his amateur days. Although entirely different in stature, style, and personality, the two were called

Lew Hoad: His strength lifted many a cup. • *UPI*

Australia's tennis twins, the prodigies who drew attention as teenagers and were rivals and teammates through 1956. Hoad was stronger, but less patient and consistent, more easygoing. His back problems cut his career short in the mid-1960s while Rosewall, whose style was less taxing, kept on going into the next decade.

His countrymen fondly remember Hoad's Davis Cup triumph of 1953 over Tony Trabert on a rainy Melbourne afternoon. At 19, he and Rosewall had been selected to defend the Cup. The U.S. led, 2–1, in the finale and seemed about to clinch the Cup when the more experienced Trabert, already the U.S. champion, caught up at two sets all. Hoad hung on to win, however, 13–11, 6–3, 3–6, 2–6, 7–5, and Rosewall beat Vic Seixas the following day to save the Cup, 3–2.

Although they lost it to the Americans the next year, Hoad and Rosewall were awesome in 1955, retaking the prize, 5–0, and defended the Davis Cup for the last time together in 1956.

Their first major titles came in 1953, when Lew and Ken were allied to win the Australian, French, and Wimbledon doubles. Lew won 13 major titles in singles and doubles, and in 1956 appeared on his way to win all four (Australian, French, Wimbledon and U.S.) singles within one year and thus achieve a rare Grand Slam. His Wimbledon final-round victory over the omnipresent Rosewall meant he was

Gonzalez in 1958 and 1959.

Despite losing out on a Grand Slam, his 1956 season was a luminous hard-working campaign that netted 32 titles: 15 victories in 26 singles tourneys on a 95–11 match record, 17 victories in 23 doubles starts on 79–5. For five straight years, beginning in 1952, he was in the World Top Ten, No. 1 1956.

Hoad (five attempts) and Bjorn Borg (10) are probably the two greatest players not to win the U.S. Open. Lew married another player, countrywoman Jenny Staley (finalist in the 1954 Australian singles). They operate a tennis resort in Spain.

MAJOR TITLES (13)—*Australian singles, 1956; French singles, 1956; Wimbledon singles, 1956–57; Australian doubles, 1953–56–57; French doubles, 1953; Wimbledon doubles, 1953–55–56; U.S. doubles, 1956; French mixed, 1954.* DAVIS CUP—*1953–54–55–56; record: 10–2 in singles, 7–2 in doubles.*

Billie Jean King
United States (1943–   )

The fireman's daughter, Billie Jean Moffitt King, began blazing through the ten-

nis world in 1960 when she first appeared in the U.S. women's rankings at No. 4. She was 17. For more than two decades she continued as a glowing force in the game as the all-time Wimbledon champion, frequently the foremost player, a crusader in building the female professional game, and a million-dollar-plus winner on the tour.

Born Nov. 22, 1943, in Long Beach,

surprising triumph in the Wimbledon women's doubles. They were the youngest team to win it. That was the first of 20 Wimbledon championships, making King the record winner of the most prestigious tourney.

In 1979 she got the 20th in her 19th Wimbledon, the doubles, in the company of Martina Navratilova, with whom she won her last major, the U.S. doubles, in 1980.

Elizabeth Ryan's 19 Wimbledon titles (between 1914 and 1934) were all in doubles and mixed doubles. King won six singles, 10 doubles, and four mixed doubles between 1961 and 1979, and in 1979 lengthened another Wimbledon record by appearing in her 27th final, the doubles. Ryan was in 24 finals.

Billie Jean's has been a career of firsts. In 1968 she was the first woman of the open era to sign a pro contract to tour with a female tournament group, with Rosie Casals, Francoise Durr and Ann Haydon Jones as the women's auxiliary of the National Tennis League, which also included six men (Rod Laver, Ken Rosewall, Pancho Gonzalez, Andres Gimeno, Fred Stolle, and Roy Emerson).

Billie Jean King: Volleying trailblazer. • *Russ Adams*

A few women before King had turned pro to make head-to-head barnstorming tours, notably Suzanne Lenglen and Mary K. Browne 1926–27; Alice Marble and Mary Hardwick, 1941; Pauline Betz and Sarah Palfrey Fabyan Cooke, 1947; Althea Gibson and Karol Fageros, 1960.

In 1971 B.J. was the first woman athlete over the 100-grand hurdle, winning $117,000. During that memorably monster season when she was toiling mightily to establish the women's tour, she played 31 tournaments in singles, winning 17, and played 26 in doubles, winning a record 21. She had a match mark of 112–13 in singles, a record number of wins, and 80–5 in doubles. Overall it added up to 38 titles on 192 match wins, both records. Imagine how many millions such a campaign would be worth today.

In 1973 Billie Jean engaged in a "Battle of the Sexes" challenge match, defeating 55-year-old ex-Wimbledon champ Bobby Riggs, 6–4, 6–3, 6–3, in a heavily publicized and nationally televised extravaganza that captured the nation's fancy and drew a record tennis crowd, 30,472, to Houston's Astrodome.

In 1974 she became the first woman to coach a professional team containing men when she served as player-coach of the Philadelphia Freedoms of World Team Tennis, a league she and her husband, Larry King, helped establish. Traded to the New York Apples, she led that team to WTT titles in 1976 and 1977 as a player.

Ten years after Riggs, B.J. was to establish a geriatric mark herself, winning Beckenham. At 39½ she was the oldest woman to take a pro title.

An aggressive, emotional player who has often said, "You have to love to guts it out to win," Billie Jean specialized in serve-and-volley tactics, aided by quickness and a highly competitive nature. She overcame several knee operations to continue as a winner into her 40th year. As a big-match player she was unsurpassed, excelling in team situations when she represented the U.S. In nine years on the Federation Cup team, she helped the U.S. gain the final each time, and win seven by winning 51 of her 55 singles and doubles. In the Wightman Cup against Britain she played on only one losing side in 10 years, winning 21 of her 26 singles and doubles.

Outspoken on behalf of women's rights, in and out of sports—and the game of tennis in particular—she was possibly the most influential player in popularizing professional tennis in the United States. She worked tirelessly to promote the Virginia Slims tour during the early 1970s when the women realized they must separate from the men to achieve recognition and significant prize money on their own. With the financial backing of Virginia Slims, the organizational acumen of Gladys Heldman and the salesmanship and winning verve of King, the women pros built an extremely profitable circuit.

Only two women, Margaret Smith (62) and Navratilova (54) won more majors than King's 39 in singles, doubles and mixed. In regard to U.S. titles on all surfaces (grass, clay, hard court, indoor), King is second at 28 behind Hazel Hotchkiss Wightman's 34. King and Rosie Casals were the only doubles team to win U.S. titles on all four surfaces. She won seven of her major doubles with Casals, her most fre-

Fla., tourney, winning a doubles match with 13-year-old pro rookie Jennifer Capriati.

In a career encompassing the amateur and open eras, she won 67 pro and 37 amateur singles titles, was a pro finalist 38 times on a 677–149 match record. Her prize money total was $1,966,487. Her marriage ended in divorce. In 1987 she entered the

gles titles. Ranked No. 1 in the U.S. seven times, she tied Molla Bjurstedt Mallory for most years at the top.

However, Navratilova would pass them both with 12. Between 1960 and 1982 Billie Jean was ranked in the U.S. Top Ten 18 times, topped only by Chris Evert's 19. Between 1963 and 1980 she was in the World Top Ten 18 times, at No. 1 in 1966–67–68–71–74, and held her last ranking, No. 13, at age 40 in 1983.

She greatly aided Owen Davidson in making his mixed doubles Grand Slam in 1967 with two partners. King and Davidson won the French, Wimbledon and U.S. after he took the Australian with Lesley Turner. She scored three major triples, winning the singles, doubles and mixed at Wimbledon in 1967 and 1973, and at the U.S. in 1967. She won the longest singles set played by women (36 games) in a 1963 Wightman Cup win over Christine Truman, 6–4, 19–17.

Billie Jean's grand swan song occurred at 39 in 1983 at Wimbledon, a semifinal finish (her 14th), losing to 18-year-old Andrea Jaeger. Seven years later she played a cameo role in the Boca Raton,

1967–71–73–74; U.S. mixed, 1967–71–73–76. OTHER U.S. TITLES—*Indoor singles, 1966–67–68–71–74; Clay Court singles, 1971; Hard Court singles, 1966; Indoor doubles, 1966–68–71–75, with Rosie Casals; 1979, with Martina Navratilova; 1983, with Sharon Walsh; Clay Court doubles, 1960, with Darlene Hard; 1971, with Judy Tegart Dalton; Hard Court doubles, 1966, with Casals; Indoor mixed, 1966–67, with Paul Sullivan.* FEDERATION CUP—*1963–64–65–66–67–76–77–78–79; record 25–4 in singles, 27–0 in doubles.* WIGHTMAN CUP—*1961–62–63–64–65–66–67–70–77–78; record: 14–2 in singles, 7–3 in doubles.*

Jack Kramer
United States (1921–)

The impact of John Albert "Jake" Kramer on tennis has been fourfold: as great player, exceptional promoter, thoughtful innovator and astute television commentator.

Kramer, born Aug. 5, 1921, in Las Vegas, Nev., grew up in the Los Angeles area. He achieved international notice as a teenager when he was selected to play doubles, alongside Joe Hunt, for the U.S. in the Davis Cup finale against Australia. At 18, Kramer was the youngest to play in the Cup title round, although John Alexander of Australia lowered the record to 17 by playing in 1968.

It was after World War II, however, that Kramer came to prominence as the dominant player in the game, so strong that he was voted fifth on a list of all-time greats selected by a panel of expert tennis journalists in 1969. The powerful right-hander was the leading practitioner of the "big game," rushing to the net constantly behind his serve, and frequently attacking on return of serve. His serve put opponents off, setting them up for the volley, as did his forcing forehand.

A blistered racket hand probably prevented the Californian from winning Wimbledon in 1946, but he took the title the following year with an awesome performance, losing only 37 games in seven matches, the most lopsided run to the championship. Kramer also won the U.S. singles title at Forest Hills in 1946 and 1947.

In December 1946 he and Ted Schroeder journeyed to Melbourne to regain the Davis Cup in the first postwar showdown. Kramer was no longer the kid who had helped lose the Cup to the Aussies seven years before. Although the home side was favored, power players Kramer and Schroeder completely overwhelmed Adrian Quist and Dinny Pails in singles, and Quist and John Bromwich in doubles in a stunning 5–0 victory over Australia.

The following summer, Jake and Ted repelled the Australian challenge for the Cup at Forest Hills, and then Kramer closed out his amateur career memorably by overhauling Frankie Parker in the U.S. final. Kramer lost the first two sets, and was in danger of losing out on a lucrative professional contract as well as his championship. Counterpunching, Kramer won, 4–6, 2–6, 6–1, 6–0, 6–3, and set off in pursuit of Bobby Riggs, the reigning pro champ.

Jack Kramer: Power player and promoter. • *UPI*

Kramer knocked Riggs off the summit by winning their odyssey of one-nighters throughout the U.S., which was the test of professional supremacy of that day. Their opener was a phenomenon: New York was buried by a blizzard that brought the city to a stop, yet 15,114 customers made it on foot to the old Madison Square Garden on Dec. 27, 1947, to watch Riggs win. Bobby couldn't keep it up. Kramer won the tour, 69–20, and stayed in action while Riggs took over as the promoter and signed Pancho Gonzalez to challenge Kramer. Nobody was up to Kramer then. He bruised the rookie Gonzalez 96–27, on the longest of the tours. Kramer made $85,000 against Riggs at his percentage, and $72,000 against Gonzalez.

In 1952 Kramer assumed the position of promoter himself, the boss of pro tennis, a role he would hold for over a decade, well past his playing days. Kramer's last tour as a principal was against the first man he recruited, Frank Sedgman, the Aussie who was tops among amateurs. Kramer won, 54–41. An arthritic back led to Kramer's retirement as a player, but he kept the tour going, resurrecting one of his victims, Gonzalez, who became the strongman.

One of the shrewdest operators in tennis, Kramer was looked to for advice when the open era began in 1968. He devised the Grand Prix for the men's game, a series of tournaments leading to a Masters Championship for the top eight finishers, and a bonus pool to be shared by more than a score of the leading players. The Grand Prix, incorporating the most attractive tournaments around the world, func-

as an analyst on tennis telecasts in many countries, notably for the British Broadcasting Corporation at Wimbledon and for all the American networks at Forest Hills, and at other events.

Kramer, winner of 13 U.S. singles and doubles titles, was named to the Hall of Fame in 1968.

U.S. Coast Guard service interrupted his career during World War II. He ranked in the U.S. Top Ten five times between 1940 and 1947, No. 1 in 1946–47 as he was in the world those two years.

MAJOR TITLES (10)—*Wimbledon singles, 1947; U.S. Singles, 1946–47; Wimbledon doubles, 1946–47; U.S. doubles, 1940–41–43–47; U.S. mixed, 1941.* OTHER U.S. TITLES—*Indoor singles, 1947; Pro singles, 1948; Pro doubles, 1948–55, with Pancho Segura; Indoor doubles, 1947, with Bob Falkenburg; Clay Court doubles, 1941, with Ted Schroeder.* DAVIS CUP—*1939–46–47; record: 6–0 in singles, 1–2 in doubles.*

Rod Laver
Australia (1938–   )

Rod Laver was so scrawny and sickly as a child in the Australian bush that no one could guess he would become a left-

handed whirlwind who would conquer the tennis world and be known as possibly the greatest player ever.

A little more than a month before Don Budge completed the first Grand Slam, Rodney George "Rocket" Laver was born Aug. 9, 1938, at Rockhampton, Queensland, Australia. Despite lack of size and early infirmities, Laver grew strong and tough on

and pro during the 1960s. An incessant attacker, he was nevertheless a complete player who glowed in backcourt and at the net. Laver's 145-pound body seemed to dangle from a massive left arm that belonged to a gorilla, an arm with which he bludgeoned the ball and was able to impart ferocious topspin. Although others had used topspin, Laver may have inspired a wave of heavy-hitting topspin practitioners of the 1970s such as Bjorn Borg and Guillermo Vilas. The stroke became basic after Laver.

As a teenager he was sarcastically nicknamed "Rocket" by Australian Davis Cup captain Harry Hopman. "He was anything but a Rocket," Hopman recalled. "But Rod was willing to work harder than the rest, and it was soon apparent to me that he had more talent than any other of our fine Australian players."

His first international triumph came during his first trip abroad in 1956, when he won the U.S. Junior Championship at 17. Three years later he was ready to take his place among the world's best when he won the Australian singles and, with Bob Mark, the doubles, and was runner-up to Alex Olmedo for the Wimbledon champi-

Rod Laver: Ferocious attacker. • *UPI*

onship. The Australian victories were the first of Laver's 20 major titles in singles, doubles and mixed, placing him fifth among all-time male winners behind Roy Emerson (28), John Newcombe (25), Frank Sedgman (22), Bill Tilden (21). Jean Borotra also won 20. His 11 singles (equaled by Bjorn Borg) were second to Emerson's 12.

The losing Wimbledon final of 1959 was the beginning of an incredible run of success in that tournament. He was a finalist six straight times he entered, losing in 1960 to Neale Fraser, winning in 1961 and 1962, and—after a five-year absence because professionals were barred until 1968—winning again in 1968 and 1969. Only two others had played in six successive finals, back before the turn of the century: Willie Renshaw, 1881 through 1886 and Wilfred Baddely, 1891 through 1896. Borg played in six straight, 1976 through 1981. While winning Wimbledon four straight times (the only man since World War I to win four prior to Borg) and proceeding to the fourth round in 1970, Laver set a male tournament record of 31 consecutive match wins, ended by his loss to Roger Taylor, and eclipsed by Borg in 1980.

The year 1969 was Laver's finest, perhaps the best experienced by any player, as he won an open-era record 17 singles tournaments (tied by Guillermo Vilas in 1977) of 32 played on a 106–16 match record. In 1962 he won 19 of 34 on 134–15.

Unlike his Grand Slam year of 1962 as an amateur, he was playing in tournaments that were open to all, amateur and pro, and this Slam was all the more impressive. It was endangered only a few times—Tony Roche forcing him to a fifth set in an exhausting 90-game semifinal in the Australian championships; Dick Crealy winning the first two sets of a second-rounder in the French; Premjit Lall winning the first two sets of a second-rounder at Wimbledon; Stan Smith threatening in the fifth set of a fourth-rounder at Wimbledon; Arthur Ashe and John Newcombe pushing him to four sets in the Wimbledon semifinal and final, respectively; Dennis Ralston leading 2 sets to 1 in the fourth round of the U.S.; Roche winning the opening set of the U.S. final.

But that year Laver could always accelerate to a much higher gear and bang his way out of trouble. The closest anyone came to puncturing either Slam was Marty Mulligan, who held a match point in the fourth set of their French quarterfinal in 1962.

After his second year running as the No. 1 amateur, 1962, and helping Australia win a fourth successive Davis Cup, Laver turned pro. It was a life of one-nighters, but Pancho Gonzalez was no longer supreme. Kenny Rosewall was at the top and gave Laver numerous beatings as their long, illustrious rivalry began. Rosewall beat Laver to win the U.S. Pro singles in 1963, but the next year Laver defeated Rosewall and Gonzalez to win the first of his five crowns, four of them in a row beginning in 1966. He had a record streak of 19 wins in the U.S. Pro until losing the 1970 final to Roche.

When open tennis dawned in 1968, Laver was ready to resume where he'd left off at the traditional tournaments, whipping Roche in less than an hour, 6–3, 6–4, 6–2, to take the first open Wimbledon.

In 1971 Laver won $292,717 in tournament prize money (a season record that stood until Arthur Ashe won $338,337 in 1975), the figure enabling him to become

himself for one last effort, after 11 years away. He was brilliant, teaming with John Newcombe to end a five-year U.S. reign, 5–0. Laver beat Tom Gorman in five sets on the first day and paired with Newcombe for a crushing straight-set doubles victory over Stan Smith and Erik van Dillen that clinched the Cup, Laver's fifth. Of all the marvelous Aussie Davis Cup performers he was the only one never to play in a losing match.

He was also a factor in winning three World Cups (1972–74–75) for Australia in the since disbanded team competition against the U.S. In 1976, as his tournament career was winding down, Laver signed with San Diego in World Team Tennis and was named the league's Rookie of the Year at age 38!

During a 23-year career that spanned the amateur and open eras he won 47 pro titles in singles, and was runner-up 21 times. Laver was elevated to the Hall of Fame in 1981.

His 13 years in the World Top Ten ranged from 1959 to 1975, No. 1 in 1961–62–68–69. His last year there he was No. 10 at age 37.

MAJOR TITLES (20)—*Australian singles, 1960–62–69; French singles, 1962–69; Wimbledon singles, 1961–62–68–69; U.S. singles, 1962–69; Australian doubles, 1959–60–61–69; French doubles, 1961; Wimbledon doubles, 1971; French mixed, 1961; Wimbledon mixed, 1959–60.* DAVIS CUP— *1959–60–61–62–73; record: 16–4 in singles, 4–0 in doubles.*

Ivan Lendl

He won two other French (1986–87) and two Australian (1989–90).

Until 1984, at 24, his competitive zeal in big finals had been questioned, particularly after his U.S. Open losses to Jimmy Connors in 1982–83. But Lendl dispelled all that, and had the first of his three U.S. titles (also over McEnroe) in 1985, the second and third over Miloslav Mecir and Mats Wilander in 1986 and 1987.

His U.S. Open conquest of McEnroe hoisted him past the New Yorker to No. 1 in the world, a position he held until losing the Open in 1988 to Wilander—156 straight weeks, three short of Jimmy Connors's open era record. He returned to No. 1 for 1989 and has spent a record total 269 weeks at the peak during 13 seasons in the Top Ten.

His Flushing Meadow time has been spectacular: appearing in eight successive finals (from 1982), he equalled the record of Big Bill Tilden (1918–25). His loss of the 1988 final to Wilander halted a 27-match winning streak in the U.S. championship, second only to Tilden's string of 42 between 1920 and the quarters of 1926.

Ivan Lendl: Relentless baseline basher.
• *Mitchell Reibel*

Born March 7, 1960, in Ostrava, Czechoslovakia, and reared there, he has an excellent tennis bloodlines. His mother, Olga Lendlova, was a Top Ten player in their homeland, ranking as high as No. 2. His father, Jiri Lendl, also was a fine player, ranking as high as No. 15, and who, in 1990, became president of the Czechoslovak Tennis Federation.

Unlike countrywoman Martina Navratilova, he did not announce his defection, but left no doubt when he settled in the U.S. in 1984, and declined to play further Davis Cup after 1985. He became a U.S. citizen in 1992.

In 1980 Lendl, unbeaten in seven singles and three doubles, led Czechoslovakia to its lone Davis Cup. Before an uproarious final round crowd in Prague, he anchored the 4–1 triumph over Italy. He won both his singles, beating Corrado Barazzutti, 3–6, 6–1, 6–1, 6–2, on the first day. Then he and Tom Smid 6–1, clinched

with a stirring 3–6, 6–3, 3–6, 6–3, 6–4, doubles decision over Adriano Panatta and Paolo Bertolucci.

A tall, right-handed paragon of hard work and fitness, he amassed stunning numbers campaigning tirelessly between 1980 and 1983 when he won 36 of 101 tournaments. He played 32 in 1980, winning three on a 113–29 match record, and won 15 of 23 in 1982 on 107–9. He won 11 of 17 in 1985 on 84–7. His last big production year was 1989: 10 of 17 on 79–7. His 92nd pro singles title in 1992, leaves him second only to Connors' 109 in the open era. In 1982 he put together the third longest winning streak of the open era, 44 straight matches, six shy of Guillermo Vilas's 1977 record.

A basher from the baseline, relying on strength and topspin, Lendl isn't particularly stylish, but gets the job done with determination. He has striven mightily to make himself into a volleyer, hopeful of landing the one big prize to elude him: Wimbledon. Two losing finals, to Boris Becker in 1986 and Patrick Cash in 1987, are as close as he's come in 13 tries. After 15 years as a pro he was the all-time male leader in prize money with $19,172,627 at the close of 1992 and he had a 1,007–192 match record, second only to Connors (1,331–274).

MAJOR TITLES (8)—*Australian singles, 1989–90; French singles, 1984–86–87; U.S. singles, 1985–86–87.* OTHER U.S. TITLE—*Clay Court singles, 1985; Pro singles, 1992.* DAVIS CUP— *1978–79–80–81– 82–83–84–85; record: 18–11 in singles, 4–4 in doubles.*

John McEnroe
United States (1959–   )

Right from the start, in his 1977 introduction to pro tennis, John Patrick McEnroe, Jr., was a hit.

An 18-year-old amateur (he would not turn pro until winning the National

John McEnroe: Playing with fire. • *Russ Adams*

per, the last leading to fines, suspensions and a singular disqualification during the 1990 Australian Open for abusive language directed at court officials.

A magnificent volleyer with a feathery touch, he is an attacker whose fast court style netted four U.S. Open and three Wimbledon singles. But he has the baselining strength to have done well on clay at

again as the 19-year-old took both his singles in a 4–1 championship-round victory over Britain. He was the youngest American to do so well in the Cup round, although Lew Hoad, a younger 19 by eight months for victorious Australia, also took both his singles in 1953.

McEnroe continued as a mainstay in helping the U.S. win four more Cups through 1992, and set numerous of his country's records: years played (12), ties (30), singles win (41), singles and doubles wins altogether (59). A workhorse, he played both singles and doubles in 13 matches, and he and Peter Fleming won 14 of 15 Cup doubles together.

As epic was his 6-hour-32 minute, five-set victory over Mats Wilander in St. Louis (9–7, 6–2, 15–17, 3–6, 8–6), clinching a 1982 quarterfinal 3–2 win over Sweden. Another thriller was his five-set win over Jose-Luis Clerc of Argentina (7–5, 5–7, 6–3, 3–6, 6–3) to send the Cup to the U.S. in the 1981 final at Cincinnati. In 1982 France built a home-court advantage for the final, especially to counter McEnroe, installing clay indoors at Grenoble. But Mac beat Yannick Noah and Henri Leconte in singles, and paired with

Intercollegiate singles as a Stanford freshman in 1978), McEnroe made his first splash in Paris, a boy edging into man's territory. He won his first of 17 major titles there, the French mixed with childhood pal, Mary Carillo, as well as the French junior singles.

Soon after, electrifying Wimbledon, he went through the qualifying tourney and all the way to the semis, losing to Jimmy Connors. It was a major tourney record for a qualifier. It was also a record for an amateur in the open era. Immediately he was a player to reckon with.

Born on Feb. 16, 1959, in Wiesbaden, Germany, where his father was stationed with the U.S. Air Force, he grew up in the Long Island suburb of Douglaston, N.Y.

A left-hander, McEnroe stands as perhaps the most skilled—and controversial—of all players. Brilliant in doubles and singles, he is distinguished by shotmaking artistry, competitive fire and a volatile tem-

Fleming for the doubles win. A decade later he was on another Cup winner as doubles partner of Pete Sampras in the triumph over Switzerland at Ft. Worth, Tex.

At 20 he won the U.S. title for the first time over fellow New Yorker Vitas Gerulaitis, the youngest winner since Pancho Gonzalez, also 20, 31 years before. He repeated in dramatic battles with Bjorn Borg in 1980 and 1981, the latter seeming the straw that broke the Swede's sensational career. Borg retired shortly thereafter. McEnroe won for the last time in 1984, over Lendl. But he was defeated in the Flushing Meadow rematch 12 months later, relinquishing to Lendl the No. 1 ranking McEnroe had held for four years.

His most celebrated result may have been a loss, the 1980 Wimbledon final called by many the greatest of all. Beaten, 1–6, 7–5, 6–3, 6–7 (16–18), 8–6, McEnroe nervelessly staved off five match points during the monumental fourth-set tie-breaker to fight Borg to the fifth-set wire. A year later he cut down Borg on Centre Court, 4–6, 7–6 (7–1), 7–6 (7–4), 6–4, ending Bjorn's incredible five-year, 41-match Wimbledon run.

McEnroe won again in 1983 and 1984, and he won the doubles five times, four with Fleming, and, after an eight-year interval, in 1992 with German Michael Stich.

Three intense rivalries stand out during his career. He had the edge on Connors (20–31), but not Lendl (15–21), and was even with Borg (7–7).

Except for the French Open lapse against Lendl, he was virtually unbeatable in 1984, winning 13 of 15 singles tournaments on an 82–3 record. Other big seasons were 1979 (10 titles on a 94–12 record), 1980 (10 titles on 88–18). In 1979 he set an open-era record with 27 overall tournament victories, 17 in doubles, winning a record total of 177 matches. He

won the season-climaxing Masters singles thrice, 1978 and 1983–84, and is the all-time overall professional leader with 152 tournament victories: a 77–75 singles-doubles split. He is third in singles titles behind Connors's 109 and Lendl's 92, second in doubles behind Tom Okker's 78. His career singles match record is 849–183.

Ten years he ranked in the World Top Ten, and 16 in the U.S. (No. 1 there seven times).

His brother, Patrick McEnroe, younger by seven years, followed him as a standout pro, winning the French doubles (with Jim Grabb) in 1989. In 1991 they met in the Chicago final, the second such clash of brothers (Emilio Sanchez defeated Javier Sanchez, 6–3, 3–6, 6–2, in the 1987 Madrid final). John won, 3–6, 6–2, 6–4. John's prize money for 15 years as a pro was $12,227,622 at the close of 1992. He married movie actress Tatum O'Neal and they have three children.

MAJOR TITLES (17)—*Wimbledon singles, 1981–83–84; U.S. singles, 1979–80–81–84; Wimbledon doubles, 1979–81–83–84–92; U.S. doubles, 1979–81–83–84; French mixed, 1977.* OTHER U.S. TITLES—*Indoor singles, 1980; Hard Court singles, 1989; Indoor doubles, 1980, with Brian Gottfried; Clay Court doubles, 1979, with Gene Mayer.* DAVIS CUP—*1978–79–80–81–82–83–84–87–88–89–91–92; record: 41–8 in singles, in 18–2 in doubles.*

Ilie Nastase
Romania (1946–   )

No player in history has been more gifted or mystifying than the Bucharest Buffoon, Ilie Nastase, noted both for his sorcery with the racket and his bizarre, even objectionable behavior. He was an entertainer second to none, amusing spectators with his antics and mimicry, also infuriating them with gaucheries and walkouts.

Despite a fragile nervous system and erratic temperament, Nastase—slender,

Ilie Nastase: The sorcerer's apprentice. • *Jack Mecca*

quick, leggy and athletic—could do everything, and when his concentration held together he was an artist creating with great originality and panache. His record in the season-closing Masters was spectacular. He won four times, 1971 through 1973 and 1975, and was finalist to Guillermo Vilas in five sets in 1974.

Born July 19, 1946, in Bucharest, he was the first Romanian of international prominence, and largely through his play that small country rose to the Davis Cup final on three occasions, 1969, 1971, and 1972, losing each time to the U.S. At the end of 1985 after playing Davis Cup since 1966, Nastase ranked second among the most active players in Cup history, having won 109 of 146 singles and doubles engagements in 52 ties.

Romania was favored to lift the Cup from the U.S. in the 1972 finale on the friendly slow clay of Nastase's hometown. However, his nervousness combined with an inspirational performance by Stan

Smith added up to an 11–9, 6–2, 6–3 victory for the American in the crucial opening singles, and the U.S. kept the Cup, 3–2. Nastase's foremost disappointment occurred three months prior, when Smith narrowly defeated him in the Wimbledon final, 4–6, 6–3, 6–3, 4–6, 7–5, one of the most exciting championship matches there. Nastase was in another Wimbledon singles final in 1976, but was beaten easily

1969 during Romania's Davis Cup semifinal against the favored British when he beat Mark Cox in the decisive singles, and cooperated with Tiriac in a doubles win, putting Romania in the final against the U.S., where they lost, 5–0. Two years later Romania came closer against the U.S., 3–2, but it was Nastase's failure in the critical opener against Smith that was the difference, as it would be again in 1972.

By 1970 Nastase began to assert himself as a champion. He won the Italian singles and jolted Cliff Richey in the final of the U.S. Indoor, 6–8, 3–6, 6–4, 9–7, 6–0, the only instance of a victor making up so big a deficit including two match points, in the title match.

Despite his Davis Cup and Wimbledon heartaches of 1972, Nastase had the immeasurable consolation of winning the U.S. Open at Forest Hills from a seeming losing position, down 2–4 in the fourth set and a service break to open the fifth against Arthur Ashe. The score: 3–6, 6–3, 6–7 (1–5), 6–4, 6–3. It was his only major grass-court singles prize.

His finest season was 1973, when he was regarded as No. 1 in the world after winning the Italian, French and 13 other tournaments, and downing Tom Okker in the Masters final, 6–3, 7–5, 4–6, 6–3. That season he won 15 of 31 tourneys on a 118–17 match record, also eight doubles for an overall total of 23, tying Rod Laver's open-era record (17 singles, 6 doubles), broken in 1979 by John McEnroe's 27.

Though he provoked controversy, and his career was marred by fines, disqualifications, and suspensions, Nastase was good-natured and friendly off-court. He had a sense of humor in his oncourt shenanigans, but frequently did not know when to stop and lost control of himself. "I am a little crazy," he said, "but I try to be a good boy."

He was expert at putting the ball just beyond an opponent's reach, and applying discomfiting spin. He lobbed and retrieved splendidly, in his prime possibly the fastest player of all, and he could play either baseline or serve-and-volley. In 1976 he was the first European to exceed $1 million in career prize money, and had a career total of $2,076,761. Nastase played World Team Tennis for Hawaii in 1976 and Los Angeles in 1977–78, leading the latter to the league title in 1978 as player-coach.

Eight times between 1970 and 1977 he was ranked in the World Top Ten, No. 1, in 1973, the year he won the French and Italian back-to-back, an unusual coupling.

In a career begun in the amateur era and continued in the open era, he was one of five players to win more than 100 pro titles in singles (57) and doubles (51). He was inducted into the Hall of Fame in 1991.

MAJOR TITLES (7)—*French singles, 1973; U.S. singles, 1972; French doubles, 1970; Wimbledon doubles, 1973; U.S. doubles, 1975; Wimbledon mixed, 1970–72.* DAVIS CUP—*1966–67–68–69–70–71–72–73–74–75–76–77–79–80–82–83–84–85; record: 74–22 in singles, 35–15 in doubles.*

Martina Navratilova
Czechoslovakia/United States (1956–   )

As the game's most prolific winner of the open era—probably ever—Martina Navratilova, the puissant left-hander, continues to add to her record totals. Nobody has as glittering a trove of numbers. As a pro, at the close of 1992, she had played (352) and won (161) the most singles tournaments and matches, with a won-lost mark of 1,359–190, and amassed more prize money ($18,396,526) than all but Ivan Lendl.

Her doubles feats were as sparkling: played (270) and won (157) the most matches with a 943–111 won-lost mark. Overall: 318 titles in 622 tournaments, a 2,302–301 won-lost mark. Thus she batted .877 in singles, .895 in doubles, .844 for everything.

A sure shot for the Hall of Fame, arguably the greatest player of all time, Martina was born on Oct. 18, 1956, in Prague, Czechoslovakia, and became a U.S. citizen in 1981, after defecting six years earlier. She was raised by her mother, Jana, and stepfather, Mirek Navratil, whose name she took.

Despite her upbringing on slow clay in the small town of Revnice, outside of Prague, she has always been a tornado-like attacker, a net-rusher. She attracted notice at 16 in Paris, the French Open of 1973, by serving-and-volleying a clay specialist and former champ, Nancy Richey, to defeat, and reaching the quarters unseeded.

Her lustrous 16-year rivalry with Chris Evert was launched that year in Akron, Ohio, an indoor defeat. "She was overweight, but eager and gifted," Evert remembered. "It was a close match (7–6, 6–3). Even though I'd never heard of her, and couldn't pronounce or spell her name, I could tell she'd be trouble. Especially if she got in shape."

Martina Navratilova: Greatest of all? • *Russ Adams*

Navratilova, yet pudgy, began her run at Moody by coming from behind in the third set to beat top-seeded Evert, 2–6, 6–4, 7–5, in the 1978 final. She repeated over Evert, but was deterred, momentarily, in the 1980 and 1981 semis by Evert and Hana Mandlikova.

Rebounding, she reeled off championships in six successive years, snapping

She was trouble, and eventually Navratilova made extreme fitness her trademark in chasing and overcoming Evert, who became her good friend. Although Evert led in the rivalry, 21–4, at the high point of her dominance, Navratilova won their last encounter, Chicago, in 1988, 6–2, 6–2, to wind up with a 43–37 edge. Three years later, also in Chicago, Martina scaled Evert's seemingly unattainable record of 157 pro tournament victories. By beating Jana Novotna from two match points down, 7–6 (7–4), 4–6, 7–5, she nailed victory No. 158, and kept going. She had unknowingly begun to stalk Evert at home with her initial title, Pilsen, in 1973.

Her proudest times were spent in the game's temple, Centre Court, Wimbledon, where she became the all-time singles champ by defeating Zina Garrison, 6–4, 6–1, in 1990—her ninth championship. The record of eight had been achieved more than a half-century before when Helen Wills Moody beat Helen Jacobs in 1938.

Graf beat her for the title in 1991, too, but lost to Garrison in the 1990 semis. Thus Martina triumphed again in her 11th final. Also Wimbledon records: her nine consecutive final round appearances (1982–90) and 108 match wins. At the Big W through 1992 she was 108–11 in singles, 76–13 in doubles, 29–8 in mixed.

That, of course, has been her masterpiece, but Navratilova also won four U.S., three Australian and two French singles for a total of 18 majors, tying her with Evert, one behind Moody and eight behind Margaret Court whose record total (62 singles, doubles, mixed) she yet threatens with 54.

Winning the U.S. was her most frustrating trial. Not until her 11th try, in 1983 (having lost the 1981 final in a tie-breaker to Tracy Austin) did Navratilova make it: 6–1, 6–3, over Evert. In 1991, almost 35 she was the tourney's oldest losing finalist since 40-year-old Molla Mallory in 1924.

Only one prize, a singles Grand Slam, has eluded her—barely in 1983 and 1984. Although 1983 was her most overpowering season (16 victories in 17 tournaments on an 86–1 match record), it was 1984 (13 victories in 15 tourneys on 78–2) when the Slam seemed certain. With three of the titles in her satchel, she reached the semis of the last that year, the Australian, on a record 74-match winning streak, eclipsing Evert's 55 of 1974. However, Helena Sukova intervened, 1–6, 6–3, 7–5. After that Martina took off on a 54-match streak, severed by Hana Mandlikova. Mandlikova also snipped her second longest streak, 56, in the Australian final of 1987.

In 1983 a Slam never got started. Kathy Horvath, ranked 33rd, upset Navratilova in the fourth round of the first major, the French. Thereafter Martina won the next three, and so Sukova ended her string of six major titles.

Navratilova did, however, register a doubles Grand Slam with Pam Shriver in 1984. Perhaps the greatest of all teams, Navratilova-Shriver won 20 majors (equaling the record total of Louise Brough and Margaret duPont, 1942–1957). The Navratilova-Shriver combine produced 79 tournament victories, including 10 season-climaxing Virginia Slims titles, and a record 109-match winning streak between 1983 and a 1985 loss in the Wimbledon final to Liz Smylie and Kathy Jordan.

As a tireless all-round campaigner, Martina piled up awesome singles and doubles totals. She won more than 20 titles in singles and doubles six years: 29 in 1982 (15 singles) and 1983 (16 singles). Twelve years she won more than 100 matches overall, singles and doubles, a high of 160 (against seven losses) in 1982.

During 1985–86–87 she was in the final of all 11 majors (Australian not held in 1986), winning six, a singular feat until Steffi Graf played in 12 straight between 1987 and 1990, winning 10.

In 1987 she made a rare triple at the U.S. Open (singles, doubles, mixed), the third of the open era.

From 1973 through 1982 Navratilova was no worse than No. 4 in the world rankings, attaining No. 1 1978, keeping it in 1979. She returned for a record run of 150 weeks, 1982 into 1987, until supplanted by Graf in 1987, who broke the record with 186 straight weeks. She has ranked in the U.S. Top Ten 14 years, no worse than No. 3 (1980–81), and at No. 1 a record 12 years, 11 straight since 1982, also a record.

Disapproving of what was termed Navratilova's increasing "Americanization," sports federation authorities in the communist Czechoslovak government reportedly planned to curtail her travel. "Learning this," she said, "I knew I had to defect." She announced her intention of becoming a U.S. citizen at the U.S. Open of 1975. For years after she was considered a "non-person," her results never printed or announced in Czechoslovakia.

Returning to her homeland in triumph (and to the government's discomfort) as a U.S. citizen in 1986, she led her adopted country's team to a Federation Cup victory, as she had Czechoslovakia 11 years before.

Playing for the U.S., she was peerless, unbeaten, and helped win two other Federation as well as one Wightman Cup.

MAJOR TITLES (54)—*Australian singles, 1981–83–85; French singles, 1982–84; Wimbledon singles, 1978–79–82–83–84–85–86–87–90; U.S. singles, 1983–84–86–87; Australian doubles, 1980–82–83–84–85–87–88–89; French doubles, 1975–82–84–85–86–87–88; Wimbledon doubles, 1976–79–81–82–83–84–86; U.S. doubles, 1977–78–80–83–84–86–87–89–90; French mixed, 1974–85; Wimbledon mixed; 1985; U.S. mixed, 1985–87.* OTHER U.S. TITLES—*Indoor singles, 1976–81–84–86; Indoor doubles, 1979, with Billie Jean King; 1981–84–85, with Pam Shriver.* FEDERATION CUP—*1975–82–86–89; record: 20–0 in singles, 16–0 in doubles.* WIGHTMAN CUP—*1983; record: 2–0 in singles, 1–0 in doubles.*

John Newcombe
Australia (1944–   )

When John Newcombe and Tony Roche, an Australian pair, won the Wimbledon doubles of 1965, it was the start not only of an extraordinary string of major titles for Newcombe but also for the two of them as a unit.

Two years earlier, though, Newcombe,

hard sets in the decisive fifth match.

Newcombe and the left-handed Roche, one of the great doubles teams in history, won five Wimbledons together, a modern record (topped only by the English Doherty brothers, who won eight between 1897 and 1905, and the English Renshaw brothers, who won seven between 1880 and 1889). Newcombe and Roche also won the U.S. in 1967, the French in 1967–69, and the Australian in 1965–67–71–76, standing as one of only four teams to win all the Big Four titles during a career. Their three successive Wimbledons, 1968–69–70, enabled them to set a tourney record of 18 straight doubles match wins.

It was in singles, though, that Newcombe made his name. He and Rod Laver are the only players to win the men's singles at Forest Hills and Wimbledon as amateurs and pros. Newcombe was the last amateur champion at Wimbledon in 1967, and repeated in 1970 and 1971 during the open era.

In all Newcombe, a right-hander, won 25 major titles in singles, doubles, and mixed doubles to stand second behind Roy Emerson (28) in the list of all-time male championships.

John Newcombe: Best server of his time.
• *Peter Mecca*

John David Newcombe was born May 23, 1944, in Sydney, and was more interested in other sports as a youngster. Not until he was 17 did a career in tennis appeal to him. But he was powerful, athletic and extremely competitive, and Australian Davis Cup captain Harry Hopman was glad when Newcombe turned his full attention to tennis. Newcombe helped Hopman win four Cups, 1964–67, and then returned to Cup play in 1973, when all pros were reinstated, to be part of perhaps the strongest team ever, alongside Laver, Ken Rosewall and Mal Anderson. In the finale that year Newcombe and Laver were overpowering. Both beat Stan Smith and Tom Gorman in singles, and teamed in crushing Smith and Erik van Dillen in the doubles during a 5–0 Australian victory that ended five-year possession of the Cup by the U.S.

Newcombe also played in the World Cup in 1970, the inaugural of the since disbanded team match between the Aussies and the U.S., and helped win five of those Cups for his country.

Newcombe's serve, forehand and volleying were the backbone of his attacking game, which was at its best on grass. His heavy serve was possibly the best of his era. Grass was the setting for his foremost singles wins, the three Wimbledons plus two U.S. Championships at Forest Hills in 1967 and 1973.

Newcombe regretted missing successive Wimbledons of 1972–73 when he felt he might have added to his string. In 1972 he was a member of the World Championship Tennis pro troupe that was banned because of the quarrels between its leader, Lamar Hunt, and the International Tennis Federation. In 1973 Newcombe was a member of the players union, Association of Tennis Pros, which boycotted Wimbledon in another dispute with the ITF. The following year he stretched his Wimbledon match win streak to 18 before losing to Rosewall in the quarterfinals. That year Newcombe won the World Championship Tennis singles over an adolescent Bjorn Borg, 17.

Newcombe felt, "I'm at my best in a five-set match, especially if I get behind. My adrenalin starts pumping." This was evident in two of his outstanding triumphs, both over Stan Smith, a strong rival for world supremacy in the early 1970s. Newcombe beat Smith, 6–3, 5–7, 2–6, 6–4, 6–4, in the 1971 Wimbledon title match, and 6–1, 3–6, 6–3, 3–6, 6–4, during the 1973 Davis Cup finale, rating the latter as his finest performance.

In 1967 he was the No. 1 amateur in the world, and in 1970 and 1971 No. 1 of all. He was one of the first to sign a contract to play World Team Tennis (with Houston) in 1974, his presence helping give the new league credibility, although he played just that one season. His best pro season was 1971, when he won five of 19 singles tourneys on a 53–14 match record.

He totaled 73 pro titles, 32 in singles, 41 in doubles, and won $1,062,408. Newcombe was named to the Hall of Fame, along with Roche, in 1986. He is married to former German player Angelika Pfannenburg.

MAJOR TITLES (25)—*Australian singles, 1973–75; Wimbledon singles, 1967–70–71; U.S. singles, 1967–73; Australian doubles, 1965–67–71–73–76; French doubles, 1967–69–73; Wimbledon doubles, 1965–66–68–69–70–74; U.S. doubles, 1967–71–73; U.S. mixed, 1964.* DAVIS CUP—*1963–64–65–66–67–73–75–76; record: 16–7 in singles, 9–2 in doubles.*

Ken Rosewall
Australia (1934–   )

As the Doomsday Stroking Machine, the remarkable Kenneth Robert "Muscles" Rosewall was a factor in three decades of tennis, winning his first major titles, the Australian and French singles in 1953, and continuing as a tournament winner past his 43rd birthday.

He was yet a tough foe into 1978. At the close of the 1977 season, he was still ranked as one of the top 15 players in the game on the ATP computer, having won two of 24 tournaments on a 44–23 match record.

"It's something I enjoy and find I still do well," was his simple explanation of his prowess in 1977, "but I never imagined myself playing so long when I turned pro in 1957."

The son of a Sydney, New South Wales, Australia, grocer, Rosewall was born in that city Nov. 2, 1934, and grew up there. A natural left-hander, he was taught to play right-handed by his father, Robert Rosewall, and developed a peerless backhand. Some felt his lack of size (5-foot-7, 135 pounds) would impede him, but it was never a problem. He moved quickly, with magnificent anticipation and perfect balance, and never suffered a serious injury.

• UPI

Though his serve wasn't formidable, he placed it well, and backed it up with superb volleying. Rosewall was at home on any surface, and at the baseline or the net. He had an even temperament, was shy and reticent, but good-natured.

Although Rosewall, the little guy, always seemed overshadowed by a rival, first Lew Hoad, then Pancho Gonzalez and Rod Laver, he outlasted them all, and had the last competitive word. Even when Laver was acknowledged as the best in the world, Rosewall could bother him, and twice shocked Rod in the rich World Championship Tennis finals in Dallas in 1971 and 1972, snatching the $50,000 first prize from the favorite's grasp. The latter match, thought by many to be the greatest ever played—a 3½-hour struggle watched by millions on TV—went to Rosewall, 4–6, 6–0, 6–3, 6–7, 7–6, when he stroked two magnificent backhand returns to escape a seemingly untenable position in the decisive tie-breaker and win by two points (7 points to 5), the closest finish of an important championship until Boris Becker beat Ivan Lendl, also 7–5, in a fifth-set tie-breaker, for the 1988 Masters title.

Rosewall and Hoad, born only 21 days apart, Ken the elder, were linked as teammates and rivals almost from their first days on court. In 1952 as 17-year-olds they made an immediate impact on their first overseas tour, both reaching the quarterfinals of the U.S. Championships at Forest Hills, Ken beating the No. 1 American, Vic Seixas. Late the following year (having won the Wimbledon doubles together), shortly after "Muscles" by his countrymen, Ken always managed to keep up in the early days and often surpass. Hoad beat Rosewall in the 1956 Wimbledon final, but his bid for a Grand Slam was spoiled when Rosewall knocked him off in the U.S. final at Forest Hills, 4–6, 6–2, 6–2, 6–3.

After helping Australia win the Davis Cup over the U.S. in 1956, Rosewall turned pro to take on the professional king, Pancho Gonzalez. Gonzalez stayed on top, winning their head-to-head tour, 50–26, but it was apparent that Rosewall belonged at the uppermost level. Thus began one of the longest active professional careers, certainly the most distinguished in regard to significant victories over so long a span. Rosewall won the first of his three U.S. Pro singles titles over Laver in 1963, the second by beating Gonzalez and Laver in succession in 1965 and the third over Cliff Drysdale in 1971.

He holds several longevity records. Fourteen years after his 1956 Forest Hills triumph over Hoad he beat the favored Tony Roche, 10 years his junior, 2–6, 6–4, 7–6, 6–3, to win the U.S. Championship again. Eighteen years after, he was the finalist (having beaten favored John

Newcombe) but lost in 1974 to Jimmy Connors. Twenty years after appearing in the first of four Wimbledon finals, he lost the 1974 final to Connors. The only big one Rosewall missed out on was Wimbledon singles, but he won the doubles twice. Nineteen years after his first major title, the Australian, he won it again, in 1972. Twenty years after his first Davis Cup appearance he returned to help Australia win once again in 1973, and played his last cup match in 1975. He played on four Australian Davis Cup winners and three World Cup winners in the since disbanded team match against the U.S.

Altogether, Rosewall won 18 major titles in singles, doubles and mixed, the sixth-highest male total. In 1974 he tried World Team Tennis for a season, serving as player-coach of the Pittsburgh Triangles. He was the second tennis player to cross $1 million in prize money, following Laver, and had a career total of $1,600,300.

Like Laver, Gonzalez and Hoad, and a few others, he had one of those rare careers spanning the amateur era, pro one-night stand years and the open era. His victories were innumerable, but in the last section, begun at age 33, he won 50 titles, 32 in singles, 18 in doubles. The first of those was the baptismal "Open," the British Hard Court singles at Bournemouth in April 1968; the second, the initial major open, the French, a month later—both over Laver. His last pro triumph, Hong Kong in 1977 over Tom Gorman, was recorded two weeks after his 43rd birthday, making him the second oldest (just shy of Gonzalez) to win an open-era title.

Rosewall was named to the Hall of Fame in 1980, along with Hoad.

MAJOR TITLES (18)—*Australian singles, 1953–55–71–72; French singles, 1953–68; U.S. singles, 1956–70; Australian doubles, 1953–56–72; French doubles, 1953–68; Wimbledon doubles,* *1953–56; U.S. doubles, 1956–69; U.S. mixed, 1956.* DAVIS CUP—*1953–54–55–56–73–75; record: 17–2 in singles, 2–1 in doubles.*

Manolo Santana
Spain (1938–   )

One of the masters of legerdemain, Manuel Martinez "Manolo" Santana was the first post-World War II European to gain universal respect because he not only won the most difficult clay-court event, the French singles in 1961 and 1964, but also the grass-court gems, Wimbledon of 1966 and the U.S. Championship of 1965 at Forest Hills. In doing so, the engaging Spaniard was the first European champ at Forest Hills since Frenchman Henri Cochet in 1928.

"He was a magician on clay," said Rod Laver. "Manolo could hit the most incredible angles, drive you crazy with topspin lobs or drop shots. And he improved his volleying so that he was dangerous on grass, too."

In 1965 Santana became a national hero in Spain and was decorated by the country's leader, Francisco Franco, with the coveted Medal of Isabella, qualifying for the title *Ilustrissimo*. That year Santana spearheaded the 4–1 upset of the U.S. at Barcelona during the Davis Cup campaign and led Spain all the way to the finale for the first time. Although the Spaniards were turned back, 4–1, Santana gave Roy Emerson his only defeat in 12 title-round singles. Two years later he drove Spain to the finale again, salvaging the only point in a 4–1 defeat by beating John Newcombe.

Only Italian Nicola Pietrangeli (164 singles and doubles in 66 ties) and Romanian Ilie Nastase played more Davis Cup than Santana, who played 120 singles (69–16) and doubles (24–9) in 46 matches between 1958 and 1973. He set Cup records by win-

Manolo Santana: Magician on clay. • *UPI*

Less than a month later a similarly jubilant celebration was staged at Forest Hills after Santana jolted Cliff Drysdale in the U.S. final, 6–2, 7–9, 7–5, 6–1. A troupe of dancers from the World's Fair's Spanish Pavilion toted him from stadium to clubhouse, whereupon they serenaded him.

The following year was Santana's at Wimbledon, where he beat Ralston in the

U.S. Championship at Forest Hills a decade after his own, though the surface had by then been transformed to clay.

Beginning in 1961, Santana was in the World Top Ten seven years, No. 1 in 1966. His career was virtually over when the open era arrived, but he did elate his countrymen by winning Barcelona in 1970, his last singles victory, plus three pro doubles titles.

Santana came out of retirement briefly in 1973 to play his last season of Davis Cup, and again in 1974 to act as player-coach for New York in the new World Team Tennis League. He was named to the Hall of Fame in 1984, the second Spaniard, following Manuel Alonso.

MAJOR TITLES (5)—*French singles, 1961–64; Wimbledon singles, 1966; U.S. singles, 1965; French doubles, 1963.* DAVIS CUP—*1958–59–60–61–62–63–64–65–66–67–68–69–70–73; record: 69–7 in singles, 23–11 in doubles.*

ning 13 singles matches in 1967 (equalled by Nastase in 1971), and also by winning 17 singles and doubles in 1965 and 19657 (topped by Nastase's 18 in 1971).

Born May 10, 1938, in Madrid, he worked as a ball boy at a local club and picked up the game. He was a very appealing player, a right-hander, who frequently smiled at play and was an admirable sportsman. His racket control was phenomenal, enabling him to hit with touch and power. He had great flair, the ability to improvise and to inspire himself and his partners and teammates. Never losing heart in the doubles of the 1965 Davis Cup against the U.S., he rallied partner Luis Arilla as they stormed back to beat Dennis Ralston and Clark Graebner, 4–6, 3–6, 6–3, 6–4, 11–9, in an emotional battle that clinched the decision. Cushions showered down on the two Spaniards as they were carried about the stadium court of the Real Club de Tennis in the manner of bullfighters. Santana and Arilla wept with joy at the most tremendous victory in Spanish tennis annals.

Frank Sedgman
Australia (1927–)

The beginning of the most powerful dynasty in tennis history was in the strokes of Frank Allan Sedgman, the Australian savior of 1950.

Australia was sagging in the Davis Cup after World War II, losing four successive finales to the U.S. Then, in 1950, 22-year-old Sedgman—loser of both his singles the previous year—startled crowds at Forest Hills by beating Tom Brown and Ted Schroeder in singles, joining John Bromwich for the doubles win to spearhead a 4–1 victory for the Aussies.

Not since 1911—Norman Brookes—had an Aussie won three matches in a Cup triumph. In the company of Ken McGregor that year, Mervyn Rose and McGregor the next, and McGregor again in 1952, Sedgman led the way to three straight Cups. In 1951 Sedgman became the first of nine Aussie men to win 15 U.S. championships at Forest Hills, and he repeated the following year.

Those Cup successes were the start of captain Harry Hopman's stewardship under which Australia won the Davis trophy 15 times between 1950 and 1967. And also the start of Sedgman's nearly three years as the premier amateur.

Sedgman, tall, extremely athletic, right-handed, was born Oct. 29, 1927, in Mount Albert, Victoria, Australia, and was such an acquisitive winner of major titles during the late 1940s and early 1950s that he stands third among all-time male champions with 22 major victories in singles, doubles and mixed doubles, three behind John Newcombe and six behind Roy Emerson.

In 1951 Sedgman and McGregor scored the only Grand Slam in men's doubles by winning all the Big Four (Australian, Wimbledon, French and U.S.) within a calendar year. In 1952, his last season as an amateur, Sedgman was the last man to make a rare Wimbledon triple, adding the doubles (with McGregor) and mixed (with Doris Hart) to his singles conquest.

Frank Sedgman: The first $100,000-a-year man.
• *New York Herald Tribune*

Speed, brilliant volleying and a heavy forehand were his chief assets, plus a fighting—yet good-natured—spirit.

Jack Kramer, proprietor of the professional tour and its foremost player, enticed Sedgman to become his challenger in 1953, and they played the customary head-to-head tour between the amateur-king-turned-pro-rookie and the incumbent, Kramer, who stayed on top, 54–41. However, Sedgman's share of the gate was $102,000, and he was the first male player to earn more than 100 grand in a season.

Sedgman continued to barnstorm with the pros into the 1960s. He was finalist to Pancho Gonzalez for the U.S. Pro singles championship in 1954 and won the U.S. Pro doubles with Andres Gimeno in 1961. Keeping himself unusually fit, he was able to launch a second professional career in 1974 when promoter Al Bunis formed the Grand Masters tour for ex-champs over 45. Sedgman won the Grand Masters championship in a season's-end playoff among the top eight players in 1975 and 1977–78, and in this second phase of professionalism won more than $250,000 over six seasons.

His fleeting residency in the World Top Ten covered 1949 through 1952, No. 1 the last two years. Sedgman was named to the Hall of Fame in 1979.

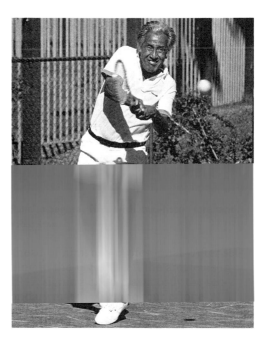

Pancho Segura: First with two-fisted forehand.
• *Russ Adams*

Pancho Segura
Ecuador (1921–   )

A strange sight was Francisco "Pancho" Segura when he appeared on the American scene in 1942 and seized the No. 4 U.S. ranking. He had an unorthodox two-fisted forehand, and flimsy-looking bowed legs that seemed incapable of holding him up. Yet the little guy (5-foot-6) was quick, nimble, and extremely effective.

Segura was born June 20, 1921, in Guayaquil, Ecuador, and was raised there. A childhood attack of rickets deformed his legs but his will was strong, and he drove himself to play tennis well, even though he was so weak at first that he had to grip the racket with both hands. A right-hander, he was likely the first to utilize a two-fisted forehand.

Entering the University of Miami on a tennis scholarship, he won the U.S. Intercollegiate singles in 1943–44–45, the only man in this century to take three straight. He won the U.S. Indoor title of 1946 and the U.S. Clay Court of 1944, was a U.S. semifinalist 1942–43–44–45 and a member of the U.S. Top Ten six times, No. 3 in 1943–44–45. But his best days were

ahead of him, as a professional. After settling in the U.S., he left the amateurs in 1947, signing on to play mostly the secondary matches on the tour of one-nighters. Unfortunately for Segura, he was out of the limelight once he became a professional, but while he beat Dinny Pails, Frank Parker, and Ken McGregor in their series, sharpening his strokes and tactics and becoming one of the great players, he received little recognition. Jack Kramer and Pancho Gonzalez were the stars, but Segura was making his mark in a small circle as a shrewd strategist, a cunning lobber, and a killer with a forehand.

He toured for nearly two decades and stands as one of the prominent figures in the history of the U.S. Pro Championships. Segura won the singles title three times in a row, first in 1950 over Frank Kovacs, then in 1951 and 1952 over Gonzalez. Segura lost the title to Gonzalez on three occasions, 1955, 1956 and 1957, and a fourth time, at age 41, to Butch Buchholz in 1962.

Segura also won the doubles with Jack Kramer in 1948 and 1955, and with Gonzalez in 1954 and 1958.

Hardy and good-natured, Segura was a favorite with crowds. He could always smile and crack a joke, yet was thoroughly professional and a constant competitor. He never made big money. Open tennis arrived too late for him, but he entered the doubles of the first open Wimbledon in 1968 with Alex Olmedo, and in the second round they won the longest doubles match of Wimbledon's open era, 94 games, over Abe Segal and Gordon Forbes, 32–30, 5–7, 6–4, 6–4. The 62-game set was the longest ever at Wimbledon.

Segura was elected to the Hall of Fame in 1984 and he concentrates on teaching as tennis director at the LaCosta Resort in Carlsbad, Cal.

U.S. TITLES (14)—*Intercollegiate singles, 1943–44–45; Indoor singles, 1946; Clay Court singles, 1944; Pro singles, 1950–51–52; Clay Court doubles, 1944–45 with Bill Talbert; Pro doubles, 1948–55 with Jack Kramer; 1954–58 with Pancho Gonzalez.*

Stan Smith
United States (1946–)

One of the great Davis Cup competitors, Stan Smith added the U.S. (1971) and Wimbledon (1972) titles to his laurels, and, with Bob Lutz, was part of one of the preeminent doubles teams. Smith, who overcame teenage awkwardness, to become a feared 6-foot-3 foe, with crashing serves and volleys, may have hit his zenith on alien clay. That was in Bucharest in 1972 as the U.S. won a fifth consecutive Cup, and he supplied the clinching victory—the insuperable third point—for a fifth time. That's a Davis Cup record to which he added in 1979, with Bob Lutz, in the 5–0 victory over Italy at San Francisco.

Stan was in at the finish of seven Cup victories, tying him with Bill Tilden for a

Stan Smith: His Cup runneth over. • *UPI*

U.S. high. And he had a smaller share of an eighth Cup, in 1981, when he and Lutz took a doubles over Ivan Lendl and Tom Smid—the Cup adieu for Stan and Bob, at Flushing Meadow—in the win over Czechoslovakia en route to the final.

A notable sportsman, he had to "concentrate so hard I got a headache," he said after the three-day ordeal at the hands of a loud partisan crowd and overly patriotic line judges in Bucharest. It was an extended, rocky campaign during which Smith won seven of eight singles and, with Erik van Dillen, all five doubles. Stan scored the clinching point in each of five matches and nailed down two of the most dramatic singles victories ever by an American in the finale. Romania, loser to the U.S. in the 1969 and 1971 showdowns, appeared the favorite on home earth, but Smith shocked Ilie Nastase on the slow court, 11–9, 6–2, 6–3, to lead off, and then out-battled the shrewd, combative Ion Tiriac in a tense five-set struggle, 4–6, 6–2, 6–4, 2–6, 6–0.

Knowing that he had to hit outright winners well away from the lines to make sure of the points, Smith did just that to storm through a last-set bagel and send the U.S. safely ahead, 3–1, in the 3–2 victory.

Born Dec. 4, 1946, in Pasadena, Cal., he grew up there and was an All-American at the University of Southern California, where he won the U.S. Intercollegiate sin-

Indoor singles, 1972; Indoor doubles, 1966–69 with Bob Lutz; 1970, with Arthur Ashe; Clay Court doubles, 1968, with Lutz; Hard Court singles, 1966–67–68; Hard Court doubles, 1966, with Lutz; Pro doubles, 1973, with Erik van Dillen; 1974–77, with Bob Lutz; Intercollegiate singles, 1968; Intercollegiate doubles, 1967–68 with Lutz. DAVIS CUP—*1968–69–70–71–72–73–75–77–78–79–81; record; 15–5 in singles, 20–3 in doubles.*

Cup matches together. As the U.S. ran up a record Cup streak of 17 victories from 1968 to the finale of 1973, Smith was involved in 14, the clincher in 12.

His 1972 Wimbledon triumph over Nastase, 4–6, 6–3, 6–3, 4–6, 7–5 was one of the outstanding finals, and his 1971 defeat of Jan Kodes at Forest Hills, 3–6, 6–3, 6–2, 7–6 (5–3), was the first U.S. final to conclude in a tie-breaker. Smith and Lutz won the U.S. doubles four times, the Australian once. In a career spanning the amateur and open eras, he was one of five centurions, winning at least 100 pro titles overall in singles and doubles. Stan hit the century with 39 singles, 61 doubles, and made $1,774,881 in career prize money. Eleven times between 1967 and 1980 he was in the U.S. Top Ten, No. 1 four years, 1969–71–72–73. Six straight times from 1970 he was in the World Top Ten, No. 1 in 1972.

Stan entered the Hall of Fame in 1987. He served in the U.S. Army and is director of coaching for the USTA.

MAJOR TITLES (7)—*Wimbledon singles, 1972; U.S. singles, 1971; Australian doubles, 1970; U.S. doubles, 1968–74–78–80.* OTHER U.S. TITLES—

to their Grand Slams, have won those three uppermost championships within a calendar year.

Moreover, Trabert also won the U.S. Indoor and U.S. Clay Court titles, adding them to the pre-eminent American championships on grass at Forest Hills.

For that year, probably the most productive ever by an American man, he won 18 of 23 singles tourneys on a 106–7 match record. Included was a winning streak of 36 matches. He also won 12 doubles titles (with Vic Seixas).

An exceptional athlete, Marion Anthony Trabert was born Aug. 16, 1930, in Cincinnati, where he grew up. He was a standout basketball player at the University of Cincinnati, for which he also won the U.S. Intercollegiate singles title in 1951.

The French Championships has traditionally been the most difficult battleground for American men. Trabert won five titles in Paris, the singles in 1954 and 1955. Thirty-four years passed before another American, Michael Chang, won in 1989. Trabert also won the doubles in 1950 (with Bill Talbert) and in 1954 and

Tony Trabert: A champ for all surfaces. • *UPI*

1955 (with Vic Seixas). Only a defeat by Ken Rosewall (the eventual champ) in the semifinals of the Australian Championships ruined Trabert's chance at a Grand Slam in 1955.

For five years Trabert was a mainstay of the U.S. Davis Cup team, along with Seixas. In each of those years the U.S. reached the challenge round finale, and Trabert's best-remembered match may have been a defeat, a tremendous struggle against Lew Hoad on a rainy afternoon in 1953 at Melbourne. Hoad won out, 7–5, in the fifth, and Australia kept the Cup. However, Trabert and Seixas returned to Australia a year later, where Trabert beat Hoad on the opening day in singles and he and Seixas won the doubles over Hoad and Rex Hartwig in a 3–2 triumph, the only U.S. seizure of the Cup from the Aussies during an eight-year stretch.

Though an attacker with a powerful backhand and strong volley, the competitive right-hander also had exceptional

groundstrokes. In winning the U.S. Singles at Forest Hills twice, 1953 and 1955, and Wimbledon, he did not lose a set, a rare feat.

Amassing 15 U.S. titles in singles and doubles, he was one of two Americans (the other was Art Larsen) to win singles championships on all four surfaces: grass at Forest Hills, indoor, clay court and hard court.

Following the custom of the time, Trabert, as the top amateur, signed on with the professionals to challenge the ruler, Pancho Gonzalez, on a head-to-head tour in 1956. Gonzalez won, 74–27. Trabert was runner-up to Alex Olmedo for the U.S. Pro singles title in 1960, having won the doubles with Hartwig in 1956.

When his playing career ended, Trabert worked as a teaching pro and as a television commentator on tennis. In 1976 he returned to the Davis Cup scene as the U.S. captain, leading the Cup-winning teams of 1978–79.

He had four years in the U.S. and World Top Ten, 1951–53–54–55, No. 1 in each in 1953 and 1955, before turning pro. His amateur career was interrupted by service in the U.S. Navy. He was named to the Hall of Fame in 1978.

MAJOR TITLES (10)—*French singles, 1954–55; Wimbledon singles, 1955; U.S. singles, 1953–55; Australian doubles, 1955; French doubles, 1950–54–55; U.S. doubles, 1954.* OTHER U.S. TITLES—*Intercollegiate singles, 1951; Indoor singles, 1955; Clay Court singles, 1951–55; Hard Court singles, 1953; Indoor doubles, 1954, with Bill Talbert; 1955, with Vic Seixas; Clay Court doubles, 1951–55, with Hamilton Richardson; 1954, with Seixas; Hard Court doubles, 1950–53, with Tom Brown; Pro doubles, 1956, with Rex Hartwig.* DAVIS CUP (*As player*)—*1951–52–53–54–55; record: 16–5 in singles, 11–3 in doubles; DAVIS CUP (As captain)—1953–76–77–78–79–80; Record: 14-3, 2 Cups.*

Mats Wilander
Sweden (1964–)

No sooner had Swedes grieved the retirement of Bjorn Borg, and wistfully thought of his sixth French title in 1981, than an unheralded kid countryman conquered Paris the following year. That was unseeded 17-year-old Mats Arne Wilander, a rugged 6-footer, who beat the powerful one-time champ, Guillermo Vilas, at his

Mats Wilander: All but a Grand Slam. • *Mitchell Reibell*

record for the majors, Wilander won the French again in 1985 (dethroning Ivan Lendl, 6–2 in the fourth) and 1988, the Australian, on grass, in 1983–84.

But it was 1988, an all-time season, that stands as his masterwork. He won three of the majors, starting with a magnificent Australian final-round victory over home-towner Patrick Cash in Melbourne's newly opened Flinders Park, 6–3, 6–7 (3–7), 2–6, 6–1, 8–6. It was the Aussie Open's first year on hard courts, and victory meant that Mats was only the second man (emulating Jimmy Connors) to win majors on grass, clay and hard.

He won the French without too much trouble, but whatever dreams he had of a Grand Slam were pierced by Miloslav Mecir in the Wimbledon quarters. An arduous U.S. backcourt duel with Lendl (who'd beaten him for the title the year before) lasted more than four hours. At last Wilander showed more offensive initiative to win, 6–4, 4–6, 6–3, 5–7, 6–4. As the first winner of three majors in a year since Connors in 1974, he completed 1988 with six victories in 15 tournament on a 53–11 match record, and with a personal prize-

money high, $1,726,731. (His career total was $7,377,193.)

But after that, having attained the No. 1 ranking, he seemed to lose motivation. He was through as a factor, and by 1991 he retired. His last of 33 career titles was at Itaparica (Brazil) in 1990. But, in some ways, Wilander outdid Borg. Bjorn never won three majors in a year, and led Sweden to but one Davis Cup to Mats' three. Stunning Connors, 6–1, 6–3, 6–3, on opening day in Goteborg in 1984, Wilander launched Sweden to a 4–1 upset of the U.S. He backboned a 3–2 win over Germany in 1985 in Munich, and a 5–0 win over India in 1987 in Goteborg.

Speedy afoot and an unrelenting competitor through 1988, he was at first a pure topspinning grind-it-out baseliner, a right-hander with a two-fisted backhand. But Mats developed attacking skills and a good volley, winning the Wimbledon doubles in 1986 with Joakim Nystrom.

Two memorable matches were Davis Cup losses, the longest and third-longest played: 6:32 against John McEnroe (9–7, 6–2, 15–17, 3–6, 8–6) in 1982; 6:04 against Horst Skoff of Austria (6–7, 7–6, 1–6, 6–4, 9–7) in 1989. His career figures: 33 wins in 220 tournaments on a 524–164 match record.

He was born Aug. 22, 1964, in Vaxjo, Sweden, grew up there, and lives with his wife, Sonya, in Greenwich, Conn.

MAJOR TITLES (8)—*Australian singles, 1983–84–88; French singles, 1982–85–88; U.S. singles, 1988; Wimbledon doubles, 1986.* DAVIS CUP—*1981–82–83–84–85–86–87–88–89–90; record: 36–14 in singles, 7–2 in doubles.*

7: THE OFFICIALS

The chair umpire is the most vulnerable of all. He or she sits in a shaky chair some eight feet above the court, an open target to personal insult from the players and derisive taunts from the fans.

A crafty conniver such as Jimmy Connors was a master at orchestrating a crowd into a ranting rage, creating a frenzy of fury directed on the head of a single official. The umpire, in turn, is virtually defenseless, unable to run away, has nowhere to hide and is sometimes reluctant to enforce the disciplinary powers as regulated.

Nevertheless, the person perceived by many fans as a sitting symbol of scorn is in fact a strong and secure individual, one able to endure personal attack without upstaging the players or seeking retribution.

"We're very conscious of the situation," says Jay Snyder, chief umpire for the USTA. "That's the reason there are so few top level, full-time umpires. You must be able to completely disregard what is going on around you and to have the ability to with-around them, and the top officials are able to do the same thing."

Sandy Schwan, a long-time official with the USTA, says the key to handling an abusive situation is to not take it personally.

"What you really focus on is the match and what the players are doing," she says. "Just as you deal with people in real life if you have the ability to communicate well and be sensitive to what's happening around you, you must tune out the bad things that are happening and focus on what the players are feeling.

"You make sure the players are being treated fairly, but at the same time be sure that you're being treated fairly."

The adversarial relationship between player and official is woefully one-sided, and has only become more vitriolic as the stakes have magnified.

Since the advent of the open era in 1968, officials have been sadly underpaid and subject to extraordinary pressure and antagonism. Million-dollar tournament purses no longer are unusual, and a personal fortune for a player can ride on a single call.

In contrast, when Arthur Ashe defeated Tom Okker in the first U.S. Open in 1968, the top prize was $14,000, and Ashe didn't even take a penny since he was an amateur. Twenty-four years later, Stefan Edberg and Monica Seles each earned $500,000 as 1992 champions.

Compounding the problem, tennis officials traditionally wield less authority than arbiters of other major sports. Unlike a team sport, where there is always someone sitting on the bench to replace a banished teammate, a tennis player stands alone. Disqualify him and the match is over, leaving a lot of unhappy paying customers.

But a major breakthrough occurred on a hot, humid Sunday in Melbourne on the seventh day of the 1990 Australian Open. On that day, years of shoddy, sophomoric behavior caught up to John McEnroe, and he was disqualified from his fourth-round match against Mikael Pernfors for verbal abuse and an audible obscenity.

It was the first time ever a top-rated player had been booted from a Grand Slam tournament. More important, the disqualification delivered a definite message to the players that if it can happen to McEnroe, it can happen to anyone.

Ken Farrar, a former hockey referee who went on to become a tennis referee and then a supervisor for the Men's Tennis Council, was working his first tournament as head supervisor for the Grand Slams when he ordered English umpire Gerry Armstrong to default McEnroe.

"I've never discussed it with other players, but there's no question they now recognize they can possibly be disqualified and it's applicable to anyone, not just to a little guy," Farrar says.

The players, for their part, insist they need an outlet to express their feelings,

and the only targets in sight are the officials.

"Nobody's fighting for our rights out there," says Jimmy Connors, who was still playing championship caliber tennis past the age of 40. "I don't have a coach, I don't have a team captain, I don't have anyone.

"If I don't stand up for my rights, then who will? I just can't go out there and let them take full advantage of me. I've got to be able to project a little bit, but as the rules go today, you can't even project."

Farrar is sympathetic to this plea.

"We recognize that players have to vent their frustration or anger at times on court," he says. "The officials are taught to accept this, within limits. But when those limits are transgressed, then the Code of Conduct comes into effect.

"We don't mind players shouting and yelling on court, but when they use profanity or verbally abuse an official, that's not acceptable."

If a situation is developing, umpires are instructed to discuss it with the player during a changeover. This is called "a soft warning." The more experienced officials are better able to placate the player while issuing a word of warning such as "stop throwing your racket around, or the next time it's going to cost you."

"You try to let a player blow off steam," says Snyder, who has worked as an official more than 25 years. "You've got a pressure situation that is escalating, and instead of allowing it to blow up, your top umpires will allow that player to blow off a little bit of steam before they say 'let's play,' which means it's time to go back to play."

On one major point both players and officials are in agreement: mistakes are

Classic confrontation: John McEnroe arguing a call with the umpire at Wimbledon in 1980. • *Wide World*

made on court. The players certainly are guilty of their share, and officials contribute a few of their own.

The speed of the game can blur the eyesight, and a serve rocketing by at 130 mph can deceive the senses.

"You very seldom get mistakes on a point of tennis law because everyone knows the rules," player Pam Shriver says. "But when it comes to the human eye, a tennis ball is very difficult to call. Is it a quarter of an inch beyond the line or is it just nipping the line? I don't care how good your eyes are, there are going to be mistakes involved.

"When you get on a clay court and they check the mark, it's amazing how many times they change the call."

Farrar doesn't dispute this.

"We recognize mistakes are made," he says. "They're made in all walks of life, and officials are no different than anybody else. Mostly you hope they're minimized, but if we see a pattern developing we talk to an official.

"While we don't chart mistakes, we evaluate officials constantly. Every official gets an evaluation."

Prior to the open era, when it could be said tennis was more of a game than a business, officiating was a lark. People literally were picked out of the stands to work a match, and even at a Grand Slam championship the caliber was poor.

"I can't even tell you the number of tournaments I worked where officials were paid in food chits and drank alcoholic beverages throughout the day," Snyder says. "As the day wore on the calls got worse. You had people who were totally untrained who sat on the courts more interested in

who was in the stands as opposed to what they were doing on court."

Farrar recalls that when he started as a chair umpire, he'd work two or three tournaments a year and think that was a lot. He adds, "We now have umpires who work as many as 300 matches a year and they've developed a rapport with the players and the players respect them."

A top official now can earn a decent living, although certainly not in the class of million-dollar players. Contracts are individually negotiated and payment varies considerably around the world.

The average fee for a chair umpire ranges from $1,000 to $1,200 a week, with umpires earning more and line judges a little less. At both Wimbledon and the U.S. Open, officials will earn about $4,000 for working the qualifying and the main draw, about 17 days work.

There were more than 3,000 officials in the United States at the start of 1993, the great majority of whom worked on the local level, which serves as a training and developmental ground. The best of those are chosen to work professional matches.

At the top level, the ITF classifies chair umpires into three categories—gold badge, silver badge and bronze badge—according to ability, skills and experience. There are two categories for international umpires—gold badge and silver badge.

Indisputably, the quality of officiating has improved immeasurably during the open era, to the point that at the start of 1993 there were 10 full-time professional chair umpires on the ATP Tour and another seven employed by the ITF.

There is a formalized educational school system with beginner, intermediate, advanced and refresher schools for officials. These schools are a prerequisite for any official who expects to work in professional tennis. The program is universal and is supported by all the national federations.

"The officials are better trained, they're better paid, we attract higher quality people and they operate on a professional basis, where before it was strictly amateur," Farrar says. "With the advent of

for tennis.

"There were 23 of us, and the most important thing we did was to declare uniformity with everyone doing the same thing, the same way, just like football officials and basketball officials," Korff said. "That's really where it started. We've been improving the system ever since.

"The single element that has made the biggest difference is the Code of Conduct. This limited the obscenity and has penalized players for undignified action. Each year officiating gets tighter and tighter because players realize they're going to be hurt by more than a slap on the wrist. This makes the sponsors happy and the fans are happy."

The Code of Conduct was adopted by the Men's International Tennis Council in 1975, and its first full year of implementation was in 1976.

The women have used a Code of Conduct since the founding of the Women's Tennis Association in 1973.

Along with the Code of Conduct and the point penalty system came the imple-

mentation of a fine system, and all this had brought a significant amount of control back into the game. At first the code violation had four stages: first violation, warning; second, point penalty; third, game penalty; fourth, disqualification. Now it's three stages: warning, point penalty, disqualification.

All officials constantly are being evaluworks as an evaluator for the USTA. "I'm not here to spy on anybody or downgrade them. I talk to the umpires at the morning meeting and I always make a point of communicating with them."

Evaluation grades range from 0 to 6, with 6 being perfect. Realistically, the points range from 2 to 5, with 2 being unacceptable.

The three categories evaluators address are competence and ability, technique and attitude, and appearance.

"When a Frank Hammond was up there, he used to put on a show," Thomson said of one of the more flamboyant umpires the game has known. "But this is no longer what is wanted. The whole philosophy toward umpiring now is that good umpires should not be obvious. The word is firm, but not aggressive. A good job by a good umpire means he was in control of the match and was not noticed by the crowd."

Hammond, an all-time umpire with a booming voice and a commanding personality, once enjoyed a reputation for controlling a match better than anyone.

The annual meeting in the 1920s of the National Umpires' Association at Forest Hills. The man in the white suit is the association's first president, Edward C. Conlin. In the second row, second from the left, is F.P.A. (Franklin P. Adams), noted columnist ("The Conning Tower") and friend and admirer of Bill Tilden. F.P.A., according to notes in the photo album of the late William M. Fischer, was "a good umpire." • *Fischer Collection/SPS*

"I think an umpire is very much like a conductor, without being hammy, and before you can concentrate on the players you'd better have great empathy with the people who are paying the money to come in," Hammond said of his technique. "They're your reeds and your brass and your timpani, and the two players are your soloists."

Hammond once asserted that he umpired more than 5,000 matches and ran 500 tournaments as a referee without a single major incident. However, this all changed for him at the 1979 U.S. Open when he lost control of a match between McEnroe and Ilie Nastase.

The rules of the game are fairly uniform around the world, although individual circuits among the men and women

may apply their unique interpretations. For example, there's nothing written in the rules referring to toilet breaks, but the men are allowed one during a three-set match or two in a five-setter.

A woman is entitled to two breaks during a three-set match, and this can consist of any combination of a change of apparel or a visit to the bathroom.

Both men and women are permitted time-outs for injury incurred during a match, but not loss of condition, such as cramps.

A full complement of officials (11) for a feature match at a Grand Slam championship would include the chair umpire, a net judge and 10 line judges (two baseline, four sideline, two center line, one service line). A foot-fault judge and another service judge could be added, swelling the crew to 13. But sometimes skeleton crews of seven are used: two sideline and one center line, calling the line the length of the court; two baseline, one service line and the chair umpire.

A certain harbinger of the future, is the use of machines to replace officials.

of machines.

"When I was playing I didn't mind having human beings call a match," says Chris Evert, who is a spokesperson for Wilson. "Over a tournament or over a career the calls even out. Now I'm in favor of an electronic system because the prize money is so great and so much is at stake. But it's going to be very expensive to implement, and different organizations like the WTA and ATP will have to chip in."

Martina Navratilova agrees with her longtime friend and rival, saying, "What a player wants is consistency, and a machine doesn't make that many mistakes. It's very difficult for the human eye to measure the progress of the ball. I sat on the sidelines at Team Tennis matches and three of us would say of a shot, 'It's in,' and three of us would say, 'it's out.'

"A machine obviously is quicker than the human eye, so it would be great."

Taking a contrary view is Jimmy Connors, who says half-jokingly, "I'd rather have somebody to argue with. If they don't want you to argue with the umpire or linesman now, how am I going to be arguing with a machine?"

A preliminary review of the test at the U.S. Open showed there were three or four calls a match where the electronic system

see something and overrule? I know a ball going 130 mph and landing on a line is difficult to spot. I would not like that job, not one bit.

"But that's what they're doing, that's what they want to do. They're sitting there, so they must pay attention. All the players really want is to know officials are out there doing their job, paying attention and giving it the best effort they can."

Mistakes will continue to be made, players will continue to vent their anger and frustration on a sitting target, and the crowds will continue to add their collective voice to the confrontation. But great strides have been made in the integrity of officiating during the open era, and the quality improves each year.

Soon, comes the electronic age, adding an intriguing twist to the age-old conflict between player and official.

8: Equipment and Technology

fronted with a bewildering array of different tennis rackets of several shapes, sizes and materials. Not only are they styled so as to be visually attractive, but claims are made to cover every conceivable measure of playability and performance.

The consumer is inundated with an abundance of technical and pseudotechnical information, which, by and large, is more confusing than illuminating. Against such a background, one needs a guidebook to help one steer clear of misconceptions and wrong choices, and arrive at what is best for one's game.

On the other hand, the choices that are now available to the tennis player are exciting indeed. Clearly the trend has been one of pushing the state of the art in the technology of tennis, which has surely become a high-tech sport. Compared to the bygone days of wood rackets, we now have rackets which are well designed and engineered, and deliver high performance. Generally, however, they are more expensive than before, but the enhanced performance is often worth the increase in price.

What is presented here is a general description of the growth in tennis technology and some guidelines in facilitating the choices of equipment. Clearly, in order to become a good tennis

Nothing can really make up for the lack of talent. However, while talent and skill are essential, using the correct equipment will considerably enhance one's playing capability and performance and add to the joy of play. To some extent, a highly skilled player can often overcome the inadequacies of equipment such as a racket. But the right equipment would make him/her an even more formidable player and lead to greater enjoyment of the game.

Rackets

The most dramatic and significant changes in tennis technology have involved the design of rackets. The shape and design of tennis rackets remained largely unchanged for a long time, from the early stirrings at the beginning of the sport to the latter half of this century. Wood rackets were made with different kinds of wood with multiple laminations to minimize warping and other changes due to aging, humidity and varying temperatures. They had to be kept in presses to prevent warping.

The rackets were governed by rather loose specifications regarding shape, size, materials, etc. From the early days of wood

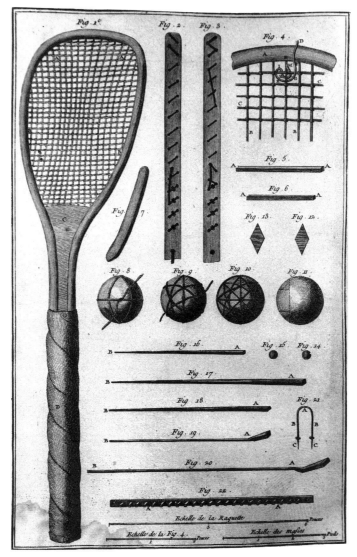

The way it was. • *USTA*

and standard size (85–90 square inches) frames, racket technology has experienced quantum jumps in size, materials and shape. Three main advances in the state-of-the art in technology can be recognized. They are: (1) large head size, (2) use of graphite and (3) widebody design.

Size

The first real change was introduced in 1976 by Howard Head in making the racket head much larger than the earlier designs. While at first there was a certain degree of resistance to his Prince Classic on the part of the playing public in accepting the unusually large rackets, this gave way to acceptance and even enthusiasm, because of the advantages of the large frame. The average recreational player as well as professional tennis player felt that the larger head area was more forgiving in not requiring great precision in ball contact.

This established a new trend in racket design, and head sizes of rackets were made larger and larger. Today, there are now rackets of several sizes, loosely classified as: standard size (less than 90 sq. in.),

Materials

Concurrently with changing head size, designers were experimenting with the use of different materials. Early new designs incorporated metal, such as the Wilson T-2000, a steel frame with open throat used by Jimmy Connors for many years. Different metals were used including aluminum (Spalding), magnesium (Prince), and even the extremely light and strong, if expensive, titanium (Matchmate). Then came other materials such as boron, ceramics, graphite and composites. The choices of the materials were dictated by considerations of desirable properties such as, predominantly, stiffness, but also others such as vibration damping, ease of workmanship, etc. Of these, graphite and composites survived and have become preeminent as the materials of choice in racket design.

Weight

Years ago the rackets weighed generally in the range of 12-14 ounces, plus about one-half ounce for the strings. This provided greater racket mass in the hand of the player and therefore imparted greater momentum and speed to the ball. However, this requires a strong forearm to use the heavier frames. The current trend

is towards light rackets, even among professionals, with some modern designs weighing less than 10 ounces! The rackets are very powerful because of the design and materials, and are also highly maneuverable because of the light weight.

Generally speaking, lighter rackets cause less arm strain for the same stroke motion than heavier ones. It is important

rackets provide more momentum and thus more power, on ground strokes and especially on serve, but also require greater arm strength. Head light rackets are more maneuverable. Some new rackets are designed head heavy but with low overall weight (less than 10 ounces) to combine both advantages—greater power and maneuverability.

Grip Size

This measures the perimeter around the racket handle. Again the trend in recent years is toward smaller grips. Earlier, the practice was to use relatively large grips, like 4⅞ or 4¾ inches. Some well-known world-class players even used 5-inch grips—Hall of Famer Roy Emerson for one. The modern practice is to use grips of 4⅜ or 4½ inches, with 4⅜ inches being the average. Again, in purchasing a racket, it is prudent to try different grip sizes to decide what is best for one's needs.

Shape

Most modern rackets have open throats to reduce air resistance and increase mobility. The head shapes vary from elliptic, oval, circular, quasi-rectangular with rounded corners, and so on.

Appearance and Cosmetics

The rackets are aesthetically very attractive, with multiple overlays of glossy finish in eye-catching colors. Protective racket covers and bags are available with multiple features including pockets with zippers and velcro fasteners.

Engineering Design

Having addressed the aforementioned issues, the racket manufacturers turned to the engineering design of rackets. Indeed, this is the area where the major thrust has occurred and warrants the use of high technology. It has led to the design of the so-called *widebody* rackets. They have resulted in the most dramatic improvements in racket performance. The reason for this change can be traced to technical considerations.

In tennis, power and control—the ability to hit the ball with high speed, and to place the ball within the court at a desired location—have always been the principal goals of tennis players. This is essentially because: the faster the ball is hit, the less time available to the opponent to execute a good shot in reply, and the greater opportunity for opponent errors.

It is now clear from the physics of tennis that power essentially comes from a property of the racket frame, called "stiffness." It is a measure of how much force is needed to bend the frame by a certain amount; or equivalently, the amount of deflection (in inches or centimeters) of the head caused by a certain force (i.e., a prescribed weight in pounds). The greater the deflection for a given weight, the less stiff (or more flexible) the racket.

Therefore, in an effort to squeeze more power from the racket, the designers started making the rackets stiffer than before. At first, this was done using new stiffer materials such as graphite. However, it soon became clear that the choices of new materials are limited. Accordingly, rackets were made stiffer by increasing the cross-section of the frames. They became thicker, prompting the use of the term *widebodies*. Thus, being very stiff, the widebody rackets provide greater power by propelling the ball faster.

One may wonder why frame stiffness affects power. When a ball is struck, essentially three things happen: (1) the ball deforms, (2) the strings deform, and (3) the frame bends. At the moment of impact the ball is totally flattened against the string bed which stretches. Most of the energy that goes into ball deformation is unrecoverable. It goes into what is technically termed *hysteresis*, and turns into heat. There is not much anyone can do about this. The strings give back most of the energy.

The racket frame absorbs some of the energy and is not as efficient as the strings in returning the energy to the ball. Therefore, in order to achieve high ball velocities after impact, more energy must be given to the strings than the racket. This is done by lowering the string tension and increasing the frame stiffness (either by using stiffer materials or thicker sections, as in widebodies). Compared to earlier thinking, what is clear now is that greater frame thickness yields greater power, as do *lower* string tensions (*not* tighter string).

In regard to racket preferences, there is a clear distinction between professionals and recreational players. The professionals are highly skilled, physically fit and young. They practice long and hard and make a living in tennis. The recreational players are not necessarily young, and have different levels of playing skills, physical fitness and preparation. This class includes most of the playing public. Players in this group look for performance enhancement from rackets. Typically, they use rackets which give them great power.

On the other hand, most of the professionals have resisted the use of widebodies in spite of their great power. They argue that professionals do not need the extra power given by the rackets and can generate as much power as they need by swinging the rackets fast. So only a few professionals, especially the younger ones, have started using the widebodies.

like to use widebodies, whereas professionals mostly use rackets of conventional thickness.

In the development of new materials, some have potential application to tennis equipment. Most of these have been in the aerospace field under the sponsorship of NASA and the Department of Defense. For applications in space the new materials offered high strength and light weight. Many of these, such as kevlar, spectra and some thermoplastic materials, have eventually found their way into commercial applications and tennis rackets.

In particular, a racket has been developed by Prince, using a thermoplastic. According to the manufacturer, the material provides self-adjusting properties in the sense that if the racket is swung fast, it plays like a stiff frame at ball impact; if it is swung slowly, it plays like a flexible frame. This property is termed *dynamic stiffness.* Thus one interpretation could be that the racket adjusts to suit the purpose of the stroke, either power or touch.

Some people feel that this feature is advantageous to the player. However, another interpretation, especially shared

by the professionals, is that the racket does not give a constant predictable response from shot to shot and is, therefore, more difficult to master. In any case, technologically it is a step in the direction of extracting more performance from the rackets.

Another new material that offers much promise is the polyethylene spectra fiber. It is one of the lightest high-strength com-

While the rackets are of high quality and high performance, they are also quite expensive. The price depends on the design, ranging from less than $100 at the low end, $100–$200 in the midrange and $200–$300 at the high end. There are some rackets that are priced even above $300. High performance is costly.

Racket Testing

In the early days, and even as recently as 20 years ago, no systematic engineering tests were employed to evaluate the performance of tennis rackets. Indeed, all the manufacturers claimed high performance for their own rackets. This left the consumer at a great disadvantage wondering about the proper choice of a racket.

A most comprehensive and rigorous engineering testing methodology for rackets was developed by Radrupatna Ramnath and his associates at Massachusetts Institute of Technology in 1978 under the sponsorship of *World Tennis* magazine. This work involved the conceptualization, identification, definition and measurement of the significant parameters that characterize the performance of a racket, both in the laboratory and play-testing on the tennis court.

They developed precise tests and the instrumentation required to perform the tests.

Ramnath has continued to refine and enlarge the tests under the sponsorship of *World Tennis* at first and subsequently *Tennis* magazine. He has maintained a large data base on tennis rackets comprising most of the existing designs which have been published in these magazines. As a result, the current reader is more able to interpret this data, which will help in choosing a suitable racket.

Other than the simple quantities such as length, weight, head area, grip size and balance point, the main parameters that characterize the performance of a racket are: (1) stiffness, (2) stability, (3) vibration damping (4) maneuverability and (5) power.

(1) Stiffness is the amount of deflection through which a clamped racket bends when a prescribed weight is placed on the racket head. As discussed earlier, a stiffer racket yields high power.

(2) Stability is the property of a racket that describes its resistance to twisting as a result of off-center hits. Technically, it is related to what is called *polar moment of inertia.*

(3) Vibration damping. This describes the rate at which the vibratory energy decays with time. Thus, in a racket with high damping, the vibrations decay rapidly and are not felt after a very short time.

(4) Maneuverability is a measure of the resistance of the racket to changes in position or orientation. Thus a racket is said to be maneuverable if it can be moved from one position to another (such as from a ground stroke to a volley) quickly and easily.

(5) Power. This measures the velocity after striking the ball with a racket moving at a prescribed, constant head speed. If this after-impact velocity is high, the racket is said to have high power. Experimental measurements involve firing a ball at a particular spot on the racket face and measuring the ball velocity after impact. An area on the racket face which results in high ball velocities is termed the *power zone* of the racket. Ball velocities are measured by a number of techniques using, for example, lasers, infra-red beams, stroboscopic photography, etc.

After measurements, the data is appropriately scaled on a scale of 1 to 10 so that 10 is the maximum value of a particular parameter. Thus, all that one has to do to compare two rackets is to compare the two index values of a particular parameter such as stiffness, for the two rackets. This data is widely in use today among the general tennis-playing public.

Strings

The changes in the technology of strings, though not as dramatic as with rackets, have undergone much improvement. The overall goal is still to produce synthetic strings that would play like natural gut, but also have other desirable properties: low cost, durability and long life, insensitivity to environmental conditions such as moisture, heat, humidity. Many types of strings have been developed recently and offer great choices to players. The modern synthetic strings are very good and provide a degree of playability almost as good as that of natural gut, but at much lower cost. Many of the synthetics have variations with different materials, wire wound, some specifically for widebody rackets, some for conventional rackets. Generally, a thinner gauge string is more elastic and plays more responsively, so that for tournament play, thinner gauge strings are recommended. For practice, thicker gauge strings are adequate.

Price

The price for stringing has not increased by the same proportion as for frames. Natural cow gut is still the most expensive, costing in the range of $50. Synthetic strings cost in the range of $15–$30, depending on where the stringing is done.

Balls

The ball has not changed much over

Price

The price on balls has not changed much over the years. The best balls by Wilson or Penn are available in many stores for a little more than $2. However, the balls used in an electronic line-calling system are likely to cost more because of the modifications made to the ball. They are not yet available commercially.

Shoes

Tennis shoes have undergone much improvement. They are lightweight, well-cushioned, afford better tread. However, they tend to be quite expensive. The tread provides good traction, desirable on a clay court. However, on a hard surface the same tread could lead to greater strain and perhaps joint injury because of the friction with the court surface. A sole with less friction might slip slightly and thus help reduce injuries. Some of the more innovative shoes are even inflatable, with more or less air as desired.

Price

While the shoes currently available are of high quality, they come at high price.

The top-of-the-line shoes from well-known companies cost more than $100, although shoes are also available for about $50–$75, and can be quite good. However, it is important to get the best shoes one can afford because they are protective of one's feet and ankles and help avoid injuries.

Electronic Line-Calling

this that a number of systems have been proposed to solve this problem by means of technology. Indeed, the USTA, with an eye to the U.S. Open, and the ATP Tour, for male professionals, are evaluating the different systems in regard to their technical viability and general acceptability. The various systems consider the problem and propose several ingenious solutions.

Generally they can be classified into two types: those that require a modification of the ball, and those that do not. The physical phenomena upon which the systems are based include many areas, such as sensitivity to pressure, magnetic field interaction, infrared beam interruption, electrical contact formation, video imaging technology. In the Cyclops system, in use since 1980 to judge service lines, an infrared beam is aligned with the line. When a ball crosses the beam, it sets off a signal. By carefully aligning the beam, an out ball is determined. This system works only on the service line and has been used in some tournaments, such as Wimbledon and the U.S. Open, if rather sporadically.

The Australian TEL system makes use of the magnetic field interaction between the ball and antennas embedded underneath the court surface below the lines. The signal generated by the moving ball is tracked and an accurate determination is made as to whether the ball is in or out. This system is sophisticated and has built-in features to aid discrimination between the ball and other spurious signals, so that the system is resistant to tampering. The Canadian Accucall system relies on the completion of an electrical circuit when a ball lands outside the court. An advanced system is being developed by an Israeli company by means of video technology.

The balls used in these systems are modified. In the TEL system, a small part of the rubber in the ball is replaced by a magnetic material (such as iron powder), during the manufacturing process. The ball will look, feel and play like a regular ball, and in all ways is totally indistinguishable from a regular ball. The Accucall system calls for a modification of the ball that incorporates thin electrical wires to make contact upon hitting the ground. Further work is going on in these and related systems to improve the ball process as well.

9: INTERNATIONAL TENNIS HALL OF FAME

Design and construction of the Casino as an exclusive men's club was commissioned by James Gordon Bennett, Jr., publisher of the New York Herald. In this case "casino" was to adhere to one of its definitions as a place of entertainment, and not, the more familiar, gambling emporium.

Renowned New York architect Stanford White was the designer of the handsome wooden complex (now an historic landmark). It includes the two-story building with clock tower and horseshoe piazza that housed the club and is now devoted to the Hall of Fame and its museum. There is also a building containing a theatre, court tennis court and dressing rooms. The landscaped grounds include a 5,000-seat lawn tennis stadium and a dozen grass courts.

As the cradle of American tennis, the Casino was the scene of the first U.S. Championships, the Nationals for men in 1881, and continued as the site of that tournament through 1914. Thereafter, the Casino Invitational for men was played

Davis Cup matches were played at the Casino in 1921 (Japan over Australia) and 1991 (U.S. over Spain.)

It was here that innovator Van Alen developed and put into play VASSS (Van Alen Streamlined Scoring System) that included the tie-breaker.

At the suggestion of his wife, Candy, Van Alen, as president of the Casino, proposed in 1952 the formation of a National Tennis Hall of Fame to the USTA, which sanctioned its establishment in 1954. The first class of tennis immortals was posthumously inducted in 1955.

Their entry has been followed almost annually by the installment of great players as well as such prominent off-court contributors to the game as administrators, organizers and journalists.

In 1975 the concept broadened, and the name was changed to the International Tennis Hall of Fame. Fred Perry of Britain was, that year, the first non-U.S. inductee.

Newport, R.I., 1891, site of the National Championships in which Oliver Campbell successfully defended his title against Clarence Hobart in five sets. • *Fischer Collection/SPS*

Players

Fred Alexander
United States (1880–1969)

As the first foreigner to win the Australian titles, Frederick Beasley Alexander beat Alf Dunlop in 1908 and joined with native Dunlop to take the doubles, too. That year he and Beals Wright were the U.S. Davis Cup team in an unsuccessful attempt to pry the Cup away from Australasia (Norman Brookes and Tony Wilding), 3–2 in Melbourne. He lost a tough opener to Brookes, 6-3 in the fifth, and the decisive match to Wilding in three. Right-handed, a New Yorker and Princeton man, he won the U.S. Intercollegiate singles (1901) and doubles (1900).

He ranked six times in the U.S. Top Ten between 1904 and 1918, the last, at 38, his highest, No. 3. He was Harold Hackett's partner in a standout doubles team, U.S. finalists a record seven straight times, beginning in 1905, winning in 1907–08–09–10. In 1917, at 37, he won a fifth U.S. title, shepherding 19-year-old Harold Throckmorton to the championship. Lean and lanky, a smooth stroker, he was born in New York Aug. 14, 1880, and died in Beverly Hills, Cal., March 3, 1969. Inducted into the Hall of Fame in 1961.

MAJOR TITLES (7)—*Australian singles, 1908; Australian doubles, 1908; U.S. doubles, 1907–08–09–10–17.* OTHER U.S. TITLES—*Indoor doubles, 1906–07–08, with Harold Hackett; 1911–12, with Theodore Pell; 1917, with William Rosenbaum; Intercollegiate singles, 1901; Intercollegiate doubles, 1900, with Raymond Little.* DAVIS CUP—*1908; record: 0–2 in singles, 1–1 in doubles.*

Wilmer Allison
United States (1904–77)

Although the firm of Allison & Van Ryn was synonymous with doubles excellence, Texan Wilmer Lawson Allison, who played the left court, had several singles triumphs at the top of the game. Foremost, he won the U.S. Championship in 1935 when, at 32, he shot through not only 23-year-old ex-Wimbledon champ Sidney Wood, 6–2, 6–2, 6–3, in one of the most lopsided finals, but 1933–34 champ Fred Perry in the semis, 7–5, 6–3, 6–3. That ended a Forest Hills streak of 18 matches for Perry, and eased

McEnroe's 14–1. Their 24 team matches (tied with Stan Smith and Vic Seixas) are second only to McEnroe's 30 in U.S. annals. They beat the topnotch French teams in Cup finals in Paris (Jean Borotra-Henri Cochet in 1929, Cochet-Jacques Brugnon in 1932) but could do no more than prolong successful French defenses.

A 5-foot-11 right-hander, Allison experienced two extraordinary Cup singles matches in Paris in 1931–32. Opening the 4–1 semifinal victory over Italy he made an all-time comeback to beat ambidextrous Giorgio de Stefani, 4–6, 7–9, 6–4, 8–6, 10–8. Allison squandered four set points of his own in the second, but the most exciting was to come; from 2–5 down in the fourth he saved two match points, and in the last set, from 1–5 down, 16 more.

The following year, with France ahead, 2–1, and the Cup at stake, he lost a controversial match to Borotra, 1–6, 3–6, 6–4, 6–2, 7–5, after the Frenchman saved five match points in the fifth set. On the sixth, at 4–5 advantage out, Borotra apparently double–faulted by a considerable margin. But the local linesman made no call, and it was an ace against Allison, who was on his way to the net to shake hands.

Objective Al Laney wrote for the consumption of U.S. readers: "The U.S. has won the Cup, but the trophy remains in France. A linesman [Gerard de Ferrier] kept Allison from his just victory." Ellsworth Vines beat Cochet in the fifth match, to make the score 3–2, France, but nobody can know how that match would have gone had it been decisive.

had been in the U.S. Top Ten from 1928, eight straight years, No. 1 in 1934–35, and the World Top Ten five times between 1930 and 1935, No. 4 in 1932 and 1935. He was born Dec. 8, 1904, in San Antonio, and won the U.S. Intercollegiate title for his alma mater, Texas, in 1927. He entered the Hall of Fame in 1963, and died April 20, 1977, in Austin, Tex.

MAJOR TITLES (6)—*U.S. singles, 1935; Wimbledon doubles, 1929–30; U.S. doubles, 1931–35; U.S. mixed, 1930.* OTHER U.S. TITLE—*Intercollegiate singles, 1927.* DAVIS CUP—*1928–29–30–31–32–33–35–36; record: 18–10 in singles, 14–2 in doubles.*

Manuel Alonso
Spain (1895–1984)

As the first Spanish male of international stature, Manolo Alonso de Areyzaga made his country's best showing at Wimbledon and the U.S. Championships before Manolo Santana won them in 1966 and 1965, respectively. He beat Zenzo Shimidzu in a terrific battle, 8–6 in the fifth, to reach the Wimbledon all-comers final of 1921, where he lost to Babe Norton in another tense struggle, 6–3, in the fifth. A U.S. resident for several years during the

1920s he was a U.S. Championships quarterfinalist in 1922–23–25–27 and was ranked in the U.S. Top Ten in 1925–26–27, No. 2 in 1926. He was also in the World Top Ten three years, 1925–26–27, No. 5 the last year.

A right-hander, he played Davis Cup for Spain. He was born Nov. 12, 1895, in San Sebastian and died Oct. 11, 1984, in Madrid. He entered the Hall of Fame in 1977.

DAVIS CUP—*1921–22–24–25–31–36; record: 11–7 in singles, 3–4 in doubles.*

Arthur Ashe
United States (1943–93)

See page 330.

Juliette Atkinson
United States (1873–1944)

Juliette Paxton Atkinson, a right-hander who lived in Brooklyn, N.Y., was prominent in singles for four years at the U.S. Championships, a finalist, 1895—98, winning the title thrice: 1895–97–98. She did not defend in 1899, defaulting the challenge round to Californian Marion Jones, who gave her a terrific struggle for the '98 title, 6–3, 5–7, 6–4, 2–6, 7–5—one of the longest matches, in games, 51, ever played by women. But she did continue to compete through 1902.

She won the U.S. doubles seven times with five different partners between 1894 and 1902. She had five in a row with three partners (1894–98), the last two with her younger sister, Kathleen. Other than the Roosevelts, Ellen and Grace in 1900, they were the only sisters to win the title. They were the first sisters to face one another in the Championships, Juliette winning semifinals in 1895 and 1897. She was born April 15, 1873, in Rahway, N.J., died Jan. 12, 1944, in Lawrenceville, Ill., and entered the Hall of Fame in 1974.

MAJOR TITLES (13)—*U.S. singles, 1895–97–98; U.S. doubles, 1894–95–96–97–98–01–02; U.S. mixed, 1894–95–96.*

Tracy Austin
United States (1962–   )

One of the game's prodigies, Tracy Ann Austin was meteoric, an iron-willed girl whose blaze was glorious though fleeting. A variety of injuries cut short what had promised to be one of the great careers. At 14 her junior career was practically a memory.

She had won the U.S. 12s title at 10 in 1972, and added 21 more age-group titles. Arriving at Forest Hills in 1977, an unseeded amateur, she was already the youngest winner of a pro tournament, Portland (Ore.), earlier in the year. Sensationally she made her way to the last eight of the U.S. Open by beating fourth-seeded Sue Barker and Virginia Ruzici, who would win the French in 1978. Wimbledon finalist Betty Stove stopped her there, but the 5-foot, 90-pound Tracy, in ponytail and pinafore, was the youngest of all major quarterfinalists—until Jennifer Capriati, a younger 14, was a French semifinalist in 1990.

Two years later, 1979, at 16 years, 9 months, Tracy not only dethroned four-time champ Chris Evert, 6–4, 6–3, at Flushing Meadow but undercut Maureen Connolly (1951) as the youngest U.S. champ by a couple of months. Earlier that year she severed Evert's 125-match clay-court winning streak in the semis of the Italian, then won the title, her first important prize.

She won the U.S. again in 1981 in a thrilling tie-breaker finish over Martina Navratilova, 1–6, 7–6 (7–4), 7–6 (7–1). That year she won seven other tourneys and had a 58–7 match record, and in 1980 12 titles on 68–7. Having made her Wimbledon debut in 1977 (a third-round loss to Evert), she was a semifinalist in 1979 and 1980, losing to the champs, Navratilova and Evonne Goolagong.

But back maladies began to impair her effectiveness, and sideline her for long stretches. San Diego, 1982, was the last of Austin's 33 pro titles. By 1983, before her 21st birthday, she was virtually finished. Although she has tried comebacks, as

the 1980 final at Flushing, recalls, "Tracy's mental strength was scary. She had no weaknesses, she was obsessive about winning." By 1977 Austin was No. 4 in the U.S. rankings, the greenest to stand so high until Capriati's No. 3 in 1990. She continued in that elite group through 1983, No. 1 in 1980. Six straight years, from 1978, she was in the World Top Ten, No. 2 in 1980–81. Briefly in 1980 she was No. 1 on the WTA computer, breaking the Evert/Navratilova stranglehold of nearly six years. She had tremendous battles with those two whose world she invaded.

Turning pro in October 1978, she won $1,966,487 in career prize money. She played on three winning Federation Cup teams (1978–79–80) for the U.S., and two Wightman Cup winners (1979–81). Tracy was born into a tennis family Dec. 12, 1962, in Palos Verdes, Cal., and grew up in Rolling Hills. Her older sister and brothers—Pam, Jeff and John—played the pro circuit, and she and John won the Wimbledon mixed in 1980, the only brother-sister pairing to do so. She entered the Hall of Fame in 1992.

MAJOR TITLES (3)—*U.S. singles, 1979–81; Wimbledon mixed, 1980.* FEDERATION CUP—

1978–79–80; record: 13–1 in singles. WIGHTMAN CUP—*1978–79–81; record: 4–2 in singles, 2–0 in doubles.*

Karl Behr
United States (1885–1949)

A Yale man, Karl Howell Behr won the U.S. Intercollegiate doubles in 1904, and played on the 1907 U.S. Davis Cup team. He ranked seven times in the U.S. Top Ten between 1906 and 1915, No. 3 in 1914 when he was a quarterfinalist in the U.S. Championships, losing to eventual champ, Dick Williams. He beat an all-time champ, Bill Larned, and got to the final of the all-comers of the 1906 U.S. Championships, losing to eventual champ Bill Clothier. A semifinalist in 1912, he lost to Wallace Johnson. Behr, a right-hander, was born May 30, 1885, in Brooklyn, N.Y., and died Oct. 15, 1949, in New York. He entered the Hall of Fame in 1969.

U.S. TITLES—*Intercollegiate doubles, 1904, with George Bodman.* DAVIS CUP—*1907; record: 0–2 in singles, 1–0 in doubles.*

Pauline Betz
United States (1919–)

See page 334.

Bjorn Borg
Sweden (1956–)

See page 335.

Jean Borotra
France (1898–)

See page 70.

Jack Bromwich
Australia (1918–   )

Elected to the Hall of Fame in 1984 as one-half of the great Australian doubles team of Bromwich and Quist, John Edward "Jack" Bromwich missed winning Wimbledon by the narrowest of margins. In the 1948 final Bob Falkenburg escaped him at three match-point junctures, from 3–5, 15–40, then advantage out, in the fifth set, won by the Californian, 7–5. But Bromwich did win two major singles, the Australian in 1939 and 1946, and was a three-time U.S. semifinalist, 1938–39–47. He lost the last one to the only other U.S. semifinalist playing before and after World War II, Frank Parker.

A loping, big-jawed man with an unruly shock of blond hair, Bromwich was one of the most curious stylists in the game's history. A natural left-hander, he nevertheless served right-handed, stroked with two hands on his right side and one, the left, on his left side. Using an extremely loosely-strung racket, he had superb touch and chipped his returns maddeningly on his foes' shoetops. He was an attacker, his volleys well placed, and his competitive fire ever burning high.

World War II interrupted the strong partnership of himself—the right court player—and Adrian Quist, but they won their native Australian title eight straight times, a team record for majors, and gave up the title only after a tremendous struggle, 6–3 in the fifth against youngsters Frank Sedgman and Ken McGregor in 1951. Bromwich was 33, Quist 38. The two of them scored a singular triumph as the Australian Davis Cup team in 1939, rebounding from 0–2 down against the Cup-holding U.S. in Philadelphia to win. They began turning it around with a four-set doubles victory over Joe Hunt and Jack Kramer, and Bromwich clinched in the decisive fifth match, 6–0, 6–3, 6–1, over Parker.

Bromwich concluded a long, distinguished Cup career by accompanying Sedgman to a 1950 Cup-deciding victory over Ted Schroeder and Gar Mulloy of the U.S., 6–4 in the fifth at Forest Hills. He had won 20 of 21 Cup doubles. He ranked in the World Top Ten, 1938–39–46–47–48, No. 2 in 1939. He was born Nov. 14, 1918, in Kogarah, New South Wales, and served in the Australian army during the war.

MAJOR TITLES (19)—*Australian singles, 1939–46; Australian doubles, 1938–39–40–46–47–48–49–50; Wimbledon doubles, 1948–50; U.S. doubles, 1939–49–50; Australian mixed, 1938; Wimbledon mixed, 1947–48; U.S. mixed, 1947.* DAVIS CUP—*1937–38–39–46–47–49–50; record: 19–11 in singles, 20–1 in doubles.*

BROMWICH-QUIST: MAJOR TITLES (10)—*Australian doubles, 1938–39–40–46–47–48–49–50; Wimbledon doubles, 1950; U.S. doubles, 1939.* DAVIS CUP—*1938–39–46; record: 9–1 in doubles.*

Norman Brookes
Australia (1877–1968)

See page 71.

Louis Brough
United States (1923–   )

See page 337.

Mary K. Browne
United States (1891–1971)

As the first American female professional, Mary Kendall Browne left a splendid amateur record behind in 1926 to join promoter C.C. Pyle's original troupe of touring pros (France's great Suzanne Lenglen was the centerpiece. Others: Vinnie Richards, Howard Kinsey, Fred Snodgrass and Paul Feret.) During the winter of 1926–27, well past her prime, she played one-night stands across North America as "the opponent" against the invincible Lenglen.

A right-hander and staunch volleyer, Browne was born June 3, 1891, in Ventura

County, Cal., and came East to dominate the U.S. Championships at Philadelphia, scoring triples—singles, doubles, mixed titles—in 1912–13–14. Only Hazel Hotchkiss Wightman, the previous three years, and Alice Marble (1938–39–40) swept the field as thoroughly.

She was unique for an American woman in transferring her talent to golf,

tennis annals, Mary played 82 games while winning the 1912 singles, doubles and mixed finals all in the same afternoon, much of it in a downpour. "The rain was coming down in torrents, and still we went on," she later recalled, "our rackets mushy and our clothes soaked." She beat Eleo Sears, 6–4, 6–2, in the all-comers singles to become champion since Wightman didn't defend the title. With Dorothy Green she won the doubles, 6–2, 5–7, 6–0, over Maud Barger Wallach and Mrs. Frederick Schmitz. And, with Dick Williams, the soggy mixed, 6–4, 2–6, 11–9, over Evelyn Sears and Bill Clothier.

Mary ranked No. 1 in the U.S. in 1913 and 1914, the first two years of the Top Ten, returning to the select group at No. 2 in 1921 and 1924, and No. 6 in 1925. In 1926 she had a world ranking of No. 6, the USTA declining to give her a high ranking that she'd earned because she turned pro. She was later married to Kenneth Kenneth-Smith. Browne, still a fine golfer in her 70s, capable of shooting close to her age, died Aug. 19, 1971, in Laguna Hills, Cal. She was elected to the Hall of Fame in 1957.

MAJOR TITLES (13)—*U.S. singles, 1912–13–14; Wimbledon doubles, 1926; U.S. dou-*

bles, 1912–13–14–21–25; U.S. mixed, 1912–13–14–21. OTHER U.S. TITLES—*Indoor doubles, 1926, with Elizabeth Ryan; Clay Court singles, 1914; Clay Court doubles, 1914, with Mrs. Robert Williams.* WIGHTMAN CUP—*1925–26; record: 0–2 in singles, 1–1 in doubles.*

Jacques Brugnon
France (1895–1978)

Jacques "Toto" Brugnon was the old-

three other finals. He won the French five times, three with Cochet, two with Borotra, and the Australian with Borotra, plus two French mixed for a dozen major titles.

His Davis Cup career ran 11 years, and he had a hand in four of the Cup triumphs. A right-handed left-court player, he was in the Top Ten twice, No. 10 in 1926 and No. 9 in 1927. For a time he was a teaching professional in California. He was born May 11, 1895, in Paris, and died there March 20, 1978. He entered the Hall of Fame in 1976.

MAJOR TITLES (12)—*Australian doubles, 1928; French doubles, 1927–28–30–32–34; Wimbledon doubles, 1926–28–32–33; French mixed, 1925–26.* DAVIS CUP—*1921–23–24–25–26–27–30–31–32–33–34; record: 4–2 in singles, 22–9 in doubles.*

Don Budge
United States (1916–)

See page 72.

Maria Bueno
Brazil (1939–)

See page 338.

May Sutton Bundy
United States (1886–1975)

Although May Sutton was, as a U.S. citizen, the first outsider from beyond the British Isles—and first American—to win Wimbledon, she had a distinct English connection. Born in Plymouth Sept. 25, 1886, daughter of an English sea captain, she moved with the family at age six to Santa Monica, Cal., where she and her four sisters all became standout tennis players. The saying in Southern California was "It takes a Sutton to beat a Sutton" because four of them—May, Violet, Florence, Ethel—dominated that section for almost a generation through 1915.

May, a husky, highly competitive right-hander with a powerful topspin forehand, was the best known of the four, with her U.S. title of 1904, 6–1, 6–2, over defending Bessie Moore, and her two Wimbledon titles over Dorothea Douglass, in 1905 and 1907. She took the title from the Englishwoman, 6–3, 6–4, lost in the following year, and subdued Dorothea (who'd become Mrs. Lambert Chambers), 6–1, 6–4, as the two contested three successive finals. She shocked English crowds at first by rolling up her sleeves to bare her elbows, and wearing a shorter skirt than most, showing ankles.

In 1912 she married Tom Bundy, a top player who won three U.S. doubles titles (1912-13-14) with Maurice McLoughlin. She became the mother of Dorothy Bundy Cheney, Australian champ of 1938 who was still winning U.S. senior titles in her 70s. May had her best days before U.S. rankings for women were established in 1913. But her groundstrokes were formidable enough when she made a comeback in 1921 to earn her the No. 4 ranking at age 35. That made her the third of the sisters to rank in the U.S. Top Ten—a record. Ethel was No. 2 in 1913; Florence 3-2-4, 1913-14-15. Moreover May played Wightman Cup for the U.S. four years later and ranked No. 5 in 1928 at 42. She

entered the Hall of Fame in 1956, and died Oct. 4, 1975, in Santa Monica, Cal.

MAJOR TITLES (4)—*Wimbledon singles, 1905–07; U.S. singles, 1904; U.S. doubles, 1904.* OTHER U.S. TITLES—*Clay Court singles, 1912; Clay Court mixed, 1912, with Fred Harris.* WIGHTMAN CUP—*1925; record: 0–1 in doubles.*

Mabel Cahill
Ireland (1863–unknown)

Little is known of Mabel Esmonde Cahill except that, as an Irish citizen, she was the first foreigner to win one of the major championships. That was the U.S. singles of 1891 when she got even with Ellen Roosevelt, who had defeated her in the all-comers final of 1890 and gone on to win the title. In 1891, Cahill, a right-hander, decimated the Roosevelts, beating Ellen's sister, Grace, in the all-comers final, 6–3, 7–5, and then Ellen in the challenge round, 6–4, 6–1, 4–6, 6–3. She retained the title by defeating Bessie Moore in the 1892 challenge round, 5–7, 6–3, 6–4, 4–6, 6–2. That year she also won the mixed doubles with Clarence Hobart.

But she declined to return to Philadelphia for the 1893 Championships, defaulting her title to Aline Terry in the challenge round. During her residence in the U.S. she belonged to the New York Tennis Club. She was born April 2, 1863, in Ballyragget, County Kilkenny, Ireland. No details of her death, believed to have occurred in Ireland, have been found. She entered the Hall of Fame in 1976.

MAJOR TITLES (5)—*U.S. singles, 1891–92; U.S. doubles, 1891–92; U.S. mixed, 1892.*

Oliver Campbell
United States (1871–1953)

For a century Oliver Samuel Campbell had the distinction of being the youngest to win the U.S. singles title. He did it as a 19-year-old Columbia student in 1890. (Pete Sampras, a younger 19, became the youngest when he won the title in 1990.)

Four years earlier, Campbell, at 15 years, 5 months, had lost in the opening round at Newport to the man he would dethrone four years later, Henry Slocum. Oliver was the youngest entry until 1918 when Vinnie Richards undercut him by a month.

After his first exposure to Newport, Campbell determined to transform himself from a baseliner into a net-storming

Slocum again in the 1888 semis, and to lefty Quincy Shaw in the 1889 all-comers final. But in 1890 he outbattled Bob Huntington, 3–6, 6–2, 5–7, 6–2, 6–1, in the semis, and Percy Knapp, 8–6, 0–6, 6–2, 6–3, in the all-comers final. Stronger physically, he kept rushing the net, and at last beat Slocum, deposing the champ, 6–2 4–6, 6–3, 6–1.

Campbell endured another struggle in the challenge round of 1891, 2–6, 7–5, 7–9, 6–1, 6–2, over Clarence Hobart. He made it three straight, 7–5, 3–6, 6–3, 7–5, over Fred Hovey in 1892, and retired, leaving the 1893 title to Bob Wrenn by default. In 1888 he made the U.S. Top Ten for the first of five straight years, No. 1 in 1890–91–92. He was born Feb. 25, 1871, in New York, and died July 11, 1953, in Campellton, Canada. He entered the Hall of Fame in 1955.

MAJOR TITLES (6)—*U.S. single's, 1890–91–92; U.S. doubles, 1888–91–92.* OTHER U.S. TITLES—*Intercollegiate double, 1888, with Valentine Hall; 1889, with A.E. Wright.*

Malcolm Chace
United State (1875–1955)

A Rhode Islander, born in Valley Falls March 12, 1875, Malcolm Greene Chace

made his first mark in the game by winning the U.S. Interscholastic title in 1892 for University Grammar in Providence. In 1893 (for Brown) and 1894–95 (for Yale), he became the only three-straight winner of both the U.S. Intercollegiate singles and doubles titles, the only man to win both for two different colleges. He was a semifinalist at the U.S. Championships in 1894, losing to Bill Larned, and won the doubles

1893–94–95; Intercollegiate doubles, 1893, with Clarence Budlong; 1894–95, with Arthur Foote.

Dorothea Chambers
Great Britain (1878–1960)

See page 74.

Clarence Clark
United States (1859–1937)

A member of a distinguished Philadelphia family, Clarence Monroe Clark had the distinction of winning the first U.S. doubles title at Newport in 1881. He and Fred Taylor beat Alexander van Rensselaer and A.E. Newbold, 6–5, 6–4, 6–5. Earlier they eliminated the favorites, Dick Sears and James Dwight. The next year at Newport he made it to the singles final, losing to Sears, the original champ, 6–1, 6–4, 6–0. His brother, Joe Clark (named to the Hall of Fame in 1955), won the first Intercollegiate title for Harvard in 1883.

Joe and Clarence tested foreign waters for America, journeying to England in 1883, playing and losing two doubles matches against the dominant Renshaw twins, Willie and Ernest. Clarence was the first secretary of the newly formed USTA in

1881 and was, along with Dwight and Eugenius Outerbridge, a guiding light in the organization's establishment. He was born Aug. 27, 1859, in Germantown, Pa., died there June 29, 1937, and was named to the Hall of Fame in 1983.

MAJOR TITLE (1)—*U.S. doubles, 1881.*

Joe Clark
United States (1861–1956)

Two years after the first U.S. Championships at Newport, the Intercollegiate Championships was established in 1883, and won by Joseph Sills Clark of Harvard in both singles and doubles. Clark, a senior, was the Harvard champ that year, feeling justifiably proud of himself because he won the title over classmate Dick Sears, who happened to be the U.S. champion.

The first Intercollegiates, which Sears did not enter, was played on the grounds of a mental hospital in Hartford, and Clark recalled that some of the patients served as ball boys. Clark, a right-hander, was a Philadelphian, brother of Clarence Clark, who won the first U.S. doubles title with Fred Taylor. Together he and his brother were a formidable doubles team. They played in England in 1883 after beating the reigning U.S. champs, Sears and Dr. James Dwight, in matches in Boston and New York. They represented the U.S. against the foremost English pair, the Renshaw brothers, Ernest and Willie, in a series for the world championship. The Renshaws won the two matches played, losing one set in the first.

In 1885 Joe Clark joined Sears to win the U.S. doubles, 6–3, 6–0, 6–2, over Henry Slocum and Percy Knapp. Joe was a singles semifinalist in 1885–86–87 while brother Clarence lost the 1882 final to Sears. Joe ranked five straight years from 1885 in the U.S. Top Ten, No. 4 in 1888. He was born Nov. 30, 1861, in Germantown, Pa., entered the Hall of Fame in 1955, and died April

14, 1956. He was president of the USTA, 1889–91.

MAJOR TITLE (1)—*U.S. doubles, 1885.*
OTHER U.S. TITLES—*Intercollegiate singles, 1883; Intercollegiate doubles, 1883, with Howard Taylor.*

Bill Clothier
United States (1891–1962)

Another Harvard man to win the Intercollegiate championship (1902) in the early days, William Jackson Clothier was the U.S. champ four years later, ranking No. 1 in the U.S. A right-handed net rusher, Clothier said that "he never played better" than in the 1906 Championships, gaining confidence from his quarterfinal victory over Fred Alexander, 8–6, 6–2, 4–6, 1–6, 7–5, in which he came from triple match point (2–5, 0–40) to race through the last five games. He took the title from Beals Wright in the challenge round, 6–3, 6–0, 6–4.

He lost the U.S. final to Holcombe Ward in 1904 and, in a five-set battle, to Bill Larned in 1909. He held a Top Ten ranking for 11 years between 1901 and 1914, and in 1905 played on the first U.S. Davis Cup team to compete abroad, beating the French champion, Max Decugis, in a 3–0 victory over France in London. He and his son, William Clothier II, won two U.S. Father and Son doubles titles in 1935–36. He was born in Philadelphia Sept. 27, 1881, and died there Sept. 4, 1962. He was inducted into the Hall of Fame in 1956.

MAJOR TITLE (1)—*U.S. singles, 1906.*
OTHER U.S. TITLES—*Intercollegiate singles, 1902; Intercollegiate doubles, 1902, with Edward Leonard.*
DAVIS CUP—*1905–09; record: 4–1 in singles.*

Henri Cochet
France (1901–87)
See page 75.

Maureen Connolly
United States (1934–69)

See page 339.

Sarah Palfrey Cooke
United States (1912–   )

See page 76.

Ashley Cooper

Ten, No. 1 the last two years. He was born Sept. 15, 1936, in Melbourne, and entered the Hall of Fame in 1991.

MAJOR TITLES (8)—*Australian singles, 1957–58; Wimbledon singles, 1958; U.S. singles, 1958; Australian doubles, 1958; French doubles, 1957–58; U.S. doubles, 1957.* DAVIS CUP— *1957–58; record: 2–2 in singles.*

the right-handed Ash's career in the public eye was brief though very productive. His last two amateur years, 1957–58, could compare well to anyone's: six finals and four championship out of eight major starts, and two semis at the French, the only ones he didn't win.

An athletic 5-foot-10, he was of an attacking mindset, like the others of his tribe, a thorough, smooth, if not spectacular, stroker in attaining his goals at the net. He also won the Australian championship in 1958, one of only 10 men to grab three majors in one year. But whatever hopes he had for a Grand Slam were dashed in Paris by Luis Ayala. Still, he had one of the finest years with a 25–1 match record in the majors.

Cooper, who had lost the 1957 Wimbledon final to Lew Hoad, was upset in the U.S. final by unseeded Mal Anderson, but they got together three months later to successfully defend the Davis Cup against the U.S. Despite an ankle injury incurred during their final at Forest Hills in 1958, Cooper regrouped and came from behind to beat Anderson, 6–2, 3–6, 4–6, 10–8, 8–6. Cooper spent three years, 1956—58, in the World Top

Dwight Davis
United States (1879–1945)

A left-handed, big-serving Harvardian who won the Intercollegiate title in 1899, Dwight Filley Davis ranked in the U.S. Top Ten four times between 1898 and 1901, No. 2 in 1899 and 1900. But he is best known for launching in 1900 the great worldwide team competition that bears his name: Davis Cup. He intended for it to be called the International Lawn Tennis Challenge Trophy when he purchased the silver bowl at the Boston jeweler, Shreve, Crump & Low. His fellow members at Longwood Cricket Club, where the inaugural was staged in 1900, jocularly referred to it as "Dwight's pot." Soon just-plain "Davis Cup" was the accepted handle.

The original U.S. team was a Harvard production, Davis captaining, he and schoolmates Malcolm Whitman and Holcombe Ward playing a 3–0 victory over the British Isle. Davis was a member of President Coolidge's cabinet as Secretary of War, and also served his country as governor-general of the Philippines. He was born in St. Louis July 5, 1879, and died Nov. 28, 1945, in Washington, D.C. He was inducted into the Hall of Fame in 1956.

MAJOR TITLES (3)—*U.S. doubles, 1899–1900–1901.* OTHER U.S. TITLES— *Intercollegiate single, 1899; Intercollegiate doubles, 1899, with Holcombe Ward.* DAVIS CUP— *1900–02; record: 1–0 in singles, 1–1 in doubles.*

Lottie Dod
Great Britain (1871–1960)

Tall and athletic, Charlotte "Lottie" Dod became the youngest of major champions at 15 years, 10 months by winning Wimbledon in 1887, knocking off the defending champion, Blanche Bingley, 6–2, 6–0, in the challenge round. She played four other years, never lost—in 10 matches she dropped one set—though her championship foe, each time, now Mrs. Hillyard, did give her a tough match, 6–8, 6–1, 6–4, in the 1893 final. She also won the Irish title in 1887, was exceptional at ice skating, archery (an Olympic silver medalist in 1908), field hockey and golf. She represented Britain in international hockey in 1889–90 and competed in the British Women's Golf Championships in 1904. Born Sept. 24, 1871, in Lower Bebington, England, she died June 27, 1960, in Sway, England. She entered the Hall of Fame in 1983.

MAJOR TITLES (5)—*Wimbledon singles, 1887–88–91–92–93.*

Johnny Doeg
United States (1908–78)

As the fourth left-handed U.S. champ (following Bob Wrenn, Beals Wright, Lindley Murray), sixth-seeded John Thomas Godfray Hope Doeg hit the title jackpot in 1930 while, in the semis, thwarting Bill Tilden's fervent bid for a record eighth crown with 28 aces. His brilliant serving, speed and spin, made him a feared foe for five years as he ranked in the U.S. Top Ten between 1927 and 1931.

He was No. 1 in 1930 when he beat Frank Shields at Forest Hills, 10–8, 1–6, 6–4, 16–14, a record closing set of a major

singles final. It was a strenuous serve-and-volleying rush to the title: 6–4 in the fifth over Frank Hunter; 12–10 in the fourth over No. 1 seed Tilden (Big Bill's Forest Hills farewell); and Shields. He was determined to keep pressure on foes by charging the net incessantly.

In the world rankings he was No. 7 in 1929, No. 4 in 1930. He and George Lott were Wimbledon doubles finalists in 1930 and won the U.S. titles of 1929–30. He was the U.S. junior champ in 1926, the first of eight males to make the transition from the 18s to the adult championship. Johnny was born in Guayamas, Sonora, Mexico, Dec. 7, 1908, and grew up in California. He was a son of a Southern California champ, the former Violet Sutton, and a nephew of Hall of Famer May Sutton. He entered the Hall of Fame in 1962 and died April 27, 1978, in Redding, Cal.

MAJOR TITLES (3)—*U.S. singles, 1930; U.S. doubles, 1929–30.* DAVIS CUP—*1930; record: 1–0 in singles.*

Laurie Doherty
Great Britain (1875–1919)

Laurie, or "Little Do," born Hugh Laurence Doherty, was the shorter and younger, and probably better, of the Oxford-educated Doherty brothers who illuminated the tennis skies in their native England and at Wimbledon at the turn of the century. Although Laurie lost the 1898 Wimbledon final to Reggie, 6–1, in the fifth, he won the title five straight times, beginning in 1902.

The brothers carried Britain to its first four Davis Cups, beginning in 1903, by taking it from the U.S., 4–1, in Boston after falling short, 3–2, the previous year in Brooklyn. He never lost a Cup match, winning seven singles and five doubles.

As the first serious foreign contenders for the U.S. singles crown, the brothers failed in 1902 at Newport. Laurie sportingly defaulted to Reggie rather than face him in the semis, whereupon Reggie beat Malcolm Whitman in the all-comers final, 6–1, 3–6, 6–3, 6–0, but lost the challenge round to the defender, Bill Larned, 4–6, 6–2, 6–4, 8–6.

But in 1903, after Reggie returned the default courtesy to his brother in the quarters, Laurie became the initial alien male

MAJOR TITLES (16)—*Wimbledon singles, 1902–03–04–05–06; U.S. singles, 1902; Wimbledon doubles, 1897–98–99–1900–01–03–04–05; U.S. doubles, 1902–03.* DAVIS CUP—*1902–03–04–05–06; record: 7–0 in singles, 5–0 in doubles.*

Reggie Doherty
Great Britain (1872–1910)

The appealing and dominant Doherty brothers, Reggie and Laurie, Oxford men, enhanced the popularity of tennis and Wimbledon in their homeland, England, at the turn of the century, and were the backbone of Britain's first four Davis Cup triumphs, 1903—06. Reginald Frank Doherty, the older and known as "Big Do," was frequently ill with digestive problems, and wasn't considered as good as Laurie, but did win four straight Wimbledons (1897–1900), beating his sibling in the 1898 final, 6–1 in the fifth.

Contesting a record 11 straight doubles finals together (1896–1906), they won a record eight, losing only in 1896 to the Baddeley brothers, Herbert and Wilfred, and 1902–06 to Syd Smith and Frank Riseley. Reggie, who played the left court with his brother, was in 12 straight, losing

with Harold Nesbit in 1897. They won all five Davis Cup doubles together, clinching the 1904–05–06 Cups. Reggie was born Oct. 14, 1872, in London and died Dec. 29, 1910. They entered the Hall of Fame together in 1980.

MAJOR TITLES (14)—*Wimbledon singles, 1897–08–09–1900; U.S. doubles, 1902–03; Wimbledon doubles, 1897–98–99–1900–01–*

was traveling on Egyptian papers when he won Wimbledon in 1954, and five years after that became a British citizen. Although his clever game of court management, varied speeds, spins and angles worked best on the Continent's clay, his twisting serve and sharp volleying held up well on grass.

He showed up at the Big W as a 16-year-old in 1938, and, finally—on his 11th try, seeded 11th, he won the title in 1954, elating his long-time loyalists. He was the lowest-rated winner until unseeded Boris Becker in 1985 and another 11th seed, Pat Cash, in 1987. Drob was 32.

The victim, 19-year-old Ken Rosewall (13–11, 4–6, 6–2, 9–7) was in the first of his four fruitless finals. That took 2 hours, 37 minutes, the longest final at that time. But Drobny was probably better known for another, much longer match the year before, a third-rounder over Budge Patty. Slashing away at each other into the gloaming for 4:23, they went 93 games. Drobny circumvented six match points in winning, 8–6, 16–18, 3–6, 8–6, 12–10—the longest there until Pancho Gonzalez and Charlie Pasarell traveled 112 games in 5:12 in

1969—and Drob continued to the semis, losing to Kurt Nielsen.

Defending his title in 1955, he lost to the champ, Tony Trabert, in the semis. Drobny played 116 matches in 17 Wimbledons: 50–16 in singles, 26–8 in doubles, 10–6 in mixed. He won the Italian three of four years starting in 1950, but his first majors were the French of 1951–52, over Eric Sturgess and Frank Sedgman, rewards after three losing finals.

Before defecting he led Czechoslovakia to the Davis Cup European Zone title in 1947 and 1948, and within one match of the challenge round finale. Both times the Czechs lost to Australia, but it was 3–2 the second year. Ten straight years, from 1946, he was in the World Top Ten, No. 1 in 1954. Born Oct. 12, 1921, in Prague, he entered the Hall of Fame in 1983.

MAJOR TITLES (5)—*French singles, 1951, 52; Wimbledon singles, 1954; French doubles, 1948; French mixed, 1948.* DAVIS CUP—*1946–47–48–49; record: 24–4 in singles, 13–2 in doubles.*

Margaret Osborne duPont
United States (1918–   )

See page 345.

Dr. James Dwight
United States (1852–1917)

Hailed deservedly as the "Father of American Tennis," Doc Dwight, a Bostonian and graduate of Harvard and Harvard Medical, may have introduced the game to the U.S., playing with his cousin, Fred Sears, at Nahant, Mass., in 1874. It arrived from England at several locations that year. He did organize and win the initial tournament, a sociable competition at Nahant in 1876.

More importantly he was a driving force behind the organization of the USTA (then the U.S. National Lawn Tennis Association) in 1881, and its first National Championship that year at the Newport Casino, as well as the first Davis Cup match (1900) between the U.S. the British Isles at his Boston club, Longwood Cricket Club.

As a player, right-handed and short (about 5-foot-5), he was more adept at doubles, sharing five U.S. titles with his protégé, Dick Sears, who defeated him in the 1883 singles final. He was No. 2 in 1985–86, the first years of U.S. rankings, and No. 3 in 1888. He, Sears and A.L. Rives were the American pioneers at Wimbledon in 1884, Dwight the only one to win a round, losing in the second round to Herbert Chipp, 7–5 in the fifth. Dwight and Sears teamed in the doubles. In 1885 Dwight returned to the Big W to win three rounds, losing in the all-comers semi to Herbert Lawford, 6–2, 6–2, 6–3.

Shepherding the USTA through its formative years, he was president 21 years, 1882–84 and 1894–1911. He entered the Hall of Fame in 1955. Born in Boston July 14, 1852, he died July 13, 1917 in Mattapoisett, Mass. His son, Dr. Richard Dwight, also a Boston physician, continues to compete, in super-senior events for the over-85s.

MAJOR TITLES (5)—*U.S. doubles, 1882–83–84–86–87.*

Roy Emerson
Australia (1936–   )

See page 347.

Bob Falkenburg
United States (1926–   )

A gangling, dark-haired 6-foot-3 right-hander, Robert Falkenburg came from a tennis family. He and brother Tom won the U.S. Interscholastic title for Los Angeles Fairfax High in 1942, the same year Bob won the singles. Both played in the U.S. Championships at Forest Hills, as did sister Jinx. But Bob, seventh-seeded, made the family's name with a sensational Wimbledon triumph in 1948, eluding three match points while defeating second-seeded Jack Bromwich, 7–5, 0–6, 6–2, 3–6, 7–5.

He and Jack Kramer won the doubles the year before, and in 1944, at 18, he won the U.S. doubles with Don McNeill, one of the youngest to hold that title.

A slam-bang, big-serving net-charger,

that year.

A semifinalist at the U.S. Championships in 1946 and a quarterfinalist in 1947, he lost both times to the champ, Kramer. He was also a quarterfinalist in 1948.

Bromwich had his revenge as Falkenburg defended the Wimbledon title in 1949, taking their quarterfinal, 6–4 in the fifth from two sets down. Marrying a Brazilian and becoming a resident, Bob played Davis Cup for Brazil. He was born Jan. 29, 1926, in Brooklyn, N.Y., and entered the Hall of Fame in 1974.

MAJOR TITLES (3)—*Wimbledon singles, 1948; Wimbledon doubles, 1947; U.S. doubles, 1944.* OTHER U.S. TITLE—*Indoor doubles, 1947, with Jack Kramer.* DAVIS CUP—*Brazil 1954–55; record: 2–4 in singles, 1–3 in doubles.*

Neale Fraser
Australia (1933–   )

A serve-bombing lefty whose onerous delivery was flat, sliced and kicked, Neale Fraser backed it up with tough volleying and was a marvelous competitor. Solidly built and athletic at 6-foot-1, he was especially overpowering on fast surfaces.

Although he won Wimbledon in 1960 and the U.S. title in 1959–60, Fraser found team play—doubles and Davis Cup—nearest his heart. As one of the few men to win all four majors in doubles, Fraser took three each Australian, French and U.S. and two Wimbledon with three different partners: Ashley Cooper, Lew Hoad, Roy Emerson.

he beat Barry MacKay, 8–3, 3–6, 6–2, 6–4, in a tense duel interrupted by rain and carried over to the following afternoon.

His love for Davis Cup showed when he succeeded legendary Harry Hopman as non-playing captain in 1970, and held the job for a record 23 year, piloting four winners: 1973–77–83–86. and a record 49 series victories. He lost the 1990 final to the U.S. He was No. 1 in the world in 1959–60 and in the Top Ten every year between 1956 and 1962. Although he retired in 1963, he played a cameo at Wimbledon 10 years later as doubles finalist (to Jimmy Connors and Ilie Nastase) with John Cooper, younger brother of Ashley Cooper, with whom he'd won the U.S. doubles in 1957. A brother, Dr. John Fraser, a physician, was also a fine player, a Wimbledon semifinalist along with Neale in 1962. Neale was born Oct. 3, 1933, in Melbourne, where he lives, and entered the Hall of Fame in 1984.

MAJOR TITLES (19)—*Wimbledon singles, 1960; U.S. singles, 1959–60; Australian doubles, 1957–58–62; French double, 1958–60–62; Wimbledon doubles, 1959–61; U.S. doubles, 1957–59–60; Australian mixed, 1956; Wimbledon mixed, 1962; U.S. mixed, 1958–59–60.* DAVIS

CUP (As player)—1958–59–60–61–62–63; record: 11–1 in singles, 7–2 in doubles. (As captain)—1970–92; record: 49–19; 4 Cups, 1973–77–83–86.

Shirley Fry
United States (1927–   )

See page 351.

Chuck Garland
United States (1898–1971)

A Yale man who won the U.S. Intercollegiate doubles in 1919, Charles Stedman Garland joined a Harvardian, Dick Williams, the following year to beat Algernon Kingscote and James Parke, 4–6, 6–4, 7–5, 6–2, and become the first Americans to win the doubles at Wimbledon.

Ranked three times in the U.S. Top Ten, 1918–19–20 (No. 8 each time), he was selected for the Hall of Fame in 1969 as much for his service to the USTA as committeeman as player. One of his duties was captaining the 1927 Davis Cup team. Garland, a right-hander, was born Oct. 29, 1898, in Pittsburgh. He later lived in Baltimore and died there Jan. 28, 1971.

MAJOR TITLE (1)—*Wimbledon doubles, 1920.* U.S. TITLES—*Intercollegiate singles, 1919; Intercollegiate doubles, 1919, with K. N. Hawkes; Clay Court doubles, 1917–18, with Sam Hardy.*

Althea Gibson
United States (1927–   )

See page 352.

Kitty Godfree
Great Britain (1896–1992)

See page 78.

Pancho Gonzalez
United States (1928–   )

See page 354.

Evonne Goolagong
Australia (1951–   )

See page 355.

Bitsy Grant
United States (1910–86)

A scrappy little guy, 5-foot-4, 120-pound Bryan Morel "Bitsy" Grant was the smallest American man to attain championship stature. A right-handed retriever supreme, he was able to beat such heavy hitters as Don Budge and Ellsworth Vines even on grass. Between 1930 and 1941 he was ranked nine times in the U.S. Top Ten, No. 3 in 1935–36. In 1936–37 he was in the World Top Ten, Nos. 8 and 6.

Reared on the clay of his native Georgia, he won the U.S. title on that surface thrice (1930–34–35) but he had his moments on the grass at Forest Hills, reaching the U.S. semis in 1935 by beating second-seeded Budge, and in 1936, losing to eventual champion, Fred Perry, 6–4, 3–6, 7–5, 6–2. He was a quarterfinalist in 1937, losing to Gottfried von Cramm, 6–2 in the fifth, and reached the same round a year later.

He played Davis Cup 1935–36–37, helping the U.S. regain the prize in 1937 after a 10-year slump. He continued to compete as a senior, winning 19 U.S. singles titles on the four surfaces: Grass Court—45s (1956–57), 55s (1965–66–67–68); Indoor—55s (1966); Clay Court—45 (1959–60–61–63), 55s (1965–66–67–68–69), 65s (1976–77); Hard Court—65s (1976).

He was born in Atlanta, Dec. 25, 1910, and died there June 5, 1986. Named for him, the Bitsy Grant Tennis Center in his hometown is one the finest public court complexes. He entered the Hall of Fame in 1972.

U.S. TITLES—*Clay Court singles, 1930–34–35; Clay Court doubles, 1932, with George Lott.* DAVIS CUP—*1935–36–37; record: 8–2 in singles.*

Clarence Griffin
United States (1888–1973)

Clarence James "Peck" Griffin ranked in the U.S. Top Ten three times (1915–16–20), No. 6 the last two, but made his mark in doubles alongside fellow Californian Bill Johnston. They won the U.S. title thrice, 1915–16–20. He was also in the 1913 final with John Strachan. He and Strachan won the U.S. Clay Court title

Jan. 19, 1888, in San Francisco, and died March 28, 1973, in Santa Barbara Cal. He entered the Hall of Fame in 1970.

MAJOR TITLES (3)—*U.S. doubles, 1915–16–20.* OTHER U.S. TITLES—*Clay Court singles, 1914; Clay Court doubles, 1913, with John Strachan.*

Harold Hackett
United States (1878–1937)

A New Yorker, Harold Humphrey Hackett was best known as the partner of Fred Alexander in one of the most successful doubles teams. Hackett was the softer, more deceptive stroker of the two. Beginning in 1905 they were U.S. finalists a record seven successive years, winning in 1907–08–09–10. A Yale man, and right-handed, he was born July 12, 1878, in Hingham, Mass. He and Alexander won the U.S. Indoor doubles thrice (1906–08), and he completed a sweep of the surface titles available then by taking the Clay doubles in 1912 with Walter Hall.

The following year, 1913, he was player-captain of the U.S. Davis Cup team that broke a decade drought by seizing the Cup in a 3–2 beating of Britain. He and Maurice McLoughlin won the vital go-

ahead point over H. Roper Barrett and Charles Dixon, 6–4 in the fifth. He was ranked in the U.S. Top Ten twice, 1902–06, No. 7 in 1906 when he was a U.S. quarterfinalist. He was inducted into the Hall of Fame in 1961. He died in New York Nov. 20, 1937.

MAJOR TITLES (4)—*U.S. doubles, 1907–08–09–10.* OTHER U.S. TITLES—*Indoor*

her hometown, not long before her 18th birthday. She beat Laura Knight, 6–1, 6–0, at the Philadelphia Cricket Club, but lost the title the following year to Bertha Townsend, and wasn't a factor again. A right-hander, she served sidearm, as, she said, did most of the women in that inaugural.

Forty-four years later she recalled that she had been an anemic child, who showed some "enthusiasm and aptitude" for tennis. Her mother was advised by the family doctor to take Ellen out of school and put her on a court daily to build herself up. She remembered her mother making her tennis dresses of red plaid gingham: "A red felt hat topped the tight-collared and be-corseted body. I also wore a blazer of red and blue stripes...we did now and then grip our overdraped, voluminous skirts with our left hand to give us a bit more limb freedom when dashing to make a swift, snappy stroke, every bit as well placed as today, but lacking the force and great physical strength of the modern girl. Is it possible for you to envision the gallery? A loving, but openly prejudiced crowd standing within two feet of the court lines, calling out hurrahs of applause plus groans of disappointment, and some suggestive criticism, such as: 'Run to the net.' 'Place it to her left.' 'Don't dare lose this game.'"

She was born Sept, 18, 1869, in Philadelphia, and died, Mrs. Taylor Allderdice, May 11, 1937, in Pittsburgh. Induction into the Hall of Fame came in 1965.

MAJOR TITLE (1)—*U.S. singles, 1887.*

Darlene Hard
United States (1936–   )

An all-out attacking Californian with a splendid serve, volley and overhead, Darlene Ruth Hard nevertheless won the French singles on slow clay (1960) as well as the U.S. title on grass at Forest Hills (1960–61), and was a Wimbledon finalist twice (1957–59). A stocky blonde right-hander, she was born Jan. 6, 1936, in Los Angeles and attended Pomona. She won the U.S. Intercollegiate title in 1958.

She played with considerable zest, inspiring a variety of doubles partners, winning the U.S. title five straight years (1958–62) and again in 1969 with four different accomplices, the French twice with different partners and four Wimbledons with three different partners. The 1969 triumph with Francoise Durr—a last-minute amalgamation—may have been her most sensational in that Darlene, no longer competing, looked so out of place in the final. But after a disastrous start, losing the first eight games, she recalled the old moves to beat Margaret Court and Virginia Wade, 0–6, 6–3, 6–4.

Between 1954 and 1963 she ranked in the U.S. Top Ten 10 times, No. 1 four straight years (1960–63), and in the World Top Ten nine times, No. 2 in 1960–61. She was a standout Wightman and Federation Cup player. She had 21 major titles in singles, doubles and mixed, and entered the Hall of Fame in 1973. She married Richard Waggoner in 1977.

MAJOR TITLES (21)—*French singles, 1960; U.S. singles, 1960–61; French doubles, 1955–57–60; Wimbledon doubles, 1957–59–60–63; U.S. doubles, 1958–59–60–61–62–69; French mixed, 1955–61; Wimbledon mixed, 1957–59–60.* OTHER U.S. TITLES—*Clay Court doubles, 1957, with Althea Gibson; 1960, with Billie Jean Moffitt King; 1962, with Sue Behlmar; 1963, with Maria Bueno; Hard Court singles, 1963; Hard Court doubles, 1963, with Paulette Verzin; Intercollegiate singles, 1958.* FEDERATION CUP—*1963; record: 3–1 in singles, 3–0 in doubles.* WIGHTMAN CUP—*1957–59–60–62–63; record: 6–3 in singles, 4–1 in doubles.*

Doris Hart
United States (1925–   )

See page 358.

Bob Hewitt
Australia/South Africa (1940–   )

Tapped for the Hall of Fame in 1992 in harness with his partner, Robert Anthony John Hewitt was the right-court player in the alignment of Hewitt and Frew McMillan. They combined for five major championships and were one of the shrewdest, strongest of all teams, men whose prowess spanned the amateur and open eras. In 1974 they were central to South Africa's winning the Davis Cup, the fifth member of the exclusive club, and first newcomer since France in 1927.

Hewitt was a born and bred Aussie, beginning life Jan. 12, 1940, in Dubbo, New South Wales. He became one of a tribe that terrorized the tennis world, and first came to attention winning the Wimbledon doubles in 1962 and 1964 with compatriot Fred Stolle. But love broke up that potent alliance. Hewitt fell for a South African lass named Dalaille, and moved to Johannesburg to wed. Since he hadn't played Davis Cup for Australia, Hewitt was eligible, as a resident, to compete for South Africa.

In 1966 he and McMillan were put together as teammates, and they stayed together for much of the next 15 years to win Wimbledon thrice (1967–72–78), the French (1972), the U.S. (1977) plus 60 other titles. Hewitt, bald, bearded and sometimes volatile on court, was a blocky 6-footer with surprisingly delicate touch, an accurate and seldom failing returner.

He was the better singles player, taking seven pro titles in singles, along with 65 in doubles, the latter total placing him sixth

amounted to more than $1 million.

MAJOR TITLES (15)—*Australian doubles, 1963–64; French doubles, 1972; Wimbledon doubles, 1962–64–67–72–78; U.S. doubles, 1977; Australian mixed, 1961; French mixed, 1970–79; Wimbledon mixed, 1977–79 U.S. mixed, 1979.* DAVIS CUP—*1967–68–69–74–78; record: 22–3 in singles, 16–1 in doubles.*

HEWITT-McMILLAN: MAJOR TITLES (5)— *French doubles, 1972; Wimbledon doubles, 1967–72–78; U.S. doubles, 1977.* DAVIS CUP— *1967–68–69–74–78; record: 16–1 in doubles.*

Lew Hoad
Australia (1934–)
See page 360.

Harry Hopman
Australia (1906–85)

A fine player, particularly in doubles, at which he won seven major titles, Henry Christian Hopman made his name as the most successful of all Davis Cup captains, piloting Australia to 16 Cups between 1939 and 1967. His was the era of perhaps the greatest players of all, the Hall of Fame Aussies from Frank Sedgman through Lew Hoad, Ken Rosewall, Ashley Cooper, Neale Fraser, Roy Emerson, Rod Laver, John Newcombe, Fred Stolle, Tony Roche.

He drove and inspired them, and built pride in their underpopulated country's beating up on the rest of the world. The first of his 22 teams, 1938, reached the challenge round final, losing to the U.S. But he was back with the same pair, Adrian Quist and Jack Bromwich, to win a singular

sters, Sedgman and Ken McGregor, he won the Cup in New York in 1950, and the Down Under-takers were in business for a glorious near-quarter-century. His teams compiled a 38–6 record.

As a player he won the Australian doubles with Jack Crawford in 1929–30 and four mixed titles with his wife, the former Nell Hall, a record for married couples. In singles his high point was the U.S. Championships of 1938 when he beat fifth-seeded Elwood Cooke and future U.S. and French champ Don McNeill to reach the quarters, where he was an historic footnote in Don Budge's original Grand Slam, 6–3, 6–1, 6–3.

Following his last Davis Cup match as captain, a loss to Mexico at Mexico City in 1969, he emigrated to the U.S. to become a highly successful teaching pro, counseling such champions-to-be as Vitas Gerulaitis and John McEnroe at the Port Washington (N.Y.) Tennis Academy. He later opened his own Hopman Tennis Academy at Largo, Fla. Hop was born Aug. 12, 1906, in Sydney and died Dec. 27, 1985, in Largo, Fla. He entered the Hall of Fame in 1978.

MAJOR TITLES (7)—*Australian doubles, 1929–30; U.S. mixed, 1939; Australian mixed,*

1930–36–37–39. DAVIS CUP (*As player*)—*1928–30–32; record: 4–5 in singles, 4–3 in doubles.* (*As captain*)—*1938–39–50–51–52–53–54–55–56–57–58–59–60–61–62–63–64–65–66–67–68–69; record: 38–6, 16 Cups.*

Fred Hovey
United States (1868–1945)

Frederick Howard Hovey, a Bostonian and Harvardian, won the U.S. Intercollegiate singles in 1890 and 1891 as well as the doubles with Bob Wrenn the second year. Four years later he, a right-hander, beat lefty Wrenn, 6–3, 6–2, 6–4, to end his fellow Bostonian's two-year reign at the U.S. Championships. Wrenn returned the favor the next year, 1896, 6–1 in the fifth set of the challenge round.

Between 1890 and 1896 he was in the U.S. Top Ten seven times, No. 1 in 1895. In 1893 he and Clarence Hobart, twice U.S. champs in doubles, won the championship of the World Columbian Exposition at Chicago. He was born Oct. 7, 1868, in Newton Centre, Mass., and died Oct. 18, 1945, in Miami Beach. He entered the Hall of Fame in 1974.

MAJOR TITLES (3)—*U.S. singles, 1895; U.S. doubles, 1893–94.* OTHER U.S. TITLES—*Intercollegiate singles, 1890–91; Intercollegiate doubles, 1891, with Robert Wrenn.*

Joe Hunt
United States (1919–44)

Fifteen days short of his 25th birthday, Lt. Joseph Raphael Hunt of the U.S. Navy, was a victim of World War II, a pilot-in-training killed in an on-duty crash near Daytona Beach, Fla., Feb. 2, 1944. Thus he was the shortest-lived of the Hall of Famers.

He was a Californian who reveled in the attacking game, and won the U.S. singles at Forest Hills in 1943 while on leave from the Atlantic fleet. It was a unique all-service final in which he beat ex-Davis Cup doubles partner, Seaman Jack Kramer of

the Coast Guard, 6–3, 6–8, 10–8, 6–0. That was the end of Joe's tennis.

In 1938 at Southern Cal (doubles) and 1941 at the Naval Academy (singles), Hunt was the only player other than Malcolm Chace (Brown and Yale, 1893–94–95), to win U.S. Intercollegiate titles for two different schools. Husky and athletic, Hunt also played football at Navy. He, 20, and Kramer, 18, were the second youngest Davis Cup doubles pair for the U.S., losing in 1939 at Philadelphia to Australians Jack Bromwich and Adrian Quist, the first domino in the only final-round 3–2 loss from a 2–0 lead.

Seemingly headed for a great career, he was one of the youngest ever to rank in the U.S. Top Ten, 17 when he was No. 9 in 1936. He was also there in 1937–38–43, No. 1 posthumously in 1943. He was born Feb. 17, 1919, in San Francisco and was inducted into the Hall of Fame in 1966.

MAJOR TITLES (1)—*U.S. singles, 1943.* OTHER U.S. TITLES—*Intercollegiate singles, 1941; Clay Court doubles, 1938, with Lew Wetherell; Intercollegiate doubles, 1938, with Wetherell.* DAVIS CUP—*1939; record: 0–1 in doubles.*

Frank Hunter
United States (1894–1981)

As one of the earlier touring pros, Francis Townsend Hunter joined the nomad ranks in 1931 after a distinguished amateur career. A right-handed New Yorker, he was born there June 28, 1894. He played extremely well for his country, taking a 1924 Olympic gold medal in doubles alongside Vinnie Richards, and helping build a 2–1 lead in the losing Davis Cup 1927 finale, yoked to Bill Tilden in a five-set win over France's Jacques Brugnon and Jean Borotra.

He came close, as finalist, to the U.S. title twice in succession: 1928 final, 6–3 in the fifth to Henri Cochet, and 1929, 6–4 in the fifth to Tilden. He also lost the 1923 Wimbledon final to Bill Johnston. And he was one of those unlucky three victims in a row who built two-set leads over 1927 champ Cochet, Hunter in the quarterfinals, preceding Tilden and Borotra. But he won the Wimbledon doubles twice, 1924 with Olympic sidekick Richards and 1927 with Tilden.

Wimbledon doubles, 1924–27; Wimbledon mixed, 1927-28-29. OTHER U.S. TITLES—*Indoor singles, 1922–30; Indoor doubles, 1923–24, with Vincent Richards; 1929, with Bill Tilden.* DAVIS CUP—*1927-28-29; record: 3–1 in singles, 1–1 in doubles.*

Helen Jacobs
United States (1908–   )

See page 79.

Bill Johnston
United States (1894–1946)

See page 80.

Ann Haydon Jones
Great Britain (1938–   )

The first left-handed woman to win Wimbledon, Adrianne Shirley Haydon Jones had to cool a rampaging Billie Jean King to do it in the 1969 final, 3–6, 6–3, 6–2. King had won three straight times and 24 straight matches. Before that, Ann had shown her all-around value and steadiness by winning the French in 1961 and 1966. She could attack or stay back, and had a compact service motion with little windup. In 1967, despite a leg injury that hobbled her, she pushed King hard (11–9,

6–4) in the U.S. final. Jones, King, Francoise Durr and Rosie Casals became the first professional female touring troupe, signing with George MacCall, promoter of the National Tennis League.

Jones was born Oct. 7, 1938, in Birmingham, England, to parents who were outstanding table tennis players. She followed in their paddling steps as a five-

national play, Federation and Wightman Cup, coming back in 1975 at age 37 to help win the Wightman over the U.S. Her Wimbledon triumph was a gem of persistence—Ann won on her 14th try, and, fourth-seeded, beat the 5–1–2 seeds in the stretch to do so: Nancy Richey, 6–2, 7–5; Margaret Court, 10–12, 6–3, 6–2; and King. Jones played 157 matches at Wimbledon: 57–13 in singles, 33–15 in doubles, 29–10 in mixed. She married P.F. Jones in 1962 and entered the Hall of Fame in 1985.

MAJOR TITLES (7)—*French singles, 1961–66; Wimbledon singles, 1969; French doubles, 1963-68-69; Wimbledon mixed, 1969.* FEDERATION CUP—*1963-64-65-66-67-71; record: 11–8 in singles, 13–7 in doubles.* WIGHTMAN CUP—*1957-58-59-60-61-62-63-64-65-66-67-70-75; record: 10–11 in singles, 6–5 in doubles.*

Billie Jean King
United States (1943–   )

See page 361.

Jan Kodes
Czechoslovakia (1945–   )

Determination marked the grim-faced Jan Kodes, who clawed and battled to many a victory though seemingly exhausted. As a sportsman he was even more a hero to many of his countrymen for his refusal to leave the repressed country as Jaroslav Drobny, Martina Navratilova and Ivan Lendl had done. Thus they shared more fully in his major triumphs: Wimbledon of 1973, and the French of 1970 and 1971.

A compact, muscular 5-foot-9 right-hander, Kodes was a standout and dogged groundstroker. He volleyed well, too, but was disdainful of grass even though he signalled his ability there in 1971 by knocking top-seeded John Newcombe out of the U.S. Open in the first round, and going all the way, unseeded, to a final-round defeat by Stan Smith. Two years later he was the Wimbledon champ, defeating Alex Metreveli in straight sets, and fought Newcombe through a brilliant five-set U.S. final, losing the last set, 6–3.

Kodes, seventh-seeded, beat Zeljko Franulovic easily to win the French in 1970, countered the artistry of Ilie Nastase, 8–6, 6–2, 2–6, 7–5, the following year, but fell to Patrick Proisy in the 1972 quarters, ending a 17-match run at Roland Garros.

As a devoted Davis Cupper, he played 15 years and 39 series for Czechoslovakia beginning in 1966, and was among the top 20 players in matches played (97) and won (60): 39–22 in singles, 21–15 in doubles. He led the team to the 1975 Cup round, a 3–2 defeat by Sweden at Stockholm, and played a cameo doubles role along the way in 1980 as he realized a dream—the Cup for Czechoslovakia, Lendl-powered.

Besides his three majors he won six pro titles in singles, 17 in doubles, and accumulated $693,197 in career prize money. Jan was in the World Top Ten in 1971 and 1973, No. 5 in the former. Born March 1, 1945, in Prague, he has served as his country's national coach and Davis Cup captain, and entered the Hall of Fame in 1990.

MAJOR TITLES (3)—*French singles, 1970–71; Wimbledon singles, 1973.* DAVIS CUP—*1966–67–68–69–70–71–72–73–74–75–76–77–78–79–80; record: 39–20 in singles, 21–15 in doubles.*

Jack Kramer
United States (1921–   )
See page 363.

René Lacoste
France (1905–   )
See page 81.

Bill Larned
United States (1872–1926)

One of the Big Three of the U.S. men's championship, William Augustus Larned won seven times, as did Dick Sears before him and Bill Tilden after. Like Tilden, he was a late achiever, 28 years old when, after failing in the final before Malcolm Whitman the previous year, he won the title in 1901 for a first time, over Beals Wright. His last, ending a five-year run, in 1911, made him the oldest male singles champ, 38.

He began playing the Championships in 1891 and in 19 years, through 1911, fell short of the semis only twice, making a 61–12 match record. He was ranked in the U.S. Top Ten 19 times, starting with No. 6 in 1892, and probably would have been there 20 straight years if he hadn't missed the 1898 season serving with the Rough Riders in the Spanish-American War. Nineteen years was a record for eight decades until topped by Jimmy Connors.

He was No. 1 eight times, tied by Connors, topped by Tilden's 10. Three of those years his younger brother, Edward Larned, was also in the Top Ten, No. 6 in 1903. He was a member of five Davis Cup teams, in 1902 a Cup winner. He was a powerful groundstroker with an oppressive topspinning right-handed forehand.

Bill was born Dec. 30, 1872, in Summit, N.J., and attended Cornell. He committed suicide on Dec. 16, 1926, in New York. He was inducted into the Hall of Fame in 1956.

MAJOR TITLES (7)—*U.S. singles, 1901–02–07–08–09–10–11.* OTHER U.S. TITLE—*Intercollegiate singles, 1892.* DAVIS CUP—*1902–03–05–08–09–11; record: 9–5 in singles.*

in a long-shot final—they were seeded No. 5 and No. 2 respectively—to win at Forest Hills, 6–3, 4–6, 5–7, 6–4, 6–3.

A combat veteran of the U.S. Army in World War II, Larsen was delayed in his start in big-time tennis, making the U.S. Top Ten the first of eight successive times at No. 6 in 1949, at age 24. He was No. 1 in 1950, and ranked in the World Top Ten thrice, 1950–51–54, No. 3 the first year.

By adding the U.S. Clay and Hard Court (1952) and Indoor (1953) titles to this Forest Hills prize he became the first man to take the championships on the four surfaces. Only he and Tony Trabert have done so. Losing the French to Trabert in 1954, he was only the ninth of 15 American men to attain that final. Larsen was born April 17, 1925, in Hayward, Cal., and entered the Hall of Fame in 1969.

MAJOR TITLE (1)—*U.S. singles, 1950.* OTHER U.S. TITLES—*Indoor singles, 1953; Clay Court singles, 1952; Hard Court singles, 1950–52; Indoor doubles, 1953, with Kurt Nielsen; Clay Court doubles, 1950, with Herb Flam; 1952, with Grant Golden; Hard Court doubles, 1952, with Tom Brown.* DAVIS CUP—*1951–52; record: 4–0 in singles.*

Rod Laver
Australia (1938–   )
See page 365.

Suzanne Lenglen
France (1899–1938)
See page 82.

George Lott

joined the touring pros in 1934.

He was a U.S. Davis Cup stalwart between 1928 and 1934, going undefeated in 11 doubles matches. He ranked in the U.S. Top Ten nine times between 1924 and 1934, No. 2 in 1931 when he lost the final at Forest Hills to Ellie Vines, 7–5 in the fourth. He won the Wimbledon doubles in 1931 with Johnny Van Ryn and 1934 with Stoefen. A right-hander, he was born Oct. 16, 1906, in Springfield Ill., and died Dec. 2, 1991, in Chicago, where he was still active as varsity coach of Loyola University. He was inducted into the Hall of Fame in 1964.

MAJOR TITLES (12)—*French doubles, 1931; Wimbledon doubles, 1931–34; U.S. doubles, 1928–29–30–33–34; Wimbledon mixed, 1931; U.S. mixed, 1929–31–34.* OTHER U.S. TITLES—*Clay Court singles, 1932; Indoor doubles, 1932, with John Van Ryn; 1934, with Lester Stoefen; Clay Court doubles, 1932, with Bryan "Bitsy" Grant; Pro doubles, 1935, with Stoefen; 1937, with Vincent Richards.* DAVIS CUP—*1928–29–30–31–33–34; record: 7–4 in singles, 11–0 in doubles.*

Gene Mako
United States (1916–   )
Though brief, the career of Hungarian-born Constantine Gene Mako

was one of the most remarkable in that he achieved his foremost results after sustaining a devastating and painful right-shoulder injury that would have finished most men as competitors. As a teenager he had one of the most powerful serves, but he injured himself by overdoing it. This was compounded by a 1936 tumble in London that finished the job of wrecking his right (playing) shoulder, and kept him out of Wimbledon that year.

"I continued only because my friend and doubles partner, Don Budge, asked me to do so," Mako says. "I told him I'd be serving like a little old lady and would have to shovel the ball around, but it was okay with him."

Despite the sometimes puny appearance of his strokes, 6-footer Mako, in the right court alongside Budge, was a canny playmaker, a man who knew the angles and where to put the ball—and competed fiercely—as they became one of the greatest teams. They won Wimbledon in 1937–38, and were in four successive U.S. finals from 1935, triumphing in 1936 and 1938.

A formidable singles player as well, he performed on four Davis Cup teams (two winners), seizing the go-ahead point with Budge in the 1937 lifting of the Cup from Britain, 4–1, to end a 10-year U.S. dry spell. They beat Charles Tuckey and Frank Wilde, 6–3, 7–5, 7–9, 12–10. Just as vital was their go-ahead win in the previous round, a 3–2 thriller over Germany—a 4–6, 7–5, 8–6, 6–4 squeeze past Henner Henkel and Gottfried von Cramm.

Mako was in the U.S. Top Ten in 1937–38, No. 3 the second year, and No. 9 in the world ranking of 1938. That year he was the last obstacle between Budge and the original Grand Slam in the U.S. final at Forest Hills. Unseeded, Mako dashed to his only major singles final on victories over sixth-seed Frank Kovacs and the third and first foreign seeds, Franjo Puncec and

Jack Bromwich. He resisted Budge well, holding off the inevitable for four sets, 6–3, 6–8, 6–2, 6–1. Mako had one of the four sets Budge lost during the Slam.

Gene had a brief fling at pro tennis while serving in the Navy during World War II, winning the U.S. pro doubles in 1943 with Bruce Barnes. Upon discharge, he made another sort of sporting name on the West Coast as a semipro basketball player. Born in Budapest Jan. 24, 1916, he moved with his family to Buenos Aires, then to Los Angeles when he was seven. There he remained, today a gregarious art dealer. He entered the Hall of Fame in 1973.

MAJOR TITLES (5)—*Wimbledon doubles, 1937–38; U.S. doubles, 1936–38; U.S. mixed, 1936.* OTHER U.S. TITLES—*Clay Court doubles, 1933, with Jack Tidball; 1934, with Don Budge; 1939, with Frank Parker; Pro doubles, 1943, with Bruce Barnes; Intercollegiate singles, 1934; Intercollegiate doubles, 1934, with Philip Castlen.* DAVIS CUP—*1935–36-37–38; record: 0–1 in singles, 6–2 in doubles.*

Molla Mallory
United States (1884–1959)
See page 84.

Alice Marble
United States (1913–90)
See page 85.

Chuck McKinley
United States (1941–86)
Bubbling with energy and grit, Charles Robert McKinley, Jr., was a tough little guy who hustled every minute and died tragically of a brain tumor shortly after learning, in 1986, that he had been named to the Hall of Fame. But he had achieved his utmost tennis goals, both in 1963—winning Wimbledon, and leading the U.S. to the Davis Cup with a 3–2 victory over the holder, Australia, at Adelaide.

A stubby, chesty 5-foot-9 Missourian, he learned to play at a St. Louis YMCA, where he was already proficient at table tennis. He was a crowd-wowing player, hurling himself about the court, leaping for smashes at which he was expert since so many opponents tried to lob him. Although favored to win the U.S. Intercollegiate title in 1963 for Trinity in San Antonio, Chuck obtained permission from the college president to go for the larger prize, Wimbledon, and, seeded

Wimbledon splash in 1961, until losing the final to second-seeded Rod Laver in straight sets. As the defender in 1964, he was paid back by Stolle in a four-set semi. As the left-court player, he blended splendidly with Dennis Ralston in three U.S. doubles championships, 1961–63–64. They beat Mexico's Rafe Osuna and Tonio Palafox the first two times, McKinley serving out of two match points in the exciting 11–9 fifth set in 1963.

During the long Cup campaign of 1963 he won six of eight singles, all four doubles matches with Ralston. The Cup round was McKinley's *tour de force* although he lost to Roy Emerson the first day. He and Ralston got the go-ahead point over Emerson and Neale Fraser, but after Ralston lost to Emerson on the third day it "was up to me. That's the way I wanted it, the Cup riding on one match."

It was a rare position for an American. None since Malcolm Whitman, beating Britain's Reggie Doherty in 1902, had come through in the decisive fifth match. McKinley did, despite being down a service break in the fourth to the thunder-serving Aussie rookie John Newcombe, 10–12, 6–2, 9–7, 6–2, as the Memorial Drive stadium

rocked with patriotic fervor for Newc. The following year, however, in Cleveland, McKinley couldn't repeat, losing the decisive fifth to Emerson, 3–6, 6–2, 6–4, 6–4, as Australian regained the Cup, 3–2.

More intent on getting a college degree and establishing himself in business, McKinley resisted professional offers, and his career was relatively brief without a

1941, in St. Louis, and died Aug. 10, 1986, in Dallas.

MAJOR TITLES (4)—*Wimbledon singles, 1963; U.S. doubles, 1961–63–64.* OTHER U.S. TITLES—*Indoor singles, 1962–64; Clay Court singles, 1962–63; Indoor doubles, 1962, with Rod Laver; 1963–65, with Dennis Ralston; Clay Court doubles, 1961–64, with Ralston; Pro doubles, 1943, with Bruce Barnes.* DAVIS CUP—*1960–61–62–63–64–65; record: 16–6 in singles, 13–3 in doubles.*

Maurice McLoughlin
United States (1890–1957)

See page 87.

Frew McMillan
South Africa (1942–   )

Side by side again entering the Hall of Fame in 1992, Frew Donald McMillan was reunited with his one-time collaborator on the team of Hewitt and McMillan. The unorthodox McMillan—stroking with two hands on both sides in the left court—and Bob Hewitt were a dynamite blend, winning five major titles (three Wimbledons) and driving South Africa to the 1974 Davis Cup.

Love was the prime ingredient in bringing them together in 1966. It was

Hewitt's romance with his South African wife-to-be that moved the Australian westward to Johannesburg. When he became eligible to play for his new land, Hewitt was yoked to McMillan in 1966, and they were an immediate hit. They won their first start together late that year, and didn't lose until the quarters of the French the following year, a 45-match streak.

In 1967 they won Wimbledon, and repeated in 1972 and 1978. A springy 6-foot-1, the slim McMillan was born in Springs, South Africa, May 20, 1942, and grew up there.

"We were touch and thrust," he says of the combination that was so winning over a 15-year period. "Right from the start each of us knew what the other would do. Bob had wonderful returning touch from the first court." McMillan, a right-hander, handled the racket like a cricket bat and could slug or chip. Distinctive beneath a tiny white cap that partially covered his shining dark hair, Frew was the first player of international prominence of two-way two-fisted swinging.

A straight-set Wimbledon quarterfinal win over five-time champs John Newcombe and Tony Roche en route to the 1978 title showed them at their very best. They continued lethally through the final, 6–1, 6–4, 6–2, over Peter Fleming and John McEnroe. Spanning the amateur and open eras, they added 60 titles to their five majors. McMillan's individual total of pro doubles titles was 74, third on the all-time list behind Tom Okker (78) and McEnroe (75). Frew won two pro singles titles. He also had five major mixed titles, two Wimbledons and two U.S. with Betty Stove, for a career total of 10 majors.

MAJOR TITLES (10)—*French doubles, 1972; Wimbledon doubles, 1967–72–78; U.S. doubles, 1977; French mixed, 1966; Wimbledon mixed, 1979–81; U.S. mixed, 1977–78.* DAVIS CUP— *1965–66–67–68–69–73–74–75–76–77–78; record: 2–0 in singles, 23–5 in doubles.*

MCMILLAN-HEWITT: MAJOR TITLES (5)— *French doubles, 1972; Wimbledon doubles, 1967–72–78; U.S. doubles, 1977.* DAVIS CUP—*1967–68–69–74–78; record: 16–1 in doubles.*

Don McNeill
United States (1918–   )

William Donald McNeill may have lost his best years to World War II in which he served in the U.S. Navy. A right-hander with an all-around game, he is one of only four American men to win the U.S. on grass at Forest Hills (1940) and the French on clay at Roland Garros (1939), succeeding Don Budge and preceding Frank Parker and Tony Trabert. Don stopped the year's No. 1 player, Bobby Riggs, to win the French, 7–5, 6–0, 6–3.

Born April 30, 1918, in Chickasha, Okla., he attended Kenyon College in Ohio and won the U.S. Intercollegiate title in 1940. He and Ted Schroeder (1942) are the only men to wear the college and national crowns in the same year. In beating defender Riggs for the 1940 title at Forest Hills, 7–5 in the fifth (following a semis win over Jack Kramer), McNeill was the third of five players in the Championship finals to rebound from two sets down. He ranked in the U.S. Top Ten six times between 1937 and 1946, No. 1 in 1940, and was No. 7 in the world in 1939. On leave from the Navy, he won the U.S. doubles in 1944 with Bob Falkenburg. He was elected to the Hall of Fame in 1965.

MAJOR TITLES (4)—*French singles, 1939; U.S. singles, 1940; French doubles, 1939; U.S. doubles, 1944.* OTHER U.S. TITLES—*Indoor singles, 1938–50; Clay Court singles, 1940; Intercollegiate singles, 1940; Indoor doubles, 1941–46, with Frank Guernsey; 1949–50–51, with Bill Talbert.*

Helen Wills Moody
United States (1905–   )

See page 88.

Bessie Moore
United States (1876–1959)

Elisabeth Holmes Moore, a New Yorker, was a young champ, winning the first of her U.S. titles at 20 in 1896. But four years before, she was in the final, losing the first five-set match played by women, 5–7, 6–3, 6–4, 4–6, 6–2, to Ireland's Mabel Cahill. She was the youngest U.S. finalist at 16 until Pam

Mallory's 10 and Helen Wills Moody and Chris Evert's nine. Her longevity spread between the finals of 1892 and 1905 was also a U.S. record.

In 1901, she beat Marion Jones in the all-comers final, 4–6, 1–6, 9–7, 9–7, 6–3 (58 games, the longest of all major women's finals), then ousted defender Myrtle McAteer in the challenge round, 6–4, 3–6, 7–5, 2–6, 6–2, to become the lone woman to play five-set matches on successive days.

The 105 games alarmed the men who ran the USTA. They decreed best-of-three-set finals thereafter. Moore and the other women hadn't complained about five-set matches and she said they felt "dissatisfied" by the decision and patronized by the male establishment. Moore, a right-hander, was born March 5, 1876, in Brooklyn, N.Y., and died Jan. 22, 1959, in Starke, Fla.. She was elected to the Hall of Fame in 1971.

MAJOR TITLES (8)—*U.S. singles, 1896–1901–03–05; U.S. doubles, 1896–1903; U.S. mixed, 1902–04.* OTHER U.S. TITLES—*Indoor singles, 1907; Indoor doubles, 1908, with Helen Pouch; 1909, with Erna Marcus.*

Angela Mortimer
Great Britain (1932–   )

Turning a physical impairment to her advantage, Florence Angela Margaret Mortimer Barrett capped an excellent career with a rebounding, unexpected Wimbledon triumph in 1961. She was 29 and partially deaf.

"I could hear the applause of the

Truman, 4–6, 6–4, 7–5. It was the first all-English finale in 47 years.

Born April 21, 1932, at Plymouth, Mortimer didn't start playing tennis until she was 15. But her resolve, speed and intelligence combined to produce a strong all-around game, with emphasis on ground-strokes, particularly a battering forehand.

Mortimer lost the Wimbledon final to Althea Gibson in 1958 and was a quarterfinalist in 1953–54–56–59–60. She won the French in 1955 and Australian in 1958. And the Wimbledon doubles in 1955.

She played Wightman Cup six years, helping Britain win, 4–3, in 1960 with a critical victory over Janet Hopps, and captained the team seven years (1964–70), piloting the 1968 victory. She was in the World Top Ten, 1953–62, Nos. 1–4–4 in 1961–55–56. Following the 1961 season, in which she was a U.S. semifinalist, she underwent a stapedectomy, improving her hearing significantly. But she was never again the player of her Wimbledon glory.

She is married to John Edward Barrett, former British Davis Cup player and captain. They live in London.

MAJOR TITLES (4)—*Australian singles, 1958; French singles, 1955; Wimbledon singles, 1961; Wimbledon doubles, 1955.* WIGHTMAN CUP—*1953–55–56–59–60–61; record: 3–7 in singles, 1–4 in doubles.*

Gardnar Mulloy
United States (1913–   )

Seemingly an eternal beacon in the game, Gardnar Putnam Mulloy held his first U.S. national ranking in 1936 (No. 11 in men's doubles) and his most recent in 1992, No. 9 and No. 4, respectively, in 75s singles and doubles. As a slim 6-footer seemingly fit as ever, he continues to play effortlessly—a man with a complete game, whose volleying and smashes lit up the left court as he and Bill Talbert became one of the finest teams.

They won the U.S. title four times (1942–45–46–48), and were finalists in 1950 and 1953. Their six final-round appearances are one short of Fred Alexander and Harold Hackett's team record. He and Talbert won the clinching point in the 1948 Davis Cup victory over Australia at Forest Hills, beating Billy Sidwell and Colin Long. Gar was on the team six other years, helping also to win the Cups of 1946 and 1949, and was a winning playing-captain in two zone matches, 1952–53. Playing on the 1957 team at 43, he was the oldest U.S. Cupper.

Ranking in the U.S. Top Ten 14 times between 1939 and 1954, he was No. 1 in 1952, when he was U.S. finalist at Forest Hills, losing to 24-year-old Frank Sedgman. At 38, Mulloy was the oldest to attain that eminence, five weeks older than 38-year-old Bill Larned in 1911. He ranked in the World Top Ten thrice: 1946–49–52, No. 7 the last year. His most startling triumph may have been the Wimbledon doubles in 1957, at 43, joined with Budge Patty, 33. Unseeded, they became the oldest championship team of the post-World War I era by stunning the top-seeded Lew Hoad, 22, and Neale Fraser, 23, 8–10, 6–4, 6–4, 6–4.

A right-hander, he was born Nov. 22, 1913, in Washington, D.C., but has been a lifelong Miamian, a graduate of the University of Miami and its law school, organizer-coach-leading player of its first tennis team. His first U.S. Championships were the Father and Son doubles with his father, Robin Mulloy, in 1939–41–42, but they have continued to flow from his rackets unceasingly for more than a half-century. Campaigning among the seniors since he won the Grass Court 45s singles in 1960, he has racked up 37 U.S. titles in singles through the age groups and 31 in doubles including the Grass 45s of 1963–64–65–67 with his old sidekick, Talbert. He served in the U.S. Navy in World War II and entered the Hall of Fame in 1972.

MAJOR TITLES (5)—*Wimbledon doubles, 1957; U.S. doubles, 1942–45–46–48.* OTHER U.S. TITLES—*Clay Court doubles, 1946, with Bill Talbert.* DAVIS CUP—*1946–48–49–50–52–53–57; record: 3–0 in singles, 8–3 in doubles.*

Lindley Murray
United States (1892–1970)

A big-serving lefty out of California, Robert Lindley Murray was born Nov. 3, 1892, in San Francisco. He had a brief, bright run in the U.S. Championships, losing in the 1916 semis to Bill Johnston and taking the title in 1917 (over Nat Niles) and 1918 (over Bill Tilden).

He was ranked No. 1 in the U.S. in 1918, No. 4 in 1916 and 1919. A chemical engineer who graduated from Stanford, he was working on explosives production during World War I and had no intention of entering the 1917 Championships, billed as a "patriotic" tournament to raise money for the Red Cross. His employer, Elon Hooker of Hooker Chemical, talked Murray into it and he had an explosive tourney—the only one he played that summer.

"My strong points were a vicious serve, a quick dash to the net and the ability to volley decisively anything that came near me," he said.

He settled in the Buffalo area and died Jan. 17, 1970, in Lewiston Heights, N.Y. He was named to the Hall of Fame in 1958.

MAJOR TITLES (2)—*U.S. singles, 1917–18.* OTHER U.S. TITLE—*Indoor singles, 1916.*

Betty Nuthall
Great Britain (1911–   )

See page 89.

Alex Olmedo
Peru (1936–   )

Alexandro Olmedo, called "Chief" at the University of Southern California because of his regal bearing at 6-foot-1 and Incan features, was an aggressive volleyer who constantly sought the net. He fared best on the quickest terrain: concrete (U.S. Intercollegiate titles in singles and doubles for USC in 1956 and 1958); boards (U.S. Indoor titlist in 1959) and grass (Wimbledon and Australian chieftain in 1959). His was a quick but huge splash that covered two years.

Born March 24, 1936, in Arequipa, Peru, he picked up the game in his homeland as an extremely agile athlete. But it was refined when he came to USC where he was thrust into the limelight—and controversy—by one of his patrons, Southern California tennis czar Perry Jones. Jones, the U.S. Davis Cup captain in 1958–59, saw in Olmedo the chance for victory after three lean years.

Lobbying successfully for Olmedo's inclusion on the basis that the Peruvian was a U.S. resident whose own country had no team, Jones installed him for the semifinal victory over Italy on grass at Perth. Alex won his debut over Nicola Pietrangeli, 5–7, 10–8, 6–0, 6–1. This launched a storm of press criticism over the U.S. using a non-citizen for the first time. Another hassle developed at the Cup round when the

by beating Anderson, 8–6, 2–6, 9–7, 8–6, and clinched over Wimbledon champ Ashley Cooper, 6–3, 4–6, 6–4, 8–6.

A half-year later Wimbledon belonged to Olmedo, 6–4, 3–6, 9–7, 7–5, over Rod Laver. Although he beat Laver again in the Cup round the following month, the U.S. lost the Cup to Australia, 3–2, at Forest Hills. Fraser, his conqueror in that series, also beat him for the U.S. title, 6–3, 5–7, 6–2, 6–4. In 1960 Olmedo turned pro and joined the nomads on their odyssey of one-night stands. His brief mention in the rankings were in 1958, No. 2 in the U.S.; 1959, No. 1 in the U.S., No. 2 in the world. His daughter, Amy Olmedo, won the U.S. Public Parks Championship for 12s in 1975. He entered the Hall of Fame in 1987.

MAJOR TITLES (2)—*Wimbledon singles, 1959; Australian singles, 1959.* OTHER U.S. TITLES—*Indoor singles, 1959; Pro singles, 1960; Pro doubles, 1960, with Ashley Cooper; Indoor doubles, 1959, with Barry MacKay; Clay Court doubles, 1956, with Francisco Contreras; Hard Court singles, 1956; Hard Court doubles, 1957, with Mike Franks; Intercollegiate singles, 1956–58; Intercollegiate doubles, 1956, with Contreras; 1958, with Ed Atkinson.* DAVIS CUP—*1958–59 record: 5–1 in singles, 2–1 in doubles.*

Rafe Osuna
Mexico (1938–69)

Mexico's greatest player, Rafael Herrera Osuna, died tragically in an air crash near Monterey, June 6, 1969—shortly after one of his brightest performances. He had spearheaded Mexico's lone Davis Cup triumph over Australia, 3–2, in Mexico City by winning both his singles (the exciting fifth-match clincher over Bill Bowrey, 6–2, 3–6, 8–6, 6–3) as well as the doubles with Vicente Zarazua over John Alexander and Phil Dent. Ironically it was not only his last match, but the last appearance in the Australian captain's chair of the man whose side he defeated, legendary Harry Hopman.

Long the anchor of Mexico's team, the super-quick and clever Osuna, was the better known half of an extraordinary combine. He and Antonio Palafox showed what two good men could do for their country in 1962, taking Mexico past the U.S. for the first time, 3–2; Yugoslavia, 4–1; Sweden, 3–2; India, 5–0, all the way to the finale at Brisbane, where they lost to Cup-holding Australia, 5–0.

During that campaign en route to Australia, Osuna was 5–1 in singles, and with Palafox, 4–0 in doubles. Twice he came through in emotional and decisive fifth sets of fifth matches, beating Jack Douglas of the U.S., 6–1 at the wire, and Jan-Erik Lundquist of Sweden, likewise, 6–3, both at Mexico City.

Twice he won the doubles at Wimbledon, his country's only triumphs there, 1960 and 1963. The first time, at 21, with his University of Southern California pal and partner, Dennis Ralston, 17, they were unseeded, and the second-youngest champs, beating Mike Davies and Bobby Wilson, 7–5, 6–3, 10–8. In 1963 he and Palafox beat Pierre Darmon and Jean Claude Barclay. The two of them had a terrific series with Ralston and Chuck McKinley in three straight U.S. finals,

1961–63, the Mexicans winning in 1962 and holding fifth-set match points in 1963.

Ubiquitous on court, confusing to foes, ever seeking the net, he reached a zenith in singles by winning the U.S. title at Forest Hills in 1963, bewildering huge-serving Frank Froehling III, 7–5, 6–4, 6–2, with lobs, chips, angles and footspeed. Slouching, unimposing until his feet and hands whirred in action, he had a beguiling smile and a court manner that endeared him to galleries. At Southern Cal, where he was an All-American, he won the U.S. Intercollegiate singles in 1962 and was the first player since World War I to take the doubles three times: 1961–62 with Ramsey Earnhart, 1963 with Ralston. Osuna was in the World Top Ten thrice, 1962–64, No. 1 in 1963. He was born Sept. 15, 1938, in Mexico City and he made it into the Hall of Fame in 1979.

MAJOR TITLES (4)—*U.S. singles, 1963; U.S. doubles, 1962; Wimbledon doubles, 1960–63.* DAVIS CUP—*1958–60–61–62–63–64–65–66–67–68–69; record: 23–13 in singles, 14–8 in doubles.*

Frank Parker
United States (1916–   )

Frank Andrew Parker, a marvelous groundstroker, particularly on the backhand side, was a paragon of durability, ranking in the U.S. Top Ten 17 straight years (1933–49), a male record until Jimmy Connors surpassed it in 1988. One of the youngest to rank with the elite, 17 in 1933, he was No. 1 in 1944 and 1945, and the oldest ever to play in the U.S. Championships, 52 in 1968.

He entered in 1968 on a lark, this man who had teamed with Don Budge and Gene Mako to win the Davis Cup for the U.S. in 1937, saying he wanted to be part of yet another era, the "open." He lost his first match to eventual champion, Arthur Ashe, thus completing a championship career that began with a third-round defeat by fourth-seeded George Lott, 6–2 in the fourth, at Forest Hills in 1932. In between, as Sgt. Parker, Frankie won the U.S. title on his 13th try in 1944, again in 1945, both while on leave from the U.S. Army during World War II. He beat civilian Bill Talbert both times. A five-set quarterfinal defeat in 1946 by Tom Brown busted his dream of winning three straight. But he nearly jolted Jack Kramer by winning the first two sets of their 1947 final. After the 1949

in the successful defense against Australia. Coupled with his singles win while the U.S. heisted the Cup from Britain in 1937, this made him the only man to help win the Cup with singles victories at either end of World War II. He was ranked in the World Top Ten six times between 1937 and 1949, No. 1 in 1948. Born in Milwaukee Jan. 31, 1916, he was christened Frank Andezej Pajkowski. He entered the Hall of Fame in 1966.

MAJOR TITLES (6)—*French singles, 1948–49; U.S. singles, 1944–44; Wimbledon doubles, 1949; French doubles, 1949.* OTHER U.S. TITLES—*Clay Court singles, 1933–39–41–46–47; Clay Court doubles, 1939, with Gene Mako; Indoor doubles, 1937, with Greg Mangin.* DAVIS CUP—*1937–39–46–48; record: 12–2 in singles.*

Gerald Patterson
Australia (1895–1967)

A strapping 6-footer, Gerald Leighton Patterson followed Norman Brookes as Australia's second international tennis star. A heroic Military Cross winner with the Australian army in World War I, he played the game with daring, too, charging the net behind an explosive serve, both flat and twisting. His exemplary smash, stiff volleying and good forehand rewarded him with two Wimbledon championships.

An all-or-nothing outlook never was displayed more glaringly than in his Australian championship victory in 1927. Beating Jack Hawkes, 6–3 in the fifth, he blasted 29 aces and 29 doubles faults. In 1919 Patterson took the Wimbledon title from Brookes, who had to wait five years.

the only point against the U.S. at Forest Hills, joining Pat O'Hara Wood for a doubles victory over Tilden and Vinnie Richards in 1922. In 1925 he was considerably ahead of his time, using for a while a steel racket strung with wire. His best U.S. showings were semifinal finishes at Forest Hills in 1922 and 1924, losing to the champ, Tilden, the first time.

Five Aussie doubles titles were his between 1914 and 1927, three with Hawkes. He was among the World Top Ten six times between 1919 and 1925, No. 1 in 1919. Patterson was born Dec. 17, 1895, in Melbourne, and died there June 13, 1967.

MAJOR TITLES (9)—*Australian singles, 1927; Wimbledon singles, 1919–22; Australian doubles, 1922–25–26–27; U.S. doubles, 1919; Wimbledon mixed, 1920.* DAVIS CUP—*1919–20–22–24–25–28; record: 21–10 in singles, 11–4 in doubles.*

Budge Patty
United States (1924–   )

A rare combination for an American male was "Budge" Patty's French-Wimbledon double of 1950. Only Don Budge (for whom John Edward Patty was nicknamed as a youngster in California) in

1938 and Tony Trabert achieved such a double.

Born Feb. 11, 1924, at Ft. Smith, Ark., a right-hander, Patty has lived in Europe since serving in the U.S. Army in World War II. His smooth groundstroking game played well on the Continent's clay. He won the Italian in 1954. But he was a sharp volleyer, too, a fine doubles player. Seeded fifth, Patty beat second-seeded Bill Talbert in the quarters and top-seeded Frank Sedgman for the Wimbledon title, 6–1, 8–10, 6–2, 6–3.

At Paris he overcame lefty Jaroslav Drobny for the title, 6–1, 6–2, 3–6, 5–7, 7–5. Defending in 1952, he was upset by Ham Richardson in the second round at Wimbledon, and by Lennart Bergelin in the fourth round at Paris. Probably his two most renowned matches, both at Wimbledon, were a singles defeat and a doubles victory. In the third round of 1953, despite six match points, he fell to Drobny at dusk in a 93-game classic, 8–6, 16–18, 3–6, 8–6, 12–10. Four years later, he, 33, and Gar Mulloy, 43—unseeded— were the oldest team of the post-World War I era to win at the Big W, beating top-seeded Lew Hoad, 22, and Neale Fraser, 23, 8–10, 6–4, 6–4, 6–4.

They reached the title round of the U.S. Championships that year, the oldest finalists there, losing to Fraser and Ashley Cooper. Patty is also remembered in Paris for an incredible defeat, a 1958 fourth-rounder in which Robert Haillet revived from 5–0, 40–0 down, Patty serving, in the fifth set, to win, 5–7, 7–5, 10–8, 4–6, 7–5, saving four match points. Seldom appearing in the U.S., Patty was a quarterfinalist in the 1951 Championships, and played Davis Cup briefly, to get his only U.S. Top Ten ranking, No. 10. But he was ranked seven times in the World Top Ten between 1947 and 1957, No. 1 in 1950. He entered the Hall of Fame in 1977.

MAJOR TITLES (4)—*French singles, 1950; Wimbledon singles, 1950; Wimbledon doubles, 1957; French mixed, 1946.* U.S. TITLES—*Indoor doubles, 1952, with Bill Talbert; Indoor mixed, 1950, with Nancy Chaffee.* DAVIS CUP—*1951; record: 1–0 in singles, 1–0 in doubles.*

Teddy Pell
United States (1879–1967)

Theodore Roosevelt Pell made his mark inside, winning the U.S. Indoor singles in 1907–09–11, and the doubles four times between 1905 and 1912. A right-hander, he had a particularly strong backhand, and was ranked in the U.S. Top Ten five times between 1910 and 1918, No. 5 in 1913 and 1915. Born in New York, May 12, 1879, he died Aug. 18, 1967, in Sands Point, N.Y. He was elected to the Hall of Fame in 1966.

U.S. TITLES—*Indoor singles, 1907–09–11; Indoor doubles, 1905, with H.F. Allen; 1909, with Wylie Grant; 1911–12, with Fred Alexander.*

Fred Perry
Great Britain (1909–   )

See page 91.

Nicky Pietrangeli
Italy (1933–   )

Nicola "Nicky" Pietrangeli was Signor Davis Cup. That team competition seemed Nicky's private preserve, although he won his only Cup from the sidelines as Italy's non-playing captain in 1976. Before that, as a smooth touch operator, winner of the French (1957 over Beppe Merlo, 1961 over Rod Laver), he had made his name synonymous with Italy. He did it in Davis Cup by playing (164) and winning (120) more matches than anyone before or since during a Cup career that reached from 1954 through 1972. In 66 ties for his country he was 78–32 in singles, 42–12 in doubles.

Twice he carried Italy all the way to the Cup round, 1960–61, but on alien grass in

Australia, and during the reign of Aussie powerhouses, he and 6-foot-7 accomplice Orlando Sirola were unable to come closer to the Cup than a good look. Still, to get there in 1960 they pulled off one of Italy's greatest victories, 3–2 from 0–2, over the U.S. in the semifinal at Perth. Despite their discomfort on grass, Pietrangeli and Sirola, perhaps the finest doubles team developed in post-World War II Europe,

Rome as he beat both Whitney Reed and Jack Douglas, teamed with Sirola again triumphantly in a 4–1 victory. But in the two finales, only Pietrangeli's third-day win over Neale Fraser could be salvaged as Australia won, 5–0 and 4–1.

Solidly built, possessing exceptional instincts for the game and anticipation, Nicky was an all-around performer who moved with grace and purpose. He was in four French finals, losing to Manolo Santana in 1961 and 1964, and four Italian. His best showing away from compatible clay was a 1960 Wimbledon semifinal which he lost to Laver, 6–4 in the fifth. His was a career of the amateur era during which he was in the World Top Ten five times between 1957 and 1964, No. 3 in 1959–60. Retired from the court, he captained Italy to the Cup round twice, defeating Chile in 1976 but losing to Australia in 1977. A right-hander, born Sept. 11, 1933, in Tunis, he entered the Hall of Fame in 1986.

MAJOR TITLES (4)—*French singles, 1959–60 French doubles, 1959; French mixed, 1958.* DAVIS CUP—*1954–55–56–57–58–59–60–61–62–63–64– 65–66–67–68–69–71–72; record 78–32 in singles, 42–12 in doubles.*

Adrian Quist
Australia (1913–91)

Elected to the Hall of Fame in 1984 as the left-court half of the great Australian doubles team of Bromwich and Quist, Adrian Karl Quist also won three major singles, the Australian, 1936–40–48. Quist was the only man to win a major before and after World War II, in which he served in the Australian army.

He and Brom registered a unique triumph in lifting the Davis Cup from the U.S. in 1939. Losing their singles the first day in Philadelphia (Quist to Frank Parker, 7–5 in the fifth), they began the unparalleled comeback by beating Jack Kramer and Joe Hunt in a four-set doubles, even though they lost the first set and trailed 1–3 in the third. Hunt led 3–2, 30–15 on serve in the third when the turnabout began. Quist, a short, bouncy right-hander with an all-court game and telling volleys, then hung on after losing the third and fourth sets to beat Wimbledon champ Bobby Riggs, 6–4 in the fifth, even though Riggs saved a match point at 5–2 and reached 4–5. Bromwich beat Frank Parker in a groundstroking duel to ice it in the fifth match.

Quist and Bromwich won the U.S. doubles, too, in 1939, and, well beyond expectations, took their lone Wimbledon crown together in 1950, beating Billy Sidwell and Geoff Brown, 6–2 in the fifth. Quisty was within a month of his 37th birthday, Brom 31. Having won the French title with Jack Crawford in 1935, Quist—holder of 17 majors altogether—was one of few to win all four in doubles. Quist first appeared in the World Top Ten in 1936 at No. 4, No. 6 in 1938 and No. 3 in 1939. He was born Aug. 4, 1913, in Medindia, South Australia, and died Nov. 17, 1991, in Sydney.

MAJOR TITLES (17)—*Australian singles, 1936–40–48; Australian doubles, 1936–37–38–39–40–46–47–48–49–50; French doubles, 1935; Wimbledon doubles, 1935–50; U.S. doubles, 1939.* DAVIS CUP—*1933–34–35–36–37–38–39–46–48; record: 24–10 in singles, 19–3 in doubles.*

QUIST-BROMWICH: MAJOR TITLES (10)— *Australian doubles, 1938–39–40–46–47–48–49–50; Wimbledon doubles, 1950; U.S. doubles, 1939. Davis Cup—1938–39–46; record: 9–1 in doubles.*

Denny Ralston
United States (1942–   )

Robert Dennis Ralston was one of those rare men who was a Davis Cup winner both as player and captain. He was considered a stormy figure early in his career although his actions seem tame in comparison with numerous who came after, and he has made a name as an outstanding educator and influence as the varsity tennis coach at Southern Methodist University.

It was as a doubles player, in the right court alongside Chuck McKinley, that he made his strongest showing. They won the U.S. title thrice (1961–63–64) and were in the final in 1962.

Wimbledon and the tennis public first heard from him in 1960. As a 17-year-old joined with his University of Southern California teammate, 21-year-old Rafe Osuna, he took the doubles prize. Unseeded, they were the second-youngest to win at the Big W, 7–5, 6–3, 10–8, over Mike Davies and Bobby Wilson. He suffered many frustrations as a Davis Cup player, but it all came together for him and McKinley as they pried the punchbowl away from Australia, 3–2, at Adelaide in 1963.

During an arduous campaign he won six of seven singles and all five doubles,

four with McKinley. He led off in a difficult win over rookie John Newcombe, firming up when all seemed lost, 6–4, 6–1, 3–6, 4–6, 7–5, and teamed with McKinley for the go-ahead doubles point. After he lost to Roy Emerson, McKinley clinched against Newcombe. They lost the Cup to the Aussies the following year, 3–2, though winning the doubles—he and McKinley were 8–2 in Cup doubles.

Between 1968 and 1971 he served as coach of winning U.S. teams, and in 1972 he became captain for a four-year term. His coolness and calming manner in the face of an uproarious crowd and patriotic local line judges in Bucharest was a highlight of the 1972 Cup victory over Romania.

A slim 6-footer, Ralston was a stylish stroker with a piercing backhand, a fine server and excellent volleyer who was in the U.S. Top Ten for seven straight years from 1960. He was, the first to be No. 1 three straight years (1963—65) since Don Budge (1936—38). His career spanned the amateur and open eras and he made the World Top Ten in both: 1963–64–65–66 and 1968, No. 5 in 1966 when he lost the Wimbledon final to Manolo Santana.

He had one pro singles title, five in doubles. Denny was an unseeded U.S. semifinalist in 1960, losing to the champ, Neale Fraser. But his best Forest Hills moment was a 7–6, 7–5, 5–7, 4–6, 6–3 triumph over No. 1 Rod Laver, the defender, to reach the quarters, where he lost to Cliff Richey. He and his dad, Bob Ralston, won the U.S. Father and Son title in 1964. He was born July 27, 1942, in Bakersfield, Cal., and entered the Hall of Fame in 1987.

MAJOR TITLES (5)—*French doubles, 1966; U.S. doubles, 1961–63–64; Wimbledon doubles, 1960.* OTHER U.S. TITLES—*Indoor singles, 1963; Clay Court singles, 1964–65; Hard Court singles, 1964–65; Indoor doubles, 1963–65, with Chuck*

McKinley; Clay Court doubles, 1961–64, with McKinley; 1966, with Clark Graebner; Hard Court doubles, 1964, with Bill Bond; 1965, with Tom Edlefsen; Pro Doubles, 1967, with Ken Rosewall. DAVIS CUP *(As player)—1960–61–62–63–64–65–66; record: 14–5 in singles, 11–4 in doubles; (As captain)—1972–73–74–75; record: 9–3, 1 Cup.*

Ernest Renshaw
Great Britain (1861–99)

Reggie.

Ernest, who made the singles title round five times, won in 1888, and might have done better if brother hadn't been in the way, losing the prize to Willie thrice, 1882–83–89, and to Herbert Lawford in 1887. Like the Dohertys, the Renshaws were miserable playing against one another. A right-hander, Ernest was born Jan. 3, 1861, in Leamington, England, and died Sept. 2, 1899, in Twyford, England. He entered the Hall of Fame in 1983.

MAJOR TITLES (8)—*Wimbledon singles, 1888; Wimbledon doubles, 1880–81–84–85–86–88–89.*

Willie Renshaw
Great Britain (1861–1904)

Bjorn Borg said in 1981, "Yes, I know who Mr. Willie Renshaw was." Few others did. Borg, who had won five straight Wimbledons, was trying to overtake that bygone luminary, but couldn't make it. Nobody has. Not only did William Charles Renshaw, a forceful right-handed aggressor, win an unequaled six straight Wimbledons from 1881, wresting the title from John Hartley, 6–0, 6–2, 6–1, but he

added a record seventh title in 1889, defeating older (by 15 minutes) brother, Ernest Renshaw, in the title round, 6–4, 6–1, 3–6, 6–0.

In the all-comers final against Harry Barlow, Willie made an all-time recovery. He ducked six match points in the fourth set, trailing 5–2, and came back from 0–5 in the fifth to win, 3–6, 5–7, 8–6, 10–8, 8–6

Big W are the male record. The offense-minded Renshaws played doubles as never before, rushing the net and volleying more frequently and effectively than their predecessors, helped by the lowering of the net to its present three feet in 1882.

Willie, noted particularly for his serve and overhead smash, was a third-round loser to O.E. Woodhouse in his Wimbledon debut, 1880. He lost only twice after that, to nemesis Willoughby Hamilton in the 1888 quarters, and again in the 1890 challenge round, 6–8, 6–2, 3–6, 6–1, 6–1. He won 23 of 26 Wimbledon matches in singles, and had a 13-match streak from 1881 to the 1888 defeat by Hamilton, having declined to defend in 1887 because of an elbow injury. That mark wasn't broken until after the challenge round system was abandoned and Fred Perry recorded a 14th straight match win by taking the 1935 title.

The Renshaws seemed to be the first to take the game really seriously, playing a full English summer schedule, and then competing on the Riviera during the winter. Willie was born Jan. 3, 1861, in Leamington, England, and died Aug. 12, 1904, in

Swanage, England. He entered the Hall of Fame in 1983.

MAJOR TITLES (14)—*Wimbledon singles, 1881–82–83–84–85–86–89; Wimbledon doubles, 1880–81–84–85–86–88–89.*

Vinnie Richards
United States (1903–59)

Vincent Richards was the boy wonder of his day, and hasn't lost that luster: the youngest male to win any of the major championships. A volleying master all his life, he was 15 when Big Bill Tilden, on the verge of greatness, selected the kid as partner in the U.S. doubles championships of 1918 at Longwood Cricket Club in Boston. They marched through the field, and Vinnie must have felt as though he were in the geriatric ward.

He and Tilden, 25, beat a couple of 38-year-old ex-champs, Fred Alexander and Beals Wright, for the title, 6–3, 6–4, 3–6, 2–6, 6–2. They won twice more in 1921–22, beating Davis Cup teammates Dick Williams and Watty Washburn, then the Australian Cup pair, Gerald Patterson and Pat O'Hara Wood. Fittingly, the last national title Richards and Tilden won was a valedictory together, the U.S. Pro doubles 27 years after, in 1945.

Richards was a pro pioneer, signing on with promoter C.C. Pyle as leading man of the original professional touring troupe in 1926. His mates barnstorming North America during the winter of 1926–27 were the star attraction, Suzanne Lenglen of France, Paul Feret of France and fellow Americans Howard Kinsey and Harvey Snodgrass.

It was tough to break into the Davis Cup lineup in singles with Little Bill Johnston and Tilden around. But Vinnie got his chance in 1924, and beat both Patterson and O'Hara Wood in straight sets during the 5–0 victory over Australia. That year he won two Olympic golds (sin-gles, doubles) and a silver (mixed). He was on four Cup-winning teams, losing only a doubles with Tilden in 1922. In 1918 Richards was also the youngest ever to play or win a match in the U.S. singles, and he steadily advanced toward the top, a 19-year-old semifinalist in 1922, losing to Johnston. He was back in the semis in 1924, battling the champ, Tilden, to 6–4 in the fifth, repeating the next year but losing to Big Bill, 6–1 in the fourth. In 1926 he was generally acknowledged as the best American, losing to Jean Borotra in the semis, 6–2 in the fifth while Tilden lost in the quarters to Henri Cochet.

Many felt that Richards, who had refined his game well beyond his teen-age volleying skills, deserved the No. 1 U.S. ranking. Instead, because he turned pro, the USTA unfairly awarded him no ranking for that year when he was No. 6 in the world rankings. He had been in the U.S. and World Top Ten five straight years from 1921, No. 2 in both in 1924.

Once the initial Pyle tour was disbanded, he was active in trying to find other opportunities for the fledgling professionals, no longer welcome at the traditional events. Vinnie, who championed the pros during those difficult years, even after his playing days were over, helped organize the first U.S. Pro Championships in New York in 1927, an event that continues as the longest-running pro tournament. The purse was $2,000. Richards beat Kinsey for that title and a first prize of $1,000, and was its singles victor three more times. Born March 20, 1903, and raised in Yonkers, N.Y., he died Sept. 28, 1959, in New York, shortly after entering the Hall of Fame.

MAJOR TITLES (9)—*French doubles, 1926; Wimbledon doubles, 1924; U.S. doubles, 1918–21–22–25–26; U.S mixed, 1919–24.* OTHER U.S TITLES—*Indoor singles, 1919–23–24; Indoor doubles, 1919–20, with Bill Tilden; 1921, with Howard Voshell; 1923–24, with Frank Hunter; Clay Court doubles, 1920, with Roland Roberts; Pro singles, 1927–28–30–33; Pro doubles, 1929, with Karel Kozeluh; 1930–31, with Howard Kinsey; 1933, with Charles Wood; 1937, with George Lott; 1938, with Fred Perry, 1945, with Bill Tilden.* DAVIS CUP—*1922–24–25–26; record: 2–0 in singles, 2–1 in doubles.*

Bobby Riggs
United States (1918–   )

and 1967, alongside John Newcombe, he'd won the Cup-clinching doubles, both years against Spain. Ten years later he was recalled for singles duty before his friends and neighbors in Sydney, and came through.

In a stunning opening-day victory, he turned back Adriano Panatta (6–3, 6–4, 6–4), who had led Italy to the 1976 Cup. That set the tone for a 3–1 Australian victory. His yoking with Newcombe (Roche in the left court) was one of the all-time teams. They won Wimbledon five times (1965–68–69–70–74), the best showing of any 20th century male pair. Roche, with his wicked left-handed serve and magnificent volleying took 11 major doubles, all in the company of Newcombe. They were among only four male teams to win all four majors.

But Tony, broad-shouldered and barrel-chested, had the groundstrokes to succeed on clay, winning the difficult Continental double in 1966, the Italian and French singles. Paradoxically he lost three major finals on his best surface, grass, and to older countrymen whom he'd idolized: Wimbledon, 1968, and the U.S., 1969, to Rod Laver; U.S., 1970, to Ken Rosewall.

Shoulder trouble curtailed a career that spanned the amateur and open eras, but he was in the World Top Ten in both, six straight years from 1965. No. 2 in 1969, and won 12 pro titles in singles, 27 in doubles. In 1968 he turned pro, signing with World Championship Tennis as one of the so-called "Handsome Eight" along with other rookies Newcombe, Cliff Drysdale, Nikki Pilic and Roger Taylor. His prize

MAJOR TITLES (14)—*French singles, 1966; Australian doubles, 1967–71–76; French doubles, 1967–69–73; Wimbledon doubles, 1965–68–69– 70–74; U.S. doubles, 1967; Australian mixed, 1966.* DAVIS CUP—*1964–65–66–67–74–75–76–77–78; record; 7–3 in singles, 7–2 in doubles.*

Ellen Roosevelt
United States (1868–1954)

The Roosevelt sisters, Ellen, 20, and Grace, believed to be 22, played in the U.S. Championships in 1888, and two years later both were champions. Ellen Crosby Roosevelt won the 1890 singles over defending champ Bertha Townsend in the challenge round, 6–2, 6–2 and joined with Grace for the doubles championship, 6–1, 6–2, over Townsend and Margarette Ballard.

The Roosevelts, who were born and raised in Hyde Park N.Y., and were first cousins of U.S. President Franklin D. Roosevelt, were the first sisters to win a major title. They were emulated only by Juliette and Kathleen Atkinson at the U.S. of 1897–98. In 1891, however, the Roosevelts were done in by an Irishwoman, Mabel Cahill. Cahill beat Grace, 6–3, 7–5, in the final of the all-comers, then deposed

Ellen, 6–4, 6–1, 4–6, 6–3, in the challenge round. In the doubles Cahill and Mrs. Emma Leavitt Morgan unseated the sisters, 2–6, 8–6, 6–4.

The only Roosevelt reappearance in the Championships was Ellen's mixed-doubles title with Clarence Hobart in 1893. The Roosevelts, reared on a private court at home, may have been the first to be prodded by a tennis parent. Recalled original champ Ellen Hansell: "Their father [John Roosevelt] coached and treated them as if they were a pair of show ponies. We silly, non-serious-mixed players giggled at their early-to-bed and careful food habits."

Ellen, a right-hander, was born in August 1868 and died in Hyde Park Sept 26, 1954. She entered the Hall of Fame in 1975. Grace Walton Roosevelt, also a right-hander, who became Mrs. Appleton Clark, was born in either 1866 or 1867 in Hyde Park and died there Nov. 29, 1945.

MAJOR TITLES (3)—*U.S. singles, 1890; U.S. doubles, 1890; U.S. mixed, 1893.*

Ken Rosewall
Australia (1934–   )
See page 376.

Dorothy Round
Great Britain (1909–   )
See page 93.

Elizabeth Ryan
United States (1892–1979)
Elizabeth Montague "Bunny" Ryan, a magnificent doubles player who long held the major tournament record for total championships—19 at Wimbledon between 1914 and 1934—dearly wished to win a major in singles. But she missed out in three finals, losing to Suzanne Lenglen (1921) and Helen Mills Moody (1930) at Wimbledon, and coming closest in 1926, a heartbreaker at the U.S.

In the most elderly of major finals, Ryan, 34, led Molla Mallory, 42, 4–0 in the third, and had a match point in the 13th game only to fall, 4–6, 6–4, 9–7, at Forest Hills.

It may be that she was a bit too stout and slow of foot to equal her doubles success on the singles court. Still, with superb anticipation and tactics, she won numerous singles titles, including the last played in Imperial Russia in 1914. "I got the last train out as the war [World War I] descended," she later recalled.

Her 12 Wimbledon doubles titles (and 13 finals) are the tourney records, as are five straight with Lenglen (1919–23), plus 1925, and personally six straight (1914–23; no play World War I, 1915–18). She won a record seven mixed (of a record 10 finals) with five different partners, three with Randolph Lycett. She and Lenglen never lost (31–0) at the Big W.

Yet standing is Ryan's Wimbledon doubles record of 50 straight match victories from 1914 to the 1928 final. She first played Wimbledon in 1912, reaching the quarters in singles, and was to set a championship longevity record: 20 years between first and last titles (1914–34). Only Billie Jean King (224) and Martina Navratilova (209) won more matches at Wimbledon, where Ryan was 189–29: 61–15 in singles, 77–4 in doubles, 80–10 in mixed.

Ryan, a right-hander with a severe chop, volley and drop shot, was born Feb. 8, 1892, in Anaheim, Cal., and played Wightman Cup for her native land, but spent most of her life as a London resident. She did work as a teaching pro for a time in the U.S. Intensely protective of her Wimbledon record of 19 titles (of 25 finals), she was uncomfortable sharing it with King when Billie Jean overtook her by winning the singles in 1975. She was undoubtedly pleased not to see herself eclipsed.

Ryan collapsed and died July 8, 1979, at her beloved Wimbledon, the day before King got No. 20 by winning the doubles with Navratilova. Twice she played enough in the U.S. to make the Top Ten rankings, No. 2 in 1925–26. She was in the World Top Ten five times between 1924 and 1930, No. 3 in 1927. She entered the Hall of Fame in 1972.

See page 378.

Dick Savitt
United States (1927–   )

Only three American men have won the Australian and Wimbledon titles in one year. Richard "Dick" Savitt was the second in 1951 (following Don Budge, 1938, and preceding Jimmy Connors, 1974). He beat Ken McGregor in both, four sets in the Aussie's lair and straight sets at Wimbledon.

Any hopes he had of a Grand Slam were squelched by Eric Sturgess in a five-set quarterfinal of the French. Defending his Aussie title, Savitt was beaten in the 1952 semis by McGregor, and at Wimbledon by Mervyn Rose in a five-set quarterfinal. In the U.S. Championships he was a semifinalist in 1950, losing to the champ, Art Larsen; a semifinalist in 1951, losing to Vic Seixas; and a quarterfinalist in 1952, 1956 and 1958. In 1956 he lost a stirring five-set baseline slugfest to the champ, Ken Rosewall.

A large, broad-shouldered right-hander, 6-foot-2, 180 pounds, he was a powerful groundstroker and stubborn competitor. He demonstrated quick reflexes and volleying skills in winning the U.S. Indoor singles thrice, 1952–58–61. He ranked six times in the U.S. Top Ten between 1950 and 1959, No. 2 in 1951, and four times in the World Top Ten between 1951 and 1957, No. 2 in 1951.

A Cornell graduate, Dick was born March 4, 1927, in Bayonne, N.J., and lives

Ted Schroeder
United States (1921–   )

Emulating Don McNeill in 1940, Frederick Rudolph "Ted" Schroeder of Stanford became in 1942 only the second player to win the U.S. Intercollegiate and the U.S. singles in the same year. A stand-out big-situation competitor—especially in Davis Cup—volleying wizard Schroeder, along with his pal, Jack Kramer, recovered the Cup for the U.S. in 1946 after it had spent seven years in Australia during World War II.

Their teammates, Gar Mulloy and Frank Parker, weren't happy when captain Walter Pate selected attack-minded Kramer and Schroeder to play all the way against the favored Aussies in Melbourne. But Schroeder led off by stopping Jack Bromwich, 3–6, 6–1, 6–2, 0–6, 6–3, and the 5–0 sweep was on. A daring right-hander, Ted helped the U.S. keep the Cup in 1947–48–49 by winning both his singles against Australia each year.

But he was beaten by both Frank Sedgman and Ken McGregor as the Aussies lifted the Cup in 1950, and though he tied the 1951 finale at Sydney at 2–2 by beating

Mervyn Rose, the U.S. was tipped, 3–2, and he retired. A part-time player, taking vacations from business to compete, Ted rose to his peak in 1949 when he won Wimbledon by overcoming Jaroslav Drobny, 6–4 in the fifth. In the quarters he dodged two match points in the fifth set to beat Sedgman, 9–7.

Seven years after winning Forest Hills, he reappeared in the U.S. final and seemed the winner after taking the first two sets from Pancho Gonzalez, but faded. He and Kramer formed one of the great doubles teams, winning the U.S. title thrice, 1940–41–46. He refused several offers to join Kramer as a pro. A Californian, he was born July 20, 1921, in Newark, N.J., and was ranked in the U.S. Top Ten nine times between 1940 and 1951, No. 1 in 1942. He was in the World Top Ten six straight times from 1946, No. 2 the first four years. He served in the U.S. Navy in World War II and entered the Hall of Fame in 1966. His son, John, was an accomplished professional golfer.

MAJOR TITLES (6)—*Wimbledon singles, 1949; U.S. singles, 1942; U.S. doubles, 1940–41–47; U.S. mixed, 1942* OTHER U.S. TITLES—*Intercollegiate singles, 1942; Intercollegiate doubles, 1942, with Larry Dee; Hard Court singles, 1948–49–51; Clay Court doubles, 1941, with Jack Kramer; 1947, with Jack Tuero; Hard Court doubles, 1948, with Vic Seixas; 1949, with Eric Sturgess.* DAVIS CUP—*1946–47–48–49–50–51; record: 11–3 in singles, 2–3 in doubles.*

Eleo Sears
United States (1881–1968)

Eleonora Randolph Sears, though of a proper Bostonian background, was noted for her athleticism and vigor. She was an equestrian, golfer and determined walker (frequently striding the 40 miles between her Boston home and Providence, R.I.), and maintained a trim, healthful figure into old age.

The right-handed Eleo was from a tennis-playing family. Her father, Fred Sears, was one of the first (if not the first) to play tennis in the U.S., with Dr. James Dwight in 1874. Her uncle, Dick Sears, was the original U.S. champion.

Eleo made it to the U.S. singles final in 1912, losing to Mary K. Browne, and won four U.S. doubles, two with Hazel Hotchkiss Wightman (1911–15) and Molla Bjurstedt Mallory (1916–17), as well as the mixed with Willis Davis (1916). She ranked in the U.S. Top Ten twice, 1914–16, No. 6 in the first year. She was born Sept. 28, 1881, in Boston, died March 16, 1968, in Palm Beach, Fla., and entered the Hall of Fame in 1968.

MAJOR TITLES (5)—*U.S. doubles, 1911–15–16–17; U.S. mixed, 1916.*

Dick Sears
United States (1861–1943)

Never beaten in the U.S. Championships, the original singles champ, Richard Dudley Sears, won his first of seven titles in 1881 while still a Harvard ('83) student. As one of 24 entries he, a Bostonian, ventured onto the lawn of the Newport (R.I.) Casino in knickerbockers, long wool socks, a necktie and cap, and wielding a slightly lop-sided racket (similar to those for court tennis) that weighed 16 ounces.

Beating first-round opponent Powell, 6–0, 6–2, Dick was off on an 18-match streak that would carry him through the Championships of 1887, after which he retired from the game. Not until the challenge round format was abandoned and 1920–21 champion Bill Tilden beat Zenzo Shimidzu to reach the 1922 semis, and register a 19th successive win in the Championships, was Sears' record eclipsed.

Sears later recalled the Championships' launching in '81: "...the nets were four-feet at the posts and three-feet at center. This led to a scheme of attack by playing, whenever possible, across court to avoid lifting drives over the highest part of the net at the sidelines. This method just suited me. I had taken up a mild form of volleying, and all I had to do was to tap the balls, as they came over, first to one side and then to the other, running my opponent all over the court."

A few of the players served underhand,

in that year he began to hit a topspin forehand that he'd seen used in England by the originator, Herbert Lawford. Since the challenge round was instituted in 1884 he had to play but one match, against the victor in the all-comers tournament, to retain the title the last four years. Then he lost one set each to Howard Taylor in '84, Godfrey Brinley in '85 and Livingston Beeckman in '86.

Those last four years he used a prized racket given to him in England by the all-time Wimbledon champ, Willie Renshaw, and won four singles and doubles titles with it. He and Dwight won the doubles five times together, and he won once with Joseph Clark, 1885. Sears was the first of the 19-year-olds to conquer the U.S., slightly older than Oliver Campbell in 1890, and the very youngest, Pete Sampras, in 1990. He was No. 1 in the U.S. 1885–86–87, the first years of national rankings. Scion of a prominent Boston family, he was born there Oct. 16, 1861, and died there April 8, 1943. His older brother, Fred, played with Dwight, possibly the first tennis in the U.S., in 1884, and a younger brother, Philip, was in the U.S. Top Ten five years. A cousin, Eleo Sears, is also in the Hall of Fame. After giving up

lawn tennis, Sears won the U.S. Court Tennis singles title in 1892. He served as USTA president in 1887 and 1888 and was elected to the Hall of Fame in 1955.

MAJOR TITLES (13)—*U.S. singles, 1881–82–83–84–85–86–87; U.S. doubles, 1882–83–84–85–86–87.*

Frank Sedgman

United States (1923–   )

When Vic Seixas played—and won—the fifth-longest singles match in tennis history, he was 42. That was in 1966, when Vic went 94 games to beat a 22-year-old Australian Davis Cup player, Bill Bowrey, 32–34, 6–4, 10–8, during the Pennsylvania Grass Championships at Philadelphia. It took nearly four hours.

Elias Victor Seixas, Jr., born Aug 30, 1923, in Philadelphia, played the U.S. Championships at Forest Hills a record 28 times between 1939 and 1969, winning the singles in 1954. He played more Davis Cup matches than any other American, until John McEnroe, winning 38 of 55 singles and doubles encounters during his seven years on the team between 1951 and 1957. Thirteen times he was ranked in the Top Ten in the U.S. between 1942 and 1966, setting an American longevity record of a 24-year span between his first and last entries (later equaled by Pancho Gonzalez, 1948–72).

In 1954, when Seixas won the Wimbledon singles and led the U.S. to the Davis Cup, a brief cracking of the Australian monopoly of the time, he was considered No. 1 in the amateur world.

Although he helped the U.S. attain the finale every year he played Davis Cup, the team could win only once, the high spot of 1954 when he and Tony Trabert were victorious. After Trabert opened with a win over Lew Hoad, Seixas followed with a stunning 8–6, 6–8, 6–4, 6–3 triumph over his nemesis, Ken Rosewall. That put the U.S. ahead, 2–0, on the first day, and Seixas and Trabert clinched the Cup the following day with a doubles victory over Hoad and Rex Hartwig, 6–2, 4–6, 6–2, 10–8, before a record outdoor crowd of 25,578 at Sydney.

Seixas won 15 of the Big Four titles in singles doubles and mixed, setting a Wimbledon record by winning the mixed four successive years, 1953–54–55 with Doris Hart, and 1956 with Shirley Fry.

Among his 13 U.S. titles were the Clay Court singles in 1953 and 1957, the Hard Court doubles (with Ted Schroeder) in 1948, and the Indoor doubles (with Trabert) in 1955, making Seixas one of the few to win national titles on all four surfaces. In 1971 he was named to the Hall of Fame.

The right-handed Seixas was an attacker who won more on determination and conditioning than on outstanding form. His volleying was exceptional, and he had an excellent match temperament. His career was interrupted for three years by World War II, during which he served as a pilot in the U.S. Air Force. He graduated from the University of North Carolina. Seixas was one of the few extraordinary amateurs who did not join the pro tour. Eventually, though, after the age of 50, he did become a pro to compete on the Grand Masters circuit.

MAJOR TITLES (15)—*Wimbledon singles, 1953; U.S. singles, 1954; French doubles, 1954–55; U.S. doubles, 1952–54; Australian doubles, 1955; French mixed, 1953; Wimbledon mixed, 1953–54–55–56; U.S. mixed, 1953–54–55.*

OTHER U.S. TITLES—*Clay Court singles, 1953–57; Clay Court doubles, 1949, with Sam Match; 1954, with Tony Trabert; Hard Court doubles, 1948; with Ted Schroeder; Indoor doubles, 1955, with Trabert; 1956 with Sam Giammalva.* DAVIS CUP (*As player*)—*1951–52–53–54–55–56–57; record: 24–12 in singles, 14–5 in doubles; (As captain)—1952–57–64; record: 3–2.*

Frank Shields
United States (1909–75)

A dashing, handsome performer who spent some time in Hollywood in bit movie roles, unseeded Francis Xavier Shields was the only Wimbledon finalist to lose without going onto the court. Frank defaulted the 1931 final to Sidney Wood beforehand, sidelined by an ankle injury suffered in the semis when he beat Jean Borotra, the 1924–26 champ, 7–5, 3–6, 6–4, 6–4.

The 6-foot-3 right-hander came closer to a major title the year before at Forest Hills, losing the 1930 final to Johnny Doeg, 16–14 in the fourth. Between 1928 and 1945 he was ranked eight times in the U.S. Top Ten, No. 1 in 1933, No. 2 in 1930. In 1928 and 1933 he was singles semifinalist at the U.S. Championships, in 1934 at Wimbledon. He was a U.S. Davis Cupper in 1931–32–34, winning 19 of 25 matches, and was non-playing captain in 1951 when the team won four matches, then lost the finale in Australia, 3–2. In 1934 he sent the U.S. into the finale (a 4–1 loss to Britain) by winning the decisive fifth match in straight sets over Viv McGrath to clinch a 3–2 victory over Australia at Wimbledon. It was the only time the U.S. came back from 0–2 to win a Cup match.

Shields was born in New York Nov. 18, 1909, and died there Aug. 19, 1975. Movie actress Brooke Shields is his grand-daughter. He was inducted into the Hall of Fame in 1964.

DAVIS CUP—*1931–32–34; record: 16–6 in singles, 3–0 in doubles.*

Henry Slocum
United States (1862–1949)

A football and tennis player at Yale, Henry Warner Slocum played in the first Intercollegiate Championships, in 1883, as partner of the great footballer, Walter Camp. He took time out from his New York law practice to refine his tennis (to the disapproval of his father), and on his third try at the U.S. title in Newport, 1887,

comers final, to decide the championship, Slocum, a right-hander, was sharper against the quick 5-foot-4 Taylor, and became the second champion of the U.S., 6–4, 6–1, 6–0. He successfully defended in 1889 over lefty Quincy Shaw, 6–3, 6–1, 4–6, 6–2.

That year he and Taylor beat Valentine Hall and Oliver Campbell for the doubles crown, 6–1, 6–3, 6–2. It was Slocum's third time in the doubles final. He lost in 1885 with Percy Knapp and 1887 with Ollie Taylor. But Slocum, 28, was overtaken by 19-year-old collegian, Campbell, in the 1890 challenge round, 6–2, 4–6, 6–3, 6–1.

Slocum had realized his tennis ambitions, and immersed himself in law. But he returned to Newport for an 1892 cameo, registering one of the Championships' rare triple bagels—6–0, 6–0, 6–0, over W.N. Ryerson. He played again in 1903 and in a stretch from 1905 through 1913, when he made his last appearance.

Henry won 15 of 19 matches in the Championships, and, in the 1888 quarters, gave the godfather, James Dwight, 36, his last singles defeat, 4–6, 6–3, 6–0, 6–2. Five straight years, from 1886, he was in the U.S. Top Ten, No. 1 in 1888–89. Slocum was born May 28, 1862, died Jan. 22, 1949,

and entered the Hall of Fame in 1955. He was president of the USTA in 1892–93.

MAJOR TITLES (3)—*U.S. singles, 1888–89; U.S. doubles, 1889.*

Stan Smith
United States (1946–   )

See page 382.

or fiery to his teammates for his outspoken competitiveness, he became also known as the "Old Hacker" at the U.S. Championships of 1966. A proven grass-court player for some time, member of winning Australian Davis Cup teams, and thrice Wimbledon runner-up (1963–64–65), he was outraged on arriving at Forest Hills, fresh from winning the German title, to find himself unseeded.

"I guess they think I'm just an old hacker," said he, almost 28. Then he proceeded to win the title, the second unseeded man to do so, over unseeded John Newcombe, chortling, "Well, I guess the Old Hacker can still play a bit."

He had won the French in 1965, showing that he could be patient at the baseline, too, although his strengths were a high-velocity serve, stinging volleys and a splendid backhand. These paid off in his 16 major doubles titles. He is one of few men to win all four majors, and had his greatest success with Bob Hewitt (two Wimbledons, two Australian), Roy Emerson (two U.S. and an Australian), Ken Rosewall (a U.S. and French).

As a member of three victorious Australian Davis Cup teams, 1964–65–66, he scored his most memorable win the first year in the Cup round at Cleveland, 7–5, 6–3, 3–6, 9–11, 6–4, over Dennis Ralston. Down a break in the fifth, with his side trailing the U.S. 2–1, Stolle pulled it out so that Emerson could win the Cup-lifting clincher over Chuck McKinley. Perhaps his lead-off win in the following year's Cup finale meant more since it came in his hometown, Sydney, and he had to dig himself from a very deep hole to beat the Spanish ace, Manolo Santana, 10–12, 3–6, 6–1, 6–4, 7–5, to send the Aussies on their way.

His career spanned the amateur and open eras, and he was in the World Top Ten four years, starting with 1963, No. 2 in 1964 and 1966. He turned pro in 1967, and as a pro won two singles and 13 doubles titles, and about $500,000 in career prize money. He had a last U.S. fling in 1972, at 33, beating 5 and 11 seeds Newcombe and Cliff Drysdale to gain the quarters, where he lost to the champ, Ilie Nastase.

Born Oct. 8, 1938, in Hornsby, New South Wales, Fred has worked as a teaching pro, was player-coach of the title-winning New York Apples of World Team Tennis in 1976–77, and of Australia 10 times (5–5) in the since disbanded World Cup against the U.S., 1970–79. His son, Sandon, is a touring pro, and has played the major championships. For some time Fred has been a successful TV commentator on tennis. He entered the Hall of Fame in 1985.

MAJOR TITLES (18)—*French singles, 1965; U.S. singles, 1966; French doubles, 1965–68; U.S. doubles, 1965–66–69; Australian doubles, 1963–64–66; Wimbledon doubles, 1962–64; Australian mixed, 1962; U.S. mixed, 1962–65; Wimbledon mixed, 1961–64–69.* DAVIS CUP—*1964–65–66; record: 10–2 in singles, 3–1 in doubles.*

Bill Talbert
United States (1918–)

Adapting to life as a diabetic, William Franklin Talbert was an outstanding player,

U.S. Davis Cup captain and administrator as director of the U.S. Open. Thwarted twice in U.S. singles finals, 1944–45, by Frank Parker, the right-handed Talbert made his strongest showing in doubles in the right court alongside Gardnar Mulloy.

They were in the U.S. final six times, one short of Fred Alexander and Harold Hackett's team record, winning four, 1942–45–46–48. Bill himself was in the final nine times. He and Mulloy won the clinching point in the Davis Cup victory over Australia in 1948 at Forest Hills, defeating Billy Sidwell and Colin Long. He was on the team six years, winning nine of 10 matches, and captained it to the victory over Australia in 1954, as well as the full seasons of 1955–56–57 and portions of 1952–53, compiling a 13–4 record.

A stylish groundstroker and excellent volleyer and tactician, he ranked in the U.S. Top Ten 13 times between 1941 and 1954, No. 2 in 1944–45. He was in the World Top Ten in 1949–50, No. 3 the first year. An Ohioan, born Sept. 4, 1918, in Cincinnati, he grew up there, moving to New York during his playing career. He and Margaret Osborne duPont won the U.S. mixed a record four straight years, 1943–46. In 1970, the first of 10 years in charge of the U.S. Open, he was instrumental in obtaining acceptance of the tie-breaker for its first use in a major tournament.

With Bruce Old, Talbert wrote definitive books, *The Game of Singles in Tennis* and *The Game of Doubles in Tennis*. He also wrote an autobiography, *Playing for Life* and a history of the U.S. men's singles championships, *Tennis Observed*. He has been involved in the financial printing business for many years, and entered the Hall of Fame in 1967.

MAJOR TITLES (9)—*French doubles, 1950; U.S. doubles, 1942–45–46–48; U.S. mixed, 1943–44–45–46;* OTHER U.S. TITLES—*Indoor singles, 1948–51; Clay Court singles, 1945; Indoor doubles, 1949–50–51, with Don McNeill; 1952, with Budge Patty; 1954, with Tony Trabert; Clay Court doubles, 1942, with Bill Reedy; 1944–45, with Pancho Segura; 1946, with Gardnar Mulloy; Indoor mixed, 1947–48, with Doris Hart.* DAVIS CUP (*As player*)—*1946–48–49–51–52–53; record: 2–0 in singles, 7–1 in doubles.* (*As captain*)—*1952–53–54–55–56–57; record: 13–4.*

Bill Tilden

times. She won in 1888, unseating original champ, Ellen Hansell, in the challenge round, 6–3, 6–5. She fought off the challenge of Lida Vorhees, 7–5, 6–3, to become the first repeating female champ, but then fell to Ellen Roosevelt, 6–2, 6–2, in the 1890 challenge round.

She reappeared, married, in 1894, to reach the final of the all-comers, losing to Helen Hellwig, who became champion. The following year she was a semifinalist, and that ended her career.

She was born March 7, 1869, died May 12, 1909, in Haverford, Pa. as Mrs. Harry Toulmin, and was inducted into the Hall of Fame in 1974.

MAJOR TITLES (2)—*U.S. singles, 1888–89.*

Tony Trabert
United States (1930–   )

See page 383.

Johnny Van Ryn
United States (1905–   )

Allison and Van Ryn were a headline combination during their bright career between 1929 and 1936 as one of the most formidable U.S. Davis Cup partnerships.

Wilmer Allison and John William Van Ryn won 14 of 16 Cup matches together, the best for Americans until Peter Fleming and John McEnroe's 14–1.

Their 24 team matches (tied with Stan Smith and Vic Seixas) are second only to McEnroe's 30 in U.S. annals. Van Ryn's 24 doubles matches and 22 wins are highs for the U.S. They beat the splendid French

Allison and Van Ryn were in the U.S. final six times, one behind Fred Alexander and Harold Hackett's record, winning in 1931 and 1935. They also won Wimbledon in 1929–30. In 1931 Van Ryn teamed with George Lott to win the French and Wimbledon, the only American to win the latter three successive times. He ranked in the U.S. Top Ten six times between 1927 and 1932, No. 4 in 1931 when he was a five-set quarterfinal loser at Forest Hills to George Lott. He was also a quarterfinalist in 1929–30, losing to Bill Tilden each time in four sets, and 1936–37. In 1929 and 1931 he was in the World Top Ten. He was born June 30, 1905, in Newport News, Va., and resides at Palm Beach, Fla. He was inducted into the Hall of Fame in 1963.

MAJOR TITLES (6)—*French doubles, 1931; Wimbledon doubles, 1929–30–31; U.S. doubles, 1931–35.* OTHER U.S. TITLES—*Indoor doubles, 1932, with George Lott; Intercollegiate doubles, 1927, with Kenneth Appel.* DAVIS CUP—*1929–30–31–32–33–34–35–36; record: 7–1 in singles, 22–2 in doubles.*

Guillermo Vilas
Argentina (1952–   )

Seldom has a player found such empathy beyond his own borders as did

Guillermo Vilas, the "Young Bull of the Pampas," during his pro career. It is a career that has not yet ended since he was still playing on the satellite circuit for enjoyment in 1992. As the foremost Latin-American male, he is the only Argentine to be tapped for the Hall of Fame (1991), and the first to win major titles (four of them).

The burly left-hander captivated audiences everywhere with his sportsmanship and sensitivity of a poet—which he is. An appealing headbanded figure of the 1970s and early 1980s, his chestnut hair flowing below his shoulders, Vilas was the epitome of strength and fitness, endurance and patience on court, outlasting opponents from the baseline with his high-rolling top-spinning strokes—hour after hour, a destructive metronome.

His 1977 was a monumental year in the game's history: he won a Rod Laver record-tying 17 of 33 tournaments on a record of 145 match wins against 14 losses. Among his souvenirs were an open-era winning streak of 50 matches and the French and U.S. titles. His streak, begun after Wimbledon, was stopped at Aix-en-Provence in September by Ilie Nastase, who used one of the controversial "spaghetti" rackets that produced weird strokes and bounces. Vilas quit in disgust; such rackets were shortly banned.

Although he reveled in the backcourt, Vilas startled Jimmy Connors with volleying forays that turned the U.S. Open his way, and set off a wild celebration after he'd won the last championship match in the 54-year-old Forest Hills Stadium. Joyous fans carried him on victory laps within the concrete arena, as though he were a triumphant bullfighter.

Though grass seemed anathema to the clay-loving Villas, he did win the Australian twice (1978–79) and the Masters of 1974 at the same place, Melbourne's Kooyong. Perhaps he wasn't a serve-volley smoothy,

but his Australian Open record is excellent: two titles plus a final-round loss to Roscoe Tanner in 1977, and a 16-match streak to a semis loss to Kim Warwick in 1980.

As Argentina's foremost Davis Cupper he took great satisfaction in bulwarking three American Zone wins over the U.S. (1977–80–83). Vilas won all six of his singles on the Buenos Aires loam, including victories over John McEnroe the last two years. In 1981 he led Argentina to the Cup round, a narrow 3–1 defeat by the U.S. in Cincinnati where, in the fifth set, Guillermo actually served for an improbable doubles victory, and an unrealized 2–1 lead (with Jose-Luis Clerc) against McEnroe and Peter Fleming. Vilas and Clerc were hardly a team, or doubles players; McEnroe and Fleming were the best. But the match, lost 11–9 in the fifth, showed Guillermo's heart and desire on behalf of his homeland.

He was in four French finals, but couldn't get past the Swedes, losing to Bjorn Borg in 1975–78 and, wearing down before 17-year-old Mats Wilander in 1982. It was his last major final in a career that landed him in fifth place among the all-time pro winners headed by Connors: 61 singles titles, one behind Borg. His career prize money amounted to $4,904,922. It was in Paris, 1973, that he first gained notice, removing defending champ Andres Gimeno from the French in the second round.

Beginning in 1974 he graced the World Top Ten for nine straight years, No. 2 in 1977. He was born Aug. 17, 1952, in Mar del Plata, Argentina, where he grew up.

MAJOR TITLES (4)—*Australian singles, 1978–79; French singles, 1977; U.S. singles, 1977.* DAVIS CUP—*1970–71–72–73–75–76–77–78–79–80–81–82–83–84; record: 45–10 in singles, 12–14 in doubles.*

Ellsworth Vines
United States (1911–   )

See page 96.

Gottfried von Cramm
Germany (1909–76)

See page 98.

Virginia Wade

sent the women's prize. Ginny had set the stage by deposing 1976 champ Chris Evert in the semis, 6–2, 4–6, 6–1.

Attacking incessantly, heedless of whatever mistakes she made, Wade finished strongly to beat Betty Stove for the title, 4–6, 6–3, 6–1, nine days short of her 32nd birthday. An extraordinary jubilant Centre Court crowd of more than 14,000, unaccustomed to homegrown success, became a chorus in singing "For She's a Jolly Good Fellow!" A tennis queen was saluted by her Queen.

Dark-haired Wade was slender (5-foot-8) and nimble, of elegant bearing. She had the longest and, considering the highly competitive age in which she sparkled, the most fruitful career of any Englishwoman. Her career spanned the amateur and open eras, and in 1968 she scored two notable firsts. As an amateur she won the inaugural open, the British Hard Court at Bournemouth, turning down the £300 first prize, and five months later, as a pro, she captured the initial U.S. Open (and $6,000), upending the favored defender and Wimbledon champ, Billie Jean King, 6–4, 6–4.

As a pro she won 29 singles titles, seventh among the all-time leaders, and amassed $1,542,278 in career prize money. She won the Australian title in 1972, only the third Brit to do so, following Dorothy Round (1935) and Angela Mortimer (1958). With her severely sliced backhand approach and splendid volleying, right-handed Ginny was a natural on grass. But she showed her clay mettle in winning the

ers in matches played there (212): 64–23 in singles, 53–24 in doubles, 24–24 in mixed. She entered the World Top Ten in 1967 and was there 13 straight years, No. 2 in 1968. She set records for participation in Federation Cup (18 years) and singles wins (35–20); and, for Britain, Wightman Cup (21 years) and total wins (12–23 in singles, 7–13 in doubles).

She was born July 10, 1945 in Bournemouth, England, learned to play tennis in South Africa, where she lived, and was inducted into the Hall of Fame in 1989.

MAJOR TITLES (7)—*Australian singles, 1972; Wimbledon singles, 1977; U.S. singles. 1967; Australian doubles, 1973; French doubles, 1973; U.S. doubles, 1973–75.* FEDERATION CUP—*1967–68–69–70–71–72–73–74–75–76–77–78–79 –80–81–82–83; record: 35–20 in singles, 27–12 in doubles.* WIGHTMAN CUP—*65–66–67–68–69– 70–71–72–73–74–75–76–77–78–79–80–81–82–8 3–84–85; record: 12–23 in singles, 7–13 in doubles.*

Marie Wagner
United States (1883–1975)

Queen of the boards, Marie Wagner, a New Yorker, was the scourge of Manhattan's Seventh Regiment Armory where she won the U.S. Indoor singles a record six times (1908–09–11–13–14–17), and the doubles four times. She was also singles finalist in 1915 to Molla Mallory. Her best outdoor showing was as the 1914 U.S. finalist to Mary K. Browne, losing, 6–2, 1–6, 6–1.

She ranked No. 6 in 1913 when the U.S. Top Ten was established, and was in that select group every year through 1920—No. 3 in 1914—as well as 1922 when she was No. 9 at age 39. A right-hander, she was born Feb. 2, 1883, in Freeport, N.Y., and died April 1, 1975. She entered the Hall of Fame in 1969.

U.S. TITLES (10)—*Indoor singles, 1908–09–11–13–14–17; Indoor doubles, 1910–13 with Clara Kutroff; 1916, with Molla Bjurstedt; 1917, with Margaret Taylor.*

Maud Barger Wallach
United States (1870–1954)

A late-in-life tennis success, Maud Barger Wallach—"I started to play at about 30"—became the oldest major champion in 1908. She was 38 when she toppled the defending U.S. champ, lefty Evelyn Sears, 6–3, 1–6, 6–3, in the challenge round, after having beaten Marie Wagner, 4–6, 6–1, 6–3, in the all-comers. Molla Mallory, winning in 1926 at 42, took away her old-age record.

In her first shot at the title, 1906, Maud lost the final to Helen Homans, 6–4, 6–3. Hazel Hotchkiss Wightman, who took the crown from her in the 1909 challenge round, recalled that Mrs. Richard Wallach had a good forehand "but not much of backhand. I concentrated on it until I was well ahead"—winning, 6–1, 6–0.

Maud was a New Yorker, a right-hander, born there June 15, 1870. She was a familiar summer figure at Newport, R.I., generally playing beneath a distinctive wide-brimmed straw hat. "Mine was not a great career," she recalled, "but a long and happy one."

At 46 she made the U.S. quarterfinals of 1916 (losing to runner-up Louise Raymond) and ranked No. 10, the oldest to do so well in the tournament and the rankings. National rankings for women weren't instituted until 1913, then largely because of her lobbying. But she was No. 5 in 1915. After dying in Baltimore, April 2, 1954, she was buried at Newport, not far from her beloved Casino, and was placed there eternally on her 1958 induction into the Hall of Fame.

MAJOR TITLE (1)—*U.S. singles, 1908.*

Holcombe Ward
United States (1878–1967)

One of the originals, the Harvard Three forming the first U.S. Davis Cup team, Holcombe Ward is also credited with originating the American twist serve which bedeviled the British invaders as the Cup was put into play in 1900. He accompanied donor Dwight Davis—his partner in two subsequent U.S. doubles championships—to the clinching doubles win in the 3–0 victory over the British Isles.

The right-hander played for the Cup-winners again in 1902, and the losers, to the Brits in 1905–06. At Harvard, Ward partnered Davis to the Intercollegiate doubles title in 1899, and broke through as U.S. singles champ in 1904. That year he was ranked No. 1, the acme of his seven years in his country's Top Ten. In 1922 Ward and Davis reunited to win the U.S. Veterans doubles title. He served as president of the USTA between 1937 and 1947.

A New Yorker, he was born there Nov. 23, 1878, and died Jan. 23, 1967, in Red Bank, N.J. He was inducted into the Hall of Fame in 1956.

MAJOR TITLES (7)—*U.S. singles, 1904; U.S. doubles, 1899–1900–01–04–05–06.* OTHER U.S. TITLES—*Indoor singles, 1901; Intercollegiate doubles, 1899, with Dwight Davis.* DAVIS CUP—*1900–02–05–06; record: 3–4 in singles, 4–3 in doubles.*

Watty Washburn
United States (1894–1973)

A New Yorker and a Harvard man, Watson McLean Washburn had a hand early on in the U.S. record run of seven Davis Cups that began in 1920. Watty played in the first defense, at Forest Hills in 1921, where he and Dick Williams won the Cup-clinching match over Japan's Zenzo Shimidzu and Ichiya Kumagae, 7–5 in the

U.S. 45s singles in 1940 and the doubles in that category thrice, 1940–42–44.

He was born June 13, 1894, in New York, was a committeeman for the USTA, and died in New York, Dec. 2, 1973. He was inducted into the Hall of Fame in 1965.

U.S. TITLES (2)—*Indoor doubles, 1915, with Gus Touchard; Intercollegiate doubles, 1913, with Joe Armstrong.* DAVIS CUP—*1921; record: 1–0 in doubles.*

Mal Whitman
United States (1877–1932)

One of the Harvard Three, the original U.S. Davis Cup team, Malcolm Douglass Whitman led off in the initial clash—U.S. vs. British Isles—in 1900 by beating Arthur Gore, 6–1, 6–3, 6–2. Classmate Dwight Davis, the Cup donor, won a singles and joined Holcombe Ward for the doubles clincher for the 3–0 triumph at Boston's Longwood Cricket Club.

A quarterfinalist in the 1896 and 1897 U.S. Championships, Whitman came through at Newport in 1898 with the first of his three straight championships. In the all-comers title match he beat Davis, 3–6,

6–3, 6–2, 6–1, and was crowned champion because 1897 victor Bob Wrenn, off to the Spanish-American War, didn't defend in the challenge round.

After another successful defense in 1899, Whitman had to first win a fight with his father, who wanted him to concentrate on law school (Harvard) and put away his racket. The son won, and that enabled

once more, and he reached the U.S. all-comers final, only to be stung by Reggie Doherty, 6–1, 3–6, 6–3, 6–0.

In the Davis Cup showdown he won both his matches (over Joshua Pim, 6–1, 6–1, 1–6, 6–0, and over Doherty, 6–1, 7–5, 6–4) and the U.S. kept the Cup, 3–2.

Whitman was through, after posting an unbeaten Cup record and a 19–3 match record at Newport. He was in the U.S. Top Ten six times from 1896, No. 1 1898–99–1900, and No. 2 in 1902. Ever absorbed by the game's history, he wrote *Tennis Origins and Mysteries*, published in 1931. Born March 15, 1877, in New York, he committed suicide there Dec. 28, 1932. He was named to the Hall of Fame in 1955.

MAJOR TITLES (3)—*U.S. singles, 1898–99–1900.* OTHER U.S. TITLES—*Intercollegiate singles, 1896; Intercollegiate doubles, 1897–98 with Leo Ware.* DAVIS CUP—*1900–02; record: 3–0 in singles.*

Hazel Hotchkiss Wightman
United States (1886–1974)

"Lady Tennis," as she came to be known, remembered herself as a shy, somewhat awed and fascinated college girl when she arrived at the Philadelphia Cricket Club in 1909 for the U.S. Championships. A Californian, Hazel Virginia Hotchkiss hadn't played on grass, but with her attacking style and rock-ribbed volleying—she was the first woman to rely so heavily on the volley—22-year-old Hazel, a right-hander, scythed through the field to lift the title effortlessly (6–0, 6–1) from 39-year-old Maud Barger Wallach in the challenge round.

She lost only one set, in the all-comers final over Louise Hammond, 6–8, 6–1, 6–4. That was the start of the first of the three U.S. triples (singles, doubles, mixed titles) registered by American women. Hazel repeated in 1910–11, and was emulated by Mary K. Browne (1912–13–14) and Alice Marble (1938–39–40). Hazel had no trouble with Hammond in the 1910 challenge round, but an old West Coast rival, May Sutton—champion in 1904—pushed her hard in 1911, 8–10, 6–4, 9–7.

Marrying Bostonian George Wightman in 1912, she didn't defend. But, responding to a challenge from her father—to win after becoming a mother, a U.S. first—she reappeared in 1915 to lose the singles final to Molla Mallory, and win the doubles and mixed. But papa's wish came true in another comeback, 1919. At 32, she won her fourth singles title. She lost only one set, beating Marion Zinderstein, 6–1, 6–2, in the final, and reaching the doubles final. Thereafter her long-lived and unapproached success (U.S. adult titles between 1909 and 1943) was confined to doubles, at which she was one of the supremes.

Hazel, devoted to the game in all aspects, generously instructed innumerable players, at no charge, throughout her life, and was able to win important titles with two of her protégés who would join her in the Hall of Fame: Wimbledon, U.S. and Olympic doubles with Helen Wills in 1924; U.S. Indoor doubles with Sarah Palfrey 1928 through 1931. Her second Olympic

gold in 1924 came in the mixed with Dick Williams.

She envisioned a team tournament for women similar to the Davis Cup, and offered a silver vase as prize. In 1923 British women were the strongest apart from Americans, and Julian Myrick of the USTA decided that a U.S.-Britain competition would be in order for the Wightman Cup. The event, with Hazel captaining and playing for a winning U.S. side, opened the newly constructed stadium at Forest Hills. A treasured series, it lasted through 1989, disbanded unfortunately with the Brits no longer able to offer competition.

The last of Hazel's record 34 U.S. adult titles was recorded in 1943 as she, 56, and Pauline Betz won the Indoor doubles. Though a short woman, no more than 5–2, she anticipated and moved extremely well and competed fiercely though undemonstrably. She perfected her volleying early, hitting the ball against the family home in Berkeley, where she grew up and graduated from the University of California. She refused to let the ball bounce because the yard was so uneven. She used to play against her four brothers and then the proud and spiky Sutton sisters.

As the Bostonian Mrs. Wightman, she was in the U.S. Top Ten in 1915–18–19, No. 1 the last. She was born Dec. 20, 1886, in Healdsburg, Cal., and died Dec. 5, 1974, in Chestnut Hill, Mass. She entered the Hall of Fame in 1956.

MAJOR TITLES (17)—*U.S. singles, 1909–10–11–19; Wimbledon doubles, 1924; U.S. doubles, 1909–10–11–15–24–28; U.S. mixed, 1909–10–11–15–18–20.* OTHER U.S. TITLES— *Indoor singles, 1919–27; Indoor doubles, 1919–21–24–27, with Marion Zinderstein Jessup; 1928–29–30–31–33, with Sarah Palfrey; 1943, with Pauline Betz; Indoor mixed, 1923–24–26–27–28; Clay Court mixed, 1915; Grass 40 doubles, 1940–41–44–46–47, with Edith Sigourney; 1942, with Molly Fremont Smith; 1948, with Jessup; 1949–50–52–53, with Marjorie Gladman Van Ryn Buck; 1954, with Nell Hall Hopman.*

Tony Wilding
New Zealand (1883–1915)

See page 99.

Dick Williams
United States (1891–1968)

second-youngest champion of Centre Court, and without stepping onto the hallowed sod. Frank Shields, with an injured ankle, withdrew, marking the only time Wimbledon has had a defaulted final.

Born Nov. 1, 1911, in Black Rock, Conn., a right-hander, Wood never reached that 1931 eminence again, although he did get to play a major final, losing the U.S. to Wilmer Allison in 1935. A slim, nimble blond, he ranked in the U.S. Top Ten 10 times between 1930 and 1945, No. 2 in 1934, and was in the World Top Ten five times between 1931 and 1938, No. 5 in 1938, No. 6 in 1931.

He was a Davis Cupper in 1931 and 1934, and in the latter year was part of the most astounding U.S. comeback, from 0–2 against Australia in London. Having lost the first day to Viv McGraw, Wood knocked off Jack Crawford to open the third day and tie the score at 2–2. Then Shields beat McGrath, and the U.S. entered the finals, losing, 4–1, to Britain. There, on opening day, Wood battled the Cup-holder's main man, Fred Perry, losing 6–3 in the fifth, and also lost to Bunny Austin on the third day. An inventive man, he was a developer of Supreme Court, the synthetic carpet on

which most indoor events are played. He was inducted into the Hall of Fame in 1964.

MAJOR TITLE (1)—*Wimbledon singles, 1931.* DAVIS CUP—*1931–34; record: 5–6 in singles, 3–0 in doubles.*

Bob Wrenn
United States (1873–1925)

He came from a prominent Chicago family of several fine athletes, and became a topflight football, baseball and tennis player at Harvard. Noted for swiftness and court coverage, a defensive star featuring devilish lobs, he was the first left-hander to win the U.S. singles. He beat Fred Hovey for the 1893 title, 7–5, 3–6, 6–3, 7–5, and kept it by repelling Manliffe Goodbody in the 1894 challenge round.

Hovey took it from him easily in 1895. But Bob wrested it back, 6–1 in the fifth in the 1896 challenge round, and fended off Wilberforce Eaves, 6–2 in the fifth set of the 1897 challenge round. War service prevented him from defending in 1898. He did team with his right-handed younger brother, George Wrenn, as the U.S. Davis Cup doubles pair in 1903 when they lost to the British Dohertys, Laurie and Reggie, 7–5, 9–7, 2–6, 6–3, the only instance of brothers clashing for the Cup.

They were the only brothers to play for the U.S., and to rank together in the U.S. Top Ten: Bob was No. 1 in 1893–94–96–97, No. 8 in 1892 and 1900; George four times No. 6 during his five years up there between 1896 and 1900. Another brother, Everts, ranked No. 18 in 1896. In Bob's last thrust for the U.S. singles title he was beaten by George in a 1900 quarterfinal, 6–4, 6–1, 6–4, the only such brotherly battle in the Championships. George then lost the all-comers, 6–3, 6–2, 6–2, to Larned.

After leaving Harvard, Bob became a stockbroker in New York, and was president of the USTA from 1912 through 1915. Born Sept. 20, 1873, in Highland Park, Ill., he died in New York Nov. 12, 1925, and was named to the Hall of Fame in 1955.

MAJOR TITLES (5)—*U.S. singles, 1893-94-96-97; U.S. doubles, 1895.* OTHER U.S. TITLES—*Intercollegiate doubles, 1892, with F.B. Winslow.* DAVIS CUP—*1903; record: 0–2 in singles, 0–1 in doubles.*

Beals Wright
United States (1879–1961)

Before the turn of the century, Beals Coleman Wright was a national champion, winning the Interscholastic singles for Boston's Hopkinson School in 1898 at 18, and repeating the following year when he made his first of 11 entries in the U.S. Top Ten at No. 8. In 1900 his brother, Irving, won the Interscholastic for the same school.

In 1905, dethroning Holcombe Ward, he was the second lefty to win the U.S. singles, following Bob Wrenn. He had to beat the future champ, Bill Clothier, and an ex-champ, Bill Larned, plus Clarence Hobart, to reach the challenge round to topple Ward, 6–2, 6–1, 11–9.

Extremely aggressive, Wright received inside the baseline and approached with his returns and serves. Few liked to play against his fiendish chop and wide-spinning serve.

His biggest year was 1905. It included one of his three U.S. doubles titles (with Ward), and Davis Cup victories over

Australian greats Tony Wilding and Norman Brookes, that sent the U.S. into a losing Cup round against Britain. In 1908 he beat those two again, even more stunning victories since it was the Davis Cup finale at Melbourne, their home turf. But it wasn't enough in a 3–2 defeat. He was born Dec. 19, 1879, in Boston, lived in Brookline, Mass., and died Aug. 23, 1961, in Alton, Ill. He was inducted into the Hall of Fame in 1956.

MAJOR TITLES (4)—*U.S. singles, 1905; U.S. doubles, 1904–05–06.* DAVIS CUP—*1905–07–08–11; record: 6–4 in singles, 3–3 in doubles.*

Court Tennis

Pierre Etchebaster
France (1894–1980)

A Basque maestro of the racket in the complex game of court tennis, the short, trim, elegant Pierre Etchebaster, a professional, was probably the greatest to roam the arcane concrete cubicle. Migrating to New York from his French homeland, he became the resident paragon at the Racquet & Tennis Club on Park Avenue, as player and instructor. Traveling to London to challenge for the world title in 1927, he lost to the champion G.F. Covey, 7-sets-to-5 in Prince's Club.

However, a year later on the same court he dethroned Covey, 7–5. Thereafter, he repelled seven challenges himself, the first at Prince's, the remainder on his home paving, Racquet & Tennis: 1930, Walter Kinsella, 7–1; 1937, Ogden Phipps, 3–1, injured; 1948, Phipps, 7–2; 1948; James Deal, 7–4; 1949, Phipps, 7–1; 1950, Alastair Martin, 7–0; 1952, Martin, 7–2.

He retired as unbeaten champion in 1954 at age 60. A right-hander, he was born in May 1894, in St. Jean de Luz, France, and died there March 24, 1980. He entered the Hall Fame in 1978.

Tom Pettit
Great Britain (1859–1946)

As a youngster, 17, English-born Tom Pettit migrated to Boston. He became a wizard at racket sports, and was immensely popular as teaching professional of court tennis at Boston's Tennis & Racquet Club, and that game as well as lawn tennis at the Newport (R.I.) Casino, where he was a familiar walrus-mustachioed figure until his

Court, outside of London. In an 1890 defense he turned back Charles Saunders, 7–5, at St. Stephens Green, Ireland, resigning the title later unbeaten. In the earliest pro lawn tennis tour, he and Irish pro champ George Kerr played a series of three well-attended matches in New England in 1889. Kerr, won at Boston, Springfield (Mass.), and Newport. Pettit was born Dec. 19, 1859, in Beckenham, England, and died Oct. 17, 1946, in Newport, R.I.

Journalists

Allison Danzig
United States (1898–1987)

His familiar and authoritative byline appeared in *The New York Times* for 45 years through 1967. Before that he was a sportswriter for the *Brooklyn Eagle*, developing an incisive, perceptive style that made him the widest regarded literary voice of the game in the U.S. Al Danzig, the first journalist to enter the Hall of Fame (1968), was a thoroughgoing gentleman respected throughout the game and his profession. He covered the game from its first great impact during the Tilden, Wills and Lenglen days of the 1920s to the dawn of

the open era, and also was a nationally known chronicler of college football, rowing and the Olympic Games.

He was one of the few who could write knowledgeably about court tennis, ancestor of lawn tennis. Born in Waco, Tex., Feb. 27, 1898, he graduated from Cornell, where he played football despite a diminu-

tennis writers, and is presented periodically during the U.S. Pro Championships.

David Gray
Great Britain (1927–83)

David Gray was such a fine chronicler of the game for an exceptional English newspaper, *The Guardian*, that many regretted his departure from journalism in 1976 to become an official of the ITF. A well-educated and witty man, he showed his grasp of tennis, its figures, matches, history and politics in his literate daily reports from across the world. But he served the game well, even without byline, as the ITF's diplomatic general secretary from 1976 until his untimely death of cancer in 1983. He was also secretary of the Men's International Professional Tennis Council.

As a journalist he strongly advocated the abolition of phony amateurism and the adoption of open tennis in 1968. Gray was influential in reorganizing the Davis Cup, returning tennis to the Olympics in 1988 and broadening the game's base, especially by encouraging its development on the African continent. Among the large and competitive British press contingent he was a standout, and he brought to the game's administration a keen overall view and perception, much wider than that of most tennis officials.

He was born Dec. 31, 1927, in Kingswinford, England, and died Sept 6, 1983, in London. He was named to the Hall of Fame in 1985.

Gladys Heldman
United States (1922–   )

For more than two decades, brilliant Gladys Medalie Heldman was the game's anchor, first as founder-owner-publisher-editor-chief writer of *World Tennis* magazine (launched in 1953), later as the instigator and housemother of a separate professional circuit for women, begun in 1970. Under her guidance, WT became the international literary voice of tennis. A slim, petite dynamo, who often seemed shy, she came to tennis through marriage to a first-flight player, left-handed Julius Heldman, who was the U.S. junior champ in 1936.

She, a previously non-athletic New Yorker, quickly absorbed his enthusiasm for the game, becoming a maven. Their two daughters, Trixie and Julie, held national junior rankings, and Julie went on to win the Italian Open in 1969, and rank No. 5 in the world that year and in 1974. In 1970, Gladys and her magazine became the allies of disgruntled female players— Billie Jean King and Rosie Casals foremost—who felt, justifiably, that they were being demeaned, financially and attitudinally, by the game's male establishment. They believed it was necessary to break away from the traditional dual-sex tournament format and go it alone.

Heldman encouraged them, and urged a close friend, Joe Cullman, head of Philip Morris, to provide an initial bankroll. Joined by the "Houston Eight" (King, Casals, daughter Julie, Peaches Bartkowicz, Valerie Ziegenfuss, Nancy Richey, Kristy Pigeon, Judy Tegart), Heldman staged the first Virginia Slims tournament in that city late in 1970. Although the Americans among the Eight risked (and received brief) suspensions from the USTA, that tourney, and another in Richmond, Va., succeeded.

They prompted Virginia Slims to underwrite a 1971 tour, and the stunning progress of the "Long Way Babies" commenced. Heldman counseled and editorially backed the circuit which she first dubbed "Women's Lob" featuring "The Little Broads."

Heldman, who became a better-than-average player herself, sold the magazine and withdrew from tennis politics in the mid-1970s, and now lives with her husband in Santa Fe, N.M. She was born May 13, 1922, in New York, and entered the Hall of Fame in 1972.

Al Laney
United States (1895–1988)

A fine writer who made his name covering sports, Albert Gillis Laney was usually associated with tennis and golf, but he covered everything on the menu, from big league baseball to football to championship fights, with his usual understanding of what was at foot, and a keen reportorial touch. Laconic, mustachioed, usually beneath a gray fedora, he settled in Paris for a time after World War I, worked for James Joyce as secretary, and joined the staff of the renowned *Paris Herald* (now the *International Herald Tribune*).

He had an eye for compelling features, and his coverage of the epic 1926 showdown of Suzanne Lenglen and Helen Wills at Cannes graces several anthologies. He spanned the generations, having observed another epic, the Maurice McLoughlin-Norman Brookes Davis Cup duel at Forest Hills in 1914, and worked as a reporter until his last newspaper, the *New York Herald Tribune*, folded in 1966. That paper had a legendary sports staff headed by Stanley Woodward, who felt Laney's story on blind, down-and-out Sam Langford, onetime great boxer, was an American masterpiece.

His *Courting the Game*, a tennis memoir, remains one of the splendid tennis books. Laney was born Jan. 11, 1895, in Pensacola, Fla., retained a Southern lilt in his speech, and died Jan. 31, 1988, in Spring Valley, N.Y. He entered the Hall of Fame in 1979.

Lance Tingay
Great Britain (1915–90)

As the dean of a sizeable platoon of

1980, writing his dispatches from across the world.

Ever good humored, even while pounding his typewriter on deadline, he was a leading historian of the game, the author of *History of Lawn Tennis in Pictures, One Hundred Years of Wimbledon, Royalty and Lawn Tennis*, and wrote for numerous tennis publications and yearbooks. Tingay was born in London July 15, 1915, and died there March 10, 1990. He was named to the Hall of Fame in 1982.

Innovators

Ted Tinling
Great Britain (1910–90)

The Leaning Tower of Pizzaz, 6-foot-5 Cuthbert Collingwood Tinling entered the Hall of Fame in 1986 as a many-faceted benefactor of the game. Witty and literate, a man who had served in intelligence for the British army during World War II, Tinling, a right-hander, was a good enough player to compete on the English circuit after the war. But it was as an involved bystander that he served the game well, first as a teenager on the Riviera where he,

spending winters for reasons of ill health, umpired matches, including some for the great Suzanne Lenglen.

He was master of ceremonies at Wimbledon until one of his careers, that of designer-dressmaker, made him for a time *persona non grata*. That occurred in 1949 when he scandalously (or so it seemed to the tournament committee) equipped

he was counselor for the newly formed Virginia Slims circuit, and later the Slimsies' minister of protocol and emcee, a strong advocate of the women's game. An unmistakable bald-headed beacon, he was of immeasurable value late in life as historian and writer who had observed most of the game's luminaries, and as liaison between the players and Wimbledon. Outspoken, generous in informing and counseling newcomers to the game, Ted could make light of his own death, remarking on one of his last days: "Send me a fax to hell to let me know if Jennifer [Capriati] wins Wimbledon." He was born June 23, 1910, in Eastbourne, England, and died May 23, 1990, in Cambridge, England.

Mary Outerbridge
United States (1852–86)

Celebrated as the "Mother of Tennis," Mary Ewing Outerbridge was undoubtedly one of the pioneers, but the claims by her adherents that she introduced the game to the U.S. are undocumented. The story is that she, a New Yorker, saw soldiers of the British garrison playing tennis in Bermuda, where she was vacationing in 1874, the year of the game's patenting and early marketing. Intrigued, she is said to have taken a set home where her brother, Emilius

Outerbridge, and friends set up a court at the Staten Island Cricket and Baseball Club.

Tennis was indeed introduced to the U.S. at several locations in 1874, the first documented instance in Arizona. Outerbridge was born March 9, 1852, in Philadelphia, died May 3, 1886, on Staten Island five years after the first U.S. Championships, and entered the Hall of Fame in 1981.

Jimmy Van Alen
United States (1902-91)

James Henry Van Alen, born Sept. 19, 1902, in his beloved Newport, R. I., was intimately involved with tennis as player, organizer and—best known—innovator whose pet idea, the tie-breaker, radically altered the game, making it more televisable in the U.S. As a U.S. singles champ at court tennis in 1933–38–40 he was good enough at that abstruse ancestor of lawn tennis to warrant a Hall of Fame spot as a player. He played tennis well enough to have won his blue at his alma mater, Cambridge, appeared in the Wimbledon and U.S. Championships, and played in the Newport Casino Invitational, where he had a win over fellow Hall of Famer George Lott.

He would become director of that tournament, a leader in the preservation of the aging wooden Casino (the cradle of U.S. tennis), and, at the instigation of his wife, Candy, the guiding light in founding the Hall of Fame to which he was elected in 1965.

Feeling the game's scoring should be simplified and deuce done away with, he lobbied tirelessly on behalf of his creation, VASSS: Van Alen Simplified/Streamlined Scoring System. Among the elements were single point scoring and 21-point or 31-point matches (à la table tennis), no-ad (games scored 1-2-3-4, maximum 7–points, sudden death at 3–3), medal play (à la golf,

based on single point totals for specific numbers of rounds), and, the most celebrated—tie-breakers.

Unveiled in 1965 at the Casino Pro Championships, which he personally sponsored for $10,000 prize money, the seminal tie-breaker needed retooling. That he did with veteran referee Mike Blanchard. Eventually it became sudden death (best-of-9 points).

Amazingly this breaker was accepted by the USTA, and used in U.S. championship events from 1970 through 1974. Thereafter the USTA embraced the current ITF-approved "lingering death," as Van Alen disparagingly called the best-of-12 point version that requires a 2-point margin for victory, thus can extend into double figures. Between 1970 and 1977, at "Newport Bolshevik" Jimmy's suggestion, red flags were raised wherever a tie-breaker was played at the U.S. Open. Sadly this custom wasn't continued at Flushing Meadow.

A man of old family wealth, Jimmy hoped to give the game a common touch, and became an avuncular, almost cherubic figure in planter's straw hat and burgundy blazer at the Casino. His love for tennis was endless, as well as his delight in shaking up the establishment with his brainstorms. He served in the U.S. Navy during World War II, and died July 3, 1991, in Newport. Jimmy would have enjoyed the irony: That semifinal day at Wimbledon Michael Stich deposed champion Stefan Edberg by winning three breakers while Edberg never lost his serve. Such a match could not have been played during nearly a century before Van Alen.

Administrators

George Adee
United States (1874–1948)

George T. Adee made his sporting name as an All-American quarterback at

Yale in 1894. He was elevated to the Hall of Fame in 1964, for his contributions to tennis on the administrative side. He was president of the USTA four years, 1916–19, and was also a member of the Davis Cup and Amateur Rules committees. A New Yorker, he was an enthusiastic tennis player, good enough to appear six times in the U.S. Championships singles between 1903 and 1909. He was born Jan. 4, 1874, in Stonington, Conn., and died July 26,

paign to restore tennis to the Olympic Games, a goal realized in 1988 after a 64-year interval.

Championing the Grand Slam concept, he worked hard to ally the four major championships in staying at the pinnacle. He is a member of the International Olympic Committee. An intelligent chronicler of the game, he was a Paris newspa-

Foundation, and captained the U.S. Davis Cup team for its 1953 win over Canada at Montreal. He sponsored the Baker Cup, a U.S. vs. Canada event for seniors. Baker was born June 20, 1890, in Lowdensville, S.C., lived in East Hampton, N.Y., and died there Oct. 15, 1980. He entered the Hall of Fame in 1975.

ager in tennis, a moonlighter away from his principal position as chairman and CEO of the Philip Morris Co. As such he benefitted tennis extraordinarily in several ways. He was chairman of the U.S. Open at Forest Hills in 1969 and 1970, formative years, and was instrumental in getting the original Open, 1968, televised.

Philippe Chatrier
France (1926–   )

As player, journalist and administrator Philippe Chatrier, a Parisian, made a tremendous impact on the game, and was instrumental in its growth and success, particularly during the open era. He was a good enough player to win the French junior titles in singles and doubles in 1945, play internationally for France, and later captained the Cup team.

Serving dual roles as president of the French Federation of Tennis (1972–92) and the ITF (1977–91) he was largely responsible for the renaissance of the French Open, placing it on par with the other three majors and overseeing the splendid updating of Stade Roland Garros. He fought valiantly against over-commercialization of the game, and led a cam-

In 1970, at the behest of another Hall of Fame member, Gladys Heldman, he came to the financial and spiritual rescue of the women, up to then second-class citizens of tournament tennis. With the backing of one of his products, Virginia Slims, a separate women's professional circuit was born. It continues.

He was president and chairman of the International Tennis Hall of Fame 1982–88, a period during which the Hall's home, the revered and historic Newport Casino, made a recovery from years of neglect, and became a sound and viable institution. A Yale alumnus, he built a tennis complex, the Cullman Center, for his alma mater. A fervent player, he enjoys nothing more than a game on the Casino lawn. Joe is a New Yorker, born there April 9, 1912, and entered the Hall of Fame in 1990.

Slew Hester
United States (1912–93)

A fine athlete, a football player at Millsaps College in his native Mississippi, William E. Hester won numerous tennis trophies. Among them were U.S. senior doubles titles such as the Grass Court 45s with Alex Wellford in 1957. But, as one of the most thoughtful and forceful USTA presidents, burly Slew made an indelible mark on the game by determining to expand the scope and potential of the U.S. Open by moving the event from Forest Hills after the 1977 Championships.

He took the Open a few miles away to Flushing Meadow and the swiftly constructed, Hester-inspired-and-overseen U.S. National Tennis Center in time for the 1978 Open. There the event annually set tennis attendance records. A gregarious cigar-smoking oilman from Jackson, Hester earned a bronze star while serving in the U.S. Army in World War II.

He was a USTA officer from 1969 to 1977 when he became president for a critical two-year term. Born May 8, 1912, in Hazlehurst, Mass., he was inducted into the Hall of Fame in 1981, and died Feb. 8, 1993, in Jackson, Miss.

Lamar Hunt
United States (1932–   )

A man about Halls of Fame, Texan Lamar Hunt entered the tennis valhalla in 1993, having been inducted previously into the Professional Football Hall of Fame and the Soccer Hall of Fame.

Although he played football—"I sat on the bench"—at Southern Methodist, Hunt, scion of a prominent Dallas oil industry family, made his mark in American and international sport with his organizational and promotional strengths.

He was a leading founder of the American Football League, which eventu- ally merged with the NFL. And with his daughter, Hunt has been credited with the naming of the Super Bowl. He is owner of the Kansas City Chiefs and launched the Dallas Tornados in the North American Soccer League.

It was as a partner in the establishment of World Championship Tennis (WCT)— and later its guiding light—that he was a strong global influence in transforming and professionalizing the tournament game. In 1967, a New Orleans friend, Dave Dixon, enlisted Hunt's aid in forming WCT. Headquartered in Dallas, WCT has- tened the dawn of open tennis with the signing of the elite of the amateurs.

WCT developed a circuit and season of its own, leading the way to increased pay- days for the pros that forced the rest of the tennis world to catch up.

Unfortunately (and ungratefully), the Association of Tennis Professionals, in reorganizing the men's tour in 1990, froze WCT out, and Hunt's organization ceased operations after 23 years of raising stan- dards within the professional game. Hunt was born Aug. 2, 1932, in Eldorado, Ark., and lives in Dallas.

Perry T. Jones
United States (1890–1970)

A powerful figure in making Southern California a tennis vineyard of champions, Perry Thomas Jones oversaw the game from his office at the Los Angeles Tennis Club for well over a quarter-century. As president of the Southern California Association and director of the Pacific Southwest Championships, he was active in the game from bottom to top, singling out promising juniors for attention and travel and making his tournament one of the best in the U.S.

In short, Perry T., or Mr. Jones, as he was called, stood imposingly as Mr. Tennis of the West Coast, an exceptional fundraiser whose judgment and help forwarded the careers of numerous stars, including Jack Kramer, Billie Jean King and Dennis Ralston.

The last was Alex Olmedo, the Peruvian student at the University of Southern California. Maneuvering controversially, Jones got him, the only non-citizen to play for the U.S., approved for the Davis Cup team in 1958, citing the fact that

Alastair Martin
United States (1915–)

A mild yet determined man, Alastair Bradley Martin qualified for 1973 induction to the Hall of Fame on two counts: He was a progressive vice president and president of the USTA during the critical transition period between the amateur and open eras. And he was one of the finest of all court tennis players, U.S. amateur champion in singles eight times, doubles 10 times. He also challenged the great pro Pierre Etchebaster (a fellow Hall of Fame member) for Etchebaster's world title, vainly in 1950 and 1952.

Alastair was a good enough lawn tennis player to have competed in the U.S. Championships at Forest Hills several times before and after World War II. As vice president of the USTA in 1967–68, he worked closely with president Bob Kelleher, advocating, with the British, the revolutionary adoption of open tennis.

He was USTA president in the trying days of 1969–70 as the game became professionalized, and the amateur associations maintained their standing. He founded the Eastern Tennis Patrons in 1951 and

served as president of the National Tennis Foundation. A New Yorker, he was born there March 11, 1915, and resides in Katonah, N.Y.

Bill Martin
United States (1906–)

A distinguished figure in finance and government when Chairman of the Federal Reserve Board for 20 years (1951–70),

make sure that its home, the historic Newport Casino (imperiled by age and apathy), was preserved and put into fine condition.

He married into an honored tennis family, wedding Cynthia Davis, daughter of Dwight Davis, donor of the Cup bearing his name. Like the Davises, he was raised in St. Louis, born there Dec. 17, 1906. He entered the Hall of Fame in 1982 and resides in Washington, D.C.

Julian Myrick
United States (1880–1969)

A New Yorker, though born March 1, 1880, in Murfreesboro, N.C., Julian Southall Myrick was inducted into the Hall of Fame in 1963 on the basis of his administrative ability and contributions to the game in the U.S. Known as "Uncle Mike" to friends and associates, he was president of the USTA 1920–21–22 and an active committeeman. He was a leader in enlarging the U.S. Championships, influential in construction of the Forest Hills Stadium in 1923, and launching the Wightman Cup competition between U.S. and British women, the first edition of which inaugurated the stadium. He died in New York, Jan. 4, 1969.

Patrons

King Gustav V
Sweden (1858–1950)

A grand patron of the game and an enthusiastic player into his 90s, King Gustav V of Sweden learned to play during a visit to Britain in 1878, and founded his country's first tennis club on his return home. In 1936 he founded the King's Cup. Eventually disbanded during the open era, it was a men's indoor team competition for European countries. He became king on Dec. 8, 1907, ruled for 43 years and was often seen playing friendly events on the Riviera.

Entered under the pseudonym, Mr. G., he frequently took part in handicap tourneys, partnered by famous players such as Suzanne Lenglen. During World War II this widely respected ruler interceded to obtain better treatment for the Nazi-imprisoned Davis Cup stars, Jean Borotra of France and Gottfried von Cramm of Germany, and may have saved their lives.

Gustav was born June 16, 1858, in Drottningholm, Sweden and died Oct. 29, 1950. He was elected to the Hall of Fame in 1980.

Arthur Nielsen
United States (1897–1980)

Arthur Charles Nielsen's name is synonymous with television —the Nielsen Ratings—but he was long an avid player and a generous patron, contributing much time and money to the construction of tennis courts. One such monument to his memory is the Nielsen Center at his alma mater, the University of Wisconsin, where he was captain of the tennis varsity three years, 1916–18.

He continued playing after graduation, teaming with Arthur Nielsen, Jr., to win the U.S. Father and Son doubles titles of 1946 and 1948. A Chicagoan, he was born there Sept. 5, 1897, and died in Chicago June 1, 1980. He entered the Hall of Fame in 1971.

10: THEY ALSO SERVE

(1914-19 and 1946-92), numerous others during 117 years of tournament tennis have made distinctive/unusual marks and contributions. A select number may be found here—such as the eventually unlovable St. Leger Goold. Some players may be said to have gotten away with murder but he is the only Wimbledon finalist to be convicted of same.

ABBREVIATIONS USED: LH, LEFT-HANDER; RH, RIGHT-HANDER; B., BORN; D., DIED. DENOTING TOURNAMENT FINISH: RD., ROUND; QF, QUARTERFINAL, SF, SEMIFINAL; F, FINAL.

Agassi, Andre

Andre Kirk Agassi, long-haired flamboyant American RH, with two-handed backhand, b. April 29, 1970, Las Vegas. Forceful groundstroker registered startling Wimbledon win, 1992, after losing three major F—French, 1990–91; U.S., 1990. Davis Cup, 1988 through 1992, helping U.S. win twice, 1990–92. First impact, French SF, 1988. U.S. SF, 1988–89. Wimbledon QF, 1991. Biggest winning season, 1988 (six titles, 63–11 match record). Pro since 1986, 17 career singles titles, $5,351,203 through 1992. World rank, Nos. 3–7–4–10–9 from 1988.

Andre Agassi celebrates his Wimbledon title in 1992. •*Russ Adams*

Akhurst, Daphne

Daphne Akhurst Cozens, Australian RH, country's first prolific champ, first to make World Top Ten (No. 3, 1928), though had short career and life. B. April 22, 1903, d. Jan. 9, 1933. Between 1925 and 1931, won 14 majors, all Australian: five singles, five doubles, four mixed. Last doubles, 1931, won as Mrs. Roy Cozens. French QF, Wimbledon SF 1928, QF 1925.

Alvarez, Lili de

Spain's most accomplished female until Arantxa Sanchez Vicario, Lili de Alvarez, later Comtesse de la Valdene, was World No. 2, 1927–28; No. 3, 1926, No. 8, 1930–31. RH, b. May 9, 1905, Rome. Lost Wimbledon F to Kitty McKane, 1926; to Helen Wills, 1928. French QF, 1927, SF 1930–31. Lives in Madrid.

Ampon, Felicismo

Felicismo Hermoso Ampon, speedy, popular miniature, barely 5 feet, 100 pounds, smallest world-class man. Philippines' finest, RH, b. Oct. 27, 1920, Manila. Splendid retriever, made mark at French: QF 1952 (beat Tony Trabert), 1953 (beat Budge Patty). Incredible Davis Cup career over 29-year span (played 16)— from Philippines' initial team, 1939, to farewell victory, age 47, 1968. Led team to 22–16 record, was 32–26, singles. Nadir: 6–0, 6–0, 6–0, Cup beating by Frank Parker, U.S., 1946.

Amritraj, Vijay; Anand; Ashok

Three rangy, RH brothers, pros, from India with attacking styles, all born and raised in Madras. Vijay and Anand played Davis Cup together 15 years between 1973–88, led India to two title rounds, 1974–87. All live in Los Angeles.

Vijay Amritraj, b., Dec. 14, 1953, graceful 6-3, superb volleyer, Best World rank, No. 20, 1980. Won 16 singles, 13 doubles pro titles, $1,325,833 career. Winning Bretton Woods, N.H., 1973, saved three match points each vs. Humphrey Hose, Rod Laver, two more in F over Jimmy Connors. QF Wimbledon, U.S., 1973 (beating No. 2 seed Laver in latter.)

Anand Amritraj, 6-1, b. March 20, 1952. Best World rank, No. 87, 1974. Won 13 pro doubles titles, eight with Vijay, $331,698 career.

Ashok Amritraj, 6-1, b. Feb 22, 1957. Best World rank, No. 206, 1976.

Anderson, Jim; Mal

Australian Davis Cuppers, RH, not related.

James Outram "Greyhound" Anderson, b. Sept. 17, 1895, Enfield, d. July 19, 1960, Sydney. Best World rank, No. 3, 1923–24. Swift afoot, with husky, damaging forehand, won Australian singles, 1922–24–25; doubles, 1924. Led Aussies to Cup finale 1922, gave Bill Johnston, U.S., first Cup defeat.

Malcolm James "Cowboy" Anderson, b. March 5, 1935, Rockhampton. Willowy, 6-1, serve-and-volleyer, came off Queensland ranch. First unseeded player to win U.S., beat 2–3–1 seeds Dick Savitt, Sven Davidson, then Ashley Cooper in F. Lost F, 1958, to Cooper. World rank No. 2, 1957–58. Wimbledon QF, 1956–58. Lost Australian F, 1958–72. Won French doubles, Australian mixed, 1957; Australian doubles, 1973. Davis Cup, 1957–58–73, with 1957–73 winners. Turned pro, 1959.

Asboth, Josef

Probably Hungary's finest player, Josef Asboth was clever performer on clay, won French, 1947. Wimbledon SF, 1948. B. Sept. 18, 1917, Szombathely. Davis Cup seven years, between 1938 and 1957. World rank, No. 8, 1947–48. Turned pro, 1958.

Aussem, Cilly

Until Steffi Graf, Cilly Aussem was Germany's most successful woman. Tiny 5-foot RH baseliner. Won French, Wimbledon, 1931 (latter over Hilde Krahwinkel, only all-German female final). Wimbledon SF, 1930. French SF,

1929–30–34. Won French mixed, 1930. World rank, 1928–30–31, Nos. 7–2–2. B. Jan. 4, 1909, Cologne; d. March 22, 1963, Portofino.

Austin, Bunny; Joan

English brother, sister, RH.

Henry Wilfred "Bunny" Austin liberated male legs, first internationalist to wear

London. Lost Wimbledon doubles F, 1923. A liberator herself, first to play on Centre Court without stockings, 1931. Was married to Randolph Lycett, winner Wimbledon doubles, 1921–22–23.

Ayala, Luis

Chile's most successful male, Luis Ayala stocky RH, best on clay. B. Sept. 18, 1932, Santiago. Won Italian, 1959. French F, 1958–60; SF 1959. Won French mixed, 1956. Wimbledon QF, 1959–61. U.S. QF, 1957–59. Davis Cup four years between 1952 and 1957, captained team to title round, 1976, losing to Italy. Turned pro, 1961. World rank, No. 5, 1958, Nos. 6–7–7, 1959–60–61.

Baddeley, Herbert; Wilfred

English twins, Herbert and Wilfred Baddeley, RH, b. Jan. 11, 1872, Bromley. Made names at Wimbledon. In 1891 Wilfred, 19 years, 5 months, youngest singles champ for almost century, until Boris Becker, younger 19, 1985. Made F six straight years, winning also 1892–95. Linked as doubles team, twins made F seven straight years from 1891, winning 1891–94–95–96. In 1895 they beat English Doherty brothers for the title, lost it in a

reversal in 1897—only brotherly teams to square off for major title. Wilfred d. Jan. 30, 1929; Herbert d. July 20, 1931.

Barrett, Herbert

Herbert Roper Barrett, English RH, b. Nov. 24, 1873, Upton. An original Davis Cupper with losing British, 1900. Also played 1907–12–13–14, captained Cup winners of 1933–36. Had good long run...

French LH, Marcel Bernard had no intention winning French, 1946. He was 32, rusty, planned to play only doubles, but said OK when they wanted to put him in the draw—and startled everyone, including himself, by making F, beating favored Jaroslav Drobny, 5 sets. Also won doubles with Yvon Petra, 11 years after first French title, 1935, mixed with Lolette Payot. Davis Cup 10 years between 1935–56. World rank, No. 5, 1946. B. May 18, 1914, La Madeleine, France.

Bollettieri, Nick

Most renowned coach, effervescent Nicholas James Bollettieri, b. July 31, 1931, Pelham, N.Y., runs assembly line for champs, Bollettieri Tennis Academy, Bradenton, Fla. Ex-U.S. Army paratrooper, became teaching pro, 1958. Among pupils to make pro Top Ten: Andre Agassi, Jimmy Arias, Carling Bassett, Jim Courier, Aaron Krickstein, Monica Seles, David Wheaton.

Bolton, Nancye

Nancye Meredith Wynne Bolton, RH Australian, career extended around World War II. B. June 10, 1917, Melbourne, prodigious winner of Australian titles (record 20 until topped by Margaret

Court—six singles, 10 doubles, four mixed). First Aussie woman in U.S. F, lost to Alice Marble, 1938. Won first Aussie title, 1936, last, 1952, both doubles. Won record 10 doubles with Thelma Coyne Long, first singles, 1937. Beat Long for singles title, 1940, again for title, 1951. Wimbledon QF, 1947. U.S. SF, 1947. Australian F, 1936–49; SF, 1938–50–52; QF, 1939. World rank, No. 10, 1938; No. 4, 1947–48–49.

Boothby, Penelope

Penelope Dora Harvey Boothby, later Mrs. A.C. Geen, leading English player of her day. Won Wimbledon singles, 1909, doubles, 1913. But poor Dora, twice singles finalist, only double-bagel victim, losing 1911 title to Dorothea Douglass Lambert Chambers, 6–0, 6–0—two weeks after Lambert Chambers double-bageled her at Beckenham. RH, b. Aug. 2, 1881, Finchley, d. Feb. 22, 1970, London.

Bowrey, Lesley; Bill

Australian husband, wife, RH, scored singularly year of marriage, 1968, he winning Australian, she Italian.

Lesley Rosemary Turner Bowrey, b. Aug. 16, 1942, Sydney, had the stronger record, 12 major titles, including two French singles, 1963–65, all four major doubles. World rank, No. 2, 1963; No. 3, 1964–65; Top Ten four other years. Played for Australian Federation Cup winners, 1964–65.

William Walter "Tex" Bowrey, b. Dec. 25, 1943, Sydney. Australian QF, 1965–67. U.S. QF, 1966. Doubles F Wimbledon, 1966; Australian, U.S., 1967, with Owen Davidson. Davis Cup, losing finale, 1968.

Bundy, Dorothy

Dorothy May "Dodo" Bundy Cheney, a most enduring champ, flowing from teens into super-seniors. American RH, B. Sept. 1, 1916, Los Angeles, grew up in Santa Monica. Won Australian, 1938—still winning. First U.S. title, 1941, Indoor doubles, with Pauline Betz. Most recent, 1992: 70-singles, doubles; 75-singles, doubles, all four surfaces. End of '92, total record 232 U.S. senior titles, from 40s age group up (45, 50, 55, 60, 65, 70, 75); beginning 1957. Hard Court-40 singles, 13 straight years. Included, 18 U.S. Senior Grand Slams: Grass, Clay, Hard, Indoor singles/doubles within calendar year, five in 70-singles, 1986–87–88–89–92. Great genes: Mother, Hall of Famer May Sutton Bundy, won Wimbledon, 1904; father, Tom Bundy, U.S. doubles champ, 1912–13–14.

Capriati, Jennifer

Jennifer Marie Capriati, American prodigy, RH with two-fisted backhand, b. March 29, 1976, New York, grew up in Florida. Attracted great attention as youngest pro (and pro finalist), making debut at 13 years, 11 months, Boca Raton, Fla., 1990, losing F to Gabriela Sabatini. Made numerous "youngest" marks: Federation Cupper (and winner), 1990; Wightman Cupper (and winner), 1989; Wimbledon SF, 1991; in U.S. Top Three (Nos. 3–2–3), 1990–90–91. World rank (Nos. 8–6–7), 1990–91–92. Olympic gold medalist, singles, 1992. Powerful 5-7 groundstroker, dethroned two major champs, 1991—Martina Navratilova, Wimbledon; Sabatini, U.S. Five career singles titles, $1,134,715 through 1992.

Carillo, Mary

Mary Jean Carillo Bowden, LH, b. March 15, 1957, New York. Played women's tour, collaborated with John McEnroe, his first major title, French mixed, 1977. Best known as tennis telecaster, ESPN, CBS, refreshingly informative, uninhibited style.

Casals, Rosie

Rosemary "Rosebud" Casals, whirling, shotmaking sorceress, 5-2 RH, dazzling quick hands, feet during career over two decades, spanning amateur, open eras.

Played record 685 singles, doubles tournaments. Acrobatic volleyer made larger mark in doubles—12 majors over 15 years—especially with Billie Jean King, partner in seven, including open-era record five Wimbledons. Won 56 pro titles together. QF or better all major singles, doubles. Last obstacle to Margaret Court Grand Slam, lost U.S. F, 1970. U.S. Top Ten, 11 years, 1966–75, No. 2, 1970–71. World rank, Top Ten 11 years,

life, unprecedented penalty. Ban later rescinded but had ended exceptional career of Top Ten amateur. Cochell, Nos. 8–6–7–7 in U.S., 1947–50, was no longer ranked, though 1951 play warranted another Top Ten spot. A Californian, won Intercollegiate doubles for USC, 1951. B. May 18, 1922, Sacramento.

Courier, Jim

Chang, Michael

Diminutive (5-7), tenacious Michael Chang, RH American, with two-handed backhand. Tireless retriever. B. Feb. 22, 1972, Hoboken, N.J., of Chinese-American parentage, reared in Southern California. Electrified French, 1989, as youngest male champ, 17, and first American victor since 1955 (Tony Trabert). Beat favorite Ivan Lendl from 2-sets down 4th rd., Stefan Edberg in 5-set F. Lost longest major match (5:26) to Edberg, SF, U.S., 1992. Youngest to help U.S. win Davis Cup, 1990. In SF that year (3–2 over Austria at Vienna), won extraordinary deciding match from 2-sets down over Horst Skoff. Turned pro 1988. Eight career singles titles, $3,677,821 through 1992. Coached by brother, Carl, who played for U. of California, Berkeley.

Cochell, Earl

Earl Cochell, RH American, created stir at U.S., Forest Hills, 1951, behaving erratically, disruptively, verbally assaulted referee Ellsworth Davenport, other court officials, while losing 4th rd. to Gardnar Mulloy. USTA reacted by banning him for

25-match win streak. Through 1992, $4,846,451 prize money, nine singles, three doubles pro titles. Turned pro, 1988.

Cox, Mark

English LH, Cambridge graduate, Mark Cox has niche as first amateur to beat a pro in open competition. Defeated Pancho Gonzalez, Roy Emerson successive April afternoons, gained SF, British Hard Court Championships, Bournemouth 1968, inaugural open. B. July 5, 1943, Leicester. Davis Cup, helped Britain reach F, 1978.

Dalton, Judy

Judith Anne Marshall Tegart Dalton, Australian RH, b. Dec. 12, 1937, Melbourne. Tall, sturdy, excellent doubles player, won all majors—Australian, 1964–67–69–70; French, 1966; Wimbledon, 1969; U.S., 1970–71; five with Margaret Court. Wimbledon singles F, 1968. Helped Australia win 1970 Federation Cup. World rank Nos. 10–7–9, 1967–68–71.

Davidson, Owen

Owen Keir Davidson, LH Australian ladies man—mixed doubles ace. B. Oct. 4,

1943, Melbourne. Mixed Grand Slam, 1967, with Lesley Turner (Australian), Billie Jean King other three. Won eight major mixed plus two doubles: U.S., with John Newcombe, 1973; Australian, with Ken Rosewall, 1972. Wimbledon SF, 1966. Rookie pro, 1968, played, won first open match over amateur John Clifton, inaugural open, British Hard Courts.

Davidson, Sven

B. July 13, 1928, Boras, Sweden, Sven Viktor Davidson was first Swede to win majors: French singles, 1957, after losing 1955–56 F; Wimbledon doubles, 1958, with Ulf Schmidt. World rank No. 3, 1957, in Top Ten six straight years from 1953. Sweden's foremost prior to Bjorn Borg.

Drysdale, Cliff

Eric Clifford Drysdale, best South African male, RH, with two-handed backhand. B. May 26, 1941, Nelspruit, Transvaal. Slim 6-2, deceptive groundstroker, good volleyer. First to use double-handed stroke in U.S. F, 1965, lost to Manolo Santana. Career spanned amateur, open eras. Wimbledon, French SF, 1965–66, became pro, 1968, WCT "Handsome Eight." U.S. QF, 1968 (beat favorite Rod Laver). Australian QF, 1971. Davis Cup, 1962–67, 1974, 30–12 in singles, helped South Africa win Cup, 1974. Became U.S. citizen. Won five singles, seven doubles (including U.S., 1972), pro titles. World rank, Top Ten five times, 1965–66–68–69–71, No. 4, 1965.

Durr, Frankie

Francoise Durr Browning. Best Frenchwoman since Suzanne Lenglen; last to win her country's singles title, 1967. RH. Deceptive. Unorthodox grips, strokes, puffball serve made her seem harmless, but combative nature, pinpoint accuracy atoned for lack of power. B. Dec. 25, 1942, Algiers. Married Boyd Browning, 1975, lives in U.S. Turned pro, 1968, joining first female touring troupe (with Rosie Casals, Ann Jones, Billie Jean King). Excellent

volleyer, won 11 majors in doubles, mixed, five straight French doubles (1967–71), a record tied by Martina Navratilova, plus two U.S. World rank, Top Ten nine times, 1965–76, No. 3, 1967. Had 41 career pro titles (eight singles, 33 doubles).

Edmondson, Mark

Mark "Eddo" Edmondson, husky 6-1 Aussie RH, long-shot winner of men's major, Australian, 1976. B. June 24, 1954, Gosford. From obscurity (supported himself as janitor), unseeded, ranked No. 212 won homeland title. Beat all-timers, 2–1 seeds, Ken Rosewall, SF, John Newcombe, F. Thereafter, fine career. Wimbledon SF, 1982. Serve-and-volleyer, best at doubles: won French, 1985, Australian, 1980–81. Davis Cup, 1979–85, helping win 1983 Cup (4–0 doubles, 2–0 singles). Won six singles, 35 doubles pro titles, $1,449,486 prize money. Best World rank, No. 20, 1981.

Fibak, Wojtek

Best Polish man, Wojtek Fibak, RH, b. Aug. 30, 1952, Poznan. Trained as lawyer. Late starter, first Polish pro, 22, despite opposition of Polish Federation, solid 13-year career. Davis Cup. Agile 6-footer, superb volleyer, best at doubles, won 48 titles; also 15 singles titles; made $2,725,133. Lost Masters F, 1976. Wimbledon, U.S. QF, 1980; French QF, 1977–80. Best World rank, No. 13, 1977. Only Pole to win major: Australian doubles, 1978.

Garrison, Zina

Zina Lynna Garrison Jackson, American RH from Houston Public parks, won Olympic gold (doubles with Pam Shriver), bronze (singles), 1988. Gave Chris Evert her last defeat, QF U.S., 1989. First black woman in major F, Wimbledon, 1990, since Althea Gibson won there, 1958. Lost first pro F between two blacks, Largo, Fla., 1988, to childhood pal, Lori McNeil. Aggressive, quick, fine volleyer, b. Nov. 16, 1963, Houston. Married Willard Jackson,

1989. U.S. SF, 1988–89; QF, 1987–90. Wimbledon SF, 1985; QF, 1985–91. World rank, seven times Top Ten, 1983–84–85–87–88–89–90, No. 4, 1989. Turned pro, 1982. Through 1992, has 11 career singles, 16 doubles titles, $3,574,576.

Gerulaitis, Vitas

Vitas Kevin Gerulaitis, speedy, RH, lean 6-footer, determined attacker, only

won five of six singles helping U.S. keep Davis Cup (including incredible SF escape from Mark Edmondson at Australia, triple match point at 7–8, 0–40 in 3rd to win, 6–8, 14–16, 10–8, 6–3, 6–3). Also helped win Cup, 1978, played 1977–80. Lost sensational 1977 5-set Wimbledon SF, Bjorn Borg, 8–6. French SF, 1979; QF, 1982. Wimbledon QF, 1976–82. U.S. SF, 1978–81. Won Wimbledon doubles, 1975. Lost Masters F, 1979–81. Won 27 singles, nine doubles pro titles, $2,778,748. World rank, Top Ten, 1977–82, No. 4, 1977–79. B. July 26, 1954, Brooklyn, N.Y. Father, Vitas, champion of native Lithuania. Sister, Ruta, was on women's pro tour, No. 31, 1980; French QF, 1979.

Gimeno, Andres

Spanish RH, Andres Gimeno, oldest male winner French, 34, 1972. Best years as touring pro, from 1961, prior to open era. Graceful, slender 6-2, solid groundstrokes, good serve, competent volley. B. Aug. 3, 1937, Barcelona. Won seven singles, four doubles pro titles. Australian F, 1969; QF, 1959. French SF, 1968; QF, 1969. Davis Cup, five years, 1958–60, 1972–73, 17–4 singles. World rank, No. 10, 1969–70–72.

Gore, Arthur

Arthur William Charles Gore (unrelated to first champ, Spencer Gore). English RH, became Wimbledon's most enduring player, thrice singles victor (1901–08–09), oldest major male champ last year, 41½. First entered 1888, continued in singles through 1922, age 54 (oldest such), doubles through 1927, totaling 156 matches over record 35 years. Was most

Ex-rackets champ, not overly taken by tennis.

Gottfried, Brian

Brian Edward Gottfried, hard-working, energetic 6-foot RH. Sound groundstrokes, preferred serve-and-volley. B. Jan. 27, 1952, Baltimore, raised in Florida, All-American, Trinity (Tex.), 1971–72, lost F Intercollegiate singles, doubles, 1972. Davis Cup, 1976–77–78–80–82, with 1978 winner. QF or better all majors but Aussie, lost F French, 1977, to Guillermo Vilas. Heavy-duty 1977: won five of 27 tournaments, 109–23 record. U.S. Top Ten, 11 years, 1972–83, Nos. 2–3, 1977–78. World Top Ten, 1976–77–78, Nos. 10–5–7. With Raul Ramirez won 39 doubles, including Wimbledon. French, Italian. Won 25 singles, 54 doubles pro titles, $2,782,514.

Goold, St. Leger

Vere Thomas St. Leger Goold, Wimbledon F, 1879, RH. Personal finale, death in prison, was most ignominious for a champ. Won native, Irish, championship, 1879,, skilled volleyer. Played as "St. Leger" (pseudonyms not uncommon at time), lost F, Wimbledon, to John

Hartley before crowd of 1,100. In 1907, with French wife, Violet Girodin, convicted in French court of murdering Emma Levin, given life sentence. D. Sept. 8, 1909, Devils Island, French Guiana. B. Oct. 2, 1853, Waterford.

Graebner, Carole; Clark

American couple, Carole and Clark Graebner, only husband-wife to rank World Top Ten, play major F while married. Second couple ranked U.S. Top Ten same years, following Cookes, Sarah, Elwood (1940–45). RH. Teammates, Cleveland, World Team Tennis, 1974. However, during divorce proceedings he, player-coach, traded her to Pittsburgh for Laura DuPont, a unique divestiture.

Carole Caldwell Graebner, b. June 24, 1943, Pittsburgh, grew up in Southern California. Baseliner, good volleyer. U.S., lost F, 1964, to Maria Bueno, 6–1, 6–0 (equaling worst such beating, original F, 1884, Ellen Hansell over Laura Knight). World rank, Nos. 4–9, 1964–65. U.S. Top Ten, 1961–65, 1967, No. 3, 1964–65. Federation Cup, 1963–65–66, on 1963–65 winners (won 12 of 13 matches, 10 doubles). Wightman Cup, 1964–65–67–71, all winning years (2–2, singles; 2–0, doubles).

Clark Edward Graebner, b. Nov. 4, 1943, Cleveland, grew up there. Strong, 6-2, serve-and-volleyer. Lost U.S. F, 1967. World rank, Nos. 8–7, 1967–68. U.S. Top Ten, 1964, 1966–72, No. 2, 1968, No. 3, 1966–71. Davis Cup, 1965–68 (9–2, singles; 5–2, doubles), with 1968 winner. Won U.S. Indoor, 1971; Clay, 1966.

Gullickson, Tim; Tom

Identical twins, RH Timothy Edward, LH Thomas Robert Gullikson, b. Sept. 8, 1951, LaCrosse, Wis., Tom elder by minutes. Graduates, Northern Illinois. Lost Wimbledon F, 1983, first twins in major F since English Baddeleys, 1897. Sturdy, 5-11, 185, attackers, won 10 pro doubles titles

together. Tim, best World rank No. 18, 1978, won four singles, 16 doubles pro titles, $1,120,570. Tom, best World rank, No. 56, 1981, won one singles, 12 doubles pro titles, $889,042. Each won U.S. original, Newport, Tim, 1977, Tom, 1985.

Hadow, Frank

Patrick Francis Hadow, English RH, b. Jan. 24, 1855, Regents Park; d. June 29, 1946, Bridgwater. Loftiest Wimbledon champ: introduced the lob to thwart, bring down volleyer Spencer Gore, defender, second Wimbledon F, 1878. Lost no sets in tourney, played on holiday from his tea plantation in Ceylon. Didn't return to defend, may never have played again.

Heath, Rod

Wilfrid Rodney Heath, First Australian male champ, RH, won at 21 in hometown, Melbourne, 1905, conquering field of 17 at Warehousemen's Cricket Ground, beating Dr. A.H. Curtis' volleying with forehand drives. Won again, 1910. Davis Cup, 1911–12. After aviation duty, World War I, lost Wimbledon doubles F, 1919, with Randolph Lycett, SF victim in 1905 Aussie. B. June 15, 1884, Melbourne, d. there Oct. 6, 1936.

Hillyard, Blanche Bingley

Hardy, enthusiastic Englishwoman, Blanche Bingley Hillyard played first female Wimbledon, 1884, still around 29 years later, 1913, her last of 17. Won six, a record 14-year spread from 1886 to last, 1900, at 36, second-oldest female champ. RH, b. Nov. 3, 1863, Greenford, d. Aug. 6, 1946, Pulborough. At Wimbledon, 48–18, singles. Also won three Irish, two German. Her 1912 victim, rookie Bunny Ryan, made Hall of Fame.

Ivanisevic, Goran

Spindly yet powerful Croatian, Goran Ivanisevic, 6-4 LH. Huge server, streaky, strong strokes. B. Sept. 13, 1971, Split. Only man his country to play Wimbledon

F, 1992, losing to Andre Agassi. First in major F since fellow townsman, Nikki Pilic, French, 1973. Served Wimbledon record 206 aces, 1992; season total, 1,017, also record. Won Olympic bronzes, singles, doubles (with Goran Prpic), 1992. SF, Wimbledon, 1990. QF French, 1990–92, Australian, 1989. Won six singles, six doubles pro titles $2,908,258 career. World rank, Nos. 9–4, 1990–92.

U.S., 1937, lost first all-foreign F to Anita Lizana, Chile; French, 1939, won doubles with Simone Mathieu. Husky, good-natured baseliner with battering forehand. World rank, Top Ten, 1936–1939, No. 3, 1937.

Jordan, Barbara; Kathy

American sisters, Barbara and Kathy Jordan, King of Prussia, Pa. RH, All-Americans, Stanford, then winners major titles. Only sisters in major singles F (both in Australian) since Maud and Lillian Watson clashed for first Wimbledon title, 1884. Kathy higher rated.

Barbara Jordan, b. April 2, 1957, Milwaukee. Smooth-stroking serve-and-volleyer. Long-shot winner Australian, 1979 (unseeded, ranked No. 68), only American champ 1970s, beat favorite Hana Mandlikova (1980–87 champ), Sharon Walsh, won $10,000, high in career $135,534. Only pro singles title; won two doubles, plus major mixed, French, 1983. Best World rank, No. 37, 1980.

Katherine "KJ" Jordan, b. Dec. 3, 1959, Bryn Mawr, Pa. Willowy, 5-8, attacker, awkward-looking but effective stroker, extreme Western forehand, excellent volleyer. Won

Intercollegiate singles, doubles, 1979, then turned pro. QF or better all major singles, doubles. Wimbledon SF, 1984; QF, 1983, beating Chris Evert, 3rd rd., only time 19 years Evert failed to make SF. Lost Australian F, 1983, to Martina Navratilova. Won all major doubles: Australia, U.S., 1981; French, 1980; Wimbledon, 1980–85, latter, with Liz Smylie, ended Navratilova-Pam Shriver 109-match streak. Won one

Kelleher, Bob

Robert Joseph Kelleher progressive president USTA—right man at right time—shepherded U.S. into open era, 1968, overcoming past organizational objections to "open" concept, backed British revolt against ITF. B. March 5, 1913, New York. Graduate Williams, Harvard Law ('38). Longtime residents Los Angeles, appointed federal judge, 1970. U.S. Davis Cup captain, 1962–63, won 1963. Good player. Wife, Gracyn Wheeler Kelleher (1914–80), U.S. No. 5, 1941.

Kormoczi, Suzi

Hungary's best woman, Suzi Kormoczi was persistent baseliner, patient pursuing success. RH, b. Aug. 25, 1924, Budapest. First entered French, 1947, won 1958, oldest champ, almost 34. Oldest champ Italian, 1960. Wimbledon SF, 1958; French F, 1959; SF, 1956–61. World rank, Top Ten seven times 1953–55–56–58–59–60–61, No. 2, 1958.

Krishnan, Ramanathan; Ramesh

Father, son, Ramanathan and Ramesh Krishnan, possibly India's best. Unique, both helping homeland to Davis Cup finales, reaching QF, Wimbledon. RH, clever, deceptive. Born, raised in Madras.

Ramanathan Krishnan, b. April 11, 1932, World Top Ten, 1959–62, No. 6, 1961. Davis Cup 16 years, 1953–69, one of few to play 100 matches, led India to finale, 1966. Wimbledon SF, 1960–61.

Ramesh Krishnan, b. June 5, 1961, pro since 1976, best World rank, No. 24, 1980. QF, Wimbledon, 1986; U.S., 1981–87. Davis Cup 11 years, 1978–92; won five of singles, leading India to 1987 final. Won eight singles, one doubles pro titles, $1,235,548.

Langrishe, May

Mary Isabella Langrishe, original female champ—and youngest, 14, to win national title. Won her own, Irish, 1879 (the inaugural, Dublin's Fitzwilliam Club, first to welcome women). RH, b. Dec. 31, 1864, Ireland. Beat D. Meldon, 6–2, 0–6, 8–6, to rule field of seven. Also won first female doubles title, Northern Championship, Manchester, England, 1882, with older sister. D. Jan. 24, 1939.

Lawford, Herb

Herbert Fortescue Lawford, English RH innovator, Wimbledon champ, 1887. Introduced topspin—known as "Lawford Stroke"—around 1880, first of his six years in title round. B. May 15, 1851, Bayswater; d. April 20, 1925, Dess, Scotland.

Lizana, Anita

Chilean RH Anita Lizana, a significant blip—played U.S. Championships once, 1937, and won, over Pole Jadwiga Jedrzejowska, first all-foreign F. First Latin American to win a major. B. 1915, Santiago, married Ronald Ellis, settled in England. Wimbledon QF, 1936 (led champ Helen Jacobs, 4–2, 30–0 in 3rd) and 1937. Solid groundstroker with good passing shots, drop shot, admirable footwork. World rank, Nos. 8–1, 1936–37.

Long, Thelma

Thelma Dorothy Coyne Long, sturdy Australian RH, b. Oct. 14, 1918, Sydney. Had one of longest careers, fine volleyer, winning first of record 12 Australian doubles, 1936, last, 1958. Also won singles, 1952–54, mixed four times; French mixed, 1956—total 19 majors. World rank, No. 7, 1952.

Main, Lorne

Lorne Garnet Main, inadvertent father of rare two-way, two-handed style, both forehand and backhand. Foremost proponent today, Monica Seles. "Seemed natural to me as a boy since I was a baseball switch-hitter." Canadian RH, 5-8, 145, b. July 9, 1930, Vancouver. Davis Cup, 1949–55, No. 1, Canada, 1951–54. Biggest title, Monte Carlo, 1954.

Maleeva, Manuela; Katerina; Magdalena

Internationally most exceptional trio of sisters ever, clearly greatest in Bulgaria annals. All three—baselining RH with two-handed backhands, born and brought up in Sofia—have played for Bulgarian in Federation Cup, Olympics. Mother, Yulia Berberian, champion of Bulgaria nine years; father, Gyorgy Maleev, Olympic basketball player, 1956. Unique accomplishments: Katerina, Manuela in World Top Ten together, 1990, have been in QF every major, together at French, 1990, only sisters to do so. Manuela's 1992 U.S. QF win over Maggie (winner over Martina Navratilova) first such sisterly encounter since 1897 champ Juliette Atkinson beat sibling, Kathleen, SF. Manuela, Katerina in 1988 U.S. QF, first sisters there since Atkinsons. Manuela in U.S. QF five times, 1990 by beating Navratilova.

Manuela Maleeva Fragniere, b. Feb. 14, 1967. Won rain-delayed Italian, 1984, three wins last day, F over Chris Evert. Won Olympic bronze, singles, 1988. Married Swiss tennis coach Francois Fragniere, 1987, became a citizen, played Federation Cup, 1992 Olympics for Switzerland.

Through 1992 has 16 career singles, three doubles titles, $2,574,032. World rank, Top Ten nine straight years from 1984, No. 6, 1984–88.

Katerina Maleeva, b. May 7, 1969, won Japan Open, 1987, has 11 career singles, two doubles titles, $1,653,319. Best World rank, No. 6, 1990.

Magdalena "Maggie" Maleeva, B. April

slick racket-handling attacker. Won four major singles (Australian, 1980–87; U.S., 1985; French, 1981), one doubles (U.S., 1989). Rare feat, beat Chris Evert, Martina Navratilova in succession to win U.S. Stopped Navratilova 56-match streak to win Aussie, 1987. Lost F, Wimbledon, 1981–86; U.S., 1980–82. Led Czechoslovakia to three Federation Cups, 1983–84–85. Retired, 1990, with 23 singles, six doubles titles, $ 3,340,959, World rank, Top Ten seven times 1980–81–82–84–85–86–87, No. 3, 1984–85.

Maskell, Daniel

England's gracious, informed Voice of Wimbledon, first on radio, then TV, Dan Maskell was a national auditory treasure. Pre-commentary career: topflight teaching pro, RH, All England club, coached British Davis Cup winners, 1933–36, won 16 British Pro singles between 1928 and 1950. Awarded OBE for wartime service rehabilitating wounded airmen. B. April 11, 1908; d. Dec. 12, 1992.

Mathieu, Simone Passemard

Following Suzanne Lenglen, Simone Passemard Mathieu was best French woman prior to World War II. b. Jan. 11,

1908, Neuilly-sur-Seine; d. Jan. 7, 1980, Paris. Married Rene Mathieu, 1925. Steady, accurate, maintained consistently high level. Won French, 1938–39, after losing F, 1932–33–36–37. Wimbledon SF, 1930–31–32–34–36–37; QF, 1933–35–38–39. U.S. QF, 1938. Also won nine major doubles (Wimbledon, 1933–34–37, six French, 1933–34–36–37–38–39, record until Martina Navratilova's seven). World

only brothers to rank together U.S. Top Ten, 1983 (Gene higher, 4–8), World Top Fifteen, 1981 (Gene higher, 7–14), and make Wimbledon QF open era. Family total, 65 pro singles, doubles titles. Stanford grads, All-Americans.

Alexander "Sandy" Meyer, b. April 5, 1952, Flushing, N.Y., sleek 5-10 attacker, excellent volleyer, won Intercollegiate singles, 1973, doubles, 1972–73. Wimbledon SF, 1973 (rookie pro beat top seed Ilie Nastase, 4th rd., huge upset); QF, 1978–83. Won Wimbledon doubles, 1975. Best World rank, No. 14, 1981. Won 11 singles, 24 doubles pro titles, $1,057,783.

Eugene Mayer, b. April 11, 1956, New York, slender 6-footer, rare unorthodox style: both-handed backhand, forehand. Solid groundstroker, good volleyer. Davis Cup, 1982–83, helped win 1982 (3–1, singles). Wimbledon QF, 1980–82; U.S. QF, 1982. World rank, Top Ten four straight years from 1980, No. 4, 1980, winning five titles. Won 14 singles, 16 doubles pro titles, $1,381,562.

McGrath, Viv

Vivian "Viv" McGrath, pronounced "McGraw," Australian original: RH, introduced two-handed backhand to international game, considered strongest pre-war shot among Aussies. B. Feb. 17, 1916, Mudgee; d. 1978, Buradee. Called "Wonder Boy," at 16, beat World No. 1 Ellie Vines, QF, Australian. Won that title, 1937, over another rising double-hander, Jack Bromwich. Also Australian SF, 1934–35–39–40; QF, 1932–36–38. Wimbledon QF, 1935–37. Youngest Aussie Davis Cupper, 1933, 4–4 singles as team lost European Zone F, 3–2, at Britain, eventual winner. World rank, Nos. 8–10, 1935–36. Unable to regain form after army service in war.

Metreveli, Alexander

Foremost Soviet man, Alexander Metreveli gained prominence open era, beating Pancho Gonzalez, Wimbledon, 1968. Georgian RH, b. Feb. 11, 1944, Tblisi. Atypical Soviet, serve-and-volleyer, poised 5-10. Only USSR male in major F, lost Wimbledon, 1973. Also, with Olga Morozova, lost F Wimbledon mixed, 1968–70. In career overlapping amateur, open eras, QF or better all majors. Davis Cup standout, 14 years, spanning 1963 to 1980, one of select few to have played 100 matches or more (56–14, singles; 24–11, doubles). Best World rank, No. 9, 1974. Won eight singles, two doubles pro titles.

Molesworth, Mall

Margaret "Mall" Mutch Molesworth, first Australian women's champ. RH, b. 1894, Brisbane; d. July 9, 1985. Might have exceeded two singles, 1922–23; three doubles, 1930–33–34, had Championships welcomed women prior to 1922, Sydney. Won first title at 27, with complete game, feared serve. Remained factor for some time: lost F, 1934 to Joan Hartigan.

Morozova, Olga

Preeminent Soviet woman, Olga Morozova, RH, b. Feb. 22, 1949, Moscow. Unusual Soviet, preferred serve-and-volley. Quick, athletic, 5-7. Only USSR female in Wimbledon F, 1974, (beat defender Billie Jean King). QF or better all majors. Won 15 singles, 11 doubles pro titles. World rank, Top Ten, four straight years from 1973, No. 4, 1974. Federation Cup. First Soviet winner of a U.S. title—Indoor doubles, 1973, with compatriot Marina Kroshina.

Mottram, Tony; Joy; Buster; Linda

Internationalist English family: father, Tony; mother, Joy; son, Buster; daughter, Linda. All RH.

Anthony John Mottram, b. June 8, 1920, Coventry, Davis Cup, 1947–1955 (25–13, singles; 11–7, doubles). Wimbledon QF, 1948; lost doubles F, 1947. Best Brit immediate post-war.

Joy Gannon Mottram, b. March 21, 1928, Enfield. Wightman Cup, 1947–48–51–52. Won German, 1954. Wimbledon 3rd rd., 1946–47–49. French QF, 1952.

Christopher John "Buster" Mottram, b. April 25, 1955, Kingston, lanky 6-3, free-swinging big hitter. Wimbledon 4th rd., 1982; French 4th rd., 1977. High point, 1978, led Britain to first Davis Cup finale since 1937 (8–2, singles; 1–0, doubles). Also played, 1975–76, 1979–83 (27–8, singles; 4–2, doubles). Won two singles, five doubles pro titles, about $500,000. Best World rank, No. 19, 1982.

Linda Mottram, b. May 17, 1957, Wimbledon. Played Wimbledon six straight years from 1974, lost 3rd rd., 1975. Won German Indoor, 1976.

Noah, Yannick

Yannick Simone Camille Noah, b. May 18, 1960, Sedan France. Foremost Frenchman in accomplishment, popularity since Four Musketeers, attained all-time renown with countrymen winning French, 1983 (over Mats Wilander), first male title for Frenchman since Marcel Bernard, 1945. Imposing physical specimen, 6-4,

190, RH. Led French (6–2, singles; 2–2 doubles) to first Davis Cup F in 49 years, 1982, lost to U.S.; as non-playing captain to first Cup in 59 years, 3–1 over U.S., 1991. Offspring Cameroonian father, French mother, discovered in Yaounde, Cameroon, 1971, recommended to French Federation for development by touring Arthur Ashe. Appealing net-rushing gambler, acrobatic volleyer, big server. World

When she defected to the U.S. in 1982, she became the initial Chinese pro. Slim, 5-8, RH, a serve-and-volleyer. B. April 16, 1963, Chengdu, No. 1 Peoples Republic. Federation Cup, 1981–82. Best World rank, No. 58, 1987. High point, five wins at Wimbledon, 1985, qualifying, reaching 3rd rd. Won one pro title, doubles, $213,220. U.S. citizen, 1989.

O'Hara Wood, Arthur; Pat

Australian brothers, Arthur and Pat O'Hara Wood, RH, both winners homeland's singles title, only brothers to do so. First brothers to win majors since Dohertys, 1906, Wimbledon.

Dr. Arthur O'Hara Wood, killed, World War I, Australian army, Melbourne physician with all-round game. Defeated future Hall of Famer Gerald Patterson, 1914 F, then went to war.

Patrick O'Hara Wood also served, Aussie army, survived to win Australian twice, 1920–23, plus four Aussie doubles, Wimbledon doubles and, with Suzanne Lenglen, mixed, 1922. Short, quick, consistent, effortless strokemaker. Davis Cup, 1922–24, helped Australia gain F both

years. B. April 30, 1891. Melbourne; d. there, Dec. 3, 1961. World rank No. 7, 1922. Wife, Meryl Wood, won Australian doubles, 1926–27.

Okker, Tom

Flying Dutchman Tom Samuel Okker, Netherlands' finest male. RH, b. Feb. 22, 1944, Amsterdam. Slight (5-9, 145), speedy, excellent volleyer, one of five men 1968 and 1973, No. 5, 1968–69. Davis Cup, 11 years between 1964 and 1981.

O'Neil, Chris

Six-foot Aussie Chris O'Neil, RH, longest shot to win women's major, Australian, 1978. Unseeded, ranked No. 111, she went through weak field, beat No. 68 Betsy Nagelsen in F, 6–3, 7–6, winning $6000. Only pro title. B. March 19, 1956, Newcastle, serve-and-volleyer. Highest World rank, No. 80, 1978.

Orantes, Manolo

Manuel "Manolo" Orantes, stocky, prestidigitating, gracious Spanish LH, master of spin and placement. Won U.S., 1975, sensationally, beating ex-champ Ilie Nastase, 2–1 seeds Guillermo Vilas, defender Jimmy Connors, in succession. Great SF comeback over Vilas: 4–6, 1–6, 6–2, 7–5, 6–4, from 0–5, three match points, then 5–1, two match points 4th. B. Feb. 6, 1949, Granada. Davis Cup, 14 years, helped Spain to finale, 1967, Career, 16 years, spanned amateur, open eras. Won 32 singles, 24 doubles pro titles, including Masters, 1976, U.S. Pro, 1977–78, $1,338,601. World rank, Top Ten 1975–77, No. 4, 1976.

Palfrey, Polly; Lee; Mianne; Sarah; Joey

Five remarkable Palfrey sisters—Joey, Lee, Mianne, Polly, Sarah—all won U.S. junior titles. Sarah won 16 majors, made the Hall of Fame. In 1945, with second husband, Elwood Cooke, permitted to enter men's doubles Tri-State tourney, Cincinnati, because of wartime shortage of male players, lost F to Hal Surface-Bill Talbert. Sisters, RH, b., Boston, except Sarah, Sharon, Mass.

Margaret Germaine "Polly" Palfrey Woodrow, b. Oct. 7, 1906. Won one: 18-doubles, 1924, with Fanny Curtis.

Elizabeth Howland "Lee" Palfrey Fullerton, b. Jan. 14, 1909; d. Jan. 5, 1987. Won one: 18-Indoor doubles, 1926, with Midge Morrill.

Mary Ann "Mianne" Palfrey Dexter, b. March 6, 1911. Won seven: 18-Indoor singles, 1929: 18-doubles, 1926–28–29, with sister Sarah; 18-Indoor doubles, 1927–28–29, with Sarah. Also won adult U.S. Indoor singles, 1930.

Sarah Hammond Palfrey Fabyan Cooke Danzig, b. Sept. 18, 1912. Won 13: 18-singles, 1928–29–30; 18-Indoor singles, 1927–28–29–30; six doubles with Joey.

Joanna "Joey" Oakes Palfrey Brown, b. Jan. 30, 1915. Won one: 18-Indoor doubles, 1930, with Sarah.

Panatta, Adriano

Best Italian open era, Adriano Panatta, RH, b. July 9, 1950, Rome. Slick 6-foot god at Il Foro Italico, Rome, responding winningly to feverish chants, "AD-REE-ANNO!" Strong serve, whipping forehand, called "Goaltender" for brilliant volleying saves. Spectacular 1976: won Italian, French, 45–15 match record, led Italy to lone Davis Cup (10–1, singles: 5–1 doubles). Also to F, 1977–79–80. Cup record, 1970–83; 37–26, singles; 27–10, doubles,

one of few to play 100 matches. Match point escapes in big titles, 1976: 11, vs. Kim Warwick, Italian; one, Pavel Hutka, French. Best World rank, No. 7, 1976. Won 10 singles, 18 doubles pro titles, $776,187. Younger brother, Claudio Panatta (b. Feb. 2, 1960, Rome) played Davis Cup, pro tour.

Petra, Yvon

Yvon Francoise Marie Petra, French RH, at 6-5 tallest winner major singles, Wimbledon, 1946, a surprise, rising above 5th seed to beat 3rd Geoff Brown. B. March 8, 1916, Cholun, IndoChina, d. Sept. 12, 1984, Paris. Won French doubles twice, 1938–46. Davis Cup, 1937–38–39–46–47, led France to SF, 1946. Turned pro, 1948. Strong server, last man to win a major Wimbledon in long trousers. World rank, No. 4, 1946.

Pilic, Nikki

Nikola "Nikki" Pilic, slim 6-3 LH, Yugoslavia's best of post-war, country's first pro athlete, 1968, with WCT "Handsome Eight." Cause of famous Wimbledon boycott, 1973: most ATP colleagues walked out, protesting Wimbledon honoring his suspension by Yugoslav Federation. Solidarity on Pilic's behalf established year-old union. B. Aug. 27, 1939, Split. Big serve, forehand. French F, 1973 (second oldest finalist), QF, 1967. Wimbledon SF, 1967. U.S. QF, 1973. Won U.S. doubles, 1970. World rank, No. 7, 1967. Davis Cup 11 years, spanning 1961 to 1977. Won four singles, seven doubles pro titles. Became German citizen, captain Davis Cup team, winner 1988–89.

Rahim, Haroon

Foremost player of Pakistan, Haroon Rahim, RH, b. Nov. 12, 1949, Lahore, one of 14 children. Quick, fine volleying All-American, Intercollegiate doubles champ, UCLA, 1971. Youngest ever Davis Cupper, 15 years, 109 days, 1965, against Vietnam (beat Vo Van Bay, 6–1 in 5th). Beat Tom Gorman in closest match ever, 6–7 (3–5),

7–6 (5–1), 7–6 (5–4), Pennsylvania Grass, 1970. Won one singles, six doubles pro titles. Best World rank, No. 49, 1976.

Ramirez, Raul

Raul Carlos Ramirez, Mexico's premier player open era, got tennis education in U.S. All-American, USC, combined with Brian Gottfried in superb doubles team (39 titles). RH, b. June 20, 1953, Ensenada.

World Top Ten, 1976–77–78, Nos. 5–8–8. Won 17 singles, 62 doubles pro titles, $2,213,671.

Redl, Hans

Austrian Hans Redl, RH (subsequently only-hander) of extraordinary grit. B. Jan. 19, 1914, Vienna. Davis Cup, Austria, 1937, then Germany, 1938–39, when his country absorbed. Lost left arm, World War II, fighting with German army in Russia. Amazingly resumed play at upper level, Davis Cup, Austria, 1948–55. Reached 4th rd. Wimbledon, 1947. Because of him, rules amended to permit one-armed players to make service toss with racket.

Richards, Renée

American LH, 6–1, ophthalmological surgeon, b. Richard Raskind, Aug. 19, 1934, New York. Graduate Yale, Rochester Medical. Unique: Played U.S. as amateur male (1955–56–57–60), pro female (1977–81). Lost F U.S. doubles, 1977, with Bettyann Stuart. Strong server, clever tactician. Following 1975 sex change surgery, sought to play women's pro tour, faced opposition, resorted to courts of law to gain entry. New York Supreme Court ruling, August 1977, cleared way to enter

WTA, USTA events. Age 43, lost 1st rd., U.S., 1977, to Wimbledon champ Virginia Wade, reached 3rd rd., 1979, lost to Chris Evert. Reasonable pro career, five years, winning one pro singles title. Returned to medicine. Best World rank, No. 22, 1977.

Richey, Nancy; Cliff

American brother, sister, Nancy and Cliff Richey, RH, out of San Angelo, T___ ___

___, ____ ___, b. Aug. 23, 1942, San Angelo, Tex. Powerful baseliner despite slight physique (5–6, 130), but good volleyer, winning doubles, Australian, Wimbledon, 1966; U.S., 1965–66. Best on clay, winning first French Open, 1968, over Ann Jones, record six straight U.S. Clay Courts (33 straight matches) from 1963. Tough on grass, too, winning Australian, 1967, making U.S. F, 1966–69; SF, 1968; QF, 1964–65–66–69. U.S. Top Ten, 16 years, 1960–76. World Top Ten, 11 years spanning 1963 to 1975, No. 3, 1968–72; No. 4, 1967–69–70. Played for eight Wightman Cup winners plus Federation Cup winner, 1969. One of greatest comebacks, rebounded from 1–5, match point, 2nd set, to win 12 straight games, beat Billie Jean King, 4–6, 7–5, 6–0, SF New York International, 1968.

George Clifford Richey, Jr., b. Dec. 31, 1946, San Angelo, Tex. Quick, stocky (5-7, 170), scrappy, hard worker, strong groundstroker, good volleyer. Led U.S. to 1970 Davis Cup over Germany. Also played 1966–67. Biggest season, 1970, won eight titles (including U.S. Clay), 93–19 record, SF, French, US; World rank, No. 7. Took U.S. No. 1 rank by narrowest margin: 1-point victory—beating No. 2 Stan Smith in

5–4 5th set tie-breaker, Pacific Coast SF—decided order of rank.

Ruzici, Virginia

Romania's standout woman, Virginia Ruzici, b. Jan. 31, 1955, Cimpa-Turzil, grew up in Bucharest. Lissome, 5-8, RH, baseliner with lusty forehand. Won French singles, doubles, 1978. QF or better all majors. Won U.S. Clay, 1982. Federation Cup. Over 13-year career won 14 singles, eight doubles pro titles, $1,184,228. Best World rank, No. 11, 1980; 12, 1978–81–82.

Sabatini, Gabriela

Argentinean Gabriela Sabatini, RH, finest Latin American female since Maria Bueno. Tall, 5-9, dark-haired beauty, the "Divine Argentine." Powerful topspin, groundstroker, showed attacking qualities to win U.S., 1990, over defender Steffi Graf, reach Wimbledon F, 1991. B. May 16, 1970, Buenos Aires, lives in Florida, where spent formative years. Won Olympic silver, singles, 1988, runner-up to Graf. First impact at 14: three-match day at rain-compressed Hilton Head, beat Pam Shriver, Manuela Maleeva, lost F, Chris Evert. Won Italian, 1988–89–91–92. SF all majors. Painful loss to Graf, Wimbledon F, 1990, led 3rd set, 6–5, 30–15. Australian SF, 1992, QF, 1991. French SF, 1985–87–89–91–92. Wimbledon SF, 1986–90–92, QF, 1987. U.S. F, 1988; SF, 1989; QF, 1987–91–92. World rank, Top Ten, 1986–92, No. 3, 1988–89–91. Won 25 singles, 12 doubles pro titles, $6,056,672.

Sampras, Pete

Pete Sampras, fluid-stroking California RH, 6-footer with all-court game, basically an attacker, b. Aug. 12, 1971, Washington, D.C., grew up in Palos Verdes, lives in Tampa, Fla. Broke century-old record, winning U.S., 1990, younger 19 than Oliver Campbell, champ 1890. In World rank rose from No. 81 to No. 5 that year, Nos. 6–3, 1991–92. Painful Davis Cup debut, 1991: lost both singles (Henri Leconte, Guy Forget) in 3–1 F loss to France, but helped U.S. win, 1992, in doubles role. French QF, Wimbledon SF, U.S. F, 1992. First to win Grand Slam Cup, with $2 million prize 1990. Won ATP title, 1991. Through 1992, 12 career titles, $6,557,225. Turned pro 1988. Sister, Stella, is pro on female circuit.

Sanchez, Arantxa; Emilio; Javier

Probably most accomplished family combination ever at uppermost level: two brothers, one sister, RH from Barcelona. All represented Spain, Davis/Federation Cup, two in Olympics.

Arantxa Sanchez Vicario, b. Dec. 18, 1971, Barcelona. Best Spanish woman in more than half-century. Peppery, strong-legged 5-5, with two-fisted backhand. Youngest French champ, 17, 1989 (until Monica Seles, 1990), beating Steffi Graf in F. U.S. F, 1992; SF, 1990. French F, 1991; SF, 1992. Led Spain to first Federation Cup, 1991. Won Olympic bronze (singles), silver (doubles), 1992. Speedy, marvelous retriever. Strong at doubles, improving volley, won Australian, 1992. Through 1992 had eight career singles, 18 doubles pro titles, $3,436,112. World rank, Nos. 5–7–5–4 from 1989. Sister, Marisa, played at Pepperdine.

Emilio Sanchez, quick, smooth-stroking 5-10, b. May 29, 1965, Madrid. Won Italian, 1991. Excellent at doubles. With Sergio Casal won U.S., 1988; Italian and French, 1990; Olympic silver medal, 1988. Davis Cupper since 1984. Through 1992 had 15 career singles, 42 doubles (36 with Casal, three with Javier), $3,948,131. Best World rank, No. 8, 1990.

Javier Sanchez, speedy, 5-10, b. Feb. 1, 1968, Pamplona. Consistent winner singles, doubles. Through 1992, had two career singles titles, 15 doubles (three with Emilio), $1,368,485 prize money. Davis Cup, 1989. Best World rank, No. 32 in 1991.

Sawamatsu, Kazuko; Junko

Sisters, Kazuko, Junko Sawamatsu, RH, first Japanese women to make mark pro tour. Federation Cup together, 1970–71. Kazuko only Japanese woman to win major, Wimbledon doubles, 1975. Both made QF, Australian, Junko, 1973, Kazuko, 1975.

Kazuko Sawamatsu, sturdy 5-7, b. Jan. 5, 1951, Nishinomiya. Solid groundstroker,

Nishinomiya. Daughter, Naoko Sawamatsu (RH with two-handed backhand, b. March 23, 1973, Nishinomiya), is on pro tour, best World rank, No. 24, 1992.

Seles, Monica

Yugoslav Monica Seles, LH, all-time prodigy, unique World No. 1 (1991–92), with both-handed groundstrokes both sides. B. Dec. 2, 1973, Novy Sad, resides Sarasota, Fla., spent formative years in Florida. Tall, 5-11, all-out slugger, tremendous power from baseline. First to win three majors successive years (Australian, French, U.S., 1991–92) since Margaret Court (three and four, 1969–70). Lost Wimbledon F, 1992, to Steffi Graf. Fourth woman in all major F one year. Won first major, French, 1990, over Graf, stopped Graf's 66-match streak, Berlin F, 1990. Youngest to hold seven majors. Through 1992, 30 career singles, four doubles titles (first, Houston, over Chris Evert, 1989), $6,971,393. Other World rank, Nos. 6–2, 1989–90. She was target of a shocking attack by a knife-wielding fan on April 30, 1993, at the Citizen Cup tournament in Hamburg, Germany. While sitting during a changeover in her quarterfinal match against Magdalena Maleeva of Bulgaria, a

deranged German, Gunter Parche, stabbed her in the back with a nine-inch boning knife. While not seriously injured, she was expected to be out of tournament competition for several months.

Shimidzu, Zenzo

Zenzo "Shimmy" Shimidzu, first Japanese of note, attained highest male level. B. March 25, 1891, Tokyo; d. April 19

entered F vs. U.S., Forest Hills; astoundingly came within two points, 3rd set, of beating Tilden, losing, 5–7, 4–6, 7–5, 6–2, 6–1. Davis Cup also, 1923–24–25–27, not with fortune of 1921. World rank, Nos. 9–4, 1920–21.

Shriver, Pam

Pamela Howard "Pam" Shriver, RH American, extraordinary early splash in singles, but her place in history is in doubles, including Olympic gold medal (alongside Zina Garrison), 1988. Joined with Martina Navratilova as all-time team: between 1981–87 they won record 20 majors (tying Louise Brough-Margaret duPont), Grand Slam in 1984, 79 titles altogether. Their record 109-match win streak ended 1985. B. July 4, 1962, Baltimore, grew up in Lutherville, Md. Rangy 6-footer, expert serve-and-volleyer, fine smash, lob. As amateur, went to F, first U.S., 1978. First to do so since Anita Lizana, champ, 1937. Was youngest finalist at 16 years, 2 months. Only amateur U.S. female finalist open era. Wimbledon SF, 1981–87–88. U.S. SF, 1982–83; QF, 1980–84–85–86–87. Turned pro, 1979. Through 1992, won $4,870,516, 129 titles (21 singles, 108 doubles), one of five women to win more than 100 overall. U.S. Top Tenner 12 times between

1978–92, No. 3, 1984–88. World rank, Top Ten nine times, 1980–88, No. 4, 1983–84–85–87.

Sirola, Orlando

Gaunt, towering Italian RH Orlando Sirola was tallest (6-6) to play in Davis Cup finale (1960–61), major finals (won French doubles, 1959, lost Wimbledon, 1956, with Nicola Pietrangeli). B. April 30, 1928, Fiume. Self-taught, late starter, 1950. Huge serve, overhead, good volleyer, streaky. Joined Cup team, 1953, with Pietrangeli, 1955, playing, winning as pair most doubles in Cup history (34–8) through 1963. Among most active Cuppers: 22–25, singles; 35–8, doubles. High point, 1960 SF, 3–2 comeback from 0–2 over U.S.: won pivotal doubles, 13–11, 4th, over Butch Buchholz-Chuck McKinley, decider in singles over Barry MacKay, 9–7, 6–3, 8–6.

Stove, Betty

Netherlands' Betty Flippina Stove, 6-foot RH, her country's foremost woman since 1920s. Powerful server, fine volleyer, erratic. Only Hollander in Wimbledon F, 1977 (lost to Virginia Wade), and won most major doubles (nine): three U.S., 1972, with Francoise Durr; 1977, with Martina Navratilova; 1979, with Wendy Turnbull; Wimbledon, French, 1972, with Billie Jean King. Plus two U.S., Wimbledon mixed, with Frew McMillan. Rarity: lost all three Wimbledon F, 1977. B. June 24, 1945, Rotterdam. Federation Cup 11 straight years, from 1966: 20–4, singles; 20–8, doubles. World rank, Nos. 7–8–7, 1976–77–78.

Suk/Sukova, Vera; Helena; Cyril

Great name in Czechoslovak game. Mother, Vera; son, Cyril; daughter, Helena, all RH champions played for country in Federation/Davis Cup. Only mother, daughter in major singles F, World Top Ten. Father, Cyril Suk, was president Czechoslovak Federation.

Vera Puzejova Sukova, b. June 13, 1931, Uherske Hradiste; d. May 13, 1982, Prague. Married Suk, 1961. Unimpressive serve, strokes, but strong, persistent, competitive. Stolid baseliner, fine passing shots: French SF, 1957, losing to champ Shirley Bloomer, 6–4, 3rd; QF, 1959–60–63–64. Unseeded, had stunning Wimbledon, 1962, beat 6–2–3 seeds—defender Angela Mortimer, Darlene Hard, ex-champ Maria Bueno—lost F, Karen Susman. Also QF, U.S., 1962. World rank, Nos. 6–5–10, 1957–62–63. Was Czechoslovak national coach, early tutor of Martina Navratilova.

Helena Sukova, b. Feb. 23, 1965, Prague. At 6-2 tallest ever female player of consequence, standout serve-and-volleyer, possessing sound groundies. QF or better, all majors. Ended Navratilova's record 74-match streak, Grand Slam bid, SF, Australian, 1984, lost F, Chris Evert. Also Australian, 1989, lost F, Steffi Graf. Beat Evert, U.S. SF, 1986, LF to Navratilova. Wimbledon QF, 1985–88. French SF, 1986; QF, 1988. U.S. SF, 1987; QF, 1984–85–89. World rank, Top Ten, 1984–89, No. 5, 1985. Superior at doubles, won eight majors: Wimbledon, 1987, with Claudia Kohde Kilsch; 1989–90, with Jana Novotna; Australian, 1990–92, with Novotna, Arantxa Sanchez Vicario; French, 1990, with Novotna; U.S., 1985, with Kohde Kilsch. Also French mixed, 1991, with Suk, only brother-sister to win. Missed Grand Slam with Novotna, lost U.S. F to Navratilova-Gigi Fernandez. Through 1992, won 10 singles, 53 doubles pro titles, $4,343,033 prize money. Federation Cup mainstay, helping Czechoslovakia win, 1983–84–85–88.

Cyril Suk, b. Jan. 19, 1967, Prague. Quick, clever, 5–11, singles (best World rank, No. 184, 1988) overshadowed by doubles expertise. Through 1992, $532,706 prize money. Davis Cup, 1992.

Tapscott, Billie

South African Ruth Daphne "Billie" Tapscott, b. May 31, 1903, Kimberly; d.

1970. Emancipated female legs, shocked Wimbledon, 1929, appearing without stockings. "It's just the way we do it at home." With bared gams, made QF, probably inspired Joan Austin Lycett, first bold peeler of hose for Centre Court match, 1931, as stockings went way of corsets. RH, won South African, 1930. Married South African player Collin John James Robbins, 1930.

‾‾ ‾ ‾

play tennis. Davis Cup, 1959–77, led way for protégé Ilie Nastase. Together carried Romania to three F, all lost to U.S.: 1969–71–72, Sixth all-time Cup matches played, 109 (40–28, singles: 30–11, doubles). Highest World rank No. 72, 1974 (best years pre-computer). Won two singles, 27 doubles pro titles.

Ulrich, Einer; Torben; Jorgen

Davis Cup workhorses for Denmark. Father, Einer, two sons, Torben and Jorgen Ulrich all b. in Copenhagen, played 232 Cup matches between 1924 and 1978.

Einer Ulrich, RH, b. May 6, 1896. Cup, 1924–38: 23–23, singles: 16–12, doubles.

Torben Ulrich, free-spirited, bearded LH, b. Oct. 4, 1928; family's most promi-nent, strong serve, delicate touch. Career spanned amateur, open eras, 4th rd. French, 1959; 3rd rd., U.S., 1969, at 40. Cup, 1948–61, 1964–68, 1978, one of few in over 100 matches: 31–35, singles; 15–21, doubles. Oldest of all Cuppers, 48 years, 11 months, 1978.

Jorgen Ulrich, RH. b. Aug. 21, 1935. Cup, 1955, 1958–71: 17–21, singles: 8–11

ney (15 entered), 1884. Also won Irish, 1884–85; Welsh, 1887. RH, b. Oct. 9, 1864, Harrow; died June 6, 1946, Charmouth.

Weir, Reginald

Racial pioneer, New York physician, Dr. Reginald S. Weir, overcame early dis-crimination to win U.S. titles. Though Althea Gibson received much attention entering Forest Hills, 1950, Weir RH, was first black to play national championship sanctioned by USTA: U.S. Indoor, 1948, New York, 7th Regt. Armory. Also first to win U.S. title, Senior singles, 1956–57–59 (doubles, 1961–62), at 7th Regt., gratifying turnaround where he'd been refused entry U.S. Junior Indoor, 1929. Beat Ed Tarangioli, 5–7, 6–3, 6–1, first title. B. 1911; d. Aug. 21, 1987, Fairlawn, N.J.

Davis Cup: The first U.S. team comprised (from left) Malcolm Whitman, Dwight Davis and Holcombe Ward. • *USTA*

11: TENNIS LINGO

ADVANTAGE: The point following deuce. The umpire generally calls the same of the player holding advantage (example, "Advantage Connors") whether he is server or receiver. Also called ad in informal play; ad-in is the score called when the server has the advantage; ad-out refers to the advantage being held by the receiver; ad-court refers to the left court, from which the advantage is always played.

AGE-GROUP TENNIS: Diaper-to-doomsday competition is available in the U.S., where sectional and national championships are determined for males and females of practically every age. It starts with the 14s (for those 14 years and under), and continues through the 16s and 18s. After that come the adult tournaments. Then, for older adults, the 30s, 35s, 40s, 50s, 55s, 60s, 65s. Then, the "Super Seniors"—70s, 75s, 80s, 85s. These are contested on four surfaces; grass, clay, hard, indoor.

ALL: The score is even. It can be 15–all, 30–all in a game; or 2–all, 3–all in set score.

ALLEY; A 4½-foot-wide addition to the singles court on both sides in order to provide

no monetary reward involved, although some living expenses may be reimbursed. Prior to the advent of open tennis and the prize-money boom in 1968, the word was much abused. Amateurs at top tournaments were frequently referred to as "Shamateurs": players who accepted compensation under the well-known table and did not take checks or report their earnings as income. Alleged amateurs at the top sometimes earned more than the few outright touring professionals. "Pro" was considered a dirty word in most tennis circles until open tennis and a flood of prize money made the profession respectable. There was a semantic problem with "amateur" in the countries of eastern Europe when they formed the Communist bloc. Their state-supported players were labeled "amateurs" but were pros in everything but name. They were permitted to keep prize money in varying amounts, and depending on the outlook of the national federation. In some cases—notably that of the USSR—players had to turn prize money over to the national federation, and then were granted subsidies. This ended in 1990, largely due to the complaints of Soviet players Andrei Chesnokov and Natalia Zvereva, who lobbied publicly to keep the money they earned.

AMBIES: Those aberrational few of bi-sockual habits—the ambidextrous. Unable to tolerate backhands, they switch racket from hand to hand, swatting only forehands. Two most notable were right-handers: Italian Giorgio de Stefani (1904–1992) and American Beverly Baker Fleitz (born March 13, 1930). De Stefani, a Davis Cupper, was World No. 9, 1934, when he may have blotted a Grand Slam for Fred Perry (who won the other three majors), beating him at the French. Fleitz was No. 1 in the U.S., No. 4 in the World, 1959, lost the Wimbledon final that year, only such creature to fly so high. At Wimbledon, 1972, two ambies clashed in the only major backhands-banned battle, Lita Liem, Indonesia, beating Marijke Schaar, Netherlands, 7–5, 7–9, 6–3, a first-rounder.

AMERICAN FORMATION: *See* I Formation.

AMERICAN TWIST: A top-spinning serve that takes a high bounce and can present difficulties for the receiver, particularly on grass, where the bounce is tricky. It was originated by Holcombe Ward, a Harvard man, and developed by him with his college friend, Dwight Davis, around the turn of the century. Their use of the stroke during the first Davis Cup match in 1900 was a revelation to their English opponents, whom they baffled and beat. *See* Kicker.

APPROACH SHOT: A drive followed to the net.

AROUND THE POST: A stroke hit by a player drawn so wide that it goes into the opposing court without clearing the net. In this rare case the shot is within the rules even if the flight of the ball is not higher than the net.

ATA: American Tennis Association. Founded in 1916, a time when tournament tennis was restricted to whites in the U.S., to provide sectional and national championships for blacks. The most famous ATA champs were Althea Gibson, who broke the color barrier in major events by entering the U.S. Championships in 1950, and Arthur Ashe. The organization continues to hold tournaments, open to all.

ATP: Association of Tennis Pros, an organization of male touring pros comparable to a union, embracing most of the leading pros. Founded in 1972, it has been influential in governing tournament conditions, conduct, prize-money amounts, and structure. Rebelling against the ITF and the MIPTC in 1989, and led by executive director Hamilton Jordan, the ATP took over organization and control of the men's worldwide circuit, with the exception of the four majors (Australian, French, Wimbledon, U.S.). After 20 years beneath the umbrella of the Grand Prix, it became in 1990 the ATP Tour.

ATP TOUR: Since 1990 the men's professional circuit has been under the jurisdiction of the ATP Tour, with the exception of the Grand Slams (or four majors—Australian, French, Wimbledon, U.S.). This tour follows the same path as the Grand Prix, replacing it. The top eight finishers, on a point system, qualify for cash bonuses and a year-climaxing tournament called the ATP World Championship, formerly the Masters.

AUSTRALIAN FORMATION: *See* I Formation.

AVON CIRCUIT: A series of women's prize money tournaments that operated from 1979 through 1982, sponsored by Avon cosmetics between the sponsorship of Virginia Slims (1970–78 and 1983–92).

BACKHAND: The stroke from the side of the body opposite the normal serving side—from the left for the right-handed and from the right for the left-handed.

BAGEL, BAGEL JOB: A shutout set, 6–0. The loser's score looks like a bagel. A double bagel or triple bagel could be a shutout match. Also used as a verb: to bagel, or shut out. The term was coined by Eddie Dibbs, a leading American player, in 1973.

BALL: The bouncing object hit back and forth over the net by the players. It is two-and-a-half inches in diameter and two ounces in weight. Balls are pressurized, with the pressure varying slightly according to national origin. The American ball is

grass. Balls were uniformly white until 1972 when yellow, offering increased visibility, began to take over.

BALL BOY, GIRL: Youngsters who retrieve balls during tournament matches. Must be as unobtrusive as possible in retrieving balls and throwing to server. For the U.S. Open there are tryouts (minimum age 14), with candidates tested for throwing arm, speed, agility, and knowledge of tennis. They are paid the prevailing minimum wage, receive free uniforms, and get a chance to see the matches free.

BASELINE: The court's back line, joining the sidelines, from which the serve is delivered.

BASELINER: A player who hangs back at the rear of the court, generally quite steady, keeping the ball in play with groundstrokes:

BELL CUP: A team competition between Australian and U.S. women, named for the donor, cosmetic manufacturer Jesse Bell, and held for three years, 1971–73–74. Australia won two of the matches. Discontinued.

BIG FOUR: The major championships—Australian, French, Wimbledon, U.S. Also called the Grand Slams because winning all four within a calendar year constitutes a Grand Slam. Came to be called the Big Four because only those countries had won the Davis Cup for the first 73 years of its existence. Then South Africa (1974), Sweden (1975), Italy (1976), Czechoslovakia (1980) and Germany (1988) joined the

BREAK POINT: Potentially the last point of a game being won by the receiver. If the receiver wins it, he breaks. If the server wins it, he prolongs the game and may eventually pull it out. Obviously a critical point. The following are break points (with the server's score first): 0–40, 15–40, 30–40, advantage out.

BREAKFAST AT WIMBLEDON: A repast for American televiewers since 1979 when NBC first provided live coverage of the Big W, arriving at 9 A.M. on the East Coast, earlier in the West. Roscoe Tanner saved the day, and concept, for nervous network officials, worried whether anyone would watch at that hour. He pushed Bjorn Borg for five exciting sets before losing at 6–4. The promo come-on, "Breakfast at Wimbledon," was coined by Bob Basche, then of NBC Sports.

CANNONBALL: An extraordinarily swift serve. Maurice McLoughlin, who won the U.S. title 1912–13, was the first of the cannonballing big servers. Bill Tilden was known for his cannonball. Pancho Gonzalez was said to be the fastest in his day, clocked at 117 MPH. Later, in the 1960s, Englishman Mike Sangster was timed at 154 MPH. Colin Dibley, an Aussie, was clocked at 148 MPH, American Roscoe Tanner at 140 in 1974—all those times with wooden rackets in serving demonstrations. Timing devices have changed, apparently, and even with the high-tech thundersticks of today, seemingly producing the highest speeds, the clockings don't register as high. But today's clockings are taken in actual matches, which may make a difference. David Pate, an American, was timed at 138 MPH in Indianapolis in 1988, Michael Stich, a German, at 128 MPH in Memphis. Female cannonballers of recent years, Brenda Schultz of the Netherlands, and Jennifer Capriati of the U.S., have been timed at 100-plus MPH.

CARRY: *See* Double Hit.

CENTRE COURT: This is the cathedral of tennis, a covered stadium surrounding the principal court at Wimbledon, a structure much like an Elizabethan theater. On this grass court the championship finals are played along with the most important matches of the Wimbledon fortnight. It was built in 1922 to hold 14,000 spectators, 1,500 of them on each side in the open standing-room areas. That capacity was increased to about 15,000 in 1979. However, the imposition of stricter crowd control in Britain, following soccer stadium disasters, eliminated standing room in 1991, and lowered Centre Court capacity, 13,107 as of 1992. Also center court can mean the main court in any tennis complex.

CHALLENGE ROUND: A type of final once common to tennis, particularly the Davis Cup, and now out of use, whereby the champion was privileged to stand aside the following year, waiting for a challenger to be determined by an elimination "all-comers" tournament. Then the challenger would face the reigning champion for the title. This format was discarded by the U.S. Championships for men in 1912, women in 1919, by Wimbledon in 1921, and by the

Davis Cup in 1972. That year the Cup-holding U.S. played through the tournament along with the other nations entered, reached the final against Romania, and retained the title.

CHANGE GAME: At the completion of each odd game of a match, beginning with the first game, the players change sides in order to equalize playing conditions—sun, wind, court surface, etc.

CHIP: *See* Dink.

CHOKING: What a player is doing who can't perform to his normal ability when the going gets rough and the pressure is on. Most players recognize that it can happen to the best of them, and they are not ashamed to admit it. Also called gagging.

CHIP AND CHARGE: Attacking tactic—following a sliced approach to the net.

CHOP: A severe, slicing stroke that imparts underspin.

COMPUTER RANKINGS: A separate rating system used by male (ATP) and female (WTA) professional tours in both singles and doubles, based on data of results in tournament play. Rankings, revised and released at regular intervals, are used to determine who gets into which tournaments, and who is seeded. Data covers performance over the 12-month period preceding the release of rankings. The computers began making their printout pronouncements in 1973.

COURT: The surface on which the game is played. A tennis court can be surfaced with anything from anthill sand (in Australia) to dried cow dung (in India) to wood, clay, grass, linoleum, canvas, concrete, asphalt or synthetic carpets. The dimensions are always the same: 78 feet long and 27 feet wide (36 feet wide for doubles). The game began on grass courts in England. That is an uncommon surface now, although the biggest tournament of all, Wimbledon, is still a grass event.

COURT SPEED: The "fastest" courts are those producing quick, low bounces such as grass and wood, and smooth, hard surfaces such as canvas stretched over wood or concrete, or concrete itself, or similar compositions such as asphalt. The "slowest" courts are those producing high, lazy carpets. Outdoors, a damp court of clay or grass generally plays slower. Manufacturers of synthetic carpets can change the speed, as can manufacturers of outdoor hard courts by altering the texture, following the principle that the smoother a court the faster it plays. As of 1988, the Big Four were played on three different surfaces: U.S. and Australia on hard courts, Wimbledon on grass, French on clay. All but the French, the premier clay-court event in the world, favor power players. U.S. titles are determined on three surfaces: indoor, clay, and hard court (the U.S. Open), although a few grass-court titles remain, such as the Girls' 18 at Philadelphia.

CROSSCOURT: Diagonal shot across the court from the left or the right.

DAVIS CUP: Men's competition for teams representing nations throughout the world. It was originated at Boston's Longwood Cricket Club in 1900 by Dwight Filley Davis, who was a student at Harvard and played on the first team, competing against the top players from Great Britain. The Americans won in the inaugural year and have won a record 30 times through 1992. The competition has broadened from those two countries in 1900 to more than 90 in 1993, and is played over the course of nine or 10 months. Only 16 countries actually compete annually for the Cup now, in a section called the World Group, instituted in 1981. The remainder play annually in geographically separated zones (European, African, American, Asian-Oceanian), and hope for promotion to the World Group through a system of World Group in 1989. The format is for four-man teams to meet in a best-of-five match series (formally called a tie) over three days (four singles, one doubles.) Two singles the first day, doubles the second, two singles the third with the opponents reversed. Two men must play two singles each. The doubles team may be made up of any combination among the four players. The country with choice of ground selects the site and surface, usually a "home-court advantage." All matches are best-of-five sets. Since 1989, tie-breakers have been used, except for the ultimate fifth set. Referee and umpires are neutrals. Only nine countries have won: U.S., leading Australia, 30–26, as well as Britain (9), France (7), Sweden (4), Germany (2), South Africa (1) and Italy (1).

DEUCE: A game or set score meaning the opponents are even at a certain point. The deuce factor provides that games and sets can go on and on. In a game the score is deuce at 40–all or three points each. To win, a player must take two straight points from deuce. The first point after deuce is advantage, and the score keeps reverting to deuce unless one player wins the two straight points. A set is deuced when the score becomes five games apiece. To win the set, a player must be two games ahead, thus winning two straight games from 5–all, 6–all, 7–all, etc. The longest deuce set ever played was 49–47 during the longest match ever played: Dick Leach and Dick Dell beat Tom Mozur and Len Schloss, 3–6, 49–47, 22–20—147 games—in the 1967 Newport (R.I.) Invitation.

DINK: A softly sliced stroke intended to fall in the forecourt, between the net and service line at a net-rusher's feet. Sometimes called a chip.

DONKEYS: Once fashionable term for consistent losers when the pro tour was principally an odyssey of one-night stands. Coiner was probably Pancho Segura.

DOUBLE CHRISSIE: Rare bird, player who emulates Chris Evert not only with two-handed backhand but also two-handed forehand. Lorne Main, a Canadian, on scene in 1940s–50s is believed to have been first such. Monica Seles is most successful. In between a handful have doubled up, such as Japanese Federation Cupper Akiko Kijimuta, U.S. Davis Cuppers Jim Pugh and Gene Mayer. Best of the early specimens was Hall of Famer Frew McMillan.

DOUBLE FAULT: When the server misses with both serves, thus losing the point.

DOUBLE HIT: Striking the ball twice during the same stroke, a misfortune that used to mean automatic loss of the point but now only if judged "intentional." Also called a carry.

DOUBLES: A team game with two players on each side of the net.

DOWN-THE-LINE: A shot along either sideline.

DOWN UNDERTAKERS: Sometimes called Godfather Hopman's Aussie Mafia, they buried the rest of the male world. Most successful tennis mob ever, led and moti-

vated by Australian Davis Cup captain Harry Hopman, dominant from 1950 (Cup-grabbers Frank Sedgman and Ken McGregor) for almost a quarter-century through 1973, John Newcombe's U.S. triumph and his and Rod Laver's Davis Cup heist. Starting with Sedgman's Aussie titles, 1949–50, the gang accounted for 62 major singles: Sedgman (5), McGregor (1), Ken Rosewall (8), Lew Hoad (4), Mervyn Rose (2), Ashley Cooper (4), Mal Anderson (1), Rod Laver (11), Neale Fraser (3), Roy Emerson (12), Bill Bowrey (1), Newcombe (7), Tony Roche (1) Fred Stolle (2).

DRAW: The lineup for a customary elimination tournament. Names of the non-seeded players are drawn blindly, usually from a cup, and placed in the order drawn, from top to bottom on a bracketed draw sheet that indicates who opposes whom.

DROP SHOT: A softly hit shot, intentionally aimed to barely clear the net in order to win a point outright, or to pull the opponent in close.

ELBOW: Getting the elbow is choking or tightening up at a critical point, a bad reaction to pressure. However, "tennis elbow" is an actual physical affliction, a painful mal-functioning of the elbow that strikes not only tennis players. Physicians have not found a sure cure.

ERROR: A mistake that loses a point during a rally, such as hitting the ball out or into the net.

FAST COURT: *See* Court Speed.

FAULT: Failing to put the ball into play with the serve, either by serving into the net or beyond the confines of the service court. It is also a fault to step on the baseline while serving or to swing and miss the ball altogether. One fault isn't disastrous, but two lose the point.

FEDERATION CUP: An annual worldwide women's team competition among nations comparable to the Davis Cup for men, which began in 1963, honoring the 50th anniversary of the founding of the ITF (International Tennis Federation). The format is a best-of-three match series for four-woman teams (two singles and a doubles). Two different players compete in singles, but the doubles may be made up of

Germany (2), Spain (1), South Africa (1).

FIFTEEN: The first point either player or side wins.

FIRST TEN OR TOP TEN: Select groups worldwide and nationally. The ATP and WTA issue computerized worldwide rankings weekly, based on play over the preceding 12-month period. Countries issue Top Ten rankings at the end of each year for play in that year, some based on computerized data, some based on the outlook of ranking committees. In the U.S. this began in 1894 for men when Bob Wrenn was No. 1, and in 1913 for women with Mary K. Browne at the top. In 1895 the USTA published retroactive rankings for 1885 through 1893, collected as consensus from various sources. Prior to the advent of the computers in 1973, informal world rankings were based on the judgment of various journalists covering the sport. In the U.S. the most frequent Top Ten residents have been Jimmy Connors (20 times between 1971 and 1991, eight times at No. 1) and Chris Evert (19 times between 1971 and 1989, No. 1 six times). Bill Tilden and Martina Navratilova were No. 1 12 times each.

On the worldwide ATP computer, Connors has ranked No. 1 in the year-end rankings five times and was in the Top Ten every year from 1973 through 1988. The WTA computer over the same period has listed Navratilova No. 1 seven times and in the Top Ten every year between 1975 and 1992.

FLINDERS PARK: Location of Australia's

time in 1978. It is named the USTA National Tennis Center, and is located in the borough of Queens in New York City. The principal court, Louis Armstrong Stadium, is the largest tennis arena in the world, seating 19,500. The courts are hard, an asphalt composition called DecoTurf. *See* U.S. Open.

FOOT FAULT: An infraction by the server, stepping on the baseline or serving from the wrong side of the center line. On a first serve it is not serious. On the second it's a double fault and loss of point.

FOREHAND: The stroke hit from the right side of the body for a right-hander, and the left for a left-hander.

FOREST HILLS: Scene of the U.S. National Championships (from 1968 the U.S. Open) for 63 years until the event moved to Flushing Meadow in 1978. Although the championship was played at the West Side Tennis Club, the tournament was generally referred to as Forest Hills, the section of the New York borough of Queens where the club is situated. The men's tournament moved from its original site, the Casino at Newport, R.I., to Forest Hills in 1915 and was played there every year through 1977 with the exception of 1921–23, when it was shifted to Germantown Cricket Club at Philadelphia while the Forest Hills Stadium was constructed on the West Side grounds. The women's tournament moved here from the Philadelphia Cricket Club in 1921. This stadium was opened in 1923 by the inaugural Wightman Cup match between the U.S. and Great Britain, and became one of the world's great tennis arenas, whose record crowd was 16,253 for the 1976 finals. The tournament was played on grass at Forest Hills until 1975, when clay courts were installed for the Open. *See* U.S. Open.

FORO ITALICO: Scene of the Italian Championships in Rome. A bastion of marble and pines alongside the Tiber, it is the world's most handsome setting for an important event and was built as Foro Mussolini during the dictator's reign in 1935.

FORTY: The score for three points won by a side.

GAME: The contest within a set and a match. One player serves throughout a game. To win a game, the player must win four points, unless the score is three points apiece, known as deuce. Then the player must get two points ahead of his opponent to win the game. The points in a game are called, 15, 30, 40, and game—in that order. To win a set, the player must win six games, unless the score is five games apiece. Then it is a deuce set, and the player must take two straight games from deuce to win. In some cases a tiebreaker game is played to determine the winner of a set at six games apiece. *See* Tiebreaker.

GRAND MASTERS: A prize-money tournament circuit inaugurated in 1973 for the cream of the crocks—ex-champs over 45—by Cincinnati businessman Al Bunis. Dealing in nostalgia and featuring such yet imposing players as Pancho Gonzalez, Frank Sedgman and Torben Ulrich, it was a financial success. Sedgman won the championship tournament in 1975, 1977 and 1978, Ulrich in 1976, and Sven Davidson in 1979. Ken Rosewall had the greatest fortune, winning in 1982, and 1985 through 1989. After that the Grand Masters was discontinued, but had spawned such other enterprises for elders as the ATP Senior Tour and the Legends.

GRAND PRIX: Between 1970 and 1989, this was the worldwide tournament structure for men. Conceived by Hall of Famer Jack Kramer, it embraced all the consequential tournaments, offering points for each win, cash bonuses for the leading finishers, and spots in the season-climaxing tournament, the Masters, for the top eight finishers. This system is continued, but as the ATP Tour, begun in 1990, except that the majors (Australian, French, Wimbledon, U.S.) are not included. The ATP World Championship replaces the Masters.

GRAND SLAM: The rare feat of winning the four major championships (Australian, French, Wimbledon, U.S.) all in the same year. Don Budge did it in 1938, Maureen Connolly in 1953, Rod Laver in 1962 and 1969, Margaret Smith Court in 1970, Steffi Graf in 1988. Grand Slams have also been made in doubles: Frank Sedgman and Ken McGregor, 1951; Martina Navratilova and Pam Shriver, 1984; Maria Bueno (with two partners, Christine Truman and Darlene Hard), 1960. And mixed doubles: Margaret Smith and Ken Fletcher, 1963; Owen Davidson (with two partners, Lesley Turner and Billie Jean King), 1967.

GRAND SLAM CUP: An event initiated in 1989 by the ITF for the 16 top male finishers in the four majors/Grand Slams (Australian, French, Wimbledon, U.S.). Played at the close of the season, it is the richest of all tournaments, offering a $6-million purse with $2 million for the victor. Played in Munich 1990–92, and won in its first three years by Pete Sampras, David Wheaton, Michael Stich.

GRAND SLAMS: The four major tournaments (Australian, French, Wimbledon, U.S.) In recent years it has become popular to refer to any of the majors as a Grand Slam tournament. Formerly the usage was Big Four. Put four Grand Slams together in one year and you have a feat called the G̲ ̲d Sl̲ ̲

and Bjorn Borg in the early 1970s, two-handed strokes were rare. But those three influenced so many players with their two-handed backhand baseball grip that one-handed backhands now are rare. Left-handed Monica Seles, gripping the racket with both hands on both sides, may be an influence, too. Pancho Segura of Ecuador, right-handed, was one of the earlier two-fisted strokesmen in the 1940s, his shot a forehand. Vivian McGrath, a right handed-Australian Davis Cup player and champion of his country in 1937, at 20, was the first to use a two-handed backhand at the world-class level.

GROUNDIES: *See* Groundstroke.

GROUNDSTROKE: A stroke hit after the ball bounces, usually from the backcourt.

GUT: Animal intestines used to string rackets. The best gut comes from cows.

HACKER: An ordinary player—a term applying to most of us; the tennis equivalent of the golfing duffer. Also used in good-natured ribbing by the pros. It came into vogue in 1966 when Aussie Fred Stolle, Wimbledon runner-up and German champion, arrived at Forest Hills to find

himself surprisingly unseeded. "I guess they think I'm just an old hacker," he said. After he won the title, Fred said, "There's still some life in the old hacker." He was 27 and has been the Old Hacker since.

HALF VOLLEY: The stroke by which the ball is blocked as soon as it hits the ground. Like trapping a baseball.

̲̲ ̲ ̲ ̲̲

That year the name and scope went worldwide as the International Tennis Hall of Fame with the induction of Englishman Fred Perry. The first class of inductees was tapped in 1955.

HANDSOME EIGHT: The appellation given his World Championship Tennis troupe by promoter Dave Dixon, who raided the traditional game as seldom before, turning five outstanding amateurs professional in 1968: Cliff Drysdale, South Africa; Wimbledon and U.S. champ John Newcombe, Australia; Nikki Pilic, Yugoslavia; Tony Roche, Australia; Roger Taylor, England. To those he added established pros Pierre Barthes, France; Butch Buchholz and Dennis Ralston, U.S. These signings, depleting the amateur ranks, hastened the advent of open tennis that year. Roche, a rugged type, joked that in handsomeness he ranked 15th among the eight.

HARD COURT: This can be confusing because in the U.S. "hard court" means concrete, asphalt or similar paving, such as U.S. Open courts at Flushing Meadow, while in Europe, Australia and most other countries the term applies to clay courts. Beginning in 1948 the USTA held a National Hard Court Championships for men and women. This ran through 1969. With the exception of a men's championships in 1971, it was abandoned between 1970 and 1987, resuming in separate locations in 1988. *See* Court Speed.

I FORMATION: An unorthodox doubles alignment with the netman standing in the service court directly ahead of his partner, the server, instead of in the adjoining court. The purpose is to confuse the receiver. Also called the tandem formation, as well as the Australian formation (in the U.S.) and the American formation (in Australia).

IN THE ZONE: A state of great confidence when one is playing sensationally, even above expected ability. "I'm sure in the zone today." From "The Twilight Zone," a TV program about other-worldly behavior and situations.

IPA: Independent Players' Association, an organization founded in opposition to the ATP by Bill Riordan, tournament promoter, and then manager of Jimmy Connors. Connors appeared to be the only member of his private union, of which nothing has been heard since 1975.

ITF: International Tennis Federation (originally the International Lawn Tennis Federation). Since 1913 it has been the world governing body of tennis, embracing the amateur bodies of nearly 100 countries. The ITF has little control over professional tennis but does have the major championships, (Australian, French, Wimbledon, U.S.) beneath its umbrella, administers the Davis Cup, Federation Cup and Olympic competitions as well as a worldwide network of junior and senior events.

JAG: A verb coined by Aussies meaning "to hit the ball unstylishly but somehow getting it over the net," as in Rod Laver remarking, "I just made up my mind to jag a few, keep it in play, until I found my timing."

JOHNSTON AWARD: An award for outstanding sportsmanship presented annually to an American male by the U.S. Tennis Association. It was named for a short but indomitable competitor, the late Bill Johnston (1894–1946), who was national champion, 1915–19.

JUNKBALLER: Player using a variety of speeds, spins, change-of-pace, soft stuff—a mixture of "junk," ("garbage")—usually intended to throw off a superior, hard-hitting foe. A standout, Julie Heldman, No. 5 in the world, 1974, called herself "Junkball Julie," relished driving opponents to distraction. An outstanding junkballing feat was Michael Chang's fourth-round befuddlement of favorite Ivan Lendl at the French, 1989 (en route to the title), his repertory of trash including an underhand serve.

KICKER: An American twist serve taking a high bounce to the right if served by a right-hander and to the left if served by a left-hander. *See* American Twist.

KILL: To put a ball away, usually by hitting an overhead smash that blasts the ball well out of the opponent's reach.

KING'S CUP: An indoor team competition for European nations, along the lines of the Davis Cup. It was named for the 1936 donor, King Gustav V of Sweden, the tennis fanatic who played into his nineties. Discontinued.

KOOYONG: A stadium at a private club in Melbourne, Australia, where the third-largest crowds in tennis history, 22,000, gathered for the Australian-U.S. Davis Cup finale in 1957. An aboriginal word, kooyong means "haunt of the wild fowl." Built in 1927. Customary site of Australian Open, whose surface was grass. In 1988 the championships moved to the newly constructed National Tennis Center at Melbourne's Flinders Park, and hard courts.

KRAFT TOUR: Since 1990, the women's professional circuit, including the Grand Slams (the four majors—Australian, French, Wimbledon, U.S.), has been under the sponsorship banner of the Kraft Foods Tour. Top 16 finishers in a points system qualify for cash bonuses and a year-climaxing event, the Virginia Slims Championships, at New York's Madison Square Garden.

LINER: A shot landing on or touching a line. It is a good shot.

LINE JUDGE: A court official who judges whether a shot is out or in play. Sometimes known as line umpire or linesman/lineswoman. To indicate "out" an arm-extended signal and vocal call are given ("Fault!" if it is a service line call.) On a shot close to the line a "safe" signal—hands extended parallel to the court—is given to indicate that the ball in play. A "skeleton crew" of six may officiate, with a chair umpire (covering service line, baselines, and center and sidelines the length of the court). Eleven make up a full officiating crew: umpire, net judge, two baseline judges, six (three at either end) for side and center lines, one to handle both service lines. A crew can be expanded to 13 with the addition of another service-line judge and a foot-fault judge.

LINGERING DEATH: A tie-breaker based on Jimmy Van Alen's original theme, but adhering to the deuce principle of winning only if ahead by two or more points. The goal is to reach seven points, but the winner must be two points ahead; thus at 6 points-all the tie-breaker could continue indefinitely. This form is usually called the 12-point tie-breaker, a misnomer since it may stretch well beyond 12. *See* Tie-breaker.

LOB: A high, arching stroke meant either as a defensive shot (enabling the hitter to regain position) or to go over the head of an opponent at net. Frank Hadow, the Wimbledon champion in 1878, is generally credited with originating this stroke.

oldest). Located in the Boston suburb of Chestnut Hill, Longwood has been the scene of top-flight tennis almost since its beginning. The first Davis Cup match was played there in 1900, the National Doubles Championships from 1917 through 1967, the U.S. Pro from 1964 to date. Among members were such tennis pioneers as Dwight Davis, donor of the Davis Cup; Hazel Wightman, donor of the Wightman Cup; Richard Sears, first U.S. champion; Dr. James Dwight, "Father of the Game" in the U.S. Courts are grass, hard and clay.

LOVE: A zero score. A love game is a blitz, with the winner taking four straight points. A love set is six games to nothing (*See* Bagel Job). Probably derived from the French word l'oeuf, meaning the egg—and implying the old goose egg.

LUCKY LOSER: A player who loses in the quallies (qualifying tournament), yet gets into the main draw because a vacancy opens through a withdrawal. The lucky loser filling such a vacancy is the loser in the quallies with the highest computer ranking. In earlier days of the open era such a winning loser was genuinely lucky since he/she was picked at random from a hat containing the names of all the defeated. Rarest of the rare is a lucky loser who actually slips into the tournament and wins it; Heinz Gunthardt at Springfield (Mass.) in 1978 was the first of five such champs.

MASTERS: The climax of the tennis year was the eight-man Masters playoff among the top eight finishers in the Grand Prix. Begun in 1970 at Tokyo, where Stan Smith won, the Masters moved from city to city, settling in New York in 1977, and stayed at Madison Square Garden through 1989 when the Masters, under that name, was discontinued. The format went on as the ATP Tour World Championship in Frankfort, Germany, in 1990. Ivan Lendl won the Masters five times (1981–82–85–86–87) and Ilie Nastase four (1971–72–73–75).

MATCH: The overall contest. It may be a two-out-of-three-sets match or a three-out-of-five-sets match, meaning one player must win either two sets or three sets to be the victor. The number of matches needed to win a tournament is determined by the size of the draw in a conventional elimination tournament, or by whatever rules prevail, as in a round-robin or medal-play event.

MATCH POINT: The point prior to completion of a match. The player in the lead needs only one more point to win. This can be a very dramatic spot, and sometimes the player behind in the score saves numerous match points and goes on to victory. Pancho Gonzalez saved seven match points in a dramatic five-set victory over Charlie Pasarell during the 1969 Wimbledon, the longest match ever played there: 22–24, 1–6, 16–14, 6–3, 11–9—112 games.

MIPTC: Men's International Professional Tennis Council, a board of control for the male pro tournament game. Formed in 1974, it governed the men's game through 1989 with representation from the ATP, ITF and tournament directors. Abandoned in 1990 when the ATP Tour supplanted the Grand Prix.

MIXED DOUBLES: Doubles with one male and one female on each side.

MOONBALL: A high, floating groundstroke used in baseline rallying to slow down the pace. It's not as high as a lob and is usually hit with topspin. It is most associated with a leading American, Harold Solomon, who hit them forever and who coined the term in 1972 when his moonballing epic, a marathon victory over Guillermo Vilas during the French Open, consumed more than five hours.

NET: The webbed barrier dividing the court at middle and over which the ball is to be hit. At the center point it is three feet high and at either end three-and-a-half feet.

NET CORD: A shot that hits the top of the net and drops into the opposite court. Also, the cord or wire cable that supports a net.

NET JUDGE: An official seated at one end of the net, usually below the umpire's chair, to detect lets on serve. During the serve he rests one hand on the net cord to feel whether the ball hits the top of the net. If it does, he calls "Net!" and the serve is replayed as a let if the ball lands in the proper court.

NET RUSHER: An attacking player who follows his serve to the net and continually seeks the closeup position to make winning volleys.

NEWPORT CASINO: Oldest of the world's active tennis grounds. The Newport Casino was built in Rhode Island in 1880 as a private club by James Gordon Bennett, Jr., becoming the cradle of American tournament tennis, playing host to the first U.S. Championships (for men only) on its grass courts in 1881. The tourney site through 1914, it remains a busy club and location of the International Tennis Hall of Fame. Prominent tournament tennis has continued on the grass courts, including a men's amateur event from 1915 through 1967, and professional tournaments since 1965, recently an ATP Tour stopover, the last American pro tourney on grass.

NO-AD: A form of scoring originated by Jimmy Van Alen that eliminates deuce and replaces love–15–30–40 with 0–1–2–3. The maximum points for a game are seven. At

what a non-brainer!" after being served out of Wimbledon by Kevin Curren (33 aces) in 1983.

NOT UP: The call when a player hits the ball just as it has bounced the second time on a close play. Usually the net judge makes the ruling, but if there are no officials, it is up to the offending player to call it against himself and accept loss of the point.

NTL: National Tennis League, an organization formed by George MacCall in 1967 to promote professional tournaments. Under contract were Rod Laver, Ken Rosewall, Pancho Gonzalez, Andres Gimeno, Fred Stolle, Roy Emerson, Billie Jean King, Rosie Casals, Ann Jones and Francoise Durr. By 1970 NTL had been put out of business and absorbed by rival WCT.

OPEN: A tournament that may be entered by both amateurs and professionals, generally offering prize money. Not until 1968 did the ITF permit opens. The first, the British Hard Court Championships, was won by pro Ken Rosewall and amateur Virginia Wade. Now all the leading national title events are open.

OVERHEAD: A stroke, usually a smash, executed like a serve by raising the racket above the head and swinging down hard.

PASSING SHOT: A ball hit past the opposing netman on either side beyond his reach.

PHILADELPHIA CRICKET CLUB: This pri-

can't touch it.

POACH: In doubles, a net player, hoping to make a winning volley, crosses in front of his partner.

POINT: The smallest unit of scoring. A game is won by a player winning four points, except in the case of deuce. The first point of a game is called 15, the second 30, the third 40, and the fourth is game. At 40–all the score is deuce. Each point is begun with the serve, and one player serves an entire game. In keeping score, the server's score is called first—e.g., in 15–40, 15 is the server, and 40 is the receiver.

PROFESSIONAL: A player who plays prize-money events for money or a teacher who gives tennis lessons for money.

PUSHER: A player who hopes to wear down the opponent by maddeningly returning everything with soft looping strokes. A pusher hangs back at the baseline, a good retriever, patiently waiting for a big hitter to blow his cool and the match. Also known as a pooper, puddler, or puffball artist.

QUALLIES: The qualifying tournament preceding every professional tournament. The rewards for winners (qualifiers) are spots in the main draw. Entrance is based on computer ranking.

QUALIFIER: One who wins the required number of matches in a qualifying tournament to be admitted to the main draw. Most celebrated qualifier was John McEnroe, then an 18-year-old at Wimbledon in 1977. He won three qualifying matches to enter the main draw, and won five more matches to reach the semis. Occasionally a qualifier even wins the tournament—longest-shot example was Yahiya Doumbia of Senegal, who won Lyon, 1988, ranked No. 453. The women's longest-shot was Catrin Jexel of Sweden, who ranked No. 146 in winning Hong Kong in 1982. Quallies for the four majors, and some other tournaments, offer prize money.

RACKET: The implement used in hitting the ball. Originally the frame—handle and relatively oval head—was made of wood, and remained that way for nearly a century. Metal began making serious inroads with the introduction of the Wilson "steelie," T2000 in 1967, notably in the right hand of Billie Jean King winning the U.S. title. Conceived by French great, Hall of Famer René Lacoste, the steelie was given its greatest prominence a few years after King by Jimmy Connors, who won almost all of his male-record 109 titles with it. Steel had been used sporadically in the early days of the game, and the durable Dayton Steel racket, with steel strings, enjoyed some popularity in the 1920s and '30s. Aluminum made a hit in 1968 as Arthur Ashe used the Head "snowshoe" to win the U.S. Open. Others took up that metal including Rod Laver. A high-tech breakthrough was scored in 1976 by ski designer and tennis enthusiast Howard Head, introducing for Prince a revolutionary composition model with abnormally oversized head and much more hitting area. Wood's days were numbered then,

and all sorts of high-tech materials were introduced, such as graphite, magnesium, boron, fiberglass. Rackets grew in head size, frame thickness and strength. Players hit with more power and speed. Not until 1981 did the ITF decide that rules should be made governing racket size. It was then decreed that it must not exceed 32 inches from bottom of handle to top of head, or 12½ inches in overall width. The strung surface must not exceed 15½ inches in overall length and 11½ inches in overall width. The best strings are made of cow's intestines, but synthetics are efficient, cheaper, more widely used.

RALLY: An exchange of shots during a point.

RIORDAN CIRCUIT: The first viable indoor circuit for men in the U.S., organized by the late Bill Riordan, dynamic promoter from Salisbury, Md., and then manager of Jimmy Connors. He started in earnest in 1964 by transferring the nearly defunct U.S. Indoor Championships from New York to Salisbury, where it became a thriving event. He expanded to eight tournaments by 1975, its last year. A combative type, Riordan fought the growth of WCT and the ATP; founded his own players' organization, called the IPA (Independent Players' Association); and kept his series of winter tournaments going as a one-man operation under the aegis of the USTA that he called the Independent circuit but was generally known as the Riordan circuit. *See* IPA.

REFEREE: The official in charge of tournament play, making the draw, scheduling of matches, interpreting the rules and adjudicating disputes between players and umpires.

ROLAND GARROS: The 17,000-seat stadium and tennis complex in Paris where the French Championships has been played yearly since 1928. Built primarily for the first French defense of the Davis Cup that year, it was named for a heroic

French aviator killed in World War I. Surface is clay. In 1968 the French was the first major open. Although the tournament dates to 1891, it did not become an international championship, welcoming non-French citizens, until 1925. Nearly 30,000 spectators are on the grounds daily and total attendance is around 350,000, testimony of its preeminence among the country's sporting occasions.

pusher.

SEEDING: The deliberate, instead of chance, placing of certain strong players so that they will not meet in the earlier rounds of an elimination tournament. It was introduced to major tennis at Wimbledon in 1924 and soon became standard procedure, adopted at Forest Hills in 1927. Seeded players (those judged by a tournament committee or according to computerized rankings to be the leaders on the basis of performance and ability) are listed in numbered order prior to the draw. Then the seeds are separated by being planted in positions specified by tournament regulations. Thus the top two players, Nos. 1 and 2, are located at opposite ends of the draw, and if the seeding runs true, they will meet in the final.

SERVICE OR SERVE: The act of putting the ball into play and beginning a point by hitting the ball from the baseline diagonally over the net and into the opponent's service court. Any motion (underhand, sidearm, or whatever) is permissible. However, the overhead stroke is nearly universal.

SERVICE BREAK: Winning the opponent's service.

SERVICE COURT(S): There are two, since the server alternates from the right to the left side of the court with each point. The service courts are bounded by the sidelines, the net, and the service line, which is 21 feet from the net; they are divided from one another by the center line. Each court is 13½ feet wide by 21 feet deep.

SERVICE WINNER: An unreturned serve

of the set, whose score would be 7–6.

SET POINT: The point prior to the completion of a set. The player needs only one more point to win the set. But the player behind may still save the set point and go on to win the set himself, thanks to the deuce factor.

SITTER: An easy opportunity; a ball softly hit close to the net and well within reach, which can be smashed away for a point.

SLICE: Hitting under the ball, which produces underspin and a low bounce.

SLIMS CIRCUIT: The first notable attempt to bring women into the prize-money era of tennis was made successfully by Gladys Heldman, publisher of *World Tennis* magazine, who in 1970 began forming a circuit for the women separate from that of the men and backed by Virginia Slims cigarettes, a sponsorship lasting through 1978, and returning in 1983. Although the tour has been sponsored by Kraft since 1990, Slims maintains a presence, particularly as the sponsor of the season-closing Championships in New York. With Heldman as the organizational wizard and Billie Jean King as spokeswoman and all-conquering champion, the women's game took off in 1971. By going it alone, the women no longer played second racket to the men in cash or publicity, and the women's prize money rose dramatically.

SLOW COURT: *See* Court Speed.

SMASH: An overhead stroke brought down hard like a serve.

SPIKES: Spiked shoes with ⅜ inch metal spikes were in common usage years ago when grass-court tennis was preeminent, usually on wet courts to aid footing. Their last notable appearance was on the feet of Rod Laver, completing his 1969 Grand Slam with a U.S. Open final victory over sneaker-shod Tony Roche at damp and mushy Forest Hills.

SPIN: Pronounced rotation of the ball according to how it is struck by the racket, and divided into three categories: topspin (overspin); slice (underspin); and sidespin. For topspin the racket brushes the ball from low to high producing a high bouncing ball, enabling one to hit the ball harder and still keep it deep but within the court. For slice the racket brushes from high to low, producing a low bounce. A sewing slice is a chop, causing the ball to bounce to the receiver's right if server is right-handed and to the left if server is left-handed. For sidespin the racket brushes across the ball on either side, producing a bounce to the left if ball is struck on the right side, and vice versa.

SUDDEN DEATH: A tie-breaker of definite length, either nine-point or 13-point, settled by a sudden-death point when the score is 4–4, or 6–6. It was conceived by Jimmy Van Alen. *See* Tie-breaker.

SUPERVISOR: The person in charge of officiating at an ATP Tour or Grand Slam tournament. Working in cooperation with the referee, the supervisor is the highest court of appeal, levying fines, if need be,

and issuing or approving disqualifications by umpire or referee.

SUPREME COURT: The trade name for a synthetic carpet court favored for a majority of professional indoor tournaments.

TANDEM FORMATION: *See* I Formation.

THIRTY: Two points.

THROAT: The thin part of the racket between the handle and the head, when rackets were wood, Now it's an open triangular throat.

TIE: A team match between countries, such as Davis Cup or Federation Cup. It is an old expression, used mainly in Britain and Europe, seldom in the U.S. In the Davis Cup a tie is composed of five rubbers. *See* Rubber.

TIE-BREAKER, TIE-BREAK: An overtime game to end a set at 6-games all, rather than continuing in a theoretically interminable deuce set in which one side must be ahead by two games to win a set that has been tied at 5-games all. It's another scoring innovation—the most revolutionary rules change in the game's first century—from the fertile mind of the late Jimmy Van Alen, sometimes called the "Newport Bolshevik." He unveiled it at the pro tourney he sponsored at the Newport (R.I.) Casino in 1965 as a feature of his radical scoring plan, VASSS. Mike Davies defeated Ken Rosewall, 5-points-to-3 in the initial breaker. This evolved to the Sudden Death, best-of-9-points breaker, in use at the U.S. Open between 1970 and 1974, on the Virginia Slims circuit and in U.S. colleges. Following the U.S. in adopting the breaker were Australia and Italy in 1971, France in 1973 and Wimbledon in 1972, although Wimbledon cautiously put it into effect at 8-games all. That lasted until 1979. Those three majors, as well as Italy and most other countries, didn't approve of Sudden Death, however, and were using the ITF's variation on Van Alen's theme, the so-called 12-point tie-break, in universal use today. This version is actually "Lingering Death," as Van Alen called it. Although generally won by the first side to reach 7 points, it could theoretically run interminably since a two-point margin is required. The longest thus has lingered 50 points (a 26–24 breaker won by Jan Gunnarson and Michael Mortensen over

After one side serves the first point from the right court, serve alternates for two-point sequences, each beginning from the left court. Players change ends at every six-point juncture. The score of a tie-breaker set is 7–6. Only one match at the U.S. Open has been settled by a tie-breaker in every set: Steffi Graf over Pam Shriver, 7–6 (7–4), 6–7 (4–7), 7–6 (7–4), in 1985. The closest consequential matches ending with a two-point margin (7–5 fifth-set breakers) were the 1972 WCT final in Dallas, Rosewall over Rod Laver, and the 1988 Masters at New York, Boris Becker over Ivan Lendl. The closest consequential match in the "sudden death" days with a one-point margin (5–4 fifth-set breaker) was the 1970 Pacific Coast semifinal at Berkeley, Cliff Richey over Stan Smith. Scoring the last point—simultaneous match point—with a diving volley, Richey not only won the match but barely (by one point) assured himself of the No. 1 U.S. ranking over No. 2 Smith as the season concluded. Because of the similarity of their records for the year, the outcome of that meeting was to determine No. 1.

TOPSPIN: An overspin produced by brushing the ball from low to high. This enables one to hit the ball very hard and high over

the net and still keep it in court. It creates a high bounce, and also a ball difficult to volley. Originated by Englishman Herbert Lawford in the early days of the game, helping him to gain the Wimbledon final six times, and win in 1887. Called the "Lawford stroke" during the 1880s in the U.S. *See* Spin.

TOP TEN: *See* First Ten.

Opens—normally have draws of 128 men and women, with seven rounds of play.

U.E.: Dreaded initials for unforced error, a loss of a point on a shot that should have been put in play.

UMPIRE: The official in charge of a match, keeping and calling score, usually from a high chair at one end of the net.

U.S. OPEN: *See* Forest Hills and Flushing Meadow.

TREE-ING: A fantastic performance where everything goes right—"He was tree-ing: I couldn't get into it." Particularly serving overpoweringly. "The guy was serving from a tree."

U.S. PRO CHAMPIONSHIPS: Longest running tournament for male professionals, won at its launching in 1927 by Vinnie Richards on the clay of long-since vanished Notlek Tennis Club in Manhattan. The purse was $2000, half of it won by Richards for his victory over Howard Kinsey. Largely unnoticed and unsuccessful during the heyday of amateurism, it was played all over the country, indoors and out, until moving to its present location, Longwood

Cricket Club in Boston in 1964, where it has prospered and was the fountainhead for the solid growth of the pro game. In Boston it has been played outdoors, on grass (1964–68), synthetic carpet (1969–73), clay (1974–91) and hard court, from 1992. Pancho Gonzalez won a record eight times between 1952 and 1961, all in Cleveland. Rod Laver won five times, between 1964 and 1969, all in Boston. Prize money rose from $10,000 (first prize $2,200) in 1964 to $400,000 in 1992 (first prize $50,000).

USTA: The United States Tennis Association (formerly U.S. Lawn Tennis Association), the governing organization of amateur tennis in the United States. It also operates the U.S. Open. Founded in 1881 as the U.S. National Lawn Tennis Association, it embraces seventeen sectional associations from New England to Southern California, with about 450,000 members. In 1975 the "L" was dropped from the association abbreviation as dated, since so little tennis is now played on grass.

VASSS: Van Alen Streamlined Scoring System. Devised by Jimmy Van Alen, who was anxious to make the game more readily understood by the general public and to eliminate long drawn-out matches. VASSS replaced love–15–30–40 with 0–1–2–3 and eliminated deuce altogether. He devised the tie-breaker to avoid deuce sets. In VASSS no-ad the first player to win four points wins the game. In VASSS single-point the scoring is changed altogether. The first player to reach 31 points wins the set, with the tie-breaker to be used if the score reaches 30–30. Few tournaments have adopted Van Alen's system, although World Team Tennis and the National Collegiate Athletic Association did use no-ad.

VOLLEY: To hit the ball during play before it touches the ground, usually at the net.

WCT: World Championship Tennis. This most ambitious and successful organization

to promote professional tennis was formed in late 1967 by Dave Dixon of New Orleans in partnership with Dallas sportsman-oil millionaire Lamar Hunt. Dixon signed eight players. (*See* Handsome Eight.) The firm was in business, though shakily, and Hunt and his nephew, Al Hill, Jr., bought out Dixon after a few months' operation and huge losses. Gradually, under director Mike Davies, the concept of the World Championship of Tennis developed—a series of tournaments throughout the world involving most of the leading men and pointing to playoffs in May among the top eight finishers in singles and doubles. Ken Rosewall won the first WCT playoff over Rod Laver in Dallas in 1971 and collected the $50,000 first prize. WCT broadened its operations by constructing tennis resorts (Lakeway World of Tennis outside Austin, Tex., and Peachtree World of Tennis outside Atlanta), marketing tennis clothing, and opening tennis academies. ATP Tour squeezed WCT out of a business it led in creating, and, sadly John McEnroe's victory over Brad Gilbert in 1989 was farewell to WCT and its trailblazing championship.

WEST SIDE TENNIS CLUB: This facility was long the scene of championship tennis, the site of the U.S. Championships for 63 years between 1915 and 1977 as well as 10 Davis Cup finales. This private club was founded in 1892 when situated in Manhattan on Central Park West between 88th Street and 89th Street, thus the name West Side. It occupied two other locations in Manhattan before moving to Forest Hills in 1913. *See* Forest Hills.

WHITE CITY: A stadium in Sydney, Australia, where the second-largest crowd in tennis history, 25,578, attended the Australia-U.S. Davis Cup finale in 1954. The tournament courts were grass, but have been paved to conform to the hard courts of the Aussie circuit in line with those for the Open at Flinders Park.

WIDE: To be out of the court on either side, thus a loss of a point.

WIGHTMAN CUP: The annual women's team competition between Great Britain and the U.S. begun in 1923. The format: best-of-seven matches—five singles and two doubles. The Cup was donated by Mrs. Hazel Hotchkiss Wightman of Boston

slots in a draw are reserved for wild cards. A wild card may be granted for a variety of reasons. It may go to a once prominent name (usually a gate attraction) whose computer ranking doesn't warrant admission, or to a star who decides to enter at the last minute. Or to a local attraction. Perhaps as a favor to a player who has helped the tournament in the past, or is on the way up. A player is limited in the number of wild cards permitted. Under ATP rules, however, a player over 30 who has won at least one major may accept unlimited wild cards. Wild cards are also issued for qualifying tournaments. A spectacular wild carding was that of then 174th-ranked Jimmy Connors at the U.S. Open of 1991. Jimmy, in on a pass, romped to the semifinals.

WIMBLEDON: The game's leading tournament, considered by many the world championship. Entitled formally, and simply, The Lawn Tennis Championships. Played on the grounds of the All England Lawn Tennis & Croquet in the London suburb of Wimbledon. Between the tourney's 1877 inception and 1921, the Championships was played at the "old Wimbledon" on Worple Road. The "new Wimbledon," the present complex, was opened on Church Road in 1922. Grass has always been the

surface. The tournament, begun as an amateur event, has been open to pros as well since 1968. Championships are decided in men's and women's singles and doubles, mixed doubles, junior boys and girls singles and doubles, veterans (45s and 35s) doubles. Always a sellout, the tournament draws well over 400,000 for 13 days. The single-day record was 38,290 in 1978 (a world high). The grounds embrace the

control for the female pro tournament game. Formed in 1975, it seeks to regulate schedules, conditions of play, and conduct. It is made up of representatives of the ITF, WTA, and various tournaments. *See MIPTC.*

WORLD CUP: An annual team competition between Australia and U.S. male pros, begun in 1970. The event had been played at Hartford, Conn., since 1972, and Australia led, 5–4, following a 6–1 victory in 1978. Discontinued after the 1980 meeting with U.S. leading, 6–5.

WTA: The Women's Tennis Association, an organization of the leading female pros, similar to a union and comparable to the ATP. Billie Jean King was the guiding light in the 1974 founding, and she was the first president.

WORLD TEAM TENNIS, TEAM TENNIS: City team franchises, the foundation of major pro sports in the U.S., came to tennis with the establishment of WTT (World Team Tennis), which lasted for five years, folding because of large financial losses after the 1978 season. Founded by Dennis Murphy, Jordan Kaiser and Larry King (then husband of Billie Jean King), WTT operated with 16 cities between Boston and Honolulu in 1974, a high point, and involved most of the game's leading players during its lifespan. They were well paid to ignore the summer season and play team tennis, a new concept in which teams had both male and female players. It was single-set tennis, five sets (men's and women's singles and doubles plus mixed doubles) constituting a match, the score based on total games won. Fearing the summer competition, the ITF (International Tennis Federation) railed against WTT, and the French Open barred players from the league in 1974, one of them, Jimmy Connors of Baltimore (who won the other three majors) thus deprived of a chance at a Grand Slam. A feature of the first season was the unprecedented appearance of women coaching professional teams containing men. Billie Jean King led the Philadelphia Freedoms, Rosie Casals the Detroit Loves. Billie Jean King revived the concept modestly under the masthead of Team Tennis in 1981, with shorter season, lesser players, although Connors and Martina Navratilova came aboard in 1991 with Los Angeles and Atlanta respectively. In 1992 Team Tennis assumed the name World Team Tennis. These were the championship rounds:

1974 Denver d. Philadelphia, 27–21, 28–24

1975 Pittsburgh d. Oakland-San Francisco, 25–26, 28–25, 21–14

1976 New York d. Oakland-San Francisco, 31–23, 29–21, 31–13

1977 New York d. Phoenix, 27–22, 28–17

1978 Los Angeles d. Boston, 24–21, 30–20, 26–27, 28–25

1981 Los Angeles finished first

1982 Dallas finished first

1983 Chicago d. Los Angeles, 26–20

1984 San Diego d. Long Beach, 30–13

1985 San Diego d. St. Louis, 25–24

1986 San Antonio d. Sacramento, 25–23

1987 Charlotte d. San Antonio, 25–20

1988 Charlotte d. New Jersey, 27–22

1989 San Antonio d. Sacramento, 27–25

1990 Los Angeles d. Raleigh, 27–16

1991 Atlanta d. Los Angeles, 27–16

1992 Atlanta d. Newport Beach, 30–17

APPENDIX A: RULES

Except where otherwise stated, every reference in these Rules to the masculine includes the feminine gender.

THE SINGLES GAME

RULE 1 • The Court

The court shall be a rectangle 78 feet (23.77 m.) long and 27 feet (8.23 m.) wide.

USTA COMMENT: See *Rule 34 for a doubles court.*

It shall be divided across the middle by a net suspended from a cord or metal cable of a maximum diameter of one-third of an inch (0.8 cm.), the ends of which shall be attached to, or pass over, the tops of two posts, which shall be not more than 6 inches (15 cm.) square or 6 inches (15 cm.). in diameter. These posts shall not be higher than 1 inch (2.5 cm.) above the top of the net cord. The centres of the posts shall be 3 feet (0.914 m.) outside the court on each side and the height of the posts shall be such that the top of the cord or metal cable shall be 3 feet 6 inches (1.07 m.) above the ground.

When a combined doubles (*see* Rule 34) and singles court with a doubles net is used for singles, the net must be supported to a height of 3 feet 6 inches (1.07 m.) by means of two posts, called "singles sticks," which shall be not more than 3 inches (7.5 cm.) square or 3 inches (7.5 cm.) in diameter. The centres of the singles sticks shall be 3 feet (0.914 m.) outside the singles court on each side.

The net shall be extended fully so that it fills completely the space between the two posts and shall be of sufficiently small mesh to prevent the ball passing through. The height of the net shall be 3 feet (0.914 m.) at the centre, where it shall be held down taut by a strap not more than 2 inches (5 cm.) wide and completely white in colour. There shall be a band covering the cord or metal cable and the top of the net of not less than 2½ inches (5 cm.) nor more than 2½ inches (6.3 cm.) in depth on each side and completely white in colour.

There shall be no advertisement on the net, strap, band or singles sticks.

The lines bounding the ends and sides of the Court shall respectively be called the base-lines and the side-lines. On each side of the net, at a distance of 21 feet (6.40 m.) from it and parallel with it, shall be drawn the service-lines. The space on each side of the net between the service-line and the side-lines shall be divided into two equal parts called the service-courts by the centre service-line, which must be 2 inches (5 cm.) in width, drawn half-way between, and parallel with, the side-lines. Each base-line shall be bisected by an imaginary continuation of the centre service-line to a line 4 inches (10 cm.) in length and 2 inches (5 cm.) in width called the centre mark drawn inside the Court, at right angles to and in contact with such base-lines. All other lines shall be not less than 1 inch (2.5 cm.) nor more than 2 inches (5 cm.) in width except the base-line, which may be not more than 4 inches (10 cm.) in width, and all measurements shall be made to the outside of the lines. All lines shall be of uniform colour.

If advertising or any other material is placed at the back of the court, it may not contain white, or yellow. A light colour may only be used if this does not interfere with the vision of the players.

If advertisements are placed on the chairs of the Linesmen sitting at the back of the court, they may not contain white, or yellow. A light colour may only be used if this does not interfere with the vision of the players.

ITF NOTE: *In the case of the Davis Cup or other Official Championships of the International Tennis Federation, there shall be a space behind each base-line of not less than 21 feet (6.4 m.), and the sides of not less than 12 feet (3.66 m.). The chairs of the linesmen may be placed at the back of the court within the 21 feet or at the side of the court within the 12 feet, provided they do not protrude into that area more than 3 feet (0.914 m.).*

USTA COMMENT: *An approved method for obtaining proper net tautness is this: Loosen the center strap; tighten the net cord until it is approximately 40 inches above the ground, being careful not to over-tighten the net; tighten the center strap until the center of the net is 36 inches above the ground. These measurements should always be made before the first match of the day.*

RULE 2 • Permanent Fixtures

The permanent fixtures of the Court shall include not only the net, posts, singles sticks, cord or metal cable, strap and band, but also, where there are any such, the back and side stops, the stands, fixed or movable seats and chairs round the Court, and their occupants, all other fixtures around and above the Court, and the Umpire, Net-cord Judge, Foot-fault Judge, Linesmen and Ball Boys when in their respective places.

ITF NOTE: *For the purpose of this Rule, the word "Umpire" comprehends the Umpire, the persons entitled to a seat on the Court, and all those persons designated to assist the Umpire in the conduct of a match.*

RULE 3 • The Ball

The ball shall have a uniform outer surface and shall be white or yellow in colour. If there are any seams, they shall be stitchless.

The ball shall be more than two and a half inches (6.35 cm.) and less than two and five-eighths inches (6.67 cm.) in diameter, and more than two ounces (56.7 grams) and less than two and one-sixteenth ounces (58.5 grams) in weight.

The ball shall have a bound of more than 53 inches (135 cm.) and less than 58 inches (147 cm.) when dropped 100 inches (254 cm.) upon a concrete base.

The ball shall have a forward deformation of more than 0.220 of an inch (0.56 cm.) and less than 0.290 of an inch (0.74 cm.) and a return deformation of more than 0.350 of an inch (0.89 cm.) and less than 0.425 of an inch (1.08 cm.) at 18 lb. (8.165 kg.) load. The two deformation figures shall be the averages of three individual readings along three axes of the ball and no two individual readings shall differ by more than 0.030 of an inch (0.08 cm.) in each case.

For play above 4,000 feet (1219 m.) in altitude above sea level, two additional

described above except that they shall have a bound of more than 53 inches (135 cm.) and less than 58 inches (147 cm.) and shall have an internal pressure that is approximately equal to the external pressure and have been acclimatized for 60 days or more at the altitude of the specific tournament. This type of tennis ball is commonly known as a zero-pressure or non-pressurized ball.

RULE 4 • The Racket

Rackets failing to comply with the following specifications are not approved for play under the Rules of Tennis:

(a) The hitting surface of the racket shall be flat and consist of a pattern of crossed strings connected to a frame and alternately interlaced or bonded where they cross; and the stringing pattern shall be generally uniform, and in particular not less dense in the centre than in any other area. The strings shall be free of attached objects and protrusions other than those utilized solely and specifically to limit or prevent wear and tear or vibration and which are reasonable in size and placement for such purposes.

(b) The frame of the racket shall not exceed 32 inches (81.28 cm.) in overall length, including the handle and 12½ inches (31.75 cm.) in overall width. The strung surface shall not exceed 15½ inches (39.37 cm.) in overall length, and 11½ inches (29.21 cm.) in overall width.

(c) The frame, including the handle, shall be free of attached objects and devices other than those utilized solely and specifically to limit or prevent wear and tear or of a point.

The International Tennis Federation shall rule on the question of whether any racket or prototype complies with the above specifications or is otherwise approved, or not approved, for play. Such ruling may be undertaken on its own initiative, or upon application by any party with a bona fide interest therein, including any player, equipment manufacturer or National Association or members thereof. Such rulings and applications shall be made in accordance with the applicable Review and Hearing Procedures of the International Tennis Federation, copies of which may be obtained from the office of the Secretary.

Case 1. Can there be more than one set of strings on the hitting surface of a racket? **Decision.** No. The rule clearly mentions a pattern, and not patterns, of crossed strings.

Case 2. Is the stringing pattern of a racket considered to be generally uniform and flat if the strings are no more than one plane? **Decision.** No.

Case 3. Can a vibration dampening device be placed on the strings of a racket and if so, where can it be placed?

Decision. Yes; but such devices may only be placed outside the pattern of crossed strings.

RULE 5 • Server and Receiver

The players shall stand on opposite sides of the net; the player who first delivers the ball shall be called the Server, and the other the Receiver.

Case 1. Does a player, attempting a stroke, lose the point if he crosses an imaginary line in the extension of the net,
(a) before striking the ball,
(b) after striking the ball?
Decision. He does not lose the point in either case by crossing the imaginary line and provided he does not enter the lines bounding his opponent's Court (Rule 20 (e)). In regard to hindrance, his opponent may ask for the decision of the Umpire under Rules 21 and 25.

Case 2. The Server claims that the Receiver must stand within the lines bounding his Court. Is this necessary?
Decision. No. The Receiver may stand wherever he pleases on his own side of the net.

RULE 6 • Choice of Ends and Service

The choice of ends and the right to be Server or Receiver in the first game shall be decided by toss. The player winning the toss may choose or require his opponent to choose:
(a) The right to be Server or Receiver, in which case the other player shall choose the end; or
(b) The end, in which case the other player shall choose the right to be Server or Receiver.

USTA COMMENT: *These choices should be made promptly after the toss and are irrevocable, except that if the match is postponed or suspended before the start of the match. See* Case 1 below.

Case 1. Do players have the right to new choices if the match is postponed or suspended before it has started?

Decision. Yes. The toss stands, but new choices may be made with respect to service and end.

RULE 7 • The Service

The service shall be delivered in the following manner. Immediately before commencing to serve, the Server shall stand with both feet at rest behind (i.e. further from the net than) the base-line, and within the imaginary continuations of the centre-mark and side-line. The Server shall then project the ball by hand into the air in any direction and before it hits the ground strike it with his racket, and the delivery shall be deemed to have been completed at the moment of the impact of the racket and the ball. A player with the use of only one arm may utilize his racket for the projection.

USTA COMMENT: *The service begins when the Server takes a ready position (i.e., both feet at rest behind the baseline) and ends when his racket makes contact with the ball, or when he misses the ball in attempting to serve it.*

Case 1. May the Server in a singles game take his stand behind the portion of the base-line between the side-lines of the Singles Court and the Doubles Court?
Decision. No.

USTA COMMENT: *The Server may stand anywhere in back of the baseline between the imaginary extensions of the center mark and the singles sideline.*

Case 2. If a player, when serving, throws up two or more balls instead of one, does he lose that service?
Decision. No. A let should be called, but if the Umpire regards the action as deliberate he may take action under Rule 21.

USTA COMMENT: *There is no restriction regarding the kind of services which may be used; that is, the player may use an underhand or overhand service at his discretion.*

RULE 8 • Foot Fault

(a) The Server shall throughout the delivery of the service:

(i) Not change his position by walking or running. The Server shall not by slight movements of the feet which do not materially affect the location originally taken up by him, be deemed "to change his position by walking or running."

(ii) Not touch, with either foot, any area other than that behind the base-line within the imaginary extensions of the cen...

RULE 10 • Service Fault

The Service is a fault:

(a) if the Server commits any breach of Rules 7, 8 or 9(b);

(b) if he misses the ball in attempting to strike it;

(c) if the ball served touches a permanent

...no official has the right to instruct any umpire to disregard violations of it. *In a non-officiated match, the Receiver, or his partner, may call foot faults after all efforts (appeal to the server, request for an umpire, etc.) have failed and the foot faulting is so flagrant as to be clearly perceptible from the Receiver's side.*

It is improper for any officials to warn a player that he is in danger of having a foot fault called on him. On the other hand, if a player, in all sincerity, asks for an explanation of how he foot faulted, either the line Umpire or the Chair Umpire should give him that information.

RULE 9 • Delivery of Service

(a) In delivering the service, the Server shall stand alternately behind the right and left Courts beginning from the right in every game. If service from a wrong half of the Court occurs and is undetected, all play resulting from such wrong service or services shall stand, but the inaccuracy of station shall be corrected immediately it is discovered.

(b) The ball served shall pass over the net and hit the ground within the Service Court which is diagonally opposite, or upon any line bounding such Court, before the Receiver returns it.

USTA COMMENT: *See Rule 18.*

...attempt to strike the ball, it is immaterial whether he catches it in his hand or on his racket or lets it drop to the ground.*

Case 2. In serving in a singles game played on a Doubles Court with doubles posts and singles sticks, the ball hits a singles stick and then hits the ground with the lines of the correct Service Court. Is this a fault or a let?
Decision. In serving it is a fault, because the singles stick, the doubles post, and that portion of the net, or band between them are permanent fixtures. (Rules 2 and 10, and note to Rule 24.).

USTA COMMENT: *The significant point governing Case 2 is that the part of the net and band "outside" the singles sticks is not part of the net over which this singles match is being played. Thus such a serve is a fault under the provisions of Article (c) above... By the same token, this would be a fault also if it were a singles game played with permanent posts in the singles position. (See Case 1 under Rule 24 for difference between "service" and "good return" with respect to a ball's hitting a net post.)*

USTA COMMENT: *In a non-officiated singles match, each player makes calls for all balls landing on, or aimed at, his side of the net. In doubles, normally the Receiver's partner makes the calls with respect to the service line, with the Receiver calling the side and center lines, but either partner may have the call on any ball he clearly sees out.*

RULE 11 • Second Service

After a fault (if it is the first fault) the Server shall serve again from behind the same half of the Court from which he served that fault, unless the service was from the wrong half, when, in accordance with Rule 9, the Server shall be entitled to one service only from behind the other half.

Case 1. A player serves from a wrong Court. He loses the point and then claims it was a fault because of his wrong station.
Decision. The point stands as played and the next service should be from the correct station according to the score.

Case 2. The point score being 15 all, the Server, by mistake, serves from the left-hand Court. He wins the point. He then serves again from the right-hand Court, delivering a fault. This mistake in station is then discovered. Is he entitled to the previous point? From which Court should be next serve?
Decision. The previous point stands. The next service should be from the left-hand Court, the score being 30/15, and the Server has served one fault.

RULE 12 • When to Serve

The Server shall not serve until the Receiver is ready. If the latter attempts to return the service, he shall be deemed ready. If however, the Receiver signifies that he is not ready, he may not claim a fault because the ball does not hit the ground within the limits fixed for the service.

USTA COMMENT: *The Server must wait until the Receiver is ready for the second service as well as the first, and if the Receiver claims to be not ready and does not make any effort to return a service, the Server's claim for the point may not be honored even though the service was good. However, the Receiver, having indicated he is ready, may not become unready unless some outside interference takes place.*

RULE 13 • The Let

In all cases where a let has to be called under the rules, or to provide for an inter-

ruption to play, it shall have the following interpretations:

(a) When called solely in respect of a service that one service only shall be replayed.

(b) When called under any other circumstance, the point shall be replayed.

Case 1. A service is interrupted by some cause outside those defined in Rule 14. Should the service only be replayed?
Decision. No, the whole point must be replayed.

USTA COMMENT: *If a delay between first and second serves is caused by the Receiver, by an official or by an outside interference the whole point shall be replayed; if the delay is caused by the Server, the Server has one serve to come. A spectator's outcry (of "out," "fault" or other) is not a valid basis for replay of a point, but action should be taken to prevent a recurrence.*

USTA COMMENT: *Case 1 refers to a second serve, and the decision means that if the interruption occurs during delivery of the second service, the Server gets two serves.* EXAMPLE: *On a second service a linesman calls "fault" and immediately corrects it, the Receiver meanwhile having let the ball go by. The Server is entitled to two serves, on this ground: The corrected call means that the Server has put the ball into play with a good service, and once the ball is in play and a let is called, the point must be replayed. Note, however, that if the serve is an unmistakable ace—that is, the Umpire is sure the erroneous call had not part in the Receiver's inability to play the ball—the point should be declared for the Server.*

Case 2. If a ball in play becomes broken, should a let be called?
Decision. Yes.

USTA COMMENT: *A ball shall be regarded as having become "broken" if, in the opinion of the Chair Umpire, it is found to have lost compression to the point of being unfit for further play, or unfit for any reason, and it is clear the defective ball was the one in play.*

RULE 14 • The "Let" in Service

The service is a let:

(a) If the ball served touches the net, strap or band, and is otherwise good, or, after touching the net, strap or band, touches the Receiver or anything which he wears or carries before hitting the ground.

(b) If a service or a fault is delivered when the Receiver is not ready (*see* Rule 12).

In case of a let, that particular service shall not count, and the Server shall serve again, but a service let does not annul a

the mistake is discovered, but all points scored before such discovery shall be reckoned. If a game shall have been completed before such discovery, the order of service remains as altered. A fault served before such discovery shall not be reckoned.

RULE 16 • When Players Change Ends

The players shall change ends at the end of the first, third and every subsequent alternate game of each set, and at the end of each set unless the total number of games in such set is even, in which case the change is not made until the end of the first game of the next set.

If a mistake is made and the correct sequence is not followed the players must take up their correct station as soon as the discovery is made and follow their original sequence.

RULE 17 • The Ball in Play

A ball is in play from the moment at which it is delivered in service. Unless a fault or a let is called it remains in play until the point is decided.

USTA COMMENT: *A point is not decided simply when, or because, a good shot has clearly passed a player, or when an apparently bad shot passes over a baseline or sideline. An outgoing ball is still definitely*

in play until it actually strikes the ground, backstop or a permanent fixture (other than the net, posts, singles sticks, cord or metal cable, strap or band), or a player. The same applies to a good ball, bounding after it has landed in the proper court. A ball that becomes imbedded in the net is out of play.

Case 1. A player fails to make a good return. No call is made and the ball remains in play. May his opponent later claim the point after the

See Case 5 under Rule 29.

USTA COMMENT: *When a ball is hit into the net and the player on the other side, thinking the ball is coming over, strikes at it and hits the net he loses the point if his touching the net occurs while the ball is still in play.*

RULE 18 • Server Wins Point

The Server wins the point:

(a) If the ball served, not being a let under Rule 14, touches the Receiver or anything which he wears or carries, before it hits the ground;

(b) If the Receiver otherwise loses the point as provided by Rule 20.

RULE 19 • Receiver Wins Point

The Receiver wins the point:

(a) If the Server serves two consecutive faults;

(b) If the Server otherwise loses the point as provided by Rule 20.

RULE 20 • Player Loses Point

A player loses the point if:

(a) He fails, before the ball in play has hit the ground twice consecutively, to return it directly over the net (except as provided in Rule 24(a) or (c)); or

(b) He returns the ball in play so that it hits the ground, a permanent fixture, or other object, outside any of the lines which bound his opponent's Court (except as provided in Rule 24(a) or (c)); or

USTA COMMENT: *A ball hitting a scoring device or other object attached to a net post results in loss of point to the striker.*

(c) He volleys the ball and fails to make a good return even when standing outside the Court; or

(d) In playing the ball he deliberately carries or catches it on his racket or deliberately touches it with his racket more than once; or

USTA COMMENT: *Only when there is a definite "second push" by the player does his shot become illegal, with consequent loss of point. The word 'deliberately' is the key word in this rule. Two hits occurring in the course of a single continuous swing are not deemed a double hit.*

(e) He or his racket (in his hand or otherwise) or anything which he wears or carries touches the net, posts, singles sticks, cord or metal cable, strap or band, or the ground within his opponent's Court at any time while the ball is in play; or

USTA COMMENT: *Touching a pipe support that runs across the court at the bottom of the net is interpreted as touching the net; See USTA Comment under Rule 23.*

(f) He volleys the ball before it has passed the net; or

(g) The ball in play touches him or anything that he wears or carries, except his racket in his hand or hands; or

USTA COMMENT: *This loss of point occurs regardless of whether the player is inside or outside the bounds of his court when the ball touches him.*

(h) He throws his racket at and hits the ball; or

(i) He deliberately and materially changes the shape of his racket during the playing of the point.

Case 1. In serving, the racket flies from the Server's hand and touches the net before the ball has touched the ground. Is this a fault, or does the player lose the point?
Decision. The Server loses the point because his racket touches the net while the ball is in play (Rule 20(e)).

Case 2. In serving, the racket flies from the Server's hand and touches the net after the ball has touched the ground outside the proper court. Is this a fault, or does the player lose the point?
Decision. This is a fault because the ball was out of play when the racket touched the net.

Case 3. A and B are playing against C and D, A is serving to D, C touches the net before the ball touches the ground. A fault is then called because the service falls outside the Service Court. Do C and D lose the point?
Decision. The call "fault" is an erroneous one. C and D had already lost the point before "fault" could be called, because C touched the net while the ball was in play (Rule 20(e)).

Case 4. May a player jump over the net into his opponent's Court while the ball is in play and not suffer penalty?
Decision. No. He loses the point (Rule 20(e)).

Case 5. A cuts the ball just over the net, and it returns to A's side. B, unable to reach the ball, throws his racket and hits the ball. Both racket and ball fall over the net on A's Court. A returns the ball outside of B's Court. Does B win or lose the point?
Decision. B loses the point (Rule 20(e) and (h)).

Case 6. A player standing outside the service Court is struck by a service ball before it has touched the ground. Does he win or lose the point?
Decision. The player struck loses the point (Rule 20(g)), except as provided under Rule 14(a).

Case 7. A player standing outside the Court volleys the ball or catches it in his hand and claims the point because the ball was certainly going out of court.

Decision. In no circumstances can he claim the point:

(1) If he catches the ball he loses the point under Rule 20(g).

(2) If he volleys it and makes a bad return he loses the point under Rule 20(c).

rally has started constitutes a distraction (hindrance), the Umpire, if he deems the claim valid, shall require the server to make some other and satisfactory disposition of the ball. Failure to comply with this instruction may result in loss of point(s) or disqualification.

RULE 22 • Ball Falls on Line

A ball falling on a line is regarded as falling in the Court bounded by that line.

USTA COMMENT: *'Deliberate' means a player did what he intended to do, although the resulting effect on his opponent might or might not have been what he intended.* EXAMPLE: *A player, after his return is in the air, gives advice to his partner in such a loud voice that his opponent is hindered. 'Involuntary' means a non-intentional act such as a hat blowing off or a scream resulting from a sudden wasp sting.*

Case 1. Is a player liable to a penalty if in making a stroke he touches his opponent?

Decision. No, unless the Umpire deems it necessary to take action under Rule 21.

Case 2. When a ball bounds back over the net, the player concerned may reach over the net in order to play the ball. What is the ruling if the player is hindered from doing this by his opponent?

Decision. In accordance with Rule 21, the Umpire may either award the point to the player hindered, or order the point to be replayed. (*See also* Rule 25).

Case 3. Does an involuntary double hit constitute an act which hinders an opponent within Rule 21?

Decision. No.

USTA COMMENT: *Upon appeal by a competitor that the server's action in discarding a "second ball" after a*

. . . the ball in play touches a permanent fixture (other than the net, posts, singles sticks, cord or metal cable, strap or band) after it has hit the ground, the player who struck it wins the point; if before it hits the ground, his opponent wins the point.

Case 1. A return hits the Umpire or his chair or stand. The player claims that the ball was going into Court.

Decision. He loses the point.

USTA COMMENT: *A ball in play that after passing the net strikes a pipe support running across the court at the base of the net is regarded the same as a ball landing on clear ground. See also* Rule 20(e).

RULE 24 • A Good Return

It is a good return:

(a) If the ball touches the net, posts, singles sticks, cord or metal cable, strap or band, provided that it passes over any of them and hits the ground within the Court; or

(b) If the ball, served or returned, hits the ground within the proper Court and rebounds or is blown back over the net, and the player whose turn it is to strike reaches over the net and plays the ball, provided that he does not contravene Rule

20(e), and that the stroke be otherwise good; or

(c) If the ball is returned outside the posts, or singles sticks, either above or below the level of the top of the net, even though it touches the posts or singles sticks, provided that it hits the ground within the proper Court; or

(d) If a player's racket passes over the net after he has returned the ball, provided the ball passes the net before being played and is properly returned; or

(e) If a player succeeds in returning the ball, served or in play, which strikes a ball lying in the Court.

USTA COMMENT: *Paragraph (e) of the rule refers to a ball lying on the court at the start of the point, as a result of a service let or fault, or as a result of a player dropping it. If a ball in play strikes a rolling or stationary "foreign" ball that has come from elsewhere after the point started, a let should be played. See Case 7 under Rule 25 and note that it pertains to an object other than a ball that is being used in the match.*

ITF NOTE: *In a singles match, if, for the sake of convenience, a doubles court is equipped with singles sticks for the purpose of a singles game, then the doubles posts and those portions of the net, cord or metal cable and the band outside such singles sticks shall at all times be permanent fixtures, and are not regarded as posts or parts of the net of a singles game.*

A return that passes under the net cord between the singles stick and adjacent doubles post without touching either net cord, net or doubles post and falls within the court, is a good return.

USTA COMMENT: *But in doubles this would be a "through"—Loss of point.*

Case 1. A ball going out of Court hits a net post or singles stick and falls within the lines of the opponent's Court. Is the stroke good?
Decision. If a service: no, under Rule 10(c). If other than a service: yes, under Rule 24 (a).

Case 2. Is it good return if a player returns the ball holding his racket in both hands?
Decision. Yes.

Case 3. The service, or ball in play, strikes a ball lying in the Court. Is the point won or lost thereby?

USTA COMMENT: *A ball that is touching a boundary line is considered to be "lying in the court."*

Decision. No. Play must continue. If it is not clear to the Umpire that the right ball is returned a let should be called.

Case 4. May a player use more than one racket at any time during play?
Decision. No; the whole implication of the Rules is singular.

Case 5. May a player request that a ball or balls lying in his opponent's Court be removed?
Decision. Yes, but not while a ball is in play.

USTA COMMENT: *This request must be honored.*

RULE 25 • Hindrance of a Player

In case a player is hindered in making a stroke by anything not within his control, except a permanent fixture of the Court, or except as provided for in Rule 21, a let shall be called.

Case 1. A spectator gets into the way of a player, who fails to return the ball. May the player then claim a let?
Decision. Yes, if in the Umpire's opinion he was obstructed by circumstances beyond his control, but not if due to permanent fixtures of the Court or the arrangements of the ground.

Case 2. A player is interfered with as in Case No. 1, and the Umpire calls a let. The Server had previously served a fault. Has he the right to two services?
Decision. Yes: as the ball is in play, the point, not merely the stroke, must be replayed as the Rule provides.

Case 3. May a player claim a let under Rule 25 because he thought his opponent was being hindered, and consequently did not expect the ball to be returned?
Decision. No.

Case 4. Is a stroke good when a ball in play hits another ball in the air?
Decision. A let should be called unless the other ball is in the air by the act of one of the players, in which case the Umpire will decide under Rule 21.

Case 5. If an Umpire or other judge erroneously calls "fault" or "out," and then corrects himself, which of the calls shell prevail?

remove the ball from the Court and negligently failed to do so, he may not claim a let.

Case 7. Is it a good stroke if the ball touches a stationary or moving object on the Court?
Decision. It is a good stroke unless the stationary object came into Court after the ball was put into play in which case a let must be called. If the ball in play strikes an object moving along or above the surface of the Court a let must be called.

Case 8. What is the ruling if the first service is a fault, the second service correct, and it becomes necessary to call a let either under the provision of Rule 25 or if the Umpire is unable to decide the point?
Decision. The fault shall be annulled and the whole point replayed.

USTA COMMENT: See *Rule 13 with its USTA Comments.*

RULE 26 • Score in a Game

If a player wins his first point, the score is called 15 for that player; on winning his second point, the score is called 30 for that player; on winning his third point, the score is called 40 for that player, and the fourth point won by a player is scored game for that player except as below:

If both players have won three points, the score is called deuce; and the next point won by a player is scored advantage for that player. If the same player wins the next point, he wins the game; if the other player wins the next point the score is again called deuce; and so on, until a player wins the two points immediately following the score at deuce, when the game is scored for that player.

(a) A player (or players) who first wins six games wins a set; except that he must win by a margin of two games over his opponent and where necessary a set is extended until this margin is achieved.

(b) The tie-break system of scoring may be adopted as an alternative to the advantage set system in paragraph (a) of this Rule provided the decision is announced in advance of the match. In this case, the following Rules shall be effective:

The tie-break shall operate when the score reaches six games all in any set except in the third or fifth set of a three set or five set match respectively when an ordinary advantage set shall be played, unless otherwise decided and announced in advance of the match.

The following system shall be used in a tie-break game:

Singles

(i) A player who first wins seven points shall win the game and the set provided he leads by a margin of two points. If the score reaches six points all the game shall be extended until this margin has been achieved. Numerical scoring shall be used throughout the tie-break game.

(ii) The player whose turn it is to serve shall be the server for the first point. His opponent shall be the server for the second and third points and thereafter each player shall serve alternately for two consecutive points until the winner of the game and set has been decided.

(iii) From the first point, each service shall be delivered alternately from the right and left courts, beginning from the right court. If service from a wrong half of the court occurs and is undetected, all play resulting from such wrong service or services shall stand, but the inaccuracy of station shall be corrected immediately it is discovered.

(iv) Players shall change ends after every six points an at the conclusion of the tie-break game.

(v) The tie-break game shall count as one game of the ball change, except that, if the balls are due to be changed at the beginning of the tie-break, the change shall be delayed until the second game of the following set.

Doubles

In doubles the procedure for singles shall apply. The player whose turn is to serve shall be the server for this point. Thereafter each player shall serve in rotation for two points, in the same order as previously in that set, until the winners of the game and set have been decided.

Rotation of Service

The player (or pair in the case of doubles) whose turn it was to serve first in the tie-break game shall receive service in the first game of the following set.

Case 1. At six all the tie-breaker is played, although it has been decided and announced in advance of the match that an advantage set will be played. Are the points already played counted?
Decision. If the error is discovered before the ball is put in play for the second point, the first point shall count but the error shall be corrected immediately. If the error is discovered after the ball is put in play for the second point the game shall continue as a tie-break game.

Case 2. At six all, an advantage game is played, although it has been decided and announced in advance of the match that a tie-break will be played. Are the points already played counted?
Decision. If the error is discovered before the ball is put in play for the second point, the first point shall be counted but the error shall be corrected immediately. If the error is discovered after the ball is put in play for the second point an advantage set shall be continued. If the score thereafter reaches eight games all or a higher even number, a tie-break shall be played.

Case 3. If during a tie-break in a singles or doubles game, a player serves out of turn, shall the order of service remain as altered until the end of the game?
Decision. If a player has completed his turn of service the order of service shall remain as altered. If the error is discovered before a player has completed his turn of service the order of service shall be corrected immediately and any points already played shall count.

RULE 28 • Maximum Number of Sets

The maximum number of sets in a match shall be 5, or, where women take part, 3.

RULE 29 • Role of Court Officials

In matches where an Umpire is appointed, his decision shall be final; but where a Referee is appointed, an appeal shall lie to him from the decision of an Umpire on a question of law, and in all such cases the decision of Referee shall be final.

In matches where assistants to the Umpire are appointed (Linesmen, Net-cord Judges, Foot-fault Judges) their decisions shall be final on questions of fact except that if in the opinion of an Umpire a clear mistake has been made he shall have the right to change the decision of an assistant or order a let to be played. When such an assistant is unable to give a decision he shall indicate this immediately to the Umpire who shall give a decision. When an Umpire is unable to give a decision on a question of fact he shall order a let to be played.

In Davis Cup matches or other team competitions where a Referee is on Court,

only overrule a Linesman if he does so immediately after the mistake has been made.

USTA COMMENT: See *Rule 17, Case 1.*

Case 4. A Linesman calls a ball out. The Umpire was unable to see clearly, although he thought the ball was in. May he overrule the Linesman?
Decision. No. An Umpire may only overrule if he considers that a call was incorrect beyond all

Referee and the players unanimously agree otherwise.

USTA COMMENT: See *second USTA Comment under Rule 30.*

Case 1. The Umpire orders a let, but a player claims that the point should not be replayed. May the Referee be requested to give a decision?
Decision. Yes. A question of tennis law, that is an issue relating to the application of specific facts, shall first be determined by the Umpire. However, if the Umpire is uncertain or if a player appeals from his determination, then the Referee shall be requested to give a decision, and his decision is final.

Case 2. A ball is called out, but a player claims that the ball was good. May the Referee give a ruling?
Decision. No. This is a question of fact, that is an issue relating to what actually occurred during a specific incident, and the decision of the on-court officials is therefore final.

Case 3. May an Umpire overrule a Linesman at the end of a rally if, in his opinion, a clear mistake has been made during the course of a rally?
Decision. No, unless in his opinion the opponent was hindered. Otherwise an Umpire may

Decision. Yes. If a Linesman realizes he has made an error, he may make a correction provided he does so immediately.

Case 6. A player claims his return shot was good after a Linesman called "out." May the Umpire overrule the Linesman?
Decision. No. An Umpire may never overrule as a result of a protest or an appeal by a player.

RULE 30 • Continuous Play and Rest Periods

Play shall be continuous from the first service until the match is concluded, in accordance with the following provisions:

(a) If the first service is a fault, the second service must be struck by the Server without delay.

The Receiver must play to the reasonable pace of the Server and must be ready to receive when the Server is ready to serve.

When changing ends, a maximum of one minute thirty seconds shall elapse from the moment the ball goes out of play at the end of the game to the time the ball is struck for the first point of the next game.

The Umpire shall use his discretion when there is interference which makes it impractical for play to be continuous.

The organizers of international circuits and team events recognized by the ITF may determine the time allowed between points, which shall not at any time exceed 25 seconds.

(b) Play shall never be suspended, delayed or interfered with for the purpose of enabling a player to recover his strength, breath, or physical condition.

However, in the case of accidental injury, the Umpire may allow a one-time three minute suspension for that injury.

The organizers of international circuits and team events recognized by the ITF may extend the one-time suspension period from three minutes to five minutes.

(c) If, through circumstances outside the control of the player, his clothing, footwear or equipment (excluding racket) becomes out of adjustment in such a way that it is impossible or undesirable for him to play on, the Umpire may suspend play while the maladjustment is rectified.

USTA COMMENT: *Loss of, or damage to, a contact lens or eyeglasses shall be treated as equipment maladjustment. All players must follow the same rules with respect to suspending play, even though in misty, but playable, weather a player who wears glasses may be handicapped.*

(d) The Umpire may suspend or delay play at any time as may be necessary and appropriate.

USTA COMMENT: *When a match is resumed after a suspension of more than ten minutes, it is permissible for the players to engage in a re-warm-up that may be of the same duration as that at the start of the match. The preferred method is to warm-up with other used balls and then insert the match balls when play starts. If the match balls are used in the re-warm-up, then the next ball change will be two games sooner. There shall be no re-warm-up after an authorized intermission or after a suspension of ten minutes or less.*

(e) After the third set, or when women take part the second set, either player is entitled to a rest, which shall not exceed 10 minutes, or in countries situated between latitude 15 degrees north and latitude 15 degrees south, 45 minutes and furthermore, when necessitated by circumstances not within the control of the players, the Umpire may suspend play for such a period as he may consider necessary. If play is suspended and is not resumed until a later day the rest may be taken only after the third set (or when women take part the second set) of play on such a later day, completion of an unfinished set being counted as one set.

If play is suspended and is not resumed until 10 minutes have elapsed in the same day, the rest may be taken only after three consecutive sets have been played without interruption (or when women take part two sets), completion of an unfinished set being counted as one set.

Any nation and/or committee organizing a tournament, match or competition, other than the International Tennis Championships (Davis Cup and Federation Cup), is at liberty to modify this provision or omit it from its regulations provided this is announced before the event commences.

(f) A tournament committee has the discretion to decide the time allowed for a warm-up period prior to a match but this may not exceed five minutes and must be announced before the event commences.

USTA COMMENT: *When there are no ball persons this time may be extended to 10 minutes.*

(g) When approved point penalty and non-accumulative point penalty systems are in operation, the Umpire shall make his decisions within the terms of those systems.

(h) Upon violation of the principle that play shall be continuous the Umpire may, after giving due warning, disqualify the offender.

RULE 31 • Coaching

During the playing of a match in a team competition, a player may receive coaching from a captain who is sitting on the court only when he changes ends at the end of a game, but not when he changes ends during a tie-break game.

A player may not receive coaching during the playing of any other match.

by signals in an unobtrusive manner?
Decision. The Umpire must take action as soon as he becomes aware that coaching is being given verbally or by signals. If the Umpire is unaware that coaching is being given, a player may draw his attention to the fact that advice is being given.

Case 2. Can a player receive coaching during an authorized rest period under Rule 30(e), or when play is interrupted and he leaves the court?
Decision. Yes. In these circumstances, when the player is not on the court, there is no restriction on coaching.

ITF NOTE: *The word "coaching" includes any advice or instruction.*

RULE 32 • Changing Balls

In cases where balls are to be changed after a specified number of games, if the balls are not changed in the correct sequence, the mistake shall be corrected when the player, or pair in the case of doubles, who should have served with new balls is next due to serve. Thereafter the balls shall be changed so that the number of games between changes shall be that originally agreed.

THE DOUBLES GAME

RULE 33

The above Rules shall apply to the Doubles Game except as below.

RULE 34 • The Doubles Court

For the Doubles Game, the Court shall be 36 feet (10.97 m) in width, i.e., 4½ feet

omitted if desired.

USTA COMMENT: *The Server has the right in doubles to stand anywhere back of the baseline between the center mark imaginary extension and the doubles sideline imaginary extension.*

RULE 35 • Order of Service in Doubles

The order of serving shall be decided at the beginning of each set as follows:

The pair who have to serve in the first game of each set shall decide which partner shall do so and the opposing pair shall decide similarly for the second game. The partner of the player who served in the first game shall serve in the third; the partner who served in the second game shall serve in the fourth, and so on in the same order in all the subsequent games of a set.

Case 1. In doubles, one player does not appear in time to play, and his partner claims to be allowed to play single-handed against the opposing players. May he do so?
Decision. No.

RULE 36 • Order of Receiving in Doubles

The order of receiving the service shall be decided at the beginning of each set as follows:

The pair who have to receive the service in the first game shall decide which partner shall receive the first service, and that partner shall continue to receive the first service in every odd game throughout that set. The opposing pair shall likewise decide which partner shall receive the first service in the second game and that partner shall continue to receive the first service in every even game throughout that set. Partners shall receive the service alternately throughout each game.

Case 1. Is it allowable in doubles for the Server's partner or the Receiver's partner to stand in a position that obstructs the view of the Receiver? **Decision.** Yes. The Server's partner or the Receiver's partner may take any position on his side of the net in or out of the Court that he wishes.

RULE 37 • Service Out of Turn in Doubles

If a partner serves out of his turn, the partner who ought to have served shall serve as soon as the mistake is discovered, but all points scored, and any faults served before such discovery, shall be reckoned. If a game shall have been completed before such discovery, the order of service remains as altered.

USTA COMMENT: *For an exception to Rule 37, see Case 3 under Rule 27.*

RULE 38 • Error in Order of Receiving in Doubles

If during a game the order of receiving the service is changed by the Receivers it shall remain as altered until the end of the game in which the mistake is discovered, but the partners shall resume their original order of receiving in the next game of that set in which they are Receivers of the service.

RULE 39 • Service Fault in Doubles

The service is a fault as provided for by Rule 10, or if the ball touches the Server's partner or anything which he wears or carries; but if the ball served touches the partner of the Receiver, or anything which he wears or carries, not being a let under Rule 14(a) before it hits the ground, the Server wins the point.

RULE 40 • Playing the Ball in Doubles

The ball shall be struck alternately by one or other player of the opposing pairs, and if a player touches the ball in play with his racket in contravention of this Rule, his opponents win the point.

USTA COMMENT: *This means that, in the course of making one return, only one member of a doubles team may hit the ball. If both of them hit the ball, either simultaneously or consecutively, it is an illegal return. The partners themselves do not have to "alternate" in making returns. Mere clashing of rackets does not make a return illegal unless it is clear that more than one racket touched the ball.*

ITF NOTE: *Except where otherwise stated, every reference in these rules to the masculine includes the feminine gender.*

Queen Mary congratulates the queen of Wimbledon, Suzanne Lenglen, in 1926. • *UPI*

APPENDIX B: RECORDS

National Tennis Center, Flushing Meadow, New York, had separate beginnings for men and women. The first Championships, men only, was staged at the Newport Casino in 1881, and held there through 1914. The doubles championship was played along with the singles between 1881 and 1886. From 1887 through 1914, sectional doubles tournaments, East and West, sometimes North and South as well, were staged at various locations with the winners playing off for the title at Newport.

In 1915 the men's singles moved to the West Side Tennis Club, Forest Hills, New York, as did the doubles final for sectional winners. In 1917 the men's doubles championship, a complete tournament, was installed at the Longwood Cricket Club, Boston, and remained there through 1967, with two exceptions (1934 at Germantown Cricket Club, Philadelphia, and 1942 through 1945 at Forest Hills, during World War II).

The men's singles departed briefly from Forest Hills for a three-year stay at Germantown Cricket, 1921 through 1923, and thereafter was staged at West Side where the newly constructed Stadium was ready in 1924.

through 1920, along with the mixed doubles, begun in 1892. In 1921 the women's singles and doubles moved to Forest Hills, but as an event prior to and separate from the men's championship, while the mixed doubles moved to Longwood to be played concurrently with the men's doubles.

In 1935 the men's and women's singles championships were united at Forest Hills while the women's doubles moved to Longwood as part of the National Doubles with men's and mixed events.

During World War II (1942–45) all five events—men's and women's singles and doubles and mixed—were played at Forest Hills. In 1946 the men's and women's doubles returned to Longwood but the mixed remained at West Side until 1967 when it was played again at Longwood.

In 1968, with the advent of open tennis, the Championships, an amateur event closed to professionals since inception, was moved to Longwood where men's and women's singles and doubles and mixed were played as amateur events in 1968–69. Forest Hills thus became the scene of the first U.S. Open in 1968, and remained so until the move to Flushing Meadow in 1978. Men's and women's singles and doubles and mixed were thereby open to professionals and amateurs alike, and prize money was offered from 1968 on. The original amateurs-only event was abandoned in Boston after 1969, eliminating the confusion of two U.S. championships on successive dates on the calendar.

The Championships began on grass courts and continued that way until 1975 when the Forest Hills surface was changed to clay. The present surface at Flushing Meadow is hard, an asphalt composition. Night play began with the installation of floodlights in 1975 at Forest Hills.

The following is a list of champions and finalists in men's and women's singles and doubles, and champions in mixed doubles. The challenge round system was in force from 1884 through 1911, meaning that the defending champion played only one match, waiting for a challenger to emerge from an all-comers tournament. Sometimes the champion did not defend, and the winner of the all-comers became champion. The system has not been used since 1911 by the men, but continued until 1919 for women.

Separate U.S. championships are also determined on clay, hard and indoor courts at various locations for men and women. The indoor championships began in 1898 for men and 1907 for women; the clay court in 1910 for men, 1912 for women. Hard court championships for men and women, begun in 1948, were discontinued after 1971, but restored in 1988, seemingly redundant since the foremost championship, the U.S. Open at Flushing Meadow, is played on identical courts.

Men's Singles

Year

1881	Richard Sears d. William Glyn 6–0 6–3, 6–2
1882	Richard Sears d. Clarence Clark 6–1, 6–4, 6–0
1883	Richard Sears d. James Dwight 6–2, 6–0, 9–7
1884	Richard Sears d. Howard Taylor 6–0, 1–6, 6–0, 6–2
1885	Richard Sears d. Godfrey Brinley 6–3, 4–6, 6–0, 6–3
1886	Richard Sears d. R. Livingston Beeckman 4–6, 6–1, 6–3, 6–4
1887	Richard Sears d. Henry Slocum 6–1, 6–3, 6–2
1888	Henry Slocum d. Howard Taylor 6–4, 6–1, 6–0
1889	Henry Slocum d. Quincy Shaw 6–3, 6–1, 4–6, 6–2
1890	Oliver Campbell d. Henry Slocum 6–2, 4–6, 6–3, 6–1
1891	Oliver Campbell d. Clarence Hobart 2–6, 7–5, 7–9, 6–1, 6–2
1892	Oliver Campbell d. Fred Hovey 7–5, 3–6, 6–3, 7–5
1893	Robert Wrenn d. Fred Hovey 6–4, 3–6, 6–4, 6–4
1894	Robert Wrenn d. Manliffe Goodbody 6–8, 6–1, 6–4, 6–4
1895	Fred Hovey d. Robert Wrenn 6–3, 6–2, 6–4
1896	Robert Wrenn d. Fred Hovey 7–5, 3–6, 6–0, 1–6, 6–1
1897	Robert Wrenn d. Wilberforce Eaves 4–6, 8–6, 6–3, 2–6, 6–2
1898	Malcolm Whitman d. Dwight Davis 3–6, 6–2, 6–2, 6–1
1899	Malcolm Whitman d. Parmly Paret 6–1, 6–2, 3–6, 7–5
1900	Malcolm Whitman d. Bill Larned 6–4, 1–6, 6–2, 6–2
1901	Bill Larned d. Beals Wright 6–2, 6–8, 6–4, 6–4
1902	Bill Larned d. Reggie Doherty 4–6, 6–2, 6–4, 8–6
1903	Laurie Doherty d. Bill Larned 6–0, 6–3, 10–8
1904	Holcombe Ward d. Bill Clothier 10–8, 6–4, 9–7
1905	Beals Wright d. Holcombe Ward 6–2 6–1, 11–9
1906	Bill Clothier d. Beals Wright 6–3, 6–0, 6–4
1907	Bill Larned d. Bob LeRoy 6–2, 6–2, 6–4
1908	Bill Larned d. Beals Wright 6–1, 6–2, 8–6
1909	Bill Larned d. Bill Clothier 6–1, 6–2, 5–7, 1–6, 6–1
1910	Bill Larned d. Tom Bundy 6–1, 5–7, 6–0, 6–8, 6–1
1911	Bill Larned d. Maurice McLoughlin 6–4, 6–4, 6–2
1912	Maurice McLoughlin d. Wallace Johnson 3–6, 2–6, 6–2, 6–4, 6–2

1913 Maurice McLoughlin d. Dick Williams 6–4, 5–7, 6–3, 6–1

1914 Dick Williams d. Maurice McLoughlin 6–3, 8–6, 10–8

1915 Bill Johnston d. Maurice McLoughlin 1–6, 6–0, 7–5, 10–8

1916 Dick Williams d. Bill Johnston 4–6, 6–4, 0–6, 6–2, 6–4

1917 R. Lindley Murray d. Nathaniel Niles 5–7, 8–6, 6–3, 6–3

1918 R. Lindley Murray d. Bill Tilden 6–3, 6–1, 7–5

1919 Bill Johnston d. Bill Tilden 6–4, 6–4, 6–3

1927 Rene Lacoste d. Bill Tilden 11–9, 6–3, 11–9

1928 Henri Cochet d. Francis Hunter 4–6, 6–4, 3–6, 7–5, 6–3

1929 Bill Tilden d. Francis Hunter 3–6, 6–3, 4–6, 6–2, 6–4

1930 John Doeg d. Frank Shields 10–8, 1–6, 6–4, 16–14

1931 Ellsworth Vines d. George Lott 7–9, 6–3, 9–7, 7–5

1932 Ellsworth Vines d. Henri Cochet 6–4, 6–4, 6–4

1933 Fred Perry d. Jack Crawford 6–3, 11–13, 4–6, 6–0, 6–1

1934 Fred Perry d. Wilmer Allison 6–4, 6–3, 1–6, 8–6

1935 Wilmer Allison d. Sidney Wood 6–2, 6–2, 6–3

1936 Fred Perry d. Don Budge 2–6, 6–2, 8–6, 1–6, 10–8

1937 Don Budge d. Gottfried von Cramm 6–1, 7–9, 6–1, 3–6, 6–1

1938 Don Budge d. Gene Mako 6–3, 6–8, 6–2, 6–1

1939 Bobby Riggs d. Welby Van Horn 6–4, 6–2, 6–4

1940 Don McNeill d. Bobby Riggs 4–6, 6–8, 6–3, 6–3, 7–5

1941 Bobby Riggs d. Frank Kovacs 5–7, 6–1, 6–3, 6–3

1942 Ted Schroeder d. Frank Parker 8–6, 7–5, 3–6, 4–6, 6–2

1943 Joe Hunt d. Jack Kramer 6–3, 6–8, 10–8, 6–0

1944 Frank Parker d. Bill Talbert 6–4, 3–6, 6–3, 6–3

1945 Frank Parker d. Bill Talbert 14–12, 6–1, 6–2

1946 Jack Kramer d. Tom Brown 9–7, 6–3, 6–0

1947 Jack Kramer d. Frank Parker 4–6, 2–6, 6–1, 6–0, 6–3

1948 Pancho Gonzalez d. Eric Sturgess 6–2, 6–3, 14–12

1949 Pancho Gonzales d. Ted Schroeder 16–18, 2–6, 6–1, 6–2, 6–4

1950 Art Larsen d. Herbie Flam 6–3, 4–6, 5–7, 6–4, 6–3

1951 Frank Sedgman d. Vic Seixas 6–4, 6–1, 6–1

1952 Frank Sedgman d. Gardnar Mulloy 6–1, 6–2, 6–3

1953 Tony Trabert d. Vic Seixas 6–3, 6–2, 6–3

1954 Vic Seixas d. Rex Hartwig 3–6, 6–2, 6–4, 6–4

1955 Tony Trabert d. Ken Rosewall 9–7, 6–3, 6–3

1963 Rafael Osuna d. Frank Froehling 7–5, 6–4, 6–2

1964 Roy Emerson d. Fred Stolle 6–4, 6–1, 6–4

1965 Manuel Santana d. Cliff Drysdale 6–2, 7–9, 7–5, 6–1

1966 Fred Stolle d. John Newcombe 4–6, 12–10, 6–3, 6–4

1967 John Newcombe d. Clark Graebner 6–4, 6–4, 8–6

1968 Arthur Ashe d. Bob Lutz 4–6, 6–3, 8–10, 6–0, 6–4

1968* Arthur Ashe d. Tom Okker 14–12, 5–7, 6–3, 3–6, 6–3

1969 Stan Smith d. Bob Lutz 9–7, 6–3, 6–1

1969* Rod Laver d. Tony Roche 7–9, 6–1, 6–3, 6–2

1970 Ken Rosewall d. Tony Roche 2–6, 6–4, 7–6, 6–3

1971 Stan Smith d. Jan Kodes 3–6, 6–3, 6–2, 7–6

1972 Ilie Nastase d. Arthur Ashe 3–6, 6–3, 6–7, 6–4, 6–3

1973 John Newcombe d. Jan Kodes 6–4, 1–6, 4–6, 6–2, 6–3

1974 Jimmy Connors d. Ken Rosewall 6–1, 6–0, 6–1

1975 Manuel Orantes d. Jimmy Connors 6–4, 6–3, 6–3

1976 Jimmy Connors d. Bjorn Borg 6–4, 3–6, 7–6, 6–4

1977 Guillermo Vilas d. Jimmy Connors 2–6, 6–3, 7–6, 6–0

1978 Jimmy Connors d. Bjorn Borg 6–4, 6–2, 6–2

1979 John McEnroe d. Vitas Gerulaitis 7–5, 6–3, 6–3

*Open champions. In 1968 and 1969 both Amateur and Open Championships were held. Thereafter there was only the Open as principal Championship.

1980	John McEnroe d. Bjorn Borg 7–6, 6–1, 6–7, 5–7, 6–4

1980   John McEnroe d. Bjorn Borg 7–6, 6–1, 6–7,
        5–7, 6–4
1981   John McEnroe d. Bjorn Borg 4–6, 6–2, 6–4,
        6–3
1982   Jimmy Connors d. Ivan Lendl 6–3, 6–2, 4–6,
        6–4
1983   Jimmy Connors d. Ivan Lendl 6–3, 6–7, 7–5,
        6–0
1984   John McEnroe d. Ivan Lendl 6–3, 6–4, 6–1
1985   Ivan Lendl d. John McEnroe 7–6, 6–3, 6–4
1986   Ivan Lendl d. Miloslav Mecir 6–4, 6–2, 6–0
1987   Ivan Lendl d. Mats Wilander 6–7, 6–0, 7–6,
        6–4
1988   Mats Wilander d. Ivan Lendl 6–4, 4–6, 6–3,
        5–7, 6–4
1989   Boris Becker d. Ivan Lendl 7–6, 1–6, 6–3, 7–6
1990   Pete Sampras d. Andre Agassi 6–4, 6–3, 6–2
1991   Stefan Edberg d. Jim Courier 6–2, 6–4, 6–0
1992   Stefan Edberg d. Pete Sampras 3–6, 6–4, 7–6,
        6–2

Women's Singles

Year

1887   Ellen Hansell d. Laura Knight 6–1, 6–0
1888   Bertha Townsend d.Ellen Hansell 6–3, 6–5
1889   Bertha Townsend d. Lida Voorhees 7–5, 6–2
1890   Ellen Roosevelt d. Bertha Townsend 6–2, 6–2
1891   Mabel Cahill d. Ellen Roosevelt 6–4, 6–1, 4–6,
        6–3
1892   Mabel Cahill d. Elisabeth Moore 5–7, 6–3,
        6–4, 4–6, 6–2
1893   Aline Terry d. Augusta Schultz 6–1, 6–3
1894   Helen Hellwig d. Aline Terry 7–5, 3–6, 6–0,
        3–6, 6–3
1895   Juliette Atkinson d. Helen Hellwig 6–4, 6–1,
        6–2
1896   Elisabeth Moore d. Juliette Atkinson 6–4,
        4–6, 6–2, 6–2
1897   Juliette Atkinson d. Elisabeth Moore 6–3,
        6–3, 4–6, 3–6, 6–3
1898   Juliette Atkinson d. Marion Jones 6–3, 5–7,
        6–4, 2–6, 7–5
1899   Marion Jones d. Maud Banks 6–1, 6–1, 7–5
1900   Myrtle McAteer d. Edith Parker 6–2,6–2, 6–0
1901   Elisabeth Moore d. Myrtle McAteer 6–4, 3–6,
        7–5, 2–6, 6–2
1902   Marion Jones d. Elisabeth Moore 6–1, 1–0
        default
1903   Elisabeth Moore d. Marion Jones 7–5, 8–6
1904   May Sutton d. Elisabeth Moore 6–1, 6–2
1905   Elisabeth Moore d. Helen Homans 6–4, 5–7,
        6–1
1906   Helen Homans d. Maud Barger–Wallach 6–4,
        6–3

1907   Evelyn Sears d. Carrie Neely 6–3, 6–2
1908   Maud Barger Wallach d. Evelyn Sears 6–2,
        1–6, 6–3
1909   Hazel Hotchkiss d. Maud Barger Wallach
        6–0, 6–1
1910   Hazel Hotchkiss d. Louise Hammond 6–4,
        6–2
1911   Hazel Hotchkiss d. Florence Sutton 8–10,
        6–1, 9–7
1912   Mary K. Browne d. Eleonora Sears 6–4, 6–2
1913   Mary K. Browne d. Dorothy Green 6–2, 7–5
1914   Mary K. Browne d. Marie Wagner 6–2, 1–6,
        6–1
1915   Molla Bjurstedt d. Hazel Hotchkiss Wightman
        4–6, 6–2, 6–0
1916   Molla Bjurstedt d. Louise Hammond
        Raymond 4–6, 6–2, 6–0
1917   Molla Bjurstedt d. Marion Vanderhoef 4–6,
        6–0, 6–2
1918   Molla Bjurstedt d. Eleanor Goss 6–4, 6–3
1919   Hazel Hotchkiss Wightman d. Marion
        Zinderstein 6–1, 6–2
1920   Molla Bjurstedt Mallory d. Marion
        Zinderstein 6–3, 6–1
1921   Molla Bjurstedt Mallory d. Mary K. Browne
        4–6, 6–4, 6–2
1922   Molla Bjurstedt Mallory d. Helen Wills 6–3,
        6–1
1923   Helen Wills d. Molla Bjurstedt Mallory 6–2,
        6–1
1924   Helen Wills d. Molla Bjurstedt Mallory 6–1,
        6–3
1925   Helen Wills d. Kitty McKane 3–6, 6–0, 6–2
1926   Molla Bjurstedt Mallory d. Elizabeth Ryan
        4–6, 6–4, 9–7
1927   Helen Wills d. Betty Nuthall 6–1, 6–4
1928   Helen Wills d. Helen Jacobs 6–2, 6–1
1929   Helen Wills Moody d. Phoebe Watson 6–4,
        6–2
1930   Betty Nuthall d. Anna McCune Harper, 6–1,
        6–4
1931   Helen Wills Moody d. Eileen Whitingstall
        6–4, 6–1
1932   Helen Jacobs d. Carolin Babcock 6–2, 6–2
1933   Helen Jacobs d. Helen Wills Moody 8–6, 3–6,
        3–0, default
1934   Helen Jacobs d. Sarah Palfrey Fabyan 6–1,
        6–4
1935   Helen Jacobs d. Sarah Palfrey Fabyan 6–2,
        6–4
1936   Alice Marble d. Helen Jacobs 4–6, 6–3, 6–2
1937   Anita Lizana d. Jadwiga Jedrzejowska 6–4, 6–2
1938   Alice Marble d. Nancye Wynne Bolton 6–0,
        6–3
1939   Alice Marble d. Helen Jacobs 6–0, 8–10, 6–4
1940   Alice Marble d. Helen Jacobs 6–2, 6–3
1941   Sarah Palfrey Cooke d. Pauline Betz 7–5, 6–2
1942   Pauline Betz d. Louise Brough 4–6, 6–1, 6–4

1943	Pauline Betz d. Louise Brough 6–3, 5–7, 6–3
1944	Pauline Betz d. Margaret Osborne 6–3, 8–6
1945	Sarah Palfrey Cooke d. Pauline Betz 3–6, 8–6, 6–4
1946	Pauline Betz d. Doris Hart 11–9, 6–3
1947	Louise Brough d. Margaret Osborne duPont 8–6, 4–6, 6–1
1948	Margaret Osborne duPont d. Louise Brough 4–6, 6–4, 15–13
1949	Margaret Osborne duPont d. Doris Hart 6–4, 6–1
1950	Margaret Osborne duPont d. Doris Hart 6–8

1959	Maria Bueno d. Christine Truman 6–1, 6–4
1960	Darlene Hard d. Maria Bueno 6–4, 10–12, 6–4
1961	Darlene Hard d. Ann Haydon 6–3, 6–4
1962	Margaret Smith d. Darlene Hard 9–7, 6–4
1963	Maria Bueno d. Margaret Smith 7–5, 6–4
1964	Maria Bueno d. Carole Caldwell Graebner 6–1, 6–0
1965	Margaret Smith d. Billie Jean Moffitt 8–6, 7–5
1966	Maria Bueno d. Nancy Richey 6–3, 6–1
1967	Billie Jean Moffitt King d. Ann Haydon Jones 11–9, 6–4
1968	Margaret Smith Court d. Maria Bueno 6–2, 6–2
1968*	Virginia Wade d. Billie Jean Moffitt King 6–4, 6–2
1969	Margaret Smith Court d. Virginia Wade 4–6, 6–3, 6–0
1969*	Margaret Smith Court d. Nancy Richey 6–2, 6–2
1970	Margaret Smith Court d. Rosemary Casals 6–2, 2–6, 6–1
1971	Billie Jean Moffitt King d. Rosemary Casals 6–4, 7–6
1972	Billie Jean Moffitt King d. Kerry Melville 6–3, 7–5
1973	Margaret Smith Court d. Evonne Goolagong 7–6, 5–7, 6–2
1974	Billie Jean Moffitt King d. Evonne Goolagong 3–6, 6–3, 7–5
1975	Chris Evert d. Evonne Goolagong 5–7, 6–4, 6–2
1976	Chris Evert d. Evonne Goolagong 6–3, 6–0
1977	Chris Evert d. Wendy Tumbull 7–6, 6–2
1978	Chris Evert d. Pam Shriver 7–5, 6–4
1979	Tracy Austin d. Chris Evert Lloyd 6–4, 6–3

1980	Chris Evert d. Hana Mandlikova 5–7, 6–1, 6–1
1981	Tracy Austin d. Martina Navratilova 1–6, 7–6, 7–6
1982	Chris Evert d Hana Mandlikova 6–3, 6–1
1983	Martina Navratilova d. Chris Evert 6–1, 6–3
1984	Martina Navratilova d. Chris Evert Lloyd 4–6, 6–4, 6–4
1985	Hana Mandlikova d. Martina Navratilova 7–6, 1–6, 7–6
1986	Martina Navratilova d. Helena Sukova 6–3, 6–2
1987	Martina Navratilova d. Steffi Graf 7–6, 6–1

Open Championships were held. Thereafter there was only the Open as principal Championship.

Men's Doubles

Year

1881	Clarence Clark–Fred Taylor d. Alexander Van Rensselaer–A. Newbold 6–5, 6–4, 6–5
1882	Richard Sears–James Dwight d. C. Nightingale–G. Smith 6–2, 6–4, 6–4
1883	Richard Sears–James Dwight d. Alexander Van Rensselaer–A. Newbold 6–0, 6–2, 6–2
1884	Richard Sears–James Dwight d. A. Van Rensselaer–W. Berry 6–4, 6–1, 8–10, 6–4
1885	Richard Sears–Joseph Clark d. Henry Slocum–Percy Knapp 6–3, 6–0, 6–2
1886	Richard Sears–James Dwight d. Howard Taylor–Godfrey Brinley 7–5, 5–7, 7–5, 6–4
1887	Richard Sears–James Dwight d. Howard Taylor–Henry Slocum 6–4, 3–6, 2–6, 6–3, 6–3
1888	Oliver Campbell–Valentine Hall d. Clarence Hobart–E. MacMullen 6–4, 6–2, 6–4
1889	Henry Slocum–Howard Taylor d. Valentine Hall–Oliver Campbell 14–12, 10–8, 6–4
1890	Valentine Hall–Clarence Hobart d. J. Carver–J. Ryerson 6–3, 4–6, 6–2, 2–6, 6–3
1891	Oliver Campbell–Bob Huntington d. Valentine Hall–Clarence Hobart 6–3, 6–4, 8–6
1892	Oliver Campbell–Bob Huntington d. Valentine Hall–Edward Hall 6–4, 6–2, 4–6, 6–3

1893 Clarence Hobart–Fred Hovey d. Oliver Campbell–Bob Huntington 6–4, 6–4, 4–6, 6–2

1894 Clarence Hobart–Fred Hovey d. Carr Neel–Sam Neel 6–3, 8–6, 6–1

1895 Malcolm Chace–Robert Wrenn d. Clarence Hobart–Fred Hovey 7–5, 6–1, 8–6

1896 Carr Neel–Sam Neel d. Robert Wrenn–Malcolm Chace 6–3, 1–6, 6–1, 3–6, 6–1

1897 Leo Ware–George Sheldon d. Harold Mahony–Harold Nisbet 11–13, 6–2, 9–7, 1–6, 6–1

1898 Leo Ware–George Sheldon d. Holcombe Ward–Dwight Davis 1–6, 7–5, 6–4, 4–6, 7–5

1899 Holcombe Ward–Dwight Davis d. Leo Ware–George Sheldon 6–4, 6–4, 6–3

1900 Holcombe Ward–Dwight Davis d. Fred Alexander–Ray Little 6–4, 9–7, 12–10

1901 Holcombe Ward–Dwight Davis d. Leo Ware–Beals Wright 6–3, 9–7, 6–1

1902 Reggie Doherty–Laurie Doherty d. Holcombe Ward–Dwight Davis 11–9, 12–10, 6–4

1903 Reggie Doherty–Laurie Doherty d. Kriegh Collins–Harry Waidner 7–5, 6–3, 6–3

1904 Holcombe Ward–Beals Wright d. Kriegh Collins–Ray Little 1–6, 6–2, 3–6, 6–4, 6–1

1905 Holcombe Ward–Beals Wright d. Fred Alexander–Harold Hackett 6–2, 6–1, 6–3

1906 Holcombe Ward–Beals Wright d. Fred Alexander–Harold Hackett 6–3, 3–6, 6–3, 6–3

1907 Fred Alexander–Harold Hackett d. Nat Thornton–Bryan "Bitsy" Grant 6–2, 6–1, 6–1

1908 Fred Alexander–Harold Hackett d. Ray Little–Beals Wright 6–1, 7–5, 6–2

1909 Fred Alexander–Harold Hackett d. Maurice McLoughlin–George Janes 6–4, 6–4, 6–0

1910 Fred Alexander–Harold Hackett d. Thomas Bundy–Trowbridge Hendrick 6–1, 8–6, 6–3

1911 Ray Little–Gus Touchard d. Fred Alexander–Harold Hackett 7–5, 13–15, 6–2, 6–4

1912 Maurice McLoughlin–Tom Bundy d. Ray Little–Gus Touchard 3–6, 6–2, 6–1, 7–5

1913 Maurice McLoughlin–Tom Bundy d. John Strachan–Clarence Griffin 6–4, 7–5, 6–1

1914 Maurice McLoughlin–Tom Bundy d. George Church–Dean Mathey 6–4, 6–2, 6–4

1915 Bill Johnston–Clarence Griffin d. Maurice McLoughlin–Tom Bundy 2–6, 6–3, 6–4, 3–6, 6–3

1916 Bill Johnston–Clarence Griffin d. Maurice McLoughlin–Ward Dawson 6–4, 6–3, 5–7, 6–3

1917 Fred Alexander–Harold Throckmorton d. Harry Johnson–Irving Wright 11–9, 6–4, 6–4

1918 Bill Tilden–Vinnie Richards d. Fred Alexander–Beals Wright 6–3, 6–4, 3–6, 2–6, 6–2

1919 Norman Brookes–Gerald Patterson d. Bill Tilden–Vinnie Richards 8–6, 6–3, 4–6, 6–2

1920 Bill Johnston–Clarence Griffin d. Willis Davis–Roland Roberts 6–2, 6–2, 6–3

1921 Bill Tilden–Vinnie Richards d. Dick Williams–Watson Washburn 13–11, 12–10, 6–1

1922 Bill Tilden–Vinnie Richards d. Gerald Patterson–Pat O'Hara Wood 4–6, 6–1, 6–3, 6–4

1923 Bill Tilden–Brian Norton d. Dick Williams–Watson Washburn 3–6, 6–2, 6–3, 5–7, 6–2

1924 Howard Kinsey–Robert Kinsey d. Gerald Patterson–Pat O'Hara Wood 7–5, 5–7, 7–9, 6–3, 6–4

1925 Dick Williams–Vinnie Richards d. Gerald Patterson–John Hawkes 6–2, 8–10, 6–4, 11–9

1926 Dick Williams–Vinnie Richards d. Bill Tilden–Al Chapin 6–4, 6–8, 11–9, 6–3

1927 Bill Tilden–Francis Hunter d. Bill Johnston–Dick Williams 10–8, 6–3, 6–3

1928 George Lott–John Hennessey d. Gerald Patterson–John Hawkes 6–2, 6–1, 6–2

1929 George Lott–John Doeg d. Berkeley Bell–Lewis White 10–8, 16–14, 6–1

1930 George Lott–John Doeg d. John Van Ryn–Wilmer Allison 8–6, 6–3, 4–6, 13–15, 6–4

1931 Wilmer Allison–John Van Ryn d. Greg Mangin–Berkeley Bell 6–4, 8–6, 6–3

1932 Ellsworth Vines–Keith Gledhill d. Wilmer Allison–John Van Ryn 6–4, 6–3, 6–2

1933 George Lott–Lester Stoefen d. Frank Shields–Frank Parker 11–13, 9–7, 9–7, 6–3

1934 George Lott–Lester Stoefen d. Wilmer Allison–John Van Ryn 6–4, 9–7, 3–6, 6–4

1935 Wilmer Allison–John Van Ryn d. Don Budge–Gene Mako 6–4, 6–2, 3–6, 2–6, 6–1

1936 Don Budge–Gene Mako d. Wilmer Allison–John Van Ryn 6–4, 6–2, 6–4

1937 Gottfried von Cramm–Henner Henkel d. Don Budge–Gene Mako 6–4, 7–5, 6–4

1938 Don Budge–Gene Mako d. Adrian Quist–John Bromwich 6–3, 6–2, 6–1

1939 Adrian Quist–John Bromwich d. Jack Crawford–Harry Hopman 8–6, 6–1, 6–4

1940 Jack Kramer–Ted Schroeder d. Gardnar Mulloy–Henry Prusoff 6–4, 8–6, 9–7

1941 Jack Kramer–Ted Schroeder d. Wayne Sabin–Gardnar Mulloy 9–7, 6–4, 6–2

1942 Gardnar Mulloy–Bill Talbert d. Ted Schroeder–Sidney Wood 9–7, 7–5, 6–1

1943 Jack Kramer–Frank Parker d. Bill Talbert–David Freeman 6–2, 6–4, 6–4

1944   Don McNeill–Bob Falkenburg d. Bill Talbert–
        Pancho Segura 7–5, 6–4, 3–6, 6–1

1945   Gardnar Mulloy–Bill Talbert d. Bob
        Falkenburg–Jack Tuero 12–10, 8–10,
        12–10, 6–2

1946   Gardnar Mulloy–Bill Talbert d. Don McNeill–
        Frank Guernsey 3–6, 6–4, 2–6, 6–3, 20–18

1947   Jack Kramer–Ted Schroeder d. Bill Talbert–
        Bill Sidwell 6–4, 7–5, 6–3

1948   Gardnar Mulloy–Bill Talbert d. Frank Parker–
        Ted Schroeder 1–6, 9–7, 6–3, 3–6, 9–7

1949   John Bromwich–Billy Sidwell d. Frank

1954   Vic Seixas–Tony Trabert d. Lew Hoad–Ken
        Rosewall 3–6, 6–4, 8–6, 6–3

1955   Kosei Kamo–Atsushi Miyagi d. Gerald Moss–
        Bill Quillan 6–2, 6–3, 3–6, 1–6, 6–4

1956   Lew Hoad–Ken Rosewall d. Ham Richardson–
        Vic Seixas 6–2, 6–2, 3–6, 6–4

1957   Ashley Cooper–Neale Fraser d. Gardnar
        Mulloy–J. Edward "Budge" Patty 4–6, 6–3,
        9–7, 6–3

1958   Alex Olmedo–Ham Richardson d. Sammy
        Giammalva–Barry MacKay 3–6, 6–3, 6–4,
        6–4

1959   Neale Fraser–Roy Emerson d. Alex Olmedo–
        Earl "Butch" Buchholz 3–6, 6–3, 5–7, 6–4,
        7–5

1960   Neale Fraser–Roy Emerson d. Rod Laver–Bob
        Mark 9–7, 6–2, 6–4

1961   Chuck McKinley–Dennis Ralston d. Rafael
        Osuna–Tony Palafox 6–3, 6–4, 2–6, 13–11

1962   Rafael Osuna–Tony Palafox d. Chuck
        McKinley–Dennis Ralston 6–4, 10–12,
        1–6, 9–7, 6–3

1963   Chuck McKinley–Dennis Ralston d. Rafael
        Osuna–Tony Palafox 9–7, 4–6, 5–7, 6–3,
        11–9

1964   Chuck McKinley–Dennis Ralston d. Graham
        Stilwell–Mike Sangster 6–3, 6–2, 6–4

1965   Roy Emerson–Fred Stolle d. Frank
        Froehling–Charlie Pasarell 6–4, 10–12,
        7–5, 6–3

1966   Roy Emerson–Fred Stolle d. Clark Graebner–
        Dennis Ralston 6–4, 6–4, 6–4

1967   John Newcombe–Tony Roche d. Bill Bowrey–
        Owen Davidson 6–8, 9–7, 6–3, 6–3

1968   Bob Lutz–Stan Smith d. Bob Hewitt–Ray

        Moore 6–4, 6–4, 9–7

1968*   Bob Lutz–Stan Smith d. Arthur Ashe–Andres
        Gimeno 11–9, 6–1, 7–5

1969   Dick Crealy–Allan Stone d. Bill Bowrey–
        Charlie Pasarell 9–11, 6–3, 7–5

1969*   Ken Rosewall–Fred Stolle d. Charlie Pasarell–
        Dennis Ralston 2–6, 7–5, 13–11, 6–3

1970   Pierre Barthes–Nikki Pilic d. Roy Emerson–
        Rod Laver 6–3, 7–6, 4–6, 7–6

1971** John Newcombe–Roger Taylor d. Stan Smith–
        Erik van Dillen 6–7, 6–3, 7–6, 4–6, 5–3

1972   Cliff Drysdale–Roger Taylor d. Owen

        Gottfried–Raul Ramirez 6–4, 6–6

1978   Bob Lutz–Stan Smith d. Marty Riessen–
        Sherwood Stewart 1–6, 7–5, 6–3

1979   John McEnroe–Peter Fleming d. Bob Lutz–
        Stan Smith 6–2, 6–4

1980   Bob Lutz–Stan Smith d. Peter Fleming–John
        McEnroe 7–5, 3–6, 6–1, 3–6, 6–3

1981   Peter Fleming–John McEnroe d. Heinz
        Gunthardt–Peter McNamara 7–6, 7–6,
        6–4

1982   Kevin Curren–Steve Denton d. Victor Amaya–
        Hank Pfister 6–2, 6–7, 5–7, 6–2, 6–4

1983   Peter Fleming–John McEnroe d. Fritz
        Buehning–Van Winitsky 6–3, 6–4, 6–2

1984   John Fitzgerald–Tomas Smid d. Stefan
        Edberg–Anders Jarryd 7–6, 6–3, 6–3

1985   Ken Flach–Robert Seguso d. Henri Leconte–
        Yannick Noah 6–7, 7–6, 7–6, 6–0

1986   Andres Gomez–Slobodan Zivojinovic d.
        Joakim Nystrom–Mats Wilander 4–6, 6–3,
        6–3, 4–6, 6–3

1987   Stefan Edberg–Anders Jarryd d. Ken Flach–
        Robert Seguso 7–6, 6–2, 4–6, 5–7, 7–6

1988   Sergio Casal–Emilio Sanchez d. Rick Leach–
        Jim Pugh, default

1989   John McEnroe–Mark Woodforde d. Ken
        Flach–Robert Seguso 6–4, 4–6, 6–3, 6–3

*Open champions. In 1968 and 1969 both Amateur and
Open Championships were held. Thereafter there was only
the Open as principal Championships.

**at nightfall, by mutual agreement, a tie–breaker was
played to decide the title, Newcombe–Taylor winning
5–points–to–3.

1990 Pieter Aldrich–Danie Visser d. Paul
     Annacone–David Wheaton 6–2, 7–6, 6–2
1991 John Fitzgerald–Anders Jarryd d. Scott Davis–
     David Pate 6–3, 3–6, 6–3, 6–3
1992 Jim Grabb–Richey Reneberg d. Kelly Jones–
     Rick Leach 3–6, 7–6, 6–3, 6–3

Women's Doubles

Year

1889 Margarette Ballard–Louise Townsend d.
     Marion Wright–Laura Knight 6–0, 6–2
1890 Ellen Roosevelt–Grace Roosevelt d. Bertha
     Townsend–Margarette Ballard, 6–1, 6–2
1891 Mabel Cahill–Emma Leavitt Morgan d. Grace
     Roosevelt–Ellen Roosevelt 2–6, 8–6, 6–4
1892 Mabel Cahill–Adeline McKinlay d. Helen Day
     Harris–Amy Williams 6–1, 6–3
1893 Aline Terry–Hattie Butler d. Augusta Shultz–
     Stone 6–4, 6–3
1894 Helen Hellwig–Juliette Atkinson d. Annabella
     Wistar–Amy Williams 6–4, 8–6, 6–2
1895 Helen Hellwig–Juliette Atkinson d. Elisabeth
     Moore–Amy Williams 6–2, 6–2, 12–10
1896 Elisabeth Moore–Juliette Atkinson d.
     Annabella Wistar–Amy Williams 6–3, 9–7
1897 Juliette Atkinson–Kathleen Atkinson c. Mrs. F
     Edwards–Elizabeth Rastall 6–2, 6–1, 6–1
1898 Juliette Atkinson–Kathleen Atkinson d. Marie
     Wimer–Carrie Neely 6–1, 2–6, 4–6, 6–1,
     6–2
1899 Jane Craven–Myrtle McAteer d. Maud Banks–
     Elizabeth Rastall 6–1, 6–1, 7–5
1900 Edith Parker–Hallie Champlin d. Marie
     Wimer–Myrtle McAteer 9–7, 6–2, 6–2
1901 Juliette Atkinson–Myrtle McAteer d. Marion
     Jones–Elisabeth Moore, default
1902 Juliette Atkinson–Marion Jones d. Maud
     Banks–Nona Closterman 6–2, 7–5
1903 Elisabeth Moore–Carrie Neely d. Miriam
     Hall–Marion Jones 4–6, 6–1, 6–1
1904 May Sutton–Miriam Hall d. Elisabeth Moore–
     Carrie Neely 3–6, 6–3, 6–3
1905 Helen Homans–Carrie Neely d. Marjorie
     Oberteuffer–Virginia Maule 6–0, 6–1
1906 Ann Burdette Coe–Mrs. D. Platt d. Helen
     Homans–Clover Boldt 6–4, 6–4
1907 Marie Wimer–Carrie Neely d. Edna Wildey–
     Natalie Wildey 6–1, 2–6, 6–4
1908 Evelyn Sears–Margaret Curtis d. Carrie
     Neely–Marion Steever 6–3, 5–7, 9–7
1909 Hazel Hotchkiss–Edith Rotch d. Dorothy
     Green–Lois Moyes 6–1, 6–1
1910 Hazel Hotchkiss–Edith Rotch d. Adelaide
     Browning–Edna Wildey 6–4, 6–4

1911 Hazel Hotchkiss–Eleonora Sears d. Dorothy
     Green–Florence Sutton 6–4, 4–6, 6–2
1912 Dorothy Green–Mary K. Browne d. Maud
     Barger Wallach–Mrs. Frederick Schmitz
     6–2, 5–7, 6–0
1913 Mary K. Browne–Louise Williams d. Dorothy
     Green–Edna Wildey 12–10, 2–6, 6–3
1914 Mary K. Brown–Louise Williams d. Louise
     Hammond Raymond–Edna Wildey 8–6,
     6–2
1915 Hazel Hotchkiss Wightman–Eleonora Sears
     d. Helen Homans McLean–Mrs. G. L.
     Chapman 10–8, 6–2
1916 Molla Bjurstedt–Eleonora Sears d. Louise
     Hammond Raymond–Edna Wildey 4–6,
     6–2, 10–8
1917 Molla Bjurstedt–Eleonora Sears d. Phyllis
     Walsh–Mrs. Robert LeRoy 6–2, 6–4
1918 Marion Zinderstein–Eleanor Goss d. Molla
     Bjurstedt–Mrs. Johan Rogge 7–5, 8–6
1919 Marion Zinderstein–Eleanor Goss d.
     Eleanora Sears–Hazel Hotchkiss
     Wightman 10–8, 9–7
1920 Marion Zinderstein–Eleonor Goss d. Eleanor
     Tennant–Helen Baker 6–3, 6–1
1921 Mary K. Browne–Mrs. R. H. Williams d. Helen
     Gilleaudeau–Mrs. L. G. Morris 6–3, 6–2
1922 Marion Zinderstein Jessup–Helen Wills d.
     Edith Sigourney–Molla Bjurstedt Mallory
     6–4, 7–9, 6–3
1923 Kitty McKane–Phyllis Hawkins Covell d. Hazel
     Hotchkiss Wightman–Eleanor Goss 2–6,
     6–2, 6–1
1924 Hazel Hotchkiss Wightman–Helen Wills d.
     Eleanor Goss–Marion Zinderstein Jessup
     6–4, 6–3
1925 Mary K. Browne–Helen Wills d. May Sutton
     Bundy–Elizabeth Ryan 6–4, 6–3
1926 Elizabeth Ryan–Eleanor Goss d. Mary K.
     Browne–Charlotte Hosmer Chapin 3–6,
     6–4, 12–10
1927 Kitty McKane Godfree–Ermyntrude Harvey
     d. Betty Nuthall–Joan Fry 6–1, 4–6, 6–4
1928 Hazel Hotchkiss Wightman–Helen Wills d.
     Edith Cross–Anna McCune Harper 6–2,
     6–2
1929 Phoebe Watson–Peggy Michell d. Phyllis
     Hawkins Covell–Dorothy Shepherd
     Barron 2–6, 6–3, 6–4
1930 Betty Nuthall–Sarah Palfrey d. Marjorie
     Morrill Painter–Alice Marble 8–6, 6–1
1931 Betty Nuthall–Eileen Bennett Whittingstall d.
     Helen Jacobs–Dorothy Round 6–2, 6–4
1932 Helen Jacobs–Sarah Palfrey d. Edith Cross–
     Anna McCune Harper 3–6, 6–3, 7–5
1933 Betty Nuthall–Freda James d. Helen Wills
     Moody–Elizabeth Ryan, default
1934 Helen Jacobs–Sarah Palfrey d. Carolin

Babcock–Dorothy Andrus 4–6, 6–3, 6–4

1935 Helen Jacobs–Sarah Palfrey Fabyan d.
Carolin Babcock–Dorothy Andrus 6–4,
6–2

1936 Marjorie Gladman Van Ryn–Carolin Babcock
d. Helen Jacobs–Sarah Palfrey Fabyan
9–7, 2–6, 6–4

1937 Sarah Palfrey Fabyan–Alice Marble d. Marjorie
Gladman Van Ryn–Carolin Babcock 7–5,
6–4

1938 Sarah Palfrey Fabyan–Alice Marble d. Simone
Passemard Mathieu–Iadwiga Iedrzeiowska

1943 Louise Brough–Margaret Osborne d. Pauline
Betz–Doris Hart 6–4, 6–3

1944 Louise Brough–Margaret Osborne d. Pauline
Betz–Doris Hart 4–6, 6–4, 6–3

1945 Louise Brough–Margaret Osborne d. Pauline
Betz–Doris Hart 6–3, 6–3

1946 Louise Brough–Margaret Osborne d. Patricia
Canning Todd–Mary Arnold Prentiss 6–1,
6–3

1947 Louise Brough–Margaret Osborne d. Patricia
Canning Todd–Doris Hart 5–7, 6–3, 7–5

1948 Louise Brough–Margaret Osborne duPont d.
Patricia Canning Todd–Doris Hart 6–4,
8–10, 6–1

1949 Louise Brough–Margaret Osborne duPont d.
Doris Hart–Shirley Fry 6–4, 10–8

1950 Louise Brough–Margaret Osborne duPont d.
Doris Hart–Shirley Fry 6–2, 6–3

1951 Shirley Fry–Doris Hart d. Nancy
Chaffee–Patricia Canning Todd 6–4, 6–2

1952 Shirley Fry–Doris Hart d. Louise Brough–
Maureen Connolly 10–8, 6–4

1953 Shirley Fry–Doris Hart d. Louise Brough–
Margaret Osborne duPont 6–2, 7–9, 9–7

1954 Shirley Fry–Doris Hart d. Louise Brough–
Margaret Osborne duPont 6–4, 6–4

1955 Louise Brough–Margaret Osborne duPont d.
Doris Hart Shirley Fry 6–3, 1–6, 6–3

1956 Louise Brough–Margaret Osborne duPont d.
Betty Rosenquest Pratt–Shirley Fry 6–3,
6–0

1957 Louise Brough–Margaret Osborne duPont d.
Althea Gibson–Darlene Hard 6–2, 7–5

1958 Jeanne Arth–Darlene Hard d. Althea Gibson–
Maria Bueno 2–6, 6–3, 6–4

1959 Jeanne Arth–Darlene Hard d. Maria Bueno–
Sally Moore 6–2, 6–3

1960 Maria Bueno–Darlene Hard d. Ann Haydon–
Deidre Catt 6–1, 6–1

1961 Darlene Hard–Lesley Turner d. Edda Buding–
Yola Ramirez 6–4, 5–7, 6–0

1962 Darlene Hard–Maria Bueno d. Karen Hantze
Susman–Billie Jean Moffitt 4–6, 6–3, 6–2

1963 Robyn Ebbern–Margaret Smith d. Darlene
Hard–Maria Bueno 4–6, 10–8, 6–3

1964 Billie Jean Moffitt–Karen Hantze Susman d.
Margaret Smith–Lesley Turner 3–6, 6–2, 6–4

Wade–Joyce Barclay Williams 6–3, 7–5

1968* Maria Bueno–Margaret Smith Court d. Billie
Jean Moffitt King–Rosemary Casals 4–6,
9–7, 8–6

1969 Virginia Wade–Margaret Court Smith d. Mary
Ann Eisel Curtis–Valerie Ziegenfuss 6–1,
6–3

1969* Francoise Durr–Darlene Hard d. Margaret
Smith Court–Virginia Wade 0–6, 6–4, 6–4

1970 Margaret Smith Court–Judy Tegart Dalton d.
Rosemary Casals–Virginia Wade 6–3, 6–4

1971 Rosemary Casals–Judy Tegart Dalton d. Gail
Sherriff Chanfreau–Francoise Durr 6–3,
6–3

1972 Francoise Durr–Betty Stove d. Margaret
Smith Court–Virginia Wade 6–3, 1–6, 6–3

1973 Margaret Smith Court–Virginia Wade d.
Billie Jean Moffitt King–Rosemary Casals
3–6, 6–3, 7–5

1974 Rosemary Casals–Billie Jean Moffit King d.
Francoise Durr–Betty Stove 7–6, 6–7, 6–4

1975 Margaret Smith Court–Virginia Wade d. Billie
Jean Moffitt King–Rosemary Casals 7–5,
2–6, 7–5

1976 Delina Boshoff–Ilana Kloss d. Olga Morozova–
Virginia Wade 6–1, 6–4

1977 Martina Navratilova–Betty Stove d. Renée
Richards–Bettyann Grubb Stuart 6–1, 7–6

1978 Billie Jean Moffitt King–Martina Navratilova
d. Kerry Melville Reid–Wendy Turnbull
7–6, 6–4

---

*Open champions. In 1968 and 1969 both Amateur and
Open Championships were held. Thereafter there was only
the Open as principal Championship.*

1979 Betty Stove–Wendy Turnbull d. Billie Jean
Moffit King–Martina Navratilova 7–5, 6–3

1980 Billie Jean Moffitt King–Martina Navratilova
d. Pam Shriver–Betty Stove 7–6, 7–5

1981 Anne Smith–Kathy Jordan d. Rosemary
Casals–Wendy Turnbull 6–3, 6–3

1982 Rosemary Casals–Wendy Turnbull d. Sharon
Walsh–Barbara Potter 6–4, 6–4

1983 Pam Shriver–Martina Navratilova d. Rosalyn
Fairbank–Candy Reynolds 6–7, 6–1, 6–3

1984 Pam Shriver–Martina Navratilova d. Anne
Hobbs–Wendy Turnbull 6–2, 6–4

1985 Claudia Kohde-Kilsch–Helena Sukova d.
Martina Navratilova–Pam Shriver 6–7,
6–2, 6–3

1986 Martina Navratilova–Pam Shriver d. Hana
Mandlikova–Wendy Turnbull 6–4, 3–6,
6–3

1987 Martina Navratilova–Pam Shriver d. Kathy
Jordan–Elizabeth Sayers Smylie 5–7, 6–4,
6–2

1988 Beatrice "Gigi" Fernandez–Robin White d.
Patty Fendick–Jill Hetherington 6–4, 6–1

1989 Hana Mandlikova–Martina Navratilova d.
Mary Joe Fernandez–Pam Shriver 5–7,
6–4, 6–4

1990 Beatrice "Gigi" Fernandez–Martina
Navratilova d. Jana Novotna–Helena
Sukova 6–2, 6–4

1991 Pam Shriver–Natalia Zvereva d. Jana Novotna–
Larisa Savchenko 6–4, 4–6, 7–6

1992 Beatrice "Gigi" Fernandez–Natalia Zvereva d.
Jana Novotna–Larisa Savchenko Neiland
7–6, 6–1

Mixed Doubles

Year

1892 Mabel Cahill–Clarence Hobart d. Elisabeth
Moore–Rod Beach 5–7, 6–1, 6–4

1893 Ellen Roosevelt–Clarence Hobart d. Ethel
Bankson–Robert Willson, Jr. 6–1, 4–6,
10–8, 6–1

1894 Juliette Atkinson–Edwin Fischer d. Mrs.
McFadden–Gustav Remack, Jr. 6–3, 6–2,
6–1

1895 Juliette Atkinson–Edwin Fischer d. Amy
Williams–Mantle Fielding 4–6, 8–6, 6–2

1896 Juliette Atkinson–Edwin Fischer d. Amy
Williams–Mantle Fielding 6–2, 6–3, 6–3

1897 Laura Henson–D. L. Magruder d. Maud
Banks–R. A. Griffin 6–4, 6–3, 7–5

1898 Carrie Neely–Edwin Fischer d. Helen
Chapman–J. A. Hill 6–2, 6–4, 8–6

1899 Elizabeth Rastall–Albert Hoskins d. Jennie
Craven–James Gardner 6–4, 6–0, default

1900 Margaret Hunnewell–Alfred Codman d. T.
Shaw–George Atkinson 11–9, 6–3, 6–1

1901 Marion Jones–Raymond Little d. Myrtle
McAteer–Clyde Stevens 6–4, 6–4, 7–5

1902 Elisabeth Moore–Wylie Grant d. Elizabeth
Rastall–Albert Hoskins 6–2, 6–1

1903 Helen Chapman–Harry Allen d. Carrie
Neely–W. H. Rowland 6–4, 7–5

1904 Elisabeth Moore–Wylie Grant d. May Sutton–
Trevanion Dallas 6–2, 6–1

1905 Augusta Schultz Hobart–Clarence Hobart d.
Elisabeth Moore–Edward Dewhurst 6–2,
6–4

1906 Sarah Coffin–Edward Dewhurst d. Margaret
Johnson–Wallace Johnson 6–3, 7–5

1907 May Sayers–Wallace Johnson d. Natalie
Wildey–W. Morris Tilden 6–1, 7–5

1908 Edith Rotch–Nat Niles d. Louise Hammond–
Raymond Little 6–4, 4–6, 6–4

1909 Hazel Hotchkiss–Wallace Johnson d. Louise
Hammond–Raymond Little 6–2, 6–0

1910 Hazel Hotchkiss–Joseph Carpenter, Jr. d.
Edna Wildey–Herbert M. Tilden 6–2, 6–2

1911 Hazel Hotchkiss–Wallace Johnson d. Edna
Wildey–Herbert M. Tilden 6–4, 6–4

1912 Mary K. Browne–Dick Williams d. Eleanora
Sears–Bill Clothier 6–4, 2–6, 11–9

1913 Mary K. Browne–Bill Tilden d. Dorothy
Green–C. S. Rogers 7–5, 7–5

1914 Mary K. Browne–Bill Tilden d. Margarette
Myers–J. R. Rowland 6–1, 6–4

1915 Hazel Hotchkiss Wightman–Harry Johnson d.
Molla Bjurstedt–Irving Wright 6–0, 6–1

1916 Eleanora Sears–Willis Davis d. Florence
Ballin–Bill Tilden 6–4, 7–5

1917 Molla Bjurstedt–Irving Wright d. Florence
Ballin–Bill Tilden 10–12, 6–1, 6–3

1918 Hazel Hotchkiss Wightman–Irving Wright d.
Molla Bjurstedt–Fred Alexander 6–2, 6–4

1919 Marion Zinderstein–Vincent Richards d.
Florence Ballin–Bill Tilden 2–6, 11–9, 6–2

1920 Hazel Hotchkiss Wightman–Wallace Johnson
d. Molla Bjurstedt Mallory–Craig Biddle
6–4, 6–3

1921 Mary K. Browne–Bill Johnston d. Molla
Bjurstedt Mallory–Bill Tilden 3–6, 6–4, 6–3

1922 Molla Bjurstedt Mallory–Bill Tilden d. Helen
Wills–Howard Kinsey 6–4, 6–3

1923 Molla Bjurstedt Mallory–Bill Tilden d. Kitty
McKane–John Hawkes 6–3, 2–6, 10–8

1924 Helen Wills–Vincent Richards d. Molla
Bjurstedt Mallory–Bill Tilden 6–8, 7–5,
6–0

1925 Kitty McKane–John Hawkes d. Ermyntrude
Harvey–Vincent Richards 6–2, 6–4

1926 Elizabeth Ryan–Jean Borotra d. Hazel
Hotchkiss Wightman–Renè Lacoste 6–4,
7–5

1927 Eileen Bennett–Henri Cochet d. Hazel
    Hotchkiss Wightman–René Lacoste 6–2,
    0–6, 6–2

1928 Helen Wills–John Hawkes d. Edith Cross–Gar
    Moon, 6–1, 6–3

1929 Betty Nuthall–George Lott d. Phyllis Covell–
    Henry Austin 6–3, 6–3

1930 Edith Cross–Wilmer Allison d. Marjorie
    Morrill–Frank Shields 6–4, 6–4

1931 Betty Nuthall–George Lott d. Anna McCune
    Harper–Wilmer Allison 6–3, 6–3

1932 Sarah Palfrey–Fred Perry d. Helen Jacobs–
    Henroth–Ivon Petra 6–2, 8–10, 6–0

1938 Alice Marble–Donald Budge d. Thelma
    Coyne–John Bromwich 6–1, 6–2

1939 Alice Marble–Harry Hopman d. Sarah Palfrey
    Fabyan–Elwood Cooke 9–7, 6–1

1940 Alice Marble–Robert Riggs d. Dorothy
    Bundy–Jack Kramer 9–7, 6–1

1941 Sarah Palfrey Cooke–Jack Kramer d. Pauline
    Betz–Bobby Riggs 4–6, 6–4, 6–4

1942 Louise Brough–Ted Schroeder d. Patricia
    Canning Todd–Alejo Russell 3–6, 6–1, 6–4

1943 Margaret Osborne–Bill Talbert d. Pauline
    Betz–Francisco "Pancho" Segura, 10–8, 6–4

1944 Margaret Osborne–Bill Talbert d. Dorothy
    Bundy–Lt. Don McNeill 6–2, 6–3

1945 Margaret Osborne–Bill Talbert d. Doris
    Hart–Bob Falkenburg 6–4, 6–4

1946 Margart Osborne–Bill Talbert d. Louise
    Brough–Robert Kimbrell 6–3, 6–4

1947 Louise Brough–John Bromwich d. Gertrude
    Moran–Francisco "Pancho" Segura 6–3,
    6–1

1948 Louise Brough–Tom Brown d. Margaret
    Osborne dupont–Bill Talbert 6–4, 6–4

1949 Louise Brough–Eric Strugess d. Margaret
    duPont–Bill Talbert 4–6, 6–3, 7–5

1950 Margaret Osborne duPont–Ken McGregor d.
    Doris Hart–Frank Sedgman 6–4, 3–6, 6–3

1951 Doris Hart–Frank Sedgman d. Shirley Fry–
    Mervyn Rose 6–3, 6–2

1952 Doris Hart–Frank Sedgman d. Thelma Coyne
    Long–Lew Hoad 6–3, 7–5

1953 Doris Hart–Vic Seixas d. Julia Sampson–Rex
    Hartwig 6–2, 4–6, 6–4

1954 Doris Hart–Vic Seixas d. Margaret Osborne
    duPont–Ken Rosewall 4–6, 6–1, 6–1

1955 Doris Hart–Vic Seixas d. Shirley Fry–Gardnar
    Mulloy 7–5, 5–7, 6–2

1956 Margaret Osborne duPont–Ken Rosewall d.
    Darlene Hard–Lew Hoad 9–7, 6–1

1957 Althea Gibson–Kurt Nielsen d. Darlene Hard–
    Bob Howe 6–3, 9–7

1958 Margaret Osborne duPont–Neale Fraser d.
    Maria Bueno–Alex Olmedo 6–4, 3–6, 9–7

1959 Margaret Osborne duPont–Neale Fraser d.
    Janet Hopps–Bob Mark 7–5, 13–15, 6–2

1960 Margaret Osborne duPont–Neale Fraser d.
    Maria Bueno–Antonio Palafox 6–3, 6–2

1965 Margaret Smith–Fred Stolle d. Judy Tegart–
    Frank Froehling III 6–2, 6–2

1966 Donna Floyd Fales–Owen Davidson d. Carol
    Hanks Aucamp–Ed Rubinoff 6–1, 6–3

1967 Billie Jean Moffitt King–Owen Davidson d.
    Rosemary Casals–Stan Smith 6–3, 6–2

1968 Mary Ann Eisel–Peter Curtis d. Tory Ann
    Fretz–Robert Perry 6–4, 7–5

1969 Patti Hogan–Paul Sullivan d. Kristy Pigeon–
    Terry Addison 6–4, 2–6, 12–10

1969* Margaret Smith Court–Marty Riessen d.
    Francoise Durr–Dennis Ralston 7–5, 6–3

1970 Margaret Smith Court–Marty Riessen d. Judy
    Tegart Dalton–Frew McMillan 6–4, 6–4

1971 Bilie Jean Moffitt King–Owen Davidson d.
    Betty Stove–Rob Maud, 6–3, 7–5

1972 Margaret Smith Court–Marty Riessen d.
    Rosemary Casals–Ilie Nastase 6–3, 7–5

1973 Billie Jean Moffitt King–Owen Davidson d.
    Margaret Smith Court–Marty Riessen 6–3,
    3–6, 7–6

1974 Pam Teeguarden–Geoff Masters d. Chris
    Evert–Jimmy Connors 6–1, 7–6

1975 Rosemary Casals–Dick Stockton d. Billie Jean
    Moffitt King–Fred Stolle 6–3, 7–6

1976 Billie Jean Moffitt King–Phil Dent d. Betty
    Stove–Frew McMillan 3–6, 6–2, 7–6

1977 Betty Stove–Frew McMillan d. Billie Jean
    Moffitt King–Vitas Gerulatis 6–2, 3–6, 6–3

1978 Betty Stove–Frew McMillan d. Billie Jean
    Moffitt King–Ray Ruffels 6–3, 7–6

*Open champions. In 1969 both Amateur and Open
Championships were held. Thereafter there was only the
Open as principal Championship.*

1979	Greer Stevens–Bob Hewitt d. Betty Stove–Frew McMillan 6–3, 7–5
1980	Wendy Turnbull–Marty Riessen d. Betty Stove–Frew McMillan, 7–5, 6–2
1981	Anne Smith–Kevin Curren d. JoAnne Russell–Stove Denton 6–4, 7–6
1982	Anne Smith–Kevin Curren d. Barbara Potter–Ferdi Taygan 6–7, 7–6 7–6
1983	Elizabeth Sayers–John Fitzgerald d. Barbara Potter–Ferdi Taygan 3–6 6–3, 6–4
1984	Manuela Maleeva–Tom Gulikson d. Elizabeth Sayers–John Fitzgerald 2–6, 7–5, 6–4
1985	Martina Navratilova–Heinz Gunthardt d. Elizabeth Sayers Smylie–John Fitzgerald 6–3, 6–4
1986	Raffaella Reggi–Sergio Casal d. Martina Navratilova–Peter Fleming 6–4, 6–4
1987	Martina Navratilova–Emilio Sanchez d. Betsy Nagelson–Paul Annacone 6–4, 6–7, 7–6
1988	Jana Novotna–Jim Pugh d. Elizabeth Sayers Smylie–Patrick McEnroe 7–5, 6–3
1989	Robin White–Shelby Cannon d. Meredith McGrath–Rick Leach 3–6, 6–2, 7–5
1990	Elizabeth Sayers Smylie–Todd Woodbridge d. Natalia Zvereva–Jim Pugh 6–4, 6–2
1991	Manon Bollegraf–Tom Nijssen d. Arantxa Sanchez Vicario–Emilio Sanchez 6–2, 7–6
1992	Nicole Provis–Mark Woodforde d. Helena Sukova–Tom Nijssen 4–6, 6–3, 6–3

All–Time United States Championships Records

Most men's singles: 7—Dick Sears, 1881–87; Bill Larned, 1901–11 Bill Tilden, 1920–29

Most men's doubles: 6—Sears, 1882–87; Holcombe Ward, 1895–1906

Most men's mixed: 4—Edwin Fischer, 1894–98; Wallace Johnson, 1907–20; Tilden, 1913–23; Bill Talbert, 1943–46; Owen Davidson, 1966–73; Marty Riessen 1969–80

Most men's altogether: 16—Tilden, 1913–30

Most women's singles: 8—Molla Bjurstedt Mallory, 1915–26

Most women's doubles: 13—Margaret Osborne duPont, 1941–57

Most women's mixed: 9—duPont, 1943–60

Most women's altogether: 25—duPont, 1941–60

Most men's doubles team: 5—James Dwight and Sears, 1882–87

Most women's doubles, team: 12—Louise Brough and duPont, 1942–57

Most mixed doubles, team: 4—duPont and Talbert, 1943–46

Youngest Champions

Women's singles—Tracy Austin, 1979, 16 years 9 months

Women's doubles—May Sutton, 1904, 17–11

Women's mixed—Manuela Maleeva Fragniere, 1984, 17–7

Men's singles—Pete Sampras, 1990, 19–1

Men's doubles—Vinnie Richards, 1916, 15–4

Men's mixed—Vinnie Richards, 1919, 16–3

Oldest Champions

Women's singles—Molla Bjurstedt Mallory, 1926, 42–5

Women's doubles—Hazel Hotchkiss Wightman, 1928, 41–8

Women's mixed—Margaret Osborne duPont, 1960, 42–5

Men's singles—Bill Larned, 1911, 38–8

Men's doubles—Bob Hewitt, 1977, 37–8

Men's mixed—Bob Hewitt, 1979, 39–8

Longest Matches (Total Games)

Women's singles—51 games, Juliette Atkinson d. Marion Jones 6–3, 5–7, 6–4, 2–6, 7–5. Challenge round, 1898

Women's doubles—48 games, Mrs. George L. Chapman–Marion Chapman (mother–daughter) d. Dorothy Green Brigge–Corinne Stanton Henry 10–8, 6–8, 9–7, 1st. rd., 1922

Mixed doubles—71 games, Margaret Osborne duPont–Bill Talbert d. Gussy Moran–Bob Falkenburg 27–25, 5–7, 6–1, semis, 1948

Men's singles—100 games, F. D. Robbins d. Dick Dell 22–20, 9–7, 6–8, 8–10, 6–4, 1st rd., 1969

Men's doubles—105 games Marcelo Lara–Joaquin Loyo–Mayo d. Luis Garcia–Manolo Santana 10–12, 24–22, 11–9, 3–6, 6–2, 3rd rd., 1966. 105 games, Cliff Drysdale–Ray Moore d. Ronnie Barnes–Roy Emerson 29–31, 8–6, 3–6, 8–6, 6–2, quarters, 1967

Longest Match (Playing Time)

5 hours 26 minutes—Stefan Edberg d. Michael Chang 6–7 (3–7), 7–5, 7–6, (7–3), 5–7, 6–4, semis, 1992

Individual Singles Career Records

Women

Tournaments played—20, Virginia Wade, 1964—70, 1978—84

Men

Tournaments played—28, Vic Seixas, 1940—43, 1946—69

Matches played—115, Jimmy Connors, 1970—89, 1991–92

Matches won—98, Jimmy Connors, 1970—89, 1991–92

Matches won consecutively—42, Bill Tilden, 1920 through 3rd rd., 1926, lost quarters to Henri Cochet

Match winning percentage—1.000, Dick Sears 18–0, 1881—87; .910, Bill Tilden 71–7, 1916—30

U.S. NATIONAL INTERCOLLEGIATE CHAMPIONS

Men's Singles

Year		College
1883	Joseph Clark (spring)	Harvard
1883	Howard Taylor (fall)	Harvard
1884	Percy Knapp	Yale
1885	Percy Knapp	Yale
1886	Godfrey Brinley	Trinity (CT)
1887	Philip Sears	Harvard
1888	Philip Sears	Harvard
1889	Bob Huntingdon	Yale
1890	Fred Hovey	Harvard
1891	Fred Hovey	Harvard
1892	Bill Larned	Cornell
1893	Malcolm Chace	Brown
1894	Malcolm Chace	Yale
1895	Malcolm Chace	Yale
1896	Malcolm Whitman	Harvard
1897	Samuel Thomson	Princeton
1898	Leo Ware	Harvard
1899	Dwight Davis	Harvard
1900	Ray Little	Princeton
1901	Fred Alexander	Princeton
1902	Bill Clothier	Harvard
1914	George Church	Princeton
1915	Dick Williams	Harvard
1916	Colket Caner	Harvard
1917–18	Not held; World War I	
1919	Chuch Garland	Yale
1920	Maxwell Banks	Yale
1921	Phil Neer	Stanford
1922	Lucien Williams	Yale
1923	Carl Fischer	Philadelphia Osteopathic
1924	Wallace Scott	Washington
1925	Edward Chandler	California
1926	Edward Chandler	California
1927	Wilmer Allison	Texas
1928	Julius Seligson	Lehigh
1929	Berkeley Bell	Texas
1930	Cliff Sutter	Tulane
1931	Keith Gledhill	Stanford
1932	Cliff Sutter	Tulane
1933	Jack Tidball	UCLA
1934	Gene Mako	USC
1935	Wilbur Hess	Rice
1936	Ernie Sutter	Tulane
1937	Ernie Sutter	Tulane
1938	Frank Guernsey	Rice
1939	Frank Guernsey	Rice
1940	Don McNeill	Kenyon
1941	Joe Hunt	U.S. Naval Academy
1942	Ted Schroeder	Stanford
1943	Francisco "Pancho" Segura	Miami
1944	Francisco "Pancho" Segura	Miami
1945	Francisco "Pancho" Segura	Miami
1946	Bob Falkenburg	USC
1947	Gardner Larned	William & Mary
1948	Harry Likas	San Francisco
1949	Jack Tuero	Tulane

1950	Herbie Flam	UCLA
1951	Tony Trabert	Cincinnati
1952	Hugh Stewart	USC
1953	Ham Richardson	Tulane
1954	Ham Richardson	Tulane
1955	Jose Aguero	Tulane
1956	Alex Olmedo	USC
1957	Barry MacKay	Michigan
1958	Alex Olmedo	USC
1959	Whitney Reed	San Jose State
1960	Larry Nagler	UCLA
1961	Allen Fox	UCLA
1962	Rafael Osuna	USC
1963	Dennis Ralston	USC
1964	Dennis Ralston	USC
1965	Arthur Ashe	UCLA
1966	Charlie Pasarell	UCLA
1967	Bob Lutz	USC
1968	Stan Smith	USC
1969	Joaquin Loyo–Mayo	USC
1970	Jeff Borowiak	UCLA
1971	Jimmy Connors	UCLA
1972	Dick Stockton	Trinity (TX)
1973	Alex Mayer	Stanford
1974	John Whitlinger	Stanford
1975	Billy Martin	UCLA
1976	Bill Scanlon	Trinity
1977	Matt Mitchell	Stanford
1978	John McEnroe	Stanford
1979	Kevin Curren	Texas
1980	Robert Van't Hof	USC
1981	Tim Mayotte	Stanford
1982	Mike Leach	Michigan
1983	Greg Holmes	Utah
1984	Mikael Pernfors	Georgia
1985	Mikael Pernfors	Georgia
1986	Dan Goldie	Stanford
1987	Andrew Burrow	Miami
1988	Robbie Weiss	Pepperdine
1989	Donni Leaycraft	LSU
1990	Steve Bryan	Texas
1991	Jared Palmer	Stanford
1992	Alex O'Brien	Stanford

Women's Singles

Year		College
1958	Darlene Hard	Pomona
1959	Donna Floyd	William & Mary
1960	Linda Vail	Oakland City College
1961	Tory Fretz	Occidental
1962	Roberta Allison	Alabama
1963	Roberta Allison	Alabama
1964	Jane Albert	Stanford
1965	Mimi Henreid	UCLA

1966	Cecilia Martinez	San Francisco State
1967	Patsy Rippy	Odessa JC
1968	Emilie Burrer	Trinity (TX)
1969	Emilie Burrer	Trinity (TX)
1970	Laura DuPont	North Carolina
1971	Pam Richmond	Arizona State
1972	Janice Metcalf	Redlands
1973	Janice Metcalf	Redlands
1974	Carrie Meyer	Marymount
1975	Stephanie Tolleson	Trinity (TX)
1976	Barbara Hallquist	USC
1977	Barbara Hallquist	USC
1978	Stacy Margolin	USC
1979	Kathy Jordan	Stanford
1980	Wendy White	Rollins College
1981	Anna Maria Fernandez	USC
1982	Alycia Moulton	Stanford
1983	Beth Herr	USC
1984	Lisa Spain	Georgia
1985	Linda Gates	Stanford
1986	Patty Fendick	Stanford
1987	Patty Fendick	Stanford
1988	Shaun Stafford	Florida
1989	Sandra Birch	Stanford
1990	Debbie Graham	Stanford
1991	Sandra Birch	Stanford
1992	Lisa Raymond	Florida

Men's Doubles

Year		College
1883	Joseph Clark–Howard Taylor (spring)	Harvard
1883	Howard Taylor–Palmer Presbrey (fall)	Harvard
1884	Percy Knapp–William Thorne	Yale
1885	Percy Knapp–Arthur Shipman	Yale
1886	Percy Knapp–William Thacker Shipman	Yale
1887	Philip Sears–Quincy Shaw	Harvard
1888	Valentine Hall–Oliver Campbell	Columbia
1889	Oliver Campbell–A. Wright	Columbia
1890	Quincy Shaw–Sam Chase	Harvard
1891	Fred Hovey–Robert Wrenn	Harvard
1892	Robert Wrenn–Fred Winslow	Harvard
1893	Malcolm Chace–Clarence Budlong	Brown
1894	Malcolm Chace–Arthur Foote	Yale
1895	Malcolm Chace–Arthur Foote	Yale
1896	Leo Ware–William Scudder	Harvard
1897	Leo Ware–Malcolm Whitman	Harvard
1898	Leo Ware–Malcolm Whitman	Harvard
1899	Holcombe Ward–Dwight Davis	Harvard
1900	Fred Alexander–Ray Little	Princeton
1901	Howard Plummer–Sam Russell	Yale
1902	Bill Clothier–Edgar Leonard	Harvard
1903	Fred Colston–Edwin Clapp	Yale

1904	Karl Behr–George Bodman	Yale
1905	Ed Dewhurst–H. Register	Pennsylvania
1906	E. Wells–Alfred Spaulding	Yale
1907	Nathaniel Niles–Alfred Dabney	Harvard
1908	Herbert Tilden–Alex Thayer	Pennsylvania
1909	Wallace Johnson–Alex Thayer	Pennsylvania
1910	Dean Mathey–Burnham Dell	Princeton
1911	Dean Mathey–Charles Butler	Princeton
1912	George Church–Winifred Mace	Princeton
1913	Watson Washburn–Joe Armstrong	Harvard
1914	Dick Wiliams–Richard Harte	Harvard

1927	John Van Ryn–Ken Appel	Princeton
1928	Ralph McElevenny–Alan Herrington	Stanford
1929	Benjamin Gorchakoff–Arthur Kussman	Occidental
1930	Dolf Muehleisen–Bob Muench	California
1931	Bruce Barnes–Karl Kamrath	Texas
1932	Keith Gledhill–Joe Coughlin	Stanford
1933	Joe Coughlin–Sam Lee	Stanford
1934	Gene Mako–Phil Castlen	USC
1935	Paul Newton–Richard Bennett	California
1936	Bennett Dey–Bill Seward	Stanford
1937	Richard Bennett–Paul Newton	California
1938	Joe Hunt–Lewis Wetherell	USC
1939	Doug Imhoff–Bob Peacock	California
1940	Larry Dee–Jim Wade	Stanford
1941	Charles Olewine–Charles Mattmann	USC
1942	Ted Schroeder–Larry Dee	Stanford
1943	John Hickman–Walt Driver	Texas
1944	John Hickman–Felix Kelly	Texas
1945	Francisco "Pancho" Segura–Tom Burke	Miami
1946	Bob Falkenburg–Tom Falkenburg	USC
1947	Sam Match–Bobby Curtis	Rice
1948	Fred Kovaleski–Bernard "Tut" Bartzen	William & Mary
1949	Jim Brink–Fred Fisher	Washington
1950	Herbie Flam–Gene Garrett	UCLA
1951	Earl Cochell–Hugh Stewart	USC
1952	Hugh Ditzler–Clif Mayne	California
1953	Larry Huebner–Bob Perry	UCLA
1954	Ron Livingston–Bob Perry	UCLA
1955	Francisco Contreras–Joaquin Reyes	USC
1956	Francisco Contreras–Alex Olmedo	USC
1957	Crawford Henry–Ron Holmberg	Tulane
1958	Ed Atkinson–Alex Olmedo	USC

1959	Crawford Henry–Ron Holmberg	Tulane
1960	Larry Nagler–Allen Fox	UCLA
1961	Rafael Osuna–Ramsey Earnhart	USC
1962	Rafael Osuna–Ramsey Earnhart	USC
1963	Rafael Osuna–Dennis Ralston	USC
1964	Bill Bond–Dennis Ralston	USC
1965	Arthur Ashe–Ian Crookenden	UCLA
1966	Ian Crookenden–Charlie Pasarell	UCLA
1967	Bob Lutz–Stan Smith	USC
1968	Bob Lutz–Stan Smith	USC
1969	Joaquin Loyo-Mayo–Marcelo Lara	USC

1981	David Pate–Karl Richter	TCU
1982	Peter Doohan–Pat Serrett	Arkansas
1983	Ole Malmqvist–Allen Miller	Georgia
1984	Jerome Jones–Kelly Jones	Pepperdine
1985	Carlos DiLaura–Kelly Jones	Pepperdine
1986	Rick Leach–Tim Pawsat	USC
1987	Rick Leach–Scott Melville	USC
1988	Patrick Galbraith–Brian Garrow	UCLA
1989	Eric Amend–Byron Black	USA
1990	Doug Eisenman–Matt Lucena	California
1991	Matt Lucena–Bengt Pederson	California
1992	Alex O'Brien–Chris Cocotos	Stanford

Women's Doubles

Year		College
1958	Sue Metzger–Erika Puetz Webster	St. Mary's–Notre Dame
1959	Joyce Pniewski–Phyllis Saganski	Michigan State
1960	Susan Butt–Linda Vail	British Columbia–Oakland City
1961	Tory Fretz–Mary Sherar	Occidental–Yakima Valley
1962	Linda Yeomans–Carol Hanks	Stanford
1963	Roberta Alison–Justina Bricka	Alabama–Washington (MO)
1964	Connie Jaster–Carol Loop	Cal State (L.A.)
1965	Nancy Falkenburg–Cynthia Goeltz	Mary Baldwin
1966	Yale Stockwell–Libby Weiss	USC
1967	Jane Albert–Julie Anthony	Stanford
1968	Emilie Burrer–Becky Vest	Trinity (TX)

1969	Emilie Burrer–Becky Vest ....Trinity (TX)
1970	Pam Farmer–Connie Capozzi ....Odessa JC
1971	Pam Richmond–Peggy Michel..Arizona State
1972	Pam Richmond–Peggy Michel..Arizona State
1973	Cathy Beene–Linda Rupert..................Lamar
1974	Ann Lebedeff–Karen Reinke ....
	San Diego State
1975	JoAnne Russell–Donna Stockton ....
	Trinity (TX)
1976	Susie Hagey–Diane Morrison ....Stanford
1977	Jodi Applebaum–Terry Saiganik ....Miami
1978	Sherry Acker–Judy Acker ....Florida State
1979	Kathy Jordan–Alycia Moulton ....Stanford
1980	Trey Lewis–Anne White ....USC
1981	Alycia Moulton–Caryn Copeland .....Stanford
1982	Heather Ludloff–Lynn Lewis ....UCLA
1983	Louise Allen–Gretchen Rush.....Trinity (TX)
1984	Elise Burgin–Linda Gates ....Stanford
1985	Leigh Ann Eldredge–Linda Gates....Stanford
1986	Lise Gregory–Ronni Reis ....Miami
1987	Katrina Adams–Diana Donnelly ....
	Northwestern
1988	Allyson Cooper–Stella Sampras...........UCLA
1989	Jackie Holden–Claire Pollard ....
	Mississipi State
1990	Meredith McGrath–Teri Whitlinger...............
	Stanford
1991	Jillian Alexander–Nicole Arendt ....Florida
1992	Mamie Ceniza–Iwalina McCalla ....UCLA

U.S. INTERSCHOLASTIC CHAMPIONS

Boys

Year	School
1891	Robert Wrenn ....Cambridge Latin (MA)
1892	Malcolm Chace..............Univ. Grammar (RI)
1893	Clarence Budlong................Providence (RI)
1894	Gordon Parker.............................Tutor (NY)
1895	Leo Ware......................Roxbury Latin (MA)
1896	Rex Fincke...........................Hotchkiss (CT)
1897	Rex Fincke...........................Hotchkiss (CT)
1898	Beals Wright......................Hopkinson (MA)
1899	Beals Wright......................Hopkinson (MA)
1900	Irving Wright.....................Hopkinson (MA)
1901	Edward Larned.................Lawrenceville (NJ)
1902	Hendricks Whitman ....Noble's (MA)
1903	Karl Behr ....Lawrenceville (NJ)
1904	Nathaniel Niles ....Boston Latin (MA)
1905	Nathaniel Niles...................Volkmann (MA)
1906	J. Allen Ross...........................Hyde Park (IL)
1907	Wallace Johnson ....Haverford (PA)
1908	Dean Mathey................................Pingry (PA)
1909	Maurice McLoughlin ......San Francisco (CA)

1910	Edwin Whitney ....Stone's (MA)
1911	George Church ....Irving (MA)
1912	Clifton Herd ....Exeter (NH)
1913	Colket Caner ....St. Mark's (MA)
1914	Leonard Beekman....................Pawling (NY)
1915	Harold Throckmorton ....Woodridge (NY)
1916–22	Not held
1923	John Whitbeck ....Loomis (CT)
1924	Horace Orser......................Stuyvesant (NY)
1936	Robert Low ....Choate (CT)
1937	William Gillespie................Scarborough (RI)
1938	Jack Kramer.......................Montebello (CA)
1939	Ted Olewine ....Santa Monica (CA)
1940	Bob Carothers ....Coronado (CA)
1941	Vic Seixas.........................Penn Charter (PA)
1942	Bob Falkenburg ....Fairfax (CA)
1943	Chuck Oliver ....Perth Amboy (NJ)
1944	Bernard "Tut" Bartzen ....San Angelo (TX)
1945	Herbie Flam.......................Beverly Hills (CA)
1946	Hugh Stewart ....So. Pasadena (CA)
1947	Herb Behrens...............Fort Lauderdale (FL)
1948	Gil Bogley ....Landon (MD)
1949	Keston Deimling ....Oak Park (IL)
1950	Ham Richardson...
	Univ. High Baton Rouge (LA)
1951	Herb Browne...............................Dreher (SC)
1952	Ed Rubinoff.......................Miami Beach (FL)
1953	Mike Green ....Miami Beach (FL)
1954	Greg Grant ....South Pasadena (CA)
1955	Crawford Henry ....Grady (GA)
1956	Clarence Sledge...........Highland Park (TX)
1957	Butch Buchholz ....
	John Burroughs St. Louis (MO)
1958	Ray Senkowski.....................Hamtramck (MI)
1959	Bill Lenoir ....Tucson (AR)
1960	Bill Lenoir ....Tucson (AR)
1961	Arthur Ashe ....Sumner St. Louis (MO)
1962	Jackie Cooper.........St. Xavier Louisville (KY)
1963	Mike Belkin ....Miami Beach (FL)
1964	Bob Goeltz................................Landon (MD)
1965	Bob Goeltz................................Landon (MD)
1966	Bob Goeltz................................Landon (MD)
1967	Zan Guerry.................................Baylor (TN)
1968	Charlie Owens ....Tuscaloosa (AL)
1969	Fred McNair ....Landon (MD)
1970	Harold Solomon ....Springbrook (CT)
1971	John Whitlinger ....Shattuck (WI)
1972	Bill Matyastik ....Univ. High (LA)
1973	Dave Parker...........................Galesburg (IL)
1974	Chris Delaney...................Georgetown (MD)
1975	Pem Guerry................................Baylor (TN)
1976	Jim Hodges ....Landon (MD)
1977	Jay Lapidus.....................Lawrenceville (NJ)
1978	Jeff Turpin ....St. Mark's (TX)
1979	Mike DePalmer ....Bradenton Acad. (FL)
1980	Mike DePalmer ....Bradenton Acad. (FL)
1981	Chris Kennedy ....Ravencroft (NC)
1982	John Zahurak ....Calvert Hall (MD)

1983	Bryan Shelton ....Randolph School (AL)
1984	Ashley Rhoney ....S. Caldwell (NC)
1985	Al Parker................Pinewood Christian (GA)
1986	Jim Courier.....St. Stephen's Bradenton (FL)
1987	Jack Frierson...................................Vista (CA)
1988	John Yancey...............................Liggett (MI)
1989	William Webb.........................Durham (NC)
1990	Chris Woodruff.......................Bearden (TN)
1991	Craig Baskin ....Walker School (GA)
1992	Jim Thomas ....Canton Catholic (IA)

	St. Stephen's Bradenton (FL)
1982	Beverly Bowes.................St. Mary's Hall (TX)
1983	Juliet Kaczmarek ....St. Mary's Hall (TX)
1984	Trisha Laux ....Marist (GA)
1985	Jennifer Young............Bradenton Acad. (FL)
1986	Jennifer Young............Bradenton Acad. (FL)
1987	Jennifer Young............Bradenton Acad. (FL)
1988	Audra Keller ....Bartlett (TN)
1989	Lihini Weerasuriya ......Bradenton Acad.(FL)
1999	Tracee Lee ....Punahou (HI)
1991	Jean Okada ....Lahaina Luna (HI)
1992	Angela Nelson ....Highland (UT)

WIMBLEDON

Men's Singles

Year

1877	Spencer Gore d. William Marshall 6–1, 6–2, 6–4
1878	Frank Hadow d. Spencer Gore 7–5, 6–1, 9–7
1879	John Hartley d. V. St. Leger Goold 6–2, 6–4, 6–2
1880	John Hartley d. Herbert Lawford 6–3, 6–2, 2–6, 6–3
1881	Willie Renshaw d. John Hartley 6–0, 6–1, 6–1
1882	Willie Renshaw d. Ernest Renshaw 6–1, 2–6, 4–6, 6–2, 6–2
1883	Willie Renshaw d. Ernest Renshaw 2–6, 6–3, 6–3, 4–6, 6–3
1884	Willie Renshaw d. Herbert Lawford 6–0, 6–4, 9–7

1885	Willie Renshaw d. Herbert Lawford 7–5, 6–2, 4–6, 7–5
1886	Willie Renshaw d. Herbert Lawford 6–0, 5–7, 6–3, 6–4
1887	Herbert Lawford d. Ernest Renshaw 1–6, 6–3, 3–6, 6–4, 6–4
1888	Ernest Renshaw d. Herbert Lawford 6–3, 7–5, 6–0
1889	Willie Renshaw d. Ernest Renshaw 6–4, 6–1, 3–6, 6–0
1890	Willoughby Hamilton d. Willie Renshaw 6–8,
	6–8, 5–7, 8–6, 6–3
1897	Reggie Doherty d. Harold Mahony 6–4, 6–4, 6–3
1898	Reggie Doherty d. Laurie Doherty 6–3, 6–3, 2–6, 5–7, 6–1
1899	Reggie Doherty d. Arthur Gore 1–6, 4–6, 6–2, 6–3, 6–3
1900	Reggie Doherty d. Sidney Smith 6–8, 6–3, 6–1, 6–2
1901	Arthur Gore d. Reggie Doherty 4–6, 7–5, 6–4, 6–4
1902	Laurie Doherty d. Arthur Gore 6–4, 6–3, 3–6, 6–0
1903	Laurie Doherty d. Frank Riseley 7–5, 6–3, 6–0
1904	Laurie Doherty d. Frank Riseley 6–1, 7–5, 8–6
1905	Laurie Doherty d. Norman Brookes 8–6, 6–2, 6–4
1906	Laurie Doherty d. Frank Riseley 6–4, 4–6, 6–2, 6–3
1907	Norman Brookes d. Arthur Gore 6–4, 6–2, 6–2
1908	Arthur Gore d. Roper Barrett 6–3, 6–2, 4–6, 3–6, 6–4
1909	Arthur Gore d. M.J.G. Ritchie 6–8, 1–6, 6–2, 6–2, 6–2
1910	Tony Wilding d. Arthur Gore 6–4, 7–5, 4–6, 6–2
1911	Tony Wilding, d. Roper Barrett 6–4, 4–6, 2–6, 6–3 retired
1912	Tony Wilding d. Arthur Gore 6–4, 6–4, 4–6, 6–4
1913	Tony Wilding d. Maurice McLoughlin 8–6, 6–3, 10–8
1914	Norman Brookes d. Tony Wilding 6–4, 6–4, 7–5
1915–18	Not held; World War I
1919	Gerald Patterson d. Norman Brookes 6–3, 7–5, 6–2

1920	Bill Tilden d. Gerald Patterson 2–6, 6–3, 6–2, 6–4
1921	Bill Tilden d. Brian Norton 4–6, 2–6, 6–1, 6–0, 7–5
1922	Gerald Patterson d. Randolph Lycett 6–3, 6–4, 6–2
1923	Bill Johnston d. Francis Hunter 6–0, 6–3, 6–1
1924	Jean Borotra d. René Lacoste 6–1, 3–6, 6–1, 3–6, 6–4
1925	René Lacoste d. Jean Borotra 6–3, 6–3, 4–6, 8–6
1926	Jean Borotra d. Howard Kinsey 8–6, 6–1, 6–3
1927	Henri Cochet d. Jean Borotra 4–6, 4–6, 6–3, 6–4, 7–5
1928	René Lacoste d. Henri Cochet 6–1, 4–6, 6–4, 6–2
1929	Henri Cochet d. Jean Borotra 6–4, 6–3, 6–4
1930	Bill Tilden d. Wilmer Allison 6–3, 9–7, 6–4
1931	Sidney Wood d. Frank Shields, default
1932	Ellsworth Vines d. Henry "Bunny" Austin 6–4, 6–2, 6–0
1933	Jack Crawford d. Ellsworth Vines 4–6, 11–9, 6–2, 2–6, 6–4
1934	Fred Perry d. Jack Crawford 6–3, 6–0, 7–5
1935	Fred Perry d. Gottfried von Cramm 6–2, 6–4, 6–4
1936	Fred Perry d. Gottfried von Cramm 6–1, 6–1, 6–0
1937	Don Budge d. Gottfried von Cramm 6–3, 6–4, 6–2
1938	Don Budge d. Henry "Bunny" Austin 6–1, 6–0, 6–3
1939	Bobby Riggs d. Elwood Cooke 2–6, 8–6, 3–6, 6–3, 6–2
1940–45	Not held; World War II
1946	Yvon Petra d. Geoff Brown 6–2, 6–4, 7–9, 5–7, 6–4
1947	Jack Kramer d. Tom Brown 6–1, 6–3, 6–2
1948	Bob Falkenburg d. John Bromwich 7–5, 0–6, 6–2, 3–6, 7–5
1949	Ted Schroeder d. Jaroslav Drobny 3–6, 6–0, 6–3, 4–6, 6–4
1950	J.E. "Budge" Patty d. Frank Sedgman 6–1, 8–10, 6–2, 6–3
1951	Dick Savitt d. Ken McGregor 6–4, 6–4, 6–4
1952	Frank Sedgman d. Jaroslav Drobny 4–6, 6–2, 6–3, 6–2
1953	Vic Seixas d. Kurt Nielsen 9–7, 6–3, 6–4
1954	Jaroslav Drobny d. Ken Rosewall 13–11, 4–6, 6–2, 9–7
1955	Tony Trabert d. Kurt Nielsen 6–3, 7–5, 6–1
1956	Lew Hoad d. Ken Rosewall 6–2, 4–6, 7–5, 6–4
1957	Lew Hoad d. Ashley Cooper 6–2, 6–1, 6–2
1958	Ashley Cooper d. Neale Fraser 3–6, 6–3, 6–4, 13–11
1959	Alex Olmedo d. Rod Laver 6–4, 6–3, 6–4
1960	Neale Fraser d. Rod Laver 6–4, 3–6, 9–7, 7–5
1961	Rod Laver d. Chuck McKinley 6–3, 6–1, 6–4

1962	Rod Laver d. Marty Mulligan 6–2, 6–2, 6–1
1963	Chuck McKinley d. Fred Stolle 9–7, 6–1, 6–4
1964	Roy Emerson d. Fred Stolle 6–4, 12–10, 4–6, 6–3
1965	Roy Emerson d. Fred Stolle 6–2, 6–4, 6–4
1966	Manuel Santana d. Dennis Ralston 6–4, 11–9, 6–4
1967	John Newcombe d. Willie Bungert 6–3, 6–1, 6–1
1968	Rod Laver d. Tony Roche 6–3, 6–4, 6–2
1969	Rod Laver d. John Newcombe 6–4, 5–7, 6–4, 6–4
1970	John Newcombe d. Ken Rosewall 5–7, 6–3, 6–2, 3–6, 6–1
1971	John Newcombe d. Stan Smith 6–3, 5–7, 2–6, 6–4, 6–4
1972	Stan Smith d. Ilie Nastase 4–6, 6–3, 6–3, 4–6, 7–5
1973	Jan Kodes d. Alex Metreveli 6–1, 9–8, 6–3
1974	Jimmy Connors d. Ken Rosewall 6–1, 6–1, 6–4
1975	Arthur Ashe d. Jimmy Connors 6–1, 6–1, 5–7, 6–4
1976	Bjorn Borg d. Ilie Nastase 6–4, 6–2, 9–7
1977	Bjorn Borg d. Jimmy Connors 3–6, 6–2, 6–1, 5–7, 6–4
1978	Bjorn Borg d. Jimmy Connors 6–2, 6–2, 6–3
1979	Bjorn Borg d. Roscoe Tanner 6–7, 6–1, 3–6, 6–3, 6–4
1980	Bjorn Borg d. John McEnroe 1–6, 7–5, 6–3, 6–7, 8–6
1981	John McEnroe d. Bjorn Borg 4–6, 7–6, 7–6, 6–4
1982	Jimmy Connors d. John McEnroe 3–6, 6–3, 6–7, 7–6, 6–4
1983	John McEnroe d. Chris Lewis 6–2, 6–2, 6–2
1984	John McEnroe d. Jimmy Connors 6–1, 6–2, 6–2
1985	Boris Becker d. Kevin Curren 6–3, 6–7, 7–6, 6–4
1986	Boris Becker d. Ivan Lendl 6–4, 6–3, 7–5
1987	Pat Cash d. Ivan Lendl 7–6, 6–2, 7–5
1988	Stefan Edberg d. Boris Becker 4–6, 7–6, 6–4, 6–2
1989	Boris Becker d. Stefan Edberg 6–0, 7–6, 6–4
1990	Stefan Edberg d. Boris Becker 6–2, 6–2, 3–6, 3–6, 6–4
1991	Michael Stich d. Boris Becker 6–4, 7–6, 6–4
1992	Andre Agassi d. Goran Ivanisevic 6–7, 6–4, 6–4, 1–6, 6–4

Women's Singles

Year

| 1884 | Maud Watson d. Lillian Watson 6–8, 6–3, 6–3 |
| 1885 | Maud Watson d. Blanche Bingley 6–1, 7–5 |

1886	Blanche Bingley d. Maud Watson 6–3, 6–3
1887	Lottie Dod d. Blanche Bingley Hillyard 6–2, 6–0
1888	Lottie Dod d. Blanche Bingley Hillyard 6–3, 6–3
1889	Blanche Bingley Hillyard d. Helena Rice 4–6, 8–6, 6–4
1890	Helena Rice d. M. Jacks 6–4, 6–1
1891	Lottie Dod d. Blanche Bingley Hillyard 6–2, 6–1
1892	Lottie Dod d. Blanche Bingley Hillyard 6–1, 6–1
1893	Lottie Dod d. Blanche Bingley Hillyard 6–8,

Cooper 6–2, 6–3
1900	Blanche Bingley Hillyard d. Charlotte Cooper 4–6, 6–4, 6–4
1901	Charlotte Cooper Sterry d. Blanche Bingley Hillyard 6–2, 6–2
1902	Muriel Robb d. Charlotte Cooper Sterry 7–5, 6–1
1903	Dorothea Douglass d. Ethel Thomson 4–6, 6–4, 6–2
1904	Dorothea Douglass d. Charlotte Cooper Sterry 6–0, 6–3
1905	May Sutton d. Dorothea Douglass 6–3, 6–4
1906	Dorothea Douglass d. May Sutton 6–3, 9–7
1907	May Sutton d. Dorothea Douglass Lambert Chambers 6–1, 6–4
1908	Charlotte Cooper Sterry d. Agnes Morton 6–4, 6–4
1909	Dora Boothby d. Agnes Morton 6–4, 4–6, 8–6
1910	Dorothea Douglass Lambert Chambers d. Dora Boothby 6–2, 6–2
1911	Dorothea Douglass Lambert Chambers d. Dora Boothby 6–0, 6–0
1912	Ethel Thomson Larcombe d. Charlotte Cooper Sterry 6–3, 6–1
1913	Dorothea Douglass Lambert Chambers d. Winifred Slocock McNair 6–0, 6–4
1914	Dorothea Douglass Lambert Chambers d. Ethel Thomson Larcombe 7–5, 6–4
1915–18	Not held; World War I
1919	Suzanne Lenglen d. Dorothea Douglass Lambert Chambers 10–8, 4–6, 9–7
1920	Suzanne Lenglen d. Dorothea Douglass Lambert Chambers 6–3, 6–0
1921	Suzanne Lenglen d. Elizabeth Ryan 6–2, 6–0
1922	Suzanne Lenglen d. Molla Bjurstedt Mallory 6–2, 6–0

1923	Suzanne Lenglen d. Kitty McKane 6–2, 6–2
1924	Kitty McKane d. Helen Wills 4–6, 6–4, 6–4
1925	Suzanne Lenglen d. Joan Fry 6–2, 6–0
1926	Kitty McKane Godfree d. Lili de Alvarez 6–2, 4–6, 6–3
1927	Helen Wills d. Lili de Alvarez 6–2, 6–4
1928	Helen Wills d. Lili de Alvarez 6–2, 6–3
1929	Helen Wills d. Helen Jacobs 6–1, 6–2
1930	Helen Wills Moody d. Elizabeth Ryan 6–2, 6–2
1931	Cilly Aussem d. Hilde Krahwinkel 6–2, 7–5
1932	Helen Wills Moody d. Helen Jacobs 6–3, 6–1

1939 Alice Marble d. Kay Stammers 6–2, 6–0
1940–45	Not held; World War II
1946	Pauline Betz d. Louise Brough 6–2 6–4
1947	Margaret Osborne d. Doris Hart 6–2, 6–4
1948	Louise Brough d. Doris Hart 6–3, 8–6
1949	Louise Brough d. Margaret Osborne duPont 10–8, 1–6, 10–8
1950	Louise Brough d. Margaret Osborne duPont 6–1, 3–6, 6–1
1951	Doris Hart d. Shirley Fry 6–1, 6–0
1952	Maureen Connolly d. Louise Brough 7–5, 6–3
1953	Maureen Connolly d. Doris Hart 8–6, 7–5
1954	Maureen Connolly d. Louise Brough 6–2, 7–5
1955	Louise Brough d. Beverly Baker Fleitz 7–5, 8–6
1956	Shirley Fry d. Angela Buxton 6–3, 6–1
1957	Althea Gibson d. Darlene Hard 6–3, 6–2
1958	Althea Gibson d. Angela Mortimer 8–6, 6–2
1959	Maria Bueno d. Darlene Hard 6–4, 6–3
1960	Maria Bueno d. Sandra Reynolds 8–6, 6–0
1961	Angela Mortimer d. Christine Truman 4–6, 6–4, 7–5
1962	Karen Hantze Susman d. Vera Sukova 6–4, 6–4
1963	Margaret Smith d. Billie Jean Moffitt 6–3, 6–4
1964	Maria Bueno d. Margaret Smith 6–4, 7–9, 6–3
1965	Margaret Smith d. Maria Bueno 6–4, 7–5
1966	Billie Jean Moffitt King d. Maria Bueno 6–3, 3–6, 6–1
1967	Billie Jean Moffitt King d. Ann Haydon Jones 6–3, 6–4
1968	Billie Jean Moffitt King d. Judy Tegart 9–7, 7–5
1969	Ann Haydon Jones d. Billie Jean Moffitt King 3–6, 6–3, 6–2
1970	Margaret Smith Court d. Billie Jean Moffitt King 14–12, 11–9

1971	Evonne Goolagong d. Margaret Smith Court 6–4, 6–1
1972	Billie Jean Moffitt King d. Evonne Goolagong 6–3, 6–3
1973	Billie Jean Moffitt King d. Chris Evert 6–0, 7–5
1974	Chris Evert d. Olga Morozova 6–0, 6–4
1975	Billie Jean Moffitt King d. Evonne Goolagong Cawley 6–0, 6–1
1976	Chris Evert d. Evonne Goolagong Cawley 6–3, 4–6, 8–6
1977	Virginia Wade d. Betty Stove 4–6, 6–3, 6–1
1978	Martina Navratilova d. Chris Evert 2–6, 6–4, 7–5
1979	Martina Navratilova d. Chris Evert Lloyd 6–4, 6–4
1980	Evonne Goolagong Cawley d. Chris Evert Lloyd 6–1, 7–6
1981	Chris Evert Lloyd d. Hana Mandlikova 6–2, 6–2
1982	Martina Navratilova d. Chris Evert Lloyd 6–1, 3–6, 6–2
1983	Martina Navratilova d. Andrea Jaeger 6–0, 6–3
1984	Martina Navratilova d. Chris Evert Lloyd 7–6, 6–2
1985	Martina Navratilova d. Chris Evert Lloyd 4–6, 6–3, 6–2
1986	Martina Navratilova d. Hana Mandlikova 7–6, 6–3
1987	Martina Navratilova d. Steffi Graf 7–5, 6–3
1988	Steffi Graf d. Martina Navratilova 5–7, 6–2, 6–1
1989	Steffi Graf d. Martina Navratilova 6–2, 6–7, 6–1
1990	Martina Navratilova d. Zina Garrison 6–4, 6–1
1991	Steffi Graf d. Gabriela Sabatini 6–4, 3–6, 8–6
1992	Steffi Graf d. Monica Seles 6–2, 6–1

Men's Doubles

Year

1884	William Renshaw–Ernest Renshaw d. Ernest Lewis–Edward Williams 6–3, 6–1, 1–6, 6–4
1885	William Renshaw–Ernest Renshaw d. Claude Farrar–Arthur Stanley 6–3, 6–3, 10–8 (challenge round instituted)
1886	William Renshaw–Ernest Renshaw d. Claude Farrar–Arthur Stanley 6–3, 6–3, 4–6, 7–5
1887	Herbert Wilberforce–P.B. Lyon d. J. Hope Crisp–Barratt Smith 7–5, 6–3, 6–2
1888	William Renshaw–Ernest Renshaw d. Herbert Wilberforce–P.B. Lyon 2–6, 1–6, 6–3, 6–4, 6–3
1889	William Renshaw–Ernest Renshaw d. Ernest Lewis–George Hillyard 6–4, 6–4, 3–6, 0–6, 6–1
1890	Joshua Pim–Frank Stoker d. Ernest Lewis–George Hillyard 6–0, 7–5, 6–4
1891	Wilfred Baddeley–Herbert Baddeley d. Joshua Pim–Frank Stoker 6–1, 6–3, 1–6, 6–2
1892	Ernest Lewis–Harry Barlow d. Wilfred Baddeley–Herbert Baddeley 4–6, 6–2, 8–6, 6–4
1893	Joshua Pim–Frank Stoker d. Ernest Lewis–Harry Barlow 4–6, 6–3, 6–1, 2–6, 6–0
1894	Wilfred Baddeley–Herbert Baddeley d. Harry Barlow–Charles Martin 5–7, 7–5, 4–6, 6–3, 8–6
1895	Wilfred Baddeley–Herbert Baddeley d. Ernest Lewis–Wilberforce Eaves 8–6, 5–7, 6–4, 6–3
1896	Wilfred Baddeley–Herbert Baddeley d. Reggie Doherty–Harold Nisbet 6–4, 4–6, 8–6, 6–4
1897	Reggie Doherty–Laurie Doherty d. Wilfred Baddeley–Herbert Baddeley 6–4, 4–6, 8–6, 6–4
1898	Reggie Doherty–Laurie Doherty d. Harold Nisbet–Clarence Hobart 6–4, 6–4, 6–2
1899	Reggie Doherty–Laurie Doherty d. Harold Nisbet–Clarence Hobart 7–5, 6–0, 6–2
1900	Reggie Doherty–Laurie Doherty d. H. Roper Barrett–Harold Nisbet 9–7, 7–5, 4–6, 3–6, 6–3
1901	Reggie Doherty–Laurie Doherty d. Dwight Davis–Holcombe Ward 4–6, 6–2, 6–3, 9–7
1902	Sidney Smith–Frank Riseley d. Reggie Doherty–Laurie Doherty 4–6, 8–6, 6–3, 3–6, 11–9
1903	Reggie Doherty–Laurie Doherty d. Sidney Smith–Frank Risely 6–4, 6–2, 6–4
1904	Reggie Doherty–Laurie Doherty d. Sidney Smith–Frank Riseley 6–2, 6–4, 6–8, 6–3
1905	Reggie Doherty–Laurie Doherty d. Sidney Smith–Frank Riseley 6–2, 6–4, 6–8, 6–3
1906	Sidney Smith–Frank Riseley d. Reggie Doherty–Laurie Doherty 6–8, 6–4, 5–7, 6–3, 6–3
1907	Norman Brookes–Tony Wilding d. Beals Wright–Karl Behr 6–4, 6–4, 6–2
1908	Tony Wilding–Major Ritchie d. Arthur Gore–H. Roper Barrett 6–1, 6–2, 1–6, 1–6, 9–7
1909	Arthur Gore–H. Roper Barrett d. Stanley Doust–Harry Parker 6–2, 6–1, 6–4
1910	Tony Wilding–Major Ritchie d. Arthur Gore–H. Roper Barrett 6–1, 6–1, 6–2
1911	Andre Gobert–Max Decugis d. Tony Wilding–Major Ritchie 9–7, 5–7, 6–3, 2–6, 6–2
1912	H. Roper Barrett–Charles Dixon d. Andre Gobert–Max Decugis 3–6, 6–3, 6–4, 7–5
1913	H. Roper Barrett–Charles Dixon d. Friedrich Rahe–Heinrich Kleinschroth 6–2, 6–4, 4–6, 6–2

1914	Norman Brookes–Tony Wilding d. H. Roper
	Barrett–Charles Dixon 6–1, 6–1, 5–7, 8–6
1915–18 Not held; World War I
1919	Ronald Thomas–Pat O'Hara Wood d.
	Randolph Lycett–Rodney Heath 6–4, 6–2,
	4–6, 6–2
1920	Dick Williams–Chuck Garland d. Algernon
	Kingscote–James Parke 4–6, 4–7, 7–5, 6–2
1921	Randolph Lycett–Max Woosnam d. Arthur
	Lowe–Frank Lowe 6–3, 6–0, 7–5 (chal-
	lenge round abolished)

	6–3
1926	Jacques Brugnon–Henri Cochet d. Howard
	Kinsey–Vinnie Richards 7–5, 4–6, 6–3, 6–2
1927	Frank Hunter–Bill Tilden d. Jacques
	Brugnon–Henri Cochet 1–6, 4–6, 8–6,
	6–3, 6–4
1928	Jacques Brugnon–Henri Cochet d. Gerald
	Patterson–John Hawkes 13–11, 6–4, 6–4
1929	Wilmer Allison–John Van Ryn d. Colin
	Gregory–Ian Collins 6–4, 5–7, 6–3, 10–12,
	6–4
1930	Wilmer Allison–John Van Ryn d. John Doeg–
	George Lott 6–3, 6–3, 6–2
1931	George Lott–John Van Ryn d. Jacques
	Brugnon–Henri Cochet 6–2, 10–8, 9–11,
	3–6, 6–3
1932	Jean Borotra–Jacques Brugnon d. Fred
	Perry–Pat Hughes 6–0, 4–6, 3–6, 7–5, 7–5
1933	Jean Borotra–Jacques Brugnon d. Ryosuki
	Nunoi–Jiro Satoh 4–6, 6–3, 6–3, 7–5
1934	George Lott–Les Stoefen d. Jean
	Borotra–Jacques Brugnon 6–2, 6–3, 6–4
1935	Jack Crawford–Adrian Quist d. Wilmer
	Allison–John Van Ryn 6–3, 5–7, 6–2, 5–7,
	7–5
1936	Pat Hughes–Raymond Tuckey d. Charles
	Hare–Frank Wilde 6–4, 3–6, 7–9, 6–1, 6–4
1937	Don Budge–Gene Mako d. Pat Hughes–
	Raymond Tuckey 6–0, 6–4, 6–8, 6–1
1938	Don Budge–Gene Mako d. Henner Henkel–
	Georg von Metaxa 6–4, 3–6, 6–3, 8–6
1939	Elwood Cooke–Bobby Riggs d. Charles
	Hare–Frank Wilde 6–3, 3–6, 6–3, 9–7
1940–45 Not held; World War II
1946	Tom Brown–Jack Kramer d. Geoff
	Brown–Dinny Pails 6–4, 6–4, 6–2

1947	Bob Falkenburg–Jack Kramer d. Tony
	Mottram–Billy Sidwell, 8–6, 6–3, 6–3
1948	John Bromwich–Frank Sedgman d. Tom
	Brown–Gardnar Mulloy 5–7, 7–5, 7–5, 9–7
1949	Richard "Pancho" Gonzalez–Frank Parker d.
	Gardnar Mulloy–Ted Schroeder 6–4, 6–4,
	6–2
1950	John Bromwich–Adrian Quist d. Geoff Brown–
	Billy Sidwell 7–5, 3–6, 6–3, 3–6, 6–2
1951	Ken McGregor–Frank Sedgman d. Jaroslav
	Drobny–Eric Sturgess 3–6, 6–2, 6–3, 3–6,

1957	J. E. "Budge" Patty–Gardnar Mulloy d. Neale
	Fraser–Lew Hoad 8–10, 6–4, 6–4, 6–4
1958	Sven Davidson–Ulf Schmidt d. Ashley Cooper–
	Neale Fraser 6–4, 6–4, 8–6
1959	Roy Emerson–Neale Faser d. Rod Laver–Bob
	Mark 8–6, 6–3, 14–16, 9–7
1960	Rafael Osuna–Dennis Ralston d. Mike Davies–
	Bobby Wilson 7–5, 6–3, 10–8
1961	Roy Emerson Neale Fraser d. Bob
	Hewitt–Fred Stolle 6–4, 6–8, 6–4, 6–8, 8–6
1962	Bob Hewitt–Fred Stolle d. Boro
	Jovanovic–Nikki Pilic 6–2, 5–7, 6–2, 6–4
1963	Rafael Osuna–Antonio Palafox d. Jean-
	Claude Barclay–Pierre Darmon 4–6, 6–2,
	6–2, 6–2
1964	Bob Hewitt–Fred Stolle d. Roy Emerson–Ken
	Fletcher 7–5, 11–9, 6–4
1965	John Newcombe–Tony Roche d. Ken
	Fletcher–Bob Hewitt 7–5, 6–3, 6–4
1966	Ken Fletcher–John Newcombe d. Bill Bowrey–
	Owen Davidson 6–3, 6–4, 3–6, 6–3
1967	Bob Hewitt–Frew McMillan d. Roy Emerson–
	Fletcher 6–2, 6–3, 6–4
1968	John Newcombe–Tony Roche d. Ken
	Rosewall–Fred Stolle 3–6, 8–6, 5–7, 14–12,
	6–3
1969	John Newcombe–Tony Roche d. Tom Okker–
	Mary Riessen 7–5, 11–9, 6–3
1970	John Newcombe–Tony Roche d. Ken
	Rosewall–Fred Stolle 10–8, 6–3, 6–1
1971	Roy Emerson–Rod Laver d. Arthur Ashe–
	Dennis Ralston 4–6, 9–7, 6–8, 6–4, 6–4
1972	Bob Hewitt–Frew McMillan d. Stan Smith–
	Eric van Dillen 6–2, 6–2, 9–7
1973	Jimmy Connors–Ilie Nastase d. John Cooper–
	Neale Fraser 3–6, 6–3, 6–4, 8–9, 6–1

1974	John Newcombe–Tony Roche d. Bob Lutz–Stan Smith 8–6, 6–4, 6–4

1974 John Newcombe–Tony Roche d. Bob Lutz–
Stan Smith 8–6, 6–4, 6–4

1975 Vitas Gerulaitis–Alex Mayer d. Colin
Dowdeswell–Allan Stone 7–5, 8–6, 6–4

1976 Brian Gottfried–Raul Ramirez d. Ross Case–
Geoff Masters 3–6, 6–3, 8–6, 2–6, 7–6

1977 Geoff Masters–Ross Case d. John Alexander–
Phil Dent 6–3, 6–4, 3–6, 8–9, 6–4

1978 Bob Hewitt–Frew McMillan d. Peter Fleming–
John McEnroe 6–1, 6–4, 6–2

1979 Peter Fleming–John McEnroe d. Brian
Gottfried–Raul Ramirez 4–6, 6–4, 6–2, 6–2

1980 Peter McNamara–Paul McNamee d. Bob
Lutz–Stan Smith 7–6, 6–3, 6–7, 6–4

1981 Peter Fleming–John McEnroe d. Bob Lutz–
Stan Smith 6–4, 6–4, 6–4

1982 Peter McNamara–Paul McNamee d. Peter
Fleming–John McEnroe 6–3, 6–2

1983 Peter Fleming–John McEnroe d. Tim
Gullikson–Tom Gullikson 6–4, 6–3, 6–4

1984 Peter Fleming–John McEnroe d. Patrick Cash–
Paul McNamee 6–2, 5–7, 6–2, 3–6, 6–3

1985 Heinz Gunthardt–Balazs Taroczy d. Patrick
Cash–John Fitzgerald 6–4, 6–3, 4–6, 6–3

1986 Joakim Nystrom–Mats Wilander d. Gary
Donnelly–Peter Fleming 7–6, 6–3, 6–3

1987 Ken Flach–Robert Seguso d. Sergio Casal–
Emilio Sanchez 3–6, 6–7, 7–6, 6–1, 6–4

1988 Ken Flach–Robert Seguso d. John Fitzgerald–
Anders Jarryd 6–4, 2–6, 6–4, 7–6

1989 John Fitzgerald–Anders Jarryd d. Rick Leach–
Jim Pugh 3–6, 7–6, 6–4, 7–6

1990 Rick Leach–Jim Pugh d. Pieter Aldrich–Danie
Visser 7–6, 7–6, 7–6

1991 John Fitzgerald–Anders Jarryd d. Javier
Frana–Leonardo Lavalle 6–3, 6–4, 6–7, 6–1

1992 John McEnroe–Michael Stich d. Jim Grabb–
Richey Reneberg 5–7, 7–6, 3–6, 7–6, 19–17

Women's Doubles

Year

1913 Winifred Slocock McNair–Dora Boothby d.
Charlotte Cooper Sterry–Dorothea
Douglass Lambert Chambers 4–6, 2–4,
retired

1914 Agnes Morton–Elizabeth Ryan d. Edith
Boucher Hannam–Ethel Thompson
Larcombe 6–1, 6–3

1915–18 Not held; World War I

1919 Suzanne Lenglen–Elizabeth Ryan d. Dorothea
Douglass Lambert Chambers–Ethel
Thompson Larcombe 4–6, 7–5, 6–3

1920 Suzanne Lenglen–Elizabeth Ryan d. Dorothea
Douglass Lambert Chambers–Ethel
Thompson Larcombe 6–4, 6–0

1921 Suzanne Lenglen–Elizabeth Ryan d.
Geraldine Ramsey Beamish–Irene
Peacock 6–1, 6–2

1922 Suzanne Lenglen–Elizabeth Ryan d. Kitty
McKane–Margaret McKane Stocks 6–0,
6–4

1923 Suzanne Lenglen–Elizabeth Ryan d. Joan
Austin–Evelyn Colyer 6–3, 6–1

1924 Hazel Hotchkiss Wightman–Helen Wills d.
Phyllis Howkins Covell–Kitty McKane 6–4,
6–4

1925 Suzanne Lenglen–Elizabeth Ryan d. Kathleen
Lidderdale Bridge–Mary McIlquham 6–2,
6–2

1926 Mary K. Browne–Elizabeth Ryan d. Kitty
McKane Godfree–Evelyn Colyer 6–1, 6–1

1927 Helen Wills–Elizabeth Ryan d. Bobbie
Heine–Irene Peacock 6–3, 6–2

1928 Peggy Saunders–Phoebe Holcroft Watson d.
Eileen Bennett–Ermyntrude Harvey 6–2,
6–3

1929 Peggy Saunders Michell–Phoebe Holcroft
Watson d. Phyllis Howkins Covell–Dorothy
Shepherd Barron 6–4, 8–6

1930 Helen Wills Moody–Elizabeth Ryan d. Edith
Cross–Sarah Palfrey 6–2, 9–7

1931 Dorothy Shepherd Barron–Phyllis Mudford
d. Doris Metaxa–Josane Sigart 3–6, 6–3,
6–4

1932 Doris Metaxa–Josane Sigart d. Helen Jacobs–
Elizabeth Ryan 6–4, 6–3

1933 Simone Passemard Mathieu–Elizabeth Ryan
d. Freda James–Adeline Yorke 6–2, 9–11,
6–4

1934 Simone Passemard Mathieu–Elizabeth Ryan
d. Dorthy Andrus–Sylvie Jung Henrotin
6–3, 6–3

1935 Freda James–Kay Stammers d. Simone
Passemard Mathieu–Hilde Krahwinkel
Sperling 6–1, 6–4

1936 Freda James–Kay Stammers d. Sarah Palfrey
Fabyan–Helen Jacobs 6–2, 6–1

1937 Simone Passemard Mathieu–Adeline Yorke d.
Phyllis Mudford King–Elsie Goldsack
Pittman 6–3, 6–3

1938 Sarah Palfrey Fabyan–Alice Marble d. Simone
Passemard Mathieu–Adeline Yorke 6–2,
6–3

1939 Sarah Palfrey Fabyan–Alice Marble d. Helen
Jacobs–Adeline Yorke 6–1, 6–0

1940–45 Not held; World War II

1946 Louise Brough–Margaret Osborne d. Pauline
Betz–Doris Hart 6–3, 2–6, 6–3

1947 Doris Hart–Patricia Canning Todd d. Louise
Brough–Margaret Osborne 3–6, 6–4, 7–5

1948 Louise Brough–Margaret Osborne duPont d.
Doris Hart–Patricia Canning Todd 6–3,
3–6, 6–3

1949	Louise Brough–Margaret Osborne duPont d. Gertrude Moran–Patricia Canning Todd 8–6, 7–5
1950	Louise Brough–Margaret Osborne duPont d. Shirley Fry–Doris Hart 6–4, 5–7, 6–1
1951	Shirley Fry–Doris Hart d. Louise Brough–Margaret Osborne duPont 6–3, 13–11
1952	Shirley Fry–Doris Hart d. Louise Brough–Maureen Connolly 8–6, 6–3
1953	Shirley Fry–Doris Hart d. Maureen Connolly–Julia Sampson 6–0, 6–0

Fleitz–Christine Truman 2–6, 6–2, 6–3

1960	Maria Bueno–Darlene Hard d. Sandra Reynolds–Renee Schuurman 6–4, 6–0
1961	Karen Hantze–Billie Jean Moffitt d. Jan Lehane–Margaret Smith 6–3, 6–4
1962	Billie Jean Moffitt–Karen Hantze Susman d. Sandra Reynolds Price–Renee Schuurman 5–7, 6–3, 7–5
1963	Maria Bueno–Darlene Hard d. Robyn Ebbern–Margaret Smith 8–6, 9–7
1964	Margaret Smith–Lesley Turner d. Billie Jean Moffitt–Karen Hantze Susman 7–5, 6–2
1965	Maria Bueno–Billie Jean Moffitt d. Francoise Durr–Jeanine Lieffrig 6–2, 7–5
1966	Maria Bueno–Nancy Richey d. Margaret Smith–Judy Tegart 6–3, 4–6, 6–4
1967	Rosie Casals–Billie Jean Moffitt King d. Maria Bueno–Nancy Richey 9–11, 6–4, 6–2
1968	Rosie Casals–Billie Jean Moffitt King d. Francoise Durr–Ann Haydon Jones 3–6, 6–4, 7–5
1969	Margaret Smith Court–Judy Tegart d. Patty Hogan–Peggy Michel 9–7, 6–2
1970	Rosie Casals–Billie Jean Moffitt King d. Francoise Durr–Virginia Wade 6–2, 6–3
1971	Rosie Casals–Billie Jean Moffitt King d. Margaret Smith Court–Evonne Goolagong 6–3, 6–2
1972	Billie Jean Moffitt King–Betty Stove d. Judy Tegart Dalton–Francoise Durr 6–2, 4–6, 6–3
1973	Rosie Casals–Billie Jean Moffitt King d. Francoise Durr–Betty Stove 6–1, 4–6, 7–5
1974	Evonne Goolagong–Peggy Michel d. Helen Gourlay–Karen Krantzcke 2–6, 6–4, 6–3
1975	Ann Kiyomura–Kazuko Sawamatsu d. Francoise Durr–Betty Stove 7–5, 1–6, 7–5
1976	Chris Evert–Martina Navratilova d. Billie Jean Moffitt King–Betty Stove 6–1, 3–6, 7–5
1977	Helen Gourlay Cawley–JoAnne Russell d. Martina Navratilova–Betty Stove 6–3, 6–3
1978	Kerry Melville Reid–Wendy Turnbull d. Mima Jausovec–Virginia Ruzici 4–6, 9–8, 6–3
1979	Billie Jean Moffitt King–Martina Navratilova d. Betty Stove–Wendy Turnbull 5–7, 6–3, 6–2
1980	Kathy Jordan–Anne Smith d. Rosie Casals–

6–3, 6–4

1986	Martina Navratilova–Pam Shriver d. Hanas Mandlikova–Wendy Turnbull 6–1, 6–3
1987	Claudia Kohde-Kilsch–Helena Sukova d. Betsy Nagelsen–Elizabeth Sayers Smylie 7–5, 7–5
1988	Steffi Graf–Gabriela Sabatini d. Larisa Savchenko–Natalia Zvereva 6–3, 1–6, 12–10
1989	Jana Novotna–Helena Sukova d. Larisa Savchenko–Natalia Zvereva 6–1, 6–2
1990	Jana Novotna–Helena Sukova d. Kathy Jordan–Elizabeth Sayers Smylie 6–3, 6–4
1991	Larisa Savchenko–Natalia Zvereva d. Beatrice "Gigi" Fernandez–Jana Novotna 6–4, 3–6, 6–4
1992	Beatrice "Gigi" Fernandez–Natalia Zvereva d. Jana Novotna–Larisa Savchenko Neiland 6–4, 6–1

Mixed Doubles

Year

1913	Agnes Daniell Tuckey–J. Hope Crisp d. Ethel Thompson Larcombe–James Parke 3–6, 5–3 (retired)
1914	Ethel Thomson Larcombe–Cecil Parke d. Marguerite Broquedis–Tony Wilding 4–6, 6–4, 6–2
1915–18	Not held; World War I
1919	Elizabeth Ryan–Randolph Lycett d. Dorothea Douglass Lambert Chambers–Albert Prebble 6–0, 6–0

1920	Suzanne Lenglen–Gerald Patterson d. Elizabeth Ryan–Randolph Lycett 7–5, 6–3

1920 Suzanne Lenglen–Gerald Patterson d.
Elizabeth Ryan–Randolph Lycett 7–5, 6–3

1921 Elizabeth Ryan–Randolph Lycett d. Phyllis
Howkins–Max Woosnam 6–3, 6–1

1922 Suzanne Lenglen–Pat O'Hara Wood d.
Elizabeth Ryan–Randolph Lycett 6–4, 6–3

1923 Elizabeth Ryan–Randolph Lycett d. Dorothy
Shepherd Barron–Lewis Deane 6–4, 7–5

1924 Kitty McKane–J. Brian Gilbert d. Dorothy
Shephard Barron–Leslie Godfree 6–3,
3–6, 6–3

1925 Suzanne Lenglen–Jean Borotra d. Elizabeth
Ryan–Umberto de Morpurgo 6–3, 6–3

1926 Kitty McKane Godfree–Leslie Godfree d.
Mary K. Browne–Howard Kinsey 6–3, 6–4

1927 Elizabeth Ryan–Frank Hunter d. Kitty
McKane Godfree–Leslie Godfree 8–6, 6–0

1928 Elizabeth Ryan–Pat Spence d. Daphne
Akhurst–Jack Crawford 7–5, 6–4

1929 Helen Wills–Frank Hunter d. Joan Fry–Ian
Collins 6–1, 6–4

1930 Elizabeth Ryan–Jack Crawford d. Hilde
Krahwinkel–Daniel Prenn 6–1, 6–3

1931 Anna McCune Harper–George Lott d. Joan
Ridley–Ian Collins 6–3, 1–6, 6–1

1932 Elizabeth Ryan–Enrique Maier d. Josane
Sigart–Harry Hopman 7–5, 6–2

1933 Hilde Krahwinkel–Gottfried von Cramm d.
Mary Heeley–Norman Farquharson 7–5,
8–6

1934 Dorothy Round–Ryuki Miki d. Dorothy
Shepherd Barron–Henry "Bunny" Austin
3–6, 6–4, 6–0

1935 Dorothy Round–Fred Perry d. Nell Hall
Hopman–Harry Hopman 7–5, 4–6, 6–2

1936 Dorothy Round–Fred Perry d. Sarah Palfrey
Fabyan–Don Budge 7–9, 7–5, 6–4

1937 Alice Marble–Don Budge d. Simone
Passemard Mathieu–Yvon Petra 6–4, 6–1

1938 Alice Marble–Don Budge d. Sarah Palfrey
Fabyan–Henner Henkel 6–1, 6–4

1939 Alice Marble–Bobby Riggs d. Nina Brown–
Frank Wilde 9–7, 6–1

1940–45 Not held; World War II

1946 Louise Brough–Tom Brown d. Dorothy
Bundy–Goeff Brown 6–4, 6–4

1947 Louise Brough–John Bromwich d. Nancye
Wynne Bolton–Colin Long 1–6 6–4 6–2

1948 Louise Brough–John Bromwich d. Doris
Hart–Frank Sedgman 6–2, 3–6, 6–3

1949 Sheila Piercey Summers–Eric Sturgess d. Louise
Brough–John Bromwich 9–7, 9–11, 7–5

1950 Louise Brough–Eric Sturgess d. Pat Canning
Todd–Geoff Brown 11–9, 1–6, 6–4

1951 Doris Hart–Frank Sedgman d. Nancye Wynne
Bolton–Mervyn Rose 7–5, 6–2

1952 Doris Hart–Frank Sedgman d. Thelma Coyne
Long–Enrique Morea 4–6, 6–3, 6–4

1953 Doris Hart–Vic Seixas d. Shirley Fry–Enrique
Morea 9–7, 7–5

1954 Doris Hart–Vic Seixas d. Margaret Osborne
duPont–Ken Rosewall 5–7, 6–4, 6–3

1955 Doris Hart–Vic Seixas d. Louise Brough–
Enrique Morea 8–6, 2–6, 6–3

1956 Shirley Fry–Vic Seixas d. Althea Gibson–
Gardnar Mulloy 2–6, 6–2, 7–5

1957 Darlene Hard–Mervyn Rose d. Althea
Gibson–Neale Fraser 6–4, 7–5

1958 Lorraine Coghlan–Bob Howe d. Althea
Gibson–Kurt Nielsen 6–3, 13–11

1959 Darlene Hard–Rod Laver d. Maria Bueno–
Neale Fraser 6–4, 6–3

1960 Darlene Hard–Rod Laver d. Maria Bueno–
Bob Howe 13–11, 3–6, 8–6

1961 Lesley Turner–Fred Stolle d. Edda Buding–
Bob Howe 11–9, 6–2

1962 Margaret Osborne duPont–Neale Fraser d.
Ann Haydon–Dennis Ralston 2–6, 6–3,
13–11

1963 Margaret Smith–Ken Fletcher d. Darlene
Hard–Bob Hewitt 11–9, 6–4

1964 Lesley Turner–Fred Stolle d. Margaret
Smith–Ken Fletcher 6–4, 6–4

1965 Margaret Smith–Ken Fletcher d. Judy Tegart–
Tony Roche 12–10, 6–3

1966 Margaret Smith–Ken Fletcher d. Billie Jean
Moffitt King–Dennis Ralston 4–6, 6–3, 6–3

1967 Billie Jean Moffitt King–Owen Davidson d.
Maria Bueno–Ken Fletcher 7–5, 6–2

1968 Margaret Smith Court–Ken Fletcher d. Olga
Morozova–Alex Metreveli 6–1, 14–12

1969 Ann Haydon Jones–Fred Stolle d. Judy
Tegart–Tony Roche 6–3, 6–2

1970 Rosemary Casals–Ilie Nastase d. Olga
Morozova–Alex Metreveli 6–3, 4–6, 9–7

1971 Billie Jean Moffitt King–Owen Davidson d.
Margaret Smith Court–Martin Riessen
3–6, 6–2, 15–13

1972 Rosemary Casals–Ilie Nastase d. Evonne
Goolagong–Kim Warwick 6–4, 6–4

1973 Billie Jean Moffitt King–Owen Davidson d.
Janet Newberry–Raul Ramirez 6–3, 6–2

1974 Billie Jean Moffitt King–Owen Davidson d.
Lesley Charles–Mark Farrell 6–3, 9–7

1975 Margaret Smith Court–Martin Riessen d.
Betty Stove–Allan Stone 6–4, 7–5

1976 Francoise Durr–Tony Roche d. Rosemary
Casals–Dick Stockton 6–3, 2–6, 7–5

1977 Greer Stevens–Bob Hewitt d. Betty Stove–
Frew McMillan 3–6, 7–5, 6–4

1978 Betty Stove–Frew McMillan d. Billie Jean
Moffitt King–Ray Ruffels 6–2, 6–2

1979 Greer Stevens–Bob Hewitt d. Betty Stove–
Frew McMillan 7–5, 7–6

1980 Tracy Austin–John Austin d. Dianne
Fromholtz–Mark Edmondson 4–6, 7–6, 6–3

1981 Betty Stove–Frew McMillan d. Tracy Austin–John Austin 4–6, 7–6, 6–3

1982 Anne Smith–Kevin Curren d. Wendy Turnbull–John Lloyd 2–6, 6–3, 7–5

1983 Wendy Turnbull–John Lloyd b. Billie Jean Moffitt King–Steve Denton 6–7, 7–6, 6–5

1984 Wendy Turnbull–John Lloyd d. Kathy Jordan–Steve Denton 6–3, 6–3

1985 Martina Navratilova–Paul McNamee d. Elizabeth Sayers Smylie–John Fitzgerald 7–5, 4–6, 6–2

1986 Kathy Jordan–Ken Flach d. Martina

1992 Larisa Savchenko Neiland–Cyril Suk d. Miriam Oremans–Jacco Eltingh 7–6, 6–2

All–Time Wimbledon Championship Records

Most men's singles: 7—Willie Renshaw, 1881–89

Most men's doubles: 8—Reggie Doherty, 1897–1905; Laurie Doherty, 1897–1905

Most men's, mixed: 4—Ken Fletcher, 1963–68; Owen Davidson, 1967–74

Most men's altogether: 13—Laurie Doherty, 1897–1905

Most women's singles: 9—Martina Navratilova, 1978–90

Most women's doubles: 12—Elizabeth Ryan, 1914–34

Most women's mixed: 7—Ryan, 1919–32

Most women's altogether: 20—Billie Jean Moffitt King, 1961–79

Most men's doubles, team: 8—Reggie and Laurie Doherty (brothers), 1897–1905

Most women's doubles, team: 6—Suzanne Lenglen and Ryan, 1919–25

Most mixed doubles, team: 4—Court and Fletcher, 1963–68; King and Davidson, 1967–74

Youngest Champions

Women's singles—Lottie Dod, 1887, 15 years 9 months

Women's doubles—Billie Jean Moffitt (King), 1961, 17–6

Women's mixed—Tracy Austin, 1980, 17–7

Men's singles—Boris Becker, 1985, 17–7

Men's doubles—Dennis Ralston, 17–10

Men's mixed—Rod Laver, 1959, 20–10

Oldest Champions

Women's singles—Charlotte Cooper Sterry, 1908, 37–9

Individual Career Singles Records

Women

Tournaments played—24, Blanche Bingley Hillyard, 1884—89, 1891—94, 1897, 1899—1902, 1904—10, 1912–13

Matches played—119, Martina Navratilova, 1973—92

Matches won—108, Navratilova

Matches won consecutively—50, Helen Wills Moody, 1927–30, 1932–33, 1935, 1938

Match winning percentage—1,000, Suzanne Lenglen (28–0), 1919—23, 1925–26 .982 , Moody (55–1), 1924, 1927–30, 1932–33, 1935, 1938

Men

Tournaments played—29, Arthur Gore, 1888—1922

Matches played—102, Jimmy Connors, 1972—89, 1991–92

Matches won—84, Connors, 1972—89, 1991

Matches won consecutively—41, Bjorn Borg, 1976 through semis, 1981, lost final to John McEnroe

Match winning percentage—.927, Bjorn Borg (51–4), 1973—81

Longest Matches (Total Games)

Women's singles—54 games, Alice Weiwers d. Rita Anderson 8–10, 14–12, 6–4, 2nd rd., 1948

Women's doubles—48 games, Pat Brazier–Christabel Wheatcroft d. Mildred Nonwiler–Betty Soames 11–9, 5–7, 9–7, 1st rd., 1933. 48 games, Svetlana Cherneva–Larisa Savchenko (Neiland) d. Catherine Tanvier–Chris Evert Lloyd 3–6, 7–6, 14–12, 3rd rd., 1984.

Mixed doubles—77 games, Brenda Schultz–Michiel Schapers d. Andrea Temesvari Tom Nijssen 6–3, 5–7, 29–27, 1st rd., 1991

Men's singles—112 games, Pancho Gonzalez d. Charlie Pasarell 22–24, 1–6, 16–14, 6–3, 11–9, 1st rd., 1969

Men's doubles—98 games, Nikki Pilic–Gene Scott d. Cliff Richey–Torben Ulrich 19–21, 12–10, 6–4, 4–6, 9–7, 1st rd., 1966

Longest Match (Playing Time)

5 hours, 12 minutes—Pancho Gonzalez d. Charlie Pasarell, 1969

AUSTRALIAN CHAMPIONSHIPS

Men's Singles

There were two championships held in 1977 when the tournament was switched from January to December.

Year

1905	Rodney Heath d. A.H. Curtis 4–6, 6–3, 6–4, 6–4
1906	Tony Wilding d. Harry Parker 6–0, 6–4, 6–4
1907	Horace Rice d. Harry Parker 6–3, 6–4, 6–4
1908	Fred Alexander d. Alfred Dunlop 3–6, 3–6, 6–0, 6–2, 6–3
1909	Tony Wilding d. Ernie Parker 6–1, 7–5, 6–2
1910	Rodney Heath d. Horace Rice 6–4, 6–3, 6–2
1911	Norman Brookes d. Horace Rice 6–1, 6–2, 6–3
1912	J. Cecil Parke d. Alfred Beamish 3–6, 6–3, 1–6, 6–1, 7–5
1913	Ernie Parker d. Harry Parker 2–6, 6–1, 6–3, 6–2
1914	Arthur O'Hara Wood d. Gerald Patterson 6–4, 6–3, 5–7, 6–1
1915	Gordon Lowe d. Horace Rice 4–6, 6–1, 6–1, 6–4
1916–18	Not held; World War 1
1919	Algernon Kingscote d. E. O. Pockley 6–4, 6–0, 6–3
1920	Pat O'Hara Wood d. Ron Thomas 6–3, 4–6, 6–8, 6–1, 6–3

1921	Rice Gemmell d. A.H. Hedemann 7–5, 6–1, 6–4
1922	Pat O'Hara Wood d. Gerald Patterson 6–0, 3–6, 3–6, 6–3, 6–2
1923	Pat O'Hara Wood d. C.B. St. John 6–1, 6–1, 6–3
1924	James Anderson d. Bob Schlesinger 6–3, 6–4, 3–6, 5–7, 6–3
1925	James Anderson d. Gerald Patterson 11–9, 2–6, 6–2, 6–3
1926	John Hawkes d. Jim Willard 6–1, 6–3, 6–1
1927	Gerald Patterson d. John Hawkes 3–6, 6–4, 3–6, 18–16, 6–3
1928	Jean Borotra d. R. O. Cummings 6–4, 6–1, 4–6, 5–7, 6–3
1929	John Gregory d. Bob Schlesinger 6–2, 6–2, 5–7, 7–5
1930	Gar Moon d. Harry Hopman 6–3, 6–1, 6–3
1931	Jack Crawford d. Harry Hopman 6–4, 6–2, 2–6, 6–1
1932	Jack Crawford d. Harry Hopman 4–6, 6–3, 3–6, 6–3, 6–1
1933	Jack Crawford d. Keith Gledhill 2–6, 7–5, 6–3, 6–2
1934	Fred Perry d. Jack Crawford 6–3, 7–5, 6–1
1935	Jack Crawford d. Fred Perry 2–6, 6–4, 6–4, 6–4
1936	Adrian Quist d. Jack Crawford 6–2, 6–3, 4–6, 3–6, 9–7
1937	Vivian McGrath d. John Bromwich 6–3, 1–6, 6–0, 2–6, 6–1
1938	Don Budge d. John Bromwich 6–4, 6–2, 6–1
1939	John Bromwich d. Adrian Quist 6–4, 6–1, 6–3
1940	Adrian Quist d. Jack Crawford 6–3, 6–1, 6–2
1941–45	Not held; World War II
1946	John Bromwich d. Dinny Pails 5–7, 6–3, 7–5, 3–6, 6–2
1947	Dinny Pails d. John Bromwich 4–6, 6–4, 3–6, 7–5, 8–6
1948	Adrian Quist d. John Bromwich 6–4, 3–6, 6–3, 2–6, 6–3
1949	Frank Sedgman d. Ken McGregor 6–3, 6–3, 6–2
1950	Frank Sedgman d. Ken McGregor 6–3, 6–4, 4–6, 6–1
1951	Dick Savitt d. Ken McGregor 6–3, 2–6, 6–3, 6–1
1952	Ken McGregor d. Frank Sedgman 7–5, 12–10, 2–6, 6–2
1953	Ken Rosewall d. Mervyn Rose 6–0, 6–3, 6–4
1954	Mervyn Rose d. Rex Hartwig 6–2,0–6, 6–4, 6–2
1955	Ken Rosewall d. Lew Hoad 9–7, 6–4, 6–4
1956	Lew Hoad d. Ken Rosewall 6–4, 3–6, 6–4, 7–5
1957	Ashley Cooper d. Neale Fraser 6–3, 9–11, 6–4, 6–2
1958	Ashley Cooper d. Mal Anderson 7–5, 6–3, 6–4
1959	Alex Olmedo d. Neale Fraser 6–1, 6–2, 3–6, 6–3

1960	Rod Laver d. Neale Fraser 5–7, 3–6, 6–3, 8–6, 8–6
1961	Roy Emerson d. Rod Laver 1–6, 7–5, 6–3 6–4
1962	Rod Laver d. Roy Emerson 8–6, 0–6, 6–4 6–4
1963	Roy Emerson d. Ken Fletcher 6–3, 6–3, 6–1
1964	Roy Emerson d. Fred Stolle 6–3, 6–4 6–2
1965	Roy Emerson d. Fred Stolle 7–9, 2–6, 6–4 7–5 6–1
1966	Roy Emerson d. Arthur Ashe 6–4, 6–8, 6–2, 6–3
1967	Roy Emerson d. Arthur Ashe 6–4, 6–1, 6–4
1968	Bill ... d. ... Gib... 7–5, 2–6, 9–7 6–4

1924	Sylvia Lance d. Esna Boyd 6–3, 3–6, 6–4
1925	Daphne Akhurst d. Esna Boyd 1–6, 8–6, 6–4
1926	Daphne Akhurst d. Esna Boyd 6–1, 6–3
1927	Esna Boyd d. Sylvia Lance Harper 5–7, 6–1, 6–2
1928	Daphne Akhurst d. Esna Boyd 7–5, 6–2
1929	Daphne Akhurst d. Louie Bickerton 6–1, 5–7, 6–2
1930	Daphne Akhurst d. Sylvia Lance Harper 10–8, 2–6, 7–5
1931	Coral McInnes Buttsworth d. Marjorie Cox ...

1976	Mark Edmondson d. John Newcombe 6–7, 6–3, 7–6 6–1
1977	(January) Roscoe Tanner d. Guillermo Vilas 6–3, 6–3, 6–3
1977	(December) Vitas Gerulaitis d. John Lloyd 6–3, 7–6, 5–7 3–6, 6–2
1978	Guillermo Vilas d. John Marks 6–4, 6–4, 3–6, 6–3
1979	Guillermo Vilas d. John Sadri 7–6, 6–3, 6–2
1980	Brian Teacher d. Kim Warwick 7–5, 7–6, 6–3
1981	Johan Kriek d. Steve Denton 6–3, 7–6, 6–7, 6–4
1982	Johan Kriek d. Steve Denton 6–3, 6–3, 6–2
1983	Mats Wilander d. Ivan Lendl 6–1, 6–4, 6–4
1984	Mats Wilander d. Kevin Curren 6–7, 6–4, 7–6, 6–2
1985	Stefan Edberg d. Mats Wilander 6–4, 6–3, 6–3
1986	Not held due to change in dates
1987	Stefan Edberg d. Pat Cash 6–3, 6–4, 3–6, 5–7, 6–3
1988	Mats Wilander d. Pat Cash 6–3, 6–7, 3–6, 6–1, 8–6
1989	Ivan Lendl d. Miloslav Mecir 6–2, 6–2, 6–2
1990	Ivan Lendl d. Stefan Edberg 4–6, 7–6, 5–2 ret.
1991	Boris Becker d. Ivan Lendl 1–6, 6–4, 6–4, 6–4
1992	Jim Courier d. Stefan Edberg 6–3, 3–6, 6–4 6–2

Women's Singles

Year

| 1922 | Mall Molesworth d. Esna Boyd 6–3, 10–8 |
| 1923 | Mall Molesworth d. Esna Boyd 6–1, 7–5 |

1938	Dorothy Bundy d. Dorothy Stevenson 6–3, 6–2
1939	Emily Hood Westacott d. Nell Hall Hopman 6–1, 6–2
1940	Nancye Wynne Bolton d. Thelma Coyne 5–7, 6–4, 6–0
1941–45	Not held; World War II
1946	Nancye Wynne Bolton d. Joyce Fitch 6–4, 6–4
1947	Nancye Wynne Bolton d. Nell Hall Hopman 6–3, 6–2
1948	Nancye Wynne Bolton d. Marie Toomey 6–3, 6–1
1949	Doris Hart d. Nancye Wynne Bolton 6–3, 6–4
1950	Louise Brough d. Doris Hart 6–4, 3–6, 6–4
1951	Nancye Wynne Bolton d. Thelma Coyne Long 6–1, 7–5
1952	Thelma Coyne Long d. Helen Angwin 6–2, 6–3
1953	Maureen Connolly d. Julia Sampson 6–3, 6–2
1954	Thelma Coyne Long d. Jenny Staley 6–3, 6–4
1955	Beryl Penrose d. Thelma Coyne Long 6–4, 6–3
1956	Mary Carter d. Thelma Coyne Long 3–6, 6–2, 9–7
1957	Shirley Fry d. Althea Gibson 6–3, 6–4
1958	Angela Mortimer d. Lorraine Coghlan 6–3, 6–4
1959	Mary Carter Reitano d. Renee Schuurman 6–2, 6–3
1960	Margaret Smith d. Jan Lehane 7–5, 6–2
1961	Margaret Smith d. Jan Lehane 6–1, 6–4
1962	Margaret Smith d. Jan Lehane 6–0, 6–2
1963	Margaret Smith d. Jan Lehane 6–2, 6–2
1964	Margaret Smith d. Lesley Turner, 6–3, 6–2
1965	Margaret Smith d. Maria Bueno 5–7, 6–4, 5–2, ret.

1966	Margaret Smith d. Nancy Richey, default
1967	Nancy Richey d. Lesley Turner 6–1, 6–4
1968	Billie Jean Moffitt King d. Margaret Smith 6–1, 6–2
1969	Margaret Smith Court d. Billie Jean Moffitt King 6–4, 6–1
1970	Margaret Smith Court d. Kerry Melville 6–1, 6–3
1971	Margaret Smith Court d. Evonne Goolagong 2–6, 7–6, 7–5
1972	Virginia Wade d. Evonne Goolagong 6–4, 6–4
1973	Margaret Smith Court d. Evonne Goolagong 6–4, 7–5
1974	Evonne Goolagong d. Chris Evert 7–5, 4–6, 6–0
1975	Evonne Goolagong d. Martina Navratilova 6–3, 6–2
1976	Evonne Goolagong d. Renata Tomanova 6–2, 6–2
1977	(January) Kerry Melville Reid d. Dianne Fromholtz Balestrat 7–5, 6–2
1977	(December) Evonne Goolagong Cawley d. Helen Gourlay Cawley 6–3, 6–0
1978	Chris O'Neil d. Betsy Nagelsen 6–3, 7–6
1979	Barbara Jordan d. Sharon Walsh 6–3, 6–3
1980	Hana Mandlikova d. Wendy Turnbull 6–0, 7–5
1981	Martina Navratilova d. Chris Evert Lloyd 6–7, 6–4, 7–5
1982	Chris Evert Lloyd d. Martina Navratilova 6–3, 2–6, 6–3
1983	Martina Navratilova d. Kathy Jordan 6–2, 7–6
1984	Chris Evert Lloyd d. Helena Sukova 6–7, 6–1, 6–3
1985	Martina Navratilova d. Chris Evert Lloyd 6–2, 4–6, 6–2
1986	Not held due to change in dates
1987	Hana Mandlikova d. Martina Navratilova 7–5, 7–6
1988	Steffi Graf d. Chris Evert 6–1, 7–6
1989	Steffi Graf d. Helena Sukova 6–4, 6–4
1990	Steffi Graf d. Mary Joe Fernandez 6–3, 6–4
1991	Monica Seles d. Jana Novotna 5–7, 6–3, 6–1
1992	Monica Seles d. Mary Joe Fernandez 6–2, 6–3

Men's Doubles

Year

1905	Randolph Lycett–Tom Tachell d. E.T. Banard–B. Spence 11–9, 8–6, 1–6, 4–6, 6–1
1906	Rodney Heath–Tony Wilding d. Harry Parker–C.C. Cox 6–2, 6–4, 6–2
1907	Bill Gregg–Harry Parker d. Horace Rice–George Wright 6–2, 3–6, 6–2, 6–2
1908	Fred Alexander–Alfred Dunlop d. G.G. Sharp–Tony Wilding 6–3, 6–2, 6–1

1909	J.P. Keane–Ernie Parker d. L. Crooks–Tony Wilding 1–6, 6–1, 6–1, 9–7
1910	Ashley Campbell–Horace Rice d. Rodney Heath–J. L. O'Dea 6–3, 6–3, 6–2
1911	Rodney Heath–Randolph Lycett d. J.J. Addison–Norman Brookes 6–2, 7–5, 6–0
1912	James Parke–Charles Dixon d. Alfred Beamish–Gordon Lowe 4–0, 6–4, 6–2
1913	A. H. Hedemann–Ernie Parker d. Harry Parker–Roy Taylor 8–6, 4–6, 6–4, 6–4
1914	Ashley Campbell–Gerald Patterson d. Rodney Heath–Arthur O'Hara Wood 7–5, 3–6, 6–3, 6–3
1915	Horace Rice–Clarrie Todd d. Gordon Lowe–C.B. St. John 8–6, 6–4, 7–9, 6–3
1916–18	Not held; World War 1
1919	Pat O'Hara Wood–Ron Thomas d. James Anderson–Arthur Lowe 7–5, 6–1, 7–9, 3–6, 6–3
1920	Pat O'Hara Wood–Ron Thomas d. Horace Rice–R. Taylor 6–1, 6–0, 7–5
1921	S.H. Eaton–Rhys Gemmell d. N. Breasley–E. Stokes 7–5, 6–3, 6–3
1922	John Hawkes–Gerald Patterson d. James Anderson–Norman Peach 8–10, 6–0, 6–0, 7–5
1923	Pat O'Hara Wood–C.B. St. John d. J. Bullough–Horace Rice 6–4, 6–3, 3–6, 6–0
1924	James Anderson–Norman Brookes d. Gerald Patterson–Pat O'Hara Wood 6–2, 6–4, 6–3
1925	Pat O'Hara Wood–Gerald Patterson d. James Anderson–Fred Kalms 6–4, 8–6, 7–5
1926	John Hawkes–Gerald Patterson d. James Anderson–Pat O'Hara Wood 6–1, 6–4, 6–2
1927	John Hawkes–Gerald Patterson d. Pat O'Hara Wood–Ian McInnes 8–6, 6–2, 6–1
1928	Jean Borotra–Jacques Brugnon d. Jim Willard–Gar Moon 6–2, 4–6, 6–4, 6–4
1929	Jack Crawford–Harry Hopman d. R.O. Cummings–Gar Moon 6–1, 6–8, 4–6, 6–1, 6–3
1930	Jack Crawford–Harry Hopman d. John Hawkes–T. Fitchett 8–6, 6–1, 2–6, 6–3
1931	Charles Donohoe–Ray Dunlop d. Jack Crawford–Harry Hopman 8–6, 6–2, 5–7 7–9, 6–4
1932	Jack Crawford–Gar Moon d. Harry Hopman–Gerald Patterson 12–10, 6–3, 4–6 6–4
1933	Keith Gledhill–Ellsworth Vines d. Jack Crawford–Gar Moon 6–4 10–8, 6–2
1934	Fred Perry–Pat Hughes d. Adrian Quist–Don Turnbull 6–8, 6–3, 6–4, 3–6, 6–3
1935	Jack Crawford–Viv McGrath d. Pat Hughes–Fred Perry 6–4, 8–6, 6–2
1936	Adrian Quist–Don Turnbull d. Jack Crawford–Viv McGrath 6–8, 6–2 6–1, 3–6, 6–2
1937	Adrian Quist–Don Turnbull d. John Bromwich–Jack Harper 6–2, 9–7, 1–6, 6–8, 6–4

1938　John Bromwich–Adrian Quist d. Gottfried von Cramm–Henner Henkel 7–5, 6–4, 6–0

1939　John Bromwich–Adrian Quist d. Don Turnbull–Colin Long 6–4, 7–5, 6–2

1940　John Bromwich–Adrian Quist d. Jack Crawford–Viv McGrath 6–3, 7–5, 6–1

1941–45　Not held; World War II

1946　John Bromwich–Adrian Quist d. Max Newcombe–Len Schwartz 6–3, 6–1, 9–7

1947　John Bromwich–Adrian Quist d. Frank Sedgman–George Worthington 6–1, 6–3, 6–1

Candy–Mervyn Rose 6–4, 7–5, 6–3

1953　Lew Hoad–Ken Rosewall d. Don Candy–Mervyn Rose 9–11, 6–4, 10–8, 6–4

1954　Rex Hartwig–Mervyn Rose d. Neale Fraser–Clive Wilderspin 6–3, 6–4, 6–2

1955　Vic Seixas–Tony Trabert d. Lew Hoad–Ken Rosewall 6–3, 6–2, 2–6, 3–6, 6–1

1956　Lew Hoad–Ken Rosewall d. Don Candy–Mervyn Rose 10–8, 13–11, 6–4

1957　Neale Fraser–Lew Hoad d. Mal Anderson–Ashley Cooper 6–3, 8–6, 6–4

1958　Ashley Cooper–Neale Fraser d. Roy Emerson–Bob Mark 7–5, 6–8, 3–6, 6–3, 7–5

1959　Rod Laver–Bob Mark d. Don Candy–Bob Howe 9–7, 6–4, 6–2

1960　Rod Laver–Bob Mark d. Roy Emerson–Neale Fraser 1–6, 6–2, 6–4, 6–4

1961　Rod Laver–Bob Mark d. Roy Emerson–Marty Mulligan 6–3, 7–5, 3–6, 9–7, 6–2

1962　Roy Emerson–Neale Fraser d. Bob Hewitt–Fred Stolle 4–6, 4–6, 6–1, 6–4, 11–9

1963　Bob Hewitt–Fred Stolle d. Ken Fletcher–John Newcombe 6–2, 3–6, 6–3, 3–6, 6–3

1964　Bob Hewitt–Fred Stolle d. Roy Emerson–Ken Fletcher 6–4, 7–5, 3–6, 4–6, 14–12

1965　John Newcombe–Tony Roche d. Roy Emerson–Fred Stolle 3–6, 4–6, 13–11, 6–3, 6–4

1966　Roy Emerson–Fred Stolle d. John Newcombe–Tony Roche 7–9, 6–3, 6–8, 14–12, 12–10

1967　John Newcombe–Tony Roche d. Bill Bowrey–Owen Davidson 3–6, 6–3, 7–5, 6–8, 8–6

1968　Dick Crealy–Allan Stone d. Terry Addison–Ray Keldie 10–8, 6–4, 6–3

1969　Roy Emerson–Rod Laver d. Ken Rosewall–Fred Stolle 6–4, 6–4, 6–4

1970　Bob Lutz–Stan Smith d. John Alexander–Phil Dent 6–3, 8–6

1971　John Newcombe–Tony Roche d. Tom Okker–Marty Riessen 6–2, 7–6

1972　Owen Davidson–Ken Rosewall d. Ross Case–Geoff Masters 3–6, 7–6, 6–2

1973　Mal Anderson–John Newcombe d. John Alexander–Phil Dent 6–3, 6–4, 7–6

1974　Ross Case–Geoff Masters d. Syd Ball–Bob Giltinan 6–7, 6–3, 6–4

1975　John Alexander–Phil Dent d. Bob Carmichael, Allan Stone 6–8, 7–6

1980　Mark Edmondson–Kim Warwick d. Peter McNamara–Paul McNamee 7–5, 6–4

1981　Mark Edmondson–Kim Warwick d. Hank Pfister–John Sadri 6–3, 6–7, 6–3

1982　John Alexander–John Fitzgerald d. Andy Andrews–John Sadri 6–4, 7–6

1983　Mark Edmondson–Paul McNamee d. Steve Denton–Sherwood Stewart 6–3, 7–6

1984　Mark Edmondson–Sherwood Stewart d. Joakim Nystrom–Mats Wilander 6–2, 6–2, 7–5

1985　Paul Annacone–Christo Van Rensburg d. Mark Edmondson–Kim Warwick 3–6, 7–6, 6–4, 6–4

1986　Not held due to change in dates

1987　Stefan Edberg–Anders Jarryd d. Peter Doohan–Laurie Warder 6–4, 6–4, 7–6

1988　Rick Leach–Jim Pugh d. Jeremy Bates–Peter Lundgren 6–3, 6–2, 6–3

1989　Rick Leach–Jim Pugh d. Darren Cahill–Mark Kratzmann 6–4, 6–4, 6–4

1990　Pieter Aldrich–Danie Visser d. Grant Connell–Glenn Michibata 6–4, 4–6, 6–1, 6–4

1991　Scott Davis–David Pate d. Patrick McEnroe–David Wheaton 6–7, 7–6, 6–3 7–5

1992　Todd Woodbridge–Mark Woodforde d. Kelly Jones–Rick Leach 6–4, 6–3, 6–4

Women's Doubles

Year

1922　Esna Boyd–Marjorie Mountain d. Floris St. George–Lorna Utz 1–6, 6–4, 7–5

1923	Esna Boyd–Sylvia Lance d. Mall Molesworth–H. Turner 6–1, 6–4

1923 Esna Boyd–Sylvia Lance d. Mall Molesworth–
H. Turner 6–1, 6–4

1924 Daphne Akhurst–Sylvia Lance d. Kathrine
LeMesurier–Meryl O'Hara Wood 7–5, 6–2

1925 Sylvia Lance Harper–Daphne Akhurst d. Esna
Boyd–Kathrine LeMesurier 6–4, 6–3

1926 Meryl O'Hara Wood–Esna Boyd d. Daphne
Akhurst–Marjorie Cox 6–3, 6–8, 8–6

1927 Meryl O'Hara Wood–Louie Bickerton d.
Esna Boyd–Sylvia Lance Harper 6–3, 6–3

1928 Dahpne Akhurst–Esna Boyd d. Kathrine
LeMesurier–Dorothy Weston 6–3, 6–1

1929 Daphne Akhurst–Louie Bickerton d. Sylvia
Lance Harper–Meryl O'Hara Wood 6–2,
3–6, 6–2

1930 Mall Molesworth–Emily Hood d. Marjorie
Cox–Sylvia Harper 6–3, 0–6, 7–5

1931 Daphne Akhurst Cozens–Louie Bickerton d.
N. Lloyd–Lorna Utz 6–0, 6–4

1932 Coral Buttsworth–Marjorie Cox d. Kathrine
LeMesurier–Dorothy Weston 6–2, 6–2

1933 Mall Molesworth–Emily Hood Westacott d.
Joan Hartigan–Marjorie Gladman Van
Ryn 6–3, 6–2

1934 Mall Molesworth–Emily Hood Westacott d.
Joan Hartigan–Ula Valkenburg 6–8, 6–4,
6–4

1935 Evelyn Dearman–Nancye Wynne Lyle d. Louie
Bickerton–Nell Hall Hopman 6–3, 6–4

1936 Thelma Coyne–Nancye Wynne d. May Blick–
K. Woodward 6–2, 6–4

1937 Thelma Coyne–Nancye Wynne d. Nell Hall
Hopman–Emily Hood Westacott 6–2, 6–2

1938 Thelma Coyne–Nancye Wynne d. Dorothy
Bundy–Dorothy Workman 9–7, 6–4

1939 Thelma Coyne–Nancye Wynne Bolton d. May
Hardcastle–Emily Hood Westacott 7–5,
6–4

1940 Thelma Coyne–Nancye Wynne Bolton d.
Joan Hartigan–Emily Nieymeyer 7–5, 6–2

1941–45 Not held; World War II

1946 Joyce Fitch–Mary Bevis d. Nancye Wynne
Bolton–Thelma Coyne Long 9–7, 6–4

1947 Thelma Coyne Long–Nancye Wynne Bolton
d. Mary Bevis–Joyce Fitch 6–3, 6–3

1948 Thelma Coyne Long–Nancye Wynne Bolton
d. Mary Bevis–P. Jones 6–3, 6–3

1949 Thelma Coyne Long–Nancye Wynne Bolton
d. Doris Hart–Marie Toomey 6–0, 6–1

1950 Louise Brough–Doris Hart d. Nancye Wynne
Bolton–Thelma Coyne Long 6–2, 2–6, 6–3

1951 Thelma Coyne Long–Nancye Wynne Bolton
d. Joyce Fitch–Mary Hawton 6–2, 6–1

1952 Thelma Coyne Long–Nancye Wynne Bolton
d. R. Baker–Mary Hawton 6–1, 6–1

1953 Maureen Connolly–Julia Sampson d. Mary
Hawton–Beryl Penrose 6–4, 6–2

1954 Mary Hawton–Beryl Penrose d. Hazel Redick-
Smith–Julia Wipplinger 6–3, 8–6

1955 Mary Hawton–Beryl Penrose d. Nell Hall
Hopman–Gwen Thiele 7–5, 6–1

1956 Mary Hawton–Thelma Coyne Long d. Mary
Carter–Beryl Penrose 6–2, 5–7, 9–7

1957 Althea Gibson–Shirley Fry d. Mary Hawton–
Fay Muller 6–2, 6–1

1958 Mary Hawton–Thelma Coyne Long d. Lorraine
Coghlan–Angela Mortimer 7–5, 6–8, 6–2

1959 Renee Schuurman–Sandra Reynolds d.
Lorraine Coghlan–Mary Carter Reitano
7–5, 6–4

1960 Maria Bueno–Christine Truman d. Lorraine
Coghlan Robinson–Margaret Smith 6–2,
5–7, 6–2

1961 Mary Carter Reitano–Margaret Smith d. Mary
Hawton–Jan Lehane 6–4, 3–6, 7–5

1962 Margaret Smith–Robyn Ebbern d. Darlene
Hard–Mary Carter Reitano 6–4, 6–4

1963 Margaret Smith–Robyn Ebbern d. Jan
Lehane–Lesley Turner 6–1, 6–3

1964 Judy Tegart Dalton–Lesley Turner d. Robyn
Ebbern–Margaret Smith 6–4, 6–4

1965 Margaret Smith–Lesley Turner d. Robyn
Ebbern–Billie Jean Moffitt King 1–6, 6–2,
6–3

1966 Carole Caldwell Graebner–Nancy Richey d.
Margaret Smith–Lesley Turner 6–4, 7–5

1967 Lesley Turner–Judy Tegart Dalton d. Lorraine
Coghlan Robinson–Evelyn Terras 6–0, 6–2

1968 Karen Krantzcke–Kerry Melville d. Judy Tegart
Dalton–Lesley Turner 6–4, 3–6, 6–2

1969 Margaret Smith Court–Judy Tegart Dalton d.
Rosie Casals–Billie Jean Moffitt King 6–4,
6–4

1970 Margaret Smith Court–Judy Tegart Dalton d.
Karen Krantzcke–Kerry Melville 6–3, 6–1

1971 Margaret Smith Court–Evonne Goolagong d.
Joy Emerson–Lesley Hunt 6–0, 6–0

1972 Kerry Harris–Helen Gourlay d. Patricia
Coleman–Karen Krantzcke 6–0, 6–4

1973 Margaret Smith Court–Virginia Wade d.
Kerry Harris–Kerry Melville 6–4, 6–4

1974 Evonne Goolagong–Peggy Michel d. Kerry
Harris–Kerry Melville 7–5, 6–3

1975 Evonne Goolagong–Peggy Michel d. Margaret
Smith Court–Olga Morozova 7–6, 7–6

1976 Evonne Goolagong–Helen Gourlay d. Lesley
Turner Bowrey–Renata Tomanova 8–1
(one set by mutual agreement)

1977 (January) Diane Fromholtz–Helen Gourlay d.
Betsy Nagelsen–Kerry Melville Reid

1977 (December) Evonne Goolagong Cawley–
Helen Gourlay and Mona Schallau
Guerrant–Kerry Melville Reid shared title
due to rained-out final

1978 Betsy Nagelsen–Renata Tomanova d. Naoko
Sato–Pam Whytcross 7–5, 6–2

1979	Judy Chaloner–Dianne Evers d. Leanne Harrison–Marcella Mesker 6–1, 3–6, 6–0
1980	Martina Navratilova–Betsy Nagelsen d. Ann Kiyomura–Candy Reynolds 6–4, 6–4
1981	Kathy Jordan–Anne Smith d. Martina Navratilova–Pam Shriver 6–2, 7–5
1982	Martina Navratilova–Pam Shriver d. Claudia Kohde Kilsch–Eva Pfaff 6–4, 6–2
1983	Martina Navratilova–Pam Shriver d. Anne Hobbs–Wendy Turnbull 6–4, 6–7, 6–2
1984	Martina Navratilova–Pam Shriver d. Claudia Kohde Kilsch–Helena Sukova 6–3, 6–4

| 1991 | Patty Fendick–Mary Joe Fernandez d. Beatrice "Gigi" Fernandez 7–6, 6–1 |
| 1992 | Arantxa Sanchez Vicario–Helena Sukova d. Mary Joe Fernandez–Zina Garrison 6–4, 7–6 |

Mixed Doubles

Year

1922	Esna Boyd–John Hawkes d. Lorna Utz–H.S. Utz 6–1, 6–1
1923	Sylvia Lance-Horace Rice d. Mall Molesworth–C.B. St. John 2–6, 6–4, 6–4
1924	Daphne Akhurst–John Willard d. Esna Boyd–Gar Hone 6–3, 6–4
1925	Daphne Akhurst–John Willard d. Sylvia Lance Harper–Bob Schlesinger 6–4 6–4
1926	Esna Boyd–John Hawkes d. Daphne Akhurst–Jim Willard 6–2, 6–4
1927	Esna Boyd–John Hawkes d. Youtha Anthony–Jim Willard 6–1, 6–3
1928	Daphne Akhurst–Jean Borotra d. Esna Boyd–John Hawkes, default
1929	Daphne Akhurst–Gar Moon d. Marjorie Cox–Jack Crawford 6–0, 7–5
1930	Nell Hall–Harry Hopman d. Marjorie Cox–Jack Crawford 11–9, 3–6, 6–3
1931	Marjorie Cox Crawford–Jack Crawford d. Emily Hood Westacott–A. Willard 7–5, 6–4
1932	Marjorie Cox Crawford–Jack Crawford d. Meryl O'Hara Wood–Jiri Satoh 6–8, 8–6, 6–3

1933	Marjorie Cox Crawford–Jack Crawford d. Marjorie Gladman Van Ryn–Ellsworth Vines 3–6, 7–5, 13–11
1934	Joan Hartigan–Gar Moon d. Emily Hood Westacott–Ray Dunlop 6–3, 6–4
1935	Louie Bickerton–Christian Boussus d. Mrs. Bond–Vernon Kirby 1–6, 6–3, 6–3
1936	Nell Hall Hopman–Harry Hopman d. May Blick–A.A. Kay 6–2, 6–0
1937	Nell Hall Hopman–Harry Hopman d. Dorothy Stevenson–Don Turnbull 3–6, 6–3, 6–2

1947	Nancye Wynne Bolton–Colin Long d. Joyce Fitch–John Bromwich 6–3, 6–3
1948	Nancye Wynne Bolton–Colin Long d. Thelma Coyne Long–Billy Sidwell 7–5, 4–6, 8–6
1949	Doris Hart–Frank Sedgman d. Joyce Fitch–John Bromwich 6–1, 5–7, 12–10
1950	Doris Hart–Frank Sedgman d. Joyce Fitch–Eric Sturgess 8–6, 6–4
1951	Thelma Coyne Long–George Worthington d. Clare Proctor–J. May 6–4, 3–6
1952	Thelma Coyne Long–George Worthington d. Mrs. A.R. Thiele–T. Warhurst 9–7, 7–5
1953	Julia Sampson–Rex Hartwig d. Maureen Connolly–Hamilton Richardson 6–4, 6–3
1954	Thelma Coyne Long–Rex Hartwig d. Beryl Penrose–John Bromwich 4–6, 6–1, 6–2
1955	Thelma Coyne Long–George Worthington d. Jenny Staley–Lew Hoad 6–2, 6–1
1956	Beryl Penrose–Neale Fraser d. Mary Bevis Hawton–Roy Emerson 6–2, 6–4
1957	Fay Muller–Mal Anderson d. J. Langley–Billy Knight 7–5, 3–6, 6–1
1958	Mary Bevis Hawton–Bob Howe d. Angela Mortimer–Peter Newman 9–11, 6–1, 6–2
1959	Sandra Reynolds–Bob Mark d. Renee Schuurman–Rod Laver 4–6, 13–11, 6–1
1960	Jan Lehane–Trevor Fancutt d. Mary Carter Reitano–Bob Mark 6–2, 7–5
1961	Jan Lehane–Bob Hewitt d. Mary Carter Reitano–J. Pearce 9–7, 6–2
1962	Lesley Turner–Fred Stolle d. Darlene Hard–Roger Taylor 6–3, 9–7
1963	Margaret Smith–Ken Fletcher d. Lesley Turner–Fred Stolle 7–5, 5–7, 6–4
1964	Margaret Smith–Ken Fletcher d. Jan Lehane–Mike Sangster 6–1, 6–2

1965	Margaret Smith–John Newcombe shared title with Robyn Ebbern–Owen Davidson; final not played
1966	Judy Tegart–Tony Roche d. Robyn Ebbern–Bill Bowery 6–1, 6–3
1967	Lesley Turner–Owen Davidson d. Judy Tegart–Tony Roche 9–7, 6–4
1968	Billie Jean Moffitt King–Dick Crealy d. Margaret Smith Court–Allan Stone 6–2, 9–7
1969	Margaret Smith Court–Marty Riessen shared title with Ann Haydon Jones–Fred Stolle; final not played
1970–86	Not held
1987	Zina Garrison–Sherwood Stewart d. Anne Hobbs–Andrew Castle 3–6, 7–6, 6–3
1988	Jana Novotna–Jim Pugh d. Martina Navratilova–Tim Gullikson 5–7, 6–2, 6–4
1989	Jana Novotna–Jim Pugh d. Zina Garrison–Sherwood Stewart 6–3, 6–4
1990	Natalia Zvereva–Jim Pugh d. Zina Garrison–Rick Leach 4–6, 6–2, 6–3
1991	Jo Durie–Jeremy Bates d. Robin White–Scott Davis 2–6, 6–4, 6–4
1992	Nicole Provis–Mark Woodforde d. Arantxa Sanchez Vicario–Todd Woodbridge 6–3, 4–6, 11–9

All–Time Australian Championship Records

Most men's singles: 6—Roy Emerson, 1961–67

Most men's doubles: 10—Adrian Quist, 1936–50

Most men's, mixed: 4—Colin Long, 1940–48; Harry Hopman, 1930–39

Most men's altogether: 13—Quist, 1936–50

Most women's singles: 11—Margaret Court, 1960–73

Most women's doubles: 12—Thelma Long, 1936–58

Most women's mixed: 4—Nell Hopman, 1930–39; Long, 1951–55; Nancye Bolton, 1940–48

Most women's altogether: 21—Court, 1960–75

Most men's doubles, team: 8—Quist and John Bromwich, 1938–50

Most women's doubles, team: 10—Long and Bolton, 1936–52

Most mixed doubles, team 4—Nell and Harry Hopman (husband–wife), 1930–39; Bolton and Colin Long, 1940–48

Youngest Champions

Women's singles—Monica Seles, 1991, 17, years, 2 months

Women's doubles—Thelma Coyne (Long), 1936, 17–7

Women's mixed—Jan Lehane, 1960, 18–6

Men's singles—Ken Rosewall, 1953, 18–2

Men's doubles—Lew Hoad–Rosewall, 1953, 18–2 (Hoad 19 days younger)

Men's mixed—Tony Roche, 1966, 20–8

Oldest Champions

Women's singles—Long, 1954, 35–7

Women's doubles—Long, 1956, 37–7

Women's mixed—Long, 1955, 36–7

Men's singles—Rosewall, 1972, 37–2

Men's doubles—Norman Brookes, 1924, 46–2

Men's mixed—Sherwood Stewart, 1987, 40–7

Individual Career Singles Records

Men

Tournaments played—15, Roy Emerson, 1954—56, 1958—67, 1969, 1971

Matches played—56, Emerson

Matches won—47, Emerson; Stefan Edberg, 1983—93

Matches won consecutively—27, Emerson, 1963 through 2nd rd. 1969, lost 3rd rd. to Rod Laver

Match winning percentage—.870, Edberg (47–7) .839, Emerson (47–9)

Women

Tournaments played—14, Margaret Smith Court, 1959—66, 1968—71, 1973, 1975

Matches played—60, Court

Matches won—57, Court

Matches won consecutively—37, Court, 1960 through semis, 1968, lost final to Billie Jean King

Match winning percentage—.950, Court (57–3)

Longest Matches (total games)

Women's singles—45 games, Celine Cohen d. Catherine Suire 6–7, 7–5, 11–9, 2nd rd., 1988

Women's doubles—42 games, Linda Gates–Alycia Moulton d. Katerina Maleeva–Manuela Maleeva 4–6,

6–2, 13–11, 2nd rd., 1985. 42 games, Lise Gregory–
Manon Bollegraf d. Elise Burgin–Roslyn Fairbank
Nideffer 5–7, 6–4, 11–9, 3rd rd., 1991

Mixed—47 games, Joe-Anne Faull–Jason Stoltenberg
d. Paula Smith–Mike Bauer 7–6 (7–5), 4–6, 13–11, 1st
rd., 1988

Men's singles—94 games, Dennis Ralston d. John
Newcombe 19–17, 20–18, 4–6, 6–4, quarters, 1970

Men's doubles—94 games, Max Senior–Paul Avery d.
Warren Jacques–Cedric Mason 4–6, 18–16, 7–9,

1946	Marcel Bernard d. Jaroslav Drobny 3–6, 2–6, 6–1, 6–4, 6–3
1947	Joseph Asboth d. Eric Sturgess 8–6, 7–5, 6–4
1948	Frank Parker d. Jaroslav Drobny 6–4, 7–5, 5–7, 8–6
1949	Frank Parker d. J.E. "Budge" Patty 6–3, 1–6, 6–1, 6–4
1950	J.E. "Budge" Patty d. Jaroslav Drobny 6–1, 6–2, 3–6, 5–7, 7–5
1951	Jaroslav Drobny d. Eric Sturgess 6–3, 6–3, 6–3
1952	Jaroslav Drobny d. Frank Sedgman 6–2, 6–0,

French Championships

Only French nationals were eligible prior to 1925.

Men's Singles

Year

1925	René Lacoste d. Jean Borotra 7–5, 6–1, 6–4
1926	Henri Cochet d. René Lacoste 6–2, 6–4, 6–3
1927	René Lacoste d. Bill Tilden 6–4, 4–6, 5–7, 6–3, 11–9
1928	Henri Cochet d. René Lacoste 5–7, 6–3, 6–1, 6–3
1929	René Lacoste d. Jean Borotra 6–3, 2–6, 6–0, 2–6, 8–6
1930	Henri Cochet d. Bill Tilden 3–6, 8–6, 6–3, 6–1
1931	Jean Borotra d. Christian Boussus 2–6, 6–4, 7–5, 6–4
1932	Henri Cochet d. Giorgio de Stefani 6–0, 6–4, 4–6, 6–3
1933	Jack Crawford d. Henri Cochet 8–6, 6–1, 6–3
1934	Gottfried von Cramm d. Jack Crawford 6–4, 7–9, 3–6, 7–5, 6–3
1935	Fred Perry d. Gottfried von Cramm 6–3, 3–6, 6–1, 6–3
1936	Gottfried von Cramm d. Fred Perry 6–0, 2–6, 6–2, 2–6, 6–0
1937	Henner Henkel, d. Henry "Bunny" Austin 6–1, 6–4, 6–3
1938	Don Budge d. Roderic Menzel 6–3, 6–2, 6–4
1939	Don NcNeill d. Bobby Riggs 7–5, 6–0, 6–3
1940–45	Not held; World War II

	3–6, 6–3
1961	Manuel Santana d. Nicola Pietrangeli 4–6, 6–1, 3–6, 6–0, 6–2
1962	Rod Laver d. Roy Emerson 3–6, 2–6, 6–3, 9–7, 6–2
1963	Roy Emerson d. Pierre Darmon 3–6, 6–1, 6–4, 6–4
1964	Manuel Santana d. Nicola Pietrangeli 6–3, 6–1, 4–6, 7–5
1965	Fred Stolle d. Tony Roche 3–6, 6–0, 6–2, 6–3
1966	Tony Roche d. Istvan Gulyas 6–1, 6–4, 7–5
1967	Roy Emerson d. Tony Roche 6–1, 6–4, 2–6, 6–2
1968	Ken Rosewall d. Rod Laver 6–3, 6–1, 2–6, 6–2
1969	Rod Laver d. Ken Rosewall 6–4, 6–3, 6–4
1970	Jan Kodes d. Zeljko Franulovic 6–2, 6–4, 6–0
1971	Jan Kodes d. Ilie Nastase 8–6, 6–2, 2–6, 7–5
1972	Andres Gimeno d. Patrick Proisy 4–6, 6–3, 6–1, 6–1
1973	Ilie Nastase d. Nikki Pilic 6–3, 6–3, 6–0
1974	Bjorn Borg d. Manuel Orantes 2–6, 6–7, 6–0, 6–1, 6–1
1975	Bjorn Borg d. Guillermo Vilas 6–2, 6–3, 6–4
1976	Adriano Panatta d. Harold Solomon 6–1, 6–4, 4–6, 7–6
1977	Guillermo Vilas d. Brian Gottfried 6–0, 6–3, 6–0
1978	Bjorn Borg d. Guillermo Vilas 6–1, 6–1, 6–3
1979	Bjorn Borg d. Victor Pecci 6–3, 6–1, 6–7, 6–4
1980	Bjorn Borg d. Vitas Gerulaitis 6–4, 6–1, 6–2
1981	Bjorn Borg d. Ivan Lendl 6–1, 4–6, 6–2, 3–6, 6–1
1982	Mats Wilander d. Guillermo Vilas 1–6, 7–6, 6–0, 6–4
1983	Yannick Noah d. Mats Wilander 6–2, 7–5, 7–6
1984	Ivan Lendl d. John McEnroe 3–6, 2–6, 6–4, 7–5, 7–5

1985	Mats Wilander d. Ivan Lendl 3–6, 6–4, 6–2, 6–2
1986	Ivan Lendl d. Mikael Pernfors 6–3, 6–2, 6–4
1987	Ivan Lendl d. Mats Wilander 7–5, 6–2, 3–6, 7–6
1988	Mats Wilander d. Henri Leconte 7–5, 6–2, 6–1
1989	Michael Chang d. Stefan Edberg 6–1, 3–6, 4–6, 6–4, 6–2
1990	Andres Gomez d. Andre Agassi 6–3, 2–6, 6–4, 6–4
1991	Jim Courier d. Andre Agassi 3–6, 6–4, 2–6, 6–1, 6–4
1992	Jim Courier d. Petr Korda 7–5, 6–2, 6–1

Women's Singles

Year

1925	Suzanne Lenglen d. Kitty McKane 6–1, 6–2
1926	Suzanne Lenglen d. Mary K. Browne 6–1, 6–0
1927	Kea Bouman d. Irene Peacock 6–2, 6–4
1928	Helen Wills d. Eileen Bennett 6–1, 6–2
1929	Helen Wills d. Simone Passemard Mathieu 6–3, 6–4
1930	Helen Wills Moody d. Helen Jacobs 6–2, 6–1
1931	Cilly Aussem d. Betty Nuthall 8–6, 6–1
1932	Helen Wills Moody d. Simone Passemard Mathieu 7–5, 6–1
1933	Margaret Scriven d. Simone Passemard Mathieu 6–2, 4–6, 6–4
1934	Margaret Scriven d. Helen Jacobs 7–5, 4–6, 6–1
1935	Hilde Krahwinkel Sperling d. Simone Passemard Mathieu 6–2, 6–1
1936	Hilde Krahwinkel Sperling d. Simone Passemard Mathieu 6–3, 6–4
1937	Hilde Krahwinkel Sperling d. Simone Passemard Mathie 6–2, 6–4
1938	Simone Passemard Mathieu d. Nelly Adamson Landry 6–0, 6–3
1939	Simone Passemard Mathieu d. Jadwiga Jerdzejowska 6–3, 8–6
1940–45	Not held; World War II
1946	Margaret Osborne d. Pauline Betz 1–6, 8–6, 7–5
1947	Patricia Canning Todd d. Doris Hart 6–3, 3–6, 6–4
1948	Nelly Landry d. Shirley Fry 6–2, 0–6, 6–0
1949	Margaret Osborne duPont d. Nelly Adamson 7–5, 6–2
1950	Doris Hart d. Patricia Canning Todd 6–4, 4–6, 6–2
1951	Shirley Fry d. Doris Hart 6–3, 3–6, 6–3
1952	Doris Hart d. Shirley Fry 6–4, 6–4
1953	Maureen Connolly d. Doris Hart 6–2, 6–4

1954	Maureen Connolly d. Ginette Bucaille 6–4, 6–1
1955	Angela Mortimer d. Dorothy Head Knode 2–6, 7–5, 10–8
1956	Althea Gibson d. Angela Mortimer 6–0, 12–10
1957	Shirley Bloomer d. Dorothy Head Knode 6–1, 6–3
1958	Suzi Kormoczy d. Shirley Bloomer 6–4, 1–6, 6–2
1959	Christine Truman d. Suzi Kormoczi 6–4, 7–5
1960	Darlene Hard d. Yola Ramirez 6–3, 6–4
1961	Ann Haydon d. Yola Ramirez 6–2, 6–1
1962	Margaret Smith d. Lesley Turner 6–3, 3–6, 7–5
1963	Lesley Turner d. Ann Haydon Jones 2–6, 6–3, 7–5
1964	Margaret Smith d. Maria Bueno 5–7, 6–1, 6–2
1965	Lesley Turner d. Margaret Smith 6–3 6–4
1966	Ann Haydon Jones d. Nancy Richey 6–3, 6–1
1967	Francoise Durr d. Lesley Turner 4–6, 6–3, 6–4
1968	Nancy Richey d. Ann Haydon Jones 5–7, 6–4, 6–1
1969	Margaret Smith Court d. Ann Jones 6–1, 4–6, 6–3
1970	Margaret Smith Court d. Helga Niessen 6–2, 6–4
1971	Evonne Goolagong d. Helen Gourlay 6–3, 7–5
1972	Billie Jean Moffitt King d. Evonne Goolagong 6–3, 6–3
1973	Margaret Smith Court d. Chris Evert 6–7, 7–6, 6–4
1974	Chris Evert d. Olga Morozova 6–1, 6–2
1975	Chris Evert d. Martina Navratilova 2–6, 6–2, 6–1
1976	Sue Barker d. Renata Tomanova 6–2, 0–6, 6–2
1977	Mima Jausovec d. Florenta Mihai 6–2, 6–7, 6–1
1978	Virginia Ruzici d. Mima Jausovec 6–2, 6–2
1979	Chris Evert Lloyd d. Wendy Turnbull 6–2, 6–0
1980	Chris Evert Lloyd d. Virginia Ruzici 6–0, 6–3
1981	Hana Mandlikova d. Sylvia Hanika 6–2, 6–4
1982	Martina Navratilova d. Andrea Jaeger 7–6, 6–1
1983	Chris Evert Lloyd d. Mima Jausovec 6–1, 6–2
1984	Martina Navratilova d. Chris Evert Lloyd 6–3, 6–1
1985	Chris Evert Lloyd d. Martina Navratilova 6–3, 6–7, 7–5
1986	Chris Evert Lloyd d. Martina Navratilova 2–6, 6–3, 6–3
1987	Steffi Graf d. Martina Navratilova 6–4, 4–6, 8–6
1988	Steffi Graf d. Natalia Zvereva 6–0, 6–0
1989	Arantxa Sanchez Vicario d. Steffi Graf 7–6, 3–6, 7–5
1990	Monica Seles d. Steffi Graf 7–6, 6–4
1991	Monica Seles d. Arantxa Sanchez Vicario 6–3, 6–4
1992	Monica Seles d. Steffi Graf 6–2, 3–6, 10–8

Men's Doubles

Year

1925 Jean Borotra–René Lacoste d. Henri Cochet–Jacques Brugnon 7–5, 4–6, 6–3, 2–6, 6–3
1926 Vinnie Richards–Howard Kinsey d. Henri Cochet–Jacques Brugnon 6–4, 6–1, 4–6, 6–4
1927 Henri Cochet–Jacques Brugnon d. Jean Borotra–Renè Lacoste 2–6, 6–2, 6–0, 1–6, 6–4

1933 Pat Hughes–Fred Perry d. Adrian Quist–Viv McGrath 6–2, 6–4, 2–6, 7–5
1934 Jean Borotra–Jacques Brugnon d. Jack Crawford–Viv McGrath 11–9, 6–3, 2–6, 4–6, 9–7
1935 Jack Crawford–Adrian Quist d. Viv McGrath–Don Turnbull 6–1, 6–4, 6–2
1936 Jean Borotra–Marcel Bernard d. Charles Tuckey–Pat Hughes 6–2, 3–6, 9–7, 6–1
1937 Gottfried von Cramm–Henner Henkel d. Norman Farquharson–Vernon Kirby 6–4, 7–5, 3–6, 6–1
1938 Bernard Destremau–Yvon Petra d. Don Budge–Gene Mako 3–6, 6–3, 9–7, 6–1
1939 Don McNeill–Charles Harris d. Jean Borotra–Jacques Brugnon 4–6, 6–4, 6–0, 2–6, 10–8
1940–45 Not held; World War II
1946 Marcel Bernard–Yvon Petra d. Enrique Morea–Francisco (Pancho) Segura 7–5, 6–3, 0–6, 1–6, 10–8
1947 Eustace Fannin–Eric Sturgess d. Tom Brown–Billy Sidwell 6–4, 4–6, 6–4, 6–3
1948 Lennart Bergelin–Jaroslav Drobny d. Harry Hopman–Frank Sedgman 8–6, 6–1, 12–10
1949 Richard "Pancho" Gonzalez–Frank Parker d. Eustace Fannin–Eric Sturgess 6–3, 8–6, 5–7, 6–3
1950 Bill Talbert–Tony Trabert d. Jaroslav Drobny–Eric Sturgess 6–2, 1–6, 10–8, 6–2
1951 Ken McGregor–Frank Sedgman d. Gardnar Mulloy–Dick Savitt 6–2, 2–6, 9–7, 7–5
1952 Ken McGregor–Frank Sedgman d. Gardnar Mulloy–Dick Savitt 6–3, 6–4, 6–4
1953 Lew Hoad–Ken Rosewall d. Mervyn Rose–Clive Wilderspin 6–2, 6–1 6,1

1954 Vic Seixas–Tony Trabert d. Lew Hoad–Ken Rosewall 6–4, 6–2, 6–1
1955 Vic Seixas–Tony Trabert d. Nicola Pietrangeli–Orlando Sirola 6–1, 4–6, 6–2, 6–4
1956 Don Candy–Robert Perry d. Ashley Cooper–Lew Hoad 7–5, 6–3, 6–3
1957 Mal Anderson–Ashley Cooper d. Don Candy–Mervyn Rose 6–3, 6–0, 6–3
1958 Ashley Cooper–Neale Fraser d. Bob Howe–Abe Segal 3–6, 8–6, 6–3, 7–5
1959 Orlando Sirola–Nicola Pietrangeli d. Roy Emerson–Neale Fraser 6–3, 6–9, 14–12

1965 Roy Emerson–Fred Stolle d. Ken Fletcher–Bob Hewitt 6–8, 6–3, 8–6, 6–2
1966 Clark Graebner–Dennis Ralston d. Ilie Nastase–Ion Tiriac 6–3, 6–3, 6–0
1967 John Newcombe–Tony Roche d. Roy Emerson–Ken Fletcher 6–3, 9–7, 12–10
1968 Ken Rosewall–Fred Stolle d. Roy Emerson–Rod Laver 6–3, 6–4, 6–3
1969 John Newcombe–Tony Roche d. Roy Emerson–Rod Laver 4–6, 6–1, 3–6, 6–4, 6–4
1970 Ilie Nastase–Ion Tiriac d. Arthur Ashe–Charles Pasarell 6–2, 6–4, 6–3
1971 Arthur Ashe–Marty Riessen d. Tom Gorman–Stan Smith 6–8, 4–6, 6–3, 6–4, 11–9
1972 Bob Hewitt–Frew McMillan d. Patricio Cornejo–Jaime Fillol 6–3, 8–6, 3–6, 6–1
1973 John Newcombe–Tom Okker d. Jimmy Connors–Ilie Nastase 6–1, 3–6, 6–3, 5–7, 6–4
1974 Dick Crealy–Onny Parun d. Stan Smith–Bob Lutz 6–3, 6–2, 3–6, 5–7, 6–1
1975 Brian Gottfried–Raul Ramirez d. John Alexander–Phil Dent 6–2, 2–6, 6–2, 6–4
1976 Fred McNair–Sherwood Stewart d. Brian Gottfried–Raul Ramirez 7–6, 6–3, 6–1
1977 Brian Gottfried–Raul Ramirez d. Wojtek Fibak–Jan Kodes 7–6, 4–6, 6–3, 6–4
1978 Gene Mayer–Hank Pfister d. Jose Higueras–Manuel Orantes 6–3, 6–2, 6–2
1979 Gene Mayer–Alex Mayer d. Ross Case–Phil Dent 6–4, 6–4, 6–4
1980 Victor Amaya–Hank Pfister d. Brian Gottfried–Raul Ramirez 1–6, 6–4, 6–4, 6–3
1981 Heinz Gunthardt–Balazs Taroczy d. Terry Moor–Eliot Teltscher 6–2, 7–6, 6–3

FRENCH CHAMPIONSHIPS 555

| 1982 | Sherwood Stewart–Ferdi Taygan d. Hans Gildemeister–Belus Prajoux 7–5, 6–3, 1–1, ret. |

1982   Sherwood Stewart–Ferdi Taygan d. Hans Gildemeister–Belus Prajoux 7–5, 6–3, 1–1, ret.

1983   Anders Jarryd–Hans Simonsson d. Mark Edmondson–Sherwood Stewart 7–6, 6–4, 6–2

1984   Henri Leconte–Yannick Noah d. Pavel Slozil–Tomas Smid 6–4, 2–6, 3–6, 6–3, 6–2

1985   Mark Edmondson–Kim Warwick d. Schlomo Glickstein–Hans Simonsson 6–3, 6–4, 6–7, 6–3

1986   John Fitzgerald–Tomas Smid d. Stefan Edberg–Anders Jarryd 6–3, 4–6, 6–3, 6–7, 14–12

1987   Anders Jarryd–Robert Seguso d. Guy Forget–Yannick Noah 6–7, 6–7, 6–3, 6–4, 6–2

1988   Andres Gomez–Emilio Sanchez d. John Fitzgerald–Anders Jarryd 6–3, 6–7, 6–4, 6–3

1989   Jim Grabb–Patrick McEnroe d. Mansour Bahrami–Eric Winogradsky 6–4, 2–6, 6–4, 7–5

1990   Sergio Casal–Emilio Sanchez d. Goran Ivanisevic–Petr Korda 7–5, 6–3

1991   John Fitzgerald–Anders Jarryd d. Rick Leach–Jim Pugh 6–0, 7–6

1992   Jakob Hlasek–Marc Rosset d. David Adams–Andrei Olhovskiy 7–6, 6–7, 7–5

Women's Doubles

Year

1925   Suzanne Lenglen–Didi Vlasto d. Evelyn Colyer–Kitty McKane 6–1, 9–11, 6–2

1926   Suzanne Lenglen–Didi Vlasto d. Evelyn Colyer–Kitty McKane Godfree 6–1, 6–1

1927   Irene Peacock–Bobbie Heine d. Peggy Saunders–Phoebe Watson 6–2, 6–1

1928   Phoebe Watson–Eileen Bennett d. Suzanne Deve–Sylvia Lafaurie 6–0, 6–2

1929   Lili de Alvarez–Kea Bouman d. Bobbie Heine–Alida Neave 7–5, 6–3

1930   Helen Wills Moody–Elizabeth Ryan d. Simone Barbier–Simone Passemard Mathieu 6–3, 6–1

1931   Eileen Bennett Whittingstall–Betty Nuthall d. Cilly Aussem–Elizabeth Ryan 9–7, 6–2

1932   Helen Wills Moody–Elizabeth Ryan d. Betty Nuthall–Eileen Bennett Whittingstall 6–1, 6–3

1933   Simone Passemard Mathieu–Elizabeth Ryan d. Sylvie Jung Henrotin–Colette Rosambert 6–1, 6–3

1934   Simone Passemard Mathieu–Elizabeth Ryan d. Helen Jacobs–Sarah Palfrey 3–6, 6–4, 6–2

1935   Margaret Scriven–Kay Stammers d. Ida Adam-off–Hilde Krahwinkel Sperling 6–4, 6–0

1936   Simone Passemard Mathieu–Adeline Yorke d. Susan Noel–Jadwiga Jerdzejowska 2–6, 6–4, 6–4

1937   Simone Passemard Mathieu–Adeline Yorke d. Dorothy Andrus–Sylvia Henrotin 3–6, 6–2, 6–2

1938   Simone Passemard Mathieu–Adeline Yorke d. Arlette Halff–Nelly Adamson Landry 6–3, 6–3

1939   Simone Passemard Mathieu–Jadwiga Jerdzejowska d. Alice Florian–Hella Kova 7–5, 7–5

1940–45   Not held; World War II

1946   Louise Brough–Margaret Osborne d. Pauline Betz–Doris Hart 6–4, 0–6, 6–1

1947   Louise Brough–Margaret Osborne d. Doris Hart–Patricia Canning Todd 7–5, 6–2

1948   Doris Hart–Patricia Canning Todd d. Shirley Fry–Mary Arnold Prentiss 6–4, 6–2

1949   Margaret Osborne duPont–Louise Brough d. Joy Gannon–Betty Hilton 7–5, 6–1

1950   Doris Hart–Shirley Fry d. Louise Brough–Margaret Osborne duPont 1–6, 7–5, 6–2

1951   Doris Hart–Shirley Fry d. Beryl Bartlett–Barbara Scofield 10–8, 6–3

1952   Doris Hart–Shirley Fry d. Hazel Redick-Smith–Julie Wipplinger 7–5, 6–1

1953   Doris Hart–Shirley Fry d. Maureen Connolly–Julia Sampson 6–4, 6–3

1954   Maureen Connolly–Nell Hall Hopman d. Maude Galtier–Suzanne Schmitt 7–5, 4–6, 6–0

1955   Beverly Baker Fleitz–Darlene Hard d. Shirley Bloomer–Pat Ward 7–5, 6–8, 13–11

1956   Angela Buxton–Althea Gibson d. Darlene Hard–Dorothy Head Knode 6–8, 8–6, 6–1

1957   Shirley Bloomer–Darlene Hard d. Yola Ramirez–Rosie Reyes 7–5, 4–6, 7–5

1958   Rosie Reyes–Yola Ramirez d. Mary Hawton–Thelma Coyne Long 6–4, 7–5

1959   Sandra Reynolds–Renee Schuurman d. Yola Ramirez–Rosie Reyes 2–6, 6–0, 6–1

1960   Maria Bueno–Darlene Hard d. Pat Ward Hales–Ann Haydon 6–2, 7–5

1961   Sandra Reynolds–Renee Schuurman d. Maria Bueno–Darlene Hard default

1962   Sandra Reynolds Price–Renee Schuurman d. Justina Bricka–Margaret Smith 6–4, 6–4

1963   Ann Haydon Jones–Renee Schuurmann d. Robyn Ebbern–Margaret Smith 7–5, 6–4

1964   Margaret Smith–Lesley Turner d. Norma Baylon–Helga Schultze 6–3, 6–1

1965   Margaret Smith–Lesley Turner d. Francoise Durr–Jeanine Lieffrig 6–3, 6–1

1966   Margaret Smith–Judy Tegart d. Jill Blackman–Fay Toyne 4–6, 6–1, 6–1

1967	Fancoise Durr–Gail Sherriff d. Annette Van Zyl–Pat Walkden 6–2, 6–2
1968	Francoise Durr–Ann Haydon Jones d. Rosemary Casals–Billie Jean Moffitt King 7–5, 4–6, 6–4
1969	Francoise Durr–Ann Haydon Jones d. Margaret Smith–Nancy Richey 6–0, 4–6, 7–5
1970	Gail Sherriff Chanfreau–Francoise Durr d. Rosemary Casals–Billie Jean Moffitt King 6–1, 3–6, 6–3
1971	Gail Sherriff Chanfreau–Francoise Durr d. Helen Gourlay–Kerry Harris 6–4, 6–1

6–4, 1–6, 6–3

1977	Regina Marsikova–Pam Teeguarden d. Rayni Fox–Helen Gourlay 5–7, 6–4, 6–2
1978	Mima Jausovec–Virginia Ruzici d. Lesley Turner Bowery–Gail Sherriff Lovera 5–7, 6–4, 8–6
1979	Betty Stove–Wendy Turnbull d. Francoise Durr–Virginia Wade 6–4, 7–6
1980	Kathy Jordan–Anne Smith d. Ivanna Madruga–Adriana Villagran 6–1, 6–0
1981	Rosalyn Fairbank–Tayna Harford d. Candy Reynolds–Paula Smith 6–1, 6–3
1982	Martina Navratilova–Anne Smith d. Rosemary Casals–Wendy Turnbull 6–3, 6–4
1983	Rosalyn Fairbank–Candy Reynolds d. Kathy Jordan–Anne Smith 5–7, 7–5, 6–2
1984	Martina Navratilova–Pam Shriver d. Claudia Kohde Kilsch–Hana Mandlikova 5–7, 6–3, 6–2
1985	Martina Navratilova–Pam Shriver d. Claudia Kohde Kilsch–Helena Sukova 4–6, 6–2, 6–2
1986	Martina Navratilova–Andrea Temesvari d. Steffi Graf–Gabriela Sabatini 6–1, 6–2
1987	Martina Navratilova–Pam Shriver d. Steffi Graf–Gabriela Sabatini 6–2, 6–1
1988	Martina Navratilova–Pam Shriver d. Claudia Kohde Kilsch–Helena Sukova 6–2, 7–5
1989	Larisa Savchenko–Natalia Zvereva d. Steffi Graf–Gabriela Sabatini 6–4, 6–4
1990	Jana Novotna–Helena Sukova d. Larisa Savchenko–Natalia Zvereva 6–4, 7–5
1991	Beatrice "Gigi" Fernandez–Jana Novotna d. Larisa Savchenko–Natalia Zvereva 6–4, 6–0
1992	Beatrice "Gigi" Fernandez–Natalia Zvereva d. Conchita Martinez–Arantxa Sanchez Vicario 6–3, 6–2

Mixed Doubles

<u>Year</u>

1925	Suzanne Lenglen–Jacques Brugnon d. Didi Vlasto–Henri Cochet 6–2, 6–2
1926	Suzanne Lenglen–Jacques Burgnon d. Mme. LeBesnerais–Jean Borotra 6–4, 6–3
1927	Marguerite Broquedis Bordes–Jean Borotra d. Lili de Alvarez–Bill Tilden 6–4, 2–6, 6–2
1928	Eileen Bennett–Henri Cochet d. Helen Wills–Frank Hunter 3–6, 6–3, 6–3

Nuthall–Fred Perry 6–2, 6–3

1934	Colette Rosambert–Jean Borotra d. Elizabeth Ryan–Adrian Quist 6–2, 6–4
1935	Lolette Payot–Marcel Bernard d. Sylvie Jung Henrotin–Martin Legeay 4–6, 6–2 6–4
1936	Adeline York–Marcel Bernard d. Sylvie Jung Henrotin–Martin Legeay 7–5, 6–8 6–3
1937	Simone Passemard Mathieu–Yvon Petra d. M. Horne–R. Journu 7–5, 7–5
1938	Simone Passemard Mathieu–Dragutin Mitic d. Nancye Wynne–Christian Boussus 2–6, 6–3 6–4
1939	Sarah Palfrey Fabyan–Elwood Cooke d. Simone Passemard Mathieu–Franjo Kukuljevic 4–6, 6–1, 7–5
1940–45	Not held; World War II
1946	Pauline Betz–J.E. "Budge" Patty d. Dorothy Bundy–Tom Brown 7–5, 9–7
1947	Sheila Piercey Summers–Eric Sturgess d. Jadwiga Jedrzejowska–Christian Caralulis 6–0, 6–0
1948	Patricia Canning Todd–Jaroslav Drobny d. Doris Hart–Frank Sedgman 6–3, 3–6, 6–3
1949	Sheila Piercey Summers–Eric Sturgess d. Jean Quertier–Gerry Oakley 6–1, 6–1
1950	Barbara Scofield–Enrique Morea d. Patricia Canning Todd–Bill Talbert default
1951	Doris Hart–Frank Sedgman d. Thelma Coyne Long–Mervyn Rose 7–5, 6–2
1952	Doris Hart–Frank Sedgman d. Shirley Fry–Eric Sturgess 6–8, 6–3 6–3
1953	Doris Hart–Vic Seixas d. Maureen Connolly–Mervyn Rose 4–6, 6–4, 6–0
1954	Maureen Connolly–Lew Hoad d. J. Patorni–Rex Hartwig 6–4, 6–3
1955	Doris Hart–Gordon Forbes d. Jenny Staley–

Luis Ayala 5–7, 6–1, 6–2

1956 Thelma Coyne Long–Luis Ayala d. Doris Hart–Bob Howe 4–6, 6–4, 6–1

1957 Vera Puzejova–Jiri Javorsky d. Edda Buding–Luis Ayala 6–3, 6–4

1958 Shirley Bloomer–Nicola Pietrangeli d. Lorraine Coghlan–Bob Howe 9–7, 6–8, 6–2

1959 Yola Ramirez–Billy Knight d. Renee Schuurman–Rod Laver 6–4, 6–4

1960 Maria Bueno–Bob Howe d. Ann Haydon–Roy Emerson 1–6, 6–1, 6–2

1961 Darlene Hard–Rod Laver d. Vera Puzejova–Jiri Javorsky 6–0, 2–6, 6–3

1962 Renee Schuurman–Bob Howe d. Lesley Turner–Fred Stolle 3–6, 6–4, 6–4

1963 Margaret Smith–Ken Fletcher d. Lesley Turner–Fred Stolle 6–1, 6–2

1964 Margaret Smith–Ken Fletcher d. Lesley Turner–Fred Stolle 6–3, 6–4

1965 Margaret Smith–Ken Fletcher d. Maria Bueno–John Newcombe 6–4, 6–4

1966 Annette Van Zyl–Frew McMillan d. Ann Haydon Jones–Clark Graebner 1–6, 6–3, 6–2

1967 Billie Jean Moffitt King–Owen Davidson d. Ann Haydon Jones–Ion Tiriac 6–3, 6–1

1968 Francoise Durr–Jean Claude Barclay d. Billie Jean Moffitt King–Owen Davidson 6–1, 6–4

1969 Margaret Smith Court–Marty Riessen d. Francoise Durr–Jeanne Claude Barclay 7–5, 6–4

1970 Billie Jean Moffitt King–Bob Hewitt d. Francoise Durr–Jean Claude Barclay 3–6, 6–3, 6–2

1971 Francoise Durr–Jean Claude Barclay d. Winnie Shaw–Tomas Lejus 6–2, 6–4

1972 Evonne Goolagong–Kim Warwick d. Francoise Durr–Jean Claude Barclay 6–2, 6–4

1973 Francoise Durr–Jean Claude Barclay d. Betty Stove–Patrice Dominguez 6–1, 6–4

1974 Martina Navratilova–Ivan Molina d. Rosie Reyes Darmon–Marcelo Lara 6–3, 6–3

1975 Fiorella Bonicelli–Tom Koch d. Pam Teeguarden–Jaime Fillol 6–4, 7–6

1976 Ilana Kloss–Kim Warwick d. Delina Boshoff–Colin Dowdeswell 5–7, 7–6, 6–2

1977 Mary Carillo–John McEnroe d. Florenta Mihai–Ivan Molina 7–6, 6–3

1978 Renata Tomanova–Pavel Slozil d. Virginia Ruzici–Patrice Dominguez 7–6 ret.

1979 Wendy Turnbull–Bob Hewitt d. Virginia Ruzici–Ion Tiriac 6–3, 2–6 6–3

1980 Anne Smith–Billy Martin d. Renata Tomanova–Stanislav Birner 2–6, 6–4, 8–6

1981 Andrea Jaeger–Jimmy Arias d. Betty Stove–Fred McNair 7–6, 6–4

1982 Wendy Turnbull–John Lloyd d. Claudia Monteiro–Cassio Motta 6–2, 7–6

1983 Barbara Jordan–Eliot Teltscher d. Lesley Allen–Charles Strode 6–2, 6–3

1984 Anne Smith–Dick Stockton d. Anne Minter–Laurie Warder 6–2, 6–4

1985 Martina Navratilova–Heinz Gunthardt d. Paula Smith–Francisco Gonzalez 2–6, 6–3 6–2

1986 Kathy Jordan–Ken Flach d. Rosalyn Fairbank–Mark Edmondson 3–6, 7–6, 6–3

1987 Pam Shriver–Emilio Sanchez d. Lori McNeil–Sherwood Stewart 6–3, 7–6

1988 Lori McMeil–Jorge Lozano d. Brenda Schultz–Michiel Schapers 7–5, 6–2

1989 Manon Bollegraff–Tom Nijssen d. Arantxa Sanchez Vicario–Horacio de la Pena 6–3, 6–7, 6–2

1990 Arantxa Sanchez Vicario–Jorge Lozano d. Nicole Provis–Danie Visser 7–6, 7–6

1991 Helena Sukova–Cyril Suk d. Caroline Vis–Paul Haarhuis 3–6, 6–4 6–1

1992 Arantxa Sanchez Vicario–Mark Woodforde d. Lori McNeil–Bryan Shelton 6–2, 6–3

All-Time French Championship Records

(Only since 1925, when championships were opened to non-French)

Most men's singles: 6—Bjorn Borg, 1974–81

Most men's doubles: 6—Roy Emerson, 1960–65

Most men's mixed: 3—Ken Fletcher, 1963–65

Most men's altogether: 9—Henri Cochet, 1926–32

Most women's singles: 7—Chris Evert, 1974–86

Most women's doubles: 7—Martina Navratilova—Simone Mathieu 1975–88

Most women's mixed: 4—Margaret Smith Court, 1932–69

Most women's altogether: 13—Court, 1960–75

Most men's doubles, team: 4—Cochet and Jacques Brugnon, 1927–32

Most women's doubles, team: 4—Doris Hart and Shirley Fry, 1950–53; Martina Navratilova and Pam Shriver, 1984–88

Most mixed doubles, team: 3—Francoise Durr and Jean Claude Barclay, 1968–73; Court and Ken Fletcher, 1963–65

Youngest Champions

Women's singles: Monica Seles, 1990, 16 years 6 months

Women's doubles: Natalia Zvereva, 1989, 18–2

Women's mixed: Andrea Jaeger, 1981, 15–11

Men's singles: Michael Chang, 1989, 17–4

Men's doubles: Lew Hoad–Ken Rosewall, 1953, 18–7 (Lew Hoad 19 days younger)

Men's doubles: Jacques Brugnon, 1934, 39

Men's mixed: Bob Hewitt, 1979, 39–5

Individual Career Singles Records

Women

Tournaments played: 19, Andree Varin, 1932–64; Anne-Marie Seghers, 1936–66

Matches played: 78, Chris Evert, 1973–75, 1979–88

Matches won: 72, Evert

Matches won consecutively: 29, Evert, 1974–75, 1979 through quarters, 1981, lost semis to Hana Mandlikova

Match winning percentage: .963, Seles, (26–1), 1989–92, .901, Evert (72–6)

Men

Tournaments played: 20, Francoise Jauffret, 1961–80; Ben Berthet, 1929–55; Antoine Gentien, 1929–53

Matches played: 74, Guillermo Vilas, 1972–89

Matches won: 57, Vilas

Matches won consecutively: 28, Bjorn Borg, 1978—81

Match winning percentage: .961, Borg (49–2), 1973—1976, 1978 81

Longest Matches (total games)

Women's singles: 56 games, Kerry Melville (Reid) d. Pam Teeguarden 9–7, 4–6, 16–14, 3rd rd., 1972

Women's doubles: 50 games, Beverly Baker Fleitz–Darlene Hard d. Shirley Bloomer (Brasher)–Pat Ward (Hale) 7–5, 6–8, 13–11, final, 1955

Mixed: 48 games, Rosie Reyes Darmon–Bob Howe d. Marina Tshuvirina–Tim Kakulia 5–7, 10–8, 10–8, 1st rd., 1972. 48 games, Lucia Bassi–Pancho Contreras d. Edda Buding–Ingo Buding, 10–12, 9–7, 6–4, 2nd rd., 1960

Men's singles: 76 games, Eric Sturgess d. Ken McGregor 10–8, 7–9, 8–6, 5–7, 9–7, semis, 1951

ITALIAN CHAMPIONSHIPS

Men's Singles

<u>Year</u>

1930	Bill Tilden d. Umberto de Morpurgo 6–1, 6–1, 6–2
1931	Pat Hughes d. Henri Cochet 6–4, 6–3, 6–2
1932	Andre Merlin d. Pat Hughes 6–1, 5–7, 6–0, 8–6
1933	Emanuele Sertorio d. Martin Legeay 6–3, 6–1, 6–3
1934	Giovanni Palmieri d. Giorgio de Stefani 6–3, 6–0, 8–6
1935	Wilmer Hines d. Giovanni Palmieri 6–3, 10–8, 9–7
1936–49	Not held
1950	Jaroslav Drobny d. Bill Talbert 6–4, 6–3, 7–9, 6–2
1951	Jaroslav Drobny d. Gianni Cucelli 6–3, 10–8, 6–0
1952	Frank Sedgman d. Jaroslav Drobny 7–5, 6–3, 1–6, 6–4
1953	Jaroslav Drobny d. Lew Hoad 6–2, 6–1, 6–2
1954	J. E. "Budge" Patty d. Enrique Morea 11–9, 6–4, 6–4
1955	Fausto Gardini d. Giuseppe Merio 1–6, 6–1, 3–6, 6–6, (ret.)
1956	Lew Hoad d. Sven Davidson 7–5, 6–2, 6–0
1957	Nicola Pietrangeli d. Giuseppe Merlo 8–6, 6–2, 6–4
1958	Mervyn Rose d. Nicola Pietrangeli 5–7, 8–6, 6–4, 1–6, 6–2

1959	Luis Ayala d. Neale Fraser 6–3, 3–6, 6–3, 6–3
1960	Barry MacKay d. Luis Ayala 7–5, 7–5, 0–6, 0–6, 6–1
1961	Nicola Pietrangeli d. Rod Laver 6–8, 6–1, 6–1, 6–2
1962	Rod Laver d. Roy Emerson 6–2, 1–6, 3–6, 6–3, 6–1
1963	Marty Mulligan d. Boro Jovanovic 6–2, 4–6, 6–3, 8–6
1964	Jan Erik Lundquist d. Fred Stolle 1–6, 7–5, 6–3, 6–1
1965	Marty Mulligan d. Manuel Santana 1–6, 6–4, 6–3, 6–1
1966	Tony Roche d. Nicola Pietrangeli 11–9, 6–1, 6–3
1967	Marty Mulligan d. Tony Roche 6–3, 0–6, 6–4, 6–1
1968	Tom Okker d. Bob Hewitt 10–8, 6–8, 6–1, 1–6, 6–0
1969	John Newcombe d. Tony Roche 6–3, 4–6, 6–2, 5–7, 6–3
1970	Ilie Nastase d. Jan Kodes 6–3, 1–6, 6–3, 8–6
1971	Rod Laver d. Jan Kodes 7–5, 6–3, 6–3
1972	Manuel Orantes d. Jan Kodes 4–6, 6–1, 7–5, 6–2
1973	Ilie Nastase d. Manuel Orantes 6–1, 6–1, 6–1
1974	Bjorn Borg d. Ilie Nastase 6–3, 6–4, 6–2
1975	Raul Ramirez d. Manuel Orantes 7–6, 7–5, 7–5
1976	Adriano Panatta d. Guillermo Vilas 2–6, 7–6, 6–2, 7–6
1977	Vitas Gerulaitis d. Antonio Zugarelli 6–2, 7–6, 3–6, 7–6
1978	Bjorn Borg d. Adriano Panatta 1–6, 6–3, 6–1, 4–6, 6–3
1979	Vitas Gerulaitis d. Guillermo Vilas 6–7, 7–6, 6–7, 6–4, 6–2
1980	Guillermo Vilas d. Yannick Noah 6–0, 6–4, 6–4
1981	Jose Luis Clerc d. Victor Pecci 6–3, 6–4, 6–0
1982	Andres Gomez d. Eliot Teltscher 6–2, 6–3, 6–2
1983	Jimmy Arias d. Jose Higueras 6–2, 6–7, 6–1, 6–4
1984	Andres Gomez d. Aaron Krickstein 2–6, 6–1, 6–2, 6–2
1985	Yannick Noah d. Miloslav Mecir 6–3, 3–6, 6–2, 7–6
1986	Ivan Lendl d. Emilio Sanchez 7–5, 4–6, 6–1, 6–1
1987	Mats Wilander d. Martin Jaite 6–3, 6–4, 6–4
1988	Ivan Lendl d. Guillermo Perez–Roldan 2–6, 6–4, 6–2, 4–6, 6–4
1989	Alberto Mancini d. Andre Agassi 6–3, 4–6, 2–6, 7–6, 6–1
1990	Thomas Muster d. Andrei Chesnokov 6–1, 6–3, 6–1
1991	Emilio Sanchez d. Alberto Mancini 6–3, 6–1, 3–0, (ret.)
1992	Jim Courier d. Carlos Costa 7–6, 6–0, 6–4.

Women's Singles

Year

1930	Lili de Alvarez d. Lucia Valerio 3–6, 8–6, 6–0
1931	Lucia Valerio d. Dorothy Andrus 2–6, 6–2, 6–2
1932	Ida Adamoff d. Lucia Valerio 6–4, 7–5
1933	Elizabeth Ryan d. Ida Adamoff 6–1, 6–1
1934	Helen Jacobs d. Lucia Valerio 6–3, 6–0
1935	Hilde Krahwinkel Sperling d. Lucia Valerio 6–4, 6–1
1936–49	Not held
1950	Annalisa Bossi d. Joan Curry 6–4, 6–4
1951	Doris Hart d. Shirley Fry 6–3, 8–6
1952	Susan Partridge d. Betty Harrison 6–3, 7–5
1953	Doris Hart d. Maureen Connolly 4–6, 9–7, 6–3
1954	Maureen Connolly d. Pat Ward 6–3, 6–0
1955	Pat Ward d. Erika Vollmer 6–4, 6–3
1956	Althea Gibson d. Suzi Kormoczy 6–3, 7–5
1957	Shirley Bloomer d. Dorothy Head Knode 1–6, 9–7, 6–2
1958	Maria Bueno d. Lorraine Coghlan 3–6, 6–3, 6–3
1959	Christine Truman d. Sandra Reynolds 6–0, 6–1
1960	Suzi Kormoczy d. Ann Haydon 6–4, 4–6, 6–1
1961	Maria Bueno d. Lesley Turner 6–4, 6–4
1962	Margaret Smith d. Maria Bueno 8–6, 5–7, 6–4
1963	Margaret Smith d. Lesley Turner 6–3, 6–4
1964	Margaret Smith d. Lesley Turner 6–1, 6–1
1965	Maria Bueno d. Nancy Richey 6–1, 1–6, 6–3
1966	Ann Haydon Jones d. Annette van Zyl 8–6, 6–1
1967	Lesley Turner d. Maria Bueno 6–3, 6–3
1968	Lesley Turner Bowrey d. Margaret Smith Court 2–6, 6–2, 6–3
1969	Julie Heldman d. Kerry Melville 7–5, 6–4
1970	Billie Jean Moffitt King d. Julie Heldman 6–1, 6–3
1971	Virginia Wade d. Helga Niessen Masthoff 6–4, 6–4
1972	Linda Tuero d. Olga Morozova 6–4, 6–3
1973	Evonne Goolagong d. Chris Evert 7–6, 6–0
1974	Chris Evert d. Martina Navratilova 6–3, 6–3
1975	Chris Evert d. Martina Navratilova 6–1, 6–0
1976	Mima Jausovec d. Lesley Hunt 6–1, 6–3
1977	Janet Newberry d. Renata Tomanova 6–3, 7–6
1778	Regina Marsikova d. Virginia Ruzici 7–5, 7–5
1979	Tracy Austin d. Sylvia Hanika 6–4, 1–6, 6–3
1980	Chris Evert Lloyd d. Virginia Ruzici 5–7, 6–2, 6–2

1981   Chris Evert Lloyd d. Virginia Ruzici 6–1, 6–2
1982   Chris Evert Lloyd d. Hana Mandlikova 6–0, 6–3
1983   Andrea Temesvari d. Bonnie Gadusek 6–1, 6–0
1984   Manuela Maleeva d. Chris Evert Lloyd 6–3, 6–3
1985   Raffaela Reggi d. Vicki Nelson 6–4, 6–4
1986   Not held
1987   Steffi Graf d. Gabriela Sabatini 7–5, 4–6, 6–0
1988   Gabriela Sabatini d. Helen Kelesi 6–1, 6–7, 6–1

1930   Wilbur Coen–Bill Tilden d. Umberto de Morpurgo–Placido Gaslini 6–0, 6–3
1931   Alberto DelBono–Pat Hughes d. Henri Cochet–Andre Merlin 3–6, 8–6, 4–6, 6–4, 6–3
1932   Pat Hughes–Giorgio de Stefani d. J. Bonte–Andre Merlin 6–2, 6–2, 6–4
1933   Jean Lesuer–A. Martin Legeay d. Giovanni Palmieri–Emanuele Sertori 6–2, 6–4, 2–6, 6–2
1934   Giovanni Palmieri–George Rogers d. Pat Hughes–Giorgio de Stefani 3–6, 6–4, 9–7, 0–6, 6–2
1935   Jack Crawford–Viv McGrath d. Jean Borotra–Jacques Brugnon 4–6, 4–6, 6–4, 6–2, 6–2
1936–49 Not held
1950   Bill Talbert–Tony Trabert d. J.E. "Budge" Patty–Billy Sidwell 6–3, 6–1, 4–6, 5–5 (ret.)
1951   Jaroslav Drobny–Dick Savitt d. Gianni Cucelli–Marcello Del Bello 6–2, 7–9, 6–3, 6–3
1952   Jaroslav Drobny–Frank Sedgman d. Gianni Cucelli–Marcello Del Bello 3–6, 7–5, 3–6, 6–3, 6–2
1953   Lew Hoad–Ken Rosewall d. Jaroslav Drobny–J.E. "Budge" Patty 6–2, 6–4, 6–2
1954   Jaroslav Drobny–Enrique Morea d. Vic Seixas–Tony Trabert 6–4, 0–6, 3–6, 6–3, 6–4
1955   Art Larsen–Enrique Morea d. Nicola Pietrangeli–Orlando Sirola 6–1, 6–4, 4–6, 7–5
1956   Jaroslav Drobny–Lew Hoad d. Nicola Pietrangeli–Orlando Sirola 11–9, 6–2, 6–3

1957   Neale Fraser–Lew Hoad d. Nicola Pietrangeli–Orlando Sirola 6–1, 6–8, 6–0, 6–2
1958   Anton Jancso–Kurt Nielsen d. Luis Ayala–Don Candy 8–10, 6–3, 6–2, 1–6, 9–7
1959   Roy Emerson–Neale Fraser d. Nicola Pietrangeli–Orlando Sirola 8–6, 6–4, 6–4
1960   Nicola Pietrangeli–Orlando Sirola d. Roy Emerson–Neale Fraser 3–6, 7–5, 2–6, 11–11, (ret.)
1961   Roy Emerson–Neale Fraser d. Nicola Pietrangeli–Orlando Sirola 6–2, 6–4, 11–9

1967   Bob Hewitt–Frew McMillan d. Bill Bowrey–Owen Davidson 6–3, 2–6, 6–3, 9–7
1968   Tom Okker–Marty Riessen d. Allan Stone–Nicky Kalogeropoulos 6–3, 6–4, 6–2
1969   Tony Roche–John Newcombe d. Tom Okker–Marty Riessen 6–4, 1–6, (suspended)
1970   Ilie Nastase–Ion Tiriac d. Bill Bowrey–Owen Davidson 0–6, 10–8, 6–3, 6–8, 6–1
1971   Tony Roche–John Newcombe d. Andres Gimeno–Roger Taylor, 6–4, 6–4
1972   Ilie Nastase–Ion Tiriac d. Lew Hoad–Frew McMillan 3–6, 3–6, 6–4, 6–3, 5–3, retired
1973   John Newcombe–Tom Okker d. Ross Case–Geoff Masters 6–2, 6–3, 6–4
1974   Brian Gottfried–Raul Ramirez d. Juan Gisbert–Ilie Nastase 6–3, 6–2, 6–3
1975   Brian Gottfried–Raul Ramirez d. Jimmy Connors–Ilie Nastase 6–4, 7–6, 2–6, 6–1
1976   Brian Gottfried–Raul Ramirez d. Geoff Masters–John Newcombe, 7–6, 5–7, 6–3, 3–6, 6–3
1977   Brian Gottfried–Raul Ramirez d. Fred McNair–Sherwood Stewart 7–6, 6–7, 7–5
1978   Victor Pecci–Belus Prajoux d. Jan Kodes–Tomas Smid 6–7, 7–6, 6–1
1979   Peter Fleming–Tomas Smid d. Jose-Luis Clerc–Ilie Nastase 4–6, 6–1, 7–5
1980   Mark Edmondson–Kim Warwick d. Balazs Taroczy–Eliot Teltscher 7–6, 7–6
1981   Hans Gildemeister–Andres Gomez d. Bruce Manson–Tomas Smid 7–5, 6–2
1982   Heinz Gunthardt–Balazs Taroczy d. Wojtek Fibak–John Fitzgerald 6–4, 4–6, 6–3
1983   Francisco Gonzalez–Victor Pecci d. Jan Gunnarsson–Mike Leach 6–2, 6–7, 6–4

1984	Ken Flach–Robert Seguso d. John Alexander–Mike Leach 3–6, 6–3, 6–4
1985	Anders Jarryd–Mats Wilander d. Ken Flach–Robert Seguso 4–6, 6–3, 6–2
1986	Guy Forget–Yannick Noah d. Mark Edmondson–Sherwood Stewart 7–6, 6–2
1987	Guy Forget–Yannick Noah d. Miloslav Mecir–Tomas Smid 6–2, 6–7, 6–3, 7–6, 8–2
1988	Jorge Lozano–Todd Witsken d. Anders Jarryd–Tomas Smid 6–3, 6–3
1989	Jim Courier–Pete Sampras d. Danilo Marcelino–Mauro Menezes 6–4, 6–3
1990	Sergio Casal–Emilio Sanchez d. Jim Courier–Marty Davis 7–6, 7–5
1991	Omar Camporese–Goran Ivanisevic d. Luke Jensen–Laurie Warder 6–2, 6–3
1992	Jakob Hlasek–Marc Rosset d. Wayne Ferreira–Mark Kratzmann 6–4, 3–6, 6–1

Women's Doubles

Year

1930	Lili de Alvarez–Lucia Valerio d. Claude Anet–M. Neufeld 7–5, 5–7, 8–6
1931	Anna Luzzatti–Rosetta Gagliardi Prouse d. Dorothy Andrus Burke–Lucia Valerio 6–3, 1–6, 6–3
1932	Colette Rosambert–Lolette Payot d. Dorothy Andrus Burke–Lucia Valerio 7–5, 6–3
1933	Ida Adamoff–Dorothy Andrus Burke d. Elizabeth Ryan–Lucia Valerio 6–2, 1–6, 6–4
1934	Helen Jacobs–Elizabeth Ryan d. Ida Adamoff–Dorothy Andrus Burke 7–5, 9–7
1935	Evelyn Dearman–Nan Lyle d. Cilly Aussem–Elizabeth Ryan 6–2, 6–4
1936–49	Not held
1950	Jean Quertier–Jean Walker-Smith d. Betty Hilton–Kay Tuckey 1–6, 6–3, 6–2
1951	Shirley Fry–Doris Hart d. Louise Brough–Thelma Coyne Long 6–1, 7–5
1952	Nell Hall Hopman–Thelma Coyne Long d. Nicla Migliori–V. Tonilli 6–2, 6–8, 6–1
1953	Maureen Connolly–Julia Sampson d. Shirley Fry–Doris Hart 6–8, 6–4, 6–4
1954	Pat Ward–Elaine Watson d. Nelly Adamson–Ginette Bucaille 3–6, 6–3, 6–4
1955	Christiane Mercellis–Pat Ward d. Fay Muller–Beryl Penrose 6–4, 10–8
1956	Mary Bevis Hawton–Thelma Coyne Long d. Angela Buxton–Darlene Hard 6–4, 6–8, 9–7
1957	Mary Bevis Hawton–Thelma Coyne Long d. Yola Ramirez–Rosie Reyes 6–1, 6–1
1958	Shirley Bloomer–Christine Truman d. Mary Bevis Hawton–Thelma Coyne Long 6–3, 6–2

1959	Yola Ramirez–Rosie Reyes d. Maria Bueno–Janet Hopps 4–6, 6–4, 6–4
1960	Margaret Hellyer–Yola Ramirez d. Shirley Bloomer Brasher–Ann Haydon 6–4, 6–4
1961	Jan Lehane–Lesley Turner d. Mary Carter Reitano–Margaret Smith 2–6, 6–1, 6–1
1962	Maria Bueno–Darlene Hard d. Silvana Lazzarino–Lea Pericoli 6–4, 6–4
1963	Robyn Ebbern–Margaret Smith d. Silvana Lazzarino–Lea Pericoli 6–2, 6–3
1964	Lesley Turner–Margaret Smith d. Silvana Lazzarino–Lea Pericoli 6–1, 6–2
1965	Madonna Schacht–Annette van Zyl d. Silvana Lazzarino–Lea Pericoli 2–6, 6–2, 12–10
1966	Norma Baylon–Annette van Zyl d. Ann Haydon Jones–Liz Starkie 6–3, 1–6, 6–2
1967	Rosemary Casals–Lesley Turner d. Silvana Lazzarino–Lea Pericoli 7–5, 7–5
1968	Margaret Smith Court–Virginia Wade d. Annette van Zyl–Pat Walkden 6–2, 7–5
1969	Francoise Durr–Ann Haydon Jones d. Rosemary Casals–Billie Jean Moffitt King 6–3, 3–6, 6–2
1970	Rosemary Casals–Billie Jean Moffitt King d. Francoise Durr–Virginia Wade 6–2, 3–6, 9–7
1971	Helga Niessen Masthoff–Virginia Wade d. Lesley Turner–Helen Gourlay 5–7, 6–2, 6–2
1972	Lesley Hunt–Olga Morozova d. Gail Sherriff Chanfreau–Rosalba Vido 6–3, 6–4
1973	Olga Morozova–Virginia Wade d. Martina Navratilova–Renata Tomanova 3–6, 6–2, 7–5
1974	Chris Evert–Olga Morozova d. Helga Niessen Masthoff–Heidi Orth, (default)
1975	Chris Evert–Martina Navratilova d. Sue Barker–Glynis Coles 6–1, 6–2
1976	Delina Boshoff–Ilana Kloss d. Mariana Simionescu–Virginia Ruzici 6–1, 6–2
1977	Brigitte Cuypers–Marise Kruger d. Bunny Bruning–Sharon Walsh 6–4, 7–5, 6–2
1978	Mima Jausovec–Virginia Ruzici d. Florenta Mihai–Betsy Nagelsen 6–2, 2–6, 7–5
1979	Betty Stove–Wendy Turnbull d. Evonne Goolagong–Kerry Melville Reid 6–3, 6–4
1980	Hana Mandlikova–Renata Tomanova d. Ivanna Madruga–Adriana Villigran 6–4, 6–4
1981	Candy Reynolds–Paula Smith d. Chris Evert Lloyd–Virginia Ruzici 7–5, 6–1
1982	Kathy Horvath–Yvonne Vermaak d. Billie Jean Moffitt King–Ilana Kloss 2–6, 6–4, 7–6
1983	Virginia Ruzici–Virginia Wade d. Ivanna Madruga Osses–Catherine Tanvier 6–3, 2–6, 6–1
1984	Iva Budarova–Marcela Skuherska d. Kathy Horvath–Virginia Ruzici 7–6, 1–6, 6–4
1985	Sandra Cecchini–Raffaela Reggi d. Patricia Murgo–Barbara Romano 1–6, 6–4, 6–3
1986	Not held

1987   Martina Navratilova–Gabriela Sabatini d. Claudia Kohde–Kilsch–Helena Sukova 6–4, 6–1

1988   Jana Novotna–Catherine Suire d. Jenny Byrne–Janine Thompson 6–3, 4–6, 7–5

1989   Liz Sayers Smylie–Janine Thompson d. Manon Bollegraf–Mercedes Paz 6–4, 6–3

1990   Helen Kelesi–Monica Seles d. Laura Garrone–Laura Golarsa 6–3, 6–4

1991   Jennifer Capriati–Monica Seles d. Nicole Provis–Elna Reinach 7–5, 6–2

1999   Monica Seles–Helena Sukova d. Katerina

1962   Lesley Turner–Fred Stolle d. Madonna Schacht–Sven Davidson 6–4, 6–1

1963   Not held

1964   Margaret Smith–John Newcombe d. Maria Bueno–Tom Koch 3–6, 7–5, 6–2

1965   Carmen Coronado–Edison Mandarino d. Elena Subirats–Vicente Zarazua 6–1, 6–1

1966   Not held

1967   Lesley Turner–Bill Bowrey d. Francoise Durr–Frew McMillan 6–2, 7–5

1968*   Margaret Smith Court–Martin Riessen d. Virginia Wade–Tom Okker 8–6, 6–3

1931   Lucia Valerio–Pat Hughes d. Dorothy Andrus Burke–Alberto Del Bono 6–0, 6–1

1932   Lolette Payot–J. Bonte d. Dorothy Andrus Burke–Alberto Del Bono 6–1, 6–2

1933   Dorothy Andrus Burke–Martin Legeay d. Y. Orlandini–E. Gabrowitz 6–4, 6–3

1934   Elizabeth Ryan–Henry Culley d. Rollin Couquerque–Franjo Puncec 6–1, 6–3

1935   Jadwiga Jedrzejowska–Harry Hopman d. Evelyn Dearman–Pat Hughes 6–4, 1–6, 6–3

1936–49   Not held

1950   Gertrude Moran–Adrian Quist divided title with Annalies Bossi–Gianni Cucelli 6–3, 1–1 unfinished

1951   Shirley Fry–Felicisimo Ampon d. Doris Hart–Lennart Bergelin 8–6, 3–6, 6–4

1952   Arvilla McGuire–Kurt Nielsen d. M.J. de Riba–E. Migone 4–6, 6–3, 6–3

1953   Doris Hart–Vic Seixas d. Maureen Connolly–Mervyn Rose 6–4, 6–4

1954   Maureen Connolly–Vic Seixas divided title with Barbara Kimbrell–Tony Trabert 3–6, 11–9, 3–3 unfinished

1955   Pat Ward–Enrique Morea divided title with Beryl Penrose–Mervyn Rose not played

1956   Thelma Coyne Long–Luis Ayala d. Shirley Bloomer–Georgio Fachini 6–4, 6–3

1957   Thelma Coyne Long–Luis Ayala d. Shirley Bloomer–Bob Howe 6–1, 6–1

1958   Shirley Bloomer–Giorgio Fachini d. Thelma Coyne Long–Luis Ayala 4–6, 6–2, 9–7

1959   Rosie Reyes–Francisco Contreras d. Yola Ramirez–Billy Knight 9–7, 6–1

1960   Not held

1961   Margaret Smith–Roy Emerson d. Jan Lehane–Bob Hewitt 6–1, 6–1

the international team competition for men that eventually bore his name: the Davis Cup. Davis was just out of Harvard in 1900 when he commissioned a sterling bowl for $750 from a Boston jeweler and offered it for competition among nations. That year only Great Britain, whose team was called British Isles, showed interest, and sent a team to Boston to challenge the United States on the grass of Longwood Cricket Club.

Davis himself, along with schoolmates Holcombe Ward and Malcolm Whitman, formed the U.S. team that defeated the Britons, 3–0. In the first three years of the competition (1900, 1902–03), only Britain and the U.S. entered, and their match determined who would hold the Cup. In 1904 other nations showed interest, and Belgium and France entered (the U.S. did not). It was then that the Challenge Round format was put into use. Belgium defeated France for the right to challenge the defender, Britain, for the Cup. Gradually more nations entered and the prize, entitled the International Lawn Tennis Challenge Trophy, became known as the Davis Cup.

In 1981 the World Group of 16 countries was instituted. Only those 16 annually are eligible to compete for the Cup itself.

Remaining countries engage in zonal competition with the possibility of being promoted to the World Group the following year, replacing four first-round World Group losers who are relegated to zonal play.

It became necessary to divide the world into zones for preliminary tournaments to determine one challenger for the championship nation. The champion was required to play only the title match—the Challenge Round—the following year against the winner of the preliminary tournament. That system was changed in 1972, when all nations were required to play in the eliminations in their respective zones: American (North and South sections), European (A and B sections) and Eastern. That year the Cup–defending U.S. reached the final against Romania in Bucharest and won, 3–2.

A total of 101 nations have appeared in the competition. But only eight have won the Cup: the U.S. (30 times), Australia (26), Britain (9), France (7), Sweden (4), Germany (2), Italy (1), South Africa (1), Czechoslovakia (1). Eight nations besides the nine winners have qualified for the Challenge Round and/or Final: Romania (3 times), India (2), Spain (2), Belgium (1), Japan (1), Mexico (1), Chile (1), Switzerland (1).

The competition was confined to amateurs until 1969, when certain professionals, those with ties to their national federations, became eligible. In 1973 it became a truly open event, with all players welcome, and Australia won with possibly the strongest team ever, a group of pros who had been away from Davis Cup for years: Rod Laver, Ken Rosewall, John Newcombe, Mal Anderson.

The format for a match (or tie) is four singles and one doubles, a best-of-five series over three days. A team may be composed of no more than four players. Two players are nominated for singles and each faces the two men from the opposing team.

A draw determines who plays whom. Opponents on the first day are reversed on the third. The doubles is played on the second day.

Nations visit one another for matches, a scheduling formula determining which of two opponents has choice of ground.

By 1923, when 17 nations entered, it was necessary to divide the world into two zones, American and European. In 1955 an Eastern Zone was added, and in 1966 the European Zone was split into sections A and B. In 1967 the American Zone was split into North and South sections.

Early Australian success was achieved under the banner of Australasia, a joint effort by Australia and New Zealand. This ended in 1924, when each county began to enter separate teams.

Through 1992 the competition had been held 81 times, the annual flow interrupted only by two world wars and a hiatus in 1901 and 1910.

Title–Round Standings

	Final Rounds		(Since 1972)		Total	
	W	L	W	L	W	L
United States	24	24	6	3	30	27
Australia	22	15	4	1	26	16
Britain	9	7	0	1	9	8
France	6	3	1	1	7	4
Italy	0	2	1	3	1	5
Sweden	0	0	1	0	4	4
South Africa	0	0	1	0	1	0
Romania	0	2	0	1	0	3
Spain	0	2	0	0	0	2
India	0	1	0	2	0	3
Belgium	0	1	0	0	0	1
Japan	0	1	0	0	0	1
Mexico	0	1	0	0	0	1
West Germany	0	1	2	1	2	2
Czechoslovakia	0	0	1	1	1	1
Chile	0	0	0	1	0	1
Argentina	0	0	0	1	0	1
Switzerland	0	0	0	1	0	1

Davis Cup Final Round Results

1900   United States d. British Isles 3–0 (Boston)
        Malcolm Whitman d. Arthur Gore 6–1,
            6–3, 6–2
        Dwight Davis d. Black 4–6, 6–2, 6–4, 6–4
        Holcombe Ward–Dwight Davis d. Black–
            Herbert Roper Barrett 6–4, 6–4, 6–4
        Malcolm Whitman vs. Black (not played)
        Dwight Davis vs. Arthur Gore 9–7, 9–9 abon

        6–3, 6–4
        Bill Larned d. Joshua Pim 6–3, 6–2, 6–3
        Malcolm Whitman d. Reggie Doherty 6–1,
            7–5, 6–4

1903   British Isles d. United States 4–1 (Boston)
        Laurie Doherty d. Robert Wrenn 6–0, 6–3,
            6–4
        Bill Larned (US) d. Reggie Doherty (default)
        Reggie Doherty–Laurie Doherty d. Robert
            Wrenn–George Wrenn 7–5, 9–7, 2–6, 6–3
        Laurie Doherty d. Bill Larned 6–3, 6–8, 6–0,
            2–6, 7–5
        Reggie Doherty d. Robert Wrenn 6–4, 3–6,
            6–3, 6–8, 6–4

1904   British Isles d. Belgium 5–0 (Wimbledon)
        Laurie Doherty d. Paul de Borman 6–4, 6–1,
            6–1
        Frank Riseley d. Willie Lemairie 6–1, 6–4, 6–2
        Reggie Doherty–Laurie Doherty d. Paul de
            Borman–Willie Lemaire 6–0, 6–1, 6–3
        Laurie Doherty d. Willie Lemaire (default)
        Frank Riseley d. Paul de Borman 4–6, 6–2,
            8–6, 7–5

1905   British Isles d. United States 5–0 (Wimbledon)
        Laurie Doherty d. Holcombe Ward 7–9, 4–6,
            6–1, 6–2, 6–0
        Sidney Smith d. Bill Larned 6–4, 6–4, 5–7, 6–4
        Reggie Doherty–Laurie Doherty d. Holcombe
            Ward–Beals Wright 8–10, 6–2, 6–2, 4–6, 8–6
        Sidney Smith d. Bill Clothier 6–1, 6–4, 6–3
        Laurie Doherty d. Bill Larned 6–4, 2–6, 6–8,
            6–4, 6–2

1906   British Isles d. United States 5–0 (Wimbledon)
        Sidney Smith d. Ray Little 6–4, 6–4, 6–1

        Laurie Doherty d. Holcombe Ward 6–2, 8–6,
            6–3
        Reggie Doherty–Laurie Doherty d. Holcombe
            Ward–Ray Little 3–6, 11–9, 9–7, 6–1
        Sidney Smith d. Holcombe Ward 6–1, 6–0, 6–4
        Laurie Doherty d. Ray Little 3–6, 6–3, 6–8,
            6–1, 6–3

1907   Australasia d. British Isles 3–2 (Wimbledon)
        Norman Brookes d. Arthur Gore 7–5, 6–1,
            7–5
        Tony Wilding d. Roper Barrett 1–6, 6–4, 6–3,

        Beals Wright (US) d. Tony Wilding 3–6, 7–5,
            6–3, 6–1
        Norman Brookes–Tony Wilding (A) d. Beals
            Wright–Fred Alexander 6–4, 6–2, 5–7,
            1–6, 6–4
        Tony Wilding d. Fred Alexander 6–3, 6–4, 6–1
        Beals Wright d. Norman Brookes 0–6, 3–6,
            7–5, 6–2, 12–10

1909   Australia d. United States 5–0 (Sydney)
        Norman Brookes d. Maurice McLoughlin
            6–2, 6–2, 6–4
        Tony Wilding d. Melville Long 6–2, 7–5, 6–1
        Norman Brookes–Tony Wilding d. Maurice
            McLoughlin–Melville Long 12–10, 9–7,
            6–3
        Norman Brookes d. Melville Long 6–4, 7–5,
            8–6
        Tony Wilding d. Maurice McLoughlin 3–6,
            8–6, 6–2, 6–3

1910   No competition

1911   Australia d. United States 5–0 (Christ church,
            New Zealand)
        Norman Brookes d. Beals Wright 6–4, 2–6,
            6–3, 6–3
        Rod Heath d. Bill Larned 2–6, 6–1, 7–5, 6–2
        Norman Brookes–Alfred Dunlop d. Beals
            Wright–Maurice McLoughlin 6–4, 5–7,
            7–5, 6–4
        Norman Brookes d. Maurice McLoughlin
            6–4, 3–6, 4–6, 6–3, 6–4
        Rod Heath d. Wright (default)

1912   British Isles d. Australia 3–2 (Melbourne)
        Cecil Parke d. Norman Brookes 8–6, 6–3,
            5–7, 6–2

Charles Dixon d. Rod Heath 5–7, 6–4, 6–4, 6–4

Norman Brookes–Alfred Dunlop (A) d. Cecil Parke–Alfred Beamish 6–4, 6–1, 7–5

Cecil Parke d. Rod Heath 6–2, 6–4, 6–4

Norman Brookes (A) d. Charles Dixon 6–2, 6–4, 6–4

1913   United States d. British Isles 3–2 (Wimbledon)

Cecil Parke (B) d. Maurice McLoughlin 8–10, 7–5, 6–4, 1–6, 7–5

Dick Williams d. Charles Dixon 8–6, 3–6, 6–2, 1–6, 7–5

Harold Hackett–Maurice McLoughlin d. Roper Barrett–Charles Dixon 5–7, 6–1, 2–6, 7–5, 6–4

Maurice McLoughlin d. Charles Dixon 8–6, 6–3, 6–2

Cecil Parke (B) d. Dick Williams 6–2, 5–7, 5–7, 6–4, 6–2

1914   Australasia d. United States 3–2 (Forest Hills)

Tony Wilding d. Dick Williams 7–5, 6–2, 6–3

Maurice McLoughlin (US) d. Norman Brookes 17–15, 6–3, 6–3

Norman Brookes–Tony Wilding d. Maurice McLoughlin–Tom Bundy 6–3, 8–6, 9–7

Norman Brookes d. Dick Williams 6–1, 6–2, 8–10, 6–3

Maurice McLoughlin d. Tony Wilding 6–2, 6–3, 2–6, 6–2

1915–18 Not held

1919   Australia d. British Isles 4–1 (Sydney)

Gerald Patterson d. Arthur Lowe 6–4, 6–3, 2–6, 6–3

Algernon Kingscote (B) d. Jim Anderson 7–5, 6–2, 6–4

Norman Brookes–Gerald Patterson d. Algernon Kingscote–Alfred Beamish 6–0, 6–0, 6–2

Gerald Patterson d. Algernon Kingscote 6–4, 6–4, 8–6

Jim Anderson d. Arthur Lowe 6–4, 5–7, 6–3, 4–6, 12–10

1920   United States d. Australasia 5–0 (Auckland)

Bill Tilden d. Norman Brookes 10–8, 6–4, 1–6, 6–4

Bill Johnston d. Gerald Patterson 6–3, 6–1, 6–1

Bill Tilden–Bill Johnston d. Norman Brookes–Gerald Patterson 4–6, 6–4, 6–0, 6–4

Bill Tilden d. Gerald Patterson 5–7, 6–2, 6–3, 6–3

Bill Johnston d. Norman Brookes 5–7, 7–5, 6–3, 6–3

1921   United States d. Japan 5–0 (Forest Hills)

Bill Tilden d. Zenzo Shimidzu 5–7, 4–6, 7–5, 6–2, 6–1

Bill Johnston d. Ichiya Kumagae 6–2, 6–4, 6–2

Dick Williams–Watson Washburn d. Zenzo Shimidzu–Ichiya Kumagae 6–2, 7–5, 4–6, 7–5

Bill Tilden d. Ichiya Kumagae 9–7, 6–4, 6–1

Bill Johnston d. Zenzo Shimidzu 6–3, 5–7, 6–2, 6–4

1922   United States d. Australasia 4–1 (Forest Hills)

Bill Tilden d. Gerald Patterson 7–5, 10–8, 6–0

Bill Johnston d. Jim Anderson 6–1, 6–2, 6–3

Gerald Patterson–Pat O'Hara Wood (A) d. Bill Tilden–Vinnie Richards 6–3, 6–0, 6–4

Bill Johnston d. Gerald Patterson 6–2, 6–2, 6–1

Bill Tilden d. Jim Anderson 6–4, 5–7, 3–6, 6–4, 6–2

1923   United States d. Australasia 4–1 (Forest Hills)

Jim Anderson (A) d. Bill Johnston 4–6, 6–2, 2–6, 7–5, 6–2

Bill Tilden d. John Hawkes 6–4, 6–2, 6–1

Bill Tilden–Dick Williams d. Jim Anderson–John Hawkes 17–15, 11–13, 2–6, 6–3, 6–2

Bill Johnston d. John Hawkes 6–0, 6–2, 6–1

Bill Tilden d. Jim Anderson 6–2, 6–3, 1–6, 7–5

1924   United States d. Australasia 5–0 (Philadelphia)

Bill Tilden d. Gerald Patterson 6–4, 6–2, 6–2

Vincent Richards d. Pat O'Hara Wood 6–3, 6–2, 6–4

Bill Tilden–Bill Johnston d. Gerald Patterson–Pat O'Hara Wood 5–7, 6–3, 6–4, 6–1

Bill Tilden d. Pat O'Hara Wood 6–2, 6–1, 6–1

Vincent Richards d. Gerald Patterson 6–3, 7–5, 6–4

1925   United States d. France 5–0 (Philadelphia)

Bill Tilden d. Jean Borotra 4–6, 6–0, 2–6, 9–7, 6–4

Bill Johnston d. René Lacoste 6–1, 6–1, 6–8, 6–3

Vincent Richards–Dick Williams d. René Lacoste–Jean Borotra 6–4, 6–4, 6–3

Bill Tilden d. René Lacoste 3–6, 10–12, 8–6, 7–5, 6–2

Bill Johnston d. Jean Borotra 6–1, 6–4, 6–0

1926   United States d. France 4–1 (Philadelphia)

Bill Johnston d. René Lacoste 6–0, 6–4, 0–6, 6–0

Bill Tilden d. Jean Borotra 6–2, 6–3, 6–3

Dick Williams–Vincent Richards d. Henri Cochet–Jacques Brugnon 6–4, 6–4, 6–2

Bill Johnston d. Jean Borotra 8–6, 6–4, 9–7

René Lacoste (F) d. Bill Tilden 4–6, 6–4, 8–6, 8–6

1927   France d. United States 3–2 (Philadelphia)

René Lacoste d. Bill Johnston 6–3, 6–2, 6–2

Bill Tilden (US) d. Henri Cochet 6–4, 2–6, 6–2, 8–6
Bill Tilden–Frank Hunter (US) d. Jean Borotra–Jacques Brugnon 3–6, 6–3, 6–3, 4–6, 6–0
René Lacoste d. Bill Tilden 6–3, 4–6, 6–3, 6–2
Henri Cochet d. Bill Johnston 6–4, 4–6, 6–2, 6–4

1928   France d. United States 4–1 (Paris)
Bill Tilden (US) d. René Lacoste 1–6, 6–4, 6–4, 2–6, 6–3
Henri Cochet d. John Hennessey 5–7, 9–7,

Ellsworth Vines (U.S.) d. Henri Cochet 4–6, 0–6, 7–5, 8–6, 6–2

1933   Great Britain d. France 3–2 (Paris)
Bunny Austin d. Andre Merlin 6–3, 6–4, 6–0
Fred Perry d. Henri Cochet 8–10, 6–4, 8–6, 3–6, 6–1
Jean Borotra–Jacques Brugnon (F) d. Pat Hughes–Harold Lee 6–3, 8–6, 6–2
Henri Cochet (F) d. Henry "Bunny" Austin 5–7, 6–4, 4–6, 6–4, 6–4
Fred Perry d. Andre Merlin 4–6, 8–6, 6–2, 7–5

1934   Great Britain d. United States 4–1 (Wimbledon)

John Van Ryn–Wilmer Allison (US) d. Henri Cochet–Jean Borotra 6–1, 8–6, 6–4
Bill Tilden (US) d. Jean Borotra 4–6, 6–1, 6–4, 7–5
Henri Cochet d. George Lott 6–1, 3–6, 6–0, 6–3

1930   France d. United 4–1 (Paris)
Bill Tilden (US) d. Jean Borotra 2–6, 7–5, 6–4, 7–5
Henri Cochet d. George Lott 6–4, 6–2, 6–2
Henri Cochet–Jacques Brugnon d. Wilmer Allison–John Van Ryn 6–3, 7–5, 1–6, 6–2
Jean Borotra d. George Lott 5–7, 6–3, 2–6, 6–2, 8–6
Henri Cochet d. Bill Tilden 4–6, 6–3, 6–1, 7–5

1931   France d. Great Britain 3–2 (Paris)
Henri Cochet d. Henry "Bunny" Austin 3–6, 11–9, 6–2, 6–4
Fred Perry (B) d. Jean Borotra 4–6, 10–8, 6–0, 4–6, 6–4
Henri Cochet–Jacques Brugnon d. Pat Hughes–Charles Kingsley 6–1, 5–7, 6–3, 8–6
Bunny Austin (B) d. Jean Borotra 7–5, 6–3, 3–6, 7–5
Henri Cochet d. Fred Perry 6–4, 1–6, 9–7, 6–3

1932   France d. United States 3–2 (Paris)
Jean Borotra d. Ellsworth Vines 6–4, 6–2, 3–6, 6–4
Henri Cochet d. Wilmer Allison 5–7, 7–5, 7–5, 6–2
Wilmer Allison–John Van Ryn (US) d. Henri Cochet–Brugnon 6–3, 11–13, 7–5, 4–6, 6–4
Jean Borotra d. Wilmer Allison 1–6, 3–6, 6–4, 6–2, 7–5

1935   Great Britain d. United States 5–0 (Wimbledon)
Bunny Austin d. Wilmer Allison 6–2, 2–6, 4–6, 6–3, 7–5
Fred Perry d. Don Budge 6–0, 6–8, 6–3, 6–4
Pat Hughes–Charles Tuckey d. Wilmer Allison–John Van Ryn 6–2, 1–6, 6–8, 6–3, 6–3
Bunny Austin d. Don Budge 6–2, 6–4, 6–8, 7–5
Fred Perry d. Wilmer Allison 4–6, 6–4, 7–5, 6–3

1936   Great Britain d. Australia 3–2 (Wimbledon)
Henry "Bunny" Austin d. Jack Crawford 4–6, 6–3, 6–3, 6–1
Fred Perry d. Adrian Quist 6–3, 4–6, 7–5, 6–2
Jack Crawford–Adrian Quist d. Pat Hughes–Charles Tuckey 6–4, 2–6, 7–5, 10–8
Adrian Quist (A) d. Henry "Bunny" Austin 6–4, 3–6, 7–5, 6–3
Fred Perry d. Jack Crawford 6–2, 6–2, 6–3

1937   United States d. Great Britain 4–1 (Wimbledon)
Henry "Bunny" Austin (B) d. Frank Parker 6–3, 6–2, 7–5
Don Budge d. Charlie Hare 15–13, 6–1, 6–2
Don Budge–Gene Mako d. Charles Tuckey–Frank Wilde 6–3, 7–5, 7–9, 12–10
Frank Parker d. Charlie Hare 6–2, 6–4, 6–2
Don Budge d. Henry "Bunny" Austin 8–6, 3–6, 6–4, 6–3

1938   United States d. Australia 3–2 (Philadelphia)
Bobby Riggs d. Adrian Quist 4–6, 6–0, 8–6, 6–1

Don Budge d. John Bromwich 6–2, 6–3, 4–6,
7–5
Adrian Quist–John Bromwich (A.) d. Don
Budge–Gene Mako 0–6, 6–3, 6–4, 6–2
Don Budge d. Adrian Quist 8–6, 6–1, 6–2
John Bromwich (A) d. Bobby Riggs 6–4, 4–6,
6–0, 6–2

1939   Australia d. United States 3–2 (Haverford, Pa.)
Bobby Riggs (US) d. John Bromwich 6–4,
6–0, 7–5
Frank Parker (US) d. Adrian Quist 6–3, 2–6,
6–4, 1–6, 7–5
Adrian Quist–John Bromwich d. Jack Kramer–
Joe Hunt 5–7, 6–2, 7–5, 6–2
Adrian Quist d. Bobby Riggs 6–1, 6–4, 3–6,
3–6, 6–4
John Bromwich d. Frank Parker 6–0, 6–3, 6–1

1940–45 No competition

1946   United States d. Australia 5–0 (Melbourne)
Ted Schroeder d. John Bromwich 3–6, 6–1,
6–2, 0–6, 6–3
Jack Kramer d. Dinny Pails 8–6, 6–2, 9–7
Jack Kramer–Ted Schroeder d. John
Bromwich–Adrian Quist 6–2, 7–5, 6–4
Jack Kramer d. John Bromwich 8–6, 6–4, 6–4
Gardnar Mulloy d. Dinny Pails 6–3, 6–3, 6–4

1947   United States d. Australia 4–1 (Forest Hills)
Jack Kramer d. Dinny Pails 6–2, 6–1, 6–2
Ted Schroeder d. John Bromwich 6–4, 5–7,
6–3, 6–4
John Bromwich–Colin Long (A) d. Jack
Kramer–Ted Schroeder 6–4, 2–6, 6–2, 6–4
Ted Schroeder d. Dinny Pails 6–3, 8–6, 4–6,
9–11, 10–8
Jack Kramer d. John Bromwich 6–3, 6–2, 6–2

1948   United States d. Australia 5–0 (Forest Hills)
Frank Parker d. Bill Sidwell 6–4, 6–4, 6–4
Ted Schroeder d. Adrian Quist 6–3, 4–6, 6–0,
6–0
Bill Talbert–Gardnar Mulloy d. Bill Sidwell–
Colin Long 8–6, 9–7, 2–6, 7–5
Ted Schroeder d. Bill Sidwell 6–2, 6–1, 6–1
Frank Parker d. Adrian Quist 6–2, 6–2, 6–3

1949   United States d. Australia 4–1 (Forest Hills)
Ted Schroeder d. Bill Sidwell 6–1, 5–7, 4–6,
6–2, 6–3
Pancho Gonzalez d. Frank Sedgman 8–6, 6–4,
9–7
Bill Sidwell–John Bromwich (A) d. Bill
Talbert–Gardnar Mulloy 3–6, 4–6, 10–8,
9–7, 9–7
Ted Schroeder d. Frank Sedgman 6–4, 6–3,
6–3
Pancho Gonzalez d. Bill Sidwell 6–1, 6–3, 6–3

1950   Australia d. United States 4–1 (Forest Hills)
Frank Sedgman d. Tom Brown 6–0, 8–6, 9–7

Ken McGregor d. Ted Schroeder 13–11, 6–3,
6–4
Frank Sedgman–John Bromwich d. Ted
Schroeder–Gardnar Mulloy 4–6, 6–4, 6–2,
4–6, 6–4
Frank Sedgman d. Ted Schroeder 6–2, 6–2,
6–2
Tom Brown (US) d. Ken McGregor 9–11,
8–10, 11–9, 6–1, 6–4

1951   Australia d. United States 3–2 (Sydney)
Vic Seixas (US) d. Mervyn Rose 6–3, 6–4, 9–7
Frank Sedgman d. Ted Schroeder 6–4, 6–3,
4–6, 6–4
Ken McGregor–Frank Sedgman d. Ted
Schroeder–Tony Trabert 6–2, 9–7, 6–3
Ted Schroeder (US) d. Mervyn Rose 6–4,
13–11, 7–5
Frank Sedgman d. Vic Seixas 6–4, 6–2, 6–2

1952   Australia d. United States 4–1 (Adelaide)
Frank Sedgman d. Vic Seixas 6–3, 6–4, 6–2
Ken McGregor d. Tony Trabert 11–9, 6–4, 6–1
Ken McGregor–Frank Sedgman d. Vic Seixas–
Tony Trabert 6–3, 6–4, 1–6, 6–2
Frank Sedgman d. Tony Trabert 7–5, 6–4, 10–8
Vic Seixas (US) d. Ken McGregor 6–3, 8–6,
6–3

1953   Australia d. United States 3–2 (Melbourne)
Lew Hoad d. Vic Seixas 6–4, 6–2, 6–3
Tony Trabert (US) d. Ken Rosewall 6–3, 6–4,
6–4
Vic Seixas–Tony Trabert (US) d. Rex Hartwig–
Lew Hoad 6–2, 6–4, 6–4
Lew Hoad d. Tony Trabert 13–11, 6–3, 2–6,
3–6, 7–5
Ken Rosewall d. Vic Seixas 6–2, 2–6, 6–3, 6–4

1954   United States d. Australia 3–2 (Sydney)
Tony Trabert d. Lew Hoad 6–4, 2–6, 12–10,
6–3
Vic Seixas d. Ken Rosewall 8–6, 6–8, 6–4, 6–3
Vic Seixas–Tony Trabert d. Lew Hoad–Ken
Rosewall 6–2,4–6, 6–2, 10–8
Ken Rosewall (A) d. Tony Trabert 9–7, 7–5,
6–3
Rex Hartwig (A) d. Vic Seixas 4–6, 6–3, 6–2,
6–3

1955   Australia d. United States 5–0 (Forest Hills)
Ken Rosewall d. Vic Seixas 6–3, 10–8, 4–6, 6–2
Lew Hoad d. Tony Trabert 4–6, 6–3, 6–3, 8–6
Lew Hoad–Rex Hartwig d. Tony Trabert–Vic
Seixas 12–14, 6–4, 6–3, 3–6, 7–5
Lew Hoad d. Vic Seixas 7–9, 6–1, 6–4, 6–4
Ken Rosewall d. Ham Richardson 6–4, 3–6,
6–1, 6–4

1956   Australia d. United States 5–0 (Adelaide)
Lew Hoad d. Herbie Flam 6–2, 6–3, 6–3
Ken Rosewall d. Vic Seixas 6–1, 6–4, 4–6, 6–1

Lew Hoad–Ken Rosewall d. Sammy Giamalva–
Vic Seixas 1–6, 6–1, 7–5, 6–4
Ken Rosewall d. Sammy Giammalva 4–6, 6–1,
8–6, 7–5
Lew Hoad d. Vic Seixas 6–2, 7–5, 6–3

1957 Australia d. United States 3–2 (Melbourne)
Mal Anderson d. Barry MacKay 6–3, 7–5, 3–6,
7–9, 6–3
Ashley Cooper d. Vic Seixas 3–6, 7–5, 6–1,
1–6, 6–3
Mal Anderson–Mervyn Rose d. Barry MacKay–

Anderson–Neale Fraser 10–12, 3–6,
16–14, 6–3, 7–5
Alex Olmedo d. Ashley Cooper 6–3, 4–6, 6–4,
8–6
Mal Anderson d. Barry MacKay 7–5, 13–11,
11–9

1959 Australia d. United States 3–2 (Forest Hills)
Neale Fraser d. Alex Olmedo 8–6, 6–8, 6–4,
8–6
Barry MacKay (US) d. Rod Laver 7–5, 6–4, 6–1
Neale Fraser–Roy Emerson d. Alex Olmedo–
Earl "Butch" Buchholz 7–5, 7–5, 6–4
Alex Olmedo (US) d. Rod Laver 9–7, 4–6,
10–8, 12–10
Neale Fraser d. Barry MacKay 8–6, 3–6, 6–2,
6–4

1960 Australia d. Italy 4–1 (Sydney)
Neale Fraser d. Orlando Sirola 4–6, 6–3, 6–3,
6–3
Rod Laver d. Nicola Pietrangeli 8–6, 6–4, 6–3
Neale Fraser–Roy Emerson d. Nicola
Pietrangeli–Orlando Sirola 10–8, 5–7,
6–2, 6–4
Rod Laver d. Orlando Sirola 9–7, 6–2, 6–3
Nicola Pietrangeli (I) d. Neale Fraser 11–9,
6–3, 1–6, 6–2

1961 Australia d. Italy 5–0 (Melbourne)
Roy Emerson d. Nicola Pietrangeli 8–6, 6–4,
6–0
Rod Laver d. Orlando Sirola 6–1, 6–4, 6–3
Neale Fraser–Roy Emerson d. Nicola
Pietrangeli–Orlando Sirola 6–2, 6–3, 6–4
Rod Laver d. Nicola Pietrangeli 6–3, 3–6, 4–6,
6–3, 8–6

Roy Emerson d. Orlando Sirola 6–3, 6–3, 4–6,
6–2

1962 Australia d. Mexico 5–0 (Brisbane)
Rod Laver d. Rafael Osuna 6–2, 6–1, 7–5
Neale Fraser d. Tony Palafox 7–9, 6–3, 6–4, 11–9
Roy Emerson–Rod Laver d. Rafael Osuna–
Tony Palafox 7–5, 6–2, 6–4
Neale Fraser d. Rafael Osuna 3–6, 11–9, 6–1,
3–6, 6–4
Rod Laver d. Tony Palafox 6–1, 4–6, 6–4, 8–6

1963 United States d. Australia 3–2 (Adelaide)

1964 Australia d. United States 3–2 (Cleveland)
Chuck McKinley (US) d. Fred Stolle 6–1, 9–7,
4–6, 6–2
Roy Emerson d. Dennis Ralston 6–3, 6–4, 6–2
Chuck McKinley–Dennis Ralston (US) d. Roy
Emerson–Fred Stolle 6–4, 4–6, 4–6, 6–3,
6–4
Fred Stolle d. Dennis Ralston 7–5, 6–3, 3–6,
9–11, 6–4
Roy Emerson d. Chuck McKinley 3–6, 6–2,
6–4, 6–4

1965 Australia d. Spain 4–1 (Sydney)
Fred Stolle d. Manuel Santana 10–12, 3–6,
6–1, 6–4, 7–5
Roy Emerson d. Juan Gisbert 6–3, 6–2, 6–2
John Newcombe–Tony Roche d. Luis Arilla–
Manuel Santana 6–3, 4–6, 7–5, 6–2
Manuel Santana (S) d. Roy Emerson 2–6,
6–3, 6–4, 15–13
Fred Stolle d. Juan Gisbert 6–2, 6–4, 8–6

1966 Australia d. India 4–1 (Melbourne)
Fred Stolle d. Ramanathan Krishnan 6–3,
6–2, 6–4
Roy Emerson d. Jai Mukerjea 7–5, 6–4, 6–2
Ramanathan Krishnan–Jai Mukerjea (I) d.
John Newcombe–Tony Roche 4–6, 7–5,
6–4, 6–4
Roy Emerson d. Ramanathan Krishnan 6–0,
6–2, 10–8
Fred Stolle d. Jai Mukerjea 7–5, 6–8, 6–3, 5–7,
6–3

1967 Australia d. Spain 4–1 (Brisbane)
Roy Emerson d. Manuel Santana 6–4, 6–1, 6–1
John Newcombe d. Manuel Orantes 6–3, 6–3,
6–2

John Newcombe–Tony Roche d. Manuel
Santana–Manuel Orantes 6–4, 6–4, 6–4
Manuel Santana (S) d. John Newcombe 7–5,
6–4, 6–2
Roy Emerson d. Manuel Orantes 6–1, 6–1,
2–6, 6–4

1968   United States d. Australia 4–1 (Adelaide)
Clark Graebner d. Bill Bowrey 8–10, 6–4, 8–6,
3–6, 6–1
Arthur Ashe d. Ray Ruffels 6–8, 7–5, 6–3, 6–3
Bob Lutz–Stan Smith d. John Alexander–Ray
Ruffels 6–4, 6–4, 6–2
Clark Graebner d. Ray Ruffels 3–6, 8–6, 2–6,
6–3, 6–1
Bill Bowrey (A) d. Arthur Ashe 2–6, 6–3,
11–9, 8–6

1969   United States d. Romania 5–0 (Cleveland)
Arthur Ashe d. Ilie Nastase 6–2, 15–13, 7–5
Stan Smith d. Ion Tiriac 6–8, 6–3, 5–7, 6–4,
6–4
Bob Lutz–Stan Smith d. Ilie Nastase–Ion
Tiriac 8–6, 6–1, 11–9
Stan Smith d. Ilie Nastase 4–6, 4–6, 6–4, 6–1,
11–9
Arthur Ashe d. Ion Tiriac 6–3, 8–6, 3–6, 4–0
default

1970   United States d. Germany 5–0 (Cleveland)
Arthur Ashe d. Willie Bungert 6–2, 10–8, 6–2
Cliff Richey d. Christian Kuhnke 6–3, 6–4,
6–2
Bob Lutz–Stan Smith d. Christian Kuhnke–
Willie Bungert 6–3, 7–5, 6–4
Cliff Richey d. Willie Bungert 6–4, 6–4, 7–5
Arthur Ashe d. Christian Kuhnke 6–8, 10–12,
9–7, 13–11, 6–4

1971   United States d. Romania 3–2 (Charlotte,
N.C.)
Stan Smith d. Ilie Nastase 7–5, 6–3, 6–1
Frank Froehling d. Ion Tiriac 3–6, 1–6, 6–3,
6–1, 8–6
Ilie Nastase–Ion Tiriac (R) d. Stan Smith–
Erik van Dillen 7–5, 6–4, 8–6
Stan Smith d. Ion Tiriac 8–6, 6–3, 6–0
Ilie Nastase (R) d. Frank Froehling 6–3, 6–1,
4–6, 6–4

1972   United States d. Romania 3–2 (Bucharest)
Stan Smith d. Ilie Nastase 11–9, 6–2, 6–3
Ion Tiriac (R) d. Tom Gorman 4–6, 2–6, 6–4,
6–3, 6–2
Stan Smith–Erik van Dillen d. Ilie Nastase–
Ion Tiriac 6–2, 6–0, 6–3
Stan Smith d. Ion Tiriac 4–6, 6–2, 6–4, 2–6, 6–0
Ilie Nastase (R) d. Tom Gorman 6–1, 6–2,
5–7, 10–8

1973   Australia d. United States 5–0 (Cleveland)

John Newcombe d. Stan Smith 6–1, 3–6, 6–3,
3–6, 6–4
Rod Laver d. Tom Gorman 8–10, 8–6, 6–8,
6–3, 6–1
John Newcombe–Rod Laver d. Erik van
Dillen–Stan Smith 6–1, 6–2, 6–4
John Newcombe d. Tom Gorman 6–2, 6–1,
6–3
Rod Laver d. Stan Smith 6–3, 6–4, 3–6, 6–2

1974   South Africa d. India (default—India refused
to play, a protest against the South
African government's policy of apartheid.
The South African team was Bob Hewitt,
Fred McMillan, Ray Moore, and Rob
Maud. The Indian team was Vijay
Amritraj, Anand Amritraj, Jasjit Singh,
and Sashi Menon.)

1975   Sweden d. Czechoslovakia 3–2 (Stockholm)
Bjorn Borg d. Jiri Hrebec 6–1, 6–3, 6–0
Jan Kodes (C) d. Ove Bengston 4–6, 6–2, 7–5,
6–4
Bjorn Borg–Ove Bengtson d. Jan Kodes–
Vladimir Zednik 6–4, 6–4, 6–4
Bjorn Borg d. Jan Kodes 6–4, 6–2, 6–2
Jiri Hrebec (C) d. Ove Bengston 1–6, 6–3,
6–1, 6–4

1976   Italy d. Chile 4–1 (Santiago)
Corrado Barazzutti d. Jaime Fillol 7–5, 4–6,
7–5, 6–1
Adriano Panatta d. Pat Cornejo 6–3, 6–1, 6–3
Adriano Panatta–Paolo Bertolucci d. Pat
Cornejo–Jaime-Fillol 3–6, 6–2, 9–7, 6–3
Adriano Panatta d Jamie Fillol 8–6, 6–4, 3–6,
10–8
Belus Prajoux (C) d Antonio Zugarelli 6–4,
6–4, 6–2

1977   Australia d. Italy 3–1 (Sydney) Tony Roche d.
Adriano Panetta 6–3, 6–4, 6–4
John Alexander d. Corrado Barazzutti 6–4,
8–6, 4–6, 6–2
Adriano Panatta–Paolo Bertolucci (I) d. John
Alexander–Phil Dent 6–4, 6–4, 7–5
John Alexander d. Adriano Panatta 6–4, 4–6,
2–6, 8–6, 11–9
Tony Roche vs. Corrado Barazzutti 12–12
abandoned

1978   United States d. Great Britain 4–1 (Rancho
Mirage)
John McEnroe d. John Lloyd 6–1, 6–2, 6–2
Buster Mottram (B) d. Brian Gottfried 4–6,
2–6, 10–8, 6–4, 6–3
Stan Smith–Bob Lutz d. David Lloyd–Mark
Cox 6–2, 6–2, 6–3
John McEnroe d. Buster Mottram 6–2, 6–2,
6–1
Brian Gottfried d. John Lloyd 6–1, 6–2, 6–4

1979   United States d. Italy 5–0 (San Francisco)
Vitas Gerulaitis d. Corrado Barazzuti 6–2, 3–2
    (default, injury)
John McEnroe d. Adriano Panatta 6–2, 6–3,
    6–4
Stan Smith–Bob Lutz d. Paolo Bertolucci–
    Adriano Panatta 6–4, 12–10, 6–2
John McEnroe d. Antonio Zugarelli 6–4, 6–3,
    6–1
Vitas Gerulaitis d. Adriano Panatta 6–1, 6–3,
    6–3

1980   Czechoslovakia d. Italy 4–1 (Prague)

United States d. Argentina 3–1 (Cincinnati)
John McEnroe d. Guillermo Vilas 6–3, 6–3,
    6–2
Jose-Luis Clerc d. Roscoe Tanner 7–5, 6–3,
    8–6
Peter Fleming–John McEnroe d. Jose-Luis
    Clerc–Guillermo Vilas 6–3, 4–6, 6–4, 4–6,
    11–9
John McEnroe d. Jose-Luis Clerc 7–5, 5–7,
    6–3, 3–6, 6–3
Roscoe Tanner vs. Guillermo Vilas (sus-
    pended at 11–10, first set)

1982   United States d. France 4–1 (Grenoble)
John McEnroe d. Yannick Noah 12–10, 1–6,
    3–6, 6–3, 6–2
Gene Mayer d. Henri Leconte 6–2, 6–2, 7–9,
    6–4
Peter Fleming–John McEnroe d. Henri
    Leconte–Yannick Noah 6–3, 6–4, 9–7
Yannick Noah d. Gene Mayer 6–1, 6–0
John McEnroe d. Henri Leconte 6–2, 6–3

1983   Australia d. Sweden 3–2 (Melbourne)
Mats Wilander (S) d. Pat Cash 6–3, 4–6, 9–7,
    6–3
John Fitzgerald d. Joakim Nystrom 6–4, 6–2,
    4–6, 6–4
Mark Edmondson–Paul McNamee (A) d.
    Anders Jarryd–Hans Simonsson 6–4, 6–4,
    6–2
Pat Cash d. Joakim Nystrom 6–4, 6–1, 6–1
Mats Wilander d. John Fitzgerald 6–8, 6–0, 6–1

1984   Sweden d. United States 4–1 (Goteborg)
Mats Wilander (S) d. Jimmy Connors 6–1,
    6–3, 6–3

Henrik Sundstrom (S) d. John McEnroe
    13–11, 6–4, 6–3
Stefan Edberg–Anders Jarryd d. Peter
    Fleming–John McEnroe 7–5, 5–7, 6–2,
    7–5
John McEnroe d. Mats Wilander 6–3, 5–7, 6–3
Henrik Sundstrom d. Jimmy Arias 3–6, 8–6,
    6–3

1985   Sweden d. Germany 3–2 (Munich)
Mats Wilander (S) d. Michael Westpal 6–3,
    6–4, 10–8
Boris Becker (G) d. Stefan Edberg 6–3, 3–6,

Mikael Pernfors (S) d. Paul McNamee 6–3,
    6–1, 6–3
Pat Cash–John Fitzgerald d. Stefan Edberg–
    Anders Jarryd 6–3, 6–4, 4–6, 6–1
Pat Cash d. Mikael Pernfors 2–6, 4–6, 6–3,
    6–4, 6–3
Stefan Edberg d. Paul McNamee 10–8, 6–4

1987   Sweden d. India 5–0 (Goteborg, Sweden)
Mats Wilander d. Ramesh Krishnan 6–4, 6–1,
    6–3
Anders Jarryd d. Vijay Amritraj 6–3, 6–3, 6–1
Joakim Nystrom–Mats Wilander d. Anand
    Amritraj–Vijay Amritraj 6–2, 3–6, 6–1, 6–2
Anders Jarryd d. Ramesh Krishnan 6–4, 6–3
Mats Wilander d. Vijay Amritraj 6–2, 6–0

1988   Germany d. Sweden 4–1 (Goteberg, Sweden)
Carl–Uwe Steeb (G) d. Mats Wilander 8–10,
    1–6, 6–2, 6–4, 8–6
Boris Becker (G) d. Stefan Edberg 6–3, 6–1,
    6–4
Boris Becker–Eric Jelen d. Stefan Edberg–
    Anders Jarryd 3–6, 2–6, 7–5, 6–3, 6–2
Stefan Edberg d. Carl Uwe–Steeb 6–4 8–6
Patrick Kuhnen d. Kent Carlsson w/o

1989   Germany d. Sweden 3–2 (Stuttgart,
    Germany)
Mats Wilander (S) d. Carl Uwe–Steeb 5–7,
    7–6, 6–7, 6–2, 6–3
Boris Becker (G) d. Stefan Edberg 6–2, 6–2,
    6–4
Boris Becker–Eric Jelen d. Jan Gunnarson–
    Anders Jarryd 7–6, 6–4, 3–6, 6–7, 6–4
Boris Becker d. Mats Wilander 6–2, 6–0, 6–2
Stefan Edberg d. Carl Uwe–Steeb 6–2, 6–4

1990   United States d. Australia 3–2 (St. Petersburg)
        Andre Agassi (US) d. Richard Fromberg 4–6,
           6–2, 4–6, 6–2, 6–4
        Michael Chang (US) d. Darren Cahill 6–2,
           7–6, 6–0
        Rick Leach–Jim Pugh (US) d. Pat Cash–Jon
           Fitzgerald 6–4, 6–2, 3–6, 7–6
        Darren Cahill d. Andre Agassi 6–4, 4–6 ret.
        Richard Fromberg d. Michael Chang 7–5,
           2–6, 6–3

1991   France d. United States 3–1 (Lyon)
        Andre Agassi (US) d. Guy Forget 6–7, 6–2,
           6–1, 6–2
        Henri Leconte (F) d. Pete Sampras 6–4, 7–5,
           6–4
        Guy Forget–Henri Leconte d. Ken Flach–
           Robert Seguso 6–4, 6–4, 4–6, 6–2
        Guy Forget d. Pete Sampras 7–6, 3–6, 6–3, 6–4

1992   United States d. Switzerland 3–1 (Forth
           Worth)
        Andre Agassi (US) d. Jakob Hlasek 6–1, 6–2,
           6–2
        Marc Rosset (S) d. Jim Courier 6–3, 6–7, 3–6,
           6–4, 6–4
        John McEnroe–Pete Sampras d. Hlasek–
           Rosset 6–7, 6–7, 7–5, 6–1, 6–2
        Jim Courier d. Jakob Hlasek 6–3, 3–6, 6–3, 6–4

All–Time Davis Cup Records

Individual

Most Cup–winning years: 8—Roy Emerson, Australia,
1959–67

Most Years in challenge round and/or final: 11–Bill
Tilden, U.S., 1920–30

Most years played: 21—Torben Ulrich, Denmark,
1948–68

Most matches played: 164—Nicola Pietrangeli, Italy,
1954–72

Most singles played: 110—Pietrangeli

Most singles won: 78—Pietrangeli

Most doubles played: 54—Pietrangeli

Most doubles won: 42—Pietrangeli

Most singles and doubles altogether: 164—Pietrangeli

Most singles and doubles won altogether: 120—
Pietrangeli

Most consecutive singles wins: 33—Bjorn Borg,
Sweden, 1973–79

Longest singles: 100 games—Harry Fritz, Canada, d.
Jorge Andrew, Venezuela, 16–14, 11–9, 9–11, 4–6,
11–9. American Zone, 2nd rd., Caracas, 1982.

Longest doubles: 122 games—Stan Smith and Erik
van Dillen, U.S., d. Jaime Fillol and Pat Cornejo,
Chile, 7–9, 37–39, 8–6, 6–1, 6–3; zone match, Little
Rock, Ark., 1973

Best record in challenge round and/or finals: 7–0 in
singles, 5–0 in doubles—Laurie Doherty, Britain,
1902–06

Most Cups won as captain: 16—Harry Hopman,
Australia, 1938–67

Team

Most Cups won: 30—United States

Most matches won: 175—U.S.

Most consecutive Cups won: 7—U.S., 1920–26

Most consecutive matches won: 17—U.S., 1968–73

U.S. Davis Cup Records

Individual

Most Cup–winning years: 7—Bill Tilden, 1920–26;
Stan Smith, 1968—79

Most years played: 12—John McEnroe, 1978–92

Most team matches played: 30—McEnroe, 1978–92

Most singles played: 49—McEnroe, 1978–91

Most singles won: 41—McEnroe, 1978–91

Most doubles played: 23—John Van Ryn

Most doubles won: 22—John Van Ryn

Most singles and doubles played altogether: 69—
McEnroe, 1978–92

Most singles and doubles won altogether: 59—
McEnroe, 1978–92

Most consecutive singles won: 16—Tilden, 1920–27

**Best winning percentage, 25 or more wins, singles and
doubles altogether:** .903—Van Ryn, 28 wins, 3 losses

Best doubles team record: 14–1—McEnroe–Peter
Fleming

Best winning percentage singles, 15 or more wins:
1.000—Bernard Bartzen, 1952–61, 15 wins

Best winning percentage doubles 10 or more wins:
.923—Bob Lutz, 1968, 78, 12 wins, 1 loss

Most Cups won as captain: 6—Dick Williams, 1921–26

Most matches won as captain: 17—Tom Gorman,
1986—92

Players with More Than 100 Davis Cup Matches

Matches	W–L	Singles W–L	Doubles W–L	Ties W–L
Nicola Pietrangeli, Italy (1954–72)				
164	120–44	78–32	42–12	66
Ilie Nastase, Romania (1966–85)				
146	109–37	74–22	35–15	52
Jacques Brichant, Belgium (1949–65)				
120	71–49	52–27	19–22	42
Manuel Santana, Spain (1958–73)				
105	80–25	56–14	24–11	38
Wilhelm Bungert, Germany (1958–71)				
102	67–35	53–26	14–9	43
Ulf Scmidt, Sweden (1955–64)				
102	66–36	46–18	20–18	39
Torben Ulrich, Denmark (1948–77)				
102	46-56	31–35	15–21	40
Philippe Washer, Belgium (1946–61)				
102	66–36	46–18	20–18	39
Gottfried Von Cramm, Germany (1932–53)				
101	82-19	58-10	24–9	37
Ramanathan Krishnan, India (1953–70)				
100	71–29	52–20	19–9	45
Adriano Panatta, Italy (1970–83)				
100	64–36	37–26	27–10	38

FEDERATION CUP

In response to a growing interest a world-wide women's team competition similar to the men's Davis Cup, the International Tennis Federation put the Federation Cup into play in 1963, marking the ITF's 50th birthday. Sixteen countries entered the competition that year in London at Queen's Club, and the United States edged Australia for the Cup, 2–1, as Billie Jean King and Darlene Hard beat Margaret Court and Lesley Turner in the decisive doubles, 3–6, 13–11, 6–3.

The format differs from the Davis Club in that all teams gather at one location each year for an elimination tournament to be played within one week. Each one-day engagement is best-of-three matches, two singles and a doubles. A team consists of a minimum of two players and a maximum of four, with players nominated for Nos. 1 and 2 singles facing respective opponents. The competition has grown to a 32 draw annually, with a qualifying tournament if more than that number enter. It was con-

	W	L
United States	14	6
Australia	7	9
Czechoslovakia	5	1
Germany	2	4
South Africa	1	1
Spain	1	2
Netherlands	0	1
USSR	0	2
Great Britain	0	4

Federation Cup Final Round Results

Year

1963   United States d. Australia 2–1 (London, England)
Margaret Smith (A) d. Darlene Hard 6–3, 6–0
Billie Jean Moffitt d. Lesley Turner 5–7, 6–0, 6–3
Darlene Hard–Billie Jean Moffitt d. Margaret Smith–Lesley Turner 3–6, 13–11, 6–3

1964   Australia d. United States 2–1 (Philadelphia)
Margaret Smith d. Billie Jean Moffitt 6–2, 6–3
Lesley Turner d. Nancy Richey 7–5, 6–1
Billie Jean Moffitt–Karen Susman (US) d. Margaret Smith–Lesley Turner 4–6, 7–5, 6–1

1965   Australia d. United States 2–1 (Melbourne)
Lesley Turner d. Carole Caldwell Graebner 6–3, 2–6, 6–3
Margaret Smith d. Billie Jean Moffitt 6–4, 8–6

Billie Jean Moffitt–Carole Caldwell Graebner
(US) d. Margaret Smith–Judy Tegart 7–5,
4–6, 6–4

1966   United States d. Germany 3–0 (Turin)
Julie Heldman d. Helga Niessen 4–6, 7–5, 6–1
Billie Jean Moffitt King d. Edda Buding 6–3,
3–6, 6–1
Carole Caldwell Graebner–Billie Jean Moffitt
King d. Helga Schultze–Edda Buding 6–4,
6–2

1967   United States d. Great Britain 2–0 (Berlin)
Rosie Casals d. Virginia Wade 9–7, 8–6
Billie Jean Moffitt King d. Ann Jones 6–3, 6–4
Doubles match called at set–all

1968   Australia d. Netherlands 3–0 (Paris)
Kerry Melville d. Marijke Jansen 4–6, 7–5, 6–3
Margaret Court d. Astrid Suurbeek 6–1, 6–3
Margaret Court–Kerry Melville d. Astrid
Suurbeek–Lidy Venneboer 6–3, 6–8, 7–5

1969   United States d. Australia 2–1 (Athens)
Nancy Richey d. Kerry Melville 6–4, 6–3
Margaret Court (A) d. Julie Heldman 6–1, 8–6
Jane "Peaches" Bartkowicz–Nancy Richey d.
Margaret Court–Judy Tegart 6–4, 6–4

1970   Australia d. Germany 3–0 (Freiburg, West
Germany)
Karen Krantzcke d. Helga Schultze Hoesl
6–2, 6–3
Judy Tegart Dalton d. Helga Niessen 4–6,
6–3, 6–3
Karen Krantzcke–Judy Dalton d. Helga
Hoesl–Helga Niessen 6–2, 7–5

1971   Australia d. Great Britain 3–0 (Perth, Australia)
Margaret Court d. Ann Jones 6–3, 6–8, 6–2
Evonne Goolagong d. Virginia Wade 6–4, 6–1
Margaret Court–Lesley Hunt d. Virginia
Wade–Winnie Shaw 6–4, 6–4

1972   South Africa d. Great Britain 2–1
(Johannesburg)
Virginia Wade (GB) d. Pat Walkden Pretorious
6–3, 6–2
Brenda Kirk d. Winnie Shaw 4–6, 7–5, 6–0
Brenda Kirk–Pat Pretorious d. Winnie
Shaw–Virginia Wade 6–1, 7–5

1973   Australia d. South Africa 3–0 (Bad Homburg,
West Germany)
Evonne Goolagong d. Pat Walkden
Pretorious 6–0, 6–2
Patti Coleman d. Brenda Kirk 10–8, 6–0
Evonne Goolagong–Janet Young d. Brenda
Kirk–Pat Pretorious 6–1, 6–2

1974   Australia d. United States 2–1 (Naples, Italy)
Evonne Goolagong d. Julie Heldman 6–1, 7–5
Jeanne Evert (US) d. Dianne Fromholtz 2–6,
7–5, 6–4

Evonne Goolagong–Janet Young d. Julie
Heldman–Sharon Walsh 7–5, 8–6

1975   Czechoslovakia d. Australia 3–0 (Aix–En–
Provence, France)
Martina Navratilova d. Evonne Goolagong
6–3, 6–4
Renata Tomanova d. Helen Gourlay 6–4, 6–2
Martina Navratilova–Renata Tomanova d.
Dianne Fromholtz–Helen Gourlay 6–3,
6–1

1976   United States d. Australia 2–1 (Philadelphia)
Kerry Melville Reid (A) d. Rosie Casals 1–6,
6–3, 7–5
Billie Jean Moffitt King d. Evonne Goolagong
7–6, 6–4
Billie Jean Moffitt King–Rosie Casals d.
Evonne Goolagong–Kerry Melville Reid
7–5, 6–3

1977   United States d. Australia 2–1 (Eastbourne,
England)
Billie Jean Moffitt King d. Dianne Fromholtz
6–1, 2–6, 6–2
Chris Evert d. Kerry Melville Reid 7–5, 6–3
Kerry Melville Reid–Wendy Turnbull (A) d.
Chris Evert–Rosie Casals 6–3, 6–3

1978   United States d. Australia 2–1 (Melbourne)
Kerry Melville Reid (A) d. Tracy Austin 6–3,
6–3
Chris Evert d. Wendy Turnbull 3–6, 6–1, 6–1
Chris Evert–Billie Jean Moffitt King d. Wendy
Turnbull–Kerry Melville Reid 4–6, 6–1,
6–4

1979   United States d. Australia 3–0 (Madrid)
Tracy Austin d. Kerry Melville Reid 6–3, 6–0
Chris Evert Lloyd d. Dianne Fromholtz 2–6,
6–3, 8–6
Billie Jean King–Rosie Casals d. Wendy
Turnbull–Kerry Melville Reid 3–6, 6–3,
8–6

1980   United States d. Australia 3–0 (Berlin)
Chris Evert Lloyd d. Dianne Fromholtz 4–6,
6–1, 6–1
Tracy Austin d. Wendy Turnbull 6–2, 6–3
Rosie Casals–Kathy Jordan d. Dianne
Fromholtz–Susan Leo 2,6 6–4, 6–4

1981   United States d. Great Britain 3–0 (Tokyo)
Chris Evert Lloyd d. Sue Barker 6–2, 6–1
Andrea Jaeger d. Virginia Wade 6–3, 6–1
Kathy Jordan–Rosie Casals d. Sue Barker–
Virginia Wade 6–4, 7–5

1982   United States d. Germany 3–0 (Santa Clara,
Cal.)
Chris Evert Lloyd d. Claudia Kohde 2–6, 6–1,
6–3
Martina Navratilova d. Bettina Bunge 6–4, 6–4

Martina Navratilova–Chris Evert Lloyd d. Claudia Kohde–Bettina Bunge 3–6, 6–1, 6–2

1983   Czechoslovakia d. Germany 2–1 (Zurich, Switzerland)
Helena Sukova (C) d. Claudia Kohde 6–4, 2–6, 6–2
Hana Mandlikova (C) d. Bettina Bunge 6–2, 3–0 ret.
Claudia Kohde–Eva Pfaff d. Iva Budarova–Marcela Skuherska 3–6 6–2, 6–1

Elise Burgin–Sharon Walsh d. Regina Marsikova–Andrea Holikova 6–2, 6–3

1986   United States d. Czechoslovakia 3–0 (Prague, Czechoslovakia)
Chris Evert Lloyd d. Helena Sukova 7–5, 7–6
Martina Navratilova d. Hana Mandlikova 7–5, 6–1
Martina Navratilova–Pam Shriver d. Hana Mandlikova–Helena Sukova 6–4, 6–2

1987   Germany d. United States 2–1 (West Vancouver, British Columbia)
Pam Shriver d. Claudia Kohde Kilsch 6–0, 7–6
Steffi Graf d. Chris Evert 6–2, 6–1
Steffi Graf–Claudia Kohde Kilsh d. Chris Evert–Pam Shriver 1–6, 7–5 6–4

1988   Czechoslovakia d. U.S.S.R. 2–1 (Melbourne)
Radka Zrubakova (C) d. Larisa Savchenko 6–1, 7–6
Helena Sukova d. Natalia Zvereva 6–3, 6–4
Larisa Savchenko–Natalia Zvereva d. Jana Novotna–Jana Pospislova 7–6, 7–5

1989   United States d. Spain 3–0 (Tokyo)
Chris Evert d. Conchita Martinez 6–3, 6–2
Martina Navratilova d. Arantxa Sanchez Vicario 0–6, 6–3, 6–4
Zina Garrison–Pam Shriver d. Conchita Martinez–Arantxa Sanchez Vicario 7–5, 6–1

1990   United States d. U.S.S.R. 2–1 (Atlanta)
Jennifer Capriati d. Leila Meshki 7–6, 6–2
Natalia Zvereva d. Zina Garrison 4–6, 6–3, 6–3
Zina Garrison–Gigi Fernandez d. Natalia Zvereva–Larisa Savchenko 6–4, 6–3

1991   Spain d. United States 2–1 (Nottingham, England)
Jennifer Capriati d. Conchita Martinez 4–6, 7–6, 6–1
Arantxa Sanchez Vicario d. Mary Joe Fernandez 6–3, 6–4
Conchita Martinez–Arantxa Sanchez Vicario d. Gigi Fernandez–Zina Garrison 3–6, 6–1, 6–1

1992   Germany d. Spain 2–1 (Frankfurt)
Steffi Graf d. Arantxa Sanchez Vicario 6–4,

U.S. 1963–79

Most years played: 17—Virginia Wade, Britain, 1967–83

Most team matches played: 56—Wade

Most singles played: 55—Wade

Most singles won: 40—Chris Evert, U.S.

Most singles and doubles played together: 94—Wade

Most singles and doubles won together: 62—Wade

Most consecutive singles won: 29—Chris Evert Lloyd, U.S., 1977–86

WIGHTMAN CUP

Hoping to stimulate international interest in women's tennis as the Davis Cup did in men's, Hazel Hotchkiss Wightman, an all-time champion from Boston, donated a sterling vase to the USTA as a prize for such a team competition. It was decided to invite Great Britain to challenge for the prize in 1923 to open the new Forest Hills Stadium at the West Side Tennis Club in New York. With Mrs. Wightman as player-captain, the U.S. won the inaugural, 7–0. The rivalry was rewarding to both countries and initially developed into a close competition, an annual match between the two with the prize soon known as the Wightman Cup. The matches were played in even years in Britain and in odd years in the U.S.

Interrupted only by World War II, the series became dominated by the U.S., which mounted a 50–10 record through 1989, when both sides mutually agreed to suspend what was no longer a competition.

Wightman Cup Results

Year

1923   United States d. Great Britain 7–0 (Forest Hills)
Helen Wills d. Kitty McKane 6–2, 7–5
Molla Bjurstedt Mallory d. M. H. Davey Clayton 6–1, 8–6
Eleanor Goss d. Geraldine Beamish 6–2, 7–5
Helen Wills d. M. H. Clayton 6–2, 6–3
Molla Bjurstedt Mallory d. Kitty McKane 6–2, 6–3
Hazel Hotchkiss Wightman–Eleanor Goss d. Kitty McKane–Phyllis Covell 10–8, 5–7, 6–4
Molla Bjurstedt Mallory–Helen Wills Moody d. Geraldine Beamish–M. H. Clayton 6–3, 6–2

1924   Great Britain d. United States 6–1 (Wimbledon)
Phyllis Howkins Covell d. Helen Wills 6–2, 6–4
Kitty McKane d. Molla Bjurstedt Mallory 6–3, 6–3
Kitty McKane d. Helen Wills 6–2, 6–2
Phyllis Covell d. Molla Bjurstedt Mallory 6–2, 5–7, 6–3
Geraldine Beamish d. Eleanor Goss 6–1, 8–10, 6–3
Phyllis Covell–Dorothy Shepherd Barron d. Marion Jessup–Eleanor Goss 6–2, 6–2
Hazel Hotchkiss Wightman–Helen Wills (US) d. Kitty McKane–Evelyn Colyer 2–6, 6–2, 6–4

1925   Great Britain d. United States 4–3 (Forest Hills)
Kitty McKane d. Molla Bjurstedt Mallory 6–4, 5–7, 6–0
Helen Wills (US) d. Joan Fry 6–0, 7–5
Dorothea Douglass Lambert Chambers d. Eleanor Goss 7–5, 3–6, 6–1
Helen Wills (US) d. Kitty McKane 6–1, 1–6, 9–7

Molla Bjurstedt Mallory (US) d. Joan Fry 6–3, 6–0
Dorothea Douglass Lambert Chambers–Ermyntrude Harvey (GB) d. Molla Bjurstedt Mallory–May Sutton Bundy 10–8, 6–1
Kitty McKane–Evelyn Colyer (GB) d. Helen Wills–Mary K. Browne 6–0, 6–3

1926   United States d. Great Britain 4–3 (Wimbledon)
Elizabeth Ryan d. Joan Fry 6–1, 6–3
Kitty McKane Godfree (GB) d. Mary K. Browne 6–1, 7–5
Joan Fry (GB) d. Mary K. Browne 3–6, 6–0, 6–4
Kitty McKane Godfree (GB) d. Elizabeth Ryan 6–1, 5–7, 6–4
Marion Zinderstein Jessup d. Dorothy Shepherd Barron 6–1, 5–7, 6–4
Marion Jessup–Eleanor Goss d. Dorothea Douglass Lambert Chambers–Dorothy Shepherd Barron 6–4, 6–2
Mary K. Browne–Elizabeth Ryan d. Kitty McKane Godfree–Evelyn Colyer 3–6, 6–2, 6–4

1927   United States d. Great Britain 5–2 (Forest Hills)
Helen Wills d. Joan Fry 6–2, 6–0
Molla Bjurstedt Mallory d. Kitty McKane Godfree 6–4, 6–2
Betty Nuthall (GB) d. Helen Jacobs 6–3, 2–6, 6–1
Helen Wills d. Kitty McKane Godfree 6–1, 6–1
Molla Bjurstedt Mallory d. Joan Fry 6–2, 11–9
Gwendolyn Sterry–Betty Hill (GB) d. Eleanor Goss–Charlotte Hosmer Chapin 5–7, 7–5, 7–5
Helen Wills–Hazel Hotchkiss Wightman d. Kitty McKane Godfree–Ermyntrude Harvey 6–4, 4–6, 6–3

1928   Great Britain d. United States 4–3 (Wimbledon)
Helen Wills (US) d. Phoebe Holcroft Watson 6–1, 6–2
Eileen Bennett d. Molla Bjurstedt Mallory 6–1, 6–3
Helen Wills (US) d. Eileen Bennett 6–3, 6–2
Phoebe Holcroft Watson d. Molla Bjurstedt Mallory 2–6, 6–1, 6–2
Helen Jacobs (US) d. Betty Nuthall 6–3, 6–1
Ermyntrude Harvey–Peggy Saunders d. Eleanor Goss–Helen Jacobs 6–4, 6–1
Eileen Bennett–Phoebe Holcroft Watson d. Helen Wills–Penelope Anderson 6–2, 6–1

1929   United States d. Great Britain 4–3 (Forest Hills)
Helen Wills d. Phoebe Holcroft Watson 6–1, 6–4

Helen Jacobs d. Betty Nuthall 7–5, 8–6
Phoebe Watson (GB) d. Helen Jacobs 6–3, 6–2
Edith Cross d. Peggy Saunders Michell 6–3, 3–6, 6–3
Helen Wills d. Betty Nuthall 8–6, 8–6
Phoebe Watson–Peggy Michell (GB) d. Helen Wills–Edith Cross 6–4, 6–1
Phyllis Howkins Covell–Dorothy Shepherd Barron (GB) d. Hazel Hotchkiss Wightman–Helen Jacobs 6–2, 6–1

1930   Great Britain d. United States 4–3 (Wimbledon)

1931   United States d. Great Britain 5–2 (Forest Hills, N.Y.)
Helen Wills Moody d. Betty Nuthall 6–4, 6–2
Anna McCune Harper d. Dorothy Round 6–3, 4–6, 9–7
Helen Jacobs d. Phyllis Mudford 6–4, 6–2
Helen Moody d. Phyllis Mudford 6–1, 6–4
Helen Jacobs d. Betty Nuthall 8–6, 6–4
Phyllis Mudford–Dorothy Shepherd Barron (GB) d. Sarah Palfrey–Hazel Hotchkiss Wightman 6–4, 10–8
Betty Nuthall–Eileen Bennett Whittingstall (GB) d. Helen Moody–Anna Harper 8–6, 5–7, 6–3

1932   United States d. Great Britain 4–3 (Wimbledon)
Helen Jacobs d. Dorothy Round 6–4, 6–3
Helen Wills Moody d. Eileen Bennett Whittingstall 6–4, 6–2
Helen Moody d. Dorothy Round 6–2, 6–3
Eileen Bennett Whittingstall (GB) d. Helen Jacobs 6–4, 2–6, 6–4
Phyllis Mudford King (GB) d. Anna McCune Harper 3–6, 6–3, 6–1
Anna Harper–Helen Jacobs d. Peggy Saunders Michell–Dorothy Round 6–4, 6–1
Eileen Whittingstall–Betty Nuthall (GB) d. Helen Moody–Sarah Palfrey 6–3, 1–6, 10–8

1933   United States d. Great Britain 4–3 (Forest Hills)
Helen Jacobs d. Dorothy Round 6–4, 6–2
Sarah Palfrey d. Margaret Scriven 6–3, 6–1

Betty Nuthall (GB) d. Carolin Babcock 1–6, 6–1, 6–3
Dorothy Round (GB) d. Sarah Palfrey 6–4, 10–8
Helen Jacobs d. Margaret Scriven 5–7, 6–2, 7–5
Helen Jacobs–Sarah Palfrey d. Dorothy Round–Mary Heeley 6–4, 6–2
Betty Nuthall–Freda James (GB) d. Alice Marble–Marjorie Gladman Van Ryn 7–5, 6–2

1934   United States d. Great Britain 5–2

Helen Jacobs–Sarah Palfrey d. Kitty McKane Godfree–Betty Nuthall 5–7, 6–3, 6–2

1935   United States d. Great Britain 4–3 (Forest Hills)
Kay Stammers (GB) d. Helen Jacobs 5–7, 6–1, 9–7
Dorothy Round (GB) d. Ethel Burkhardt Arnold 6–0, 6–3
Sarah Palfrey Fabyan d. Phyllis Mudford King 6–0, 6–3
Helen Jacobs d. Dorothy Round 6–3, 6–2
Ethel Arnold d. Kay Stammers 6–2, 1–6, 6–3
Helen Jacobs–Sarah Palfrey Fabyan d. Kay Stammers–Freda James 6–3, 6–2
Nancy Lyle–Evelyn Dearman (GB) d. Dorothy Andrus–Carolin Babcock 3–6, 6–4, 6–1

1936   United States d. Great Britain 4–3 (Wimbledon)
Kay Stammers (GB) d. Helen Jacobs 12–10, 6–1
Dorothy Round (GB) d. Sarah Palfrey Fabyan 6–3, 6–4
Sarah Palfrey Fabyan d. Kay Stammers 6–3, 6–4
Dorothy Round (GB) d. Helen Jacobs 6–3, 6–3
Carolin Babcock d. Mary Hardwick 6–4, 4–6, 6–2
Carolin Babcock–Marjorie Gladman Van Ryn d. Evelyn Dearman–Nancy Lyle 6–2, 1–6, 6–3
Helen Jacobs–Sarah Palfrey Fabyan d. Kay Stammers–Freda James 1–6, 6–3, 7–5

1937   United States d. Great Britain 6–1 (Forest Hills)

Alice Marble d. Mary Hardwick 4–6, 6–2, 6–4
Helen Jacobs d. Kay Stammers 6–1, 4–6, 6–4
Helen Jacobs d. Mary Hardwick 2–6, 6–4, 6–2
Alice Marble d. Kay Stammers 6–3, 6–1
Sarah Palfrey Fabyan d. Margot Lumb 6–3, 6–1
Alice Marble–Sarah Palfrey Fabyan d. Evelyn
  Dearman–Joan Ingram 6–3, 6–2
Kay Stammers–Freda James (GB) d. Marjorie
  Gladman Van Ryn–Dorothy Bundy 6–3,
  10–8

1938   United States d. Great Britain 5–2
          (Wimbledon)
        Kay Stammers (GB) d. Alice Marble 3–6, 7–5,
          6–3
        Helen Wills Moody d. Margaret Scriven 6–0,
          7–5
        Sarah Palfrey Fabyan d. Margot Lumb 5–7,
          6–2, 6–3
        Alice Marble d. Margaret Scriven 6–3, 3–6, 6–0
        Helen Moody d. Kay Stammers 6–2, 3–6, 6–3
        Alice Marble–Sarah Palfrey Fabyan d. Margot
          Lumb–Freda James 6–4, 6–2
        Evelyn Dearman–Joan Ingram (GB) d. Helen
          Moody–Dorothy Bundy 6–2, 7–5

1939   United States d. Great Britain 5–2 (Forest
          Hills)
        Alice Marble d. Mary Hardwick 6–3, 6–4
        Kay Stammers (GB) d. Helen Jacobs 6–2, 1–6,
          6–3
        Valerie Scott (GB) d. Sarah Palfrey Fabyan
          6–3, 6–4
        Alice Marble d. Kay Stammers 3–6, 6–3, 6–4
        Helen Jacobs d. Mary Hardwick 6–2, 6–2
        Dorothy Bundy–Mary Arnold d. Betty
          Nuthall–Nina Brown 6–3, 6–1
        Alice Marble–Sarah Palfrey Fabyan d. Kay
          Stammers–Freda James Hammersley 7–5,
          6–2

1940–45 Not held

1946   United States d. Great Britain 7–0
          (Wimbledon)
        Pauline Betz d. Jean Bostock 6–2, 6–4
        Margaret Osborne d. Jean Bostock 6–1, 6–4
        Margaret Osborne d. Kay Stammers Menzies
          6–3, 6–2
        Louise Brough d. Joan Curry 8–6, 6–3
        Pauline Betz d. Kay Menzies 6–4, 6–4
        Margaret Osborne–Louise Brough d. Jean
          Bostock–Mary Halford 6–2, 6–1
        Pauline Betz–Doris Hart d. Betty
          Passingham–Molly Lincoln 6–1, 6–3

1947   United States d. Great Britain 7–0 (Forest Hills)
        Margaret Osborne d. Jean Bostock 6–4, 2–6,
          6–2
        Louise Brough d. Kay Stammers Menzies 6–4,
          6–2

Doris Hart d. Betty Hilton 4–6, 6–3, 7–5
Louise Brough d. Jean Bostock 6–4, 6–4
Margaret Osborne d. Kay Menzies 7–5, 6–2
Doris Hart–Pat Canning Todd d. Joy Gannon–
  Jean Quertier 6–1, 6–2
Margaret Osborne–Louise Brough d. Jean
  Bostock–Betty Hilton 6–1, 6–4

1948   United States d. Great Britain 6–1
          (Wimbledon)
        Margaret Osborne duPont d. Jean Bostock
          6–4, 8–6
        Louise Brough d. Betty Hilton 6–1, 6–1
        Margaret duPont d. Betty Hilton 6–3, 6–4
        Louise Brough d. Jean Bostock 6–2, 4–6,
          7–5
        Doris Hart d. Joy Gannon 6–1, 6–4
        Louise Brough–Margaret duPont d. Kay
          Stammers Menzies–Betty Hilton 6–2, 6–2
        Jean Bostock–Molly Lincoln Blair (GB) d.
          Doris Hart–Pat Canning Todd 6–3, 6–4

1949   United States d. Great Britain 7–0
          (Haverford, Pa.)
        Doris Hart d. Jean Walker Smith 6–3, 6–1
        Margaret Osborne duPont d. Betty Hilton
          6–1, 6–3
        Doris Hart d. Betty Hilton 6–1, 6–3
        Margaret duPont d. Jean Smith 6–4, 6–2
        Beverly Baker d. Jean Quertier 6–4, 7–5
        Doris Hart–Shirley Fry d. Jean Quertier–
          Molly Lincoln Blair 6–1, 6–2
        Gussy Moran–Pat Canning Todd d. Betty
          Hilton–Kay Tuckey 6–4, 8–6

1950   United States d. Great Britain 7–0
          (Wimbledon)
        Margaret Osborne duPont d. Betty Hilton
          6–3, 6–4
        Doris Hart d. Joan Curry 6–2, 6–4
        Louise Brough d. Betty Hilton 2–6, 6–2, 7–5
        Margaret duPont d. Jean Walker Smith 6–3,
          6–2
        Louise Brough d. Jean Smith 6–0, 6–0
        Pat Canning Todd–Doris Hart d. Jean Smith–
          Jean Quertier 6–2, 6–3
        Louise Brough–Margaret duPont d. Betty
          Hilton–Kay Tuckey 6–2, 6–0

1951   United States d. Great Britain 6–1 (Chestnut
          Hill, Mass.)
        Doris Hart d. Jean Quertier 6–4, 6–4
        Shirley Fry d. Jean Walker Smith 6–1, 6–4
        Maureen Connolly d. Kay Tuckey 6–1, 6–3
        Doris Hart d. Jean Smith 6–4, 2–6, 7–5
        Jean Quertier (GB) d. Shirley Fry 6–3, 8–6
        Pat Canning Todd–Nancy Chaffee d. Pat
          Ward–Joy Gannon Mottram 7–5, 6–3
        Shirley Fry–Doris Hart d. Jean Quertier–Kay
          Tuckey 6–3, 6–3

1952   United States d. Great Britain 7–0
          (Wimbledon)
        Doris Hart d. Jean Quertier-Rinkel 6–3, 6–3
        Maureen Connolly d. Jean Walker Smith 3–6,
          6–1, 7–5
        Doris Hart d. Jean Smith 7–5, 6–2
        Maureen Connolly d. Jean Rinkel 9–7, 6–2
        Shirley Fry d. Susan Partridge 6–0, 8–6
        Shirley Fry-Doris Hart d. Helen Fletcher-
          Jean Rinkel 8–6, 6–4
        Louise Brough-Maureen Connolly d. Joy
          Gannon Mottram-Pat Ward 6–0, 6–3

                    Fletcher 6–2, 6–1

1954   United States d. Great Britain 6–0
          (Wimbledon)
        Maureen Connolly d. Helen Fletcher 6–1, 6–3
        Doris Hart d. Ann Shilcock 6–4, 6–1
        Doris Hart d. Helen Fletcher 6–1, 6–8, 6–2
        Louise Brough d. Angela Buxton 8–6, 6–2
        Maureen Connolly d. Ann Shilcock 6–2, 6–2
        Louise Brough-Margaret Osborne duPont d.
          Angela Buxton-Pat Hird 2–6, 6–4, 7–5
        Helen Fletcher-Ann Shilcock vs Shirley Fry-
          Doris Hart not played

1955   United States d. Great Britain 6–1 (Rye, N.Y)
        Angela Mortimer (GB) d. Doris Hart 6–4,
          1–6, 7–5
        Louise Brough d. Shirley Bloomer 6–2, 6–4
        Louise Brough d. Angela Mortimer 6–0, 6–2
        Dorothy Head Knode d. Angela Buxton 6–3,
          6–3
        Doris Hart d. Shirley Bloomer 7–5, 6–3
        Louise Brough-Margaret duPont d. Shirley
          Bloomer-Pat Ward 6–3, 6–3
        Doris Hart-Shirley Bloomer d. Angela
          Mortimer-Angela Buxton 3–6, 6–2, 7–5

1956   United States d. Great Britain 5–2
          (Wimbledon)
        Louise Brough d. Angela Mortimer 3–6, 6–4,
          7–5
        Shirley Fry d. Angela Buxton 6–2, 6–8, 7–5
        Louise Brough d. Angela Buxton 3–6, 6–3, 6–4
        Shirley Bloomer (GB) d. Dorothy Head
          Knode 6–4, 6–4
        Angela Mortimer (GB) d. Shirley Fry 6–4, 6–3

        Dorothy Knode-Beverly Baker Fleitz d.
          Shirley Bloomer-Pat Ward 6–1, 6–4
        Louise Brough-Shirley Fry d. Angela Buxton-
          Angela Mortimer 6–2, 6–2

1957   United States d. Great Britain 6–1 (Sewickley,
          Pa.)
        Althea Gibson d. Shirley Bloomer 6–4, 4–6,
          6–2
        Dorothy Head Knode d. Christine Truman
          6–2, 11–9
        Ann Haydon (GB) d. Darlene Hard 6–3, 3–6,

        Althea Gibson (US) d. Shirley Bloomer 6–3,
          6–4
        Christine Truman d. Dorothy Head Knode
          6–4, 6–4
        Dorothy Knode (US) d. Shirley Bloomer 6–4,
          6–2
        Christine Truman d. Althea Gibson 2–6, 6–3,
          6–4
        Ann Haydon d. Mimi Arnold 6–3, 5–7, 6–3
        Christine Truman-Shirley Bloomer d. Karol
          Fageros-Dorothy Knode 6–2, 6–3
        Althea Gibson-Janet Hopps (US) d. Anne
          Shilcock-Pat Ward 6–4, 3–6, 6–3

1959   United States d. Great Britain 4–3 (Sewickley,
          Pa.)
        Beverly Baker Fleitz d. Angela Mortimer 6–2,
          6–1
        Christine Truman (GB) d. Darlene Hard 6–4,
          2–6, 6–3
        Darlene Hard d. Angela Mortimer 6–3, 6–8,
          6–4
        Beverly Fleitz d. Christine Truman 6–4, 6–4
        Ann Haydon (GB) d. Sally Moore 6–1, 6–1
        Darlene Hard-Jeanne Arth d. Shirley
          Bloomer Brasher-Christine Truman 9–7,
          9–7
        Ann Haydon-Angela Mortimer (GB) d. Janet
          Hopps-Sally Moore 6–2, 6–4

1960   Great Britain d. United States 4–3
          (Wimbledon)
        Ann Haydon d. Karen Hantze 2–6, 11–9, 6–1
        Darlene Hard (US) d. Christine Truman 4–6,
          6–3, 6–4
        Darlene Hard (US) d. Ann Haydon 5–7, 6–2,
          6–1

Christine Truman d. Karen Hantze 7–5, 6–3

Angela Mortimer d. Janet Hopps 6–8, 6–4, 6–1

Karen Hantze–Darlene Hard (US) d. Ann Haydon–Angela Mortimer 6–0, 6–0

Christine Truman–Shirley Bloomer Brasher d. Janet Hopps–Dorothy Head Knode 6–4, 9–7

1961   United States d. Great Britain 6–1 (Chicago)

Karen Hantze d. Christine Truman 7–9, 6–1, 6–1

Billie Jean Moffitt d. Ann Haydon 6–4, 6–4

Karen Hantze d. Ann Haydon 6–1, 6–4

Christine Truman (GB) d. Billie Jean Moffitt 6–3, 6–2

Justina Bricka d. Angela Mortimer 10–18, 4–6, 6–3

Karen Hantze–Billie Jean Moffitt d. Christine Truman–Deidre Catt 7–5, 6–2

Margaret Osborne duPont–Margaret Varner d. Angela Mortimer–Ann Haydon default

1962   United States d. Great Britain 4–3 (Wimbledon)

Darlene Hard d. Christine Truman 6–2, 6–2

Ann Haydon (GB) d. Karen Hantze Susman 10–8, 7–5

Deidre Catt (GB) d. Nancy Richey 6–1, 7–5

Darlene Hard d. Ann Haydon 6–3, 6–8, 6–4

Karen Susman d. Christine Truman 6–4, 7–5

Margaret Osborne duPont–Margaret Varner d. Deidre Catt–Elizabeth Starkie 6–2, 3–6, 6–2

Christine Truman–Ann Haydon (GB) d. Darlene Hard–Billie Jean Moffitt 6–4, 6–3

1963   United States d. Great Britain 6–1 (Cleveland)

Ann Haydon Jones (GB) d. Darlene Hard 6–1, 0–6, 8–6

Billie Jean Moffitt d. Christine Truman 6–4, 19–17

Nancy Richey d. Deidre Catt 14–12, 6–3

Darlene Hard d. Christine Truman 6–3, 6–0

Billie Jean Moffitt d. Ann Jones 6–4, 4–6, 6–3

Darlene Hard–Billie Jean Moffitt d. Christine Truman–Ann Jones 4–6, 7–5, 6–2

Nancy Richey–Donna Floyd Fales d. Deidre Catt–Elizabeth Starkie 6–4, 6–8, 6–2

1964   United States d. Great Britain 5–2 (Wimbledon)

Nancy Richey d. Deidre Catt 4–6, 6–4, 7–5

Billie Jean Moffitt d. Ann Haydon Jones 4–6, 6–2, 6–3

Carole Caldwell d. Elizabeth Starkie 6–4, 1–6, 6–3

Nancy Richey d. Ann Jones 7–5, 11–9

Billie Jean Moffitt d. Deidre Catt 6–3, 4–6, 6–3

Deidre Catt–Ann Jones (GB) d. Carole Caldwell–Billie Jean Moffitt 6–2, 4–6, 6–0

Angela Mortimer–Elizabeth Starkie (GB) d. Nancy Richey–Donna Floyd Fales 2–6, 6–3, 6–4

1965   United States d. Great Britain 5–2 (Cleveland)

Ann Haydon Jones (GB) d. Billie Jean Moffitt 6–2, 6–4

Nancy Richey d. Elizabeth Starkie 6–1, 6–0

Carole Caldwell Graebner d. Virginia Wade 3–6, 10–8, 6–4

Billie Jean Moffitt d. Elizabeth Starkie 6–3, 6–2

Ann Jones (GB) d. Nancy Richey 6–4, 8–6

Carole Graebner–Nancy Richey d. Nell Truman–Elizabeth Starkie 6–1, 6–0

Billie Jean Moffitt–Karen Hantze Susman d. Ann Jones–Virginia Wade 6–3, 8–6

1966   United States d. Great Britain 4–3 (Wimbledon)

Ann Haydon Jones (GB) d. Nancy Richey 2–6, 6–4, 6–3

Billie Jean Moffitt King d. Virginia Wade 6–2, 6–3

Winnie Shaw (GB) d. Mary Ann Eisel 6–3, 6–3

Nancy Richey d. Virginia Wade 2–6, 6–2, 7–5

Billie Jean King d. Ann Jones 5–7, 6–2, 6–3

Ann Jones–Virginia Wade (GB) d. Billie Jean King–Jane Albert 7–5, 6–2

Nancy Richey–Mary Ann Eisel d. Rita Bentley–Elizabeth Starkie 6–1, 6–2

1967   United States d. Great Britain 6–1 (Cleveland)

Billie Jean Moffitt King d. Virginia Wade 6–3, 6–2

Nancy Richey d. Ann Haydon Jones 6–2, 6–2

Christine Truman (GB) d. Rosie Casals 3–6, 7–5, 6–1

Nancy Richey d. Virginia Wade 3–6, 8–6, 6–2

Billie Jean Kind d. Ann Jones 6–1, 6–2

Rosie Casals–Billie Jean King d. Ann Jones–Virginia Wade 10–8, 6–4

Mary Ann Eisel–Carole Caldwell Graebner d. Winnie Shaw–Joyce Barclay Williams 8–6, 12–10

1968   Great Britain d. United States 4–3 (Wimbledon)

Nancy Richey (US) d. Christine Truman Janes 6–1, 8–6

Virginia Wade d. Mary Ann Eisel 6–0, 6–1

Jane "Peaches" Bartkowicz (US) d. Winnie Shaw 7–5, 3–6, 6–4

Mary Ann Eisel (US) d. Christine Janes 6–4, 6–3

Virginia Wade–Winnie Shaw d. Nancy Richey–Mary Ann Eisel 5–7, 6–4, 6–3

Nell Truman–Christine Janes d. Stephanie DeFina–Kathy Harter 6–3, 2–6, 6–3

1969   United States d. Great Britain 5–2 (Cleveland)

Julie Heldman d. Virginia Wade 3–6, 6–1, 8–6

Nancy Richey d. Winnie Shaw 8–6, 6–2
Jane "Peaches" Bartkowicz d. Christine
   Truman Janes 8–6, 6–0
Christine Janes–Nell Truman (GB) d. Mary
   Ann Eisel Curtis Val–Ziegenfuss 6–1, 3–6,
   6–4
Virginia Wade (GB) d. Nancy Richey 6–3,
   2–6, 6–3
Julie Heldman d. Winnie Shaw 6–3, 6–4
Julie Heldman–Jane "Peaches" Bartkowicz d.
   Winnie Shaw–Virginia Wade 6–4, 6–2

Eisel Curtis–Julie Heldman 6–3, 6–2
Billie Jean King–Jane "Peaches" Barkowitz d.
   Virginia Wade–Winnie Shaw 7–5, 6–8, 6–2

1971   United States d. Great Britain 4–3
          (Cleveland)
       Chris Evert d. Winnie Shaw 6–0, 6–4
       Virginia Wade (GB) d. Julie Heldman 7–5, 7–5
       Joyce Barclay Williams (GB) d. Kristy Pigeon
          7–5, 3–6, 6–4
       Mary Ann Eisel Curtis–Val Ziegenfuss d.
          Christine Truman Janes–Nell Truman
          6–1, 6–4
       Val Ziegenfuss d. Winnie Shaw 6–4, 4–6, 6–3
       Chris Evert d. Virginia Wade 6–1, 6–1
       Virginia Wade–Joyce Williams (GB) d. Carole
          Caldwell Graebner–Chris Evert 10–8, 4–6,
          6–1

1972   United States d. Great Britain 5–2
          (Wimbledon)
       Joyce Barclay Williams (GB) d. Wendy
          Overton 6–3, 3–6, 6–3
       Chris Evert d. Virginia Wade 6–4, 6–4
       Chris Evert–Patti Hogan d. Winnie Shaw–
          Nell Truman 7–5, 6–4
       Patti Hogan d. Corinne Molesworth 6–8, 6–4,
          6–2
       Chris Evert d. Joyce Williams 6–2, 6–3
       Virginia Wade (GB) d. Wendy Overton 8–6,
          7–5
       Val Ziegenfuss–Wendy Overton d. Virginia
          Wade–Joyce Willams 6–3, 6–3

1973   United States d. Great Britain 5–2 (Brookline,
          Mass.)
       Chris Evert d. Virginia Wade 6–4, 6–2

Patti Hogan d. Veronica Burton 6–4, 6–3
Linda Tuero d. Glynis Coles 7–5, 6–2
Virginia Wade–Glynis Coles (GB) d. Chris
   Evert–Marita Redondo 6–3, 6–4
Chris Evert d. Veronica Burton 6–3, 6–0
Virginia Wade (GB) d. Patti Hogan 6–2, 6–2
Patti Hogan–Jeanne Evert d. Lindsey Beaven–
   Lesley Charles 6–3, 4–6, 8–6

1974   Great Britain d. United States 6–1,
          (Queensferry, North Wales)
       Virginia Wade d. Julie Heldman 5–7, 9–7, 6–4
       Glynis Coles d. Janet Newberry 4–6, 6–1, 6–3

Sue Barker d. Janet Newberry 6–4, 7–5
Virginia Wade–Ann Haydon Jones d. Janet
   Newberry–Julie Anthony 6–2, 6–3, 7–6
Chris Evert d. Virginia Wade 6–3, 7–6
Glynis Coles d. Mona Schallau 6–3, 7–6
Glynis Coles–Sue Barker d. Chris Evert–Mona
   Schallau 7–5, 6–4

1976   United States d. Great Britain 5–2
          (Wimbledon)
       Chris Evert d. Virginia Wade 6–2, 3–6, 6–3
       Sue Barker (GB) d. Rosie Casals 1–6, 6–3, 6–2,
       Terry Holladay d. Glynis Coles 3–6, 6–1, 6–4
       Chris Evert–Rosie Casals d. Virginia Wade–
          Sue Barker 6–0, 5–7, 6–1
       Virginia Wade (GB) d. Rosie Casals 3–6, 9–7,
          ret.
       Chris Evert d. Sue Barker 2–6, 6–2, 6–2
       Ann Kiyomura–Mona Schallau Guerrant d.
          Sue Mappin–Lesley Charles 6–2, 6–2

1977   United States d. Great Britain 7–0 (Oakland)
       Chris Evert d. Virginia Wade 7–5, 7–6
       Billie Jean Moffitt King d. Sue Barker 6–1, 6–4
       Rosie Casals d. Michele Tyler 6–2, 3–6, 6–4
       Billie Jean King–Jo Anne Russell d. Sue
          Mappin–Lesley Charles 6–0, 6–1
       Billie Jean King d. Virginia Wade 6–4, 3–6, 8–6
       Chris Evert d. Sue Barker 6–1, 6–2
       Chris Evert–Rosie Casals d. Virginia Wade–
          Sue Barker 6–2, 6–4

1978   Great Britain d. United States 4–3 (London)
       Chris Evert (US) d. Sue Barker 6–2, 6–1
       Michele Tyler d. Pam Shriver 5–7, 6–3, 6–3
       Virginia Wade d. Tracy Austin 3–6, 7–5, 6–3
       Billie Jean King–Tracy Austin (US) d. Sue
          Mappin–Anne Hobbs 6–2, 4–6, 6–2

Chris Evert (US) d. Virginia Wade 6–0, 6–1
Sue Barker d. Tracy Austin 6–3, 3–6, 6–0
Virginia Wade–Sue Barker d. Chris Evert–
Pam Shriver 6–0, 5–7, 6–4

1979   United States d. Great Britain 7–0 (Palm
        Beach, Fla.)
        Chris Evert Lloyd d. Sue Barker 7–5, 6–2
        Kathy Jordan d. Anne Hobbs 6–4, 6–7, 6–2
        Tracy Austin d. Virginia Wade 6–1, 6–4
        Tracy Austin–Ann Kiyomura d. Jo Durie–
            Debbie Jevans 6–3, 6–1
        Tracy Austin d. Sue Barker 6–4, 6–2
        Chris Evert Lloyd d. Virginia Wade 6–1, 6–1
        Chris Evert Lloyd–Rosie Casals d. Virginia
            Wade–Sue Barker 6–0, 6–1

1980   United States d. Great Britain 5–2 (London)
        Chris Evert Lloyd d. Sue Barker 6–1 6–2
        Anne Hobbs d. Kathy Jordan 4–6, 6–4, 6–1
        Andrea Jaeger d. Virginia Wade 3–6, 6–3, 6–2
        Rosie Casals–Chris Evert Lloyd d. Glynis
            Coles–Anne Hobbs 6–3, 6–3
        Chris Evert Lloyd d. Virginia Wade 7–5, 3–6,
            7–5
        Sue Barker d. Andrea Jaeger 5–7, 6–3, 6–3
        Kathy Jordan–Anne Smith d. Sue Barker–
            Virginia Wade 6–4, 7–5

1981   United States d. Great Britain 8–1 (Chicago)
        Tracy Austin d. Sue Barker 7–5, 6–3
        Andrea Jaeger d. Anne Hobbs 6–0, 6–0
        Chris Evert Lloyd d. Virginia Wade 6–1, 6–3
        Andrea Jaeger–Pam Shriver d. Anne Hobbs–
            Jo Durie 6–1, 6–3
        Tracy Austin d. Virginia Wade 6–3, 6–1
        Chris Evert Lloyd d. Sue Barker 6–3, 6–0
        Chris Evert Lloyd–Rosie Casals d. Glynis
            Coles–Virginia Wade 6–3, 6–3

1982   United States d. Great Britain 6–1 (London)
        Barbara Potter d. Sue Barker 6–2, 6–2
        Anne Smith d. Virginia Wade 3–6, 7–5, 6–3
        Chris Evert Lloyd d. Jo Durie 6–2, 6–2
        Jo Durie–Anne Hobbs d. Rosie Casals–Anne
            Smith 6–3, 2–6, 6–2
        Barbara Potter d. Jo Durie 5–7, 7–6, 6–2
        Chris Evert Lloyd d. Sue Barker 6–4, 6–3
        Barbara Potter–Sharon Walsh d. Sue Barker–
            Virginia Wade 2–6, 6–4, 6–4

1983   United States d. Great Britain 6–1
        (Williamsburg, Va.)
        Martina Navratilova d. Sue Barker 6–2, 6–0
        Kathy Rinaldi d. Virginia Wade 6–2, 6–2
        Pam Shriver d. Jo Durie 6–3, 6–2
        Sue Barker–Virginia Wade d. Candy
            Reynolds–Paula Smith 7–5, 3–6, 6–1
        Pam Shriver d. Sue Barker 6–0, 6–1
        Martina Navratilova d. Jo Durie 6–3, 6–3

Martina Navratilova–Pam Shriver d. Annabel
    Croft–Jo Durie 6–2, 6–1

1984   United States d. Great Britain 5–2 (London)
        Chris Evert Lloyd d. Anne Hobbs 6–2, 6–2
        Annabel Croft d. Alycia Moulton 6–1, 5–7, 6–4
        Jo Durie d. Barbara Potter 6–3, 7–6
        Chris Evert Lloyd–Alycia Moulton d. Virginia
            Wade–Amanda Brown 6–2, 6–2 Barbara
            Potter d. Anne Hobbs 6–1, 6–3
        Chris Evert Lloyd d. Jo Durie 7–6, 6–1
        Barbara Potter–Sharon Walsh d. Jo Durie–
            Anne Hobbs 7–6, 4–6, 9–7

1985   United States d. Great Britain 7–0
        (Williamsburg, Va.)
        Chris Evert Lloyd d. Jo Durie 6–2, 6–3
        Kathy Rinaldi d. Anne Hobbs 7–5, 7–5
        Pam Shriver d. Annabel Croft 6–0, 6–0
        Betsy Nagelsen–Anne White d. Annabel
            Croft–Virginia Wade 6–4, 6–1
        Pam Shriver d. Jo Durie 6–4, 6–4
        Chris Evert Lloyd d. Annabel Croft 6–3, 6–0
        Chris Evert Lloyd–Pam Shriver d. Jo Durie–
            Anne Hobbs 6–3, 6–7, 6–2

1986   United States d. Great Britain 7–0 (London)
        Kathy Rinaldi d. Sara Gomer 6–3, 7–6
        Stephanie Rehe d. Annabel Croft 6–3, 6–1
        Bonnie Gadusek d. Jo Durie 6–2, 6–4
        Bonnie Gadusek–Kathy Rinaldi d. Annabel
            Croft–Sara Gomer 6–3, 5–7, 6–3
        Bonnie Gadusek d. Anne Hobbs 2–6, 6–4, 6–4
        Kathy Rinaldi d. Jo Durie 6–4, 6–2
        Elise Burgin–Anne White d. Jo Durie–Anne
            Hobbs 7–6, 6–3

1987   United States d. Great Britain 5–2
        (Williamsburg, Va.)
        Zina Garrison d. Anne Hobbs 7–5, 6–2
        Lori McNeil d. Sara Gomer 6–2, 6–1
        Pam Shriver d. Jo Durie 6–1, 7–5
        Beatrice Fernandez–Anne White d. Sara
            Gomer–Clare Wood 6–4, 6–1
        Pam Shriver d. Anne Hobbs 6–4, 6–3
        Jo Durie d. Zina Garrison 7–6, 6–3
        Jo Durie–Anne Hobbs d. Zina Garrison–Lori
            McNeil 0–6, 6–4, 7–5

1988   United States d. Great Britain 7–0 (London)
        Zina Garrison d. Jo Durie 6–2, 6–4
        Patty Fendick d. Monique Javer 6–2, 6–1
        Lori McNeil d. Sara Gomer 6–7, 6–4, 6–4
        Lori McNeil–Betsy Nagelsen d. Sara Gomer–
            Julie Salmon 6–3, 6–2
        Zina Garrison d. Claire Wood 6–3, 6–2
        Lori McNeil d. Jo Durie 6–1, 6–2
        Beatrice Fernandez–Zina Garrison d. Jo
            Durie–Clare Wood 6–1, 6–3

1989   United States d. Great Britain 7–0
        (Williamsburg, Va.)

Lori McNeil d. Jo Durie 7–5, 6–1
Jennifer Capriati d. Clare Wood 6–0, 6–0
Mary Joe Fernandez d. Sara Gomer 6–1, 6–2
Mary Joe Fernandez–Betsy Nagelsen d. Sara
   Gomer–Clare Wood 6–2 7–6
Lori McNeil d. Sara Gomer 6–4, 6–2 Mary Joe
   Fernandez d. Jo Durie 6–1, 7–5
Patty Fendick–Lori McNeil d. Jo Durie–Anne
   Hobbs 6–3, 6–3

Most doubles played: 20—Wade

Most doubles won: 10—Louise Brough, U.S., 1946–57

Most singles and doubles together: 55–Wade

Most singles and doubles won together: 34—Evert

Most consecutive singles won: 26—Evert

Best winning percentage, 15 or more wins, singles and doubles altogether: 1.000—Evert, 26 wins, 0 losses.

Best winning percentage singles, 10 or more wins: 1.000—Evert, 26–0.

Best winning percentage doubles, 5 or more wins: 1.000—Brough, 10 wins, 0 losses

Best doubles team record: 7–0—Margaret Osborne duPont and Brough, 1946–57

Longest singles: 46 games—Billie Jean Moffitt King, U.S. d. Christine Truman, 19–17, 6–4, 1963

Longest doubles: 40 games—Hazel Hotchkiss Wightman and Eleanor Goss, U.S., d. Kitty McKane and Phyllis Howkins Covell, 10–8, 5–7, 6–4, 1923

Most Cups won by captain: 12—Wightman, 1923–48

GRAND PRIX MASTERS/ATP WORLD CHAMPIONSHIP

The Grand Prix Masters was a playoff for the top eight players at the end of a year-long series of Grand Prix tournaments.

The players earned the right to play the Masters by accumulating points in tournaments throughout the year. It became a prestigious event from the time the first Masters was played under the sponsorship of Pepsi in 1970. Commercial Union sponsored the Grand Prix and the Masters from 1972 through 1976, and then Colgate 1977–79, Volvo from 1980-84, and Nabisco from 1985–89. When the MIPTC (Men's

Meanwhile, Colgate established the Colgate International Series for women in 1976. This meant that the women had their own Grand Prix, and when the top eight women assembled in Palm Springs for the Colgate Series Championship, the tournament was a female version of the Masters.

In 1981 Toyota replaced Colgate as the primary sponsor for the women's tour and in 1981 and 1982 they held the year-end championship. The top eight players of the year continued to compete in a round-robin, eight-player format. In 1982 the top 16 were invited for a conventional, single elimination event.

Men

<u>Year</u>

1970	(Tokyo) Stan Smith, won a round-robin among six players with 4-1 record.
1971	(Paris) Ilie Nastase, won a round-robin among seven players with 6-0 record
1972	(Barcelona) Ilie Nastase d. Stan Smith 6-3, 6-2, 3-6, 2-6, 6-3

1973	(Boston) Ilie Nastase d. Tom Okker 6-3, 7-5, 4-6, 6-3
1974	(Melbourne) Guillermo Vilas d. Ilie Nastase 7-6, 6-2, 3-6, 3-6, 6-4
1975	(Stockholm) Ilie Nastase d. Bjorn Borg 6-2, 6-2, 6-1
1976	(Houston) Manuel Orantes d. Wojtek Fibak 5-7, 6-2, 0-6, 7-6, 6-1
1977	(New York) Jimmy Connors d. Bjorn Borg 6-4, 1-6, 6-4
1978	(New York) John McEnroe d. Arthur Ashe 6-7, 6-3, 7-5
1979	(New York) Bjorn Borg d. Vitas Gerulaitis 6-2, 6-2
1980	(New York) Bjorn Borg d. Ivan Lendl 6-4, 6-2, 6-2
1981	(New York) Ivan Lendl d. Vitas Gerulaitis 6-7, 2-6, 7-6, 6-2, 6-4
1982	(New York) Ivan Lendl d. John McEnroe 6-4, 6-4, 6-2
1983	(New York) John McEnroe d. Ivan Lendl 6-3, 6-4, 6-4
1984	(New York) John McEnroe d. Ivan Lendl 7–5, 6–0, 6–4
1985	(New York) Ivan Lendl d. Boris Becker 6-2, 7-6, 6-3
1986	(New York) Ivan Lendl d. Boris Becker 6-4, 6-4, 6-4
1987	(New York) Ivan Lendl d. Mats Wilander 6-2, 6-2, 6-3
1988	(New York) Boris Becker d. Ivan Lendl 5-7, 7-6, 3-6, 6-2, 7-6
1989	(New York) Stefan Edberg d. Boris Becker 4-6, 7-6, 6-3, 6-1
1990	(Frankfurt) Andre Agassi d. Stefan Edberg 5-7, 7-6, 7-5, 6-2
1991	(Frankfurt) Pete Sampras d. Jim Courier 3-6, 7-6, 6-3, 6-4
1992	(Frankfurt) Boris Becker d. Jim Courier 6-4, 6-3, 7-5

Colgate Series/Toyota Series Champions (Women)

Year

1976	(Palm Springs, Cal.) Chris Evert d. Francoise Durr 6-1, 6-2
1977	(Palm Springs, Cal.) Chris Evert d. Billie Jean King 6-2, 6-2
1978	(Palm Springs, Cal.) Chris Evert d. Martina Navratilova 6-3, 6-3
1979	(Landover, Md.) Martina Navratilova d. Tracy Austin 6-2, 6-1
1980	(Landover, Md.) Tracy Austin d. Andre Jaeger 6-2, 6-2

| 1981 | (East Rutherford, N.J.) Tracy Austin d. Martina Navratilova 2-6, 6-4, 6-2 |
| 1982 | (East Rutherford, N.J.) Martina Navratilova d. Chris Evert Lloyd 4-6, 6-1, 6-2 |

VIRGINIA SLIMS/AVON

In the fall of 1970, eight leading women (including Billie Jean King) signed pro contracts with Gladys Heldman, founder of *World Tennis* magazine. They played a few small events that fall but by 1971 the Virginia Slims circuit had quickly expanded and the women competed for almost $200,000 in prize money. With interest growing faster than the players could ever have imagined, the first Virginia Slims Championship was played in Boca Raton, Florida in October of 1972. The top 32 players played the initial event. Eventually the Slims became a winter indoor circuit.

The field was reduced to sixteen players in 1974, when the tournament was moved to Los Angeles, and the format was changed to a round-robin with two groups of four players in 1976. The format remained the same through 1978, but a political struggle between the Women's Tennis Association and Virginia Slims resulted in the women electing to establish a new circuit with a new sponsor.

Avon, which had begun a Futures circuit designed to help young players get the opportunity to move up to the big tour, signed an agreement with the WTA to take over the Virginia Slims, and the sponsor continued the tradition of a circuit championship for the top eight players when it launched the first Avon Championship at Madison Square Garden in New York in March 1979.

In 1983, Virginia Slims was brought back in with the approval of the WTA to take over the tour sponsorship. They did not hold an official season-ending tournament that year but beginning in 1984, the Virginia Slims Championships became again one of the premier tournaments in the sport. In 1986, due to switch in dates from March to November, two Virginia Slims Championships were held at Madison Square Garden in New York. Thereafter, the event remained an authentic conclud-

1983	(New York) Martina Naratilove d. Chris Evert 6–2, 6–0
1984	(New York) Martina Navratilova d. Chris Evert Lloyd 6–3, 7–5, 6–1
1985	(New York) Martina Navratilova d. Helena Sukova 6–3, 7–5, 6–4
1986	(spring) (New York) Martina Navratilova d. Hana Mandlikova 6–2, 6–0, 3–6, 6–1
1986	(fall) (New York) Martina Navratilova d. Steffi Graf 7–6, 6–3, 6–2
1987	(New York) Steffi Graf d. Gabriela Sabatini 4–6, 6–4, 6–0, 6–4

Virginia Slims Championships

Year

1972	(Boca Raton, Fla.) Chris Evert d. Kerry Melville Reid 7–5, 6–4
1973	(Boca Raton, Fla.) Chris Evert d. Nancy Richey 6–3, 6–3
1974	(Los Angeles) Evonne Goolagong d. Chris Evert 6–3, 6–4
1975	(Los Angeles) Chris Evert d. Martina Navratilova 6–4, 6–2
1976	(Los Angeles) Evonne Goolagong d. Chris Evert 6–3, 5–7, 6–3
1977	(New York) Chris Evert d. Sue Barker 2–6, 6–1, 6–1
1978	(Oakland) Martina Navratilova d. Evonne Goolagong 7–6, 6–4

Avon Champions

Year

1979	(New York) Martina Navratilova d. Tracy Austin 6–3, 3–6, 6–2
1980	(New York) Tracy Austin d. Martina Navratilova 6–2, 2–6, 6–2
1981	(New York) Martina Navratilova d. Andrea Jaeger 6–3, 7–6
1982	(New York) Sylvia Hanika d. Martina Navratilova 1–6, 6–3, 6–4

WORLD CHAMPIONSHIP TENNIS

World Championship Tennis (WCT) was a Dallas-based professional tennis organization headed by Lamar Hunt. WCT became involved in tennis in 1967, the year before open tennis, when it signed up eight leading players to pro contracts and called them "The Handsome Eight." What began as a small pro circuit with these eight players (Dennis Ralston, Butch Buchholz, John Newcombe, Tony Roche, Nikki Pilic, Cliff Drysdale, Pierre Barthes, and Roger Taylor) grew into an important part of the international game.

WCT established a circuit of its own, and starting in 1971 the top eight players on the basis of points earned throughout the circuit came to Dallas for the WCT finals, the circuit championship. The first WCT finals was played in November 1971, but thereafter WCT established a May date for the annual event in Dallas. The WCT tournaments were eventually incorporated into the Grand Prix before they went on their own again. The last WCT Championship was held in 1989.

WCT Finals

Year

1971	Ken Rosewall d. Rod Laver 6–4, 1–6, 7–6, 7–6
1972	Ken Rosewall d. Rod Laver 4–6, 6–0, 6–3, 6–7, 7–6
1973	Stan Smith d. Arthur Ashe 6–3, 6–3, 4–6, 6–4
1974	John Newcombe d. Bjorn Borg 4–6, 6–3, 6–2, 6–3
1975	Arthur Ashe d. Bjorn Borg 3–6, 6–4, 6–4, 6–0
1976	Bjorn Borg d. Guillermo Vilas 1–6, 6–1, 7–5, 6–1
1977	Jimmy Connors d. Dick Stockton 6–7, 6–1, 6–4, 6–3
1978	Vitas Gerulaitis d. Eddie Dibbs 6–3, 6–2, 6–1
1979	John McEnroe d. Bjorn Borg 7–5, 4–6, 6–2, 7–6
1980	Jimmy Connors d. John McEnroe 2–6, 7–6, 6–1, 6–2
1981	John McEnroe d. Johan Kriek 6–1, 6–2, 6–4
1982	Ivan Lendl d. John McEnroe 6–2, 3–6, 6–3, 6–3
1983	John McEnroe d. Ivan Lendl 6–2, 4–6, 6–3, 6–7, 7–6
1984	John McEnroe d. Jimmy Connors 6–1, 6–2 6–3
1985	Ivan Lendl d. Tim Mayotte 7–6, 6–4, 6–1
1986	Anders Jarryd d. Boris Becker 6–7 6–1, 6–1, 6–4
1987	Miloslav Mecir d. John McEnroe 6–0, 3–6, 6–2 6–2
1988	Boris Becker d. Stefan Edberg 6–4, 1–6, 7–5, 6–2
1989	John McEnroe d. Brad Gilbert 6–3, 6–3 7–6

UNITED STATES
TENNIS ASSOCIATION RANKINGS

(Editor's Note: Every year the United States Tennis Association, formerly the U.S. Lawn Tennis Association, releases annual rankings for the leading male and female players in the country. Until 1972, these rankings included only amateur players, but when open tennis arrived in 1968, bringing the pros and amateurs together under the same roof, it was inevitable that the American rankings would soon include all players.)

USTA Men's Rankings

#Indicates foreign citizens residing in the U.S.
*Indicates tie

1885

1. Richard Sears
2. James Dwight
3. Walter Berry
4. Godfrey Brinley
5. Joseph Clark
6. Alex Moffat
7. Livingston Beeckman
8. Howard Taylor
9. Fred Mansfield
10. Percy Knapp

1886

1. Richard Sears
2. James Dwight
3. Livingston Beeckman
4. Howard Taylor
5. Joseph Clark
6. Henry Slocum
7. Godfrey Brinley
8. Fred Mansfield
9. Alex Moffat
10. Richard Conover

1887

1. Richard Sears
2. Henry Slocum
3. Livingston Beeckman
4. Howard Taylor
5. Joseph Clark
6. Fred Mansfield
7. Philip Sears
8. Godfrey Brinley
9. E. P. MacMullen
10. Quincy Shaw

1888

1. Henry Slocum
2. Howard Taylor
3. James Dwight
4. Joseph Clark
5. Charles Chase
6. Philip Sears
7. E. P. MacMullen
8. Oliver Campbell
9. Livingston Beeckman
10. Fred Mansfield

1889

1. Henry Slocum
2. Quincy Shaw
3. Oliver Campbell
4. Howard Taylor
5. Charles Chase
6. Joseph Clark
7. Percy Knapp
8. Bob Huntington
9. Philip Sears
10. Fred Mansfield

6. Clarence Hobart
7. Philip Sears
8. Howard Taylor
9. Charles Chase
10. Valentine Hall

1891

1. Oliver Campbell
2. Clarence Hobart
3. Bob Huntington
4. Fred Hovey
5. Edward Hall
6. Valentine Hall
7. Philip Sears
8. Samuel Chase
9. Charles Lee
10. Marmaduke Smith

1892

1. Oliver Campbell
2. Edward Hall
3. Percy Knapp
4. Clarence Hobart
5. Fred Hovey
6. Bill Larned
7. Malcolm Chace
8. Robert Wrenn
9. Richard Stevens
10. Charles Hubbard

1893

1. Robert Wrenn
2. Clarence Hobart
3. Fred Hovey
4. Malcolm Chace
5. Bill Larned
6. Edward Hall
7. Richard Stevens
8. Arthur Foote
9. John Howland
10. Clarence Budlong

6. Clarence Hobart
7. Richard Stevens
8. Clarence Budlong
9. Arthur Foote
10. Gordon Parker

1895

1. Fred Hovey
2. Bill Larned
3. Malcolm Chace
4. John Howland
5. Robert Wrenn
6. Carr Neel
7. Clarence Hobart
8. Richard Stevens
9. Arthur Foote
10. Clarence Budlong

1896

1. Robert Wrenn
2. Bill Larned
3. Carr Neel
4. Fred Hovey
5. Edwin Fischer
6. George Wrenn
7. Richard Stevens
8. Malcolm Whitman
9. Leo Ware
10. George Sheldon

1897

1. Robert Wrenn
2. Bill Larned
3. # Wilberforce Eaves
4. # Harold Nisbet
5. Harold Mahony
6. George Wrenn
7. # Malcolm Whitman
8. Kreigh Collins
9. Edwin Fischer
10. William Bond

1898

1. Malcolm Whitman
2. Leo Ware
3. William Bond
4. Dwight Davis
5. Clarence Budlong
6. Edwin Fischer
7. George Wrenn
8. Richard Stevens
9. Stephen Millett
10. George Belden

1899

1. Malcolm Whitman
2. Dwight Davis
3. Bill Larned
4. Parmly Paret
5. Kreigh Collins
6. George Wrenn
7. Leo Ware
8. Beals Wright
9. Holcombe Ward
10. Bob Huntington

1900

1. Malcolm Whitman
2. Dwight Davis
3. Bill Larned
4. Beals Wright
5. Kreigh Collins
6. George Wrenn
7. Holcolmbe Ward
8. Leo Ware
9. John Allen
10. Ray Little

1901

1. Bill Larned
2. Beals Wright
3. Dwight Davis
4. Leo Ware
5. Clarence Hobart
6. Ray Little
7. Holcombe Ward
8. Kreigh Collins
9. Edwin Fischer
10. Bill Clothier

1902

1. Bill Larned
2. Malcolm Whitman
3. Beals Wright
4. Holcolmbe Ward
5. Bill Clothier
6. Leo Ware
7. Ray Little
8. Kreigh Collins
9. Harold Hackett
10. Clarence Hobart

1903

1. Bill Larned
2. Holcolmbe Ward
3. Bill Clothier
4. Beals Wright
5. Kreigh Collins
6. Edward Larned
7. Harry Allen
8. Edgar Leonard
9. Richard Carleton
10. Ken Horton

1904

1. Holcombe Ward
2. Bill Clothier
3. Bill Larned
4. Beals Wright
5. Kreigh Collins
6. Ray Little
7. Fred Alexander
8. Richard Stevens
9. Alphonzo Bell
10. Edgar Leonard

1905

1. Beals Wright
2. Holcombe Ward
3. Bill Larned
4. Bill Clothier
5. Fred Alexander
6. Clarence Hobart
7. Richard Stevens
8. Kreigh Collins
9. Ray Little
10. Fred Anderson

6. Ray Little
7. Harold Hackett
8. Fred Anderson
9. Ed Dewhurst
10. Irving Wright

1907

1. Bill Larned
2. Beals Wright
3. Karl Behr
4. Ray Little
5. Bob LeRoy
6. Clarence Hobart
7. Edward Larned
8. Robert Seaver
9. Irving Wright
10. Fred Colston

1908

1. Bill Larned
2. Beals Wright
3. Fred Alexander
4. Bill Clothier
5. Ray Little
6. Bob LeRoy
7. Nat Emerson
8. Nat Niles
9. Wallace Johnson
10. Richard Palmer

1909

1. Bill Larned
2. Bill Clothier
3. Wallace Johnson
4. Nat Niles
5. Ray Little
6. Maurice McLoughlin
7. Melville Long
8. Karl Behr
9. Edward Larned
10. Bob LeRoy

6. Nat Niles
7. Gus Touchard
8. Theodore Pell
9. Fred Colston
10. Carlton Gardner

1911

1. Bill Larned
2. Maurice McLoughlin
3. Tom Bundy
4. Gus Touchard
5. Melville Long
6. Nat Niles
7. Theodore Pell
8. Ray Little
9. Karl Behr
10. Walter Hall

1912

1. Maurice McLoughlin
2. Dick Williams
3. Wallace Johnson
4. Bill Clothier
5. Nat Niles
6. Tom Bundy
7. Karl Behr
8. Ray Little
9. George "Peebo" Gardner
10. Gus Touchard

1913

1. Maurice McLoughlin
2. Dick Williams
3. Bill Clothier
4. Bill Johnston
5. Theodore Pell
6. Nat Niles
7. Wallace Jonhson
8. Gus Touchard
9. George "Peebo" Gardner
10. John Strachan

1914

1. Maurice McLoughlin
2. Dick Williams
3. Karl Behr
4. R. Lindley Murray
5. Bill Clothier
6. Bill Johnston
7. George Church
8. Fred Alexander
9. Watson Washburn
10. Elia Fottrell

1915

1. Bill Johnston
2. Dick Williams
3. Maurice McLoughlin
4. Karl Behr
5. Theodore Pell
6. Nat Niles
7. Clarence Griffin
8. Watson Washburn
9. George Church
10. Walter Hall

1916

1. Dick Williams
2. Bill Johnston
3. George Church
4. R. Lindley Murray
5. # Ichiya Kumagae
6. Clarence Griffin
7. Watson Washburn
8. Wallace Davis
9. Joseph Armstrong
10. Dean Mathey

1917 No rankings

1918

1. R. Lindley Murray
2. Bill Tilden
3. Fred Alexander
4. Walter Hall
5. Walter Hayes
6. Nat Niles
7. # Ichiya Kumagae
8. Chuck Garland
9. Howard Voshell
10. Theodore Pell

1919

1. Bill Johnston
2. Bill Tilden
3. # Ichiya Kumagae
4. R. Lindley Murray
5. Wallace Johnson
6. Dick Williams
7. Roland Roberts
8. Chuck Garland
9. Walter Hayes
10. Watson Washburn

1920

1. Bill Tilden
2. Bill Johnston
3. Dick Williams
4. # Ichiya Kumagae
5. Willis Davis
6. Clarence Griffin
7. Watson Washburn
8. Chuck Garland
9. Nat Niles
10. Wallace Johnson

1921

1. Bill Tilden
2. Bill Johnston
3. Vinnie Richards
4. Wallace Johnson
5. Watson Washburn
6. Dick Williams
7. # Ichiya Kumagae
8. Howard Voshell
9. Larry Rice
10. Nat Niles

1922

1. Bill Tilden
2. Bill Johnston
3. Vinnie Richards
4. Dick Williams
5. Wallace Johnson
6. Bob Kinsey
7. # Zenzo Shimidzu
8. Howard Kinsey
9. Frank Hunter
10. Watson Washburn

6. Howard Kinsey
7. Carl Fischer
8. # Brian Norton
9. Harvey Snodgrass
10. Bob Kinsey

1924

1. Bill Tilden
2. Vinnie Richards
3. Bill Johnston
4. Howard Kinsey
5. Wallace Johnson
6. Harvey Snodgrass
7. John Hennessey
8. # Brian Norton
9. George Lott
10. Clarence Griffin

1925

1. Bill Tilden
2. Bill Johnston
3. Vinnie Richards
4. Dick Williams
5. # Manuel Alonso
6. Howard Kinsey
7. # Takeichi Harada
8. Cranston Holman
9. # Brian Norton
10. Wray Brown

1926

1. Bill Tilden
2. # Manuel Alonso
3. # Takeichi Harada
4. Bill Johnston
5. Ed Chandler
6. Lewis White
7. Al Chapin
8. # Brian Norton
9. George Lott
10. George King

6. John Van Ryn
7. Arnold Jones
8. John Doeg
9. Lewis White
10. Cranston Holman

1928

1. Bill Tilden
2. Frank Hunter
3. George Lott
4. John Hennessey
5. Wilmer Allison
6. John Van Ryn
7. Fred Mercur
8. John Doeg
9. Julius Seligson
10. Frank Shields

1929

1. Bill Tilden
2. Frank Hunter
3. John Doeg
4. George Lott
5. John Van Ryn
6. Fred Mercur
7. Wilmer Allison
8. Wilbur Coen
9. Berkeley Bell
10. Greg Mangin

1930

1. John Doeg
2. Frank Shields
3. Wilmer Allison
4. Sidney Wood
5. Cliff Sutter
6. Greg Mangin
7. George Lott
8. Ellsworth Vines
9. John Van Ryn
10. Bryan "Bitsy" Grant

1931

1. Ellsworth Vines
2. George Lott
3. Frank Shields
4. John Van Ryn
5. John Doeg
6. Cliff Sutter
7. Sidney Wood
8. Keith Gledhill
9. Wilmer Allison
10. Berkeley Bell

1932

1. Ellsworth Vines
2. Wilmer Allison
3. Cliff Sutter
4. Sidney Wood
5. Frank Shields
6. Lester Stoefen
7. Greg Mangin
8. Keith Gledhill
9. John Van Ryn
10. David Jones

1933

1. Frank Shields
2. Wilmer Allison
3. Lester Stoefen
4. Cliff Sutter
5. Greg Mangin
6. Sidney Wood
7. Bryan "Bitsy" Grant
8. Frank Parker
9. Keith Gledhill
10. George Lott

1934

1. Wilmer Allison
2. Sidney Wood
3. Frank Shields
4. Frank Parker
5. Lester Stoefen
6. George Lott
7. Berkeley Bell
8. Cliff Sutter
9. Don Budge
10. Bryan "Bitsy" Grant

1935

1. Wilmer Allison
2. Don Budge
3. Bryan "Bitsy" Grant
4. Frank Shields
5. Sidney Wood
6. Greg Mangin
7. Frank Parker
8. Gilbert Hall
9. Wilmer Hines
10. Berkeley Bell

1936

1. Don Budge
2. Frank Parker
3. Bryan "Bitsy" Grant
4. Bobby Riggs
5. Greg Mangin
6. John Van Ryn
7. John McDiarmid
8. Charlie Harris
9. Joe Hunt
10. Arthur Hendrix

1937

1. Don Budge
2. Bobby Riggs
3. Frank Parker
4. Bryan "Bitsy" Grant
5. Joe Hunt
6. Wayne Sabin
7. Harold Surface
8. Gene Mako
9. Don McNeill
10. John Van Ryn

1938

1. Don Budge
2. Bobby Riggs
3. Gene Mako
4. Sidney Wood
5. Joe Hunt
6. Bryan "Bitsy" Grant
7. Elwood Cooke
8. Frank Parker
9. Gilbert Hunt
10. Frank Kovacs

1942

1. Ted Schroeder
2. Frank Parker
3. Gardnar Mulloy
4. Francisco "Pancho" Segura
5. Bill Talbert
6. Sidney Wood
7. Seymour Greenberg
8. George Richards
9. Vic Seixas
10. Ladislav Hecht

6. Elwood Cooke
7. Bryan "Bitsy" Grant
8. Gardnar Mulloy
9. Gilbert Hunt
10. Henry Prusoff

6. Sidney Wood
7. Bob Falkenburg
8. Frank Parker
9. Jim Brink
10. Jack Tuero

1940

1. Don McNeill
2. Bobby Riggs
3. Frank Kovacs
4. Joe Hunt
5. Frank Parker
6. Jack Kramer
7. Gardnar Mulloy
8. Henry Prusoff
9. Elwood Cooke
10. Ted Schroeder

1944

1. Frank Parker
2. Bill Talbert
3. Francisco "Pancho" Segura
4. Don McNeill
5. Seymour Greenberg
6. Bob Falkenburg
7. Jack Jossi
8. Charles Oliver
9. Jack McManis
10. Gilbert Hall

1941

1. Bobby Riggs
2. Frank Kovacs
3. Frank Parker
4. Don McNeill
5. Ted Schroeder
6. Wayne Sabin
7. Gardnar Mulloy
8. Bryan "Bitsy" Grant
9. Jack Kramer
10. Bill Talbert

1945

1. Frank Parker
2. Bill Talbert
3. Francisco "Pancho" Segura
4. Elwood Cooke
5. Sidney Wood
6. Gardnar Mulloy
7. Frank Shields
8. Hal Surface
9. Seymour Greenberg
10. Jack McManis

1946

1. Jack Kramer
2. Ted Schroeder
3. Frank Parker
4. Tom Brown
5. Gardnar Mulloy
6. Bill Talbert
7. Don McNeill
8. Bob Falkenburg
9. Eddie Moylan
10. Francisco "Pancho" Segura

1947

1. Jack Kramer
2. Frank Parker
3. Ted Schroeder
4. Gardnar Mulloy
5. Bill Talbert
6. Francisco "Pancho" Segura
7. Bob Falkenburg
8. Eddie Moylan
9. Earl Cochell
10. Seymour Greenberg

1948

1. Richard "Pancho" Gonzalez
2. Ted Schroeder
3. Frank Parker
4. Bill Talbert
5. Bob Falkenburg
6. Earl Cochell
7. Vic Seixas
8. Gardnar Mulloy
9. Herbie Flam
10. Harry Likas

1949

1. Richard "Pancho" Gonzalez
2. Ted Schroeder
3. Bill Talbert
4. Frank Parker
5. Gardnar Mulloy
6. Art Larsen
7. Earl Cochell
8. Sammy Match
9. Eddie Moylan
10. Herbie Flam

1950

1. Art Larsen
2. Herbie Flam
3. Ted Schroeder
4. Gardnar Mulloy
5. Bill Talbert
6. Dick Savitt
7. Earl Cochell
8. Vic Seixas
9. Tom Brown
10. Sammy Match

1951

1. Vic Seixas
2. Dick Savitt
3. Tony Trabert
4. Herbie Flam
5. Bill Talbert
6. Art Larsen
7. Ted Schroeder
8. Gardnar Mulloy
9. Ham Richardson
10. Budge Patty

1952

1. Gardnar Mulloy
2. Vic Seixas
3. Art Larsen
4. Dick Savitt
5. Herbie Flam
6. Bill Talbert
7. Ham Richardson
8. Tom Brown
9. Noel Brown
10. Harry Likas

1953

1. Tony Trabert
2. Vic Seixas
3. Art Larsen
4. Gardnar Mulloy
5. Straight Clark
6. Ham Richardson
7. Bernard "Tut" Bartzen
8. Tom Brown
9. Noel Brown
10. Grant Golden

1954

1. Vic Seixas
2. Tony Trabert
3. Ham Richardson
4. Art Larsen
5. Gardnar Mulloy
6. Tom Brown
7. Eddie Moylan
8. Bernard "Tut" Bartzen
9. Bill Talbert

6. Gilbert Shea
7. Ham Richardson
8. Herbie Flam
9. Sammy Giammalva
10. Tom Brown

1956

1. Ham Richardson
2. Herbie Flam
3. Vic Seixas
4. Eddie Moylan
5. Bernard "Tut" Bartzen
6. Bob Perry
7. Sammy Giammalva
8. Art Larsen
9. Gilbert Shea
10. Grant Golden

1957

1. Vic Seixas
2. Herbie Flam
3. Dick Savitt
4. Gilbert Shea
5. Barry MacKay
6. Ron Holmberg
7. Tom Brown
8. Whitney Reed
9. Bernard "Tut" Bartzen
10. William Quillian

1958

1. Ham Richardson
2. # Alex Olmedo
3. Barry MacKay
4. Bernard "Tut" Bartzen
5. Herbie Flam
6. Dick Savitt
7. Sammy Giammalva
8. Vic Seixas
9. Earl "Butch" Buchholz

6. Earl "Butch" Buchholz
7. Mike Franks
8. Noel Brown
9. Whitney Reed
10. Vic Seixas

1960

1. Barry MacKay
2. Bernard "Tut" Bartzen
3. Earl "Butch" Buchholz
4. Chuck McKinley
5. Dennis Ralston
6. Jon Douglas
7. Ron Holmberg
8. Whitney Reed
9. Donald Dell
10. Chris Crawford

1961

1. Whitney Reed
2. Chuck McKinley
3. Bernard "Tut" Bartzen
4. Jon Douglas
5. Donald Dell
6. Frank Froehling III
7. Ron Holmberg
8. Allen Fox
9. Jack Frost
10. Bill Bond

1962

1. Chuck McKinley
2. Frank Froehling III
3. Ham Richardson
4. Allen Fox
5. Jon Douglas
6. Whitney Reed
7. Donald Dell
8. Gene Scott
9. Marty Riessen
10. Charlie Pasarell

1963

1. Chuck McKinley
2. Dennis Ralston
3. Frank Froehling III
4. Gene Scott
5. Marty Riessen
6. Arthur Ashe
7. Ham Richardson
8. Allen Fox
9. Tom Edlefsen
10. Charlie Pasarell

1964

1. Dennis Ralston
2. Chuck McKinley
3. Arthur Ashe
4. Frank Froehling III
5. Gene Scott
6. Ron Holmberg
7. Ham Richardson
8. Allen Fox
9. Clark Graebner
10. Marty Riessen

1965

1. Dennis Ralston
2. Arthur Ashe
3. Cliff Richey
4. Chuck McKinley
5. Charlie Pasarell
6. Ham Richardson
7. # Mike Belkin
8. Marty Riessen
9. Ron Holmberg
10. Tom Edlefsen

1966

1. Dennis Ralston
2. Arthur Ashe
3. Clark Graebner
4. Charlie Pasarell
5. Cliff Richey
6. Ron Holmberg
7. Marty Riessen
8. Frank Froehling III
9. Vic Seixas
10. Chuck McKinley

1967

1. Charlie Pasarell
2. Arthur Ashe
3. Cliff Richey
4. Clark Graebner
5. Marty Riessen
6. Ron Holmberg
7. Stan Smith
8. Allen Fox
9. Gene Scott
10. Bob Lutz

1968

1. Arthur Ashe
2. Clark Graebner
3. Stan Smith
4. Cliff Richey
5. Bob Lutz
6. Ron Holmberg
7. Charlie Pasarell
8. Jim Osborne
9. Jim McManus
10. Gene Scott

1969

1. Stan Smith
2. Arthur Ashe
3. Cliff Richey
4. Clark Graebner
5. Charlie Pasarell
6. Bob Lutz
7. Tom Edlefsen
8. Roy Barth
9. Jim Osborne
10. Jim McManus

1970

1. Cliff Richey
2. Stan Smith
3. Arthur Ashe
4. Clark Graebner
5. Bob Lutz
6. Tom Gorman
7. Jim Osborne
8. Jim McManus
9. Barry MacKay
10. Charlie Pasarell

1972

1. Stan Smith
2. Tom Gorman
3. Jimmy Connors
4. Dick Stockton
5. Roscoe Tanner
6. Harold Solomon
7. Erik van Dillen
8. Clark Graebner
9. Richard "Pancho" Gonzalez
10. Brian Gottfried

9. Alex Olmedo
10. Harold Solomon

6. Charlie Pasarell
7. Marty Riessen
8. Erik van Dillen
9. Brian Gottfried
10. Bob Lutz

All-American Ranking, 1970–71

(In 1970 and 1971 contract professionals were not included in the traditional rankings. In those years an additional All-American ranking was made to include professionals of every status.)

1974

1. Jimmy Connors
2. Stan Smith
3. Marty Riessen
4. Roscoe Tanner
5. Arthur Ashe
6. Tom Gorman
7. Dick Stockton
8. Harold Solomon
9. Charlie Pasarell
10. Jeff Borowiak

1970

1. Cliff Richey
2. Stan Smith
3. Martin Riessen
4. Arthur Ashe
5. Dennis Ralston
6. Richard "Pancho" Gonzalez
7. Clark Graebner
8. Robert Lutz
9. Tom Gorman
10. Earl " Butch" Buchholtz

1975

1. Arthur Ashe
2. Jimmy Connors
3. Roscoe Tanner
4. Vitas Gerulaitis
5. Eddie Dibbs
6. Brian Gottfried
7. Harold Solomon
8. Bob Lutz
9. Cliff Richey
10. Dick Stockton

1971

1. Stan Smith
2. Arthur Ashe
3. Martin Riessen
4. Cliff Richey
5. Clark Graebner
6. Tom Gorman
7. Jimmy Connors
8. Erik van Dillen
9. Frank Froehling III
10. Robert Lutz

1976

1. Jimmy Connors
2. Eddie Dibbs
3. Arthur Ashe
4. Harold Solomon
5. Brian Gottfried
6. Roscoe Tanner
7. Dick Stockton
8. Stan Smith
9. Vitas Gerulaitis
10. Bob Lutz

1977

1. Jimmy Connors
2. Brian Gottfried
3. Vitas Gerulaitis
4. Eddie Dibbs
5. Dick Stockton
6. Harold Solomon
7. Stan Smith
8. Roscoe Tanner
9. Bob Lutz
10. John McEnroe

1978

1. Jimmy Connors
2. Vitas Gerulaitis
3. Brian Gottfried
4. Eddie Dibbs
5. John McEnroe
6. Alex "Sandy" Mayer
7. Roscoe Tanner
8. Harold Solomon
9. Arthur Ashe
10. Dick Stockton

1979

1. John McEnroe
2. Jimmy Connors
3. Roscoe Tanner
4. Vitas Gerulaitis
5. Arthur Ashe
6. Eddie Dibbs
7. Harold Solomon
8. Peter Fleming
9. Gene Mayer
10. Brian Gottfried

1980

1. John McEnroe
2. Jimmy Connors
3. Gene Mayer
4. Vitas Gerulaitis
5. Harold Solomon
6. Brian Gottfried
7. Eddie Dibbs
8. Roscoe Tanner
9. Eliot Teltscher
10. Stan Smith

1981

1. John McEnroe
2. Jimmy Connors
3. Gene Mayer
4. Brian Teacher
5. Vitas Gerulaitis
6. Eliot Teltscher
7. Roscoe Tanner
8. Brian Gottfried
9. Bill Scanlon
10. Mel Purcell

1982

1. Jimmy Connors
2. John McEnroe
3. Vitas Gerulaitis
4. Gene Mayer
5. Alex "Sandy" Mayer
6. Johan Kriek
7. Eliot Teltscher
8. Brian Teacher
9. Steve Denton
10. Brian Gottfried

1983

1. John McEnroe
2. Jimmy Connors
3. Jimmy Arias
4. Gene Mayer
5. Bill Scanlon
6. Eliot Teltscher
7. Johan Kriek
8. Alex "Sandy" Mayer
9. Brian Teacher
10. Brian Gottfried

1984

1. John McEnroe
2. Jimmy Connors
3. Johan Kriek
4. Eliot Teltscher
5. Jimmy Arias
6. Aaron Krickstein
7. Vitas Gerulaitis
8. Gene Mayer
9. Brad Gilbert

6. Paul Annacone
7. Brad Gilbert
8. Eliot Teltscher
9. Scott Davis
10. Greg Holmes

1986

1. Jimmy Connors
2. John McEnroe
3. Brad Gilbert
4. Tim Mayotte
5. Kevin Curren
6. Robert Seguso
7. Aaron Krickstein
8. Johan Kriek
9. David Pate
10. Tim Wilkison

1987

1. Jimmy Connors
2. John McEnroe
3. Tim Mayotte
4. Brad Gilbert
5. David Pate
6. Eliot Teltscher
7. Paul Annacone
8. Jimmy Arias
9. Kevin Curren
10. Andre Agassi

1988

1. Andre Agassi
2. Jimmy Connors
3. John McEnroe
4. Tim Mayotte
5. Aaron Krickstein
6. Kevin Curren
7. Brad Gilbert
8. Michael Chang
9. Robert Seguso
10. Dan Goldie

6. Tim Mayotte
7. Jay Berger
8. Jimmy Connors
9. Kevin Curren
10. Jim Courier

1990

1. Andre Agassi
2. Pete Sampras
3. Brad Gilbert
4. John McEnroe
5. Jay Berger
6. Michael Chang
7. Jim Courier
8. David Wheaton
9. Aaron Krickstein
10. Richey Reneberg

1991

1. Jim Courier
2. Pete Sampras
3. Andre Agassi
4. Michael Chang
5. David Wheaton
6. Derrick Rostagno
7. Jimmy Connors
8. Brad Gilbert
9. John McEnroe
10. Richey Reneberg

1992

1. Jim Courier
2. Pete Sampras
3. Michael Chang
4. Andre Agassi
5. Ivan Lendl
6. John McEnroe
7. Aaron Krickstein
8. MaliVai Washington
9. David Wheaton
10. Brad Gilbert

USTA Women's Rankings

1913

1. Mary K. Browne
2. Ethel Sutton Bruce
3. Florence Sutton
4. Helen Homans McLean
5. Louise Riddell Williams
6. Marie Wagner
7. Dorothy Green Briggs
8. Edith Rotch
9. Anita Myers
10. Gwendolyn Rees

1914

1. Mary K. Browne
2. Florence Sutton
3. Marie Wagner
4. Louise Hammond Raymond
5. Edith Rotch
6. Eleonora Sears
7. Louise Riddell Williams
8. Sarita Van Vliet Wood
9. Mrs H. Niemeyer
10. Sara Livingston

1915

1. Molla Bjurstedt
2. Hazel Hotchkiss Wightman
3. Helen Homans McLean
4. Florence Sutton
5. Maud Barger Wallach
6. Marie Wagner
7. Anita Myers
8. Sara Livingston
9. Clare Cassel
10. Eleonora Sears

1916

1. Molla Bjurstedt
2. Louise Hammond Raymond
3. Evelyn Sears
4. Anita Myers
5. Sara Livingston
6. Marie Wagner
7. Adelaide Browning Green
8. Martha Guthrie
9. Eleonora Sears
10. Maud Barger Wallach

1917

No rankings

1918

1. Molla Bjurstedt
2. Hazel Hotchkiss Wightman
3. Adelaide Browning Green
4. Eleanor Goss
5. Marie Wagner
6. Carrie Neely
7. Corinne Gould
8. Helene Pollak
9. Edith Handy
10. Clare Cassel

1919

1. Hazel Hotchkiss Wightman
2. Eleanor Goss
3. Molla Bjurstedt Mallory
4. Marion Zinderstein
5. Helen Baker
6. Louise Hammond Raymond
7. Helen Gilleaudau
8. Marie Wagner
9. Corinne Gould
10. Helene Pollak

1920

1. Molla Bjurstedt Mallory
2. Marion Zinderstein
3. Eleanor Tennant
4. Helen Baker
5. Eleanor Goss
6. Louise Hammond Raymond
7. Helene Pollack
8. Edith Sigourney
9. Florence Ballin
10. Marie Wagner

1921

1. Molla Bjurstedt Mallory
2. Mary K. Browne
3. Marion Zinderstein Jessup
4. May Sutton Bundy
5. Eleanor Goss
6. Helen Gilleaudeau
7. Anne Sheafe Cole
8. Leslie Bancroft
9. Louise Hammond Raymond
10. Margaret Grove

6. Martha Bayard
7. Helen Gilleaudeau
8. Mollie Thayer
9. Marie Wagner
10. Florence Ballin

1923

1. Helen Wills
2. Molla Bjurstedt Mallory
3. Eleanor Goss
4. Lillian Scharman
5. Helen Gilleaudeau Lockhorn
6. Mayme MacDonald
7. Edith Sigourney
8. Leslie Bancroft
9. Martha Bayard
10. Helen Hooker

1924

1. Helen Wills
2. Mary K. Browne
3. Molla Bjurstedt Mallory
4. Eleanor Goss
5. Marion Zinderstein Jessup
6. Martha Bayard
7. Mayme MacDonald
8. Anne Sheafe Cole
9. Mollie Thayer
10. Leslie Bancroft

1925

1. Helen Wills
2. Elizabeth Ryan
3. Molla Bjurstedt Mallory
4. Marion Zinderstein Jessup
5. Eleanor Goss
6. Mary K. Browne
7. Martha Bayard
8. May Sutton Bundy
9. Charlotte Hosmer
10. Edith Sigourney

6. Betty Corbiere
7. Margaret Blake
8. Penelope Anderson
9. Edna Hauslett Roeser
10. Mrs. Ellis Endicott

1927

1. Helen Wills
2. Molla Bjurstedt Mallory
3. Charlotte Hosmer Chapin
4. Helen Jacobs
5. Eleanor Goss
6. Betty Corbiere
7. Penelope Anderson
8. Margaret Blake
9. Edna Roeser
10. Alice Francis

1928

1. Helen Wills
2. Helen Jacobs
3. Edith Cross
4. Molla Bjurstedt Mallory
5. May Sutton Bundy
6. Marjorie Morrill
7. Marjorie Gladman
8. Anna McCune Harper
9. Charlotte Hosmer Chapin
10. Betty Corbiere

1929

1. Helen Wills Moody
2. Helen Jacobs
3. Edith Cross
4. Sarah Palfrey
5. Anna McCune Harper
6. Mary Greef
7. Eleanor Goss
8. Ethel Burkhardt
9. Marjorie Gladman
10. Josephine Cruickshank

1930

1. Anna McCune Harper
2. Marjorie Morrill
3. Dorothy Weisel
4. Virginia Hilleary
5. Josephine Cruickshank
6. Ethel Burkhardt
7. Marjorie Gladman Van Ryn
8. Sarah Palfrey
9. Mary Greef
10. Edith Cross

1931

1. Helen Wills Moody
2. Helen Jacobs
3. Anna McCune Harper
4. Marion Zinderstein Jessup
5. Mary Greef
6. Marjorie Morrill
7. Sarah Palfrey
8. Marjorie Gladman Van Ryn
9. Virginia Hilleary
10. Dorothy Andrus Burke

1932

1. Helen Jacobs
2. Anna McCune Harper
3. Carolin Babcock
4. Marjorie Morrill Painter
5. Josephine Cruickshank
6. Virginia Hilleary
7. Alice Marble
8. Marjorie Gladman Van Ryan
9. Virginia Rice
10. Marjorie Sachs

1933

1. Helen Jacobs
2. Helen Wills Moody
3. Alice Marble
4. Sarah Palfrey
5. Carolin Babcock
6. Josephine Cruickshank
7. Maud Rosenbaum Levi
8. Marjorie Gladman Van Ryn
9. Virginia Rice
10. Agnes Sherwood Lamme

1934

1. Helen Jacobs
2. Sarah Palfrey Fabyan
3. Carolin Babcock
4. Dorothy Andrus
5. Maude Rosenbaum Levi
6. Jane Sharp
7. Marjorie Morrill Painter
8. Mary Greef Harris
9. Marjorie Sachs
10. Catherine Wolf

1935

1. Helen Jacobs
2. Ethel Burkhardt Arnold
3. Sarah Palfrey Fabyan
4. Carolin Babcock
5. Marjorie Gladman Van Ryn
6. Gracyn Wheeler
7. Mary Greef Harris
8. Agnes Lamme
9. Dorothy Andrus
10. Catherine Wolf

1936

1. Alice Marble
2. Helen Jacobs
3. Sarah Palfrey Fabyan
4. Gracyn Wheeler
5. Carolin Babcock
6. Helen Pedersen
7. Marjorie Gladman Van Ryn
8. Dorothy Bundy
9. Katherine Winthrop
10. Mary Greef Harris

1937

1. Alice Marble
2. Helen Jacobs
3. Dorothy Bundy
4. Marjorie Gladman Van Ryn
5. Gracyn Wheeler
6. Sarah Palfrey Fabyan
7. Dorothy Burke Andrus
8. Helen Pedersen
9. Carolin Babcock Stark
10. Katherine Winthrop

6. Dorothy Workman
7. Margaret Osborne
8. Helen Pedersen
9. Virginia Wolfenden
10. Katherine Winthrop

1939

1. Alice Marble
2. Helen Jacobs
3. Sarah Palfrey Fabyan
4. Helen Bernhard
5. Virginia Wolfenden
6. Dorothy Bundy
7. Dorothy Workman
8. Pauline Betz
9. Katherine Winthrop
10. Mary Arnold

1940

1. Alice Marble
2. Helen Jacobs
3. Pauline Betz
4. Dorothy Bundy
5. Gracyn Wheeler Kelleher
6. Sarah Palfrey Cooke
7. Virginia Wolfenden
8. Helen Bernhard
9. Mary Arnold
10. Hope Knowles

1941

1. Sarah Palfrey Cooke
2. Pauline Betz
3. Dorothy Bundy
4. Margaret Osborne
5. Helen Jacobs
6. Helen Bernhard
7. Hope Knowles
8. Mary Arnold
9. Virginia Wolfenden Kovacs
10. Louise Brough

6. Doris Hart
7. Pat Canning Todd
8. Helen Pedersen Rihbany
9. Madge Harshaw Vosters
10. Katherine Winthrop

1943

1. Pauline Betz
2. Louise Brough
3. Doris Hart
4. Margaret Osborne
5. Dorothy Bundy
6. Mary Arnold
7. Dorothy Head
8. Helen Bernhard
9. Helen Pedersen Rihbany
10. Katherine Winthrop

1944

1. Pauline Betz
2. Margaret Osborne
3. Louise Brough
4. Dorothy Bundy
5. Mary Arnold
6. Doris Hart
7. Virginia Wolfenden Kovacs
8. Shirley Fry
9. Pat Canning Todd
10. Dorothy Head

1945

1. Sarah Palfrey Cooke
2. Pauline Betz
3. Margaret Osborne
4. Louise Brough
5. Pat Canning Todd
6. Doris Hart
7. Shirley Fry
8. Mary Arnold Prentiss
9. Dorothy Bundy
10. Helen Pedersen Rihbany

1946

1. Pauline Betz
2. Margaret Osborne
3. Louise Brough
4. Doris Hart
5. Pat Canning Todd
6. Dorothy Bundy Cheney
7. Shirley Fry
8. Mary Arnold Prentiss
9. Virginia Wolfenden Kovacs
10. Dorothy Head

1947

1. Louise Brough
2. Margaret Osborne duPont
3. Doris Hart
4. Pat Canning Todd
5. Shirley Fry
6. Barbara Krase
7. Dorothy Head
8. Mary Arnold Prentiss
9. Gertrude "Gussy" Moran
10. Helen Pedersen Rihbany

1948

1. Margaret Osborne duPont
2. Louise Brough
3. Doris Hart
4. Gertrude "Gussy" Moran
5. Beverly Baker
6. Pat Canning Todd
7. Shirley Fry
8. Helen Pastall Perez
9. Virginia Wolfenden Kovacs
10. Helen Pedersen Rihbany

1949

1. Margaret Osborne duPont
2. Louise Brough
3. Doris Hart
4. Pat Canning Todd
5. Helen Pastall Perez
6. Shirley Fry
7. Gertrude "Gussy" Moran
8. Beverly Baker Beckett
9. Dorothy Head
10. Barbara Scofield

1950

1. Margaret Osborne duPont
2. Doris Hart
3. Louise Brough
4. Beverly Baker
5. Pat Caning Todd
6. Nancy Chaffee
7. Barbara Scofield
8. Shirley Fry
9. Helen Pastall Perez
10. Muareen Connolly

1951

1. Maureen Connolly
2. Doris Hart
3. Shirley Fry
4. Nancy Chaffee Kiner
5. Pat Canning Todd
6. Beverly Baker Fleitz
7. Dorothy Head
8. Betty Rosenquest Pratt
9. Magda Rurac
10. Mercedes "Baba" Madden Lewis

1952

1. Maureen Connolly
2. Doris Hart
3. Shirly Fry
4. Louise Brough
5. Nancy Chaffee Kiner
6. Anita Kanter
7. Pat Canning Todd
8. Mercedes "Baba" Madden Lewis
9. Althea Gibson
10. Julie Sampson

1953

1. Maureen Connolly
2. Doris Hart
3. Shirley Fry
4. Louise Brough
5. Margaret Osborne duPont
6. Helen Pastall Perez
7. Althea Gibson
8. Mercedes "Baba" Madden Lewis
9. Anita Kanter

6. Barbara Breit
7. Darlene Hard
8. Lois Felix
9. Helen Pastall Perez
10. Barbara Scofield Davidson

1955

1. Doris Hart
2. Shirley Fry
3. Louise Brough
4. Dorothy Head Knode
5. Beverly Baker Fleitz
6. Barbara Scofield Davidson
7. Barbara Breit
8. Althea Gibson
9. Darlene Hard
10. Dorothy Bundy Cheney

1956

1. Shirley Fry
2. Althea Gibson
3. Louise Brough
4. Margaret Osborne duPont
5. Betty Rosenquest Pratt
6. Dorothy Head Knode
7. Darlene Hard
8. Karol Fageros
9. Janet Hopps
10. Miriam Arnold

1957

1. Althea Gibson
2. Louise Brough
3. Dorothy Head Knode
4. Darlene Hard
5. Karol Fageros
6. Miriam Arnold
7. Jeanne Arth
8. Sally Moore
9. Janet Hopps
10. Mary Ann Mitchell

6. Jeanne Arth
7. Janet Hopps
8. Sally Moore
9. Gwyneth Thomas
10. Mary Ann Mitchell

1959

1. Beverly Baker Fleitz
2. Darlene Hard
3. Dorothy Head Knode
4. Sally Moore
5. Janet Hopps
6. Karen Hantze
7. Barbara Green Weigandt
8. Karol Fageros
9. Miriam Arnold
10. Lois Felix

1960

1. Darlene Hard
2. Karen Hantze
3. Nancy Richey
4. Billie Jean Moffitt
5. Donna Floyd
6. Janet Hopps
7. Gwyneth Thomas
8. Vicki Palmer
9. Kathy Chabot
10. Carol Hanks

1961

1. Darlene Hard
2. Karen Hantze
3. Billie Jean Moffitt
4. Kathy Chabot
5. Justina Bricka
6. Gwyneth Thomas
7. Marilyn Montgomery
8. Judy Alvarez
9. Carole Caldwell
10. Donna Floyd

1962

1. Darlene Hard
2. Karen Hantze Susman
3. Billie Jean Moffitt
4. Carole Caldwell
5. Donna Floyd Fales
6. Nancy Richey
7. Vicki Palmer
8. Gwyneth Thomas
9. Justina Bricka
10. Judy Alvarez

1963

1. Darlene Hard
2. Billie Jean Moffitt
3. Nancy Richey
4. Carole Caldwell
5. Gwyneth Thomas
6. Judy Alvarez
7. Carol Hanks
8. Tory Fretz
9. Donna Floyd Fales
10. Julie Heldman

1964

1. Nancy Richey
2. Billie Jean Moffitt
3. Carole Caldwell Graebner
4. Karen Hantze Susman
5. Carol Hanks Aucamp
6. Jane Albert
7. Julie Heldman
8. Justina Bricka
9. Tory Fretz
10. Mary Ann Eisel

1965

1. * Nancy Richey
2. * Billie Jean Moffitt
3. Carole Caldwell Graebner
4. Jane Albert
5. Mary Ann Eisel
6. Carol Hanks Aucamp
7. Kathy Harter
8. Julie Heldman
9. Tory Fretz
10. Donna Floyd Fales

1966

1. Billie Jean Moffitt King
2. Nancy Richey
3. Rosie Casals
4. Tory Fretz
5. Jane "Peaches" Bartkowicz
6. Mary Ann Eisel
7. Donna Floyd Fales
8. Carol Hanks Aucamp
9. Stephanie DeFina
10. Fern "Peachy" Kellmeyer

1967

1. Billie Jean Moffitt King
2. Nancy Richey
3. Mary Ann Eisel
4. Jane "Peaches" Bartkowicz
5. Rosie Casals
6. Carole Caldwell Graebner
7. Stephanie DeFina
8. Kathy Harter
9. Lynne Abbes
10. Vicky Rogers

1968

1. Nancy Richey
2. Julie Heldman
3. Vicky Rogers
4. Mary Ann Eisel
5. Kathy Harter
6. Kristy Pigeon
7. Jane "Peaches" Bartkowicz
8. Linda Tuero
9. Stephanie DeFina
10. Patti Hogan

1969

1. Nancy Richey
2. Julie Heldman
3. Mary Ann Eisel Curtis
4. Jane "Peaches" Bartkowicz
5. Patti Hogan
6. Kristy Pigeon
7. Betty Ann Grubb
8. Denise Carter
9. Val Ziegenfuss

6. Jane "Peaches" Bartkowicz
7. Val Ziegenfuss
8. Kristy Pigeon
9. Stephanie DeFina Johnson
10. Denise Carter Triolo

1971

1. Billie Jean Moffitt King
2. Rosie Casals
3. Chris Evert
4. Nancy Richey Gunter
5. Mary Ann Eisel
6. Julie Heldman
7. Jane "Peaches" Bartkowicz
8. Linda Tuero
9. Patti Hogan
10. Denise Carter Triolo

1972

1. Billie Jean Moffitt King
2. Nancy Richey Gunter
3. Chris Evert
4. Rosie Casals
5. Wendy Overton
6. Patti Hogan
7. Linda Tuero
8. Julie Heldman
9. Pam Teeguarden
10. Janet Newberry

1973

1. Billie Jean Moffitt King
2. Chris Evert
3. Rosie Casals
4. Nancy Richey Gunter
5. Julie Heldman
6. Pam Teeguarden
7. Kristien Kemmer
8. Janet Newberry
9. Val Ziegenfuss

6. Kathy Kuykendall
7. Pam Teeguarden
8. Val Ziegenfuss
9. Jeanne Evert
10. Marcie Louie

1975

1. Chris Evert
2. Nancy Richey Gunter
3. Julie Heldman
4. Wendy Overton
5. Marcie Louie
6. Mona Schallau
7. Kathy Kuykendall
8. Janet Newberry
9. Terry Holladay
10. Rosie Casals

1976

1. Chris Evert
2. Rosie Casals
3. Nancy Richey Gunter
4. Terry Holladay
5. Marita Redondo
6. Mona Schallau Guerrant
7. Kathy May
8. JoAnne Russell
9. Janet Newberry
10. Kathy Kuykendall

1977

1. Chris Evert
2. Billie Jean Moffitt King
3. Rosie Casals
4. Tracy Austin
5. JoAnne Russell
6. Kathy May
7. Terry Holladay
8. Kristien Kemmer Shaw
9. Janet Newberry
10. Laura duPont

1978

1. Chris Evert
2. Billie Jean Moffitt King
3. Tracy Austin
4. Rosie Casals
5. Pam Shriver
6. Marita Redondo
7. Kathy May Teacher
8. Anne Smith
9. JoAnne Russell
10. Jeanne DuVall

1979

1. Martina Navratilova
2. Chris Evert Lloyd
3. Tracy Austin
4. Billie Jean Moffitt King
5. Kathy Jordan
6. Ann Kiyomura
7. Caroline Stoll
8. Kathy May Teacher
9. Kate Latham
10. Terry Holladay

1980

1. Tracy Austin
2. Chris Evert Lloyd
3. Martina Navratilova
4. Andrea Jaeger
5. Billie Jean Moffitt King
6. Pam Shriver
7. Kathy Jordan
8. # Bettina Bunge
9. Terry Holladay
10. Mary Lou Piatek

1981

1. Chris Evert Lloyd
2. Tracy Austin
3. Martina Navratilova
4. Andrea Jaeger
5. Pam Shriver
6. Barbara Potter
7. Bettina Bunge
8. Kathy Jordan
9. Mary Lou Piatek
10. Pam Casale

1982

1. Martina Navratilova
2. Chris Evert Lloyd
3. Andrea Jaeger
4. Tracy Austin
5. Pam Shriver
6. Barbara Potter
7. Billie Jean Moffitt King
8. Anne Smith
9. Zina Garrison
10. Kathy Rinaldi

1983

1. Martina Navratilova
2. Chris Evert Lloyd
3. Andrea Jaeger
4. Pam Shriver
5. Tracy Austin
6. Zina Garrison
7. Kathy Jordan
8. Kathy Rinaldi
9. Kathy Horvath
10. Bonnie Gadusek

1984

1. Martina Navratilova
2. Chris Evert Lloyd
3. Pam Shriver
4. Kathy Jordan
5. Zina Garrison
6. Bonnie Gadusek
7. Barbara Potter
8. Pam Casale
9. Lisa Bonder
10. Kathy Rinaldi

1985

1. Martina Navratilova
2. Chris Evert Lloyd
3. Pam Shriver
4. Bonnie Gadusek
5. Zina Garrison
6. Kathy Rinaldi
7. Kathy Jordan
8. Barbara Potter
9. Stephanie Rehe
10. Marcie Louie

6. Kathy Jordan
7. Bonnie Gadusek
8. Stephanie Rehe
9. Lori McNeil
10. Robin White

1987

1. Martina Navratilova
2. Chris Evert
3. Pam Shriver
4. Zina Garrison
5. Lori McNeil
6. Mary Joe Fernandez
7. Barbara Potter
8. Kate Gompert
9. Elly Hakami
10. Kathy Jordan

1988

1. Martina Navratilova
2. Chris Evert
3. Pam Shriver
4. Zina Garrison
5. Mary Joe Fernandez
6. Lori McNeil
7. Barbara Potter
8. Stephanie Rehe
9. Patty Fendick
10. Susan Sloane

1989

1. Martina Navratilova
2. Zina Garrison
3. Chris Evert
4. Mary Joe Fernandez
5. Pam Shriver
6. Gretchen Rush Magers
7. Patty Fendick
8. Beatrice "Gigi" Fernandez
9. Amy Frazier
10. Susan Sloane

6. Meredith McGrath
7. Gretchen Rush Magers
8. Patty Fendick
9. Beatrice "Gigi" Fernandez
10. Susan Sloane

1991

1. Martina Navratilova
2. Jennifer Capriati
3. Mary Joe Fernandez
4. Zina Garrison
5. Amy Frazier
6. Lori McNeil
7. Beatrice "Gigi" Fernandez
8. Mary Pierce
9. Pam Shriver
10. Marianne Werde

1992

1. Martina Navratilova
2. Jennifer Capriatti
3. Mary Joe Fernandez
4. Lori McNeil
5. Amy Frazier
6. Zina Garrison Jackson
7. Beatrice "Gigi" Fernandez
8. Pam Shriver
9. Patty Fendick
10. Ann Grossman

WORLD RANKINGS

World rankings always provide good controversy in tennis, all the more because there is no official ranking of the tennis players in the world. The national associations of each of the countries customarily issue rankings that include only their own players. There are a number of unofficial world ranking lists produced by magazines and newspaper people, and since 1973 the Association of Tennis Professionals (ATP) and Women's Tennis Association (WTA) each issue computer ranking lists, which add to the debate.

What is fact is that since 1913 there have been men's ratings, and in 1921 and since 1925 there have been women's ratings, all unofficial but rendered by respected tennis journalists. From 1913 through 1938, with time off for *World War I*, A. Wallis Myers of the London *Daily Telegraph* was the ratings master. In the years since through 1951, except for World War II (1940–45), F. Gordon Lowe, Pierre Gillou and John Olliff were the sources for the world rankings. Starting in 1952, Lance Tingay of the London *Daily Telegraph* made the rankings, and these are included here through 1967. The rankings for the open era, from 1968 on, are those of Bud Collins of the *Boston Globe*.

---

* indicates tie

Men

1913

1. Tony Wilding, New Zealand
2. * Norman Brookes, Australia
3. * Maurice McLoughlin, U.S.
4. Jim Parke, Ireland
5. Dick Williams, U.S.
6. Percy Dixon, England
7. Otto Froitzheim, Germany
8. Stanley Doust, Australia
9. Andre Gobert, France
10. Max Decugis, France

1914

1. Maurice McLoughlin, U.S.
2. Norman Brookes, Australia
3. Tony Wilding, New Zealand
4. Otto Froitzheim, Germany
5. Dick Williams, U.S.
6. Jim Parke, Ireland
7. Arthur Lowe, England
8. Frank Lowe, England
9. R. Kleinschroth, Germany
10. Max Decugis, France

1919

1. * Gerald Patteron, Australia
2. * Bill Johnston, U.S.
3. André Gobert, France
4. Bill Tilden, U.S.
5. Norman Brookes, Australia
6. Algernon Kingscote, England
7. Dick Williams, U.S.
8. Percival Davson, England
9. Willis Davis, U.S.
10. William Laurentz, France

1920

1. Bill Tilden, U.S.
2. Bill Johnston, U.S.
3. Algernon Kingscote, England
4. Jim Cecil Parke, England
5. André Gobert, France
6. Norman Brookes, Australia
7. Dick Williams, U.S.
8. William Laurentz, France
9. Zenzo Shimidzu, Japan
10. Gerald Patterson, Australia

1921

1. Bill Tilden, U.S.
2. Bill Johnston, U.S.
3. Vincent Richards, U.S.
4. Zenzo Shimidzu, Japan
5. Gerald Patterson, Australia
6. Jim Anderson, Australia
7. Brian Norton, S. Africa
8. Manuel Alonso, Spain
9. Dick Williams, U.S.
10. André Gobert, France

1922

1. Bill Tilden, U.S.
2. Bill Johnston, U.S.
3. Gerald Patterson, Australia
4. Vincent Richards, U.S.
5. Jim Anderson, Australia
6. Henri Cochet, France
7. Pat O'Hara Wood, Australia
8. Dick Williams, U.S.
9. Algernon Kingscote, England
10. Andres Gobert, France

6. Vincent Richards, U.S.
7. Brian Norton, S. Africa
8. Manuel Alonso, Spain
9. Jan Washer, Belgium
10. Henri Cochet, France

1924

1. Bill Tilden, U.S.
2. Vincent Richards, U.S.
3. Jim Anderson, Australia
4. Bill Johnston, U.S.
5. René Lacoste, France
6. Jean Borotra, France
7. Howard Kinsey, U.S.
8. Gerald Patterson, Australia
9. Henri Cochet, France
10. Manuel Alonso, Spain

1925

1. Bill Tilden, U.S.
2. Bill Johnston, U.S.
3. Vincent Richards, U.S.
4. René Lacoste, France
5. Dick Williams, U.S.
6. Jean Borotra, France
7. Gerald Patterson, Australia
8. Manuel Alonso, Spain
9. Brian Norton S. Africa
10. Takeichi Harada, Japan

1926

1. René Lacoste, France
2. Jean Borotra, France
3. Henri Cochet, France
4. Bill Johnston, U.S.
5. Bill Tilden, U.S.
6. Vincent Richards, U.S.
7. Takeichi Harada, Japan
8. Manuel Alonso, Spain
9. Howard Kinsey, U.S.
10. Jacques Brugnon, France

6. Frank Hunter, U.S.
7. George Lott, U.S.
8. John Hennessey, U.S.
9. Jacques Brugnon, France
10. Karel Kozeluh, Czechoslovakia

1928

1. Henri Cochet, France
2. René Lacoste, France
3. Bill Tilden, U.S.
4. Frank Hunter, U.S.
5. Jean Borotra, France
6. George Lott, U.S.
7. Henry "Bunny" Austin, England
8. John Hennessey, U.S.
9. Umberto de Morpurgo, Italy
10. John Hawkes, Australia

1929

1. Henri Cochet, France
2. René Lacoste, France
3. Jean Borotra, France
4. Bill Tilden, U.S.
5. Frank Hunter, U.S.
6. George Lott, U.S.
7. John Doeg, U.S.
8. John Van Ryn, U.S.
9. Henry "Bunny" Austin, England
10. Umberto de Morpurgo, Italy

1930

1. Henri Cochet, France
2. Bill Tilden, U.S.
3. Jean Borotra, France
4. John Doeg, U.S.
5. Frank Shields, U.S.
6. Wilmer Allison, U.S.
7. George Lott, U.S.
8. Umberto de Morpurgo, Italy
9. Christian Boussus, France
10. Henry "Bunny" Austin, England

1931

1. Henri Chochet, France
2. Henry "Bunny" Austin, England
3. Ellsworth Vines, U.S.
4. Fred Perry, England
5. Frank Shields, U.S.
6. Sidney Wood, U.S.
7. Jean Borotra, France
8. George Lott, U.S.
9. Jiro Satoh, Japan
10. John Van Ryn, U.S.

1932

1. Ellsworth Vines, U.S.
2. Henri Cochet, France
3. Jean Borotra, France
4. Wilmer Allison, U.S.
5. Cliff Sutter, U.S.
6. Daniel Prenn, Germany
7. Fred Perry, England
8. Gottfried von Cramm, Germany
9. Henry "Bunny" Austin, England
10. Jack Crawford, Australia

1933

1. Jack Crawford, Australia
2. Fred Perry, England
3. Jiro Satoh, Japan
4. Henry "Bunny" Austin, England
5. Ellsworth Vines, U.S.
6. Henri Cochet, France
7. Frank Shields, U.S.
8. Sidney Wood, U.S.
9. Gottfried von Cramm, Germany
10. Lester Stoefen, U.S.

1934

1. Fred Perry, England
2. Jack Crawford, Australia
3. Gottfried von Cramm, Germany
4. Henry "Bunny" Austin, England
5. Wilmer Allison, U.S.
6. Sidney Wood, U.S.
7. Roderic Menzel, Czechoslovakia
8. Frank Shields, U.S.
9. Giorgio de Stefani, Italy
10. Christian Boussus, France

1935

1. Fred Perry, England
2. Jack Crawford, Australia
3. Gottfried, von Cramm, Germany
4. Wilmer Allison, U.S.
5. Henry "Bunny" Austin, England
6. Don Budge, U.S.
7. Frank Shields, U.S.
8. Viv McGrath, Australia
9. Christian Boussus, France
10. Sidney Wood, U.S.

1936

1. Fred Perry, England
2. Gottfried von Cramm, Germany
3. Don Budge, U.S.
4. Adrian Quist, Australia
5. Henry "Bunny" Austin, England
6. Jack Crawford, Australia
7. Wilmer Allison, U.S.
8. Bryan "Bitsy" Grant, U.S.
9. Henner Henkel, Germany
10. Viv McGrath, Australia

1937

1. Don Budge, U.S.
2. Gottfried von Cramm, Germany
3. Henner Henkel, Germany
4. Henry "Bunny" Austin, England
5. Bobby Riggs, U.S.
6. Bryan "Bitsy" Grant, U.S.
7. Jack Crawford, Australia
8. Roderic Menzel, Czechoslovakia
9. Frank Parker, U.S.
10. Charlie Hare, England

1938

1. Don Budge, U.S.
2. Henry "Bunny" Austin, England
3. John Bromwich, Australia
4. Bobby Riggs, U.S.
5. Sidney Wood, U.S.
6. Adrian Quist, Australia
7. Roderic Menzel, Czechoslovakia
8. Jiro Yamagishi, Japan
9. Gene Mako, U.S.
10. Franjo Punčec, Yugoslavia

6. Henner Henkel, Germany
7. Don McNeill, U.S.
8. Elwood Cooke, U.S.
9. Welby Van Horn, U.S.
10. Joseph Hunt, U.S.

1946

1. Jack Kramer, U.S.
2. Ted Schroeder, U.S.
3. Jaroslav Drobny, Czechoslovakia
4. Yvon Petra, France
5. Marcel Bernard, France
6. John Bromwich, Australia
7. Tom Brown, U.S.
8. Gardnar Mulloy, U.S.
9. Frank Parker, U.S.
10. Geoff Brown, Australia

1947

1. Jack Kramer, U.S.
2. Ted Schroeder, U.S.
3. Frank Parker, U.S.
4. John Bromwich, Australia
5. Jaroslav Drobny, Czechoslovakia
6. Dinny Pails, Australia
7. Tom Brown, U.S.
8. J. Edward "Budge" Patty, U.S.
9. Jozsef Asboth, Hungary
10. Gardnar Mulloy, U.S.

1948

1. Frank Parker, U.S.
2. Ted Schroeder, U.S.
3. Richard "Pancho" Gonzalez, U.S.
4. John Bromwich, Australia
5. Jaroslav Drobny, Czechoslovakia
6. Eric Sturgess, S. Africa
7. Bob Falkenburg, U.S.
8. Jozsef Asboth, Hungary
9. Lennart Bergelin, Sweden
10. Adrian Quist, Australia

6. Eric Sturgess, S. Africa
7. Jaroslav Drobny, Czechoslovakia
8. J. Edward "Budge" Patty, U.S.
9. Gardnar Mulloy, U.S.
10. Billy Sidwell, Australia

1950

1. J. Edward "Budge" Patty, U.S.
2. Frank Sedgman, Australia
3. Art Larsen, U.S.
4. Jaroslav Drobny, Egypt
5. Herbie Flam, U.S.
6. Ted Schroeder, U.S.
7. Vic Seixas, U.S.
8. Ken McGregor, Australia
9. Bill Talbert, U.S.
10. Eric Sturgess, S. Africa

1951

1. Frank Sedgman, Australia
2. Dick Savitt, U.S.
3. Jaroslav Drobny, Egypt
4. Vic Seixas, U.S.
5. Tony Trabert, U.S.
6. Ted Schroeder, U.S.
7. Ken McGregor, Australia
8. Herbie Flam, U.S.
9. Art Larsen, U.s.
10. Mervyn Rose, Australia

1952

1. Frank Sedgman, Australia
2. Jaroslav Drobny, Egypt
3. Ken McGregor, Australia
4. Mervyn Rose, Australia
5. Vic Seixas, U.S.
6. Herbie Flam, U.S.
7. Gardnar Mulloy, U.S.
8. Eric Sturgess, S. Africa
9. Dick Savitt, England
10. *Ken Rosewall, Australia
    *Lew Hoad, Australia

1953

1. Tony Trabert, U.S.
2. Ken Rosewall, Australia
3. Vic Seixas, U.S.
4. Jaroslav Drobny, Egypt
5. Lew Hoad, Australia
6. Mervyn Rose, Australia
7. Kurt Nielsen, Denmark
8. J. Edward "Budge" Patty, U.S.
9. Sven Davidson, Sweden
10. Enrique Morea, Argentina

1954

1. Jaroslav Drobny, Egypt
2. Tony Trabert, U.S.
3. Ken Rosewall, Australia
4. Vic Seixas, U.S.
5. Rex Hartwig, Australia
6. Mervyn Rose, Australia
7. Lew Hoad, Australia
8. J. Edward "Budge" Patty, U.S.
9. Art Larsen, U.S.
10. * Enrique Morea, Argentina
    *Ham Richardson, U.S.
    *Sven Davidson, Sweden

1955

1. Tony Trabert, U.S.
2. Ken Rosewall, Australia
3. Lew Hoad, Australia
4. Vic Seixas, U.S.
5. Rex Hartwig, Australia
6. J. Edward "Budge" Patty, U.S.
7. Ham Richardson, U.S.
8. Kurt Nielsin, Denmark
9. Jaroslav Drobny, Egypt
10. *Sven Davidson, Sweden
    *Mervyn Rose, Australia

1956

1. Lew Hoad, Australia
2. Ken Rosewall, Australia
3. Ham Richardson, U.S.
4. Vic Seixas, U.S.
5. Sven Davidson, Sweden
6. Neale Fraser, Australia
7. Ashley Cooper, Australia
8. Dick Savitt, U.S.
9. Herbie Flam, U.S.
10. * J. Edward "Budge" Patty, U.S.
    * Nicola Pietrangeli, Italy

1957

1. Ashley Cooper, Australia
2. Mal Anderson, Australia
3. Sven Davidson, Sweden
4. Herbie Flam, U.S.
5. Neale Fraser, Australia
6. Mervyn Rose, Australia
7. Vic Seixas, U.S.
8. J. Edward "Budge" Patty, U.S.
9. Nicola Pietrangeli, Italy
10. Dick Savitt, U.S.

1958

1. Ashley Cooper, Australia
2. Mal Anderson, Australia
3. Mervyn Rose, Australia
4. Neale Fraser, Australia
5. Luis Ayala, Chile
6. Ham Richardson, U.S.
7. Nicola Pietrangeli, Italy
8. Ulf Schmidt, Sweden
9. Barry MacKay, U.S.
10. Sven Davidson, Sweden

1959

1. Neale Fraser, Australia
2. Alex Olmedo, Peru
3. Nicola Pietrangeli, Italy
4. Barry MacKay, U.S.
5. Rod Laver, Australia
6. Luis Ayala, Chile
7. Roy Emerson, Australia
8. Bernard "Tut" Bartzen, U.S.
9. Ramanathan Krishnan, India
10. Ian Vermaak, S. Africa

1960

1. Neale Fraser, Australia
2. Rod Laver, Australia
3. Nicola Pietrangeli, Italy
4. Barry MacKay, U.S.
5. Earl "Butch" Buchholz, U.S.
6. Roy Emerson, Australia
7. Luis Ayala, Chile
8. Ramanathan Krishnan, India
9. Jan Erik Lundquist, Sweden

6. Ramanathan Krishnan, India
7. Luis Ayala, Chile
8. Neale Fraser, Australia
9. Jan Erik Lundquist, Sweden
10. Ulf Schmidt, Sweden

1962

1. Rod Laver, Australia
2. Roy Emerson, Australia
3. Manolo Santana, Spain
4. Neale Fraser, Australia
5. Chuck McKinley, U.S.
6. Rafael Osuna, Mexico
7. Marty Mulligan, Australia
8. Bob Hewitt, Australia
9. Ramanathan Krishnan, India
10. Willie Bungert, Germany

1963

1. Rafael Osuna, Mexico
2. Chuck McKinley, U.S.
3. Roy Emerson, Australia
4. Manolo Santana, Spain
5. Fred Stolle, Australia
6. Frank Froehling III, U.S.
7. Dennis Ralston, U.S.
8. Boro Jovanovic, Yugoslavia
9. Mike Sangster, England
10. Marty Mulligan, Australia

1964

1. Roy Emerson, Australia
2. Fred Stolle, Australia
3. Jan Erik Lundquist, Sweden
4. Willie Bungert, Germany
5. Chuck McKinley, U.S.
6. Manolo Santana, Spain
7. Nicola Pietrangeli, Italy
8. Christian Kuhnke, Germany
9. Dennis Ralston, U.S.
10. Rafael Osuna, Mexico

6. Jan Erik Lundquist, Sweden
7. Tony Roche, Australia
8. John Newcombe, Australia
9. Dennis Ralston, U.S.
10. Arthur Ashe, U.S.

1966

1. Manolo Santana, Spain
2. Fred Stolle, Australia
3. Roy Emerson, Australia
4. Tony Roche, Australia
5. Dennis Ralston, U.S.
6. John Newcombe, Australia
7. Arthur Ashe, U.S.
8. Istvan Gulyas, Hungary
9. Cliff Drysdale, S. Africa
10. Ken Fletcher, Australia

1967

1. John Newcombe, Australia
2. Roy Emerson, Australia
3. Manolo Santana, Spain
4. Marty Mulligan, Australia
5. Tony Roche, Australia
6. Bob Hewitt, S. Africa
7. Nikki Pilic, Yugoslavia
8. Clark Graebner, U.S.
9. Arthur Ashe, U.S.
10. * Jan Leschley, Denmark
    * Willie Bungert, Germany
    * Cliff Drysdale, S. Africa

1968

1. Rod Laver, Australia
2. Arthur Ashe, U.S.
3. Ken Rosewall, Australia
4. Tony Roche, Australia
5. Tom Okker, Netherlands
6. John Newcombe, Australia
7. Clark Graebner, U.S.
8. Dennis Ralston, U.S.
9. Cliff Drysdale, S. Africa
10. Richard "Pancho" Gonzalez, U.S.

1969

1. Rod Laver, Australia
2. Tony Roche, Australia
3. John Newcombe, Australia
4. Ken Rosewall, Australia
5. Tom Okker, Netherlands
6. Richard "Pancho" Gonzalez, U.S.
7. Stan Smith, U.S.
8. Arthur Ashe, U.S.
9. Cliff Drysdale, S. Africa
10. Andres Gimeno, Spain

1970

1. John Newcombe, Australia
2. Ken Rosewall, Australia
3. Tony Roche, Australia
4. Rod Laver, Australia
5. Ilie Nastase, Romania
6. Tom Okker, Netherlands
7. Cliff Richey, U.S.
8. Stan Smith, U.S.
9. Arthur Ashe, U.S.
10. Andres Gimeno, Spain

1971

1. John Newcombe, Australia
2. Stan Smith, U.S.
3. Ken Rosewall, Australia
4. Rod Laver, Australia
5. Jan Kodes, Czechoslovakia
6. Arthur Ashe, U.S.
7. Ilie Nastase, Romania
8. Tom Okker, Netherlands
9. Cliff Drysdale, S. Africa
10. Marty Riessen, U.S.

1972

1. Stan Smith, U.S.
2. Ken Rosewall, Australia
3. Ilie Nastase, Romania
4. Rod Laver, Australia
5. Arthur Ashe, U.S.
6. John Newcombe, Australia
7. Bob Lutz, U.S.
8. Tom Okker, Netherlands
9. Marty Riessen, U.S.
10. Andres Gimeno, Spain

1973

1. Ilie Nastase, Romania
2. John Newcombe, Australia
3. Stan Smith, U.S.
4. Rod Laver, Australia
5. Ken Rosewall, Australia
6. Jimmy Connors, U.S.
7. Tom Okker, Netherlands
8. Jan Kodes, Czechoslovakia
9. Arthur Ashe, U.S.
10. Manolo Orantes, Spain

1974

1. Jimmy Connors, U.S.
2. Guillermo Vilas, Argentina
3. John Newcombe, Australia
4. Bjorn Borg, Sweden
5. Rod Laver, Australia
6. Ilie Nastase, Romania
7. Ken Rosewall, Australia
8. Stan Smith, U.S.
9. Manolo Orantes, Spain
10. Arthur Ashe, U.S.

1975

1. Arthur Ashe, U.S.
2. Bjorn Borg, Sweden
3. Manolo Orantes, Spain
4. Jimmy Connors, U.S.
5. Ilie Nastase, Romania
6. Guillermo Vilas, Argentina
7. Rod Laver, Australia
8. Raul Ramirez, Mexico
9. John Alexander, Australia
10. Ken Rosewall, Australia

1976

1. Jimmy Connors, U.S.
2. Bjorn Borg, Sweden
3. Ilie Nastase, Romania
4. Manolo Orantes, Spain
5. Adriano Panatta, Italy
6. Harold Solomon, U.S.
7. Raul Ramirez, Mexico
8. Roscoe Tanner, U.S.
9. Eddie Dibbs, U.S.
10. Wojtek Fibak, Poland

6. Manolo Orantes, Spain
7. Dick Stockton, U.S.
8. Eddie Dibbs, U.S.
9. Ilie Nastase, Romania
10. Raul Ramirez, Mexico

1978

1. Bjorn Borg, Sweden
2. Jimmy Connors, U.S.
3. John McEnroe, U.S.
4. Vitas Gerulaitis, U.S.
5. Eddie Dibbs, U.S.
6. Guillermo Vilas, Argentina
7. Brian Gottfried, U.S.
8. Raul Ramirez, Mexico
9. Harold Solomon, U.S.
10. Arthur Ashe, U.S.

1979

1. Bjorn Borg, Sweden
2. John McEnroe, U.S.
3. Jimmy Connors, U.S.
4. Vitas Gerulaitis, U.S.
5. Roscoe Tanner, U.S.
6. Guillermo Vilas, Argentina
7. Harold Solomon, U.S.
8. Jose Higueras, Spain
9. Victor Pecci, Paraguay
10. Wojtek Fibak, Poland

1980

1. Bjorn Borg, Sweden
2. John McEnroe, U.S.
3. Jimmy Connors, U.S.
4. Ivan Lendl, Czechoslovakia
5. Gene Mayer, U.S.
6. Guillermo Vilas, Argentina
7. Jose-Luis Clerc, Argentina
8. Vitas Gerulaitis, U.S.
9. Harold Solomon, U.S.
10. Brian Gottfried, U.S.

6. Guillermo Vilas, Argentina
7. Gene Mayer, U.S.
8. Eliot Teltscher, U.S.
9. Peter McNamara, Australia
10. Roscoe Tanner, U.S.

1982

1. Jimmy Connors, U.S.
2. Ivan Lendl, Czechoslovakia
3. John McEnroe, U.S.
4. Mats Wilander, Sweden
5. Guillermo Vilas, Argentina
6. Vitas Gerulaitis, U.S.
7. Jose-Luis Clerc, Argentina
8. Yannick Noah, France
9. Johan Kriek, U.S.
10. Jose Higueras, Spain

1983

1. John McEnroe, U.S.
2. Mats Wilander, Sweden
3. Jimmy Connors, U.S.
4. Yannick Noah, France
5. Ivan Lendl, Czechoslovakia
6. Jimmy Arias, U.S.
7. Jose Higueras, Spain
8. Jose-Luis Clerc, Argentina
9. Bill Scanlon, U.S.
10. Guillermo Vilas, Argentina

1984

1. John McEnroe, U.S.
2. Ivan Lendl, Czechoslovakia
3. Jimmy Connors, U.S.
4. Mats Wilander, Sweden
5. Andres Gomez, Ecuador
6. Henrik Sundstrom, Sweden
7. Aaron Krickstein, U.S.
8. Anders Jarryd, Sweden
9. Joakim Nystrom, Sweden
10. Pat Cash, Australia

1985

1. Ivan Lendl, Czechoslovakia
2. Boris Becker, Germany
3. Mats Wilander, Sweden
4. John McEnroe, U.S.
5. Stefan Edberg, Sweden
6. Jimmy Connors, U.S.
7. Yannick Noah, France
8. Anders Jarryd, Sweden
9. Kevin Curren, U.S.
10. Joakim Nystrom, Sweden

1986

1. Ivan Lendl, Czechoslovakia
2. Boris Becker, Germany
3. Stefan Edberg, Sweden
4. Mats Wilander, Sweden
5. Joakim Nystrom, Sweden
6. Miloslav Mecir, Czechoslovakia
7. Yannick Noah, France
8. Henri Leconte, France
9. Andres Gomez, Ecuador
10. Brad Gilbert, U.S.

1987

1. Ivan Lendl, Czechoslovakia
2. Mats Wilander, Germany
3. Stefan Edberg, Sweden
4. Pat Cash, Australia
5. Miloslav Mecir, Czechoslovakia
6. Boris Becker, Germany
7. Jimmy Connors, U.S.
8. Tim Mayotte, U.S.
9. John McEnroe, U.S.
10. Brad Gilbert, U.S.

1988

1. Mats Wilander, Sweden
2. Stefan Edberg, Sweden
3. Boris Becker, Germany
4. Ivan Lendl, Czechoslovakia
5. Andre Agassi, U.S.,
6. Miloslav Mecir, Czechoslovakia
7. Jimmy Connors, U.S.
8. Tim Mayotte, U.S.
9. Pat Cash, Australia
10. Jakob Hlasek, Switzerland

1989

1. Boris Becker, Germany
2. Ivan Lendl, Czechoslovakia
3. Stefan Edberg, Sweden
4. John McEnroe, U.S.
5. Michael Chang, U.S.
6. Brad Gilbert, U.S.
7. Aaron Krickstein, U.S.
8. Jay Berger, U.S.
9. Andre Agassi, U.S.
10. Jimmy Connors, U.S.

1990

1. Stefan Edberg, Sweden
2. Ivan Lendl, Czechoslovakia
3. Pete Sampras, U.S.
4. Andre Agassi, U.S.
5. Boris Becker, Germany
6. Thomas Muster, Austria
7. Andres Gomez, Ecuador
8. Brad Gilbert, U.S.
9. Michael Chang, U.S.
10. John McEnroe, U.S.

1991

1. Stefan Edberg, Sweden
2. Michael Stich, Germany
3. Jim Courier, U.S.
4. Boris Becker, Germany
5. Guy Forget, France
6. Pete Sampras, U.S.
7. Ivan Lendl, Czechoslovakia
8. Andre Agassi, U.S.
9. Petr Korda, Czechoslovakia
10. Karel Novacek, Czechoslovakia

1992

1. Jim Courier, U.S.
2. Stefan Edberg, Sweden
3. Andre Agassi, U.S.
4. Pete Sampras, U.S.
5. Michael Chang, U.S.
6. Goran Ivanisevic, Yugoslavia
7. Peter Korda, Czechoslovakia
8. Boris Becker, Germany
9. Wayne Ferreira, S. Africa

1927

1. Helen Wills, U.S.
2. Lili de Alvarez, Spain
3. Elizabeth Ryan, U.S.
4. Molla Bjurstedt Mallory, U.S.
5. Kitty McKane Godfree, England
6. Betty Nuthall, England
7. Esther "Bobbie" Heine, S. Africa
8. Joan Fry, England
9. Kea Bouman, Holland

5. Kitty McKane, England
6. May Sutton Bundy, U.S.
7. Irene Peacock, India
8. Winifred Beamish, England
9. Eleanor Goss, U.S.
10. Marion Zinderstein Jessup, U.S.

6. Elizabeth Ryan, U.S.
7. Cilly Aussem, Germany
8. Kea Bouman, Holland
9. Helen Jacobs, U.S.
10. Esna Boyd, Australia

1929

1925

1. Suzanne Lenglen, France
2. Helen Wills, U.S.
3. Kitty McKane, England
4. Elizabeth Ryan, U.S.
5. Molla Bjurstedt Mallory, U.S.
6. Eleanor Goss, U.S.
7. Dorothea Douglass Lambert Chambers, England
8. Joan Fry, England
9. Marguerite Billout, France
10. Marion Zinderstein Jessup, U.S.

1. Helen Wills Moody, U.S.
2. Phoebe Holcroft Watson, England
3. Helen Jacobs, U.S.
4. Betty Nuthall l, England
5. Esther "Bobby" Heine, S. Africa
6. Simone Passemard Mathieu, France
7. Eileen Bennett, England
8. Paula von Reznicek, Germany
9. Peggy Saunders Michell, England
10. Elsie Goldsack, England

1930

1926

1. Suzanne Lenglen, France
2. Kitty McKane Godfree, England
3. Lili de Alvarez, Spain
4. Molla Bjurstedt Mallory, U.S.
5. Elizabeth Ryan, U.S.
6. Mary K. Browne, U.S.
7. Joan Fry, England
8. Phoebe Holcroft Watson, England
9. Marion Zinderstein Jessup, U.S.
10. Didi Vlasto, France

1. Helen Wills Moody, U.S.
2. Cilly Aussem, Germany
3. Phoebe Holcroft Watson, England
4. Elizabeth Ryan, U.S.
5. Simone Passemard Mathieu, France
6. Helen Jacobs, U.S.
7. Phyllis Mudford, England
8. Lili de Alvarez, Spain
9. Betty Nuthall, England
10. Hilde Krahwinkel, Germany

1931

1. Helen Wills Moody, U.S.
2. Cilly Aussem, Germany
3. Eileen Bennett Whittingstall, England
4. Helen Jacobs, U.S.
5. Betty Nuthall, England
6. Hilde Krahwinkel, Germany
7. Simone Passemard Mathieu, France
8. Lili de Alvarez, Spain
9. Phyllis Mudford, England
10. Elsie Goldsack Pittman, England

1935

1. Helen Wills Moody, U.S.
2. Helen Jacobs, U.S.
3. Kay Stammers, England
4. Hilde Krahwinkel Sperling, Germany
5. Sarah Palfrey Fabyan, U.S.
6. Dorothy Round, England
7. Mary Arnold, U.S.
8. Simone Passemard Mathieu, France
9. Joan Hartigan, Australia
10. Margaret Scriven, England

1932

1. Helen Wills Moody, U.S.
2. Helen Jacobs, U.S.
3. Simone Passemard Mathieu, France
4. Lolette Payot, Switzerland
5. Hilde Krahwinkel, Germany
6. Mary Heeley, England
7. Eileen Bennett Whittingstall, England
8. Marie Louise Horn, Germany
9. Kay Stammers, England
10. Josane Sigart, Belgium

1936

1. Helen Jacobs, U.S.
2. Hilda Krahwinkel Sperling, Germany
3. Dorothy Round, England
4. Alice Marble, U.S.
5. Simone Passemard Mathieu, France
6. Jadwiga Jedrzejowska, Poland
7. Kay Stammers, England
8. Anita Lizana, Chile
9. Sarah Palfrey Fabyan, U.S.
10. Carolin Babcock, U.S.

1933

1. Helen Wills Moody, U.S.
2. Helen Jacobs, U.S.
3. Dorothy Round, England
4. Hilde Krahwinkel, Germany
5. Margaret Scriven, England
6. Simone Passemard Mathieu, France
7. Sarah Palfrey, U.S.
8. Betty Nuthall, England
9. Lolette Payot, Switzerland
10. Alice Marble, U.S.

1937

1. Anita Lizana, Chile
2. Dorothy Round Little, England
3. Jadwiga Jedrzejowska, Poland
4. Hilde Krahwinkel Sperling, Germany
5. Simone Passemard Mathieu, France
6. Helen Jacobs, U.S.
7. Alice Marble, U.S.
8. Mary Louise Horn, Germany
9. Mary Hardwick, England
10. Dorothy Bundy, U.S.

1934

1. Dorothy Round, England
2. Helen Jacobs, U.S.
3. Hilde Krahwinkel Sperling, Germany
4. Sarah Palfrey, U.S.
5. Margaret Scriven, England
6. Simone Passemard Mathieu, France
7. Lolette Payot, Switzerland
8. Joan Hartigan, Australia
9. Cilly Aussem, Germany
10. Carolin Babcock, U.S.

1938

1. Helen Wills Moody, U.S.
2. Helen Jacobs, U.S.
3. Alice Marble, U.S.
4. Hilde Krahwinkel Sperling, Germany
5. Simone Passemard Mathieu, France
6. Jadwiga Jedrzejowska, Poland
7. Sarah Palfrey Fabyan, U.S.
8. Esther "Bobbie" Heine Miller, S. Africa
9. Kay Stammers, England
10. Nancye Wynne, Australia

1939

1. Alice Marble, U.S.
2. Kay Stammers, England
3. Helen Jacobs, U.S.
4. Hilda Krahwinkel Sperling, Germany
5. Simone Passemard Mathieu, France
6. Sarah Palfrey Fabyan, U.S.
7. Jadwiga Jerzejowska, Poland
8. Mary Hardwick, England
9. Valerie Scott, England

6. Dorothy Bundy, U.S.
7. Nelly Adamson Landry, France
8. Kay Stammers Menzies, England
9. Shirley Fry, U.S.
10. Virginia Wolfenden Kovacs, U.S.

1947

1. Margaret Osborne duPont, U.S.
2. Louise Brough, U.S.
3. Doris Hart, U.S.
4. Nancye Wynne Bolton, Australia
5. Pat Canning Todd, U.S.
6. Sheila Piercey Summers, S. Africa
7. Jean Bostock, England
8. Barbara Krase, U.S.
9. Betty Hilton, England
10. Magda Rurac, Romania

1948

1. Margaret Osborne duPont, U.S.
2. Louise Brough, U.S.
3. Doris Hart, U.S.
4. Nancye Wynne Bolton, Australia
5. Pat Canning Todd, U.S.
6. Jean Bostock, England
7. Sheila Piercey Summers, S. Africa
8. Shirley Fry, U.S.
9. Magda Rurac, Romania
10. Nelly Adamson Landry, France

1949

1. Margaret Osborne duPont, U.S.
2. Louise Brough, U.S.
3. Doris Hart, U.S.
4. Nancye Wynne Bolton, Australia
5. Pat Canning Todd, U.S.
6. Betty Hilton, England
7. Sheila Summers, S. Africa
8. Anna Bossi, Italy
9. Joan Curry, England
10. Jean Walker Smith, England

6. Nancy Chaffee, U.S.
7. Beverly Baker, U.S.
8. Shirley Fry, U.S.
9. Anna Bossi, Italy
10. Maria Weiss, Argentina

1951

1. Doris Hart, U.S.
2. Maureen Connolly, U.S.
3. Shirley Fry, U.S.
4. Nancy Chaffee Kiner, U.S.
5. Jean Walker Smith, England
6. Jean Quertier, England
7. Louise Brough, U.S.
8. Beverly Baker Fleitz, U.S.
9. Pat Canning Todd, U.S.
10. Kay Tuckey Maule, England

1952

1. Maureen Connolly, U.S.
2. Doris Hart, U.S.
3. Louise Brough, U.S.
4. Shirley Fry, U.S.
5. Pat Canning Todd, U.S.
6. Nancy Chaffee Kiner, U.S.
7. Thelma Coyne Long, Australia
8. Jean Walker Smith, England
9. Jean Quertier Rinkel, U.S.
10. Dorothy Head Knode, U.S.

1953

1. Maureen Connolly, U.S.
2. Doris Hart, U.S.
3. Louise Brough, U.S.
4. Shirley Fry, U.S.
5. Margaret Osborne duPont, U.S.
6. Dorothy Head Knode, U.S.
7. Suzi Kormoczi, Hungary
8. Angela Mortimer, England
9. Helen Fletcher, England
10. Jean Quertier Rinkel, England

1954

1. Maureen Connolly, U.S.
2. Doris Hart, U.S.
3. Beverly Baker Fleitz, U.S.
4. Louise Brough, U.S.
5. Margaret Osborne duPont, U.S.
6. Shirley Fry, U.S.
7. Betty Rosenquest Pratt, U.S.
8. Helen Fletcher, England
9. Angela Mortimer, England
10. * Ginette Bucaille, France
    * Thelma Coyne Long, Australia

1955

1. Louise Brough, U.S.
2. Doris Hart, U.S.
3. Beverly Baker Fleitz, U.S.
4. Angela Mortimer, England
5. Dorothy Head Knode, U.S.
6. Barbara Breit, U.S.
7. Darlene Hard, U.S.
8. Beryl Penrose, Australia
9. Pat Ward, England
10. * Suzie Kormoczi, Hungary
    * Shirley Fry, U.S.

1956

1. Shirley Fry, U.S.
2. Althea Gibson, U.S.
3. Louise Brough, U.S.
4. Angela Mortimer, England
5. Suzi Kormoczi, Hungary
6. Angela Buxton, England
7. Shirley Bloomer, England
8. Pat Ward, England
9. Betty Rosenquest Pratt, Jamaica
10. *Margaret Osborne duPont, U.S.
    *Darlene Hard, U.S.

1957

1. Althea Gibson, U.S.
2. Darlene Hard, U.S.
3. Shirley Bloomer, England
4. Louise Brough, U.S.
5. Dorothy Head Knode, U.S.
6. Vera Puzejova, Czechoslovakia
7. Ann Haydon, England
8. Yola Ramirez, Mexico
9. Christine Truman, England
10. Margaret Osborne duPont, U.S.

1958

1. Althea Gibson, U.S.
2. Suzi Kormoczi, Hungary
3. Beverly Baker Fleitz, U.S.
4. Darlene Hard, U.S.
5. Shirley Bloomer, England
6. Christine Truman, England
7. Angela Mortimer, England
8. Ann Haydon, England
9. Maria Bueno, Brazil
10. Dorothy Head Knode, U.S.

1959

1. Maria Bueno, Brazil
2. Christine Truman, England
3. Darlene Hard, U.S.
4. Beverly Baker Fleitz, U.S.
5. Sandra Reynolds, S. Africa
6. Angela Mortimer, England
7. Ann Haydon, England
8. Suzi Kormoczi, Hungary
9. Sally Moore, U.S.
10. Yola Ramirez, Mexico

1960

1. Maria Bueno, Brazil
2. Darlene Hard, U.S.
3. Sandra Reynolds, S. Africa
4. Christine Truman, England
5. Suzi Kormoczi, Hungary
6. Ann Haydon, England
7. Angela Mortimer, England
8. Jan Lehane, Australia
9. Yola Ramirez, Mexico
10. Renee Schuurman, S. Africa

1961

1. Angela Mortimer, England
2. Darlene Hard, U.S.
3. Ann Haydon, England
4. Margaret Smith, Australia
5. Sandra Reynolds, S. Africa
6. Yola Ramirez, Mexico
7. Christine Truman, England
8. Suzi Kormoczi, Hungary
9. Renee Schuurman, S. Africa

6. Sandra Reynolds Price, S. Africa
7. Lesley Turner, Australia
8. Ann Haydon, England
9. Renee Schuurman, S. Africa
10. Angela Mortimer, England

1963

1. Margaret Smith, Australia
2. Lesley Turner, Australia
3. Maria Bueno, Brazil
4. Billie Jean Moffitt, U.S.
5. Ann Haydon Jones, England
6. Darlene Hard, U.S.
7. Jan Lehane, Australia
8. Renee Schuurman, S. Africa
9. Nancy Richey, U.S.
10. Vera Puzejova Sukova, Czechoslovakia

1964

1. Margaret Smith, Australia
2. Maria Bueno, Brazil
3. Lesley Turner, Australia
4. Carole Caldwell Graebner, U.S.
5. Helga Schultze, Germany
6. Nancy Richey, U.S.
7. Billie Jean Moffitt, U.S.
8. Karen Hantze Susman, U.S.
9. Robyn Ebbern, Australia
10. Jan Lehane, Australia

1965

1. Margaret Smith, Australia
2. Maria Bueno, Brazil
3. Lesley Turner, Australia
4. Billie Jean Moffitt King, U.S.
5. Ann Haydon Jones, England
6. Annette Van Zyl, S. Africa
7. Christine Truman, England
8. Nancy Richey, U.S.
9. Carole Caldwell Graebner, U.S.

6. Annette Van Zyl, S. Africa
7. Norma Baylon, Argentina
8. Francoise Durr, France
9. Rosie Casals, U.S.
10. Kerry Melville, Australia

1967

1. Billie Jean Moffitt King, U.S.
2. Ann Haydon Jones, England
3. Francoise Durr, France
4. Nancy Richey, U.S.
5. Lesley Turner, Australia
6. Rosie Casals, U.S.
7. Maria Bueno, Brazil
8. Virginia Wade, England
9. Kerry Melville, Australia
10. Judy Tegart, Australia

1968

1. Billie Jean Moffitt King, U.S.
2. Virginia Wade, England
3. Nancy Richey, U.S.
4. Margaret Smith Court, Australia
5. Maria Bueno, Brazil
6. Ann Haydon Jones, England
7. Judy Tegart, Australia
8. Lesley Turner Bowrey, Australia
9. Annette Van Zyl duPlooy, S. Africa
10. Rosie Casals, U.S.

1969

1. Margaret Smith Court, Australia
2. Ann Haydon Jones, England
3. Billie Jean Moffitt King, U.S.
4. Nancy Richey, U.S.
5. Julie Heldman, U.S.
6. Rosie Casals, U.S.
7. Kerry Melville, Australia
8. Mary Ann Eisel, U.S.
9. Virginia Wade, England
10. Lesley Turner Bowrey, Australia

1970

1. Margaret Smith Court, Australia
2. Billie Jean Moffitt King, U.S.
3. Rosie Casals, U.S.
4. Nancy Richey, U.S.
5. Virginia Wade, England
6. Helga Niessen Masthoff, Germany
7. Ann Haydon Jones, England
8. Kerry Melville, Australia
9. Karen Krantzcke, Australia
10. Francoise Durr, France

1971

1. Billie Jean Moffitt King, U.S.
2. Evonne Goolagong, Australia
3. Margaret Smith Court, Australia
4. Rosie Casals, U.S.
5. Kerry Melville, Australia
6. Francoise Durr, France
7. Virginia Wade, England
8. Helga Niessen Masthoff, Germany
9. Judy Tegart, Australia
10. Chris Evert, U.S.

1972

1. Billie Jean Moffitt King, U.S.
2. Margaret Court, Australia
3. Nancy Richey Gunter, U.S.
4. Chris Evert, U.S.
5. Virginia Wade, England
6. Evonne Goolagong, Australia
7. Rosie Casals, U.S.
8. Kerry Melville, Australia
9. Francoise Durr, France
10. Olga Morozova, U.S.S.R.

1973

1. Margaret Smith Court, Australia
2. Billie Jean Moffitt King, U.S.
3. Evonne Goolagong, Australia
4. Chris Evert, U.S.
5. Rosie Casals, U.S.
6. Virginia Wade, England
7. Kerry Melville, Australia
8. Nancy Richey Gunter, U.S.
9. Julie Heldman, U.S.
10. Helga Niessen Masthoff, Germany

1974

1. Billie Jean Moffitt King, U.S.
2. Evonne Goolagong, Australia
3. Chris Evert, U.S.
4. Virginia Wade, England
5. Julie Heldman, U.S.
6. Rosie Casals, U.S.
7. Kerry Melville, Australia
8. Olga Morozova, U.S.S.R.
9. Lesley Hunt, Australia
10. Francoise Durr, France

1975

1. Chris Evert, U.S.
2. Billie Jean Moffitt King, U.S.
3. Evonne Goolagong, Australia
4. Martina Navratilova, Czechoslovakia
5. Virginia Wade, England
6. Margaret Smith Court, Australia
7. Olga Morozova, U.S.S.R.
8. Nancy Richey Gunter, U.S.
9. Francoise Durr, France
10. Rosie Casals, U.S.

1976

1. Chris Evert, U.S.
2. Evonne Goolagong, Australia
3. Virginia Wade, England
4. Martina Navratilova, Czechoslovakia
5. Sue Barker, England
6. Betty Stove, Netherlands
7. Dianne Fromholtz, Australia
8. Mima Jausovec, Yugoslavia
9. Rosie Casals, U.S.
10. Francoise Durr, France

1977

1. Chris Evert, U.S.
2. Billie Jean Moffitt King, U.S.
3. Virginia Wade, England
4. Martina Navratilova, Czechoslovakia
5. Sue Barker, England
6. Wendy Turnbull, Australia
7. Betty Stove, Netherlands
8. Rosie Casals, U.S.
9. Dianne Fromholtz, Australia

6. Tracy Austin, U.S.
7. Pam Shriver, U.S.
8. Virginia Ruzici, Romania
9. Wendy Turnbull, Australia
10. Kerry Melville Reid, Australia

1979

1. Martina Navratilova, U.S.
2. Tracy Austin, U.S.
3. Chris Evert Lloyd, U.S.
4. Evonne Goolagong, Australia
5. Billie Jean Moffitt King, U.S.
6. Wendy Turnbull, Australia
7. Dianne Fromholtz, Australia
8. Kerry Melville Reid, Australia
9. Virginia Wade, England
10. Regina Marsikova, Czechoslovakia

1980

1. Chris Evert Lloyd, U.S.
2. Tracy Austin, U.S.
3. Martina Navratilova, U.S.
4. Hana Mandlikova, Czechoslovakia
5. Andrea Jaeger, U.S.
6. Evonne Goolagong, Australia
7. Billie Jean Moffitt King, U.S.
8. Wendy Turnbull, Australia
9. Pam Shriver, U.S.
10. Virginia Ruzici, Romania

1981

1. Tracy Austin, U.S.
2. Martina Navratilova, U.S.
3. Chris Evert Lloyd, U.S.
4. Hana Mandlikova, Czech.
5. Pam Shriver, U.S.
6. Andrea Jaeger, U.S.
7. Sylvia Hanika, Germany
8. Mima Jausovec, Yugoslavia
9. Barbara Potter, U.S.

6. Tracy Austin, U.S.
7. Wendy Turnbull, Australia
8. Sylvia Hanika, Germany
9. Pam Shriver, U.S.
10. Bettina Bunge, Germany

1983

1. Martina Navratilova, U.S.
2. Chris Evert Lloyd, U.S.
3. Pam Shriver, U.S.
4. Andrea Jaeger, U.S.
5. Jo Durie, England
6. Wendy Turnbull, Australia
7. Hana Mandlikova, Czechoslovakia
8. Andrea Temesvari, Hungary
9. Sylvia Hanika, Germany
10. Kathy Jordan, U.S.

1984

1. Martina Navratilova, U.S.
2. Chris Evert Lloyd, U.S.
3. Hana Mandlikova, Czechoslovakia
4. Helena Sukova, Czechoslovakia
5. Manuela Maleeva, Bulgaria
6. Pam Shriver, U.S.
7. Claudia Kohde Kilsch, Germany
8. Zina Garrison, U.S.
9. Wendy Turnbull, Australia
10. Carling Bassett, Canada

1985

1. Martina Navratilova, U.S.
2. Chris Evert Lloyd, U.S.
3. Hana Mandlikova, Czechoslovakia
4. Claudia Kohde Kilsch, Germany
5. Pam Shriver, U.S.
6. Zina Garrison, U.S.
7. Helena Sukova, Czechoslovakia
8. Steffi Graf, Germany
9. Kathy Rinaldi, U.S.
10. Gabriela Sabatini, Argentina

1986

1. Martina Navratilova, Czechoslovakia
2. Chris Evert Lloyd, U.S.
3. Steffi Graf, Germany
4. Helena Sukova, Czechoslovakia
5. Pam Shriver, U.S.
6. Hana Mandlikova, Czechoslovakia
7. Claudia Kohde Kilsch, Germany
8. Gabriela Sabatini, Argentina
9. Lori McNeil, U.S.
10. Manuela Maleeva, Bulgaria

1987

1. Steffi Graf, Germany
2. Martina Navratilova, U.S.
3. Chris Evert, U.S.
4. Pam Shriver, U.S.
5. Hana Mandlikova, Czechoslovakia
6. Gabriela Sabatini, Argentina
7. Helena Sukova, Czechoslovakia
8. Manuela Maleeva, Bulgaria
9. Lori McNeil, U.S.
10. Zina Garrison, U.S.

1988

1. Steffi Graf
2. Martina Navratilova, U.S.
3. Gabriela Sabatini, Argentina
4. Chris Evert, U.S.
5. Pam Shriver, U.S.
6. Natalia Zvereva, Russia
7. Manuela Maleeva, Bulgaria
8. Helena Sukova, Czechoslovakia
9. Zina Garrison, U.S.
10. Katerina Maleeva, Bulgaria

1989

1. Steffi Graf, Germany
2. Martina Navratilova, U.S.
3. Arantxa Sanchez Vicario, Spain
4. Gabriela Sabatini, Argentina
5. Monica Seles, Yugoslavia
6. Zina Garrison, U.S.
7. Chris Evert, U.S.
8. Helena Sukova, Czechoslovakia
9. Manuela Maleeva, Bulgaria
10. Mary Joe Fernandez, U.S.

1990

1. Monica Seles, Yugoslavia
2. Gabriela Sabatini, Argentina
3. Steffi Graf, Germany
4. Martina Navratilova, U.S.
5. Jennifer Capriati, U.S.
6. Arantxa Sanchez Vicario, Spain
7. Mary Joe Fernandez, U.S.
8. Katerina Maleeva, Bulgaria
9. Manuela Maleeva Fragniere, Bulgaria
10. Zina Garrison, U.S.

1991

1. Monica Seles, Yugoslavia
2. Steffi Graf, Germany
3. Gabriela Sabatini, Argentina
4. Martina Navratilova, U.S.
5. Jennifer Capriati, U.S.
6. Arantxa Sanchez Vicario, Spain
7. Jana Novotna, Czechoslovakia
8. Mary Joe Fernandez, U.S.
9. Manuela Maleeva Fragniere, Bulgaria
10. Conchita Martinez, Spain

1992

1. Monica Seles, Yugoslavia
2. Steffi Graf, Germany
3. Arantxa Sanchez Vicario, Spain
4. Jennifer Capriati, U.S.
5. Martina Navratilova, U.S.
6. Gabriela Sabatini, Argentina
7. Mary Joe Fernandez, U.S.
8. Conchita Martinez, Spain
9. Manuela Maleeva Fragniere, Bulgaria
10. Anke Huber, Germany

MISCELLANEOUS ALL-TIME RECORDS

MEN

Singles

Match

Aces—42, John Feaver vs. John Newcombe,
Wimbledon, 1976
40, Bryan Shelton vs. Paolo Cane, Australian
~~Open, 1991~~

Career

Tournaments played—399, Connors, 1970—92
305, Lendl, 1979—82

Finals—163, Connors, 1971—89
141, Lendl, 1979—92

Tournaments won—109, Connors, 1972—89
92, Lendl, 1982—92
77, McEnroe, 1978—91
62, Bjorn Borg, 1974—81
62, Vilas, 1973—86
~~57, Nastase, 1970—81~~

Season

Aces—1,017, Ivanisevic, 1992

Double faults—362, Petr Korda, 1992

Winning streaks—50, Guillermo Vilas, 1977
45, Bjorn Borg, 1979—80
44, Ivan Lendl, 1982
42, John McEnroe, 1984

Losing streak—20, Garry Donnelly, 1986—87

Tournaments played—40, Ross Case; Onny Parun, 1973
39, Dick Crealy, 1974
38, Bob Carmichael, Frew McMillan, 1973
37, Onny Parun, 1972; Colin Dibley, Ray
Moore, 1973; Dick Crealy, 1975
36, Gerald Battrick, 1973; Barry Phillips-
Moore, 1974; Ray Moore, 1975
35, Phil Dent, 1971; Brian Gottfried, Dick
Crealy, 1973; Harold Solomon, 1974 and
1975

Tournaments won—17, Rod Laver (of 32), 1969
17, Vilas (of 33), 1977
15, Lendl (of 23), 1982; Ilie Nastase (of 31),
1973

Matches played—159, Vilas, 1977
142, Lendl, 1980
135, Nastase, 1973
123, Arthur Ashe, 1975

Matches won—145, Vilas (of 159), 1977
118, Nastase (of 135), 1973
113, Lendl (of 142), 1980
107, Lendl (of 116), 1982
106, Laver (of 122), 1969

Season

Tournaments played—38, David Adams, 1992

Tournaments won—17, John McEnroe, 1979
15, Bob Hewitt, Frew McMillan, both 1977

Matches played—86, McEnroe, 1979

Matches won—83, McEnroe, 1979

Tournaments played, team—19, Peter Fleming–
McEnroe, 1979

Tournaments won, team—
15, Fleming–McEnroe, 1977
13, Hewitt–McMillan, 1977

Matches played team—78, Fleming–McEnroe, 1979

Matches won, team—74, Fleming–McEnroe, 1979

Career

Finals—125, Tom Okker, 1968–80
119, McMillan, 1968–81

Tournaments won—78, Okker, 1968–80
75, McEnroe, 1978—92
74, McMillan, 1968–81
66, Peter Fleming, 1978—87
65, Hewitt, 1968–80
62, Raul Ramirez, 1973—83

Tournaments won, team—
57, Fleming–McEnroe; Hewitt–McMillan
39, Brian Gottfried–Ramirez
36, Sergio Casal–Emilio Sanchez
34, Bob Lutz–Stan Smith

Overall (Singles and Doubles together)

Season

Singles and doubles tournaments played—
44, Vilas, 1977
43, McEnroe, 1979

Singles and doubles tournaments won—
27, McEnroe (10–17), 1979
23, Nastase, (15–8), 1973; Laver (17–6), 1969
21, Vilas (17–4), 1977

Singles and doubles matches played—
221, Vilas, 1977 (159–62)
192, McEnroe, 1979 (106–86)

Singles and doubles matches won—
187, Vilas, 1977 (145 singles, 42 doubles)
177, McEnroe, 1979 (94 singles, 83 doubles)

Career

Singles and doubles tournaments won—
152, McEnroe (77–75), 1978—92
128, Connors (109–19), 1972—89
108, Nastase (57–51) 1968—81
108, Okker (30–78), 1968—80
100, Stan Smith (39–61), 1968—80

WOMEN

Singles

Match

Aces—16, Brenda Schultz vs. Monica Seles,
Wimbledon, 1989

Double faults—16, Helena Sukova vs. Chris Evert,
Eastbourne, 1987

Season

Winning streaks—74, Martina Navratilova, 1984
66, Steffi Graf, 1990
58, Navratilova, 1986–87
55, Evert, 1974
54, Margaret Smith Court, 1972–73;
Navratilova, 1983–84

Tournaments played—32, Rosie Casals, 1971
31, Billie Jean King, 1971
30, Kim Steinmetz, 1985
29, Camille Benjamin, 1985
28, Benjamin, 1986

Tournaments won—21, Court, 1970
18, Court, 1973
17, King, 1971
16, Evert, 1974–1975; Navratilova, 1983

Matches played—126, King, 1971
116, Casals, 1971
110, Court, 1970
108, Court, 1973; Evert, 1974
103, Navratilova, 1981
102, Navratilova, 1979

Matches won—112, King, 1971
104, Court, 1970
102, Court, 1973
100, Evert, 1974
90, Navratilova, 1979

Career

Tournaments played—350, Navratilova, 1973–92
304, Casals, 1968–82
303, Evert, 1969–89
242, Pam Shriver, 1978–92
216, King, 1968–83
130, Court, 1968–77

Tournaments won—161, Navratilova
157, Evert
79, Court
69, Graf
67, King

Matches played—1,549, Navratilova
1,455, Evert
892, Court
826, King
824, Casals

Matches won—1,359, Navratilova
1,309, Evert
789, Court
677, King
528, Casals

Doubles

Season

Tournaments played—31, Casals, 1979
30, Casals, 1980, 1982
28, Casals, 1971, 1981
26, King, 1971; McNeil, 1985–87; Jana
Novotna, 1987
25, McNeil, 1984–86
24, McNeil, 1988
23, Navratilova, 1975

Tournaments won—21, King, 1971; Casals, 1971
14, Navratilova, 1982
13, Shriver, 1982 and 1983; Casals 1970, 1973

Matches played—99, Casals, 1982
96, Casals, 1981
89, Casals, 1971

85, King, 1971
84, Arantxa Sanchez Vicario, 1992
80, Novotna, 1991
75, Shriver, 1982
72, Navratilova, 1982

Matches won—82, Casals, 1971
80, King, 1971
74, Casals, 1981, 1982
73, Sanchez Vicario, 1992
68, Navratilova, 1982; Shriver, 1982; Novotna, 1991

Overall (Singles and Doubles Together)

Season

Singles and doubles tournaments played—
60, Casals, 1971
57, King, 1971
56, Casals, 1979
55, Casals, 1980
48, Navratilova, 1975
45, Court, 1970
44, Novotna, 1987

17, Casals–King, 1969
16, Casals–King, 1973
14, Navratilova–Shriver, 1982

Tournaments won, team—19, Casals–King, 1971
12, Navratilova–Shriver, 1982
11, Navratilova–Shriver, 1983–84
10, Casals–King, 1973

166, Court, 1970
165, Navratilova, 1982
157, Court, 1973

Singles and doubles matches won—
192, King (of 210), 1971
169, Casals (of 205), 1971
158, Navratilova (of 165), 1982
150, Court (of 166), 1970
144, Court (of 157), 1973
139, Sanchez Vicario, 1992 (of 167)

Career

Tournaments played—381, Casals, 1968–91
270, Navratilova, 1973–92
216, King, 1968–90
215, Shriver, 1978–92

Tournaments won—157, Navratilova
112, Casals
106, Shriver
101, King

Matches played—1,054, Navratilova
1,125 Casals
789, Shriver
725, King

Matches won—943, Navratilova
856, Casals
679, Shriver
611, King

Tournaments played, team—101, Navratilova–Shriver
98, Casals–King

Tournaments won, team—79, Navratilova–Shriver
56, Casals–King

Matches won, team—390 (of 415), Navratilova–Shriver
294 (of 335), Casals–King

Career

Singles and doubles tournaments played—685, Casals
662, Navratilova
567, Casals
442, Evert
432, King
231, Court

Singles and doubles tournaments won—318, Navratilova
189, Evert
168, King
127, Court
123, Casals

Singles and doubles matches played—2,603, Navratilova
1,949 Casals
1,875, Evert
1,551, King
892 Court

Singles and doubles matches won—2,302, Navratilova
1,631, Evert
1,384, Casals
1,288, King

Longest Matches

Men's singles: 126 games—Roger Taylor, Britain, d. Wieslaw Gasiorek, Poland, 27–29, 31–29, 6–4. King's Cup match, Warsaw, 1966.

Men's doubles: 147 games—Dick Leach, Arcadia, Calif., and Dick Dell, Bethesda, Md., d. Len Schloss, Baltimore, and Tom Mozur, Sweetwater, Tenn., 3–6, 49–47, 22–20. Second round, Newport (R.I.) Casino Invitation, 1967.

Women's singles: 62 games—Kathy Blake, Pacific Palisades, Calif., d. Elena Subirats, Mexico, 12–10, 6–8, 14–12. First round, Piping Rock Invitation, Locust Valley, N.Y., 1966.

Women's doubles: 81 games—Nancy Richey, San Angelo, Tex., and Carole Graebner, New York, d. Carol Hanks and Justina Bricka, both St. Louis, 31–33, 6–1, 6–4. Semifinal, Eastern Grass Championship, South Orange, N.J., 1964.

Mixed doubles: 77 games—Brenda Schultz and Michiel Schapers, Netherlands, d. Andrea Temesvari, Hungary, and Tom Nijssen, Netherlands, 6–3, 5–7, 29–27, first round, Wimbledon, 1991.

Longest Matches (playing time)

Men

6 hours 32 minutes: John McEnroe, U.S., d. Mats Wilander, Sweden, 9–7, 6–2, 15–17, 3–6, 8–6. Davis Cup, quarters, St. Louis, 1982.

Women

6 hours 31 minutes: Vicki Nelson-Durbar d. Jean Hepner, 6–4, 7–6 (13–11). Richmond, (Va.), 1st rd., 1984 (tie-breaker alone lasted 1:47, one point of which lasted 29 minutes, a rally of 643 strokes).

Longest Sets

Men's singles: 70 games—John Brown, Australia, d. Bill Brown, Omaha, Neb., 36–34, 6–1. Third Round, Heart of America tourney, Kansas City, Mo., 1968.

Men's doubles: 96 games—Dell and Leach d. Schloss and Mozur, 3–6, 49–47, 22–20 (see above).

Women's singles: 36 games—Billie Jean King, U.S., d. Christine Truman, Britain, 6–4, 19–17. Wightman Cup, Cleveland, 1963.

Women's doubles: 64 games—Richey and Graebner d. Hanks and Bricka, 31–33, 6–1, 6–4 (see above).

Mixed doubles: 52 games—Margaret duPont, Wilmington, Del., and Bill Talbert, N.Y., d. Gussy Moran, Santa Monica, Cal., and Bob Falkenburg Los Angeles, 27–25, 5–7, 6–1. Semifinal, U.S. Championships, Forest HIlls, N.Y.

Longest Tie-Breaks

Men's singles: 24–22—First set, Aki Rahunen, Finland, d. Peter Nyborg, Denmark, 7–6, 2–6, 6–3, 1st rd., qualifying Copenhagen Open, 1992.

Men's doubles: 26–24—Fourth set, Jan Gunnarson, Sweden, and Michael Mortensen, Denmark, d. John Frawley, Australia, and Victor Pecci, Paraguay, 6–4, 6–4, 3–6, 7–6, 1st rd., Wimbledon, 1985.

Women's singles: 19–17—First set, Pat Medrado, Brazil, d. Laura Arraya (Gildemeister), 7–6, 6–7, 6–1, round-robin, Sao Paulo, Brazil, 1981

Women's doubles: 20–18—Third set, Rosie Casals, Sausalito, Calif., and Kathy Horvath, Largo, Fla., d. Sandy Collins, Odessa, Tex., and Beth Herr, Dayton, Ohio, 5–7, 6–1, 7–6, 2nd rd., Amelia Island, Fla., 1984.

Mixed doubles: 18–16—Third set, Marcie Louie, San Francisco, and Andy Lucchesi d. Diane Desfor, Long Beach, Calif., and Horace Reid, New York, 6–2, 6–7, 7–6. Second round, U.S. Open, Flushing Meadow, N.Y., 1978.

Championships

(This pertains to the major titles, the Big Four championships of Australia, France, Britain/Wimbledon, and the United States, with years between first and last championship indicated.)

Most men's singles: 12—Roy Emerson, 1961–67 (6 Aus., 2 Fr., 2 Wim., 2 U.S.)

Most men's doubles: 17—John Newcombe, 1965–76 (5 Aus., 3 Fr., 6 Wim., 3 U.S.)

Most men's mixed: 8—Vic Seixas, 1953–56 (1 Fr., 4 Wim., 3 U.S.); Frank Sedgman, 1949–52 (2 Aus., 2 Fr., 2 Wim., 2 U.S.)

Most men's altogether: 28—Emerson, 1959–71.

Most women's singles: 24—Margaret Smith Court, 1960–73 (11 Aus., 4 Fr., 2 Wim. 7 U.S.)

Most women's doubles: 31—Martina Navratilova (8 Aus., 7 Fr., 7 Wim., 9 U.S.)

Most women's mixed: 19—Court, 1961–75 (2 Aus., 4 Fr., 5 Wim., 8 U.S.)

Most women's altogether: 62—Court, 1960–75

Most men's doubles, team: 12—Newcombe and Tony Roche, 1965–75 (4 Aus., 2 Fr., 5 Wim., 1 U.S.)

Most women's doubles, team: 20—Margaret Osborne duPont and Louise Brough, 1942–57 (3 Fr., 5 Wim., 12 U.S.); Navratilova and Pam Shriver, 1982—89 (7 Aus., 4 Fr., 5 Wim., 4 U.S.)

Most mixed doubles, team: 10—Court and Ken Fletcher, 1963–68 (2 Aus., 3 Fr., 4 Wim., 1 U.S.)

1991

Men's career high: $19,172,627—Ivan Lendl

Women's career high: $18,396,526—Martina Navratilova

Men's tournament high: $2,000,000—Pete Sampras, 1990 Compaq Grand Slam Cup, Munich; David Wheaton, 1991 Compaq Grand Slam Cup, Munich; Michael Stitch, 1992 Compaq Grand Slam Cup, Munich.

Women's tournament high: $500,000—Monica Seles, 1992 U.S. Open, Flushing Meadow, N.Y.

Career Prize Money Leaders

Men

1.	Ivan Lendl	1978–92	$19,172,627
2.	Stefan Edberg	1984–92	$13,339,075
3.	John McEnroe	1978–92	$12,227,622
4.	Boris Becker	1984–92	$11,670,442
5.	Jimmy Connors	1972–92	$8,471,435
6.	Mats Wilander	1982–90	$7,377,193
7.	Andre Agassi	1986–92	$5,351,203
8.	Guillermo Vilas	1972–92	$4,923,132
9.	Jim Courier	1988–92	$4,846,459
10.	Pete Sampras	1988–92	$4,557,225
11.	Anders Jarryd	1980–92	$4,388,749
12.	Andres Gomez	1979–92	$4,257,500
13.	Emilio Sanchez	1984–92	$3,948,131
14.	Brad Gilbert	1982–92	$3,904,698
15.	Guy Forget	1982–92	$4,257,500
16.	Tomas Smid	1978–89	$3,699,738
17.	Bjorn Borg	1973–92	$3,644,826
18.	Jakob Hlasek	1983–92	$3,453,525
19.	Yannick Noah	1978–91	$3,295,395
20.	Kevin Curren	1979–92	$2,951,195

Women

1.	Martina Navratilova	1973–92	$18,396,526
2.	Steffi Graf	1982–92	$10,332,673
3.	Chris Evert	1973–89	$8,896,195
4.	Monica Seles	1989–92	$6,671,393
5.	Gabriela Sabatini	1985–92	$6,056,672
		1978–92	$4,870,516
15.	Mary Joe Fernandez	1986–92	$2,255,521
16.	Claudia Kohde Kilsch	1980–92	$2,224,887
17.	Lori McNeil	1983–92	$2,073,795
18.	Billie Jean Moffitt King	1968–83	$1,966,487
19.	Tracy Austin	1978–89	$1,925,415
20.	Beatrice "Gigi" Fernandez	1983–92	$1,871,589

WTA YEAR-END COMPUTER TOP 10 1973–92

1973

1. Margaret Smith Court
2. Billie Jean Moffitt King
3. Evonne Goolagong Cawley
4. Chris Evert
5. Rosie Casals
6. Virginia Wade
7. Kerry Melville
8. Nancy Richey Gunter
9. Julie Heldman
10. Helga Niessen Masthoff

1974

1. Billie Jean Moffitt King
2. Evonne Goolagong Cawley
3. Chris Evert
4. Virginia Wade
5. Julie Heldman

6. Rosie Casals
7. Kerry Melville
8. Olga Morozova
9. Lesley Hunt
10. Francoise Durr

1975

1. Chris Evert
2. Billie Jean Moffitt King
3. Evonne Goolagong Cawley
4. Martina Navratilova
5. Virgina Wade
6. Margaret Smith Court
7. Olga Morozova
8. Nancy Richey Gunter
9. Francoise Durr
10. Rosie Casals

1976

1. Chris Evert
2. Evonne Goolagong Cawley
3. Virginia Wade
4. Martina Navratilova
5. Sue Barker
6. Betty Stove
7. Dianne Fromholtz
8. Mima Jausovec
9. Rosie Casals
10. Francoise Durr

1977

1. Chris Evert
2. Billie Jean Moffitt King
3. Martina Navratilova
4. Virginia Wade
5. Sue Barker
6. Rosie Casals
7. Betty Stove
8. Dianne Fromholtz
9. Wendy Turnbull
10. Kerry Melville Reid

1978

1. Martina Navratilova
2. Chris Evert
3. Evonne Goolagong Cawley
4. Virgina Wade
5. Billie Jean Moffitt King
6. Tracy Austin
7. Wendy Turnbull
8. Kerry Melville Reid
9. Betty Stove
10. Dianne Fromholtz

1979

1. Martina Navratilova
2. Chris Evert Lloyd
3. Tracy Austin
4. Evonne Goolagong Cawley
5. Billie Jean Moffitt King
6. Dianne Fromholtz
7. Wendy Turnbull
8. Virginia Wade
9. Kerry Melville Reid
10. Sue Barker

1980

1. Chris Evert Lloyd
2. Tracy Austin
3. Martina Navratilova
4. Hana Mandlikova
5. Evonne Goolagong Cawley
6. Billie Jean Moffitt King
7. Andrea Jaeger
8. Wendy Turnbull
9. Pam Shriver
10. Greer Stevens

1981

1. Chris Evert Lloyd
2. Tracy Austin
3. Martina Navratilova
4. Andrea Jaeger
5. Hana Mandlikova
6. Sylvia Hanika
7. Pam Shriver
8. Wendy Turnbull
9. Bettina Bunge
10. Barbara Potter

1982

1. Martina Navratilova
2. Chris Evert Lloyd
3. Andrea Jaeger
4. Tracy Austin
5. Wendy Turnbull
6. Pam Shriver
7. Hana Mandlikova
8. Barbara Potter
9. Bettina Bunge
10. Sylvia Hanika

1983

1. Martina Navratilova
2. Chris Evert Lloyd
3. Andrea Jaeger
4. Pam Shriver
5. Sylvia Hanika
6. Jo Durie
7. Bettina Bunge
8. Wendy Turnbull
9. Tracy Austin

6. Manuela Maleeva
7. Helena Sukova
8. Claudia Kohde-Kilsch
9. Zina Garrison
10. Kathy Jordan

1985

1. Martina Navratilova
2. Chris Evert Lloyd
3. Hana Mandlikova
4. Pam Shriver
5. Claudia Kohde-Kilsch
6. Steffi Graf
7. Manuela Maleeva
8. Zina Garrison
9. Helena Sukova
10. Bonnie Gadusek

1986

1. Martina Navratilova
2. Chris Evert Lloyd
3. Steffi Graf
4. Hana Mandlikova
5. Helena Sukova
6. Pam Shriver
7. Claudia Kohde-Kilsch
8. Manuela Maleeva
9. Kathy Rinaldi
10. Gabriela Sabatini

1987

1. Steffi Graf
2. Martina Navratilova
3. Chris Evert
4. Pam Shriver
5. Hana Mandlikova
6. Gabriela Sabatini
7. Helena Sukova
8. Manuela Maleeva
9. Zina Garrison
10. Claudia Kohde-Kilsch

6. Manuela Maleeva Fragniere
7. Natalia Zvereva
8. Helena Sukova
9. Zina Garrison
10. Barbara Potter

1989

1. Steffi Graf
2. Martina Navratilova
3. Gabriela Sabatini
4. Zina Garrison
5. Arantxa Sanchez Vicario
6. Monica Seles
7. Conchita Martinez
8. Helena Sukova
9. Manuela Maleeva Fragniere
10. Chris Evert

1990

1. Steffi Graf
2. Monica Seles
3. Martina Navratilova
4. Mary Joe Fernandez
5. Gabriela Sabatini
6. Katerina Maleeva
7. Aranxta Sanchez Vicario
8. Jennifer Capriati
9. Manuela Maleeva Fragniere
10. Zina Garrison

1991

1. Monica Seles
2. Steffi Graf
3. Gabriela Sabatini
4. Martina Navratilova
5. Aranxta Sanchez Vicario
6. Jennifer Capriati
7. Jana Novotna
8. Mary Joe Fernandez
9. Conchita Martinez
10. Manuela Maleeva Fragniere

1992

1. Monica Seles
2. Steffi Graf
3. Gabriela Sabatini
4. Arantxa Sanchez Vicario
5. Martina Navratilova
6. Mary Joe Fernandez
7. Jennifer Capriati
8. Conchita Martinez
9. Manuela Maleeva Fragniere
10. Jana Novotna

ATP Tour Year-End Computer Top 10 1973–92

1973

1. Ilie Nastase
2. John Newcombe
3. Jimmy Connors
4. Tom Okker
5. Stan Smith
6. Ken Rosewall
7. Manuel Orantes
8. Rod Laver
9. Jan Kodes
10. Arthur Ashe

1974

1. Jimmy Connors
2. John Newcombe
3. Bjorn Borg
4. Rod Laver
5. Guillermo Vilas
6. Tom Okker
7. Arthur Ashe
8. Ken Rosewall
9. Stan Smith
10. Ilie Nastase

1975

1. Jimmy Connors
2. Guillermo Vilas
3. Bjorn Borg
4. Arthur Ashe
5. Manuel Orantes
6. Ken Rosewall
7. Ilie Nastase
8. John Alexander
9. Roscoe Tanner
10. Rod Laver

1976

1. Jimmy Connors
2. Bjorn Borg
3. Ilie Nastase
4. Manuel Orantes
5. Raul Ramirez
6. Guillermo Vilas
7. Adriano Panatta
8. Harold Solomon
9. Eddie Dibbs
10. Brian Gottfried

1977

1. Jimmy Connors
2. Guillermo Vilas
3. Bjorn Borg
4. Vitas Gerulaitis
5. Brian Gottfried
6. Eddie Dibbs
7. Manuel Orantes
8. Raul Ramirez
9. Ilie Nastase
10. Dick Stockton

1978

1. Jimmy Connors
2. Bjorn Borg
3. Guillermo Vilas
4. John McEnroe
5. Vitas Gerulaitis
6. Eddie Dibbs
7. Brian Gottried
8. Raul Ramirez
9. Harold Solomon
10. Corrado Barazzutti

1979

1. Bjorn Borg
2. Jimmy Connors
3. John McEnroe
4. Vitas Gerulaitis
5. Roscoe Tanner
6. Guillermo Vilas
7. Arthur Ashe
8. Harold Solomon
9. Jose Higueras

6. Ivan Lendl
7. Harold Solomon
8. Jose-Luis Clerc
9. Vitas Gerulaitis
10. Eliot Teltscher

1981

1. John McEnroe
2. Ivan Lendl
3. Jimmy Connors
4. Bjorn Borg
5. Jose-Luis Clerc
6. Guillermo Vilas
7. Gene Mayer
8. Eliot Teltscher
9. Vitas Gerulaitis
10. Peter McNamara

1982

1. John McEnroe
2. Jimmy Connors
3. Ivan Lendl
4. Guillermo Vilas
5. Vitas Gerulaitis
6. Jose–Luis Clerc
7. Mats Wilander
8. Gene Mayer
9. Yannick Noah
10. Peter McNamara

1983

1. John McEnroe
2. Ivan Lendl
3. Jimmy Connors
4. Mats Wilander
5. Yannick Noah
6. Jimmy Arias
7. Jose Higueras
8. Jose-Luis Clerc
9. Kevin Curren
10. Gene Mayer

6. Anders Jarryd
7. Henrik Sundstrom
8. Pat Cash
9. Eliot Teltscher
10. Yannick Noah

1985

1. Ivan Lendl
2. John McEnroe
3. Mats Wilander
4. Jimmy Connors
5. Stefan Edberg
6. Boris Becker
7. Yannick Noah
8. Anders Jarryd
9. Miloslav Mecir
10. Kevin Curren

1986

1. Ivan Lendl
2. Boris Becker
3. Mats Wilander
4. Yannick Noah
5. Stefan Edberg
6. Henri Leconte
7. Joakim Nystrom
8. Jimmy Connors
9. Miloslav Mecir
10. Andres Gomez

1987

1. Ivan Lendl
2. Stefan Edberg
3. Mats Wilander
4. Jimmy Connors
5. Boris Becker
6. Miloslav Mecir
7. Pat Cash
8. Yannick Noah
9. Tim Mayotte
10. John McEnroe

1988

1. Mats Wilander
2. Ivan Lendl
3. Andre Agassi
4. Boris Becker
5. Stefan Edberg
6. Kent Carlsson
7. Jimmy Connors
8. Jakob Hlasek
9. Henri Leconte
10. Tim Mayotte

1989

1. Ivan Lendl
2. Boris Becker
3. Stefan Edberg
4. John McEnroe
5. Michael Chang
6. Brad Gilbert
7. Andre Agassi
8. Aaron Krickstein
9. Alberto Mancini
10. Jay Berger

1990

1. Stefan Edberg
2. Boris Becker
3. Ivan Lendl
4. Andre Agassi
5. Pete Sampras
6. Andres Gomez
7. Thomas Muster
8. Emilio Sanchez
9. Goran Ivanisevic
10. Brad Gilbert

1991

1. Stefan Edberg
2. Jim Courier
3. Boris Becker
4. Michael Stich
5. Ivan Lendl
6. Pete Sampras
7. Guy Forget
8. Karel Novacek
9. Petr Korda
10. Andre Agassi

1992

1. Jim Courier
2. Stefan Edberg
3. Pete Sampras
4. Goran Ivanisevic
5. Boris Becker
6. Michael Chang
7. Petr Korda
8. Ivan Lendl
9. Andre Agassi
10. Richard Krajicek

ITF WORLD CHAMPIONS

Since 1978 the ITF has crowned world champions in men's and women's singles. Until 1992 these were subjective, chosen by committees. That year a computerized ranking was adopted.

Men

1978	Bjorn Borge, Sweden
1979	Bjorn Borg, Sweden
1980	Bjorn Borg, Sweden
1981	John McEnroe, U.S.
1982	Jimmy Connors, U.S.
1983	John McEnroe, U.S.
1984	John McEnroe, U.S.
1985	Ivan Lendl, Czechoslovakia
1986	Ivan Lendl, Czechoslovakia
1987	Ivan Lendl, Czechoslovakia
1988	Mats Wilander, Sweden
1989	Boris Becker, Germany
1990	Ivan Lendl, Czechoslovakia
1991	Stefan Edberg, Sweden
1992	Jim Courier, U.S.

Women

1978	Chris Evert Lloyd, U.S.
1979	Martina Navratilova, Czechoslovakia
1980	Chris Evert Lloyd, U.S.
1981	Chris Evert Lloyd, U.S.
1982	Martina Navratilova, Czechoslovakia
1983	Martina Navratilova, Czechoslovakia
1984	Martina Navratilova, Czechoslovakia
1985	Martina Navratilova, Czechoslovakia
1986	Martina Navratilova, Czechoslovakia

6–1; Len Schwartz, 6–4, 6–3, 10–8; Adrian Quist , 5–7, 6–4, 6–1, 6–2; Jack Bromwich, 6–4, 6–2, 6–1.

French at Roland Garros, Paris—d. Antoine Gentien, 6–1, 6–2, 6–4; Ghaus Mohammed, 6–1, 6–1, 5–7, 6–0; Franjo Kukuljevic, 6–2, 8–6, 2–6, 1–6, 6–1; Bernard Destremau, 6–4, 6–3, 6–4; Josip Pallada, 6–2, 6–3, 6–3; Roderich Menzel, 6–3, 6–2, 6–4.

British, at Wimbledon, London—d. Kenneth Gandar Dower, 6–2, 6–3, 6–3; Henry Billington, 7–5, 6–1, 6–1; George Lyttleton Rogers, 6–0, 7–5, 6–1; Ronald Shayes, 6–3, 6–4, 6–1; Franz Cejnar, 6–3, 6–0, 7–5;

First to win a Grand Slam—the championships of Australia, France, Britain (Wimbledon) and the United States in the same season—was Don Budge of the U.S. Then came Maureen Connolly of the U.S. in 1953 and Rod Laver of Australia, in 1962 as an amateur, again in 1969 when the Slam first became open to all competitors. In 1970 Margaret Smith Court of Australia made the second female Slam and in 1988 Steffi Graf of Germany became the fifth to claim a Slam.

Slams have also been made in doubles by Frank Sedgman and Ken McGregory of Australia in 1951; Martina Navratilova and Pam Shriver of the U.S. in 1984; and in mixed doubles by Margaret Smith (Court) and Ken Fletcher in 1963. A Slam in doubles with two partners was made by Maria Bueno in 1960, and in mixed by Owen Davidson of Australia in 1967.

The complete record of all Grand Slams follows:

SINGLES

Don Budge, 1938

Australian, at Memorial Drive, Adelaide—d. Les Hancock, 6–2, 6–3, 6–4; Harold Whillans, 6–1, 6–0,

Australian at Kooyong, Melbourne—d. Carmen Boreilli, 6–0, 6–1; Alison Burton Baker, 6–1, 6–0; Pam Southcombe, 6–0, 6–1; Mary Bevis Hawton, 6–2, 6–1; Julie Sampson, 6–3, 6–2.

French, at Roland Garros, Paris—d. Christine Mercelis, 6–1, 6–3; Raymonde Verber Jones, 6–3, 6–1; Susan Partridge Chatrier, 3–6, 6–2, 6–2; Dorothy Head Knode, 6–3, 6–3; Doris Hart, 6–2, 6–4.

British, at Wimbledon, London—d. D. Killian, 6–0, 6–0; J. M. Petchell, 6–1, 6–1; Anne Shilcock, 6–0, 6–1; Erika Vollmer, 6–3, 6–0; Shirley Fry, 6–1, 6–1; Doris Hart, 8–6, 7–5.

United States, at Forest Hills, New York—d. Jean Fallot, 6–1, 6–0; Pat Stewart, 6–3, 6–1; Jeanne Arth, 6–1, 6–3; Althea Gibson, 6–2, 6–3; Shirley Fry, 6–1, 6–1; Doris Hart, 6–2, 6–4.

Rod Laver, 1962

Australian, at White City, Sydney—d. Fred Sherriff, 8–6, 6–2, 6–4; Geoff Pares, 10–8, 18–16, 7–9, 7–5; Owen Davidson, 6–4, 9–7, 6–4; Bob Hewitt, 6–1, 4–6, 6–4, 7–5; Roy Emerson, 8–6, 0–6, 6–4, 6–4.

French, at Roland Garros, Paris—d. Michele Pirro, 6–4, 6–0, 6–2; Tony Pickard, 6–2, 9–7, 4–6, 6–1; Sergio Jacobini, 4–6, 6–3, 7–5, 6–1; Marty Mulligan, 6–4, 3–6, 2–6, 10–8, 6–2; Neale Fraser, 3–6, 6–3, 6–2, 7–5; Roy Emerson, 3–6, 2–6, 6–3, 9–7, 6–2.

British, at Wimbledon, London—d. Naresh Kumar, 7–5, 6–1, 6–2; Tony Pickard, 6–1, 6–2, 6–2; Whitney Reed, 6–4, 6–1, 6–4; Pierre Darmon, 6–3, 6–2, 13–11; Manolo Santana, 14–16, 9–7, 6–2, 6–2; Neale Fraser, 10–8, 6–1, 7–5; Marty Mulligan, 6–2, 6–2, 6–1.

United States, at Forest Hills, New York—d. Eleazar Davidman, 6–3, 6–2, 6–3; Eduardo Zuleta, 6–3, 6–3, 6–1; Bodo Nitsche, 9–7, 6–1, 6–1; Antonio Palafox, 6–1, 6–2, 6–2; Frank Froehling, 6–3, 13–11, 4–6, 6–3; Rafe Osuna, 6–1, 6–3, 6–4; Roy Emerson, 6–2, 6–4, 5–7, 6–4.

Rod Laver, 1969

Australian, at Milton Courts, Brisbane—d. Massimo di Domenico, 6–2, 6–2, 6–3; Roy Emerson, 6–2, 6–3, 3–6, 9–7; Fred Stolle, 6–4, 18–16, 6–2; Tony Roche, 7–5, 22–20, 9–11, 1–6, 6–3; Andres Gimeno, 6–3, 6–4, 7–5.

French, at Roland Garros, Paris—d. Koji Watanabe, 6–1, 6–1, 6–1; Dick Crealy, 3–6, 7–9, 6–2, 6–2, 6–4; Pietro Marzano, 6–1, 6–0, 8–6; Stan Smith, 6–4, 6–2, 6–4; Andres Gimeno, 3–6, 6–3, 6–4, 6–3; Tom Okker, 4–6, 6–0, 6–2, 6–4; Ken Rosewall, 6–4, 6–3, 6–4.

British, at Wimbledon, London—d. Nicola Pietrangeli, 6–1, 6–2, 6–2; Premjit Lall, 3–6, 4–6, 6–3, 6–0, 6–0; Jan Leschly, 6–3, 6–3, 6–3; Stan Smith, 6–4, 6–2, 7–9, 3–6, 6–3; Cliff Drysdale, 6–4, 6–2, 6–3; Arthur Ashe, 2–6, 6–2, 9–7, 6–0; John Newcombe, 6–4, 5–7, 6–4, 6–4.

United States, at Forest Hills, New York—d. Luis Garcia, 6–2, 6–4, 6–2; Jaime Pinto-Bravo, 6–4, 7–5, 6–2; Jaime Fillol, 8–6, 6–1, 6–2; Dennis Ralston, 6–4, 4–6, 4–6, 6–2, 6–3; Roy Emerson, 4–6–8–6, 13–11, 6–4; Arthur Ashe, 8–6, 6–3, 14–12; Tony Roche, 7–9, 6–1, 6–2, 6–2.

Margaret Smith Court, 1970

Australian, at White City, Sydney—d. R. Langsford, 6–0, 6–0, K. Wilkinson, 6–0, 6–1; Evonne Goolagong, 6–3, 6–1; Karen Krantzke, 6–1, 6–3; Kerry Melville, 6–3, 6–1.

French, at Rolando Garros, Paris—d. Marijke Jansen Scharr, 6–1, 6–1; Olga Morozova, 3–6, 8–6, 6–1; Lesley Hunt, 6–2, 6–1; Rosie Casals, 7–5, 6–2; Julie Heldman, 6–0, 6–2; Helga Niessen, 6–2, 6–4.

British, at Wimbledon, London—d. Sue Alexander, 6–0, 6–1, Maria Guzman, 6–0, 6–1; Vlasta Vopickova, 6–3, 6–3; Helga Niessen, 6–8, 6–0, 6–0; Rosie Casals, 6–4, 6–1; Billie Jean King, 14–12, 11–9.

United States, at Forest Hills, New York—Pam Austin, 6–1, 6–0; Patti Hogan, 6–1, 6–1; Pat Faulkner, 6–0, 6–2; Helen Gourlay, 6–2, 6–2; Nancy Richey, 6–1, 6–3; Rosie Casals, 6–2, 2–6, 6–1.

Steffi Graf, 1988

Australian, at Flinders Park, Melbourne—d. Amy Jonsson, 6–3, 6–1; Janine Thompson, 6–0, 6–1; Cammy MacGregor, 6–1, 6–2; Catarina Lindqvist, 6–0, 7–5; Hana Mandlikova, 6–2, 6–2; Claudia Kohde Kilsch, 6–2, 6–3; Chris Evert, 6–1, 7–6.

French, at Roland Garros, Paris—d. Natalie Guerree, 6–0, 6–4, Ronni Reis, 6–1, 6–0, Susan Sloane, 6–0, 6–1; Nathalie Tauziat, 6–1, 6–3; Bettina Fulco, 6–0, 6–1; Gabriela Sabatini, 6–3, 7–6; Natalia Zvereva, 6–0, 6–0.

British, at Wimbledon, London—d. Hu Na, 6–0, 6–0; Karine Quentrec, 6–2, 6–0; Terry Phelps, 6–3, 6–1; Mary Joe Fernandez, 6–2, 6–2; Pascale Paradis, 6–3, 6–1; Pam Shriver, 6–1, 6–2; Martina Navratilova, 5–7, 6–2, 6–1.

United States, at Flushing Meadow, New York—d. Elizabeth Minter 6–1, 6–1; Manon Bollegraf, 6–1, 6–0; Nathalie Herreman, 6–0, 6–1; Patty Fendick, 6–4, 6–2; Katerina Maleeva, 6–3, 6–0; Chris Evert, default (illness); Gabriela Sabatini, 6–3, 3–6, 6–1.

DOUBLES

Frank Sedgman–Ken McGregor, 1951

Australian, at White City, Sydney—d. Don Rocavert–Jim Gilchrist, 6–1, 6–3, 13–11; John Mehaffey–Clive Wilderspin, 6–4, 6–4, 6–3; Merv Rose–Don Candy, 8–6, 6–4, 6–3; Adrian Quist–Jack Bromwich, 11–9, 2–6, 6–3, 4–6, 6–3.

French, at Roland Garros, Paris—d. Antoine Gentien–Pierre Grandquillot, 6–0, 6–0, 6–0; Biddy Bergamo–Beppe Merlo, 6–2, 7–5, 6–1; Bob Abdesselam–Paul Remy, 6–2, 6–2, 4–6, 6–3; Merv Rose–Ham Richardson, 6–3, 7–5, 6–2; Gardnar Mulloy–Dick Savitt, 6–2, 2–6, 9–7, 7–5.

British, at Wimbledon, London—d. Vladimir Petrovic–P. Milojkovic, 6–1, 6–1, 6–3; Raymundo Deyro–Gene Garrett, 6–4, 6–4, 6–3; Bernard Destremeau–Torsten Johansson, 3–6, 6–3, 6–2, 9–7; Gianni Cucelli–Marcello del Bello, 6–4, 7–5, 16–14; Budge Patty–Ham Richardson, 6–4, 6–2, 6–3; Eric Sturgess–Jaroslav Drobny, 3–6, 6–2, 6–3, 3–6, 6–3.

United States, at Longwood Cricket Club, Boston—d. Harrison Rowbotham–Sumner Rodman, 6–2, 6–3, 6–3; Dave Mesker–Ed Wesely, 6–1, 6–1; Earl Cochell–Ham Richardson, default; Budge Patty–Tony Trabert, 6–3, 6–1, 6–4; Don Candy–Merv Rose, 10–8, 4–6, 6–4, 7–5 (final-round match played at Forest Hills, moved from Boston due to heavy rains).

Martina Navratilova–Pam Shriver, 1984

French, at Roland Garros, Paris—d. Heather Crowe–Kim Steinmetz, 6–2, 6–1; Carling Bassett—Andrea Temesvari, 6–4, 6–2; Sandy Collins–Alycia Moulton, 6–2, 6–4; Brenda Remilton–Naoko Sato, 6–2, 6–2; Kathleen Horvath–Virginia Ruzici, 6–0, 7–6; Claudia Kohde-Kilsch–Hana Mandlikova, 5–7, 6–3, 6–2.

British, at Wimbledon, London—d. Pam Casale–Lucia Romanov, 6–1, 6–1; Peanut Louie–Heather Ludloff, 6–4, 6–1; Lisa Bonder–Susan Mascarin, 6–0, 6–0; Claudia Kohde Kilsch–Hana Mandlikova, 6–7, 6–4, 6–2; Jo Durie–Ann Kiyomura Hayashi, 6–3, 6–3; Kathy Jordan–Anne Smith, 6–3, 6–4.

United States, at Flushing Meadow, New York—d. Jennifer Mundel–Felicia Raschiatore, 6–2, 6–1; Leslie Allen–Kim Shaefer, 6–1, 7–6; Rosalyn Fairbank–Candy Reynolds, 6–3, 6–4; Betsy Nagelsen–Anne White, 6–4, 7–5; Anne Hobbs–Wendy Turnbull, 6–2, 6–4.

French, at Roland Garros, Paris—d. C. Rouire–M. Lagard, 6–2, 6–1; Marie Dusapt–Ion Tiriac, 6–0, 6–2; Mary Habicht–Peter Strobl, 6–3, 6–0; Margaret Hunt–Cliff Drysdale, 7–5, 4–6, 6–1; Judy Tegart–Ed Rubinoff, 6–3, 6–1; Lesley Turner–Fred Stolle, 6–1, 6–2.

British, at Wimbledon, London—d. Judy Tegart–Ed Rubinoff, 6–2, 6–2; Judy Alvarez–John Fraser, 9–7; Alfonso and Yola Ramirez Ochoa, 6–4, 6–4; Rene Schuurman–Wilhelm Bungert, 6–2, 6–1; Ann Jones–Dennis Ralston, 6–1, 7–5; Darene Hard–Bob Hewitt, 11–9, 6–4.

with Darlene Hard at the French, Wimbledon and U.S.)

Australian, at Milton Courts, Brisbane—Christine Truman–Bueno d. Val Craig–Hortense Saywell, 6–2, 6–1; Betty Holstein–Sapphire Shipton, 6–3, 6–4; Fay Muller–Mary Hawton, 6–4, 11–9; Margaret Smith–Lorraine Coughlan Robinson, 6–3, 5–7, 6–2.

French, at Roland Garros, Paris—Darlene Hard–Bueno d. Jacqueline Kermina–P. Seghers, 6–22, 6–2; Jacqueline Rees Lewis–Jacqueline Morales, 6–2, 6–0; Josette Billaz–Suzanne Le Besnerais, 6–4, 6–4; Mary Hawton–Jan Lehane, 6–3, 7–5; Pat Ward Hales–Ann Haydon, 6–2, 7–5.

British, at Wimbledon, London—Hard–Bueno d. Myrtle Cheadle–Gem Hoahing, 6–1, 6–2; Pat Hird–Caroline Yates Bell, 6–2, 7–5; Edna Buding–Vera Puzejova, 6–2, 6–3; Karen Hantze–Janet Hopps, 3–6, 6–1, 6–4; Renee Schuurman–Sandra Reynolds, 6–4, 6–0.

United States at Longwood Cricket Club, Boston—Hard–Bueno d. Lorraine Carder–Polly Knowlton, 6–0, 6–2; Linda Vail–Marilyn Montgomery, 6–1, 7–5; Carole Loop–Carole Wright, 6–2, 6–4; Mary Hawton–Jan Lehane, 8–6, 6–4; Ann Haydon–Deirdre Catt, 6–1, 6–1.

MIXED DOUBLES

Margaret Court Smith–Ken Fletcher, 1963

Australian, at Memorial Drive, Adelaide—d. Faye Toyne–Bill Bowrey, 6–2, 6–2; Jill Blackman–Roger Taylor, 6–3, 6–3; Liz Starkie–Mark Cox, 7–5, 6–4; Lesley Turner–Fred Stolle, 7–5, 5–7, 6–4.

Australian, at Memorial Drive, Adelaide—Lesley Turner–Davidson d. Melba Foster–Brenton Higgins, 6–1, 7–5; Margaret Starr–Paul McPherson, 6–2, 6–4; Jan Lehane O'Neill–Ray Ruffels, 7–5, 6–4; Judy Tegart–Tony Roche, 9–7, 6–4.

French, at Roland Garros, Paris—Billie Jean Moffitt King–Davidson d. Maria Zuleta–Eduardo Zuleta, 6–2, 6–4; Pat Walkden–Colin Stubs, 6–2, 2–6, 6–3; Trudy Groenman–Tom Okker, 6–1, 6–2; Christine Truman–Bob Howe, 6–2, 6–4; Ann Haydon Jones–Ion Tiriac, 6–3, 6–1.

British, at Wimbledon, London—King–Davidson d. Betty Stove–Bob Howe, 6–1, 6–1; Ingrid Lofdahl–Pat Cornejo, 6–4, 6–1; Mr. and Mrs. John Cottrill, 6–4, 6–1; Annette van Zyl–Frew McMillan, 6–3, 3–6, 6–1; Maria Bueno–Ken Fletcher, 7–5, 6–2.

United States, at Longwood Cricket Club, Boston—King–Davidson d. Joyce Barclay Williams–George Seewagen, Jr., 6–4, 6–4; Donna Floyd Fales–Paul Sullivan, 6–2, 6–2; Mary Ann Eisel–Peter Curtis, 6–4, 6–3; Kristy Pigeon–Terry Addison, 6–4, 6–4; Rosie Casals–Stan Smith, 6–3, 6–2.]

ALL-TIME MAJOR CHAMPIONS

The following is based on the four major championships—Australian, French, Wimbledon and U.S. The dates indicate years of first and last championships.

Overall

Men

Player	Aust.	Fr.	Wim.	U.S.	S–D–M	Total
Roy Emerson, 1959–71	6–3–0	2–6–0	2–3–0	2–4–0	12–16–0	28
John Newcombe, 1965–76	2–5–0	0–3–0	3–6–0	2–3–1	7–17–1	25
Frank Sedgman, 1949–52	2–2–2	0–2–2	1–3–2	2–2–2	5–9–8	22
Bill Tilden, 1913–30	–	0–0–1	3–1–0	7–5–4	10–6–5	21
Rod Laver, 1959–71	3–4–0	2–1–1	4–1–2	2–0–0	11–6–3	20
John Bromwich, 1938–50	2–8–1	0–0–0	0–2–2	0–3–1	2–13–4	19
Jean Borotra, 1925–36	1–1–1	1–5–2	2–3–1	0–0–1	4–9–5	18
Fred Stolle, 1962–69	0–3–1	1–2–0	0–2–3	1–3–2	2–10–6	18
Ken Rosewall, 1953–72	4–3–0	2–2–0	0–2–0	2–2–1	8–9–1	18
Neale Fraser, 1957–62	0–3–1	0–3–0	1–2–0	2–3–3	3–11–5	19
Adrian Quist, 1936–50	3–10–0	0–1–0	0–2–0	0–1–0	3–14–0	17
John McEnroe, 1977–92	0–0–0	0–0–1	3–5–0	4–4–0	7–9–1	17
Jack Crawford, 1929–35	4–4–3	1–1–1	1–1–1	0–0–0	6–6–5	17
Laurie Doherty, 1897–06	–	–	5–8–0	1–2–0	6–10–0	16
Henri Cochet, 1926–32	–	4–3–2	2–2–0	1–0–1	7–5–3	15
Vic Seixas, 1952–56	0–1–0	0–2–1	1–0–4	1–2–3	2–5–8	15
Bob Hewitt, 1961–79	0–2–1	0–1–2	0–5–2	0–1–1	0–9–6	15
Reggie Doherty, 1897–05	–	–	4–8–0	0–2–0	4–10–0	14
Fred Perry, 1933–36	1–1–0	1–1–1	3–0–2	3–0–1	8–2–4	14
Don Budge, 1936–38	1–0–0	1–0–0	2–2–2	2–2–2	6–4–4	14
Tony Roche, 1965–76	0–7–1	1–2–0	0–5–1	0–1–0	1–11–2	14
Willie Renshaw, 1880–1889	–	–	7–7–0	–	7–5–0	12
Lew Hoad, 1953–57	1–3–0	1–1–1	2–3–0	0–1–0	4–8–1	13

Mens (cont'd.)

Player	Aust.	Fr.	Wim.	U.S.	S–D–M	Total
Jacques Brugnon, 1925–34	0–1–0	0–5–2	0–4–0	0–0–0	0–10–2	12
George Lott, 1928–34	0–0–0	0–1–0	0–2–1	0–5–3	0–8–4	12
Owen Davidson, 1966–74	0–1–1	0–0–1	0–0–4	0–1–4	0–2–10	12
Ken Fletcher, 1963–68	0–0–2	0–1–3	0–1–4	0–0–1	0–2–10	12
Tony Wilding, 1906–14	2–1–0	–	4–4–0	–	6–5–0	11
Bjorn Borg, 1975–81	0–0–0	6–0–0	5–0–0	0–0–0	11–0–0	11
Jimmy Connors, 1973–83	1–0–0	0–0–0	2–1–0	5–1–0	8–2–0	10
René Lacoste, 1925–29	–	3–2–0	2–1–0	2–0–0	7–3–0	10
Jack Kramer, 1940–47	–	–	1–2–0	2–4–1	3–6–1	10
Tony Trabert, 1950–55	0–1–0	2–3–0	1–0–0	2–1–0	5–5–0	10
Frew McMillan, 1968–81	0–0–0	0–1–1	0–3–2	0–1–2	0–5–5	10

Women

Player	Aust.	Fr.	Wim.	U.S.	S–D–M	Total
Margaret Court, 1960–75	11–8–2	5–4–4	3–2–5	5–5–8	24–19–19	62
Martina Navratilova, 1974–90	3–8–0	2–7–2	9–7–1	4–9–2	18–31–5	54
Billie Jean Moffitt King, 1961–81	1–0–1	1–1–2	6–10–4	4–5–4	12–16–11	39
Margaret Osborn duPont, 1941–60	–	2–3–0	1–5–1	3–13–9	6–21–10	37
Louise Brough, 1942–57	1–1–0	0–3–0	4–5–4	1–12–4	6–21–8	35
Doris Hart, 1948–55	1–1–2	2–5–3	1–4–5	2–4–5	6–14–15	35
Helen Wills Moody, 1923–38	–	4–2–0	8–3–1	7–4–2	19–9–3	31
Elizabeth Ryan, 1914–34	–	0–4–0	0–12–7	0–1–2	0–17–9	26
Pam Shriver, 1981–91	0–7–0	0–4–1	0–5–0	0–5–0	0–21–1	22
Darlene Hard, 1958–69	–	1–3–2	0–4–3	2–6–0	3–15–5	21
Suzanne Lenglen, 1919–26	–	2–2–2	6–6–3	0–0–0	8–8–5	21

	Aust.	Fr.	Wim.	U.S.	S–D–M	Total
Chris Evert, 1974–86	2–0–0	7–2–0	3–1–0	6–0–0	18–3–0	21
Nancye Bolton, 1935–52	6–10–4	0–0–0	0–0–0	0–0–0	6–10–4	20
Maria Bueno, 1958–68	0–1–0	0–1–1	3–5–0	4–5–0	7–13–1	19
Thelma Long, 1936–58	2–12–4	0–0–1	0–0–0	0–0–0	2–12–5	19

money, particularly in France and Britain, with teaching professionals/ coaches as entries, the U.S. Pro Championships stands as the oldest continous such event. It began in 1927 on courts of the small, since vanished, Notlek Tennis Club on the West Side of Manhattan, starring the newly avowed touring pros, Vinnie Richards and Howard Kinsey, from the Pyle troupe, and was filled out by teaching pros, playing for a $2000 ⸻ ⸻

	Aust.	Fr.	Wim.	U.S.	S–D–M	Total
	5–5–4	0–0–0	0–0–0	–	5–5–4	14
Evonne Goolagong, 1971–81	4–4–0	1–0–1	2–1–0	0–0–0	7–5–1	13
Simone Mathieu, 1933–39	–	2–6–2	0–3–0	0–0–0	2–9–2	13
Molla Bjurstedt Mallory, 1915–26	–	0–0–0	0–0–0	8–2–3	8–2–3	13
Mary K. Browne, 1912–26	–		0–1–0	3–5–4	3–6–4	13
Maureen Connolly, 1951–54	1–1–0	2–1–1	3–0–0	3–0–0	9–2–1	12
Francoise Durr, 1967–76	0–0–0	1–5–3	0–0–1	0–2–0	1–7–4	12
Lesley Turner, 1961–67	0–3–2	2–2–0	0–1–2	0–1–0	2–7–4	13
Rosie Casals, 1967–82	0–0–0	0–0–0	0–5–2	0–4–1	0–9–3	12
Steffi Graf, 1987–92	3–0–0	2–0–0	4–1–0	2–0–0	11–1–0	12
Althea Gibson, 1956–58	0–1–0	1–1–0	2–3–0	2–0–1	5–5–1	11
Anne Smith, 1980–84	0–1–0	0–2–2	0–1–1	0–1–2	0–5–5	10

prior guarantees, got 8 and ⸻ ished at last. But in 1964 the tournament was revived at Boston's Longwood Cricket Club through the efforts of Ed Hickey, public relations officer for the sponsoring New England Merchants Bank, and John Bottomley, Longwood president, with an assist from ex-promoter, Jack Kramer, and has thrived thereafter at that location.

U.S. PRO CHAMPIONSHIPS

Although there were earlier instances of professional tournaments offering prize

Year	Winner Score	Runner-up
1927	Vincent Richards 11–9, 6–4, 6–3	Howard Kinsey
1928	Vincent Richards 8–6, 6–3, 0–6, 6–2	Karel Kozeluh
1929	Karel Kozeluh 6–4, 6–4, 4–6, 4–6, 7–5	Vincent Richards
1930	Vincent Richards 2–6, 10–8, 6–3, 6–4	Karel Kozeluh
1931	Bill Tilden 7–5, 6–2, 6–1	Vincent Richards
1932	Karel Kozeluh 6–2, 6–2, 7–5	Hans Nusslein
1933	Vincent Richards 6–3, 6–0, 6–2	Frank Hunter
1934	Hans Nusslein 6–4, 6–2, 1–6, 7–5	Karel Kozeluh
1935	Bill Tilden 0–6, 6–1, 6–4, 0–6, 6–4	Karel Kozeluh
1936	Joseph Whalen 4–6, 4–6, 6–3, 6–2, 6–3	Charles Wood
1937	Karel Kozeluh 6–2, 6–3, 4–6, 4–6, 6–1	Bruce Barnes

1938	Fred Perry 6–3, 6–2, 6–4	Bruce Barnes
1939	Ellsworth Vines 8–6, 6–8, 6–1, 20–18	Fred Perry
1940	Don Budge 6–3, 5–7, 6–4, 6–3	Fred Perry
1941	Fred Perry 6–4, 6–8, 6–2, 6–3	Dick Skeen
1942	Don Budge 6–2, 6–2, 6–2	Bobby Riggs
1943	Lt. Bruce Barnes 6–1, 7–9, 7–5, 4–6, 6–3	John Nogrady
1944	Not Held	
1945	Welby Van Horn 6–4, 6–2, 6–2	John Nogrady
1946	Bobby Riggs 6–3, 6–1, 6–1	Don Budge
1947	Bobby Riggs 3–6, 6–3, 10–8, 4–6,6–3	Don Budge
1948	Jack Kramer 14–12, 6–2, 3–6, 7–5	Bobby Riggs
1949	Bobby Riggs 9–7, 3–6, 6–3, 6–3	Don Budge
1950	Pancho Segura 6–4, 1–6, 8–6, 4–4 retired	Frank Kovacs
1951	Pancho Segura 6–3, 6–4, 6–2	Pancho Gonzalez
1952	Pancho Segura 3–6, 6–4, 3–6, 6–4, 6–0	Pancho Gonzalez
1953	Pancho Gonzalez 4–6, 6–4, 7–5, 6–2	Don Budge
1954	Pancho Gonzalez 6–3, 9–7, 3–6, 6–2	Frank Sedgman
1955	Pancho Gonzalez 21–16, 19–21, 21–8, 20–22, 21–19*	Pancho Segura
1956	Pancho Gonzalez 21–15, 13–21, 21–14, 22–20*	Pancho Segura
1957	Pancho Gonzalez 6–3, 3–6, 7–5, 6–1	Pancho Segura
1958	Pancho Gonzalez 3–6, 4–6, 14–12, 6–1, 6–4	Lew Hoad
1959	Pancho Gonzalez 6–4, 6–2, 6–4	Lew Hoad
1960	Alex Olmedo 7–5, 6–4	Tony Trabert
1961	Pancho Gonzalez 6–3, 7–5	Frank Sedgman
1962	Butch Buchholz 6–4, 6–3, 6–4	Pancho Segura
1963	Ken Rosewall 6–4, 6–2, 6–2	Rod Laver
1964	Rod Laver 4–6, 6–3, 7–5, 6–4	Pancho Gonzalez
1965	Ken Rosewall 6–4, 6–3, 6–3	Rod Laver
1966	Rod Laver 6–4, 4–6, 6–2, 8–10, 6–3	Ken Rosewall
1967	Rod Laver 4–6, 6–4, 6–3, 7–5	Andres Gimeno
1968	Rod Laver 6–4, 6–4, 9–7	John Newcombe
1969	Rod Laver 7–5, 6–2, 4–6, 6–1	John Newcombe
1970	Tony Roche 3–6, 6–4, 1–6, 6–2, 6–2	Rod Laver
1971	Ken Rosewall 6–4, 6–3, 6–0	Cliff Drysdale
1972	Bob Lutz 6–4, 2–6, 6–1, 6–4	Tom Okker
1973	Jimmy Connors 6–3, 4–6, 6–4, 3–6, 6–2	Arthur Ashe
1974	Bjorn Borg 7–6, 6–1, 6–1	Tom Okker
1975	Bjorn Borg 6–3, 6–4, 6–2	Guillermo Vilas
1976	Bjorn Borg 6–7, 6–4, 6–1, 6–2	Harold Solomon
1977	Manuel Orantes 7–6, 7–5, 6–4	Eddie Dibbs
1978	Manuel Orantes 6–4, 6–3	Harold Solomon
1979	Jose Higueras 6–3, 6–1	Hans Gildemeister
1980	Eddie Dibbs 6–2, 6–1	Gene Mayer
1981	Jose-Luis Clerc 0–6, 6–3, 6–2	Hans Gildemeister
1982	Guillermo Vilas 6–4, 6–0	Mel Purcell
1983	Jose-Luis Clerc 6–3, 6–1	Jimmy Arias
1984	Aaron Krickstein 7–6, 3–6, 6–4	Jose–Luis Clerc
1985	Mats Wilander 6–2, 6–4	Martin Jaite
1986	Andres Gomez 7–5, 6–4	Martin Jaite
1987	Mats Wilander 7–6, 6–1	Kent Carlsson
1988	Thomas Muster 6–2, 6–2	Lawson Duncan
1989	Andres Gomez 6–1, 6–4	Mats Wilander
1990	Martin Jaite 7–5, 6–3	Libor Nemecek
1991	Andres Gomez 7–5, 6–3	Andrei Cherkasov
1992	Ivan Lendl 6–3, 6–3	Richey Reneberg

VASSS Scoring

One-Night Stands of the Bygone Pros

Until the dawn of open tennis in 1968, the usual format for the handful of playing pros—outlaws beyong the boundaries of traditional amateur tourneys—was a tour of one-night stands, indoors on a portable canvas court, across the U.S., and some-

After resisting promoters for several years, Tilden finally turned pro having failed to extricate the Davis Cup from France or win a long-desired eighth U.S. title. He then toured victoriously against the Czech master, Karel Kozeluh, and repeated the next winter against German Hans Nusslein before Vines unseated him. That left Vines in charge to fend off the next rookie, Fred Perry, 1937–38. Tilden stuck around, as did a few others, to play secondary roles.

Whoever the promoter, he lured the leading amateur with a guarantee against a percentage of gate receipts, making a similar type of deal with the champion, and generally paying the others' salaries. It all began in November 1926 as promoter C. C. Pyle transformed the first troupe—Suzanne Lenglen, Mary K. Browne, Vinnie Richards, Howard Kinsey, Harvey Snodgrass, Paul Feret—from amateurs to pros en masse, principally to capitalize on Lenglen's gate appeal on a North American tour. The last tour, 1963, was Australian-dominated as pros Ken Rosewall and Lew Hoad personally guaranteed 1962 Grand Slammer Rod Laver $110,000 over three years to give up his amateur status, and put them back in business.

Although the pros grew slightly in numbers and began leaning toward tournament formats in 1964, hastening the day of opens, tours continued into 1968, but merely as exhibitions, lacking the king-of-the-hill aspect. Pancho Gonzalez, challenger, and loser, in his first tour against player-promoter Jack Kramer, 1949–50, was relegated to the scrap heap. But he got a second chance when Kramer retired from

1940–41—Budge d. Tilden, 51–7
1946–47—Bobby Riggs d. Budge, 23–21
1947–48—Jack Kramer d. Riggs, 69–20
1949–50—Kramer d. Richard "Pancho" Gonzalez, 96–27
1950–51—Kramer d. Francisco "Pancho" Segura, 64–28
1953—Kramer d. Frank Sedgman, 54–41
1954—Gonzalez d. Sedgman and Segura, round-robin
1955–56—Gonzalez d. Tony Trabert, 74–27
1957—Gonzalez d. Ken Rosewall, 50–26
1957–58—Gonzalez d. Lew Hoad, 51–36
1959—Gonzalez d. Hoad, Mal Anderson and Ashley Cooper, round-robin
1958–59—Althea Gibson d. Karol Fageros, 114–4
1959–60—Gonzalez d. Alex Olmedo, Rosewall and Segura, round-robin
1961—Gonzalez leading winner in tour involving Butch Buchholz, Barry MacKay, Andres Gimeno, Hoad, Olmedo, Sedgman, Trabert, Cooper.
1963—Rosewall, Laver finished 1–2 on tour also including Luis Ayala, Buchholz, Gimeno, MacKay.

Olympic Games

Although tennis could hardly be termed a staple of the Olympic Games—having disappeared from the Olympic calendar for 64 years—it is very much back in the lineup of medal sports.

First played when the Games were revived in Athens in 1896, tennis was a fixture on the program through the 1924 edition in Paris—when the Americans swept all four events on the program.

Friction arose after 1924 between the Olympic Committee and the International Tennis Federation. It centered on the definition of amateurism and it led to the absence of tennis—except as a demonstration sport in Mexico City in 1968 and Los Angeles in 1984—until ITF president Philippe Chatrier led the successful drive toward return of the sport to the 1988 Olympics in Seoul, Korea.

Players from the United States have won two gold medals in men's singles, two in women's singles, two in men's doubles, three in women's doubles and one in mixed doubles. A highlight of the 1992 Games in Barcelona was Jennifer Capriati's upset of Steffi Graf. Summaries of the finals:

1896, Athens

Men's singles—John Pius Boland (Great Britain/Ireland) d. Kasdaglis (Greece) 7–5, 6–4, 6–1

Men's doubles—Boland (Great Britain/Ireland)–Fritz Traun (Germany) d. Demis Kasdaglis–Demetrios Petrokokkinos (Greece) 6–2, 6–4

1900, Paris

Men's singles—Laurie Doherty (Great Britain) d. Harold Segerson Mahony (Great Britain/Ireland) 6–4, 6–2, 6–3

Women's singles—Charlotte Cooper (Great Britain) d. Helene Prevost (France) 6–3, 6–3, 7–5

Men's doubles—Reggie Doherty–Laurie Doherty (Great Britain) d. Spalding de Garmendia (U.S.)–Max Decugis (France) 6–3, 6–3, 7–5

Mixed doubles—Cooper–Reggie Doherty (Great Britain) d. Helene Prevost (France)–Mahony (Great Britain/Ireland) 6–2, 6–4

1904, St. Louis

Men's singles—Beals Wright (U.S.) d. Robert LeRoy (U.S.) 6–4, 6–4

Men's doubles—Edgar Welch Leonard–Wright (U.S.) d. Alphonso Edward Bell–LeRoy (U.S.) 6–4, 6–4, 6–2

1906, Athens

Men's singles—Max Decugis (France) d. Maurice Germot (France) 7–5, 6–2, 6–4

Women's singles—Esmee Simiriotou (Greece) d. Sophia Marinou (Greece) 6–1, 6–4

Men's doubles—Decugis–Germot (France) d. Xenophon Kasdaglis–Ionnis Ballis (Greece) 6–4, 6–2, 6–1

Mixed doubles—Marie Decugis–Max Decugis (France) d. Marinou–Georgios Simiriotis (Greece) 6–1, 6–2

1908, London

Men's singles—Wilberforce Vaughan Eaves (Great Britain) d. Ivie John Richardson (South Africa) 6–2, 6–2, 6–3

Women's singles—Dorothea Lambert Chambers (Great Britain) d. Penelope Dora Boothby (Great Britain) 6–1, 7–5

Men's doubles—George Whiteside Hillyard–Reggie Doherty (Great Britain) d. Major Josiah George Richie–James Cecil Parke (Great Britain/Ireland) 9–7, 7–5, 9–7

1908, London (Indoor)

Men's singles—Arthur Wentworth Gore (Great Britain) d. George Caridia (Great Britain) 6–3, 7–5, 6–4

Women's singles—Gwendoline Eastlake Smith (Great Britain) d. Angela Greene (Great Britain) 6–2, 4–6, 6–0

Men's doubles—Gore–Herbert Roper Barrett (Great Britain) d. George Mieville Simond-Caridia (Great Britain) 6–2, 2–6, 6–3, 6–3

1912, Stockholm

Men's singles—Charles Lyndhurst Winslow (South Africa) d. Harold Austin Kitson (South Africa) 7–5, 4–6, 10–8, 8–6

Women's singles—Marguerite Broquedis (France) d. Dora Koring (Germany) 4–6, 6–3, 6–4

Men's doubles—Winslow–Kitson (South Africa) d. Felix Pipes–Arthur Zborzil (Austria) 4–6, 6–1, 6–2, 6–2

Mixed doubles—Koring–Heinrich Schomburgk (Germany) d. Sigrid Fick-Gunnar Setterwall (Sweden) 6–4, 6–0

1912, Stockholm (Indoor)

Men's singles—Andre Gobert (France) d. Charles Percy Dixon (Great Britain) 8–6, 6–4, 6–4

Women's singles—Edith Margaret Hannam (Great Britain) d. Thora Gerda Sophy Castenschiold (Denmark) 6–4, 6–3

Men's doubles—Gobert–Maurice Germot (France) d. Gunnar Setterwall-Carl Kempe (Sweden) 6–4, 12–14, 6–2, 6–4

Mixed doubles—Hannam–Dixon (Great Britain) d.

Men's doubles—Noel Turnbull (South Africa) Max Woosnam (Great Britain) d. Seiichiro Kashio–Kumagae (Japan) 6–2, 7–5, 7–5

Women's doubles—Kitty McKane-Winifred McNair (Great Britain) d. Geraldine Beamish-Holman (Great Britain) 8–6, 6–4

Mixed doubles—Lenglen-Max Decugis (France) d. McKane-Woosnam (Great Britain) 6–4, 6–2

1924, Paris

Men's singles—Vinnie Richards (U.S.) d. Henri Cochet (France) 6–4, 6–4, 4–6, 5–7, 6–2

Women's singles—Helen Wills (U.S.) d. Didi Vlastro (France) 6–2, 6–2

Men's doubles—Frank Hunter–Richards (U.S.) d. Jacques Brugnon-Cochet (France) 4–6, 6–2, 6–3, 2–6, 6–3

Women's doubles—Hazel Hotchkiss Wightman-Wills (U.S.) d. Kitty McKane-Dorothy Covell (Great Britain) 7–5, 8–6

Mixed doubles—Wightman-Dick Williams (U.S.) d. Marion Zinderstein Jessup-Richards (U.S.) 6–2, 6–3

1988, Seoul

Men's singles—Miloslav Mecir (Czechoslovakia) d. Tim Mayotte (U.S.) 3–6, 6–2, 6–4, 6–2

1992, Barcelona

Men's singles—Marc Rosset (Switzerland) d. Jordi Arrese (Spain) 7–6 (7–2), 6–4, 3–6, 4–6, 8–6

Women's singles—Jennifer Capriati (U.S.) d. Steffi Graf (Germany) 3–6, 6–3, 6–4

Men's doubles—Boris Becker-Michael Stich (Germany) d. Wayne Ferreira-Piet Norval (South Africa) 7–6 (7–5), 4–6, 7–6 (7–5), 6–3

Women's doubles—Gigi Fernandez-Mary Joe Fernandez (U.S.) d. Conchita Martinez-Arantxa Sanchez Vicario (Spain) 7–5, 2–6, 6–2

(Events not held: Women's singles, 1896, 1904; mixed doubles, 1896, 1904, 1908, 1988, 1992; women's doubles, 1896, 1904, 1908, 1912)

INDEX

(1968), 167; earnings (1975), 203, 205; first U.S. Open
(1968), 167; and Gimeno, U.S. Open (1968), 167; missed
season (1978), 230; South African Open (1973), 197; U.S.
Clay Court (1967), 160; U.S. Open (1968), 164, *164;* vs.
Connors, Wimbledon (1975), 203; vs. Emerson, Forest Hills
(1965), 153; win record (1975), 202-203
Association of Tennis Professionals (ATP), **484**; formation of,
189
Association of Tennis Pros (ATP): computer rankings (1973-92),
633-636; and Pilic Affair, 193-194; and self-managed men's
tour, 307
ATA. *See* American Tennis Association
Atkinson, Juliette Paxton, **406**
ATP. *See* Association of Tennis Professionals
ATP Tour, **484**
ATP World Championships, 583
Aussem, Cilly, **464-465**; vs. Krahwinkel, 47
Austin, Bunny, **465**
Austin, Bunny, on Ellsworth Vines, 47
Austin, Joan Winifred, **465**
Austin, Tracy, **406-407**; (1980), 240; turns pro, 231-232;
U.S. Open (1979), 239; U.S. Open (1981), *251,* 252; vs.
Evert; Rome (1979), 235; U.S. Open (1979), 239; vs.
Navratilova; U.S. Open (1981), 252; Virginia Slims (1978),
231; Wimbledon (1977), 217; Wimbledon (1981), 251; win
record (1979), 233, *234;* youngest in Top Ten (1977), 222
Australasia, defined, 18-19
Australian Championships, 546-553; all-time records, 552;
career records, 552; early, 23; longest matches, 552-553;
Men's Doubles, 548-549; Men's Singles, 546-547; Mixed
Doubles, 551-552; Women's Doubles, 549-551; Women's
Singles, 547-548; youngest and oldest champions, 552
Australian formation. *See* I formation
Avon, 233
Avon Circuit, **484**, 584-585
Award, Johnston, 492
Ayala, Luis, **465**

B

Backhand, defined, 484
Baddeley, Herbert, **465**
Baddeley, Wilfred, 14, **465**
Bagel, defined, 484-485
Bagel job, defined, 484-485
Bagnal-Wild, R.B., 8

Baker, Larry, **459**
Ball(s): changing during match, 517; defined, 485; dimensions
of, 504-505; in doubles, 518; for high-altitudes, 505; in
play, 509, 511; in play, in doubles, 518; during service,
507; yellow at Wimbledon, 282
Ball boy (girl), defined, 485
Barger, Maud. *See* Wallach, Maud Barger
Barker, Sue, Virginia Slims (1977), 222
Barrett, Herbert Roper, **465**
Barrett, Mrs. John Edward. *See* Mortimer, Angela
Bartkowicz, Jane "Peaches," 173, *173,* 174
Bartzen, Bernard, vs. Dell, U.S. Clay Court (1961), 143
Baseline, defined, 485
Baseliner, defined, 485
Baselines, dimensions of, 504
"Battle of the Sexes," 191, *191*
Beamish, Geraldine, *32*
Becker, Boris, *306,* **332-334**, *333;* Australian Open (1991),
315; and British press, 275; Davis Cup (1988), 300; and
Stich, Olympic tournament (1992), 327; vs. Courier, ATP
World Championships (1992), 322; vs. Curren, Wimbledon
(1985), 273, 275; vs. Edberg, Wimbledon (1989), 305; vs.
Lendl; Masters (1988), 300; U.S. Open (1989), 305;
Wimbledon (1986), 283; Wimbledon (1989), 305; vs.
McEnroe, Davis Cup playoff (1987), 287; Wimbledon
(1985), 273, *273,* 275-276; win record (1986), 280; win
record (1988), 294; win record (1989), 305-306
Behind the Scenes at Wimbledon (Macaulay), 33, 51, 104-105
Behr, Karl Howell, **407**
Bellamy, Rex: on Becker, 275; on first open French
Championships, 165; on Gonzalez vs. Sedgman, 131; on
Santana vs. Pietrangeli, 142
Bell Cup, **485**
Belmont (Phila.) Cricket Club, 13
Bennett, James Gordon, Jr., 403
Bernard, Marcel, **465**
Betz, Pauline, *334,* **334-335**; as pro, 117; U.S.
Championships, Wimbledon (1946), 105
Bicycle, 8
Big Bill Tilden (Deford), 27
Big Four, **485**
Big W. *See* Wimbledon
Bingley Hillyard, Blanche, 13, 18, **470**
Bjurstedt, Molla. *See* Mallory, Molla
Bloomer, Shirley, 133
Bollettieri, Nick, **465**

292; vs. Lendl, Wimbledon (1987), 292; Wimbledon (1987), 286, *287*

Cawley, Evonne Goolagong. *See* Goolagong, Evonne

Centre Court (Wimbledon), **486**; bombing of, 275

Chace, Malcolm Greene, **411**

Chair, position of umpire's, 504

Chair umpire(s), 387

Chair umpires(s): fees for, 390; ITF classification of, 390

Challenge round, defined, 486

Chambers, Dorothea Douglass. *See* Lambert Chambers, Dorothea

Chambers, Dorothea Douglass (Mrs. Robert Lambert Chambers), **74**, *74*

Champions, all-time, 639-640. *See also* Big Four

Championship records. *See* specific championships and individuals

Championships: career prize leaders, 630-631; early, 12; highest total prize money from, 630; prize money statistics for, 630-631; statistics on, 630

Chang, Michael, **467**; Davis Cup (1990), 308; French Open (1989), 300, *300*, 301, 303-304; ranking improvement (1988), 295; U.S. Open (1987), 292-293; vs. Edberg, French Open (1989), 304

Change game, defined, 486

Changeover, umpire's use of, 388

Chapacu, Hugo, 287

Chatrier, Philippe, **459**

Chatrier, Susan Partridge. *See* Partridge, Susan

Cheney, Dorothy Bundy, **466**

Chesnokov, Andre, 304

Chestnut Hill (Phila.) Tennis Club Ladies Open, 13-14

Chip. *See* Dink

Chip and charge, defined, 486

Choking, defined, 486

Chop, defined, 486

Circuit: Riordan, **496**; Slims, **497-498**

Clapp, Mrs. A. T.. *See* Brough, Louise

Clark, Clarence, 9, **411-412**

Clark, Joe, 9, **412**

Clark brothers, vs. Renshaws, 9

Clayton, Mrs. R., *32*

Clothier, Bill, **412**

Coaching, during match, 517

Cochell, Earl, **467**; suspended for life, 120

Cochet, Henri, 32-33, *75*, **75-76**; as also-ran at Wimbledon (1932), 47; first Wimbledon title (1927), 39-40, *40;* Forest Hills (1928), 42; vs. Tilden; U.S. Championships (1926), 37-39; Wimbledon (1927), 39; Wimbledon (1925), 34-35;

Wimbledon (1929), 43

Code of Conduct, 213, 388, 391; stages in violation of, 391

Coles, Glynis, 209

Colgate International Series, 212

Commercial Union Assurance, Grand Prix sponsorship, 183

Commercial Union Masters, format of, 189

Computer rankings: ATP (1973-92), 633-636; defined, 486; WTA (1973-92), 631-633

Conduct: Code of, 213; deterioration of, 250. *See also* by specific individual, e.g., McEnroe, John

Conlin, Edward C., **392**

Connolly, Maureen ("Little Mo"), **339-340**, *340;* disastrous injury (1954), 125-126; Forest Hills (1951), 119, *120;* Grand Slam (1953), 123-124; vs. Hart, Wimbledon and Forest Hills (1953), 124; Wimbledon (1952), 122-123

Connors, Jimmy, **340-343**, *341;* barred from Grand Slam (1974), 198; comeback at U.S. Open (1991), 315; Davis Cup (1975), 206-207; Davis Cup (1984), 271; earnings and win record (1977), 220; first World Cup appearance, 214; in Heavyweight Championship of Tennis, 202; marries Patti McGuire, 234; and Nastase, U.S. Open (1975), 206; No. 1 ranking (1978), 228; No. 1 U.S. ranking with Smith (1973), 193; No. 1 world ranking, 210-211; split from Riordan, 205; suspended through French Open (1986), 281; triple-surface record (1978), 227; U.S. Clay Court (1979), 238; U.S. Open (1978), 227, *227;* U.S. Open (1982), 253, *253;* U.S. Open (1983), 260; on use of electronic line-calling systems, 393; vs. Ashe, U.S. Indoor and Pro Indoor (1979), 234; vs. Borg, U.S. Open (1978), 227; vs. Laver, Heavyweight Championship of Tennis (1975), 203; vs. Lendl; U.S. Open (1982), 259; U.S. Open (1983), 265; vs. McEnroe; Wimbledon (1977), 217; Wimbledon (1982), 258; vs. Navratilova, Caesars Palace (1992), 323, *323;* vs. Newcombe, Heavyweight Championship of Tennis (1975), 203; vs. Panatta, U.S. Open (1978), 227; vs. Pernfors, Wimbledon (1987), 292; vs. Rosewall, 198, 199; vs. umpire, 387, 388; as wild card at U.S. Open (1991), 320; as wild card in French Open (1991), 318-319; Wimbledon (1982), 258; win and earnings record (1976), 211; win record (1973), 193; win record (1974), 198-199; win record (1975), 204-205; win record (1979), 234

Continuous play, rules for, 515-516

Contract professional, 163-164

Cooke, Sarah Palfrey, 54, *76*, **76-77**; U.S. Championships (1941), 66, *66*

Coolidge, Calvin, *34*

Double Chrissie, defined, 486

Double fault, defined, 486

Double hit, defined, 486

Doubles: defined, 486; introduction of, 8; mixed, 494; rules for, 517-518; scoring tie-break in, 514; at Wimbledon (1913), 22

Doubles game, rules for, 503-517

"Double-strung" racket, 216, 223, *223*

Douglass, Dorothea. *See* Chambers, Dorothea Douglass; Lambert Chambers, Dorothea

Down-the-line, defined, 488

Down Undertakers, **488**

Draw, defined, 488

Dress, tennis. *See* Tennis dress

Drobny, Jaroslav, 115, 118, 121, 126, **415-416**; vs. Patty, 124, *125;* vs. Rosewall, Wimbledon (1954), 126

Drop shot, defined, 488

Drysdale, Cliff, 152, 153, **468**

duPont, Margaret, 105, 106, 112, 116, *345,* **345-346**

Durr, Frankie, **468**; French Championships (1967), 158; and Sherriff, French Championships (1967), 158

Dwight, James, 9, **416**; and Davis Cup, 10; visits Europe, 9-10

E

Earnshill, as test site for lawn tennis, 5

Ecuador, Davis Cup win (1967), 160

Edberg, Stefan, *346,* **346-347**; on Connors, 320; Davis Cup (1992), 328; earnings (1992), 328; earnings and win record (1991), 315; U.S. Open (1991), 320, *321;* U.S. Open (1992), 321, *321;* vs. Becker, Wimbledon (1988), 299; Wimbledon (1990), 312-313; vs. Chang, U.S. Open (1992), 328; vs. Courier, U.S. Open (1991), 320; vs. Lendl, Wimbledon (1990), 312; vs. Sampras, U.S. Open (1992), 328; vs. Westphal, Davis Cup (1985), 277; vs. Wilander, Australian Open (1985), 277; Wimbledon (1988), 299; win record (1989), 302-303

Edmondson, Mark, **468**; Australian Open (1976), 211

Education, of officials, 390-391

Edwards, Vic, 184

Elbow, defined, 488

Electronic line-calling systems, 393, 401-402

Elizabeth, Queen (Great Britain), 108, 218

Emerson, Roy, 142, **347-349**, *348;* Australian, French Championships (1963), 147; Australian, Wimbledon, Forest Hills (1964), 150, *150;* Australian Championship (1966), 155; Australian Championship (1967), 158; Davis Cup (1967), 161; Forest Hills (1961), 144; French Championships (1967), 158-159; injured at Wimbledon (1966), 155-156; and Osuna, Forest Hills (1961), 144; and Stolle, Davis Cup (1965), 152-153; suspended by LTAA (1964), 149-150; Wimbledon (1965), 153; win record (1965), 153

Ends: change of, rules for, 8, 509; choice of, rules for, 506

England, early lawn tennis in, 1-8

Equipment, **395-402**; balls, 401; early sales of, 3, 5; electronic line-calling, 401-402; rackets, 395-401, *396;* shoes, 401; strings, 400-401

Error: defined. *See* U.E.

Etchebaster, Pierre, **454**

Evans, Richard, on Emerson injury at Wimbledon, 155-156

Evert, Chris, *349,* **349-351**; Australian Open (1984), 267; awards and win record (1978), 232; earnings (1975), 208; earnings and ranking (1977), 221-222; earnings and win record (1976), 214; fails to reach U.S. Open semifinals, 288; Federation Cup (1989), 302; final U.S. Open (1989), 300-301, 302; Forest Hills (1971), 185; French Open (1985), 274; French Open (1986), 280; and John Lloyd, 234, 288; last U.S. Open, 306; lifetime percentage, 306; No. 1 U.S. ranking (1974), 201; No. 3 U.S. ranking (1972), 190; team play (1980), 245; team play (1982), 258; U.S. Clay Court (1975), 209; U.S. Clay Court (1979), 238; U.S. Open, *231,* 232; U.S. Open (1975), 208; U.S. Open (1982), 253, *253;* on use of electronic line-calling systems, 393; vs. Austin, Flushing Meadow (1980), 245; vs. Gadusek, U.S. Open (1982), 258; vs. Jaeger, U.S. Open (1982), 258; vs. King, Wimbledon (1982), 257; vs. Mandlikova, 252; U.S. Open (1982), 258; Wimbledon (1981), 251; vs. Navratilova, French Open (1985), 278; French Open (1986), 282; U.S. Open (1982), 253; vs. Sukova, Australian Open (1984), 272; Wimbledon (1974), 201; Wimbledon (1981), 251; Wimbledon (1985), 278; win record (1973), 196; win record (1975), 203; win record (1976), 215, 216; win record (1977), 221-222; win record (1979), 234, 235; win record (1980), 240, 244-245, *245;* win record (1981), 252; win record (1983), 262, 263

Evert, Jeanne, 202

Evert, Jim, 245

F

Fabyan, Sarah Palfrey. *See* Cooke, Sarah Palfrey

Falkenburg, Bob, **416-417**; vs. Bromwich, Wimbledon (1948), 111; Wimbledon (1948), 110-111

Mark Cox, 165; Pro tour (1956), 131; serve of, 47; top money winner (1969), 172; turns pro, 114-115; U.S. Pro title, 125, 127; vs. Hoad, pro tour (1958), 136; vs. Pasarell, Wimbledon (1969), 172; vs. Schroeder, Forest Hills (1949), 114; vs. Sedgman, Wembley (1956), 131; vs. Trabert, Pro tour (1956), 131

Goodbody, Manliffe, 14-15

Goolagong, Evonne, **355-357**, *356;* Australian Open (1975), 207-208; fall comeback (1977), 222-223; French Open, Wimbledon (1971), *180,* 184; vs. Evert, Forest Hills (1974), 201; vs. Evert, Virginia Slims (1974), 202; vs. Evert, Wimbledon (1972), 190; Wimbledon (1980), 240, *241,* 244; win record (1974), 201; win record (1976), 214-215

Goold, V. St. Leger, 12, **469-470**

Gore, Arthur William Charles, **468**

Gore, Spencer, **468**; on tennis, 11; vs. W.C. Marshall (1877), 7, 11

"Gorgeous Gussy." *See* Moran, Gertrude

"Gorgo," 114. *See* Gonzalez, Pancho

Gottfried, Brian, 220, **468**; and Ramirez, (1977), 220; and Ramirez, Italian Open (1976), 213

Gottfried-Ramirez, win record (1975), 206

Graebner, Carole Caldwell, 151, **470**

Graebner, Clark, 173, **470**; Davis Cup (1968), 167; and steel racket, 159

Graf, Peter, 293

Graf, Steffi, **357-358**, *358;* Federation Cup (1987), 290; first Grand Slam (1987), 286; French Open (1987), 289, *289;* French Open (1991), 316; and German measles, 323; Grand Slam (1988), 293-294, *296;* Olympic gold metal, 294; U.S. Open (1985), 274, 279; vs. Evert, Australian Open, 296; vs. Evert, Wimbledon (1989), 305; vs. Fernandez, Australian Open, 308; vs. McNeil, U.S. Open (1987), 290; vs. Navratilova, French Open (1987), 289; vs. Navratilova, International Players Championship (1987), 288-289; vs. Navratilova, U.S. Open (1989), 305; vs. Navratilova, Wimbledon (1988), 297; vs. Navratilova, Wimbledon (1989), 304-305; vs. Sabatini, U.S. Open (1988), 297-298; vs. Sabatini, Virginia Slims (1987), 288; vs. Sabatini, Wimbledon (1991), 317; vs. Sanchez Vicario, French Open (1992), 324; vs. Seles, Wimbledon (1992), 322, 326; vs. Zvereva, French Open (1988), 297; winning streak (1986), 282

Grand Masters, **490**

Grand Prix, 174-175, **490**; dissolution of, 306-307; prize money, 212-213; sponsorship change, 212; vs. WCT, 175

Grand Prix (Colgate), prize money (1977), 221

Grand Prix Masters, 174, 180, 182

Grand Prix Masters/ATP World Championships, 583; Men's records, 583; Women's records (Colgate Series/Toyota Series Champions), 584

Grand Slam Cup, 307-308, **490**

Grand Slams, **490**; officials for, 392-393; record of champions, 636-639

Grange, Red, *37*

Grant, Bitsy, *58*, **418**

Gray, David, **455-456**; on Court vs. King (1970), 176

Green, Mrs. A.C. *See* Boothby, Penelope

Griffin, Clarence James "Peck," **419**

Grimsley, Will: on Budge vs. von Cramm, 59; on Moody default, 49

Grip, 491. *See also* Racket

Groundies. *See* Groundstroke

Groundstroke, defined, 491

Grunters, 310

Gullickson, Tim (Timothy Edward), **470**

Gullickson, Tom (Thomas Robert), **470**

Gunter, Mrs. Kenneth. *See* Richey, Nancy

Gustav V, King (Sweden), 120, **462**

Gut, 491. *See also* Racket

Guzman, Pancho, 160

H

Haas, Robert, 268

Hacker, defined, 491

Hackett, Harold Humphrey, **419**

Hadow, Frank (Patrick Francis), **470**

Hailley, Robert, 135

Half volley, defined, 491

Hall of Fame, **491**

Hammond, Frank, 391-392

Handle, racket, 505

Handsome Eight, 161, 164, **491**

Hansell, Ellen Forde, 14, **419-420**

Hantze, Karen. *See* Susman, Karen Hantze

Hantze-Moffitt, Wimbledon doubles (1961), 143, *143*

Hard, Darlene, 143, **420**; and Arth, Wimbledon (1959), 139; doubles Grand Slam, 139; and Durr, U.S. Open (1969), 174; Forest Hills (1961), 144; French, Forest Hills Championships (1960), 139, *140*

Hard court, defined, 491-492

Lloyd, French Open (1982), 256; vs. King, Wimbledon (1983), 262

Jag, defined, 492

Jargon, tennis, 483-502

Jarryd, Anders, 287; and Edberg, Davis Cup (1984), 271

Jedrzejowska, Jadwiga ("JaJa"), 60, **471**

Jessup, Marion, *28*

Johnston, Bill ("Little Bill"), 26*27*, **80-81**, *81;* on Tilden, 35; vs. Hunter, Wimbledon (1923), 31; vs. Tilden, Forest Hills (1919), 26, *26*

Johnston Award, **492**

Jones, Ann Haydon, 160, **423**; French Championships, 157; in open era, 165

Jones, Henry, 6

Jones, Marian, 17, *120*

Jones, Mrs. Pip, Wimbledon (1969), 171

Jones, Perry Thomas (Perry T., Mr. Jones), **460-461**

Jordan, Barbara, **471**

Jordan, Kathy, vs. Evert, Wimbledon (1983), 262

Jordan, Kathy (Katherine "KJ"), **471**

Jorgensen, Gordon, 294

Journalists, in Hall of Fame, 455-457

Judge, net, 494

Junkballer, defined, 492

Jusserand, J.J., 1

K

Kamo, Kosei, and Atsushi Miyagi, U.S. National Doubles, 129

Kelleher, Bob (Robert Joseph), **471**

Kenneth-Smith, Mrs. Kenneth. *See* Browne, Mary K.

Kerr, George, vs. Tom Pettit (1889), 14

Kicker: defined, 492. *See also* American twist

Kill, defined, 492

Kilsch, Kohde, and Sukova, U.S. Open (1985), 274

King, Billie Jean, 143, *143*, 146, **361-363**, *362;* and Bobby Riggs, 191, *191;* co-ranked with Richey (1965), 154; Federation Cup (1976), 215-216; French Open, U.S. Open (1972), 190; and prize money inequity, 177; Top Ten ranking (1980), 245-246; triple victories (1967), *158*, 159-160; turns pro, 168; and Virginia Slims Circuit, 183; vs. Austin, Wimbledon (1982), 257; vs. Casals, double default, 185; vs. Fairbank, Edgbaston Cup (1982), 256; vs. Goolagong, Forest Hills (1974), 201-202; Wightman Cup (1970), 179-180; Wimbledon (1966), 156, 157; Wimbledon (1968), 166-167; Wimbledon (1975), 208; Wimbledon (1982), 256;

Wimbledon triple (1973), 196; win record (1972), 190; win record (1973), 196; win record (1977), 222

King's Cup, 120, **492**

Kinsey, Howard, 39

Kloss, Ilana, 215

Kodes, Jan, 177; vs. Nastase, French Open (1971), 181; Wimbledon (1973), 194

Kooyong, **492**

Korda, Petr, 325

Korff, Norman, 391

Kormoczi, Suzi, **471**

Kovacs, Frank, turns pro, 67, *68*

Kozeluh, Karel, 42, 43, *44*, 47

Kraft Tour, **493**

Kramer, Jack, 67, 103-104, *104*, **363-365**, *364;* Davis Cup (1946), 106-107; as first "jet-setter," 107; and Grand Prix, 174; on Hoad vs. Gonzalez, 132; mass amateur signings by, 141-142; as pro, 108, *109*, 109-110, 125; pro debut, 109, *109;* as promoter, 123, 127, 131; retires as promoter, 146; on Riggs, 109-110; and "shamateur" era, 137; U.S. Nationals (1946), 106; and U.S. Pro Championships (1964), 151-152; vs. Parker, Forest Hills (1948), 108-109; vs. Segura, pro tour (1950), 117; Wimbledon, U.S. Championships and Davis Cup (1947), 107-109, *107*

Krickstein, Aaron, 287; Davis Cup (1990), 308; U.S. Open (1983), 265

Kriek, Johan, 242-243; Australian Open, 254, *254;* Australian Open (1981), 250

Krishnan, Ramanathan, **471-472**

Krishnan, Ramesh, 288, **471-472**

Kuhn, Ferdinand, on Perry vs. Crawford (1934), 53

L

Lacoste, (Jean) René, **81-82**, *82;* (1924), 32-33, *33;* Forest Hills (1927), 40; and steel racket, 159; on Tilden, 41, 42-43; U.S. Championships (1926), 38, *38;* vs. Tilden, (1927), 40

Ladbrokes, 275

Ladies' tennis, introduction of, 8

"Lady Tennis." *See* Wightman, Hazel Hotchkiss

Lall, Premjit, 170

Lambert Chambers, Dorothea, 22, 27, 35, **74**, *74*

Laney, Al, **456-457**; on Kramer vs. Budge, 110; on Suzanne Lenglen, 28; on Tilden, 33

Langrishe, May, 12, **472**; and Maud Watson, 13

(1922), 30

Mancini, Albert, 304

Mandlikova, Hana, **473**; (1980), 240-241; Federation Cup (1985), 279; Grand Slam (1981), 251; U.S. Open (1985), 274, 279, *279;* vs. Navratilova, Australian Open (1987), 288; Wimbledon (1981), 251

Marble, Alice, 49, 62, **85-87**, *86;* turns pro, 66-67; U.S. Championship (1936), 57; U.S. Nationals (1940), 65-66; Wimbledon (1939), 63

Marshall, Julian, 1-2

Martin, Alastair Bradley, **461**

Martin, Bill, **461**

Martinez, Conchita, 302

Mary, Queen (Great Britain), 25, 53, *520;* and Suzanne Lenglen, *520*

Marylebone Cricket Club (M.C.C.), rules of for lawn tennis, 6

Maskell, Daniel (Dan), **473**

Master of Ceremonies (Wimbledon). *See* Tinling, Ted

Masters. *See* Grand Prix; Grand Prix Masters: defined, 494

Match, defined, 494

Match, longest tournament, 160

Matches: all-time records, 626-629; longest, 629; longest top-level, 157

Match point, defined, 494

Mathieu, Simone Passemard, **473**

Maureen Connolly Brinker Cup, 340

Maureen Connolly Brinker Indoor, 190

Mayer, Gene (Eugene), **473**

Mayer, Sandy, **473**

Mayer, Sandy, and Vitas Gerulaitis, Wimbledon (1975), 206

Mayotte, Tim, 283, 287; as Rookie of the Year (1981), 251

McEnroe, John, **368-370**, *369;* Australian Open default, 308-309; on Borg at Wimbledon (1980), 242; Davis Cup (1982), 259; Davis Cup (1984), 271; default and suspension (1987), 286-287; disqualification of (Aus. Open, 1990), 388; doubles titles (1984), 267-268; and Fleming; Masters (1983), 266; Masters doubles (1984), 271; U.S. Open (1979), 239; and Fleming, vs. Newcombe and Stolle at U.S. Open (1981), 250; French Open (1984), 268-269; French Open (1988), 298; granted All England Club membership, 259; Masters (1980), 244; Masters (1984), 271; misbehavior of, 236-237, 238, 247-248; off tour (1986), 281; and Stich, Wimbledon (1992), 326; Stockholm suspension (1984); suspended during U.S. Open (1987), 293; suspended through Masters (1986), 285; U.S. Open (1979), 238, *238;* U.S. Open (1981), 249-250; U.S. Open (1984), 270-271; vs.

Borg, Stockholm (1978), 228; vs. Borg, U.S. Open (1980), 240, 242, 243; vs. Borg, U.S. Open (1981), 249-250; vs. Borg, Wimbledon (1980), 247-249; vs. Connors, U.S. Open (1980), 243; vs. Connors, U.S. Open (1984), 270-271; vs. Connors, Wimbledon (1984), 269-270; vs. Lendl, Masters (1983), 265-266; vs. Lendl, U.S. Open (1984), 271; vs. Lewis, Wimbledon (1983), 264; vs. Nastase, U.S. Open (1979), 238; vs. umpire, *389;* vs. Wilander, Flushing Meadow (1985), 276; WCT final (1979), 234-235; Wimbledon (1984), 269-270; winning percentage (1984), 266; win record (1978), 228, *228;* win record (1979), 233; win record (1981), 250; win record (1984), 268, *268*

McEnroe, Patrick, 318; Australian Open (1991), 315

McGeehan, W.O., on Helen Wills, 42

McGrath, Vivian ("Viv"), **473-474**

McGregor, Ken, doubles Grand Slam, 119

McKane, Kitty. *See* Godfree, Kitty McKane: vs. Wills, Wimbledon (1924), 34

McKay, Barry: Italian, U.S. Indoor (1960), 140; turns pro, 141; vs. Olmedo, Davis Cup (1959), 138, *138*

McKinley, Chuck, **426-427**; and Ralston, Longwood, Davis Cup (1963), 149; Wimbledon (1963), *147,* 148

McKinley-Ralston, U.S. Doubles (1961), 144

McLoughlin, Maurice, *19,* 19-20, *87,* **87-88**

McMillan, Frew Donald, **427-428**

McNamee, Paul, 293

McNeil, Lori: U.S. Open (1987), 288; vs. Evert, U.S. Open (1987), 290, *291;* vs. Garrison, U.S. Open (1987), 290

McNeill, Don, *68,* **428**; U.S. Nationals (1940), 65; vs. Riggs, U.S. Nationals (1940), 65

Mecir, Miloslav, 285-286, 294; vs. Mayotte, Olympics (1988), 300; vs. Wilander, Wimbledon (1988), 299

Meers, E. G., 14

Meissner, Nicole, 310

Melville, Kerry, South African Open (1974), 202

Men's International Professional Tennis Council (MIPTC), 494

Men's International Professional Tennis Council (MIPTC), formation of, 206

Merion Cricket Club, 10

Merlo, Beppe, and Fausto Gardini, 128

Metreveli, Alexander, **474**

"Mexican Thumping Beans." *See* Osuna, Rafael; Palafox, Tony

Mexico, and Davis Cup default, 213-214

Minton, Robert: on Perry, 52; on Riggs vs. Van Horn, 63

MIPTC. *See* Men's International Professional Tennis Council

Mixed doubles, defined, 494

Moffitt, Billie Jean. *See* King, Billie Jean

Molesworth, Mall (Margaret Mutch), **474**

Montreal Cricket Club, 23

Moonball, defined, 494

Moore, Bessie (Elizabeth Holmes), **429**

Moran, Gertrude ("Gorgeous Gussy"), *112*, 112-113; as pro, 117

Morozova, Olga, **474**

Mortimer, Angela, **429-430**; vs. Truman, Wimbledon (1961), 143

Doubles (1946), 105, *106*

Murphy, Dennis, 193

Murray, (Robert) Lindley, **430-431**

Myers, A.T., 12

Myrick, Julian, 30, **461-462**

N

Na, Hu, **475**

Nahant tournament, 9

Nantclwyd, as test site for lawn tennis, 5

Nastase, Ilie, 172, **370-372**, *372;* conduct and win record (1975), 205-206; conduct violations (1976), 213; earnings (1971), 182-183; Forest Hills (1972), 188, *188;* Grand Prix Masters (1971), 182; No. 1 ranking (1973), 192-193; and spaguetti racket, 223; U.S. Indoor (1970), 178; vs. Ashe, Forest Hills (1972), 188; win record (1976), 213

National Championships (U.S.), inaugural, 13

National Tennis Center (Flushing, New York), 224-226, *225*

National Tennis League (NTL), **495**; formed (1967), 157, 161

Nations Cup (ATP), 207

Navratilova, Martina, 201, **372-374**, *373;* Avon Series, 235; conditioning of, 268; defects from Czechoslovakia, 208-209, *209;* defects to United States, 208-209, *209*, 230; doubles titles (1984), 268; earnings and win record, 260, 261; earnings and win record (1987), 288; ends doubles with Shriver, 328; Federation Cup (1986), 280, 283-284; frustrated by Graf (1989), 302; Grand Slam (1984), 271;

granted U.S. citizenship, 246; on Horvath at French Open, 261; and King, Wimbledon (1979), 237; mother at Wimbledon (1979), 237; and Shriver, doubles competitions (1985), 274; and Shriver, Slims Championships (1991), 318; and Shriver, win record (1988), 296; single loss (1983), 259, *261;* U.S. Open (1981), 252; U.S. Open (1983), 263; U.S. Open (1986), 284-285; U.S. Open triple (1987), 288; on use of electronic line-calling systems, 393; Virginia Slims (1977), 222; vs. Connors, Caesars Palace (1992), 323, *323;* vs. Evert, Australian Open (1985), 277-278; vs. Evert, U.S. (1982), 256; vs. Jaeger, Wimbledon (1983), 262; vs. Mandlikova, Australian Open (1985), 279; vs. Mandlikova, Wimbledon (1986), 282-283; vs. Sukova, U.S. Open (1986), 285, *285;* Wimbledon (1984), 272; Wimbledon (1985), 278; Wimbledon (1986), 280; Wimbledon (1990), 310; win record (1978), 230-231; win record (1981), 246, *247,* 252; win record (1982), 254, 255-256; win record (1984), 267; win record (1991), 315; win record and team play (1983), 263; wins after fitted with eyeglasses, 278

Neighborhood Club (West Newton, Mass.), British at (1895), 15

Nelson, Judy, 272; 315

Net: defined, 494; dimensions of, 503; tautness of, 504; tightening of, 504

Net cord, defined, 494

Net judge, defined, 494

Net rusher, defined, 494

Newcombe, John, 149, *375,* **375-376**; Australian Open (1975), 203; earnings (1971), 182; and Laver, Davis Cup (1973), 194-195; and Roche, Australian doubles title (1965), 152-153; and Roche, Davis Cup (1967), 161; and Roche, default at U.S. Open (1969), 174; and Taylor, U.S. Open (1971), 182; U.S. doubles and singles (1967), 159; U.S. Open (1973), 194; vs. Smith, Wimbledon (1971), 181; WCT tournaments (1974), 199-200; Wimbledon (1967), 159; Wimbledon (1970), 178; win record (1973), 192, *192;* on younger players, 250

New Orleans Lawn Tennis Club, 10

Newport Casino (Newport, R.I.), 20, **494-495**; British at

(1897), 15; International Hall of Fame at, 403-404;
  National Championships at, 13
Nielsen, Arthur Charles, **462**
Nielsen, Kurt, 124; Trabert vs. (1955), 128
Niessen, Helga, 176
Night play, at Forest Hills, 209
Nixon, Richard M., 172, 185
No-ad, defined, 495
Noah, Yannick, **474-475**; vs. Wilander, French Open (1983),
  264
Noah, Yannick, French Open (1983), 260, *260*, 264
No-brainer, defined, 495
Noel, E.B., 2
Non-pressurized ball, 505
North America, early tennis in, 8-9
Northern Lawn Tennis Association, 8
Not up, defined, 495
NTL. *See* National Tennis League
Nunez, Juan, on Sanchez Vicario, 303
Nunneley, K. M., 23
Nuthall, Betty Kay, **89-91**, *90*

O

O'Brien, Bill, as promoter, 57
Odizor, Nduka "Duke," Wimbledon (1983), 264
Officials, **387-393**; court, role of, 514-515; education of,
  390-391; evaluation of, 391; fees for, 390; and foot fault,
  507; for Grand Slam match, 392-393; rules on role of,
  514-515; vs. player, in open era, 387
O'Hara Wood, Arthur, **475**
O'Hara Wood, Patrick, **475**
Okker, Tom, **475**
Okker, Tom, as registered player, 164
"Old Hacker." *See* Stolle, Fred
Olliff, John, on Kramer, 108
Olmedo, Alejandro "Alex," **431**; Australian singles, U.S. Indoor
  (1959), 137, *137;* Davis Cup (1958), 135-136; Wimbledon
  (1959), 137
Olvera, Miguel, 160
Olympic Games: records, 643-645; tennis in (1896-1924), 21
O'Neil, Chris, **475**
Onslow Hall, as test site for lawn tennis, 5
Open, defined, 495
Open championship, first event advertised as, 60
Open competition, issue of, 134

Open era, and ITF, 139
Open era, player vs. official in, 387-388
Open tennis: advent of, 163; initial classification of players,
  163; stage set for (1967), 161-162
Open tournament, first, 164
Orantes, Manuel ("Manolo"), **475**; Forest Hills (1975), 204, *204;*
  U.S. Clay Court (1977), 220; vs. Connors, Forest Hills (1975),
  204; win record (1975), 205; win record (1976), 212
Osborne, Margaret. *See* duPont, Margaret
Osuna, Rafael, **432**; death of, 173; Forest Hills (1963),
  148-149; and Palafox, U.S. Doubles (1962), 145-146; vs.
  Froehling, 148-149
"Our Ginny." *See* Wade, Virginia
Outerbridge, Mary, 2, 9, **457-458**
Overhead, defined, 495
Overrule, 393

P

Pacific Southwest, as open tournament, 167
Pails, Dinny, 104, 107; as pro, 109, *109*
Palafox, Tony, 313
Palfrey (Brown), Joey (Joanna Oakes), **476**
Palfrey (Fullerton), Lee (Elizabeth Howland), **476**
Palfrey (Dexter), Mianne (Mary Ann), **476**
Palfrey (Woodrow), Polly (Margaret Germaine), **476**
Palfrey, Sarah, (1935), 54
Palfrey (Fabyan Cooke Danzig), Sarah Hammond, **476**
Panatta, Adriano, **476**; French Open (1976), 211-212
Parker, Frank, *58*, 67, *67*, **432-433**
Partridge, Susan, 123, 124
Passing shot, defined, 495
Pate, Walter, *58*
Patent, for lawn tennis, 3, 6
Patterson, Gerald, **433**; and O'Hara Wood, Davis Cup (1922),
  30; vs. Lycett, Wimbledon (1922), 29, *30*
Patterson, Gerald, (1919), 26
Patty, Budge (John Edward), 115, **433-434**
Pecci, Victor, 287; French Open (1979), 236
Pell, Teddy, **434**
Pelota, 5, 6
Penalty system, 391
Permanent fixtures, of court, 504
Pernfors, Mikael, French Open (1986), 281-282
Perry, Fred, *91*, **91-92**; championship year (1934), 52-53;
  Forest Hills (1933), 51, *52;* Forest Hills (1934), 53; injury

Championships (1970), 179; win record (1966), 156-157

Riggs, Bobby, **92-93**, *93;* and Billie Jean King, 191, *191;* characteristics of, 63; Davis Cup, Wimbledon and Forest Hills (1939), 62-63, *64;* as pro, 109, *109;* as promoter, 114, 117, 123; turns pro, 67, 106; vs. Court (1973), 191; vs. Van Horn, Forest Hills (1939), 63

Rinaldi, Kathy, 278; French Open (1981), 251

Riordan, Bill, 181; antitrust suit against ATP, 198; and ITF-WCT agreement, 187-188

Riordan Circuit, **496**. *See also* Independent Players' Association (IPA)

Riviera, tennis at, 22

Rizici, Virginia, **478**

Robbins, F. D., vs. Dick Dell, record number of games in match (1969), 174

Robertson, Max: on Brough vs. Fleitz, 128-129; on Crawford, 51; on Jacobs, 54; on Nielsen, 128

Roche, Tony, 153, 156, **439**

"Rockhampton Rocket." *See* Laver, Rod

Roger-Vasselin, Christophe, *223, 264*

Roland Garros (Stadium), 41, **496-497**; golden anniversary of, 226

Romance of Wimbledon, The (Olliff), 108

Roosevelt, Ellen Crosby, **439-440**

Roosevelt, Grace (Mrs. Appleton Clark), 439-440

Roosevelt, Theodore, 1

Rose, Merv, 135

Rose, Mervyn, 126

Rosewall, Ken, 124, *376*, **376-378**; Australian Open (1972), 187; continued wins (1970), 180; earnings (1971), 182; Forest Hills (1970), 178; in open era, 165; signs Laver, 146-147; vs. Hoad (1956), 129, *129;* vs. Hoad, Forest Hills (1956), 129-130; vs. Laver, U.S. Pro Championships (1963), 149; vs. Laver, WCT final (1972), 186

Rosset, Marc, vs. Arrese, Olympic tournament (1992), 327

Rostagno, Derrick, 305

Round, challenge, defined, 486

Round, Dorothy, **93-94**, *94;* Wimbledon (1934), 53

Rubber, defined, 497

Rules, **503-519**; for doubles game, 517-519; for early tennis, 6, 7-8; in early women's competition, 14; ITF and USTA, 503-518; for singles game, 503-517

Rules (and Cases and Decisions), **503-518**

Rusher, net, 494

Russian Championships (1913), 22

Ryan, Elizabeth ("Bunny"), 22, **440-441**; death of,

237-238; doubles record, 53; Mathieu, Wimbledon (1934), 53; at Wimbledon Centenary, 217

S

Sabatini, Gabriela, **478**; French Open semifinals (1985), 274; Hilton Head (1985), 278; U.S. Open (1984), 272; vs. Graf, Boca Raton (1991), 316; vs. Graf, U.S. Open (1990), 313-314; vs. Seles, French Open (1992), 323-324; vs. Shriver, Slims Championships (1988), 298; Wimbledon (1985), 278; win record (1988), 296

Sampras, Pete, **478**; (1991), 315-316; U.S. Open (1990), 313; vs. Agassi, U.S. Open (1990), *312,* 313; vs. Courier, ATP World Championships (1991), 320; vs. McEnroe, U.S. Open (1990), 312-313

Sanchez, Emilio, **478**

Sanchez, Javier, **478-479**

Sanchez Vicario, Arantxa, 296, **478**; vs. Graf, French Open (1989), 301, *301,* 302, 303

Santana, Manuel ("Manolo"), **378-379**, *379;* Forest Hills (1965), *152,* 152-153, 153; vs. Pietrangeli, French Championships (1961), 142; Wimbledon (1966), 156

Savitt, Dick, 118, *119,* 137, *137,* **441**

Sawamatsu, Junko, **479**

Sawamatsu, Kazuko, **479**

Schooling, for officials, 390

Schroeder, Ted, 67, 106, 119, **441-442**; Davis Cup (1946), 106-107; as first "jet-setter," 107; Wimbledon (1949), 113, *114*

Schwam, Sandy, 387

Scoring, 509-511; in game, 513; rules for, 513-514; in set, 513; in tie-break game, 513-514

Scott, Gene, 159

Scottish Championships, 12

Scrambler, defined, 497

Sears, Dick, **442-443**; early record of, 13; vs. William E. Glyn, 9

Sears, Eleo, **442**

Sears, Fred, 9

Sedgman, Frank, **379-380**, *380;* in all "Big Four" finals (1952), *121,* 121-122; Forest Hills (1951), 118; Grand Slam (1949), 113; and McGregor, doubles Grand Slam (1951), 119; and McGregor, doubles Grand Slam (1952), 122; as pro, 125; turns pro, 123

Seeding, defined, 497

Segura, Pancho (Francisco), *381,* **381-382**; as pro, 109, *109*

Suk, Cyril, **480**

Sukova, Helen, vs. Navratilova, Australian Open (1984), 272

Sukova, Helena, **480**

Sukova, Vera Puzejova, **480**

Sullivan Award, for Don Budge, 59

Summerhayes, Martha, 9

Supervisor, defined, 498

Supreme Court, defined, 498

Susman, Karen Hantze, 151; Wimbledon (1962), 146

Suspension of play, 516

Suspensions, for poor conduct (1981), 250

Sutter, Cliff, 48; vs. Vines, Forest Hills (1932), 48

Sutton, May, *17*, 17-18, *21*, *120*, **409**

Swedes, male sweep by (1988), 294

T

Talbert, Bill, **446-447**

Tandem Formation. *See* I formation

Tanner, Roscoe: U.S. Open (1974), 199; vs. Borg, U.S. Open (1979), 238-239

Tapscott, Billie, 43, **480-481**

Team Tennis (World Team Tennis), **501-502**

TEL. *See* Tennis Electronics Line system

Television, tennis and, 186, 219

Temesvari, Andrea, 263

Tennant, Eleanor "Teach," 122-123, 340

Tennis: age-group, defined, 483; early strokes in, 10; as entertainment for the masses, 191-192; etymology of, 1; in high altitude, balls for, 505; long (*longue paume*), 5; origins of, 1-9, *4*, *7*; popularity of, 197-198; pro vs. amateur, 483; women's, 8. *See also* Lawn tennis

Tennis ball. *See* Ball

Tennis dress, 46, 108; of Agassi, 310, 313, 319; Bermuda shorts as, 49; and "Gorgeous Gussy" Moran, *112*, 112-113; sans stockings, 43; shorts as, 51, 53, 57; of Suzanne Lenglen, 25; Ted Tinling and, *112*, 112-113, 457

Tennis elbow. *See* Elbow

Tennis Electronics Line (TEL) system, 393, 401-402

Tennis equipment, 395-402

Tennis Origins and Mysteries (Noel and Crawley), 2

Tennis racket. *See* Racket

Tennis terms, defined, 483-502

Thirty, defined, 498

Throat, defined, 498

Tie, defined, 498

Tie-breaker: defined, 498-499; Jimmy Van Alen and, 458; longest, 630; rotation of service in, 514; scoring of, 513-514; at U.S. Open, 178; U.S. Open adopts, 209

Tilden, Bill ("Big Bill"), 24, *27*, **94-96**, *95*; (1920), 27, *27*; Bill Johnston vs. (1919), 26; Cochet vs., at U.S. Championships (1926), 37-38; Davis Cup (1923), 32; as Davis Cup coach for Germany, 59; and Johnston, Davis Cup (1920), 27, *27*, 29; on loss at Wimbledon (1927), 39; pro debut, 47; retires (1930), 43-44; U.S. Championships (1929), 43; U.S. Championships record, 44-45; and USTA conflict, 33, 41; vs. Borotra, Wimbledon (1930), 44; vs. Johnston, at Forest Hills, 33; vs. Johnston, U.S. Championships (1920), 27; vs. Johnston, U.S. Nationals (1922), 30; vs. Johnston, U.S. Nationals (1925), 35; vs. Lacoste, French Championships (1928), 41; vs. Norton, Wimbledon (1921), 29; vs. Patterson, Wimbledon (1920), 27; and Williams, Davis Cup (1923), 32; Wimbledon (1930), 43-44, *45*

Time-outs, 392

Tingay, Lance, **457**; on Bueno, 140; on Connolly, 125; on Drobny, 126; on Laver at Wimbledon, 166; on Maureen Connolly, 121, 340; on Schroeder, Ted, 113; on Seixas, 124

Tinling, Ted, **457**; and Evonne Goolagong, 184; and Gorgeous Gussy's lace, 112-113; on McEnroe's trophies, 258

Tiriac, Ion, 172, **481**; on Becker, 275

Titanic, and Dick Williams, 100

"To cough and quit," 29

Todd, Pat Canning, 107

Toilet breaks, 392

Topspin, **472**; defined, 499. *See also* Spin

Top Ten: defined, 489; for 1941, 66

Toulmin, Mrs. Harry. *See* Townsend, Bertha

Tour, Kraft, **493**

Tournament(s): age-group, 483; defined, 499; early control of, 8; Nahant, 9

Townsend, Bertha, 14, **447**

Trabert, Tony, 124, 126, *214*, **383-384**, *384*; on Chang, 304; and Davis Cup (1954), 127; Forest Hills (1955), 128; French, Wimbledon and U.S. (1955), *127*, 127-128; vs. Seixas, Forest Hills (1953), 124

Tree-ing, defined, 499

Truman, Christine, 138; vs. Gibson, Wightman Cup (1958), 136

Turnbull, Wendy, U.S. Open (1977), 222

Turner, Lesley. *See* Bowrey, Lesley

Twist, American, defined, 484

U

U.E., defined, 499
Ulrich, Einer, **481**
Ulrich, Jorgen, **481**
Ulrich, Torben, **481**
Umpire, 504; defined, 499; defined, in ITF Rule, 504; education of, 390; evaluation of, 391; fees for, 390; ITF classification of, 390; role of, 514-515; rules on role of, 514-515

United States Interscholastic Champions, 536-537
United States National Intercollegiate Champions, 533-536
United States Tennis Association (USTA), **500**; All-American rankings (1970-71), 596; comment on foot fault rule, 507; and ITF rules, 503-518; men's rankings, 585-599; and National Tennis Center, 224-226; and open tennis, 163, 169; Women's rankings, 599-609
U.S. Lawn Tennis Association (USLTA), becomes USTA, 209
U.S. National Lawn Tennis Association, 9; formation of, 13. *See also* United States Tennis Association (USTA)
U.S. Open. *See* United States Championships
U.S. Pro Championships, **499-500**; revival of (1964), 151-152
U.S. Women's Championship, first, 13-14
U.S. Pro Championships, 640-642
USTA. *See* United States Tennis Association
USTA Indoor Circuit, 192

V

Van Alen, Candy, and National Tennis Hall of Fame, 403
Van Alen, Jimmy, **458**; hosts pro tournament, 153-154; and Newport Casino, 403
Van Alen Streamlined Scoring System (VASSS), 458, **500**
Van Horn, Welby, 63
Vanished Arizona (Summerhayes), 9
Van Nostrand, Molly, 278
Van Ryn, Johnny (John William), **447**
VASSS. *See* Van Alen Streamlined Scoring System

Vilas, Guillermo, **447-448**; defaults vs. Nastase, 219; earnings and win record (1977), 220; Forest Hills (1977), 219, *219*; Grand Prix (1974), 200; suspended by MIPTC (1983), 265; win record (1975), 205; win record (1977), 218-219; win record (1978), 229
Vines, Ellsworth, **96-98**, *97*; pro debut, 45; technique of, 48; U.S. Championships (1931), 46; vs. Austin, Wimbledon (1932), 47; vs. Cochet, Forest Hills (1932), 48-49; Wimbledon and Forest Hills (1932), 47-49, *48*
Virginia Slims, withdrawal from sponsorship, 232-33

W

Wade, Virginia, **449**; U.S. Open (1968), 167; Wimbledon (1977), 217-218; Wimbledon (1985), 278-279; and Wimbledon Centenary, 218
Wagner, Marie, **449-450**
Wales, Prince of (Great Britain), approves of shorts as tennis dress, 53
Wallach, Maud Barger, 20, **450**
Ward, Holcombe, *64*, **450**, *482*
Warning, "soft," 388
Warwick, Kim, 212
Washburn, Watty (Watson McLean), **451**
Watson, Maud, 13, **481**
WCT. *See* World Championship Tennis
Weir, Reginald S., **481**
West Hants Lawn Tennis Club (Bournemouth), 164
West Side Tennis Club (New York), **500**; as championship host, 20; first Davis Cup at, 20. *See also* Forest Hills
Wheaton, David, Wimbledon (1991), 319
White, Stanford, 403
White City (Sydney, Australia), **500**
Whitman, Mal, **451**, *482*
Wide, defined, 501
Wightman, Hazel Hotchkiss, 26, *173*, **451-453**; and "all-white" rule, 112; death of, 202; and Sarah Palfrey Cooke, 76; and Wightman Cup, 30-31, *32*
Wightman Cup, **501**, 575-582; (1927), 41; (1930), 45-46;